Constitutional Government

THE AMERICAN EXPERIENCE

Ninth Edition

James A. Curry
Department of Political Science
Baylor University

Richard M. Battistoni
Department of Political Science
Providence College

Chapter opener photos by Betsy A. Ritz.
Cover image © Shutterstock, Inc.

Kendall Hunt
publishing company

www.kendallhunt.com
Send all inquiries to:
4050 Westmark Drive
Dubuque, IA 52004-1840

Copyright © 1989 by West Publishing Company
Copyright © 1994, 1997, 1999, 2003, 2006, 2009, 2011, 2013 by Kendall Hunt Publishing Company

ISBN 978-1-4652-5356-9

All rights reserved. No part of this publication may be reproduced,
stored in a retrieval system, or transmitted, in any form or by any means,
electronic, mechanical, photocopying, recording, or otherwise,
without the prior written permission of the copyright owner.

Printed in the United States of America
10 9 8 7 6 5 4 3 2 1

CONTENTS

About the Authors xix
Table of Cases xxi
Preface To The Ninth Edition xxxiii

PART 1
The Constitutional Text and Context 1

1. THE PRINCIPLES AND ORIGINS OF AMERICAN CONSTITUTIONALISM 3

An Introductory Conversation between John Locke and Jean-Jacques Rousseau 4
Introduction: The Basic Theory of Constitutionalism 6
Brief 1.1 The Legacy of the Universal Declaration of Human Rights 7
Comparative Constitutions and Constitutionalism 8
Brief 1.2 Constitution Writing Over Time 8
Brief 1.3 Keeping the Spread of Democracy in Perspective 9
The Preamble: A Statement of Purpose and Goals 10
Organizational Chart 11
    Separation of Powers 12
    Federalism 12
    Judicial Review 13
Amendatory Articles and a Supreme Law 13
Brief 1.4 The "Unwritten" British Constitution 14
Bills of Rights: Limits on Government 16
The Twin Pillars of American Constitutionalism 16
The Individualist Theory of Politics 18
The Communitarian Theory of Politics 19
Brief 1.5 Contemporary Liberals and Conservatives 21
Historical Influences on American Constitutionalism 21
    Ancient Constitutionalism 21
    Medieval Constitutionalism 22
    English Common Law and Parliamentary Practice 23
Colonial Influences on American Constitutionalism 24
    Religious Ideas and Practices 24
Brief 1.6 Sir Edward Coke's Legacy 24
    Structure of Government: Colonial Experience 26

Brief 1.7 The English Bill of Rights 27
Conclusion 27

2, AMERICAN CONSTITUTIONALISM: THE FOUNDING GENERATION 29

Introductory Remarks by President and Secretary of State James Madison 30
Introduction: Constitutionalism and the American Revolution 32
Emerging American Constitutionalism (1760–1776) 32
The Declaration of Independence 34
    Post-Revolutionary Constitutionalism 35
The Revolutionary State Constitutions 36
The Articles of Confederation 38
Brief 2.1 The Northwest Ordinance: A Legacy of the Articles of Confederation 40
The "Critical Period" and the State Governments 41
    The Constitutional Convention and Its Aftermath 42
Brief 2.2 Roll Call at the Constitutional Convention 43
The Virginia Plan and the Problem of Representation 43
Powers of Congress Under the New Constitution 44
Separation of Powers and the Presidency 45
The Federal Judiciary and Individual Rights 47
Ratification of the Constitution 47
    The Anti-Federalist Argument Against Ratification 48
    The Federalist Response 49
Brief 2.3 The Difficult Struggle Over Ratification 51
Conclusion 52
Brief 2.4 Historical Critiques of the U.S. Constitution 52

PART 2
Structures and Process of American Constitutional Government 55

3, THE NATURE AND SCOPE OF JUDICIAL POWER 57

Introductory Remarks by Chief Justice Rehnquist 58
A Brief History of the Federal Judiciary 60
The Constitution, Congress, and Federal Court Jurisdiction 61
Organizational Structure of the Federal Judicial System 62
United States District Courts 63
United States Courts of Appeal 63
United States Supreme Court 64

Brief 3.1 The Men and Women of October 65
Brief 3.2 Clerking at the Supreme Court 66
Limitations on Federal Judicial Power 70
The Appointment of Judges and Justices 72
    Judicial Selection: An Inherently Political Process 72
Brief 3.3 Two Historic Battles Over Supreme Court Confirmation 73
Judicial Selection Variables 74
Brief 3.4 The Contentious Confirmation Process: From Clinton to Obama 75
    Professional Competence 76
    Political Affiliation 76
    Ideological or Policy Views 77
Brief 3.5 Judicial Appointments . . . and Disappointments: What Is a President to Do? 78
Other Selection Variables: Race, Gender, and Ethnic Origin 79
Brief 3.6 President Obama's First Two Supreme Court Appointees: Sonia Sotomayor and Elena Kagan 79
The Roberts Court and Ongoing Judicial Confirmation Concerns 82
Conclusion 82
Brief 3.7 The Seventeenth Chief Justice: John G. Roberts 83

4. THE ORIGINS AND PRACTICE OF JUDICIAL REVIEW IN THE AMERICAN SYSTEM 85

Introductory Remarks by Chief Justice John Marshall 86
Judicial Review: Continuing Paradox in a Democratic System 88
The Policymaking Function of the U.S. Supreme Court 88
    Some Thoughts on Constitutional Interpretation 88
Brief 4.1 Competing Visions of the Judicial Role 89
The Restraint–Activism Dimension of Judicial Decision Making 90
    Judicial Restraint and the Thayer-Frankfurter-Harlan Prescription 91
    Judicial Restraint and the Holmes-Brandeis-Stone Prescription 92
Brief 4.2 The Supreme Court Revolution of 1937 93
    Judicial Activism from John Marshall to John Roberts 94
Roots of Judicial Review: Theory and Practice 95
    The Framers' Intentions and Judicial Review 95
    Historical Acceptance of Judicial Review 97
    Judicial Review as a Check on Majority Rule 98
Brief 4.3 A Classic Confrontation: *Marbury v. Madison* (1803) 99
    Judicial Review and the Articulation of Neutral Principles 101

Brief 4.4 *Bush v. Gore*: **One for the Textbooks?** 102
Conclusion 103

5, SEPARATION OF POWERS AND THE AMERICAN PRESIDENCY 105

Introductory Remarks by President Theodore Roosevelt 106
The Separation of Powers 108
    Early Writings on Separated Powers 108
Early American Writings and the Founding 109
The United States Presidency: An Overview 110
    Electing the President 112
Brief 5.1 Constitutional Amendments and The Presidency 112
    Removing the President 113
    Presidential Powers: Theory and Practice 113
Brief 5.2 Anatomy of the 2012 Presidential Election 113
    Contrasting Theories of Executive Power 114
Brief 5.3 The President's Constitutional Powers: Article II 114
President as Legislative Leader 116
    The Veto Power 116
Providing Information on the State of the Union 116
President as Chief Executive 117
    Appointment and Removal Powers 117
Brief 5.4 The Rise and Fall of the Line-Item Veto 118
Brief 5.5 The Executive Branch of Government 119
Brief 5.6 The Controversy Over "Recess" Appointments 120
    Presidential Power to Pardon 121
President as Chief Diplomat 121
    Treaties and Executive Agreements 121
Brief 5.7 Pardon Me?: Some Controversial Pardons 122
    Receiving Ambassadors and Public Ministers 123
President as Commander in Chief 124
    Executive War Power and National Emergencies 124
    Inherent Powers in the Twentieth Century 125
        World War II and the Internment of Japanese-Americans 126
        The Korean War and the Steel Seizure Case 127
Brief 5.8 A Nation Struggles with Its Conscience 127
    The Vietnam War 128
Brief 5.9 The War Powers Resolution 130

Brief 5.10 Presidential War Power and the Persian Gulf Conflict 130
    September 11 and the War on Terror 131
Brief 5.11 The USA PATRIOT Act of 2001 132
    The Second Iraq War 133
    The Constitution and Detainees' Rights 134
Brief 5.12 What Is Guantanamo Bay? 134
Brief 5.13 The Military Commissions Act of 2006 137
Conclusion 138

6, SEPARATION OF POWERS AND CONGRESS 139

Introductory Remarks by Senator Robert C. Byrd 140
Congress: An Overview 141
    Congress Then and Now: Comparing the 1st and 112th Congresses 142
    The Constitution and Congress 143
Brief 6.1 Members of the 113th Congress 144
The Powers of Congress 144
    The Legislative Power of Congress 145
Brief 6.2 The Filibuster: Protecting Minority Rights or Wasting Time? 145
    The Investigative Power of Congress 146
    The Impeachment Power of Congress 149
        The Nixon Presidency: Executive Privilege and the Threat of Impeachment 150
Brief 6.3 What Was Watergate? 151
    The Clinton Presidency and Impeachment 152
Brief 6.4 The Starr Report and the Clinton Impeachment 153
Congress at Work: An Overview 154
    Organizing and Staffing Government 155
Brief 6.5 The Rise of Government Corporations 156
    The Power of the Purse: Taxing, Spending, and Borrowing 156
        Taxation 157
        Spending 158
        Borrowing and Debt 158
Conclusion 161

7, FEDERALISM: THE INTERACTION OF NATIONAL AND STATE GOVERNMENTS 163

Introductory Remarks by Vice President and Senator John C. Calhoun 164
The Theory of Federalism 165

Federalism: A Comparative Perspective   165

Origins of American Federalism   166

Brief 7.1 Horizontal Federalism: Legacy of the Articles of Confederation   167

National Supremacy: The Federalist Position   168

    The Judiciary Act of 1789   168

    The Hamiltonian Economic Program   168

    John Marshall's Federalism: *McCulloch v. Maryland* (1819)   169

States' Rights: The Anti-Federalist Position   170

    Whiskey Rebellion (1794)   170

    Jeffersonianism and the Virginia and Kentucky Resolutions (1798)   170

Brief 7.2 Jeffersonians as Nationalists, Federalists as States'-Righters   171

    State Sovereignty: The Extension of States' Rights   172

    The Missouri Compromise   172

Brief 7.3 States, Territories, and Federalism   172

    John C. Calhoun: State Sovereignty and Nullification   173

Brief 7.4 The Webster–Hayne Debate   173

    Secession: The Nature of the Union   174

Brief 7.5 The Constitution of the Confederate States of America   175

Federalism in the Post–Civil War Era   175

    The New Deal and Federalism   175

    LBJ and the "Great Society"   176

    Ronald Reagan's Federalism and "Devolution"   176

Other Federalism Issues   177

    The Eleventh Amendment and Sovereign Immunity   177

Brief 7.6 Sovereign Immunity in a Democracy?   178

    Federal Preemption of State Law   180

    Federalism and September 11, 2001   181

Conclusion   181

Brief 7.7 Federal Homeland Security Grants to States   182

8, FEDERALISM: THE GROWTH OF FEDERAL POWER AND ECONOMIC REGULATION   183

An Introductory Conversation between Presidents Franklin D. Roosevelt and Ronald Reagan   184

Property Rights and Economic Liberty in the United States   186

Brief 8.1 Can Government Take Your Property? 186
Brief 8.2 The Contract Clause: Only a Shadow of Its Former Self 187
    The Early View of Due Process and Property: The Slaughterhouse Cases 188
Brief 8.3 United States Citizenship 188
    The Rise and Fall of the Freedom of Contract 189
Brief 8.4 Women and Wages: Challenges to the Freedom of Contract 190
The Regulation of Commerce 191
    Chief Justice John Marshall and the Commerce Power 193
Brief 8.5 The Shreveport Rate Cases: Offspring of the Marshall Legacy 194
    Chief Justice Roger Taney and Dual Federalism 194
    Commerce: Manufacturing, Monopolies, and the Economy 195
Brief 8.6 The Sherman Anti-trust Act and Monopolies 196
Brief 8.7 The Federal Minimum Wage 198
    Commerce as a Federal Police Power 198
Brief 8.8 Child Labor: Freedom of Contract or a National Shame? 199
    Recent Developments in Commerce and Spending Powers 200
    The Fight over "Obamacare:" *National Federation of Independent Business, et al. v. Sebelius* (2012) 201
The Congressional Power to Tax and Spend 202
Brief 8.9 Direct Taxes and the Federal Income Tax 202
Brief 8.10 Limitations on the Spending Power: *National Federation of Independent Business, et al. v. Sebelius* 204
Conclusion 205

PART 3
Constitutional Rights and Liberties 207

9. RACIAL EQUALITY UNDER THE CONSTITUTION 209

Introductory Remarks by Frederick Douglass 210
Racial Equality: An American Dilemma 211
Slavery, Race, and the Constitution 212
The Post–Civil War Amendments and Racial Equality 213
Brief 9.1 Slavery Under the Constitution: The Pre–Civil War Years 214
Race and Constitutional Equality: The Court's Original Understanding 215
Brief 9.2 Laundries and Jury Boxes: An Expansive Vision of Equal Protection 216

Narrowing the Intention of the Framers   218
Brief 9.3 Rationality Scrutiny Defined   218
Toward Color Blindness: The Struggle for Racial Equality   219
Racial Discrimination in Housing   219
Brief 9.4 Congressional Authority Under the Thirteenth Amendment: The *Jones* Case and Beyond   222
Racial Discrimination in Education   222
    School Desegregation Under the Separate-But-Equal Doctrine: *Sweatt v. Painter* (1950)   223
    Brown v. Board of Education and the End of Segregation in Education   224
    The Positive Duty to Desegregate and Court-Ordered Busing   225
Brief 9.5 Enforcing and Implementing the *Brown* Decision   226
    School Desegregation after Fifty Years: Advance or Retreat?   228
Brief 9.6 School Desegregation Today: An Ongoing "American Dilemma"   231
Racial Discrimination in Employment: The "Purposeful-Discrimination" Test Examined   232
Racial Discrimination and the Franchise   233
    Methods of Disenfranchisement   234
        Literacy Tests   234
        White Primary Laws   234
Congressional Action: The Voting Rights Act of 1965   235
    Electoral System Discrimination   236
Brief 9.7 Black Voting Power: Representation or Influence?   237
Conclusion   237
Brief 9.8 Equal Protection Challenges to State Legislative Redistricting   238

10, THE NEW EQUAL PROTECTION   241

Introductory Remarks by Elizabeth Cady Stanton   242
Introduction: Equal Protection Old and New   243
Origins of the New Equal Protection   243
The Two-Tier Approach   244
Suspect Classifications and the Equal Protection Clause   245
Affirmative Action: Denial of Equal Protection to Whites?   245
Brief 10.1 What Makes a Classification Suspect?   246
The Court's First Answer: The *Bakke* Decision   247
Affirmative Action Resolved: The *Croson* and *Adarand* Decisions   248
Brief 10.2 *Bakke* Revisited: Affirmative Action in Higher Education   250
Gender-Based Discrimination and the Constitution   251

Brief 10.3 The Long History of Women's Legal Inequality   251

The Court's First Steps: *Reed v. Reed* and Progeny   253

Sex Discrimination in Employment   254

Brief 10.4 Is Differential Treatment of Pregnancy Sex Discrimination?   255

Brief 10.5 The Expansion of Sexual Harassment Law in the 1990s   256

Brief 10.6 The Equal Rights Amendment and Constitutional Equality for Women   257

Age Discrimination and Equality   257

Noncitizens and the Equal Protection Clause   258

Disabled Persons and the Equal Protection Clause   259

Sexual Orientation and the Constitution   260

Brief 10.7 The Scope and Enforcement of the ADA   261

Brief 10.8 Equal Protection and Same-Sex Marriage   262

The Equal Protection Clause and the Poor: Wealth Classifications, Poverty, and the Fundamental "Necessities of Life"   262

Poverty as a Potentially Suspect Class: The Warren Court   263

The Return to Rationality Scrutiny: The Burger Court   264

Rationality Scrutiny Confirmed: *San Antonio School District v. Rodriguez*   265

Equal Protection and Reform of the Electoral System: *Bush v. Gore*   267

Brief 10.9 Electoral Reform in the Aftermath of the 2000 Election   268

Conclusion   268

11. THE BILL OF RIGHTS AND DUE PROCESS OF LAW   271

Introductory Remarks by Justice Thurgood Marshall   272

The Bill of Rights   274

Brief 11.1 The Twenty-Seventh Amendment   274

The Fourteenth Amendment and Due Process of Law   275

The Doctrine of Selective Incorporation   279

Incorporation of the First Amendment   279

Brief 11.2 The Case for Total Incorporation   280

Incorporation of the Second Amendment   280

Incorporation of the Third Amendment   283

Incorporation of the Fourth Amendment   283

Incorporation of the Fifth Amendment   285

Incorporation of the Sixth Amendment   285

Incorporation of the Eighth Amendment   286

Beyond the Bill of Rights: Fundamental Rights and Due Process of Law   287

Brief 11.3 What Does the Ninth Amendment Mean? 287
Brief 11.4 What Makes a Right Fundamental? 288
The Right to Vote 289
Legislative Apportionment 289
Equal Access to the Franchise 290
Brief 11.5 Can College Students Be Restricted From Voting on Campus? 291
Equal Access to the Ballot: *Williams v. Rhodes* (1968) 291
Brief 11.6 The Right to Vote and Convicted Felons 292
The Right to Interstate Travel: *Shapiro v. Thompson* 292
The Right to Privacy 294
Right to Privacy: Origins and Foundations 294
The Right to Privacy and Abortion 296
Limitations on Abortion Rights: State and Federal Funding Restrictions 298
Brief 11.7 Using Restrictions on Speech to Restrict Abortion: *Rust v. Sullivan* 299
Limitations on Abortion Rights: Government Regulations on Abortion Procedures 300
Brief 11.8 Restrictions on Abortion Rights: The Webster and Casey Decisions 301
The Right to Sexual Privacy: *Lawrence v. Texas* 303
Fundamental Rights of Parents 305
Conclusion 306

12. THE FOURTH AMENDMENT: SEARCHES, SEIZURES, AND PRIVACY 307

Introductory Remarks by James Otis 308
Liberty and Security in a Free Society 309
Brief 12.1 Crime in the United States: The Uniform Crime Report 309
Fourth Amendment 310
    The Fourth Amendment and Warrants 310
Brief 12.2 Executing a Search Warrant 312
    The Exclusionary Rule and the Fourth Amendment 312
Brief 12.3 The "Good-Faith" Exception to the Exclusionary Rule 314
    Exceptions to the Fourth Amendment's Warrant Requirements 315
        The "Automobile" Exception 315
Brief 12.4 Two Cases on the Common Law and Arrests 316
        The "Border Exception" 318
Brief 12.5 Police Checkpoints and Reasonable Suspicion 319

The "Hot-Pursuit" Exception   319
The "Stop-and-Frisk" Exception   319

Brief 12.6 When Police Come to the Door   320

Brief 12.7 Would You Call This "Reasonable Suspicion"?   321

The "Search-Incident-to-Arrest" Exception   322

Brief 12.8 "Stop and Frisk" in New York City   322

Brief 12.9 Searches and Citations: Knowles v. Iowa (1998) and Virginia v. Moore (2008)   324

The "Consent" Exception   324
The "Plain-View" Exception   325
Drug Testing   326

Brief 12.10 Entering the Body to Obtain Evidence   326

Wiretapping and Electronic Surveillance   328

Brief 12.11 The Expectation of Privacy in Your Home (Or Someone Else's Home)   329

Wiretapping and National Security   330

Brief 12.12 High-Tech Thermal Imaging: Kyllo v. United States (2001)   331

The Fourth Amendment and Administrative Searches   331
Conclusion   332

13. CRIMINAL PROCEDURE AND DUE PROCESS OF LAW   335

Introductory Remarks by Chief Justice Earl Warren   336
Due Process Guarantees in the Bill of Rights   337
Fifth Amendment   337
  Double Jeopardy   337

Brief 13.1 Juries and Double Jeopardy: Blueford v. Arkansas (2012)   338

Self-Incrimination   339
  Self-Incrimination and Confessions   339

Brief 13.2 Miranda Is a "Constitutional Rule". . . But It May Be Limited   342

Sixth Amendment   342
  The Nature of a Fair Trial   342

Brief 13.3 Can God Coerce a Confession?: Colorado v. Connelly (1986)   343

Jury Trials   343

Brief 13.4 What Makes a Trial "Unfair"?   344

Jury Size   344
Jury Verdicts   345
Jury Selection   345

Notice, Confrontation, and Securing of Witnesses 346
Right to Counsel 348
Brief 13.5 Forensic Analysis, Lab Reports, and CSI: See You in Court 348
Ineffective Counsel 350
Eighth Amendment 351
Preventive Detention 351
The Death Penalty 352
Brief 13.6 Some Non–Death Penalty "Cruel and Unusual Punishments" Cases 353
Sentencing Guidelines 355
Brief 13.7 Trends in the Death Penalty 356
Execution of Minors and Those with Mental Problems 356
Minors 356
Mentally Retarded 357
Victim-Impact Statements 357
Methods of Execution 358
The Changing Nature of Due Process of Law 358
Due Process for Juveniles 358
Brief 13.8 The Changing Juvenile Justice System 359
Mental Patients 360
Sex Offenders 360
Probationers, Parolees, and Prisoners 361
Conclusion 362
Brief 13.9 Due Process and the "Supermax" Prison 362

14. THE FIRST AMENDMENT IN A DEMOCRATIC SOCIETY: POLITICAL SPEECH AND OTHER FORMS OF EXPRESSION 365

An Introductory Conversation between Justices Hugo Black and Felix Frankfurter 366
The Theory and Scope of First Amendment Freedoms 368
Freedom of Expression in Historical Perspective 368
Contrasting Views of Freedom of Expression 369
Political Speech and National Security: Conflicting Standards of Regulation 371
Restricting Speech During War: "A Question of Proximity and Degree" 373
The Aftermath of Schenck: A New Standard Emerges 373
The Early Cold War and National Security Concerns: How Serious Is the Threat? 374
Brief 14.1 The American Civil Liberties Union 375
Dennis v. United States (1951) 376
Yates v. United States (1957) 377

Political Speech, the States, and Internal Security   377
    Modernization of the Bill of Rights Begins: Gitlow v. New York (1925)   378
    A New Standard: Brandenburg v. Ohio (1969)   379

Brief 14.2 The Trial and Execution of Sacco and Vanzetti   379

Other Political Expression Issues Before the Supreme Court   380
    Are Political Symbols Included in the Meaning of "Speech"?   380
    Symbolic Protest Against Federal Policies   382

Brief 14.3 The Student's Right to Free Speech Can Be Regulated   384

"Speech Plus" and the First Amendment   384
    Labor Picketing and the First Amendment   385
    Peaceful Assembly and the First Amendment   386

Brief 14.4 Anti-Abortionists and the First Amendment   389

    Commercial Speech and the First Amendment   390

Adult Entertainment and the First Amendment   393

Campaign Finance and the First Amendment: Corrupted Politics or Free Speech?   394
    Campaign Contributions versus Expenditures: Buckley v. Valeo   394
    Campaign Finance Reform, The BCRA, and the *Citizens United* Decision   397

Brief 14.5 The Struggle to Abolish "Soft Money"   397

Coerced Speech and the "Culture Wars"   399

Brief 14.6 Gay Rights and Free Speech   400

The "Fighting-Words" Doctrine: Is Some Speech Not Protected?   401

Brief 14.7 Does the First Amendment Protect False Speech?   403

Conclusion   403

15. FREEDOM OF THE PRESS   405

Introductory Remarks by Benjamin Franklin   406

The Basic Theory of Freedom of the Press   407

Brief 15.1 Freedom of the Press at Home and Around the World   407

    The Anglo-American Context of a Free Press   408

Brief 15.2 The Zenger Trial and the Quest for a Free Press   409

Brief 15.3 The "Press" Then and Now   409

    The Classic Case: Near v. Minnesota (1931)   410
    Prior Restraint and the Vietnam War: *New York Times v. United States* (1971)   410

Brief 15.4 The Students' Right to Publish Can Be Regulated   412

Free Press and Fair Trial: Problems When Rights Collide   413

Brief 15.5 Prior Restraint as a Condition for Government Employment:

Snepp v. United States (1980)   414
    Pretrial Publicity and "Gag Orders"   414
Brief 15.6 Television in the Courtroom   416
    Media Access to Pretrial Hearings   417
    Media Access at the Trial Stage   417
Free Press Issues and Criminal Justice   418
    Grand Jury Testimony   418
Brief 15.7 The Limits of Press Regulation   419
    Publishing and Profiting from Crime   419
    Intercepting Private Conversations   420
Confidentiality of Sources: Privilege for Journalists?   420
Obscenity and the First Amendment   422
    Early Attempts to Define Obscenity   422
    Search for a National Standard: The *Roth* Test   423
Brief 15.8 Animal Cruelty and Violence: Protected Or Unprotected Speech?   424
    Modifications to *Roth*   425
    Confusion, Politics, and Obscenity Law   425
Brief 15.9 Who Is the "Average Person"?   426
Brief 15.10 Private Possession of Child Pornography   426
    Advent of a New Standard: *Miller v. California* (1973)   427
    Government Subsidies and Free Expression: NEA Grants   428
    Child Pornography   428
Brief 15.11 Federal Regulation of "Dial-A-Porn"   428
The Law of Libel   431
Brief 15.12 Is "Sexting" Child Porn?   431
    Libel Law in the Twentieth Century   432
    The "Actual-Malice" Doctrine: *New York Times v. Sullivan* (1964)   432
    "Public Figures" and Actual Malice   434
    Private Citizens and Libel Law   435
    Refining the Law of Libel   436
Brief 15.13 Larry Flynt vs. The Reverend Jerry Falwell   436
Government Regulation of the Airwaves   437
Conclusion   439
Brief 15.14 Regulating "Fleeting Expletives"   440

16. FREEDOM OF RELIGION   441

    Introductory Remarks by President John F. Kennedy   442
    The Constitution, Religious Freedom, and American Culture   444

Early English and American Colonial Experience   444
American Experience During and After the Founding   444

Brief 16.1 Two Sons of Virginia Labor for Religious Freedom   445

The Bill of Rights and the Religion Clauses   446

The Free Exercise Clause and Religious Freedom   446

Early Conflicts with the Free Exercise of Religion   446
Interpreting the Free Exercise Clause: Two Competing Standards   448
Compelling State Interest Standard   448

Brief 16.2 Jehovah's Witnesses, Free Exercise, and the Flag Salute Cases   449

The "Generally Applicable Law" Standard   450

Brief 16.3 Rise and Fall of the Religious Freedom Restoration Act   452

The Issue of Exceptions to Generally Applicable Laws   452
Compulsory School Attendance and the Old Amish Order   452
The Meaning of "Religion" and Conscientious Objectors   453

Brief 16.4 May a Religious Sect Have Its Own School District?   454

The Establishment of Religion   454

Brief 16.5 Competing Theories of the Establishment Clause   455

Public Assistance to Parochial Schools: The Constitutional Foundation   455
Emergence of the Three-Pronged Test   458
The Movement Toward Neutrality and Accommodation   459

Brief 16.6 The "Ministerial Exception": Avoiding Excessive Entanglement   459

Mueller v. Allen (1983)   460
Zobrest v. Catalina Foothills School District (1993)   460
Agostini v. Felton (1997)   461
Mitchell v. Helms (2000)   461
Zelman v. Simmons-Harris (2002)   462
The Neutrality Principle in Equal Access and Taxation   463
Equal Access and Public Facilities   463

Brief 16.7 When Free Exercise and Establishment Clash: Locke v. Davey (2004)   464

Taxation and Religion: Rendering Unto Caesar   465

Brief 16.8 Hastings Christian Fellowship v. Martinez (2010)   465

Religious Activities in Public Schools and Society   467

Brief 16.9 Accommodating Religion in Prison: *Cutter v. Wilkinson* (2005)   469

The Delicate Issue of School Prayer   469
Religious Invocations and Benedictions   471

Brief 16.10 Prayer and Football Games: *Santa Fe Independent School District v. Doe*   472

Tale of Two Theories: Evolution versus Creationism   472

Brief 16.11 The Scopes "Monkey Trial": In the Image of Man or Monkey? 473
    Public Religious Displays 474
Brief 16.12 The Ten Commandments: Religious, Historical, or Both? 475
Conclusion 476

APPENDIX 479

ENDNOTES 491

GLOSSARY 509

INDEX 517

About the Authors

James A. Curry is the Bob Bullock Professor of Public Policy and Administration and Professor of Political Science at Baylor University. Dr. Curry has been recognized by Baylor University, various honorary organizations, and student groups for his teaching and service. He is Director of Baylor's Washington Internship Program and travels regularly to Washington to work with interns throughout the federal government. He also serves as the Director of the Bob Bullock Scholars Program which enables students to spend a semester working in the Texas Legislature.

Professor Curry earned a doctorate with honors in political science at the University of Kansas. He has published articles in several areas of political science, criminal justice, and public policy. Professor Curry is a member of the American Political Science Association, the Academy of Criminal Justice Sciences, and Pi Sigma Alpha.

Richard M. Battistoni is Professor of Political Science and Public and Community Service Studies at Providence College. Prior to his appointment at Providence College in 1994, he was an associate professor of political science at Baylor University and director of its Civic Education and Community Service Program. For the past 20 years, Professor Battistoni has been a leader in the field of service-learning, especially as it relates to questions of political theory and citizenship education. From 2001–2004, he directed *Project 540*, a nationwide high school civic engagement initiative.

Professor Battistoni is the author of numerous books and articles, including *Public Schooling and the Education of Democratic Citizens* and *Education for Democracy: Citizenship, Community, and Service* (co-edited with Benjamin R. Barber, also available from Kendall/Hunt). A native of Bakersfield, California, Battistoni is a graduate of the University of Southern California and earned his doctorate in political science at Rutgers University.

Table of Cases

A

Abbott Laboratories v. Gardner (1967), 71
Abington School District v. Schempp (1963), 455, 468, 470
Abrams v. United States (1919), 372, 373
Adair v. United States (1908), 96
Adams v. Williams (1972), 281
Adamson v. California (1947), 280
Adarand Constructor's Inc. v. Pena (1995), 249
Adderly v. Florida (1966), 388
AFL v. Swing (1941), 385
Agostini v. Felton (1997), 457, 461
Aguilar v. Felton (1985), 456, 461
Air Transport Association of America, Inc. v. Cuomo, et al., 180,
Al Odah v. United States (2004), 135
Alabama v. Shelton (2002), 349
Alberts v. California (1957), 422
Alden v. Maine (1999), 179
Alexander v. Holmes County Board of Education (1969), 226
Allgeyer v. Louisiana (1897), 189
Allied Structural Steel Company v. Spannaus (1978), 187
Almeida-Sanchez v. United States (1973), 318
Amalgamated Food Employees Union Local 590 v. Logan Valley Plaza (1968), 385, 386
Ambach v. Norwick (1979), 259
American Needle, Inc. v. National Football League (2010), 192, 196
Apodaca v. Oregon (1972), 345
Argersinger v. Hamlin (1972), 281, 349
Arizona v. Evans (1995), 313, 314
Arizona v. Fulminante (1991), 340, 341
Arizona v. Gant (2009), 308, 314, 323,
Arizona v. Hicks (1987), 325
Arizona v. United States (2012), 180, 259,
Arizona v. Washington (1978), 338
Arkansas v. Sanders (1979), 317
Ashcroft v. American Civil Liberties Union (ACLU-I) (2002), 429, 430
Ashcroft v. American Civil Liberties Union

Ashcroft v. Free Speech Coalition (2002), 430
Ashwander v. Tennessee Valley Authority (1936), 70, 156
Associated Press v. Walker (1967), 433, 435
Atkins v. Virginia (2002), 355, 357
Atwater v. City of Lago Vista, 316
Austin v. Michigan State Chamber of Commerce (1990), 395, 398

B

Bailey v. Drexel Furniture Co. (1922), 199
Baker v. Carr (1962), 91, 92, 100
Baker v. Carr, 336
Ballew v. Georgia (1978), 344
Barenblatt v. United States (1959), 92, 148
Barnes v. Glen Theatre, 393
Barr v. Matteo (1959), 432, 433
Barron v. Baltimore (1833), 274, 277, 306
Bartnicki v. Vopper (2001), 420
Bates v. Arizona State Bar (1977), 391
Batson v. Kentucky (1986), 345
Baze v. Rees (2008), 355, 358
Bd of Trustees of Univ. of Alabama v. Garrett (2000), 179,
Beauharnais v. Illinois (1952), 432, 433
Benton v. Maryland (1969), 281, 285
Berghuis v. Smith (2010), 345
Berghuis v. Thompkins (2010), 340, 342
Betts v. Brady (1942), 349
Bigelow v. Virginia (1975), 390, 391
Bloate v. United States (2010), 343
Blueford v. Arkansas (2012), 338
Blystone v. Pennsylvania (1990), 354
Board of Education of Independent School District No. 92 of Pottawatomie County v. Lindsay Earls (2002), 327
Board of Education of Kiryas Joel Village School District v. Grumet (1994), 454, 469
Board of Education of Westside v. Mergens (1990), 457, 463
Board of Education v. Allen (1968), 456, 458
Board of Education v. Mergens (1998), 457

Board of Regents of the University of Wisconsin v. Southworth (2000), 399
Board of Trustees of the University of Alabama v. Garrett (2000), 179
Bob Jones University v. United States (1983), 456, 466
Bond v. United States (2000), 317, 318
Booth v. Maryland (1987), 354
Boumediene v. Bush (2007), 137
Boumediene v. Bush (2008), 137
Bowers v. Hardwick, 262, 304
Bowsher v. Synar (1986), 159
Boy Scouts of America v. Dale (2000), 401
Boyde v. California (1990), 354
Bradwell v. Illinois (1873), 251, 252
Brandenburg v. Ohio (1969), 378, 379
Branzburg v. Hayes (1972), 415, 421
Braunfeld v. Brown (1961), 447, 448, 514
Bray v. Alexandria Women's Health Clinic (1993), 222
Breard v. Alexandria (1951), 419
Breedlove v. Suttles (1939), 290
Breithaupt v. Abram (1957), 326
Brendlin v. California (2007), 317, 318
Brewer v. Quarterman (2007), 355
Bridges v. California (1941), 415
Brown v. Board of Education (1954), 78, 90, 100
Brown v. Board of Education (1954–55), 470
Brown v. Board of Education (2004), 228
Brown v. Entertainment Merchants Association (2011), 424
Brown v. Louisiana (1966), 388
Brown v. Mississippi (1936), 340
Bruesewitz v. Wyeth (2011), 180
Buchanan v. Warley (1917), 219, 220
Buckley v. Valeo (1976), 395, 396, 397
Bullcoming v. New Mexico (2011), 348
Burch v. Louisiana (1979), 345
Burlington Industries Inc v. Ellerth (1998), 256
Burroughs v. United States (1934), 395
Burton v. Wilmington Parking Authority (1962), 220
Bush v. Gore (2000), 63, 71, 75, 102, 105, 267
Business, et al. v. Sebelius in 2012, 185
Butterworth v. Smith (1990), 418

C

California Federal Savings and Loan Association v. Guerra (1987), 255
California v. Acevedo (1991), 315, 317
California v. Carney (1985), 317
California v. Ciraolo (1986), 325
Cantwell v. Connecticut (1940), 280, 281, 447, 448
Carey v. Musladin (2006), 344
Carroll v. United States (1925), 315, 317
Carter v. Carter Coal Company (1936), 93, 192, 195
CBS v. Democratic National Committee (1973), 438
Chambers v. Florida (1940), 340
Champion v. Ames (1903), 192, 198
Chandler v. Florida (1981), 415, 416
Chandler v. Miller (1997), 327
Chaplinsky v. New Hampshire (1942), 401, 423, 432
Charles River Bridge Co. v. Warren Bridge Co. (1837), 187
Chavez v. Martinez (2003), 340
Chicago, Burlington & Quincy Railroad Co. v. Chicago (1897), 277, 281, 285
Chimel v. California (1969), 322, 323
Chisholm v. Georgia (1793), 14, 98, 177
Christian Legal Society Chapter of the University of California, Hastings College of Law, aka, Hastings Christian Fellowship v. Martinez (2010), 457, 465
Church of the Lukumi Babalu Aye v. City of Hialeah (1993), 448, 451, 464
Citizens United v. Federal Election Commission (2010), 96, 113, 396, 398
City of Boerne, Texas v. Flores (1997), 448, 452
City of Cuyahoga Falls v. Buckeye Community Hope Foundation (2003), 221
City of Erie v. Pap's A. M. (2000), 393
City of Indianapolis v. Edmond (2000), 319
City of Lakewood v. Plain Dealer Publishing Co. (1988), 411, 419
City of Richmond v. J.A. Croson Co. (1989), 248
Clark v. Community for Creative Non-Violence (1984), 388
Clay v. United States (1971), 447, 506
Cleburne v. Cleburne Living Center (1985), 246, 260
Clinton v. City of New York (1998), 118, 513
Clinton v. Jones (1997), 153
Cochran v. Louisiana State Board of Education (1930), 456, 506
Cohen v. California (1971), 381, 401
Coker v. Georgia (1977), 354
Cole v. Arkansas (1948), 281
Cole v. Quarterman (2007), 355
Coleman v. Alabama (1970), 350, 432

Coleman v. Court of Appeals of Maryland (2012), 179, 180
Coleman v. McLennan (1908), 432
Colgrove v. Battin (1973), 344
College Savings Bank v. Florida Prepaid Postsecondary Education Expense Bd (1999), 179
Colorado Republican CC v. Federal Election Commission (1996), 395
Colorado v. Connelly (1986), 340, 343
Committee for Public Education v. Nyquist (1973), 456
Cooley v. Board of Wardens (1851), 191
Cooley v. The Board of Wardens of the Port of Philadelphia (1851), 194
Coolidge v. New Hampshire (1971), 325
Cooper v. Aaron (1958), 226
County of Allegheny v. American Civil Liberties Union (1989), 468, 474
Cox Broadcasting v. Cohn (1975), 415, 433
Cox v. Louisiana (1965), 388
Cox v. New Hampshire (1941), 387
Coy v. Iowa (1988), 346
Craig v. Boren, 248, 253
Crawford v. Marion County Election Board (2008), 291
Crawford v. Washington (2004), 347
Curtis Publishing v. Butts (1967), 433, 435
Cutter v. Wilkinson (2005), 457, 469

D

Dames & Moore v. Regan (1981), 123
Dandridge v. Williams (1970), 264
Daniel v. Paul (1969), 200
Dartmouth College v. Woodward (1819), 187
Davis v. Federal Election Commission (2008), 396
Davis v. Mississippi (1969), 350
Davis v. United States, 314
Davis v. Washington (2005), 347
Debs v. United States (1919), 372
Deck v. Missouri (2005), 355
Defunis v. Odegaard (1974), 71
DeJonge v. Oregon (1937), 277, 281, 386, 388
Dellums v. Bush (1990), 130
Dennis v. Higgins (1991), 192
Dennis v. United States (1951), 92, 372, 376
Denver Area Edu-cational Telecommunications Consortium v. FCC (1996), 439
Dickerson v. United States (2000), 336, 340, 342
District of Columbia v. Heller (2008), 89, 282

Dixon v. Love (1977), 358
Dolan v. City of Tigard, Oregon (1994), 186
Douglas v. California (1963), 264, 350
Draper v. United States (1959), 315
Dred Scott v. Sandford (1857), 96, 173, 212, 214
Duckworth v. Eagan (1989), 340
Duncan v. Louisiana (1968), 281, 285, 344
Dunn v. Blumstein (1972), 290

E

Edwards v. Aguillard (1987), 468, 472
Edwards v. Arizona (1981), 340
Edwards v. California (1941), 263
Edwards v. S. Carolina (1963), 388
Eisenstadt v. Baird (1972), 295
Elk Grove Unified School District v. Newdow (2004), 468
Employment Division Oregon v. Smith (1990), 450
Engel v. Vitale (1962), 455, 468, 469
Epperson v. Arkansas (1968), 468, 472
Escobedo v. Illinois (1964), 340, 350
Essex v. Wolman (1972), 456
Estelle v. Williams (1976), 344
Estes v. Texas (1965), 415, 416
Evans v. Michigan (2013), 337, 338
Everson v. Board of Education (1947), 280, 281, 455, 456
Ewing v. California (2003), 353
Ex Parte Merryman (1861), 134
Ex Parte Milligan (1861), 134
Ex Parte Quirin (1942), 134

F

F.S. Royster Guano Co. v. Virginia (1920), 218
Fair Labor Standards Act (FLSA) (1938), 192
Farragher v. City of Boca Raton (1998), 256
FCC v. Fox Television Station (2009), 438, 440,
FCC v. Fox Television Station (2012), 438
Federal Communications Commission (FCC) v. League of Women Voters of Calif. (1984), 438
Federal Communications Commission (FCC) v. National Citizens Comm. for Broadcasting (1978), 438
Federal Communications Commission v. Pacifica Foundation (1978), 438
Federal Election Commission v. Beaumont (2003), 395
Federal Election Commission v. Colorado Republican CC (2001), 395

Federal Election Commission v. National Conservative PAC (1985), 395
Federal Election Commission v. Wisconsin Right to Life (2007), 396
Federal Maritime Commission v. South Carolina State Ports Authority (2002), 179
Federal Trade Commission* Act; Clayton Anti-trust Act (1914), 191
Fellers v. United States (2004), 350
Feiner v. New York (1951), 401
Ferguson v. City of Charleston (2001), 327
Ferguson v. Skrupa (1963), 190
First English Evangelical Lutheran Church of Glendale v. County of Los Angeles, 186
First National Bank of Boston v. Bellotti (1976), 398
Fiske v. Kansas (1927), 378
Flast v. Cohen (1968), 92, 203
Fletcher v. Peck (1810), 99
Flood v. Kuhn (1972), 196
Florence v. Board of the County of Burlington (2012), 361
Florence v. County of Burlington (2012), 323, 326
Florida Prepaid Postsecondary Education Expense Bd Act. v. College Savings Bank (1999), 179
Florida Star v. B. J. F. (1989), 433, 436
Florida v. Harris (2013), 310, 318
Florida v. J.L. (2000), 322
Florida v. Jardines (2013), 320
Florida v. Jimeno (1991), 324
Florida v. Nixon (2004), 350
Ford v. Wainwright (1986), 354
Frazee v. Illinois Dept. of Employment Security (1989), 447
Frohwerk v. United States (1919), 372
Frontiero v. Richardson (1973), 252, 253
Fullilove v. Klutznick (1980), 203
Furman v. Georgia (1972), 352, 354

G

Gagnon v. Scarpelli (1973), 350, 361
Gannett Company v. DePasquale (1979), 415, 417
Garcia v. San Antonio Metropolitan Transit Authority (1985), 192, 198
Garner v. Louisiana (1961), 381
Garrison v. Louisiana (1964), 433, 434
Geduldig v. Aiello (1974), 252, 255
General Electric Company v. Gilbert (1976), 255
Georgia v. Ashcroft (2003), 237

Georgia v. Randolph (2006), 325
Gertz v. Welch (1974), 433, 435, 436
Gibbons v. Ogden (1824), 170, 191, 193
Gideon v. Wainwright (1963), 281, 286, 349, 362
Gideon v. Wainwright, 375
Gillette v. United States (1971), 447
Ginzburg v. United States (1966), 422, 425
Gitlow v. New York (1925), 277, 278, 281, 378
Goldberg v. Kelly (1970), 358
Goldberg v. Sweet (1989), 192
Goldwater v. Carter (1979), 123
Gonzales v. Carhart (2007), 302
Gonzales v. O Centro Espirita Beneficente Uniao De Vegetal (2006), 448
Gonzales v. Oregon (2006), 180
Gonzalez v. Raich, 192, 201
Good News Club v. Milford Central School (2001), 457, 465
Goss v. Lopez (1975), 358
Graham v. Florida (2010), 357, 353, 359
Graham v. Richardson (1971), 258
Grand Rapids School District v. Ball (1985), 456, 461
Granholm v. Heald (2005), 192
Gratz v. Bollinger (2003), 250
Greater New Orleans Broadcasting Assoc. v. United States (1999), 392
Green v. County School Board of New Kent County (1968), 226
Gregg v. Georgia (1976), 352, 354
Gregory v. Ashcroft (1991), 180
Gregory v. City of Chicago (1969), 388
Griffin v. County School Board of Prince Edward County (1964), 226
Griffin v. Illinois (1956), 264
Griggs v. Duke Power Co. (1971), 220, 232
Griswold v. Connecticut (1965), 280, 295, 329
Grosjean v. American Press (1936), 411
Grutter v. Bollinger (2003), 250
Guinn v. United States (1915), 234
Gustafson v. Florida (1973), 323

H

Hague v. Committee for Industrial Organization (1939), 387
Halbert v. Michigan (2005), 350
Hall v. Bradshaw (1981), 468
Hamdan v. Rumsfeld (2006), 136
Hamdi v. Rumsfeld (2004), 135

Hammer v. Dagenhart (1918), 92, 96, 191, 199
Hammon v. Indiana (2005), 347
Hanlon v. Berger (1999), 329
Hannegan v. Esquire (1946), 419
Hans v. Louisiana (1890), 177, 179
Harper v. Virginia State Board of Elections (1966), 264, 290
Harris v. Alabama (1995), 354, 355
Harris v. Forklift Systems Inc. (1993), 256
Harris v. McRae (1980), 299
Harris v. New York (1971), 340, 342
Harris v. United States (1968), 325
Harte-Hanks Communications v. Connaughton (1989), 437
Hastings Christian Fellowship v. Martinez (2010), 465
Hawaii Housing Authority v. Midkiff (1984), 186
Hazelwood School District v. Kuhlmeier (1988), 411, 412
Heart of Atlanta Motel v. United States (1964), 192, 200
Heckler v. Mathews (1984), 252
Hein et.al. v. Freedom from Religion Foundation, Inc. (2007), 203, 457
Hein v. Freedom from Religion Foundation (2007), 203
Helling v. McKinney (1993), 353
Helvering v. Davis (1937), 203
Henry v. United States (1959), 311
Hepburn v. Griswold (1870), 96
Herbert v. Lando (1979), 433, 435
Herndon v. Lowry (1937), 378
Herring v. United States (2008), 313, 314,
Hildwin v. Florida (1989), 354, 355
Hill v. Colorado (2000), 389
Hipolite Egg Co. v. United States (1911), 191
Hirabayashi v. United States (1943), 126, 244
Hoffa v. United States (1966), 329
Hoke v. United States (1913), 191
Hollingsworth v. Perry, 262,
Holmes v. United States (1968), 129
Home Building & Loan Association v. Blaisdell (1934), 187
Hosanna-Tabor Evangelical Lutheran Church and School v. Equal Employment Opportunity Commission, et al. (2012), 457, 459,
Houchins v. KQED Inc. (1978), 419
Houston, East & West Texas Railway Co. v. United States (1914), 194

Houston, East & West Texas Railway Co. v. United States (1914), 194
Howes v. Fields (2012), 340, 342
Hudgens v. National Labor Relations Board (1976), 385, 386
Hudson Gas & Electric Corp. v. Public Service Commission (1980), 390
Hudson v. McMillian (1992), 353
Hudson v. Michigan (2006), 313, 316
Hughes v. Superior Ct. of Calif. (1950), 385
Humphrey's Executor v. United States (1935), 120
Hunt v. Cromartie (1999), 238
Hunt v. Cromartie (2001), 238
Hunt v. McNair (1973), 456
Hurley v. Irish-American Gay Group of Boston (1995), 400
Hurtado v. California (1884), 276, 277
Hustler v. Falwell (1988), 436
Hylton v. United States (1796), 98, 202

I

Idaho v. Coeur d'Alene Tribe of Idaho (1997), 179
Illinois v. Caballes (2005), 317, 318
Illinois v. Gates (1983), 310
Illinois v. Lidster (2004), 319
Illinois v. Perkins (1990), 340, 341
Illinois v. Rodriguez (1990), 325
Illinois v. Wardlow (2000), 322
In re Debs (1895), 191, 196
In re Gault (1967), 359
In re Oliver (1948), 281, 343
In re Pappas, 421
Ingraham v. Wright (1977), 353
International Union, UAW v. Johnson Controls, Inc. (1991), 255
Irwin v. Dowd (1961), 414, 415

J

J.D.B. v. North Carolina (2011), 340,
J.E.B. v. Alabama ex rel T.B. (1994), 346
Jacobellis v. Ohio (1964), 425
Jacobson v. Massachusetts (1905), 447, 448
Jenkins v. Georgia (1974), 422
Jimmy Swaggart Ministries v. Board of Equalization of California (1990), 457, 467
Johnson v. California (2005), 244, 345
Johnson v. Eisentrager (1950), 135
Johnson v. Louisiana (1972), 345

Johnson v. Santa Clara County (1987), 252
Jones v. Alfred H. Mayer Co. (1969), 221
Jones v. Opelika (1942), 449
Jurek v. Texas, 354

K

Kansas v. Crane (2002), 361
Kansas v. Hendricks (1997), 360
Kansas v. Marsh (2006), 355
Katz v. United States (1967), 328
Katz v. United States, 308
Katzenbach v. McClung (1964), 192, 200
Kaupp v. Texas (2003), 340
Kawananakoa v. Polyfolank (1907), 178
Kelo v. City of New London (2005), 186
Kennedy v. Louisiana (2008), 355
Kentucky v. King (2011), 320
Kilbourn v. Thompson (1881), 147
Kimel v. Florida Board of Regents (2000), 179
Kirby v. Illinois (1972), 350
Kitzmiller v. Dover Area School District (2005), 473
Klopfer v. North Carolina (1967), 281, 343
Knowles v. Iowa (1998), 323, 324
Knox v. Lee (1871), 96
Korematsu v. United States (1944), 126, 244
Kramer v. Union Free School District No. 15 (1969), 290
Kurns v. Railroad Friction Products Corp, 180
Kyllo v. United States (2001), 331

L

Lakewood v. Plain Dealer Publishing (1988), 411, 419
Lamb's Chapel v. Center Moriches Free Union School District (1993), 457, 460
Lapides v. Board of Regents of the University System of Georgia (2002), 179
Lapides v. Board of Regents of Univ. System of Georgia (2002*), 179
Lassiter v. Northampton County Board of Elections (1959), 234
Lawrence v. Texas, 262, 303, 304, 305
Ledbetter v. Goodyear Tire and Rubber Co. (2007), 255
Lee v. Weisman (1992), 468, 471
Lemon v. Kurtzman (1971), 456, 458, 473
Lewis v. United States (1980), 281
Lindsley v. Natural Carbonic Gas Co. (1911), 218

Lloyd Corp. v. Tanner (1972), 385, 388
Local Plumbers Union #10 v. Graham (1953), 385
Lochner v. New York (1905), 92, 189
Locke v. Davey (2004), 448, 464
Lockyer v. Andrade (2003), 353
Lorance v. AT & T Technologies (1991), 255
Lorillard Tobacco v. Reilly (2001), 391, 392
Lovell v. Griffin (1938), 411
Loving v. Virginia (1967), 245
Lynch v. Donnelly (1984), 468, 474

M

Mack v. United States (1997), 192, 204
Madsen v. Women's Health Center (1994), 388, 389
Maher v. Roe, 298, 299
Malloy v. Hogan (1964), 281, 285
Manual Enterprises v. Day (1962), 422, 425
Mapp v. Ohio (1961), 92, 281, 284, 313, 314, 333
Mapp v. Ohio, 308, 375
Mara v. McNamara (1967), 129
Marbury v. Madison (1803), 60, 71, 86, 91, 94, 95, 96, 98, 99, 452
Marsh v. Alabama (1946), 385
Marsh v. Chambers (1983), 468
Martin v. Hunter's Lessee (1824), 61, 98
Martin v. Mott, 71
Martin v. Struthers (1943), 419
Maryland v. Buie (1990), 323
Maryland v. Craig (1990), 346
Maryland v. King (2013), 323,
Maryland v. Pringle (2003), 310, 317
Maryland v. Shatzer (2010), 340, 342
Maryland v. Wilson (1997), 323
Mass. v. Feeney (1979), 252
Massachusetts Board of Retirement v. Murgia (1976), 257
Massachusetts v. Laird (1970), 129
Massiah v. United States (1964), 350
Masson v. New Yorker (1991), 433
Matthews v. Eldridge (1976), 358
McCleskey v. Kemp (1987), 354, 356
McCollum v. Board of Education (1948), 467, 468
McConnell v. Federal Election Commission (2003), 395, 398
McCray v. United States (1904), 203
McCreary County v. American Civil Liberties Union (2005), 468, 475
McCulloch v. Maryland (1819), 86, 170

McDonald v. City of Chicago (2008), 282
McDonald v. City of Chicago (2010), 281
McGrain v. Daugherty (1927), 147
McKoy v. North Carolina (1990), 354
Meadows v. Moon (1997), 238
Medellin v. Texas (2008), 355
Meek v. Pittenger (1975), 456
Melendez-Diaz v. Massachusetts (2009), 348
Memoirs of a Woman of Pleasure v. Massachusetts (1966), 422, 425
Meritor Savings Bank v. Vinson (1986), 252, 256
Metro Broadcasting Inc. v. Federal Communications Commission (1990), 249
Michael M. v. Superior Court of Sonoma County (1981), 252
Michigan Dept. of State Police v. Sitz (1990), 319
Michigan v. Bryant (2011), 348
Michigan v. Summers (1981), 312
Milkovich v. Lorain Journal (1990), 433, 437
Miller v. Alabama (2012), 354, 359
Miller v. California (1973), 422, 427
Miller v. Johnson (1995), 238
Miller-El v. Dretke (2005), 345
Milliken v. Bradley (1974), 220, 227
Mills v. Alabama (1966), 411, 419
Minersville School District v. Gobitis (1940), 366, 448, 449
Minnesota v. Carter (1998), 329
Minor v. Happersatt (1875), 251, 252
Miranda v. Arizona (1966), 336, 341, 350, 340, 362, 375
Mishkin v. New York (1966), 426
Mississippi University for Women v. Hogan (1982), 252, 254
Missouri v. Frye (2012), 351
Missouri v. Holland (1920), 121
Missouri v. McNeely (2013), 326
Mitchell v. Helms (2000), 457, 461, 465
Mitchell v. United States (1967), 129
Mobile v. Bolden (1980), 236
Moose Lodge No. 107 v. Irvis (1972), 220
Morrison v. Olson (1990), 329
Morrissey v. Brewer (1972), 361
Morse v. Frederick (2007), 381, 384
Muehler v. Mena (2005), 312
Mueller v. Allen (1983), 456, 460
Mulford v. Smith (1939), 96, 203
Mulford v. Smith (1939), 96

Muller v. Oregon (1908), 190, 252
Munn v. Illinois (1877), 189
Murray v. Curlett (1963), 455, 470
Myers v. United States (1926), 119

N

National Endowment for the Arts v. Finley (1998), 428
National Federation of Independent Business, et al. v. Sebelius (2012), 192, 201, 204,
National Labor Relations Board v. Jones & Laughlin Steel Corporation (1937), 197
National League of Cities v. Usery (1976), 192, 198
National Meat Association v. Harris, 180
National Organization for Women v. Scheidler (1994), 389
National Treasury Employees Union v. Von Raab (1989), 326
Near v. Minnesota (1931), 277, 279, 281, 410, 411, 439
Nebbia v. New York (1934), 190
Nebraska Press Association v. Stuart (1976), 415, 417
Nevada Department of Human Resources v. Hibbs (2003), 177, 179,
New Jersey v. T.L.O. (1985), 332
New York Times v. Sullivan (1964), 390, 432, 433, 434
New York Times v. United States (1971), 63, 406, 411, 413, 417, 439
New York v. Belton (1981), 314, 323
New York v. Ferber (1982), 422, 429
New York v. Miln (1837), 191
New York v. Quarles (1984), 340
New York v. United States (1992), 204
Newbury v. United States (1921), 395
Nix v. Williams (1984), 313
Nixon v. Fitzgerald (1982), 178
Nixon v. Shrink Mo. Gov't PAC (2000), 395
NLRB v. Jones & Laughlin Steel Corporation (1937), 93, 96, 192
Noel Canning v. NLRB (12-1115, 12-1153), 120
North Carolina v. Pearce (1969), 338
Northern Securities Company v. United States (1904), 78, 191, 196

O

O'Connor v. Donaldson (1975), 360
Ohio v. Robinette (1996), 324
Oklahoma Press Pub. Co. v. Walling (1946), 419

Olmstead v. United States (1928), 294, 328
Oncale v. Sundowner Offshore Services (1998), 256
Oregon v. Hass (1975), 340
Oregon v. Smith (1990), 447, 451
Organization for a Better Austin v. Keefe (1971), 411
Ornelas v. United States (1996), 310
Osborne v. Ohio (1990), 422, 426

P

Padilla v. Kentucky (2010), 351
Palko v. Connecticut (1937), 277, 279, 306
Panetti v. Quarterman (2007), 355
Parents Involved in Community Schools v. Seattle School District No. 1 (2007), 83, 220, 228, 231
Paris Adult Theatre v. Slaton (1973), 427
Parker v. Gladden (1966), 281
Passenger Cases (1849), 292
Patterson v. McLean Credit Union (1989), 222, 232
Payne v. Tennessee (1991), 354, 357
Pennsylvania v. Mimms (1977), 323
Pennsylvania v. Muniz (1990), 339
Penry v. Johnson (2001), 355
Penry v. Lynaugh (1989), 354, 357
People v. DeFore (1926), 313
Personnel Administrator of Massachusetts v. Feeney (1979), 255
Peters v. New York, 321
Phila. Newspapers v. Hepps (1986), 433, 436
Philadelphia Newspapers, Inc. v. Hepps, 436
Pierce v. Society of Sisters (1925), 447, 448
Pierce v. United States (1920), 372, 374
Pipefitters v. United States (1972), 395
Planned Parenthood of Central Missouri v. Danforth (1976), 501
Planned Parenthood v. Casey (1992), 301
Pleasant Grove City, Utah, et al. v. Summum (2009), 468, 475
Plessy v. Ferguson (1896), 101, 215
PLIVA, Inc. v. Mensing, et al. (2011), 180
Plyler v. Doe (1982), 246, 258
Pointer v. Texas (1965), 281, 286, 346
Pollock. v. Farmers' Loan and Trust Co. (1895), 96, 202
Porter v. McCollom (2010), 351
Powell v. Alabama (1932), 277, 278, 348
Powell v. McCormack (1969), 71
Presley v. Georgia (2010), 344
Press-Enterprise v. Superior Ct of California, 415, 417
Prigg v. Pennsylvania (1842), 214
Printz v. United States (1997), 192, 204
Proffitt v. Florida, 354
PruneYard Shopping Ctr. v. Robins (1980), 385

R

R.A.V. v. City of St. Paul (1992), 402
Randall v. Sorrell (2006), 395
Rasul v. Bush (2004), 135
Red Lion Broadcasting v. Federal Communications Commission (FCC) (1969), 438
Reed v. Reed (1971), 252, 253
Regents of the University of California v. Bakke (1978), 247
Regina v. Hicklin (1868), 422
Reid v. Georgia (1980), 321
Reno v. American Civil Liberties Union (1997), 429, 430
Reno v. Condon (2000), 201
Reynolds v. Sims (1964), 92, 101, 289
Reynolds v. United States (1878), 446, 447
Rhode Island v. Innis (1980), 340
Richards v. Wisconsin (1997), 316
Richardson v. Ramirez (1974), 291
Richmond Newspapers v. Virginia (1980), 415, 417
Ring v. Arizona (2002), 355
Robbins v. California (1981), 317
Roberts v. Louisiana (1976), 354
Robinson v. California (1962), 281, 286
Rochin v. California, 92, 313, 326
Roe v. Wade (1973), 296
Roemer v. Maryland Public Works Board (1976), 456
Romer v. Evans (1996), 261
Rompilla v. Beard (2005), 350
Roper v. Simmons (2005), 355, 357, 359
Rosenberger v. Rector and visitors of the University of Virginia (1995), 457, 464
Rosenblatt v. Baer (1966), 433
Ross v. Moffitt (1974), 350
Roth v. United States (1957), 423
Rubin v. Coors Brewing Company (1995), 391
Rumsfeld et al. v. Padilla (2004), 135
Runyon v. McCrary (1976), 222
Rust v. Sullivan (1991), 299

S

Sable Communications of California, Inc. v. F.C.C., 428
Saenz v. Roe (1999), 293

Salazar, Secretary of the Interior v. Buono (2010), 468, 476
Samson v. California (2006), 325
San Antonio School District v. Rodriguez (1973), 246, 265, 266
San Antonio v. Rodriguez, 272
Santa Clara County v. Southern Pacific Railroad (1886), 189, 277
Santa Fe Independent School District v. Doe (2000), 468, 472
Sattazahn v. Pennsylvania (2003), 337
Schaefer v. United States (1920), 372
Schechter Poultry Corp. v. United States (1935), 93, 96, 191, 195
Schenck v. Pro-Choice Network of Western New York (1997), 388, 389
Schenck v. U.S. (1919), 372, 373
Schick v. Reed (1974), 121
Schmerber v. California (1966), 326
Schneckloth v. Bustamonte (1973), 324
Schneider v. Irvington (1939), 391, 411
Scopes v. State of Tennessee (1925), 472
Scott v. Illinois (1979), 349
Sears v. Upton (2010), 351
Segura v. United States (1984), 313
Selman v. Cobb County School District (2005), 473
Seminole Tribe v. Florida (1996), 179
Shafer v. South Carolina (2001), 355
Shapiro v. Thompson (1969), 292
Shaw v. Hunt (1996) (Shaw II), 238
Shaw v. Reno (1993) (Shaw I), 238
Shelley v. Kraemer (1948), 220, 249
Sheppard v. Maxwell (1966), 414, 415
Sherbert v. Verner (1963), 447, 450
Sherman Anti-trust Act (1890), 191
Shreveport Rate Cases, 191, 194, 195
Sibron v. New York, 321
Silkwood v. Kerr-McGee (1984), 180
Simon & Schuster v. New York State Crime Victims Bd (1991), 411, 419
Skinner v. Oklahoma (1942), 243, 287
Skinner v. Railway Labor Executives' Association (1989), 326
Smith v. Allwright (1944), 221, 235
Smith v. Daily Mail Publishing Company (1979), 415
Smith v. Goguen (1974), 381
Smith v. Hooey (1969), 343
Snepp v. United States (1980), 411, 414

Snyder v. Louisiana (2008), 346
Snyder v. Phelps (2011), 388
Snyder v. Phelps, 403
Sossamon v. Texas (2011), 179,
South Carolina v. Gathers (1989), 354
South Carolina v. Katzenbach (1966), 235
South Dakota v. Dole Department of Transportation (1987), 203
Spano v. New York (1959), 336, 340, 341,
Spector v. Norwegian Cruise Line (2005), 261
Spence v. Washington (1974), 381
Springer v. United States (1881), 202
Stack v. Boyle (1951), 351
Standard Oil v. United States (1911), 191, 196
Stanford v. Kentucky (1989), 354, 356
Stanley v. Georgia (1969), 422, 425, 426
States v. Santana (1976), 319
Stenberg v. Carhart (2000), 300
Steward Machine Co. v. Davis (1937), 203
Stone v. Graham (1980), 468, 475
Stone v. Powell (1976), 315
Stop the Beach Renourishment, Inc. v. Florida Department of Environmental Protection, 186
Strauder v. West Virginia (1880), 216
Street v. New York (1969), 381, 383
Strickland v. Washington (1984), 350
Stromberg v. California (1931), 380
Swann v. Charlotte-Mecklenburg Board of Education (1971), 220, 225
Sweatt v. Painter (1950), 220, 223
Swift and Co. v. United States (1905), 191, 196
Symm v. United States (1979), 291

T

Tahoe-Sierra Preservation Council, Inc. v. Tahoe Regional Planning Agency (2002), 186,
Talley v. California (1960), 411
Tennessee v. Lane (2004), 261
Terminiello v. Chicago (1949), 401
Terry v. Ohio (1968), 308, 320, 321
Texas Monthly, Inc. v. Bullock (1989), 457, 466
Texas v. Johnson (1989), 381, 383, 404
Texas v. White (1869), 174
The Slaughterhouse Cases (1873), 188, 215, 243, 276, 277
Thompson v. Oklahoma (1988), 354, 356
Thornhill v. Alabama (1940), 385
Tilton v. Richardson (1971), 456
Time Inc. v. Firestone, 433

Time Inc. v. Hill (1967), 433
Tinker v. Des Moines Independent Community School District, (1969), 381, 382, 384
Tinker v. Des Moines Independent School District, 375, 412
Torcaso v. Watkins (1961), 447
Troxel v. Granville (2000), 305
Turner Broad Casting v. FCC (1994), 438
Turner Broadcasting System v. FCC (1997), 439
Turner v. Rogers (2011), 350
Twining v. New Jersey (1908), 277, 278

U

U.S. v. Darby (1941), 192, 197, 199
U.S. v. Morrison (2000), 192
U.S. v. Wade (1967), 350
United Haulers Assn v. Oneida-Herkimer Solid Waste Mgt Authority (2007), 192
United States Postal Service v. Flamingo Industries (USA) LTD (2004), 196
United States v. $405,089.23 (1996), 337
United States v. Alvarez (2012), 403
United States v. American Library Association (2003), 430
United States v. Arvizu (2002), 318
United States v. Ash (1973), 350
United States v. Ballard (1944), 447
United States v. Belmont (1937), 122
United States v. Butler (1936), 92, 93, 96, 203
United States v. Calandra (1974), 313, 314
United States v. Caldwell, 421
United States v. Carolene Products Co. (1938), 243, 287
United States v. Chadwick (1977), 317
United States v. Classic (1941), 395
United States v. Comstock (2010), 361
United States v. Curtiss-Wright Export Corporation (1936), 125
United States v. Darby Lumber (1941), 96
United States v. Drayton, 324
United States v. E. C. Knight Co. (1895), 191, 195
United States v. Eichmann (1990), 381, 383
United States v. Gonzalez-Lopez (2005), 351
United States v. Grubbs (2006), 312
United States v. Guest (1966), 292
United States v. Janis (1976), 314
United States v. Jones (2012), 308, 320, 329
United States v. Jorn (1971), 338

United States v. Knights (2001), 325
United States v. Knotts (1983), 329
United States v. Leon (1984), 313, 314
United States v. Lopez (1995), 192, 200
United States v. Martin Linen Supply Co (1977), 338
United States v. Martinez-Fuerte (1976), 318
United States v. Miller (1939), 281
United States v. Morrison (2000), 192, 201, 252, 254
United States v. Nixon (1974), 63, 78, 150, 151, 152
United States v. O'Brien (1968), 381, 382
United States v. Ortiz (1975), 318
United States v. Peltier (1975), 314
United States v. Pink (1942), 122
United States v. Playboy Entertainment Group, Inc. (2000), 438, 439
United States v. Rabinowitz (1950), 323
United States v. Robinson (1973), 323
United States v. Ross (1982), 315, 317
United States v. Salerno (1987), 351
United States v. Scott (1975), 338
United States v. Seeger (1965), 447, 454
United States v. Sokolow (1989), 321
United States v. Stevens (2010), 424
United States v. Tinklenberg (2011), 343
United States v. United Foods (2001), 392
United States v. Ursery (1996), 337
United States v. Virginia (1996), 252, 254
United States v. Wade (1967), 350
United States v. Williams, 431
United States v. Windsor, 167, 262
United States v. Wong Kim Ark (1898), 188
United States v. X-Citement Video, Inc. (1994), 429

V

Valentine v. Chrestensen (1942), 390, 391
Van Orden v. Perry (2005), 468, 475
Vance v. Bradley (1979), 258
Vernonia School District 47J v. Acton (1995), 327
Virginia Office for Protection and Advo-cacy v. Stewart (2011), 179,
Virginia State Board of Pharmacy v. Virginia Citizens Consumer Council (1976), 390, 391
Virginia v. Black (2003), 402
Virginia v. Moore (2008), 324

W

Wallace v. Jaffree (1985), 468, 471
Walton v. Arizona (1990), 354, 355

Walz v. Tax Commission of City of New York (1970), 456, 463, 466
Warden v. Hayden (1967), 319
Wards Cove Packing Co. v. Atonio (1989), 220, 232
Washington v. Davis (1976), 233
Washington v. Texas (1967), 281, 286
Watkins v. United States (1957), 148
Watters v. Wachovia Bank (2007), 180
Webster v. Reproductive Health Services (1989), 301
Weeks v. Angelone (2000), 354
Weeks v. United States (1914), 283, 313, 323
Weems v. United States (1910), 353
Welsh v. United States (1970), 447
West Coast Hotel Company v. Parrish (1937), 93, 190, 205
West Virginia State Board of Education v. Barnette (1943), 91, 380, 381, 399, 447, 449
Whitney v. Calif (1927), 378
Whren and Brown v. United States (1996), 323
Wickard v. Filburn (1942), 197, 192, 201
Widmar v. Vincent (1981), 456, 463
Wiggins v. Smith (2003), 350
Wilkins v. Gaddy (2010), 353
Wilkins v. Missouri (1989), 354, 356
Wilkinson v. Austin (2005), 362
Williams v. Florida (1970), 344
Williams v. North Carolina (1945), 167
Williams v. Rhodes (1968), 291

Williams v. Taylor (1986), 344
Willson v. Black Bird Creek Marsh Co. (1829), 191
Wilson v. Arkansas (1995), 316
Wilson v. Layne (1999), 329
Winston v. Lee (1985), 326
Winters v. New York (1948), 419
Wisconsin v. Yoder (1972), 447, 452, 453
Witters v. Washington Department of Services for Blind (1986), 456, 460
Wolf v. Colorado (1949), 281, 283, 313
Wolff v. McDonnell (1974), 361
Wolman v. Walter (1977), 456
Woodson v. North Carolina (1976), 354
Wooley v. Maynard (1977), 399
Wyman v. James (1971), 332
Wyoming v. Houghton (1999), 316, 317
Wyoming v. Oklahoma (1992), 192

Y

Yarborough v. Gentry (2003), 350
Yates v. United States (1957), 372, 377
Yick Wo v. Hopkins (1886), 216
Youngstown Sheet & Tube Co. v. Sawyer (1952), 63, 128

Z

Zelman v. Simmons-Harris (2002), 457, 460, 462
Zobrest v. Catalina School District, 457, 460
Zorach v. Clausen (1952), 455, 467, 468
Zurcher v. Stanford Daily (1978), 415

Preface To The Ninth Edition

The eighth edition of *Constitutional Government: The American Experience* comes twenty-five years after publication of the first edition. Throughout these years, the eight editions of this text have chronicled significant developments in the Constitution and in our nation's political system.

There are two noteworthy changes to the 8th edition. The first is the absence of one of our original co-authors. Dr. Richard B. Riley made the well-earned decision to retire from university life and also from the role of textbook author. We already miss him greatly, especially as we have been forced to assume his very sizable responsibilities. We dedicate this edition to Rich, and we hope that we have been faithful to his high standards. The second is the inauguration of *Constitutional Government* as an e-book, allowing readers to select between the traditional hard copy version and a new electronic one. We are excited about the possibilities.

The web-based component unveiled for the seventh edition has proven so successful that it continues to be part of the current edition. We have incorporated suggestions from colleagues and students to improve the web component in various ways. We believe that the electronic component adds a significant dimension to the study of American constitutional development that will be helpful to teachers and students alike.

The study of American constitutional government traditionally has been addressed in a number of different ways, ranging from detailed historical analysis to the highly legalistic casebook approach. While these approaches provide certain advantages in accounting for the development of constitutionalism in America, each by itself leaves something of the story untold. We believe that a combined emphasis upon history, politics, and law offers a productive format for examining the growth and development of the United States Constitution.

A few explanations to the reader about appendices are appropriate. First, to minimize having to document cases throughout the book, we have included a case index which lists all cases discussed in the text. In most instances, the citation refers to *United States Reports*, the official publication of decisions of the United States Supreme Court. In a few instances, commercial reporting systems are used to refer to very recent Supreme Court cases or those at the lower federal court level (e.g., *Supreme Court Reporter* or the *Federal Supplement*). Other appendices include the Constitution of the United States and a general subject index.

A project of this magnitude clearly would not be possible without the assistance and support of many people. Thanks to Betsy Ritz who provided the excellent photographs used to introduce each chapter. To our colleagues who have offered encouragement and helpful advice, we are especially indebted. Finally, to the several graduate and undergraduate students who have both served as sounding boards for our ideas in the classroom and helped with various research steps in the project, we express our thanks.

A project of this magnitude invariably requires sacrifices to be made, and large amounts of time must be spent away from home and family. This project was no exception, and, as a result, we are especially thankful to our wives, Kay and Betsy, for their patience, understanding, and continued support. This book certainly would not have been possible without them. And finally, of course, we say thank you and happy retirement to Rich Riley.

J.A.C.   R.M.B.

Part 1

THE CONSTITUTIONAL TEXT AND CONTEXT

American constitutionalism exists and flourishes within a rich historical and intellectual context. Constitutionalism in America first appeared in a rudimentary form in the seventeenth century and developed until the writing of the U.S. Constitution in 1787. The two chapters in Part 1 explore the texts and contexts of American constitutionalism. Chapter 1 introduces the subject by examining the underlying principles of constitutional government and by comparing the world's constitutions for insight into these basic principles. It goes on to delineate the two theoretical approaches to government at the heart of American Constitutionalism—individualism and communitarianism—and discusses the various historical and intellectual influences on eighteenth-century American constitutionalists. Chapter 2 chronicles the history of the founding period in American constitutionalism. It begins by addressing the major constitutional concerns of the American revolutionaries in the 1760s and 1770s and concludes with an examination of the Constitutional Convention in Philadelphia in 1787 and the document drafted there. These two chapters detail the basic themes of American constitutionalism that form the basis of the specific discussions in Parts 2 and 3.

CHAPTER 1

The Principles and Origins of American Constitutionalism

OVER TWO HUNDRED YEARS AFTER AMERICANS FIRST PUT PEN TO PAPER IN PHILADELPHIA, CONSTITUTION WRITING HAS BECOME AN INTERNATIONAL PRACTICE. AMERICAN CONSTITUTIONALISM DREW UPON A DIVERSE ARRAY OF THEORETICAL SOURCES, FROM ANCIENT THINKERS LIKE ARISTOTLE AND CICERO TO MORE MODERN IDEAS FOUND IN WRITERS LIKE LOCKE, ROUSSEAU, AND PAYNE. (PHOTOGRAPHED WITH THE COURTESY OF INDEPENDENCE NATIONAL HISTORICAL PARK.)

▼ An Introductory Conversation between John Locke and Jean-Jacques Rousseau

Background: John Locke (1632–1704) and Jean-Jacques Rousseau (1712–1778) not only were great thinkers in the history of political thought, but also influential figures in the origins of American constitutionalism. American revolutionaries of the eighteenth century extensively cited Locke in making their arguments against continued British rule, and parts of his *Second Treatise on Government* made their way almost word for word into the Declaration of Independence. Members of the founding generation such as Thomas Jefferson also were influenced by, and cited, Rousseau, particularly his arguments in *On the Social Contract*. Each author represents one of the twin pillars of American constitutionalism discussed in this chapter: Locke's thinking exemplifies the individualist strain in American political thought, whereas Rousseau's political ideas reflect a more communitarian emphasis. Their dialogue serves as a fitting introduction to the more theoretical treatment of constitutionalism found in this chapter.

John Locke: My good fellow Jean-Jacques, I am sure you have been following the ongoing debate in U.S. politics about the proper role of government in people's lives. I think you will agree that any discussion of the underlying principles of a political constitution and the proper role of government must begin with an understanding of human nature, of the condition in which individual human beings find themselves prior to the existence of society or government.

Jean-Jacques Rousseau: Yes, John, both you and I write about human beings in a hypothetical "state of nature," as a precursor to a discussion of the conditions under which individuals would be motivated to join in a **social contract** and subject themselves to political rule under government.

JL: I believe that nature invests persons with equal rights (the most fundamental of these being life, liberty, and property) and with "a perfect freedom to order their actions as they think fit, within the bounds of the Law of Nature." Each person can know and interpret the commands of natural law, the primary principle of which is "that being all equal and independent, no one ought to harm another in his Life, Health, Liberty, or Possessions." Still, free individuals pursuing their private interests are bound to come into conflict, and without some external mediator and judge, will find their rights in some jeopardy. So, government may not be intrinsically necessary to human development, but it does become necessary to mediate conflicts between individuals attempting to protect their property and to pursue their private interests. However, because individuals ought to be able to fully exercise their rights so long as such exercise brings no injury to others, government must be limited in its scope and functions.

JJR: Here's where we begin to disagree, *mon ami*. Like you, I assert that the individual in the state of nature is endowed with freedom and equality. But unlike you, I believe that people have a natural dependence on others. Because of this dependence, the political community is necessary to fulfill inherent human needs; it does not exist simply to adjudicate conflict and protect private interests. "For if the opposition of private interests made necessary the establishment of societies, it is the agreement of these same interests that made it possible." My goal was to set up a legitimate government in the face of both the natural freedom and the social needs of individuals. "[T]he fundamental problem" is to "find a form of association which defends and protects with all common forces the person and goods of each associate, and by means of which each one, while uniting with all, nevertheless obeys only himself and remains as free as before." For me, the method by which individuals can be brought together into political community without sacrificing their natural freedom and equality is what I called "the social contract."

JL: Your "social contract" makes me very nervous. I might agree that individuals "contract" with government to perform certain legislative, administrative, and judicial functions that they cannot provide for themselves. But the purpose of government is to secure individual rights and liberties, and it cannot exercise power beyond this purpose. At one point in your writing, you say that your social contract "entails the commitment" that if the majority decides on a policy with which individuals in the minority disagree, these individuals will be "forced to obey the general will;" they will be, to use your phrase, "forced to be free." This not only seems like an oxymoron, but also helps me understand how your ideas could influence someone like Robespierre and could so easily lead to the guillotine!

JJR: This isn't fair at all, my dear Locke. The key to understanding this phrase, and my entire political philosophy, is to ask, who, really, is doing the forcing? In my social contract, individuals agree to obey a government, but one in which the people themselves make the laws governing them; the only legitimate government is a democracy, where the people directly decide the rules and procedures governing their lives. This is the only way truly to secure one's freedom, "[f]or to be driven by appetite alone is slavery, and obedience to the law one has prescribed for oneself is liberty." You English with your representative government think you are free, but you are sadly mistaken. You are free "only during the election of the members of Parliament. Once they are elected, the populace is enslaved; it is nothing. The use the English people makes of that freedom in its brief moments of liberty certainly warrants their losing it."

JL: Now it is you, Rousseau, who are being unfair. In my social contract, individuals entrust government and its representatives with power. They consent to obey their rules. But when government abuses its power and goes against the people's interests or abuses their rights, the people have a right to resist. As I said in my *Second Treatise of Government*, "if a long train of abuses, prevarications, and artifices, all tending the same way, make the design visible to the people, and they cannot but feel, what they lie under, and see, whither they are going . . . they should then rouze themselves, and endeavor to put the rule into such hands, which may secure to them the ends for which government was at first erected." Under these circumstances, I would grant citizens the right to overthrow an oppressive government and to establish a new one in its place, a principle that guided the American colonists at the time of their revolution.

JJR: I can see that we may never agree on the proper role of government in people's lives. But it is clear that our different perspectives on human nature and the proper role of government lead out into different principles on how to constitute "we the people" and provide for legitimate political rule. It is always interesting to me to see how different peoples or nations, including our American friends, create their own fundamental "social contract" and constitutional systems, which is the subject of Chapter 1.

SOURCES: John Locke, *Two Treatises of Government* (Cambridge, UK: Cambridge University Press, 1960); Jean-Jacques Rousseau, *On the Social Contract* (Indianapolis, IN: Hackett, 1987); Jean-Jacques Rousseau, *The Government of Poland* (Indianapolis, IN: Bobbs-Merrill, 1972).

Introduction: The Basic Theory of Constitutionalism

On the morning of Tuesday, September 11, 2001, nineteen hijackers flew commercial airplanes into the twin towers of New York City's World Trade Center and the Pentagon in Virginia. A fourth plane crashed in Pennsylvania. That evening, President George W. Bush addressed the nation, proclaiming that America was targeted for attack "because we're the brightest beacon for freedom and opportunity in the world." The following day the president stated: "Freedom and democracy are under attack.... This enemy attacked not just our people, but all freedom-loving people everywhere in the world."

Over a decade later, the events of September 11 continue to dominate the thinking of many Americans and certainly the daily actions of the U.S. government. Whether the United States was attacked *because* of our constitutional democracy or not, international terrorism and government's response to its threat raise serious questions about freedom, democracy, and the rule of law. In the aftermath of "9/11," it is safe to conclude that many of the basic principles of U.S. constitutional government will be challenged by the government's need to protect citizens in a time of crisis. The constitutional changes and tensions resulting from the events of September 11 are discussed throughout this textbook. But before we can understand what has shifted, Americans must first appreciate the Constitution itself, by reflecting on and analyzing its principles, its content, and its contemporary meaning. The text that follows attempts to illuminate the American constitutional experience.

American constitutionalism must take into account historical, legal, and political factors that have played pivotal roles in forming a long-standing relationship between the American government and its people. The central focus, of course, must be the federal Constitution of 1787 and that document's impact on American political institutions and processes; however, an understanding of American constitutionalism is not possible by limiting inquiry solely to the written constitution. While it is difficult to overrate the significance of the 1787 Constitution, it is similarly difficult to ignore the changes the document has undergone since its drafting. Accordingly, the study of American constitutional development must consider the theory underlying the written constitution along with the practices of government that have evolved over time. In the proceeding chapters, attention is given to both the theory and practice of the American constitutional experience.

In the broadest sense, a constitution refers to a framework providing basic principles of organization and operation. In government, a constitution describes the arrangement of political and governmental institutions and the powers and functions assigned to them. The American Constitution, for example, is organized around creating and defining the powers of the major branches of government, beginning with the legislative branch in Article I, and moving to the executive and judiciary in the following articles. Yet, the American Constitution has come to be recognized as far more than just a descriptive treatment of American government; it has risen to the level of a powerful symbol to which generations of citizens defer and give allegiance. The manner in which the constitution accomplishes its roles as organizational framework and national symbol can be termed **constitutionalism**. The discussion now turns to that concept.

The distinction between a "constitution" and "constitutionalism" is more than a simple exercise in semantics. The world is full of countries with written constitutions, but relatively few possess constitutional governments. The reason for this is that constitutionalism requires a government limited in its power and accountable for its actions. In short, constitutionalism, in addition to providing the theory underlying a constitution, must include an effective limitation on governmental power.

As constitutional scholars have noted, constitutionalism is tied to a suspicion and distrust of power in general and to the concentration of power in particular. Writing in an earlier time, Englishman Lord Acton noted that "all power tends to corrupt, and absolute power corrupts absolutely."[1] Lord Acton's observation would certainly find no shortage of adherents among today's advocates of constitutionalism, although the agreement would begin to fade when the search for an acceptable solution to the problem were begun. On the one hand, it is easy to see how power in government can become concentrated and, perhaps, abused, but it is quite another thing to conclude that power should never be handed over to our leaders because of the dangers involved. In fact, for proponents of constitutionalism, Lord

Acton's statement lays the basis for a real dilemma. How is it possible to avoid the pitfalls of an overly powerful and potentially irresponsible government while at the same time providing government leaders and institutions with the ability to solve society's problems? James Madison, a key founder of the American constitutional system, recognized the dilemma of modern constitutional government in *Federalist No. 51*:

> IN FRAMING A GOVERNMENT WHICH IS TO BE ADMINISTERED BY MEN OVER MEN, THE GREAT DIFFICULTY LIES IN THIS: YOU MUST FIRST ENABLE THE GOVERNMENT TO CONTROL THE GOVERNED; AND IN THE NEXT PLACE, OBLIGE IT TO CONTROL ITSELF.[2]

Madison went on to note that while the primary method of controlling and limiting government power was reliance on the people, it was further necessary to construct "auxiliary precautions." These, of course, would provide for the division and separation of power among institutions of government, along with various devices designed to "check and balance" the actions of others (see Chapter 5 for further discussion). It should be noted, however, that the solution presented by Madison did not favor the elimination of a government's power, but merely its subordination to competing interests and to the will of the people.

The preceding discussion indicates that constitutional government means government limited in its powers and functions. Constitutionalism is also premised on the **rule of law** as opposed to the rules of everyday men and women. A constitution places a higher law above the policies and practices of transient leaders or ruling majorities, and it requires that they abide by that constitutional higher law. The general structures and principles found in a constitution reflect the long-term interests of a people and should therefore supersede the short-term wishes of even a popular leader or an overwhelming majority. Of course, everyday women and men must hold rulers accountable to these legal principles to ensure the effectiveness of the rule of law. But Americans in general possess a deep-seated belief in the rule of law, which may contribute to the strength of American constitutionalism.

In addition to emphasizing limited government and the rule of law, constitutionalism recognizes the fundamental worth of each individual and the rights and liberties that accompany each person. Across the globe, attention to human rights has increased substantially (see Brief 1.1). This is not to say that individuals possess universally recognized freedoms in all constitutional governments of present times, but it is clear that a constitutional government, by limiting the power of institutions and leaders, gives value to its citizens as individuals.

In summary, modern constitutionalism limits the power of sovereign rulers, makes leaders subject to the law, takes precautions against tyranny, and protects the rights and liberties of individuals. None of these developments occurred quickly, as is discussed later in this chapter, and none has reached its

---

Brief 1.1

THE LEGACY OF THE UNIVERSAL DECLARATION OF HUMAN RIGHTS

The world has witnessed an explosion in concern about human rights, and even the rights of nonhuman animals and the environment. Organizations dedicated to advocacy for and the protection of human rights abound. Many colleges and universities now offer courses and programs in international human rights law and policy. Governments are monitored, and foreign policy is crafted, on the basis of how individual human rights are respected.

The explosion in human rights began over sixty years ago, with the United Nations' adoption of the Universal Declaration of Human Rights. Drafted under the leadership of former first lady Eleanor Roosevelt, this document contains statements that often go beyond the proclamations found in the bills of rights of national constitutions discussed later in this chapter. For example, while traditional legal guarantees and political rights to "freedom of conscience and religion . . . opinion and expression . . . peaceful assembly and association" are mentioned, the Declaration also provides that every person has a "right to a nationality . . . to an adequate standard of living . . . to rest and leisure [and] social and cultural rights indispensable for [human] dignity and the free development of [human] personality." In separate international conventions that followed the Universal Declaration of Human Rights in 1948, more specific protections (e.g., of the rights of women and children) have also been adopted.[3]

One of the ongoing controversies surrounding international human rights involves their enforcement. Much of the discussion in later chapters of this text is devoted to how the rights found in the U.S. Constitution are enforced. But in the absence of effective international governance, the problems of human rights enforcement on the global scene are even greater.

conclusion. In fact, constitutionalism is by no means a static concept, especially where limited government and individual rights are involved. The relationship between constitutionalism and government is constantly changing, with the constitution itself the most obvious proof of that development.

COMPARATIVE CONSTITUTIONS AND CONSTITUTIONALISM

For more than two hundred years, the Constitution of the United States has served as a source of stability for Americans. As a result, Americans are accustomed to thinking of constitutions as "old" documents. In fact, however, more than half of the world's existing constitutions have been written and adopted since 1980, and more constitutions have come into existence since 2000 than those left from before 1960 (see Brief 1.2).

There seems to be little doubt that the forces of democracy and constitutionalism are currently on the march, most recently exemplified by events such as the Arab Spring. The nonprofit organization Freedom House, in a report disseminated at the end of 1999,[5] proclaimed a "dramatic expansion of democratic governance over the course of the twentieth century." Judged by a standard of "universal suffrage for competitive multiparty elections," in 1900 there were no sovereign states that qualified as democracies. Freedom House counts twenty-five states that had "restricted democratic practices" (including the United States), accounting for 12.4 percent of the world's population. By 1950, at the beginning of the "second wave" of democracy, with the defeat of Nazi totalitarianism, post-war reconstruction of Europe, and decolonization, along with changes in some nations granting women suffrage, there were twenty-two democracies (including the United States), accounting for 31 percent of the world's population. By the end of the twentieth century, the "third wave" had brought democracy to the post-Communist world, Latin America, and parts of Asia and Africa. In 2000, 120 of the world's 192 sovereign states could be judged electoral democracies by this standard, representing more than 62 percent of the world's population. Nobel Prize–winning economist Amartya Sen, when asked about the most important thing that happened in the twentieth century, concluded that it was "the emergence of democracy as the preeminently acceptable form of governance."[6]

Still, most scholars would agree that reversals are possible, even likely, and the history of the last century marks many instances where democracy was followed by the ascendance of anti-democratic forces. Many of

---

Brief 1.2
CONSTITUTION WRITING OVER TIME

The U.S. Department of State maintains "Background Notes" on all of the world's nations.[4] An analysis of 194 countries in that collection, including the United States, shows that the bulk of the world's constitutions are quite new, and even countries with established constitutions occasionally see the need to change. For example, Switzerland, with a constitution dating to 1874, adopted a new document in 2000.

In breaking down the 194 nations, some interesting trends emerge. First, only one country, the United States, has a constitution written in the eighteenth century, and only three (Norway, Luxembourg, and The Netherlands) endure from the nineteenth century. At the other end, a number of countries (including Afghanistan, Bahrain, Bolivia, Cote d'Ivoire, Iraq, and Republic of the Congo) have new constitutions since 2000, and several other states are currently writing or working to adopt new constitutions.

Only a handful of the 192 nations currently have no written constitution, and the United Kingdom is by far the most famous here. Other states, such as Angola and Somalia, operate without a constitution because of instability or transition. An examination of the past century, for example, shows the following numbers of constitutions adopted or significantly revised, by time period:

1900–1950	13	1960–1969	17	1980–1989	27	2000–2009	33
1950–1959	6	1970–1979	30	1990–1999	76		

The decade of the 1990s was a busy time for constitution writers, largely spurred on by the disintegration of the Soviet Union and the rejection of post-colonial constitutions by many African and Asian states. The turbulent conditions in many parts of the world have been the source of constitutional revision in the past decade, and make the prospect for constitutional change appear as strong as ever.

the world's citizens have begun to experience democratic rights and constitutional liberties only recently, and it remains to be seen whether progress will continue (see Brief 1.3).

What role can the American model of democratic and constitutional government play in this apparent transition? After all, the American written constitution is the world's oldest. The collapse of Communism suggests that the American model clearly has triumphed, so why should not new, aspiring democracies look toward the American system as a guide? It promises economic prosperity and political stability—or does it?

Professor Ted Gurr argues that the American model may not necessarily meet the needs of other nations.[12] While the American model is attractive to poorer countries because of what it seems to offer in terms of economic prosperity, that prosperity, even if it comes, may not translate into political stability.

Although the American constitutional system has provided stability and continuity, the process has not always been peaceful. The American federal system was ripped apart by a horrible civil war in the 1860s and took more than a century to heal completely. America's "checks and balances" and "separation of powers" have not always produced efficient governmental operation, most recently evidenced by hyperpartisanship and governmental "gridlock" in Washington over critical policy issues. Gurr argues that the American pattern of divided government involving the legislative and executive branches is the result of a faulty design and "would precipitate either a coup or a constitutional revolution" in many of the "newer democracies."

Despite these and other arguments that can be directed against the American constitutional system as a model for the world, the fact is that it appeals to people who may have very little knowledge of

---

Brief 1.3
KEEPING THE SPREAD OF DEMOCRACY IN PERSPECTIVE

While the increase in democratic regimes has been dramatic, it is premature to proclaim that democracy has triumphed, or even that it is universally desirable. Samuel P. Huntington, in his article "Democracy's Third Wave,"[7] notes that the current era is the "third wave of democratization" in the modern world, with the first wave occurring from about 1820 to 1926 and the second from the end of World War II until about 1962. Huntington's key point is that both of these earlier waves were followed by "reverse waves," in which anti-democratic forces returned to power. Although he cites many factors as important in the future expansion of democracy, Huntington believes that economic development, which "makes democracy possible," and political leadership, which "makes it real," stand out as absolutely essential. Huntington believes that we must be cautious in our expectations concerning democratic growth, especially given his conclusion that the sense of individualism and a tradition of rights and liberties that can be found in the West are "unique among civilized societies."[8] Interestingly, in the latest Freedom House annual survey, the number of electoral democracies in the world stood at 117, down from 123 five years ago, and their report documented the sixth consecutive annual decline in political rights and civil liberties among the 195 nations of the world.[9]

On the question of democracy's universal desirability, especially as it affects economic growth, Lee Kuan Yew, former prime minister of Singapore, was famous for arguing that among developing nations, nondemocratic systems are actually better at bringing about positive economic development than democracies. The "Lee thesis" in turn has sparked a cottage industry of cultural claims against the virtues of democracy. For example, following Lee's example in Singapore, scholars have claimed that Asian cultures value discipline, not traditional Western notions of political freedom.[10] However, Amartya Sen counsels against assuming that democracy follows economic prosperity and is therefore of secondary value, arguing that there are "extensive interconnections between political freedoms and the understanding and fulfillment of economic needs."[11] He reinforces this position with the observation that in the world's history no famine has ever occurred in a country where democratic elections and a free press were present.

On yet another level, some of the advanced industrial democracies are experiencing extensive political disengagement, particularly among younger generations, causing concern about democracy's enduring value in its oldest homes. Parliamentary elections in Great Britain in 2001 and 2005 yielded the lowest voter turnout the country has experienced since 1918, though turnout rose 4 percent to 65 percent in 2010. In the United States, democratic participation, as measured primarily but not exclusively by voting, has been in the midst of a fifty-year decline. Although numbers went up in the 2004 and 2008 elections, voter turnout dropped almost 5 percent in 2012, and great concern exists in this country about how many Americans, especially younger Americans, exercise their constitutional right to vote, particularly in off-year national elections. The talk of democracy and the rule of law seem universal, but in practice there are miles to go until we can proclaim democracy's global victory over the dual forces of authoritarianism and apathy.

constitutional and democratic principles. Gurr's explanation is insightful and compelling:

> THE CRUX OF THAT APPEAL, I THINK, IS INTANGIBLE RATHER THAN MATERIAL: IT IS THE BELIEF THAT IN *AMERICA ANYTHING IS POSSIBLE.* THAT FAITH IS WHAT THE AMERICAN SYSTEM HAS TO OFFER FOR FOREIGN OBSERVERS, FOR IMMIGRANTS, AND FOR THE MAJORITY OF PEOPLE LIVING HERE.[13] [ORIGINAL EMPHASIS]

Perhaps this is the best that can be expected of any constitution—that it gives its people the hope and belief that indeed anything is possible.

This discussion leads to an important question: What is the relationship between democracy and constitutionalism? Many would argue that there is an inherent tension between democracy, which calls for majority rule, and constitutionalism, which calls for the rule of law and protects the rights of all individuals. But constitutional scholar Cass Sunstein argues:

> THE CENTRAL GOAL OF A CONSTITUTION IS TO CREATE THE PRECONDITIONS FOR A WELL-FUNCTIONING DEMOCRATIC ORDER, ONE IN WHICH CITIZENS ARE GENUINELY ABLE TO GOVERN THEMSELVES. [O]NE OF THE PRINCIPAL PURPOSES OF A CONSTITUTION IS TO PROTECT NOT THE RULE OF THE MAJORITY BUT DEMOCRACY'S INTERNAL MORALITY, SEEN IN DELIBERATIVE TERMS. A SYSTEM IN WHICH MANY PEOPLE CANNOT VOTE OR VOTE EQUALLY, OR IN WHICH SOME PEOPLE HAVE FAR MORE POLITICAL POWER THAN OTHERS, VIOLATES THAT INTERNAL MORALITY.[14]

Seen this way, emerging and even long-standing democracies will always struggle to balance the immediate concerns of their people with their constitution's "internal morality," as governments respond to economic crises, violence and war, natural disasters, or threats to citizen health and safety.

It is important to note that even though the practices of constitutional government are demanding, the written constitution has continued to be adopted on a near-universal basis. Regardless of a country's commitment to constitutional government, most leaders view a written constitution as a badge of respectability and legitimacy. Consequently, the written constitution has attracted adherents from widely different backgrounds and geographical areas. Given the diversity among the world's nations, one might expect considerable difficulty in comparing the constitutions of different countries. While differences certainly exist, there are definite similarities in most constitutional arrangements, at least insofar as the structure of the constitution itself is concerned. Ivo Duchacek, a scholar of constitutional development, has identified four "core ingredients" in all national documents. These central features include a preamble or statement of purpose, an organizational chart of the government, amendatory articles that describe the manner in which the supreme law may be changed, and, finally, a bill of rights.[15] The American Constitution can be used as a guide to analyze each of these ingredients in more detail.

THE PREAMBLE: A STATEMENT OF PURPOSE AND GOALS

The Preamble to the Constitution of the United States provides a general statement of purpose and lays the foundation for a theory of governmental action. It is clear in the Preamble's first words that "We the People" are the force underlying the document's legitimacy. Government, in short, may be created by the consent of the governed, and individuals may form a compact with one another to achieve those ends considered desirable. This perspective was shared by a number of early American settlers, primarily those for whom religious factors were of paramount importance.

Having stated the premise that the people are authorized to ordain and establish a constitution, the Preamble offers a list of social and political goals: "to form a more perfect Union, establish Justice, insure domestic Tranquility, provide for the common defence, promote the general Welfare, and secure the Blessings of Liberty to ourselves and our Posterity." The degree to which these goals have been realized in the United States remains a major focus of this book.

When compared with other constitutions, the American Preamble is relatively free of ideological content and partisan rhetoric. Although it reflects the twin conceptual poles of individualism and communitarianism (outlined later in this chapter), the Preamble seems short and simple. By comparison, the preambles to the constitutions of other countries make strong political statements and are often used to promote a specific and detailed ideology. Some countries, particularly those with a history of revolution or warfare, go to elaborate lengths in their preambles to chronicle the events and accomplishments of past generations. In this category, the Cuban, Vietnamese, and Chinese constitutions provide particularly good illustrations. Other countries use their constitution's preamble to identify the regime's leading ideological foundations—the Islam of Iran, Pakistan, Bangladesh, and others; "home-grown" ideologies such as the "Pantja Sila" Democracy of Indonesia; and international orientations such as the neutrality of Switzerland and the Japanese renunciation of war. As Table 1.1 indicates, most countries combine history, ideology, and culture into their preambles, either praising glorious past accomplishments or apologizing for the wrongs of an earlier regime.

ORGANIZATIONAL CHART

According to Duchacek, constitutions serve as "the official blueprint for the uses of public power" and may be referred to as "power maps."[16] That is to say, every constitution establishes the institutions of government, lays out procedures by which rules are made, and provides in some manner for the resolution of conflicts and disputes. The manner in which these steps are taken varies widely, even among "constitutional" governments. The American Constitution addresses the functions of rulemaking (legislative), rule implementation (executive), and adjudication (judiciary) in its first three articles. Article IV moves from the national level to the states, primarily addressing the matter of relationships between states. While each of these articles are analyzed in detail in later chapters, it is important to note three key principles that provide for much of the American constitutional structure. These three principles—separation of powers, federalism, and judicial review—are not mentioned per se in the text of the document, although their presence is not difficult to infer. For many observers, these three principles perhaps more than any others truly distinguish the American style of limited government.

Table 1.1 Some Dominant Themes in Preambles of Selected National Constitutions

The Victorious Struggle Through Revolution

Vietnam (1992): "In the course of their millennia-old history, the Vietnamese people, of all nationalities in our country conducted an uninterrupted struggle, [defeating] the two wars of aggression by the colonialists and the imperialists, liberated the country, reunified the motherland, and brought to completion the people's national democratic revolution."

Cuba (1976): "We, Cuban Citizens . . . GUIDED by the victorious doctrine of Marxism-Leninism . . . AND HAVING DECIDED to carry forward the triumphant Revolution . . . under the leadership of Fidel Castro . . . AWARE . . . that only under socialism and communism . . . can full dignity of the human being be attained."

The Source of Constitutional Authority

Afghanistan (2004): "We the people of Afghanistan: With firm faith in God Almighty and relying on His lawful mercy, and Believing in the Sacred religion of Islam . . . "

Iran (1979): "The Constitution of the Islamic Republic of Iran . . . is based upon Islamic principles and standards. . . ."

Ireland (1937): "We, the people of Eire, Humbly acknowledging all our obligations to our Divine Lord, Jesus Christ, Who sustained our fathers through centuries of trial. . . ."

India (1949): "WE, THE PEOPLE OF INDIA having solemnly resolved to constitute India into a SOVEREIGN SOCIALIST SECULAR DEMOCRATIC REPUBLIC"

Apologizing and Rejecting the Past

South Africa (1996): "We, the people of South Africa, Recognise the injustices of our past; Honour those who suffered for justice and freedom in our land. . . ."

Uganda (1995): "We the people of Uganda, Recalling our history which has been characterised by political and constitutional instability; Recognising our struggles against the forces of tyranny, oppression and exploitation. . . ."

Ethiopia (1994): "We, the nations, nationalities and peoples of Ethiopia . . . Fully cognizant that our common destiny can best be served by rectifying historically unjust relationships and by further promoting our shared interests. . . ."

SOURCE: Albert P. Blaustein and Gisbert H. Flanz, eds., *Constitutions of the Countries of the World* (Dobbs Ferry, NY: Oceana, 1971).

SEPARATION OF POWERS

The three-fold delineation of political functions presented in the first three articles is generally cited as proof of the **separation of powers** among the legislature, executive, and judiciary. The separation was clearly intended by the framers of the Constitution to avoid the concentration of power in the hands of the executive. In *Federalist No. 51*, Madison expressed the logic underlying this principle with the statement that "Ambition must be made to counteract ambition."[17] This counteracting of ambition was to be accomplished by a system of checks and balances, enabling one branch of the federal government to wield some power, although not too much, over the others. In actuality, however, these checks and balances have served to produce a series of overlapping relationships among the three branches of government. Each branch of government has some intrusive powers in the affairs of another, whether in the Congress's power to restrict the appellate jurisdiction of the Supreme Court, the Court's ability to "legislate" through its powers of judicial review, or the President's powers of appointment.

If the separation of powers divides governmental functions only nominally, it does separate the branches in one key area—personnel. Members of the legislative branch, for example, do not hold positions in the other branches of the federal government. The President may not hold a seat in the Congress, presumably because such an arrangement might create a concentration of power in a single individual.

For many Americans, the separation of powers is essential to limited government, but is it a prerequisite? Strictly speaking, the answer would seem to be negative. In fact, among the many constitutional governments today, only a few employ a formal separation-of-powers system. Most democracies of Western Europe, as well as those of Japan, Canada, and Australia, use a **parliamentary system** of government. Under this arrangement, executive power is wielded by a prime minister and cabinet chosen from the members of the majority party in the legislature. Such a system actually fuses power between the legislature and executive instead of separating it. However, in keeping with the spirit of constitutionalism, even in parliamentary systems without a formal separation of powers, limits on the abuses of governmental power do exist. In recent years, critics of the American separation of powers have called for a greater "fusion" of power in line with many of the parliamentary systems, to increase the responsiveness and accountability of our democratic government.[18]

FEDERALISM

Power can also be divided and distributed along territorial lines. When a constitution recognizes the existence of subnational units such as states or provinces and leaves powers for them to exercise, the result is known as **federalism**. In a sense, federalism is a further check on the consolidation of power. As is discussed later, the early American colonies favored autonomy above unity, resulting first in a loosely structured confederation and then in a new constitutional system based on federalism. While some early architects of the Constitution saw the system as essentially a national-dominated arrangement, many others thought that the states had retained ultimate sovereignty. This was to be a key basis for disagreement throughout the development of the Constitution, as Chapter 7 explains.

Federalism as a specific form of government can be combined with either a separation of powers arrangement as in the United States or with any number of other systems. Clearly, however, federalism, much like the separation of powers and judicial review, has been viewed as a fundamental principle of limited government in the United States. But, when constitutionalism outside the United States is examined, the results are mixed. Not all federal governments are constitutional, and not all constitutional governments are federal. Countries such as France, Sweden, and Japan—all constitutional governments—have chosen a **unitary system**, whereby all powers emanate from the central government (although local subdivisions exercise some functions in these countries). The former Soviet Union, on the other hand, touted its federal system of fifteen Republics as evidence of decentralized power and local autonomy, although the republics lacked authority, and the system was not based on constitutionalism. In summary, federal systems make constitutional governments when the constitution establishes effective restraints on *all* governmental power. When this is not done, federalism becomes nothing more than a structural arrangement serving a political purpose.

JUDICIAL REVIEW

Somewhat like the separation of powers but more controversial, judicial review is not specifically mentioned in the Constitution. **Judicial review** refers to the power of the judicial branch to review and, if necessary, invalidate legislation and executive action when it is inconsistent with the Constitution. Chapter 4 examines the origins, history, and contemporary controversies of judicial review, but a brief discussion of its constitutional basis is in order here. In one sense, judicial review can be seen as a powerful check on the abuse of power because it makes government ultimately responsible to the limits of the Constitution. On the other hand, it should be remembered that every time judicial review is used, the limits of the Constitution are being defined by the judges currently serving on the federal courts. Nonetheless, judicial review has been considered an integral part of limited government in the United States for many years. But is it essential for other constitutional governments as well?

A survey of other constitutional systems quickly shows that, once again, the American pattern is not closely followed elsewhere. Japan and Germany recognize the principle of judicial review in their national documents, but their constitutions, not surprisingly, were influenced heavily by Americans during the post–World War II period. The British, with their principle of parliamentary supremacy, logically deny the practice of judicial review. Even the French, who have sought to limit legislative power drastically in the Fifth Republic, have created only a limited type of judicial review. Once again, it becomes apparent that judicial review, a powerful constitutional force in America, is not a prerequisite for constitutional government everywhere.

AMENDATORY ARTICLES AND A SUPREME LAW

By its own statement in Article VI, the American Constitution is the "supreme Law of the Land." A supreme law cannot remain supreme if it can be changed easily and informally. Therefore, some formal mechanism for amendment of the document must be established. The Constitution's framers, cognizant of their limitations in predicting the future, provided such a mechanism in Article V. But the framers were aware of the need for stability in the rule of law, so they made it difficult to change the supreme law.

The framers arranged for amendments to pass through a two-stage process prior to incorporation into the Constitution. The first stage, *proposal*, requires either a two-thirds vote of both houses of Congress or a national constitutional convention. Of the twenty-seven amendments added since 1789, all have been proposed by Congress. In fact, a constitutional convention has never been called to consider a proposed amendment, and many experts are divided over the method of calling a convention, the matter of selecting representatives, and the setting of an agenda.

Once proposed, the next stage is *ratification*. This process, based on the federal principle, lies with the states. Amendments must be ratified by three-fourths of the states, either in their legislatures or by special conventions called for this purpose (the manner is determined by Congress). Twenty-six of the twenty-seven successful amendments to the Constitution have been ratified by legislatures (the Twenty-first Amendment, repealing the Eighteenth, was ratified by state conventions). The states have refused to ratify amendments on such topics as prohibiting child labor and granting equal rights to women.

The twenty-seven amendments added to the Constitution since 1789 can largely be grouped into two broad categories. First are those amendments that establish, confirm, or create a specific right. The first nine amendments naturally fall into this group, along with the post–Civil War Thirteenth, Fourteenth, and Fifteenth Amendments concerning the rights of ex-slaves. In addition, provision for the popular election of senators (Seventeenth), expansion of the franchise to women (Nineteenth), participation in presidential elections for the District of Columbia (Twenty-third), removal of the poll tax as a barrier to voting in federal elections (Twenty-fourth), and the right of eighteen-year-olds to vote (Twenty-sixth) constitute other guarantees relating to individual rights and liberties.

A second category of five amendments might be considered "structural" changes in the institutions and procedures of the national government. In nearly all instances, the appropriate amendment was not added until events produced an obvious need for change. For example, the Supreme Court's decision in *Chisholm v. Georgia* (1793) went against state interests and resulted in the Eleventh Amendment's restriction of the Court's original jurisdiction. The rise of political parties and a deadlocked electoral vote in the presidential election of 1800 showed the need for the Twelfth Amendment and the separate listing of presidential and vice-presidential candidates on the ballot. Next, due in large part to the Progressive reform movement and a desire to reduce the power of lame-duck (defeated in the election but not yet replaced) public officials, the Twentieth Amendment in 1933 shortened the time between national elections (November) and the taking of office (changed from March to January of the year following the election). The Twenty-second Amendment (1951) limited a president to two elected terms in office. Of course, the need for this amendment was not apparent until a president had exceeded the unwritten two-term limit. Franklin Roosevelt's four election victories provided the stimulus for change. Finally, the matters of presidential succession, disability, and presidential and vice-presidential resignation were the subjects of the Twenty-fifth Amendment in 1967. Interestingly, just six years after ratification, the amendment came into play twice in a short time period: first, with the resignation of Vice President Spiro Agnew to avoid federal criminal charges and the appointment of Gerald Ford to fill the vacancy; and second, with the resignation of President Richard Nixon in the aftermath of the Watergate affair. Also interesting is that four of the five structural amendments have dealt primarily with the presidency.

A formal amending process, of course, makes little difference when the constitution does not limit the government. Amendments may be added on top of other amendments without any effect. Compared with other nations and considering its age, the United States has formally amended its Constitution very sparingly. However, it should not be assumed that the American Constitution has changed little over the years. In fact, for every formal amendment added, perhaps a hundred or more other changes have occurred. These developments constitute the main subject matter of this book.

Before leaving the topic of constitutional change, it is helpful to place the American situation in comparative perspective. Discounting the unwritten British variety (see Brief 1.4), the Constitution of the United States is by far the world's oldest. Perhaps many Americans take for granted that a constitution is an enduring document. The experiences of other countries, even those considered to have constitutional governments, suggest that constitutional change is far from rare (see Table 1.2). Often the stimulus for scrapping an existing constitution is a crisis, defeat in war, or change in leadership. Of the major powers defeated in World War II, for example, all have new constitutions (West German Basic Law, 1949, modified with German reunification in 1990; Japanese Constitution, 1947; Italian Constitution, 1948). A costly Algerian crisis and possible military coup were responsible for the French decision in 1958 to replace the Fourth

---

Brief 1.4
THE "UNWRITTEN" BRITISH CONSTITUTION

Most of the British "Constitution" is written; it is just not found in a single document. The British Constitution typically is considered to consist of four elements, only the last of which is unwritten: historical documents, such as Magna Carta (1215), the Petition of Right (1628), and the Bill of Rights (1689); fundamental acts of Parliament, such as those in 1911 and 1949 limiting the powers of the House of Lords; judicial decisions that make up the common law system protecting individual rights and liberties; and conventions or customs that form the traditional basis for the system. For example, it is convention that the government must resign or request that Parliament be dissolved if it loses a vote of no confidence in the House of Commons.

Overall, the British Constitution provides a loosely knit fabric that helps to give the people some feeling of history, unity, and consensus. According to Douglas V. Verney, the Constitution "is a somewhat abstract and foggy notion which few people fully comprehend, but which most people dimly understand because of custom and convention. . . . [T]o a nation of gardeners it appears like a venerable oak tree which has weathered many storms."[19] Obviously, the British Constitution, whether written or unwritten, has weathered many storms, and it has stood for centuries as a symbol of what constitutional government is all about.

Table 1.2 Current National Constitutions: Ages and Origins

Country	Most Recent Constitution	Reason for Constitution
United States	1787	Failure of Articles of Confederation. To strengthen the national government.
Norway	1814	Create a Norwegian state and avoid union with Sweden.
Mexico	1917	Institutionalize the 1910 Revolution.
Japan	1947	Defeat in World War II. American occupation.
Italy	1948	Defeat in World War II. Referendum abolished monarchy and called for a republic.
India	1949	Independence from Britain. Promote unity.
France	1958	Fourth Republic's failure to deal with Algerian War. Return of Charles de Gaulle to government.
Sweden	1975	Consolidate social democratic reforms. Removal of all power from King. Replaced 1809 Constitution.
Spain	1978	Death of Franco in 1975; King Juan Carlos opens the way for a constitutional monarchy.
Iran	1979	Overthrow of the Shah. Creation of Islamic Republic.
Canada	1982	Desire to "patriate" own Constitution. Amended the 1867 British North America Act.
Croatia	1990	Dissolution of Yugoslavia. Independence declared.
Czech Republic	1993	End of Communist regime. Division of Czechoslovakia into Czech and Slovak Republics.
Uganda	1995	Installation of new regime.
South Africa	1996	Replacement of white minority regime.
Rwanda	2003	End of bloody civil war; new constitution eliminates reference to ethnicity.
Afghanistan	2004	Replacement of Taliban regime with democratically elected government.
Bolivia	2009	Revised to create a unitary, "plurinational" secular state, grant more power to country's indigenous majority.
Egypt	2012	Replacement of 1971 charter, following the popular uprising that deposed President Hosni Mubarak.

Republic with the Fifth by means of a new constitution. Other constitutional governments, such as Sweden and Switzerland, have written new constitutions for reasons of efficiency and structural change.

Communist systems seemingly write new constitutions when the current leadership discredits the practices of a past regime. The 1982 "Post-Mao" Constitution in the People's Republic of China illustrates this pattern, and it is similarly questionable whether Fidel Castro's Cuban Constitution will survive much longer than he does. Many developing nations are on their second or third constitution since independence. Because constitutions are normally not much more than organization charts in these countries, a new constitution becomes necessary when the organization changes. From this perspective, the longevity of the Constitution of the United States is indeed remarkable, making the development of American constitutionalism one of the longest-running stories in the modern world.

BILLS OF RIGHTS: LIMITS ON GOVERNMENT

Most constitutions include a section that purports to list the rights of the citizens. Whether called a **bill of rights** (by the way, no mention of this term appears in the U.S. Constitution) or something similar, the listing represents those freedoms, rights, and liberties that, at least theoretically, are beyond the government's power to abridge. In reality, the true measure of individual rights and civil liberties cannot be determined from merely reading the constitution itself, but also from observing the degree to which a government actually abides by the guarantees of individual rights found in its constitution.

One of the major undertakings of the First Congress of the United States (1789–1791) was the addition of a bill of rights. A full listing of these rights is unnecessary at present, as each requires considerable attention. Suffice it to say that the liberties listed in the first ten amendments are among the best-known features of the American Constitution, and yet they have been subject to more interpretation and refinement than any other section of the document. Not all constitutional rights are found in the Bill of Rights. Americans have seen their freedoms and liberties grow with time, often, as noted previously, by means of constitutional amendment. Many other rights to be discussed in later chapters have been discovered by the Supreme Court from within the Constitution itself. Furthermore, certain guarantees that safeguard the individual from arbitrary government intrusion, such as provisions for habeas corpus and protection from ex post facto laws and bills of attainder, are found in Article I of the original Constitution of 1787.

The constitutions of most other countries also contain a chapter or section dealing with rights and liberties guaranteed to the people. A major difference between national constitutions relates to the period in which the constitution was drafted. Constitutions that were written in the eighteenth and nineteenth centuries, like that of the United States, emphasize political rights and civil liberties. The rights protected in these earlier documents place constitutional limitations on what governments can do. Thus, they have been called **negative rights** because they *prevent* governments from doing certain things that would violate the individual's political and civil liberties. Constitutions written in the last century, however, typically stress economic or social rights, such as the right to work, to decent housing, or to health care, and even to enjoy leisure. These economic and social rights place constitutional duties on government to provide for these protections. Scholars refer to the rights in these more contemporary constitutions as **positive rights** because they *require* governments to act positively to ensure the enjoyment of economic and social entitlements. Not surprisingly, the older democracies of Western Europe emphasize political rights and civil liberties, although those that have amended their original constitutions or drafted new ones also have provisions for economic and social rights. Socialist regimes and those in the developing world tend to focus on economic or social rights. Finally, a large number of constitutions, generally in the more autocratic states, identify the duties, as well as the rights, of citizens. Some routinely included duties are paying taxes, keeping state secrets, defending the nation against enemies, and serving in the armed forces. Table 1.3 provides some examples of rights, liberties, and duties found among the constitutions of the world's nations.

THE TWIN PILLARS OF AMERICAN CONSTITUTIONALISM

As an adherent to the principles of constitutionalism, the United States is a government of laws and not of men and women. However, two points in particular require further explanation.

First of all, our history shows that laws, including the "higher law" of the Constitution, can only govern through particular men and women. This textbook is devoted to discussing the historical development of various constitutional principles and provisions by particular individuals and groups. The focus is especially on the justices who have served on the U.S. Supreme Court. As Chief Justice Charles Evans Hughes once said, "We are under a constitution, but the constitution is what the judges say it is."[20] Therefore, students of the American constitutional system must look at more than the document of the Constitution itself; they must also examine its interpretation by the Supreme Court.

Countless examples prove that the American constitutional system can change without a change in the

Table 1.3 Rights and Liberties in Constitutions of the Countries of the World

Rights and Duties Relating to Work/Labor

"Everyone has the right to choose the profession he wishes, provided it is not contrary to the principles of Islam, to the public interest, or to the rights of others. . . ." Iran (Art. 28)

"Everyone has the right to rest . . . and paid annual leave shall be guaranteed by law." Kazakhstan (Art. 24)

"The State guarantees the right to safety, security, and hygienic conditions at work." Algeria (Art. 63)

"Work in a socialist society is a right and duty and a source of pride for every citizen." Cuba (Art. 45)

"All those who work have the right to rest. . . ." Cuba (Art. 46)

"Every man fit to bear arms shall be liable, up to the completion of his sixtieth year, to serve in the defence of his country in the event of emergency." Liechtenstein (Art. 44)

Education/Welfare/Culture

"Men and women of the age of eighteen years and above, have the right to marry and to found a family and are entitled to equal rights in marriage, during marriage and at its dissolution." Uganda (Art. 31)

"Academic freedom is guaranteed." Japan (Art. 23)

"The State pledges itself to guard with special care the institution of Marriage, on which the Family is founded, and to protect it against attack." Ireland (Art. 41.3.1)

"The freedom of art and science and freedom of instruction in them is affirmed." Italy (Art. 33)

"The right of individuals and communities to their cultural identity in keeping with their values, language, and customs is recognized." Guatemala (Art. 58)

Freedoms of Expression

"Citizens enjoy freedom of speech, freedom of the press. . . . No one may misuse democratic freedoms to violate the interests of the state and the people." Vietnam (Art. 67)

"Publications and the press may express ideas freely, except when they are contrary to Islamic principles. . . ." Iran (Art. 24)

"Journalism in any of its forms may be practiced freely. Press organs lacking responsible direction shall not be permitted, nor shall the publication of immoral subject matter be printed." Paraguay (Art. 73)

"The Press is free, and shall not be censored . . . Publication shall not be made in any language prohibited by law." Turkey (Art. 28)

Freedoms of the Person

"Everyone has the right to bodily and psychological integrity (and) . . . not to be subjected to medical or scientific experiments without their informed consent." South Africa (Art. 12)

"The law shall safeguard the rights of the victim. The State guarantees judicial protection and compensation to the victim." Tajikistan (Art. 21)

"Children shall have the right from birth to a name, the right to acquire a nationality and, subject to legislation . . . to know and be cared for by their parents." Gambia (Art. 29)

SOURCE: Albert P. Blaustein and Gisbert H. Flanz, eds. *Constitutions of the Countries of the World* (Dobbs Ferry, NY: Oceana, 2007).

Constitution itself. A shift in the Supreme Court's understanding, a movement within Congress, even a mood swing among the American people can drastically alter the way our government works or the rights it protects. For instance, the Fourteenth Amendment to the Constitution (passed in 1868) provides that "No State shall . . . deny to any person . . . the equal protection of the laws." The Supreme Court at first interpreted this provision to allow states to segregate transportation, education, and other public facilities on the basis of race, and to pass laws denying equality to women. Finally, in 1954, the Supreme Court reversed its position, saying that racial segregation in education was a violation of the Fourteenth Amendment. By the 1970s, the Court began to use the Fourteenth Amendment to strike down laws that discriminated on the basis of gender. With these two shifts in the Supreme Court's understanding of the Fourteenth Amendment came a revolution in American law and social life, without a single change in the wording of the Constitution itself. These and other constitutional developments caused by historic changes in judicial interpretation and legislative policy are examined by topic throughout the book.

A second and more important point that requires explanation is that constitutions are never politically neutral documents. Americans tend to regard the U.S. Constitution as being "above politics," a neutral set of rules and procedures by which people play the political "game." People with individual biases and interests may use the provisions and mechanisms of our constitution to achieve desired results, but the procedures themselves are presumed unbiased and disinterested. Such thinking ignores the fact that rules and procedures in every game make certain assumptions about the nature of the game and its players, assumptions that may bias the direction or outcome of the action. The rules of any competitive sport, for example, assume that the players will try to use the rules to beat their opponents. The rules of the game of Monopoly assume that the players will try to drive their opponents out of business. Anyone who tries to play a "friendly" game of Monopoly will not get very far!

The American Constitution is no exception here. The Constitution contains certain assumptions about human beings, their nature and goals, and the type of political system appropriate to them. An inherent bias exists in our constitutional system toward a particular notion of government and politics. The Constitution describes and tries to establish a specific kind of politics and political life—one based on certain theories of human nature and of the government's proper role in people's lives. In the *Federalist Papers*, James Madison asked:

> [W]HAT IS GOVERNMENT ITSELF BUT THE GREATEST OF ALL REFLECTIONS ON HUMAN NATURE? IF MEN WERE ANGELS, NO GOVERNMENT WOULD BE NECESSARY. IF ANGELS WERE TO GOVERN MEN, NEITHER EXTERNAL NOR INTERNAL CONTROLS ON GOVERNMENT WOULD BE NECESSARY.[21]

As Madison acknowledges, to understand the Constitution requires an understanding of the particular political theories and assumptions it embodies.

Actually, the American Constitution and American political practices embody not one but *two* different theories of politics, as the introductory conversation between John Locke and Jean-Jacques Rousseau previewed. This text refers to these two strands of political thought underlying the American Constitution as the **individualist** (or classical liberal) approach and the **communitarian** (or classical republican) approach to government. While existing alongside each other in the nation's constitutional history, these two competing philosophies of government contain somewhat different assumptions about human nature and politics. Historically, these divergent assumptions have produced conflict over which course the nation should pursue. Many of the constitutional clashes in American history have erupted between those adhering to an individualist theory of government and those following a more communitarian approach.

THE INDIVIDUALIST THEORY OF POLITICS

The individualist theory of politics appears more prominently as a foundation underlying the American constitutional system. The individualist approach assumes that individuals take precedence over government. They inherently possess certain rights that the government should preserve and promote. The individualist perspective assumes that human beings are capable of choice and development on their own, without governmental help. Government should merely provide institutions and mechanisms that will enable individuals to exercise their rights and pursue their private interests. Under this concept of politics, individuals are more important than the political community, and their rights and interests supersede those of the community.

Still, individualists see government as necessary because people may have interests that are irreconcilable. The clash of individual interests creates conflict. Individuals whose private interests conflict require institutions that can mediate and accommodate these differences. Individualists seek to create a political order that can regulate the anarchy arising from egoistic human behavior. And yet, the individualist wants to allow people the greatest possible personal freedom. The ideal government as envisioned by individualists would be one in which general, impersonal laws and disinterested judges provide the peace and security under which each person can pursue private interests. Thus, the individualist has a notion of justice that is purely procedural in nature. A **procedural** view of **justice** sees the political system as legitimate as long as it applies fair rules and procedures equally to all persons. Persons using these procedures to obtain vastly different results are not seen as being unjust. For example, a college admissions system may be based on merit. High school seniors will be admitted to college if they achieve a certain grade point average and adequate scores on college admission tests. Those who do not meet the standards are not admitted. Although this system differentiates between people, it is procedurally just because it applies what are believed to be appropriate standards equally to all persons.

For individualists, however, beyond these minimal functions, the government must be strictly limited in its scope. People only call on government to protect and secure their rights and interests. The individualist approach sees no intrinsic value fulfilled by the political order. Because the political order fills no intrinsic needs, people ought to be given the widest possible arena of unregulated activity. And because individuals only enter the public realm to secure their private interests, they have no reason to participate directly in all aspects of politics, especially as long as the leaders they choose satisfy their desires. Individuals enter the public realm as free and independent persons with particular desires, and the political system ought to allow—even guarantee—the continuation of their privacy and independence.

What has been described here as the individualist approach to politics has also been termed the liberal tradition in Western political thought. This classical theory of liberal individualism appears in the writings of such historical figures as John Locke in the seventeenth century (discussed in the introduction to this chapter) and John Stuart Mill in the nineteenth century. In contemporary American society we can find expressions of the individualist approach to politics in the writings of economist Milton Friedman or philosopher Ayn Rand,[22] as well as in the actions of organizations such as the American Civil Liberties Union.

THE COMMUNITARIAN THEORY OF POLITICS

The communitarian perspective emphasizes the positive role that government plays in the lives of its people. Whereas the individualist approach assumes that people can choose and develop on their own, the communitarian approach contends that people need the community and its values to nurture their development and enable them to make proper choices.

Under this view, democratic government exists not only to recognize and protect individual rights and to satisfy personal interests, but also to bring individuals together into a political community to solve public problems. Participation with their fellow citizens in the public realm educates and transforms people's self-interests into a larger public interest, and better fulfills them as human beings. Communitarians see the political community in a positive light, as a place where individuals come together to share common interests and to do the public's business. Politics is not a necessary evil to be limited in scope and function. Thus, communitarians recognize that the "public interest" (as defined by the majority in a political community) creates responsibilities that may override the individual's rights. Whenever a conflict occurs between individual rights and government regulation in the public interest, the communitarian resolves the conflict on the side of the public interest. Because the community is seen as intrinsically necessary to individuals, the political majority may sometimes need to impose certain values on individuals who find themselves in the minority.

Communitarians take a **substantive** view of **justice**. Whereas the individualist is satisfied with fair procedures as a measure of justice, the communitarian is more likely to look at the fairness of the results obtained. A substantive view of justice contends that vast inequalities among individuals are potentially damaging to society as a whole. Communitarians, adhering to their substantive notion of justice, are willing to use governmental power to achieve greater justice. For example, in college admissions systems, communitarian theory supports affirmative action by government to redress institutional inequalities that resulted from past discrimination and to foster the public interest. Under an affirmative action program, a college may give admissions preference to minority group members to increase their members in higher education and certain professions. Moreover, a communitarian might argue that the presence of students from different backgrounds—including different racial and ethnic ones—enhances the common good, in this instance the overall educational climate for students. Even though such action may differentiate in such a way that individuals who are not minority group members are not preferred, communitarians see the importance of government's role in obtaining just results for all elements in society, and in advancing the common good. The strict individualist, on the other hand, would be opposed to government affirmative action, arguing that affirmative action unfairly burdens individuals who had nothing to do with the past discrimination (see Chapter 10 for further discussion).

What has been described here as the communitarian theory of government has also been labeled the **republican** tradition in Western political thought. The earliest roots of this community-oriented republican theory appear in the writings of Aristotle and Cicero. More modern examples of republicanism appear in the eighteenth-century writings of Jean-Jacques Rousseau and Thomas Jefferson. In contemporary American society, we find communitarian beliefs in the writings of people such as Benjamin Barber and Robert Bellah.[23] President John F. Kennedy's famous call in his Inaugural Address to "ask not what your country can do for you, but what you can do for your country," a philosophy reflected in current national service programs, also exemplifies the communitarian approach to politics.

Admittedly, the preceding discussion of the two theories of government underlying our constitution draws each viewpoint starkly in black and white. The theories of individualism and communitarianism are set in high contrast for purposes of study and analysis (see Table 1.4). However, few Americans actually adhere to either theory in its purest form. Indeed, the Constitution fuses the classical liberal and republican traditions (see Brief 1.5). This fusion is evident in *Federalist No. 51*, where Madison talked about the importance in a constitutional democracy of balancing "the rights of individuals, or of the minority" against the regular "combinations of the majority."[24]

However, as the historical evidence will show, many constitutional conflicts in the United States have occurred between individualists and communitarians. Important clashes have occurred when the government has tried to restrict individual liberties, especially those of minorities, in the public interest. At the same time, individuals have claimed that their rights superseded the government's powers. Examples abound. In eighteenth-century New England, individual claims for religious freedom, a principle dear to many citizens, often conflicted with the community's attempt to infuse Puritan values and practices in all its people. In the nineteenth century, private enterprises seeking profit were confronted by state governments attempting to impose regulations for the general welfare. Today, especially following the tragic shootings at Sandy Hook Elementary School in Newtown, Connecticut, an issue such as gun control pits retailers seeking to sell and individuals wanting to purchase and keep weapons against communities desiring to regulate commercial gun transactions and restrict certain kinds of firearms

Table 1.4 Individualists and Communitarians Contrasted

	Individualist	Communitarian
Priority of social system Function of government	On the individual Protect property and other rights of individuals, especially those of minorities	On the community Protect human rights of community, as defined by majority
Focus of system	Fulfill private interest	Fulfill public interest
Pursuit of justice	Procedural regularity; merit-based	Substantive change in objective conditions; results orientation
View of equality	Natural inequality exists in society and should be preserved	Devoted to creating more equality of condition through government effort
General view of Government	Negative force; government must not interfere with personal freedoms	Positive force; government can realize communal development and public interest.
View of political participation	Conditional; limited participation	Essential; maximal participation

---

Brief 1.5
CONTEMPORARY LIBERALS AND CONSERVATIVES

The student used to thinking about politics in terms of the labels "liberal" and "conservative" may be confused by the terminology used in this chapter. Individualist theory and classical liberalism as used here to refer to a tradition of belief that distrusts government power and exalts individual freedom of choice in most matters. The label "liberal" in contemporary use often refers to the opposite of individualism, that is, a belief in the use of government power to regulate the affairs of individuals, especially in the economy. Communitarian theory and classical republicanism as used in this chapter refer to the tradition of belief that supports the promotion of the public interest and public virtue over individual rights, and which upholds at least some participation by citizens in self-government. This does not compare favorably with many contemporary "conservatives," who usually rule out any public involvement in economic affairs and tend to be suspicious of mass citizen participation in government.

When one considers that the labels "liberal" and "conservative" are applied loosely to a wide range of belief systems, and that there is often wide variation within the "liberal" and "conservative" camp in contemporary American politics, the confusion appears more evident. Differences exist among traditional conservatives, "New Right" conservatives, and "neoconservatives," and among traditional liberals, "New Left" liberals, and "neoliberals." Because of the dangers of using these contemporary labels, the authors of this text have relied on the more generic concepts individualist and communitarian, and have defined each fairly starkly and simply. The student should find these two conceptions of politics more useful in analyzing American constitutional development and the ongoing clash between majority rule and minority rights.

---

and/or ammunition to maintain public safety. Eventual resolution of many of these constitutional conflicts has involved a tension between individualist and communitarian concepts of politics.

While these two theories lie at the foundation of the American Constitution, describing them is not enough. Further examination of the heritage of these ideas about politics and constitutionalism is necessary. Where did Americans' ideas about constitutional government originate? How did the individualist and communitarian strands of political thought come to be expressed in the eighteenth-century American setting? Actually, the American constitutional heritage is an amalgam of intellectual influences and practical political experiences in the colonies. Each is discussed in turn here.

HISTORICAL INFLUENCES ON AMERICAN CONSTITUTIONALISM

Edward S. Corwin once said that "the American Revolution replaced the sway of a king with that of a document."[25] The document to which Corwin referred, of course, is the U.S. Constitution. The preceding chapter emphasized that constitutional government is limited government. Constitutions place limits on the day-to-day powers and activities of government in the name of more immutable general principles. A people under a constitution believe in the rule of law—specifically the rule of a law superior to the will of transient human governors. This belief in a higher law that rules daily human endeavors was not born in eighteenth-century American political thought. It originated more than two thousand years before in Greek political thought, was nurtured in the soil of Roman theory and practice, and reached fruition during medieval times, especially in England. The Protestant Reformation and the European Enlightenment both furthered the development of ideas and practices associated with modern constitutional government.

ANCIENT CONSTITUTIONALISM

Western political thought, going all the way back to fifth century B.C. Athens, has significantly affected the American constitutional system. The ancient Greek origins of American constitutional theory find their clearest expression in Aristotle's writings, particularly in *The Politics* (his foremost work on government). Aristotle argues that no matter what person or class is chosen to rule, the law ought to rule above all individuals in the well-ordered state. The law is general and thus embodies reason; human rulers are subject to passion and self-interest. In Aristotle's writings can be found the first inklings of this belief in a higher law superior to human decrees—a belief fundamental to constitutional government.

This higher-law tradition developed further in Roman political thought four centuries later. Indeed, the Romans had a much greater and more direct intellectual impact on American colonists than did the Greeks. American revolutionaries often referred to Roman history and Roman writers in justifying their cause against the crown. They saw themselves extolling the virtues of the Roman Republic against the corruption of imperial power. They viewed the English as modern-day Caesars. Americans in the 1760s and 1770s avidly read *Cato's Letters*, an anti-establishment English publication, and Joseph Addison's play, *Cato*. Both works were obvious references to the semi-mythical figure of the Roman Republic and to the similarity of conditions between ancient Rome and modern colonial life.

The colonists also read and cited the works of Cicero, a politician and political theorist at the time of the Roman Republic. With his discussion of natural law, Cicero added to Aristotle's notion of a superior higher law that ought to rule men and women. Cicero thought that universal justice and reason are found in the permanent elements of nature, including human nature. Human law, coming either from legislative bodies or individual rulers, must embody this universal justice found in the natural law to claim allegiance from the people. Existing governments must be limited by natural law. Whenever they act contrary to the natural law and its reason, they are no longer legitimate. Cicero's works also contain a rudimentary justification for the practice of judicial review, a fundamental feature of American constitutionalism. Cicero's impact appears clearly in the writings of important colonial thinkers in America. Men such as John Winthrop, Roger Williams, Thomas Hooker, John Wise, and Thomas Jefferson all refer to Cicero and other natural law theorists in making their political arguments.

Although ancient Greek and Roman thinking were important to the development of modern constitutionalism, one crucial element was missing: the idea of individual rights. As many scholars have noted, ancient constitutionalism, although committed to government limited by the rule of law, was not devoted to securing individual rights in the same way as is modern constitutional government. In this sense, Aristotle and Cicero could be called pure communitarians. For ancient thinkers, a law-abiding community where justice prevailed for all held highest importance. Individuals were expected to abide by the common good as reflected in the community's laws and rituals. The idea that individual rights might supersede the public good was alien to ancient thinkers.

MEDIEVAL CONSTITUTIONALISM

Medieval thinkers were the first to combine (although not completely) the elements of limited government with individual rights to form the crux of modern constitutional theory. In medieval England, citizens took the earliest steps toward achieving modern constitutionalism in practice.

Higher-law notions pervaded the Middle Ages. Medieval thinkers such as St. Thomas Aquinas and John of Salisbury spoke of the natural law as coming directly from God and existing as the ultimate standard of human law and conduct. But whereas ancient thinkers saw natural law as something that readily made its way into human laws and customs, medieval thinkers saw it as a higher standard outside of politics that *limited* human authority. By the medieval period, governance had become more personalized, the rule of a monarch rather than a legislative body. This made government potentially more arbitrary and autocratic. Thus, natural-law reasoning existed to set external norms for proper kingship and to judge existing rulers. For example, both Aquinas and John make a distinction between kingship and tyranny. The legitimate king is one who rules in accordance with the natural law; the tyrant rules oppressively, based on force, and is thereby an illegitimate ruler. This medieval idea that the higher natural law places inherent limits on rulers directly contributed to American notions of higher law under constitutional government. The American colonists drew specific sustenance from medieval arguments about legitimate resistance to tyranny.

This shift from ancient to medieval notions of natural law and its applications to human law was evolutionary rather than revolutionary. For the first time during the medieval period there emerged a conception of natural right to go along with that of natural law. The rise of Christianity and its emphasis on the individual as the ultimate value profoundly influenced Western European ideas about individual worth and dignity. A belief that individuals were invested by nature with certain rights that the state must, at least in theory, respect began to emerge in medieval Europe. With the Protestant Reformation, this natural rights doctrine became a stronger root of both religious and political dissent.

The earliest practical (as opposed to theoretical) steps toward modern constitutionalism were taken in England. And for all the impact continental European thought and practice had, it was from England that the founders of our constitution took most of their cues. Magna Carta, granted in 1215, is often cited as one of the first steps toward limiting the absolute power of the monarchy. In it, King John promised not to infringe on the customary feudal rights of the nobility. By the fourteenth century, the range of classes protected by Magna Carta broadened, as did the interpretation of what limits were placed on royal authority. However, the concessions originally granted in Magna Carta did not positively affect the lives of most, and the king continued to make the key decisions for the realm. Still, Magna Carta was the beginning of a gradual process of limiting governmental authority and is part of the first chapter in modern constitutional development. Moreover, references to Magna Carta and to the "ancient constitution of England" (ninth- and tenth-century Anglo-Saxon principles of government and constitutionalism) that predates it can be found in much of the colonial resistance literature of the eighteenth century.

ENGLISH COMMON LAW AND PARLIAMENTARY PRACTICE

More important to the origins of American constitutional politics, however, was the English common law and commentaries on it by English jurists. English common law, which combined indigenous customs with judicial pronouncements and interpretations, came to be seen as a higher law, containing universal precepts that existed above human authorities. Because of the case-oriented (as opposed to code-oriented) nature of British law, the British constitution came to be an unwritten higher law. The common law was used first to limit the power of kings, and later, in seventeenth-century England, to limit Parliament's power. American constitutional theory and practice received two kinds of principles from the English common law tradition. First, it inherited general concepts such as the judicial doctrines of precedent and "reasonableness." Second, the common law tradition passed along to American constitutionalism specific guarantees, such as the rights to due process of law and to a trial by jury. Both general and specific inheritances from English common law found their way into the U.S. Constitution and have been significant in shaping American historical practices over the past two hundred years.

In addition to English common law, the rise of the English Parliament as a challenger to the monarch's absolute sovereignty had an important influence on eighteenth-century American political thought. Parliament emerged as a significant force during the seventeenth century. The dispute between king and Parliament contributed to the English civil war (1642–1649). The war ended with Parliament ordering the execution of King Charles I in 1649. Later, with the Glorious Revolution of 1688, Parliament's power culminated when it declared the royal throne vacant and selected William and Mary of Holland to occupy it. Moreover, in this period, Parliament passed laws of constitutional significance, most notably the Petition of Right, the act of Habeas Corpus, and the Bill of Rights. The American colonists came to see Parliament, and by extension their own legislative assemblies, as the defender of people's rights and liberties against the Crown's incursions. Parliament's rise in power after its seventeenth-century battles with the English king taught the colonists important lessons about checking arbitrary royal authority and about the general need for a separation of governmental powers with built-in checks and balances. Ironically, the colonists would use their own conception of "the constitutional rights of Englishmen" to challenge what they considered to be oppressive Parliamentary legislation in the 1760s.

Finally, in addition to the general influence of classical authors and the English common law and Parliamentary traditions, specific political theorists in the seventeenth and eighteenth centuries directly affected the thinking of those who forged the American Revolution and the political institutions that followed. The colonists specifically identified with a number of anti-establishment English writers of the eighteenth century whose names today are relatively unknown. These writers, some of them members of Parliament, argued for greater liberty both within Parliament and against the royal court. The colonists used the arguments of the English writers to build support for their identical cause in America. Of course, French philosopher Baron de Montesquieu, whose *Spirit of the Laws* contained a strong argument for a strict separation of governmental powers, was also an important influence, as was Sir Edward Coke (see Brief 1.6). And as we see in the "conversation" that introduces this chapter, political theorists John Locke and Jean-Jacques Rousseau advanced ideas about government and politics that resonated with colonial Americans.

COLONIAL INFLUENCES ON AMERICAN CONSTITUTIONALISM

Ancient and medieval constitutionalism, English common law and practice, and the writings of political theorists constituted the basic intellectual heritage in eighteenth-century America. In addition to the intellectual heritage that informed their minds in the late 1700s, Americans drew on religious ideas and practices and over a century and a half of political experience. Religion provided a philosophical foundation for American constitutionalism, and the practices of different congregations offered insights about democracy and equality that informed those who framed the Constitution. Political conflicts between England and the colonies and within the colonies themselves informed the way Americans looked at government and how it ought to be organized.

RELIGIOUS IDEAS AND PRACTICES

The impact of religion on American constitutional development is unmistakable. For one reason, religion and constitutional theory share a belief in a higher law that orders human behavior. Both religion and constitutionalism are based on the idea that unchanging universal principles ought to exist as standards by which to judge changing human authorities. The Constitution itself is the "sacred text" containing these principles of government. In his essay *Rights of Man*, Thomas Paine said that Americans treated their written constitution like a bible:

> IT WAS THE POLITICAL BIBLE OF THE STATE. SCARCELY A FAMILY WAS WITHOUT IT. EVERY MEMBER OF THE GOVERNMENT HAD A COPY; AND NOTHING WAS MORE

Brief 1.6

SIR EDWARD COKE'S LEGACY

Seventeenth-century jurist Sir Edward Coke contributed significantly to American constitutionalism. First as a judge (rising to the rank of chief justice of the King's Bench) and later as a Member of Parliament, Coke led the fight against the British monarchy in the early 1600s. Beginning with King James I, the Stuart kings tried to bolster their authority over an unruly Parliament by asserting that God had vested kings with absolute authority to rule. Coke rejected this divine right of kings doctrine, offering instead a legal theory that placed both king and Parliament under a higher law. As a judge he argued "that the king hath no prerogative, but that which the law of the land allows," judges being the appropriate interpreters of this law. As a Member of Parliament, he asserted the power of Parliament as lawmaker over that of the king. Coke's contributions in this area of legislative supremacy and the proper separation of government powers were felt by American colonists struggling with royal authority in the eighteenth century.

More important than this were his judgments regarding the higher-law nature of the British constitution and the common law. His famous statement in Dr. Bonham's Case in 1610 was an inspiration to eighteenth-century American constitutional ideas. The London College of Physicians had punished Bonham under an act of Parliament for practicing medicine in the city without a license from the College. In vacating the action against Bonham, Coke stated:

> *And it appears in our books, that in many cases, the common law will controul acts of Parliament, and sometimes adjudge them to be utterly void: for when an act of Parliament is against common right and reason, or repugnant, or impossible to be performed, the common law will controul it and adjudge such act to be void.*[26]

Coke's argument that the English common law was fundamental, and could be used to judge the validity of acts of Parliament, is the precursor to the American principle of judicial review. Moreover, American courts, in judging the constitutionality of governmental acts, often use a standard of "reasonableness," which is the natural outgrowth of Coke's "common right and reason" standard.

Sir Edward Coke's writings and actions, especially in the area of judicial review, contributed greatly to American constitutional theory and practice. Although he proposed a theory of Parliamentary supremacy in the lawmaking area, Coke believed that both king and Parliament were answerable to the higher law of the British constitution. He thought that judges were the proper interpreters of the "law of the land" and could void governmental actions that violated the higher law. Coke's contribution of these two principles alone makes him a towering presence in American constitutional theory and practice.

> COMMON, WHEN ANY DEBATE AROSE ON THE PRINCIPLE OF A BILL, OR ON THE EXTENT OF ANY SPECIES OF AUTHORITY, THAN FOR THE MEMBERS TO TAKE THE PRINTED CONSTITUTION OUT OF THEIR POCKET, AND READ THE CHAPTER WITH WHICH SUCH MATTER IN DEBATE WAS CONNECTED. . . . IT IS THE BODY OF ELEMENTS, TO WHICH YOU CAN REFER, AND QUOTE ARTICLE BY ARTICLE; AND WHICH CONTAINS EVERYTHING THAT RELATES TO THE COMPLETE ORGANIZATION OF CIVIL GOVERNMENT, AND THE PRINCIPLES ON WHICH IT SHALL ACT, AND BY WHICH IT SHALL BE BOUND.[27]

In addition, the specific form and content of the American constitution reflects an imperative, lawgiving feature that parallels religious imperatives and laws. This parallel is no small coincidence, as many of the American colonies had strong religious foundations. The Mayflower Compact was an early colonial constitution based largely on religious ideas of covenant and compact. The compact-based communities were founded largely for religious reasons. Seeking separation from the Church of England, a number of Calvinists began forming churches on the basis of a covenant between believers. Persecuted by James I at the beginning of the seventeenth century, these separatist Calvinist churches first sought refuge in Holland, which at the time was alone in offering religious toleration. But a number of people wanted to found a new community in America. The first and most famous was the group who traveled on the *Mayflower* to settle in Plymouth, Massachusetts, in 1620. Before landing, all the male members of this "body of believers" came together and applied their notions about religious covenants to politics. The Mayflower Compact, the basis for the Plymouth government, issued from this notable ship meeting. A part of it read:

> WE WHOSE NAMES ARE UNDERWRITTEN . . . DO BY THESE PRESENTS SOLEMNLY AND MUTUALY IN THE PRESENCE OF GOD, AND ONE OF ANOTHER, COVENANT AND COMBINE OURSELVES TOGEATHER INTO A CIVILL BODY POLITICK, FOR OUR BETTER ORDERING AND PRESERVATION . . . AND BY VERTUE HEAROF ENACTE, CONSTITUTE, AND FRAME SUCH JUST AND EQUALL LAWS, ORDINANCES, ACTS, CONSTITUTIONS, AND OFFICES, FROM TIME TO TIME, AS SHALL BE THOUGHT MOST MEETE AND CONVENIENT FOR THE GENERAL GOOD OF THE COLONIE, UNTO WHICH WE PROMISE ALL DUE SUBMISSION AND OBEDIENCE.[28]

Furthermore, the combination of individualism and communitarianism found in American political thought can also be found in the Judeo-Christian religious tradition. The Christian belief in the sanctity of the individual human being, a being whose capacity for free choice and free will sets him or her apart from other beings—a belief magnified by ideas born out of the Protestant Revolution of the sixteenth and seventeenth centuries—squares nicely with the political individualist's belief in the sanctity of individual rights in the face of government power. On the other side, the Judaic tradition celebrates the community of the Jewish people, bound together both in the here and now and in the Kingdom yet to come.[29] And, the glorification in Christian doctrine of a community of fellow believers who share values and interests, who work together and sacrifice for each other, parallels the communitarian political outlook described earlier. So the religious ideals of the Judeo-Christian tradition have exerted an important influence on America's constitutional development.

In addition, a colony's religious principles often meant different laws and political institutions. For example, religion clearly informed the government's character at Massachusetts Bay. Primarily middle-class Puritans seeking refuge from Anglican Church domination, the people at Massachusetts Bay believed that God had covenanted with them to establish this distinct community. Religious belief formed the foundation for the polity and many of its laws. In addition, the colony's leaders, most notably Governor John Winthrop, saw themselves as commanded by God to rule the people in line with Calvinist principles. Winthrop's views about a people's religious "calling" and their covenant with God translated into more authoritarian political ideas. In the eighteenth century, however, John Wise would use the same Puritan foundations to argue for more democratic church and state governance.

The mode of church governance adopted was another aspect of religion affecting colonial politics. As a rule, colonies where the congregational form of church government was predominant tended toward greater decentralization and diffusion of power. On the other hand, those colonies containing more churches governed on the Presbyterian model tended to be more hierarchical and centralized in their political decision making. Baptists, Methodists, and other denominations making up the wave of Protestant evangelicalism during this period gave congregations an egalitarian spiritual and political experience within the faith community that spilled over into the governmental realm. Moreover, one of the greatest sources of American political thought at the time of the Revolution is found in the sermons of these congregational churches' preachers. These sermons, many of which advocated rebellion against English rule, were not only heard by congregations but also published and read by people throughout the colonies. Many of these sermons contained revolutionary theories of human nature and government that would be at the heart of the new constitutional system.

STRUCTURE OF GOVERNMENT: COLONIAL EXPERIENCE

It would be a mistake to see American colonial history as the same throughout the colonies. Differences between colonies were significant. Differences existed between northern and southern colonies in the degree to which the colony's legal system stuck to the English model. The northern colonies deviated more from English legal traditions than did the southern colonies, which on the whole were more traditional.

Of course, differences in colonial structure and experience would produce difficulties in bringing the former colonies together after the revolution, as the discussion in Chapter 2 indicates. Still, despite these and other significant differences, a number of factors were felt across the American colonies. Two crucial developments that ultimately ran at cross-purposes uniformly molded colonial political theory and practice: the increased coordination of colonial affairs from England and the rise of the colonial assembly as a lawmaking body. By the late 1600s, England began forcing its administrative will on all the colonies. By setting up new courts, passing navigation and tax laws, achieving greater central coordination through the royal governor, and increasing the colonies' commercial dependence, England brought the colonies more in line with the English legal system. At the same time, however, imperial England began to deny that the colonists had the same rights as those in England. Especially after the Glorious Revolution and the Parliament's passage of the Bill of Rights in 1689 (see Brief 1.7), many colonists began to press for recognition of the "constitutional rights of Englishmen." The right to full representation in elected assemblies, to initiate legislation on all matters (even fiscal matters), and to be free from arbitrary deprivation of liberty and property were continually invoked by colonists after 1688. English leaders denied these claims, viewing the colonies as royal dominions and their inhabitants as possessing no inalienable constitutional rights.

However, the rise in prominence of the colonial assemblies counteracted this imperial thrust from London. Each colony's legislative assembly had by the 1700s become a formidable power, with Pennsylvania leading the way. The colonists became used to self-rule through their local legislatures, using them to make their own laws and to challenge imperial authority. By waiting until later in the seventeenth century to assert imperial control, England may have begun too late. The ideals and practices of "home rule" were already in place, not to be dislodged without a fight.

From their experiences with England beginning in the late 1600s, the colonists learned that discretionary executive power was the greatest threat to their liberty and autonomy. Time and again the colonists had to defend themselves against arbitrary royal power, exercised by both king and royal governor alike. Having experienced the oppressiveness of royal authority, newly independent Americans wrote state constitutions designed to limit the authority of their chief executive. In these state constitutions, the former colonists also indicated a preference for legislative over executive power. (The specific problems the new republics experienced as a result of this preference are examined in the following chapter.)

Americans would ultimately emerge from their eighteenth-century battles with a constitution based on a separation-of-powers system, with a specific set of checks and balances to give each branch in the

Brief 1.7
THE ENGLISH BILL OF RIGHTS

Drafted by Parliament and accepted by William and Mary on February 13, 1689, the Bill of Rights stands as the cornerstone of the Glorious Revolution that deposed James II and returned Parliament to ultimate sovereignty. The Bill of Rights begins by documenting the crimes committed against the people and the Protestant religion by Catholic King James II. It concludes by declaring Parliament supreme, disallowing future kings from suspending any laws or their execution and from spending money without parliamentary consent.

The Bill of Rights also contains specific guarantees that would become important in the revolutionary battles in the American colonies in the 1760s and 1770s, and would be written into the U.S. Constitution. The 1689 act establishes the right of British subjects to petition the king, which the American colonists made use of on a number of occasions before 1776. It makes illegal the keeping of a standing army in a time of peace without parliamentary consent, a principle the colonists fought for vociferously, as the next chapter indicates. Moreover, the Bill of Rights exists as a precursor to our own. Specific guarantees against "excessive bail [or] fines" and "cruel and unusual punishments" found in Parliament's 1689 law are contained word for word in our own Eighth Amendment, whereas the general provisions about jury trials read much like the U.S. Constitution's wording in the Sixth and Seventh Amendments (see Chapter 13). In addition, the act protects the free speech and debate rights of members of Parliament by preventing them from being questioned or impeached over statements made during parliamentary proceedings. An identical protection for members of Congress appears in Article I, Section 6 of the U.S. Constitution.

The English Bill of Rights signaled the culmination of a revolutionary century in Great Britain and was a watershed in the historical relationship between king and Parliament, but it also existed as a precedent for the revolutionary claims of American colonists in the next century and would serve as a landmark in their adoption of constitutional provisions in 1787 and 1791.

---

government the teeth to enforce the separation of powers. This was believed to be the best method to protect liberty while still providing the necessary governmental authority. Some people have mistakenly argued that the separation of powers doctrine was already present in the colonies before 1776. On the contrary, the colonies, again borrowing from classical Roman and contemporary English practices, exhibited the principles of the "mixed constitution." Under the mixed constitution, different components (governor, council, assembly, and courts) representing different classes or interests *shared* government powers. The different branches of colonial government were not separated during the pre-Revolutionary era, but combined together to exercise authority. It was only after 1787 that a separation of powers was put into place.

The other important question about government structure was over the amount of power to give local versus central authority. Colonial experience gave more emphasis to the idea of decentralized authority. The New England township, in conjunction with the congregational church, wielded considerable authority over many local policy matters. Similarly, in the mid-Atlantic and southern colonies, the county was the principle unit of local administration. Although often dominated by elites and the upper classes, local governments thrived throughout the American colonies and provided a major impetus toward independence. By the mid-1700s many colonists had come to feel that the desired combination of liberty with meaningful political community could only flourish under a system favoring strong local government.

Conclusion

The essence of constitutionalism lies in its distrust and restraint of power. As noted throughout this chapter, limitations on government have taken many forms. In the American case, emphasis has been placed on the separation of powers and corresponding checks and balances, judicial review, and federalism, combined with an effective Bill of Rights. Other countries have selected different structural devices to organize and restrain government power, although all constitutional systems have recognized and respected the rights of individuals to liberty, equality, and participation.

In the American experience, constitutional government has been informed by a number of elements. The individualist theory of politics (or classical liberalism), as exemplified in the writings of John Locke, certainly underlies many of our constitutional principles and structures. The other theoretical pillar of American constitutionalism can be found in the communitarian theory of government (or classical republicanism), exhibited in writers such as Jean-Jacques Rousseau. In addition, a rich intellectual heritage of Western political and religious thought, beginning in ancient Greece, informs American constitutional theory and practice. Finally, over a century of historical experience in the colonies, involving political interaction within colonies, as well as between the colonies and Great Britain, influenced the molding of American political institutions.

These basic elements of American constitutionalism were all in place by the 1760s. The colonists' ideas about human nature and the proper role of government in individuals' lives had been formed by a rich intellectual and practical heritage. Specific conflicts in the 1760s and 1770s provided the final impetus toward independence. The specific actors and issues surrounding the making of the American Constitution are the subject of Chapter 2.

Chapter 2
American Constitutionalism: The Founding Generation

The meeting room in Independence Hall is arranged as it was when delegates congregated over the summer of 1787 to draft the U.S. Constitution. The document produced from this room represents the revolutionary experiment of an entire generation. (Photographed with the courtesy of Independence National Historical Park.)

▼ Introductory Remarks by President and Secretary of State James Madison

It seems fitting for me, James Madison, to introduce this book's chapter covering the historical backdrop to, and the actual creation and adoption of, the U.S. Constitution in the 1780s. I am often referred to as the "father of the U.S. Constitution," as my draft (known as the Virginia Plan) at the Constitutional Convention in 1787 proposed the basic structure of a new constitution different from the Articles of Confederation. I was not a big fan of this title, for a simple reason I relayed to a colleague years later: "This was not, like the fabled Goddess of Wisdom, the offspring of a single brain. It ought to be regarded as the work of many heads and many hands."

My involvement in crafting a new founding document, however, was central. Although I did not play a prominent role in the revolutionary events that preceded the new nation's beginnings, I did serve as a representative from Virginia to the first Congress under the Articles of Confederation. And in my home state I advocated for a number of critical provisions in Virginia's state constitution and governmental structure, including a strict separation of church and state. As you will find out later in this text, this advocacy, along with that of Thomas Jefferson, led to passage in 1786 of the Virginia Statute of Religious Freedom, a precursor to the protections found for religious liberty in our Bill of Rights (see Brief 16.1).

But it was my concern over what was happening during operation of the Articles of Confederation, particularly in the state governments, that helped precipitate a national convention that would ultimately produce a new constitution for the United States in 1787. On the eve of a general convention in Philadelphia called in May 1787 to discuss possible revisions to the Articles of Confederation, that April I wrote "The Vices of the Political System of the U.S.," aimed at pointing out key problems with the confederation government. I thought the federal government was proving too weak to conduct economic policy for the United States, allowing the states to operate in harmful ways: "The practice of many States in restricting the commercial intercourse with other States . . . is certainly adverse to the spirit of the Union, and tends to [be] destructive of the general harmony." I was most concerned, however, with the tendency in many states for tyrannical majorities to run roughshod over the liberties of those in the minority. I wrote: "In republican Government the majority however composed, ultimately give the law. Whenever therefore an apparent interest or common passion unites a majority what is to restrain them from unjust violations of the rights and interests of the minority, or of individuals?"

My draft of the Virginia Plan, presented on the first day of the Philadelphia convention, attempted to solve the problems many saw with the first U.S. constitution under the Articles of Confederation. It not only gave the federal government greater powers to act than the Confederation congress possessed, it also provided for a congressional "negative" (i.e., a veto) over any state legislation thought detrimental to the country as a whole. As you will see in reading this chapter, I did not get everything I wanted in a new constitution—including the congressional veto—as the final document reflected a compromise among different elements and interests. But my hand in this work was quite clear, and after ratification, I became the main author responsible for drafting what would become the U.S. Bill of Rights, the first ten amendments to the Constitution adopted in 1791. The Bill of Rights granted citizens fundamental liberties against the government like those found in the First Amendment, but also included the Ninth Amendment, which makes sure that citizen rights are not circumscribed to solely those enumerated in the Bill of Rights or in the Constitution itself (see Brief 11.3 for further discussion of this important constitutional provision).

Of course, I went on to become Secretary of State for two terms under President Thomas Jefferson, and served as Fourth President of the United States myself for two terms. But as you read this chapter, you will understand why my most important legacy is as "Father of the Constitution."

Sources: James Madison, "The Vices of the Political System of the United States," *http://teachingamericanhistory.org/library/index.asp?document=802*; Jack Rakove, *James Madison and the Creation of the American Republic* (Upper Saddle River, NJ: Pearson, 2006); Garry Wills, *James Madison* (New York: Times Books, 2002).

Introduction: Constitutionalism and the American Revolution

The American Constitution adopted in 1787 was actually the culmination of a revolution started in the early 1760s. A generation of rebellion against English rule and of American experiments in popular government preceded the writing of the U.S. Constitution. The revolutionary events that predated the Constitution must be examined to understand the structure and content of that document. The discussion turns first, then, to the events that comprise the American Revolution.

In one respect, the American Revolution was not all that revolutionary. The revolution of 1776 differs from revolutions in the modern world. It did not involve the violent upheaval of social forces and institutions. And, unlike twentieth-century anticolonial independence movements, the American revolutionaries were not out to create a system to guarantee political rights that were previously nonexistent. In fact, the colonists saw themselves as trying to preserve their "ancient constitutions" (which they traced all the way back to the tenth century) and the basic liberties they had enjoyed for 150 years until English rule suddenly became oppressive.

Remember that many Americans had already declared independence from their homeland by the very act of their emigration. Those of English ancestry had, like their Saxon predecessors, uprooted themselves, leaving their previous communities to find a new life in the New World. Others had come to seek asylum from religious, political, and social oppression. Upon arriving, they set up institutions based on popular consent. Emigrants sought control over those matters in which they had invested their lives and fortunes. The colonists accepted imperial rule from London, but only insofar as English governments did not trample on their basic liberties.

A look at colonial documents and writings during the 1760s and 1770s supports this perspective. References abound to the colonists' circumstances of immigrating to the New World. Resistance originally took the form of petitions to the king and Parliament to stop interfering with the colonists' fundamental rights. American revolutionaries saw America as destined to fill the role of preserving the ancient constitution, going all the way back to Saxon times. England had grown corrupt and decadent, they argued, and it was up to America to purge the English constitution of its impurities to preserve ancient liberties enjoyed in earlier times. Until the summer of 1776, American revolutionaries themselves insisted that their action was constitutional resistance to unconstitutional governance by the British Parliament. In their own minds, the colonists revolted not against the English constitution but on behalf of it. The essentially conservative nature of the American Revolution was grasped by famous English conservative Edmund Burke, who took the colonists' side in the struggle and argued that it was the British who were suddenly revolting against decades of political history and practice.

The lasting power of the colonial heritage lends further credence to the fact that the American Revolution was basically conservative. After independence was won, Americans drew liberally on their colonial charters and on English law and customs in setting up their new institutions. In fact, two states, Rhode Island and Connecticut, basically kept their colonial charters as their state constitutions well into the 1800s.

In another important sense, however, the American Revolution and what it accomplished *was* truly revolutionary. The generation that made the revolution not only sought independence from Great Britain but they wanted to create, as the Great Seal of the United States reads, "a new order of the ages." They established political institutions in line with revolutionary beliefs about human equality, popular sovereignty, and natural rights. When the colonists broke with Great Britain, an experiment began to create institutions that would truly be based on the consent of the governed. Furthermore, a revolution in constitutional thinking took place after 1776 as well.

Emerging American Constitutionalism (1760–1776)

Events in the 1760s and early 1770s brought the conflict between England and the American colonies to a head. The British Parliament first attempted to exercise power over the American colonies in navigation and trade acts beginning in 1651. But until the conclusion of the Seven Years' War (also called the Great

War for the Empire, and the French and Indian Wars) in 1763, Americans did not feel the full force of parliamentary rule. After the Treaty of Paris, which ended the war, England introduced changes in imperial policy designed to alleviate its huge war debt and make colonial administration more efficient. After closing the area west of the Alleghenies to further colonial settlement, Parliament passed two bills meant to help finance the large public debt: the Sugar Act of 1764 and the Stamp Act of 1765. These laws, and colonial resistance to them, began a decade-long fight that would culminate in a revolution.

The crisis created by British attempts to rule the colonies in this period structured the way Americans looked at politics and their constitution. Three constitutional issues emerged from this period that would lead Americans to revolution and would shape the constitutions they wrote following independence.

First, the colonists asserted that they had certain fundamental rights, found in nature as well as in the English constitution. Colonists argued that Parliament could not interfere with these rights. Any law attempting to deprive colonists of their rights was unconstitutional and could be resisted. For example, when the Townshend Acts of 1767 authorized the enforcement of new taxes through the use of writs of assistance, which gave British officials open-ended search powers in customs cases, the colonists fought this as a clear violation of their natural property rights. And when Lord Hillsborough, the English secretary of state, sent British troops to Boston to enforce the Townshend Acts, Americans challenged the quartering of troops as an affront to their natural right to liberty as well as the property in their own homes. (Memories of the abuses incurred by the forced quartering of British troops would remain through the founding period, and the colonists' initial concerns would make their way into the Third Amendment to the U.S. Constitution. It commands that "no soldier shall, in time of peace, be quartered in any house, without the consent of the owner, nor in time of war, but in a manner to be prescribed by law.")

As the conflict between Parliament and the colonies intensified, the colonists became more fervent in their defense of these natural rights. This defense culminated in the Declaration of Independence, which begins with the statement that natural rights are the foundation for all government. One of the first examples of the individualist strain in American political thought is seen in this assertion of inalienable natural rights.

The second issue related to the fact that American colonists began forming a different conception of law and legislative power. They began to distinguish between what was "constitutional" and what was "legal." The British never made this distinction, believing that the constitution, the common law, and acts of Parliament were all mixed together. The British believed that Parliament's actions were part of the constitutional heritage and could not be set against the British constitution. But as a result of laws passed by Parliament to which the colonists objected, Americans began to speak of basic principles in the constitution that stood above lawmaking authority. For example, James Otis, in his *Rights of the British Colonies Asserted and Proved*, argued that any law in violation of the constitution and "common reason" could be declared void and unenforceable. Otis claimed that, given the constitutional principle that property not be taken without consent, Parliament had violated this principle in passing the Sugar Act. Citing Coke, he argued that "acts of parliament against natural equity [or] against the fundamental principles of the British constitution are void."[1]

Americans came to believe that a constitution establishes general principles that can never be overridden by legislation, no matter how representative the legislature is of the people. Origins of American constitutionalism and the doctrine of judicial review can be seen in this distinction.

Finally, the crisis that began in the 1760s raised the issue of local colonial autonomy. As was mentioned in the preceding chapter, Americans had been accustomed to regulating their affairs locally, through town and county meetings and through their colonial assemblies. Americans had adopted the classical republican view that popular rule and public virtue were best maintained at the local level. The attempt by Parliament to control matters from London led the colonists to assert a right to colonial self-rule within the empire. Parliament's constant attempts to levy direct taxes on goods and services in the American colonies were resisted on the grounds that Britain was interfering with the colonial assembly's right to rule over internal police and taxation matters. The belief in local self-government contributed to powerful states and localities in the early post-Revolutionary years and to the peculiar brand of federalism that we find in the American constitutional system today.

Beginning in 1774 with the First Continental Congress in Philadelphia, representatives from the American colonies began to meet to discuss and press their common constitutional claims against the king and Parliament. In addition to the two continental congresses at the intercolonial level, revolutionary governments were being formed at the local level. When conflict erupted in 1775 and the British responded punitively to colonial attempts at peaceful resolution, the full-scale war that came a year later seemed inevitable.

Americans were ready for separation from England by the beginning of 1776, but the publication of Thomas Paine's *Common Sense* in January provided the catalyst for independence. Paine's pamphlet expressed brilliantly and in language easily understood what Americans were waiting to hear. In it, Paine argued that the king was as oppressive as Parliament, and that the colonists' rights were incompatible with the British monarchy. He called on Americans to throw off the yoke of monarchy and aristocracy and to take up the mantle of republican government. Asserting that "of more worth is one honest man to society, in the sight of God, than all the crowned ruffians that ever lived," Paine urged the colonists to abolish both the monarchy and the nobility in devising new political institutions. *Common Sense* was widely read throughout the colonies (it sold 120,000 copies in three months), and it changed the basis of colonial demands from the constitutional rights of Englishmen to the natural rights of humanity in general. Paine told the colonists that "the cause of America is in great measure the cause of all mankind." Conservatives recoiled from many of Paine's more radical arguments, but by April 1776, the formal establishment of independence along the lines of Paine's recommendations appeared inevitable.

THE DECLARATION OF INDEPENDENCE

Beginning in April, the Continental Congress acted swiftly to make the final separation from Great Britain. On April 6, it opened all American ports to foreign trade, thereby nullifying British trade restrictions. On May 15, Congress transferred all government power from Great Britain to the people of the colonies, and instructed each colony to end all vestiges of royal authority and create new governments. On the same day the Virginia House of Burgesses instructed its congressional delegates to propose independence. Richard Henry Lee acted on these instructions on June 7, 1776, when he introduced the following resolution before the Congress:

> RESOLVED, THAT THESE UNITED COLONIES ARE, AND OF RIGHT OUGHT TO BE, FREE AND INDEPENDENT STATES, AND THAT THEY ARE ABSOLVED FROM ALL ALLEGIANCE TO THE BRITISH CROWN, AND THAT ALL CONNECTION BETWEEN THEM AND THE STATE OF GREAT BRITAIN IS, AND OUGHT TO BE, TOTALLY DISSOLVED.[2]

Lee's resolution was referred to a five-man committee (Thomas Jefferson, John Adams, Benjamin Franklin, Roger Sherman, and Robert Livingston) to draft a declaration of independence. At this point not all Americans favored independence. The middle colonies in particular (New York, Pennsylvania, and Delaware) were initially opposed to Lee's resolution. The ease with which the radicals proposed separation from England made conservatives worry about what the result of independence might be. They feared what they might lose if the revolt were unsuccessful, or even if it succeeded, given the possibility of anarchy or mob rule.

Jefferson's Declaration of Independence was presented to the Congress on July 2, with all but three delegates voting for adoption (New York abstained from voting). It was read in Philadelphia after some revision on July 4, and signed by the members of Congress August 2, 1776. The Declaration of Independence has been aptly described as more of a propaganda device than a real declaration of independence. Congress had already declared independence, informally at least, and the colonists had been engaging in a war of independence for over two years. The Declaration stands as a formal announcement of, and more importantly as a justification to, Britain and to the world for the decision to separate from the British Empire.

But the Declaration of Independence is more than propaganda. It is also an important constitutional document. It contains ideas about human nature and the proper foundations and ends of government that would guide Americans in setting up their independent political institutions. In fact, seven of the eleven states that wrote new constitutions after 1776 attached the Declaration to their state constitutions. The Declaration reflects the bipolar elements of individualism and communitarianism discussed in Chapter 1. Although there are some dramatic differences between the Declaration of Independence and the Constitution of 1787, which have led some to call the Constitution a betrayal of the Declaration's ideals (see the critique of the Constitution at the end of this chapter), the delegates to the constitutional convention saw the Declaration as the foundation of the document they were drafting.

Furthermore, the Declaration has been used since the founding period by Americans calling for basic changes in the constitutional system. Abolitionists and women's rights advocates used the Declaration to support their causes throughout the nineteenth century; Southern secessionists referred to it in 1861; populists cited it in calling for greater social justice in the late 1800s. The Supreme Court has used the Declaration on a number of occasions to justify the expansion of civil and political rights. A brief examination of the Declaration of Independence will bear out its importance as a constitutional document.

Jefferson begins by stating the general principles that "impel . . . [the] people to dissolve the political bands which have connected them with another, and to assume among the powers of the earth the separate and equal station which the laws of nature and nature's god entitle them." The Declaration continues with the famous statement of natural rights and the ends of government, which follows the argument found in John Locke's *Second Treatise of Government*:

> WE HOLD THESE TRUTHS TO BE SELF-EVIDENT: THAT ALL MEN ARE CREATED EQUAL; THAT THEY ARE ENDOWED BY THEIR CREATOR WITH CERTAIN UNALIENABLE RIGHTS; THAT AMONG THESE ARE LIFE, LIBERTY & THE PURSUIT OF HAPPINESS.

Nature invests people with certain *inalienable* rights, which it is government's purpose to protect. Government derives its power solely from the consent of the people constituting it. The Declaration goes on to say that "when a long train of abuses and usurpations" of the people's rights occurs, "it is their right, it is their duty to throw off such government, and to provide new guards for their future security."

A seemingly straightforward individualist statement of the natural-rights foundation of politics, Jefferson's document also contains elements of the communitarian theory of government. The commitment to popular rule evident from Jefferson's words reflects the republican ideal of citizens deliberating in communities and embodying the common good in law. The bulk of the Declaration is devoted to detailing the specific "history of injuries and usurpations" done to the colonies by the king, most of which have to do with interfering with the people's right to republican self-government.

Moreover, communitarian strands can be found in the statement of "natural rights" to life, liberty, and the pursuit of happiness just cited. "Liberty" as understood by Jefferson included public or political liberty, the people's liberty to make policy in line with their conception of public virtue. "Rights" had most to do with the rights of the people against the privileged interests of the few, not the rights of the individual against the community. In conducting their state's business after the Revolution, Americans found no contradiction between liberty and government restrictions on speech, private property rights, and other private interests. Similarly, the "pursuit of happiness" meant government's pursuit of "public happiness," the good of society as a whole, rather than the individual's hedonistic pursuit of private pleasure. For Jefferson, happiness was tied to equal participation in the public realm.

The Declaration of Independence ought to be read alongside the U.S. Constitution as a statement of American constitutionalism. It not only presents both the individualist and communitarian political theories that characterize American political history, it also expresses the general principles later embodied in American political institutions. One might say that the Declaration states the ends of government, while the Constitution contains the means of achieving those ends.

POST-REVOLUTIONARY CONSTITUTIONALISM

The American colonists had established their independence by the summer of 1776. Though a war would be fought with the British to maintain this independence, Americans were constitutionally separated by Jefferson's declaration. It became the task of the revolutionaries to draft new documents to "constitute" themselves as political communities and institutionalize new power relationships. At both the state and continental levels, Americans wrote constitutions and experimented with various governmental structures. The discussion now turns to the story of the successes and failures of post-Revolutionary constitutionalism.

THE REVOLUTIONARY STATE CONSTITUTIONS

The Declaration of Independence was made on behalf of the "free and independent states." Several colonies had begun writing new constitutions before the Declaration was even approved. This might be expected since the overarching preoccupation of the American revolutionaries was the creation of healthy state governments. They were concerned that government be conducted on a small scale, close to the people. The process of forming new governments at the state level occurred with remarkable speed. New Hampshire, South Carolina, Virginia, and New Jersey drafted new constitutions before the formal Declaration of Independence on July 4, and by the end of that year, ten state governments were already in place. The war delayed the process in New York and Georgia until 1777. The people of Massachusetts put a provisional government in place in 1777, deciding to go through a different process before formally adopting a new constitution in 1780. Vermont framed a new constitution in 1777, three years before other states even recognized its independence. In addition to conducting the war against the British, then, Americans were busy engaging in state constitution writing.

Since Americans distinguished between "constitutional" and "legal" during colonial resistance, it might be expected that these new state constitutions would reflect this principle. The constitution would exist as fundamental law, separated from and superior to statutes passed by a legislature. But how to make the higher-law nature of state constitutions *effective* was a problem. Initially, the state legislatures (or provincial congresses) wrote, interpreted, and easily amended their state constitutions, thus making the distinction between constitution and statutes meaningless. Massachusetts would be the first state to call a constitutional convention, with delegates especially selected to draft a constitution by the people. Once drafted, the Massachusetts Constitution was taken back to the people for ratification (requiring a two-thirds majority of all the towns to take effect). With adoption of the Massachusetts Constitution in 1780, a new method had been devised to give authority to the principle that government should be founded on the people and be answerable for its daily actions to a higher, written law.

A second problem lay in the vesting of sovereignty. Americans agreed that the states would establish a republican form of government, vesting power in the people rather than in the Crown or Parliament. But the question was, What kind of republic should be formed? How would revolutionary leaders provide both popular governments and effective, orderly rule? The English example of mixed government no longer offered a model Americans could emulate. This model was premised on a power-sharing arrangement among three distinct classes: the monarchy, the aristocracy, and the propertied middle classes. Having deposed the monarch and having no real aristocracy in the European sense, Americans had no basis for mixed government. They relied on the separation-of-powers principle to organize their new governments.

Separation-of-powers theory divides and balances government according to function rather than according to social class. Without a method of limiting government itself and keeping it running effectively and rationally, constitutionalism cannot survive (remember the Madisonian dilemma discussed in Chapter 1). By providing for separate legislative, executive, and judicial branches, each with its own distinct powers, the proper governmental balance could be struck. A separation of powers could stop plural officeholding and prevent one branch from manipulating another—problems believed to be sources of corruption and tyranny during the colonial era.

This was how the separation-of-powers system was to work, in theory. In practice, none of the new state constitutions effectively instituted a true separation of powers. Royal governors, the colonies' chief executives, had been the sources and symbols of tyranny. These governors had the power to stop colonial legislation. They could appoint their followers to government offices, including the judiciary, and so build webs of influence from which to dominate the people. Receiving their orders from the Crown, the governors often carried into execution coercive British measures. Americans like Jefferson vowed to "destroy the kingly office . . . to absolutely divest [it] of all its rights, powers and prerogatives."[3]

The new state constitutions created governments in which the legislature reigned supreme and the governor was demoted to no more than an administrator of the law. Governors were stripped of all prerogative powers. Eleven states denied the governor veto power. The governor's appointment powers were either limited, shared with the state legislature, or taken over completely by the state legislature. In eight states the legislature elected the governor; ten states provided for annual elections and limited reelection to prevent the governor from gaining too much power. Pennsylvania's radically democratic constitution of 1776 eliminated the governor's office entirely, replacing it with a twelve-person executive council elected directly by the people.

At first people applauded the fact that governors would be completely dependent on their legislatures, since that would tie them to the "people's representatives." Only later would attempts be made to strengthen the governor against an unruly legislature. And the framers of the new state constitutions made sure the legislature would *be* representative by increasing the number of representatives and requiring them to stand for annual elections. John Adams proclaimed, "Where annual election ends, tyranny begins." Annual election to at least one house of the state legislature, a practice adopted in every state except South Carolina, was a radical departure from past colonial practices.

The states adopted one device to slow down legislative power: the bicameral legislature. Inspired by the British Parliament, the newly independent states created a lower and an upper house in their legislatures (Pennsylvania was the only state to adopt a unicameral legislature). Requiring a bill to pass through a second house of the legislature would prevent impetuous actions on the part of thoughtless and transient majorities. The second house would thus serve as a double representative of the people, tempering well-intentioned but careless and harmful acts. In addition, some believed that the upper house of the legislature could furnish a place for the "natural aristocracy," those citizens with leadership skills or special wisdom without whose authority a government would suffer. Adams had this "natural aristocracy" in mind when he proposed the idea of bicameralism to the states in 1776. However, in many states little difference existed between the requirements and qualifications in the lower and upper houses. Critics worried that bicameral legislatures were not providing in practice the wisdom and deliberative functions asked of them in theory.

In addition to the bicameral legislature, eight of the states attached bills of rights to their constitutions to check governmental power. These bills of rights, many of which read like rough drafts to the U.S. Constitution's Bill of Rights ratified in 1791, were intended in theory to check the government's power to threaten individual liberty. However, these state bills of rights did not in practice protect individuals against the state legislatures.

The state constitutions also created an independent judiciary. By the 1770s, colonists saw that an independent judiciary could provide the most important check on the executive's prerogative powers. Had an independent judiciary existed in the colonies, it could have ruled on the constitutionality of Parliament's actions. So the new constitutions moved to establish judicial independence. Governors were denied the intimidating power of exclusive judicial appointment, and legislators were denied the right to sit as judges. To further enhance independence, judges were allowed to serve during good behavior or for fixed-year terms; they were not on the bench at the pleasure of the chief magistrate.

But as with the separation-of-powers principle in general, judicial independence was present only in theory. In fact, state legislatures dominated the judiciary as they did the executive. Legislators elected judges, paid their salaries, overruled their decisions with new laws or constitutional amendments, and subjected them to impeachment if all else failed. True judicial independence would only come with the federal constitution of 1787.

The legislature reigned supreme in the early American state governments. The other branches did not provide a check on its actions. Neither did the state constitutions themselves. Republican theory placed its emphasis on the community rather than on the individual. The people, through their representatives, had the right to act for the common good.

Constitutions were not thought to place limits on what a legislature could do in the public interest. Even the eight states that attached bills of rights to their constitutions allowed the legislature to interfere with individual rights. The irony is that having based their resistance to Parliament on a differentiation between constitutional principles and legal actions, Americans immediately enshrined the kind of legislative supremacy exercised by Parliament in their new state governments. Problems caused by this state legislative supremacy are discussed later in this chapter.

A frequent question asked about the newly created state governments is, How much of a change had occurred as a result of the Revolution? Americans had proclaimed the principle of democratic equality in their Declaration of Independence—and had demonstrated a commitment to new forms of republican rule—based on the people themselves. They had separated not only from England, but also from the principles of government expressed by the British system. Historian Merrill Jensen has said that the American Revolution was not only a dispute about home rule, but also about who should rule at home.[4] The revolutionary movement brought hope to those previously excluded from politics, especially westerners, tenant farmers, city laborers, and the propertyless. Did the American Revolution actually change things in line with the expressed commitment to republican rule based on all the people?

Although there is some dispute among historians, the evidence suggests that changes in the composition of government actually did take place after 1776. State constitutions lowered requirements for participating in elections, expanding the number of people who could vote. Between 1776 and 1789, property requirements for voting were eased, and in some cases eliminated. The Pennsylvania constitution required only residency and the payment of public taxes to vote, which qualified 90 percent of its adult males. Vermont went even further, in effect instituting universal adult male suffrage. Only in the Massachusetts Constitution of 1780 was the property qualification increased. Where property qualifications for suffrage existed, they were justified on the grounds that only people with property had an independent will and a sufficient stake in the community's affairs.

At the same time, states began to eliminate religious oaths as tests for voting or holding public office, thereby bringing people who had been previously disenfranchised into state politics. Polling places were increased and added to remote locations to enhance participation in sparsely populated areas. People who would have been excluded in colonial times now participated in government and even held seats in their state legislatures.

Moreover, most government still took place at the local level, in town meetings and county courthouses. Resistance and revolutionary activities in the towns offered more people the chance to participate in community politics. Committees of Correspondence turned into Committees of Correspondence and Safety, and were important forms of direct political participation for citizens who previously had no say in government.

Still, it would be a mistake to overestimate the extent to which the Revolution democratized American politics. The circle of powerholders did not change that much after 1776, and many people were still excluded from political participation altogether. Women, men of African ancestry, adherents to unpopular religions, and very poor white males all would have to wait for American democracy to reach into their ranks.

The Articles of Confederation

While patriots in the states were busy drafting constitutions following independence in 1776, the congress was debating proposals for a new continental union of the states. At the same time that Richard Henry Lee placed a resolution for independence before Congress, he also proposed "that a plan of confederation be prepared and transmitted to the respective colonies for their consideration and approbation."[5] On June 12, 1776, a committee was appointed to draft what would later become the Articles of Confederation.

When the congress began to debate the first draft of a new federal constitution—written largely by John Dickinson—in the summer of 1776, problems with forming a more permanent national union arose. Quarrels that divided the colonies before 1763—sectional differences, philosophical arguments, territorial disputes—resurfaced. An inherent mistrust of distant central authority, even one created by Americans, added to the colonists' mutual suspicions of each other. Communal consciousness existed at the state and local levels, but not at the national level.

Despite these inherent problems, enough common ground existed to proceed with a national organization. The common fight against England that began in 1763 had contributed to a growing social and cultural interaction among the colonies. The colonists had experienced a multi-tiered united government under the British Empire and, experimentally, under the Continental Congress. And the short-term pressures of war and the need for united action further drove the colonists toward union. In November 1777, after a year and a half of sporadic debates on and revisions of the Dickinson draft, the congress finally adopted the Articles of Confederation and sent them to the states for approval.

The states, most of which had their own constitutions in place, were not that eager to ratify the document. Concern over the amount of power given to the confederation government caused many to delay. Maryland held out until 1781, when its worries about the western territories were finally assuaged. In March 1781 the Confederation was finally operating.

Unlike the state constitutions, which at least paid lip service to the separation-of-powers principle, the Articles of Confederation lodged all governmental power in the congress, a unicameral legislative body. No separate, permanent executive branch or judiciary was created by the Articles. Being suspicious of executive power, the founders of the Articles established no clear executive authority. Provision was made for Congress to create committees to deal with matters of policy, and several departments—such as foreign affairs, war, and treasury—eventually became entrenched. Nonetheless, with no single individual responsible for executive authority, such power was extremely weak. Of course, weak executives were commonplace during this period, as most states routinely subordinated their governors to legislative authority.

The Articles did not provide for a federal judicial system, although the congress was given some narrow authority to create ad hoc courts, and these courts did resolve several disputes between states and on the high seas. In the final analysis, however, the lack of a national judiciary meant that states retained full sovereignty in their dealings with the confederation and with each other.

The Articles of Confederation reflected American distrust of central authority. Furthermore, the confederation established by the Articles was simply that—a confederation of the separate states. The congress represented the separate states rather than the people directly. There were no national elections. The states sent delegates to the congress and paid their salaries, and each state had one vote in determining national questions. To further enforce state equality, the Articles provided that the vote of nine states be required to adopt all important measures, and all states had to agree before an amendment to the Articles was approved.

On paper, the Articles of Confederation granted the congress formidable powers. The congress had exclusive authority over foreign relations, including matters of war and peace, diplomacy, trade, and treaty-making powers. It had powers over coining money and establishing weights and measures, over postal communications, over disputes between states, and over admiralty cases. In addition, the Articles authorized Congress to borrow money and to requisition the states for money and soldiers.

In reality, however, the central government proved to be anything but formidable. Only expressly delegated powers could be exercised by the national government, and the Articles of Confederation gave no power whatsoever to the congress to tax or to regulate commerce. The dispute with Parliament had arisen primarily over these two powers, and to give them to the newly created central government would have caused immediate controversy and suspicion. The power over taxation was the most critical; without it, the federal government could not remain solvent. The congress could requisition the states for money, but if they refused, the Articles provided no means to enforce the request. The confederation government received only $1.5 million of the $10 million it had requested from the states from 1781 to 1787.

This lack of enforcement power over the states applied to all other areas as well. Article II, inserted into the Dickinson draft in 1777, provided the ultimate safeguard of states' rights and the final testimony to the confederation's weaknesses. It stated: "Each state retains its sovereignty, freedom, and independence, and every power, jurisdiction, and right, which is not by this confederation expressly delegated to the United States, in Congress assembled." The

Articles of Confederation failed to grant sovereignty to the new federal government. It merely established, to use its own words, "a firm league of friendship" among the states. Without crucial taxing and commerce powers, and without mechanisms to enforce the powers it did have, the confederation foundered.

Nineteenth-century historian John Fiske called the years during which the United States was governed under the Articles of Confederation "the critical period." It is still commonplace for people to refer to the period from 1781 to 1789 as a dark time in American history. But our nation also achieved great things under the Articles of Confederation. The war for independence was successfully concluded and a favorable treaty was signed with Britain. Those Americans who had supported Britain during the war were reintegrated into American society. The western-territories crisis was solved on terms that allowed further national development according to republican principles (see Brief 2.1). The country weathered a post-war depression and by the late 1780s was beginning to grow both economically and demographically. No matter how weak the central government was under its provisions, the Articles of Confederation kept alive the idea of national union and lodged formal powers with Congress. Important principles of interstate comity and relations (e.g., "full faith and credit"; see Chapter 7 for further explanation) contained in the Articles would later be put into the Constitution of 1787. The first inklings of a national civil service corps came in these years. In many ways it was a remarkable eight-year record for a new nation.

But the national government's failures outweighed its successes, and financial problems exceeded all others. The Revolutionary War required constant expenditures for soldiers and materials. Unable to tax to raise revenues, and impotent to force the states to pay what was asked to finance the war, the congress resorted to issuing paper money to support the war effort. This scheme worked well at first, but the congress eventually printed so much paper money that its value became worthless. By the end of the war the financial crisis was severe. The government owed money to army veterans, to foreign governments (France and Holland lent millions to the United States during the war), and to private citizens and supporters who had lent money. Congress could not even pay the interest that had accrued on all the loans. The states grew even less willing to fill congressional requisitions.

To solve the financial crisis, the confederation congress proposed an amendment to the Articles, giving it the power to impose a 5 percent tariff on foreign imports. But Rhode Island alone was able to

---

Brief 2.1

THE NORTHWEST ORDINANCE: A LEGACY OF THE ARTICLES OF CONFEDERATION

The year 1787 in American history is most remembered as the year in which our federal constitution was drafted. But the year also marks the passage of the Northwest Ordinance, a law of lasting significance in its own right. The Northwest Ordinance was designed to provide for government in the lands north and west of the Ohio River (acquired in 1784 by Congress as part of the peace settlement with Great Britain). At the time, some congressional support existed for two basic options: making the territory a permanent colony, or granting immediate statehood. But Congress instead decided on a compromise plan to gradually ease the territorial population into self-government.

Under the Northwest Ordinance, the entire territory would be run by a governor, secretary, and three judges—all appointed by Congress. Once the adult male population reached five thousand, an assembly could be elected to make laws for the territory, subject to the governor's veto. Eventually, from three to five states would be created out of the territory, to come into the union on an equal basis with the original states once the population totaled sixty thousand each. The congress made provisions to protect freedom of religion, due process of law, and contractual obligations from any legislative interference either before or after statehood. Slavery was permanently excluded from the Northwest Territory.

The Northwest Ordinance made important contributions beyond solving the sticky issue of the western lands. It provided a process of expansion and union that thirty-one of the fifty states eventually followed. By guaranteeing the equality of the new states, it offered a glimpse of American federalism. The protections of individual rights found in the Northwest Ordinance actually preceded those found in the Bill of Rights. And the answer the Northwest Ordinance gave to the question of slavery struck sectional chords that endured through the next century.

The Northwest Ordinance was truly a remarkable feat, accomplished by a government that would soon be replaced. It stands today as an important constitutional legacy to go along with the more famous founding-period documents: the Declaration of Independence and the U.S. Constitution.

block this proposal, since unanimity was required to amend the Articles. A year later New York would defeat a similar revenue-power amendment. So from 1781 until 1787, when the sale of western lands brought in some revenue, the congress was completely dependent on the states for money, and as a result, hovered near bankruptcy.

Moreover, the congress could not even enforce the powers it did have under the Articles of Confederation. Independently of the congress, the states waged war, provided armies of their own, and conducted negotiations with foreign nations. The states failed to carry out provisions of treaties between the United States and foreign governments, especially the peace treaty of 1783 with Great Britain. As a result, other European powers refused to enter into commercial treaties with the United States, and the British kept troops in the Northwest territories. The congress could not regulate commerce or trade among the several states, and, in the absence of federal controls, the states were engaging in trade and tax wars with each other. Robert Morris, superintendent of finance during the early years of the confederation government, accurately described the situation:

> IMAGINE THE SITUATION OF A MAN WHO IS TO DIRECT THE FINANCES OF A COUNTRY ALMOST WITHOUT REVENUE SURROUNDED BY CREDITORS WHOSE DISTRESSES, WHILE THEY INCREASE IN THEIR CLAMORS, RENDER IT MORE DIFFICULT TO APPEASE THEM; AN ARMY READY TO DISBAND OR MUTINY; A GOVERNMENT WHOSE SOLE AUTHORITY CONSISTS IN THE POWER OF FRAMING RECOMMENDATIONS.[6]

Neither resting nor operating directly on the people of the United States, the confederation government lacked the power to act as a sovereign body.

To deal with the most pressing problem for the confederation—commercial regulation—Virginia proposed an interstate convention in the fall of 1786. Delegates from five states—New York, New Jersey, Delaware, Pennsylvania, and Virginia—met in Annapolis in September to make recommendations for changes in Congress's power that would enable it to conduct trade policy for the states. The delegates agreed that the reform of the Articles of Confederation needed to go beyond mere trade matters. They called for a general convention of all the states to meet at Philadelphia in May 1787. The convention's purpose would be "to render the constitution of the Federal government adequate to the exigencies of the Union."[7] The confederation congress later endorsed the Annapolis report and urged all states to attend the convention in Philadelphia.

THE "CRITICAL PERIOD" AND THE STATE GOVERNMENTS

The states, whose authority did derive directly from the people themselves, *were* acting as sovereign bodies. Revolutionaries had been committed to the classical republican ideal of small, relatively homogeneous communities where people actively participated in the public's business.

The republican ideal soon turned sour, however. The people, represented by their state legislatures, became oppressive. Legislatures began to assume the powers normally reserved to other branches of government, and to take on matters normally considered beyond the scope of government. State legislatures were routinely confiscating property (especially from British loyalists), altering land titles, remitting fines, granting individual exemptions to standing laws, issuing pardons, modifying or suspending judges' decisions, and authorizing judicial appeals. They interfered with private financial transactions by printing paper money, suspending debts and collections, and canceling legal contracts. In some instances state legislatures even canceled scheduled executions and dissolved marriages! The British complained that state legislatures were impeding enforcement of the peace treaty with the United States by interfering with British creditors and continuing to confiscate loyalist property.

Throughout the land, cries of "majority tyranny" and "democratic despotism" rang out. Madison argued that "wherever the true power in government lies, there also lies the source of oppression." In the state governments during the 1780s, the power and source of oppression lay with popular majorities. Madison worried that "the few will be unnecessarily sacrificed to the many."[8] The pendulum had swung from monarchs abusing their power to the people abusing their liberty.

In addition, factionalism and infighting grew within the states. Political parties formed. Towns and cities vied for favorable legislation. But most importantly, creditors clashed with small farmers and merchants who were in debt due to the burdens of the war and the postwar depression. Farmers and merchants were often able to gain a sympathetic majority in the state legislature, which would then pass laws authorizing the printing of paper money and the suspension or transferal of debts. Creditors made bankrupt by these debt-relief statutes were distressed by the abrogation of their property rights and of other liberties by state legislatures.

A call for reform of the state governments went out. Steps to reform state governments were taken in the 1780s. Beginning with the Massachusetts Constitution of 1780, revolutionary leaders put measures into effect to counter legislative domination of state governments. They strengthened the governor's office. Governors now would be elected directly by the people, given longer terms in office, and granted more extensive veto and appointment powers. Concerned leaders also tried to make the judiciary more independent of the legislature. The power of judicial review was discussed by some reformers as an important check on legislative power. The principle behind all of these reforms of the 1780s was to provide a system, as Jefferson put it, "in which the powers of government should be so divided and balanced among several bodies of magistracy, as that no one could transcend their legal limits, without being effectually checked and restrained by the others."[9]

But the reforms at the state level were too little, too late. The final straw for many property owners came in Massachusetts in the autumn of 1786. Farmers and artisans, especially in the western part of the state, angered over their economic situation and the government's inability and unwillingness to come to their aid, turned to armed rebellion. Under the leadership of Daniel Shays, they closed down court proceedings, thereby preventing creditors from suing to collect their debts. They attacked and almost took the U.S. arsenal at Springfield; only the state militia prevented them from throwing the government into complete chaos. And though the armed rebellion failed, candidates sympathetic to the rebel cause won victories at the polls that November. Shays' Rebellion and its aftermath convinced many Americans who had been wavering that a stronger central government was necessary to check the excessive power of state governments. Only three states had initially responded to the call to come to Philadelphia in 1787; the news from Massachusetts helped nudge most of the others to attend. By early 1787, it was clear that something drastic needed to be done to improve the workings of government at both the state and national level. The Philadelphia convention would be the perfect vehicle for constitutional reform.

THE CONSTITUTIONAL CONVENTION AND ITS AFTERMATH

What is now called the Constitutional Convention met in session in Philadelphia's Independence Hall from May 25, 1787, until September 17, 1787, when the new constitution was signed and sent to the confederation congress for consideration. Although James Madison and four other delegates kept notes of the convention's proceedings, the delegates adopted a rule to keep the deliberations secret, which remained in effect until thirty years afterward. The secrecy rule was adopted both to encourage the delegates to speak freely and candidly, and to prevent those skeptics outside Philadelphia from misconstruing the convention's purpose and sabotaging its deliberations. Those who debated and drafted the nation's new constitution were many of America's most respected statesmen (see Brief 2.2).

Initially, differences of opinion existed over the purpose of the Philadelphia meeting. Although the Annapolis resolution granted the delegates rather broad authority to revise the national government, Congress had authorized that the delegates meet "for the sole and express purpose of revising the Articles of Confederation."[10] The majority of delegates wanted to end the anarchy resulting from the confederation's weaknesses. But they disagreed on how far to go in reforming the continental government. Roger Sherman argued that the needs of the union were few: defense, commercial regulation, treaty-making, revenue-raising, and domestic good order. He felt that revising the Articles to meet these needs would suffice.

But James Madison wanted a complete overhaul of the national government. In April 1787 he had prepared a paper, "Vices of the Political System of the United States," in preparation for Philadelphia. In it, he outlined the defects in the Articles of Confederation and in the current state governments. Madison was particularly critical of the legislative excesses of

Brief 2.2
ROLL CALL AT THE CONSTITUTIONAL CONVENTION

Seventy-four delegates were selected by their respective states to attend the Philadelphia convention. Only fifty-five of those actually attended, but twelve of the thirteen states were eventually represented, with only Rhode Island failing to send delegates. Thomas Jefferson, who was in Europe and unable to attend, referred to the convention as "an assembly of demigods." Some important names were missing, of course. In addition to Jefferson and John Adams (who was representing the U.S. in England), Sam Adams and John Hancock were absent. Patrick Henry, having been selected to go to Philadelphia, grew suspicious of the convention's purposes and chose not to attend. In fact, only eight of the fifty-six signers of the Declaration of Independence attended the convention.

On the whole, the delegates were relatively young men. Benjamin Franklin of Pennsylvania was the oldest delegate at eighty-one, but six of the delegates were under thirty-one. In addition, it was a group with considerable wealth and social position. Most were bankers, lawyers, planters, and merchants. Only one representative—William Few of Georgia—could be said to come from the yeoman farmer class (the largest social class in America at the time). No one represented back-country folk or the city mechanics (who were essentially wage-laborers). Still, some of the finest republican minds of the eighteenth century gathered at Philadelphia "to form a more perfect union." Virginia and Pennsylvania sent six of the men who would be most influential at the convention. George Washington, James Madison, and Edmund Randolph came from Virginia. In addition to Franklin, Gouverneur Morris and James Wilson ably represented Pennsylvania. Other convention notables included John Dickinson of Delaware, Roger Sherman of Connecticut, Elbridge Gerry and Rufus King of Massachusetts, John Rutledge and Charles Pinckney of South Carolina, Alexander Hamilton of New York, and William Paterson of New Jersey. On the first day, Washington was chosen to preside over the meetings.

---

the states. They had, in his mind, passed too many laws, invaded minority rights, and failed to prevent "internal violence" (an obvious reference to Shays' Rebellion). Madison sought to establish a "more extensive republic" with greater national power to solve the problem of both a weak central government and excessively strong state governments. For Madison, providing safeguards for private rights and adequate powers for the national government were two parts of the same problem. Madison's forces would ultimately win in Philadelphia.

THE VIRGINIA PLAN AND THE PROBLEM OF REPRESENTATION

The Virginia delegation came to the convention's first session armed with a new plan for governing the United States. Though written by Madison, the plan, which came to be known as the Virginia Plan, was introduced to the convention by fellow Virginian Edmund Randolph. The Virginia Plan proposed a completely different structure of government from the Articles of Confederation. In it, the central government's powers were to be separated into a bicameral legislature, an executive branch, and a judicial branch. The new national government would represent and operate directly upon the people as opposed to working through the sovereign states. The bicameral congress would be given greater powers than the congress had under the Articles of Confederation, plus the authority to veto any acts of the various state legislatures.

The Virginia Plan was a bold nationalist proposal. Randolph himself stated that his plan would establish a "strong consolidated union in which the idea of states should be nearly annihilated." Delegates from the less populous states, frightened by the prospect of diminished influence in a new national structure, put forth a proposal of their own. On June 14, William Paterson presented the New Jersey Plan, a proposal to modify the Articles of Confederation. The New Jersey Plan would give the congress taxing and commerce powers and would strengthen the federal government's enforcement powers over disobedient states. But apart from these specific powers, the New Jersey Plan contained little else significantly different from the Articles. It retained the principle of state equality in the federal legislature, and created a federal executive that was directly subject to the state legislatures. Some of the New Jersey Plan's specific provisions were eventually incorporated into the Constitution, but it was rejected as a whole early in the convention's deliberations. The only other plan presented was Alexander Hamilton's proposal on June 18 for a constitutional monarchy, but this received no delegate support. The Virginia Plan and its nationalist principles were to be the basis for a new constitution.

Representation in Congress under this new federal constitution was the first and most important problem discussed by the Philadelphia delegates. The Articles of Confederation had established a union that was not representational, but rather, territorial, in that it gave the states in their corporate capacity equal representation in Congress. Republican ideals of popular government and majority rule had already led the states to tie representation to population rather than to territorial units. Now the Virginia Plan was calling for direct popular rule at the national level, through a system whereby the people would elect a congress that represented districts in proportion to the population (at least in one house of the national legislature). Delegates to the Philadelphia convention would have to decide whether the new government would be based on the states or on the people, and whether the state legislatures or the people would elect members of the federal legislature.

Although the delegates agreed that the new government being created would have to operate directly through the people to have the enhanced authority necessary to cure the ills of the confederation, delegates from the small states wanted to ensure the continued equality of the states. They also sought protection against large-state domination in the newly composed federal legislature. A deadlock existed on the question of representation, with the small states in favor of equal state representation and the large-state faction in favor of proportional representation. A committee was chosen to draft a compromise acceptable to a majority of the states.

The Connecticut Compromise, as it was known, recommended that representation be proportional in the lower house of Congress (each state would be allowed one member for every 40,000 inhabitants), and that each state have an equal vote in the upper house. The people would directly elect members to the House of Representatives; the state legislatures would choose members of the Senate. As an added concession to republican principles and to pre-Revolutionary disputes, a provision was made to initiate all bills for raising or spending money in the lower house, with no amendments by the upper house possible. On July 16 the convention narrowly approved the Connecticut Compromise by a five-to-four vote, with Massachusetts divided and New York not voting. Although the large-state faction was temporarily displaced, it basically received what it wanted. The dual provision for representation in Congress would reflect a constitutional system that was, to use one delegate's phrase, "partly national, partly federal." The composition of Congress decided, the delegates moved on to discuss how to enhance this new legislature's powers.

POWERS OF CONGRESS UNDER THE NEW CONSTITUTION

The convention delegates wanted to make the federal government more powerful, not only over certain matters like taxation and commerce, but also in relation to the state legislatures. But how to achieve this increased power created controversy. In addition to the powers the congress had under the Articles of Confederation, the Virginia Plan granted it the power "to legislate in all cases to which the separate states are incompetent, or in which the harmony of the United States may be interrupted by the exercise of individual legislation."[11] Several delegates objected to this additional power, claiming that the language (especially the word "incompetent") was too vague and needed more "exact enumeration." After approving a general grant of congressional power with more specific language, the committee of detail scrapped the entire resolution in favor of a list of specific powers that Congress might need to exercise. The convention finally agreed on seventeen specific grants of power, beginning with the powers to tax and to regulate commerce. Article I, Section 8 of the Constitution concludes with a more general grant of authority to Congress "to make all laws that shall be necessary and proper for carrying into execution the foregoing powers, and all other powers vested, by this Constitution, in the government of the United States." The interpretation of this last provision, called the Necessary and Proper Clause, has raised a number of controversies in our nation's history, which are addressed in Chapter 7.

The granting of specific powers to Congress was the perfect solution to the problem of creating a government that would overcome the weaknesses of the confederation and yet not be too powerful (as a result of a vague, general grant of congressional power). But the delegates wanted to be sure that Congress did not overstep its legitimate bounds. Immediately following the grants of congressional power, they included provisions that would specifically *limit* congressional power. Many of the limitations resulted from conflicting sectional interests. Southern slave owners in particular feared that the new federal government would act to prohibit the slave trade or make it economically unfeasible. North Carolina, South Carolina, and Georgia all threatened to abandon the new constitution if it prohibited the slave trade or allowed excessive duties on "imported persons." Many delegates opposed the "infernal traffic" of slavery, but a compromise was reached in late August. Congress would not be allowed to prohibit the importation of slaves until 1808, and would only be allowed a minimal taxation power of $10 a person. Slave owners also worried that the new congressional taxing power would be used to levy a capitation, or head, tax that would specifically include slaves. Accordingly, Congress was prohibited from taxing directly, "unless in proportion to the census." Questions about what constituted a "direct tax" would haunt Congress and the courts until the Sixteenth Amendment was passed in 1913 (see Chapter 8 for further discussion of taxation).

Finally, differences between the northern and southern economies led to a prohibition on export taxes. The southern states, whose economy was based heavily on agricultural exports, did not want to bear the burden of a taxing program ordered by the northern majority whose trade was not as dependent on commodity exports.

These questions of federal Congressional power decided, there still remained the problem of how to assert federal power over the states and the question of federal versus state sovereignty. Theoretically, the new constitution would solve the problem of sovereignty by basing sovereignty directly on the people themselves. The new federal government would operate directly through the people rather than working through the separate states. But practically, the states would still be exercising power over their internal affairs through their **police powers** (the power to legislate for the health, safety, welfare, and morals of the people; see Chapter 8 for further details). Even ardent nationalists understood that the states would retain the largest share of power. Given this fact, the delegates needed a way to allow the federal government to exert its supremacy over the states when necessary. The Virginia Plan called for a congressional veto, the power to "negative all laws passed by the several states contravening in the opinion of the National legislature the articles of Union."[12] Madison was adamant that Congress have this veto power as a way of exercising national supremacy over the often pernicious state legislatures.

Gouverneur Morris responded that to give Congress this veto power would "disgust all the states." He understood that given the state loyalties that existed at the time, the sovereignty of the states would have to be recognized to a significant degree. Moreover, he contended, "a law that ought to be negatived will be set aside in the Judiciary Department." So the veto was dropped, and what is called the Supremacy Clause in Article VI of the Constitution was drafted to take its place as a statement of national supremacy over the states. It states that the Constitution and all federal laws made under its authority "shall be the supreme law of the land." Judges in state courts are bound by the Constitution and by federal law, regardless of what their state laws or constitutions say. The Supremacy Clause is an important assertion of national sovereignty because it makes the Constitution a law enforceable in all courts throughout the land. It has been the basis for numerous Supreme Court opinions about the locus of sovereignty (federal or state).

Of course, the Supremacy Clause only offered a general statement of national supremacy. Given the delegates' specific concerns about debt relief and paper-money legislation being passed in the states, they wanted exact language in the Constitution to forbid certain kinds of state actions. The delegates agreed, among other things, to prohibit the states from coining or printing money, from making anything other than gold or silver acceptable in the payment of debts, and from passing any law that would interfere with the obligation of contracts. These provisions are found in Article I, Section 10.

SEPARATION OF POWERS AND THE PRESIDENCY

The preceding sections have discussed the composition and the powers of Congress. Unlike the system under the Articles of Confederation, however, Congress was not to be the only branch of the federal government. Experience with both the federal and state governments in the "critical period" led the delegates to call for a true separation of governmental powers in the new Constitution. Madison complained that the states had not adequately separated the different functions of government. This had led, in his mind, to a situation where each state's legislature had become tyrannical, "absorbing all power into its vortex."[13] Madison and his colleagues had already provided for a bicameral legislature in which the Senate could deliberate and exercise restraint on an impetuous majority in the lower house. But this was not enough. Madison, Hamilton, and others also wanted to create a strong federal executive and judiciary to further divide governmental powers and provide necessary leadership.

The powers and composition of the new executive stirred controversy among the delegates. One group, which included Franklin, Randolph, and George Mason of Virginia, believed that danger lurked in a too-powerful executive. These delegates wanted a chief executive who was elected by and dependent on the legislature. Moreover, they wanted to disperse executive power by placing it in the hands of several men, who would sit as an executive council or cabinet. Experience with the British had proven to these traditional republicans that too much power in the hands of an independent executive leads to corruption and tyranny. For example, Randolph contended that a single executive was "the foetus [fetus] of monarchy." The Virginia Plan—with its call for a plural executive with limited powers, elected by the legislature—embodied these republican concerns.

But the old-line republicans were not the only voices at the convention, and they would eventually lose the battle over the presidential office. The younger group of men in Philadelphia (plus a few elder statesmen like Washington) had seen the dangers of legislative dominance and wanted to create a unified, energetic executive as a check on legislative excesses. Led by Madison and Hamilton, as well as Morris and Wilson of Pennsylvania (where a unicameral legislature virtually unchecked by an executive council had been in power), this group called for a single executive elected by the people (either directly or indirectly). They opposed an executive council that might dilute presidential leadership and "cover [rather] than prevent malpractice." They proposed that the executive have a full range of prerogative powers, including full appointing and veto powers, and those of commander in chief of the armed forces. For support, they drew on the writings of Locke and Montesquieu.

A majority of the delegates agreed on a single executive on June 4, but continued debating the issues of presidential selection and powers throughout the summer. Wilson later declared that the provisions for the executive were "the most difficult of all on which we have had to decide." Finally, the delegates sent the matter of presidential election to a committee of eleven men to work out a compromise proposal. In early September the committee reported back with a plan for election that would encompass the ideas of both sides. Presidential electors would be chosen in a manner prescribed by the state legislatures (which could include popular selection). These electors would then choose a president, with each state having a number of votes equal to their total representation in Congress. The choice of a majority of these electors would be president, with the runner-up becoming vice president. If no one person received a majority of the votes, the Senate would choose a president from among the five highest vote-getters. The members of the Committee of Eleven were certain that both the people and the legislature would participate in the presidential selection process, since they believed it would be rare for one person to gain a majority of the votes. The compromise would make for a president independent of the legislature, yet usually selected by it. With one friendly amendment giving the House of Representatives the final say rather than the Senate, the committee's proposal was approved and the now infamous electoral college was born. Of course, the founders could not foresee the rise of political parties in the presidential selection process, which quickly made the two-stage election process obsolete. Only three presidential elections (1800, 1824, and 1876) have been decided by Congress.

Along with the selection proposal came a provision for a four-year term with the possibility of reelection to additional terms. The delegates finally voted to give the president a limited veto power, in line with that given to many state governors, as well as the power to act as commander in chief. The president was also given authority to make treaties and appoint judges, ambassadors, and other government officers "with the advice and consent of the Senate" (Art. II, Sec. 2). The new president would not merely administer the laws made by Congress, but would energetically exercise restraint and control over the federal legislature.

THE FEDERAL JUDICIARY AND INDIVIDUAL RIGHTS

All delegates agreed on the need for a national judiciary as the third branch in the federal separation of powers. The judiciary's power to judge the constitutionality of federal and state laws was considered essential to check legislative and executive power. The absence of a permanent federal judiciary separate from the legislature was seen as a major weakness in the Articles of Confederation. The delegates wanted to ensure that the judiciary would truly be an independent body, and understood that to make it so, judges would serve during good behavior rather than at the command of the president or Congress.

Two major points of disagreement did exist over this new national judiciary, however. The first concerned the extent of the federal judiciary. The New Jersey Plan had only called for a supreme court. The Virginia Plan provided for inferior courts as well as for a supreme court. Some delegates contended that the presence of inferior courts would dilute state judicial power. Others, including Madison, felt that a hierarchy of federal courts was essential to an effective judiciary that could check legislative majorities. Finally, the convention compromised by providing for a supreme court and leaving the establishment of inferior federal courts up to Congress.

The second dispute arose over the selection of federal judges. The Virginia Plan called for Congress to elect federal judges. The convention's delegates, however, fearing that judges might lose their independence if elected by the legislature, rejected this proposal. Conflict ensued over whether the president or the Senate should appoint federal judges. As with other matters, the convention ultimately accepted a compromise from the Committee of Eleven. The president would appoint Supreme Court justices "by and with the Advice and Consent of the Senate" (Art. II, Sec. 2).

To many delegates, the federal judiciary would not only restrain the other branches of government, but would also defend the constitutional rights of individual citizens. The Constitution would contain a number of specific prohibitions on the federal government that the courts could enforce, most notably against Congress's passing **bills of attainder** and **ex post facto laws** (these the states were also forbidden to pass). Individuals would be guaranteed a jury trial on all federal criminal charges, and their right to petition for a **writ of habeas corpus** could not be suspended except during rebellion or invasion. But no larger bill of rights was included at the Philadelphia convention. The majority of delegates concluded that a longer declaration of rights was unnecessary, given the existence of the bills of rights attached to the separate state constitutions. The absence of a bill of rights would be remedied quickly, however, as Congress would use the amending process specified in Article V to add a bill of rights (the first ten amendments to the Constitution) in 1789.

These major issues decided, the delegates appointed a committee of style to draft the final wording and arrange the articles agreed on in an orderly fashion. Gouverneur Morris is credited with doing the bulk of this committee's work, and is therefore the man most responsible for the final wording of the Constitution. The final document was presented to the forty-two delegates still in attendance on September 17. Thirty-nine delegates signed. The document then went to the states for ratification.

RATIFICATION OF THE CONSTITUTION

The new constitution would go into effect once nine states agreed to ratify it. The delegates removed the requirement of unanimity found in the Articles of Confederation, for obvious practical reasons. Rhode Island had refused to send delegates to the Philadelphia convention, and it was thought that other states might refuse to ratify the Constitution. The delegates chose the number of states required to ratify based on the fact that nine states had been required to pass major legislation under the Articles of Confederation. The nine-state requirement was one that, to use George Mason's words, was "familiar to the people."

In addition, delegates adopted a provision in the Virginia Plan that called for ratification by conventions specifically elected for that purpose rather than by the existing state legislatures. As a matter of principle, Madison believed that a new government founded on the people and operating directly through them needed to be approved by the people. But, as a matter of practicality, those who favored the Constitution's adoption also saw that entrenched interests in the state legislatures might prevent ratification because of the Constitution's implications for their positions of power.

Under these new rules, the battle over ratification began. Victory came for the new constitution's supporters (Federalists) only after a hard struggle with its opponents (Anti-Federalists). In the end, persuasion, compromise, and a few less-than-ethical tricks were required to get the Constitution adopted by the nine required states. The fight between Federalists and Anti-Federalists partly involved a conflict between commercial and noncommercial elements in the population. In some states, the ratification battle reflected differences between urban and rural interests, between coastal and interior towns. But most importantly, the ratification debate was argued on the battleground of political principles and ideals. Federalists and Anti-Federalists stood for competing conceptions of politics and the role of government in people's lives. To understand the Constitution's purpose, as well as many of the constitutional battles that have occurred since its adoption, these differences in principles between Federalists and Anti-Federalists must be understood.

THE ANTI-FEDERALIST ARGUMENT AGAINST RATIFICATION

It is much more difficult to discuss Anti-Federalist political theory than to discuss that of the Federalists. In many states, the Constitution's opponents shared nothing beyond their contempt for this new and, in many of their minds, radical document. The opposition was often disorganized, inarticulate, and generally unimpressive compared with the Constitution's supporters. Moreover, the Anti-Federalists had the disadvantage of having no viable alternative document to defend. Very few opponents to the Constitution wanted to keep the Articles of Confederation intact. Even the name Anti-Federalists is somewhat of a misnomer, since many of the Constitution's opponents saw themselves as "true" federalists, defenders of state sovereignty against national consolidation (which points to the political skills of the Federalists, who initially grabbed the high moral ground in their name selection).

Still, the Anti-Federalists agreed on certain fundamental political ideas and were able to launch a coherent, principled attack on the Constitution. The first concern shared by most Anti-Federalists was with the radical nature of this new document being debated. Many Anti-Federalists thought the Constitution granted the federal government powers that were too broad and too ill defined. They wanted to move more cautiously, granting the new federal government limited powers above what it possessed under the Articles. The majority of Anti-Federalists favored a stronger union, but not at the expense of political liberty and state autonomy. For example, though most opponents to the Constitution admitted the need for an enhanced federal taxing power, they saw the Constitution as granting Congress an unlimited "power to lay and collect taxes, duties, imposts and excises" (Art. I, Sec. 8). They believed that this excessive taxing power would both bleed the people and leave the states with little revenue-raising power of their own. The Anti-Federalists also complained about the radical changes in the rules of the ratification game (i.e., less than unanimity, popular ratifying conventions) made by the Federalists. Richard Henry Lee, one of the most outspoken opponents of the Constitution, believed that it was better to retain the principles of state sovereignty under the old confederation than to adopt the consolidation plan of the "hot-headed" Federalists. The consolidation plan could only bring political inequality and a loss of liberty. In response to Federalists' claims about the need for new governmental institutions, he stated: "To say that a bad government must be established for fear of anarchy is really saying that we should kill ourselves for fear of dying."[14]

A second concern focused on the scale and size of the new federal government. The Anti-Federalists believed that republicanism could only flourish in small states, where the people would have greater control over and access to their governments. The "small republic" could preserve equality, homogeneity of character and custom, and civic virtue against the corruption and divisiveness that would come with large size. As one Anti-Federalist in New York put it, the federal government established by the new constitution "would be composed of such heterogeneous and discordant principles, as would constantly be contending with each other." The Anti-Federalists were opposed to the "extended republic" that the Constitution would establish, not only because it could lead to divisiveness and corruption, but also because it placed magisterial power in a distant president who could easily become "kingly." Accordingly, the Anti-Federalists wanted to leave as much power as possible in the states, where government could be most responsive to the people and most reflective of popular values and virtues.

A third constitutional concern related to democratic representation. Most Anti-Federalists wanted a government that would be responsive to its citizens' needs. Lodging most power in the state governments would accomplish this, but the federal government also needed to be directly responsible to the people. The Anti-Federalists thought that the new constitution limited popular responsibility: it removed the chief executive, the Senate, and the judiciary from direct popular control. Moreover, even members of the House of Representatives would be distant and unresponsive. The first federal House of Representatives would contain only fifty-five members, a body smaller than many of the state legislatures! By not providing for a representative federal government that would be directly responsible to the people, the Anti-Federalists felt the Constitution inclined toward aristocracy and monarchy. They thought popular government itself would be endangered by the new national government.

Finally, most Anti-Federalists opposed the Constitution's failure to contain a bill of rights. Anti-Federalist fear of a gargantuan distant government that would be corrupt and tyrannical was only enhanced by this omission. To the Anti-Federalists, it was a basic premise of government—enshrined in most state constitutions of the time—that the people's liberties could only be maintained by a written declaration of rights that would limit what the government could do. Even Thomas Jefferson, who supported the Constitution's adoption, agreed with the Anti-Federalists on this point: "A bill of rights is what the people are entitled to against every government on earth, general or particular, and what no just government should refuse, or rest on inference."[15] As it turned out, this final concern was the only one that the Anti-Federalists saw materialize in the U.S. Constitution. Nevertheless, the concerns expressed by the Anti-Federalists would remain prominent among large numbers of Americans throughout the early years of the republic.

THE FEDERALIST RESPONSE

Describing Federalist political theory is much easier than describing its counterpart. Not only were the Federalists united in support of the same document, they also had articulate leaders in many states who could buttress their position with strong supporting ideas. For example, to persuade the people of New York to adopt the Constitution, James Madison, Alexander Hamilton, and John Jay wrote a series of essays now known as *The Federalist Papers*. These essays defend the basic principles and specific provisions of the Constitution of 1787. Though other sources of Federalist thought exist, the Federalist theory of politics can be gleaned largely from this series of essays. The essays contained specific responses to the Anti-Federalist concerns just detailed.

Most Federalists saw themselves as "progressives," inheritors of the liberal, enlightenment tradition in Europe that held that political institutions could be created and major improvements in people's collective lives could be made. They believed that the abstract principles of men like Montesquieu and Locke could be embodied in positive constitutions. As such, they were not afraid of radical, new proposals for government. After all, Americans had already overturned political traditions in 1776. Why not drastically revise the federal government in line with its major defects? Furthermore, in the eyes of the Federalists, these major defects in the state and confederation governments were hampering the people's ability to progress toward their ultimate destiny.

The Federalists differed drastically from the Anti-Federalists in their views of the nature and purpose of government. To Federalists like Madison, people were motivated primarily by private interests, not by a desire to serve the public good. Moreover, people's private interests were diverse; if allowed to dominate the public arena, they could lead to a tyranny of the majority's interests over those of the rest of the population. This was the problem the Federalists saw happening in the state governments, where arbitrary and capricious majorities were trampling on individual liberties. The Federalist solution was to provide for an "extended republic" (the federal government), where majority factions could not form, and where individual liberty would thereby be protected. Under the Constitution, the federal government would take the majority, with its capacity for excesses, out of the daily picture of government operations. This would protect the rights and interests of all citizens, provide security for economic investment and growth, and make government more stable and effective in its functions.

The Federalists responded to the Anti-Federalists' concern that the new government was unrepresentative by offering their own republican theory of leadership. As mentioned above in our discussion of the Constitutional Convention, the Federalists saw indirect representation as desirable. By removing the people from a direct and intimate say in who would represent them in government, responsible leaders from the right social background could emerge and run the country. Hamilton stated:

> ALL COMMUNITIES DIVIDE THEMSELVES INTO THE FEW AND THE MANY. THE FIRST ARE THE RICH AND WELL BORN, THE OTHER THE MASS OF THE PEOPLE. THE VOICE OF THE PEOPLE HAS BEEN SAID TO BE THE VOICE OF GOD; AND HOWEVER GENERALLY THIS MAXIM HAS BEEN QUOTED AND BELIEVED, IT IS NOT TRUE IN FACT. THE PEOPLE ARE TURBULENT AND CHANGING; THEY SELDOM JUDGE OR DETERMINE RIGHT. GIVE THEREFORE TO THE FIRST CLASS A DISTINCT, PERMANENT SHARE IN THE GOVERNMENT. THEY WILL CHECK THE UNSTEADINESS OF THE SECOND, AND AS THEY CANNOT RECEIVE ANY ADVANTAGE BY A CHANGE, THEY THEREFORE WILL EVER MAINTAIN GOOD GOVERNMENT. CAN A DEMOCRATIC ASSEMBLY, WHO ANNUALLY REVOLVE IN THE MASS OF THE PEOPLE, BE SUPPOSED STEADILY TO PURSUE THE PUBLIC GOOD? NOTHING BUT A PERMANENT BODY CAN CHECK THE IMPRUDENCE OF DEMOCRACY.[16]

This elite group would have the people's best interests at heart, would protect private rights from majoritarian impulses, and would be insulated, less susceptible to corruption. Indeed, government by an elite corps chosen by the methods found in the Constitution would be more "responsible" to republican values than one directly responsive to the "mob" of citizens.

So far the Federalists appear as classic supporters of what was described in Chapter 1 as the individualist perspective of government. They sought an efficient government, one that could secure private rights rather than public virtue, one where the natural leadership of a national elite would replace the more direct popular rule of local communities. The Anti-Federalists, by contrast, were more communitarian in their approach, believing that civic virtue must override private interests. So why weren't the Federalists the ones supporting a bill of rights? Federalists had been unconcerned with such libertarian provisions because they thought the federal government would be limited to solely those powers granted it in the Constitution. All powers not granted to the government would remain in the people's hands. In addition, the people would have some specific protections in the Constitution, as mentioned above, and the state bills of rights would still operate to protect individual citizens from state governments (which to Federalist minds were the more dangerous). Here the Federalists found themselves on shaky grounds, however, given the ambiguity surrounding the actual powers granted to the new federal government. The Anti-Federalists would finally convince the Federalists to change their mind about a bill of rights—in fact, it took a promise that an attached bill of rights would be the first order of business of the new government to gain approval of the Constitution in several states. Massachusetts, Virginia, New Hampshire, South Carolina, and New York all ratified the constitution with the understanding that a list of recommended amendments be added immediately.

The Federalists won adoption of the Constitution, but not without difficulty (see Brief 2.3). After some delay, George Washington, who received one vote from every presidential elector, was finally inaugurated as the first president of the United States on April 30, 1789. For the Revolutionary generation, Washington was a symbol of the republican values that had guided the nation's struggle for independence and self-preservation. As such, he lent a legitimacy to the new government that it desperately needed in its early years. Congress's immediate work on the constitutional amendments that had been proposed at the various state ratifying conventions also won the government acceptance in many quarters. James Madison eventually pared the more than two hundred suggestions down to nineteen proposals

Brief 2.3

THE DIFFICULT STRUGGLE OVER RATIFICATION

The ratification battle began in October 1787, when several states issued their calls for ratification conventions and set the dates and rules governing the ratification procedure. It did not end until nine months later, when New Hampshire cast the clinching ninth vote required to put the Constitution into effect. By the end of July 1788, Virginia and New York, without whose presence the union of states would have failed, came into the fold by narrow margins and after long and bitter debates.

Although a few states, including Delaware (the first state to ratify on December 7, 1787), were unanimous in their approval, in many others the vote was close. In fact, not counting North Carolina and Rhode Island, where ratification did not initially succeed, in four other states (Massachusetts, New Hampshire, Virginia, and New York), a majority of the delegates were publicly *opposed* to the Constitution when they sat down to meet on the first day of their state ratifying conventions. New Hampshire and New York probably would have rejected the new document had they not felt pressured by the approval of the other states. Alexander Hamilton even threatened New York's delegates with the secession of New York City from the state if they failed to approve the Constitution, by then already ratified by ten other states. In Massachusetts, Governor John Hancock had to be bribed with the promise of the presidency or vice presidency to get his crucial support for the Federalist cause.

The states that approved the Constitution only on the condition that a list of proposed amendments be considered took that reservation seriously: the Virginia delegates attached a list of twenty-nine proposed constitutional amendments to their official convention report. As mentioned, North Carolina and Rhode Island had not approved the new document by the summer of 1788. North Carolina postponed ratification until a lengthy set of proposed constitutional amendments could be drafted, finally ratifying on November 21, 1788. Rhode Island remained obstinate, refusing even to call a state ratifying convention until 1790. In the face of threats emanating from the new United States government, Rhode Island begrudgingly voted their approval on May 29, 1790, by a vote of 34 to 32.

A breakdown of the original thirteen states, in order of their ratification, appears in Table 2.1.

---

that he wanted woven into the text of the Constitution. Congress approved twelve of these as the Bill of Rights, but only after the House insisted on placing the amendments at the end of the Constitution, and the Senate demanded that the amendments apply only to the national government—not the states.

Ten amendments received the necessary support of three-fourths of the states and became part of the Constitution on December 15, 1791. With approval of the Bill of Rights, the opening chapter in American constitutional history was complete. But the political conflict between Federalists and their opponents

Table 2.1 Ratification of the U.S. Constitution

State	Date of Ratification	Vote	Amendments proposed?
Delaware	December 7, 1787	30–0	No
Pennsylvania	December 12, 1787	46–23	Yes
New Jersey	December 18, 1787	38–0	No
Georgia	January 2, 1788	26–0	No
Connecticut	January 9, 1788	128–40	No
Massachusetts	February 6, 1788	187–168	Yes
Maryland	April 28, 1788	63–11	No
South Carolina	May 23, 1788	149–73	Yes
New Hampshire	June 21, 1788	57–47	Yes
Virginia	June 25, 1788	89–79	Yes
New York	July 26, 1788	30–27	Yes
North Carolina	November 21, 1788	194–77	Yes
Rhode Island	May 29, 1790	34–32	Yes

SOURCES: Data taken from Murray Dry, "The Case Against Ratification: Anti-Federalist Constitutional Thought," in *The Framing and Ratification of the Constitution*, ed. Leonard W. Levy & Dennis J. Mahoney (New York: Macmillan, 1987); and Joseph T. Keenan, *The Constitution of the United States: An Unfolding Story* (Chicago: Dorsey Press, 1988).

continued. Anti-Federalist principles remained salient, especially on the question of the nature of American federalism, for years to come.

CONCLUSION

The American Constitution, like the revolution for independence that preceded it, reflects the tension between the communitarian and individualist strains of political thinking outlined in Chapter 1. On the one hand, the framers drafted a document that would theoretically place government on the foundation of the people, and would allow democratic majorities to rule in the interest of the nation as a whole (as opposed to the Articles of Confederation, where minorities of states could block actions favored by the majority). On the other hand, the men in Philadelphia placed roadblocks in the way of steamrolling majorities who would threaten individual rights (e.g., separation of powers, checks and balances, and specific provisions guaranteeing individual rights against both federal and state governments). The tensions found in the original Constitution have been played out in conflicts throughout American history, as is shown in the chapters that follow.

Nevertheless, one question remains: Does the Constitution truly represent the democratic principles advanced by the American revolutionaries of 1776? Many activists and scholars throughout U.S. history would say no, and have argued that the Constitution fails to live up to the ideals announced in the Declaration of Independence (see Brief 2.4). A response to these critics would contend that the Constitution was not undemocratic, for the eighteenth century. The procedures used to ratify it allowed more people to participate than had participated in approving the Articles of Confederation or a majority of the state constitutions. Thirty of the forty-three living signers of the Declaration of Independence supported ratification, and by the time of Rhode Island's ratification in 1790, evidence shows that a majority of the people, as reflected in their representatives, supported the new constitution.

The Constitution of 1787 was the climax of a revolution begun in the 1760s, a revolution in political principles as well as political practices. The text must now turn to a discussion of these principles and practices as they have worked themselves out in the course of American constitutional history.

HISTORICAL CRITIQUES OF THE U.S. CONSTITUTION

The argument that the Constitution of 1787 reflects a betrayal of the revolutionary ideals found in the Declaration of Independence is not new. In the nineteenth century those who fought to abolish slavery—men like Frederick Douglass and William Lloyd Garrison—and those who struggled for women's rights—women like Susan B. Anthony and Elizabeth Cady Stanton—argued that the Constitution denied to certain people the Declaration's original promise of equality. And those who fought on the side of the Confederacy during the Civil War argued that the Constitution created a federal government that denied the separate states their rights and independence.

One of the most famous attacks by historians on the Constitution's framers occurred in 1913, when Charles Beard published *An Economic Interpretation of the Constitution of the United States*. Beard argued that the constitutional convention was actually an economic conspiracy by an elite to safeguard their own interests at the expense of the popular majority. The framers of the Constitution, whom Beard contended represented the economic interests of "personalty" (capital in manufacturing, trade and shipping, public securities, and other paper assets), imposed their vision of a stable and efficient national government that could protect their own economic interests against democratic majorities. Those who opposed the Constitution represented "realty" interests (landed property, the local agrarian and debtor classes). They placed greater stress on local government and the protection of personal liberties. Beard contended that the Federalists, who represented an economic elite, outmaneuvered the Anti-Federalists, who represented a majority of the population, to win approval for a government reflective of their limited economic concerns.

While Beard's thesis has been successfully challenged by historians, his critique of the Constitution persists, although in a different form. A number of critics following Beard have continued to take the position that the Constitution was an undemocratic document, radically out of step with "the spirit of '76." For example, Merrill Jensen contends that the Articles of Confederation, which lodged power in the states, was actually the true expression of the democratic spirit found in the Declaration of Independence. The Federalists, on the other hand, did all they could to stifle popular majorities in the states by framing a Constitution that would protect an economic and social elite from the masses. Jensen declared:

The Articles of Confederation were designed to prevent the central government from infringing upon the rights of the states, whereas the Constitution of 1787 was designed as a check upon the power of the states and the democracy that found expression within their bounds.[17]

The more generic critique that the Constitution is undemocratic has historical support, especially if the rhetoric of the Constitution's opponents is taken seriously. The Anti-Federalists constantly hammered away at the aristocratic tendencies they found in the Constitution. They saw the Constitution as establishing the rule of the wealthy over the people as a whole.

Looking back from our own contemporary perspective adds even further weight to the democratic critique of the Constitution. For example, prominent political scientist Robert Dahl has judged the Constitution wanting by contemporary "democratic standards."[18] Pointing to provisions like the equal representation of states in the Senate, and comparing the U.S. Constitution with those of other successful democracies today, Dahl faults the U.S. model on counts of both representational fairness and democratic accountability.

Part 2

Structures and Process of American Constitutional Government

As the chapters in Part 1 indicate, the framers were deeply concerned with the capacity of their new system of government to resolve a perplexing dilemma—how to create a government that had sufficient power to maintain stability over time, but also one that would not arbitrarily violate individual rights. The six chapters in Part 2 concentrate upon three key structural principles of American constitutional government: judicial review, separation of powers, and federalism. Chapter 3 discusses the philosophical and historical backdrop of the early federal judiciary, the evolving organizational structure of a system of federal courts, and the current operation of the Supreme Court. The chapter also gives major exposure to the selection process for federal judges and Supreme Court justices, with considerable emphasis upon some recent judicial confirmation battles. Chapter 4 concentrates upon the policy-making role of those courts, with special emphasis accorded to the doctrine of judicial review and the main reasons for its having become a key feature of the American judicial system. Chapter 5 traces some of the evolution of the American presidency in the system and the several constitutional powers exercised by chief executives. Chapter 6 discusses the manner in which Congress has evolved as an occasional check upon executive authority. In both of these chapters, emphasis is given to several developments since 9/11 that raise important questions about both executive war power and the relative effectiveness of a legislative check on presidential prerogatives. Chapters 7 and 8 focus on American federalism, the constitutional arrangement that divides

power between levels of government. Chapter 7 gives special emphasis to the sometimes rocky relationship existing between the national and state governments since the nation's founding. Chapter 8 discusses the historical struggle in American society over property rights and economic liberty, as well as the increasing level of economic and commercial regulation. The individualist versus communitarian conflict plays a major role in this chapter.

Together, these chapters in Part 2 and their emphasis upon the responsible use of political power by government will serve as an important foundation for a later consideration in Part 3 of freedom and equality in American society.

CHAPTER 3
The Nature and Scope of Judicial Power

The Supreme Court building, erected in 1935, bears above its columns the inscription "Equal Justice Under Law." Once described by Alexander Hamilton as "the least dangerous branch" of government, the Supreme Court today wields formidable power in our constitutional system.

▼ Introductory Remarks by Chief Justice Rehnquist

I may not seem like the most appropriate person to introduce this chapter on the nature and scope of judicial power, but my experiences as a Supreme Court justice and even before being nominated to the bench touch upon all of the issues covered here. I served on the Court for more than thirty-three years, not the longest tenure but certainly well above the average of fifteen years. Moreover, I presided over the Court for nineteen years, the fourth longest-serving Chief Justice in United States history. I was nominated to the highest court in the land without any prior judicial experience, a rarity I share with our most recent justice, Elena Kagan, and I survived not one but two contentious confirmation battles. As far as constitutional interpretation goes, I oversaw the accomplishment of several important objectives, and the Court, under my direction, reached a number of landmark decisions. Although controversial, I helped to bring a presidential election to a conclusion (see Brief 4.4), less than two years after skillfully overseeing a presidential impeachment trial. And perhaps most importantly, I was by all accounts an excellent Supreme Court administrator, making a lasting impact on its annual workload and the civility of its proceedings.

I was born in Wisconsin in 1924, and after being stationed in North Africa during World War II, I received most of my higher learning out west, at Stanford University, where I graduated at the top of my law school class in 1951 (my fellow justice Sandra Day O'Connor was right behind me). After serving as Justice Robert Jackson's law clerk, I went into private practice in Arizona until being asked to serve under the Nixon Administration as Assistant Attorney General in charge of the Office of Legal Counsel. There, one of my primary duties was the screening of Supreme Court nominees. In October 1971, President Nixon nominated me, along with Lewis Powell, to fill two vacant seats on the Court.

My confirmation exemplifies much of what you will learn about the judicial selection process in this chapter. The president emphasized two things in picking me for the Court: my legal skills—he praised me as "having one of the finest legal minds in this whole nation today"—and my judicial philosophy. On the latter, President Nixon stressed the "duty of a judge to interpret the Constitution . . . not twist or bend the Constitution in order to perpetuate his personal political and social views." Having learned from the failed nominations (of Harrold Carswell and Clement Haynsworth) that preceded mine, I kept my answers in the Senate confirmation hearings short, something that has been a feature of these hearings ever since, and was able to win confirmation, albeit with a large number of "no" votes.

Once on the Court, unlike other appointments discussed in this chapter (see Brief 3.5), I did not disappoint my nominating president. In addition to advocating a philosophy of "strict construction" of constitutional law, I worked to roll back many of the more sweeping rulings of the Warren Court in the area of criminal procedure, and to reinvigorate federalism by bringing a greater balance of power between states and the national government. As an associate justice, my judicial conservatism was articulated from the margins, where more than 40 percent of my written opinions were dissents. But when I became Chief Justice, I was more often in the majority, with only 5 percent of my written opinions coming in dissent. I once wrote that the way in which a Chief Justice "strike[s] a blow for the cause affords some measurement of the stature of the men who have sat in the center chair of the Court," and by this standard, my nineteen-year tenure was a success.

I am most proud of my role as an efficient and fair Supreme Court administrator, one who, to use my own characterization, "[ran] a relatively smoothly functioning Court." Not only did I create civility and respect among my colleagues as a *prius inter pares*, but I reduced an overly burdensome workload by cutting the number of cases the Court took nearly in half, from over 150 cases per year under my predecessor to a norm of between 75 and 85 that still exists today. Even my ideological opponents praised the way I oversaw the Court. Justice Marshall, who will be introducing Chapter 11, called me a "great Chief Justice," and Justice Brennan described me as "the most all-around successful chief he had known—including Earl Warren." And Senator Edward Kennedy, who vehemently opposed my confirmation (both times), eulogized me by saying, "Chief Justice Rehnquist served this country with the greatest distinction, and I respected his leadership of the federal judiciary and his strong commitment to the integrity and independence of the courts."

To bring my chapter in the history of federal judicial power full circle, I died in office in 2005, the first justice to do so since Justice Jackson, the man I clerked for, and I was replaced as Chief Justice by my own clerk, John Roberts, about whom you will read more in this chapter. As you go through the chapter, note the places where components of my own story illustrate the points the authors are making about the structures and processes of federal judicial power.

SOURCES: Martin H. Belsky, ed., *The Rehnquist Court: A Retrospective* (New York: Oxford University Press, 2002); Craig M. Bradley, ed., *The Rehnquist Legacy* (Cambridge, UK: Cambridge University Press, 2006); David L. Hudson Jr., *The Rehnquist Court: Understanding Its Impact and Legacy* (Westport, CT: Praeger, 2007); Earl M. Maltz, *Rehnquist Justice: Understanding the Court Dynamic* (Lawrence: University Press of Kansas, 2003).

A Brief History of the Federal Judiciary

The federal judiciary today—at least in terms of its operational demands and complexity—bears little resemblance to what existed in 1789, when it was first created by an act of Congress. As discussed in Chapter 2, the Framers in 1787 were well aware of the several problems under the Articles of Confederation, some of which surfaced because of the absence of either a Supreme Court or a federal system of lower courts. Article III of the Constitution sought to remedy this glaring deficiency with two provisions. The first provided that "the judicial Power of the United States shall be vested in one supreme Court, and in such inferior Courts as the Congress may from time to time ordain and establish." The language here hints at the political controversy that accompanied the creation of the federal judiciary. Article III itself authorized a supreme court, but those who met in Philadelphia in 1787 could not agree upon the shape of the rest of the federal judiciary.

The second provision dealt with the types of cases or controversies that could be considered by a federal court under its jurisdictional authorization, which is discussed later in the chapter. The framers also disagreed about the precise nature of the power to be exercised by federal courts, although early writings from *The Federalist* provide some indication of their thoughts on the matter. One of the most insistent and out-spoken of these early framers was Alexander Hamilton, who argued in *Federalist No. 78* that an independent system of national courts was "peculiarly essential" in a limited government created by the Constitution. Hamilton argued that under the Constitution, the limits devised to curtail the power of Congress

> CAN BE PRESERVED IN PRACTICE NO OTHER WAY THAN THROUGH THE MEDIUM OF COURTS OF JUSTICE, WHOSE DUTY IT MUST BE TO DECLARE ALL ACTS CONTRARY TO THE MANIFEST TENOR OF THE CONSTITUTION VOID. WITHOUT THIS, ALL THE RESERVATIONS OF PARTICULAR RIGHTS OR PRIVILEGES WOULD AMOUNT TO NOTHING.[1]

Reflected here are both his hopes for a system of federal courts that would contribute to national power and stability, as well as a clear reference to the power of judicial review, which is discussed in the next chapter. Hamilton also noted in this essay that ". . . the judiciary, from the nature of its functions, will always be the least dangerous to the political rights of the Constitution; because it will be least in a capacity to annoy or injure them." Additionally, he argued that "the judiciary is beyond comparison the weakest of the three departments . . . it is in continual jeopardy of being over-powered, awed, or influenced by its coordinate branches."[2]

Although the framers spent relatively little time debating and drafting Article III of the Constitution, the same cannot be said about early congressional efforts to structure the judicial branch of the new government. In 1789, Congress spent nearly one-half of its inaugural session discussing various legislative provisions to create the federal judiciary. The members faced several key questions regarding the new judicial branch: should they create a separate system of federal courts at all, given the concerns about state power; if created, how would the judicial personnel be selected; how much jurisdiction would the courts have; and finally, what should be the relationship between then-existing state courts and the new federal courts?

These several questions were answered in the Judiciary Act of 1789, which was largely the work of Senator Oliver Ellsworth, a former member of the Constitutional Convention from Connecticut and the second Chief Justice of the U.S. Supreme Court (1796–1800). The Act established three layers of the federal court system: a district court (one judge per district) in each of the thirteen states; three circuit courts (each consisting of two Supreme Court justices and one district judge) in separate geographical regions of the country; and a single Supreme Court (composed of one chief justice and five associate justices). Two important provisions of the Judiciary Act implied significant power for the federal courts in 1789. Section 13 added the power to issue writs of mandamus to the Supreme Court's original and appellate jurisdiction. This meant that if a citizen wanted a court to issue an order to a public official commanding the performance of some specific task, that person could go directly to the Supreme Court. Section 13 would later be declared unconstitutional in the famous case of *Marbury v. Madison* in 1803. Section 25 of the Judiciary Act stipulated that the U.S. Supreme Court would have appellate jurisdiction over decisions by state courts, which either overturned a federal law or treaty or upheld a state law alleged to violate the Constitution, federal laws, or treaties. This provision became an important foundation for the Supreme Court's decision in *Martin v. Hunter's Lessee* in 1824. Although the federal judicial system has changed immensely since 1789 with respect to institutional size, case workload, and operational complexity, the basic organizational pattern even today bears some striking similarities to the original structure of the late eighteenth century.

THE CONSTITUTION, CONGRESS, AND FEDERAL COURT JURISDICTION

Article III, Section 2 of the Constitution states that "[t]he Judicial Power shall extend to all Cases, in Law and Equity, arising under this Constitution, the Laws of the United States, and Treaties made, or which shall be made, under their Authority;. . . ." The **jurisdiction** of federal courts involves the authority to hear a case or controversy when the proper parties are present and when the point to be decided is among the issues that these courts are authorized to consider. The full reference to judicial power in Article III, Section 2 means that federal courts can act under two separate categories: cases that merit federal consideration because of their *subject matter* (i.e., a claim arising under the Constitution, federal laws or treaties, or maritime law); and cases that warrant attention because of the nature of the *parties* involved (i.e., the United States, a state, citizens of different states, or representatives of foreign countries). Figure 3.1 summarizes this important matter of federal jurisdiction as it applies to most of the federal courts.

Original jurisdiction is the authority to be the first court to hear and decide a case. As the point of entry into the legal system, trial courts normally have a single judge and usually a jury to decide matters of law and fact in a case. Deciding issues of law involves applying relevant statutes and constitutional provisions to the evidence and conduct of a trial. Deciding issues of fact involves determining what actually happened in the circumstances of the case. Within the federal judiciary, district courts are the primary trial courts. **Appellate jurisdiction** is the power of federal

Figure 3.1 Jurisdiction of the Federal Courts as Determined by Article III of U.S. Constitution

Jurisdiction of the U.S. Supreme Court

Original Jurisdiction

❏ Cases affecting ambassadors, public ministers, and consuls
❏ Cases to which a state is a party

Appellate Jurisdiction

❏ All cases falling under the jurisdiction of the lower federal courts, (and in accordance with Article III, Sec. 2, Clause 2) "with such Exceptions, and under such Regulation as the Congress shall make."

Jurisdiction of the Lower Federal Courts

Subjects: Cases (falling under lower court authority)

❏ involving the U.S. Constitution, federal laws and treaties
❏ affecting ambassadors, public ministers, and consuls
❏ involving admiralty and maritime laws

Parties: Controversies (falling under lower court authority)

❏ involving the United States
❏ between two or more states
❏ between a state and citizens of another state
❏ between citizens of different states ("diversity" cases)
❏ between citizens of the same state claiming lands under grants of different states
❏ between a state, or the citizens thereof, and foreign nations, citizens, or subjects

courts to review and, if necessary, correct errors of law that may have occurred in the trial court. Appellate courts usually involve multi-judge panels and no jury. If certain errors in interpreting or applying the law have occurred, the appellate court can order the lower court to retry the case under the prescribed new interpretation of the law. In the federal judicial system, the primary appellate courts are the U.S. Courts of Appeal and the U.S. Supreme Court.

ORGANIZATIONAL STRUCTURE OF THE FEDERAL JUDICIAL SYSTEM

The U.S. Constitution authorizes two types of federal courts: **legislative** courts and **constitutional** courts. Legislative courts are created by the Congress under Article I, Section 8, Clause 9 for the purpose of providing technical expertise on specialized subjects and a limited range of subjects. Judges appointed to these courts are nominated by the president (subject to Senate confirmation) and serve fixed, overlapping terms. Legislative courts include the U.S. Tax Court, the U.S. Court of Veterans' Appeals, the U.S. Court of Appeals for the Armed Services, and the U.S. Court of Federal Claims. Constitutional courts are those established by Congress under Article III, Section 1 of the Constitution, and include federal district courts, courts of appeal, and the U.S. Supreme Court. The judges serving on these tribunals are nominated by the president, and with the advice and consent of the Senate, must be confirmed by that body. They serve lifetime terms of office as long as they engage in "good behaviour," as noted in Article III. The formal structure of the federal judiciary is depicted in Figure 3.2. Because these constitutional courts comprise the nucleus of the federal judiciary, a more detailed discussion of their place in the federal judicial system today is necessary.

Figure 3.2 Hierarchy of the Federal Court System

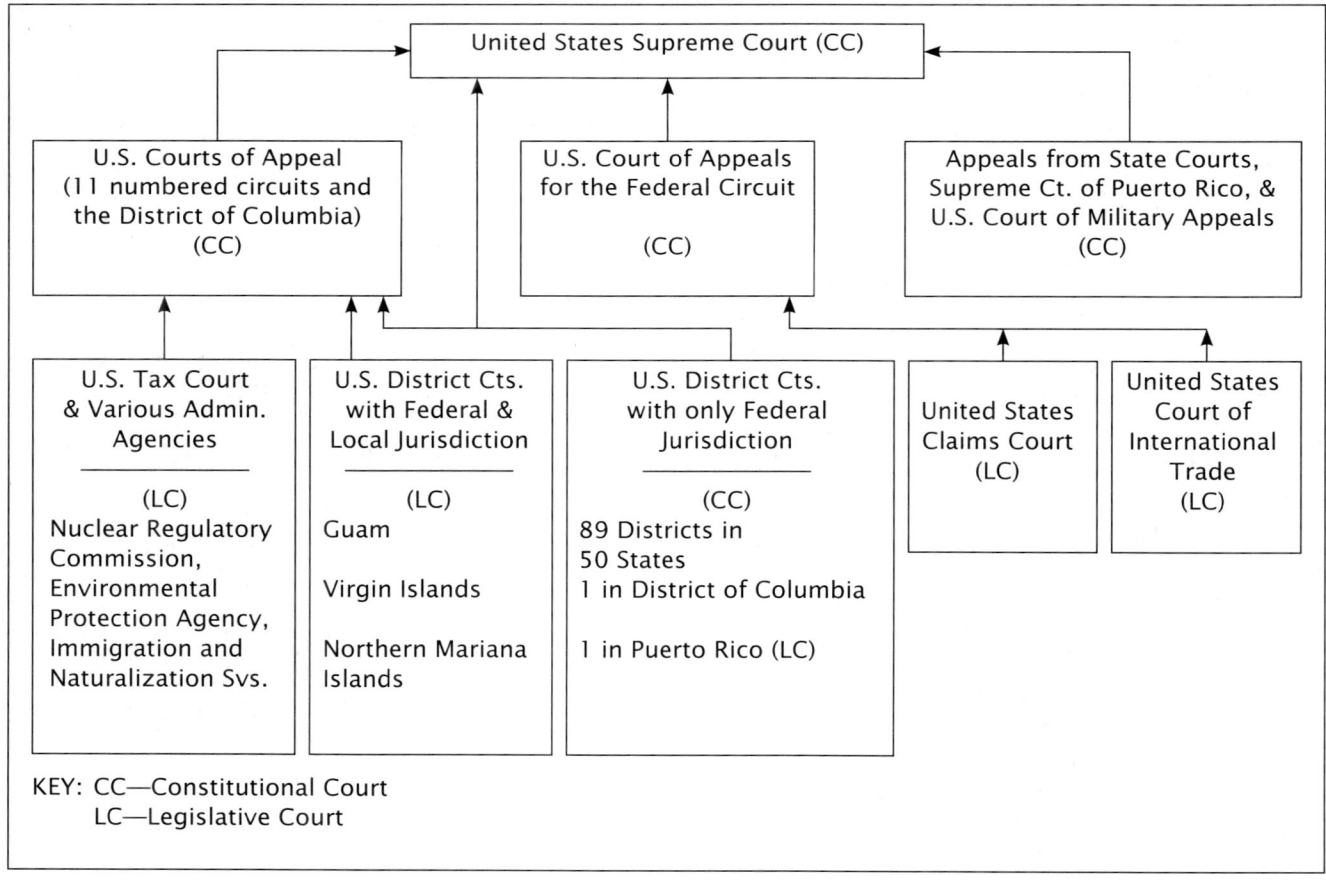

UNITED STATES DISTRICT COURTS

As noted earlier, the First Congress clearly recognized the need for federal trial courts to be established as soon as possible following ratification of the Constitution. Accordingly, it created thirteen district courts under the Judiciary Act of 1789. Today, ninety-four district courts exist throughout the United States. Eighty-nine district courts exist in the fifty states; each state contains at least one district court and the more populous states (California, Texas, and New York) each contain four district courts. Five additional district courts also exist in the District of Columbia, Guam, Puerto Rico, the Northern Mariana Islands, and the Virgin Islands. Federal district courts are the main trial courts within the federal judiciary in that they only exercise original jurisdiction, hearing cases for the first time. Although the rules governing district court jurisdiction are complex, normally the types of cases filed here usually fall into one of the categories summarized in Figure 3.1. The burden of district court activity each year tends to comprise three general categories: (1) cases involving a federal question relating to some aspect of the Constitution or federal law; (2) cases involving the United States government as a party; or (3) "diversity cases" involving citizens of different states that exceed a monetary threshold of $75,000. The losing party in a case decided at the district court level may appeal the judgment, although over 90 percent of district court decisions are never appealed to the next level.

A single judge and a federally convened jury normally determine the outcome of cases in federal district courts, although these courts occasionally use what is referred to as a "bench trial" where a single judge decides a case without the use of a jury. Each district court normally contains between two and twenty-eight federal judges, depending on the workload within the judicial territory. As a consequence of numerous laws and cost indexing practices, the annual salary of a federal district judge has been stuck at $174,000 since 2009. In 2002, Congress increased the total number of federal district judgeships throughout the United States and its territories to 679.[3] Assisting these federal judges is an extensive staff network comprised of U.S. attorneys, law clerks, court clerks, probation officers, and bankruptcy judges.

One other district court arrangement requires brief explanation—three-judge district court panels. In 1910, Congress passed legislation requiring that if a plaintiff in federal district court alleged either that a state law was unconstitutional or that the state law should not be enforced, then the case could be heard by an *ad hoc* three-judge panel (including at least one court of appeals judge), rather than by a single-judge district court. In 1976, Congress restricted the jurisdiction of these three-judge district court panels to cases involving legislative apportionment and a few other controversies dealing with individual voting rights. Over the past several decades, an appeal coming from one of these three-judge panels, or from a district court ruling where a federal law is declared unconstitutional, or when a lower court ruling is of major public significance and requires immediate resolution, could be made directly to the U.S. Supreme Court. Examples of cases appealed directly to the U.S. Supreme Court include *Youngstown Sheet & Tube Co. v. Sawyer* (1952) and *United States v. Nixon* (1974), which are discussed in Chapters 5 and 6, respectively; *New York Times v. United States* (1971), which is covered in Chapter 15; and *Bush v. Gore* (2000), which is discussed in Chapters 4 and 10.

The workload of federal district courts has grown substantially in recent decades for the same reasons that have increased demands upon the U.S. Supreme Court to hear cases upon appeal (see below). District court filings increased from 59,284 cases in 1960 to an all-time high of 402,885 in 2011 (580 percent). Criminal felony cases are much less numerous than civil cases (21 percent of total filings in 2011), but there has been a noticeable increase in recent years of felony criminal cases relating to alleged violations of federal immigration, firearms, and drug laws.[4]

UNITED STATES COURTS OF APPEAL

As stated earlier, the Judiciary Act of 1789 created three circuit courts of appeal, each of which required that two Supreme Court justices and one district court judge originally had to "ride the circuit" during the year to hear cases on appeal from one of the original thirteen district courts. Over the next century, this structure became increasingly inadequate because of judges struggling with extensive travel demands and an increasing workload of cases demanding appeal.

Finally in 1891, Congress created an intermediate appellate level in the federal judiciary that today finds the country divided into eleven numbered circuits, plus an additional appellate court in Washington, D.C. (U.S. Court of Appeals for the District of Columbia). Each circuit has a court of appeals that hears cases coming from district courts within that numbered circuit. The U.S. Court of Appeals for the District of Columbia hears cases on appeal from the U.S. District Court in the District of Columbia and most of the appeals from regulatory agencies of the federal government. Because of its location in Washington, D.C., its specialized work in administrative law and regulation, and its having been the court from which many recent Supreme Court justices have come (e.g., Justices Antonin Scalia, Clarence Thomas, and Ruth Bader Ginsburg, and Chief Justice John Roberts), this court is considered by many to be the second most important court in the federal judiciary behind the U.S. Supreme Court. Finally, the U.S. Court of Appeals for the Federal Circuit was created in 1982 and consists of twelve judges who hear appeals relating to such matters as foreign trade, monetary claims against the federal government, trademarks, and patent disputes originating in the U.S. Patent Office.

Each of these numbered courts of appeal has between six to twenty-eight appellate judges authorized by Congress, depending on the workload. The judges normally hear cases in three-judge panels, with the senior judge assigning opinions, although for particularly significant cases, all of the judges in a circuit may sit as a collective body (*en banc*) to resolve conflicting rulings among lower trial courts within the circuit. Appellate judges are currently paid $184,500 per year, a figure that has not changed since 2009.

U.S. courts of appeal, unlike normal district courts, are *collegial* courts, in that each appellate court consists of several judges who collectively hear a case only on appeal. No jury is impaneled, and no first-hand testimony is introduced at the appellate level. Just as most rulings by the federal district courts are never appealed to a higher level, the same is true with respect to decisions by these several courts of appeal. Less than 1 percent of their decisions are ever accepted for review by the U.S. Supreme Court, which means that these intermediate appellate courts are very important judicial policymakers in the judicial system.

Their primary task is to review the lower court decision to ensure that the relevant laws and procedures were interpreted and applied correctly.

The workload at the court of appeals level has also reflected increases in the overall federal caseload in recent decades. Whereas the total number of judges in the numbered circuits has more than doubled since the early 1960s (78 appellate judges in 1962, compared with 179 in 2010), the total number of appeals filed has increased eleven-fold (4,823 appeals in 1962, compared to 55,753 in 2011). Although the trend in appeals filed since the early 1960s clearly indicates a dramatic increase, the last few years have actually found modest decreases in appeals filed in the numbered circuits (68,473 in 2005, compared to 55,753 in 2011 [an 18.6 percent decrease]).[5]

UNITED STATES SUPREME COURT

At the top of the federal judiciary is the United States Supreme Court. Although in many respects the most authoritative and prestigious of the several federal courts, the Supreme Court is still only one of 108 federal constitutional courts, and it includes only nine of some 875 authorized judgeships within the federal judiciary. However, decisions by the high court carry enormous policy significance, as it seeks to resolve conflicts among the states and to ensure uniformity in the interpretation and application of the Constitution and federal laws. The Supreme Court consists of a Chief Justice and eight associate justices who, like all constitutional court judges, are nominated by the president and confirmed by the Senate with lifetime tenure (see Table 3.1 for current Supreme Court justices). The Chief Justice earns $223,500 per year, and associate justices earn $213,900 annually. Supreme Court justices can only be removed through impeachment by a majority vote in the U.S. House of Representatives and conviction by a two-thirds vote in the U.S. Senate, in accordance with Article I, Sections 2 and 3 of the Constitution. The Chief Justice presides over public sessions of the Court when cases are argued, conducts the weekly conferences among the justices, assigns the writing of the opinions if he votes with the majority, and administers the oath of office to the president and vice president every four years. (see Brief 3.1 for more detail on the operation of the Supreme Court).

Table 3.1 The United States Supreme Court, 2013

Name	Yr of Birth	Yr. of Appt.	Appointing President	Law School	Prior Judicial Experience	Prior Gov't Experience
John Roberts	1955	2005	Bush II	Harvard	US Ct. of Appeals	Dep. Solic. Gen.
Antonin Scalia	1936	1986	Reagan	Harvard	US Ct. of Appeals	————
Anthony Kennedy	1936	1988	Reagan	Harvard	US Ct. of Appeals	————
Clarence Thomas	1949	1991	Bush I	Yale	US Ct. of Appeals	Chair, EEOC
Ruth B. Ginsburg	1933	1993	Clinton	Columbia	US Ct. of Appeals	————
Stephen Breyer	1938	1994	Clinton	Harvard	US Ct. of Appeals	Justice Dept.; Senate Judiciary Committee
Samuel Alito	1950	2006	Bush II	Yale	US Ct. of Appeals	Justice Dept.
Sonia Sotomayor	1954	2009	Obama	Yale	US Ct. of Appeals	DA, New York
Elena Kagan	1960	2010	Obama	Harvard	————	Solicitor Gen.

Brief 3.1

THE MEN AND WOMEN OF OCTOBER

The Supreme Court's annual term begins on the first Monday in October and normally ends in late June the following year. The justices customarily use the summer recess to read lawyers' written briefs of cases scheduled for oral argument and decision during the upcoming term, as well as reading some of the thousands of petitions submitted by losing parties wanting their case reviewed by the high court. When in session, the justices' time is normally consumed with several tasks that involve basically two steps in a lengthy process: (1) the acceptance-of-cases phase and (2) the decision-making phase. In the acceptance phase, the justices' law clerks (see Brief 3.2) screen petitions for appeal and submit recommendations to the justices, who then confer with each other about whether a case should be scheduled for review. If four of the justices believe that sufficient reason exists to warrant review of the case (the so-called "Rule of Four"), then the case is placed on one of the Court's three (original, appellate, and miscellaneous) dockets.

When a case is scheduled for oral argument, the attorneys for both sides are asked to submit extensive written briefs that summarize the facts of the case; legal and constitutional issues that relate to the controversy; any relevant economic, sociological, psychological, or scientific data to support the legal issues; and usually some preliminary response to anticipated arguments of the opposing side. After the submittal of these written briefs, oral arguments are heard during the first three days of the first two weeks of each month beginning in October, and normally running through the following April. In most cases, each side is given only thirty minutes to address the justices, with time limits very carefully kept and controlled by the Chief Justice. Questioning from the several justices frequently interrupts allotted time for presentation of these oral arguments.

When the justices are "sitting" (i.e., hearing cases being argued), they also meet in conference (usually on Wednesday afternoons and all day Friday). In their remaining time during sittings, and when the Court is "recessed" (typically the latter two weeks of each month) the justices work in their individual chambers preparing preliminary opinions, responding to other justices' opinions, and moving toward final resolution of the cases under active consideration. While in conference, the justices discuss both sides of the case under consideration and which appeals to grant in the future. This conference occurs in total secrecy, with only the nine justices and a few Court recorders sitting in the conference room. Beginning with the Chief Justice and moving from the most senior to the most junior member of the Court, the justices indicate their views on the main issues involved in the case and why those issues should be resolved in a particular manner. Judgments expressed at this time by the justices normally suggest a preliminary vote on how the case will be decided. Some recent accounts indicate that with the advent of technology such as e-mail, the justices do not spend as much conference time together, although the dynamics of nine justices meeting physically together to discuss the main issues in the cases can affect the final outcome of many of the individual cases.

After the weekly conferences are held and the preliminary votes are taken, the chief justice (if in the majority) will assign one of the members voting in the majority to draft a preliminary **majority opinion**, which states the holding and main rationale for the Court deciding as it does in the case. On many occasions, the Chief Justice will assume the responsibility of drafting the majority opinion in the hopes of influencing the overall direction and emphasis of the Court's ruling. If the Chief Justice does not vote with the majority, the most senior justice in the majority either makes the opinion assignment or writes the majority opinion. This component of the decision-making phase of the entire process is very important because the majority opinion must be drafted in a manner that holds together the preliminary majority coalition of justices.

If a justice ruling with the majority agrees with the result reached by the Court but differs as to some of the reasoning contained in the majority opinion, then a **concurring opinion** can be written, which itself can attract other justices who may disaffiliate from the majority opinion. Generally speaking, the more concurring opinions that accompany a decision by the Court, the more diluted and weakened is the majority opinion, potentially to the point of its becoming an opinion for only a plurality rather than a majority of the Court. Finally, if a justice disagrees with the entire holding of the Court, then he or she may write a **dissenting opinion**, which speaks for either a lone justice or those justices voting in the minority who want to join in that dissent. Dissenting opinions can have particular significance for future adjudication, since they indicate a sentiment that may be accommodated later with new personnel on the Court and new circumstances that might compel reconsideration of some important constitutional issues. The months of May and June normally find the justices in chambers drafting and circulating opinions for decisions that will be announced before the end of the Court term in June.

The supporting administrative and legal staff of the Supreme Court is very small compared to other branches of the federal government, primarily because the justices and their assigned law clerks do most of the work relating to the hearing and deciding of cases. Clearly, the most important legal assistance that they receive is from their individual law clerks (see Brief 3.2).

Unlike courts at the two lower levels of the federal judiciary, the Supreme Court exercises both original and appellate jurisdiction (as indicated earlier in Figure 3.1), only the latter of which can be regulated by Congress. Its original jurisdiction can be exercised in cases between two or more states; between a state and the federal government; those involving foreign ambassadors, ministers, consuls, and their staff; or in cases initiated by a state against citizens of another state or nation. In controversies between two or more states and those filed against foreign diplomatic personnel, the Court has exclusive original jurisdiction. In all other instances, it has concurrent original jurisdiction with district courts.

Brief 3.2

CLERKING AT THE SUPREME COURT

Of all the supporting personnel employed by the Supreme Court today, only the law clerks of the individual justices assist in the all-important decisions and opinions that comprise the main body of Supreme Court activity. For the first one hundred years of the Court's existence, the justices completed all of the legal duties themselves without the benefit of legal assistants. But as the annual caseload grew in both number and complexity, the justices finally won congressional approval for law clerks to assist them. In 1882, the first law clerk was hired by Justice Horace Gray, paid out of his own personal funds. In 1886, the Congress authorized $1,600 a year to pay a "stenographer-clerk" for each of the nine justices.

Over the past century, the number of law clerks working for the individual justices has increased. Associate Justices can have four clerks, and the Chief Justice five. As one might expect, these clerkships are extremely coveted positions allotted to the top graduates of the more prestigious law schools in the country. Although some justices in the past retained the same clerks for as many as five years (Chief Justices William Howard Taft and Charles Evans Hughes, and Justice Frank Murphy), most clerks serve one-year terms and, as of 2010, were paid approximately $75,000 per year, though reports of large bonuses and salaries after finishing their Supreme Court clerkships have become common recently. The clerks perform a variety of tasks for their respective justices, but they spend most of their time reviewing *certiorari* petitions addressed to the Court, researching materials for cases scheduled for oral argument and decision, reading and summarizing cases, and helping the justices draft opinions for eventual release.

As the number of *certiorari* petitions filed with the Court has increased over the past few decades, the role of the law clerks in reviewing these petitions has changed. In 1972, Chief Justice Warren Burger and Associate Justices Byron White, Harry Blackmun, William Rehnquist, and Lewis Powell organized their assigned law clerks into a "cert" pool, and the critical task of reviewing petitions filed each year fell to these several law clerks. The participating justices agreed to rely upon the recommendations fashioned by any member of the pool. Between 1991 and 2008, Justice Stevens was the only justice not participating in the cert pool of law clerks (in 2008 Justice Alito also left the pool).

Of the nine justices serving on the Supreme Court in 2010, only three were former clerks for justices on the Court (Chief Justice John Roberts clerked for Justice William Rehnquist—the man he eventually replaced—in the 1980 term, Justice Stephen G. Breyer served as a law clerk for Justice Arthur J. Goldberg during the 1964 term, and Justice Elena Kagan clerked for Justice Thurgood Marshall in the 1988 term). Ironically, Justice Ruth Bader Ginsburg was denied a clerkship in 1960 by Justice Felix Frankfurter, who stated that he was "not ready to hire a woman."

In recent years there have been only one or two cases heard each year under the Court's original jurisdiction. The Supreme Court delivers full written opinions in only a fraction of the cases that are submitted to it each year, and this very limited involvement has become more pronounced in recent years, as is discussed below. Constitutional scholar David O'Brien has noted that during the Burger Court years (1969–86), two operational changes—reducing the oral argument time limit for each side from one hour to thirty minutes and modifying the longtime Rule of Four procedure—in effect resulted in more cases being docketed and resolved with full opinions. But as the Chief Justice indicated in the introduction to this chapter, the Rehnquist Court demonstrated a much narrower sense of what merits serious attention by the justices. As a result, the Court now accepts a much smaller number of cases for full review and decision (see Table 3.2).

Although the Supreme Court has considerable control over its agenda, Congress also has some responsibility for determining what cases the Court can review. In accordance with Article III, Section 2, Congress alone governs the appellate jurisdiction of the Supreme Court. Congress regulates the Court's appellate jurisdiction over two broad types of cases: cases coming from lower federal courts and "federal question" cases originating in state courts that involve a matter of federal statutory or constitutional law. Some cases, usually referred to as *certiorari* cases, fall within the Court's discretionary jurisdiction, meaning that the justices alone can accept or decline to review the case. Other cases historically referred to as appeal cases have customarily fallen within the Court's mandatory appellate jurisdiction, and thus the justices must hear the case.

As stated earlier, Congress in 1789 wanted to ensure that two types of controversies could be reviewed by the Supreme Court, namely, (1) state court decisions that invalidated a federal law, and (2) state court decisions upholding a state law that contradicted the U.S. Constitution or a federal law. To cover these contingencies and to make Supreme Court review mandatory, the First Congress passed Section 25 of the Judiciary Act of 1789, which for nearly two hundred years meant that the justices were required to hear and decide any state decision defined by one of these two characteristics.

In addition to these two mandatory categories of appeal cases, Congress historically required that the Supreme Court review three other types of controversies: (1) those in which a U.S. Court of Appeals had invalidated a state law; (2) civil cases in which a lower federal court had struck down a federal law; and (3) decisions by three-judge district courts that either granted or denied an injunction (referred to as equity cases). Finally, in 1988, Congress passed legislation that dramatically reduced the mandatory appellate jurisdiction of the Supreme Court. The law converted four of the five appeals case categories noted above into certiorari cases, the effect of which was to reduce dramatically the mandatory appeals and increase the certiorari jurisdiction of the Court. Presently, only the equity decisions of three-judge federal district courts must be heard by the justices, and this category of decisions has itself been substantially reduced by Congress. The practical effect of this congressional activity has been to eliminate most of the mandatory jurisdiction of the Supreme Court, leaving the justices with near total discretion over their annual docket. Figure 3.3 indicates the two main routes by which cases come to the Supreme Court each term.

Table 3.2 The Supreme Court: Shrinking Docket, Expanding Demands

Oct. Term	1995	2001	2002	2003	2004	2005	2006	2007	2008	2009
Original Docket	5	1	1	2	0	4	1	1	1	2
Appellate Docket	2,081	1,890	1,855	1,749	1,693	1,663	1,728	1,624	1,612	1,566
Miscellaneous Docket	4,511	6,133	6,486	6,030	5,808	6,537	7,173	6,749	6,210	6,519
Total petitions	6,597	8,024	8,342	7,781	7,501	8,204	8,902	8,374	7,823	8,087
Opinions of the Court	91	88	92	84	79	81	73	67	76	83
% Total petitions	1.4	1.1	1.1	1.1	1.1	.99	.82	.80	.97	1.0

Figure 3.3 The Two Primary Routes of Appeal to the United States Supreme Court

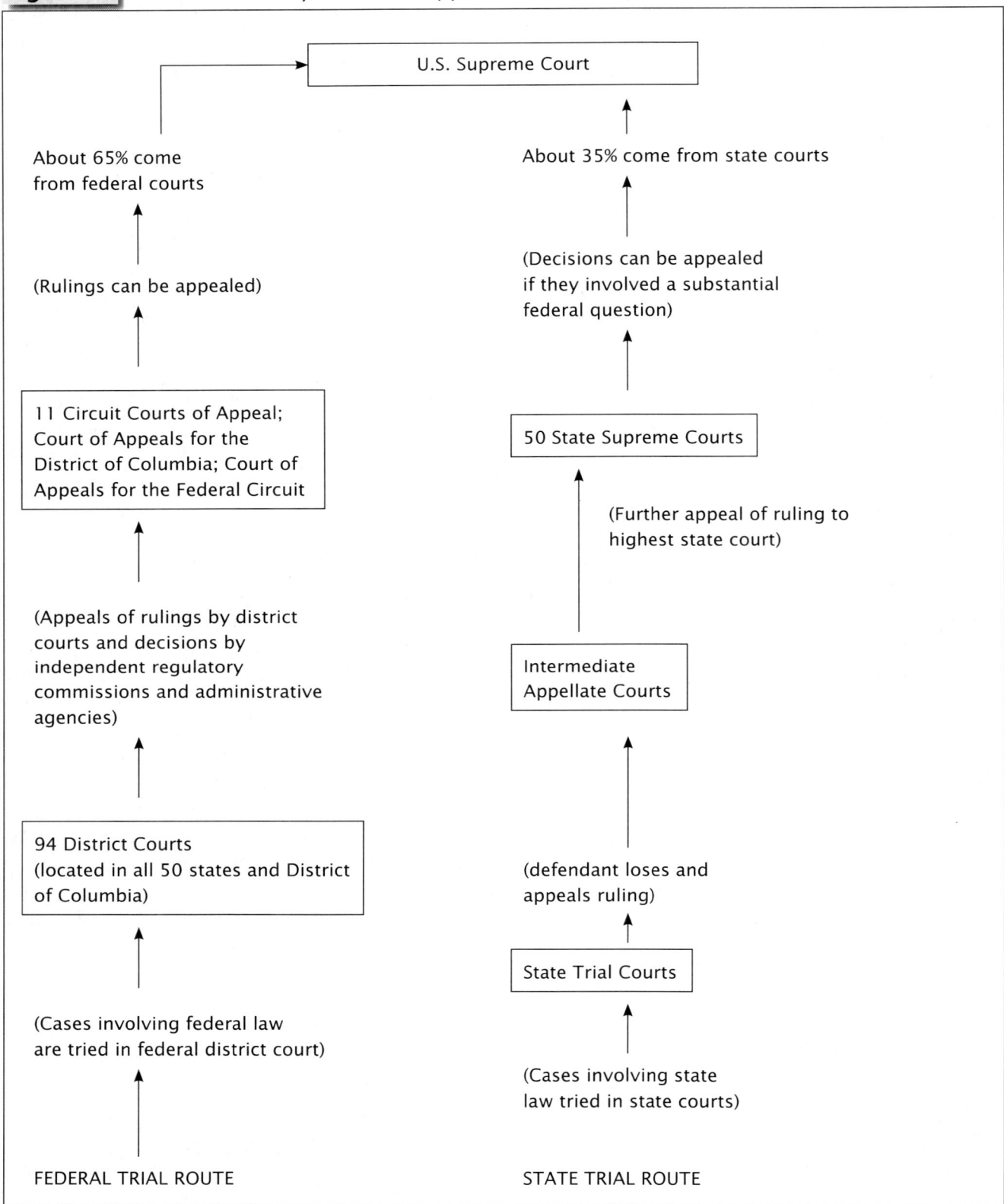

SOURCE: Adapted from Lawrence Baum, *The Supreme Court,* 9th edition (Washington, DC: CQ Press, 2007), p. 10.

It is customary to divide cases to be reviewed by the Supreme Court into three categories or dockets, two of which, until recently, were approximately equal in size. Each year, cases appealed to the Court that are accompanied by printed transcripts of the trial record and by filing fees constitute the paid cases, and are assigned to the Appellate Docket. In recent years, the Court has normally received less than two thousand paid cases for consideration annually. The rest of the Court's jurisdictional load consists of cases filed *in forma pauperis* ("in the manner of a pauper"), which require no transcripts or filing fees. Most of these cases are brought by state and federal prison inmates and comprise the Miscellaneous Docket. Until the mid-1980s, this category numbered about the same as paid cases, but over the past two decades, the number of paupers' petitions has increased dramatically. As Table 3.2 indicates, the number of cases on the Appellate Docket declined by nearly 25 percent from a high of 2,081 petitions in the 1995 Term to 1,566 petitions in the 2009 Term. The Miscellaneous Docket, which is comprised largely of prisoners' petitions, increased substantially (from a low of 4,511 petitions in the 1995 Term to a high of 7,173 petitions in the 2006 Term).

A second conclusion that can be drawn from these data is that a very small percentage of petitions submitted to the Court each year are actually granted. As mentioned earlier, beginning with the Rehnquist Court, the justices have reduced their output of opinions. In the 1985 term, the final year of the Burger Court, the justices issued 159 opinions. In the past decade, the Court has issued between sixty-seven (2007 Term) and ninety-two (2002 Term) opinions. Over the past twenty-five years, then, there has been a noticeable decline in the number of petitioners being granted full review and oral argument, along with full opinions by the Court. For whatever reason, the Court seems reasonably comfortable with its shrinking docket.

For the Supreme Court to hear a case there must be a clear collision between contending interests in a legitimate legal dispute. Article III refers specifically to "cases . . . [or] controversies." Furthermore, the parties involved in the case or controversy must have **standing** to sue in federal courts. Standing refers to a legal right to sue wherein the party must prove that he or she has suffered or will suffer direct personal injury as a result of the enforcement of some law or action. Although some rules on standing derive from statutes, judges determine most of these procedures, thus allowing for great flexibility and discretion. By the mid-twentieth century, more and more parties won "standing to sue" in federal courts, which meant that federal judges were under increasing pressure to hear suits of parties claiming denial of a constitutional right. This trend was especially apparent during the second phase of the Warren Court between 1961 and 1969. The Burger Court in the 1970s tried to restrict the number of parties finding a sympathetic court to hear their pleas by both calling for a new level of appeal prior to reaching the Supreme Court and limiting standing for parties petitioning the Court for review.[6]

As a recent example of how this limitation on "standing to sue" may play out, the two cases heard by the Court during the 2012 Term involving same-sex marriage (see Brief 10.8) raised questions regarding the legal standing of the appellants. In both cases, the government (the State of California in one case, the federal government in the other) refused to appeal after losing in the federal appeals court. So legislators advocating restrictions on same-sex marriage took up the appeal instead, raising questions about what "direct personal injury" they would face if the Court affirms the lower-court ruling. As this text goes to press, it is uncertain whether the Supreme Court will use a lack of standing in either case (or both) to limit their power to decide the issues involved on the merits.

As stated above, in many of the most recent Supreme Court terms, over eight thousand petitioners have asked the justices to review their cases, even though the actual number of cases that the justices decided annually with signed opinions comprised a very small percentage of those asking for review. In the 1890s, barely 1,800 petitions were considered by the Court, but in recent decades, the normal number of petitions for review has continued to climb noticeably. This growth in the demand for the Court to consider lower court decisions can be attributed to several developments.[7]

Lawrence Baum notes that a growing population, so-called rights consciousness, increased interest-group activity, and the massive growth in the many activities of the federal government all contributed to an increased number of petitioners before the

Supreme Court.[8] First, the workload increased in part because of the population increase of the United States since the early 1900s. Federal census data indicate that 76 million people lived in the United States in 1900, but by the end of 2012, that number increased to over 315 million Americans. With more people available either to initiate or be involved in litigation, more cases invariably filter through the federal judicial channels. Second, Congress has passed more laws in the last several decades, which has increased litigation in federal courts, especially as a consequence of new claims relating to civil rights, criminal procedure, and environmental and consumer-protection issues.

A third reason for the increased workload can be attributed to interest group activity in the American political system generally, and in federal courts in particular. Groups such as the American Civil Liberties Union, the National Association for the Advancement of Colored People's Legal Defense Fund, Common Cause, the National Rifle Association, the American Federation of Labor and Congress of Industrial Organizations, and the Natural Resources Defense Council, to name only a few, have all been active in recent years in pressing their claims through the judicial system. Many of these groups have increasingly seen their causes as legal challenges worth pursuing in court. Finally, the Court itself has enlarged the scope of legal entitlements over the past several decades by recognizing a constitutional basis for many asserted rights (e.g., abortion, procedural guarantees for criminal defendants, privacy, and First Amendment protections for private citizens). As a result, the justices have unwittingly encouraged petitions from previously isolated parties now seeking protection of their alleged rights under the law. This last factor is especially apparent with respect to paupers' petitions that have increased the size of the Miscellaneous Docket (see Table 3.2). Whereas only about six hundred such petitions from prisoners were evident in the 1950s, recent terms have witnessed a twelve-fold increase in this particular docket of the Court, as noted earlier. This increase in the Miscellaneous Docket has most likely reflected the escalating prison population in the United States over the past several years, which by 2011 exceeded 7 million.

Given the fact that nearly all of the cases that reach the Supreme Court now arrive through a petition for a **writ of certiorari** (a Latin term that means "to be made more certain"), a brief comment on this device is necessary. This appellate route involves an order by the Supreme Court to a lower court to send up the record of the case so that the justices can determine if the law were correctly interpreted and applied. For decades, the justices have followed the institutional practice of voting on all petitions for certiorari and granting only those for which at least four justices think involve a substantial federal question. This so-called "Rule of Four" dates to the era of Chief Justice William Howard Taft in the 1920s and the Judiciary Act of 1925, and it was firmly in place by the Warren Court era (1953–69).

LIMITATIONS ON FEDERAL JUDICIAL POWER

Because of the importance attached to Supreme Court decisions, great care is taken both on and beyond the Court to monitor the exercise of its judicial authority. Several internal and external limitations upon the Court's power have determined when and how the justices intervene to resolve controversies. *Internal* constraints upon the justices include what are usually referred to as the "Ashwander Rules," compiled by Justice Louis D. Brandeis in a famous concurring opinion in *Ashwander v. Tennessee Valley Authority* (1936). For many decades these self-imposed guidelines have meant that the justices will, among other things, not offer advisory opinions on hypothetical issues or questions, not rule on the validity of a statute or complaint brought by one failing to show direct injury to person or property, and not anticipate a constitutional question prior to having to decide it. These so-called Ashwander rules are still major "gatekeeping" devices that allow federal judges to refuse to hear selected disputes.

Related to the Ashwander rules are two doctrines the Court has invoked to limit its authority to hear cases: mootness and ripeness. The mootness doctrine requires that the "case" or "controversy" (see discussion of the language in Article III above) exist at all stages of judicial review, not just at the time the complaint was filed. If circumstances change and one or both parties no longer have a stake in the outcome of the case, the justices can declare the case "moot" and decide not to hear it. A classic example of mootness can be found in *Defunis v. Odegaard* (1974), an affirmative action case noted in Chapter 10, where a student originally denied admission to law school was later provisionally admitted pending the outcome of federal court decisions. By the time his case came to the Supreme Court, he was about to graduate, and nothing the Court decided would have an effect on the student's rights, so the case was dismissed as moot.

The ripeness doctrine asserts that a "case" present a "controversy" that is actual, one whose threat to the party challenging a law or regulation is real and immediate. That is, a court cannot decide a claim when the relationship between the parties is still developing or in flux, and where it would have to speculate as to contingencies that might occur in the future rather than a real set of facts. In *Abbott Laboratories v. Gardner* (1967), the Court asserted that the "basic rationale" of the ripeness doctrine "is to prevent the courts, through avoidance of premature adjudication, from entangling themselves in abstract disagreements over administrative policies, and also to protect the agencies from judicial interference until an administrative decision has been formalized and its effects felt in a concrete way by the challenging parties."

One other internal principle limiting federal courts in the exercise of their power is the **political questions** doctrine, which dates from at least 1827 and John Marshall's decision in *Martin v. Mott*. This concept maintains that courts should not intrude into disputes that are more appropriately resolved by the two popularly elected branches of the government. As elected public officials that are accountable to the popular will, state and national legislators, governors and presidents should resolve certain disputes that involve conflicting views of public issues and policies. For judges and justices to resolve these "political questions" would be to intrude into the proper domain of the other coordinate branches of government. "Political questions" have been most prominent in the policy areas of foreign affairs and national security. In these areas, the Supreme Court has frequently refused to intervene in many matters that have been thought to be within the president's policy realm. But in recent decades, the doctrine has been invoked less frequently as the Supreme Court has become involved in an increasing number of areas earlier thought to be off limits to federal courts.

Examples include legislative apportionment (Chapters 3 and 11), several areas of prisoners' rights (Chapter 13), and the seating of members of Congress [*Powell v. McCormack* (1969)]. Many critics of the Court's ruling in *Bush v. Gore* in 2000 raised the "political questions" doctrine (including Justice Breyer in his dissent), arguing that Congress has the constitutional authority to count electoral votes, and for the Court to weigh in on such a politicized matter as a presidential election threatens the integrity of the judicial branch of government.

If the Supreme Court refuses to impose certain limitations upon its own ability to hear cases and decide issues brought before it, several *external* factors have historically limited the Court's ability to exert its judicial authority. Examples of these external checks upon the Supreme Court include:

❏ The rare threat of impeachment of a Supreme Court justice (tried once unsuccessfully in 1805)
❏ The climate of public opinion
❏ Threatened changes in the size of the Court
❏ Action by Congress that changes laws that have been interpreted a certain way by the Court (e.g., passage of the Lilly Ledbetter Fair Pay Act in 2009, which is discussed in Chapter 10)
❏ Constitutional amendments that alter a Court precedent
❏ Congressional control over the dates of judicial sessions
❏ The potential body of professional criticism flowing from law reviews and other academic commentary

In addition to these external limitations upon the Supreme Court's power to act, Congress can also intervene to prevent the federal courts from exercising their appellate authority. This action by Congress involves an important distinction between original and appellate jurisdiction, especially as it affects the U.S. Supreme Court. Since *Marbury v. Madison* in 1803 (discussed in Chapter 4), one of the long-established principles in American constitutional law is that, in accordance with Article III, Section 2, Clause 2, Congress can revise only the appellate jurisdiction of the Supreme Court. Although it has seldom voted to do so, on a few prominent occasions (all in wartime), the Congress limited the ability of the Supreme Court to act by regulating its appellate jurisdiction.[9] The most recent example of this occurred in 2006 when Congress passed the Military Commissions Act, which is discussed more fully in Chapter 5.

THE APPOINTMENT OF JUDGES AND JUSTICES

One of many anomalies in the operation of the American democratic system is the fact that lifetime-tenured, appointed judges have increasingly been asked to decide some of the more critical and divisive issues in society. As a consequence, it is important to note the several stages involved in selecting personnel to serve in the federal judiciary. The selection of federal judges has always involved the same two constitutional prerequisites—nomination by the president and confirmation by the U.S. Senate. Those who successfully win confirmation to a federal judgeship enjoy lifetime tenure and significant prestige in their judicial posts. Unlike constitutional prerequisites for members of Congress or the president (e.g., age, citizenship, residence), Article III does not mention any formal requirements for federal judges or Supreme Court justices. In fact, Supreme Court justices need not even have a law degree, although in practice, only lawyers have served on the high court.

JUDICIAL SELECTION: AN INHERENTLY POLITICAL PROCESS

At first glance, the selection process for federal judges and Supreme Court justices is deceptively simple. To win appointment to the federal bench requires four basic elements: a vacancy, a presidential nomination, confirmation by a majority vote of the Senate, and a formal presidential signature and issuance of a commission. Although the delegates at the Constitutional Convention supported the creation of a national judiciary to correct a glaring weakness of the Articles of Confederation, they disagreed over how its members should be selected. Those who proposed the Virginia Plan wanted the judiciary to be chosen by Congress. An alternative proposal suggested in the New Jersey Plan was for the president to appoint judges. As happened so frequently at the Philadelphia Convention, the delegates compromised by agreeing that members of the judiciary be nominated by the president and confirmed by the Senate. Article II, Section 2 reads that "... [the President] shall nominate, and by and with the Advice and Consent of the Senate, shall appoint ... Judges of the Supreme Court, ...". Although the president can nominate individuals to fill judicial vacancies, the Senate performs an essential role when reviewing presidential nominations. Historically, the normal presumption surrounding a president's obtaining the "advice and consent" of the Senate meant that the president should be allowed considerable discretion in the selection of federal judges. Until the last few decades, when partisan politics became more pronounced and less civil, most judicial appointments, especially at the lower federal court levels, were processed without much controversy. At the Supreme Court level, presidential nominees have encountered much more scrutiny, and about one-quarter of all presidential nominations to the Supreme Court since 1793 have failed to win confirmation by the Senate.[10] Still, of the twenty-six presidential nominees to the Supreme Court that have failed to be confirmed, only five were defeated after 1900, the most recent of which was Judge Robert Bork in 1987 (see Brief 3.3).

Depending on the level at which a federal judgeship vacancy occurs, the selection process may assume different characteristics. Several potential pitfalls await a president determined to leave an imprint on the federal judiciary. Many political actors are involved—Justice Department officials, the Federal Bureau of Investigation,

U.S. senators, state and local party leaders, supporters of other potential nominees who lobby for their candidates, personnel from the American Bar Association's Standing Committee on Federal Judiciary, and members of the powerful Senate Judiciary Committee. At any one of these several levels, complications may arise for prospects desiring a seat on the federal bench, especially when it involves a Supreme Court nominee.

The first hurdle for nominees to the lower federal courts to overcome is the approval of senators from the president's party and the state in which a vacancy occurs. This important selection variable normally affects only nominees for lower federal judgeships (primarily district courts because the jurisdiction of each circuit includes at least three states) and is referred to as **senatorial courtesy**. Senatorial courtesy dates from the original design of the federal

Brief 3.3
TWO HISTORIC BATTLES OVER SUPREME COURT CONFIRMATION

From its beginnings in 1789, twenty-six individuals nominated by the president to serve on the Supreme Court failed to win Senate confirmation, but only five since 1900. Until 1929, except for the 1916 hearings on Louis D. Brandeis, Senate Judiciary Committee hearings on a Supreme Court nominee were closed to the public. Nominated by President Coolidge in 1925, Harlan Fiske Stone was the first nominee to appear personally before the Senate Judiciary Committee. Nominated by President Ronald Reagan in 1981 to replace Justice Potter Stewart, Sandra Day O'Connor was the first nominee to appear before live television cameras. In the first decade of televised coverage of confirmation hearings, two battles took place that would affect the process for years to follow.

When President Reagan in 1987 nominated Judge Robert Bork of the U.S. Court of Appeals for the District of Columbia to replace the retiring Justice Lewis Powell, it was seen as a potential turning point for the Court. Bork's criticism of a broad constitutional right to privacy, abortion rights, many free speech claims, and several legislative reapportionment precedents found several groups, including the National Organization for Women, National Abortion Rights Action League, and the Southern Christian Leadership Conference, opposing his confirmation. On October 23, 1987, the full Senate voted 58 to 42 against him, primarily on the grounds that his legal theories and judicial philosophy were not in the mainstream of prevailing constitutional norms. In a hasty attempt to avoid similar controversy and defeat, the White House then countered by nominating a little-known jurist, Judge Douglas Ginsburg, whose nomination was eventually withdrawn after embarrassing revelations about alleged conflict-of-interest charges regarding cable television regulation in cases in which he participated, and his recreational use of marijuana during his days as a Harvard Law School professor. Eventually, the Senate unanimously approved (97–0) in January 1988 the nomination of Ninth Circuit Court of Appeals Judge Anthony Kennedy after a brief hearings process that demonstrated none of the rancor of the Bork affair.

On June 27, 1991, the last remaining liberal-activist justice of the Warren Court era, Thurgood Marshall, announced that he would retire from the Court. Within a few days, President George H. W. Bush nominated Judge Clarence Thomas, a forty-three-year-old African American then serving on the U.S. Court of Appeals for the District of Columbia, to fill the vacancy. The Thomas nomination was generally seen as a carefully calculated political move by the White House to win the support of Democratic senators who would be more likely to support a minority appointment. Throughout the Senate Judiciary Committee hearings, Thomas labored to distance himself from several statements in which he had opposed affirmative action, the right to privacy, and First Amendment freedoms. In his testimony, he insisted that now as a judge he must preserve his objectivity and consider all sides of those issues likely to come before him on the bench.

The Judiciary Committee split 7–7 over the Thomas nomination in late September 1991 and was poised to send the nomination to the full Senate, but the hearings reconvened within a week in response to charges of sexual harassment against Thomas brought by Anita Hill, a law professor at the University of Oklahoma. Hill alleged that while working for Thomas in the early 1980s at the Department of Education and the Equal Employment Opportunity Commission, she had been the target on numerous occasions of sexual harassment by Thomas. He strongly denied all the charges, characterizing the allegations and media coverage as a "high-tech lynching for an uppity black who in any way deigns to think for himself." At the conclusion of the hearings, the several charges and denials came down to whether the public believed Clarence Thomas or Anita Hill. The full Senate voted 52–48 on October 15, 1991, in favor of Clarence Thomas, the slimmest approval margin for any justice in the Court's history.

Since 1991, although the six Supreme Court nominees have been questioned vigorously about their past rulings and judicial and constitutional philosophies, the ultimate Senate decision making has been less rancorous, with the smallest margin of approval coming in 2006 with Justice Samuel Alito, who received forty-two votes opposed to his confirmation to replace Justice O'Connor.

---

judicial structure in 1789, which ensured that district courts reflected the localism and federalized nature of many issues imposed by state political boundaries. The Department of Justice maintains files on potential appointments to fill vacancies within the federal judiciary, but it normally also monitors candidates recommended by U.S. senators and other key party members. In practice, it means that a nominating president extends to senators of his party "the courtesy" of first approving of prospective nominees for federal district courts in their state. As soon as a lower court vacancy is announced, the senators from the state with the vacancy begin working with their staff to compile their own list of preferred nominees. Once they have agreed upon a candidate (assuming that they are from the president's political party), the president normally submits that name to the U.S. Senate, which then assigns it to the Senate Judiciary Committee for formal hearings and an eventual full-Senate vote on the nomination. Senatorial courtesy usually affects most significantly the selection process of a prospective district court nominee, although presidents are wise to at least check with home-state senators, regardless of party, about their views on any prospective nominee for a federal judgeship, given the subsequent Senate up or down vote on that candidate.

Over the past few decades, a very secretive norm employed by the U.S. Senate involves what is called the "blue slip" procedure, which reflects an effort in the U.S. Senate to institutionalize the somewhat more informal senatorial courtesy norm.[11] When the president nominates an individual to fill a federal judicial post, the chairperson of the Senate Judiciary Committee sends "blue slips" of paper to both of the home-state senators of the nominee. If even one of the senators declines to return the blue slip, then the nomination is presumed to face greater difficulty in Senate deliberations. Although the origins and impact of the "blue slip" procedure are rather obscure, some past chairs of the Judiciary Committee have had to address criticisms of the procedure and its antidemocratic overtones. With the ideological divergence of the two parties, it has become more difficult for presidents to overcome this first hurdle, especially when at least one home-state senator is "ideologically distant" from the president. One recent study predicts that the chance of confirmation drops almost 10 percent when one of the home-state senators is ideologically distant from the president.[12]

If approved by home-state senators, the prospective candidate is then screened by administration officials in the Department of Justice, which conducts its own internal investigation and submits a list of potential nominees to the American Bar Association's Committee on Federal Judiciary. Before creation of this committee in 1946, the ABA's role in evaluating the professional credentials of judicial nominees was very informal and unsystematic. But over the next several decades, the ABA began to play an important, though not necessarily decisive, role in investigating and evaluating candidates who were nominated for a federal judgeship or Supreme Court vacancy. During this period, the ABA Committee used several different ratings systems for evaluating prospective nominees to the federal bench. For lower-court nominees, the Committee uses the categories of "Well Qualified," "Qualified," and "Not Qualified." The rating system for Supreme Court nominees has gone through three changes since 1956, when the ABA began rating high court nominees. Since 1990, two years after the fifteen-member Committee sharply divided over the Robert Bork nomination to the Supreme Court, the ABA Committee has used the same categories of "Well Qualified," "Qualified," and "Not Qualified" for its evaluation of nominees to the Supreme Court.[13]

In addition to a favorable vetting by the ABA Committee on Federal Judiciary, a lower court candidate supported by key U.S. senators and state party leaders within the president's party is normally assured nomination and confirmation if he or she also successfully meets the informal standards of the Justice Department. Depending on the president, Justice Department officials have exercised varying degrees of influence in screening prospective candidates.

If administration officials are encouraged by their preliminary internal investigation, the name of the nominee is formally announced by the president and sent to the U.S. Senate, which then assigns it to the Senate Judiciary Committee for scheduled confirmation hearings. Assuming that the home-state senators from the president's party approve of the nominee, and the Judiciary Committee finds nothing during its investigation that might prove unacceptable to its members or to the full Senate, the committee normally votes to recommend confirmation of the nominee by the full Senate. In recent years, however, Senate opposition, even by one anonymous individual placing a "hold" on a nomination, has blocked a number of nominees for the judiciary, especially on the U.S. Courts of Appeal (see Brief 3.4).

JUDICIAL SELECTION VARIABLES

A few crucial factors have historically dominated the judicial selection process. For many decades, three variables have been vital to winning eventual confirmation by the Senate: *professional*, or judicial qualifications (competency and integrity); *representational*, especially party and political activity considerations; and *doctrinal* or policy views. Although these three factors predominate in the selection of all federal judicial appointees, the following discussion also emphasizes the significant role that race and gender now play on an increasing basis.

Brief 3.4
THE CONTENTIOUS CONFIRMATION PROCESS: FROM CLINTON TO OBAMA

The confirmation of federal judges has always involved politics, but some would argue that the last two decades have exhibited an unusual degree of delay, accusation, and acrimony. During President Bill Clinton's first two years in office (1993–94), the Democratic Senate in the 103rd Congress confirmed nearly 91 percent (107 of 118) of his district-court nominees and 86 percent (18 of 21) of his circuit-court nominees. When the 104th Congress in 1995 found the Republicans in control of the confirmation process, only 73 percent (62 of 85) of Clinton's district-court nominees and 61 percent (11 of 18) of his circuit-court nominees were confirmed. The 105th Congress (1997–98) found the Republican-controlled Senate confirming approximately 80 percent of his nominees, and the length of hearings on district-court nominees was 161 days. Finally, in the 106th Congress (1999–2000), only 70 percent of Clinton's judicial nominees were confirmed and the average length of time between receipt of nomination to holding of hearings on district-court nominees was 97 days. Data on the confirmation of appellate nominations reveal even more delay before the Senate Judiciary Committee. Whereas the average length of confirmation times during the first Bush presidency and the first two years of the Clinton administration (1989–94) were between 77 and 81 days, the average length of time between receipt and hearing ballooned to between 231 days in the 105th Congress and 247 days in the 106th Congress.

Several reasons explain events in the 1990s with respect to judicial confirmations. First, the return of a divided government in 1995–96 and a partisan atmosphere in Congress in 1998–99 saw the first impeachment and Senate trial of a sitting American president since 1867. This political climate impeded President Clinton's ability to mold the federal judiciary in more representational ways. Second, the Republican-controlled 104th Congress that convened in 1995 provided the Senate with a prominent "payback" opportunity for Republicans of some still-festering wounds, such as the heated confirmation fights involving Judges Robert Bork in 1987 and Clarence Thomas in 1990 (see Brief 3.3). Finally, chairmanship of the Senate Judiciary Committee passed in 1995 from Senator Joseph Biden (D-DE) to Senator Orrin Hatch (R-UT), the latter of whom had been a vehement supporter of Judges Bork and Thomas in earlier years. Under his leadership, the Senate Judiciary Committee exhibited a more hostile environment for Clinton nominees, especially in the last two years of the Clinton presidency.

This political acrimony from the 1990s spilled over into one of the closest presidential races in American political history in 2000, which found the Supreme Court in effect declaring the winner in *Bush v. Gore* (2000). After his inauguration on January 20, 2001, George W. Bush set about to bring into the federal judiciary personnel "who would faithfully interpret the Constitution . . . and not use the courts to invent laws or dictate social policy." And looking at the record over his eight years in office, any observer would conclude that President Bush was successful in getting a large number of federal judges who fit his ideological and policy positions confirmed, with an overall confirmation rate of 77 percent from 2001 to 2009. Even in the 110th Congress, when Senate control had shifted to the Democrats, and with a presidential election in 2008 looming, George W. Bush was successful with fifty-eight of his seventy-nine district-court nominees (73 percent). He also succeeded in seating two conservative circuit-court judges—with few confirmation controversies—on the Supreme Court. But Bush II's efforts to fill judicial openings was often thwarted, especially in years where Congress was controlled by the Democrats—in his last two years, only ten of his twenty-two circuit-court nominees were confirmed (46 percent). And even when Democrats did not control the Senate, they used other tactics to block Bush judicial nominees, particularly the filibuster.

When President Barack Obama took office in 2009, Senate Republicans sent a letter to the president arguing that "the judicial appointments process has become needlessly acrimonious."[14] With a strong Democratic majority in control of the Senate, many thought the judicial "confirmation wars" might cease. But in the first two years, the process was as acrimonious as ever, and the failure and delay rate of the Obama administration reached an all-time high. Even with two successful Supreme Court nominations and a lame-duck session agreement to confirm nineteen pending federal judicial appointments, Obama ended up getting only 60 of his 103 district-court and circuit-court nominations approved during the 111th Congress (58 percent). This has improved, however, and as of March 2013, President Obama had an almost 80 percent confirmation rate (175 out of 213). Still, the number of federal judicial vacancies remains high, with almost ninety seats on the federal bench unfilled.

Several factors have been used to explain the increasingly contentious confirmation process: the rise in importance and power of the federal judiciary; an increasingly divided and polarized party politics; confirmation conditions when there is divided control of the presidency and the Senate (over the past six decades, the confirmation rate drops by 17 percent when the presidency and Senate are in different hands); the effective use of stalling and opposition tactics by the minority party; and presidential election–eve maneuvering to "save" vacancies on the courts in case party control of the White House might shift. In reality, it has been a combination of these factors that has led to the current situation, one that ultimately does not bode well for producing an efficient and effective federal judiciary.

PROFESSIONAL COMPETENCE

No president wants to nominate an individual to the Supreme Court who does not possess strong legal credentials, sound judgment and temperament, and unquestioned ethical behavior. Although political considerations may be important in attracting the initial attention of those involved in the nomination process, professional competence is an essential characteristic throughout the process. Supreme Court justices as a group have been far more likely than the average person to have attended prestigious colleges and universities, and all members of the Court in recent decades have possessed a law degree, again usually from one of the top law schools in the country. The justices serving on the Roberts Court at the beginning of 2013 come exclusively from Ivy League law schools: five Harvard Law graduates (Roberts, Scalia, Kennedy, Breyer, and Kagan), three Yale graduates (Thomas, Alito, and Sotomayor), and one Columbia graduate (Ginsburg, who attended Harvard for her first two years of law school). Prior to the early twentieth century, lawyers and judges often obtained their legal education by apprenticeship under a practicing attorney. But early in the last century, law schools quickly became the dominant source of a legal education. The last Supreme Court justice without a formal legal education to be trained by apprenticeship was James F. Byrnes, appointed to the Court by President Roosevelt in 1941.

A second aspect of professional competence that is frequently considered is whether the nominee has had previous *judicial* experience performing as a judge at some level. Approximately one-quarter of Supreme Court justices have had extensive experience as judges prior to being nominated for the high court, and yet historically some of the most famous justices on the Court never served as judges prior to their appointment. Prominent examples of the latter include John Marshall, Charles Evans Hughes, Harlan Fiske Stone, Earl Warren, Louis Brandeis, Hugo Black, William O. Douglas, Byron White, Lewis Powell, William Rehnquist, and most recently, Elena Kagan.[15] For thirty-five years up until the appointment of Kagan in 2010, every appointee to the Court had at least some judicial experience at either the state or federal level. Such experience also gives presidents more opportunity to discern the judicial philosophy of a prospective nominee if the latter has compiled a record of written opinions and decisions.

A less formalized aspect of professional competence relates to ethical standards, personal character, and integrity of the prospective nominee. A few nominees in recent decades have encountered substantial problems on this ethical dimension. In 1968, President Lyndon Johnson's attempt to elevate then–Associate Justice Abe Fortas to the chief justiceship (to succeed retiring Earl Warren) encountered some serious conflict-of-interest charges concerning Fortas's having earned legal fees while serving on the Court. Ethics charges also surrounded the nominations by President Nixon of federal judges Clement Haynsworth Jr. and G. Harrold Carswell in 1969 and 1970, respectively, both of whom were rejected by the U.S. Senate.

A significant indicator of whether a candidate is *professionally* qualified for a seat on the federal bench is the approval system devised by the American Bar Association's Standing Committee on Federal Judiciary. Ever since President Woodrow Wilson nominated Louis D. Brandeis to the Supreme Court in 1916, over the objection of the then-conservative American Bar Association, that group's role in the screening process has been an important but informal norm, as indicated earlier. Some criticisms of the ABA's role have centered on whether a private occupational group should have any say in determining who occupies high judicial office.[16] The ABA's assessment of a nominee's judicial temperament, personal integrity and professional competence neither guarantees nor precludes confirmation. Though he failed to win ABA approval, Louis Brandeis eventually was confirmed by the Senate in 1916 on a 47–22 vote after a four-month delay, and Brandeis himself went on to become one of the more distinguished justices to serve on the Court. Conversely, the ABA's endorsement of Justice Abe Fortas in 1969 was insufficient to win his confirmation, and he soon thereafter resigned his associate justice position on the Court. Both Haynsworth and Carswell received approval by the ABA Committee, but the Senate rejected both of them, by votes of 45–55 and 45–51, respectively.

POLITICAL AFFILIATION

A second important selection variable is *partisan political affiliation* of the nominee. Ever since George Washington began to nominate loyal Federalists in 1789 to the federal judiciary, presidents have wanted to reward active members of their own political party when filling court vacancies. In the modern era of party politics, this generally has meant that Republican presidents nominate Republican candidates, and Democratic presidents nominate loyal Democrats. With the notable exceptions of Presidents Taft, Hoover, Ford, Carter, Bush I, Clinton, and Bush II, presidents since 1901 (see Table 3.3) have nominated representatives of their party over 90 percent of the time when filling vacancies on the federal courts.[17]

Some might argue that political patronage should play no role in filling vacancies on the federal bench. But by nominating party loyalists, presidents can indirectly increase their chances of having their programs prevail in legislative–judicial struggles over policy. Even President Jimmy Carter, who established the U.S. Circuit Judge Nominating Commission in 1977, ostensibly to ensure that judicial selection would be based on merit rather than politics, had one of the highest judicial patronage percentages of the twentieth century, nominating Democrats 91 percent of the time to district courts (though only 82 percent of vacancies to the appellate courts).[18]

In recent decades, national political parties have declined somewhat in their ability to attract and retain party activists. As campaign and election organizations have become tied more closely to individual candidates rather than to the two major parties, judicial patronage has assumed increasing importance for presidents and party elites alike. Many Supreme Court nominees were deeply involved in politics and government prior to their nominations to the high court. Some, like Justice Hugo Black and Chief Justice Earl Warren, held high elective office before their respective nominations. Others, such as Justice Byron White, Chief Justice William Rehnquist, and Justice Elena Kagan, occupied high administrative positions in the federal government prior to being nominated to the Supreme Court.

Although over 90 percent of Supreme Court nominees have come from the same political party as the president nominating them, notable exceptions do exist. In the twentieth century, the most famous examples include Justices Benjamin Cardozo (a Democrat nominated by President Hoover in 1932), Harlan Fiske Stone (a Republican elevated to the chief justiceship by President Roosevelt in 1941), William Brennan (a Democrat appointed by President Eisenhower in 1956), and Lewis Powell (a Democrat nominated by President Nixon in 1971).

IDEOLOGICAL OR POLICY VIEWS

The third major selection variable discussed here—*policy stances* of the nominee—is easy to understand, sometimes difficult to determine, and impossible to guarantee. As one might expect, presidents invariably want persons on the federal bench who will help them achieve their major policy goals while in office. Virtually all presidents, whether they admit it publicly or not, have policy or political objectives in mind when they nominate someone to high judicial office. Democratic presidents might be expected to nominate individuals to the judiciary who have been more "individualist" in protecting civil rights and liberties, and more supportive of a collectivist or "communitarian" approach that condones government

Table 3.3 Percentage of Federal District Court and Courts of Appeal Appointments Belonging to the President's Party, 1901–2011

President	Political Party	Percentage
T. Roosevelt	Republican	95.8
Taft	Republican	82.2
Wilson	Democratic	98.6
Harding	Republican	97.7
Coolidge	Republican	94.1
Hoover	Republican	85.7
F.D. Roosevelt	Democratic	96.4
Truman	Democratic	90.1
Eisenhower	Republican	94.1
Kennedy	Democratic	90.9
Johnson	Democratic	94.4
Nixon	Republican	92.8
Ford	Republican	81.3
Carter	Democratic	89.1
Reagan	Republican	92.7
George H. W. Bush	Republican	88.6
Clinton	Democratic	87.2
George W. Bush	Republican	84.7
Obama	Democratic	89.8

intervention in the economy. Conversely, Republican presidents normally support more of an individualist approach to government that places more emphasis upon economic freedom and the free market. Likewise, they have been more willing to use governmental authority to limit civil liberties in the name of public order and national security. But the policy views of a prospective nominee may be difficult to determine, especially if the candidate lacks a lengthy, written record on particular policy issues. Furthermore, nothing guarantees that an individual, once appointed to the federal bench, will adhere to a president's predetermined image of policy positions (see Brief 3.5).

Brief 3.5

JUDICIAL APPOINTMENTS . . . AND DISAPPOINTMENTS: WHAT IS A PRESIDENT TO DO?

Although presidents intuitively want to choose nominees who, at least to some extent, reflect their policy views, the last century has seen several examples of nominees to the Supreme Court who frequently strayed from the expectations of their nominating president. When Theodore Roosevelt tapped Oliver Wendell Holmes Jr. for the Court in 1902, Roosevelt's hope was that Holmes would support his trust-busting efforts, but Holmes's dissenting opinion in *Northern Securities v. U.S.* (1904) left a narrow 5–4 majority that upheld the dissolution of the railroad holding company but jeopardized subsequent anti-trust-busting efforts. Woodrow Wilson's appointment of James McReynolds in 1914 produced a justice who differed with Wilson on virtually every issue that came before the Court, and because McReynolds stayed on the Court until 1941 and comprised one of the so-called "Four Horsemen" of the conservative Court in the 1920s and 1930s, his voting behavior haunted Democratic President Franklin D. Roosevelt's policy aims throughout the early New Deal era. President Calvin Coolidge had only one opportunity to nominate a justice to the Supreme Court: Harlan Fiske Stone, a fellow Republican in 1925. To Coolidge's dismay, Stone soon began to align with the more liberal Justices Holmes and Brandeis on the Court, against constraints upon First Amendment liberties and for governmental regulation of the economy. President Harry Truman nominated four justices to the Supreme Court during his presidency, and is reported to have been disappointed in many of their positions taken in key cases, especially the renowned Steel Seizure Case in 1952 when the Court (with the assistance of two of his appointees) ruled against his exercise of executive power.

In the latter half of the past century, additional nominations eventually disappointed four Republican presidents. Two of the most frequently cited examples of nominees whose policy orientation departed greatly from their presidential benefactor were Earl Warren and William Brennan. When President Eisenhower selected Warren from Republican ranks in 1953, it was seen as both rewarding a fellow Republican who helped him secure the presidential nomination in 1952, and containing a potential political rival in future presidential politics. As Chief Justice, Warren immediately became instrumental in molding the famous *Brown v. Board of Education* (1954) decision that overturned the "separate-but-equal" doctrine of fifty-eight years. Furthermore, Warren's later record on race relations, reapportionment, religious liberty, and the rights of criminal defendants left a judicial legacy that differed from Eisenhower's policy expectations in certain areas. The nomination of William Brennan in 1956, another disappointment to Eisenhower, placed on the Court a Democrat then serving on the New Jersey Supreme Court. Brennan quickly became a liberal legend on the Court concerning such issues as racial discrimination, gender equality, First Amendment rights, strong protection for the rights of criminal defendants, and strong opposition to the death penalty.

The four nominees who joined the Supreme Court during the Nixon years (Warren Burger, Harry Blackmun, Lewis Powell, and William Rehnquist) were ostensibly selected in an effort to reorient the Court from a presumed "soft-on-crime" stance during the Warren years to a tough "law-and-order" record. Although these justices largely conformed to Nixon's expectations initially on criminal procedure, they eventually began to show more independence in decision making, especially in the case of Justice Blackmun. On such issues as abortion, state aid to parochial schools, electronic surveillance, affirmative action, the death penalty, and court-ordered busing to achieve desegregation, with the possible exception of William Rehnquist, the Nixon appointees were unpredictable. The biggest shock to the president was undoubtedly the unanimous ruling by the Supreme Court in *United States v. Nixon* (1974), which forced him to turn over to the Special Prosecutor the White House tapes that soon forced him from office (see Brief 6.3, Chapter 6).

Finally, the Supreme Court clearly moved in a more conservative direction (pro–death penalty, anti–affirmation action, less strict separation on church–state issues) in the late 1980s, with four appointments by President Reagan (Associate Justices Sandra Day O'Connor, Antonin Scalia, and Anthony Kennedy, and the elevation of William Rehnquist to Chief Justice). But the Reagan administration's stand on curtailing abortion rights was turned back by Justices O'Connor and Kennedy, who voted to uphold the *Roe* precedent in 1992. Finally, George H. W. Bush's first appointee to the Court, the former New Hampshire attorney general and federal appellate judge David Souter, aligned himself with the more liberal bloc of justices (Stevens, Ginsburg, and Breyer) on the Rehnquist Court. A recent source on judicial behavior notes that "virtually all Supreme Court justices exhibit significant drift from their first-term preferences; and that drift occasionally manifests in doctrinal change of consequence."[19]

OTHER SELECTION VARIABLES: RACE, GENDER, AND ETHNIC ORIGIN

In addition to professional competence, party representation, and policy views, some other considerations have been factored into filling vacancies on the Supreme Court. Although it used to be fairly important, *geographical distribution* on the Court has declined since the late nineteenth century, when Supreme Court justices literally "rode the circuit" and assisted trial courts in handling cases and hearing appeals.

A nominee's *religious* affiliation is certainly less important in the appointment process than it once was. Although the Court has always been a Protestant bastion (82 percent of the 112 justices appointed to the Supreme Court, with Episcopalians and Presbyterians the most numerous of the Protestant denominations represented), the current lineup features six Roman Catholics (Roberts, Scalia, Kennedy, Thomas, Alito, and Sotomayor) and three Jewish justices (Ginsburg, Breyer, and Kagan). Historically, there have been only twelve Roman Catholics (Chief Justice Roger B. Taney being the first in 1836) and eight Jews (Louis D. Brandeis was the first, in 1916) on the Court. While the role of religion continues to affect American politics in terms of both elections and policy, it probably holds less significance with respect to judicial selection than in past decades. The most recent additions to the Court were most likely not selected primarily because of their denominational ties, as much as for other criteria, such as their race, gender, and policy views.

Racial minorities and women have been woefully underrepresented on the Supreme Court since 1789, generally reflecting the legacy of decades of discrimination. That eventually began to change in the late 1960s when racial minorities and women finally began to win federal judicial appointments. Thurgood Marshall became the first African American justice on the Supreme Court in 1967, and Sandra Day O'Connor was the first woman appointed to serve on the Court, in 1981. In 2009, Sonia Sotomayor took her oath as the first Latina justice on the Court. And with President Obama's appointment of Elena Kagan in 2010, the Supreme Court for the first time featured three women justices (see Brief 3.6).

Brief 3.6

PRESIDENT OBAMA'S FIRST TWO SUPREME COURT APPOINTEES: SONIA SOTOMAYOR AND ELENA KAGAN

When Justice David Souter announced that he would retire at the end of the 2008 Term of the Supreme Court, it gave President Obama his first opportunity to make an important judicial appointment early in his administration. On May 27, 2009, Obama nominated U.S. Court of Appeals Judge Sonia Sotomayor, which would make her the first Hispanic justice (and third woman) on the Supreme Court. The daughter of Puerto Rican parents, raised in a public housing project in the East Bronx, Sotomayor's "extraordinary journey" from low-income roots to Ivy League education and high judicial appointments was a major reason President Obama cited for appointing her: "When Sonia Sotomayor ascends those marble steps to assume her seat on the highest court of the land America will have taken another important step towards realizing the ideal that is etched above its entrance: Equal justice under the law."[22]

Sotomayor graduated as the valedictorian of Cardinal Spellman High School, then attended Princeton University and Yale Law School. After serving five years as a New York City prosecutor, she practiced law in a private firm until being appointed by President George H. W. Bush to serve as a federal district judge. President Clinton then nominated her for a vacancy on the Court of Appeals for the Second Circuit in 1997. After a delay of more than a year, part of the currently contentious judicial nomination process (see Brief 3.4), she was confirmed by a vote of 67–29 in October 1998. Her nomination to the Supreme Court drew some harsh criticism from Republicans, who called her a "liberal activist" and who worried about potential racial bias, based on comments she had made in speeches. In a law school speech that would be cited throughout her confirmation hearings, Sotomayor commented that "I would hope that a wise Latina woman with the richness of her experiences would more often than not reach a better conclusion than a white male who hasn't lived that life." (In her confirmation hearings, she backed away from that remark, as a "rhetorical flourish that fell flat."[23]) Ultimately, a distinguished background and fairly mainstream record as a federal judge (her most famous ruling was one that ended the Major League Baseball strike of 1994) overcame these initial criticisms, and Sotomayor was confirmed by a vote of 68–31 on August 6, 2009. Since Justice Souter had compiled a fairly liberal record as a Supreme Court Justice (one of the "surprises" discussed in Brief 3.5), her appointment is considered unlikely to shift the balance on the Court, as her first years of service are beginning to prove.

The following year, President Obama had another opportunity to appoint a justice to the Court, when Justice Stevens announced his retirement after thirty-five years on the bench. Stevens, at age ninety the third longest-serving Supreme Court justice and one of the most prolific opinion writers (including many scathing dissents), was regarded as one of the Court's "liberal lions." On May 10, 2010, President Obama nominated his Solicitor General, Elena Kagan, to be the 112th justice on the Supreme Court. Having served in all three branches of government, and as the first woman Dean of Harvard Law School, Kagan nonetheless was the first nominee in almost forty years without any prior experience as a judge, at any level. This brought some initial criticism, especially from Republican senators, even though an earlier nomination by President Clinton to serve as an appeals court judge was blocked by Republican Judiciary Chairman Orrin Hatch (who failed to schedule hearings on her nomination) and was allowed to expire after the 2000 election. But her distinguished background, intellectual abilities, and personal charm were able to overcome any initial hesitance at her lack of judicial experience. A native New Yorker, Kagan received her undergraduate degree from Princeton, a master of philosophy from Oxford, and her law degree from Harvard (making the Court not only an all–Ivy League team, but one where all the justices studied law at either Harvard or Yale). After clerking for Justice Thurgood Marshall, Kagan worked on a Senate staff, in the Clinton White House, as Professor and Dean of Harvard Law School, and finally as President Obama's Solicitor General.

Her confirmation hearings were mildly contentious, but with an understanding that her nomination was guaranteed, owing to the overwhelming Democratic majority in the Senate during the first two years of the Obama administration. In addition to criticizing her for a lack of prior judicial experience, Republican senators predicted that she would be a "liberal activist" in the spirit of the man she clerked for, and grilled her on abortion and gun rights, as well as her decision as dean to ban military recruiters from using the resources at Harvard Law School, in violation of federal provisions but consistent with Harvard's anti-discrimination policy (which the "don't ask, don't tell" ban in the military contradicted). In the end, Kagan was confirmed by a vote of 63–37, and took her oath of office on August 7, 2010. Once again, Justice Kagan's appointment is not thought to alter the ideological or policy balance on the Court. But as the fourth female and eighth Jewish justice, her appointment brings record numbers of both women and Jews to the Court at any one time (three each). In her early years on the Court, like her former boss and mentor Justice Marshall (who also went directly from solicitor general to Supreme Court justice), she will be forced to recuse herself from a number of cases in which she participated as the government's chief advocate before the Court.

Prior to the mid-1970s, the appointment of nonwhites or women to the lower federal judiciary was a rarity. However, beginning with the Carter years (1977–81), this pattern of traditional white-male dominance on the federal bench began to change. As Tables 3.4 and 3.5 indicate, women and racial minorities made a noticeable appearance in lower federal courts during this era. Nearly 14 percent of Carter's appointees (28 of 202) to the district courts were African-American, and approximately 7 percent (14 of 202) were Hispanic Americans. Carter also appointed eleven racial minorities and eleven women to the fifty-six vacancies at the appellate level, meaning that nearly 40 percent of his appellate appointees were "nontraditional" candidates. Neither Presidents Reagan nor Bush I approached this level of minority or female representation on the federal bench.

During his eight years in the White House, Ronald Reagan appointed women to less than 8 percent of his judicial vacancies (28 of 368 total appointments) and an even lower number of appointments (24) went to racial minorities. President George H. W. Bush (Bush I; 1989–93) appointed racial minorities to nearly 11 percent (20 of 185 total appointees) of the district and appellate court openings. With respect to female appointees, Bush appointed women 19 percent of the time to the federal bench during his four years in office (36 of 185 total appointments).

Beginning in 1993, President Bill Clinton began to build an impressive legacy of appointing an unprecedented number of racial minorities and women to the federal bench. In a genuine effort to make the federal bench look more like the American population at large, Clinton appointed a total of 305 new judges to the federal district courts and 61 to the federal courts of appeal. At the district court level, nearly 25 percent (76) were racial minorities and nearly 29 percent (87) were women. At the appellate level, over one-quarter (16) of Clinton appellate judges were racial minorities and one-third (20) were women. On January 1, 2001, as his second term was concluding, Bill Clinton could take legitimate credit for having helped increase the overall number of racial minorities and women on the federal bench. At the district court level, women comprised nearly 20 percent of the authorized judgeships and 21 percent of the appellate judgeships. Furthermore, racial minorities

Table 3.4 Comparison of U.S. District Court Appointees, by Administration—Selected Characteristics

Variable	Obama 2008–12	Bush II 2001–08	Clinton 1993–01	Bush I 1989–93	Reagan 1981–89	Carter 1977–81
Experience						
Judicial	54.5%	52.1%	52.1%	46.6%	46.2%	54%
Prosecutorial	47.7%	47.1%	41.3%	39.2%	44.1%	38.1%
Neither	29.5%	24.9%	28.9%	31.8%	28.6%	31.2%
Law School Education						
Public	45.5%	49.0%	39.7%	52.7%	44.8%	52.0%
Private	31.8%	39.1%	40.7%	33.1%	43.4%	31.2%
Ivy League	22.7%	7.7%	19.7%	14.2%	11.7%	16.8%
Gender						
Male	58.8%*	79.3%	71.5%	80.4%	91.7%	85.6%
Female	41.2%*	20.7%	28.5%	19.6%	8.3%	14.4%
Race/Ethnicity						
White	68.0%	81.6%	75.1%	89.2%	92.4%	78.2%
African American	15.0%	6.9%	17.4%	6.8%	2.1%	13.9%
Hispanic	10.0%	10.0%	5.9%	4.0%	4.8%	6.9%
Asian American	6.0%	1.5%	1.3%	—	0.7%	0.5%
Native American	1.0%	—	0.3%	—	—	0.5%
% White male	41.0%	67.4%	52.4%	73.0%	84.8%	67.8%
Total appointments	134	261	305	148	290	202

*Combined District and Appeals Court appointees, through March 2013.
Sources: Adapted from Sheldon Goldman, Sara Schiavoni, and Elliot Slotnick, "W. Bush's Judicial Legacy," *Judicature* 92, no. 6 (May–June 2009), 279; Alliance for Justice Judicial Selection Snapshot, *www.afj.org/judicial-selection/judicial-selection-snapshot.pdf*.

occupied over 15 percent of district court judgeships and 13 percent of those at the appellate level.[20]

This trend of appointing "nontraditional" judges to the federal bench was continued, though not at the same levels, during the Bush II presidency. President George W. Bush appointed a total of 261 judges to the district courts and 59 to the federal courts of appeal. Of these totals, about 18 percent (48) of his district court appointees and 15 percent (9) of his appellate judges were racial minorities. Bush had particular success in bringing in Hispanic Americans to fill 10 percent (26) of district court vacancies, a higher number and percentage than any of his predecessors. With respect to gender diversity, Bush appointed lower percentages of women than did Clinton to vacancies on the district (20.7 percent) and appellate (25.4 percent) benches. But in terms of the overall demographic shape of the federal judiciary, President Bush continued to diversify the federal judiciary, causing both a decline in "fully traditional" district courts (all white and all male) and by actually establishing nontraditional majorities on several courts. Still, most analysts have concluded that Bush II's commitment to diversifying the federal judiciary was always balanced by "the stronger commitment to his policy agenda."[21]

In his first two years, President Obama made an unparalleled commitment to racial, ethnic, and gender diversity on the federal bench. Although he had some difficulty getting federal justices confirmed (see Brief 3.4), his appointments to the district and appellate courts were the most diverse in U.S. history, with almost half being female, and nearly 45 percent African American, Hispanic, or Asian American. Through his first term as president, the total percentage of

Table 3.5 Comparison of U.S. Courts of Appeal Appointees, by Administration—Selected Characteristics

Variable	Obama 2008–12	Bush II 2001–08	Clinton 1993–01	Bush I 1989–93	Reagan 1981–89	Carter 1977–81
Experience						
Judicial	80.0%	61.0%	59.0%	62.2%	60.3%	53.6%
Prosecutorial	73.3%	33.9%	37.7%	29.7%	28.2%	30.4%
Neither	6.7%	25.4%	29.5%	32.4%	34.6%	39.3%
Law School Education						
Public	20.0%	39.0%	39.3%	32.4%	41.0%	39.3%
Private	53.3%	35.6%	31.1%	37.8%	35.9%	19.6%
Ivy League	26.7%	25.4%	29.5%	29.7%	23.1%	41.1%
Gender						
Male	58.8%*	74.6%	67.2%	81.1%	94.9%	80.4%
Female	41.2%*	25.4%	32.8%	18.9%	8.3%	19.6%
Race/Ethnicity						
White	53.0%	84.7%	73.8%	89.2%	97.4%	78.6%
African American	27.0%	10.2%	13.1%	5.4%	1.3%	16.1%
Hispanic	13.0%	5.1%	11.5%	5.4%	1.3%	3.6%
Asian American	7.0%	—	1.6%	—	—	1.8%
% White male	30.0%	64.4%	49.2%	70.3%	92.3%	60.7%
Total appointments	30	59	61	37	78	56

*Combined District and Appeals Court appointees, through March 2013.
Sources: Adapted from Sheldon Goldman, Sara Schiavoni, and Elliot Slotnick, "W. Bush's Judicial Legacy," *Judicature 92*, no. 6 (May–June 2009), 284; Alliance for Justice Judicial Selection Snapshot, www.afj.org/judicial-selection/judicial-selection-snapshot.pdf.

"nontraditional" judges appointed to the federal bench was over 60 percent. Furthermore, his first two appointments to the Supreme Court were women, with Justice Sotomayor representing the first Hispanic appointment to the Court (see Brief 3.6).

The Roberts Court and Ongoing Judicial Confirmation Concerns

As the above discussion denotes, confirming presidential nominees to serve on the federal judiciary has been a contentious and uncertain endeavor for all parties involved, especially over the past two decades. At the same time, the confirmation process for the past four Supreme Court nominations, though not without conflict and contention, has gone relatively smoothly. The current configuration of the Court led by Chief Justice John Roberts (see Brief 3.7) appears stable, notwithstanding any unforeseeable events or circumstances.

Conclusion

The federal judicial system began in an era when the Constitution's framers were searching for a more responsive and responsible government that sorely needed a judiciary to arbitrate the inevitable conflicts that would arise in a pluralistic society. Structurally, the federal judiciary has expanded greatly since its creation in 1789 to become a complex and very institutionalized apparatus that places great authority in the hands of life-tenured judges whose constitutional power is both limited and extraordinary. Although

Brief 3.7

THE SEVENTEENTH CHIEF JUSTICE: JOHN G. ROBERTS

After several weeks of considering a short list of preferred candidates, on July 19, 2005, President George W. Bush nominated John G. Roberts, a federal appeals court judge with an impressive resumé and a conservative record, to fill the vacancy on the U.S. Supreme Court created by the resignation of Justice Sandra Day O' Connor a few weeks earlier. With President Bush praising his "experience, wisdom, fairness and civility," the eventual confirmation of Judge Roberts at age fifty meant that he could serve for many decades on the high court. Soon after the death of Chief Justice William Rehnquist on September 3, 2005, the Bush White House changed the confirmation trajectory by nominating Roberts to fill the vacant chief justiceship.

Roberts's career trajectory suggested an individual with few peers in terms of legal credentials. Born in Buffalo, New York, and raised in Indiana, Roberts attended a Catholic boys' school in La Porte, Indiana, and eventually went on to graduate from Harvard College in three years and Harvard Law School with high honors. Most of his legal career was centered in Washington, with an impressive list of positions both in and outside of public service. Following law school, Roberts served first as a law clerk to Judge Henry J. Friendly on the U.S. Court of Appeals for the Second Circuit, followed by a clerkship to then–Associate Justice Rehnquist on the U.S. Supreme Court. From there he began a public career in the Reagan administration, first as an aide to Attorney General William French Smith in 1981–82, and then as an associate White House counsel to President Reagan. He developed a lucrative private law practice at Hogan & Hartson, a Washington law firm, where he attracted a long list of corporate clients from 1986 to 1989. From there, he returned to the federal service as deputy solicitor general under Judge Kenneth Starr (currently Baylor University's president) for a few years in the George H. W. Bush administration, where he was nominated by President Bush to the U.S. Court of Appeals for the D.C. Circuit but never confirmed by the Democratic Senate. From 1993 until 2003, he returned to Hogan & Hartson, where he renewed strong professional and personal ties to Washington political insiders. In 2003, with the Senate now controlled by the Republicans, George W. Bush nominated him to the D.C. Circuit Court of Appeals. He was confirmed as Chief Justice of the Supreme Court on September 29, 2005, by a vote of 78–22.

In his eighth year as Chief Justice, many Court watchers would agree that John Roberts has made an indelible mark on the Court. Although the Roberts Court, like its predecessor under Chief Justice Rehnquist, remains conservative on core constitutional issues, the Chief Justice has been willing to make significant decisions that either reversed or established precedent on important constitutional issues, such as the 2007 school desegregation decision in *Parents Involved in Community Schools* v. *Seattle School District No. 1* (see Chapter 9). But Roberts is seen as pragmatic rather than doctrinaire on jurisprudential methodology and interpretation (discussed in Chapter 4). In the 2009 Term, for example, Chief Justice Roberts was in the majority over 90 percent of the time, more than any other justice. In that term, the Court majority moved to establish strong positions on campaign finance (see Chapter 14), criminal procedure (see Chapter 13), and the right of individual citizens to bear arms (see Chapter 11). And Roberts's role in the fight over "Obamacare" may have solidified his leadership on the Court, one he is expected to lead for many years to come.

---

this book stresses primarily the role of the Supreme Court within this judicial bureaucracy, it is only one of over one hundred federal courts and includes only nine of the 875 federal judges who bear immense responsibility for interpreting all laws and their conformity to the U.S. Constitution.

This chapter should make it apparent that the process used since the beginning of the American Republic to select federal judges and Supreme Court justices is a very *political* process. While those chosen to interpret to apply the law possess impressive qualifications, federal judges are never very far from the political arena, both before they are chosen and after they assume their judicial posts. As the discussion throughout the rest of this text indicates, the American constitutional experience for more than two centuries has exhibited different patterns and preferences as to how the justices have exercised their judicial responsibility for interpreting the Constitution. These different orientations about the use of judicial power have yielded different consequences for the citizenry.

CHAPTER 4
The Origins and Practice of Judicial Review in the American System

The practice of judicial review in American Constitutionalism and the distinct role of the Supreme Court as the authoritative interpreter of the Constitution owe much to John Marshall, who will formally be introducing this chapter. His statue sits prominently in the Supreme Court building, and during his confirmation process, Chief Justice John Roberts talked about how he used to rub Marshall's foot for good luck prior to arguing a case before the Court.

▼ INTRODUCTORY REMARKS BY CHIEF JUSTICE JOHN MARSHALL

My name is John Marshall, and of all the Supreme Court justices who have attempted to interpret the Constitution, I am the one who will introduce this chapter on the origins and practice of judicial review in the U.S. constitutional system. I served as Chief Justice of the Supreme Court for thirty-four years, longer than any other in that position. Over that period of time I participated in over one thousand decisions, authoring over five hundred opinions. I am probably most known as the justice singularly responsible for establishing the power of judicial review, of the Supreme Court to determine the constitutionality of all actions taken by the other branches of the federal government as well as state legislatures, courts, and executive branch officers. It was my decision in *Marbury v. Madison* (1803), discussed thoroughly in this chapter (see Brief 4.3), that set the stage for the eventual acceptance of the principle that federal courts, and the justices of the Supreme Court at the top of the federal judiciary, have the ultimate power to interpret and enforce the dictates of the Constitution.

My argument in *Marbury* for the power of judicial review was simple, grounded in three basic propositions:

1. The framers of all written constitutions "contemplate them as forming the fundamental and paramount law of the nation, and subsequently the theory of every such government must be, that an act of the legislature, repugnant to the constitution, is void";

2. "It is emphatically the province and duty of the judicial department to say what the law is. Those who apply the rule to particular cases must of necessity expound and interpret that rule"; and

3. "If courts are to regard the constitution [as] superior to any ordinary act of the legislature; the constitution, and not such ordinary act, must govern the case to which they both apply."

In addition to being known as the first justice to explicitly articulate and apply the principle of judicial review, I also was associated with the philosophy known as **judicial nationalism**, grounded in the dual principles of popular sovereignty and the supremacy of the national government over the states. This philosophy is perhaps best expressed in my majority opinion in *McCulloch v. Maryland* (1819). In that case, I asserted that the federal government's powers are derived "directly from the people" as a whole, and as such, completely oblige and bind the governments of the states. This means that the branches of the federal government, especially Congress, must be given fairly wide latitude in determining what is necessary to legislate for the benefit of the sovereign American people (under my interpretation of the Necessary and Proper Clause in Article I, Section 8). Additionally, the Supremacy Clause of the Constitution (Article VI) means that the federal government, "though limited in its powers, is supreme" within its sphere of action, and can preempt the states from taking actions aimed at blocking or destroying federal power. Finally, I argued that the Constitution needed to be flexible enough to meet the changing demands of the American people over time. It was not the intent of the framers that the actual text of the Constitution be easily altered, as the rather cumbersome amending process embodied in Article V confirms. The primary instrument for updating the Constitution should be the frequent actions of Supreme Court justices to breathe life into it. As I famously observed in *McCulloch*, "we must never forget that it is a constitution that we are expounding."

I am excited to introduce this chapter because not even I could have anticipated that the principle of judicial review would be so broadly accepted today. There were serious assertions of legislative supremacy in constitutional interpretation, both in my time and through the nineteenth century, evidenced by this quote attributed to founding father Caesar Rodney: "Judicial supremacy may be made to bow before the strong arm of Legislative authority. We shall discover who is master of the ship." And prominent figures from Thomas Jefferson to Frederick Douglass argued vehemently for "democratic supremacy," the power of the American people in interpreting and applying the Constitution from generation to generation. Quite frankly, only a few of my opinions attracted much popular acclaim during my long tenure on the Court, so as the writers suggest here, it was more the ongoing practice of the Court over the years and the connection between judicial review and the logic of constitutionalism as laid out in Chapter 1 that has made my legacy what it is today.

SOURCES: *Marbury v. Madison*, 5 U.S. 137 (1803); *McCulloch v. Maryland*, 17 U.S. 316 (1819); Laurence Tribe, *American Constitutional Law* (Mineola, NY: Foundation Press, 1999); Charles Warren, *The Supreme Court in United States History* (Boston: Little, Brown, 1926).

Judicial Review: Continuing Paradox in a Democratic System

"Whosoever hath an absolute authority to interpret any written or spoken laws, it is he who is truly the lawgiver, to all intents and purposes, and not the person who first wrote or spoke them." Bishop Hoadley, 1717, quoted by James Bradley Thayer, *Harvard Law Review* 7, no. 3 (1893), 129, 152

"Scarcely any political question arises in the United States that is not resolved, sooner or later, into a judicial question." Alexis de Tocqueville, *Democracy in America*, Volume I (1832)

Over the past few years, the Supreme Court has issued significant rulings on issues ranging from the treatment of prisoners of war to the rights of gun owners, from the protections individuals have from police searches to campaign finance and health care reform. These rulings by the Court often involved the justices weighing the actions of another branch of the federal government or of a local or state legislative body. As Alexis de Tocqueville, the famous French observer of American democracy, noted in the 1830s, "the power vested in the American courts of justice of pronouncing a statute to be unconstitutional, forms one of the most powerful barriers which has ever been devised against the tyranny of political assemblies."[1]

However, the practice of judicial review suggests a major paradox in the American political system. Americans have consistently turned to life-tenured judges to resolve major legal issues, even allowing the U.S. Supreme Court to overrule the actions of popularly elected bodies in a democratic system. The Court has labored for more than two hundred years to resolve this paradox by diligently adhering to certain internal norms of behavior noted in the previous chapter. In so doing, it has sought to uphold, sometimes amid withering opposition to its decisions, a commitment to the rule of law and the principle of limited government.

The Policymaking Function of the U.S. Supreme Court

In remarks before the annual meeting of the American Bar Association in 1985, Attorney General Edwin Meese criticized the Supreme Court for what he viewed as a "jurisprudence of idiosyncracy." Meese placed special emphasis upon what he saw as the framers' desire for judges to "resist any political effort to depart from the literal provisions of the Constitution." In taking issue with several decisions concerning federal authority, criminal procedure, and church–state separation, Meese noted that "far too many of the Court's opinions were . . . more policy choices than articulations of constitutional principle." He recommended that the justices adopt a "jurisprudence of original intention" and place more emphasis upon the historical context of constitutional provisions.[2]

Attorney General Meese's call in 1985 for a more careful use of judicial power drew an immediate response from then-Justice William Brennan. Without mentioning Meese by name, Brennan questioned "those who find legitimacy in fidelity to what they call 'the intentions of the Framers.'" He referred to this philosophy as "little more than arrogance cloaked as humility." Brennan argued that this view of judicial decision making is suspect for several reasons. He insisted that the historical record is incomplete and imprecise on the framers' intentions, that there is disagreement over particular constitutional provisions, and that it is virtually impossible to determine whose intentions were most relevant—those who gathered in Philadelphia, the Congressional debaters, or those who ratified the Constitution in the several states. Brennan said that justices on the Supreme Court must address contemporary issues with an eye on what the Constitution means today, not that which governed the late eighteenth century.[3]

Some Thoughts on Constitutional Interpretation

The Meese–Brennan exchange highlights a debate that has raged for a long time in American law. In fact, it has been renewed with special vigor in recent years. The national Tea Party movement continues in the Meese tradition, supporting candidates who pledge, among other things, to adhere to an "originalist" interpretation of the Constitution. At the beginning of the 112th Congress in 2011, the House of Representatives—with a solid Republican majority—began with a full reading of the Constitution, and pledged that every law passed would specifically identify the constitutional provision that gives Congress the power to do what it is proposing to do. On the Supreme Court itself, two justices—Antonin Scalia and Stephen Breyer—continue the debate over how the Constitution should be interpreted and applied (see Brief 4.1).

At its core, this debate focuses on precisely *what* the Constitution says, *who* has the responsibility for interpreting the document, *how* that interpretative process should proceed, and *what techniques* are the most legitimate for authoritative interpretation. Time and space do not permit adequate treatment of these major analytical questions, but a brief outline of some key issues is necessary.[4]

One set of questions addresses what individuals see in the Constitution itself. Does interpretation deal exclusively with the actual wording and formal text of the document, or does it include certain other writings and practices that characterize the cumulative body of American political writing and practice? Should it be considered as a static, unchanging text that speaks with the same voice and specificity from age to age, or should it be seen as a more dynamic document that must be accommodated to a changing agenda of people dealing with contemporary problems? Should the Constitution be viewed as a body of strict rules for application to all public problems, or might it be seen also as an instrument that embodies larger goals, aspirations, and values, such as pursuit of human dignity and self-fulfillment?

A second set of questions deals with the different approaches for interpreting the Constitution. As one might expect, how one interprets the document is conditioned by whether one views it as an unchangeable or evolutionary statement of the law. Does one gain more by analyzing the actual words, the historic setting of when the document and its amendments were written, or the structural contradictions that appear in the Constitution (i.e., the Establishment

---

Brief 4.1
COMPETING VISIONS OF THE JUDICIAL ROLE

The two justices on the current Supreme Court who best embody a sharp contrast in judicial philosophies are Antonin Scalia and Stephen Breyer, who have served on the Supreme Court for 27 and 19 years, respectively. The former Supreme Court reporter for the *New York Times*, Linda Greenhouse, calls the contrast text versus context, with Scalia adhering to a very literal and absolute reading of original intent, and Breyer favoring a much more fluid, dynamic sense of what the law requires.[5] For Justice Scalia, it is critically important for judges to adhere to the actual text of the Constitution and prescribed law, rigidly applying the statutory language and constitutional text as stated by the original drafters. Virtually from the first year of his appointment to the Court by President Ronald Reagan in 1986, Scalia has tried to discern the precise rules and standards that he feels are embodied in the text of the Constitution and legislative statutes. As he stated in a 1995 speech at Princeton University, which was soon followed by a book, *A Matter of Interpretation*, he tends to see the Constitution as an unchanging document that compels consistent interpretation across generations. He has also been very skeptical in recognizing any emerging national or international consensus about procedural guarantees in criminal justice. He insists that international laws and customs should have no effect upon how the U.S. Constitution is interpreted or applied, particularly with respect to the death penalty, which he endorses.

In contrast to Scalia's originalism and literalism, Justice Breyer believes judges should always be sensitive to the context and effect of their decisions. In a speech at New York University Law School in October 2001, followed by his own book, *Active Liberty: Interpreting our Democratic Constitution*, he argued that three distinct principles should serve as guides to the Supreme Court's decision making. First is the purpose of the constitutional provision or law under review, second is the likely consequence of a decision (instead of a "more legalistic" approach that emphasizes the language, history, and tradition of the law), and lastly, the overall objective of the Constitution—namely, "participatory, democratic self-government."

The Court's decision in *District of Columbia v. Heller* at the close of the 2007 Term found these two justices in direct conflict, offering quite different views about the meaning of the Second Amendment and whether it embodies an individual or communal right to bear arms. The majority opinion authored by Justice Scalia insisted that the amendment "codified a pre-existing right" of individual gun ownership for private use, whereas a separate dissenting opinion by Justice Breyer insisted that the amendment protects "militia-related, not self-defense-related, interests."[6] In this and other cases over the past several years, it is clear that Scalia and Breyer hold very different views about the feasibility of achieving clarity in rules and standards, the effect that a decision might have on society, and a sharp contrast about the role of judicial power that has not been seen since the clash on the Court between Hugo Black and Felix Frankfurter in the 1940s.

and the Free Exercise Clauses of the First Amendment; the collision between government authority and individual freedom)? Are the doctrinal concepts that have evolved over two centuries of constitutional practice (i.e., judicial review, executive privilege, "one person–one vote," "wall of separation," "right to privacy," exclusionary rule) as important to defining the Constitution as the actual text itself? Finally, should those who interpret the Constitution be primarily concerned with what would be wise public policy? The Supreme Court's gradual shift toward civil rights in the 1940s, and its aggressive move against racial segregation in *Brown v. Board of Education* (1954) and its progeny reflects this type of judicial policy-making. Likewise, the Court's approval of federal intervention in the economy in the late 1930s, legislative reapportionment in the 1960s, and gender equity beginning in the early 1970s all seem to endorse this more evolutionary interpretation of what the Constitution says to contemporary society.

In addition to different approaches they take, judges use a variety of techniques to interpret the Constitution. *Literalism* is a technique that insists upon a strict interpretation of the actual words used in the Constitution (or the law in question). A literalist would suggest that the words "establishment of religion," "equal protection of the laws," "general welfare," or "unreasonable searches and seizures" presumably hold the same meaning for all people across generations. The *intent of the framers* means of analysis is another technique for determining the meaning of the Constitution. Using this technique, the judge interpreting what a phrase or provision in the Constitution means or how it ought to be applied to a case in question is interested in understanding what those who made the Constitution (or a particular amendment) meant when they wrote it. A problem with this technique, as Justice Brennan noted in 1985, is that discovering the original intentions of those who drafted the Constitution and/or its twenty-seven amendments both assumes a perfect consensus among the framers *and* lacks a complete record of what was intended. Furthermore, even if discernable, original intention may not be desirable, given evolving social changes (relating to issues like women's rights or civil rights) or technological methods (on a question such as what constitutes an "unreasonable search and seizure" under the Fourth Amendment).

A third framework for interpreting the Constitution and resolving disputes is a *balancing of interests* analysis. This technique often involves the "individualist-communitarian" continuum, since it implies that the protection of individual rights sometimes must be balanced with countervailing societal needs. Recognizing larger societal rights became more prominent in the early twentieth century as judges felt compelled to go beyond the merits of a case and anticipate the economic, sociological, or even strategic aspects of a situation (i.e., inadequate wages, unsafe working conditions, racial segregation). Likewise, the public clamor in recent years to recognize "victims' rights" involved in certain violent criminal justice claims emphasizes another swing in the pendulum of the judicial system. But the balancing-of-interests approach has been criticized for injecting social bias or emotion into decision making and skewing the balance in favor of either governmental power or selective individual freedoms.

Finally, the use of precedent, or *stare decisis* (meaning to let the previous decision stand) has been a staple of judges for resolving legal conflicts. To decide how to interpret the Constitution based on precedent means that a judge turns to previously decided cases that resemble a current controversy, and finds the rule of law that was used in those cases, applying it to the present case. Building on previous decisions both provides a cumulative body of law and ensures stability and incremental, rather than radical, change in the law. However, while precedent is almost always a component of a judge's reasoning in a case, relying on precedent alone may mean that previous court decisions will guide interpretation, rather than the goals, values, and principles behind the Constitution itself. It is like driving an automobile down a busy street while looking only through the rearview mirror. Occasionally a judge must look forward, particularly in instances wherein the previous rule of law has been widely discredited by an emerging social and political consensus for change.

THE RESTRAINT–ACTIVISM DIMENSION OF JUDICIAL DECISION MAKING

Judicial restraint and **judicial activism** is a final pair of terms that have been developed to describe constitutional interpretation.[7] Those who advocate judicial restraint argue that judges should take every precaution to avoid overturning the actions of the popularly elected branches of government—Congress, the president, or state legislatures. Judicial activists, on the other hand, are much more willing to intervene and reverse the actions of elected officials. Because these two concepts do not always reflect precise partisan or ideological alignments, a more thorough discussion of each with reference to some prominent judicial figures is necessary.

JUDICIAL RESTRAINT AND THE THAYER-FRANKFURTER-HARLAN PRESCRIPTION

The concept of judicial restraint implies that judicial authority should be very carefully used when considering the actions of popular majorities in a democratic society. Although he is normally associated with the assertion of federal judicial authority, John Marshall was one of the first to articulate a limited role for such power. In *Marbury v. Madison* (to be discussed later in the chapter), Marshall emphasized that the Supreme Court should use its power only when there is a clear conflict between a statute and the Constitution. This strategy effectively conserves the Court's time and power and preserves the legitimacy of the Court as an authoritative voice in genuine constitutional disputes. Because laws passed by a state or national legislature presumably represent the voice of a popular majority, they should not be dismissed lightly by life-tenured judges who are by definition less accountable to the people.

For much of the nineteenth century, the Supreme Court rarely overruled state or federal laws, due in part to its limited workload and the infrequency of public regulation of private economic activities (see Tables 4.1 and 4.2). One of the clearest references to judicial restraint emerged in the 1890s from the noted Harvard Law Professor James Bradley Thayer in a classic essay, "The Origin and Scope of the American Doctrine of Constitutional Law."[8] Thayer argued that by the 1890s, courts were unwisely turning away from a century of deference to legislative bodies. Before 1860, only two federal laws and thirty-five state laws or local ordinances were declared unconstitutional by the Supreme Court. However, between 1860 and 1900, the Court declared some twenty federal laws and 141 state or local laws null and void.[9] Like Marshall, Thayer insisted that laws should be declared invalid only when they were direct, blatant violations of the Constitution.

In the mid-twentieth century, Justices Felix Frankfurter and John Harlan II came to be seen as two

Table 4.1 Federal Statutes Declared Unconstitutional by the Supreme Court, 1789–2010

Decade	Number	Decade	Number
1790–1799	0	1900–1909	9
1800–1809	1	1910–1919	6
1810–1819	0	1920–1929	15
1820–1829	0	1930–1939	13
1830–1839	0	1940–1949	2
1840–1849	0	1950–1959	5
1850–1859	1	1960–1969	16
1860–1869	4	1970–1979	20
1870–1879	7	1980–1989	16
1880–1889	4	1990–1999	24
1890–1899	5	2000–2010	17
		TOTAL	**165**

Table 4.2 State and Local Statutes Declared Unconstitutional by the Supreme Court, 1789–2010

Decade	Number	Decade	Number
1790–1799	0	1900–1909	40
1800–1809	1	1910–1919	119
1810–1819	7	1920–1929	139
1820–1829	8	1930–1939	92
1830–1839	3	1940–1949	61
1840–1849	10	1950–1959	66
1850–1859	7	1960–1969	151
1860–1869	24	1970–1979	195
1870–1879	36	1980–1989	164
1880–1889	46	1990–1999	62
1890–1899	36	2000–2010	36
		TOTAL	**1,303**

SOURCE: Adapted from Lawrence Baum, *The Supreme Court*, 10th ed. (Washington, DC: Congressional Quarterly Press, 2010), p. 165.

strong advocates for judicial restraint. A one-time student of Professor Thayer at Harvard Law School, Frankfurter became a primary spokesperson for restraint during his tenure on the Court (1939–62). In many notable opinions, Frankfurter extolled the virtues of judicial deference to legislative supremacy. His dissenting opinions in *West Virginia State Board of Education v. Barnette* (1943) and *Baker v. Carr* (1962), his concurrence in *Dennis v. United States* (1951), and his opinion for the majority in *Rochin v. California* (1952) all strongly reflected his preference for judicial self-restraint and deep reservations about overturning legislative statutes. Like Frankfurter, Justice Harlan's support for judicial restraint is especially evident in several carefully crafted opinions during his distinguished career on the Supreme Court (1955–71). Of particular note are his dissenting opinions in *Mapp v. Ohio* (1961), *Baker v. Carr* (1962), *Reynolds v. Sims* (1964), and *Flast v. Cohen* (1968), as well as his opinion for the Court majority in *Barenblatt v. U.S.* (1959). Another famous dissent by Harlan in *Reynolds v. Sims* (1964), where the Court moved aggressively against legislative mal-apportionment in state legislatures, indicated Harlan's disagreement with what the Court was doing:

> THE CONSTITUTION IS NOT A PANACEA FOR EVERY BLOT UPON THE PUBLIC WELFARE, NOR SHOULD THIS COURT, ORDAINED AS A JUDICIAL BODY, BE THOUGHT OF AS A GENERAL HAVEN FOR REFORM MOVEMENTS. THE CONSTITUTION IS AN INSTRUMENT OF GOVERNMENT, FUNDAMENTAL TO WHICH IS THE PREMISE THAT IN A DIFFUSION OF GOVERNMENTAL AUTHORITY LIES THE GREATEST PROMISE THAT THIS NATION WILL REALIZE LIBERTY FOR ALL ITS CITIZENS. THIS COURT, LIMITED IN FUNCTION IN ACCORDANCE WITH THAT PREMISE, DOES NOT SERVE ITS HIGH PURPOSE WHEN IT EXCEEDS ITS AUTHORITY, EVEN TO SATISFY JUSTIFIED IMPATIENCE WITH THE SLOW WORKINGS OF THE POLITICAL PROCESS.[10]

When Justice Harlan retired in 1971, the Supreme Court lost a committed and consistent voice for judicial restraint in the exercise of judicial power. Although some might yearn for the return of justices who "interpret the law rather than make it," the Court has not seen a consistent supporter of judicial restraint since Justices Frankfurter and Harlan advanced this perspective. During the last four decades, justices appointed by Republican presidents Nixon, Reagan, Bush I, and Bush II were initially praised as being supportive of judicial restraint. But in the end, most contemporary justices have turned out to be judicial activists, at least in some areas of constitutional law.

JUDICIAL RESTRAINT AND THE HOLMES-BRANDEIS-STONE PRESCRIPTION

A more qualified version of judicial restraint emerged in the 1920s among some Supreme Court justices whose adherence to this judicial role depended on what constitutional provisions were at stake. Following World War I, Justices Oliver Wendell Holmes Jr., Louis D. Brandeis, and Harlan Fiske Stone became very protective of First Amendment rights and voted to strike down many forms of state or federal restriction on these freedoms. However, they also were quite willing to allow state legislatures and Congress to regulate aspects of a complex and changing American economy. The first hint of this qualified form of judicial restraint arose in two dissenting opinions by Holmes in the landmark decisions of *Lochner v. New York* (1905) and *Hammer v. Dagenhart* (1918). In both decisions, the Court majority struck down laws contrary to, first, the Fourteenth Amendment Due Process Clause and, second, a narrow reading of the Commerce Clause. Holmes disagreed with the Court in both instances, authoring two of his most famous dissenting opinions, both of which "disavowed the right [of the Court] to intrude its judgment upon questions of policy or morals."[11] During their long careers on the Court, Holmes (1902–32) and Brandeis (1916–39) advocated judicial restraint toward various forms of economic regulation. But they were much less deferential to the actions of popular majorities when restrictive legislation involved the important civil liberties of the First Amendment. In several rulings by the Supreme Court in the years following World War I (to be discussed more thoroughly in Chapter 14 on political speech and national security), Holmes and Brandeis frequently voted to overturn state or federal laws that unjustifiably denied individuals a right to engage in political speech and assembly.

So persuasive were these two that a third justice, Harlan Fiske Stone (1925–46), continued to support economic regulation and defend civil liberties after both Holmes and Brandeis had left the Court in the 1930s. One of the best articulations of Stone's tolerance for economic regulation is his dissenting opinion in *U.S. v. Butler* (1936), where the Supreme Court had struck down the Agricultural Adjustment Act of 1933 as an illegal delegation of legislative authority and an unwarranted exercise of commerce authority by Congress. In arguing for the Court to uphold the federal law, Stone noted in dissent that

THE ONLY CHECK UPON OUR OWN EXERCISE OF POWER IS OUR OWN SENSE OF SELF-RESTRAINT. FOR THE REMOVAL OF UNWISE LAWS FROM THE STATUTE BOOKS APPEAL LIES NOT TO THE COURTS BUT TO THE BALLOT AND TO THE PROCESSES OF DEMOCRATIC GOVERNMENT.[12]

According to Stone, the only question that courts should consider when examining government regulation of the economy is whether a legislature has the power to deal with the subject. Whether the law is wise or unwise, policy is not within the power of a court to determine. It is strictly a political matter best left to popularly elected representatives, not life-tenured judges not elected by the people. However, like Holmes and Brandeis, Stone's usual deference toward economic regulation diminished noticeably when vital civil rights or liberties were at stake. In such circumstances, he insisted that a "more exacting judicial scrutiny" was necessary to protect "discrete and insular minorities" against governmental invasion of fundamental rights (see discussion in "Origins of the New Equal Protection" in Chapter 10).

The Holmes-Brandeis-Stone model of judicial restraint reflected growing public and political disenchantment with a Supreme Court majority during the late 1930s. Since the 1890s and through the early New Deal years, the Court consistently overturned most legislative attempts to regulate aspects of the economy and to recover from the ravages of the Great Depression in the 1930s. When the Court by mid-1937 began to uphold federal efforts to deal with the economic emergencies then plaguing the country, a new deference by the justices to prevailing public opinion and political majorities forecast a new era in Supreme Court decision making (see Brief 4.2).

Brief 4.2

THE SUPREME COURT REVOLUTION OF 1937

The early years of the New Deal saw much conflict between the three branches of government. Having captured over 57 percent of the popular vote, 42 states, and 472 electoral votes in the 1932 presidential election, Franklin Roosevelt was eager to stimulate economic recovery, and the Democratic-controlled Congress was poised to assist him. The first one hundred days of the Roosevelt administration saw a flurry of legislation intended to restore public confidence and economic prosperity in the country. In 1933, Congress passed major federal statutes, including the National Industrial Recovery Act, the Bituminous Coal Conservation Act, and the Agricultural Adjustment Act, all of which attempted to regulate several aspects of the depressed national economy. However, by 1936, the Supreme Court had declared all three of these acts unconstitutional, with its rulings in *Schechter Poultry Corp. v. United States* (1935), *Carter v. Carter Coal Co.* (1936), and *United States v. Butler* (1936).

The 1936 presidential election became a de facto popular referendum on the Roosevelt New Deal and presumably the Supreme Court's refusal to recognize these new governmental tools for managing a struggling national economy. Roosevelt won 61 percent of the popular vote in 1936, which he immediately interpreted as a mandate for his policies and a substantial base from which to move against what he and many Democrats in Congress considered an obstructionist Supreme Court. His strategy for changing the judicial status quo had ironically been recommended originally by one of the Court conservatives opposing his efforts, Justice James McReynolds, when the latter had served as Attorney General under President Woodrow Wilson in 1913. Convinced that the Court held an outmoded and rigid view of the Constitution, Roosevelt sent to Congress a plan providing for voluntary retirement of all Supreme Court justices at the age of seventy. If the justice did not retire, the president could appoint a new justice for every one over seventy years that remained on the Court. If realized, the plan clearly suggested increasing the size of the Court up to a maximum of fifteen authorized seats, which might provide Roosevelt with a working majority that supported his programs. According to the president, the plan had two purposes:

> By bringing into the judicial system a steady and continuing stream of new and younger blood, I hope, first, to make the administration of all federal justice speedier and therefore less costly; secondly, to bring to the decision of social and economic problems younger men who have had personal experience and contact with modern facts and circumstances under which average men have to live and work. This plan will save our National Constitution from hardening of the judicial arteries.[13]

Congress never passed the "Court-packing" plan of Roosevelt, in part because it was not well received by the American public, which saw it as a thinly disguised plan to place on the high court ideological clones of the President. Ultimately, the plan was unnecessary. During the 168 days that Congress debated the suggested reorganization, the Supreme Court began to reverse its view of New Deal legislation. The so-called "switch in time that saved nine" in mid-1937 (upholding a state minimum wage in *West Coast Hotel v. Parrish* and a federal law regulating labor relations in *NLRB v. Jones & Laughlin Steel Corp.*) suggested a new era in Supreme Court decision making in which the justices increasingly approved of federal legislation that was intended to aid economic recovery.

JUDICIAL ACTIVISM FROM JOHN MARSHALL TO JOHN ROBERTS

Ever since John Marshall proclaimed in *Marbury v. Madison* (1803) that it is "emphatically the province and the duty of the courts to say what the law is," federal judges have frequently dealt with very controversial issues in American society while deliberating about the rule of law. In many instances, the Supreme Court is called upon to perform a major policymaking function that suggests a much more assertive role for judges and courts. It does this, in many cases, because the other branches or levels of government have been either unable or unwilling to resolve important policy issues in accordance with the Constitution.[14] Judicial intervention to change prevailing policy is normally referred to as judicial activism. As noted earlier, until the end of the nineteenth century, the Supreme Court was less likely to strike down state or federal legislation, in large part because governmental regulation of the economy was virtually nonexistent. However, as governments at all levels increasingly saw the need to intervene and regulate several facets of an industrialized economy by the early 1900s, federal courts were left with little recourse but to consider whether these governmental regulations were constitutional. Tables 4.1 and 4.2 indicate that nearly 90 percent of all legislation that has been invalidated by the Supreme Court since 1790 has been struck down since 1900. These data reflect that an activist judiciary became much more evident with the advent of the regulatory state in the last century. Activism is not unique to either Republican or Democratic justices.

Beyond these critical questions concerning the relative merits of restraint and activism, one must be careful not to ascribe political labels to the restraint–activism continuum. Judicial restraint should not be labeled as "conservative," nor should activism be interpreted as synonymous with "liberal" decision making, as Figure 4.1 suggests. So-called liberal justices of the past few decades have often been described as very protective of Bill of Rights guarantees and the Fourteenth Amendment requirements for due process and equal protection. Along the *political ideology* dimension, liberal justices might be described as activist in overturning many state or federal actions that threaten these important constitutional rights. They have also been generally more supportive of economic regulation of the past several decades. But on the *judicial role* dimension, they have reflected more support for self-restraint as they defer to the president and Congress in public programs to maintain economic prosperity through extensive governmental regulation. Justices Oliver Wendell Holmes Jr., Louis Brandeis, Harlan Stone, William Douglas, Hugo Black, Earl Warren, William Brennan, Thurgood Marshall, and Harry Blackmun fit into this category of "liberal." As a decisional group for much of its sixteen years, the Warren Court (1953–69) would best reflect this form of decision making—activist on civil rights and liberties, but restrained on economic and social management questions.

The "conservative" label has often been used to describe the Supreme Court and several justices who have been less willing to intervene to protect civil rights and liberties. These justices believe that

Figure 4.1 The Politics of Judicial Decision-Making

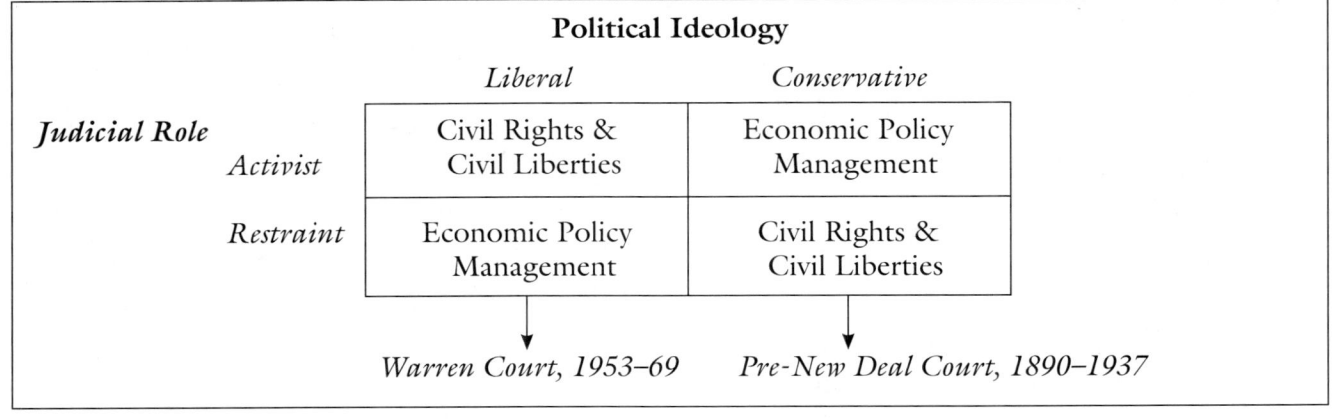

government must be given great latitude to maintain social order and stability. In this respect, they usually allow legislation regulating personal civil liberties to stand. However, they often place greater emphasis upon economic liberty and a free market unburdened by government regulations. If legislation restricts this economic liberty, it is considered suspect and frequently overturned on any of several constitutional grounds. During the 1930s, Justices Willis Van Devanter, Pierce Butler, James McReynolds, and George Sutherland in particular—the "Four Horsemen" of the pre–New Deal era—reflected this orientation, as they opposed most governmental regulation—state or federal—that regulated economic relations and private property rights. Justices Byron White, Antonin Scalia, and Clarence Thomas and Chief Justice William Rehnquist probably best reflect this mode of judicial decision making since then. Their judicial role behavior normally found them allowing government to restrict *civil* liberties (restraint) in times of national emergency, but also guarding against an intrusive government that violated *economic* liberties of the people (activism). The Supreme Court from 1890 to 1937 generally displayed this preference for a judiciary committed to the free market and economic property rights.

Over the past several decades the Supreme Court has frequently assumed a noticeably activist orientation when addressing a wide variety of societal issues. As the data in Tables 4.1 and 4.2 indicate, the invalidation of both federal and state or local laws became a common practice by the justices during the past half-century.

ROOTS OF JUDICIAL REVIEW: THEORY AND PRACTICE

If the Supreme Court can legitimately be regarded as the most powerful judicial body in the world, a primary reason for this claim may be its use of judicial review. **Judicial review** is the power of any court to hold unenforceable any law, any official action based on a law, or any other action by a public official that it considers to be in conflict with the Constitution. This power has given the U.S. Supreme Court a significant instrument for fulfilling its role as the "constitutional custodian" mentioned above. The Court's use of judicial review to invalidate legislation has varied over a long period, with most of the judicial nullifications occurring in the last century (see Tables 4.1 and 4.2). State and local actions have been overturned by the Court much more frequently than have federal laws, and these actions comprise nearly 90 percent of all laws declared unconstitutional since 1803.[15] However, as Table 4.3 indicates, only a handful of federal laws struck down have had a significant impact upon the political and economic life of the nation.

Why did judicial review evolve in the American constitutional system? Although Chapter 2 indicates evidence of the practice in early English experience, the American Constitution nowhere specifically authorizes the Supreme Court or any lower federal court to judge the constitutionality of actions taken by coordinate branches. And yet, it has evolved into the most significant instrument used by federal courts to reconcile the actions of governments with the Constitution. At least four reasons explain the development of judicial review in the American constitutional system: (1) the framers' intentions; (2) historical acceptance; (3) as a counterweight to majority rule; and (4) the continual quest for neutral "first principles" by which to resolve controversies and to effect widespread public compliance.

THE FRAMERS' INTENTIONS AND JUDICIAL REVIEW

Justifying judicial review by arguing that the Constitution's framers *intended* it is difficult, since the actual record of the Constitutional Convention is incomplete. Those regularly attending the convention generally agreed that a national judiciary should be established, given its omission under the deeply flawed Articles of Confederation, but explaining precisely what the delegates thought the nature of judicial power should be is more difficult. Probably one-half of the regular delegates to the Constitutional Convention favored judicial review, and many of the Convention's leaders, including Alexander Hamilton and Gouverneur Morris, publicly endorsed the idea.[16] Although *Marbury v. Madison* is often credited with beginning the practice of judicial review, many events forecasted this important power long before 1803.[17]

Although he had little influence at the Constitutional Convention itself (especially after advocating the adoption of a British form of centralized government),

Table 4.3 Development of Judicial Review: Significant Federal Statutes Declared Unconstitutional

Year	Case	Significance
1803	*Marbury v. Madison*	First time that Court declared a federal act unconstitutional; invalidated Section 13, Judiciary Act of 1789. Congress could not regulate original jurisdiction of Court.
1857	*Dred Scott v. Sandford*	Overturned Missouri Compromise of 1820. Ruled that slaves were property and that Congress could not regulate local property rights. Decision hastened Civil War, damaged prestige of Court, and was eventually overruled by 13th and 14th Amendments.
1870	*Hepburn v. Griswold*	Struck down Legal Tender Acts of 1862 and 1863, which made paper currency a legal substitute for gold in payment of all debts. Ruled that legislation was beyond authority of Congress, but reversed itself in *Knox v. Lee* (1871) amid public outcry and fears of economic chaos.
1883	Civil Rights Cases	Overruled Civil Rights Act of 1875. Congress could not prohibit private racial discrimination. Removed federal government from the enforcement of Reconstruction amendments; delayed passage of effective civil rights legislation until 1960s.
1895	*Pollock. v. Farmers' Loan and Trust Co.*	Overturned Wilson-Gorman Tariff Act of 1894 because it was not apportioned on basis of population; effectively denied federal government the ability to levy an income tax; decision eventually overruled by 16th Amendment in 1913.
1908	*Adair v. U.S.*	Declared void the Erdman Act (1898), which had outlawed "yellow dog" contracts, under which owners made not joining a union a condition of employment. Court finally ruled in 1937 that labor relations did fall within Congress's commerce power (*NLRB v. Jones & Laughlin Steel*).
1918	*Hammer v. Dagenhart*	Struck down Keating-Owens Child Labor Act (1916), which had prohibited interstate shipment of products manufactured with child labor; Court eventually endorsed federal prohibition of child labor in *U.S. v. Darby Lumber* (1941), which overruled *Hammer*.
1935	*Schechter Poultry v. U.S.*	Invalidated the National Industry Recovery Act of 1933; in short term, decision seriously impeded New Deal policies aimed at easing economic strain of the Great Depression.
1936	*United States v. Butler*	Declared unconstitutional the Agricultural Adjustment Act of 1933; said that Congress had no authority under its commerce power to tax and regulate agricultural production; Court soon reversed itself in *Mulford v. Smith* (1939).
1997	*Boerne v. Flores*	Struck down the Religious Freedom Restoration Act of 1993; ruled that Congress had intruded upon the judiciary's authority to interpret First Amendment religious clauses and protect sovereignty of states.
2010	*Citizens United v. FEC*	Struck down portions of the McCain-Feingold Bipartisan Campaign Reform Act of 2002; ruled that Congress could not ban political spending by corporations in elections consistent with the First Amendment.

Alexander Hamilton played a vital role in pressing the ratification fight in New York, Virginia, and Massachusetts by coauthoring *The Federalist* in 1787–88. In fact, in *Federalist No. 78*, Hamilton argued that written constitutions must be obeyed and the constitutional limits rigorously enforced by the courts:

THE INTERPRETATION OF THE LAWS IS THE PROPER AND PECULIAR PROVINCE OF THE COURTS. A CONSTITUTION IS . . . AND MUST BE REGARDED BY THE JUDGES, AS A FUNDAMENTAL LAW. IT THEREFORE BELONGS TO THEM TO ASCERTAIN ITS MEANING AS WELL AS THE MEANING OF ANY PARTICULAR PART PROCEEDING FROM THE LEGISLATIVE BODY. IF THERE SHOULD HAPPEN TO BE AN IRRECONCILABLE VARIANCE BETWEEN THE TWO, THAT WHICH HAS THE

SUPERIOR OBLIGATION AND VALIDITY OUGHT . . . TO BE PREFERRED; OR IN OTHER WORDS, THE CONSTITUTION OUGHT TO BE PREFERRED TO THE STATUTE, THE INTENTION OF THE PEOPLE TO THE INTENTION OF THEIR AGENTS.[18] (EMPHASIS ADDED)

This language eventually provided major support for John Marshall in *Marbury v. Madison*, for it says that a written constitution limits legislative power, that it is the unique function of courts to interpret the law, and that the Constitution compels the practice of judicial review. But this was somewhat of a leap of faith by both Hamilton and Marshall because, as stated earlier, the Constitution says nothing about the necessity and practice of judicial review. Furthermore, other democratic systems that have been successful with limited, constitutional government have trusted other political branches, not just the judiciary, to abide by the law. Whatever the case, Hamilton's reasoning in *Federalist No. 78* created an important precedent for this unique feature of American governmental practice.

Another claim supporting the argument that the Founding Fathers endorsed judicial review concerns the Supremacy Clause in Article VI, Clause 2. This provision states that

[T]HIS CONSTITUTION, AND THE LAWS OF THE UNITED STATES WHICH SHALL BE MADE IN PURSUANCE THEREOF AND ALL TREATIES MADE, OR WHICH SHALL BE MADE, UNDER THE AUTHORITY OF THE UNITED STATES, SHALL BE THE SUPREME LAW OF THE LAND; AND JUDGES IN EVERY STATE SHALL BE BOUND THEREBY, ANY THING IN THE CONSTITUTION OR LAWS OF ANY STATE TO THE CONTRARY NOTWITHSTANDING.

The precise meaning of the words "in pursuance thereof" is debatable; Marshall interpreted the phrase to mean "consistent with," and therefore, state judges need not enforce illegal laws. However, it is unclear as to what federal judges would do with such legislation. Again, the ambiguity of the Constitution defies precise definition.

The final piece of "founders' intent" evidence supporting the idea of judicial review concerns the Judiciary Act of 1789, passed by the First Congress to create the federal judicial system. Section 25 of this act allowed the Supreme Court to review state court decisions when the constitutionality of a federal law was challenged. This crucial provision, passed by a national legislature that was dominated by many of the original framers, indicates that those who created the federal judiciary most likely intended for the Supreme Court to oversee state court decisions affecting the new Constitution. Oliver Ellsworth, who helped draft both Article III of the Constitution and the Judiciary Act of 1789, would most likely not have contradicted himself while formulating these important documents, both of which infer that courts should rule on the constitutionality of all laws.

In summary, much evidence indicates that those attending the Constitutional Convention in 1787 anticipated that the Supreme Court might eventually have to rule on the constitutionality of actions taken by the other branches or levels of government. Why they never specifically inserted judicial review into the Constitution is unclear. It may have been omitted because of the rush to conclude the business of the Convention, the wisdom of dealing in generalities on certain subjects, or their uncertainty about how important the power of judicial review would become. Whatever the reason, this vital tool of American constitutional government eventually gained widespread acceptance, even when the Supreme Court handed down some very unpopular decisions.

HISTORICAL ACCEPTANCE OF JUDICIAL REVIEW

To say that historical acceptance explains the power of judicial review in the American system is somewhat ironic, because some Supreme Court rulings have been vilified ever since their public release. Whether it was state governments criticizing many Marshall Court rulings that advanced federal authority in the early 1800s, President Andrew Jackson criticizing Court rulings concerning the national bank or Indian removal in the 1830s, President Franklin Roosevelt criticizing the Court in the 1930s for being out of touch with the economic emergency, or angry Americans wanting to impeach Chief Justice Earl Warren in the 1950s and 1960s over desegregation and banned school prayer, the charge is frequently made that activist judges ignore the popular will when they overturn statutes passed by legislative majorities. Most recently, President Barack Obama publicly criticized the justices of the Roberts Court—in a State of the Union address, no less—for their controversial ruling on campaign finance legislation in the *Citizens United* case (see Chapter 15 for a more thorough discussion of this case).

However, this historic phenomenon of Supreme Court bashing often overlooks the extent to which judicial review has been overwhelmingly accepted as an essential device of American constitutional government. As Jesse Choper has noted, "judicial review [has] been institutionally adopted by a continuing consensus of American society as an integral rule of the system . . . ."[19] Undoubtedly, experience during the first few decades of the Supreme Court's existence was crucial to the formation of this vital social consensus.

Reference to a few cases during this early era should reinforce this point. In *Chisholm v. Georgia* (1793), the Supreme Court announced in a very unpopular decision that the Constitution allowed a citizen of one state to sue another state in federal court. The public clamor following the ruling soon led in 1798 to the ratification of the Eleventh Amendment to the Constitution, which provides that citizens of one state may not sue another state against its will. Although this amendment is one of only four constitutional amendments that directly overrules a decision by the Supreme Court,[20] it is the only one that was specifically aimed at limiting federal judicial power. In *Hylton v. United States* in 1796, in the first actual instance of the Supreme Court ruling on the constitutionality of a federal law, the justices upheld a statute levying a federal tax on horsedrawn carriages. Had the Court found the statute in question unconstitutional, the decision would have attracted far more significance in American constitutional law. Instead, the famous Marshall Court ruling in *Marbury v. Madison* (1803) became one of the landmark decisions in the history of American courts (see Brief 4.3). Still, in *Hylton* the Court assumed this authority to review and, if necessary, overturn actions of the other branches of the federal government.

One last case that supports judicial review as a practical necessity involves *Martin v. Hunter's Lessee* (1816), which presented the first important challenge to the Court's right to review state court decisions under its appellate jurisdiction. Under Virginia law and its state court practices, foreign nationals were forbidden from inheriting land in the state. After a protracted legal struggle of some three decades by a British citizen to win possession of his inheritance, the Supreme Court finally ruled in 1816 that since the controversy involved aspects of the Constitution, a federal treaty of 1794 with Great Britain, and the Judiciary Act of 1789, the Court had to review the state court judgment. Ultimately, the British citizen prevailed in the case against the state of Virginia, much to the displeasure of states' rights advocates. In retrospect, this critically important case had immense implications for the right of the Supreme Court to review state court rulings.

All of these cases demonstrate that even when the states were temporarily disadvantaged by many Marshall Court rulings, grudging historical acceptance was achieved as most parties eventually realized that some tribunal had to provide the final word on how the law was to be interpreted and applied. Undoubtedly, a major reason for these developments in early American law was the presence of John Marshall during this formative era of the American republic.

JUDICIAL REVIEW AS A CHECK ON MAJORITY RULE

One of the more famous excerpts from James Madison's *Federalist No. 51* reminds one that "[i]n framing a government which is to be administered by men over men, the great difficulty lies in this: You must first enable the government to controul the governed; and in the next place, oblige it to controul itself."[22] With respect to Madison's first concern about a government being able to "controul the governed," one question that frequently arises concerns whether the legislature, the executive, or the judiciary provides the best safeguard against what de Tocqueville observed as the tendency for majority tyranny in a democratic political system. Which of these institutions is better equipped to protect individual rights? The sad truth is that American history is littered with many instances in which popular majorities have denied important rights to vulnerable minorities. Occasionally, judges have had to intervene and curb these majoritarian tendencies that violate important principles of liberty and justice.

There is, of course, a dilemma here with respect to judges overruling popular majorities. Insisting upon a judicial corrective against majority preferences is the counterargument to those who claim that popular majorities are the best judge of what is just and preferable in a democratic society. The framers believed in representative democracy, but one limited by a rule of

Brief 4.3

A CLASSIC CONFRONTATION: *MARBURY V. MADISON* (1803)

Before leaving office following the election of 1800, the Federalists under President John Adams passed the Judiciary Act of 1801. Among other things, the law created several new judicial posts, to which Adams and the Federalist-dominated Congress were expected to appoint loyal supporters of the party. Also in January 1801, Adams named his outgoing Secretary of State, John Marshall, to become the third Chief Justice of the Supreme Court. Another law passed just prior to the inauguration of the new president authorized forty-two new justice-of-the-peace positions in the District of Columbia. Several of these minor appointments—including one for William Marbury, a loyal Federalist—had been signed by Adams and were in the office of John Marshall when Thomas Jefferson was inaugurated as president on March 4, 1801. Having just won the presidential election and eager to see the passing of the Federalist era, Jefferson was unlikely to tolerate any further entrenchment of political opponents in the federal judiciary. As a result, he ordered his incoming Secretary of State, James Madison, not to deliver the commission to Marbury.[21]

William Marbury decided to press the issue of his appointment. Relying upon a rather obscure provision of the Judiciary Act of 1789, he asked the Supreme Court to issue a writ of **mandamus** (literally, "we command") under its original jurisdiction. (Such an order, in effect, means that a court directs a lower court or another authority to perform a particular act.) In accordance with Section 13 of this act, Congress had authorized such an action "in cases warranted by the principles and usages of law, to any courts appointed, or persons holding office, under authority of the United States."

Now serving as Chief Justice, John Marshall was confronted with a major dilemma. He knew that President Jefferson was not likely to appoint Marbury to the post. Marshall also recognized that any denial by the White House of the Court's power could potentially damage the reputation and authority of the judiciary. In addressing the main questions in his opinion for the Court, Marshall argued that Marbury had a legal right to the post, that the failure to deliver the formal commission violated that right, and that a writ of *mandamus* was the proper remedy for such a situation. But he also said that Marbury's request that the Supreme Court issue such an order under its original jurisdiction was not possible because it relied upon a provision of a federal law that was unconstitutional. All but lost in this classic episode of constitutional law is the fact that, under modern standards of judicial ethics, Marshall probably should have recused himself from participating in the case, since he had served as the cabinet official most responsible for delivering the commission to Marbury.

Marshall's main argument was that, under Article III, Congress had the right to regulate the appellate jurisdiction of the Supreme Court, but not its *original* jurisdiction. Since the latter is defined solely by the Constitution, it could only be changed by a formal amendment to the Constitution, not by an ordinary act of Congress. Since Section 13 of the Judiciary Act attempted to alter this constitutional grant of original jurisdiction, the Court was left with only one option. Marshall argued that the Constitution is the supreme law of the land, and that ordinary acts of the legislature are subordinate to the Constitution. Furthermore, it is the unique duty of courts to interpret the meaning of the fundamental law. And finally, ". . . a law repugnant to the constitution is void; and . . . courts, as well as other departments, are bound by that instrument." As stated earlier, this reasoning is virtually identical to that cited by Hamilton in *Federalist No. 78*. Marshall had both avoided a potential embarrassment for the Court by not providing Jefferson with a judicial order to ignore and established a major judicial precedent for later generations.

Marbury v. Madison is significant for three reasons. First, the decision was the first time that the Court overturned an act of Congress on the principle that laws not conforming to the Constitution are null and void. By establishing this very important precedent, the *Marbury* decision established the practice of the Supreme Court reviewing legislation to ensure that it conforms to the Constitution. Second, the decision clearly held that the original jurisdiction of the Supreme Court is established on constitutional, rather than mere legislative, grounds. This principle is also important, for if the Congress could amend *both* the original and appellate jurisdiction of the Court, it could conceivably remove all power of the Court to act. Although the vast majority of Supreme Court decision making involves the Court using its appellate, rather than original, jurisdiction, Marshall's powerful commentary on the legitimacy of courts and their obligation to uphold the Constitution was a critical test of the rule-of-law principle. Finally, given the fact that the Constitutional Convention in 1787 never clearly established how the federal system could function effectively if the states passed laws that were contrary to the Constitution, the *Marbury* decision provided a very effective instrument to monitor *state* legislation and actions. True to form, Marshall wasted little time in establishing another important precedent. Seven years after the *Marbury* ruling, the Court ruled in *Fletcher v. Peck* (1810) that the repeal of a 1795 state law by the Georgia legislature was unconstitutional because it impaired a contractual obligation of the state toward individual property rights, as covered by the Contract Clause in Article I, Section 10.

law that safeguarded the rights of individuals. As cited earlier in Chapter 2, Madison recognized (again, in *Federalist No. 51*) the need for "auxiliary precautions" in order to control and limit governmental power. Examples of these checks upon the majority include the separation of powers, the Electoral College vote in presidential elections, equality of the states, the Senate filibuster, and the need for supermajorities in Congress and the states to amend the Constitution.

Judicial review is one of the most important of these "auxiliary precautions." Compared with the other deliberate departures from simple majority rule, the practice of judicial review is normally seen as less arbitrary or political, although this usually depends on how well the judges explain their decisions in sound and logical legal opinions. Granting special power to a minority in the political process—whether it is public or private—can obstruct the wishes of the majority. Whether it is a filibuster in the U.S. Senate aimed at blocking passage of a bill preferred by a clear majority, or a slim Supreme Court majority that overturns a popular law passed by Congress, the ultimate effect is the same. One difference, of course, is that a judicial ruling is more likely to be accompanied by a reasoned, logical explanation of how the judges reached their decision. The difficulty for judges or Supreme Court justices is trying to determine whether the actions of the popular majority conform to constitutional mandates, and if not, how to use judicial powers of persuasion to convince a polity that has erred to correct its mistakes as quickly as possible.

Two good examples of how Supreme Court decisions have been a vital corrective to popular majorities concern the issues of racial segregation and legislative mal-apportionment as confronted by the Warren Court. The long battle against racial discrimination is discussed in more depth in Chapter 9. For now it is important to understand how the American system has occasionally produced major policy change through judicial activity, sometimes with enormous civil resistance by popular majorities.

Before the Supreme Court acted in Brown v. Board of Education (1954) to overturn racial segregation, popular majorities in seventeen states required the segregation of black and white students in public schools. Segregation was also required in the District of Columbia, and four other states made the segregation of public schools optional. With the Court's unanimous decision on May 17, 1954, striking down the infamous separate-but-equal doctrine, the United States slowly began to emerge from more than three centuries of blatant and pervasive racial discrimination. Legislation by popular majorities reflects democratic procedures, but it may also deny basic constitutional rights to targeted minorities.

Another issue that the Supreme Court finally moved to rectify—legislative malapportionment—for decades had allowed state legislatures to distort the principle of equal representation. During the twentieth century, in increasing numbers the American people moved from rural to urban and suburban areas in many metropolitan areas of the country. But several states refused to acknowledge the new population distribution within their borders and reapportion their state legislative or congressional districts as the U.S. Constitution requires in Article I, Section 2. As a result, several state legislatures seriously underrepresented the more urbanized enclaves of their population and overrepresented less populated rural segments. In a series of decisions beginning with *Baker v. Carr* (1962), the Supreme Court finally accepted jurisdiction in legislative apportionment cases over the criticisms of many, including Justices Felix Frankfurter and John Harlan II, both of whom made the judicial restraint argument, that the Court should not interfere in areas better left to elected representatives. *Baker v. Carr* (1962) found the Court ruling for the first time that constitutional challenges to legislative malapportionment could properly be considered by federal courts. Writing for the majority in a 6–2 decision, Justice William Brennan noted that such claims involved "justiciable" issues that could be considered by federal courts because they presented a constitutional question of fairness, not mere "political questions" outside the purview of courts.

Although the Court majority in *Baker v. Carr* stopped short of addressing the merits of the specific challenge brought by Tennessee voters to the state's malapportionment scheme, the ruling soon opened the judicial doors to a succession of litigants challenging state and congressional apportionment systems across the country. A long line of Supreme Court rulings following *Baker v. Carr* finally compelled the reapportionment mandate suggested by the Court here.[23] One of the most famous reapportionment decisions (discussed further in Chapter 11) was *Reynolds v. Sims* (1964), wherein the Court decided that both houses of a state legislature had to be apportioned on an equitable population basis among all electoral districts that reflected the "one person–one vote" principle.

JUDICIAL REVIEW AND THE ARTICULATION OF NEUTRAL PRINCIPLES

The fourth and final justification for judicial review is that judicial decisions should reflect rational and unbiased decision making that articulates general principles for use in resolving later conflicts. By hearing and deciding cases, and advancing clear principles that compel compliance through logic and objectivity, the courts hope to persuade the public to comply with rational principles of law and social behavior that are grounded in fairness and equity. According to this explanation, the Supreme Court is the great educator of the body politic as it interprets and applies the law and upholds the constitutional order. Legal decisions must be seen as defined by the law, rather than the political biases of the justices.

One of the strongest reflections of this "just reasoning" argument was posed over sixty years ago by constitutional scholar Herbert Wechsler, who maintained that the essence of the law and the authority of the Supreme Court lie in the justices' ability to articulate "neutral general principles" of the law:

> . . . [T]HE MAIN CONSTITUENT OF THE JUDICIAL PROCESS IS PRECISELY THAT IT MUST BE GENERALLY PRINCIPLED, RESTING WITH RESPECT TO EVERY STEP THAT IS INVOLVED IN REACHING JUDGMENT ON ANALYSIS AND REASONS QUITE TRANSCENDING THE IMMEDIATE RESULT THAT IS ACHIEVED.[24]

A **neutral principle** is one that goes beyond the immediate case at hand, and is useful to courts in resolving future cases. If general principles of judicial neutrality are not available to use in different settings, the future resolution of conflict will be impeded by charges that personal biases of judges are the primary criteria applied to conflict resolution. As a result, a public that strongly disagrees with the Court's ruling on a particularly contentious issue will question the legitimacy of the Court's judgment, claim judicial bias has entered the equation, and disregard the decision.

"Neutral principles" historically derived from interpreting and applying provisions of the Constitution do not discriminate with respect to the content of the message or the politics of the messenger. The same First Amendment guarantees of free speech and assembly that the masses have relied upon for decades also are available to neo-Nazis, the Ku Klux Klansmen, state-militia groups, or anarchists. First Amendment rights should be accorded to all, regardless of their political or racial philosophy.

Another example of this search for principled neutrality involves the difficult issue of affirmative action, a social issue that has increasingly attracted great criticism in American society. An argument often advanced by those supporting affirmative action programs is that granting preferential treatment to racial minorities is essential in order to compensate for decades, if not centuries, of invidious discrimination (see Chapter 10 for discussion of this controversial topic). Opponents of these programs have argued that such treatment is merely reverse discrimination. If discriminating against black people in housing, employment, or public schools denies them equal protection of the laws under the Fourteenth Amendment, then critics of several different compensatory programs have insisted for several years that giving anyone preferential treatment to others denies equal protection to the nontargeted "victim." Wechsler's "neutral principles" compel complete neutrality or, to quote the first Justice John Harlan in *Plessy v. Ferguson* (1896), a Constitution that is "color-blind."

This neutral principles argument in support of judicial review is somewhat elusive, in part because American constitutional law exhibits few decisions in which the Supreme Court has provided timeless principles that are supported by a perfect consensus. As two noted constitutional scholars observed, "neutrality, save on a superficial and elementary level, is a futile quest."[25] If "neutral principles" means adherence to a value-free form of decision making, then the concept is unachievable. Furthermore, since most decisions of the Court are usually the result of collective decision making, achieving perfect neutrality among all participants is extremely rare. Majority opinions are often carefully crafted to hold together a fragile coalition of justices who may have compromised on certain points in order to achieve a convincing majority. The result is a negotiated narrative that sometimes lacks clarity and consistency. In many instances, it is the justices' dissenting opinions that provide the most crisp, impassioned, and principled reasoning. History records several justices whose reputations were forged more for their dissenting opinions than for their majority or concurring opinions. On this point, the dissents of John Harlan I, Oliver Wendell Holmes Jr., Louis Brandeis, and Harlan Fiske Stone come to mind. On the Roberts Court, many of the dissents of Justices John Paul Stevens and Antonin Scalia are equally notable.

A classic example of the elusiveness of neutral principles in judicial decision making can be found in *Bush v. Gore* (2000), one of the most controversial decisions in the Court's history (see Brief 4.4). This decision will be remembered for many things: a judicial resolution of a presidential election thirty-four days after election day; an eleventh-hour release of a decision that tested public faith in the impartiality of life-tenured judges; a ruling that revealed some surprising personal tensions between the justices; and a rationale that struggled to explain why a manual recount of the popular vote in one state should not proceed.

Brief 4.4
BUSH V. GORE: ONE FOR THE TEXTBOOKS?

On November 8, 2000, one day following the presidential election, the Florida Division of Elections reported that a razor-thin margin of 1,784 votes separated Texas Governor George W. Bush and Vice President Al Gore out of a total of some 5.8 million votes cast for both candidates. Because the vote margin was less than one-half percent of all the votes cast, under the Florida Election Code, an automatic machine recount was necessary. Following this machine recount, Bush's margin had narrowed to barely five hundred votes. Beyond the questionable accuracy of many recounts, what ultimately became the main point of contention between the two political camps in Florida were the "undervotes," ballots that did not register a clear and intentional vote for one of the presidential candidates.

A dizzying series of legal and political maneuvers then occurred, including Al Gore's request for a manual recount of all votes in disputed counties that were traditionally Democratic but which had shown large numbers of votes being registered for Bush or independent candidate Pat Buchanan. On November 11, George W. Bush petitioned the federal district court in South Florida to block manual recounts in four disputed counties, but this request was denied. On November 14, the Florida Secretary of State, Katherine Harris, a Republican supporter of Bush, certified that Bush had won the state-vote contest and therefore had won all of Florida's twenty-five electoral votes. The Gore team moved quickly to challenge the state certification, first in state court and then in federal district court. On November 16, the Florida Supreme Court ruled unanimously that the recounts in two disputed counties should proceed. By November 19, when overseas ballots were counted, Bush's slim lead increased to 930 votes, and two days later, the Florida Supreme Court issued an order supporting manual recounts in selected counties and imposed a November 26 deadline for final vote tallies and recertification by the Secretary of State on all manual recounts. On November 22, Bush's petition to the U.S. Supreme Court to review the state supreme court's decision was accepted. After oral arguments nine days later, the Court decided on December 4 not to review the federal questions being asserted in the Bush petition, and it then set aside the November 21 ruling by the Florida Supreme Court to recount manually all votes in selected counties.

On December 8, 2000, the Florida Supreme Court ruled 4–3 that recounts of all votes in two hotly contested counties—Miami-Dade and Palm Beach—should move forward and on December 9, the U.S. Supreme Court stayed that ruling and ordered both parties to submit written arguments on the matter of manual recounts. Those arguments were heard on December 11 and one day later, the high court issued a final judgment that halted further recounts of the disputed ballots in selected counties and, in effect, awarded the election to George W. Bush.

The key question that the justices had to answer in *Bush v. Gore* was whether the Florida Supreme Court was wrong in ordering a manual recount of presidential undervotes. Five of the justices (Rehnquist, O'Connor, Kennedy, Scalia, and Thomas) joined in a *per curiam* opinion that asserted that according to federal statute, all state electoral slates had to be certified by December 12, and that inadequate time remained to conduct a fair and accurate recount of all contested ballots. According to the majority, to proceed with the manual recount in the manner prescribed by the Florida Supreme Court would raise vitally important questions about equal protection of the laws (see Chapter 10 for discussion of the equal protection issues involved in the decision). While attaching great importance to fairness for the abstract voter, the Court majority seemed little interested in the thousands of real voters in selected counties whose votes were left uncounted in the Florida electoral system. In criticizing the Florida Supreme Court's effort to remedy that with a recount, the majority opposed ". . . a situation where a state court with the power to assure uniformity has ordered a statewide recount with minimal procedural safeguards." In resolving one of the most closely contested presidential elections in American history, the majority seemed both reluctant and modest about the effect of its ruling:

> *None are more conscious of the vital limits on judicial authority than are the members of this Court, and none stand more in admiration of the Constitution's design to leave the selection of the President to the people, through their legislatures, and to the political sphere. When contending parties invoke the process of the courts, however, it becomes our unsought responsibility to resolve the federal and constitutional issues the judicial system has been forced to confront.*

The four dissenting justices in this landmark decision took issue with this claim of judicial humility and the exercise of judicial activism. All four of the dissenters noted the right of state courts to interpret and apply their own laws without unwarranted interference from federal courts. Justice Souter argued that ". . . our customary respect for state interpretations of state law counsels against rejection of the Florida court's determinations in this case." He also insisted that the high court should never have reviewed the *Bush v. Gore* controversy because it lacked a substantial federal question. Justice Breyer's dissenting opinion began with the same claim—that the high court "was wrong to take this case." In his views, the justices should have allowed the Florida Supreme Court to decide whether the recount in its state should have proceeded. Justice Ginsburg observed in dissent that "[t]he extraordinary setting of this case has obscured the ordinary principle that dictates its proper resolution: [f]ederal courts defer to state high courts' interpretations of their state's own law." But perhaps the most memorable and telling dissent in the *Bush v. Gore* verdict was provided by Justice Stevens:

> *. . . Confidence in the men and women who administer the judicial system . . . is the true backbone of the rule of law. Time will one day heal the wound to that confidence that will be inflicted by today's decision. One thing, however, is certain. Although we may never know with complete certainty the identity of the winner of this year's Presidential election, the identity of the loser is perfectly clear. It is the Nation's confidence in the judge as an impartial guardian of the rule of law.*

A generous analysis of the ruling would most likely portray the decision as a sincere attempt to move beyond one of the closest and most bizarre presidential elections in American history. A more cynical assessment, perhaps best characterized by some of the dissenting justices, would say that judicial impartiality and principled objectivity were difficult to find in the ruling. But in deciding to intervene in a close presidential election, the Court raised questions about the ability of judges to reach beyond political circumstances toward neutrality and impartiality.

Conclusion

This preliminary examination of the practice of judicial review in American government has emphasized a few key points. First, several important questions must be addressed concerning what the actual words of the Constitution and laws in question actually say, what institutions of government are charged with authoritatively interpreting the law, whether it is to be interpreted in a static or evolutionary manner, and to what extent should judges seek to balance societal interests while interpreting laws that may advantage one interest while it discounts another.

Second, when justices on the Supreme Court review legislation to see if the actions of governmental officials conform to the Constitution, they engage in the practice of judicial review, a unique contribution of the United States to constitutional government. As discussed in this chapter, the dual concepts of judicial self-restraint and judicial activism raise the crucial question about whether life-tenured judges and justices who are not elected by the people should possess such immense power to invalidate policies that are enacted by government officials who are elected by the people. As this chapter has introduced, and as succeeding chapters seek to explain, how one feels about the law in question tends to determine how one evaluates a decision that sustains or overturns a law passed by a legislature.

Finally, the practice of judicial review by the U.S. Supreme Court has seen the justices operating in one of the most unique judicial bodies in the world. Few nations entrust nine judges with virtually unlimited power to resolve ongoing societal conflicts. Although scores of other nations have some form of judicial review, none of them operates in quite the same fashion as does the U.S. Supreme Court. Several factors— the intentions of the framers of the Constitution, historical acceptance of the Court's decisions, the need to check majority rule when it denies just treatment to its citizens, and the search for neutral principles—help explain why judicial review has been such a prominent feature of American constitutional experience.

After more than two centuries of interpreting the Constitution, the U.S. Supreme Court still serves as the preeminent judicial conscience of the country. As one student of judicial review stated many decades ago, the justices on the Supreme Court are "inevitably teachers in a vital national seminar . . ." that never ends.[26] They are expected to perform this noble task with intelligence, integrity, reflection, and impartiality, in a society that is still experimenting with the art of self-government.

CHAPTER 5
Separation of Powers and The American Presidency

THE CONSTITUTION PROVIDES FOR A SEPARATION OF POWERS AMONG THE BRANCHES OF THE FEDERAL GOVERNMENT, BUT THE BALANCE OF POWER HAS SHIFTED OVER THE YEARS. IN TIMES OF WAR OR INTERNATIONAL CRISIS, THE BALANCE OF POWER SKEWS IN THE DIRECTION OF THE WHITE HOUSE, GIVEN THE PRESIDENT'S POWERS AS COMMANDER-IN-CHIEF.

▼ Introductory Remarks by President Theodore Roosevelt

When I came to the United States presidency in 1901 following the assassination of President William McKinley, I was forty-three years old—the youngest person to serve as president. Now, more than one hundred years later, from my vantage point on Mount Rushmore, I see an American presidency that is in some ways similar to the one I knew but also one that has changed significantly. Allow me to explain.

The presidency is still the "bully pulpit" that I enjoyed, allowing the president sweeping powers to inform and influence the American people on a wide range of subjects. Since my presidency, my successors have used the "bully pulpit" to bring Americans into world wars, lead them through great economic depressions, and provide support during natural disasters. Presidents have always enjoyed unparalleled access to the American people, and the successful presidents have learned how to use that influence well.

I was elected to the presidency for my second term in 1904, but I failed to win as a "Bull Moose" candidate in 1912. This chapter demonstrates that mere popularity is not enough to win the office; it takes a strong organization in the states to secure the electoral vote. I watched with interest the recently concluded 2012 presidential election, in which President Barack Obama won almost 51% of the popular vote but over 60 percent of the electoral vote. It is the system our Founders devised, for better or worse. I do know that it is virtually impossible for a third-party candidate, as I was in 1912, to win the electoral vote.

The powers of the U.S. president have grown and been shaped by all forty-three men who filled the office. I like to think that I was responsible for some of that growth through my "stewardship theory" of the office. Here is what I said in my autobiography: *"I declined to adopt the view that what was imperatively necessary for the nation could not be done by the President unless he could find some specific authorization for it. My belief was that it was not only his right but his duty to do anything that the needs of the nation demanded unless such action was forbidden by the Constitution or by the laws...I did not usurp power, but I did greatly broaden the use of executive power ... whenever and in whatever manner was necessary, unless prevented by direct constitutional or legislative prohibition. ..."*

History shows us that presidents can make mistakes. We need to remember that the president is not infallible, and it is the role of the people to remain vigilant. As I noted in an editorial in 1918: *"The President is merely the most important among a large number of public servants. He should be supported or opposed exactly to the degree which is warranted by his good conduct or bad conduct, his efficiency or inefficiency in rendering loyal, able, and disinterested service to the nation as a whole. Therefore, it is absolutely necessary that there should be full liberty to tell the truth about his acts, and this means that it is exactly as necessary to blame him when he does wrong as to praise him when he does right."*

The Constitution provides each president with a wide array of powers, including the power to veto legislation, pardon individuals, appoint judges and officers of the United States, and provide information to Congress. I used all of these powers, as have my fellow presidents. But perhaps a president's most sweeping powers are those stemming from the role as commander-in-chief. In this chapter, pay particular attention to the role that the president plays in foreign affairs, looking closely at the Supreme Court's decisions relating to Franklin Roosevelt, Harry Truman, and George W. Bush.

This chapter provides numerous examples of how presidents enjoy great successes and experience significant failures. Only two of my fellow presidents have been impeached by Congress, and I am glad to report that not one has been removed from office. We did have the unfortunate Watergate scandal that led to the resignation of Richard Nixon, which is discussed in the chapter. However, it is important to remember that the institution of the United States presidency has survived despite scandals such as Teapot Dome and Watergate. Indeed, the office is greater than the individual president. Enjoy the chapter! TR

SOURCES: *The Autobiography of Theodore Roosevelt* (New York: Scribner's, 1913); "Roosevelt in the *Kansas City Star*," 149, May 7, 1918, Theodore Roosevelt Association, *www.theodoreroosevelt.org/life/quotes.htm*.

THE SEPARATION OF POWERS

Given the human tendency to pursue private interest rather than public virtue, how can power be used for effective governance in a complex world to solve public problems and also be protective of individual rights? In the judgment of many legal historians and scholars, those who created the American constitutional system tried to manage this "constitutional dilemma" by separating institutional power and equipping each unit of the new government with several tools to check the actions of the other. Because this and the next chapter concentrate on the American presidency and Congress, respectively, as key institutional actors that share power in the American system, one must begin with a discussion of this significant American contribution to constitutional government.

In the 1890s, noted British statesman and historian Lord James Bryce observed that "[t]here is little in this Constitution that is absolutely new."[1] The American Constitution is a document that contains strong traces of the European Enlightenment, with its distrust of both secular and religious power, and a corresponding attachment to the tenets of liberal democracy. As discussed in Chapter 2, a popular commitment to fundamental rights, belief in a higher law to which ordinary legislation had to conform, and growing impatience with monarchical rule all inspired the early American colonists. If drafting a constitution means controlling and containing the excesses of political conflict, the American Constitution was a direct reaction against two earlier problems: the abuse of power by the British prior to 1776 and the absence of power under the Articles of Confederation immediately after. Given these antecedents, it is natural to expect that throughout their deliberations in Philadelphia, the framers were deeply concerned about how best to manage political power.

EARLY WRITINGS ON SEPARATED POWERS

One of the primary ideas guiding the framers in their struggle to control political power was the separation-of-powers principle, which several English and European writers of the seventeenth and eighteenth centuries had earlier addressed. Such commentators as James Harrington, John Locke, and Baron de Montesquieu, as well as Thomas Hobbes and Jean-Jacques Rousseau, wrote extensively about two major themes: the growing power of the state and the assertion of individual freedoms. Both of these ideas were basic to the European Enlightenment. Although both Hobbes and Locke agreed that the source of ultimate authority should be the people, and that the purpose of government should be to manage conflict and protect private property, they disagreed about the best arrangement for accomplishing these ends. Whereas Hobbes advocated giving political power to a single office (the monarchy), Locke favored a division of power between a representative assembly and the monarchy. Although twentieth century commentators have noted the expansion of executive or judicial authority to "imperial" proportions,[2] John Locke viewed one political power as paramount: "One, Supreme Power, which is the Legislature, to which all the rest are and must be subordinate." He also suggested that the power of the sovereign, be it either the legislature or the monarchy, had the "power to act according to discretion for the public good, without prescription of law and sometimes even against it."

This assertion by Locke of supreme power in extraordinary times has special relevance to one of the prominent questions that is discussed in this chapter, Under what circumstances might ordinary restraints upon power be temporarily suspended in order to address urgent public needs? Must the rule of law and constraints upon political power be suspended on occasion in order to preserve the larger political order? Given the challenges posed by the ongoing wars in Iraq and Afghanistan, and the consolidation of political and military power in the executive branch since September 11, 2001, this perennial question about the proper balance between governmental authority and personal freedom once again demands more study.

Like Locke's *Second Treatise*, Montesquieu's primary work, *The Spirit of the Laws* (1748), was well known to the colonists who instigated the American Revolution and drafted the Constitution. Although Madison and others periodically referred to Montesquieu when writing about political power, as constitutional scholar C. Herman Pritchett observed many years ago, *Spirit of the Laws* itself may not have been that important to the delegates in Philadelphia.[3]

EARLY AMERICAN WRITINGS AND THE FOUNDING

At the Constitutional Convention itself, the eventual division of governmental power between Congress, the presidency, and the Supreme Court was primarily motivated by two realities: (1) having to address some obvious problems that existed under the failed Articles of Confederation and (2) a very skeptical population that distrusted any centralized authority. Unfortunately, memories of executive tyranny under the British were very fresh in the minds of citizens. To guard against the abuse of executive authority, the new state constitutions had given too much power to state legislatures. These bodies continued after the Revolutionary War to dominate state executives and courts, and frustrated a weak national government leading up the Constitutional Convention.

This consuming distrust of executive power and the desire that government protect "ordered liberty" sustained the framers throughout the summer of 1787. Though they were pessimistic about human nature, they remained optimistic about their own ability to structure political power in order to preserve social order and protect individual liberty. According to the new Constitution, each of the three departments was to participate in the exercise of power by the other two coordinate branches. Congress would share in the judicial power by determining the appellate jurisdiction of the courts, creating federal courts and judgeships, and with respect to the Senate, by considering judicial nominations. The president would exercise legislative power through the ability to veto legislation, address Congress annually on the state of the Union, propose legislation to Congress, and convene special legislative sessions. Finally, although the role of judicial power envisioned in Article III was very vague, the judiciary would hear all controversies arising under the new Constitution, federal laws, and federal treaties. As discussed in Chapter 4, as the concept of judicial review emerged in the early nineteenth century, it equipped the Supreme Court with a powerful instrument for judging the constitutionality of both legislative and executive actions. Each branch of the government would thus share in the exercise of power by the others, and each would have to obtain the concurrence of the others, at least in the long term, in order to accomplish anything of a lasting policy nature.

In some of his essays in *The Federalist*, James Madison spoke of the "separation of power" that the drafters of the Constitution were concerned about in Philadelphia. As discussed briefly in Chapter 2, these essays were written by Madison, Alexander Hamilton, and John Jay in order to win ratification of the new Constitution. Hamilton and Madison, in particular, argued that the new system would improve upon the Articles of Confederation without unduly infringing upon individual freedom. In *Federalist No. 37*, Madison noted that one of the crucial difficulties encountered at the Constitutional Convention dealt with "combining the requisite stability and energy in government, with the inviolable attention due to liberty and to the republican form."[4] He cautioned that "experience has instructed us that no skill in the science of government has yet been able to discriminate and define, with sufficient certainty, [government's] three great provinces—the legislative, executive, and judiciary."[5] In *Federalist No. 47* and *No. 48*, Madison again emphasized the importance of Montesquieu's maxim that "there can be no liberty where the legislative and executive powers are united in the same person or body of magistrates." But Madison's major modification of a purist separation principle in these essays was that (1) the separation should not be complete and (2) no branch should have an "overruling influence over the others in the administration of their respective power."[6]

In *Federalist No. 51*, Madison argued that separated powers are "essential to the preservation of liberty," and he provided here his most extensive prescription for avoiding tyranny. In talking about the "necessary partition of power among the several departments," he stated that the internal structure of government must be constructed so that "its several constituent parts may, by their mutual relations, be the means of keeping each other in their proper places." Although each department "should have a will of its own" and not be able to influence unduly such factors as appointment or compensation of members, the real device for ensuring responsible government goes much further than these safeguards:

> THE GREAT SECURITY AGAINST A GRADUAL CONCENTRATION OF THE SEVERAL POWERS IN THE SAME DEPARTMENT, CONSISTS IN GIVING TO THOSE WHO ADMINISTER EACH DEPARTMENT THE NECESSARY CONSTITUTIONAL MEANS AND PERSONAL MOTIVES

TO RESIST ENCROACHMENTS OF THE OTHERS.... AMBITION MUST BE MADE TO COUNTERACT AMBITION. [EMPHASIS ADDED]

And in the famous excerpt from the *Federalist No. 51* emphasizing the dilemma of constitutional government, Madison noted the need for government to control both the governed and the government. His pessimism about certain aspects of human nature was also evident when he stated the necessity for "auxiliary precautions" to counter the tendencies of concentrated power. The remainder of *Federalist No. 51* examined the checks and balances built into American government—republican government that divides the legislature into two distinct houses elected by different means, construction of a federal system that further divides power between levels of government, and the establishment of several access points for special interests to petition government for consideration of their agendas. In many respects, these counterchecks capture elements of both individualism and communitarianism, as discussed in Chapter 2.

Having discussed the historical setting for the separation of powers principle that gained prominence at the Constitutional Convention in 1787, and burnished by Madison's contributions to *The Federalist*, the emphasis now shifts to the main focus of this chapter: the American presidency. Consideration of the several constitutional powers of the presidential office is integrated with a discussion of selected political events, presidential actions, and Supreme Court precedents, all of which have important implications for American constitutional development.

THE UNITED STATES PRESIDENCY: AN OVERVIEW

When George Washington took the oath of office to become our nation's first president in 1789, he started a practice that has occurred at four-year intervals ever since. The forty-three men who have served as president (Grover Cleveland's two nonconsecutive terms make President Obama the forty-forth president), represented varying occupations, backgrounds, and religions, but until 2008 all were white. Table 5.1 provides a general overview of those individuals.

Table 5.1 Presidents of the United States

President	Dates in Office	Age*	Party	Religion	Previous Govt. Experience	Post-Presidency Legacy or Chief Accomplishment
George Washington	1789–1797	57	Federalist	Episcopal	Military General	Father of His Country
John Adams	1797–1801	61	Federalist	Unitarian	Vice-President	Founding Father and first VP
Thomas Jefferson	1801–1809	57	Dem-Rep	No formal	Vice-President	Founded University of Virginia
James Madison	1809–1817	57	Dem-Rep	Episcopal	Sec of State	Father of the Constitution
James Monroe	1817–1825	58	Dem-Rep	Episcopal	Sec of State	Monroe Doctrine
John Quincy Adams	1825–1829	57	Dem-Rep	Unitarian	Sec of State	U.S. Representative (8 terms)
Andrew Jackson	1829–1837	61	Democrat	Presby	U.S. Senator	Military hero, retired
Martin Van Buren	1837–1841	54	Democrat	Dutch Ref	Vice-President	Jackson's VP
William Henry Harrison	1841	68	Whig	Episcopal	Minister-Columbia	Died after 32 days in office
John Tyler	1841–1845	51	Whig	Episcopal	Vice-President	Annexation of Texas
James K. Polk	1845–1849	49	Democrat	Presby	Governor - TN	Mexican-American War
Zachary Taylor	1849–1850	64	Whig	Episcopal	None	Died - unusual circumstances
Millard Fillmore	1850–1853	50	Whig	Unitarian	Vice-President	Chancellor, University of Buffalo

Name	Years	Age	Party	Religion	Previous Office	Notable
Franklin Pierce	1853–1857	48	Democrat	Episcopal	U.S. Senator	Gadsden Purchase
James Buchanan	1857–1861	65	Democrat	Episcopal	Minister-England	Only bachelor president
Abraham Lincoln	1861–1865	52	Republican	No formal	U.S. Rep	Great Emancipator/assassinated
Andrew Johnson	1865–1869	56	Democrat	No formal	Vice-President	Impeached/U.S. senator
Ulysses S. Grant	1869–1877	46	Republican	Methodist	Military General	Military hero
Rutherford B. Hayes	1877–1881	54	Republican	No formal	Governor - OH	End of Reconstruction
James Garfield	1881	49	Republican	Disc of Ch	U.S. Senator	200 days in office/Assassinated
Chester A. Arthur	1881–1885	51	Republican	Episcopal	Vice-President	Civil Service Act
Grover Cleveland	1885–1889	47	Democrat	Presby	Governor - NY	Re-elected in 1893
Benjamin Harrison	1889–1893	55	Republican	Presby	U.S. Senator	Sherman Anti-Trust Act
Grover Cleveland	1893–1897	55	Democrat	Presby	U.S. President	Served 2 non-consecutive terms
William McKinley	1897–1901	54	Republican	Methodist	Governor - OH	Treaty of Paris/assassinated
Theodore Roosevelt	1901–1909	42	Republican	Dutch Ref	Vice-President	Bull Moose Party candidate-1912
William Howard Taft	1909–1913	51	Republican	Unitarian	Sec of War	Chief Justice of Supreme Court
Woodrow Wilson	1913–1921	56	Democrat	Presby	Governor - NJ	League of Nations
Warren G. Harding	1921–1923	55	Republican	Baptist	U.S. Senator	Teapot Dome/died in office
Calvin Coolidge	1923–1929	51	Republican	Congreg	Vice-President	Kellogg-Briand Pact
Herbert Hoover	1929–1933	54	Republican	Quaker	Sec of Commerce	Hoover Commissions
Franklin D. Roosevelt	1933–1945	51	Democrat	Episcopal	Governor - NY	New Deal/died in office
Harry S. Truman	1945–1953	60	Democrat	Baptist	Vice-President	Used atomic bomb to end war
Dwight D. Eisenhower	1953–1961	62	Republican	Presby	Military General	Five-star general
John F. Kennedy	1961–1963	43	Democrat	Catholic	U.S. Senator	Assassinated/25th Amendment
Lyndon B. Johnson	1963–1969	55	Democrat	Disc of Ch	Vice-President	Great Society/civil rights
Richard M. Nixon	1969–1974	56	Republican	Quaker	Vice-President	Only president to resign office
Gerald R. Ford	1974–1977	61	Republican	Episcopal	Vice-President	Never elected president or VP
James Carter	1977–1981	52	Democrat	Baptist	Governor - GA	Nobel Peace Prize, 2002
Ronald Reagan	1981–1989	69	Republican	Disc of Ch	Governor - CA	Reagan Revolution
George H.W. Bush	1989–1993	64	Republican	Episcopal	Vice-President	Operation Desert Storm
William J. Clinton	1993–2001	46	Democrat	Baptist	Governor - AR	Impeached/Clinton Initiative
George W. Bush	2001–2009	54	Republican	Methodist	Governor - TX	9-11 attacks
Barack Obama	2009–	47	Democrat	U Ch Christ	U.S. Senator	Affordable Care Act

* Upon taking office

The table illustrates the consistency with which the United States presidency has changed hands in a peaceful and predictable manner, a practice not always so consistent among some other countries of the world. The American presidents generally represented mainstream religious denominations, with Presbyterians and Episcopalians dominating the office at least during the first century or so. Only one Roman Catholic, John F. Kennedy, has held the presidency, and his candidacy pushed religion to the forefront of that campaign. The table also shows that most presidents retire from holding public office once they leave the presidency. Three exceptions stand out: John Quincy Adams went on to serve eight terms in the U.S. House of Representatives; Andrew Johnson served briefly in the U.S. Senate; and William Howard Taft ended his career as Chief Justice of the United States Supreme Court. Other retired presidents have served in numerous public capacities: Herbert Hoover chaired several important government commissions that bear his name; Jimmy Carter was awarded a Nobel Peace Prize for his peacemaking efforts after leaving the presidency; and George H. W. Bush, Bill Clinton, and George W. Bush have collaborated on several initiatives related to natural disasters across the globe. The discussion now turns to constitutional requirements surrounding the office (see Brief 5.1).

ELECTING THE PRESIDENT

The discussion in Chapter 2 explained how the Founders set up the system of electors that would choose a new president, and that system, with several adjustments and corrections, remains pretty much intact today. We continue to elect the president and vice president "indirectly," in that popular votes cast by voters actually choose "electors" that then cast the electoral votes that really elect a president. Each state has a number of electoral votes equal to its number of House of Representatives seats plus its two senators. Electors cast one electoral vote for president and one for vice president. Over time, state governments have opened up the selection process for electors to the voters, and voters often do not realize that marking an "X" next to a presidential candidate's name actually goes toward a slate of party-based electors. The Constitution requires that a winning candidate for president receive a majority of electoral votes.

CONSTITUTIONAL AMENDMENTS AND THE PRESIDENCY

The Constitution has been amended five times relating to presidential matters:

Twelfth Amendment (1804): Requires presidential electors to cast two votes, one for president and one for vice president. The amendment was proposed in response to the contested 1800 election, in which Thomas Jefferson and Aaron Burr, actually running mates on the Democratic-Republican ticket, tied with seventy-three electoral votes. Electors at that time simply cast two votes, and all of the Democratic-Republican electors cast them for Jefferson and Burr. The Twelfth Amendment now requires that presidential and vice-presidential candidates be listed separately on the ballot.

Twentieth Amendment (1933): Provides that the president's term ends at noon on the twentieth day of January, meaning that there are slightly more than two months between a presidential election and inauguration. The amendment also was a first attempt at dealing with presidential succession.

Twenty-Second Amendment (1951): Enacted in response to Franklin Roosevelt's four elections, this amendment limits a person to two elected terms in office. If filling an unexpired term, a person may be elected only once more if he serves more than two years of the unexpired term.

Twenty-Third Amendment (1961): Provided the District of Columbia with three electoral votes for president, bringing the total to the current 538.

Twenth-Fifth Amendment (1967): Following the assassination of President Kennedy, the nation grew concerned about issues relating to presidential disability and succession. The Twenty-Fifth Amendment clarified that the vice president succeeds the president and that, most significantly, a vacancy in the vice presidency must be filled by a presidential nomination and confirmation by both Houses of Congress. The amendment also laid out procedures for dealing with a disabled president and clarified presidential succession. Along with the Presidential Succession Act of 1947, the amendment makes possible the following succession: Vice President; Speaker of the House; President Pro Tempore of the Senate; and then the cabinet secretaries in order of the date their department was established. The first four, in order, are State, Treasury, Defense, and Attorney General.

In current terms, that means 50-percent-plus-1 of the 538 electoral votes (435 Representatives + 100 Senators + 3 District of Columbia), or 270.

All states except Nebraska and Maine award all electoral votes to the candidate winning the most popular votes in the state. The two exceptions assign two electoral votes on a statewide basis and the others by congressional districts. As a result, a candidate winning a majority of electoral votes and, thereby, the presidency, may quite possibly receive fewer popular votes nationwide than his opponent. That legally insignificant result actually occurred in the elections of 1876, 1888, and 2000. Finally, should no candidate receive a majority of electoral votes, the election of the president moves to the House of Representatives and that of vice president to the Senate (see Brief 5.2).

REMOVING THE PRESIDENT

The Constitution states in Article II, Section 4, that "The President, Vice President and all civil Officers of the United States, shall be removed from Office on Impeachment for, and Conviction of, Treason, Bribery, or other high Crimes and Misdemeanors." Since the impeachment function falls to Congress, detailed coverage of the matter is reserved until Chapter 6. However, several points require brief mention.

Impeachment is strictly a political remedy for wrongdoing by a president. Impeachment and conviction carry no civil or criminal penalties—they simply remove the individual from office. Of course, impeachment does have implications: an impeached and convicted president likely would not fare well in the eyes of history and, more practically, an impeached and convicted president would not be entitled to a pension.

Only two sitting presidents (Andrew Johnson and William Clinton) have actually been impeached, and neither was convicted and removed from office. One president (Nixon) resigned from office, probably just a matter of time before impeachment. Eight presidents have died in office: William Henry Harrison, Zachary Taylor, Warren Harding, and Franklin Roosevelt died of natural causes; Abraham Lincoln, James Garfield, William McKinley, and John F. Kennedy were assassinated. The discussion now turns to the heart of Article II, the powers of the president.

PRESIDENTIAL POWERS: THEORY AND PRACTICE

As noted in Chapter 2, those who drafted the U.S. Constitution had real concerns about the exercise of executive power. They first considered a plan that

ANATOMY OF THE 2012 PRESIDENTIAL ELECTION

On November 6, 2012, the nation reelected Barack Obama to be President of the United States. President Obama received 62,610,717 popular votes, or 50.6 percent, while his challenger, Republican Mitt Romney, received 59,367,717 votes, or 47.8 percent of the total. This relatively close popular vote margin translated into a fairly substantial electoral vote margin. President Obama won twenty-six states plus the District of Columbia for a total of 332 electoral votes, while Governor Romney won twenty-four states for 206 electoral votes (270 votes are required to win).

Americans turned out in record numbers throughout the nation, but the election essentially came down to a handful of so-called "swing states," in which the outcome was in doubt. As the nation watched the returns come in from Colorado, Florida, Iowa, Nevada, North Carolina, Ohio, Virginia, and Wisconsin, the outcome quickly ceased to be in doubt. President Obama prevailed in all of the "swing" states except North Carolina, and Governor Romney offered a concession speech. Observers pointed to the fact that the 2012 presidential election undoubtedly ranks as the most expensive election in American history, largely because of the effect of the Supreme Court's ruling in the *Citizens United v. FEC* decision, to be discussed later in this book. That ruling essentially lifted all restrictions against campaign spending by corporations and labor unions, and enabled wealthy donors to collectively spend an estimated $6 billion.

At the end of the election cycle, very little had changed in American government. The House of Representatives remained in the hands of the Republicans, with 233 seats to 195 for the Democrats. The United States Senate results gave Democrats fifty-three seats, Republicans forty-five seats, and two independents who are expected to caucus with the majority. In all, after three presidential debates and one vice-presidential debate, more than $6 billion in expenditures, and months and months of campaigning, the nation's politics looked remarkably similar to the preelection situation: President Obama working with a democratic Senate and a republican House—more divided government.

would have made the executive subordinate to the national legislature. Fortunately, the final draft opted for a more balanced system in which powers were to be shared by the president and Congress. When they drafted Article II dealing with the executive, they recognized certain basic things that they wanted to attain in the office of president: strong national leadership, an effective diplomat in foreign affairs, command of the nation's military forces, and administrative skill in implementing the nation's laws. Unlike Article I of the Constitution, which is quite specific in enumerating the several powers of Congress, Article II is more general in its explanation of the above-mentioned powers of the president. Whether it was their preoccupation with legislative authority, a naive faith that chief executives would always act responsibly, or their sense of urgency in finishing their work at the Convention, the precise shape and scope of presidential authority would eventually be shaped not by the confines of Article II but by the character of American presidents and the needs of the American political experience.

CONTRASTING THEORIES OF EXECUTIVE POWER

Article II of the Constitution dealing with the executive describes very briefly the powers of the president, which mainly focus on the key roles of commander-in-chief, chief executive, legislative leader, and chief diplomat (see Brief 5.3).

Although it is not mentioned in Article II of the Constitution, the president's powers with respect to legislative leadership are significantly defined by his power to veto legislation (defined in Article I, Section 7) passed by Congress, subject to an override if both houses can amass a two-thirds vote.

Debate has raged for many decades over the question of what precisely Article II of the Constitution allows for in terms of presidential power. Some have argued that the article allows the president to function in any area not specifically delegated to Congress or the judiciary. Others have contended that the relatively short list of formal powers mentioned in Article II suggests that the framers desired a more limited role for the president.[7] In other words, does Article II comprise a complete or a partial delineation of presidential power? There is little doubt that the framers viewed Congress as the more active, energetic branch of government at times, and American experience throughout most of the nineteenth century certainly confirmed that expectation of the founders of the American system. As a recent account of presidential power argues, "... the role of the presidency in nineteenth century American political theory was essentially that of carrying out the will of Congress."[8] It is important to note that the administrations of Andrew Jackson and Abraham Lincoln were important exceptions. Jackson's somewhat unique attachment to the masses in an era of

---

Brief 5.3

THE PRESIDENT'S CONSTITUTIONAL POWERS: ARTICLE II

Commander-in-Chief: Section 2, Clause 1: "The President shall be commander in chief of the Army and Navy of the United States, and of the militia of the several States."

Chief Executive: Section 2, Clause 1: "He may require the opinion, in writing, of the principal officer in each of the departments, upon any subject relating to the duties of their respective offices,...."

> Section 2, Clause 2: "... and he shall have power to grant reprieves and pardons for offences against the United States, except in cases of impeachment."
>
> "[He] shall nominate, and by and with the advice and consent of the Senate, shall appoint ambassadors, other public ministers and consuls, judges of the Supreme Court, and all other officers of the United States...."
>
> Section 2, Clause 3: "The President shall have power to fill up all vacancies that may happen during the recess of the Senate, by granting commissions which shall expire at the end of the next session."

Legislative Leader: Section 3: "He shall from time to time give to the Congress information of the state of the Union, and recommend to their consideration such measures as he shall judge necessary and expedient...."

Chief Diplomat: Section 2: "He shall have Power, and with the Advice and Consent of the Senate, to make Treaties, provided two thirds of the Senators present concur...."

> Section 3: "He shall receive Ambassadors and other public Ministers; and he shall take Care that the Laws be faithfully executed, and shall Commission all the Officers of the United States."

growing democratization of the nation and his expansive view of the presidential office served to challenge Congress's dominance over policymaking at the time. With respect to Lincoln, the obvious threat of dissolution of the Union in the midst of dire civil conflict compelled him to act beyond the confines of Article II.

At the time of the American founding, the predominant view of presidential authority was one attributed to a few of the framers themselves. Although each had somewhat different views about the scope of executive power, Alexander Hamilton and James Madison each subscribed to what has for generations been referred to as the **constitutional** or **Whig theory** of executive authority, which prevailed throughout most of the nineteenth century. This view of presidential authority said that the president was limited to the exercise of those powers expressly granted in the constitution. According to this more limiting view of the office, the president has no implied power to deal with extraordinary national problems unless specifically authorized by a grant of power from Congress or the Constitution. Hamilton, as might be expected of one favoring a constitutional monarchy, was clearly unapologetic about the need for a vigorous chief executive, noting in *Federalist No. 70* that "[e]nergy in the executive is a leading character in the definition of good government." But he did note that executive power was "subject only to the exceptions and qualifications which are expressed in [the Constitution]."[9] To Madison, presidential powers outlined in Article II were complete in themselves and did not require any further expansion in time of crisis.[10] In support of this constitutional view of executive authority, William Howard Taft, one-time president and Supreme Court Chief Justice, maintained that presidential power is limited and traceable to specific grants of power either by the Constitution or Congress:

> [T]HE PRESIDENT CAN EXERCISE NO POWER WHICH CANNOT BE FAIRLY AND REASONABLY TRACED TO SOME SPECIFIC GRANT OF POWER OR JUSTLY IMPLIED AND INCLUDED WITHIN SUCH EXPRESS GRANT AS PROPER AND NECESSARY TO ITS EXERCISE. . . . THERE IS NO UNDEFINED RESIDUUM OF POWER WHICH HE CAN EXERCISE BECAUSE IT SEEMS TO HIM TO BE IN THE PUBLIC INTEREST.[11]

A different view of presidential power, usually referred as the **stewardship theory**, is more generous than this strict adherence to constitutional wording. This second perspective emerged early in the twentieth century as the nation struggled with major challenges both at home and abroad. This theory allows the president, as Teddy Roosevelt once said, "to do anything that the needs of the nation [demand] unless such action [is] forbidden by the Constitution or by the laws."[12] According to the stewardship theory, a president functions as a steward or trustee of the people. This enables the chief executive to do whatever may be necessary for the public good unless it is specifically forbidden by the Constitution or a federal law. According to this view of presidential power, the Oval Office becomes a "bully pulpit" from which a president uses all power and prestige associated with the office to inspire and mobilize the entire nation to take extraordinary steps to meet national challenges.[13] An important point of distinction between the constitutional and stewardship theories of executive power is that the former requires the president to adhere to specific grants of power in the Constitution, whereas the latter allows a president to act in time of national emergency unless specifically forbidden from doing so by law.

A third theoretical model of presidential power, known as **prerogative** (or more recently known as unitary executive) **theory,** reflects a view articulated centuries ago by John Locke, who described "prerogative" as "the power to act according to discretion for the public good, without the prescription of the law and sometimes even against it." With an eye on real experience and presidential actions, Harvard law professor Laurence Tribe noted recently: "It is only by an extraordinary triumph of constitutional imagination that the Commander in Chief is conceived as commanded by law."[14] Several challenges faced by the American people in both domestic and foreign policy areas have found several American presidents in the last century interpreting various Article II prescriptions, noted in Brief 5.2, in a very liberal fashion. Franklin Roosevelt is said to have endorsed prerogative theory through several of his actions as president in the 1930s and 1940s. His successor, Harry Truman, who observed that "[t]he power of the President should be used in the interest of the people and in order to do that, the President must use whatever power the Constitution does not expressly deny him."[15] This would seem to mirror the stewardship theory, although some of Truman's actions toward the end of his presidency, particularly the Steel Seizure Case in 1952, contain a heavy dose of the prerogative theory rationale.

The prerogative theory has been analyzed recently by Clement Fatovic, who argues persuasively that Alexander Hamilton and Thomas Jefferson had somewhat different conceptions of what has been termed presidential prerogative.[16] Whereas both admitted to presidents on occasion having to secure vital national ends that necessitated an extra-constitutional exercise of power, they disagreed about the ultimate source of justification for such power. Hamilton looked to the implied power of the Constitution, whereas Jefferson expected presidents to look to the people for plebiscitarian approval of presidential actions, if necessary after the fact. This distinction, as Fatovic argues, is particularly relevant to the problems encountered by presidents engaged in wartime decision making, some of which will be discussed later in this chapter.

As the remainder of this chapter reflects, how American presidents seek to explain and justify their actions is very important, at least if one is to have confidence in the rule of law and the integrity of constitutional government. Whereas the Constitution allows Congress and the president to share concurrent power in several areas of policymaking, political experience has revealed that this textbook rendition of separated powers does not always reflect reality in either domestic or foreign affairs. Congress has delegated extensive legislative authority to the executive branch in several areas of activity and, with few exceptions, the Supreme Court has generally endorsed this important development over the past several decades as both Congress and the executive branch have attempted to meet a multitude of domestic and international challenges. But as will become apparent in this and the next chapter, the gradual expansion in executive authority might raise some important questions about democratic accountability in a constitutional system. The discussion of evolving presidential power in the American system first turns to the issue of lawmaking authority as it is shared by Congress and the president.

PRESIDENT AS LEGISLATIVE LEADER

THE VETO POWER

The framers of the Constitution recognized the need for a strong executive, some even arguing for a president who could exercise an *absolute* veto over acts of Congress, thereby rejecting any legislative proposal, and have it be final. Fortunately, more moderate minds prevailed at the Constitutional Convention, including those of Benjamin Franklin and James Madison, the latter of whom argued strongly in *The Federalist* for a presidential check upon unbridled legislative power. In keeping with Madison's system of checks and balances, a qualified negative veto power was conceived at the Constitutional Convention. Although the president was given the authority to veto any legislation passed by Congress (with the exception of joint resolutions that propose constitutional amendments), Congress was given the authority to override presidential vetoes by a two-thirds vote in both houses. In retrospect, the true power of the presidential veto lies in Congress's historic inability to muster enough votes to override. Since 1789, of the 2,561 presidential vetoes that have occurred, only 108 have been overridden by Congress, with over two-thirds of that total coming in the twentieth century.[17] Since 1900, with the gradual expansion of presidential power, American presidents generally have had their vetoes sustained by Congress, as data in Table 5.2 indicate.

However, as Brief 5.4 reflects, recent attempts to expand presidential power over legislation through the use of a line-item veto were thwarted by a 1998 Supreme Court decision.

PROVIDING INFORMATION ON THE STATE OF THE UNION

President George Washington carried out his constitutional obligation to "give to the Congress Information on the State of the Union" when he did so in New York City in 1790. The practice of giving the presidential address before Congress ended with Thomas Jefferson, who simply sent a written report to be read in both Houses. That ended when Woodrow Wilson again appeared before Congress in 1913. The so-called "State of the Union Address" now is considered a regular part of the president's schedule

Table 5.2 Presidential Vetoes, 1900–2012

Years	President	Regular Vetoes	Pocket Vetoes	Total Vetoes	Vetoes Overridden
1901–1909	Theodore Roosevelt	42	40	82	1
1909–1913	William H. Taft	30	9	39	1
1913–1921	Woodrow Wilson	33	11	44	6
1921–1923	Warren G. Harding	5	1	6	0
1923–1929	Calvin Coolidge	20	30	50	4
1929–1933	Herbert Hoover	21	16	37	3
1933–1945	Franklin Roosevelt	372	263	635	9
1945–1953	Harry Truman	180	70	250	12
1953–1961	Dwight D. Eisenhower	73	108	181	2
1961–1963	John F. Kennedy	12	9	21	0
1963–1969	Lyndon B. Johnson	16	14	30	0
1969–1974	Richard M. Nixon	26	17	43	7
1974–1977	Gerald R. Ford	48	18	66	12
1977–1981	Jimmy Carter	13	18	31	2
1981–1989	Ronald Reagan	39	39	78	9
1989–1993	George H. W. Bush	29	15	44	1
1993–1997	Bill Clinton	36	1	37	2
2001–2008	George W. Bush	7	1	8	1
2009–	Barack Obama	2	0	2	0
	TOTALS	1,005	680	1,684	72 (4.3%)

SOURCES: James P. Pfiffner, *The Modern Presidency*, 3rd ed. (Boston: Bedford/St. Martin's Press, 2000), p. 134; Information Please Database, Pearson Education, 2005, www.infoplease.com/ipa; www.senate.gov/reference/Legislation/Vetoes/BushGW.htm; Lyn Ragsdale, *Vital Statistics on the Presidency*, 3rd ed. (Washington, DC: Congressional Quarterly Press, 2009), pp. 517–521. John Woolley and Gerhard Peters, The American Presidency Project, www.presidency.ucsb.edu/data/vetoes.php.

and is presented around the middle of January each year. Presidents typically take the opportunity to chronicle their administration's successes and lay out the broad outlines of their agenda. The State of the Union Address also allows the president to talk directly to the American people, and technology has made this much easier. President Calvin Coolidge's 1923 address was broadcast over the radio, and President Harry Truman's 1947 speech was the first on television. According to George Edwards and Stephen Wayne:

> ...[P]RESIDENTS HAVE TIMED THE ADDRESS TO MAXIMIZE ITS PUBLIC EXPOSURE, AND TODAY IT IS AN IMPORTANT VEHICLE BY WHICH PRESIDENTS CAN ARTICULATE THE LEGISLATIVE GOALS OF THEIR ADMINISTRATIONS, RECITE THEIR ACCOMPLISHMENTS, PRESENT THEIR AGENDAS, AND TRY TO MOBILIZE SUPPORT FOR THEIR PROGRAMS.[18]

President as Chief Executive

Appointment and Removal Powers

Presidents can also greatly influence both domestic and foreign policy through their power to appoint and remove public officials. As presidential power expanded greatly in the previous century, so did the size and complexity of the vast federal bureaucracy. What began in the 1790s with three departments and a handful of officers performing all diplomatic, economic, and national defense functions has now grown to include fifteen separate departments employing over four million civilian and military personnel (see Brief 5.5). Even with a modern civil service system

Brief 5.4

THE RISE AND FALL OF THE LINE-ITEM VETO

A key component of the legislative agenda of the Republican majority in Congress in 1995, and in fact the first item in the ten-point "Contract with America," was the so-called Fiscal Responsibility Act, which contained two key proposals considered essential to controlling government spending—a balanced-budget amendment and line-item veto authority for the president. The balanced-budget amendment passed the House on January 26, 1995, with the necessary two-thirds majority vote, 300–132, but it fell two votes short in the Senate in early February on a 65–35 vote (Majority Leader Robert Dole changed his vote to "no" to allow himself the opportunity under Senate rules to call for a revote later). Ultimately, the deciding "no" vote came from Senator Mark Hatfield (R-OR), chairman of the Senate Appropriations Committee, a long-time opponent of a balanced-budget amendment.

The other major component considered critical to curtailing runaway federal spending habits—the line-item veto power—met with a different fate, but it was only a temporary victory. Ultimately, different House–Senate versions of the bill were reconciled and President Clinton, a long-time advocate of the line-item veto, signed the bill into law on April 9, 1996. In signing the legislation that took effect in 1997, Clinton noted that "the line-item veto will give us a chance to . . . better represent the public interest by cutting waste, protecting taxpayers and balancing the budget." Under the process established in the legislation, after signing a spending bill, the president would send to Congress a separate message listing the spending measures that he opposes and wants rescinded. Those rescissions would automatically take effect unless Congress passed a bill overturning them. Members in Congress also would have the choice about whether to oppose all or some of the president's rescissions. In 1997, Clinton exercised the line-item veto to rewrite eleven public laws and eliminate eighty-two budgetary items.

On June 25, 1998, in a 6–3 decision (*Clinton v. City of New York*) that found Justice John Paul Stevens writing the majority opinion, the Supreme Court declared the entire line-item veto act unconstitutional. According to Justice Stevens, the act "authorizes the President himself to effect the repeal of laws, for his own political reasons, without observing the procedures set out in Article I, Section 7 [of the Constitution]." In a concurring opinion, Justice Anthony Kennedy wrote that the line-item veto "compromises the political liberty of our citizens" by concentrating power in the hands of the president. According to Kennedy, "liberty is always at stake when one or more of the branches seek to transgress the separation of powers."

SOURCES: Alison Mitchell, "With Ceremony, Clinton Signs a Line-Item Measure," *New York Times*, April 10, 1996, p. A10; Robert Pear, "Justices, 6–3, Bar Veto of Line Items in Bills," *New York Times*, June 26, 1998, pp. A1, 16. For a complete list of the eleven public laws and eighty-two budgetary line items affected by the Clinton vetoes prior to the ruling in *Clinton v. City of New York*, see Lyn Ragsdale, *Vital Statistics on the Presidency: Washington to Clinton*, Revised ed., (Washington, DC: Congressional Quarterly, 1998), p. 409.

---

that theoretically shields the federal bureaucracy from partisan politics, American presidents still normally appoint nearly 7,000 personnel during their term of office.

This power of appointment derives from the "appointments clause," as authorized by Article II, Section 2 of the Constitution:

> . . . AND HE SHALL NOMINATE, AND BY AND WITH THE ADVICE AND CONSENT OF THE SENATE, SHALL APPOINT AMBASSADORS, OTHER PUBLIC MINISTERS AND CONSULS, JUDGES OF THE SUPREME COURT, AND ALL OTHER OFFICERS OF THE UNITED STATES, WHOSE APPOINTMENTS ARE NOT HEREIN OTHERWISE PROVIDED FOR, AND WHICH SHALL BE ESTABLISHED BY LAW; BUT THE CONGRESS MAY BY LAW VEST THE APPOINTMENT OF SUCH INFERIOR OFFICERS, AS THEY THINK PROPER, IN THE PRESIDENT ALONE, IN THE COURTS OF LAW, OR IN THE HEADS OF DEPARTMENTS.

In practice, the appointment procedure has meant that presidents normally can determine the selection of most top-level government officials. However, because Congress creates the office, determines qualifications for holding that office, and funds the position through the normal appropriations process, it can also indirectly influence executive appointments. When Senate confirmation is required for offices created by law, the president nominates and the Senate confirms by majority vote. The tradition of "senatorial courtesy," which dates to the 1840s and can be critical to nominations to the federal judiciary, can also influence appointments to the executive branch.

Brief 5.5
THE EXECUTIVE BRANCH OF GOVERNMENT

As chief executive, the president is responsible for a myriad of departments, commissions, boards, bureaus, and other offices that populate the executive branch of government. While the president's cabinet is not specifically required by the Constitution—Article II, Section 2 says that the president "may require the Opinion, in writing, of the principal Officer in each of the executive Departments"—it has evolved over time. Starting with the departments of State, Treasury, and War (now Defense), along with an attorney general (Justice), the executive branch now includes these additional cabinet-rank departments: Interior, Agriculture, Commerce, Labor, Health and Human Services, Housing and Urban Development, Transportation, Energy, Education, Veterans Affairs, and Homeland Security.

The sprawling executive branch is also home to numerous independent regulatory commissions. Well-known entities such as the Federal Communications Commission, Federal Trade Commission, Consumer Product Safety Commission, Federal Election Commission, and Securities and Exchange Commission, among others, form the regulatory core of the federal government. While members of these agencies are appointed by the president and confirmed by the Senate, their terms are not tied to the political cycle, making them "independent" of the executive branch and Congress. See the discussion below concerning the difficulties involved in removing an independent member.

The federal government has also made increasing use of government corporations, which also fall under the executive branch. The first government corporation, the Tennessee Valley Authority, was formed to provide hydroelectric power and flood control for a large area of the country. Other government corporations that are expected to seek a "profit" in their operations include the Federal Deposit Insurance Corporation, which insures individual bank accounts; the National Railroad Passenger Corporation (Amtrak), which runs passenger rail travel across the country; the Pension Benefit Guaranty Corporation, which will be responsible for preventing insolvency among pension funds; and, perhaps best known, the United States Postal Service.

Finally, the Executive Office of the President contains eleven offices that are very closely tied to the administration in power: The White House Office, Office of the Vice President, Council of Economic Advisers, Council on Environmental Quality, National Security Council, Office of Administration, Office of Management and Budget, Office of National Drug Control Policy; Office of Policy Development; Office of Science and Technology Policy; and Office of the U.S. Trade Representative. Modern presidents have expanded the size of the Executive Office of the President to bring more policymaking and evaluation under their direct control. This has led on occasion to rivalries between the Executive Office Building and cabinet departments that feel left out.

Because the appointment process involves legislative and executive agreement, it is never without controversy (see Brief 5.6).

Whereas Article II, Section 2 is fairly clear about the *appointment* process governing various public officials, it is virtually silent about the *removal* of such personnel, other than through the difficult impeachment process governing certain high-level officials. As a result, much has had to be clarified through successive executive actions, legislative provisions, and judicial interpretations. One issue that had to be confronted was whether the removal of an executive official was purely an executive function, or whether the Senate, which must confirm these appointments, also had to be consulted. For several decades, Congress showed no interest in this matter, allowing presidents sole discretion to remove executive personnel. But in 1876, Congress passed amendments to the Tenure of Office Act prohibiting presidential removal of designated executive-level officials, including postmasters, unless approved by the Senate.

Following World War I, the Supreme Court finally decided to confront the issue of the removal of executive officials by the president and the constitutionality of the 1876 amendments to the Tenure of Office Act. In 1920 President Woodrow Wilson fired a postmaster in Oregon, Frank Myers, before his four-year term had expired. The disgruntled former employee claimed that under the 1876 amendments, his removal was illegal unless approved by two-thirds of the Senate. In *Myers v. United States* (1926), the Supreme Court held in a 6–3 judgment that the 1876 provision requiring Senate approval to remove executive officials was unconstitutional. In a very long majority opinion, Chief Justice William Howard Taft, himself a former president, argued that purely executive officials performing exclusively *executive* functions can be removed at the discretion of the president, without approval by the Senate. However, the

Brief 5.6

THE CONTROVERSY OVER "RECESS" APPOINTMENTS

Article II, Section 2, of the Constitution concludes with a provision that creates what are referred to as "recess" appointments:

> *The President shall have Power to fill up all vacancies that happen during the Recess of the Senate, by granting Commissions which shall expire of their next session.*

This clause allows presidents to fill vacancies when the Senate is in "recess," and it has been used since the 1820s. In 1921, President Harding's attorney general, Harry Daugherty, issued an opinion that said the president can make legal recess appointments when "there is a real and genuine recess making it impossible for him to receive the advice and consent of the Senate." This position, followed by all presidents of both parties since Harding, effectively says that a president determines when the Senate is in recess. Presidents have used this power to make recess appointments during short breaks in the Senate's schedule and not just the formal annual recess between sessions. As of early 2013, President Obama had made thirty-two such appointments, far fewer than his predecessors, George W. Bush (171) and Bill Clinton (139).

On January 25, 2013, a three-judge panel of the U.S. Court of Appeals for the District of Columbia Circuit held that one of President Obama's appointments to the National Labor Relations Board (NLRB) violated the Constitution because it was not made during the formal "recess" period. The case, *Noel Canning v. NLRB* (12-1115, 12-1153), rejected the administration's position and held that the Constitution's definition of "recess" is limited to the period between one session and the next. The ruling directly conflicts a 2004 decision by the 11th Circuit Court of Appeals, which upheld President Bush's recess appointment of a federal judge.

The ruling also casts doubt over the decisions made by the NLRB, other federal agencies, and even federal judges who were appointed through the procedure. Because the 2013 ruling conflicts with another circuit court decision, the issue may very well end up at the Supreme Court.

SOURCES: Charlie Savage and Steven Greenhouse, "Court Rejects Obama Move to Fill Posts," *New York Times*, January 25, 2013; Melanie Trottman, Jess Bravin, and Michael R. Crittenden, "Court Throws Out Recess Picks," *Wall Street Journal*, January 25, 2013; Tom Schoenberg, "Obama Picks Rejected as Court Casts Doubt on Recess Power," *Bloomberg News*, January 27, 2013.

---

decision did not answer whether that power can be limited by legislation or whether there are any distinctions between executive offices that affect removal authority. These matters were addressed in the case of *Humphrey's Executor v. United States* (1935).

Soon after assuming the presidency in 1933, Franklin Roosevelt asked William Humphrey to resign from the Federal Trade Commission on the grounds that administration policy could be better served by a commissioner of the president's own choosing. At the time, Humphrey had already been reconfirmed by the Senate to serve a second seven-year term that would not expire until 1938. Humphrey refused to resign, was fired, and soon thereafter, died. A suit was filed by the executor of his estate for back wages during the period between his forced resignation and his death.

A unanimous Court in 1935 ruled that the president did not have unlimited power to remove commissioners on independent regulatory commissions. In striking down Roosevelt's attempt to fire Humphrey, the justices reasoned that when Congress created regulatory bodies such as the Federal Trade Commission, it intended that the officers of such bodies should be independent of executive control. Congress also expected that the commissioners would serve a fixed term in office and that they could only be removed for cause. In denying Roosevelt's action, the majority interpreted very narrowly the *Myers* precedent by saying that public officials performing purely *executive* functions serve at the will of the president, and can be removed by him alone. But the *Humphrey* case was different from *Myers* in that the former performed certain *nonexecutive* functions and therefore could only be removed for neglect of duty or malfeasance in office. Roosevelt's claim that he wanted an FTC that agreed with his policy directions was an unconvincing rationale to a Supreme Court that saw the necessity for preserving independence from executive manipulation or intimidation. Officials performing quasi-legislative or quasi-judicial tasks can only be dismissed for cause, and not merely at the president's discretion.

PRESIDENTIAL POWER TO PARDON

One final area of some controversy involving the president's executive powers concerns the Article II, Section 2 provision dealing with reprieves and pardons. A reprieve postpones punishment, a commutation reduces the sentence or punishment, and a full pardon restores all civil rights to persons and revises their legal status in all respects. In most instances, American presidents have granted limited pardons, a practice upheld by the Supreme Court in *Schick v. Reed* (1974). Unchecked by any other branch of government, the president's authority to pardon anyone charged with federal crimes historically has been exercised with great restraint to correct an injustice or to further some larger societal good. The late Justice Oliver Wendell Holmes, Jr. once characterized the pardon power as reflecting a judgment that "the public welfare will be better served" by the granting of it. Presidents in recent decades have all used this power extensively during their time in office, as Table 5.3 indicates.

Table 5.3 Presidential Pardons, Truman–Obama

President	Time in Office	Party	Pardons Granted
Truman	1945–53	Democrat	1,913
Eisenhower	1953–61	Republican	1,110
Kennedy	1961–63	Democrat	472
Johnson	1963–69	Democrat	960
Nixon	1969–74	Republican	863
Ford	1974–77	Republican	382
Carter	1977–81	Democrat	534
Reagan	1981–89	Republican	393
Bush I	1989–93	Republican	74
Clinton	1993–2001	Democrat	396
Bush II	2001–09	Republican	189
Obama	2009–	Democrat	40*
TOTAL:			**7,326**

* As of March 2013.

SOURCES: U.S. Dept. of Justice, Office of the Pardon Attorney, "Presidential Clemency Actions by Administration 1945–2001," www.usdoj.gov/pardon/actions_administraiton.htm;

"How Presidential Pardons Work," http://people.howstuffworks.com/presidential-pardon.htm; Charlie Savage, "Obama Pardons 17 Felons, First in his Second Term, *New York Times*, March 1, 2013.

With respect to these data, a few explanations are necessary. First, presidents are customarily petitioned throughout their time in office to consider clemency or commutation of sentences for persons who have been convicted of a crime or are being pursued through legal channels. Frequently, personal solicitations for a reprieve or pardon can become especially feverish just prior to a president leaving office. Second, the sheer number of pardons does not necessarily indicate much about the amount of controversy that may surround individual actions by a president under his power to pardon. For example, although President Truman granted far more pardons than did any succeeding presidents, he also denied nearly 2,900 petitions out of a total of 5,030 petitions for either pardon, commutation, or remission of fine. Third, a president's length of time in office can have an obvious effect upon the number of solicitations that he might receive from friends and advisors to intercede on behalf of affected parties who desire to be pardoned. Considerable controversy has arisen in recent years about several aspects of this legitimate constitutional power of the American president (see Brief 5.7).

PRESIDENT AS CHIEF DIPLOMAT

TREATIES AND EXECUTIVE AGREEMENTS

The Constitution reflects the framers' preference for a careful partnership involving both Congress and the president performing unique roles in the negotiation and implementation of treaties with other nations. As noted in Brief 5.2, Article II, Section 2 of the Constitution stipulates that the president "shall have power, by and with the advice and consent of the Senate, to make treaties, provided two thirds of the Senators present concur." Article VI states that the Constitution, federal laws and federal treaties "shall be the supreme Law of the Land." This means that a treaty overrides any *state* law. The principle that federal laws supersede state laws was first reflected in *Missouri* v. *Holland* (1920). The Migratory Bird Treaty of 1916 between the United States and Canada protected the migration of wild birds. Missouri tried to block this protective legislation, claiming that the law and the treaty on which it was based interfered with the rights of the states. With only two justices dissenting, the Supreme Court

Brief 5.7

PARDON ME?: SOME CONTROVERSIAL PARDONS

During less than three years in office, President Gerald Ford granted 382 pardons, nearly as many as Ronald Reagan who served a full eight years in the White House. And one of those Ford pardons—that of Richard Nixon in September 1974 for alleged crimes committed during the Watergate scandal—may well have cost him the presidential election in 1976, indicating that this unilateral presidential power can occasionally have negative consequences for the president who wields it.

Before leaving the Oval Office in January 2001, President Bill Clinton considered scores of pardon petitions, ultimately granting 395 during his time in office. But clearly the most controversial one was that granted to Marc Rich, a shadowy former commodities trader who left the United States in the early 1980s to avoid charges involving federal tax fraud and trading oil with Iran during the American hostage crisis in 1979–80 when economic sanctions against that country were in place. The circumstances of the Rich pardon also prompted considerable condemnation from the American public, the mass media, and even some of the president's political allies and supporters following Clinton's departure from the presidency in 2001.

Time magazine published a list of "The 10 Most Notorious Presidential Pardons" in 2007, and both the Nixon and Rich pardons were included. The other eight provide a snapshot of the pardon power over more than two hundred years: George Washington's pardon of the participants in the 1794 Whiskey Rebellion; Andrew Johnson's 1865 pardon of Southerners in the Confederate States who took an oath of loyalty to the Union; Richard Nixon's pardon of labor leader Jimmy Hoffa in 1971; Jimmy Carter's 1977 pardon of draft dodgers who had fled the U.S. or not registered for the draft; Ronald Reagan's pardon of Mark Felt (a.k.a. Deep Throat) and Edward Miller in 1981 for illegal actions taken as FBI agents against Vietnam protesters; Ronald Reagan's pardon of New York Yankees' owner George Steinbrenner in 1989 for obstruction of justice and making illegal campaign contributions; George H. W. Bush's 1992 pardon of former Defense Secretary Caspar Weinberger and six other defendants for his role in the Iran-Contra affair; and Bill Clinton's 2001 pardon of Patty Hearst for her bank robbery conviction stemming from her kidnapping by the Symbionese Liberation Army in 1974. While most presidential pardons do not rise to the "notorious" level, they certainly provide controversy and consternation for many.

Source: Kristina Dell and Rebecca Myers, "The 10 Most Notorious Presidential Pardons," *Time*, 2007. www.time.com/time/specials/packages/completelist/0,29569,1862257,00.html<http://www.time.com/time/specials/packages/completelist/0,29569,1862257,00.html>

---

upheld the supremacy of the federal treaty-making authority over state power. Writing for the majority, Justice Oliver Wendell Holmes, Jr. implied that federal treaties were virtually synonymous with the Constitution itself and superior to federal laws: "Acts of Congress are the supreme law of the land only when made in pursuance of the Constitution, while treaties are declared to be so when under the authority of the United States."

wIn recent decades, the diplomacy partnership involving the president and the U.S. Senate concerning treaties involving the United States and foreign countries has changed dramatically. Since 1945, American presidents have increasingly sought to achieve their international goals through a device known as the **executive agreement**. It is not entirely clear what latitude a president has in concluding such a document. Because the Constitution says nothing about executive agreements, presidents since George Washington have acted in many instances without the necessary approval of two-thirds of the Senate. The use of executive agreements grew dramatically after World War II, with all presidents showing a preference for executive agreements over treaties by a ratio of at least 4:1.[19] Ironically, this increasing use of executive agreements by presidents to avoid the political battles accompanying Senate ratification of formal treaties ultimately led in 1985 to the State Department no longer distinguishing between formal treaties and executive agreements, All are now categorized as merely "international agreements."

The practice of using executive agreements was endorsed by the U.S. Supreme Court in *United States* v. *Belmont* (1937), where the justices held that "in the case of all international compacts and agreements. . . complete power over international affairs is in the national government and is not and cannot be subject to any curtailment or interference on the part of the several states." In a similar case a few years later, the Supreme Court recognized in *United States* v. *Pink* (1942) that executive agreements, like treaties, are considered the supreme law of the land and presidents have great latitude in using them in the conduct of foreign affairs, even though they are not subject to Senate approval.

During the 1950s, conservative Republicans tried to check the extensive presidential authority to make executive agreements. In 1953, Senator John Bricker (R-OH) introduced in Congress a proposed constitutional amendment that would have required senatorial approval of such agreements. The action was strongly opposed by many liberals and some prominent conservatives, including Secretary of State John Foster Dulles, who feared that, if ratified, the constitutional change would encourage a new era of isolationism with respect to American foreign policy.

An incident during the Carter administration raised the question of whether a president can terminate a treaty ratified by the Senate without first getting the Senate's approval to do so. President Carter announced in December 1978 that he was extending full diplomatic recognition to the Peoples' Republic of China and terminating a 1954 mutual defense treaty with Taiwan as of January 1, 1980, thereby ending formal recognition of the Republic of China (Taiwan). In support of this action, Congress soon thereafter passed legislation establishing "informal relations" with Taiwan. Senator Barry Goldwater (R-AZ) and twenty-four other members of Congress filed a suit contesting the president's right to unilaterally terminate the treaty. After conflicting decisions in lower courts that first opposed and then approved the Carter move, the Supreme Court ruled in *Goldwater v. Carter* (1979) that the matter involved a "political question" not susceptible to judicial resolution. Like the appellate court, the Supreme Court refused to rule on the constitutional issue of whether a president can independently terminate a Senate-ratified treaty. Absent a definitive ruling on this larger issue, there remains a "twilight zone" of respective presidential and congressional powers in this legal aspect of foreign affairs. Under such circumstances, presidential actions tend to prevail.

When Iranian revolutionaries seized the American embassy and held American diplomatic hostages in Tehran in November 1979, President Jimmy Carter froze all Iranian assets in the United States. A Los Angeles–based engineering firm, Dames and Moore, was one of many private creditors that sought access to several Iranian assets in the United States as settlement for outstanding debts owed by Iran. The company claimed that Iran owed it $3.7 million for services provided in the development of a nuclear power plant in Iran. As part of the eventual agreement ending the American hostage crisis, President Carter signed an executive order on January 19, 1981 (the last full day of his presidency) ordering that all assets be transferred to a bank in New York for return to Iran. The Supreme Court unanimously upheld President Carter's action over the claims dispute in *Dames & Moore v. Regan* (1981). The Court held that the Hostage Act of 1868, the International Claims Settlement Act of 1949, and the International Emergency Economic Powers Act of 1977 all reflected, in the words of Chief Justice William Rehnquist, broad support "for executive action in circumstances such as those presented in this case."

RECEIVING AMBASSADORS AND PUBLIC MINISTERS

U.S. presidents have complete authority to establish or terminate relations with other countries, a practice stemming from the Constitution's grant of power to "receive Ambassadors and other public ministers." Perhaps intended as largely a "ministerial" or routine function, this power has grown to allow a president to essentially determine with which countries the United States will interact. George Washington first used this power when he accepted the credentials of Citizen Genet in 1789, as the representative of the new French Republic. President Washington later revoked Genet's credentials, thereby establishing that practice as well.

While accepting the credentials of a foreign ambassador is generally routine, the practice at times can be very controversial. After taking office in 1933, President Franklin Roosevelt announced that he was recognizing the government of the Soviet Union some fifteen years after the Soviet Union had replaced the old tsarist regime. The American distrust and dislike of communism had prevented earlier presidents from taking this controversial but realistic step. Similarly, when Mao Zedong and his Red Army swept into Beijing in 1949 and established the People's Republic of China, U.S. leaders were not willing to recognize his government.

For the next thirty years, the United States considered the Republic of China, located on the island of Taiwan, to represent the true government of China. President Jimmy Carter's 1979 decision to recognize the Beijing government drew heated protests from some in Congress, but the decision was the president's alone (see *Goldwater v. Carter*, above). Finally, Ronald Reagan took a controversial step when he announced in 1984 that the U.S. would resume formal diplomatic relations with the Vatican. The United States still does not have formal ties to Cuba as a result of President Eisenhower's reaction to the communist takeover by Fidel Castro and his followers. But occasionally presidents take small steps that stop short of actual recognition, as President Obama did in his recent reversal of the travel ban to Cuba.

PRESIDENT AS COMMANDER IN CHIEF
EXECUTIVE WAR POWER AND NATIONAL EMERGENCIES

Because major wars and foreign policy crises customarily require focused leadership and decisive action, sufficient time rarely exists for members of Congress and the president to consult at great length about what should be done to resolve these crises. In a letter to Thomas Jefferson in 1798 that was both prophetic and ironic, James Madison observed:

> THE CONSTITUTION SUPPOSES WHAT THE HISTORY OF ALL GOVERNMENTS DEMONSTRATES, THAT THE EXECUTIVE IS THE BRANCH OF POWER MOST INTERESTED IN WAR, AND MOST PRONE TO IT. IT HAS ACCORDINGLY WITH STUDIED CARE VESTED THE QUESTION OF WAR IN THE LEGISLATURE.[20]

For more than two centuries a periodic struggle between Congress and the president over which institution has preeminent power to act in time of national emergency has been apparent. Potential confrontations actually were anticipated at the Constitutional Convention in 1787. After some debate, delegates in Philadelphia finally gave to Congress the power "to declare war" in Article I, Section 8. Although they recognized that the president as commander-in-chief might need significant power to repel attacks upon American territory, they also insisted that the nation needed to be protected against unrestrained presidential power to wage war. The result was that the warmaking power envisioned in the Constitution was to be a shared power: whereas the president was to oversee all military operations as commander-in-chief (Article II), Congress would have the power to "raise and support Armies . . . [t]o provide and maintain a Navy, . . . [and] to provide for calling forth the Militia to execute the Laws of the Union, suppress Insurrections and repel Invasions" (Article I, Section 8).

Columnist William Safire identified at least two hundred instances in which the United States used armed force abroad to protect persons and property, and in only a few of these did the action involve a declared war.[21] In only five separate instances in American history—the War of 1812, the War with Mexico (1846–48), the Spanish-American War of 1898, and the two global wars of the last century—did Congress actually declare war. Every president from Theodore Roosevelt to Barack Obama has ordered military troops into real or potentially hostile situations without active congressional debate and with little or no prior notification. The half-century following World War II yielded many examples of largely unilateral presidential activity. President Truman's use of American troops on the Italian–Yugoslav border in 1946 and in Nanking/Shanghai, China in 1948–49, as well as President Eisenhower's use of troops in the 1956 Suez Crisis and in Lebanon in 1958, reflect four instances where an American president acted unilaterally to resolve perceived threats to strategic American interests overseas. President Johnson's movement of military force into the Dominican Republic in 1965, President Nixon's dispatching American troops to Cambodia in 1970 and Laos in 1971, the invasion of Grenada by American troops in 1983, the use of American forces in Panama in 1989 against the Noriega regime, and the ouster of Saddam Hussein from Kuwait in 1991, stand as additional examples of presidents using military force with the passive acquiescence of Congress. Although such actions may have been taken to achieve larger, less publicized geopolitical objectives, they were all justified at the time by the president telling the American people that vital national interests were at stake.

In the past, the only constraints upon the president's power to use military force to protect American interests have rested with either Congress or the courts, and neither has been especially anxious or effective in restraining a president who sees an immediate need for firmness and resolve, whether it be diplomatic or military. Even the most costly war in American history—the Civil War—was an internal conflict over different interpretations of ultimate sovereignty under the Constitution. Since 1789, American presidents have enjoyed great latitude in acting to protect the nation's vital interests, suggesting that such action is a practical necessity, not a mere constitutional formality. Though bound by the written law in several instances, presidents have usually acted under the mandate of national self-preservation and let history sort out whether their actions were legitimate.

Presidential power in times of national emergency or war has been recognized by Congress and the courts on many occasions, but it is not always clear precisely whether extraordinary powers of the president can be activated, or when war actually exists. More specifically, what executive war powers a president can use without a formal declaration of war is not clear. These important questions first arose immediately following the 1860 presidential election. Just prior to President Lincoln's inauguration in March 1861, several southern states seceded from the Union and Lincoln acted unilaterally, declaring the Confederate states to be in a condition of rebellion, ordering various military actions as commander-in-chief to protect federal forces and interests, and prescribing several punishments for illegal actions taken against federal law. Among other actions, Lincoln announced a military blockade of Southern ports and ordered the seizure of all ships doing business with the Confederacy following the attack upon Fort Sumter in April 1861. Lincoln justified his actions on the basis of his inherent executive power and various federal laws, all of which he felt had delegated certain war powers to the president.

Writing for a divided Supreme Court, Justice Robert Grier recognized in The Prize Cases (1863) an inherent executive power to repel an invasion or armed rebellion without first seeking congressional approval, and the right to impose a naval blockade. Applying somewhat circular reasoning, Justice Grier said that the blockade was itself "official and exclusive evidence that . . . a state of war existed which demanded and authorized a recourse to such a measure." Concerning whether the president was authorized to seize private property on the high seas, the Court said that in doing business with any one of the belligerents in a recognized civil war, private parties run the risk of federal power being used to defeat the rebellious states. As Grier observed, ". . . a civil war such as that now waged between the Northern and Southern states is properly conducted according to the humane regulations of public law as regards capture on the ocean." Four justices in dissent thought that Lincoln's actions were beyond his executive authority, that previous congressional acts did not authorize him to wage war against an individual state, and that confiscation of private property was clearly beyond his delegated power. Given the constitutional crisis of both that moment and the next four years, their views carried little force.

INHERENT POWERS IN THE TWENTIETH CENTURY

Inherent powers of the president in foreign affairs can be traced, in part, to Alexander Hamilton's claim in *Federalist No. 23*, that the powers to care for the common defense "ought to exist without limitation." Nearly 150 years later, with the precedent forged in The Prize Cases as a backdrop, the Supreme Court wrote the inherent theory into constitutional law with its landmark ruling in *United States v. Curtiss-Wright Export Corporation* (1936). This case involved a congressional joint resolution that authorized President Franklin Roosevelt to forbid American arms sales to Bolivia if, in his opinion, the sale of such arms would likely prolong hostilities between that country and its neighbor, Paraguay. Curtiss-Wright Export Corporation tried to sell arms to Bolivia despite an embargo ordered by Roosevelt. The question before the Supreme Court in 1936 was whether the congressional resolution constituted an illegal delegation of legislative authority to the president.

A seven-member Court majority said that the president had acted within his constitutional authority when implementing the congressional resolution. Writing for the majority, Justice George Sutherland, a long-time critic during the 1930s of congressional delegation of legislative authority to the executive branch, distinguished in his opinion for the Court between foreign and domestic affairs:

> THE TWO CLASSES OF POWERS ARE DIFFERENT, BOTH IN RESPECT OF THEIR ORIGIN AND THEIR NATURE. THE BROAD STATEMENT THAT THE FEDERAL GOVERNMENT CAN EXERCISE NO POWERS EXCEPT THOSE SPECIFICALLY ENUMERATED IN THE CONSTITUTION . . . IS CATEGORICALLY TRUE ONLY IN RESPECT OF OUR INTERNAL AFFAIRS. [EMPHASIS ADDED]

Sutherland maintained that when the new Constitution in 1787–88 allocated power to the national and state governments, it only did so with respect to domestic affairs. With respect to foreign affairs, the national government retained all power and prerogatives inherited from the British Crown. Sutherland further argued that executive power in foreign affairs may extend beyond the letter of the Constitution. He reasoned that to avoid embarrassment and possible damage to American interests in foreign affairs, Congress ". . . must accord to the President a degree of discretion and freedom from statutory restriction which would not be admissible were domestic affairs alone involved." National sovereignty implies that the power to formulate foreign policy must lie only with the national government, and practical necessities require that the president be the primary policymaker in this area. According to Sutherland:

> [I]T IS IMPORTANT TO BEAR IN MIND THAT WE ARE HERE DEALING NOT ALONE WITH AN AUTHORITY VESTED IN THE PRESIDENT BY AN EXERTION OF LEGISLATIVE POWER, BUT WITH SUCH AN AUTHORITY PLUS THE VERY DELICATE, PLENARY AND EXCLUSIVE POWER OF THE PRESIDENT AS THE SOLE ORGAN OF THE FEDERAL GOVERNMENT IN . . . INTERNATIONAL RELATIONS.

Within a few years, a far more treacherous time in the nation's history tested the ability of the same president to use executive war power to provide for the common defense even when it seriously threatened important civil liberties of American citizens.

WORLD WAR II AND THE INTERNMENT OF JAPANESE-AMERICANS

Following the Japanese attack on Pearl Harbor on December 7, 1941, and the subsequent declaration of war by Congress marking American entry into World War II, the federal government took various actions against persons suspected of possible disloyalty to and treasonous activity against the United States. A series of executive orders issued by President Franklin Roosevelt in early 1942, and quickly endorsed by Congress, imposed a curfew on all persons of Japanese descent and excluded them from militarily sensitive areas on the West Coast. Congress also authorized the forced relocation of these racial minorities into detention camps in several American states.

In two famous cases decided in the midst of this declared war, the Supreme Court sanctioned, in effect, racial discrimination on grounds of national security. In *Hirabayashi v. United States* (1943), the Court upheld the constitutionality of the curfew order authorized by Roosevelt. Speaking through Chief Justice Harlan Stone, a unanimous Court said that the order was entirely within both executive and congressional powers due to the grave national emergency and the "critical military situation" that existed. One year after *Hirabayashi*, a more divided Court upheld the military exclusion orders in the case of *Korematsu v. United States* (1944). Echoing the same rationale used in the previous decision, Justice Hugo Black recognized that Congress and the president had the authority in wartime to segregate those who might pose "a menace to the national defense and safety." To those who argued that such action occasioned excessive sacrifice from a small, defenseless minority, Black wrote that "[h]ardships are part of war, and war is an aggregation of hardships." When threatened by hostile forces, "the power to protect must be commensurate with the threatened danger," and therefore, the actions were legal. In dissent, Justice Frank Murphy characterized the military exclusions as falling within the "ugly abyss of racism," and Justice Robert Jackson questioned the reasonableness of the military order, the credibility of the chief military officer imposing it, and, especially, the legal precedent established by the Court's upholding the president's authority.

Korematsu is significant for at least three reasons. First, in upholding the federal actions against the internees, the Court for the first time referred to race as a "suspect" classification that demanded close scrutiny of a discriminatory law. Second, despite Justice Black's insistence to the contrary, the Court implicitly endorsed here the idea that racial minorities could be denied basic rights on grounds of military necessity and national emergency. Finally, it should be noted that the Supreme Court in *Hirabayashi* and *Korematsu* never reached the question of whether the relocation centers were themselves unconstitutional. It only dealt with the constitutionality of the specific curfews and the military exclusion orders in these two cases. Vindication of minority citizens' rights occurred decades later, when a federal appellate court in California in 1983 overturned the conviction of Fred Korematsu, and congressional hearings were held to consider whether federal compensation was due to Japanese Americans (see Brief 5.8).

THE KOREAN WAR AND THE STEEL SEIZURE CASE

One of the earliest conflicts after World War II in which the United States became involved as it confronted the Soviet Union was the Korean War (1950–53). When communist North Korea invaded non-communist South Korea in 1950, it ignited American fears of a possible communist takeover of an embattled ally in the Far East. Believing that the invasion forecast communist domination in Asia, President Harry Truman immediately sent American troops to South Korea under the auspices of the United Nations. Whatever the political and strategic merits of Truman's actions, they rested upon unclear and untested domestic and international legal grounds, since Congress never formally declared war in the Korean conflict.

The Korean War came at a time when the country was involved in both a protracted labor dispute in the steel industry and a volatile political climate involving an unpopular president and a tense public expecting political change. Unable to win a satisfactory contract

A NATION STRUGGLES WITH ITS CONSCIENCE

Following the Japanese attack on Pearl Harbor in 1941, President Franklin Roosevelt issued an executive order that affected 77,000 Japanese American citizens and 43,000 legal and illegal resident aliens of Japanese descent. These people were uprooted from their homes and businesses and forced into detention centers for the duration of the war. Decades after the last camp was closed in 1946, the United States slowly began to reexamine the actions of civilian and military officials at the time. By early 1988, both houses of Congress had debated and finally passed bills that sought to compensate survivors of the Japanese internment program. Among the several Senate sponsors of the legislation were two Democratic senators from Hawaii, Spark M. Matsunaga and Daniel K. Inouye, both of whom had fought for the United States Army in the European theater.

In commenting upon the legislation, Senator Matsunaga stated in debate that "a stigma has haunted Japanese Americans for the past 45 years. We are seeking Congressional action to remove that cloud over their heads." Another co-sponsor of the bill, Senator Ted Stevens (R-AK) said that the internees were "people who had done no wrong at all." Senator Orrin Hatch, a Republican senator from Utah, indicated his support for the compensation order by echoing Stevens, saying, "it is clear that these citizens were denied their constitutional right of due process."[22] The House and Senate worked during the summer in conference committee to reconcile different versions of the legislation. The Reagan administration finally agreed to support the conference bill, after initially insisting upon payments being made only to actual survivors of the internment. In a much publicized ceremony on August 10, 1988 (forty-three years and one day after the dropping of an atomic bomb on Nagasaki, Japan, in effect ending the war), President Reagan signed the conference bill. Referring to the internment program as a "mistake" and to the legislation as essential to "right a grave wrong," the president closed a tragic and unjust chapter in American history. Under the legislation signed into law by Reagan, a $1.25 billion trust fund for some 60,000 eligible internees and designated beneficiaries of deceased internees was established. As President Reagan observed at the signing ceremony, "no payment can make up for those lost years," in part because the purpose of the legislation and compensation "has less to do with property than with honor."[23]

from the various steel companies, the United Steelworkers of America threatened in early 1951 to walk out of contract talks, institute a labor strike, and close down the vital U.S. steel industry. President Truman argued that such action might seriously jeopardize the nation's military preparedness and its ability to defend its interests in the ongoing Korean conflict. After direct mediation efforts by the federal government failed to resolve the dispute, he eventually ordered his secretary of commerce to seize control of the steel mills and keep them open and operating in order to produce a vital national industrial resource needed in wartime. At issue in the Steel Seizure Case, formally known as *Youngstown Sheet & Tube v. Sawyer* (1952), was whether the president had the inherent right to invoke emergency powers as commander-in-chief in order to seize private property without prior congressional approval.

In the decision, Justice Black's majority opinion for the Court concluded that the president's actions were unjustified and illegal. For Truman's actions to prevail in this instance, he had to be able to point to some provision of the Constitution under his power as commander-in-chief or to some congressional delegation of authority condoning the action. Just because presidents are responsible for faithfully executing the laws, said Justice Black, does not mean that they are able to make the laws themselves. As participants in the lawmaking process, presidents are limited to recommending laws they think prudent and vetoing those they think unwise. As Black and the Court majority viewed it, "the Constitution is neither silent nor equivocal about who shall make laws which the President is to execute." That is purely a *legislative* function in which the president has an important but limited role.

In a separate concurring opinion in the Steel Seizure Case, Justice Robert Jackson stated that presidential power relies upon three sources of legitimacy: (1) if acting in response to an expressed or implied authorization by Congress, that power is at its maximum; (2) if acting without either congressional authorization or a denial of authority, a "zone of twilight" exists wherein both the president and Congress may have *concurrent* authority; and finally, (3) if a president acts against the expressed or implied will of Congress, presidential power "is at the lowest ebb." But even then, presidents may be able to rely upon some constitutional power they possess alone or with Congress. Jackson viewed Truman's actions as clearly falling within the third category and therefore, it was illegal because they were contrary to the expressed will of the Congress as provided for in the Taft-Hartley Act of 1947. As Jackson noted in closing, "With all its defects, delays, and inconvenience, men have discovered no technique for long preserving free government except that the Executive be under the law." This important principle involving the rule of law was reinforced many years later when other American presidents claimed special powers of their office in time of national crisis.[24]

THE VIETNAM WAR

In the early 1950s, as the French colonial empire in Southeast Asia was disintegrating, the United States was petitioned by France to help forestall the defeat of French military forces in Indochina (what now is Laos, Cambodia, and Vietnam). After France withdrew from the region in 1953 following its military defeat at Dienbienphu, the United States eventually found itself under four different administrations drawn deeper into the region, presumably to protect vital American interests. However, the major escalation of the conflict and American involvement in it occurred during the Johnson and Nixon administrations in the mid-1960s and early 1970s as the insurgency from North Vietnam grew more ferocious and the challenge more consuming. When the United States finally left Vietnam in 1973, the nation had suffered more than 58,000 combat deaths, years of increased doubts about the proclaimed mission and the rightness of the cause, massive public protests to end American involvement, and lingering public distrust and cynicism about national leadership.

Following an alleged, provocative attack by North Vietnamese torpedo boats against two American warships in the Gulf of Tonkin, President Lyndon Johnson asked Congress for enlarged power to defend American forces and to protect national interests. With only two dissenting votes, the U.S. Senate passed the Tonkin Gulf Resolution on August 10, 1964, which stated that "the United States is . . . prepared, as the President determines, to take all necessary steps, including the use of armed force . . . to repel any armed attack against the forces of the United States and to prevent any further aggression." Throughout the remainder of his presidency, Johnson relied upon this resolution to have legitimized subsequent American operations in Vietnam, including the saturation bombing of North Vietnam and a massive buildup of some 550,000 American combat troops in the region by the late 1960s. As military involvement increased and the chance of a clear military and political victory declined by 1967–68, members of Congress grew increasingly critical of the war and claimed that they had been manipulated by President Johnson to support unilateral, unauthorized executive actions in Southeast Asia. Public and congressional protest against the war eventually persuaded Johnson not to seek the Democratic nomination for president in 1968, which paved the way for another American president to rescue a flawed strategy for victory in the region.

Efforts by Congress to limit executive warmaking activities in Southeast Asia were greatly accelerated in 1970, when President Nixon advanced the familiar claim of protecting American forces overseas. In an effort to search for regular and guerrilla forces from North Vietnam seeking sanctuary outside South Vietnam in 1969–70, he extended American military operations into Cambodia without first consulting with Congress. The operation had only limited success and led to the Cooper-Church Amendment in 1970, which prohibited the use of funds for American combat forces in Laos, Thailand, and Cambodia. Convinced that it had been manipulated long enough, Congress voted in 1971 to repeal the Tonkin Gulf Resolution, although it had more symbolic than real effect in constraining presidential actions in Southeast Asia. Two more years would be needed to negotiate a treaty with North Vietnam and four years to remove all American personnel from South Vietnam. Unfortunately, the Vietnam experience had important consequences both at home and abroad.

An important development paralleling the growing public and congressional criticisms of the war in Southeast Asia was the role played by federal courts in addressing the legality of presidential actions in the war. As American casualties in Vietnam mounted in the late 1960s, without any formal declaration of war by Congress, the Supreme Court was frequently petitioned to rule on the constitutionality of the war, but it always declined to do so. In *Mitchell v. United States* (1967), the Supreme Court refused to hear a case involving an individual who had been sentenced to a five-year prison term for failing to report for induction into the armed forces. In *Mara v. McNamara* (1967), the Court again refused to intervene in the controversy, this time in a case involving three Army privates who were protesting their reassignment to South Vietnam on the grounds that it was an illegal war. One year later, in *Holmes v. United States* (1968), the Court refused to rule on the constitutionality of the draft in the absence of a formal declaration of war by Congress. The Court declined another opportunity to address the constitutionality of the war in what was probably the most prominent Vietnam-era case, *Massachusetts v. Laird* (1970). In all these instances, the justices followed the de facto precedent of not interfering when American presidents exercised their power as commander-in-chief in times of suspected national crisis or to defend national interests and security at home and abroad.

Congressional resolve to constrain executive war power finally emerged in 1973 with the enactment of the War Powers Resolution (see Brief 5.9). Events of the past three decades have convinced many that the legislation is seriously flawed, and the growing political debate surrounding the American invasion in Iraq in 2003 eventually prompted a commission in 2008 (discussed in Chapter 6) to propose recommendations for resolving the impasse between Congress and the White House over executive war power.

The War Powers Resolution has never worked as it was intended by its defenders, and much evidence suggests that it is more form than substance. Although it was invoked in 1975, during the brief action to free the American merchant ship USS *Mayaguez* that had been captured by the Cambodians, and again in 1982, when American troops were sent to Lebanon, the legislation has largely been dismissed by most American presidents as both unconstitutional and impractical. Every president since 1973 has considered the act to be an encroachment upon executive authority as commander-in-chief, and with the exception of President Ford in the *Mayaguez* seizure, none has officially complied with it. They consider Section 5(b) of the act requiring the withdrawal of troops within 60 days (unless Congress declares war or authorizes continuation of the commitment) to be both impractical for presidents trying to manage a crisis and an infringement upon the powers of the chief executive (see Brief 5.10).

Brief 5.9
THE WAR POWERS RESOLUTION

After many years of growing frustration with both the Johnson and Nixon administrations over the direction, justification, and costs of the Vietnam War, including extensive hearings and floor actions about executive actions in the war, members of Congress finally passed Public Law 93-148, known as the War Powers Resolution. The legislation was vetoed by President Richard Nixon, who at the time was locked in a protracted struggle involving the Watergate scandal (coverage to follow in Chapter 6), whose veto was overridden by a two-thirds vote in the House and Senate. The law had one primary purpose as stated in Section 2 (a):

> "... to fulfill the intent of the framers of the Constitution of the United States and insure that the collective judgment of both the Congress and the President will apply to the introduction of United States Armed Forces into hostilities or ... imminent involvement of hostilities...."

The legislation envisioned three main functions: presidential consultation with Congress; presidential reports to Congress; and congressional termination of military action. The act provides in Section 2 (c) that the president can commit American troops to overseas action under only three conditions: a formal declaration of war by Congress; with congressional authorization of such deployment in the absence of declared war; or an enemy attack upon the United States or its forces that creates a national emergency. The act further requires in Section 4 (a) (3) that the president report the deployment of combat troops to Congress within 48 hours. Unless Congress declares war against the aggressor state, American forces must be withdrawn from hostilities within 60 days in accordance with Section 5 (b), although an additional thirty-day period can be granted to the president before the withdrawal of American troops. After ninety days, all troops must be withdrawn at the insistence of both houses of Congress as required by Section 5 (c), and the president cannot veto such a directive.

Critics of the law maintain that the legislation severely restricts presidents in their capacity to deal responsibly with crisis situations. They also insist that Congress is poorly organized institutionally to deal with such situations and that most members have insufficient time, capability, and expertise to respond effectively and efficiently when such crises occur. These critics also argue that having the legal power to restrain an activist president in foreign affairs is not the same as having the necessary political will to invoke provisions of the law and to make difficult decisions about war and peace. Supporters of the War Powers Resolution have argued just as strongly that American presidents for too long have made major decisions affecting the lives and fortunes of the American citizens without adequately consulting with members of Congress. They insist that the legislation is necessary to restore some balance and interbranch deliberation between two major policymaking institutions, each of which is charged with protecting vital national interests.

Brief 5.10
PRESIDENTIAL WAR POWER AND THE PERSIAN GULF CONFLICT

When Iraq invaded Kuwait on August 2, 1990, some legal questions soon arose over how much President George H. W. Bush had to consult with Congress before committing American troops to the allied effort to oust Saddam Hussein from Kuwait. One issue was the relevance of the War Powers Resolution and its requirement that the president report to Congress within 48 hours after American forces are introduced "into hostilities or into situations where imminent involvement in hostilities is clearly indicated by the circumstances."

On October 1, 1990, the House of Representatives voted 380 to 29 in favor of a resolution supporting U.S. military deployment in the Gulf region. Two days later the Senate voted 96 to 3 approving a similar resolution. But members in both chambers emphasized that these two measures in no way authorized the future use of force. On December 4, 1990, fifty-four members of Congress filed suit in federal district court (*Dellums v. Bush*) to block President Bush from launching an offensive aimed at expelling Iraq from Kuwait without Congress's formal approval. On December 13, Judge Harold Greene of the D.C. District Court declined to rule in the case, saying that it was not yet "ripe" for judicial consideration because the full Congress had not yet taken a stand on the issue.

This constitutional debate became moot in the weeks that followed. On January 8, 1991, President Bush sent a formal letter to Congress asking it to support "the use of all necessary means" to expel Iraq from Kuwait, although when asked by reporters whether a congressional joint resolution was needed, he said, "I don't think I need it." On January 12, the Congress responded with divided votes (House, 250–183; Senate, 52–47) in favor of the use of armed force against the Iraqi dictator. In short order, the United States and its allies gave Iraq until January 15 to leave Kuwait. When Iraq failed to comply with the deadline and withdraw, a devastating allied air offensive was unleashed on January 16, and an American-led ground offensive began on February 23. Within less than one week, the Iraqis began a beleaguered withdrawal from Kuwait and the United States stopped the military offensive. At a joint session of Congress on March 6, 1991, President Bush announced that "the war is over."

SEPTEMBER 11 AND THE WAR ON TERROR

Everything changed both for President George W. Bush and the American public on September 11, 2001, when terrorists struck at the heart of American economic and military power with disastrous human consequences. The attacks claimed nearly 3,000 fatalities when international terrorists commandeered three commercial aircraft and crashed into the World Trade Center in New York, the Pentagon in Washington, D.C., and a deserted cornfield in Somerset County, Pennsylvania, with a plane that was most likely destined for a fiery crash into another high-profile target in the nation's capital.

The attacks left little doubt that the United States would respond with the full force of its military against Osama bin Laden, an ultra-nationalist from Saudi Arabia exiled in Afghanistan and the presumed perpetrator of the September 11 attacks. Public officials and private citizens alike exhibited a degree of resolve and unity of purpose rarely seen in American politics in recent decades. In the weeks following the attacks, the Bush administration and Congress gathered strength and purpose in the nation's darkest hour. On September 18, 2001, Congress approved Senate Joint Resolution 23, formally referred to as the Authorization for Use of Military Force (AUMF). The legislation embodied two main features. First, it granted considerable discretion to the president to use "all necessary and appropriate force" against any entity considered responsible for the 9/11 attacks. Second, it authorized the president to use that force "in order to prevent any future acts of international terrorism against the United States."

On October 8, 2001, the United States launched an attack against the al Qaeda terrorist network in Afghanistan, where it had been relatively safe for many years under the protective gaze of a fundamentalist regime known as the Taliban. Over the next seven years, numerous questions arose concerning the unfinished war in Afghanistan, the legitimacy and prosecution of a second Iraq war, the size of the military force brought to bear in the two wars, postwar reconstruction in Iraq and Afghanistan, the envisioned exit strategy for the United States, and how the U.S. was obliged to treat prisoners of war captured in the conflicts.

In a famous work on presidential power written in the early 1970s, Arthur M. Schlesinger, Jr. spoke of the emergence of an "imperial presidency" that had begun in the 1930s under Franklin Roosevelt and reached new heights by the 1960s, as successive administrations dealt with an expanding domestic and foreign policy agenda with minimal objections from Congress.[25] In many respects, the disastrous Vietnam War and a major political scandal in the Nixon administration lent credence to Schlesinger's claims. Because of several congressional efforts to curb executive power in the 1970s with such actions as the War Powers Resolution, two respected students of the American presidency—Richard Neustadt[26] and Michael Beschloss[27]—at century's end had recognized a "weakening White House" and the "end of the imperial presidency." But these assessments of the state of executive power were made just before September 11, and many developments since then suggest that on several fronts, presidential power and authority increased greatly after the 9/11 attacks.

When the United States mobilized to fight global terrorism—itself an open-ended and indefinite commitment to perpetual conflict as evidenced by the two war authorizations noted earlier—the effort quickly confirmed a long-standing reality: national security invariably trumps concerns about civil liberties. Within days of the September 11 attacks, the Bush administration sent to Congress a bill titled awkwardly "Uniting and Strengthening America by Providing Appropriate Tools Required to Intercept and Obstruct Terrorism," which allowed policymakers to refer to the legislation with a symbolic acronym, the USA PATRIOT Act of 2001. The legislation equipped the government with greatly expanded powers to gather intelligence at home and abroad in its fight against global terror and was signed into law on October 26, 2001 (see Brief 5.11).

As the government began to implement the USA PATRIOT Act, critics claimed that many provisions of the law seriously threatened basic constitutional rights of American citizens. The Justice Department soon indicated that over 1,000 persons had already been detained in connection with the September 11 attacks. The government refused to disclose the names of any

Brief 5.11
THE USA PATRIOT ACT OF 2001

The antiterrorism legislation that Congress enacted in October 2001 initially raised little concern about the reach of federal power in this hour of national challenge. An unusual alliance of conservative Republicans and liberal Democrats in both houses insisted upon some provisions that the administration opposed, such as a "sunset" provision that meant the law would expire by December 31, 2005, unless renewed by Congress. In several areas, the new law promised a much more imposing federal government that would have major new powers over citizens and foreigners alike. The law contained several provisions that seemed necessary for the tasks at hand:

- Increased Penalties: Strengthened the Antiterrorism and Effective Death Penalty Act of 1996 that prohibits "material support" to terrorists or terrorist organizations; includes committing acts of terrorism or sheltering or financing terrorists or terrorist organizations; legislation made it a federal crime to commit any terrorist act against a mass transit system;
- Bioterrorism: Made it illegal for people or groups to possess substances that can be used as biological or chemical weapons for anything other than a "peaceful" purpose;
- Detention: Authorized that the Attorney General or Commissioner of Immigration can certify an immigrant as being under suspicion of terrorist involvement; suspect can be detained for up to seven days for questioning;
- Roving Wiretaps: Amended the Foreign Intelligence Surveillance Act (FISA) by eliminating the need for the FBI to show probable cause before conducting secret searches or surveillance; FBI can obtain from the Foreign Intelligence Surveillance Court the authority for roving wiretaps on any telephone being used by any person suspected of terrorist involvement;
- Search Warrants: Allowed federal officials to obtain nationwide search warrants for terrorist investigations; authorized so-called "sneak and peek" search warrants that allow federal agents to conduct a search without notifying the owner and to delay notification indefinitely that a search has occurred;
- Computer Monitoring: Enabled officials to monitor computers and subpoena the addresses and times of all electronic mail traffic sent by terrorist suspects;
- Intelligence & Criminal Investigation: Authorized intelligence and criminal justice officials to share information gained in terrorist investigations; allowed FBI to monitor and observe religious and political groups, even in the absence of any evidence of wrongdoing;
- Money Laundering: Allowed Treasury Department to require banks to determine the sources of large overseas private banking accounts, imposing sanctions on countries that refuse to provide such information to U.S. investigators;
- Offshore Banks: Prohibited American banks from doing business with offshore "shell banks" that have no apparent connection to any regulated banking industry or operation;
- Investigative Purpose: Enabled national security investigators to obtain from the Foreign Intelligence Surveillance Court the authority to wiretap suspects in terrorism cases if they assert that foreign intelligence operations are a "significant purpose" of that investigation.
- Sunset Provisions: Expanded surveillance powers for tapping telephones and computers would expire in four years, although information obtained from expanded wiretaps could be used beyond this four-year period.

SOURCES: Adam Clymer, "Antiterrorism Bill Passes; U.S. Gets Expanded Powers," *New York Times*, October 26, 2001; "The USA PATRIOT Act: Preserving Life and Liberty," U.S. Department of Justice, www.justice.gov/archive/ll/highlights.htm.

of these individuals or the charges on which they were being detained, which raised some important questions about secret detention and concerns about due process. On November 13, 2001, President Bush issued a presidential order allowing military tribunals to try foreigners charged with terrorist activities, rather than civilian courts, and both Vice President Dick Cheney and Attorney General John Ashcroft strongly defended this order, saying that such persons "don't deserve to be treated as a prisoner of war."

The Bush administration finally proposed in June 2002 an extensive reorganization of the domestic defense establishment.[28] To correct serious organizational deficiencies and to coordinate the massive task of intelligence gathering and analysis, the administration proposed a new Department of Homeland Security that would employ 170,000 new or reassigned civil service employees, manage a proposed budget of $38 billion, and combine twenty-two different federal bureaus and agencies into one single cabinet-level department. As proposed by the administration, the plan envisioned four major new organizational sub-units that would be combined into one new federal department. What soon became known as the Department of Homeland Security was created in 2002 and charged with four primary operating functions: (1) border and transportation security, (2) emergency preparedness and response, (3) chemical–biological–nuclear countermeasures, and (4) information analysis and infrastructure protection. As elaborate as the proposed plan was in terms of size, budget, and agency reorganization, it was criticized almost from the outset as preserving the status quo with respect to the functions and power of the Federal Bureau of Investigation, the Central Intelligence Agency, the Defense Intelligence Agency, and the National Security Agency.

The Second Iraq War

The Bush administration was convinced by 2002 that Iraq posed a very serious risk to its neighbors and to the United States. Several United Nations inspections since 1991 were inconclusive as to whether Saddam Hussein possessed stockpiles of chemical, biological, or nuclear weapons, and the administration grew increasingly impatient with the ability of international sanctions and inspections to detect the threat or deter future attacks by Iraq. In October 2002, with little debate and no congressional hearings on the subject, Congress once again deferred to the administration when it passed Public Law 107-243, the Iraq Joint Resolution, providing the president broad authority to invade Iraq and depose Saddam Hussein. Section 3 (a) of the Iraq Resolution stated that the president "is authorized to use the Armed Forces of the United States as he determines to be necessary and appropriate in order to . . . defend the national security of the United States against the continuing threat posed by Iraq." On October 16, Congress extended to Bush the statutory authority to move ahead with planning for a possible military strike into Iraq.

Over the next several months, inconclusive diplomatic efforts by the United States failed to convince either the United Nations Security Council or major American allies that all had been done diplomatically to prevent war. The United States, Great Britain, and an unusual assortment of other countries launched air strikes at strategic sites in Iraq on March 20, 2003.

American military commanders characterized the battle plan in Iraq as designed to create "shock and awe" in Baghdad. An invasion force of some 140,000 American troops launched the ground offensive the following week. By mid-April, the United States occupied Baghdad and toppled the Hussein regime, while some 25,000 British forces moved up from southern Iraq. Even with Saddam's capture, trial, and execution, the war in Iraq continued to lose its popularity among Americans. Casualties mounted and costs soared, causing a surge in anti-war support to rally around the 2008 Democratic presidential candidate, Barack Obama. Mr. Obama had opposed the Iraq War since its inception, actually voting to deny statutory authority while a senator from Illinois. This would become one of his primary campaign planks, and he pledged to end American military involvement in Iraq if elected president. The Bush administration, facing growing opposition, defied conventional wisdom and initiated a "surge" strategy, which increased troops and equipment in Iraq. The results appeared to have some positive effects upon stability. Yet, the Iraq War became one of the key elements contributing to Barack Obama's victory in 2008.

The limits of presidential power are often visible, and such was the case for President Obama's pledge to end the U.S. military role in Iraq. Though troop levels began to decline in 2009 (and many of these soldiers simply went to Afghanistan), it was not until August 31, 2010, that President Obama announced that it was "time to turn the page" on Iraq. He did not proclaim victory in a conflict that had cost more than 4,400 lives, thousands more injured, and billions of dollars in costs. We would no longer have "combat" troops in Iraq, he said, but we would leave nearly 50,000 support troops in place to help train and supervise the fledgling Iraqi army.

As American troops entered their eleventh year of fighting in nearby Afghanistan, President Obama faced a situation familiar to many of his predecessors—higher body counts, escalating costs, and more public criticism. As a result, in announcing his decision to increase troop levels, he also defined the administration's goals narrowly and included an "exit strategy" for the conflict. By the beginning of 2013, numerous questions remain to be answered about Afghanistan. The 66,000 American troops currently stationed there are scheduled to withdraw by the end of 2014, but it is not clear how rapidly that can take place. Also, it is likely that a small force will remain after 2014, and estimates range from 3,000 to 20,000. However, much depends on the Afghan government's willingness to allow those troops.[29]

THE CONSTITUTION AND DETAINEES' RIGHTS

The framers of the Constitution were protective of the centuries-old concept of habeas corpus ("you have the body"), namely the right of prisoners to challenge their detention Article I, Section 9 states:

> THE PRIVILEGE OF THE WRIT OF HABEAS CORPUS SHALL NOT BE SUSPENDED, UNLESS WHEN IN CASES OF REBELLION OR INVASION THE PUBLIC SAFETY MAY REQUIRE IT.

President Abraham Lincoln suspended the writ of habeas corpus in the early stages of the Civil War in Maryland and various Midwestern states. He did so in response to riots, militia violence, and to keep Maryland possibly from seceding from the Union. His order was struck down in *Ex Parte Merryman* (1861), but Lincoln ignored the ruling. President Lincoln's later decision to try civilians in military courts was struck down by the Supreme Court in *Ex Parte Milligan* (1861). The Court reasoned that civilians cannot be tried in military tribunals unless civilian courts are closed. In more recent times, an 8–0 Supreme Court in *Ex Parte Quirin* (1942) upheld President Franklin D. Roosevelt's decision to try eight German saboteurs, including two U.S. citizens, in a military tribunal. Habeas corpus protections did not apply, said the Court, because the eight were considered "unlawful combatants."

Soon after the United States invaded Afghanistan in October 2001 in an effort to dislodge the Taliban and defeat al Qaeda, several cases were filed as hundreds of prisoners from the war in Afghanistan sought to have their claims of illegal detention, denial of legal representation, secretive hearings, and improper military tribunals addressed in federal courts. A 2003 federal appeals court ruled that federal courts lacked jurisdiction to consider these claims because the approximate 600 detainees of different nationalities were being kept at Guantanamo Naval Base, Cuba (see Brief 5.12), not in the United States, prompting the Supreme Court to become involved.

Brief 5.12
WHAT IS GUANTANAMO BAY?

Guantanamo Bay is located near the southeastern end of Cuba and is today home to one of America's most important naval bases. The naval base, nicknamed "Gitmo," was established in 1898 as a result of America's victory in the Spanish-American War. The roughly 45-square-mile base was leased to the United States by the 1903 Cuban-American Treaty in perpetuity, giving the United States "complete jurisdiction and control," while Cuba retained ultimate sovereignty. A 1934 treaty made the lease permanent unless both governments agreed to end it or unless the United States abandoned the property. The Castro regime has continued to argue that the treaty was forced upon Cuba and is invalid.

The first "enemy combatants" arrived at Gitmo in January 2002. President Barack Obama campaigned on the promise to close Guantanamo within a year of assuming office in 2009. As of the end of 2012, it remains open with a reported 166 men still imprisoned there. That number is 76 fewer than when President Obama assumed office, but little progress has been made. One key reason rests in the stringent limitations that Congress placed on transferring enemy combatants in 2010. While some 86 of the current 166 have been identified for repatriation, the limits have prohibited any transfers. In a series of decisions the Supreme Court (see the discussion in this chapter) has extended some constitutional protections to the inmates. Gitmo remains a problem for United States defense policy.

In late January 2013, the State Department announced that the special envoy in charge of closing Guantanamo Bay prison would be reassigned and his office closed. The decision appeared to indicate that the Obama administration no longer considers closing the prison to be realistic or likely. Meanwhile, the military trials continue on the base, with Khalid Shaikh Mohammed and four others facing trial over the September 11 attacks.

SOURCES: U.S. Navy, "Naval Station Guantanamo Bay," www.navy.mil/local/guantanamo/
"Close Guantanamo Prison," Editorial, *New York Times*, November 25, 2012; Charlie Savage, "Office Working to Close Guantanamo is Shuttered," *New York Times*, January 28, 2013.

The first group of cases involved sixteen detainees (two British citizens, two Australians, and twelve Kuwaitis), ironically from countries allied with the United States in its war on terror.³⁰ These cases, *Rasul v. Bush* (2004) and *Al Odah v. United States* (2004), found the U.S. Supreme Court considering the question of whether noncitizens who had never resided in the United States and who were captured outside the United States and held in military custody as a prisoner of war could be held indefinitely without access to American courts. In defending its actions to detain these prisoners and deny them access to American courts, the Bush administration relied upon the Supreme Court's precedent in *Johnson v. Eisentrager* (1950), which held that German prisoners of war from World War II who had been captured and held abroad had no legitimate access to civilian courts. In writing for a 6–3 majority, Justice John Paul Stevens distinguished the *Rasul* and *Odah* cases from *Eisentrager*:

> PETITIONERS IN THESE CASES . . . ARE NOT NATIONALS OF COUNTRIES AT WAR WITH THE UNITED STATES, AND THEY DENY THAT THEY HAVE ENGAGED IN OR PLOTTED ACTS OF AGGRESSION AGAINST THE UNITED STATES; THEY HAVE NEVER BEEN AFFORDED ACCESS TO ANY TRIBUNAL, MUCH LESS CHARGED WITH AND CONVICTED OF WRONGDOING; AND FOR MORE THAN TWO YEARS THEY HAVE BEEN IMPRISONED IN TERRITORY OVER WHICH THE UNITED STATES EXERCISES EXCLUSIVE JURISDICTION AND CONTROL.

Stevens added special historical weight to the majority opinion by emphasizing that "executive imprisonment has been considered oppressive and lawless since John, at Runnymede, pledged that no free man should be imprisoned, dispossessed, outlawed, or exiled save by the judgment of his peers or by the law of the land."

A second group of cases, argued before the Supreme Court in April 2004, involved an important distinction from the *Rasul* and *Odah* judgments. *Hamdi v. Rumsfeld* (2004) and *Rumsfeld et al. v. Padilla* (2004) involved two American citizens who were arrested soon after the September 11 attacks under rather different circumstances and treated as so-called "enemy combatants" in the war on terrorism. Yaser Esam Hamdi was captured in Afghanistan after his military unit surrendered to Northern Alliance forces in 2001, and Jose Padilla was arrested in Chicago after allegedly meeting with high-ranking al Qaeda members in Pakistan. Both Hamdi and Padilla were eventually transferred to a military brig in Charleston, South Carolina. In both cases, the detainees argued that as American citizens, they were entitled to several rights under the U.S. Constitution, including appointed defense counsel, a timely hearing of the charges against them, and access to a civilian court rather than a military tribunal. The administration alleged that as so-called "enemy combatants," neither was entitled to access of federal civilian courts.

On June 28, 2004, in *Hamdi v. Rumsfeld*, Justice O'Connor, writing for a four-member plurality, said first that the government had violated Hamdi's Fifth Amendment right to due process by holding him indefinitely and denying him access to defense counsel, and second, that the separation of powers principle did not require deference here to solely the executive branch's determination that Hamdi was an "enemy combatant." O'Connor noted that this case presented substantial interests on both sides: Hamdi's "private interest" as an American citizen and his interest in being free from physical detention by his government, and the "weighty and sensitive governmental interests in ensuring that those who have . . . fought with the enemy during a war will not return to the battle against the United States."

> [W]E BELIEVE THAT NEITHER THE PROCESS PROPOSED BY THE GOVERNMENT NOR THE PROCESS APPARENTLY ENVISIONED BY THE DISTRICT COURT BELOW STRIKES THE PROPER CONSTITUTIONAL BALANCE WHEN A UNITED STATES CITIZEN IS DETAINED IN THE UNITED STATES AS AN ENEMY COMBATANT. . . . [A] CITIZEN-DETAINEE SEEKING TO CHALLENGE HIS CLASSIFICATION AS AN ENEMY COMBATANT MUST RECEIVE NOTICE OF THE FACTUAL BASIS FOR HIS CLASSIFICATION, AND A FAIR OPPORTUNITY TO REBUT THE GOVERNMENT'S FACTUAL ASSERTION BEFORE A NEUTRAL DECISIONMAKER.

O'Connor's most succinct and emphatic verdict in this case came at the very end where she reminded all who care about the rule of law that "... a state of war is not a blank check for the President when it comes to the rights of the Nation's citizens." A 5–4 majority avoided a ruling in *Rumsfeld v. Padilla* (2004), by holding that Padilla had filed his claim for a writ of habeas corpus in the wrong court (New York).

Hamdan v. Rumsfeld (2006) involved a Yemeni national and former driver for Osama bin Laden, Salim Hamdan, who had been captured in 2001 by Afghan forces and eventually imprisoned by the American military in 2002 at Guantanamo Bay, Cuba. In July 2003, Hamdan was one of six prisoners designated by the military as an enemy combatant and made eligible for trial before a military tribunal, which eventually began in August 2004 after a military attorney had been appointed for him. Soon after it began, proceedings of the military tribunal were halted by a federal judge on the grounds that the proceedings violated various requirements under the Uniform Code of Military Justice (i.e., right of defendant to be present at trial and to examine evidence presented against him) and international treaty obligations under the Geneva Conventions. In July 2005, after the government appealed this adverse ruling, the District of Columbia Court of Appeals, on which Judge John G. Roberts sat and participated in the case, overturned the trial court judgment and allowed the tribunal proceeding to stand. By November 2005, the Supreme Court agreed to hear the case, with now Chief Justice Roberts recusing himself from the case because of his prior participation in the appellate decision.

On the last day of the Court's 2005–06 term, the justices ruled 5–3 that the plan to put Guantanamo detainees on trial before military tribunals was unauthorized by federal law and contrary to international law. For all eight of the justices, a key question was whether Section 1005 of the Detainee Treatment Act of 2005 effectively withdrew the jurisdiction of the Supreme Court (and almost all other federal courts) to hear habeas petitions on lawful detention. In a lengthy seventy-three-page opinion, Justice John Paul Stevens first dealt with this all-important question:

THE GOVERNMENT ARGUES THAT [SECTION 1005] HAD THE IMMEDIATE EFFECT, UPON ENACTMENT, OF REPEALING FEDERAL JURISDICTION NOT JUST OVER DETAINEE HABEAS ACTIONS YET TO BE FILED BUT ALSO OVER ANY SUCH ACTIONS THEN *PENDING* IN ANY FEDERAL COURT—INCLUDING THIS COURT. ... ORDINARY PRINCIPLES OF STATUTORY CONSTRUCTION SUFFICE TO REBUT THE GOVERNMENT'S THEORY—AT LEAST INSOFAR AS THIS CASE, WHICH WAS PENDING AT THE TIME THE DTA WAS ENACTED, IS CONCERNED. [EMPHASIS ADDED]

After examining congressional debates on the legislation, the majority maintained that the legislation was never intended to strip federal courts of jurisdiction with respect to pending cases like *Hamdan*. The three dissenting justices (Scalia, Alito, and Thomas) felt that the law did effectively limit the courts' power to hear both pending and future habeas petitions.

In closing, Stevens emphasized not only the need for great deference to executive decisions concerning detention of dangerous personnel but also the need to comply with basic due process guarantees. Habeas corpus protections and due process guarantees must be respected, even by the president:

[I]N UNDERTAKING TO TRY HAMDAN AND SUBJECT HIM TO CRIMINAL PUNISHMENT, THE EXECUTIVE IS BOUND TO COMPLY WITH THE RULE OF LAW THAT PREVAILS IN THIS JURISDICTION.

The administration moved quickly over the next few months to induce Congress to draw up a new set of rules for interrogating detainees and trying them before authorized military commissions. The resulting Military Commissions Act of 2006 represented an effort by the Bush administration to repair some of the damage done by the *Hamdan* ruling (see Brief 5.13).

Immediately following passage of the Military Commissions Act in 2006, the detainees were left with the limited review procedures established two years earlier following the *Hamdi v. Rumsfeld* decision in what were called Combatant Status Review

Brief 5.13
THE MILITARY COMMISSIONS ACT OF 2006

In late September 2006, Congress enacted the Military Commissions Act. The new law imposed extraordinary limits on defendants' rights in the courtroom, chief among them being the following:

- The definition of "enemy combatant" was broadened to include those who "purposefully and materially supported hostilities against the United States, and once even a legal resident of the US was so labeled, that person was subject to summary arrest and indefinite detention without access to habeas appeal."
- Habeas corpus was prohibited for all detainees in U.S. military prisons.
- The Uniform Code of Military Justice's provisions for a speedy trial and for protection against coerced self-incrimination were specifically declared inapplicable.
- No provision exists for judicial review of verdicts by the new military commissions. Furthermore, no appeals are allowed in the MCA that invoke the Geneva Conventions or other international humanitarian laws "as sources of rights and protections."
- Coerced evidence would be permissible if the military judge thought it was reliable.
- The President of the United States was given the power to "interpret the meaning and the application of the Geneva Conventions."
- Offenses enumerated in the final version of the MCA were narrowly drawn; for example, the definition of rape of a detainee as a form of torture was rejected.[31]

On October 17, 2006, three weeks before the congressional by-elections, President Bush signed the Military Commissions Act into law by claiming "it is a rare occasion when a President can sign a bill he knows will save American lives. . . . The bill I sign today helps secure this country, and it sends a clear message: This nation is patient and decent and fair, and we will never back down from the threats to our freedom."[32] Other comments on the act were not as approving. Senator Arlen Specter, Chairman of the Senate Judiciary Committee, who actually voted for the bill in spite of some of its infirmities, said that the new law was "patently unconstitutional on its face."[33] On its website, Amnesty International said that it would "work for the repeal of this legislation which violates human rights principles."[34]

Tribunals (CSRT). By early 2007, some sixty-three detainee cases were consolidated into one case known as *Boumediene v. Bush*. Lakhdar Boumediene was an Algerian arrested in Bosnia in 2001 in connection with a suspected plot to attack the U.S. embassy in Sarajevo, but like all the detainees in these consolidated cases detained at Guantanamo, Boumediene sought a writ of habeas corpus, maintaining that he was neither a member of the al Qaeda terrorist network nor the Taliban regime that supported al Qaeda.

Six months after oral arguments, the Court finally released its decision in *Boumediene v. Bush* (2008), with a 5–4 majority ruling that the prisoners had a constitutional right to challenge their continued detention in civilian courts. The court declared unconstitutional Section 7 of the Military Commissions Act, a key provision that stripped the federal courts of jurisdiction to hear habeas corpus petitions from the detainees, challenging their designation as enemy combatants. Writing for the majority, Justice Anthony Kennedy said that the procedure "falls short of being a constitutionally adequate substitute" because it fails to offer "the fundamental procedural protections of habeas corpus." After tracing the history of habeas corpus in both English and early American constitutional law, Kennedy closed his seventy-page opinion with a reminder of the importance of this sacred right and the need for judicial review of executive detention of suspects. He then noted the fundamental importance of the delicate balance between the sacred values of a free people:

> THE LAWS AND CONSTITUTION ARE DESIGNED TO SURVIVE, AND REMAIN IN FORCE, IN EXTRAORDINARY TIMES. LIBERTY AND SECURITY CAN BE RECONCILED; AND IN OUR SYSTEM THEY ARE RECONCILED WITHIN THE FRAMEWORK OF THE LAW. THE FRAMERS DECIDED THAT HABEAS CORPUS, A RIGHT OF FIRST IMPORTANCE, MUST BE A PART OF THAT FRAMEWORK, A PART OF THAT LAW.

Two quite passionate dissenting opinions by Chief Justice John Roberts and Justice Antonin Scalia criticized the majority for its judicial activism in overruling the political branches of the government. Roberts insisted that the ruling "is not really about the detainees at all, but about control of federal policy regarding enemy combatants," and that the American public will "lose a bit more control over the conduct of this nation's foreign policy to unelected, politically unaccountable judges." Justice Scalia characterized the decision as "devastating" and "disastrous," and insisted that it "will almost certainly cause more Americans to be killed."

The immediate upshot of the ruling was to accelerate the habeas petitioning process during the summer of 2008, since some 270 detainees remained at Guantanamo Naval Base. As noted elsewhere, President Obama's promise to close Guantanamo Naval Base within one year of his inauguration had not materialized as of early 2013.

Conclusion

The philosophical and historical setting in the eighteenth century of the American system found the framers concerned about how political power would be organized and exercised in the very new system that they were creating. Given their suspicions about human nature and their experiences under British colonial rule, they were determined to disperse the instruments of power by creating several mechanisms whereby executive and legislative authorities would have coordinate their agendas and actions in order to enact legislation that represented a reasonable consensus among the people. In terms of the executive apparatus of government, their handiwork in Article II envisioned several powers that could be exercised by the president relating to diplomatic, legislative, executive, and warmaking authority, all of which involved to some extent actions by Congress.

The passage of time and the challenges wrought by industrialization, social stratification, major military conflicts, economic collapse, and ideological competition altered considerably the original designs of those who constructed the American system in the late eighteenth century. A great deal of their handiwork has survived these challenges and many structural features still serve to control the exercise of power in the system. But in time of national crisis, the American people and their elected representatives in Congress have increasingly turned to the president and the executive branch to manage the business of the people, especially in foreign affairs. The twentieth century in particular found increasing deference to executive authority in times of national testing, at least initially, and the growth of presidential power has been a clear consequence of this historical development.

This chapter has attempted to trace this growth in executive authority and the implications that it may have with respect to the rule of law and the verdict of political history. The review and analysis in this chapter on several historic events, including now one of the longest wars in American history, have emphasized that the quest for national security should not sacrifice vital personal freedoms and popular consent in an open society. The next chapter extends this discussion of political power from the standpoint of legislative authority and the ability of Congress to be an effective check upon unlimited presidential power and authority.

Chapter 6
Separation of Powers and Congress

A view of the Capitol, where both houses of Congress meet to deliberate and do the legislative business of the U.S. government. Although power in the federal system has often rested with the executive branch over the past century, Congress has been able to use its legislative and budgetary authority to maintain a balance of power in the U.S. constitutional system.

▼ Introductory Remarks by Senator Robert C. Byrd

It is my distinct pleasure to introduce the chapter dealing with the finest legislative institution in the world, the United States Congress. My name is Robert C. Byrd, and when I died in 2010, I had become the longest-serving member of the United States Congress in history. I was elected to the House of Representatives in 1953 to represent my beloved home state of West Virginia. After six years, I was elected to the U.S. Senate, where I served until my death—a total of fifty-seven years on Capitol Hill.

Like many others, I saw my views evolve over those fifty-seven years. When I started, I was opposed to civil rights legislation, and I am not proud to say that—for a brief time—I was a member of the Ku Klux Klan. I regret those early mistakes, but I believe I ultimately became a champion of equal rights and liberties. True, I filibustered the Civil Rights Act of 1964, but I believe I made amends in later years.

But my real passion was defending the role of Congress against the increasingly powerful executive branch of government. I was present during the Watergate crisis, and I was proud of the way that the United States Senate investigated that scandal and ultimately forced President Nixon to resign. It was not America's finest hour, but the U.S. Senate performed admirably in its oversight and investigative roles.

I was especially upset by two episodes involving presidential power: I was a vocal opponent of the line-item veto legislation in 1993, even though a fellow Democrat, Bill Clinton, was the president at that time. I recall giving numerous speeches in opposition to the bill—comparing the action to the Roman Senate's willingness to hand over power to Julius Caesar. About ten years later, I was appalled as President George W. Bush moved toward the war with Iraq while Congress appeared willing to just hand over the warmaking power. It is the job of Congress to provide a check to unrestrained executive power.

I always took the congressional role quite seriously in matters relating to impeachment. Notice the discussion of the Clinton impeachment in this chapter, and pay close attention to the different roles played by the House and the Senate. Despite President Clinton's impeachment in the House, we in the Senate were able to prevent his conviction and removal from office.

I have always said that I am most proud of two things that I accomplished in my 57 years on Capitol Hill. The most important, by far, was my work as chair of the Appropriations Committee to help my home state of West Virginia. I publicly stated that I wanted to become "West Virginia's billion-dollar industry," and I managed to appropriate much more than that for my state. Of course, I had my critics, some of whom called me "the prince of pork," but I fulfilled my responsibilities to my constituents and to my state. That is how I saw my role. Congress is the boss when it comes to financial matters, as noted in the following sections dealing with taxation, spending, and borrowing. These are crucial powers that Congress alone must exercise, and they continue to provoke heated debate and partisan conflict. Remember the "fiscal cliff"?

My second proudest accomplishment was sponsoring legislation to require educational institutions receiving federal funding to observe Constitution Day on September 17 every year and teach students about that great document. Enjoy the chapter on Congress, and please continue to learn all you can about the United States Constitution. RCB

Sources: *Biographical Directory of the United States Congress,* http://bioguide.congress.gov/scripts/biodisplay.pl?index=b001210; "Sen. Robert Byrd Dead at 92," *Washington Post,* June 28, 2010, www.washingtonpost.com/wp-dyn/content/article/2010/06/28/AR2010062801241.html.

CONGRESS: AN OVERVIEW

By the time that the European settlers reached America's shores to establish colonies, the British Parliament had been struggling for influence against the monarch for many years. Over the course of the seventeenth century, the Parliament would ultimately win that contest and, with the Glorious Revolution of 1688, assume parliamentary supremacy over the king. Settlers in the new world followed suit by electing representatives to their own legislative bodies, and representative government established itself among the colonies. Over the next century or so, colonial legislatures became laboratories in which Americans placed their own stamp on representation and legislation.

The thirteen colonies were not much interested in joining a common legislature until forced into it by the escalating British demands for more taxes and control. Nine colonies convened in New York City in 1765 to protest the despised Stamp Act and adopt a *Declaration of Rights and Grievances*. The British response eventually led twelve colonies (all but Georgia) to send delegates to the First Continental Congress in Philadelphia in 1774, culminating in a series of actions that left America in a "state of rebellion" against England. The Second Continental Congress convened in 1775, eventually proclaiming American independence and producing the Articles of Confederation. The Articles of Confederation (discussed in Chapter 7), relied exclusively on a Congress in which all states were equal but really had very little power. Without an executive, national court, or any real way to raise funds, the Congress symbolized weakness and ineffectiveness. And so, the states decided to fix the Articles by convening in Philadelphia in May 1787.

The delegates to the Constitutional Convention in 1787 spent much of their time during the early weeks of the proceedings debating the structure, makeup, powers, size, and relative place within the overall system of what would soon become the United States Congress. Lengthy discussion surrounded especially the method of selection—appointment or popular election—of those who would serve in Congress, as well as how representation was to be determined—apportionment based on population versus a principle of state equality. These exchanges at the Convention over several aspects of the Congress forecast the eventual ratification struggle between Federalists and Anti-Federalists. To answer many of the arguments against the structure and power of Congress posed by the Anti-Federalists, several of *The Federalist* essays by Madison and Hamilton were especially relevant to the ongoing debate that spurred ratification in 1787–88: Madison's contributions in *Numbers 52–58* on the House of Representatives relating to popular election, apportionment of members, size of the body, and degree of representativeness of members; and Hamilton's essays in *Numbers 59–61, 64–66,* and *77* on the Senate contributed greatly to alleviating some of the popular concerns about how Congress would best serve popular interests, protect important freedoms, and provide stability in the new government.

As prescient as these insights were, much has changed in the nearly 220-plus years since the Constitutional Convention. The rise of a more institutionalized Congress (full-time salary and career, established committee system, standardized procedures, professional norms of behavior, division of labor to handle an increasing workload) holds both advantages and disadvantages for the modern Congress. On the plus side, Congress now has a somewhat better chance of dealing with more complex issues and expectations of the citizenry, of competing with the executive in terms of analyzing information and applying expertise on public issues, and reaching compromise on particularly contentious issues in the legislative process. As for negatives, this institutionalization has also meant that many procedural norms can become too rigid, thus frustrating and preventing the passage of legislation that is needed. The complexity of the structural and procedural features of Congress today can easily lead to delay and gridlock in both domestic and foreign policy. Whether the issue relates to energy policy, Social Security, health care reform, bankruptcy legislation, treaty ratification or immigration reform, to name only a few, the modern Congress frequently disappoints its supporters and infuriates its critics in its degree of efficiency and effectiveness.

In fairness to the legislative branch, it is important to note that some of these frustrations have involved prominent differences of opinion of what presidents and executive branch officials would prefer and whether those expectations correspond with a majority of both houses of Congress. As some of the following sections reflect, what some might see as delay and stagnation in the legislative process might also provide important checks upon unilateral executive power when a governing consensus does not exist or when other important values must be protected. In this sense, the framers of yesterday might well endorse some of the contemporary delay.

Congress Then and Now: Comparing the 1st and 112th Congresses

The 1st Congress of the United States (1789–91) met in Federal Hall at the corner of Broad and Wall Streets in New York City, the first capital of the nation. It was a far cry from what Congress would become two centuries later, and it represented a population of less than 4 million Americans at that time. Table 6.1 illustrates some of the key differences between the 1st Congress and the 112th Congress ending in 2012.

The House of Representatives consisted of sixty-five members, each of whom represented approximately 30,000 citizens in each congressional district. The Senate held twenty-six members, representing the original thirteen states. The workload of the legislative branch at that time was miniscule, compared to what it would become. In the 1790s, the federal government was extremely small and lawmaking in Congress was a very part-time occupation, with both houses in session only a few months over the two-year period of each Congress. The 1st Congress saw only 144 bills introduced, with 118 of those being enacted. The two most important were a proposed federal Bill of Rights sent to the states for ratification and the Judiciary Act of 1789, which created the first set of lower federal courts for the country. Until the 1880s, the "premodern" Congress reflected high turnover in members, many closely contested elections, short legislative sessions with a relatively light workload, chaotic floor proceedings devoid of efficient procedural rules, high turnover of committee personnel, and largely undeveloped political party structures.

Since these rather humble beginnings, the U.S. Congress has become perhaps the best known deliberative body in the world, both because of its Enlightenment period beginnings and its current status as the deliberative branch of the only super power in the world today. In contrast to the premodern Congress, today's Congress reflects low turnover in membership, few competitive elections, long legislative sessions with a heavy workload, orderly floor proceedings, low turnover of committee personnel, and well-developed political party structures. Generally speaking, Congress has become a very institutionalized, complex, and sometimes frustrating body for the public to understand.

The 112th Congress saw about 10,000 pieces of legislation introduced in both houses, only about two hundred of which were enacted into law. This is

Table 6.1 Congress Yesterday and Today

	1st Congress (1789–90)	112th Congress (2011–12)
U.S. population	4 million	300+ million
House dist. size	30,000	710,767
House members	65	435
Senate members	26	100
Standing committees (H)	0	20
Standing committees (S)	0	16
Bills introduced	144	10,000 (app.)
Bills enacted	118	200 (app.)*
Pay	$6 per diem	$174,000

* As of November 7, 2012.

Sources: Kristin D. Burnett, *Congressional Apportionment, 2010 Census Briefs*, Department of Census, November 2011, www.census.gov/prod/cen2010/briefs/c2010br-08.pdf.

down from nearly six hundred enacted laws passed in the previous session, largely due to the deep partisan division and gridlock in Congress. In part because of this explosion in legislation supporting actions of the federal government, the number of hours in which Congress is in session has roughly doubled since 1950. In addition, the number of committees has mushroomed, with twenty standing committees and 107 subcommittees in the House and sixteen standing committees and seventy-five subcommittees in the Senate. The length of time spent in a congressional career has grown substantially over the past 220 years. Between 1789 and 1901, members of the House serving at least six terms in office comprised less than 3 percent of the membership, and members of the Senate serving more than two terms made up only 11 percent of the membership.

In the 110th Congress (2007–08), 31 percent of the House membership had served at least six terms in office, and 43 percent of Senate membership had served at least two terms. Since World War II, over 90 percent of incumbent representatives and about 80 percent of incumbent senators running for reelection are reelected. In the 2007–08 election cycle, the average Senate race cost about $5.6 million and the average House race cost the candidates about $666,000, this for a job that paid each member of Congress about $174,000 per year. Of course, the fact that nearly two-thirds of senators and 39 percent of House members in 2008 were millionaires at least partly explains the seeming contradiction.[1]

Finally, although it took many years, the modern Congress is much more demographically representative of the American population than it was 220 years ago. In 1790, Congress was totally male, white, Protestant, and from the planter or professional classes. When the 111th Congress convened in January 2009, 167 members of the House and 57 senators were lawyers. Ironically, being a lawyer was a much more prominent occupational characteristic in Congress a century ago than it is today, with other professions, especially business and "career politicians," having a prominent place in both houses. Congress today is highly educated, with virtually all members holding a college degree and roughly two-thirds having graduate degrees. Nearly all members profess some religious affiliation, with membership in some Protestant denomination being the most prevalent, followed by Roman Catholicism. Historically a male institution, women have made substantial strides in winning congressional seats (see Brief 6.1).

THE CONSTITUTION AND CONGRESS

Apart from the relatively unimportant provision that revenue bills must originate in the House, the Senate's "advise and consent" function (confirming presidential appointments and ratifying treaties) represent the only significant difference between the chambers. Both houses of Congress possess identical delegated or expressed powers in the Constitution. Article I, Section 8 lays out seventeen delegations of power including the power to lay and collect taxes; to pay debts; to provide for the common defense and general welfare; to borrow money; to regulate foreign and interstate commerce; to establish a uniform rule of naturalization; to coin money and regulate its value; to punish counterfeiting; to establish post offices; to promote the progress of science and useful arts; to constitute inferior tribunals; to define and punish piracy and felonies on the high seas; to declare war; to raise and support an army and a navy; to provide for calling out the militia to execute the laws of the union; and to govern the District of Columbia. The only clarification of these powers was the Sixteenth Amendment's establishment of Congress's power to tax incomes (see Table 6.2).

While the enumerated or expressed powers described above constitute the basic framework for legislation, there is an additional provision that extends congressional power far beyond them. The final provision in Article I, Section 8 allows Congress "to make all laws which shall be necessary and proper for carrying into execution the foregoing (expressed) powers." These are the "implied" powers that allow Congress to employ numerous methods and approaches to achieving its delegated powers (see the discussion of implied powers in Chapter 7). These may include establishing a new department, commission, or government corporation, enacting new federal criminal laws, or ordering the end of certain unfair or unwise commercial practices. In short, the implied powers of Congress have allowed the federal government's reach to expand far beyond the specific language in the Constitution.

Brief 6.1

MEMBERS OF THE 113TH CONGRESS

The 2012 elections resulted in no change to the balance of power, as noted in the previous chapter, with the president winning reelection and the same party retaining control in both houses of Congress. But the 113th Congress will look a little different from its predecessors. Probably the biggest and most publicized news concerned the increase in female members of Congress. When the 113th Congress convened in January 2013, a record number of women were seated: 20 (16 Democrats and four Republicans) in the Senate and 81 (61 Democrats and 20 Republicans) in the House. The 101 (including three nonvoting) female members of Congress reached an all-time high in the 2012 elections.

But beyond the number of women, the 113th Congress has a large number of new faces in general. Eighty-four new members were elected in 2012, down slightly from the unprecedented ninety-six in 2010. Some of the 2012 winners defeated those elected just two years earlier. The 2010 and 2012 congressional elections resulted in more new faces in Congress than any two previous elections in history. Interestingly, among the new members were nine who had served previously in Congress.

The Pew Forum's analysis of the religious composition of the 113th Congress showed several interesting findings. First, the new Congress continues the trend toward more religious diversity in both chambers. While Protestants still constitute more than a majority of Congress, their numbers have been declining for years. Catholics have grown rapidly to more than 160 members, while Jewish members declined by seven in 2012. All Protestant denominations declined in numbers except for Baptists—increased to fourteen. The 2012 election produced the first Hindu member of Congress, along with the first Buddhist to serve in the Senate. Although nearly 20 percent of the U.S. population describe themselves as agnostic, atheist, or nothing in particular, eleven members of the 113th Congress do not specify a religion.

The 113th Congress maintained the same number of African American members (forty-three) as its predecessor, but Tim Scott, a Republican from North Carolina, moved from the House to the Senate, becoming that chamber's first black member since 1979. Twenty-eight Hispanics hold seats in the House, while three Hispanics (all Cuban Americans) are U.S. senators. The new class also produced changes in the area of sexual orientation, including the first openly gay U.S. senator and the first openly bisexual member of either chamber. In all, there are now a record seven openly gay or bisexual members of Congress.

SOURCE: "Faith on the Hill: The Religious Composition of the 113th Congress," *Pew Forum on Religion and Politics*, November 16, 2012; Ashley Parker, "Day of Records and Firsts as 113th Congress Opens," *New York Times*, January 3, 2013; David Sands, "113th Congress mirrors increasingly diverse U.S.," *Washington Times*, January 7, 2013. Jeremy Peters, "Openly Gay and Openly Welcomed in Congress," *New York Times*, January 25, 2013.

THE POWERS OF CONGRESS

As noted above, the Constitution vests all legislative power in Congress, so its primary function is obviously legislative. All federal laws passed in the United States come from Congress, and over the more than 220 years of its existence, Congress has enacted legislation in numerous areas. This chapter concludes with a discussion of some significant congressional legislation that relates to its responsibilities for organizing and funding government, but for now, a brief overview of the legislative process is in order.

Table 6.2 Constitutional Amendments Relating to Congress

Amendment	Date	Congressional Power
12th	1804	Specifies the manner in which the House and Senate elect the president and vice president, respectively, if no electoral vote majority exists.
16th	1913	Congress has power to levy taxes on incomes.
17th	1913	Provides for the direct popular election of U.S. senators.
20th	1933	Requires a new Congress to convene on January 3.
25th	1967	Requires majority vote by both houses to confirm the appointment of a new vice president.
27th	1992	Does not allow a congressional pay raise to take effect until the next election has occured.

THE LEGISLATIVE POWER OF CONGRESS

The legislative process requires that a bill must be approved by both Houses of Congress before it may be presented to the president for his signature or veto. The bill must be passed in identical form in both Houses. This often necessitates the convening of a permanent "conference committee" that brings together members from both chambers. This committee attempts to eliminate differences in the two different bills and provide a compromise that can be accepted by both.

Most of the legislative function occurs within an extensive committee structure. The House of Representatives employs twenty standing committees, and the Senate has sixteen. Each of the standing committees is further broken into subcommittees, with over one hundred in the House and nearly seventy-five in the Senate. These committees are run by full-time staffs that provide much-needed expertise to support congressional members. Some of the key standing committees are Senate: Appropriations; Armed Services; Budget; Finance; Foreign Relations; and Judiciary. House: Appropriations; Energy and Commerce; Foreign Affairs; Homeland Security; Judiciary; Rules; and Ways and Means.

One final distinction between the House and Senate is relevant to the legislative function. Because of its greater size, the House employs strict rules governing floor debate and speechmaking. A committed majority can move the House toward a vote and a final resolution in fairly predictable fashion. The Senate, on the other hand, allows essentially unlimited debate. The filibuster has become a tactic used successfully in the Senate as a method of stopping legislation from ever reaching a vote. Under its own rules, a filibuster may not be halted unless at least sixty senators agree to vote for "cloture," the method of shutting off debate. As a result, legislation passed by the House may never get to the voting stage in the Senate if forty senators are willing to support a filibuster (see Brief 6.2). We return to the legislative function of Congress in the final section of this chapter.

Brief 6.2

THE FILIBUSTER: PROTECTING MINORITY RIGHTS OR WASTING TIME?

The use of the filibuster (from a Dutch word meaning "pirate") to block or delay legislation has been around for a very long time. The famous Kentucky Senator Henry Clay once became so outraged when the minority tried to block a bank bill that he threatened to change Senate rules, a tactic for which he was soundly criticized by his Senate colleagues. Hollywood drew attention to the filibuster in *Mr. Smith Goes to Washington*, a film in which Jimmy Stewart held the Senate floor to prevent passage of an unpopular bill. In real life, flamboyant Louisiana Senator Huey P. Long often quoted Shakespeare and read recipes for "pot-likkers" to prevent passage of legislation that he believed favored the rich over the poor. In 1917, senators adopted Rule 22, which allowed a two-thirds vote to invoke "cloture," or the ending of debate. In 1975, the Senate reduced the number of votes for cloture from two-thirds to sixty. Supporters of the filibuster, including the late Senator Robert C. Byrd of West Virginia, argue that the filibuster is an important protector of individual and minority rights, but the record shows that filibusters have been often used against minorities. Southern senators made extensive use of filibusters to block civil rights and anti-lynching legislation (Senator Strom Thurmond of South Carolina holds the record, filibustering for twenty-four hours and eighteen minutes against the Civil Rights Act of 1957). Opponents of the filibuster point out that senators from the twenty-one smallest states are able to bring the entire Senate to a screeching halt if they choose to do so. In fairness to the filibuster, even the threat of its use often is enough to force both sides to consider compromise or negotiation to get a bill passed.

In early 2013, senators took some small steps toward reforming the filibuster. Even with the changes, the minority will still be able to force a supermajority of sixty votes to advance bills. Under the new rules, the majority will allow the minority greater opportunity to amend bills on the Senate floor, but the minority now will have less time in which to stall a motion to consider new legislation. The rules also reduce the chances for filibuster once a bill has passed the Senate. Some observers referred to the new rules as "incremental" change. Massachusetts Senator Elizabeth Warren put it this way: "It's some change in a Senate committed to no change. So that's important." Despite these minor changes, sixty members are still required for most key matters.

SOURCE: U.S. Senate: Art & History Home, www.senate.gov/artandhistory; Roger Davidson, Walter J. Oleszek, and Frances Lee. *Congress and Its Members*, 12th ed. (Washington, DC: Congressional Quarterly Press, 2010, pp. 264–266; Jeremy Peters, "New Senate Rules to Curtail the Excesses of a Filibuster," *New York Times*, January 24, 2013.

THE INVESTIGATIVE POWER OF CONGRESS

One of the more controversial powers of Congress has been its power to conduct investigations while fulfilling its legislative functions. Part of the controversy can be attributed to the fact that the Constitution nowhere specifically grants Congress the power to investigate as a corollary to its lawmaking authority. But over many decades, the authority to conduct investigations has been viewed as essential to its major purposes of passing legislation, informing the people of various public affairs, protecting the integrity of Congress, and addressing democratic accountability (see Table 6.3). It is doubtful whether Congress could ever effectively execute any of its several delegated powers in Article I, Section 8 without the authority to obtain factual information on which to base its legislative decisions. The power to investigate and inform

Table 6.3 Significant Senate Investigations Since 1860

Year	Issue	Details
1859–60	John Brown's raid	Senate Committee investigated John Brown's raid on the arsenal at Harpers Ferry, Virginia
1885–56	Interstate commerce	Select Committee to Investigate Interstate Commerce led to passage of the Interstate Commerce Act.
1912	HMS *Titanic*	Investigation into the sinking of the HMS Titanic.
1923–24	Teapot Dome	Investigation into fraud and corruption surrounding the leasing of national petroleum reserves to private parties.
1932–34	Pecora Wall Street exposé	Investigation of bank failures and stock market crash led to passage of the Securities Act of 1933, Banking Act of 1933, and Securities Exchange Act of 1934.
1950–51	Organized crime	Senate Committee to investigate organized crime in interstate commerce, chaired by Sen. Estes Kefauver, forced the FBI and the government to admit the existence of the syndicate. Televised nationally.
1953–54	Army-McCarthy hearings	First phase conducted by Sen. McCarthy charging illegal Communist influence on the federal government and the U.S. Army. Second phase investigated Sen. McCarthy's attacks on the army. Televised nationally.
1966–72	Vietnam	Hearings by Sen. J. William Fulbright and the Senate Foreign Relations Committee into the Vietnam conflict.
1973–74	Watergate	Investigation of possible corruption in the 1972 Presidential campaign. Contributed to the eventual resignation by President Nixon.
1987–89	Iran-Contra	Investigation into alleged covert sales of military equipment to Iran and diversion of the proceeds to fund the Nicaraguan contras. Embarrassed Reagan administration and led to several convictions.
1995–96	Whitewater	Investigation of White House officials and documents following death of Dep. Counsel Vincent Foster; also investigated Clinton involvement in Whitewater Development Corporation.
2002	9/11 terrorism	Senate Select Committee on Intelligence and House Permanent Committee on Intelligence investigated the U.S. intelligence community before and after 9/11.
2002	Enron scandal	Investigation of collapse of Enron and role of its Board of Directors. Contributed to passage of accounting and corporate reforms in Sarbanes-Oxley Act of 2002.
2005	Credit card industry	Investigation of practices of the credit card industry that led to passage of Credit Card Act of 2009.
2010	Financial crisis	Investigation of high-risk loans, bank regulators, credit rating agencies, and investment banks. Contributed to passage of Financial Reform Act of 2010.

SOURCE: www.senate.gov/artandhistory/history/resources/pdf/Investigations/pdf; www.Levin/senate/gov/senate/investigations/index.html.

has long been recognized. In 1885, Woodrow Wilson concluded, "the informing function of Congress should be preferred even to its legislative function."[2] Prior to his appointment to the Supreme Court in 1937, Senator Hugo Black (D-AL) referred to congressional investigations as "among the most useful and fruitful functions of the national legislature." But others have disagreed with this assertion. Columnist and presidential advisor Walter Lippmann once characterized the congressional investigation as "that legalized atrocity . . . in which congressmen, starved of their legitimate food for thought, go on a wild and feverish manhunt and do not stop at cannibalism."[3]

Given the numerous congressional investigations into alleged executive-branch wrongdoing in recent years, Congress's power to investigate has spawned both public cynicism and criticism about what some have labeled an endless process of "revelation, investigation and prosecution."[4] The fundamental question here regarding congressional investigations continues to be whether these efforts are serious efforts to investigate unwise or illegal actions by government officials, or merely partisan efforts to score political points and embarrass the opposition. Given the increasing cost and mandates of government in recent decades, congressional investigations can be viewed as either immensely important or a serious distraction for most taxpaying citizens.

Congress has historically used its investigative power as an important preliminary to the passage of legislation, oversight of the executive branch in its administration of programs, informing the public on important policy issues, and protecting its own privileges, integrity, and reputation. The Supreme Court long ago recognized the importance of the congressional power to investigate as a necessary and legitimate part of the lawmaking authority. In *Kilbourn v. Thompson* (1881), Justice Samuel Miller spoke for a majority of the Court when it upheld the investigative power of Congress, but said that the power could only be used in pursuit of purely declared *legislative* ends. Congress could only investigate those areas in which it was allowed to legislate and not in matters over which the executive or federal courts had authority.

In the twentieth century, several cases dealt with how Congress exercises its investigative power and whether it may compel private individuals to testify before Congress. A unanimous Supreme Court in *McGrain v. Daugherty* (1927) upheld a Senate committee's power to investigate why Attorney General Harry Daugherty in the Harding administration had failed to prosecute key figures in the famous Teapot Dome scandal. A majority opinion drafted by Justice Willis Van Devanter noted that two general propositions should guide congressional investigations: (1) that Congress possesses both express and delegated lawmaking power, as well as "such auxiliary powers as are necessary and appropriate to make the express powers effective"; and (2) that Congress can compel private citizens to testify when its limited power of investigation is legitimately exercised and when it is able to establish the relationship of the investigation to the legislative function.

Requiring private citizens to testify before a congressional hearing became a popular political sport in the late 1940s when Congress and the American public became consumed with the threat of international communism. Increasingly, Congress sought to compel many private citizens to answer several intrusive political questions under the threat of fine or imprisonment. By the early 1950s, committees in both houses of Congress were investigating a wide range of allegedly subversive activities aimed at the overthrow of the federal government. The House Un-American Activities Committee (HUAC) subpoenaed over 3,000 witnesses during this period, questioning them about their political beliefs, affiliations and actions deemed potentially dangerous to the United States government. Many of the witnesses invoked the Fifth Amendment protection against self-incrimination and refused to testify before the committee. Others insisted that the House committee's interrogation exceeded the Congress's legislative function and refused to appear. Nearly 150 of these uncooperative witnesses were cited for contempt of Congress.

In the Senate, this anti-Communist turmoil was dominated by the tactics and activities of Senator Joseph R. McCarthy (R-WI), who used a subcommittee of the Senate Foreign Relations Committee to make repeated, unsubstantiated charges against public officials and private individuals suspected of treason. McCarthy's allegations, along with those of the HUAC, resulted in a series of loyalty-security investigations into the backgrounds and activities of public employees, scientists, and academics, as well as imposed loyalty oaths and the passage of anti-communist legislation. Even more damaging was the distrust of public officials, the presumption of "guilt by association," and the climate of fear that gripped much of American society during the period, which for obvious reasons became known as the infamous McCarthy era.

Two of the more famous cases during this era were *Watkins v. United States* (1957) and *Barenblatt v. United States* (1959). The *Watkins* case involved a labor organizer and former union official who had been subpoenaed by a subcommittee of HUAC to testify before Congress. Although Watkins answered questions about his own relationship to the Communist party, he refused to answer anything about any personal acquaintances that might have been affiliated with the party at one time. Watkins insisted that such information was irrelevant to the committee's power and purpose, and after he refused to answer many of the questions, Congress cited him for contempt. When he appealed his contempt citation, Watkins found a Supreme Court more sympathetic to his position. Writing for a six-member majority, Chief Justice Earl Warren indicated that unless informed of the precise subject matter of the investigations, the witness could not be compelled to testify without violating due process of law. In the words of Warren, "there is no congressional power to expose for the sake of exposure."

Rather than settling the public debate over Communist subversion and Congress's right to probe, the *Watkins* decision instead merely fanned a smoldering political issue. Many in Congress threatened to limit the Supreme Court's appellate jurisdiction and criticized the justices for having "grown soft" on alleged subversive activities. Perhaps as a consequence of this public criticism, the Court retreated somewhat from its defense of civil liberties over the next few years. In *Barenblatt v. United States* (1959), the Court was confronted with a case involving a college professor who had refused to answer any questions posed by HUAC concerning his alleged past membership in the American Communist party, claiming a First Amendment right not to divulge his political affiliation.

In *Barenblatt*, the justices divided 5 to 4 and ruled that the committee had properly informed the witness of the relevance and purpose of the questioning, and therefore he could not invoke First Amendment protection or refuse to comply with the subpoena. Although recognizing the importance of preserving "academic teaching freedom and its corollary learning freedom," the majority said that a college or university is not a "constitutional sanctuary," totally immune from inquiries into matters properly within the legislative domain. Of the four justices dissenting in *Barenblatt*, the remarks of Justice Black, so reminiscent of his strong support for civil liberties in many cases, reflected his view that any limitation upon vital First Amendment rights threatens the liberty of all in a democratic order. For Black, the issue in *Barenblatt* was "whether we as a people will try fearfully and futilely to preserve democracy by adopting totalitarian methods, or whether in accordance with our traditions and our Constitution we will have the confidence and courage to be free."

The Vietnam Conflict galvanized opponents of an open-ended commitment in Southeast Asia, leading to more congressional distrust of presidential dominance in foreign policy—and more investigations. For much of the Vietnam era, the Senate Foreign Relations Committee, under the chairmanship of Senator J. William Fulbright (D-AR), held several high-profile committee hearings that compelled policymakers in the Johnson administration to justify American military policy in Southeast Asia and provide a more candid assessment of the likelihood of military victory. The hearings were a contributing factor for the United States' eventual withdrawal from South Vietnam in 1973.

In recent years, congressional investigations have ranged from relatively mundane matters to highly controversial issues. The high drama of the Watergate investigations helped to bring down a U.S. president, while the revelations of the late-1980s Iran-Contra investigation seriously wounded the Reagan administration and resulted in prison sentences for several of its members. More recently, congressional committees have called together the heads of major oil companies to explain their profit margins, so-called "fat cat" Wall Street bankers to justify the incomprehensible bonuses paid to employees, experts on global warming and carbon emissions to explain the need for either tighter or looser controls on industry, and even Major League Baseball players to answer questions about their knowledge and possible usage of performance-enhancing drugs and steroids. In all, Congress draws a lot of attention to itself by convening investigations, and the numerous committees and subcommittees virtually ensure that investigations will continue to proliferate.

THE IMPEACHMENT POWER OF CONGRESS

In an extreme sense, the ultimate form of the congressional power to investigate involves the impeachment power. First in Article I (Sections 2 and 3) and then more pointedly in Article II of the Constitution, the framers referred to the power to remove, under certain circumstances, various federal officials from office. The specific provision in Article II, Section 4 reads:

> THE PRESIDENT, VICE PRESIDENT AND ALL CIVIL OFFICERS OF THE UNITED STATES, SHALL BE REMOVED FROM OFFICE ON IMPEACHMENT FOR, AND CONVICTION OF, TREASON, BRIBERY, OR OTHER HIGH CRIMES AND MISDEMEANORS.

Removal occurs following impeachment by a majority vote in the House of Representatives and a conviction on a two-thirds vote by members present in the Senate. Stated more simply, the House serves as the grand jury to determine if charges should be brought against the suspected official, and the Senate sits as a collective body to decide the guilt or innocence of the defendant.

Two important qualifications about the impeachment power of Congress should be noted. First, under the Constitution, impeachment by the House and conviction in the Senate are purely political penalties—removal from federal office and barring the official from holding office in the future. In *Federalist No. 65*, Alexander Hamilton wrote that impeachable offenses "are of a nature which may with peculiar propriety be denominated POLITICAL, as they relate chiefly to injuries done immediately to society itself."[5] The impeachment process was not intended to require legal penalties, as is the case in Great Britain, although nothing in the Constitution prevents impeached and convicted federal officials from being tried, convicted, and punished according to civil and criminal law after being removed from federal office. Apparently, the framers wanted to encourage Congress to use impeachment against officials for gross misconduct in high office, but it also provided for due process subsequent to an official's removal from office.

The other qualification that the framers intended to place upon the power of impeachment was limiting impeachable offenses, as noted above, to "Treason, Bribery, or other High Crimes and Misdemeanors." The reference to "High Crimes and Misdemeanors" is ambiguous and open to definition by Congress. Hamilton's reference to a possible impeachable offense in *Federalist No. 65* was to an "abuse or violation of some public trust," which suggests that only very serious transgressions could trigger the impeachment process.[6] On a somewhat lower threshold, while serving as a prominent member of the House of Representatives in 1970 during an unsuccessful effort to impeach Supreme Court Justice William O. Douglas, later President Gerald Ford noted that " . . . an impeachable offense is basically whatever a majority in the House of Representatives considers it to be at a given moment in history." Although this suggests that the impeachment standard is defined largely by political rather than legal criteria, clarification of what is and what is not an impeachable offense has had to be defined over the years through a very small number of cases.

Rarely has the impeachment process been used to remove high public officials, and until the late twentieth century, only once against a sitting president. Through 1997, the House of Representatives had investigated some seventy federal officials for possible impeachment, and had impeached only seventeen of them. The Senate has convicted only seven of these persons (all federal judges), the most recent one being federal district judge Alcee Hastings in 1989 on bribery charges.[7] Before the late 1990s, the only sitting American president to be impeached was Andrew Johnson in 1868, but the Senate failed to convict Johnson by one vote.

In the twentieth century two occasions arose that forced Congress and the American public to confront the trauma of impeachment of an incumbent president. In both the Nixon and Clinton presidencies, events unfolded from two very different types of scandals involving the president—one official and the other personal. Both incidents had substantial political overtones. In each instance, the country was engaged in a protracted political and constitutional struggle that at a minimum distracted national political leaders from important policy business. The institutional presidency eventually weathered these two scandals but public trust in its leaders to "do what is right" noticeably declined. The impeachment process was certainly implicated during the Nixon presidency and aggressively pursued during the Clinton presidency.

THE NIXON PRESIDENCY: EXECUTIVE PRIVILEGE AND THE THREAT OF IMPEACHMENT

Ever since 1798, when George Washington denied the House of Representatives access to executive correspondence regarding the Jay Treaty, American presidents have periodically invoked **executive privilege** and refused to divulge various types of political, military, or diplomatic information that they think should be protected from public disclosure. Although the concept is mentioned nowhere in either the constitutional debates or the document itself, executive privilege has been a common device used by most presidents to preserve confidentiality in the Oval Office. The major rationale for the concept is that in private discussions with advisors, presidents must solicit a wide assortment of opinions and policy recommendations to maximize the chances for success in making the proper decisions. Accompanying this concept of privileged communication is the belief that candor and a full range of opinions will be less likely if advisors suspect that their views may later be the object of public disclosure. This, of course, raises the question of whether governmental secrecy is an acceptable, necessary, or sufficient precondition for candor. The historical record is probably very mixed on this matter. Like any privilege, that of presidents shielding policy advisors and their counsel from public disclosure can be abused, as it certainly was by President Nixon during the Watergate affair.

It is not possible to analyze the complex events surrounding the Watergate scandal in this limited space. As Brief 6.3 indicates, this elaborate cover-up in the early 1970s involved several illegal activities that ultimately tested the fabric of the Constitution and the power of the courts to force public officials to comply with the law. At its core, the scandal revealed continual denials by a chief executive that any of his political entourage had either participated in or had prior knowledge of an illegal break-in at Democratic Party headquarters in Washington, D.C., in 1972. It involved constant refusals by the Nixon White House to provide anything but the most grudging assistance to ongoing investigations. The inquiry also revealed that taped conversations existed that were needed to determine if this president had broken the law. But the investigation of the scandal also revealed numerous illegal activities that seriously damaged public accountability in a representative democracy: the improper use of governmental agencies, especially the Central Intelligence Agency (CIA) and the Federal Bureau of Investigation (FBI); the misuse of public money by the president to refurbish his California White House; income tax evasion; the violation of constitutional rights of American citizens; and the refusal to comply with a congressional committee's request for relevant materials needed in an ongoing investigation.

Looking back on one of the most famous political scandals in American history, it is tempting to portray the Watergate affair as a classic confrontation between a president advancing his claim of executive privilege and a Congress that by 1974 seemed committed to impeaching him. At its core, the Watergate scandal also reflected a rare clash between a chief executive's desire to protect a power base and the judiciary's need to determine guilt or innocence of criminal defendants in an ongoing criminal trial. The Supreme Court decision that finally ended this conflict between executive privilege and the judicial determination of guilt is *United States v. Nixon* (1974).

On March 1, 1974, a federal grand jury indicted seven former White House aides and campaign officials of conspiracy and obstruction of justice in connection with the 1972 break-in of the Democratic National Committee headquarters at the Watergate complex. To prepare for the trial of these individuals and pursuant to federal rules of criminal procedure, Special Watergate Prosecutor Leon Jaworski requested that President Nixon produce sixty-four White House tapes and documents relating to certain key conversations between the president and his aides. Nixon refused to turn over the requested information, insisting that this was an internal dispute between superior and subordinate offices within the executive branch and therefore not subject to judicial resolution. Furthermore, the president asserted that the concept of executive privilege was absolute and essential for preserving the confidentiality of presidential communications under all circumstances.

Brief 6.3
WHAT WAS WATERGATE?

Before June 17, 1972, the Watergate was just another rather posh apartment and office complex on the Potomac River in Washington, D.C. But after five employees of the Committee to Re-Elect the President (affectionately known by its critics as CREEP) were arrested inside the headquarters of the Democratic National Committee at the Watergate complex, it eventually became a president's Waterloo. The burglars were carrying wiretapping equipment and several sequenced $100 bills, which immediately raised questions about both their purpose and their backing. Although White House Press Secretary Ron Ziegler immediately dismissed the break-in as nothing more than a "third-rate burglary," the subsequent trial and conviction of the Watergate burglars resulted in stiff fines and prison sentences. A revealing confession by James McCord, one of the operatives in the break-in, indicated that others were involved in the incident, that certain individuals had perjured themselves at the initial trial, and that the defendants had been pressured to plead guilty and remain silent.

During the spring of 1973, due in part to increased coverage by the news media, events regarding the scandal accelerated. In April, White House Counsel John Dean was fired by the president, and H. R. Haldeman and John Ehrlichman, President Nixon's two closest personal advisors, resigned. In May 1973, the Senate Select Committee on Campaign Finance, chaired by Senator Sam Ervin (D-NC), began televised hearings into the emerging Watergate scandal. In addition to some riveting testimony by Dean, the most startling revelations were those of a former communications employee at the White House, Alexander Butterfield. Butterfield testified that a White House taping system had for some time routinely recorded all conversations between President Nixon and his advisors. With this startling revelation, a protracted struggle ensued between the president and a special prosecutor (who had been appointed in May 1973 to investigate the evolving Watergate affair) to obtain selected recordings of White House conversations between the president and his advisors.

On October 10, Vice President Spiro Agnew resigned from office after pleading "no contest" to charges of income tax evasion and reports that he had continued to accept payments from political cronies in Maryland while serving as vice president. Ten days later, in what became known as the "Saturday Night Massacre," President Nixon ordered Attorney General Elliot Richardson to fire Special Prosecutor Archibald Cox, who was vigorously pursuing the coveted taped conversations needed in the Watergate investigation. When both Richardson and Deputy Attorney General William D. Ruckelshaus refused to fire Cox, Nixon finally found the next person in charge at the Justice Department, Solicitor General Robert H. Bork, to terminate Cox. That incident occasioned a strong protest from the mass media and much of the American public. It also instigated the House Judiciary Committee, chaired by Representative Peter Rodino (D-NJ), to begin an inquiry into possible grounds for impeachment charges against the president.

By mid-January of 1974, technical experts in charge of examining some of the White House tapes reported the existence of a curious eighteen-minute gap in a recorded conversation between Nixon and Chief of Staff Haldeman on June 20, 1972, three days after the Watergate break-in. They speculated that it was probably the result of five separate manual erasures. In March, a federal grand jury handed down seven indictments of former White House and Department of Justice employees, and named President Nixon as an "un-indicted co-conspirator." By early May, the Rodino Committee convened its hearings on possible impeachment articles against President Nixon.

In July 1974, the Supreme Court publicly announced the famous *United States v. Nixon* decision, ordering the president to turn over to the special prosecutor tapes needed in the ongoing federal trials of the seven defendants. One week later the Rodino Committee voted overwhelmingly in favor of the first of three articles of impeachment against the president. The president was left with little recourse. On August 5, the Nixon White House finally released the tapes, one of which revealed a conversation of June 23, 1972, between Nixon and Haldeman in which the president was clearly overheard orchestrating a cover-up of the investigation. Four days later, Nixon resigned from the Oval Office and retired to private life. In retrospect, the Watergate scandal and its playing out over this two-year period had several significant effects upon the American political process. It clearly ended one of the most serious political scandals in American history, it precipitated significant changes in campaign finance laws, and it triggered increasing vigilance of public officials by the mass media. Unfortunately, it also led to growing public cynicism about American politics and politicians among a substantial portion of the American public.

A unanimous Supreme Court, with Justice William Rehnquist not participating (prior to being appointed to the Supreme Court in 1971, Rehnquist had served as Deputy Attorney General under John Mitchell, one of the indicted co-conspirators), disagreed with the president's claims and ruled on July 24, 1974, that the documented evidence had to be turned over to the special prosecutor. Regarding Nixon's first assertion that the dispute was internal and shielded by the separation-of-powers principle, Chief Justice Warren Burger observed that "the production or non-production of specific evidence deemed by the Special Prosecutor to be relevant and admissible in a pending criminal case" involved issues that "are traditionally justiciable." The fact that both the president and special prosecutor are part of the executive branch "cannot be viewed as a barrier to justiciability," since the Congress in 1973 granted the special prosecutor the authority to proceed in the Watergate investigation. Unless that authority was rescinded, the special prosecutor had a special responsibility to produce the necessary evidence. Regarding the president's second claim of absolute executive privilege, the Court recognized the importance of maintaining the confidentiality of high-level discussions and the necessity to protect candor and objectivity so important to presidential decision making. However, the Court stated that this necessary confidentiality must be weighed against the need for the judicial process to obtain information needed in a criminal proceeding. To facilitate the administration of law, judicial access to the requested tapes was essential. The Court thus concluded that Nixon's legitimate claim of privilege "cannot prevail over the fundamental demands of due process of law in the fair administration of justice."

The Court's decision in July 1974 ordering the president to deliver the tapes accelerated the end for the Nixon presidency. The tapes revealed that the president had clearly tried to subvert the investigation into the burglary soon after the break-in in June 1972. Within a few days of the Court's decision, the House Judiciary Committee overwhelmingly recommended three separate articles of impeachment against President Nixon for obstruction of justice, violation of the constitutional rights of American citizens, and ignoring the subpoena power of the House Judiciary Committee. The three articles never went to the full House for a vote, where undoubtedly they would have resulted in a bill of impeachment, a subsequent trial in the Senate, and a probable conviction. Richard Nixon resigned as the thirty-seventh president of the United States on August 9, 1974, thus ending one of the most famous political scandals in American history.

Notwithstanding official and public sighs of relief in the fall of 1974, that the long political nightmare was over and the constitutional system had prevailed, Nixon's resignation probably turned on the *United States v. Nixon* decision. The ruling forced him to turn over the White House tapes to the district court, the special prosecutor, and subsequently to the House Judiciary Committee. Without the evidence from this "smoking gun" and the subsequent loss of support from even Nixon's most ardent defenders on Capitol Hill, he might well have finished his second term. Even the frequently asked question, "what did he know and when did he know it," became irrelevant when, by his own words, Nixon was heard on tape as participating in a cover-up of the Watergate investigation. Ironically, *United States v. Nixon* reaffirmed the power of American presidents to use executive privilege, which, though not absolute, is essential to protect vital communications in policymaking, especially when it involves the sensitive area of foreign affairs. At the same time, the entire episode damaged congressional–presidential relations and led immediately in the post–Watergate era to some significant changes in both foreign and domestic policymaking powers of American presidents.[8]

THE CLINTON PRESIDENCY AND IMPEACHMENT

The history of the Clinton presidency needs more thorough analysis than can be provided here. What is fair to say is that one of the more politically gifted and intelligent chief executives to occupy the presidency in many decades will most likely be judged, at least in the short term, on the basis of some serious sexual dalliances, a long detachment from the truth, and a complex tendency both to seek forgiveness from an offended public and redemption in a legal strategy intended to argue against impeachment (see Brief 6.4).

Several months before the 1992 presidential election, which Bill Clinton eventually won with 43 percent of the vote, accusations were leveled by a woman named Gennifer Flowers just prior to the New Hampshire presidential primary contest in February that she and Bill Clinton had carried on a twelve-year sexual affair while he was serving as first attorney general and later governor of Arkansas. Clinton vehemently denied the charges and survived the media frenzy and public doubts created by the accusations. By 1994, rumors continued to focus upon an allegedly promiscuous Bill Clinton. Lending some credence to these reports was a federal lawsuit filed in 1994 by a woman named Paula Corbin Jones, who claimed in her suit that Bill Clinton had sexually harassed her while he was still governor of Arkansas.[9]

By 1996, the Jones suit had stalled in the judicial system, largely because President Clinton had asked to have the case dismissed, asserting presidential immunity from prosecution on charges relating to

Brief 6.4
THE STARR REPORT AND THE CLINTON IMPEACHMENT

In retrospect, November 15, 1995, might go down in presidential annals as the beginning of the unraveling of President Bill Clinton's public credibility and the roots of a tainted presidential legacy. According to a 445-page report delivered to the House of Representatives on September 9, 1998, by Independent Counsel Kenneth Starr, it was on that date that President Bill Clinton had the first of ten sexual encounters in the White House with a young intern named Monica Lewinsky. The Starr report was launched after a three-judge district court panel had found sufficient cause to investigate possible violations of federal laws relating to a speculative land deal known as Whitewater back in Arkansas while Bill Clinton was serving as governor of the state in the 1980s. The investigation lasted nearly four years and by some estimates cost some $40 million.

When shipped to Capitol Hill in September 1998, the report and supporting materials contained nothing about the Whitewater land deal, but in striking fashion it culminated eight months of accusations, denials, and grand-jury testimony from a parade of witnesses called to testify about claims of criminal wrongdoing. Delivered to the House and published the next day in newspapers throughout the nation and over the Internet, the report noted in extensive, sometimes lurid and uncensored detail what Starr's office called "substantial and credible" evidence of impeachable offenses committed by President Clinton. The report sought to substantiate four possible grounds for the House of Representatives to consider impeachment proceedings against the president:

- Perjury—that President Clinton had lied under oath to a federal grand jury about his sexual relationship with Ms. Lewinsky; and that he lied in a deposition on January 17, 1998, in an ongoing sexual harassment suit against the president brought by an Arkansas resident named Paula Jones;

- Obstruction of justice—that the President conspired with Ms. Lewinsky to protect their relationship by devising cover stories and concealing personal gifts that had been subpoenaed in the Jones suit; that he suggested to Ms. Lewinsky in early January 1998 that she should file a false affidavit in the Jones case; and that he attempted through friends to have Ms. Lewinsky obtain employment in exchange for her silence about the relationship;

- Witness tampering—that the President tried improperly to influence the grand jury testimony of his personal secretary, Betty Currie; and

- Abuse of power—that the President abused his constitutional authority by lying to the American public, Congress, and the grand jury for several months about his relationship with Lewinsky, by impeding an ongoing criminal investigation, and by invoking executive privilege to conceal personal misconduct rather than privileged communications received during performance of official duties.

By mid-September the House of Representatives voted to release the Starr Report in its entirety, 2,800 pages of supporting material, covert tape recordings by one Linda Tripp of conversations with her "friend," Monica Lewinsky, and the videotape of President Clinton's testimony before the federal grand jury of August 17, in which he was questioned for four hours about his relationship with Lewinsky. Given the cumulative impact of this massive amount of material, the clear sense was that the Clinton presidency would never be the same again. What was unclear was how the Clinton presidency would end—with a formal reprimand, with impeachment and/or conviction by Congress and his departure from office, or political vindication of his presidency.

---

alleged incidents that preceded his presidency. When this failed, the president asked to have the case delayed until he left office, arguing that the demands of the office and the distractions created by the suit interfered with the performance of his official duties. On appeal from an adverse judgment by the trial court postponing the actual trial until after Clinton left office, the 8th Circuit Court of Appeals denied Clinton's motion to dismiss and said that the case should proceed immediately. At this point, the president's lawyers appealed the case to the Supreme Court.

In *Clinton v. Jones* (1997), the justices rejected the argument for presidential immunity in this particular instance. The majority found that nothing in the history of the Constitutional Convention or in a series of cases relating to presidential immunity suggested that a president could be shielded from a lawsuit based on events or actions that took place before the person became president. The justices were also not convinced by the president's argument that by having to defend his position in this lawsuit, he would be seriously impeded from performing his official duties. They further emphasized that federal courts have jurisdiction over presidents and other federal officials in their official capacity and that there was no reason why the courts could not proceed in suits involving matters that may have occurred prior to one assuming official federal responsibilities. The significance of the Supreme Court's decision in *Clinton v. Jones* was that the case was allowed to go forward. The pace began to quicken. On August 17, President Clinton admitted to an "inappropriate relationship" with Ms. Lewinsky; the November elections in Congress cost the Republican majority five seats in the House; and the House Judiciary Committee convened impeachment hearings in November against the president.

On December 19, after two days of polarized debate on what to do and why, the full House of Representatives voted in favor of two articles of impeachment. Article I, which accused the president of providing "perjurious, false and misleading testimony to the grand jury," passed on a House vote of 228 to 206, with five Republicans voting against the charge and five Democrats voting in favor of it. On Article III, which claimed that Clinton " . . . prevented, obstructed and impeded the administration of justice . . . ," the full House voted 221 in favor and 212 against the motion to impeach the president. On this article, five Democrats voted in favor of it and twelve Republicans voted against it. Articles II and IV of the impeachment charges—lying in the Jones sexual harassment case and lying to Congress in written responses—failed passage in the House by significant margins. With this House action, William Jefferson Clinton became the first elected president in American history to be impeached by the House, and the first since Andrew Johnson in 1868 to stand trial in the Senate for "high crimes and misdemeanors." (Johnson, of course, had never been elected to the office, having succeeded to the presidency in 1865 following the assassination of President Abraham Lincoln.)

Immediately following the House action, prominent members of the Senate, the chamber that would have to consider the charges brought by the House, began to suggest publicly how that body might have several options short of a formal trial and possible conviction, which might more properly evaluate the heavily partisan charges that lay before the Senate now. On December 22, an op-ed article in the *New York Times* coauthored by former Presidents Gerald Ford and Jimmy Carter suggested that "the time has come to put aside political differences and plant seeds of justice and reconciliation." They called on the Senate to draft a bipartisan censure resolution that would require Clinton to acknowledge finally that he did not tell the truth under oath, but the resolution would also stipulate that his admission could not be used against him in any future criminal proceeding.[10]

As political events transpired in January 1999, the Senate trial displayed a very different demeanor and outcome than that which had occurred in the House. By the time the evidence was presented, the speeches made, and the final vote tallies were taken on February 12, 1999, the Senate failed to amass the two-thirds vote necessary on either of the two articles of impeachment. Article I on the perjury charge failed to pass the Senate, drawing a 45–55 vote not to convict, and the Article III charge on obstruction of justice found the Senate deadlocked 50–50.

From a constitutional standpoint, the heart of the Clinton—Lewinsky scandal amounted to a sexual relationship and an elaborate, perjured charade to conceal it. But it is arguable that it truly warranted impeachment and removal from office. Public opinion throughout the fall of 1998, even after the House voted in favor of two articles of impeachment, seemed to reflect the common wisdom of disciplining the president in some significant way but not compelling him to leave office prematurely. One can make a credible case that if a very partisan impeachment process had forced another president from office, far more damage would have been inflicted upon the constitutional order of things than having a president in power that cheated on his wife and lied about it. A parliamentary system might dispose of the Clinton—Lewinsky sex scandal in a very different way by marshalling a vote of "no confidence," but the United States chose two centuries ago not to adopt such a system, and its history and operation have most likely been the better for it.

Congress at Work: An Overview

As noted above, the Constitution contains seventeen expressed grants of authority to Congress, along with the power to pass "necessary and proper" legislation. In its more than 220 years of existence, Congress has used those enumerated powers to build a nation of laws spanning a wide area. It would be impossible in this limited space to examine all of the significant legislation enacted in that time, but it is possible to identify several key areas in which congressional authority has been most evident and influential. Other chapters in this book focus on congressional influence and are not covered here. For example, Chapter 3 examines the significant role Congress plays in establishing and structuring the federal court system, including the confirmation of its judges. Chapter 8 describes the massive presence of Congress in the regulatory state by examining its expansive commerce, taxing, and spending powers. Chapters 9 and 10 look closely at ways in which Congress has legislated to end discrimination in many areas of American life, and Chapters 11 through 18 chronicle the role played by Congress in protecting the civil liberties of Americans. Given the wide coverage of the work of Congress in nearly all other chapters, two additional topics have been selected for analysis because these two capture the core functions of Congress: organizing and staffing government and the power of the purse.

ORGANIZING AND STAFFING GOVERNMENT

The First Congress was faced with essentially a blank slate. The federal government consisted of nothing other than a president and one Supreme Court until Congress went to work. It established the federal judiciary with the Judiciary Act of 1789, creating a system of inferior courts and giving the Supreme Court some new powers (see Chapter 3). It then turned its attention to the executive branch. All cabinet departments have been established by legislation, starting with State, Treasury, and War in 1789, followed by twelve other departments: Interior (1849); Justice (1870, but the office of Attorney General had been around since 1789); Agriculture (1889); Commerce (1903); Labor (1913); Health, Education and Welfare (1953, but renamed Health and Human Services in 1979); Housing and Urban Development (1965); Transportation (1966); Energy (1977); Education (1980); Veterans Affairs (1989); and Homeland Security (2002).

To keep pace with a rapidly growing national economy, Congress began to provide additional structure to the executive branch in the nineteenth century. The passage of the Interstate Commerce Act of 1887 resulted in establishment of the Interstate Commerce Commission, the nation's first independent regulatory commission. This was followed quickly by the Sherman Anti-trust Act in 1890, a law that has governed national anti-trust policy ever since (see Chapter 8). Growing economic complexity and technological innovations have given Congress more reasons for adding to the federal bureaucratic structure. Independent agencies and commissions proliferated in the twentieth century, with Congress deciding on the focus and mission of each new entity. The Federal Trade Commission (1913) was established to address a growing problem involving truth in advertising and other unfair trade practices, and it was followed by the Federal Reserve System, the Federal Communications Commission, the National Labor Relations Board, the Securities and Exchange Commission, and numerous other boards and commissions designed to regulate and oversee specific areas of federal concern.

The New Deal produced a demand for new congressional action to oversee the burgeoning federal programs that were being created. New entities in the executive branch such as the Federal Deposit Insurance Corporation, the Social Security Administration, and the Tennessee Valley Authority, to name only a few, required Congress to delegate its power to agencies so that they could carry out specific policies aimed at achieving the desired results. Congress lacked the expertise and the time to oversee all of these new programs and technologies, and so it created more and more bureaucracy. The Great Society of Lyndon Johnson spurred Congress onward in its expansion of bureaucracy, adding new agencies such as the Consumer Product Safety Commission, Equal Employment Opportunity Commission, and the U.S. Commission on Civil Rights, and the scandal of Watergate gave rise to the Federal Election Commission. Overall, Congress has presided over the establishment of hundreds and hundreds of federal departments, agencies, boards, commissions, offices, and corporations that conduct the nation's business by carrying out Congress's own expressed powers (see Brief 6.5).

Congress also plays a substantial role in staffing the federal bureaucracy. A new president entering office has somewhere near 7,000 "patronage" or political jobs to fill. Of the total, about 1,000 must also submit themselves to confirmation by the Senate. The Senate's "advise and consent" function allows it to participate in the confirmation process and, in some cases, make things difficult for high-level appointees. Patronage appointments are, by definition, political and not always designed to produce the most qualified person for the job. The disastrous handling of the

Brief 6.5

THE RISE OF GOVERNMENT CORPORATIONS

President Franklin Roosevelt was intent on bringing new solutions to the nation's economic problems, so he asked Congress to create "a corporation clothed with the power of government but possessed of the flexibility and initiative of a private enterprise." Congress passed the Tennessee Valley Authority (TVA) Act in 1933, establishing the first government corporation. The TVA embarked on a series of activities including power generation and distribution, hydroelectric projects, and flood control, among others. The Supreme Court upheld TVA's authority over challenges by private companies in *Ashwander v. TVA* (1936). The first government corporation had been born.

Congress has leaned toward government corporations when an agency is involved essentially in commercial activities, when an agency can generate its own revenues, and when an agency requires flexibility that is not always available to government agencies. Several currently operating government corporations include the Federal Deposit Insurance Corporation (FDIC), AMTRAK, and the United States Postal Service (USPS). The FDIC was established in 1933 in response to the thousands of bank failures across the country. The FDIC takes pride in noting that no depositor in an FDIC-insured bank has ever lost a single penny of insured funds (the insured limit is currently $250,000 per depositor, per insured bank, for each account ownership category), and it also points out that it does not receive any money from Congress. It is funded by premiums from banks and other institutions to purchase insurance. AMTRAK and the USPS have not become profitable, and both rely on continued appropriations from Congress. The corporate model also has been adopted at the state and local level, with such entities as turnpikes, airports, and ports often operating in this way.

SOURCES: Jay M. Shafritz, E. W. Russell, and Christopher Borick, *Introducing Public Administration*, 6th ed. (New York: Pearson, 2009), pp. 94–95; "From the New Deal to a New Century," www.tva.com;abouttva/history.htm; "Who is the FDIC?", www.fdic.gov/about/learn/symbol/index.html.

Hurricane Katrina situation by a largely inexperienced Federal Emergency Management Agency (FEMA) director led Congress to pass the Post-Katrina Emergency Management Reform Act of 2006. In an effort to improve FEMA, Congress required that the administrator must have a "demonstrated ability in and knowledge of emergency management and homeland security; and . . . not less than 5 years of executive leadership and management experience."[11]

But the approximately 7,000 political appointees are a mere fraction of the nearly 2.7 million civil servants and 1.4 million uniformed persons that make up the federal bureaucracy. Congress has constitutional authority over the federal personnel system in general, and it has used its legislative powers to construct a large civil service system. The first step in this regard was taken with the passage of the Pendleton Act in 1883. The Act was enacted largely in response to the assassination of President James A. Garfield by a deranged office-seeker in 1881. With pressure building to take away the power of the "spoils system" based on patronage and replace it with a merit-based plan, Congress saw the Pendleton Act as a beginning. Although the Act covered only about 10 percent of the federal service, it gradually increased under each new administration to more than 70 percent by the end of World War I.[12] President Jimmy Carter further reformed the system when he signed the Civil Service Reform Act of 1978. The Act replaced the U.S. Civil Service Commission with two agencies: an Office of Personnel Management (OPM) and the independent Merit Systems Protection Board (MSPB). While the civil service system has declined somewhat in recent years, being replaced by more privatized jobs and government contractors, it remains one of Congress's most significant and enduring contributions to our federal government.

THE POWER OF THE PURSE: TAXING, SPENDING, AND BORROWING

Perhaps no responsibilities are more associated with Congress than the powers to levy taxes, spend money, and borrow money on the credit of the United States. These essential powers provide Congress with the means of financing and funding the workings of the federal (and increasingly state) government. These powers were not granted to the Congress during the Articles of Confederation era, and the result was a government without the ability to resolve financial problems as they arose. The Founders saw the clear need to equip the new Congress with a full arsenal of powers related to money, believing that the survival of a national government depended on it. The power to tax and spend as it applies to the federal police (regulatory) power is discussed in Chapter 8 and is not discussed here. That chapter also contains a thorough analysis of how the Supreme Court has ruled in both taxing and spending matters. As a result, they will not be included in this discussion. Instead, this section focuses on the ways in which taxing, spending, and borrowing powers have combined to give Congress its power of the purse.

TAXATION

The Constitution provides that Congress may "lay and collect Taxes, Duties, Imposts and Excises," and that "all Duties, Imposts and Excises shall be uniform throughout the United States." Other than the last requirement concerning uniformity throughout the country, there are no other constitutional limitations on taxation. The uniformity requirement made an income tax unconstitutional in 1895 (see Chapter 8) until Congress proposed and the states ratified the Sixteenth Amendment in 1913. That amendment allowed Congress the power to lay and collect taxes on incomes from whatever source derived, without apportionment among the states. The Sixteenth Amendment opened the money pipeline from individuals directly to the federal government, and it remains the largest source of revenue for the government. In addition to individual income taxes, the federal government relies on other sources as well: Corporate income taxes, for example, are collected on the profits of corporations; Social Retirement Taxes represent Social Security, Railroad Retirement, and Medicare taxes generally withheld from paychecks by employers or paid directly by self-employed earners; Excise Taxes are levied on specific items, including gasoline, alcohol, tobacco, and telephones; other sources of revenue come from customs duties, estate and gift taxes, and some trust funds. Table 6.4 displays the general sources of federal revenue and provides some interesting findings.

The most obvious statistic to be drawn from Table 6.4 is the tremendous increase in revenues over the past fifty years from about $93 billion to more than 2.5 trillion—a 2600% increase. Of course, the nation has grown as well, from nearly 180 million people in 1960 to more than 300 million in 2010, equal to about a 67 percent increase. Obviously, government's growth as measured through its revenues has far outstripped the grown of the population. But, of course, it is not just about total revenues. An examination of the sources of revenue reveals some interesting findings. First, at least in relative terms, the data suggests that income taxes continue to represent about the same percentage of federal revenues as they did back in 1960. The real change has been in other areas. Corporate income taxes, perhaps reflecting the power and influence of corporations, have declined as a share of federal revenues from 23 percent in 1960 to 9 percent in 2010, a reduction of over 50 percent. Meanwhile, social retirement taxes, including Social Security, Railroad Retirement, and Medicare, have more than doubled from 16 percent to more than 37 percent of the total. Excise taxes have experienced a significant, nearly five-fold drop from 16 percent to 4 percent in 2010. Overall, the statistics suggest a changing pattern of funding for the federal government, except for the consistent place of individual income taxes. Perhaps most significantly, retirement-related taxes may be on a path to eventually surpass income taxes as the major source of federal revenue.

Table 6.4 United States Revenue in Selected Years and Percentage Breakdown by Type of Tax

Source	1960	1970	1980	1990	2000	2010
Total revenues (billion $)	93	199	520	1,032	2,026	2,163
% Individual income taxes	44	46	47	45	50	42
% Corporate income taxes	23	19	13	9	10	9
% Social retirement taxes	16	23	31	37	32	37
% Excise taxes	13	8	5	3	3	4
% Others	5	5	9	5	5	6

Percentages may not equal 100% due to rounding.
SOURCES: Census Department, *Statistical Abstract of the United States, 2012.*

Spending

The congressional power to spend money and to pay the debts of the United States has been solidly established since the first Congress in 1789. In the early days of the nation, not much budget planning took place. If Congress needed money to pay for a road, a war, or a payroll, it usually just allocated the funds. Beginning in the twentieth century, reformers began to call for reform of the budget process. The Taft Commission in 1912 recommended a national budgeting system, and this led to passage of the 1921 Budget and Accounting Act. This act brought two important new components into the system: the Bureau of the Budget and the General Accounting Office, now known respectively as the Office of Management and Budget (OMB) and the General Accountability Office. The 1921 Act also introduced the concept of an executive budget and required the U.S. president to submit an annual budget to Congress for its review. In 1967, the President's Commission on Budget Concepts called for the introduction of a unified budget, one that combines receipts and outlays from federal funds and trust funds (such as Social Security), and one was adopted in 1969. Table 6.5 describes the pattern of national spending in selected functional areas.

The phenomenal growth of federal spending over the past fifty years or so can be attributed to the significant increase in federal programs, especially those that involve payments to individuals. Nearly sixty percent of all expenditures today go to payments for individuals in one form or another. Probably about 75 percent of those payments are direct payments (i.e., they go straight to individuals). Programs such as Social Security and Medicare take up the largest share of those payments. Social Security was not broken out as a separate area until 1980 in the above table, but today it accounts for more than 20 percent of all outlays. When combined with other direct payments for income security, health, and education, the total is well over 50 percent. National defense spending, once about half of all spending, now represents slightly over 20 percent of the total, having dropped to around 16 percent before the tragedy of September 11, 2001, and the subsequent military actions in Iraq and Afghanistan. Finally, the table shows how total spending for agriculture, veterans, and education do not really amount to much of the total spending by government each year. More is spent to pay the interest on the national debt than for these areas combined.

Borrowing and Debt

A comparison of Tables 6.4 and 6.5 shows that revenues and expenditures were nearly identical (hence, a balanced budget) in 1960 and 1970. They began to diverge in 1980 and have grown progressively wider ever since. As anyone on a budget knows, spending more than one earns results in a deficit; the opposite results in a surplus. Because the Constitution empowers Congress to pay the debts of the United States, it is Congress that must ultimately pay for these deficits.

Table 6.5 United States Outlays in Selected Years and Percentage Breakdown by Area

Source	1960	1970	1980	1990	2000	2010
Total outlays ($ billions)	92	198	580	1,253	1,789	3,456
% National defense	49	40	23	24	16	20
% Income security	20	22	33	12	14	18
% Health	1	7	10	5	9	25
% Social Security	–	–	20	20	23	22
% Veterans services	6	4	4	2	3	4
% Agriculture	4	3	2	1	2	1
% Education	1	4	5	3	3	4
% Net interest on debt	9	9	11	15	12	6

Percentages may not add to 100% because not all areas are listed.

SOURCES: Census Department, *Statistical Abstract of the United States*, various years.

Runaway government spending did not begin in the 1980s. Its seeds were sown many decades ago when American citizens began to rely increasingly upon the federal government to provide economic security in their lives, a strong national defense, and a prosperous economy. It was cultivated by successive presidential and congressional actions in the post-war period that courted multiple constituent interests demanding ever-larger federal outlays for an endless array of public programs and individual entitlements. By 1981, the Reagan administration had pushed through a divided Congress a budgetary package that combined large personal and corporate income tax cuts, massive increases in defense spending, and marginal decreases in entitlement spending. The immediate consequence of these economic promises was an increasing federal budget deficit each year. Prior to 1982, no budget deficits exceeded $100 billion, and after 1982, no annual deficit was less than $100 billion.

In the fall of 1985, Congress passed by overwhelming margins the Balanced Budget and Emergency Deficit Control Act, frequently referred to as GRH for the three U.S. senators responsible for its sponsorship: Phil Gramm (R-TX), Warren Rudman (R-NH), and Ernest Hollings (D-SC). As the title implies, the law was intended to eliminate the federal budget deficit by setting an annual deficit-reduction target of $36 billion in each of the five fiscal years through FY91. If the estimated budget deficit exceeded the maximum allowable amount in any fiscal year, the act required across-the-board cuts (sequestering) in federal spending to reach the targeted deficit-reduction levels, with one-half the reductions coming from domestic programs and one-half from the military budget. Some exemptions from such mandatory cuts were allowed in Social Security, Medicare, and portions of national defense.

Automatic deficit reduction was to be accomplished annually through a complicated process whereby the directors of the Office of Management and Budget (OMB) and the Congressional Budget Office (CBO) would estimate the size of the federal deficit for the upcoming fiscal year. If that estimated deficit exceeded the targeted amount, then the OMB and the CBO were to determine the necessary reductions in each program in order to meet the maximum deficit amounts. The directors of these two offices would then report the deficit estimates and the recommended cuts to the Comptroller General of the United States, who would then recommend the necessary budget reductions to the president. With much fanfare, President Reagan signed the bill into law on December 12, 1985, but several members of Congress immediately challenged the law as violating the separation of powers doctrine. When the lower courts found the law unconstitutional, the case was appealed to the Supreme Court.

On July 7, 1986, the Supreme Court ruled by a 7 to 2 vote in *Bowsher v. Synar* that the elaborate deficit-reduction process violated the Constitution because it improperly blended legislative and executive authority in the Comptroller General of the United States, an officer of the legislative branch of government. In his majority opinion Chief Justice Warren Burger wrote:

> . . . Congress cannot reserve for itself the power of removal of an officer charged with the execution of the laws . . . . To permit the execution of the laws to be vested in an officer answerable only to Congress would . . . reserve in Congress control over the execution of the laws.

Noting that the "dangers of congressional usurpation of Executive Branch functions have long been recognized," Burger said that Congress's intention to reduce the deficit could not be realized by resorting to an unconstitutional device.

The political and economic struggle over the nation's budget deficit has intensified over recent years. Table 6.6 provides a look at the pace and amount of deficit spending over the past thirty-three years. Throughout all that time, with the exception of three years at the end of the Clinton administration, Congress has neither been able to curtail its spending nor to increase revenues. Americans have become accustomed to deficit spending, demanding more entitlements from government while showing alarm at any calls for tax increases. It is a difficult cycle to break.

As 2012 drew to a close, the nation watched as Congress and the president addressed the impending "fiscal cliff." The so-called fiscal cliff was all about

Table 6.6 Budget Deficits in the United States, 1977–2010

Fiscal Year	Administration*	Deficit(−)/Surplus (+) (in billions of dollars)
1977	Carter	−53.7
1978	Carter	−59.2
1979	Carter	−40.7
1980	Carter	−73.8
1981	Reagan	−79.0
1982	Reagan	−128.0
1983	Reagan	−207.8
1984	Reagan	−185.4
1985	Reagan	−212.3
1986	Reagan	−221.3
1987	Reagan	−149.7
1988	Reagan	−155.2
1989	Bush I	−152.6
1990	Bush I	−221.2
1991	Bush I	−269.2
1992	Bush I	−290.3
1993	Clinton	−255.1
1994	Clinton	−203.2
1995	Clinton	−164.0
1996	Clinton	−107.4
1997	Clinton	−21.9
1998	Clinton	+69.3
1999	Clinton	+125.6
2000	Clinton	+236.2
2001	Bush II	+128.2
2002	Bush II	−157.8
2003	Bush II	−377.6
2004	Bush II	−412.7
2005	Bush II	−318.3
2006	Bush II	−248.2
2007	Bush II	−162.0
2008	Bush II	−458.6
2009	Obama	−1,412.7
2010	Obama	−1,293.5
2011	Obama	−1,645.1 (est.)

*A president in the first year of his administration had not participated in that year's budget.

SOURCE: Congressional Budget Office, Historical Budget Data, drawn from Table F-1, at www.cbo.gov/budget/historical.shtml; *Statistical Abstract of the United States, 2012*, Government Printing Office.

revenues and expenditures. The Bush-era tax cuts would expire on January 1, 2013, and a wide array of spending cuts would also take place on that date. Some economists predicted economic doom, and perhaps another recession, if the nation fell over the cliff. Others were not convinced that the effects would be severe. This game of political "chicken" was resolved for a short time when the two sides agreed to end the Bush-era tax cuts for single earners over $400,000 (couples over $450,000) and postponed the spending cuts. But the larger issue of the government deficit remained. Congress and the president had once again just "kicked the can down the road."

Conclusion

This chapter discussed the substantial powers exercised by Congress in pursuit of its constitutional authority with respect to investigations, budgeting, impeachment, and oversight of the executive branch. With the more extensive global responsibilities of the United States in foreign affairs in recent decades, the increasing fragmentation of power in Congress, and the prevalence of divided political control in Congress and the presidency, presidents have had more opportunity to act unilaterally in protecting national security. As the domestic and foreign policy commitments of the country have grown, it has required an enormous increase in the costs of government, and Congress and several administrations have sometimes had great difficulty mustering the political courage to remind the American public that these commitments require considerable sacrifice, both in terms of financial and human capital. As the last several decades have shown, the result has frequently been growing federal budget deficits that pay for the nation's global commitments with IOUs for future generations.

As the American people face grave new challenges in the twenty-first century, demands for a united front against global terrorism suggest a precarious balance between security and freedom. Several of the political events covered in this and the preceding chapter—the Vietnam War, the Watergate scandal and cover-up, the Iran-Contra incident, and several high-stakes clashes between Congress and the president—all inflicted significant damage upon the level of trust between the two elected branches of the government. These events have extracted a considerable toll on the American public's confidence in its leaders to do what is right. Trust is the hard currency of any institution or organization, especially in a democracy. With it, nearly everything is possible; without it virtually nothing is.

Those who drafted the American system in 1787 recognized that human wisdom and virtue frequently do not coexist in the same agent, especially when coupled with great power. It was for this very reason that the American system was constructed as it was, with numerous checks upon the exercise of power by fallible human beings. It is much better to have a government that is limited in its capacity to achieve only those goals acceptable to the people and their representatives than it is to allow supreme power to act in ways that are devoid of popular consent and substantial consensus. Unless the American public can be convinced of the virtue of a chosen foreign policy, unless its representatives in Congress can freely debate and construct a realistic, effective, and responsible strategy to accomplish clearly articulated objectives, and unless policies can be implemented by gifted leaders committed to preserving democratic consent, then a policy conceived in secret and hidden from public view has no place in a democratic system.

Ultimately, if a government is to be grounded in a democratic faith in the people, then both masses and political elites must engage in honest communication about the legitimate goals of constitutional government and the agreed-upon means to accomplish those objectives. The public must be confident about the need to communicate with government officials about public affairs, and responsible leaders must be committed to honoring the public trust that they presumably have earned. Self-government compels a people to debate the major issues of their time, and to do so openly, honestly, and thoroughly. If they cannot act accordingly, if they cannot trust each other to arrive at proximate solutions to difficult issues, then the citizenry can never lay claim to democratic self-government. In some important respects, this constitutional dynamic of deliberative democracy may well need renewal as the United States faces major challenges in the twenty-first century.

Chapter 7
Federalism: The Interaction of National and State Governments

THE FEDERAL STRUCTURE CREATED BY THE CONSTITUTION HAS CAUSED CONTINUOUS DEBATE BETWEEN THOSE ADVOCATES OF STATES' RIGHTS AND THOSE OF NATIONAL SUPREMACY. THE NEBRASKA STATE CAPITOL IN LINCOLN, SHOWN HERE, WAS THE FIRST IN THE NATION TO DEPART FROM TYPICAL STATEHOUSE DESIGN AND USE AN "OFFICE TOWER" STYLE OF ARCHITECTURE. IT HOUSES THE NATION'S LONE UNICAMERAL LEGISLATURE, ANOTHER DEPARTURE FROM THE NORM SYMBOLIZING THE DEGREE TO WHICH STATES ARE ALLOWED TO EXPERIMENT AND SET THEIR OWN COURSE WITHIN THE FRAMEWORK OF THE FEDERAL CONSTITUTIONAL SYSTEM.

▼ Introductory Remarks by Vice President and Senator John C. Calhoun

I was born in South Carolina in 1782 and remained a son of the South all my life. When I died in 1850, I had served in the South Carolina legislature, the United States House of Representatives, the United States Senate, and two terms as Vice President of the United States—serving two different presidents. Despite those many accomplishments and years of service, I seem to be remembered as the "Father of Nullification" and an opponent of the Union.

I was not always an opponent of the Union, having grown up as a strong supporter of national power and authority. I became disillusioned during my first term as Vice President under President John Quincy Adams, when I saw the northern manufacturing states gaining influence at the expense of my beloved South. The grossly unfair protective tariff that shielded American industry at the expense of other Americans proved to be the catalyst that led me to write my "Exposition" in 1828, arguing that a state could veto and refuse to enforce any law it considered to be unconstitutional. However, I did not advocate secession because I also said that a state's nullification would have to yield if three-fourths of the states upheld the law. As I stated at the time: *"I can scarcely dare hope that my friends to the North will sustain me in the positions I have taken, tho' I have the most thorough conviction that the doctrines I advanced, must ultimately become those of the Union; or that it will be impossible to preserve the Union."*

I presided over the United States Senate while my esteemed colleague from South Carolina, Robert Y. Hayne, debated Senator Daniel Webster in the Senate chamber in 1828, ostensibly over the issue of western lands, but really in a debate about the nature of the Union itself. I passed many notes to Hayne during the debate, trying to support the cause of the states.

I resigned the vice presidency and returned to the Senate in 1832, just in time for the leadership in South Carolina to issue the famous Ordinance of Nullification against the protective tariff. South Carolina stood alone, with no other states joining our cause, and we eventually achieved a kind of compromise—but the reality was that the Union was in deep trouble.

I became very ill with tuberculosis, so my last days in the Senate were difficult for me. I could see the slave trade under assault in Washington, D.C., and I opposed the Compromise of 1850 for that and other reasons. I listened to Senator Webster's famous "Seventh of March" speech, and I was able to summon enough strength to interrupt him with my fervent belief: "No sir! The Union can be broken." I knew that South Carolina and other southern states would eventually withdraw from the Union, although I did not live to see it. In this chapter, you will follow the timeline that led to secession and formation of the Confederacy and then follow the path of federalism through the twentieth century and into the twenty-first century.

As I observe today's Union, I still mourn for the lost sovereignty of the state governments, but I realize that the Civil War produced a result in which national supremacy is solidly entrenched. The Union has prospered, and national power has eclipsed state power completely. I am proud of the progress of the nation in the years since the Civil War, and I suppose I was on the wrong side of history; but our nation continues to debate the appropriate role of the national and state governments. I understand the reasoning behind the current petitions in several states calling for nullification, and I sympathize with the signers' frustrations, but that ship has sailed—the Union cannot be broken. Enjoy the chapter. JC

SOURCE: John C. Calhoun, 7th Vice President (1825–1832), United States Senate: Art and History Home, www.senate.gov/artandhistory/history/common/generic/VP_John_Calhoun.htm.

THE THEORY OF FEDERALISM

The preceding chapters have emphasized judicial review and the separation of powers, two of the most significant concepts in American constitutional government. These principles have provided distinct limits upon the power of government and ensured some degree of protection for individual rights. This chapter presents a third key principle of constitutional practice. This principle, termed **federalism**, lies at the root of the American experience.

Alexis de Tocqueville, the young Frenchman who traveled America in 1831 and 1832, found much that he admired in the United States. He saw particular promise for the American system of federalism. In his writings about the young country, Tocqueville proclaimed that Americans seemed to have a natural affinity for the federal system through their ability to easily separate national from state matters:

> I SCARCELY EVER MET WITH A PLAIN AMERICAN CITIZEN WHO COULD NOT DISTINGUISH WITH SURPRISING FACILITY THE OBLIGATIONS CREATED BY THE LAWS OF CONGRESS FROM THOSE CREATED BY THE LAWS OF HIS OWN STATE, AND WHO . . . COULD NOT POINT OUT THE EXACT LIMIT OF THE SEPARATE JURISDICTIONS OF THE FEDERAL COURTS AND THE TRIBUNALS OF THE STATE.[1]

Identifying and separating federal and state matters have not been quite as easy as Tocqueville suggested. In fact, the history of American federalism is more one of disagreement than of agreement over the proper limits of federal and state jurisdictions.

The Founding Fathers settled upon federalism as a means of creating the kind of strong national government not found in the Articles of Confederation. At the same time, federalism limited the national government by vesting significant authority in the established state governments. As a result, American constitutional development has often revolved around competing views of government power. Nationalists of the founding era, exemplified by Alexander Hamilton, drew attention to the need for a strong central government. Hamilton saw this need as especially acute in matters of defense, commerce, and foreign relations. James Madison, another early nationalist whose views later shifted toward states' rights, emphasized the fact that a federal arrangement would enable state governments to protect the liberty of their citizens by virtue of their close proximity to the people.

Federalism has produced disagreement over the exact location of **sovereignty**, or ultimate authority, in the nation. Advocates of national supremacy, or a strong central government, have been challenged by supporters of states' rights and, on occasion, state sovereignty. Although these disagreements normally could be settled peacefully through court decisions, legislation, or political compromise, they occasionally led Americans into conflict. Indeed, the massive destruction of the Civil War stands as the most obvious monument to the divisive tendencies contained in federalism. And yet, the Civil War experience actually resulted in a much strengthened federal system by removing extreme state sovereignty as a valid constitutional position.

This chapter explores the variations in federalism, ranging from the national supremacy of Alexander Hamilton and John Marshall to the states' rights of Thomas Jefferson and John C. Calhoun. The following chapter then shifts to an examination of the massive growth of national power, particularly in the areas of economic and social regulation. First, however, it is useful to examine federalism from a comparative perspective.

FEDERALISM: A COMPARATIVE PERSPECTIVE

Federalism is an arrangement in which a constitution formally establishes and divides powers between a national and "subnational" (usually state or provincial) government. Both governments are supreme within their proper sphere of authority, and both act directly on the same people. Therefore, the first characteristic of a federal system is that it guarantees at least two levels of governmental power. This can be contrasted to what is sometimes called a "unitary" system of government, in which one central government has complete sovereignty. Although local governments exist in a unitary system, they do so at the pleasure of the central government and possess only those powers granted to them by central authorities. In a federal system, on the other hand, states or provinces are "constitutionally" empowered to act in certain areas, free from national control.[2]

Since federalism was instituted in the United States more than two hundred years ago, several other countries have adopted some version of the system (see Table 7.1). The gradual expansion of federal systems

Table 7.1 Federalism in Comparative Perspective

Country	Federal Units*	Major Languages	Primary Reason for Federalism	Extent of States' Power
Brazil	26 states	One	Size/colonial history	Weak
Canada	10 provinces	Two	Size/language	Moderate
India	28 states	Many	Language/size	Moderate
United States	50 states	One	Colonial heritage/size	Moderate
Mexico	31 states	One	Colonial administration/ size	Weak
Nigeria	36 states	Several	Tribalism/size/language/colonialism	Weak/moderate
Switzerland	26 cantons	Several	History/language	Strong
Germany	16 states	One	Postwar occupation/regionalism/unification	Strong

*For some countries, state totals may include federal districts and/or other types of subdivisions.
SOURCE: *Central Intelligence Agency World Factbook.*

points up several related strengths and weaknesses of this division of governmental powers. In the first place, federalism appears to be quite popular among geographically large nations. Four of the world's six largest states—India, Canada, Brazil, and the United States—have established some form of a federal system. Even though these countries place varying degrees of emphasis on their federal systems, each has found federalism a useful way of governing a massive territory. Therefore, one perceived advantage of federalism seems to be in its ability to reduce the problems of distance in governing.

A second common pattern associated with the spread of federal systems is the use of federalism to deal with various sources of diversity among a population. Factors such as ethnicity, language, and religion have plagued many newly independent states seeking to build themselves into nations. For example, the founders of India, facing an incredibly diverse linguistic pattern, found state governments to be the answer to such diversity.[3] In Nigeria, the tribalism of the population seemed to suggest federalism as a natural solution, although the results have been disappointing. Federalism cannot be counted on to erase or eliminate ethnic and other divisions between people. Often, it may simply mask deep hatreds and animosities until they erupt into violence. The bloodshed in Bosnia, formerly a Yugoslav republic, among Serbs, Croats, and Muslims stands as a recent example of this phenomenon.

A third pattern of federalism can be traced to colonial practices of establishing territorial divisions to assist in administration. The Portuguese in Brazil and Spaniards in Mexico showed a tendency toward this type of arrangement. Among former British colonies, India and Nigeria contained colonial administrative districts that formed the basis for later federalism. In both India and Nigeria, the eventual states generally represented different language and ethnic groups. American federalism evolved from British colonial practices, as the colonies eventually formed the original thirteen states. However, America differs from other former British colonies in that American colonies were settled much more individually, for varying reasons, and over a considerably longer time span.

ORIGINS OF AMERICAN FEDERALISM

Federalism falls somewhere between the centralization of a unitary system and the decentralization of a confederation. As discussed in Chapter 2, early settlers to America had experienced unitary government in their dealings with England. In that arrangement, all power stemmed from the Crown and rested in the King and British Parliament. Laws regarding the entire British Empire were enacted in London, and the sovereignty of the Crown was indivisible. American colonies, despite attempts at some self-government, were subject to the power of the Crown and Parliament. Naturally, such an experience culminating in revolution produced little support among Americans for a unitary system of their own following independence.

In fact, early American leaders went first to the other extreme—a **confederation**—in their search for a workable governmental system. A confederation is a loose grouping of autonomous units with final authority or sovereignty resting in the individual units themselves. Central authority, to the degree that it exists, is subject to the overall sovereignty of the states that comprise it. For newly independent Americans in the late 1770s, such an arrangement was far superior to the centralized and, in their view, tyrannical British unitary system.

As Chapter 2 showed, the Articles of Confederation represented a clear departure from the centralization of a unitary system. The resulting arrangement, although often viewed as a failure, was precisely what architects of the Articles had envisioned—a loosely bound confederation of sovereign and independent states. Despite their shortcomings, the Articles left a legacy to American federalism in the area of interstate relations (see Brief 7.1).

The major critics of the Articles of Confederation were those who disapproved of such a weak national government, both in its dealings with the States and in matters of foreign affairs, trade, and defense. The Constitutional Convention produced a compromise between the centralization of a unitary system (which almost nobody wanted) and the extreme decentralization of a confederation. While the formal divisions between Federalists and anti-Federalists did not exist until after the Constitutional Convention, the Philadelphia delegates were at odds over the issue of governmental power, with some favoring a powerful national government and others pressing for continued state autonomy as practiced in the Articles of Confederation. From the two broad positions—one nationalist (Federalist), the other states' rights (Anti-Federalist)—was to come the basis for the federal system of the United States.

Brief 7.1

HORIZONTAL FEDERALISM: LEGACY OF THE ARTICLES OF CONFEDERATION

The Articles of Confederation established the importance of state-to-state relations and provided for specific areas of cooperation and "Comity," or friendship. Drawn almost exactly as written in the Articles, these provisions were incorporated in the new Constitution as Article IV. This "horizontal federalism" among states contains three key elements:

1. **Full Faith and Credit Clause**: Each state must give "full faith and credit" to the public acts, records, and judicial proceedings of the other states. This means, for example, that a marriage license or birth certificate obtained in one state is recognized as legal and authentic in another state. However, certain problems have been encountered in the area of divorce, especially in "uncontested divorces" obtained in other states. [See *Williams v. North Carolina*, 325 U.S. 226 (1945).] In 1996, the United States Congress, under its authority to declare what "effect" one State's acts, records, and judicial proceedings will have on another State, passed the Defense of Marriage Act (DOMA). This Act was prompted by the fear that Hawaii might recognize same-sex "marriage" and thereby place other states in the position of having to give them full faith and credit. It was struck down by the Supreme Court in *United States v. Windsor* (2013).

2. **Privileges and Immunities Clause**: This prohibits one state from abridging the "privileges and immunities" of citizens of the United States. Essentially, this means that a citizen of one state cannot be discriminated against in another state, especially in areas such as legal protection, access to courts, property rights, and travel. However, it should be noted that "privileges and immunities" protections do not extend to certain political rights, such as voting, nor to some privileges reserved to a state's own citizens. The college student quickly will recognize "out-of-state" tuition at state universities as such an exception.

3. **Extradition**: A term from international law that refers to the practice of returning escaped prisoners or persons wanted in another state. Although the Constitution places an obligation on states to extradite wanted persons, federal courts will not order a state governor to do so. On rare occasions a governor has refused to comply with an extradition request, but the request generally is expected to be honored on moral grounds. (Also, of course, the next time it may be the other state that is making the request for extradition.)

NATIONAL SUPREMACY: THE FEDERALIST POSITION

The Federalists—supporters of national supremacy, broad Constitutional construction, and **implied powers**—exercised influence over the federal system in two stages. In the first, from 1789 to 1801, Federalists controlled the executive, legislative, and judicial branches of government. Predictably, attention was directed toward strengthening the national government, much of it under Alexander Hamilton's direction. The second phase, brought on by the failure of the Federalists to compete politically at the polls, might be considered to span from 1801 to 1835, marking the years of Chief Justice John Marshall's tenure on the Supreme Court. During this phase, the Federalist perspective was essentially confined to the judicial branch while Congress and the president pursued different policies. As might be expected, the Supreme Court's decisions of this period were not always popular with the other branches.

Hamilton's view of federalism can be understood both from his writings before ratification and his later actions as Secretary of the Treasury. In *Federalist No. 23*, Hamilton discussed four purposes served by the new Union: common defense, public peace, regulation of commerce, and foreign relations. To accomplish these ends, said Hamilton, it was necessary to establish a unified government. While Hamilton denied any intention to abolish the state governments, he did reject any attempt to divide national from state powers. To do so, he reasoned, would unnecessarily limit the freedom of action required by a supreme national government.

Federalists controlled the presidency until Jefferson's election in 1800, although their working majority in Congress had been lost somewhat earlier. Because the government was so new, however, the Federalists wielded the immense power of filling in the blanks in the Constitution at a time when few precedents existed. For this reason, it is important to examine some key developments of the Federalist era.

THE JUDICIARY ACT OF 1789

The Judiciary Act of 1789 established a separate federal court system yet gave state courts concurrent jurisdiction in certain cases of federal law. The fundamental issue, however, involved the determination of final jurisdiction over federal law, a matter that the Constitutional Convention had left to a compromise of sorts. In Article VI, the Constitution, treaties, and national laws made in pursuance of the Constitution were declared to be the "supreme law of the land," but the "judges in every state" were to be bound by this provision. Apparently, state judges could determine the supremacy of national law—a wholly unacceptable prospect for a Federalist. In Section 25 of the Judiciary Act, Congress reasserted the sovereignty of the national government by providing for three instances in which appeal of state court decisions to the Supreme Court was possible: (1) when the state court ruled a federal treaty or law unconstitutional; (2) when a state court upheld a state law that had been alleged to conflict with the Constitution, treaties or laws of the United States; or (3) when a state court ruled against a right or privilege claimed under the Constitution or federal law. As a result of this provision, it could be inferred that final interpretation of federal law and the Constitution would henceforth come from the Supreme Court, not from the states themselves.

THE HAMILTONIAN ECONOMIC PROGRAM

Once Congress had created the executive departments of Treasury, War, and State, President Washington chose Alexander Hamilton to be his Secretary of the Treasury. In 1791, Hamilton initiated a broad program of legislation that included refunding of the Articles of Confederation debt at face value, creation of a national bank by federal charter, and passage of a protective tariff for American industry. Of these, the latter two were to stir considerable controversy on constitutional grounds.

As a staunch Federalist, Hamilton was not troubled by the prospect of Congress creating a national bank, in spite of the fact that it possessed no enumerated power to do so. In fact, Hamilton argued that Congress possessed powers beyond those delegated to it by the Constitution. Of these, Hamilton placed his greatest emphasis on the doctrine of "implied powers," which, as he reasoned, stemmed from the clause of the Constitution, which gave Congress the authority to pass laws "necessary and proper" for carrying out its enumerated powers.

Chief opponents of the national bank, fearful of increasing national dominance of the economy, rallied behind James Madison (who had become disenchanted with Hamilton's program) and Hamilton's major ideological rival, Thomas Jefferson. As Secretary of State until 1793, Jefferson was given an opportunity to express his views on the national bank, and his arguments became closely identified with a classic states'-rights, Anti-Federalist position. These opposing views are expressed in Table 7.2.

Hamilton saw the bank as closely tied to several of the Constitution's enumerated powers relating to money and commerce, while Jefferson and Madison saw no such relationship. For Hamilton and the nationalists, the power to create a national bank could be implied as "necessary and proper" for carrying out congressional enumerated powers. The states'-rights argument, on the other hand, by rejecting an enumerated power to create the bank, resorted to the Tenth Amendment's reservation of powers not delegated to the national government to the states. It was a classic case of broad versus strict construction of the Constitution. President Washington signed the law establishing the national bank in 1791. Apparently, Hamilton's views had prevailed.

While the first national bank's charter expired in 1811, a growing number of younger Republican political leaders—among them Henry Clay and John C. Calhoun—considered a national bank crucial to a strong national government. Accordingly, a law to create a second national bank was signed in 1816 by President Madison, ironically, one of the first bank's most vocal opponents. The bank's reemergence also coincided with a resurgence of states' rights and a growing resentment of federal intrusion into state affairs. For many states'-righters, the Second U.S. Bank epitomized national government interference, speculation, and mismanagement, and it quickly became a target of their anger.

JOHN MARSHALL'S FEDERALISM: *McCULLOCH V. MARYLAND* (1819)

The unpopularity of the Second U.S. Bank had spread into a number of states by 1818. Maryland levied a tax on all banks not chartered by the state, an obvious action against the U.S. bank's Baltimore branch. When Maryland courts upheld the state tax, the U.S. bank appealed to the Supreme Court. Maryland argued its case on two fronts: first, that the incorporation of a national bank was not provided for by the Constitution, thereby making the act of Congress unconstitutional; second, that Maryland, as a sovereign state, possessed the absolute power of taxation over all operations within its jurisdiction.

Maryland argued for **strict construction** of the Constitution, a position long associated with states' rights. According to this argument, no enumerated power expressly authorizes the incorporation of a bank, and Congress may not legislate beyond its enumerated powers. In his opinion, Chief Justice John Marshall acknowledged the government to be one of enumerated and, hence, limited powers, but he also argued that logic requires giving Congress the ability to execute its powers.

Having concluded that the national government's powers required execution, Marshall focused on the Necessary and Proper Clause. He stated that it was not necessary that the power to incorporate a bank be specifically delegated, provided that it served as a "necessary and proper" means to achieve a legitimate enumerated power. Because the Second U.S. Bank was an appropriate means to the attainment of a legitimate end, it was constitutional.

Maryland also argued that it possessed absolute power to tax all entities within its jurisdiction,

Table 7.2 Federalists vs. Anti-Federalists: The National Bank

Issues	Nationalists	States' Rights
Leadership	Hamilton/Marshall	Jefferson/Madison
Enumerated powers related to bank	Taxation, coin money, and regulate value thereof; regulation of commerce, etc.	No specific power
Constitutional authority	Necessary and Proper Clause	Tenth Amendment
Type of power	Implied	Reserved
Constitutional interpretation	Broad	Strict
Meaning of "necessary"	Convenient; useful, needful, incidental	Absolutely indispensable and essential

including the national bank. In this part of the opinion, Marshall leaned heavily upon the "supremacy clause" in Article VI of the Constitution and brought his reasoning down to a single premise, that "the Constitution and all laws made in pursuance thereof are supreme."[4] Marshall's logic rejected Maryland's taxation of the U.S. bank, since "the power to tax involves the power to destroy," and a supreme national government could not allow itself to be destroyed by a state. The Maryland tax was unconstitutional as applied to the national bank, although Maryland could tax anything else within its jurisidiction. This decision established the principle of **intergovernmental tax immunity**, by which federal and state governments generally may not tax each other.

From a current perspective, *McCulloch v. Maryland* stands as one of Marshall's most important opinions, but it was far from a popular decision with a majority of Americans of that era. Former Presidents Madison and Jefferson criticized the *McCulloch* decision, and several states went so far as to petition Congress unsuccessfully for a constitutional amendment allowing states to exclude the national bank from their territory. For Marshall, the constant danger to federalism lay in state encroachment of national power, strengthening his belief that the Constitution, and not the states, determines the proper balance of federalism in the nation.

STATES' RIGHTS: THE ANTI-FEDERALIST POSITION

The states'-rights position is centered in the Tenth Amendment, added to the Constitution in 1791:

> THE POWERS NOT DELEGATED TO THE UNITED STATES BY THE CONSTITUTION, NOR PROHIBITED BY IT TO THE STATES, ARE RESERVED TO THE STATES RESPECTIVELY, OR TO THE PEOPLE.

This vision of federalism shows a subordinate national government with only enumerated powers—all other powers being "reserved" to the states. The Constitution must be interpreted narrowly and strictly, making certain that the national government does not overstep its written authority and intrude upon the vast areas reserved to state control. The states'-rights view complements the Anti-Federalist position that, if government is to be responsive to the popular will, government power ought to be lodged in units closest to the people. This early communitarian perspective found among many Anti-Federalists rested on the belief that state governments were more likely to protect basic democratic values.

In spite of setbacks such as those in *McCulloch v. Maryland* and *Gibbons v. Ogden*, supporters of states' rights continued to seek alternatives to the Hamilton-Marshall concepts of national supremacy and broad constitutional construction. What remedy was available to an individual or a state when faced with an unacceptable (and allegedly unconstitutional) national law? The options available to states'-righters ranged from outright violent disobedience to more subtle forms of action. Several examples are presented below.

WHISKEY REBELLION (1794)

When Congress in 1790, as part of its "revenue program," levied a direct excise tax on whiskey, the stage was set for a test of federal power. The whiskey tax was especially odious to the small farmers and frontiersmen because it threatened a primary source of their livelihood and a major outlet for their surplus grain. When opposition to the tax began to intensify, Congress in 1792 authorized President Washington, largely at Hamilton's urging, to send the militia to restore order. In all, some 13,000 troops were dispatched to western Pennsylvania by 1794, and the insurrection was crushed. This episode was of great importance to the fledgling national government, for it demonstrated that national laws could be enforced, even against the threat of violent opposition.

JEFFERSONIANISM AND THE VIRGINIA AND KENTUCKY RESOLUTIONS (1798)

Probably the most significant Jeffersonian-inspired opposition to Federalist policies occurred in 1789 and 1798 over the issue of the Alien and Sedition Acts. The Alien Act authorized the President to order the deportation of any alien he considered dangerous to the United States, while the Alien Enemies Act authorized the President similar control over aliens from an enemy country. The Sedition Act made it illegal for any person to "defame" the government, the

President, or either house of Congress through writing, speaking, or publishing. When Jefferson's supporters quickly challenged the Sedition Act as a violation of the First Amendment, Federalist-appointed judges refused to invalidate the law. Convinced of the Act's illegality but unable to gain relief from the courts, Jeffersonian supporters sought out "states' rights" as an answer.

In secret, James Madison and Thomas Jefferson each drafted a series of resolutions and had them introduced into the legislatures of Virginia and Kentucky, respectively. Known as the Virginia and Kentucky Resolutions, they were adopted by the respective legislatures and sent to other states for their hoped-for concurrence in rejecting the Alien and Sedition Acts. The Virginia Resolution spoke of the state's duty to "interpose" itself between an invalid national law and the people. The theory of **interposition** was not spelled out further, but the implication could be drawn that state governments might exercise some duty to interpret the Constitution for themselves and their citizens. In a second declaration in 1799, Kentucky inserted the contention that states, "being sovereign and independent, have the unquestionable right to judge" an infraction of the Constitution, even pointing to "nullification" as a possible remedy. Neither Kentucky nor Virginia took action against the Alien and Sedition Acts, so a constitutional crisis was avoided.

As for the clearly unconstitutional Alien and Sedition Acts, the defeat of President Adams and the Federalists in 1800 sealed their fate. The Sedition Act was repealed by the new Jeffersonian-controlled Congress, although it appears that the act actually expired "according to its original terms" with the close of the Adams administration.[5] President Jefferson exercised his power of pardon to free all those convicted under the Sedition Act (see Brief 7.2).

Brief 7.2
JEFFERSONIANS AS NATIONALISTS, FEDERALISTS AS STATES'-RIGHTERS

While serving as president, Jefferson was called upon to exercise his authority in ways that contradicted his states'-rights and strict construction principles. Two situations stand out: the purchase of the Louisiana Territory from France in 1803, and the decision to embargo all foreign trade in 1807. When President Jefferson received information that Napoleon would sell French-owned Louisiana for $15 million, he recognized that the new territory would provide vast new areas for expansion and a plentiful supply of land -- two developments strongly favored by most Jeffersonians. Jefferson's Federalist opponents feared such a purchase because of its possible economic and political impact upon their already declining fortunes, so they resorted to constitutional arguments in support of their position: first, the lack of any enumerated power to acquire territory and, second, the compact theory of the Constitution, long supported by Jeffersonians. President Jefferson first sought to obtain a proposed constitutional amendment authorizing the purchase, but time constraints were too pressing, and he abandoned the attempt, essentially conceding that he was expanding the constitution. As for the compact theory, which held that the original states were equal members, Forrest McDonald has concluded that the Louisiana Purchase "contradicted the compact theory, with which Jefferson had been identified and which underlay the doctrine of states' rights."[6] Nonetheless, Jefferson's eventual decision to purchase Louisiana proved to be one of the single most important developments of his presidency and for the nation in general, even though it had required some reshaping of constitutional principles.

In 1807, Congress enacted the Embargo Act whereby all foreign trade, including exports and imports, was banned. This law had been motivated by the repugnant practices of Britain and France, locked in a bitter war against each other, against American shipping. Most distasteful for Jefferson and his supporters was the British practice of impressment—the seizure of American sailors on merchant ships as alleged deserters from the Royal Navy.

The Embargo Act had a devastating impact on the commercial interest of the New England states. One report holds that the value of American exports dropped from $128 million to $22 million as a result of the act.[7] Accordingly, the Act's opponents challenged it as an unconstitutional violation of the commerce clause. From a states'-rights perspective, the situation was very similar to the one that had surrounded the Alien and Sedition Acts ten years earlier. Several New England state legislatures, including Massachusetts and Connecticut, adopted resolutions reminiscent of the Virginia and Kentucky Resolutions, and Connecticut then dusted off the idea of "interposition." Despite the Embargo Act's repeal in 1809, the situation grew even worse with the decision to declare war on Britain in 1812. At the Hartford Convention, convened in 1814, the states proposed seven amendments to the Constitution that would protect New England's interests. Several of the proposed amendments were hardly subtle: No president could serve two terms; no two successive presidents could come from the same state (Jefferson and Madison, of course, were Virginians); embargoes could not extend beyond sixty days; and a two-thirds vote of Congress would be required to admit a new state, ban foreign trade, or declare war except when an actual invasion had occurred. Had the war not ended about this same time, a constitutional crisis might well have occurred.[8]

STATE SOVEREIGNTY: THE EXTENSION OF STATES' RIGHTS

By 1820, certain developments had begun to push opposition to federal policies southward. For one, the northern states' population advantage was becoming obvious, producing the fear among southerners that they would become a perpetual minority in the House of Representatives. The consequences of such a situation, according to southern interests, were potentially devastating. They were frightened by a growing, but by no means yet widespread, abolitionist movement in the northern states, threatening their ownership of slaves and, ultimately, their economic well-being. Second, the Congress seemed determined to protect American manufacturing and industry through a series of increasingly high protective tariffs on imported goods. Since most manufacturing was located in northern states, the tariff forced southern agrarian interests, as they saw it, to subsidize northern manufacturers by paying higher prices for finished goods. Finally, the country was in the process of expansion. Purchase of the Louisiana Territory in 1803 had opened up a vast new frontier, and new states had begun to join the Union as a result. These four factors—population shifts, slavery, northern protectionism, and territorial expansion—helped to produce extreme opposition to federal authority.

THE MISSOURI COMPROMISE

Due to northern domination of the House, control or at least parity in the Senate was seen as essential by slave interests. When the Missouri Territory, part of the Louisiana Purchase with a history of slavery, petitioned for statehood in 1818, it threatened to unbalance the current eleven free and eleven slave states. At issue was the constitutional procedure for admitting new states to the Union and the question of whether Congress could place restrictions on a prospective state as a condition of its admittance.

The constitutional language states that "new states may be admitted by the Congress into this Union," and Congress previously had admitted states under this provision (see Brief 7.3). However, in the previous instances, the state's geographic location and history had largely determined its status as slave or free state, and Congress had not been concerned with the issue. Anti-slave interests opposed to the expansion of slavery argued that the Constitution's use of the words "may admit" provided Congress with discretion to impose conditions on a prospective state—in this case, no slavery. Slave interests, on the other hand, favored the unconditional admission of Missouri as had been done for the nine states added to the Union since 1789. Other constitutional issues such as the status of free Negroes added to the rather confusing set of arguments.

Brief 7.3
STATES, TERRITORIES, AND FEDERALISM

The Constitution in Article IV, Section 3, dictates the rules concerning prospective states: "New states may be admitted by the Congress into this Union; but no new State shall be formed or erected within the Jurisdiction of any other State, nor any State be formed by the Junction of two or more States, or Parts of States, without the consent of the Legislatures of the States concerned as well as the Congress." Beyond the thirteen original colonies, most new states (thirty) have advanced to statehood from territorial status (generally involving the four steps of petition for statehood, an enabling act by Congress, a state Constitution, and a final act of admission). Five states (Kentucky, Maine, Tennessee, Vermont, and West Virginia) came from other states, and two—Texas, an independent republic, and California, acquired from Mexico—entered by other means.

New states have been admitted on a fairly even basis in the nation's history. Counting the original thirteen states, the Union had grown to sixteen states by 1800. Another fifteen joined by 1850, and fourteen more were admitted by 1900, bringing the total to forty-five at the beginning of the twentieth century. Since then, the pace has slowed: three new admissions by 1950, followed by Alaska and Hawaii in 1959. Currently, of the territories that could be considered prospective states, only Puerto Rico has been mentioned seriously in that regard.

Article IV, Section 3 also authorizes Congress to make rules for territories of the United States. Territorial possessions currently include Guam, Puerto Rico, Samoa, the Virgin Islands, and the Territory of the Pacific Islands. Residents of Guam, Puerto Rico, and the Virgin Islands are citizens of the United States. The District of Columbia, although neither a state nor part of any state, is not considered a territory.

Ultimately, the compromise was made possible by the admission of Maine, formerly a part of Massachusetts, as a free state and, after considerable debate, the admission of Missouri with slavery intact. In addition, slavery was to be prohibited on the remaining Louisiana Purchase north of 36° 30' latitude. Congress hoped that it had finally put the issue to rest.

The Missouri Compromise is significant in the development of American federalism, for it marked the clear delineation of northern from southern states over the issue of slavery and virtually ensured a states'-rights position for the latter. Since the 36° 30' agreement allowed for more potential states north than south of the line, slave states were cast into the minority position they had long feared. Even though the prohibition of slavery in the territories was repealed by the Kansas-Nebraska Act of 1854 and declared unconstitutional by the Supreme Court in *Dred Scott v. Sandford* (1857), it stood for nearly thirty-five years as evidence of the sectional and regional problems facing the Union.

JOHN C. CALHOUN: STATE SOVEREIGNTY AND NULLIFICATION

The extreme states'-rights position as developed in the South prior to the Civil War was primarily the work of John C. Calhoun. As a young politician, Calhoun had been an active supporter of the expansion of national power, favoring both the Second National Bank and a protective tariff as ways of bringing unity to the nation. During his tenure as Vice President of the United States from 1825 until 1832, however, Calhoun's thinking began to change. One specific cause was the increasingly unpopular protective tariff (see Brief 7.4). Drawing upon earlier states'-rights theory, Calhoun constructed the most convincing and extreme rejection of national sovereignty the nation had yet encountered. According to Calhoun, sovereignty was expressed as the highest will of the community and could not be divided. The old notion that sovereignty was vested in both national and state governments was incorrect; sovereignty existed in only one political community. Since the states had existed as sovereign entities before the Union, particularly in the Confederation, they were the logical respondents of sovereignty in the Union itself. It is easy to see how **nullification**, Calhoun's most famous concept, derived from this analysis. Because states had retained their sovereignty, they alone could render the final interpretation of the Constitution. Should a state find a violation of the Constitution, it possessed the ultimate sovereignty to nullify the unconstitutional act.

Brief 7.4

THE WEBSTER–HAYNE DEBATE

For nearly two weeks in 1830, the United States Senate galleries were crowded with onlookers as two of the nation's most skillful orators engaged in a running debate. John C. Calhoun, the Vice President of the United States at the time, presided over the proceedings and passed notes of encouragement to his South Carolina colleague, Robert Y. Hayne. The debate began over the issue of western lands but quickly escalated into a contest over the nature of the federal union. Senator Hayne attacked the 1828 "Tariff of Abominations" and traced the doctrine of nullification back through Thomas Jefferson, the Virginia and Kentucky Resolutions, and even the Hartford Convention recommendations of 1814. His statement of the problem still stands as the classic states' rights view:

If the federal government in all or any of its departments is to prescribe the limits of its own authority, and the states are bound to submit to the decision and are not allowed to examine and decide for themselves when the barriers of the Constitution shall be overleaped, this is practically "a government without limitation of powers." The states are at once reduced to mere petty corporations and the people are entirely at your mercy.[9]

Massachusetts Senator Daniel Webster defended the Union with the claim (long advanced by other nationalists) that the people and not the states had formed the Constitution of 1787. Accordingly, Webster saw the solution to unpopular and unacceptable laws to rest with the people and their power to amend the Constitution "at their sovereign pleasure." But, he added, as long as the people "are satisfied with it, and refuse to change it, . . . who can give to the state legislatures a right to alter it, either by interference, constriction, or otherwise?"

While it is unlikely that the Webster-Hayne debate changed the minds of many Americans, it is clear that the competing views of federalism were never more eloquently debated. Unfortunately, in the final resolution of the conflict between nationalists and states'-righters, guns replaced oratory, and bloodshed replaced eloquence.

Calhoun recognized the possibility that one state's nullification might be overruled by a convention of states, but this would be possible only after at least a three-fourths vote of the states. Here was Calhoun's other key concept, that of the concurrent majority. As defined by Calhoun, a concurrent majority is a series of separate majorities of the "dominant interests" (states). It is achieved by "dividing and distributing the powers of government" and giving "each division or interest, through its appropriate organ, either a concurrent voice in making and executing the laws or a veto on their execution."[10] No decision could be made unless it commanded a majority of support in a majority of the states—a far more democratic procedure than the standard principle of numerical majority (50 percent plus one) used in Congress. In fact, Calhoun saw the principle as an integral part of constitutional government "by making it impossible for any one interest or combination of interests, or class or order, or portion of the community to obtain exclusive control . . ." As such, Calhoun's views supported the position of the minority against a dominant majority.

In 1832, South Carolina's States' Rights Party, in control of the state legislature, called a state convention to consider action against the national protective tariff acts passed in 1828 and 1832. By an overwhelming vote, the convention adopted an ordinance of nullification, declaring the 1828 and 1832 tariff acts to be "null, void, and no law." The ordinance prohibited the nullification from being challenged in state courts or appealed to the Supreme Court. If the national government interfered, South Carolina would secede from the Union.

President Andrew Jackson publicly warned South Carolinians that nullification was illegal and secession was tantamount to revolution. Both would be met with force if necessary. Congress enacted the Force Bill authorizing President Jackson to dispatch troops to South Carolina. Faced with strong national opposition (no other states had taken South Carolina's side) and given the promise of future tariff reductions, South Carolina formally withdrew its ordinance of nullification in early 1833. Its leaders claimed victory but it was clear that nullification had failed as a state weapon against national supremacy. For extremists, nullification's failure simply made secession a more viable alternative.

SECESSION: THE NATURE OF THE UNION

For proponents of extreme state sovereignty the failure of nullification seemingly left only one course of action in the event of unjust national legislation. The right of **secession**, or leaving the Union, had been admitted by Calhoun in his writings, but it was left to his followers to carry it to its conclusion. With the 1860 presidential election victory of Abraham Lincoln, an anti-slavery Republican, southern states quickly began a rapid secession from the United States. Citing the compact nature of the Constitution and undivided state sovereignty as arguments, seven states of the Deep South had seceded by January 1861, several months before Lincoln's inauguration. In early March, a Confederate Constitution based on state sovereignty was adopted, and the Confederacy was born (see Brief 7.5). The stage was set for a titanic struggle.

In his inauguration address, Lincoln carefully rejected secession as a constitutional possibility, arguing that the Union was perpetual, the Constitution was supreme, and secession was illegal. Lincoln refrained from waging war on the Confederacy, and he took the position that the southern states were still part of the Union, even though some state leaders were guilty of fomenting rebellion and insurrection. Confederate spokesmen argued that the conflict was a true international war between the United States and the Confederate States of America. Of course, legal niceties aside, even without a formal declaration of war against the Confederacy, the conflict certainly resembled a war in its military aspects.

While the Confederacy's surrender in 1865 gave a *de facto* answer to the question of secession, the constitutional position did not emerge until the Supreme Court decided *Texas v. White* (1869). By this time, of course, the conquered states were in the throes of **Reconstruction**, a policy undertaken by Congress to both punish and "rebuild" the insurrectionists. At issue in *Texas v. White* was the legal right of Texas to bring suit in federal courts to recover bonds issued by the Confederate Government of that state in 1862. Underlying the issue, however, was the claim that secession had stripped Texas of the legal and constitutional remedies afforded states in the Union.

In its decision, the Supreme Court held that "The Constitution, in all of its provisions, looks to

Brief 7.5
THE CONSTITUTION OF THE CONFEDERATE STATES OF AMERICA

A side-by-side comparison of the United States and Confederate States' Constitutions yields numerous insights into the mentality of southern advocates of state sovereignty. Woodrow Wilson's classic text, *A History of the American People*, provided such a comparison.[11] Several highlights from the Confederate Constitution are presented below.

I. **The Issue of Sovereignty**
   We, the people of the Confederate States, each state acting in its sovereign and independent character, in order to form a permanent federal government . . . (Preamble)

II. **Taxation, especially the protective tariff**
   The Congress shall have power—To lay and collect taxes, duties, imposts, and excises, for revenue necessary to pay the debts, provide for the common defense, and carry on the government . . . but no bounties shall be granted from the Treasury; nor shall any duties or taxes on importations from foreign nations be laid to promote or foster any branch of industry . . . (Art. 1, Sec. 8)

III. **Slaves and Property Rights--*Dred Scott* upheld**
   No . . . law denying or impairing the right of property in negro slaves shall be passed . . . (Art. 1, Sec. 9)
   The citizens of each State shall . . . have the right of transit and sojourn in any State of this Confederacy, with their slaves and other property; and the right of property in said slaves shall not be thereby impaired . . . (Art. 4)

IV. **Executive Power**
   The President and the Vice-President shall hold their offices for the term of six years; but the President shall not be re-eligible. (Art. 2)

Other interesting provisions in the Confederate Constitution included the **line-item veto**, which allows the executive to veto selective portions of proposed legislation. The practice, held unconstitutional at the federal level in 1998, is followed in several states today. With respect to the six-year presidential term with no re-election, a proposal favored in some circles today, the Confederacy did not last long enough to allow a test of the idea.

---

an indestructible Union, composed of indestructible states." Following this reasoning, "Texas continued to be a state, and a state of the Union," during the period of the Civil War. The right of Texas to bring suit in federal courts was affirmed, and secession was, for all practical purposes, a constitutional impossibility.

FEDERALISM IN THE POST–CIVIL WAR ERA

The Civil War's primary effect upon federalism was to demonstrate the supremacy of the national government and to settle the long-standing dispute over ultimate sovereignty. Nevertheless, the rivalry between national and state governments did not end with the Civil War. The tone of federalism remained one of suspicion and distrust well into the twentieth century, as states often sought refuge from national interference in the comfort of dual federalism—a safe haven created by the Tenth Amendment into which Washington bureaucrats could not intrude.

Early in the twentieth century, several developments combined to change the existing balance of federal–state relations. Passage of the Sixteenth Amendment in 1913 opened the door to a tremendous revenue imbalance between national and state governments. By allowing the federal government to tax capital, the amendment promised an expanding revenue base—as national income rises, tax revenues follow suit. While it should be noted that states also may tax incomes (and nearly all do so), they are relegated to a distant second place behind the federal government in income tax revenues.

THE NEW DEAL AND FEDERALISM

A second critical development that contributed to changing patterns of federalism involved the major economic crisis of the Great Depression in the late 1920s and 1930s. State and local leaders who had viewed earlier federal grants-in-aid as intrusions were now forced to care for a growing number of indigent and needy Americans, and these governments were woefully short of money. Moreover, no federal policy existed to address these concerns.

President Franklin Roosevelt's "New Deal" administration began in 1933 with the rapid creation of massive new job programs to put Americans back to work. New federal agencies such as the Civilian Conservation Corps (CCC) and the Works Progress Administration (WPA) placed the national government directly into the business of creating jobs and ending unemployment. In the first few years of the New Deal, national legislation addressed matters such as unemployment compensation, child labor, public housing, wages, and old-age benefits. Programs such as Aid to Families with Dependent Children (AFDC) offered financial assistance to those Americans who could not work for a variety of reasons. Several other New Deal reforms, including the Social Security Act, the Agricultural Adjustment Act, and the Fair Labor Standards Act, initiated massive changes that continue to the present day. These are discussed in the following chapter.

World War II and its aftermath further shifted the balance of power toward the federal government, as more grant programs were undertaken. The 1957 Russian launch of *Sputnik* sent such shockwaves through American society that only the national government was regarded as strong enough to meet the challenge. Federal grants suddenly were viewed as essential for national defense and meeting the challenge mounted by *Sputnik*. As an example, the National Defense Education Act of 1957 provided federal grants and loans for students in higher education. The supremacy of the national government was unquestioned by the mid-twentieth century, and its regulatory powers over economic and social concerns had become immense.[12]

LBJ AND THE "GREAT SOCIETY"

Nearly thirty years after the New Deal, President Lyndon B. Johnson launched an extremely ambitious extension of many elements of FDR's programs. Known as the "Great Society," President Johnson's program was highlighted by the "War on Poverty," which he believed constituted the single most important problem in America. The Great Society placed emphasis on giving poor Americans opportunities for advancement through education and job training programs. New initiatives such as Head Start emphasized early childhood development as a strategy to combat the perpetuation of poverty within families.

New programs also extended the "welfare state" in significant ways. The Food Stamp Program, for example, allowed qualifying persons the opportunity to purchase food at reduced prices, while other reforms brought food and nutrition into the nation's schools, through the Elementary and Secondary Education Act. The Great Society also placed health care as a high priority and thereby moved the national government directly into the center of the problem. Congress enacted LBJ's health care proposals by creating the Medicare and Medicaid systems, two of the largest expansions of federal control in modern times.

Other U.S. presidents placed their stamp on the federal system, often claiming to be instituting a "new" form of federalism. President Richard Nixon's "new federalism" largely continued the trend toward the growth of federal power. He established the Supplemental Security Income (SSI) program and expanded federal responsibilities into the environment with the creation of the Environmental Protection Agency (EPA) in 1970. While President Nixon also sought to show that his administration favored increased state authority through the use of "revenue sharing," his administration largely maintained or expanded the extent of federal power over state governments.

RONALD REAGAN'S FEDERALISM AND "DEVOLUTION"

Ronald Reagan's 1981 inaugural address captured the new president's view of federalism: ". . . the federal government is not part of the solution, but part of the problem." President Reagan's philosophy was driven by a desire to scale back federal programs and place more responsibilities with the states. He announced that he would seek to balance the federal budget through cuts in major federal programs, but increases in defense spending and new tax cuts actually caused the budget deficit to increase. Moreover, Congress would not agree to cut the largest federal programs, Social Security and Medicare. As a result, the "Reagan Revolution" did not actually do much to limit federal power, but it did provide the basis for an expanding debate over the direction of federalism.

When the Republican Party gained control of both the U.S. Senate and House of Representatives in 1994, it marked the first time in forty years that the party had gained that position. In what some supporters referred to as a "devolution revolution," the party promised a return of power, money, and responsibility to the states. It promised, for example, to prohibit the federal government from placing requirements on states without providing the necessary funding (referred to as "unfunded mandates"). Democratic President Bill Clinton announced his administration's support for many new reforms to return power to the states, with perhaps the most significant being passage of the Personal Responsibility and Work Opportunity Act of 1996. This Act gave states significant authority to run their own welfare programs using grants from the federal government, and, importantly, it ended the system of providing direct federal payments to poor families that had existed since the New Deal.

OTHER FEDERALISM ISSUES

As the United States moved into the twenty-first century, its system of federalism faced new and, in some instances, unexpected challenges. The movement toward devolving more powers to state governments continued on several fronts, but competing forces, especially those unleashed by the devastating events of September 11, 2001, produced even more pressure for national security and safety—and a stronger national government. Some pressures seemed to pull in favor of state government authority, especially those involving attempts to sue states for violating federal laws. Others, such as the movement toward "preemption," resulted in federal laws taking precedence over state legislation. Finally, of course, the effects of September 11, 2001, on federalism have been immense. These are discussed in the following section.

THE ELEVENTH AMENDMENT AND SOVEREIGN IMMUNITY

In the late 1990s and into the 2000s, the Supreme Court protected state governments from intrusive federal laws as well as from lawsuits filed under these federal laws. Whether the Rehnquist Court initiated a "revolution" in federalism or merely a modest adjustment is the subject of considerable debate and scrutiny by constitutional scholars.[13] The Eleventh Amendment was added to the Constitution in 1798 after the state governments became incensed over the Supreme Court ruling in *Chisholm v. Georgia* (1793). That decision had enabled a person in one state to bring a lawsuit in federal court against another state. States saw themselves in great danger of being subjected to federal court orders against their will. The Eleventh Amendment prohibits federal courts from allowing suits between citizens of one state and another state, or citizens of a foreign nation and one of the states. But what about the prospect of allowing federal lawsuits brought by citizens against their own states for allegedly violating their federal rights?

The Supreme Court held in *Hans v. Louisiana* (1890) that the Eleventh Amendment prevented Congress from allowing citizens to sue a state in a federal forum for breaching federal rights. However, for much of the twentieth century, Congress enacted laws that did just that. Citizens could bring suit against their state for denial of rights under the Civil Rights Act of 1964, the Voting Rights Act of 1965, the Fair Labor Standards Act, the Age Discrimination in Employment Act, the Americans with Disabilities Act, and the Family and Medical Leave Act, to name only a few. In resisting these suits, state governments often relied on the concept of **sovereign immunity**, which generally holds that the sovereign authority cannot be sued (see Brief 7.6).

Table 7.3 lays out the development of the law relating to a state's sovereign immunity in recent years. The table clearly demonstrates a willingness on the part of the Supreme Court to protect states from lawsuits for violations of federal laws. That is, with perhaps one major exception: *Nevada Department of Human Resources v. Hibbs* (2003). The Court denied sovereign immunity from suits under the Family Medical Leave Act's family-care provisions. What was so different about this case?

In *Hibbs*, a 6–3 Court held that state employees could sue and collect money damages in federal court in the event of the State of Nevada's failure to comply with the Family and Medical Leave Act's (FMLA)

Brief 7.6

SOVEREIGN IMMUNITY IN A DEMOCRACY?

The doctrine of sovereign immunity evolved from our Anglo-Saxon heritage, and it represented one of the key pillars of early law. The doctrine rests on the argument that the king is sovereign and can do no wrong. As a result, he cannot be held accountable under the law for wrongdoing, as wrongdoing is an impossibility. While the origins of sovereign immunity are clear, the evolution of the doctrine in the United States is another matter. Why should a constitutional political system based on the rule of law hold on to a "king-can-do-no-wrong" rationale? In a system based on the rule of law, no person is supposed to be above the law.

Traditional justifications for sovereign immunity focus on the danger of allowing individuals to sue the government for damages it might cause and potentially bankrupt the state. Justice Oliver Wendell Holmes, writing for a unanimous Court in *Kawananakoa v. Polyfolank* (1907), expressed this view:

> *A sovereign is exempt from suit, not because of any formal conception or obsolete theory, but on the logical and practical ground that there can be no legal right as against the authority that makes the law on which the right depends.*

Sovereign immunity has gradually diminished in recent years, but the doctrine still continues to make it extremely difficult for injured parties to receive full and fair compensation for damages caused by government or its officials. Governments have legislated to provide some remedies for injured citizens. The Federal Tort Claims Act (1946), for example, lays out the areas in which the federal government will allow itself to be sued and the ways in which such suits must be handled. Most state governments have passed similar laws, but these laws are riddled with exceptions and limitations. Many government officials generally continue to enjoy at least "qualified immunity" for their actions, meaning that suits for damages against public officials are often problematic. Some government officials, including judges, prosecutors, and the President (see *Nixon v. Fitzgerald*, 1982), enjoy "absolute immunity."

---

family-care provision. The FMLA, passed in 1993, entitles an eligible employee to take up to twelve work weeks of unpaid leave annually for the onset of a "serious health condition" in the employee's spouse, for the birth or the adoption of a child, and for other reasons. Hibbs asked for and received twelve weeks' leave to care for his ailing wife, but the Department eventually informed him that he had exhausted the leave and had to return to work by a certain date. Hibbs then sued under the FMLA provisions that create a private right of action to seek both equitable relief and money damages "against any employer (including a public agency)" that "interfered with, restrained, or denied the exercise" of FMLA rights. The district court ruled against Hibbs on Eleventh Amendment grounds, but the Ninth Circuit Court reversed.

Chief Justice Rehnquist's majority opinion distinguished *Hibbs* from the earlier Eleventh Amendment decisions by emphasizing the unique features of the FMLA, calling it "prophylactic legislation" to deter unconstitutional conduct rather than a "substantive redefinition" of the states' legal obligations. In other words, the FMLA was different from the Religious Freedom Restoration Act, the Age Discrimination in Employment Act, and the Americans with Disabilities Act, but why?

The Chief Justice provided the following explanations:

- Valid legislation must exhibit "congruence and proportionality between the injury to be prevented or remedied and the means adopted to that end."
- The FMLA aims to protect the right to be free from gender-based discrimination in the workplace. Statutory classifications that distinguish between males and females are subject to heightened scrutiny.
- When it enacted FMLA, Congress had before it significant evidence of a long and extensive history of sex discrimination with respect to the administration of leave benefits by the States.
- The cases in which the Court reached an opposite conclusion (*Kimel*, *Garrett*) are distinguished on the ground that the issues (age and disability) are not judged under heightened scrutiny, but rather rational scrutiny.

Table 7.3 Development of the Law: The Eleventh Amendment and Sovereign Immunity

Year	Case	Ruling and Significance
1890	*Hans v. Louisiana*	Citizens may not sue states in a federal court for breaching federal rights.
1996	*Seminole Tribe v. Florida*	Held federal Indian Gaming Regulatory Act violated Florida's sovereign immunity.
1997	*Idaho v. Coeur d'Alene Tribe of Idaho*	Tribe could not sue Idaho in federal court to secure title to land; court signaled a broader sovereign immunity.
1999	*Florida Prepaid Postsecond-ary Education Expense Bd Act. v. College Savings Bank*	Held Florida immune from suit under the Patent Remedy Act.
1999	*College Savings Bank v. Florida Prepaid Postsecond-ary Education Expense Bd*	Held Florida immune for misrepresentation under the Trademark Remedy Classification Act.
1999	*Alden v. Maine*	Held that sovereign immunity extends to state courts as well as federal courts; dismissed suit under the Fair Labor Standards Act.
2000	*Kimel v. Florida Board of Regents*	The federal Age Discrimination in Employment Act (ADEA) had improperly sought to waive the state's immunity.
2000	*Bd of Trustees of Univ. of Alabama v. Garrett*	Ruled suits by citizens against states for violations of the Americans with Disabilities Act (ADA) were invalid.
2002	*Federal Maritime Comm. v. South Carolina State Ports Authority*	State sovereign immunity applies to complaints being adjudicated by an administrative agency.
2002*	*Lapides v. Board of Regents of Univ. System of Georgia*	When a state voluntarily moves a case from state to federal court, it is accepting federal jurisdiction and waiving its claims of immunity.
2003*	*Nevada Dept. of Human Resources v. Hibbs*	State employees could sue and collect money damages in federal court for Nevada's failure to comply with the Family and Medical Leave Act's (FMLA) family-care provision.
2011	*Virginia Office for Protection and Advocacy v. Stewart*	Congress authorized states to set up independent agencies to protect the mentally ill and disabled. Agencies have authority under federal law to investigate abuse and obtain state records. May an independent state agency authorized under federal law sue a state to release records? Yes, federal courts may hear suits brought by another agency of the state
2011	*Sossamon v. Texas*	States did not waive its sovereign immunity by accepting funds under the Religious Land Use and Institutional Persons Act (RLUIPA) of 2000. They did not consent to suit.
2012	*Coleman v. Court of Appeals of Maryland*	Suits against states under the FMLA self-care provision are barred by sovereign immunity.

❏ The discrimination targeted by the FMLA is based on mutually reinforcing stereotypes that only women are responsible for family caregiving and that men lack domestic responsibilities.

❏ Congress chose remedies that were "congruent and proportional" to the problem. The FMLA is narrowly targeted at the fault line between work and family, the area where "sex-based overgeneralization has been and remains strongest." Other narrowly targeted remedies include it requires only unpaid leave; it applies only to employees who have worked for the employer for at least one year and provided 1,250 hours of service within the last 12 months; and it does not apply to employees in high-ranking or sensitive positions.

To summarize, the majority in *Hibbs* saw the FMLA as different from federal laws relating to age and disability due to the use of heightened scrutiny in sex-based discrimination, the significant problem caused by the stereotypes related to family leave, and the narrowly tailored focus of the scope of the Act. Workers may sue for damages when states discriminate under the FMLA "family-care" provision, but not when states ignore federal age or disability laws. But *Hibbs* did not apply to the entire FMLA, as the Court pointed out in *Coleman v. Court of Appeals of Maryland* (2012). David Coleman, an employee of the Maryland Court of Appeals, requested sick leave under the FMLA "self-care" provision and sued when it was denied. The Supreme Court held that states are immune from suit under the "self-care" provision because Congress did not identify a pattern of constitutional violations in that area.

FEDERAL PREEMPTION OF STATE LAW

"Preemption" occurs when an act of Congress removes a state or local government's power of regulation over a particular policy area. The issue of "federal preemption" arises when a state's attempt to regulate something is supposedly prevented by federal law. When this occurs, a conflict between federal and state law must be resolved by the courts. While it would seem likely that courts would use the doctrine of national supremacy to void the state law, such is not always the case. In fact, in *Gregory v. Ashcroft* (1991), the Supreme Court held that federal preemption cannot occur unless the court is "absolutely certain" that Congress intended to preempt that area of regulation.

The doctrine of preemption stems from the Supremacy Clause, which holds that the Constitution, laws, and treaties made under the authority of the United States shall be the "supreme law of the land." Generally, preemption is said to exist when Congress has "occupied" the area of regulation. Several case examples show mixed results. In *Silkwood v. Kerr-McGee* (1984), the Court held that a $10 million award by a nuclear power plant was not preempted by federal law, despite earlier rulings showing federal preemption of nuclear power safety.

A 5–4 majority held in *Gonzales v. Oregon* (2006) that the federal Controlled Substances Act (CSA) did not preempt Oregon's Death with Dignity Act, which authorized physicians to prescribe lethal doses of controlled drugs for their patients. In *Watters v. Wachovia Bank* (2007), however, the Court said that federal banking laws preempted Michigan's efforts to regulate mortgage services.

In 2008, the 2nd U.S. Court of Appeals in New York State overturned a New York law that would have required airlines to provide food, water, and working toilets to passengers stuck inside planes on the runway. The Court stated that state law is preempted by the federal Airline Deregulation Act of 1978, which prohibits states from regulating airline routes, prices, or service. The case, *Air Transport Association of America, Inc. v. Cuomo, et al.*, complicated other efforts to pass so-called "Passenger Bills of Rights" at the state level. In April 2010, Congress approved legislation that imposed regulations protecting airline passengers stranded on runways.

Recent cases have largely upheld federal preemption. In *PLIVA, Inc. v. Mensing, et al.* (2011), a 5–4 Supreme Court held that federal drug regulations for generic drugs preempted state failure-to-warn claims by a manufacturer who meets federal standards. In short, a state cannot be held responsible for failure to warn citizens if the generic drug is properly labeled under federal law. Justice Scalia wrote for a 6–2 majority in *Bruesewitz v. Wyeth* (2011) that the National Childhood Vaccine Injury Act preempted all design and defect claims against manufacturers for injury or death. Two 2012 rulings, *Kurns v. Railroad Friction Products Corp.* and *National Meat Association v. Harris*, held that federal law occupied the fields of locomotive equipment regulation and the buying, processing, and selling of nonambulatory animals, respectively. But the most significant preemption case in recent years was yet to come.

When the State of Arizona passed S.B. 1070 into law, it made a bold statement that a state could make and enforce its own immigration laws, even when federal immigration laws were present. The federal government claimed that four provisions in the law invaded the comprehensive federal immigration regulatory scheme. Arizona argued, among other things, that the federal laws were not being enforced effectively, leaving the state no choice but to implement its own scheme to deal with the problem. The Arizona law was not put into effect, pending a Supreme Court decision. That decision came in *Arizona v. United States* (2012), and the results were not good for the Arizona law.

A five-person majority opinion by Justice Kennedy held that three of the four provisions were preempted by federal law. Those provisions did the following: authorized Arizona law enforcement officers to make a warrantless arrest whenever they have probable cause to believe that a person has committed an offense that makes that person removable from the United States; made it a state crime for an unauthorized immigrant to violate federal registration laws; and created a state misdemeanor for an unlawfully present alien to attempt to work or obtain work. According to Justice Kennedy, these provisions undermined ongoing federal immigration laws and policies, and, as a result, were preempted by federal law. The fourth provision required Arizona law enforcement officers, upon reasonable suspicion, to determine the immigration status of any person lawfully stopped, detained, or arrested. The Court upheld this provision pending actual enforcement. The majority felt that it would be premature to judge this provision because Arizona officials might enforce the provision in a way that does not conflict with federal law (perhaps by simply contacting federal authorities to check on a person's status). However, the Court also left open the possibility that it would hear lawsuits stemming from enforcement of the policy, should Arizona not comply with federal law. In summary, even if the federal government's enforcement of immigration laws is imperfect, the State of Arizona does not have the authority to substitute its policies.

Federalism and September 11, 2001

On June 6, 2002, President George W. Bush sounded the first call for a new cabinet-level Department of Homeland Security. In his speech to the nation, the president indicated that the new department would be only one part of a much broader war on terrorism—a war that would be waged largely by the national government. The Department of Homeland Security would be responsible for four primary tasks: (1) control borders to prevent terrorists and explosives from entering the country; (2) work with state and local governments in responding to emergencies; (3) lead a massive scientific effort to develop technologies to detect biological, chemical, and nuclear weapons and protect American citizens from attack; and (4) bring together law enforcement and intelligence activities under a single agency of government.

In mid-July, the president released a ninety-page strategy plan that went well beyond the Department of Homeland Security. The strategy has significant implications for federalism, calling for a series of new state laws that will provide stronger support for federal antiterrorism efforts. These include laws creating tighter minimum standards for obtaining driver's licenses; requiring states to ensure the availability of terrorism insurance for business and property owners; creating lines of succession for state judiciaries in the event of an attack; and approving new procedures for ordering quarantines in case of bioterrorism.

Along with these reforms, the president also proposed significant new federal laws to control the flow of information, facilitate the possible use of the National Guard, broaden the president's power to shift funds, and create "red teams" to act like terrorists in helping to identify possible targets and threats. In all, the package of reforms will enlarge the size of the federal government and give it greater control over the states. Any hopes for "smaller government" were diminished on September 11, 2001 (see Brief 7.7).

Conclusion

The acceptance of federalism as a method of dividing powers between the national and state governments ranks as one of America's foremost achievements in the field of constitutional government. In retrospect, federalism appears to have been a natural choice for the United States. After all, the Articles of Confederation had proven fatally weak in matters of finance and commerce, and almost nobody favored placing centralized power in the hands of a unitary government. However, before concluding that the framers were following an obvious path toward federalism, it should be recalled that such a system did not exist among the world's nations in 1787, and political thinkers had given the subject very little consideration. The compromise reached in Philadelphia seems all the more remarkable when placed in this perspective.

The development of American federalism has progressed through several identifiable periods. The early clashes between the Federalists, including such advocates as Alexander Hamilton and Chief Justice John Marshall, and the Anti-Federalists, following such leaders as Thomas Jefferson and James Madison,

---

Brief 7.7

FEDERAL HOMELAND SECURITY GRANTS TO STATES

The Department of Homeland Security has provided billions of dollars to state and local governments since its inception in 2002. These funds have become part of state government financial planning procedures. For fiscal year 2010, the Homeland Security Grant Programs (HSGP) offered more than $800 million for states, for example:

- The State Homeland Security Program (SHSP) provides over $294 million to build capabilities related to security and law enforcement, with at least 25 percent of each grant dedicated to law enforcement terrorism prevention planning.
- The Urban Areas Security Initiative (UASI) also funds more than $490 million for development of regionally integrated systems focused on prevention, protection, response, and recovery. Nearly two-thirds of the grants are given to the ten highest risk urban areas in the United States, with the remaining funds divided among the remaining fifty-four urban areas.
- Operation Stonegarden (OPSG) provides $60 million to enhance cooperation and coordination among local, state, and federal law enforcement agencies in a joint mission to secure the United States borders with both Mexico and Canada.

The impact of Homeland Security grants on federalism is obvious. Federal grants allow state and local governments to pay their bills, and they also provide the national government with a mechanism for carrying out federal policies. It is a partnership, but certainly not a partnership of equals.

SOURCE: *FY 2012 Homeland Security Grant Program (HSGP)*, www.fema.gov/government/grant/hsgp/index.shtm.

---

focused on the very nature of the Union and the critical issue of sovereignty. States' rights became more extreme in its demands under such regional spokesmen as John C. Calhoun, and the Constitution simply could not resolve the elusive problem of sovereign power. That issue was settled by the Civil War, a crucial turning point in the development of American federalism.

The Civil War's primary effect upon federalism was to demonstrate the supremacy of the national government and to settle the long-standing dispute over ultimate sovereignty. Nevertheless, the rivalry between national and state governments did not end with the Civil War. Twentieth-century federalism saw significant increases in the power of the national government. President Franklin Roosevelt's New Deal Program and the Great Society of President Lyndon Johnson, for example, paved the way for massive new federal programs and the consolidation of power in the national government, and not in the state governments.

The future of federalism is difficult to predict, especially in the aftermath of September 11. Clearly, the federal government remains the dominant partner in the relationship, but states have seen their responsibilities increase. Federal grants to state and local governments were $428 billion in 2005, $443.8 billion in 2007, $608.4 billion in 2010, and estimated to rise to $643 billion in 2014. The 2010 grants represent 17.6 percent of federal spending and 37.5 percent of total state and local expenditures. The latter figure represents the highest percentage since data was available in 1990. State and local governments have become accustomed to dependency on federal monies for their programs, and that fact is unlikely to change anytime soon.[14]

The federal system of government has faced numerous problems since its inception, and it would be naive to expect otherwise in the years ahead. The present-day conflicts between the national and state governments over such matters as immigration and health care reforms indicate that tensions inherent in federalism are not likely to subside in the near term. In some respects, in spite of the passage of two hundred years, some things are really not much different from the way they were in Philadelphia in 1787. Individualist and communitarian perspectives on the role of government, coupled with a contest between states and the federal government, are still important forces in American society.

Chapter 8

Federalism: The Growth of Federal Power and Economic Regulation

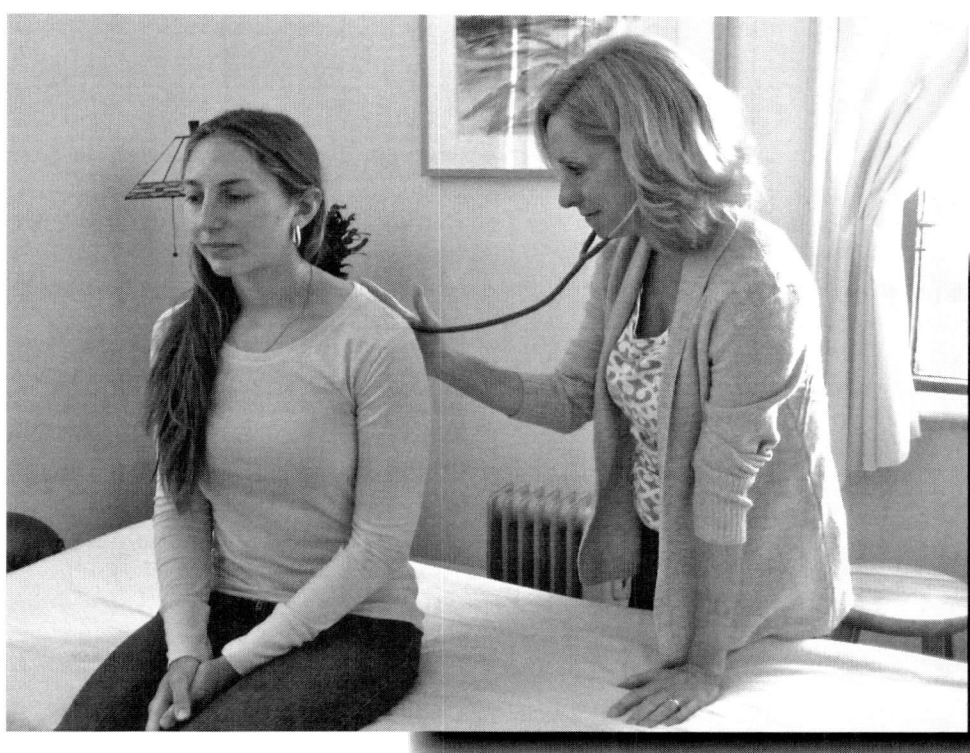

The power of the federal government to regulate all areas of economic activity has grown tremendously in the past century. The most recent controversy involving the extent of the federal commerce and taxing powers concerned federal health care legislation, which requires all to purchase health insurance and regulates many aspects of the patient's relationship with physician.

▼ An Introductory Conversation between Presidents Franklin D. Roosevelt and Ronald Reagan

Background: Franklin D. Roosevelt and Ronald Reagan served as the Thirty-Second and Fortieth Presidents of the United States, and both entered office facing severe economic problems. Roosevelt entered office in 1933 in the early years of the Great Depression, and Reagan assumed office in 1981 during a recession that most observers consider the most serious since the Great Depression. We allow these gentlemen to introduce this chapter on economic regulation. They meet in the Retired President's Club in an undisclosed location.

Franklin D. Roosevelt: Hello, Ron, it's great to see you. I assume you have been watching the ongoing debate over the current economic problems in our great nation. It reminds me—to a lesser degree, of course—of the shape of the country when I took office in 1933. Unemployment reached 25 percent of all workers and 37 percent among nonfarm workers, wages had fallen nearly 42 percent, and the gross domestic product had been cut in half, from $103 billion to $55 billion. I knew that I would have to marshal all the resources of the federal government to get us out of the difficulty. As I stated in my first inaugural address in 1933:

"Our greatest primary task is to put people to work. This is no unsolvable problem if we face it wisely and courageously. It can be accomplished in part by direct recruiting by the Government itself, treating the task as we would treat the emergency of a war, but at the same time, through this employment, accomplishing greatly needed projects to stimulate and reorganize the use of our natural resources."

I was talking about using the government to put people back to work through such successful programs as the Works Public Administration and the Civilian Conservation Corps, and it worked. Readers of this chapter will see how the constitutional powers to regulate commerce, tax, and spending have helped expand the nation's economy.

Ronald Reagan: Well, Franklin, I suppose you could argue that using the federal government to fix the economy was a good approach for you, but I think it is generally the wrong way to go. When I came to office in 1981, the United States was facing the worst economic recession since your Great Depression—inflation hit a high of 13.5 percent in 1980, and the national unemployment rate exceeded 10 percent. In my inaugural address, I made it clear that I favored less government—remember?

"In this present crisis, government is not the solution to our problem; government is *the problem. . . . We are a nation that has a government—not the other way around. . . . Our government has no power except that granted it by the people. It is time to check and reverse the growth of government, which shows signs of having grown beyond the consent of the governed. It is my intention to curb the size and influence of the Federal establishment. . . ."*

FDR: Sure, I remember hearing about the Reagan Revolution, your plan to return powers to the state and local governments, but I didn't have the luxury of waiting for states and local governments to act—they were broke. Remember my inaugural words in 1933: *"I am prepared under my constitutional duty to recommend the measures that a stricken nation in the midst of a stricken world may require. . . . But in the event that the . . . national emergency is still critical, . . . I shall ask the Congress for . . . broad Executive power to wage a war against the emergency."* As a result, we were able to implement programs such as Social Security, worker's compensation, Federal Deposit Insurance, and a national minimum wage. Readers of this chapter will see how the constitutional powers to regulate commerce, levy taxes, and spending for the general welfare have helped millions of Americans live better lives.

RR: True, and those programs helped many Americans, but the long-term result has been the explosive growth of the national government and federal programs that have continued to expand and swallow up more and more of the federal budget. Our budget deficits are escalating because of so much federal spending. Remember my words in 1981? *"Now, so there will be no misunderstanding, it's not my intention to do away with government. It is rather to make it work—work with us, not over us; to stand by our side, not ride on our back. Government can and must provide opportunity, not smother it; foster productivity, not stifle it."* Readers of this chapter also need to look at the Tenth Amendment and its clear reference to "reserved" state powers. Personally, I was disappointed in the Supreme Court's decision to uphold "Obamacare" in the *National Federation of Independent Business, et al. v. Sebelius* in 2012—just another example of more federal regulation.

FDR: Well, Ron, I suppose you are not surprised to know that I disagree. The Patient Protection and Affordable Care Act, what you call "Obamacare," reminds me of some of my "New Deal" legislation that helped solve major problems. But despite our differences, we are after the same result, aren't we? What you called "the shining city on a hill"?

RR: Absolutely, Franklin. And as you reminded us in 1933, "the only thing we have to fear is fear itself."

Sources: The Avalon Project, Documents in Law, History and Diplomacy, Yale Law School, *First Inaugural Address of Franklin D. Roosevelt, March 4, 1933; First Inaugural Address of Ronald Reagan, January 20, 1981*; Kimberly Amadeo, "The Great Depression of 1929," *About.com*; "U.S. Double-digit unemployment rate of 1980–81 vs. 2008–2009 single digit, *Investment Watch*, February 12, 2012.

PROPERTY RIGHTS AND ECONOMIC LIBERTY IN THE UNITED STATES

For more than two hundred years, issues have arisen concerning the proper role of government in relation to its citizens' property and economic freedoms, ranging from disputed land claims to employment-related matters such as minimum wage, working conditions, and job discrimination (see Brief 8.1). While no single economic explanation or theory can fully explain the framers' intentions, it is certain that they took economic matters into consideration in formulating the powers and limitations of government.[1]

The American preference for "vested" rights of property was clearly evident in the Constitution, particularly in the safeguarding of certain matters from state control. Some early leaders were fearful of radical state policies that might threaten the areas of currency, credit, and commerce, and state governments were regarded as potentially vulnerable to takeover by radical farm groups and others who might advocate such unthinkable measures as paper money and interest rate ceilings. In this respect, the Constitution's writers sought to insulate currency, credit, and commerce from state government control. Article I, Section 10 states in part:

> NO STATE SHALL ENTER INTO ANY TREATY, ALLIANCE, OR CONFEDERATION; GRANT LETTERS OF MARQUE AND REPRISAL; COIN

Brief 8.1
CAN GOVERNMENT TAKE YOUR PROPERTY?

Recent years have witnessed an increase in the number of cases coming to the Court under the following Fifth Amendment proviso: ". . . nor shall private property be taken for public use without just compensation." The concepts contained within that clause—"taking," "public use," and "just compensation"—refer to the government's power of **eminent domain**—the power to take property for public use. Recent Supreme Court rulings have held that a state may take property if it constitutes a "public use" and serves a public purpose. This line of reasoning was used in *Hawaii Housing Authority v. Midkiff* (1984), in which the Court upheld the power of a state to break up large landholdings and provide for private ownership of the smaller tracts. Despite the fact that the state itself did not intend to use the lands involved, the "taking" fell within the exercise of the state's powers and constituted a "public use," according to the Court.

In a highly controversial ruling, a 5–4 majority in *Kelo v. City of New London* (2005) expanded the meaning of "public use" by upholding a city's plan to condemn private property for commercial purposes. New London's comprehensive development plan was designed to revitalize the city's ailing economy, and it required the taking of some private property for new economic projects. Justice John Paul Stevens, speaking for the majority, held that because the "plan unquestionably serves a public purpose, the takings challenged here satisfy the Fifth Amendment." But Justice Sandra Day O'Connor's dissent viewed the precedent with alarm, noting that "Nothing is to prevent the State from replacing any Motel 6 with a Ritz-Carlton, any home with a shopping mall, or any farm with a factory." Of course, these new economic projects provide local governments with significant increases in property tax revenue. For example, the city of Arlington, Texas, used its eminent domain power to take private property for the construction of a new football stadium for the Dallas Cowboys.

The matter of "takings" will continue to occupy the Court's attention, as governments make increasing use of land-use planning, zoning, and other forms of regulatory control over private property. While it is generally true that government ordinances do not constitute a "taking" (and, thus, do not require just compensation), the Court's ruling in *First English Evangelical Lutheran Church of Glendale v. County of Los Angeles, California* (1987) held that a flood control ordinance that prohibited a church from constructing buildings on its own property, although only on a temporary basis, was a "taking" within the meaning of the constitution. But the ruling in *Tahoe-Sierra Preservation Council, Inc. v. Tahoe Regional Planning Agency* (2002) seemingly moved in a different direction. In that case, a 6–3 Court held that a temporary moratorium on residential single-family land development was not a taking of property requiring compensation under the Constitution because the property would recover its full market value when the restriction is ended.

But the Court upheld property rights in *Dolan v. City of Tigard, Oregon* (1994). When Florence Dolan asked for a building permit to expand her electrical and plumbing supply business, the city of Tigard, Oregon, demanded that she turn over 10 percent of her land for drainage improvements and a pedestrian and bicycle path. The Court called the city's 10-percent requirement "speculative," not justified by the facts, and a "taking" under the Fifth Amendment. If the city wanted some of Florence Dolan's land for drainage and recreation purposes, it would be required to pay her "just compensation."

Finally, a 2010 ruling upheld a State's power to take title to all land seaward of the "mean high water line." The decision, *Stop the Beach Renourishment, Inc. v. Florida Department of Environmental Protection*, held that beachfront owners cannot show that they have a right to contact the water that is superior to the state's right to fill in its submerged land. This ruling seemingly could impact similar legislation in other oceanfront states in their efforts to confront beach erosion often caused by hurricanes and tropical weather.

MONEY; EMIT BILLS OF CREDIT; MAKE ANY THING BUT GOLD AND SILVER COIN A TENDER IN PAYMENT OF DEBTS; PASS ANY BILL OF ATTAINDER, EX POST FACTO LAW, OR LAW *IMPAIRING THE OBLIGATION OF CONTRACTS*, OR GRANT ANY TITLE OF NOBILITY. [EMPHASIS ADDED]

Clearly, Article I, Section 10 sought to place economic limitations upon state governments. The italicized portion of Section 10 generally is referred to as the **Contract Clause**, and its prohibition upon state interference in the obligations of contracts serves as an early example of the American concern with government meddling in economic matters (see Brief 8.2).

The ratification of the Fourteenth Amendment in 1868 brought due process of law considerations to bear on property rights, despite the fact that the Fifth Amendment's Due Process of Law Clause had been around for many years. The Due Process Clauses of the Fifth and Fourteenth Amendments are identical,

---

Brief 8.2

THE CONTRACT CLAUSE: ONLY A SHADOW OF ITS FORMER SELF

The Contract Clause reached its zenith during the Federalist-era of Chief Justice John Marshall, a champion of private property rights.[2] The Marshall Court expanded the Contract Clause to its broadest point in *Dartmouth College v. Woodward* (1819), further protecting private property from state interference. In 1816, New Hampshire's Republican-dominated legislature took steps to make Dartmouth College a public institution by amending its charter. The charter, granted in 1769 by King George III, gave trustees the right to govern the institution forever. Was such a charter equivalent to a contract? Did New Hampshire's actions amount to interference in contractual obligations?

Chief Justice Marshall's characteristically broad interpretation of the Contract Clause held that the charter was a "contract within the letter of the constitution, and within its spirit also." As a result, the New Hampshire statute was found inconsistent with the Contract Clause and declared null and void. Dartmouth College would remain a private institution, of course, but the decision also indicated that charters, even those granted by state governments, would be protected from political interference.

Chief Justice Roger B. Taney, who replaced Marshall, recognized the need for some types of state regulation of property rights. *Charles River Bridge Co. v. Warren Bridge Co.* (1837) involved the right of Massachusetts to issue a charter for a bridge that would clearly undermine an existing charter. A 1785 charter gave the "Proprietors of the Charles River Bridge" authority to build a bridge, collect tolls, provide for certain construction and maintenance requirements, and to pay Harvard College an annual fee as compensation for not operating a ferry. The Charles River Bridge Company completed these requirements and in 1792 the Massachusetts legislature extended the charter for seventy years. In 1828, the Massachusetts legislature authorized the Warren Bridge Company to build a new bridge somewhat less than three hundred yards from the existing structure. This new bridge would revert to the state for the free use of its citizens once construction costs and expenses were paid. Faced with the prospect of competing against a public bridge, the Charles River Bridge Company challenged the 1828 legislation as destructive of the obligations of the exclusive ferry right granted to Harvard College and the subsequent charters of 1785 and 1792, which, they argued, gave them exclusive rights to a bridge over the Charles River.

In delivering the opinion of the court, Chief Justice Taney stated that charters must be construed narrowly, with any ambiguities or uncertainties always being resolved in favor of the state, because "the object and end of all government is to promote the happiness and prosperity of the community by which it is established." While private property must be guarded, Taney argued "that the community also have rights." A public bridge was consistent with those rights. In reality, Taney's ruling amounted to a practical decision more closely in tune with the communitarian feelings of the times. According to Benjamin Wright, Taney left the Contract Clause "a more secure and broader base for the defense of property rights in 1864 than it had been in 1835."[3]

By the late-nineteenth century, the Contract Clause had begun a decline that would run until the present time. While reasons for the decline are varied, they include an increase in police power usage by governments, the careful drafting of charters, and the emergence of the Due Process Clause to be discussed later in the chapter. Before 1889 the Contract Clause had been considered by the Court in almost 40 percent of all cases involving the validity of state legislation, and nearly half of all state laws struck down were a result of that provision. By contrast, from 1888 to 1910, less than 25 percent of all cases involving state law arose under the Contract Clause.[4] The number has declined steadily since.

In *Home Building & Loan Association v. Blaisdell* (1934) the Supreme Court let stand the Minnesota Moratorium Law, passed during the Depression to prevent massive foreclosures on mortgages of homeowners and farmers by postponing mortgage payments until conditions improved. Citing the emergency and an urgent public need for relief, the Court said that the states have the power to protect their citizens when addressing a "legitimate end" without violating the Contract Clause. Most observers concede that the *Blaisdell* case effectively limited the significance of the Contract Clause. Despite the Court's use of the Contract Clause to strike down a Minnesota law in *Allied Structural Steel Company v. Spannaus* (1978), the clause is not the source of much dispute today.

except that the former limits the national government and the latter specifically applies to states, and, for all practical purposes, both clauses have been interpreted in identical fashion by the courts. Second, due process is commonly thought of as either procedural or substantive. **Procedural due process** refers to the manner in which the law is enforced and the procedures to be followed in providing fair treatment to individuals. It is a central component of the individualist view discussed in Chapter 2. **Substantive due process**, on the other hand, refers to the existence of specific rights or liberties within the concept of due process itself. Henry J. Abraham has defined substantive due process as "referring to the content or subject matter of a law or an ordinance, (whereas) procedural due process . . . refers to the manner in which a law, ordinance, administrative practice, or judicial task is carried out."[5] While this chapter concerns itself with claims of economic substantive due process (i.e., business-related liberty), subsequent chapters examine the application of substantive due process to other matters.

THE EARLY VIEW OF DUE PROCESS AND PROPERTY: THE SLAUGHTERHOUSE CASES

The Slaughterhouse Cases (1873) stemmed from an 1869 Louisiana act regulating slaughterhouses in New Orleans, in effect giving a monopoly to one company and requiring all other slaughterhouse operators to use its facilities on a fee basis. A group of small slaughterhouse operators and butchers, the Butcher's Benevolent Association, who had been deprived of their businesses, challenged the law in state courts and lost. They contended that the statute violated the Thirteenth Amendment, as well as the Privileges and Immunities, Due Process, and Equal Protection Clauses of the Fourteenth Amendment. The Supreme Court decided three cases collectively as the *Slaughterhouse Cases.*

Writing for the majority, Justice Samuel Miller provided a strong defense of traditional state powers of regulation and found virtually no merit in the claims of the plaintiffs. The Thirteenth Amendment, he stated, was "a declaration designed to establish the freedom of millions of slaves," and did not refer to private property. As for the clauses of the Fourteenth Amendment, the Court's reasoning was somewhat more involved.

First, the Amendment's definition of citizenship identified both federal and state citizenship (see Brief 8.3). As a result, the "privileges and immunities of citizens of the United States" noted in the amendment were not identical to the "privileges and immunities" that might be associated with state citizenship.

Brief 8.3
UNITED STATES CITIZENSHIP

The Fourteenth Amendment to the Constitution confers citizenship on all persons born or naturalized in the United States, using the principle of *jus soli*—by reason of place of birth. The only exceptions to the *jus soli* principle are children born of foreign diplomatic parents stationed in the United States because these persons are not subject to the jurisdiction of the United States. American Indians, obviously native-born but long considered an exception, actually were not conferred citizenship through the Fourteenth Amendment but rather by congressional statute some years later. The principle of *jus soli* has received support from the Supreme Court as the basic rule of American citizenship. The landmark case of *United States v. Wong Kim Ark* (1898) established that even if the parents are aliens who are ineligible for citizenship themselves, children born to these parents in the United States are indeed citizens. Today, as illegal immigrants stream to the United States in search of a better life, it is not surprising to realize that many do so in order to have a child born on American soil—so-called "anchor babies." Congress has declared that American soil is found in Puerto Rico, Guam, the Virgin Islands, and the Northern Mariana Islands.

The citizenship policy has been subjected to criticism over the years, but the problem of illegal immigration has raised the debate to new heights. The debate is being driven by the number of U.S.-born children of illegal immigrants. A Pew Hispanic Center study found about 340,000 of the 4.3 million U.S.-born babies in 2008 had at least one illegal immigrant parent. Public opinion polls suggest a growing opposition to the Fourteenth Amendment–based citizenship policy. A Quinnipiac University poll in September 2010 showed that 48 percent of voters said that citizenship should not be granted to the children of illegal immigrants.

SOURCE: Greg Stohr, "Children of Illegal Immigrants Spark Clash on U.S. Citizenship," *Bloomberg L.P.,* September 13, 2010.

By holding that most privileges and immunities stem from state rather than federal citizenship, the Court effectively barred use of the Fourteenth Amendment's Privileges and Immunities Clause to oppose state regulatory legislation. Even today, the clause is largely without significance.

The Court also stated that the act did not deprive persons of property under the Fourteenth Amendment. Due process of law, rather than a substantive protection of private property rights, was to be understood as a guarantee of procedural protections before the law. As for the Equal Protection Clause, the Court simply held that it applied only to matters of race. Louisiana's legislation had denied no rights guaranteed by the Federal Constitution. In sum, the majority opinion in *The Slaughterhouse Cases* denied that the Fourteenth Amendment had changed the fundamental nature of individual rights. This view "taken as a whole, does seem to narrow considerably the scope of the first section [of the amendment] as conceived by its principal authors."[6] The Court followed essentially the same reasoning in upholding an Illinois law fixing maximum charges for grain storage by grain elevators in *Munn v. Illinois* (1877).[7]

THE RISE AND FALL OF THE FREEDOM OF CONTRACT

Business interests began to mobilize against the *Slaughterhouse* and *Munn* decisions by stepping up their level of involvement in the political process and pressuring courts to find ways to protect property rights from interference by reform-minded legislatures. As a result, substantive due process of law gradually expanded its hold on state courts during the latter decades of the nineteenth century, but it was not until 1897 that the Supreme Court invalidated state legislation on substantive due process grounds. In *Allgeyer v. Louisiana* (1897), the Court struck down an insurance regulation law and announced a new constitutional right—the **freedom of contract**. Justice Rufus Peckham's majority opinion spelled out this new freedom:

> THE "LIBERTY" MENTIONED IN THAT AMENDMENT MEANS, NOT ONLY THE RIGHT OF THE CITIZEN TO BE FREE FROM THE MERE PHYSICAL RESTRAINT OF HIS PERSON, AS BY INCARCERATION, BUT THE TERM IS DEEMED TO EMBRACE THE RIGHT OF THE CITIZEN TO BE FREE IN THE ENJOYMENT OF ALL HIS FACULTIES; TO BE FREE TO USE THEM IN ALL LAWFUL WAYS; TO LIVE AND WORK WHERE HE WILL; TO EARN HIS LIVELIHOOD BY ANY LAWFUL CALLING; TO PURSUE ANY LIVELIHOOD OR AVOCATION; AND FOR THAT PURPOSE TO ENTER INTO ALL CONTRACTS WHICH MAY BE PROPER, NECESSARY, AND ESSENTIAL TO HIS CARRYING OUT TO A SUCCESSFUL CONCLUSION THE PURPOSES ABOVE MENTIONED.

The Court elevated freedom of contract to perhaps its highest level in *Lochner v. New York* (1905). Citing health concerns, the New York legislature passed legislation that prohibited employees from working more than ten hours a day or sixty hours a week in a bakery. Joseph Lochner, the owner of a bakery, was fined $50 for violating the act. When his conviction was upheld by state courts, Lochner brought his case to the Supreme Court on a writ of error.

Justice Peckham's opinion focused on which of two powers or rights should prevail: "the power of the state to legislate or the right of the individual to liberty of person and freedom of contract." Finding that the limit of police power had been surpassed and that no solid basis existed to justify the measure as a health law, the Court reversed Lochner's conviction by 5–4 and upheld "the freedom of master and employee to contract with each other in relation to their employment."

The dissenting opinions of Justices Oliver Wendell Holmes and John Harlan took aim from different directions. Holmes, as was his practice, criticized his colleagues for their adherence to an economic theory (laissez faire), "which a large part of the country does not entertain," pointing out that the "Constitution is not intended to embody a particular economic theory." Harlan's opinion, joined by the other dissenters, focused on the problem of questioning the New York legislature's motives and substituting the judgment of the Court for that of the legislature (see Brief 8.4).

In reviewing the pattern of cases arising under the Fourteenth Amendment, several trends are evident. In the first place, the Supreme Court's *Santa Clara County v. Southern Pacific Railroad* (1886) ruling that corporations are "persons" for purposes of the

Brief 8.4

WOMEN AND WAGES: CHALLENGES TO THE FREEDOM OF CONTRACT

Reformers and women's groups, citing health, safety, and welfare concerns, had pushed through legislation in Oregon limiting work by women in certain heavy mechanical establishments and laundries to ten hours per day. Having been retained as counsel for the State, Mr. Louis Brandeis, later an associate justice of the United States Supreme Court, introduced a new form of legal brief, which has come to bear his name. The **Brandeis Brief**, first submitted in *Muller v. Oregon* (1908), contained only about two pages of legal arguments but over one hundred pages of statistical, medical, sociological, and psychological data designed to show the injurious effects of prolonged labor on females.

Apparently the tactic paid off, as the Court sustained the Oregon law. But the Court carefully carved out an exception to the freedom of contract, citing the physical differences between the sexes and the need to protect the physical well-being of women "in order to preserve the strength and vigor of the race." In short, while convinced by the Brandeis Brief, the Court would not abandon the *Lochner* precedent upholding freedom of contract. The Brandeis Brief became a standard feature of the American legal system.

The Court gave the first sign that its commitment to freedom of contract was weakening in *Nebbia v. New York* (1934), but the key step was taken in *West Coast Hotel Company v. Parrish* (1937). In that case, a 1913 Washington state minimum wage law for minors and women was challenged when Elsie Parrish, a chambermaid, brought suit against her employer to recover the difference between the wages paid her and the state minimum wage. Writing for the 5–4 Court, Chief Justice Hughes reviewed the history of the freedom of contract and concluded that freedom of contract considerations were not absolute and beyond restriction by the state legislatures. Hughes added that legislatures have the right to consider policies such as the minimum wage as a part of their responsibility toward the people. The *West Coast Hotel* decision opened the floodgates allowing numerous federal and state laws to pass through the Court's newfound acceptance of economic regulation.

Fourteenth Amendment escalated the number of corporation-related cases. From 1872 until 1910, for example, the Court heard 313 cases involving corporations under the amendment but only twenty-eight based on the claims of blacks for protection of their rights. A second trend shows the overwhelming dominance of property-related cases—property claims were litigated in 423 cases, with only twenty-four and 128 cases dealing with deprivations of life and liberty, respectively. Finally, the Court invalidated state legislation on due process grounds ninety times between 1899 and 1921.[8]

Since 1937, however, the Court has consistently refused to allow challenges to federal or state regulation of business on substantive due process grounds, as exemplified by the ruling in *Ferguson v. Skrupa* (1963). The case concerned a Kansas law that outlawed any person other than a lawyer from engaging in the business of debt adjustment. Justice Black's opinion upholding the law stated the issue very clearly:

> UNDER THE SYSTEM OF GOVERNMENT CREATED BY OUR CONSTITUTION, IT IS UP TO LEGISLATURES, NOT COURTS, TO DECIDE ON THE WISDOM AND UTILITY OF LEGISLATION.... THE DOCTRINE... THAT DUE PROCESS AUTHORIZES COURTS TO HOLD LAWS UNCONSTITUTIONAL WHEN THEY BELIEVE THE LEGISLATURE HAS ACTED UNWISELY—HAS LONG SINCE BEEN DISCARDED. WE HAVE RETURNED TO THE ORIGINAL CONSTITUTIONAL PROPOSITION THAT COURTS DO NOT SUBSTITUTE THEIR SOCIAL AND ECONOMIC BELIEFS FOR THE JUDGMENT OF LEGISLATIVE BODIES, WHO ARE ELECTED TO PASS LAWS.

At its height, substantive due process of law wielded a significant impact on the pattern of judicial review, and it opened the way for the justices in the Supreme Court to rely exclusively upon their own personal policy preferences. While the economic aspect of substantive due process did not survive much past 1937, it can be argued that the practice of judicial interpretation based on the justices' individual preferences has become commonplace.

In reality, the demise of substantive due process of law in economic matters has opened up vast new areas of authority for state and federal governments (see Chapter 11 for a discussion of substantive due process in noneconomic areas). Legislation dealing with a variety of health, safety, and welfare considerations has become commonplace in our nation since 1937, with the result that the powers of government have expanded immensely. At the national level, this expansion has been tied most closely to the phenomenal growth of congressional powers in the areas of commerce, taxation, and spending. These matters are discussed in the following sections.

THE REGULATION OF COMMERCE

No single grant of power in the Constitution has exerted such impact on our federal system as the power "[t]o regulate commerce with foreign Nations, and among the several States, and with the Indian Tribes." While regulation of foreign commerce (including with Indian Tribes) has been relatively free of controversy, the regulation of interstate commerce has been another matter entirely (see Table 8.1). The extent of controversy over such regulation can be attributed to several factors. First, the Constitution provides no definition of "commerce," with the result that a good deal of attention has been devoted over

Table 8.1 Development of the Law—The Federal Commerce Power

Year	Event	Significance
1793	Federal Coasting Act*	Requires coastal traders to obtain federal license.
1824	*Gibbons v. Ogden* *	First commerce case. C. J. Marshall defines commerce as intercourse, including both commodities and navigation.
1829	*Willson v. Black Bird Creek Marsh Co.* **	Ruling that state governments have authority over some internal matters, even if some interference in commerce results.
1837	*New York v. Miln* **	Upheld New York law requiring reports and posting of bonds by ship captains, thereby allowing state interference in commerce.
1851	*Cooley v. Board of Wardens* **	Doctrine of Selective Exclusiveness. C. J. Taney rules states may regulate interstate commerce in absence of federal laws.
1887	Interstate Commerce Act*	Interstate Commerce Commission created to regulate railroads.
1890	Sherman Anti-trust Act*	First government attempt to control trusts; makes monopolies in restraint of trade in interstate commerce illegal.
1895	*U.S. v. E.C. Knight Co.* **	First federal prosecution under Sherman Act; Court holds that commerce does not include production or manufacturing.
1895	*In Re Debs* *	Made possible future use of anti-trust laws against labor unions.
1903	*Champion v. Ames* *	First use of commerce as a "police power" to exclude materials (lottery tickets in this case) from moving in commerce.
1904	*Northern Securities Co. v. U.S.* *	First successful prosecution under Sherman Act involving railroad barons James J. Hill, E. H. Harriman, and J. P. Morgan.
1905	*Swift and Co. v. U.S.* *	Justice Holmes applies Sherman Act to buying and selling of cattle as part of a "current of commerce."
1911	*Standard Oil v. U.S.* *	Upheld the conviction of this powerful monopoly, but the Court recognized some exceptions for "reasonable" monopolies.
1911	*Hipolite Egg Co. v. U.S.* *	Upholds Pure Food and Drug Act as congressional police power.
1913	*Hoke v. U.S.* *	Upholds Mann Act, prohibiting transportation of persons for immoral purposes.
1914	Shreveport Rate Cases*	Brings intrastate rail rates into compliance with interstate rates under broad authority of Interstate Commerce Commission.
1914	Federal Trade Commission* Act; Clayton Anti-trust Act	Wilson administration steps to tighten federal control over anti-trust and unfair trade practices.
1918	*Hammer v. Dagenhart* **	Struck down First Child Labor Act on grounds that Congress may only prohibit shipment of "harmful" things in commerce.
1935	*Schechter Poultry v. U.S.* **	Struck down National Industrial Recovery Act as illegal delegation of power and improper use of commerce power.

1936	*Carter v. Carter Coal Co.***	Struck down Bituminous Coal Conservation Act under *Knight* precedent; mining precedes commerce and is not part of it.
1937	*NLRB v. Jones & Laughlin Steel Corporation**	A major ruling upholding congressional power to enact "all appropriate legislation" for advancing interstate commerce.
1938	Fair Labor Standards Act (FLSA)*	New Deal law imposing federal wage and hour requirements on companies whose workers affect interstate commerce.
1941	*U.S. v. Darby**	Court upholds FLSA, strikes down *Hammer*, and holds Congress may regulate any activity with economic effects on Commerce.
1942	*Wickard v. Filburn**	Upholds Agricultural Adjustment Act extending commerce to the production of agricultural products for use on the farm.
1964	*Heart of Atlanta Motel v. U.S.** *Katzenbach v. McClung**	Court holds Civil Rights Act of 1964 to be a legitimate use of commerce in prohibiting racial discrimination in hotels, motels, restaurants, and movie theaters.
1976	*National League of Cities v. Usery****	Court rules Fair Labor Standards Act cannot compel states to pay employees a minimum wage, citing the Tenth Amendment.
1985	*Garcia v. SAMTA**	Broad ruling upholding application of Fair Labor Standards Act to state and local government employees. Overturns *Usery*.
1989	*Goldberg v. Sweet**	Upheld state tax on all telecommunications originating or terminating in the state and billed to an Illinois address. Tax did not invade interstate commerce.
1991	*Dennis v. Higgins**	An individual injured by state action that violates an aspect of the Commerce Clause may sue for damages under §1983.
1992	*Wyoming v. Oklahoma**	Upheld a state's right to sue for loss of tax revenue when another state discriminates in favor of its own products.
1995	*United States v. Lopez****	Struck down Gun-Free School Zones Act; directly limited the Commerce Power.
1997	*Printz v. U.S.**** Mack v. U.S.*	Brady Handgun Violence Prevention Act cannot compel state officials to carry out background checks under federal law. Decided on dual federal/state sovereignty principle.
2000	*Reno v. Condon**	Unanimously upheld Driver's Privacy Protection Act restricting release of motorist records by states. Held that drivers' records are articles of interstate commerce.
2000	*U.S. v. Morrison****	Struck down Violence Against Women Act holding that Congress may not regulate noneconomic, violent criminal conduct based solely on that conduct's effect on commerce.
2005	*Granholm v. Heald**	Struck down Michigan and New York laws that prohibited out-of-state wineries from making direct sales to consumers but allowed in-state wineries to do so.
2005	*Gonzalez v. Raich**	Held that the federal commerce power can be used to prohibit the use and possession of "medical marijuana," even in the states where it is legal.
2007	*United Haulers Assn v. Oneida-Herkimer Solid Waste Mgt Authority****	Held a state "flow-control" ordinance requiring trash haulers for cities to obtain a permit and deliver waste to the authority sites rather than cheaper out-of-state sites, did not violate the Commerce Clause. Court said "flow control" laws were justified by compelling reasons.
2010	*American Needle, Inc. v. National Football League**	Held the Sherman Anti-trust Act could be applied to the NFL under a "rule of reason" because the league and its 32 teams engage in concerted activities and do not act as separate entities.
2012	*National Federation of Independent Business, et al. v. Sebelius****	Ruled that the Patient Protection and Affordable Care Act's "individual mandate" requiring all persons to purchase health insurance was not within the scope of Congress's commerce power. Persons are not engaging in an economic activity by failing to purchase health insurance.

* Expanded federal commerce power; ** Restricted federal commerce power the years to settling upon a commonly accepted view of those activities that constitute commerce. Second, changes in economic relations and technology have contributed to a demand for the regulation of certain types of commerce that did not even exist when the framers did their work. Third, in the face of ever-broadening federal control of commerce-related matters, state governments and their supporters have fought to retain their place in the federal system. It is difficult to argue with Felix Frankfurter's assessment that the Commerce Clause has "throughout the Court's history been the chief source of its adjudications regarding federalism."[9]

CHIEF JUSTICE JOHN MARSHALL AND THE COMMERCE POWER

Gibbons v. Ogden (1824) was the first commerce case to reach the Supreme Court, and it remains one of the classic rulings on the federal commerce power. The controversy began when Robert Fulton and Robert Livingstone, pioneers in the steamboat's development, obtained an exclusive right to use steam vessels in New York's waters under a grant from the state legislature in 1808. Subsequently, Aaron Ogden leased the right to navigate the waters between New York and New Jersey under this exclusive privilege. He soon faced competition in the person of Thomas Gibbons, a former partner of Ogden's, who had begun to run his two steamboats on much the same New York–New Jersey route. Gibbons had obtained a license to operate his vessel from the federal government as required by the 1793 Federal Coasting Act, a measure designed primarily to license carriers engaged in the coastal trade. Ogden, having paid for what he considered to be a monopoly, obtained an injunction from the state courts prohibiting Gibbons from engaging in direct competition on Ogden's exclusive routes. Gibbons appealed to the Supreme Court—assisted by his well-known counsel, Daniel Webster of Massachusetts.

Ogden's attorney had argued for a definition of commerce limited to "traffic, to buying and selling, or the interchange of commodities," but not including navigation. This limited definition ran counter to Marshall's expansive view of national power:

> ALL AMERICA UNDERSTANDS, AND HAS UNIFORMLY UNDERSTOOD, THE WORD "COMMERCE" TO COMPREHEND NAVIGATION. IT WAS SO UNDERSTOOD, AND MUST HAVE BEEN SO UNDERSTOOD, WHEN THE CONSTITUTION WAS FRAMED.

Marshall's view of commerce as commercial intercourse meant that the power to regulate commerce could expand to meet even unforeseen activities of an economic or commercial nature—a view that has generally prevailed since.[10] In his view, the Federal Coasting Act of 1793 fell unquestionably under the plenary power of Congress to regulate commerce. The controversy really involved two competing laws—the New York grant of monopoly versus the Federal Coasting Act. Given Marshall's well-known national supremacy preferences, the national law was to be preferred over the state law. As a result, Gibbons, and anyone else for that matter with a federal coasting license, could engage in the steamboat business in New York waters.

In deciding whether Congress might reasonably intrude into the internal affairs of states in regulating commerce, Marshall seemed to offer a strong affirmative answer. Marshall did not exclude the possibility of state involvement in matters of interstate commerce, but he implied that congressional powers of regulation were exclusive, assuming that Congress exercised its prerogative. Marshall recognized that this view could bring federal regulation of certain internal state matters:

> THE WORD "AMONG" MEANS INTERMINGLED WITH. A THING WHICH IS AMONG OTHERS, IS INTERMINGLED WITH THEM. COMMERCE AMONG THE STATES, CANNOT STOP AT THE EXTERNAL BOUNDARY LINE OF EACH STATE, BUT MAY BE INTRODUCED INTO THE INTERIOR. . . . COMPREHENSIVE AS THE WORD "AMONG" IS, IT MAY VERY PROPERLY BE RESTRICTED TO THAT COMMERCE WHICH CONCERNS MORE STATES THAN ONE.

That commerce "which is completely internal," he pointed out, would remain under the control of the states themselves. Of course, the practical application of these principles has sometimes been difficult to achieve (see Brief 8.5). John Marshall's legacy with respect to the Commerce Clause is provided by a twentieth-century Supreme Court justice:

Brief 8.5

THE SHREVEPORT RATE CASES: OFFSPRING OF THE MARSHALL LEGACY

Under pressure from reformers, radical farm groups such as Grangers, and even some railroads seeking protection from state legislatures, Congress in 1887 created the Interstate Commerce Commission (ICC), our nation's first **independent regulatory commission**. Despite some initial hostility from the Supreme Court over its rate-fixing powers, the ICC gradually came to regulate most aspects of the interstate railroad network in the country. This power occasionally brought the ICC into conflict with state commissions or boards that claimed regulatory control over railroad travel within their state boundaries.

Actually cited as *Houston, East & West Texas Railway Co. v. United States* (1914), the *Shreveport Rate Cases* involved a conflict between ICC-mandated interstate rail rates and intrastate Texas rail rates set by the Texas Railroad Commission. Three railroads, including the Houston Railway Company, were charged by the Louisiana Railroad Commission with discriminating against interstate commerce between Louisiana and Texas. As such, they were charging much lower rates between Texas cities than for routes of approximately similar distance across the state line. The lower intrastate rates were the result of the Texas Railway Commision rate structure, presumably to encourage trade among Texas cities at the expense of Shreveport, Louisiana. After hearings, the ICC set rates for both interstate and intrastate routes, and the railroads raised their intrastate rates, placing them in conflict with the maximum rates set by the Texas Railroad Commission. The Houston Railway Company brought suit to have the ICC order overturned.

Justice Charles Evans Hughes, writing for the majority, reiterated Marshall's view pertaining to the dominance of Congress in regulating interstate commerce and expanded it logically to apply to certain intrastate activities:

> *Congress is empowered to regulate,—that is, to provide the law for the government of interstate commerce. . . . Wherever the interstate and intrastate transactions of carriers are so related that the government of the one involves the control of the other, it is Congress, and not the State, that is entitled to prescribe the final and dominant rule.*

The Interstate Commerce Commission exercised regulatory power over commerce for more than one hundred years, but the deregulation movements begun in the 1980s began to question the commisson's authority and effectiveness. At the end of 1995, the ICC went out of existence, with its few remaining functions transferred to other government entities, primarily the Department of Transportation.

MARSHALL'S USE OF THE COMMERCE CLAUSE GREATLY FURTHERED THE IDEA THAT THOUGH WE ARE A FEDERATION OF STATES WE ARE ALSO A NATION, AND GAVE MOMENTUM TO THE DOCTRINE THAT STATE AUTHORITY MUST BE SUBJECT TO SUCH LIMITATIONS AS THE COURT FINDS IT NECESSARY TO APPLY FOR THE PROTECTION OF THE NATIONAL COMMUNITY. IT WAS AN AUDACIOUS DOCTRINE. . . .[11]

CHIEF JUSTICE ROGER TANEY AND DUAL FEDERALISM

Roger B. Taney was appointed Chief Justice by President Jackson upon the death of John Marshall in 1835. Taney presided over the federal judiciary for twenty-eight years during a time when the Union experienced the greatest single threat to its existence. Through this period, Chief Justice Taney sought to balance his strong attachment for states' rights (especially state control over slavery) with a recognition that national supremacy was a fundamental pillar of the federal system. The resulting philosophy has been characterized as **dual federalism**. Taney believed that both national and state governments were sovereign in their respective constitutional spheres of authority. In those areas within the states' Tenth Amendment reserved powers, the state exercised sovereignty, although Taney recognized the power of the federal courts to uphold the supremacy of the Constitution and national authority.

In regulatory matters, Taney saw the states as possessing powers in areas such as interstate commerce provided that Congress had not taken steps to regulate the matter in question. In *Cooley v. The Board of Wardens of the Port of Philadelphia* (1851), the Taney Court handed down perhaps its most important contribution to the issue of interstate commerce and the concurrent authority of states. The case originated with an 1803 Pennsylvania law requiring ships entering or leaving Philadelphia to employ a pilot for navigation purposes. Aaron Cooley's two ships had not used pilots, and Cooley was subject to the required penalty. Cooley appealed to the Supreme Court on the grounds that the Pennsylvania law was an unconstitutional regulation of commerce by the states.

Speaking for the majority, Justice Benjamin Curtis noted that Congress had not legislated on the matter of pilots, citing a 1789 law that allowed existing state pilotage laws to continue in effect. Since no federal law covering pilots had existed to conflict with Pennsylvania's statute, the question before the Court concerned whether the Constitution's delegation of interstate commerce powers to Congress excluded states from exercising any authority of their own. The resulting doctrine, known as **selective exclusiveness**, held that states could regulate aspects of interstate commerce in the absence of federal laws:

> THE MERE GRANT TO CONGRESS OF THE POWER TO REGULATE COMMERCE, DID NOT DEPRIVE THE STATES OF POWER TO REGULATE PILOTS, AND THAT ALTHOUGH CONGRESS HAS LEGISLATED ON THIS SUBJECT, ITS LEGISLATION MANIFESTS AN INTENTION, WITH A SINGLE EXCEPTION, NOT TO REGULATE THIS SUBJECT, BUT TO LEAVE ITS REGULATION TO THE SEVERAL STATES.

Justice Felix Frankfurter later summed up Taney's legacy as follows:

> TANEY'S CHIEF DIFFERENCE WITH MARSHALL WAS IN HIS CHALLENGE OF THE LATTER'S CENTRAL DOCTRINE, THAT THE 'DORMANT' COMMERCE CLAUSE OPERATED TO IMPOSE RESTRICTIONS ON STATE AUTHORITY WHICH IT WAS THE DUTY OF THE COURT TO DEFINE AND ENFORCE. . . . HE FLATLY DENIED THAT THE MERE GRANT OF THE COMMERCE POWER OPERATED TO LIMIT STATE POWER.[12]

Proponents of Taney's dual federalism in the years following *Cooley* sought to restrict federal regulation of commerce and thereby protect the states from federal intervention in their affairs. The subject of railroads, as noted above in the *Shreveport Rate Cases*, was an exception,[13] but other activities such as production and manufacturing gradually were held by dual federalist courts as falling outside the meaning of the Commerce Clause or not constituting one of the proper subjects for national regulation. In the sections that follow, attention will be given to several areas in which the competition between the Marshall and Taney views of the commerce power has been most significant.[14]

COMMERCE: MANUFACTURING, MONOPOLIES, AND THE ECONOMY

In 1890 Congress passed the Sherman Anti-trust Act, prohibiting contracts, combinations, and trusts that were in restraint of trade in interstate commerce.[15] In part, the Sherman Act provided that ". . . every contract, combination in the form of trust or otherwise, or conspiracy, in restraint of trade or commerce among the several states, or with foreign nations, is hereby declared to be illegal." (see Brief 8.6). In *United States v. E.C. Knight* (1895), the government brought suit against the American Sugar Refining Company, a large combination including the Knight Company that controlled nearly 98 percent of sugar refining in the country.

Justice Melville Fuller, writing for the 8–1 Court, held that the Sherman Act did not apply to monopolies such as the American Sugar Refining Company because Congress was authorized to regulate commerce—not manufacturing or production. According to Fuller, manufacturing was only indirectly related to commerce, stating that "Commerce succeeds to manufacture, and is not a part of it." The Court's new standard for determining whether an activity was subject to congressional control revolved around the idea of "direct" and "indirect" effects upon commerce. If an activity affected commerce directly, it was subject to federal regulation, but activities with indirect effects were beyond federal control. The artificial distinction between manufacturing and commerce resulting from the **direct–indirect effects doctrine** removed several economic activities from federal control, most notably, mining, agriculture, and oil production. The Court's opinions in *Schechter Poultry Co. v. United States* (1935) and *Carter v. Carter Coal Company* (1936), striking down the National Industrial Recovery Act (NIRA) and the Bituminous Coal Conservation Act, respectively, illustrate the problems associated with the doctrine.

The Court's refusal to consider production and manufacturing as proper subjects for congressional regulation stemmed both from a desire to protect limited state powers of control and a general aversion to government interference in the economy. In

Brief 8.6

THE SHERMAN ANTI-TRUST ACT AND MONOPOLIES

The government's celebrated first anti-trust victory occurred in *Northern Securities Company v. United States* (1904), quickly followed by the important *Swift* "current of commerce" holding. However, business interests began to fight back with some success. In the *Standard Oil v. United States* (1911) case, the Supreme Court upheld Standard Oil's conviction for violating the Act, but it opened the door for "reasonable" monopolies to avoid prosecution. In the same term, the Court ruled that the American Tobacco Company had violated the Sherman Act but should not be dissolved. The Supreme Court's "rule of reason" allowed America's corporate structure to continue its "reasonable" monopolistic practices. On the other hand, the Court opened the way for Sherman Act prosecutions of labor unions in *In re Debs* (1895).

The Clayton Anti-trust Act (1914) and the Federal Trade Commission Act of 1914 added to the federal government's anti-trust arsenal in the twentieth century. The Clayton Act was important in dealing with such matters as price discrimination, but it also stipulated that the anti-trust laws did not forbid the existence of labor unions or activities. The Federal Trade Commission was created to deal with unfair trade practices as an independent regulatory commission, able to establish rules, obtain court injunctions, and bring action against violators.

In recent years, the government's zeal for anti-trust prosecutions has varied, depending in part upon the commitment of certain key actors, including the president, attorney general and Justice Department, and even Congress. For example, the Supreme Court held that Congress had not intended Major League Baseball, although obviously a business engaged in interstate commerce, to be covered by anti-trust laws (*Flood v. Kuhn*, 1972). During the 1980s, observers pointed to the high number of mergers and acquisitions as evidence of the Reagan administration's lack of strong commitment to anti-trust prosecutions. That practice continued into the 1990s, with mergers and acquisitions in numerous areas of the economy.

Americans are familiar with the fact that the United States Postal Service (USPS) enjoys a monopoly in the residential delivery of first-class mail, so the argument that the USPS is a monopoly is hardly surprising. But is the USPS governed by the Sherman Anti-trust Act? In *United States Postal Service v. Flamingo Industries (USA) LTD* (2004), a unanimous Court held that the United States Postal Service is not a "person" within the meaning of the Sherman Anti-trust Act. For purposes of the anti-trust laws, the Postal Service is not a separate person from the United States Government, even though the Postal Service is an independent establishment of the Government. Although the Postal Service can "sue and be sued," it has different goals from private corporations, "the most important being that it does not seek profits." Finally, the Postal Service has many powers more characteristic of Government than of private business, including its monopoly on mail delivery, the power of eminent domain, and the authority to conclude international postal agreements.

Even the National Football League (NFL) could not avoid anti-trust scrutiny by arguing that its thirty-two teams were all separate entities pursuing individual ends. In *American Needle, Inc. v. National Football League* (2010), a unanimous Court held that the NFL and its teams engaged in "concerted activities." The Court did not conclude that the NFL was in violation of the Sherman Act but held that it was proper for other courts to review the NFL's actions under a 'rule of reason.'

---

support of the first objective, the Court consistently fell back upon the dual federalism of earlier years to oppose federal regulation, and the Tenth Amendment's "reserved" powers served as the primary constitutional barrier. As for the laissez-faire preferences of the Court, it need only be remembered that the justices responsible for the *Knight* ruling also constructed the "freedom of contract" doctrine discussed earlier. Professor Edward S. Corwin has noted that the Court's acceptance of laissez-faire as a constitutional doctrine after 1890 created a "no-man's land" in which business interests often escaped all regulation. He described the process as follows:

> When a State in professed exercise of its reserved powers passed a law regulative of business and the Court found it to impinge directly on interstate business, the law was pronounced void on the ground of interfering with Congress's power over Commerce among the States. Conversely, when Congress in professed exercise of its power to regulate commerce among the States, passed legislation which impinged directly upon certain processes of business which the Court held to be local, the act was pronounced void as an interference with the reserved powers of the States.[16]

A significant step toward breaking through the "no-man's land" occurred in *Swift and Co. v. United States* (1905). In *Swift*, the Court was asked to determine if the buying and selling of cattle at a stockyard was a local transaction or part of interstate commerce. According to Justice Holmes, the issues were very different than those in *Knight*. The cattle had been brought to the stockyards for sale, and they would certainly be shipped on after processing, creating what Holmes called a current of commerce:[17]

> [C]OMMERCE AMONG THE STATES IS NOT A TECHNICAL LEGAL CONCEPTION, BUT A PRACTICAL ONE, DRAWN FROM THE COURSE OF BUSINESS. WHEN CATTLE ARE SENT FOR SALE FROM A PLACE IN ONE STATE, WITH THE EXPECTATION THAT THEY WILL END THEIR TRANSIT, AFTER PURCHASE, IN ANOTHER, AND WHEN IN EFFECT THEY DO SO, WITH ONLY THE INTERRUPTION NECESSARY TO FIND A PURCHASER AT THE STOCK YARDS, AND WHEN THIS IS A TYPICAL, CONSTANTLY RECURRING COURSE, THE CURRENT THUS EXISTING IS A CURRENT OF COMMERCE AMONG THE STATES, AND THE PURCHASE OF THE CATTLE IS A PART AND INCIDENT OF SUCH COMMERCE.

The majority held that the local buying and selling of cattle was part of a larger interstate commerce in livestock, and that the stockyard conspiracy to fix prices was "in restraint of trade" in interstate commerce. Supporters hoped that the more practical view of commerce in *Swift* would open new areas of regulation, but the decision did not have an immediate impact on the meaning of the Commerce Clause.

The turning point in commerce cases came in *National Labor Relations Board v. Jones & Laughlin Steel Corporation* (1937), which concerned the 1935 National Labor Relations Act (NLRA). The act guaranteed labor the right to organize and bargain collectively and authorized the National Labor Relations Board (NLRB) to investigate and prevent unfair practices against labor. When Jones & Laughlin Steel fired ten employees for engaging in union activities, the NLRB obtained a court order compelling the reinstatement of the fired workers. Writing for a 5–4 majority, Chief Justice Hughes upheld the unfair labor practice provisions of the NLRA on the grounds that labor-management unrest posed the type of threat to interstate commerce that Congress was empowered to prevent:

> THE FUNDAMENTAL PRINCIPLE IS THAT THE POWER TO REGULATE COMMERCE IS THE POWER TO ENACT "ALL APPROPRIATE LEGISLATION" FOR "ITS PROTECTION AND ADVANCEMENT" . . .; TO ADOPT MEASURES "TO PROMOTE ITS GROWTH AND INSURE ITS SAFETY" . . .; "TO FOSTER, PROTECT, CONTROL AND RESTRAIN." . . . THAT POWER IS PLENARY AND MAY BE EXERTED TO PROTECT INTERSTATE COMMERCE "NO MATTER WHAT THE SOURCE OF THE DANGERS WHICH THREATEN IT." . . .

Whereas the *Jones & Laughlin* decision initiated a new judicial approach to commerce, it was left to later cases to complete the transformation.[18] In *United States v. Darby* (1941), the Court upheld the constitutionality of the Fair Labor Standards Act (FLSA) of 1938. This law was applicable to all employees engaged in interstate commerce or in the production of goods for interstate commerce. For those workers, a national minimum wage of twenty-five cents per hour was established, along with a forty-four-hour standard work week and provisions for overtime pay. The act also prohibited the shipment in interstate commerce of any commodities produced in violation of the minimum wage provisions. Georgia-based Darby Lumber contended that the FLSA was a regulation of wages and hours of persons engaged in manufacturing, an area reserved to the states for control. In writing for a unanimous Court, Justice Harlan Stone appropriately answered the manufacturing argument with John Marshall's well-known words from *Gibbons v. Ogden*, that the power of Congress over interstate commerce "is complete in itself, may be exercised to its utmost extent, and acknowledges no limitations other than are prescribed in the Constitution . . .". The opinion placed responsibility for assessing the motive and purpose of legislation with the legislature and not the courts, noting that the regulation "is within the constitutional authority of Congress" (see Brief 8.7).

Federal commerce power reached its zenith in *Wickard v. Filburn* (1942), when the Court upheld regulation of agricultural products that were used only on the farm. Justice Jackson's unanimous opinion provided the epitaph for the old issue of "direct" and "indirect" effects on commerce:

> WHETHER THE SUBJECT OF THE REGULATION IN QUESTION WAS "PRODUCTION,"

Brief 8.7
THE FEDERAL MINIMUM WAGE

Since passage of the FLSA, the federal minimum wage has been raised numerous times to its current level of $7.25 per hour, and millions of workers gradually have been encompassed by minimum wage legislation.[19] Amendments to the FLSA in 1974 applied the minimum wage to almost all public employees at the state and local levels. In *National League of Cities v. Usery* (1976), the amendments were ruled unconstitutional. Justice Rehnquist invoked the Tenth Amendment and state sovereignty in a manner reminiscent of past dual-federalist courts:

> One undoubted attribute of state sovereignty is the States' power to determine the wages which shall be paid to those whom they employ in order to carry out their governmental functions, what hours those persons will work, and what compensation will be provided where these employees may be called upon to work overtime.

Then, in the case of *Garcia v. San Antonio Metropolitan Transit Authority* (1985), the Court, in yet another 5–4 ruling, overturned the *Usery* precedent. The dispute in the case concerned the San Antonio Metropolitan Transit Authority (SAMTA) and several of its employees, including Mr. Garcia, who had filed suit to recover overtime pay to which they were entitled under the FLSA. Relying upon *Usery*, SAMTA claimed immunity from the overtime provisions of the act. Justice Blackmun, who switched from his position in *Usery*, began his majority opinion by noting the heavy federal subsidization of urban mass transit in the United States, with particular reference toward SAMTA. Next, Blackmun stressed the relationship between state sovereignty and the federal commerce power, noting that the Commerce Clause was limited with respect to "States as States" only by the procedural safeguards found in the federal system itself. Courts, he added, should not insert their own limitations on the federal commerce power. As a result, SAMTA would face the same FLSA provisions with respect to overtime pay as any other employer, public or private. Justice Powell's dissenting opinion painted a dismal picture of the decision's effect on the federal system: "Today's decision effectively reduces the Tenth Amendment to meaningless rhetoric when Congress acts pursuant to the Commerce Clause." However, the Rehnquist Court's revitalization of the Eleventh Amendment would make suits such as Garcia's difficult at best (see Chapter 7).

"CONSUMPTION," OR "MARKETING" IS, THEREFORE, NOT MATERIAL FOR PURPOSES OF DECIDING THE QUESTION OF FEDERAL POWER BEFORE US. . . . BUT EVEN IF APPELLEE'S ACTIVITY BE LOCAL AND THOUGH IT MAY NOT BE REGARDED AS COMMERCE, IT MAY STILL, WHATEVER ITS NATURE, BE REACHED BY CONGRESS IF IT EXERTS A *SUBSTANTIAL ECONOMIC EFFECT ON INTERSTATE COMMERCE*, AND THIS IRRESPECTIVE OF WHETHER SUCH EFFECT IS WHAT MIGHT AT SOME EARLIER TIME HAVE BEEN DEFINED AS "DIRECT" OR "INDIRECT." [EMPHASIS ADDED]

The distinction between production and commerce, long a standard dual federalist doctrine, was gone. The proper regulation of interstate commerce would henceforth be determined by analyzing the practical economic effects of an activity, and such determinations would generally be left to legislative and not judicial consideration. However, the Rehnquist Court's recent rulings have placed some clear restrictions on the commerce power and is discussed below.

COMMERCE AS A FEDERAL POLICE POWER

While the Constitution contains no specific federal "police power," a broad interpretation of the Commerce Clause has allowed the federal government to become involved in matters related to society's health, safety, morals, and welfare. The first wave of commerce-based "police power" legislation began in the late nineteenth century and continued through the first decade or so of the twentieth century. During this era, attention was focused on problems that some considered to require a national solution. For example, a powerful anti-gambling lobby succeeded in convincing Congress to pass an 1895 law prohibiting the transportation of lottery tickets in interstate commerce. In reality, the law's central aim was the abolition of gambling through lotteries, rather than the regulation of commerce.

The law was upheld in *Champion v. Ames* (1903), and Justice Harlan, who spoke for a 5–4 majority, emphasized the plenary nature of congressional power over commerce. As for the possibility that this decision might open up the power of Congress to "arbitrarily exclude" any commodity or thing from commerce that it chose, Harlan did not seem overly alarmed, indicating that the Court could "consider the constitutionality of such legislation when we must do so." The growth of a federal police power had begun.

In the early years of the twentieth century, the public became increasingly aware of numerous problems, often through the work of enterprising journalists and writers bent on exposing society's ills and evils. Termed "muckrakers" by President Theodore Roosevelt, these writers aroused public opinion to demand some federal protective legislation. Their efforts can be seen clearly in a number of laws: the Pure Food and Drug Act (1906); the Meat Inspection Act (1906); the White Slave Traffic Act of 1910 (Mann Act); and the Child Labor Act of 1916. Each of these except child labor (see Brief 8.8), was upheld by the Court as part of a broadened federal police power.20

A final example of a commerce police power involves the protection of civil rights and liberties of many Americans. Detailed treatment of civil rights is found in Chapters 9 and 10, but the relationship to the commerce power requires some treatment in this section. With passage of the Civil Rights Act of 1964, Congress sought to sweep away the years of segregation and discrimination in American life. The crucial section of the Act was Title II:

> SECTION 201 (A): ALL PERSONS SHALL BE ENTITLED TO THE FULL AND EQUAL ENJOYMENT OF THE GOODS, SERVICES, FACILITIES, PRIVILEGES, ADVANTAGES, AND ACCOMMODATIONS OF ANY PLACE OF PUBLIC ACCOMMODATION, AS DEFINED IN THIS SECTION WITHOUT DISCRIMINATION OR SEGREGATION ON THE GROUND OF RACE, COLOR, RELIGION, OR NATIONAL ORIGIN.

The Act identified four classes of business establishments that were termed "public accommodations" and covered by the law "if its operations affect commerce, or if discrimination or segregation by it is supported by State action." The covered establishments included inns, hotels, motels; restaurants and cafeterias; motion picture houses; and any establishment located within one of the others listed. Symbolically, the Act went into effect on July 4, 1964.

Brief 8.8

CHILD LABOR: FREEDOM OF CONTRACT OR A NATIONAL SHAME?

Congress passed the Child Labor Act of 1916 to deal with the widespread use and exploitation of child labor in American industry and manufacturing. The Act barred from interstate commerce the products of establishments that employed children under the age of fourteen and banned factory shipments when children between fourteen and sixteen were employed more than eight hours a day or more than six days a week. Mr. Dagenhart, the father of two minor sons who worked in a cotton mill, filed suit against United States Attorney W. C. Hammer to stop the act's enforcement. Hammer appealed to the Supreme Court following a district court ruling against the act.

Writing for a 5–4 majority in *Hammer v. Dagenhart* (1918), Justice William Day found the Child Labor Act of 1916 to be an unconstitutional use of the commerce power. According to Day, the products in the present case "are of themselves harmless," and do not justify the congressional prohibition on their shipment. Congress may use its powers to prohibit the movement of interstate commerce only with regard to harmful products. In striking down the act, the Court ignored the "current of commerce" doctrine and returned to the principles of dual federalism. Congress could not meddle in local matters.

Child labor legislation was unacceptable to the Supreme Court despite growing popular support for such policies. In fact, the entire child labor odyssey represented an ongoing conflict between what Stephen Wood has termed "popular sovereignty and judicial supervision."[21] Child labor pitted the communitarian and individualist theories of government against each other. For communitarians, society's interests in matters of health and welfare were paramount; individualists held tightly to the concept of individual liberty in the workplace and laissez-faire economic theory.

In *Bailey v. Drexel Furniture Co.* (1922), the Court struck down the Child Labor Tax Law, which imposed a 10 percent tax on the net profits of any firm that employed children under the age of fourteen. In classic dual federalist reasoning, Chief Justice William Howard Taft, speaking for an 8–1 Court, held the regulation to be a penalty that Congress had imposed to indirectly regulate an area (child labor) it had no authority to reach.

Reformers refused to give up on child labor, however, and it was readdressed in the Fair Labor Standards Act of 1938. That statute, known primarily for its minimum-wage and maximum-hour provisions, virtually restated the Child Labor Act of 1916, making it unlawful to ship goods in interstate commerce that had been produced in factories employing child labor within the previous thirty days. The Court's sweeping *U.S. v. Darby* (1941) ruling (see text) ensured that child labor would not survive in the expanded view of interstate commerce.

The Supreme Court ruled on the constitutionality of the Civil Rights Act of 1964 in the case of *Heart of Atlanta Motel, Inc. v. United States* (1964). The case was tailor-made for government prosecutors, given that the motel was located on a busy interstate highway, solicited convention business in magazine advertisements, and rented the bulk of its rooms to out-of-state or transient guests. In a unanimous opinion, Justice Thomas Clark reviewed more than one hundred years of Commerce Clause cases in which the power of Congress had been used for noncommercial purposes. He found racial discrimination to fall within the category of disruptive effects upon commerce over which Congress has regulatory power. Upholding the Act, Justice Clark gave the following, and now virtually unanimous, view of interstate commerce:

> WE, THEREFORE, CONCLUDE THAT THE ACTION OF THE CONGRESS IN THE ADOPTION OF THE ACT, AS APPLIED HERE TO A MOTEL WHICH CONCEDEDLY SERVES INTERSTATE TRAVELERS IS WITHIN THE POWER GRANTED IT BY THE COMMERCE CLAUSE OF THE CONSTITUTION, AS INTERPRETED BY THIS COURT FOR 140 YEARS.... HOW OBSTRUCTIONS IN COMMERCE MAY BE REMOVED—WHAT MEANS ARE TO BE EMPLOYED—IS WITHIN THE SOUND AND EXCLUSIVE DIRECTION OF THE CONGRESS.

The same day, in *Katzenbach v. McClung* (1964), the Court upheld the Act in even more sweeping terms by applying it to Ollie's Barbeque, a small, family-owned restaurant located far from a major highway and not frequented by out-of-state travelers. Nonetheless, the Court agreed with the government's finding that the restaurant's annual purchase of more than $70,000 worth of food was sufficient to place the establishment under the terms of the Act. Finally, in *Daniel v. Paul* (1969), the Court upheld the application of the Civil Rights Act to a rural amusement park in the Arkansas hills. In solitary dissent, Justice Hugo Black argued that applying the commerce power to "this country people's recreation center" risked giving "the Federal Government complete control over every little remote country place of recreation in every nook and cranny of each precinct and county in every one of the 50 states." The ruling showed that Congress could use its plenary power over commerce to reach broad social objectives.

RECENT DEVELOPMENTS IN COMMERCE AND SPENDING POWERS

In *United States v. Lopez* (1995), a 5–4 majority struck down the Gun-Free School Zones Act of 1990 as a violation of the interstate Commerce Clause. The Act, which forbids "any individual knowingly to possess a firearm at a place that [he] knows . . . is a school zone," was based on Congress's power to regulate interstate commerce in firearms, and it imposed criminal penalties on individuals who were in violation. When Alfonso Lopez, Jr. was arrested in a San Antonio, Texas, school with a firearm in his possession, the federal prosecutors sought to make it a federal offense. Could the congressional power to regulate commerce be used to reach into a community and apply national standards to a traditionally local criminal matter?

Chief Justice Rehnquist's majority opinion held that the Act exceeded congressional Commerce Clause authority. The Chief noted that the Court historically had given "great deference" to federal commerce laws, but he added that the possession of a gun in a local school zone is not an economic activity with a substantial economic effect upon interstate commerce. To uphold this law, he added, would require the Court to conclude "that there never will be a distinction between what is truly national and what is truly local." Justice Clarence Thomas, concurring, called for an overhaul of the Commerce Clause by making future jurisprudence "more faithful to the original understanding of that Clause."[22]

Justice John Paul Stevens dissented, noting that guns are articles of commerce that can also be used to "restrain commerce," and their possession is either directly or indirectly related to commerce. He added a strong appeal for using the commerce power to regulate guns:

> IN MY JUDGMENT, CONGRESS' POWER TO REGULATE COMMERCE IN FIREARMS INCLUDES THE POWER TO PROHIBIT POSSESSION OF GUNS AT ANY LOCATION BECAUSE OF THEIR POTENTIALLY HARMFUL USE, IT NECESSARILY FOLLOWS THAT CONGRESS MAY ALSO PROHIBIT THEIR POSSESSION IN PARTICULAR MARKETS. THE MARKET FOR THE POSSESSION OF HANDGUNS BY SCHOOL-AGE CHILDREN IS, DISTRESSINGLY, SUBSTANTIAL. WHETHER OR NOT THE NATION IN ELIMINATING THAT

MARKET WOULD HAVE JUSTIFIED FEDERAL LEGISLATION IN 1789, IT SURELY DOES TODAY.

The Court used the *Lopez* precedent to further restrict the commerce power in *United States v. Morrison* (2000). The case involved the "civil rights provision" of the 1994 Violence Against Women Act that guaranteed the right to be free from gender-motivated violence. Unlike *Lopez*, Congress had held numerous hearings on the issue, studying the effects of rape and domestic violence on employment and other activities related to interstate commerce. According to Chief Justice Rehnquist's majority opinion, "gender-motivated crimes of violence are not, in any sense of the phrase, economic activity." The Court could see no commercial relationship in what was essentially a criminal matter. As a result, women who are victims of gender-based violence may not file federal lawsuits against the perpetrators.

The Court did not restrict the commerce power in all cases. In *Reno v. Condon* (2000), the Court was unanimous in upholding the 1994 Driver's Privacy Protection Act (DPPA), which prohibits state motor-vehicle departments from disclosing personal information about drivers without permission. The Court's opinion distinguished this case from *Printz* in that the DPPA did not require states to enact laws or assist in enforcing federal statutes.

Finally, in *Gonzalez v. Raich* (2005), a 6–3 Court upheld the use of the Commerce Power to prohibit and prosecute the possession and use of "medical" marijuana. The ruling applies as well to the eleven states in which such use is legal. The decision in this case overturned a federal appeals court ruling that had shielded California's Compassionate Use Act, that state's medical marijuana law, from the reach of federal drug enforcement. Mrs. Raich, one of the plaintiffs, had been prosecuted for growing six marijuana plants, which she intended to use for her own medical needs. The majority justices placed heavy emphasis on earlier rulings such as *Wickard v. Filburn* (1942), involving the use of commerce power to regulate several hundred bushels of "home-grown" wheat destined for consumption on the family farm.

Justice Stevens, a longtime supporter of federal commerce power, defended the "power to regulate purely local activities that are part of an economic 'class of activities' that have a substantial effect on interstate commerce." Justices Kennedy and Scalia, who had consistently voted against broadening federal commerce power in the earlier *Lopez* and *Morrison* cases, switched sides in this case. Justice Scalia distinguished the marijuana case from the others by arguing that federal drug laws are part of a far more "comprehensive scheme of regulation" than the federal laws in the other cases.

Justice O'Connor, an opponent of an expanding commerce power, appeared to be dismayed by the Court's shift. She said in her dissent that the decision "threatens to sweep all of productive human activity into federal regulatory reach." While she said that she did not support the medical marijuana initiative *per se*, she argued that it clearly belongs within the realm of activity that the Constitution allows the States.

THE FIGHT OVER "OBAMACARE:" *NATIONAL FEDERATION OF INDEPENDENT BUSINESS, ET AL. V. SEBELIUS* (2012)

The most anticipated Commerce Power case in decades, *National Federation of Independent Business, et al. v. Sebelius* (2012), turned out to have very little to do with commerce. Although the Supreme Court upheld the Patient Protection and Affordable Care Act by a 5–4 vote, it did not do so on Commerce Clause grounds, despite the fact that the United States Government had stressed that argument. Instead, it relied on the Federal Taxing Power to uphold the "individual mandate" requirement that each person must purchase health insurance or pay a penalty. The Court rejected the applicability of such precedents as *Wickard v. Filburn* and *Gonzalez v. Raich*, ruling that an individual's failure to purchase health insurance is not an economic activity that can be regulated under the Commerce Power. Essentially, the justices were saying that Congress can regulate commercial activity but not inactivity.

Opponents of so-called "Obamacare" were thrilled with the first part of the opinion, but they did not like what came next. Once Chief Justice Roberts, writing for Justices Ginsburg, Breyer, Sotomayor, and Kagan, held that the penalty was really a tax and thereby subject to the congressional taxing power, the provision was constitutional. The "individual mandate" required a person to purchase health insurance or pay a 1 percent of income (or $95) penalty in 2014 up to a 2 percent (or $325) penalty in 2015 and beyond. How could this be viewed as a tax?

The Chief Justice identified the core elements of a tax: it is paid into the Treasury by taxpayers when they file their returns; it does not apply to taxpayers below certain income levels; the amount is determined by factors such as taxable income, dependents, and joint filing status; it is found in the Internal Revenue Code and enforced by the Internal Revenue Service; and, the "process yields the essential feature of any tax: It produces at least some revenue for the Government."

But what about the obvious reality that the payment is intended to influence individual conduct? According to the Chief Justice, "Although the payment will raise considerable revenue, it is plainly designed to expand health insurance coverage. But taxes that seek to influence conduct are nothing new. Some of our earliest Federal taxes sought to deter the purchase of imported manufactured goods in order to foster the growth of domestic industry."

As for the holding that the "individual mandate" can be upheld as a tax and that taxes are often used to influence individual conduct, the 5–4 majority was not breaking new ground. As the following section demonstrates, the federal taxing power has been well established and recognized by the Court for many years. Since 1936, not one law based on Congress's taxing power has been struck down by the courts.

THE CONGRESSIONAL POWER TO TAX AND SPEND

In Article I, Section 8, the Constitution provides that "Congress shall have power To lay and collect Taxes, Duties, Imposts and Excises, to pay the Debts and provide for the common Defence and general Welfare of the United States; but all Duties, Imposts and Excises shall be uniform throughout the United States." This grant of power to Congress contains both taxing and spending authority. The taxing power is conditioned by the requirement that "duties, imposts and excises shall be uniform" across the nation. By this qualification, Congress is prohibited from setting different rates for, say, excise taxes on tires or duties on imported cars in different states. The Constitution establishes two additional limitations upon taxation in Article I, Section 9:

> NO CAPITATION, OR OTHER DIRECT, TAX SHALL BE LAID, UNLESS IN PROPORTION TO THE CENSUS OR ENUMERATION HEREIN BEFORE DIRECTED TO BE TAKEN. NO TAX OR DUTY SHALL BE LAID ON ARTICLES EXPORTED FROM ANY STATE.

To summarize, the congressional power to tax may not be applied to exports, must be uniform throughout the nation, and direct taxes must be based on population (see Brief 8.9). Despite these seemingly simple limitations, the taxing power has stirred considerable controversy over two hundred years.

Brief 8.9
DIRECT TAXES AND THE FEDERAL INCOME TAX

The issue of direct taxes has arisen several times, although the Constitution offers little guidance in the matter apart from the linkage of "capitation" (head tax) with "direct" taxes. In *Hylton v. United States* (1796) the Supreme Court held that a congressional tax upon carriages was an "indirect" tax, with capitation and land taxes being the only direct taxes. In *Springer v. United States* (1881), the Court ruled that the income tax enacted during the Civil War was not a direct tax.

The most significant decision concerning direct taxes came in *Pollock v. Farmer's Loan and Trust Company* (1895), in which the Court voided an income tax in the Wilson-Gorman Tariff Act of 1894. The primary argument against the law's constitutionality was that a tax on income derived from land was actually a direct tax and should be apportioned among the states on the basis of population.

In a narrow 5–4 decision, the Court accepted the contention that a tax on income from land was a direct tax and declared the income tax law to be unconstitutional. However, as Congress could find no realistic fashion in which to apportion an income tax by population, it was unable to tax incomes until the passage of the Sixteenth Amendment in 1913:

> *The Congress shall have power to lay and collect taxes on incomes, from whatever source derived, without apportionment among the several States, and without regard to any census or enumeration.*

The amendment removed the "direct tax" issue from future consideration and opened up vast untapped sources of revenue for the federal government.

Most constitutional disagreements over the taxing power have concerned its use as a regulating device. Quite simply, while a tax raises revenue for government, it also imposes restrictions that allow government to shape public policies, consumer and corporate behavior, and production decisions. In a study of regulatory taxation, R. Alton Lee identified three schools of interpretation associated with the federal taxing power. The conservative interpretation, associated with persons such as John C. Calhoun, holds that taxation may be imposed only for revenue-raising purposes. A middle view accepts taxation for purposes other than raising revenue but rejects an "all-purpose grant of power." The liberal, or loose-constructionist, position recognizes taxation as a sweeping power, including the power to regulate or even destroy.[23] The central point of contention among these perspectives is the use of taxation as a police power enabling government to regulate matters of health, safety, and welfare. This issue was presented to the Supreme Court early in the twentieth century.

The case of *McCray v. United States* (1904) established the congressional police power in taxation. The case stemmed from a congressional tax of one-fourth-cent per-pound tax on uncolored margarine and a ten-cents-per-pound tax on colored margarine. When Leo McCray, a licensed retail dealer in oleomargarine, was fined for having failed to pay the proper tax, he challenged the tax as a transparent attempt by Congress to regulate the manufacture and sale of margarine, powers that rest with the States. In upholding the constitutionality of the tax, Justice Edward White stated that the congressional power to tax was "unrestrained, except as limited by the Constitution."[24]

The erosion of dual federalism after 1937 produced changes in the congressional taxing power much as it had done in commerce matters. In *Mulford v. Smith* (1939), the Court upheld the Second Agricultural Adjustment Act, quite similar to the law struck down three years earlier in *United States v. Butler* (1936). The new act allowed a penalty to be imposed for overproduction of tobacco beyond a quota established by Congress's control over interstate commerce. The Court's decision in *Steward Machine Co. v. Davis* (1937) upheld a portion of the Social Security Act of 1935 requiring employers of eight or more workers to pay a federal excise tax based on their employees' wages. If the employer contributed to an approved state unemployment program, however, he was permitted to credit those payments against up to 90 percent of the federal tax. Obviously, the law was designed to encourage states to create acceptable unemployment programs. Justice Benjamin Cardoza's majority opinion rejected the contention that the act coerced the states and invaded their powers. In *Helvering v. Davis* (1937), a companion case, a 5–4 Court upheld a Social Security tax for paying old-age benefits. Congress would henceforth be able to determine the proper subjects for which it could tax and spend to promote the general welfare.

A common thread running through many of these examples involves the federal government's ability to place conditions on states that receive federal funds. The ruling in *Fullilove v. Klutznick* (1980), for example, demonstrated how Congress could promote affirmative action through its federal spending rules. However, the Court's decision in *South Dakota v. Dole, Secretary, United States Department of Transportation* (1987) provided even more direct evidence of an expanding federal spending power. The case stemmed from a highway spending bill in which Congress decided that states not wishing to conform to a minimum drinking age of twenty-one simply forfeited their eligibility for 5 percent of their federal highway funds. South Dakota, with a policy of allowing nineteen-year-olds to purchase beer with no more than 3.2 percent alcohol content, challenged the federal legislation as an attempt by Congress to create a national drinking age—something that falls clearly outside the enumerated powers of Congress.

Speaking for the Court, Chief Justice William Rehnquist upheld the federal law under the Spending Clause. He indicated that Congress may attach conditions to federal funds and use its power to spend money as an "encouragement to state action." As long as the federal government does not compel or "commandeer" the states, such uses of spending power are likely to be allowable (see Brief 8.10). The decision in *Dole* suggests that Congress will continue to influence state governments through its control of the federal purse strings.

In recent years, the Court has upheld the possibility of taxpayer suits against specific uses of federal spending (*Flast v. Cohen*, 1968), but subsequent rulings (see *Hein v. Freedom from Religion Foundation*, 2007) do not offer much hope to the taxpayer who hopes to challenge federal expenditures.

Brief 8.10

LIMITATIONS ON THE SPENDING POWER: *NATIONAL FEDERATION OF INDEPENDENT BUSINESS, ET AL. V. SEBELIUS*

Despite the wide-ranging reach of the commerce and spending powers, the Courts have drawn the line on some congressional efforts to force state compliance. In *New York v. United States* (1992), Justice O'Connor's majority opinion restricted the use of congressional spending to force states to adopt regulations to deal with low-level radioactive waste. Although Justice O'Connor acknowledged that Congress has Commerce Clause authority to regulate low-level radioactive waste, she rejected efforts to "commandeer" the states' legislative process. She was particularly opposed to the provision of the act that compelled states that did not develop facilities to "take title" or ownership of radioactive wastes and assume liability for all damages. This, she said, was evidence that the federal authorities were "commandeering" the legislative process of the states.

In 1997, the "anti-commandeering" principle was applied to administrative functions performed by state officers. The Brady Handgun Violence Prevention Act of 1993 required the Attorney General to establish a national instant background check system by November 30, 1998. Until that time, chief law enforcement officers (CLEOs) in the states were required to perform background checks for prospective gun purchasers. The CLEO was directed to make a "reasonable" effort to determine in five business days if it would be unlawful to sell a handgun to a named prospective purchaser. Two sheriffs challenged the background-check provisions of the Act, contending that the federal government cannot compel state officers to enforce federal law no matter how laudable the federal law might be. They were successful in district court but lost in the Ninth Circuit Court of Appeals.

In *Printz v. United States* (1997) and *Mack v. United States* (1997), a 5–4 Supreme Court majority reversed the Ninth Circuit, holding that the Brady Act, even if temporary, violates the principle of dual federal–state sovereignty established by the Constitution. Justice Antonin Scalia, writing for the majority, referred extensively to portions of the *Federalist Papers* to support his view that the federal government may not compel states to carry out federal regulatory programs. Justice Scalia noted that the Constitution established a system of dual sovereignty, under which states surrendered many of their powers to the federal government. However, he noted that the states retained "residuary and inviolable sovereignty." This sovereignty was violated by the Brady Act's obligation on state officers to execute federal laws.

The dissenting justices found the historical evidence to lead in an opposite direction. Justice Stevens stated:

> When Congress exercises the powers delegated to it by the Constitution, it may impose affirmative obligations on executive and judicial officers of state and local governments as well as ordinary citizens. This conclusion is firmly supported by the text of the Constitution, the early history of the Nation, decisions of this Court, and a correct understanding of the basic structure of the Federal Government.

Justice Stevens also chided the majority for making a policy judgment that would be more properly left to "the elected representatives of the people."

The Supreme Court also found that Congress crossed the line from persuading to compelling the states through its spending power in *National Federation of Independent Business, et al. v. Sebelius* (2012). Portions of this decision are discussed in earlier sections dealing with commerce and taxation, but the spending power played a large role in the decision as well. In passing the Patient Protection and Affordable Care Act, Congress required the states to expand their Medicaid programs by 2014 to cover all persons under the age of sixty-five with incomes below 133 percent of the federal poverty line. The national government would pay all of the costs of covering the newly insured individuals through 2016, after which the federal share would drop to 90 percent. States could refuse to participate in the expanded program, but a state that did so would lose not only the new federal funding for the expansion but also its entire Medicaid allotment.

Seven justices agreed that the Medicaid expansion provision went far beyond simple encouragement of state participation and crossed over into compulsion. In two opinions, one by Chief Justice Roberts and another by the four dissenting justices—Scalia, Thomas, Kennedy, and Alito—the Court found that by cutting off a state's entire federal Medicaid allotment, it was, as the Chief Justice noted, putting "a gun to the head" of the states. Significantly, the five justices taking this position believed that the Medicaid expansion provision should be saved and not struck down. So, in a fairly unusual step, the five justices agreed that the Medicaid expansion was a "new" program and not part of the existing Medicaid scheme. As a result, states that refused to participate in the expansion would simply lose the federal funding for that Medicaid program—not their entire Medicaid funding. Whether the Court's approach will affect future spending bills that relate to established federal programs remains to be seen.

Conclusion

The Civil War's primary effect upon federalism was to demonstrate the supremacy of the national government and to settle the long-standing dispute over ultimate sovereignty. Nevertheless, the rivalry between national and state governments did not end with the Civil War. Nowhere has this arrangement been more visible than in the realm of government regulation of the economy. The debate between economic liberty and property rights, on the one hand, and governmental powers of regulation, on the other, has fluctuated throughout the two hundred years since our nation's founding. These two positions, generally associated with individualist and communitarian perspectives on government, have each held the upper hand at various stages of American constitutional development. As a result, our nation has embraced elements of both positions—a strong individualistic belief in rights of property ownership blended with a communitarian concern with safeguarding society's interests in matters of health, safety, morals, and welfare. Four constitutional clauses have played pivotal roles in the process.

The Contract Clause provided the earliest constitutional conflict over property rights. Written primarily to prevent state government interference in financial and commercial matters, the Contract Clause became a source of bitter dispute between the Federalist-dominated judiciary led by Chief Justice John Marshall and the emerging strength of more communitarian-minded state governments. Despite some recent signs of a revival of the Contract Clause as a limitation on state legislation, it is clear that the Contract Clause has not fulfilled the expectations of those early American individualists who envisioned it as a bastion against state control and regulation of contractual and property law.

The Due Process of Law Clauses of the Fifth and Fourteenth Amendments came to replace the Contract Clause as the foremost constitutional protection against government interference. Coupled with the growing popularity of a *laissez-faire* economic theory, the Due Process Clause effectively throttled both federal and state attempts to legislate wages, hours, working conditions, and production. The catastrophic effects of the Great Depression greatly weakened the sanctity of freedom of contract and other laissez-faire doctrines. When *West Coast Hotel v. Parrish* was decided in 1937, the Supreme Court had signaled a clear change in direction: the Due Process of Law Clause no longer would serve as a shield against all forms of economic policymaking by governments. Today, property-related disputes continue to occur, but the most controversial constitutional issue appears to be in the area of "takings."

The Commerce Clause, perhaps more so than any other constitutional vehicle, has extended the power of the national government over virtually every economically related activity in the nation. The full impact of the congressional commerce power has become evident in a wide range of areas, and nearly all working Americans are covered by federal wage and hour legislation, with significant national regulation of such areas as labor relations, job discrimination, and employee safety. While the commerce power remains strong, a few rulings have demonstrated the Court's unwillingness to expand it into areas such as gun possession and violence against women.

Finally, the Taxing and Spending Clause has opened vast new areas to federal government regulation. Through taxation policy, Congress has combined the raising of revenue with a police-power orientation. Proposals to levy tariffs on items such as imported oil and increased taxes on cigarettes serve as illustrations of the role of taxation in policy formulation. The power to spend also has resulted in considerable legislation, including, of course, Social Security and a large number of entitlement programs. In promoting the general welfare through taxing and spending, Congress has enacted programs that affect most Americans on a regular basis.

Part 3

Constitutional Rights and Liberties

Constitutionalism requires that individual rights and liberties be protected from encroachment by government. At the same time, however, the broader interests of society often must be balanced against individual concerns. As a result, the preservation of individual rights and liberties along with the protection of the public interest stand as major tasks facing American constitutional government. The eight chapters in Part 3 address this relationship from several perspectives. Chapters 9 and 10 examine the fundamental issue of equality through the Constitution's equal protection guarantees. Racial equality is discussed in Chapter 9, while the "new" equal protection is covered in Chapter 10. Chapter 11 explores the Bill of Rights, the process of "selective incorporation," and the question of whether other "fundamental rights" should be protected beyond those listed in the first ten amendments. Chapter 12 focuses on issues related to privacy and the government's power to engage in searches and seizures under the terms of the Fourth Amendment. Chapter 13 analyzes the complex areas of due process of law and criminal procedure, with primary emphasis on the Fifth, Sixth, and Eighth Amendments. The final three chapters address different aspects of the First Amendment. Chapter 14 deals with freedom of speech and assembly, in the context of the government's national security concerns as well as whether the Constitution protects other forms of free expression that do not raise such security concerns, such as labor protests, commercial speech, and campaign finance regulation. Chapter 15 delves into the complexities of freedom of the press, examining issues such as prior restraint, the conflict between a free press and criminal due process concerns, obscenity, libel, and the federal regulation of broadcast media. The text concludes with Chapter 16, which analyzes the rights and liberties protected in the religion clauses of the First Amendment. In these chapters, attention is directed toward the individualist and communitarian perspectives that help to define the most fundamental rights and liberties of Americans, as well as the limits that government can place upon them for the common good.

CHAPTER 9
Racial Equality Under the Constitution

THE RIGHT TO VOTE AND TO EQUAL REPRESENTATION HAS BEEN ONE OF THE MOST HEAVILY CONTESTED QUESTIONS OF RACIAL EQUALITY UNDER THE CONSTITUTION. ALTHOUGH THE FIFTEENTH AMENDMENT—ADOPTED IN 1870—GUARANTEED THAT THE RIGHT TO VOTE "SHALL NOT BE DENIED . . . ON ACCOUNT OF RACE, COLOR, OR PREVIOUS CONDITION OF SERVITUDE," IT WOULD TAKE THE NEXT CENTURY TO EFFECTIVELY GUARANTEE VOTING RIGHTS FOR RACIAL MINORITIES IN THE UNITED STATES.

▼ Introductory Remarks by Frederick Douglass

Who better to introduce this chapter on racial equality under the Constitution than a man born into slavery, a system that "often pierced my soul with a sense of its horrors?" For it is slavery and its legacy of racial inequality that has raised some of the greatest questions for a constitutional system grounded in the idea that "all men are created equal." In fact, a century after I railed against the "revolting barbarity and shameless hypocrisy" of slavery, a Swedish observer, Gunnar Myrdal, coined the phrase "American dilemma" to account for the existence—side by side—of a powerful ideal of equality at the heart of the nation with the systemic subordination of groups of people based on race.

Consistent with this American dilemma, I was often ambivalent about what our founders intended. In a famous speech I at once applauded the American revolutionaries for the courage they showed in throwing off oppression felt at the hands of the English, and yet decried the fact that I was "not included within the pale" of Fourth of July and its celebration:

What, to the American slave, is your 4th of July? I answer: a day that reveals to him, more than all other days in the year, the gross injustice and cruelty to which he is the constant victim. To him, your celebration is a sham; your boasted liberty, an unholy license; your national greatness, swelling vanity; your sounds of rejoicing are empty and heartless; your denunciations of tyrants, brass fronted impudence; your shouts of liberty and equality, hollow mockery; your prayers and hymns, your sermons and thanksgivings, with all your religious parade, and solemnity, are, to him, mere bombast, fraud, deception, impiety, and hypocrisy—a thin veil to cover up crimes which would disgrace a nation of savages. There is not a nation on the earth guilty of practices, more shocking and bloody, than are the people of these United States, at this very hour.

But unlike my contemporary and fellow abolitionist William Lloyd Garrison, I was not ambivalent about the promise of the Constitution for ending slavery and promoting equality. I once proclaimed that "the Constitution is a glorious liberty document" and "vindicated [it] from any design to support slavery for an hour." Although it was a protracted struggle, even after the passage of the Thirteenth, Fourteenth, and Fifteenth Amendments, I believe my view of the Constitution's promise has largely been justified.

I was able to escape slavery—literally—and spend most of my life speaking and writing on behalf of emancipation and equality, not only for slaves and former slaves, but also on behalf of women. I joined with Elizabeth Cady Stanton, who introduces the next chapter, and others at the Seneca Falls convention demanding women's equality under the Constitution. As you will see in reading this chapter, much progress has been made toward ensuring that race will cease to be a barrier to legal equality—the historic election and reelection of an African American to the highest office in the land is a testament to this fact. But in other areas (racial profiling, continuing racial disparities in educational opportunity, employment, and basic health care) the ideal of equality found in the Declaration and Constitution has been more difficult to satisfy.

SOURCES: Frederick Douglass, *Narrative of the Life of Frederick Douglass: An American Slave, Written by Himself* (Cambridge, MA: Harvard University Press, 2009); Gunnar Myrdal, *An American Dilemma: The Negro Problem and American Democracy* (New York: Harper & Row, 1944); Frederick Douglass, "What to a Slave is the Fourth of July," Speech given in Rochester, NY, July 5, 1852, http://teachingamericanhistory.org/library/index.asp?document=162.

RACIAL EQUALITY: AN AMERICAN DILEMMA

Along with liberty, the ideal of equality buttresses the American constitutional system. The banner of equality is raised by both the individualist and communitarian traditions in American political thought. The individualist sees equality of opportunity as essential to individuals seeking to maximize their goods. Equality under the law is also valued because it guarantees the kind of procedural justice individualists support. For the communitarian, political equality is a prerequisite for the values mentioned in Chapter 1 of majority rule and maximum citizen participation. In addition, communitarian concerns over substantive justice dictate that society's institutions be judged by whether they achieve relative equality for all citizens.

But the ideal of equality is capable of a wide range of meanings. Throughout the nation's history, citizens have interpreted the demands of constitutional equality differently. One view, which has been termed the "anti-discrimination principle,"[1] holds that equality's command is a negative one: Equality merely means that the government and law should not discriminate against individuals in an arbitrary fashion. Government and the law must always distinguish between individuals, their characteristics, and their behavior. For example, a law that sets the speed limit at twenty-five miles per hour will draw a line between people who drive twenty-five miles per hour and those who drive forty-five miles per hour, and law enforcement officials will discriminate against the latter. This poses no obvious problem for equality. The anti-discrimination principle merely forbids governmental discrimination against individuals on *irrational* grounds unrelated to any legitimate state purpose. Discrimination based on race and ethnic origin best exemplifies the kind of impermissible distinctions covered by the anti-discrimination principle. In the following chapter, we examine the attempt to expand the categories covered by the anti-discrimination principle to include gender, age, and sexual orientation, among others.

However, this first definition of equality leaves a wide range of distinctions between individuals acceptable. To illustrate, Shelby Steele has written that, as "a middle-class black," his children

HAVE ENDURED RACIAL INSENSITIVITY FROM WHITES. THEY HAVE BEEN CALLED NAMES, HAVE SUFFERED SLIGHTS, AND HAVE EXPERIENCED FIRSTHAND THE PECULIAR MALEVOLENCE THAT RACISM BRINGS OUT IN PEOPLE. YET, THEY HAVE NEVER EXPERIENCED RACIAL DISCRIMINATION.[2]

The anti-discrimination principle is thus perfectly compatible with vast inequalities between individuals in the society. For example, the economic inequalities resulting from a history of race- or sex-segregated employment cannot be remedied simply by an end to government discrimination. That has led some citizens to argue for a more positive, substantive, results-oriented approach to constitutional equality. Under this approach, which constitutional scholar Owen Fiss has termed the "group-disadvantaging principle,"[3] the government would have the positive duty to address inequalities between people and could operate from a group-based as opposed to an individual-based perspective. The law could take account of groups or classes of people who had been historically denied the advantages and opportunities society has to offer.

An additional question about equality relates to the area its commands cover. Is equality under the Constitution limited to governmental and legal actions, or does it extend to other areas of public life? Is discrimination carried out by individuals in the private sector subject to constitutional prohibitions in the same way that state-based discrimination is? If so, how can private individuals be monitored to determine whether the ideal of equality has been subverted?

Many of these questions have been present from the beginning of the nation's history. Documents of the founding period abound with mention of equality. Of course, Thomas Jefferson proclaimed in the Declaration of Independence that "all men are created equal." A great debate exists over what Jefferson meant by equality. Most political theorists and historians would agree that he did not intend the statement to endorse a sameness of condition on the American people. But they disagree over whether the Declaration of Independence promotes the ideal of equality of opportunity (a more individualist notion most compatible with the anti-discrimination principle just mentioned) or the notion that all citizens be effectively granted equal legal and political status (a more communitarian understanding of equality). Some have even noted that Jefferson's phrase reflects the classical republican concern over equal participation in public life, where any inequalities among citizens—economic, cultural, or social—can skew political decisions and thus damage the pursuit of a common good created out of the equally articulated voices of all the citizenry.

In addition to Jefferson's controversial statement, Chapter 2 pointed out that many of the early state constitutions granted greater political equality than did their colonial counterparts. And the Constitution itself is permeated with the ideal of equality, though it is not always explicitly stated. For example, the Preamble announces that one of the new Constitution's foremost purposes is to "establish Justice," which is given meaning by the motto inscribed on the Supreme Court Building: "Equal Justice Under Law." The writers of the Preamble understood that justice cannot be brought about unless all are treated equally.

However, no one can honestly say that this underlying ideal of equality has been consistently applied to all people. At the time of the founding, all women, native Americans, black men, and the propertyless were excluded from the promises of equal justice. Over the past two hundred years these groups and others have struggled to secure equality. This chapter examines the struggle for racial equality under the American Constitution, while the following chapter looks at similar struggles for equality by groups other than racial minorities. It will be important to keep in mind the controversy surrounding equality and its meaning, how equality's meaning has changed over time, and the role of the federal government, especially the Supreme Court, in directing those changes.

SLAVERY, RACE, AND THE CONSTITUTION

The legal treatment of black people in particular has contradicted the principle of equality found in the Declaration of Independence. With the initial arrival of African slaves at Jamestown in 1619, the principle of universal equality found in the Declaration was severely compromised. Historians disagree about the extent of chattel slavery in the seventeenth century, but at the time of independence in 1776, slavery was indeed an essential institution in the southern colonies (by historians' accounts, black slaves constituted about 40 percent of the southern colonial population in 1776). Even in the seven northern states that formally abolished slavery after the Revolution, laws discriminated against people of African ancestry, restricting suffrage and travel and segregating local schools. There is no denying the unequal treatment accorded to African Americans during the founding period. Under law, slaves were treated not as persons, but as property. They could be bought and sold, compelled to work for their owner, and even physically abused. Laws prohibited slaves from being taught to read or write. Moreover, the institution was hereditary: a slave's children also belonged absolutely to her or his master.

The Constitution, while not specifically authorizing slavery, at least condoned its continued practice and the gross inequality that resulted from slavery. Although never mentioning slavery by name, ten clauses in the original Constitution accommodated slavery, either directly or indirectly. Three constitutional provisions in particular helped protect the institution of slavery. The first, the so-called Three-fifths Compromise, provided that slaves (actually designated as "other Persons" in Article I, Section 2) would count as three-fifths of a person for the purposes of determining representatives and direct taxation. This provision is called a "compromise" because, on the question of taxation, northerners wanted slaves to count fully while southerners wanted them to be excluded completely on the grounds that they were mere property. But for the purpose of determining representation, the stakes were reversed and southerners wanted slaves to count equally with freemen, whereas northerners wanted to exclude them from the total census count. The Three-fifths Compromise resolved the conflict on both issues and had the effect of augmenting southern representation in the new House of Representatives by one-third.

A second provision, the 1808 Compromise, as mentioned briefly in Chapter 2, concerned the future of the slave trade itself. The delegates at Philadelphia decided to prevent Congress from prohibiting the slave trade until 1808 (Art. I, Sec. 9). This clause has been interpreted two ways. Chief Justice Roger B. Taney, in his infamous opinion in *Dred Scott v. Sandford* (1857), said it meant that "the right to purchase and hold this property is directly sanctioned and authorized for twenty years." But historian Don Fehrenbacher has argued that the clause actually "authorized the future abolition of the slave trade and thus amounted . . . to a delayed repudiation of the slave system."[4]

The third provision was the Fugitive-Slave Clause, found in Article IV, Section 2. It commands: "No Person held to Service or Labor in one State, under the Laws thereof, escaping into another, shall, in Consequence of any Law or Regulation therein, be discharged from such Service or Labor, but shall be delivered up on Claim of the Party to whom such service or labor may be due." This clause actually nationalized slave property, obliging even free states to assist in enforcing the slave system. It would later provide the basis for federal intervention on behalf of the institution of slavery through two fugitive slave laws passed by Congress.

The Constitution's remarks about slavery can be read in two ways. From one perspective, those who framed the Constitution justified slavery. Abolitionist William Lloyd Garrison called the sectional compromise over slavery "a covenant with death and an agreement with hell."[5] Luther Martin—a delegate to the Constitutional Convention from Maryland who not only refused to sign the Constitution but also opposed its ratification—viewed the slavery "compromises" as "a solemn mockery of, and insult to that God whose protection we had then implored, and who views with equal eye the poor African slave and his American master."[6] From this perspective, the Constitution allowed slaves to be treated as property, thus compromising the concept of equal human dignity.

But from another perspective, the ambiguous wording and limited acceptance of the institution lent itself to the eventual abolition of slavery. After all, the founders did purposely avoid using the words "slave" or "slavery." Two New Jersey delegates to the Constitutional Convention, William Paterson and Jonathan Dayton, claimed that the convention "had been ashamed to use the term 'Slaves' and had therefore substituted a description" to avoid a "stain" on the new government.[7] Madison indicated in *Federalist No. 54* that the ambiguous treatment of slavery in the Constitution reflects a sectional compromise necessary to keep all interests together in 1787. Political scientist Herbert Storing represents this perspective, arguing that, overall, the founders saw slavery as "an evil to be tolerated, allowed to enter the Constitution only by the back door, grudgingly, unacknowledged, on the presumption that the house would be truly fit to live in only when it was gone, and that it would ultimately be gone."[8]

THE POST–CIVIL WAR AMENDMENTS AND RACIAL EQUALITY

The Constitution may have been ambiguous on the question of slavery. But the federal government's actions often protected slavery as an institution (see Brief 9.1). It would take the Civil War to put an end to slavery and to the Constitution's acceptance of it. In December 1865, the Thirteenth Amendment to the Constitution was ratified, declaring that "neither slavery nor involuntary servitude . . . shall exist within the United States." The Reconstruction Congress acted quickly over the next decade to ensure that newly freed blacks were granted the full equality that the abolition of slavery promised. Richard Kluger believes that "viewed as a unit, the decade of legislation beginning with the adoption of the Thirteenth Amendment in 1865 and culminating in passage of the Civil Rights Act of 1875, may reasonably be said to have closed the gap between the promise of the Declaration and the tactful tacit racism of the Constitution."[9]

The newly reconstituted southern states did not participate in this push for racial equality, however. White southerners enacted what were called "Black Codes" beginning late in 1865. These codes restricted blacks from carrying arms or using the courts, compelled them to work, and segregated them in all public facilities. In response to the Black Codes and other prejudicial action, Congress used its legislative authority under the Thirteenth Amendment to pass the Civil Rights Act of 1866. In it, Congress specifically repudiated not only the Black Codes but also Justice Taney's view of race and citizenship, by declaring that "all persons born in the United States . . . are . . . citizens of the United States," and conferring upon

Brief 9.1

SLAVERY UNDER THE CONSTITUTION: THE PRE–CIVIL WAR YEARS

From its very beginnings under the Constitution of 1787, the U.S. Government was implicated in the institution of slavery. The mere location of the nation's capital in a slaveholding community, governed by slavery-influenced local laws, contributed to federal support of slavery. So, too, did Congress, through both territorial management and its passage of laws designed to give authority to the Fugitive-Slave Clause in Article IV.[10] Finally, the Supreme Court's rulings during this era also enhanced slavery's position.

Two cases in particular, *Prigg v. Pennsylvania* (1842) and *Dred Scott v. Sandford* (1857), deserve brief mention. Edward Prigg, a lawyer acting on behalf of a Maryland slave owner, had forcibly returned a fugitive slave who had escaped to Pennsylvania. Prigg was convicted on kidnapping charges in Pennsylvania because he had removed the slave without proper state judicial authority. The Supreme Court unanimously reversed his conviction and, in so doing, made significant concessions to slave owners (although the overall ruling itself is somewhat ambiguous). Justice Joseph Story announced for the Court that the Constitution "contains a positive and unqualified recognition of the right of the owner in the slave, unaffected by any state law or legislation whatsoever." Justice Smith Thompson concurred, stating that the Fugitive Slave Clause "affirms, in the most unequivocal manner, the right of the master to the service of his slave [and] it prohibits the states from discharging the slave from such service."

The *Dred Scott* case involved a number of issues, including the power of judicial review, the fundamental property rights of slave owners, and the nature of the federal system. But in terms of racial equality, the questions about slavery and the extent of the black man's constitutional rights are paramount. Dred Scott, a black slave born of slave parents, had sued for his freedom based on his five-year residence on free soil. As a result of the Missouri Compromise of 1820, Congress had banned slavery in Wisconsin Territory. Scott maintained that Congress's conferral of nonslave status on the Wisconsin Territory gave him a title to freedom based on his residence there. The Supreme Court ruled that the Missouri Compromise had been unconstitutional because Congress did not have the authority to restrict slavery in the territories, thereby depriving slave owners of their constitutional right to property under the Due Process Clause of the Fifth Amendment.

But the Supreme Court also dealt with Dred Scott's very right to bring suit in the federal courts. The first question Scott's suit raised was whether a black man of slave origins was a citizen and had the constitutional right to bring a suit against a citizen of another state in the federal courts. The Court answered this question with a resounding no. Chief Justice Taney proclaimed that neither Dred Scott nor any other black man (let alone woman) could be considered a citizen under the U.S. Constitution. Looking back to the founding period, Taney wrote that black men

> *had for more than a century before been regarded as beings of an inferior order, and altogether unfit to associate with the white race, either in social or political relations; and so far inferior, that they had no rights which the white man was bound to respect; and that the negro might justly and lawfully be reduced to slavery for his benefit. He was bought and sold, and treated as an ordinary article of merchandise and traffic, whenever a profit could be made by it. This opinion was at that time fixed and universal in the civilized race.*

Justice Taney's denial to blacks of any citizenship rights was the culmination of the Supreme Court's pre–Civil War rulings regarding slavery, race, and the Constitution. The decision also figured in the tension-creating events that brought the nation to civil war four years later. But in terms of jurisprudence, the Court's interpretation of the Constitution would not last very long after these two cases, as the Constitution itself would be changed after the Civil War.

THE INHABITANTS OF EVERY RACE . . . THE SAME RIGHT TO MAKE AND ENFORCE CONTRACTS, TO SUE, BE PARTIES, AND GIVE EVIDENCE, TO INHERIT, PURCHASE, LEASE, SELL, HOLD, AND CARRY REAL AND PERSONAL PROPERTY, AND TO THE FULL AND EQUAL BENEFIT OF ALL LAWS AND PROCEEDINGS FOR THE SECURITY OF PERSON AND PROPERTY, AND SHALL BE SUBJECT TO LIKE PUNISHMENT, PAINS, AND PENALTIES, AND TO NONE OTHER, ANY LAW, STATUTE, ORDINANCE, REGULATION, OR CUSTOM TO THE CONTRARY NOTWITHSTANDING.

At the same time, Representative John Bingham of New York led the fight to make permanent the guarantees of racial equality by introducing in Congress what would come to be the Fourteenth Amendment to the Constitution. This amendment would be the crowning achievement in these post–Civil War years. Ratified in 1868, the Fourteenth Amendment contains three specific provisions aimed at guaranteeing the rights of African Americans. It forbids the states from making laws that (1) "abridge the privileges or immunities of citizens of the United States"; (2) "deprive any person of life, liberty, or property, without due process of law"; or (3) "deny to any person within its jurisdiction the equal protection of the laws." Moreover, the amendment gives Congress the power to pass laws enforcing these provisions. Chapter 8 contained a discussion of the Supreme Court's early weakening of the Privileges and Immunities Clause in its ruling in the Slaughterhouse Cases (1873). Full coverage of the Due Process Clause as it pertains to issues of economic liberty and to the nationalization of the Bill of Rights appear in Chapters 8 and 11. The focus in this chapter and the next is on the Equal Protection Clause.

RACE AND CONSTITUTIONAL EQUALITY: THE COURT'S ORIGINAL UNDERSTANDING

What did the Equal Protection Clause mean? The intentions of those who framed it are not completely clear. The Fourteenth Amendment's sponsors saw it as a necessary federal protection of former slaves' civil rights against those in the states who might deny them equality under the law. The framers of the amendment clearly had in mind the Black Codes and other examples of racially biased state laws. "Equal protection," then, was designed for newly freed blacks, to provide "that no discrimination shall be made against them by law because of their color."[11]

The Supreme Court announced this primary purpose of the Fourteenth Amendment in the Slaughterhouse Cases (1873). Justice Samuel Miller announced that "the one pervading purpose" of all the post–Civil War amendments was to protect the newly freed slave "from the oppression of those who had formerly exercised unlimited dominion over him. . . . We doubt very much whether any action of a state not directed by way of discrimination against the negroes as a class, or on account of their race, will ever be held to come within the purview of this provision."

But what specific rights did the Equal Protection Clause protect? Section 2 of the Fourteenth Amendment and later the Fifteenth Amendment, ratified in 1870, were designed to guarantee *political* equality to blacks, specifically the right to vote. And it seems clear, given the backdrop of the Civil Rights Act of 1866, that Congress intended the Fourteenth Amendment to guarantee black people equality in their *civil* rights. It would eliminate the Black Codes and any other laws that specified criminal offenses for blacks only or limited their right to hold property, make contracts, or seek legal justice in the courts.

Beyond these political and civil rights, the original purpose of the Equal Protection Clause remains somewhat uncertain. Was it meant to end discrimination against other racial groups besides those of African ancestry? This question was raised by the amendment's language, which protects "any person" rather than black men specifically. Was the amendment meant to guarantee blacks "social" as opposed to "civil" equality? Did it apply to racial segregation or discrimination in education, in transportation facilities, and in privately owned places of public accommodation (i.e., hotels, restaurants, theaters)? All of these questions were raised because the amendment spoke in broad generalities, such as "equal protection" and "privileges and immunities," rather than the more specific wording and provisions of the 1866 Civil Rights Act.

The Supreme Court was left with the task of tackling these difficult issues of constitutional interpretation. At first, its decisions seemed to offer an expansive vision of the ideal of equality protected under the Fourteenth Amendment (see Brief 9.2). However, Court watchers in this period would see a rapid narrowing of the Fourteenth Amendment's application, even to African Americans. The cases that stand out in this early period are the Civil Rights Cases (1883) and *Plessy v. Ferguson* (1896).

In the Civil Rights Act of 1875, Congress had asserted its authority to legislate positively on behalf of racial minorities whom the states might not protect from racial discrimination conducted by private individuals. Congress had made it illegal to deny any persons "full and equal enjoyment of the accommodations, advantages, facilities, and privileges of inns, public conveyances on land or water, theaters, and other places of public amusement." Acting under its perceived authority in Section 5 of the Fourteenth Amendment, Congress had moved to prohibit discriminatory actions by private individuals operating services subject to public regulation. In the five companion cases decided together as the Civil Rights Cases, the Supreme Court held the Civil Rights Act of 1875 to be unconstitutional.

Justice Joseph Bradley's opinion focused narrowly on the exact wording of the Fourteenth Amendment. In response to the amendment's

Brief 9.2

LAUNDRIES AND JURY BOXES: AN EXPANSIVE VISION OF EQUAL PROTECTION

Two cases following passage of the Fourteenth Amendment signaled the Supreme Court's willingness to view the Equal Protection Clause quite expansively. In *Strauder v. West Virginia* (1880), the Court ruled that state laws that excluded blacks from serving on juries violated the Equal Protection Clause. Justice William Strong wrote:

> *The very fact that colored people are singled out and expressly denied by a statute all rights to participate in the administration of the law, as jurors, because of their color, though they are citizens, and may be in other respects fully qualified, is practically a brand upon them, affixed by the law; an assertion of their inferiority, and a stimulant to that race prejudice which is an impediment to securing to individuals of the race that equal justice which the law aims to secure to all others.*

Strong further argued that the Fourteenth Amendment itself "speaks in general terms, and those are as comprehensive as possible."[12]

In *Yick Wo v. Hopkins* (1886), the Court continued this expansive vision, striking down a law that had been applied in a discriminatory fashion against Asians. A San Francisco municipal ordinance required special permission to operate a laundry in a building constructed of wood. Of the approximately three hundred laundries made of wood, the municipality granted all but one application for such special permission filed by whites, but had denied all two hundred made by Chinese. Though the law itself did not discriminate, its unequal administration based solely on racial prejudice violated the Equal Protection Clause. Justice Stanley Matthews, delivering the Court's opinion, wrote:

> *Though the law itself be fair on its face and impartial in appearance, yet, if it is applied and administered by public authority with an evil eye and an unequal hand, so as practically to make unjust and illegal discriminations between persons in similar circumstances, material to their rights, the denial of equal justice is still within the prohibition of the Constitution.*

So in *Yick Wo* the Court not only applied the dictates of equal protection to persons of Asian ancestry but also ruled against the discriminatory implementation of a facially neutral law.

Unfortunately, *Strauder* and *Yick Wo* were, as one author put it, "islands in a sea of judicial indifference to the rights of persons who were not white males."[13] Most of the Court's nineteenth-century equal protection rulings interpreted the demands of equality quite narrowly.

---

wording that "no State" shall deny equal protection, Justice Bradley wrote, "It is State action of a particular character that is prohibited. Individual invasion of individual rights is not the subject matter of the amendment." Congress was limited under the Fourteenth Amendment to correcting state laws or actions that denied equal protection or discriminated against persons on the basis of their race. The attempt by Congress to correct private racial discrimination was based on a misconstruction of the Fourteenth Amendment, Bradley said, and was therefore an invalid exercise of federal power. In rather telling comments near the end of his opinion, Justice Bradley admitted that Congress had authority under the Thirteenth Amendment to abolish "all badges and incidents of slavery," but he denied that the individual discrimination prohibited by the Civil Rights Act constituted a "badge of slavery." Bradley went on to say that legislative aid to newly freed blacks had its limits. There has to be some point, he stated, at which the black man "ceases to be the special favorite of the laws" and takes on "the rank of a mere citizen."

In a lone dissenting opinion, Justice John Harlan, an ex-slave owner from Kentucky, stressed the breadth of congressional authority under the Thirteenth and Fourteenth Amendments. He contended that the subjects legislated by Congress in the Civil Rights Act of 1875 certainly "constitute badges of slavery and servitude" and fell legitimately under federal authority to prohibit. Harlan also thought, unlike the majority, that the racial discrimination legislated against in the act involved private "corporations and individuals in the exercise of *their public or quasi-public functions* [emphasis added]," and thus could be reached by Congress. Furthermore, he disputed Bradley's contention that the black man was being "favored" by such legislation: "The statute of 1875 is for the benefit of citizens of every race and color." Harlan bitterly concluded that "the substance and spirit of the recent amendments of the Constitution have been sacrificed by a subtle and ingenious verbal criticism."

Historian C. Vann Woodward argued that the Civil Rights Cases were the judicial ratification of the Compromise of 1877, which ended Reconstruction and transferred authority to protect civil rights from federal to state officials.[14] But regardless of how the Court's complicity in the matter of sectional politics is viewed, its decision in the Civil Rights Cases narrowly construed the Fourteenth Amendment. It also removed congressional authority to directly protect the black man's right to equal treatment, as Justice Bradley's opinion left the protection against private discrimination up to the states. This created a vacuum that a resurgent white southern elite would fill, capitalizing on hostility toward Reconstruction and the newly freed slaves to catapult themselves back into power. Once in power, southern legislatures began passing a bevy of "Jim Crow" laws, requiring racial segregation in a number of areas. The Supreme Court was asked to rule on the constitutionality of these Jim Crow laws in *Plessy v. Ferguson*.

In 1890, the Louisiana legislature passed a law titled "An Act to Promote the Comfort of Passengers." It required railroads to "provide equal but separate accommodations for the white and colored races" and made it a criminal offense for any passenger to occupy "a coach or compartment to which by race he does not belong." A group of African American citizens in New Orleans organized a committee to test the constitutionality of this Jim Crow law. They arranged for Homer Plessy, a light-complexioned mulatto, to get arrested for refusing to relinquish his seat in the white section of a train leaving New Orleans. Plessy challenged the law on the grounds that it violated the Fourteenth Amendment. Here the state was enforcing a law that discriminated on the basis of race.

The Supreme Court upheld Louisiana's separate train-car statute. Justice Henry Brown, speaking for a 7–1 majority, ruled that the Fourteenth Amendment had not been offended by this "Jim Crow" law. He wrote:

> THE OBJECT OF THE AMENDMENT WAS UNDOUBTEDLY TO ENFORCE THE ABSOLUTE EQUALITY OF THE TWO RACES BEFORE THE LAW, BUT IN THE NATURE OF THINGS IT COULD NOT HAVE BEEN INTENDED TO ABOLISH DISTINCTIONS BASED UPON COLOR, OR TO ENFORCE SOCIAL, AS DISTINGUISHED FROM POLITICAL EQUALITY, OR A COMMINGLING OF THE TWO RACES UPON TERMS UNSATISFACTORY TO EITHER.

"Social" inequalities such as those represented in this Jim Crow law were beyond the purview of the Fourteenth Amendment. Justice Brown declared, "If one race be inferior to the other socially, the Constitution of the United States cannot put them upon the same plane." Given this interpretation of the Fourteenth Amendment, the only question the Court had to address was whether the law was a "reasonable regulation." In determining reasonableness, Justice Brown said, the Court must grant legislatures "a large discretion." The legislature must be "at liberty to act with reference to the established usages, customs, and traditions of the people, and with a view to the promotion of their comfort, and the preservation of the public peace and good order."

"Gauged by this standard," Brown concluded, "we cannot say that a law which authorizes or even requires the separation of the two races in public conveyances is unreasonable." The Court discounted as "fallacy" Plessy's claim that "the enforced separation of the two races stamps the colored race with a badge of inferiority. If this be so, it is not by reason of anything found in the act, but solely because the colored race chooses to put that construction upon it."

Again a lone dissenter, Justice Harlan wrote an opinion that did not convince his peers but would later be referred to by justices up to this day. After attacking the notion that racial segregation did not imply any inferiority of blacks, Harlan launched into a ringing defense of racial equality:

> THE WHITE RACE DEEMS ITSELF TO BE THE DOMINANT RACE IN THIS COUNTRY. AND SO IT IS, IN PRESTIGE, IN ACHIEVEMENTS, IN EDUCATION, IN WEALTH AND IN POWER.... BUT IN VIEW OF THE CONSTITUTION, IN THE EYE OF THE LAW, THERE IS IN THIS COUNTRY NO SUPERIOR, DOMINANT, RULING CLASS OF CITIZENS. THERE IS NO CASTE HERE. OUR CONSTITUTION IS COLOR-BLIND, AND NEITHER KNOWS NOR TOLERATES CLASSES AMONG CITIZENS. IN

RESPECT OF CIVIL RIGHTS, ALL CITIZENS ARE EQUAL BEFORE THE LAW.

The Court's decision in Plessy rendered state-imposed racial segregation compatible with the demands of equality under the Constitution. What would come to be known as the **separate-but-equal doctrine** was to be the formula the Court used to reconcile a system of state-enforced segregation with the demands of equal protection under the Fourteenth Amendment. It would take fifty-eight years for the Court as a whole to agree with Justice Harlan about the incompatibility of racial segregation and equality under the laws.

NARROWING THE INTENTION OF THE FRAMERS

What can be said about this early history of Supreme Court interpretation, exemplified by the Civil Rights Cases and *Plessy*? The Court had moved rather quickly to narrowly construe the meaning of the post–Civil War amendments—and the requisite demands of racial equality that they imposed—in three important ways. First of all, the Court distinguished between public and private discrimination. The Court decided that these amendments would only apply to "state action." Only those discriminatory actions "done under state authority" or "sanctioned in some way by the state" could be attacked by the Constitution. The idea that state action was required to trigger the Court's constitutional scrutiny had a negative impact. The states had no positive duty to prevent racial discrimination; they only had to avoid being the direct agents of such discrimination itself.

A second way in which the Court initially limited the scope of the Fourteenth Amendment lay in the criteria it applied to examine legislative classification schemes. The problem, as mentioned in the beginning of this chapter, is that the Equal Protection Clause demands equality under the laws, but all laws classify persons and things, allowing for differential treatment. With the passage of the Fourteenth Amendment, then, the Court had to resolve the demands of equality with the legislative need to classify. In its early rulings, the Court did this by applying **rationality scrutiny** to all state laws. The state would only have to show that the classification drawn in a statute was "reasonable" in light of some legitimate public purpose. "Reasonableness" has usually required that "all persons similarly circumstanced shall be treated alike" (see Brief 9.3). This rationality scrutiny gives the states broad discretion in passing laws that may discriminate or differentiate between people and requires the individual challenging legal classifications to show that they are *unreasonable*. The separate-but-equal doctrine arises out of such rationality scrutiny, with the Court ruling that it was not unreasonable for Louisiana to segregate its train

---

Brief 9.3
RATIONALITY SCRUTINY DEFINED

Two early-twentieth-century cases set out the standards of rationality review used by the Supreme Court in Fourteenth Amendment cases. The general formulation of rationality scrutiny is found in *F.S. Royster Guano Co. v. Virginia* (1920): "[The government's] classification must be reasonable, not arbitrary, and must rest upon some ground of difference having a fair and substantial relation to the object of the legislation, so that all persons similarly circumstanced shall be treated alike." A more specific rendering of this standard occurs in *Lindsley v. Natural Carbonic Gas Co.* (1911):

1. The equal protection clause of the Fourteenth Amendment does not take from the State the power to classify in the adoption of police laws, but admits the exercise of a wide scope of discretion in that regard, and avoids what is done only when it is without any reasonable basis and therefore is purely arbitrary.

2. A classification having some reasonable basis does not offend against that clause merely because it is not made with mathematical nicety or because in practice it results in some inequality.

3. When the classification in such a law is called into question, if any state of facts reasonably can be conceived that would sustain it, the existence of that state of facts at the time the law was enacted must be assumed.

4. One who assails the classification in such a law must carry the burden of showing that it does not rest upon any reasonable basis, but is essentially arbitrary.

passengers "with a view to the promotion of their comfort." Similarly, the Court in 1883 ruled that an Alabama law prohibiting blacks and whites from marrying was reasonable, especially because it applied evenly to both blacks and whites (thus treating similarly situated people similarly).[15]

The third way in which the Court narrowly interpreted the Fourteenth Amendment was by requiring a showing of "purposeful discrimination" in order to act. In these early rulings, the Court would only invoke the Equal Protection Clause if there was proof of a racially discriminatory purpose on the part of the state. This discrimination could appear either on the face of the law itself, as in the *Strauder* case, or in the administration of the law, as in *Yick Wo*. Nevertheless, a finding of purposeful discrimination was necessary. The importance of this requirement will also be seen in more recent rulings discussed later in this chapter.

TOWARD COLOR BLINDNESS: THE STRUGGLE FOR RACIAL EQUALITY

By the turn of the twentieth century, then, the justices of the Supreme Court had abandoned the intention of the post–Civil War amendments' framers.[16] They had denied congressional authority to legislate positively on behalf of blacks facing racial discrimination. They had refused to apply the ideal of equality to a number of areas, including racial segregation in public facilities and in education.[17] The majority of the justices had rejected the expansive view of the Fourteenth Amendment proclaimed by the Reconstruction Congress and by one of their colleagues. But Justice Harlan's vision would eventually triumph. In 1910, the National Association for the Advancement of Colored People (NAACP), a civil rights organization dedicated to achieving equal justice for black people, was formed. Fueled by the NAACP's legal and political action, the courts slowly began to bring the promise of racial equality to fruition.

Table 9.1 presents the important cases, events, and laws that have contributed to the struggle for civil rights and racial equality. Much of the narrative that follows elaborates on the material found in the table, and the reader should find the chronological approach quite helpful in sorting through the numerous court decisions. The examination of this history will begin with racial discrimination in housing, moving on to the very crucial areas of education, employment, and the franchise.

RACIAL DISCRIMINATION IN HOUSING

As mentioned earlier in this chapter, the Equal Protection Clause was clearly meant to cover equal rights in the buying and selling of property. Congressional intent was made manifest by the Civil Rights Act of 1866, which granted racial minorities "the same right in every state and territory as is enjoyed by white citizens thereof to inherit, purchase, lease, sell, hold and convey real and personal property." However, bolstered by the separate-but-equal ruling in *Plessy*, some cities began passing ordinances requiring geographic segregation of the races. Baltimore apparently began this process in 1910, followed by more than a dozen other cities. In Louisville, the city council passed a municipal ordinance in 1914 that provided for "separate blocks for residence, places of abode, and places of assembly by white and colored people respectively." The ordinance prohibited blacks from moving into neighborhoods where whites constituted the majority, and vice versa. Louisville's leaders believed the statute met the demands of the Fourteenth Amendment because it imposed the same restrictions equally on both races. But in 1917 the Supreme Court, in *Buchanan v. Warley*, invalidated the ordinance as an unconstitutional interference with property owners' rights to dispose of real estate as they saw fit. Later rulings confirmed this opinion, so that by 1930 the Court had firmly established the illegitimacy of municipal segregation laws.

This did not stop segregation in housing, however. Property owners wanting to prevent blacks from buying property in their neighborhoods used the device known as the **restrictive covenant** to continue racial segregation. Restrictive covenants are agreements entered into by property owners binding themselves not to sell or lease their property to blacks and other racial or ethnic minorities. Because these covenants resulted from actions by private individuals as opposed to state action, this method of residential segregation at first succeeded in meeting equal protection challenges.[18] The Federal Housing Administration even drew up a "model" racially restrictive

Table 9.1 Development of the Law: Racial Equality, Post-*Plessy*

Year	Event	Significance
1917	*Buchanan v. Warley*	Ruled unconstitutional a municipal ordinance attempting to segregate housing by race.
1944	*Smith v. Allwright*	Disallowed racial exclusion by a political party, calling it a form of "state action" under the Fourteenth Amendment.
1948	*Shelley v. Kraemer*	Ruled against state court enforcement of racially restrictive covenants in property deeds.
1950	*Sweatt v. Painter*	Using the separate but equal doctrine, ruled unconstitutional racially segregated facilities in state university legal education.
1954–55	*Brown v. Board of Education*	Overturning Plessy, ruled unconstitutional state-enforced racial segregation in public schools.
1962	*Burton v. Wilmington Parking Authority*	Ruled a privately run coffee shop located in a public facility fell under the state action guidelines of the Fourteenth Amendment.
1964	Civil Rights Act	Made illegal discrimination in public accommodations and in employment and programs receiving federal funds.
1965	Voting Rights Act	Eliminated voting qualifications and tests used to discriminate against minority voters.
1967	*Loving v. Virginia*	Law forbidding interracial marriage ruled unconstitutional.
1968	Civil Rights Act	Prohibited all racial and religious discrimination in the sale or rental of housing.
1971	*Swann v. Charlotte-Mecklenburg Board of Education*	Approved court-ordered busing to achieve school desegregation.
1971	*Griggs v. Duke Power Co.*	Began looking at discriminatory impact in employment cases.
1972	*Moose Lodge No. 107 v. Irvis*	Private club can discriminate on the basis of race.
1974	*Milliken v. Bradley*	Limited impact of Swann school desegregation ruling by distinguishing between *de jure* and *de facto* segregation.
1988	Civil Rights Restoration Act	Congress returned broad interpretation to civil rights laws by determining that an institution receiving federal funds may not discriminate in *any* of its programs.
1989	*Wards Cove v. Atonio*	Abandoned disparate-impact analysis in employment discrimination decisions, overturning *Griggs*.
2001	*Hunt v. Cromartie*	After a decade of challenges, state redistricting plan creating additional black representation in Congress ruled constitutional.
2007	*Parents Involved in Community Schools v. Seattle School District No. 1*	Invalidated district plans using race to assign pupils to schools to maintain racial balance in district.

covenant of the type approved by the Supreme Court for use in housing projects the federal government underwrote.

In 1948, the Supreme Court reconsidered its position regarding restrictive covenants in the case of *Shelley v. Kraemer*. The Shelleys, a black family, purchased a house from Josephine Fitzgerald in a St. Louis neighborhood covered by a racially restrictive covenant. The agreement, in force since 1911, bound property owners in the area from selling their property to "people of the Negro or Mongolian race" for fifty years. Louis Kraemer, a resident of the neighborhood with a similar racial restriction in his deed, sued to stop the Shelleys from taking possession of the property. The Missouri State Supreme Court eventually granted Kraemer's request, and the Shelleys were ordered to vacate their newly purchased home. J. D. Shelley appealed to the U.S. Supreme Court, who heard his case along with a similar one coming from Michigan.

In a unanimous decision, the Court began by reiterating its earlier position that "restrictive agreements standing alone cannot be regarded as violative of any rights guaranteed by the Fourteenth Amendment." But the case involved more than just a racially restrictive covenant "standing alone." The state courts had aided private discrimination by enforcing "the restrictive terms of the agreements." The Court decided that such judicial enforcement amounted to state action in violation of the Equal Protection Clause:

> WE HAVE NO DOUBT THAT THERE HAS BEEN STATE ACTION IN THESE CASES IN THE FULL AND COMPLETE SENSE OF THE PHRASE. THE UNDISPUTED FACTS DISCLOSE THAT PETITIONERS WERE WILLING PURCHASERS OF PROPERTIES UPON WHICH THEY DESIRED TO ESTABLISH HOMES. THE OWNERS OF THE PROPERTIES WERE WILLING SELLERS; AND CONTRACTS OF SALE WERE ACCORDINGLY CONSUMMATED. IT IS CLEAR THAT BUT FOR THE ACTIVE INTERVENTION OF THE STATE COURTS, SUPPORTED BY THE FULL PANOPLY OF STATE POWER, PETITIONERS WOULD HAVE BEEN FREE TO OCCUPY THE PROPERTIES IN QUESTION WITHOUT RESTRAINT.

The fact that the state courts were enforcing a purely private agreement did not matter: "It is still the judicial branch of the state government carrying out the discrimination . . . [and] state action, as that phrase is understood for the purposes of the Fourteenth Amendment, refers to exertions of the state power in all forms."

The Supreme Court's decision in *Shelley v. Kraemer* left restrictive covenants constitutional, but unenforceable.[19] The *Shelley* decision not only opened up residential neighborhoods to African Americans and other racial minorities but also signaled a shift in the Court's interpretation of the state-action requirement. In *Shelley* (as well as in *Smith v. Allwright* decided four years before, discussed in a later section of this chapter) the Court indicated that it would take a more expansive view of the kind of state action it would consider violative of the Equal Protection Clause. As is shown later, however, the Court has moved in recent years to read *Shelley* more narrowly.

The *Shelley* decision may have aided black people in their quest for fairness in buying and selling property, but the housing problem continued. As black populations in the cities increased, whites fled to the suburbs to make their homes. There, through private agreements and "understandings" (often tacitly involving realtors and local officials), these suburban residents sought to keep their communities white. Nevertheless, black people fought for and won open-housing legislation prohibiting racial discrimination in the sale or rental of housing in numerous states and cities.[20] This culminated in 1968, when Congress for the first time passed a federal act containing wide-ranging open-housing provisions. The Civil Rights Act of 1968, passed following the assassination of Martin Luther King, Jr., prohibited all racial and religious discrimination in the sale or rental of housing. And a few weeks later the Supreme Court, in *Jones v. Alfred H. Mayer Co.* (1969), ruled that private discrimination in the sale or rental of housing was also prohibited by the Civil Rights Act of 1866 (see Brief 9.4).

The combination of Supreme Court decisions and federal and state legislation has made it more difficult to discriminate in the sale or rental of housing, especially where the intent on the part either of government or private citizens is clear. But the circumstances involving claims of housing discrimination today tend to be far more subtle, as a more recent case demonstrates. In question was an equal protection challenge to a city's attempt to block the construction of a low-income housing unit through the use of the referendum process. In June 1995, the Buckeye Community Hope Foundation attempted to begin constructing a low-income housing complex in Cuyahoga Falls, Ohio. Residents of the city immediately expressed opposition and eventually passed a referendum repealing the city council's ordinance approving the building project.

Buckeye filed suit in federal court, claiming that the city and its officials violated the Equal Protection Clause by allowing the voters to reject the building permit, the impact of which was particularly felt by low-income and minority citizens. In *City of Cuyahoga*

Brief 9.4

CONGRESSIONAL AUTHORITY UNDER THE THIRTEENTH AMENDMENT: THE *JONES* CASE AND BEYOND

Jones v. Alfred H. Mayer Co. (1968) was a landmark Supreme Court decision. As mentioned earlier in this chapter, Congress passed the Civil Rights Act of 1866 under its Thirteenth Amendment authority to eliminate the "badges of servitude." In this act, Congress prohibited racial discrimination in a number of areas, including buying, selling, or renting property. But the Supreme Court, in the Civil Rights Cases (1883), seemed to narrow the applicability of Congress's legislative authority over *private* discriminatory action.

The *Jones* case involved the Mayer Company's refusal to sell Joseph Lee Jones, a black man, a home near St. Louis. Jones filed suit under the 1866 law, and the question was whether congressional authority extended to this kind of private, as opposed to public, racial discrimination. Justice Potter Stewart, for the majority, ruled that the Thirteenth Amendment conferred broad authority on Congress "to eliminate all racial barriers to the acquisition of real and personal property." Thus, the Court had in effect overruled the decision in the Civil Rights Cases and reopened the possibility of litigation under the somewhat dormant 1866 statute. Saying in effect that the Reconstruction Era statutes ought to be accorded "a sweep as broad as their language," the Court's decision also opened the door for future Congresses to deal broadly with private acts of racial discrimination under Section 2 of the Thirteenth Amendment. Since *Jones*, the Court has allowed a number of legal actions to be taken to prevent private racial discrimination under the Civil Rights Act of 1866. For example, in *Runyon v. McCrary* (1976), a seven-justice majority decided that black people could use the 1866 Civil Rights Act to sue privately owned, nonsectarian schools that discriminated against them. The Court has even held that Jews, Arabs, and other ethnic groups racially regarded as Caucasians could sue under the provisions of the 1866 law.[21]

Since these decisions, however, the Court has placed limits on the broad use of post–Civil War civil rights laws. In *Patterson v. McLean Credit Union* (1989), discussed later in this chapter, the Court ruled that the 1866 Civil Rights Act could not be used by a black woman claiming racial harassment and promotional discrimination on the job. And in *Bray v. Alexandria Women's Health Clinic* (1993), the Court disallowed the use of the Civil Rights Act of 1871 (also known as the Ku Klux Act) by women to protect their legal right to abortion against right-to-life groups trying to block access to abortion clinics. Still, the *Jones* legacy is one of broadening the scope of civil rights protections, demonstrating two things: (1) that congressional authority under the Constitution is often broader than that of the Court's; and (2) that constitutional interpretation sometimes involves the Court's going back into history to retrieve a previously dormant law or precedent.

Falls v. Buckeye Community Hope Foundation (2003), the justices decided in favor of the city and issued a unanimous ruling concerning what is needed to invoke the Fourteenth Amendment's protections against discrimination. The Court rejected the idea that "discriminatory voter sentiment" expressed by private individuals constituted "state action" in violation of the Fourteenth Amendment. The justices also ruled against the claim on the grounds that the discriminatory impact of an action was not enough to run afoul of the Equal Protection Clause; only "proof of racially discriminatory intent or purpose" by a state actor can trigger the Court's equal protection jurisprudence.

Racial Discrimination in Education

Educational segregation presented a much more difficult problem. A judicial precedent supporting racially segregated schools in Massachusetts was set almost twenty years before the passage of the Fourteenth Amendment.[22] In the District of Columbia, separate schools were established for black children during the Civil War, and in 1864, Congress gave legal authorization for racially segregated public education in the nation's capital. By the time the Court announced the separate-but-equal doctrine in the *Plessy* decision in 1896, thirty states had some type of separate-but-equal public-school law in force. In fact, the existence of racially segregated schools in Boston, as well as the southern states, made up an important part of the Court's rationale in the Plessy decision.

In the years following *Plessy*, the Court consolidated its position favoring segregated schools. On three separate occasions, without directly ruling on the issue of racial segregation in education, the Court nonetheless sanctioned this widespread practice.[23] The problem for the Supreme Court was that even the *Plessy* doctrine required *equality* within a segregated system. By the 1920s, the southern states were spending between five and ten times as much money on the education of white children as they were spending on black children. The actual conditions of separate-but-equal schools were not lost on the NAACP.

By the 1930s, the NAACP had risen to a place of prominence in the eyes of African Americans and sympathetic white citizens. Armed with the Margold Report, a study it had commissioned in 1931 detailing the actual inequalities in segregated school systems, the NAACP established the Legal Defense and Education Fund, out of which it would bring legal actions to end educational segregation. With Thurgood Marshall at the helm, the Legal Defense Fund started its efforts by working to desegregate education at the graduate and professional school level. At the time, black students were denied any access to public graduate schools in many southern states. The NAACP determined that faced with a court order, segregationist states would not be able to afford separate-but-equal graduate facilities. They would be forced to break down and admit qualified black students to previously all-white state university law and graduate schools. This early litigation strategy focused on the *equality* of separate-but-equal education. The NAACP was not yet ready to attack segregated education head on.

School Desegregation Under the Separate-But-Equal Doctrine: *Sweatt v. Painter* (1950)

The strategy worked. After some early victories primarily involving state university professional schools,[24] the NAACP won perhaps the most important of these early decisions from the Supreme Court in *Sweatt v. Painter* (1950). Herman Marian Sweatt, a black mailman from Houston, applied to the University of Texas Law School in 1946. He was rejected on racial grounds, the university being restricted by the state legislature to whites only. Sweatt sued for admission, and the district court ordered the state either to establish a black law school within six months or admit Sweatt to the white law school in Austin. Almost overnight, the state set up a Negro law school in a downtown office building. Sporting three basement rooms, three part-time faculty members, and a ten-thousand-volume library, the new law school invited Sweatt to attend. Instead, he went back to the district court. This time the court ruled against Sweatt, saying that the new Negro law school offered him "privileges, advantages, and opportunities for the study of law substantially equivalent to those offered by the State to white students at the University of Texas." He appealed to the U.S. Supreme Court, backed by the NAACP and Thurgood Marshall.

The Supreme Court unanimously ordered Sweatt's admission to the University of Texas as a requirement of the Equal Protection Clause. Chief Justice Fred Vinson, writing for the Court, declared, "We cannot find substantial equality in the educational opportunities offered white and Negro law students by the state." Vinson compared the two schools' faculty, administration, alumni, library, reputation, traditions, and prestige. "It is difficult to believe," he said, "that one who had a free choice between these law schools would consider the question close." Vinson went on to argue that to separate Sweatt from educational contact with whites, who made up 85 percent of the state's population and almost all of its lawyers, judges, and other legal officials, was to deny him equality in his legal education.

Sweatt v. Painter was a tremendous victory for the NAACP because it was the first time that the Court had ordered a black student admitted to a previously all-white school even though a separate black school was in place. But though seeming to suggest that segregation in education was inherently unequal, the Supreme Court refused to reexamine the *Plessy* doctrine. The Court's decision in *Sweatt* stuck to the standards of the separate-but-equal doctrine, focusing on the inequalities between the separate law school facilities in Texas as the basis for its decision.

Nevertheless, *Sweatt* was a landmark case. The Court had begun to reinterpret the separate-but-equal doctrine by looking at the inequality of segregated educational facilities and, in so doing, had considered intangible factors (e.g., the future importance of Sweatt's educational contact with white students in law school) as well as physical resources. The implications of the decision were clear. In fact, many segregated school systems began pumping money into their black primary and secondary schools to head off a future challenge like the one in *Sweatt*. Meanwhile, buoyed by victories in Sweatt and other cases, the NAACP decided to press school desegregation to the limits. Suits were brought in five public school districts across the country to gain admission for black children into the white primary and secondary schools. The NAACP was challenging the constitutionality of segregation itself, asking the courts to overturn the long-standing separate-but-equal doctrine.

BROWN V. BOARD OF EDUCATION AND THE END OF SEGREGATION IN EDUCATION

The five school segregation cases that made their way to the Supreme Court in 1952 originated in Clarendon County, South Carolina; Topeka, Kansas; Prince Edward County, Virginia; Claymont, Delaware; and Washington, D.C. The NAACP filed suits in the name of local black children demanding their admission to the white public schools. Their claim was not only that the black schools were inferior to the white schools (the *Sweatt* argument), but that educational segregation itself violated the Equal Protection Clause of the Fourteenth Amendment (or, in the Washington, D.C., case, the Due Process Clause of the Fifth Amendment). To support their claims, the NAACP presented current psychological and sociological findings about the negative impact of segregated schools on black children. In their defense, the segregated school districts invoked *Plessy* and either claimed that the black schools and white schools were equal or promised to immediately bring the black schools up to a state of equality. In all five cases, U.S. District Courts continued to rely on the separate-but-equal doctrine; all five were appealed to the Supreme Court.

The Supreme Court heard arguments in the school segregation cases in December 1952. After a six-month silence, the Court set the case for reargument in the fall of 1953 and asked both sides to prepare answers to a set of historical and practical questions. Among other things, the Court was interested in hearing evidence about the original intention of the Fourteenth Amendment's framers and ratifiers. Did the Congress that drafted and the state legislatures that ratified the Fourteenth Amendment "understand that it would abolish segregation in public schools"? If not, did they nevertheless understand that either future Congresses or the judiciary would "construe the amendment as abolishing such segregation"?

Answers to these questions were presented to the Supreme Court in December 1953. After six months of discussion, deliberation, and even coalition-building, the recently arrived Chief Justice Earl Warren announced the Court's unanimous opinion on May 17, 1954. In the case of *Brown v. Board of Education of Topeka*, the Court declared segregated public schools to be a violation of the Constitution. Chief Justice Warren's opinion was brief, a mere thirteen paragraphs. And after all the arguments presented concerning the intention of those who framed and ratified the Fourteenth Amendment, Warren decided that the historical arguments were "inconclusive." "[What] Congress and the state legislatures had in mind cannot be determined with any degree of certainty." The Court had actually declared the historical question to be irrelevant. Warren wrote:

> [W]E CANNOT TURN THE CLOCK BACK TO 1868 WHEN THE [FOURTEENTH] AMENDMENT WAS ADOPTED, OR EVEN TO 1896 WHEN *PLESSY V. FERGUSON* WAS WRITTEN. WE MUST CONSIDER PUBLIC EDUCATION IN THE LIGHT OF ITS FULL DEVELOPMENT AND ITS PRESENT PLACE IN AMERICAN LIFE THROUGHOUT THE NATION.

The Court ultimately made its decision about the basic inequality of segregated schools based on the sociological and psychological evidence. Warren agreed with the NAACP position that to separate blacks "from others of similar age and qualifications solely because of their race generates a feeling of inferiority as to their status in the community that may affect their hearts and minds in a way unlikely ever to be undone." Citing the lower court's finding in the Topeka case, Warren stated:

> SEGREGATION OF WHITE AND COLORED CHILDREN IN PUBLIC SCHOOLS HAS A DETRIMENTAL EFFECT UPON THE COLORED CHILDREN. THE IMPACT IS GREATER WHEN IT HAS THE SANCTION OF THE LAW; FOR THE POLICY OF SEPARATING THE RACES IS USUALLY INTERPRETED AS DENOTING THE INFERIORITY OF THE NEGRO GROUP. A SENSE OF INFERIORITY AFFECTS THE MOTIVATION OF A CHILD TO LEARN. SEGREGATION WITH THE SANCTION OF LAW, THEREFORE, HAS A TENDENCY TO [RETARD]

THE EDUCATIONAL AND MENTAL DEVELOPMENT OF NEGRO CHILDREN AND TO DEPRIVE THEM OF SOME OF THE BENEFITS THEY WOULD RECEIVE IN A RACIAL[LY] INTEGRATED SCHOOL SYSTEM.

The Court concluded "that in the field of public education the doctrine of 'separate but equal' has no place. Separate educational facilities are inherently unequal." With this short stroke of its collective pen, the Supreme Court had voided fifty-eight years of constitutional precedent and over one hundred years of educational practice.

The Court determined that racial segregation in education was unconstitutional; however, it postponed ruling on the question of how to implement school desegregation. After hearing arguments from a number of different parties the next year,[25] the Court in what is called *Brown II* outlined its plan of action. Chief Justice Warren announced that the Court would send each case back to the district courts where it had originated, leaving it up to them to fashion decrees enforcing the Court's desegregation ruling. These lower courts would be guided by "constitutional principles" (the black children's right to be admitted to public schools on a nondiscriminatory basis), but they would be allowed to consider the local district's situation in deciding how rapidly and in what manner desegregation would proceed. The justices of the Supreme Court recognized that some flexibility might be required to ensure that school desegregation took place in an effective and peaceful manner. But they wanted the lower courts to oversee the implementation of the *Brown* decision to make sure that black children were being admitted "to public schools on a nondiscriminatory basis *with all deliberate* speed [emphasis added]." The Court hoped that their delicate blend of principle and practicality in *Brown II* would solve the problems they expected their desegregation decision would create.

THE POSITIVE DUTY TO DESEGREGATE AND COURT-ORDERED BUSING

The years following the *Brown* decision proved to be tumultuous, with the process of enforcing and implementing school desegregation far from easy (see Brief 9.5). Ultimately, in a series of decisions in the 1960s, the Court would rule that school districts not only had to stop segregating on the basis of race but also had a positive duty to integrate their previously segregated schools.[27] In addition, the Court suggested that it would look at the *effects* of desegregation plans to see if the "transition to unitary schools" was proceeding adequately. By 1970, the Court's school desegregation rulings were having an impact on formerly segregated rural and small-town school districts. Remaining problems existed in large metropolitan areas with a substantial amount of residential segregation, where nonracial attendance zoning of a unitary school system was not enough to break racial segregation. The Court began to tackle this problem in 1971, in *Swann v. Charlotte-Mecklenburg Board of Education* (1971).

The Charlotte, North Carolina, metropolitan area (whose black student population was approximately 30 percent) had been operating for several years under court-approved desegregation plans that brought about half the black students into formerly white schools. The rest remained in all-black schools. After the *Green* decision (see Brief 9.5), the district court judge overseeing desegregation in Charlotte ordered a new plan that would achieve more complete racial integration. Because of extensive residential segregation, the new plan called for the "pairing" of outlying white schools with inner-city black schools, with busing in both directions as the means to accomplish school integration. The Supreme Court upheld the busing plan.

Chief Justice Warren Burger began his decision for a unanimous Court by stressing the breadth of the federal courts' authority "to remedy past wrongs" in light of the *Brown* decision. But Burger admitted that such judicial authority can only extend to cases in which there has been a "constitutional violation." Given the state-action and purposeful-discrimination requirements to trigger the Equal Protection Clause, Burger contended that federal courts could only act on a showing of de jure segregation, that is, segregation that is positively sanctioned by the state. But what beyond intentionally discriminatory school district policies could be considered by federal judges in reaching a verdict about the presence of *de jure* segregation? Burger announced that among other methods, judges could point to the presence of predominantly one-race schools in a system with a history of racial segregation (as in the Charlotte school district) as evidence of a constitutional

Brief 9.5

ENFORCING AND IMPLEMENTING THE *BROWN* DECISION

The Court's decision in *Brown II* initiated the nationwide process of school desegregation. However, having no real enforcement mechanisms of its own, the Supreme Court had to rely on its own prestige and help from other branches of government to enforce its desegregation decision. No such aid came from the other branches of the federal government. In fact, as Chapter 8 mentioned, ninety-six members of Congress from the eleven former Confederate states signed a Southern Manifesto, which called the *Brown* decision "a clear abuse of judicial power" and "commend[ed] . . . those States which have declared the intention to resist forced integration by any lawful means." In addition, President Eisenhower seemed reticent to organize executive branch support for the desegregation ruling. While he eventually sent federal troops to Little Rock to ensure the peaceful carrying out of a court-ordered desegregation of Central High School, he maintained that "it is difficult through law and through force to change a man's heart."[26] The Supreme Court itself held off from ruling on the implementation of *Brown* for a number of years.

A campaign of massive resistance to the *Brown* decision was launched throughout the South. Eight state legislatures (Alabama, Arkansas, Florida, Georgia, Louisiana, Mississippi, South Carolina, and Virginia) passed resolutions that formally nullified the *Brown* decision and adopted laws that frustrated efforts to achieve integration. School districts either delayed or drew up plans that did little to effect dramatic changes in the racial composition of the schools. Many federal district judges were unsympathetic to the *Brown* decision and delayed the process even further. Where school districts were unwilling to desegregate voluntarily, local citizens would have to incur the financial and even physical risks of bringing a lawsuit to have the schools desegregated. And where legal attempts to resist integration failed, white resisters resorted to violence in places such as Little Rock, New Orleans, and Clinton, Tennessee.

The case of Little Rock is particularly instructive, as it drives home the point that the Supreme Court cannot enforce its own decisions, especially when, as in school desegregation, it takes the lead on an issue rather than responding to majority opinion. The Little Rock School Board, in its effort to comply with the *Brown* ruling, devised a plan in 1955 to completely desegregate the city's schools by 1963. As the first stage of this plan, nine black students were admitted to previously all-white Central High School for the fall of 1957. On the day before the black students were to attend their first class, Arkansas Governor Orval Faubus dispatched National Guard units to Central High to prevent the black students from attending. This and other obstructive action by the state government energized local citizen opposition to integration. The combined citizen and state resistance made it impossible to carry out the first stage of the school board's plan until President Eisenhower sent federal troops on September 23.

In light of all the disruption caused at Central High, the Little Rock School Board petitioned the federal courts for a two-and-one-half-year suspension of their desegregation program to allow things to calm down. The Supreme Court, in *Cooper v. Aaron* (1958), rejected the school board's application and blamed hostile conditions in Little Rock on the failure of state officials to do their duty in enforcing the law. Although the justices admitted that they were powerless to enforce their judgments, they warned government officials about the serious implications of noncompliance: "No state legislator or executive or judicial officer can war against the Constitution without violating his undertaking to support it."

The Supreme Court's opinion in *Cooper v. Aaron*, however forceful, did not stop the region-wide fight against desegregation. So much legal and extra-legal resistance occurred that by 1965, ten years after the *Brown* rulings, only 2 percent of black students in the eleven former confederate states were enrolled in previously all-white schools.

The Supreme Court decided more forcefully to step back into the legal fray in 1964. The big legal question it had to answer by this time was this: Did the *Brown* ruling merely mean that school districts would have to stop using discriminatory practices in administering the schools, or did *Brown* impose on them a positive duty to achieve racial integration? During the 1960s the Court answered this question in a series of cases involving southern attempts to avoid true compliance with *Brown*.

In *Griffin v. County School Board of Prince Edward County* (1964), the Supreme Court ruled that one of the five original Brown defendants, which had closed the public schools rather than comply with *Brown*, had acted with a discriminatory intent, in effect ordering the public schools reopened on an integrated basis that fall.

A more commonplace response to the *Brown* decision was for school districts to use "freedom-of-choice" plans. Freedom-of-choice plans allowed children in a school district to attend the school of their choice. The district would no longer discriminate on the basis of race and would exert no pressure on children's choices. Freedom-of-choice plans were widely adopted by school districts wanting to remain eligible for federal aid (in 1964, the federal government had stipulated that school districts practicing racial discrimination could not receive federal funds) and yet retain basically segregated school systems. In *Green v. County School Board of New Kent County* (1968), the Court invalidated freedom-of-choice plans. Although no intent to discriminate on the part of the school district could be found, the Court decided that freedom-of-choice plans were inadequate methods of compliance with the *Brown* decision. Justice William Brennan's opinion stated that the goal of *Brown* was the achievement of "a unitary, nonracial system of public education . . . in which racial discrimination would be eliminated root and branch." Because freedom-of-choice plans effectively failed to achieve this goal, school districts would have to do more. The time for "all deliberate speed" had ended. One year later in *Alexander v. Holmes County Board of Education* (1969), the Court made this clear, announcing that "allowing 'all deliberate speed' for desegregation is no longer constitutionally permissible. . . . [E]very school district is to terminate dual school systems at once and to operate now and hereafter only unitary schools."

violation that would need to be remedied. In such an instance, Burger wrote, "The burden upon the school authorities will be to satisfy the court that their racial composition is not the result of present or past discriminatory action on their part."

Once a constitutional violation is found, courts can order plans like the one in Charlotte that grouped noncontiguous school zones to achieve better integration. The concept of the neighborhood school would have to be sacrificed to the demands of racial equality:

> ALL THINGS BEING EQUAL, WITH NO HISTORY OF DISCRIMINATION, IT MIGHT WELL BE DESIRABLE TO ASSIGN PUPILS TO SCHOOLS NEAREST THEIR HOMES. BUT ALL THINGS ARE NOT EQUAL IN A SYSTEM THAT HAS BEEN DELIBERATELY CONSTRUCTED AND MAINTAINED TO ENFORCE RACIAL SEGREGATION.

For Burger and the Court, this meant that busing, as ordered in this case, was certainly an appropriate means to achieve racial integration. "Desegregation plans cannot be limited to the walk-in school," asserted the Court. Busing had previously been used by authorities to maintain racially separate schools; now the bus could be part of a plan to desegregate them.

The only limitation the Court imposed on court-ordered remedies for segregated schools was that there be a finding of *de jure* segregation. This limitation had resulted in a distinction between *de jure* segregation, which had to be remedied, and *de facto* segregation (resulting not from legally imposed segregation, but usually from a combination of residential segregation and neighborhood schools), which did not require court-imposed remedies. After *Swann*, the *de jure/de facto* distinction meant that most southern school systems would have the affirmative duty to achieve complete integration, given past policies of school segregation, while most northern and western school systems, which were just as segregated, would be left alone. By the 1970s it was the large northern and western urban areas that had the biggest problem with segregated public schools. According to a 1971 Department of Health, Education, and Welfare estimate, 44 percent of black students in the South attended majority white schools as opposed to only 28 percent in the North and West; 57 percent of all black students in the North and West attended primarily minority schools, as opposed to only 32 percent who did so in the South.

In *Milliken v. Bradley* (1974), the Court was confronted with a case of *de facto* segregation in the North. At issue was a desegregation plan ordered for the Detroit metropolitan area. The area comprised the city school district (75 percent black) and a number of separate school districts for the suburban communities (predominantly white) surrounding Detroit. After finding that the Detroit school system had been guilty of official actions that constituted de jure segregation, a federal judge decided that a Detroit-only plan would be ineffective in achieving desegregation. He combined the Detroit school district with fifty-three surrounding suburban school districts to create a "desegregation area" and ordered "an effective desegregation plan" for the entire area.

By a slim majority, the Supreme Court reversed the lower court order, ruling that the scope of the remedy was not required by the extent of constitutional violations. The Court could find no evidence of *de jure* segregation on the part of the outlying suburban school districts. The suburban districts did not discriminate in their enrollment practices, and there were no claims that district lines had been drawn to foster segregation. The situation was a matter of *de facto* segregation. For the district court to order such an intervention into the policies of the various school districts, the Court argued, violated deeply rooted traditions of local control over education. Chief Justice Burger's majority opinion concluded that such judicial intervention is unwarranted without evidence of *de jure* segregation. "Without an inter-district violation and inter-district effect, there is no constitutional wrong calling for an inter-district remedy."

In a bitter dissent, Justice Marshall called the *Milliken* decision "a giant step backwards" in the process of guaranteeing minority children an equal educational opportunity. Marshall concluded that the Court's ruling "is more a reflection of a perceived public mood that we have gone far enough in enforcing the Constitution's guarantee of equal justice than it is the product of neutral principles of law." Justice White also dissented, claiming that the state had "successfully insulated itself from its duty to provide effective desegregation remedies" because of the Court's "arbitrary rule that remedies for constitutional violations occurring in a single Michigan school district must stop at the school district line."

With the *Milliken* case, then, the Supreme Court maintained the distinction between *de jure* and *de facto* segregation, one that remains solidly in place today and raises a number of questions about racial segregation in public schooling and how to remedy it (see Brief 9.6). For instance, going back to the *Brown* decision, if the Court's purpose in 1954 was to grant equal educational opportunities that they thought were lost as a result of school segregation, then does not *de facto* segregation cause the same constitutional problems as *de jure* segregation? In making this distinction, has the Court abandoned the original purposes announced in *Brown*? Can meaningful judicial distinctions be made between discriminatory intent and impact? And if there is no real distinction between *de jure* and *de facto* segregation, does that force the local districts and the Court to make results-oriented rulings as opposed to procedural ones? And when they do this using race, doesn't this run afoul of the ideal of a "color-blind" Constitution? These and other questions have continued to haunt the Court, and its changing composition has rendered answers that would seem to ratify Justice Marshall's concerns.

SCHOOL DESEGREGATION AFTER FIFTY YEARS: ADVANCE OR RETREAT?

Many Americans observed the fiftieth anniversary of *Brown v. Board of Education* in 2004 by reflecting on the entire project of school desegregation. Shortly after the *Brown* decision, Thurgood Marshall predicted to reporters that "by the time the 100th anniversary of the Emancipation Proclamation was observed in 1963, segregation in all its forms would have been eliminated from the nation."[28] We can look back at Marshall's optimism, understandable given his personal investment, as obviously premature. Significant racial segregation still exists, despite the Court's ruling in *Brown*.

In the South, the steady decrease in public school segregation, observed for two decades beginning in the mid-1960s, has more recently reversed itself in many areas. Peaking in the late 1980s, the percentage of black students attending majority-white schools has declined over the last twenty-five years. In other parts of the country, particularly the Northeast, racial segregation has increased significantly. This increased racial segregation is due in part to a declining percentage of white students in public schools (owing itself to immigration and other changing national demographics). But more important, racial segregation in our nation's schools is usually the result of residential racial concentration in separate school districts,[29] something the Court has said—maintaining its *de jure/de facto* distinction—cannot be remedied judicially. Ironically, although the *Brown* decision continues to captivate our public imagination, the Court's decision in *Milliken* may present the stronger legacy.

During the 1990s, the federal courts clearly lost their appetite for enforced school desegregation, and the Supreme Court even made it easier for school districts to phase out busing or other programs designed to achieve racial integration.[30] But the culmination of this growing trend of antipathy toward racially based school desegregation plans would come in 2007, when the Court invalidated the efforts of two school districts to voluntarily (i.e., not under a court-imposed mandate) achieve racial balance among their schools.

In *Parents Involved in Community Schools v. Seattle School District No. 1* (2007), the Court majority ruled that the Constitution strictly limits the use of individual students' race in assigning them to particular schools. The decision involved school assignment plans in Seattle and Louisville. Seattle's high school enrollment plan asked students their preferences among the ten high schools in the district, but used a series of "tiebreakers" to assign students in cases in which a school was oversubscribed, one of which focused on whether a school was "racially imbalanced" given the overall demographics of the district. In Louisville, a district with a 34 percent African American population in its schools, a voluntary plan put in place to maintain racially balanced schools after court-ordered desegregation ended would ensure that each elementary school in the district would be composed of at least 15 percent and no more than 50 percent African American students.

Justice Roberts would write the opinion representing the five-justice majority. In it, he reiterated the Court's current opinion, most forcefully argued in its affirmative action decisions of the past two decades (see Chapter 10), that any use of race to make distinctions between individuals would be considered suspect and would be subjected to strict judicial scrutiny. Stating that "the way to stop discrimination on the basis of race is to stop discriminating on the basis of race," he argued that public authorities seeking to use racial classification schemes would have to show a "compelling interest" and would have to demonstrate that the plan in question was "narrowly tailored" to achieve the compelling governmental interest. In these cases, Roberts concluded, the school districts could do neither. Unlike the most recent affirmative action ruling, where the Court majority allowed the University of Michigan to use race as one aspect in a larger effort to achieve diversity in its law school (see discussion of the *Grutter* decision in Chapter 10), the two districts in this case deployed a very blunt understanding of student diversity, one that could not be considered compelling, let alone narrowly tailored. In Louisville, students were divided only into "blacks" and "others" for the purposes of achieving racial balance under their school assignment plan; in Seattle, students were characterized as "white" or "nonwhite" in cases in which the tiebreaker rules were used. The impact of this narrow use of racial classifications, according to Roberts, achieved not only limited results but also results in contradiction of the stated goal of educational diversity:

> UNDER THE SEATTLE PLAN, A SCHOOL WITH 50 PERCENT ASIAN-AMERICAN STUDENTS AND 50 PERCENT WHITE STUDENTS BUT NO AFRICAN-AMERICAN, NATIVE-AMERICAN, OR LATINO STUDENTS WOULD QUALIFY AS BALANCED, WHILE A SCHOOL WITH 30 PERCENT ASIAN-AMERICAN, 25 PERCENT AFRICAN-AMERICAN, 25 PERCENT LATINO, AND 20 PERCENT WHITE STUDENTS WOULD NOT. IT IS HARD TO UNDERSTAND HOW A PLAN THAT COULD ALLOW THESE RESULTS CAN BE VIEWED AS BEING CONCERNED WITH ACHIEVING ENROLLMENT THAT IS "BROADLY DIVERSE."

Invoking a standard of "colorblindness" and the Court's requirement in *Brown II*, that students be admitted to public schools "on a nonracial basis," Roberts concluded his opinion by looking back at the history of school desegregation efforts:

> BEFORE *BROWN*, SCHOOLCHILDREN WERE TOLD WHERE THEY COULD AND COULD NOT GO TO SCHOOL BASED ON THE COLOR OF THEIR SKIN. THE SCHOOL DISTRICTS IN THESE CASES HAVE NOT CARRIED THE HEAVY BURDEN OF DEMONSTRATING THAT WE SHOULD ALLOW THIS ONCE AGAIN— EVEN FOR VERY DIFFERENT REASONS.

In a separate concurrence, Justice Thomas sought to amplify the Court's application of "color-blind" constitutional standards, not only citing Justice Harlan's dissent in *Plessy* but also accusing the four dissenters of using a similar logic to that of the *Plessy* segregationist majority in supporting the two districts' plans.

Justice Kennedy would write a separate concurrence, and while he agreed with the other four justices' position striking down the Seattle and Louisville plans, he made clear that he was more sympathetic to the ends of achieving racial diversity and balancing, albeit through different means than those used here, than his four colleagues. In an opinion that has been compared with that of Justice Powell in the *Bakke* decision (see Chapter 10), Kennedy took great pains to distinguish between the legitimate compelling interests a school district might have, of "avoiding racial isolation" or of "bringing students together of diverse backgrounds and races," and the illegitimate means used by these two districts in failing to narrowly tailor their plans to potentially legitimate ends. He also sought to maintain the Court's distinction between *de jure* and *de facto* segregation, and stated that because neither Seattle nor Louisville were currently under court order to desegregate based on past practices, mere "racial imbalances" could not constitute a compelling reason to use race so blatantly in student assignment to public schools. He concluded his opinion with an attempt to balance educational diversity with constitutional limitations on how to achieve it:

> THIS NATION HAS A MORAL AND ETHICAL OBLIGATION TO FULFILL ITS HISTORIC COMMITMENT TO CREATING AN INTEGRATED SOCIETY THAT ENSURES EQUAL OPPORTUNITY FOR ALL OF ITS CHILDREN. A COMPELLING INTEREST EXISTS IN AVOIDING RACIAL ISOLATION, AN INTEREST THAT

A SCHOOL DISTRICT, IN ITS DISCRETION AND EXPERTISE, MAY CHOOSE TO PURSUE. LIKEWISE, A DISTRICT MAY CONSIDER IT A COMPELLING INTEREST TO ACHIEVE A DIVERSE STUDENT POPULATION. RACE MAY BE ONE COMPONENT OF THAT DIVERSITY, BUT OTHER DEMOGRAPHIC FACTORS, PLUS SPECIAL TALENTS AND NEEDS, SHOULD ALSO BE CONSIDERED. WHAT THE GOVERNMENT IS NOT PERMITTED TO DO, ABSENT A SHOWING OF NECESSITY NOT MADE HERE, IS TO CLASSIFY EVERY STUDENT ON THE BASIS OF RACE AND TO ASSIGN EACH OF THEM TO SCHOOLS BASED ON THAT CLASSIFICATION. CRUDE MEASURES OF THIS SORT THREATEN TO REDUCE CHILDREN TO RACIAL CHITS VALUED AND TRADED ACCORDING TO ONE SCHOOL'S SUPPLY AND ANOTHER'S DEMAND.

In an important signal to the nation's school districts, Justice Kennedy laid out other methods that might be deployed by districts to constitutionally achieve racial diversity (or avoid racial isolation) in their schools (see Brief 9.6).

In separate dissents, Justices Stevens and Breyer took the majority to task for its misreading of *Brown* and other Court precedents and for stripping these and other districts of tools that have long been used to prevent racial segregation (or resegregation) in their schools. Justice Stevens rejected the Court's attempt to equate the Brown decision and its progeny with situations involving affirmative action, stating that "a decision to exclude a member of a minority because of his race is fundamentally different from a decision to include a member of a minority for that reason." He ended by lamenting that "no justice of the court that I joined in 1975 would have agreed with today's decision."

In a lengthy dissent, Justice Breyer provided a different reading of the *Brown* decision, arguing that districts ought to be allowed more latitude in fashioning local remedies to the ongoing problems of racial isolation and segregation in their school communities. He concluded by warning his fellow justices about the dangers of "so quickly changing" the Constitution's interpretation and thereby threatening the legacy of the historic *Brown* ruling:

FOR MUCH OF THIS NATION'S HISTORY, THE RACES REMAINED DIVIDED. IT WAS NOT LONG AGO THAT PEOPLE OF DIFFERENT RACES DRANK FROM SEPARATE FOUNTAINS, RODE ON SEPARATE BUSES, AND STUDIED IN SEPARATE SCHOOLS. IN THIS COURT'S FINEST HOUR, *BROWN V. BOARD OF EDUCATION* CHALLENGED THIS HISTORY AND HELPED TO CHANGE IT. FOR *BROWN* HELD OUT A PROMISE. IT WAS A PROMISE EMBODIED IN THREE AMENDMENTS DESIGNED TO MAKE CITIZENS OF SLAVES. IT WAS THE PROMISE OF TRUE RACIAL EQUALITY—NOT AS A MATTER OF FINE WORDS ON PAPER, BUT AS A MATTER OF EVERYDAY LIFE IN THE NATION'S CITIES AND SCHOOLS. IT WAS ABOUT THE NATURE OF A DEMOCRACY THAT MUST WORK FOR ALL AMERICANS. IT SOUGHT ONE LAW, ONE NATION, ONE PEOPLE, NOT SIMPLY AS A MATTER OF LEGAL PRINCIPLE BUT IN TERMS OF HOW WE ACTUALLY LIVE. . . . THE LAST HALF-CENTURY HAS WITNESSED GREAT STRIDES TOWARD RACIAL EQUALITY, BUT WE HAVE NOT YET REALIZED THE PROMISE OF *BROWN*. TO INVALIDATE THE PLANS UNDER REVIEW IS TO THREATEN THE PROMISE OF *BROWN*. THE PLURALITY'S POSITION, I FEAR, WOULD BREAK THAT PROMISE. THIS IS A DECISION THAT THE COURT AND THE NATION WILL COME TO REGRET.

The Court's decision in the Seattle and Louisville cases leaves a number of questions unanswered, especially given the separate concurrence by Justice Kennedy. In the wake of the *Parents Involved* decision, hundreds of school districts must now determine whether their current policies aimed at achieving greater integration and diversity are invalid and, if so, how they might change them to meet the standards announced in 2007 (see Brief 9.6). Perhaps most important, can the Supreme Court truly address a problem—school segregation—that is more deep-seated than legal decrees can change? If, as has been argued, persistent segregation is more the result of socioeconomic factors and residual racism than it is the result of current legally sanctioned discrimination,

Brief 9.6
SCHOOL DESEGREGATION TODAY: AN ONGOING "AMERICAN DILEMMA"

The history of racial inequality in the United States and the growing racial and ethnic diversity in the nation makes school desegregation in general a goal with which few citizens would argue, at least in theory. In addition to the educational benefits of racial diversity, many would agree with Thurgood Marshall, who introduces Chapter 11, about the civic virtues of integration. Right after his confirmation as Supreme Court justice, Marshall proclaimed that "unless our children begin to learn together, then there is little hope that our people will ever learn to live together." However, increasing public school segregation, reinforced by Supreme Court decisions, along with the competing demands of parent choice, make the task both more urgent and more difficult.

In light of the Court's ruling in *Parents Involved in Community Schools v. Seattle School District* (2007), school districts—especially those in metropolitan areas—have been scrambling to square their interests in racial integration with the constitutional standards set down in the Seattle and Louisville cases. Well over two hundred school districts across the country remain under court order to desegregate their schools, and hundreds more have voluntarily implemented a variety of methods to achieve educational diversity among students, including diversity based on race and ethnicity. Given the nature of the 4-1-4 ruling in *Parents Involved*, districts will be carefully reading Justice Kennedy's concurring opinion, which would seem to control the issue, in much the same way colleges and universities interested in continuing efforts to achieve racial diversity after 1978 had to read Justice Powell's lone opinion in the *Bakke* decision (see Chapter 10). A number of organizations have given guidance to school districts in the wake of the decision, including the NAACP Legal Defense Fund, the College Board, and the National School Board Association.

How will the Court's ruling change school district practices? Just two months after the *Parents Involved* decision was handed down, the Tucson, Arizona, school board was forced to change a policy that included a prohibition on student transfers when such transfers would throw off the racial or ethnic balance of either school. But most other districts have taken more deliberate steps to ensure that their practices do not run afoul of the Court's recent ruling. The first thing a school board considering a voluntary plan for achieving greater diversity in its schools needs to do is ensure that the educational rationale for such a plan can meet the "compelling interest" standard laid down by the Court majority. Justice Kennedy and the other four justices comprising the majority in *Parents Involved* clearly ruled out policies designed solely to achieve racial balance in accordance with the district's demographics, but a well-crafted desegregation plan that lays out the clear pedagogical benefits of student diversity should be able to pass constitutional muster, at least with the current Court majority. One of the benefits of the Seattle and Louisville cases is the vast array of social science research documenting the academic and social effects of diversity that was brought together in the various *amici* briefs assembled to support the districts in question, documentation that districts can use in the future to support their case for a compelling interest in achieving educational diversity.

The second question for any school district is ensuring that the plan adopted meets the "narrowly tailored" means test used by the Court. Justice Kennedy, and presumably the four dissenting justices in *Parents Involved*, would find no constitutional problem with race-neutral policies aimed at achieving greater educational diversity (or avoiding racial isolation) in public schools. The most popular among these race-neutral tools is the use of socioeconomic status to make pupil assignments (although data from different districts indicate that socioeconomic integration plans do not always achieve positive results in terms of racial integration of schools). One district that uses such a race-neutral plan to achieve both higher academic achievement and racial diversity, often cited as an exemplar for others, is Wake County, North Carolina. The district's plan draws attendance zones with a view to limiting the number of students who receive free or reduced-price lunch benefits, as well as the number of students who read below grade level. Similar socioeconomic factors are used in places such as La Crosse, Wisconsin, and Cambridge, Massachusetts, and have achieved positive results in maintaining racial diversity in schools. Other schools deploy a multifactor "diversity index" in assigning students to schools, which could include indicators such as socioeconomic status, geographic location, record of academic achievement, parental educational attainment, and English language learner status. This method of achieving a district's interest in educational diversity would also seem safe constitutionally, given the Court's recent ruling.

In addition, Justice Kennedy's opinion suggested that certain race-conscious policies could be used to meet a compelling interest in achieving racial diversity or avoiding racial isolation, as long as they "address the problem in a general way" and avoid using race as the sole determining factor in assigning an individual student to a school. Such race-conscious general policies could include strategic site selection of new schools, the drawing of attendance lines with the demographics of neighborhoods in mind, student and faculty recruitment, magnet schools, and the direction of resources to special programs. Still, it would be wise for districts attempting to adopt even generalized race-conscious methods of achieving school integration to exhaust, or at least seriously consider, race-neutral means of achieving their compelling educational goals first.

Districts currently under court-ordered desegregation mandates may be free from strict constitutional scrutiny, as Justice Kennedy's concurrence implies that the ruling in the Seattle and Louisville cases does not apply directly to school districts under court order to remedy prior *de jure* segregation. This would be especially true if the use of race in a court-mandated desegregation plan is only one of several dimensions to student assignment.

Whatever direction districts choose to go in fashioning remedies to the problem of increasingly separate and unequal public schools, the *Parents Involved* decision leaves specific questions unanswered and guarantees that there will be more litigation in the near future. Already, legal challenges have been mounted to desegregation plans—both voluntary and court ordered—in a number of districts, and the Court will likely be asked to provide clear direction on what might and might not be acceptable efforts to continue the *Brown* legacy.

then can the courts constitutionally mandate the desired outcome? These are difficult questions, ones that are raised again in the discussion of affirmative action in the next chapter.

Racial Discrimination in Employment: The "Purposeful-Discrimination" Test Examined

In Title VII of the Civil Rights Act of 1964, Congress prohibited employers from depriving individuals of employment opportunities "because of such individuals' race, color, sex, or national origin." Along with the Fifth and Fourteenth Amendments, which presumably make racial discrimination in employment unconstitutional if conducted "under color of law" or exhibited by the government itself, fairly strong federal protections against overt employment discrimination exist. But the Supreme Court has had to decide what constitutes illegitimate racial discrimination in employment. The main question has centered around the distinction between discriminatory "intent" on the part of the employer and discriminatory "impact" of employment policies.

The Court's early answers, primarily in discrimination claims under Title VII, suggested that discriminatory effect or impact would be just as illegitimate as discriminatory intent. In *Griggs v. Duke Power Company* (1971), a unanimous court ruled that Title VII of the Civil Rights Act of 1964

> PROSCRIBES NOT ONLY OVERT DISCRIMINATION BUT ALSO PRACTICES THAT ARE FAIR IN FORM, BUT DISCRIMINATORY IN OPERATION. THE TOUCHSTONE IS BUSINESS NECESSITY. IF AN EMPLOYMENT PRACTICE WHICH OPERATES TO EXCLUDE NEGROES CANNOT BE SHOWN TO BE RELATED TO JOB PERFORMANCE, THE PRACTICE IS PROHIBITED.

The Court decided that an employer's requirement that employees have a high school diploma and pass a general intelligence test before being eligible for jobs was unrelated to successful job performance and had the effect of disadvantaging black applicants in violation of Title VII. Chief Justice Burger concluded for the Court that

> [GOOD] INTENT OR ABSENCE OF DISCRIMINATORY INTENT DOES NOT REDEEM EMPLOYMENT PROCEDURES OR TESTING MECHANISMS THAT OPERATE AS 'BUILT-IN HEADWINDS' FOR MINORITY GROUPS AND ARE UNRELATED TO MEASURING JOB CAPABILITY. CONGRESS DIRECTED THE THRUST OF THE ACT TO THE *CONSEQUENCES* OF EMPLOYMENT PRACTICES, NOT SIMPLY THEIR MOTIVATION. MORE THAN THAT, CONGRESS HAS PLACED ON THE EMPLOYER THE BURDEN OF SHOWING THAT ANY GIVEN REQUIREMENT MUST HAVE A MANIFEST RELATIONSHIP TO THE EMPLOYMENT IN QUESTION. [ORIGINAL EMPHASIS]

The Court continued to use "disparate-impact" analysis in examining Title VII discrimination claims until 1989, when it decided a number of cases restricting the application of federal laws dealing with employment discrimination. The most important of these was *Wards Cove Packing Co. v. Atonio* (1989), where a five-justice majority handed down a ruling overturning the *Griggs* precedent. This case involved a disparate-impact lawsuit by nonwhite cannery workers in a salmon processing facility in Alaska. The minority workers claimed that various employer policies resulted in a racially stratified workforce denying them opportunities for skilled, higher-paying positions in the company. The Court rejected the workers' challenges, thus abandoning the kind of disparate-impact analysis that had typified employment discrimination cases for two decades, and narrowing the enforcement of Title VII. Writing for the majority, Justice White wrote that "[a]s long as there are no barriers or practices deterring qualified nonwhites from applying for [skilled] positions," an employer is not accountable for a "racially imbalanced" workforce he or she did not directly cause.

A few days after *Wards Cove*, the Court, by the same five-justice majority, ruled against a black woman who claimed that her employer had harassed her, failed to promote her, and then discharged her, all on the basis of race. In *Patterson v. McLean Credit Union* (1989), Justice Kennedy wrote for the majority that the 1866 Civil Rights Act's prohibition of racial discrimination in the making and enforcement of private contracts did not apply to claims of racial harassment and promotional discrimination once a person was employed.

Following these decisions, a coalition of civil rights advocates moved quickly to counter what it saw as a major and abrupt departure from past Court rulings dealing with workplace discrimination. A majority in Congress was persuaded to pass the Civil Rights Act of 1990 to respond to these and other 1989 Court rulings, but President Bush vetoed the legislation, concerned that it would encourage racial hiring quotas. After another year of wrangling over statutory language, the president and Congress came to agreement and the Civil Rights Act of 1991 was passed. The statute's goal was "to respond to recent decisions by the Supreme Court by expanding the scope of relevant civil rights statutes to provide adequate protection to victims of discrimination." Title I specifically codifies concepts "enunciated by the Supreme Court in *Griggs* and in the other Supreme Court decisions prior to *Wards Cove*" by providing authority and guidelines for disparate-impact lawsuits by minorities and women under Title VII of the Civil Rights Act of 1964.[31] Also, in response to the *Patterson* decision, the Act provides expanded remedies to those who have been discriminated against or harassed in the workplace on the basis of race, ethnic origin, sex, or religion. Title II of the 1991 civil rights law creates a Glass Ceiling Commission to remedy the significant underrepresentation of women and minorities at the management and decision-making levels in the U.S. workforce.

When it comes to judging *constitutional* (as opposed to statutory) claims about denial of equality in employment, the Court has consistently used the "purposeful discrimination" test. As with the school desegregation rulings of the 1970s discussed earlier, minorities challenging employment classifications or criteria have had to show not only a discriminatory impact or effect but also a discriminatory purpose or intent on the part of the employer. The Court's decision in *Washington v. Davis* (1976) illustrates this principle.

Washington v. Davis involved a suit brought by African Americans challenging the constitutionality of hiring practices in the District of Columbia's police department. The D.C. police department required that a candidate seeking acceptance into the police training program receive a passing grade on a federal civil service test (one that gauged verbal ability, vocabulary, reading, and comprehension). Black applicants failed this test at a rate four times that of their white counterparts, which was the basis for the litigants' constitutional claim. Black plaintiffs asked the courts to invalidate the use of the test because it excluded a disproportionately high number of black people and was unrelated to job performance.

The Supreme Court upheld the use of the employment test. Justice White's opinion for the majority stressed that a practice is not unconstitutional "solely because it has a racially disproportionate impact" unless it can be proven that it "reflects a racially discriminatory purpose." A year later the Court clarified its position, stating that while disproportionate impact may "provide an important starting point . . . racially discriminatory intent or purpose is required to show a violation of the Equal Protection Clause."[32] Decisions regarding employment indicate that while Congress may have the power to use an "effect" criterion in employment discrimination cases, the Court adheres to a purposeful-discrimination test wherever equal protection claims under the Constitution are involved. This means that the constitutional burden of proof as a rule lies initially with the individuals claiming that racial discrimination in employment has taken place.

RACIAL DISCRIMINATION AND THE FRANCHISE

Black males were first made eligible to vote by Congress in 1867. The former Confederate states were ordered to form new constitutions that would guarantee black suffrage, and Congress tried to protect the black man's right to vote in both the Fourteenth Amendment and in a series of federal laws passed during Reconstruction. When it appeared that all of this still might not be enough, the Fifteenth Amendment to the Constitution was adopted in 1870, specifically stating that "the right of citizens of the United States to vote shall not be denied or abridged by the United States or by any state on account of race, color, or previous condition of servitude." Southern whites reacted swiftly to black voting rights, practicing violence and intimidation to prevent blacks from voting. But the mixture of federal guarantees protected black suffrage for almost thirty years. Throughout the

Reconstruction period, blacks voted and were elected to public office (one black senator and ten representatives were elected in this period). But at the turn of the century, southern blacks were suddenly and effectively disenfranchised and remained so for over sixty years. For instance, in Louisiana in 1896, 130,334 blacks were registered to vote; eight years later only 1,342 remained on the registrar's rolls!

METHODS OF DISENFRANCHISEMENT

How was this disenfranchisement of black people effected? In addition to "private" practices of violence and intimidation, southern states used "legal" methods to keep black citizens from voting. It must be noted at the outset that while the Constitution and federal law determine the broad parameters of citizen voting rights, the states can set specific qualifications for voting. As early as 1875, the Supreme Court announced that "the Fifteenth Amendment does not confer the right of suffrage upon anyone," and that states have the power to regulate elections and determine voting qualifications.[33] Beginning around 1890, southern states used this power to construct barriers to black suffrage. A discussion of some of the methods used by the states and the Supreme Court's response to them follows.

LITERACY TESTS

By 1900, almost all the former Confederate states had enacted literacy and other tests designed to prevent blacks from being eligible to vote. State laws required potential voters to be able to read and write, and in many cases to be capable of understanding or interpreting provisions of the state or federal constitution. These laws were based on the fact that in the South at the turn of the century more than two-thirds of black adults were illiterate while less than one-fourth of white adults could not read or write. These voting tests were thus effective means of removing most blacks from the voter rolls. And they were administered in such a way as to keep illiterate whites eligible. Evidence indicates that voter registrars administered these tests differently to white and black citizens, giving whites easier versions and providing aid in answering questions, while blacks were asked difficult questions and often disqualified for inconsequential errors, such as mispronouncing words. Nevertheless, the Supreme Court allowed the use of literacy and other such tests as requirements for voting. In *Lassiter v. Northampton County Board of Elections* (1959), a unanimous Court emphasized the broad discretion states had in setting voting qualifications:

> RESIDENCE REQUIREMENTS, AGE, PREVIOUS CRIMINAL RECORD [ARE] OBVIOUS EXAMPLES INDICATING FACTORS WHICH A STATE MAY TAKE INTO CONSIDERATION IN DETERMINING THE QUALIFICATIONS OF VOTERS. THE ABILITY TO READ AND WRITE LIKEWISE HAS SOME RELATION TO STANDARDS DESIGNED TO PROMOTE INTELLIGENT USE OF THE BALLOT. LITERACY AND ILLITERACY ARE NEUTRAL ON RACE, CREED, COLOR AND SEX. ILLITERATE PEOPLE MAY BE INTELLIGENT VOTERS, YET IN OUR SOCIETY WHERE NEWSPAPERS, PERIODICALS, BOOKS, AND OTHER PRINTED MATTER CANVASS AND DEBATE CAMPAIGN ISSUES, A STATE MIGHT CONCLUDE THAT ONLY THOSE WHO ARE LITERATE SHOULD EXERCISE THE FRANCHISE.

The Court *did* declare invalid an attempt by Oklahoma to deny blacks the right to vote while keeping whites eligible. Oklahoma amended its constitution after admittance to the Union in 1908 by imposing a literacy test for voting. However, all men lineally descended from ancestors entitled to vote in 1866 were exempt from taking the test. The purpose of this "grandfather clause" was clear, because no black man was entitled to vote prior to 1867. In *Guinn v. United States* (1915), the Supreme Court unanimously decided that the Fifteenth Amendment prevented this discriminatory practice. However, the victory for black citizens was short-lived, as Oklahoma passed a new election law bestowing permanent voting rights on all who voted in 1914 under the grandfather clause law and requiring all others (namely, black men) to register within twelve days or be disenfranchised for life. This obvious discrimination in black voting rights was not ruled invalid by the Court until 1939.[34]

WHITE PRIMARY LAWS

In their attempt to disenfranchise black citizens, southern states also used the power of the dominant one-party system to regulate the primary election process. Texas was exemplary in this regard. The Texas legislature in 1923 passed a statute declaring that "in no event shall a negro be eligible to participate in a Democratic primary election in the State of Texas." Using the Fourteenth Amendment's grant of equal protection, the Supreme Court ruled against this blatantly discriminatory action. Texas Democrats thought the Court's opinion meant that only direct state action disqualifying black people from primary voting was prohibited. The Texas legislature passed a law giving the power to set primary voting qualifications to the state executive committee of each political party. The Democratic Party responded by limiting primary voting to "all white Democrats." The Court held this practice to be unconstitutional as well because the law in effect made the party's executive committee an agent of the state.

Undaunted by these setbacks, the Texas Democratic Party, without any state authorizing legislation, adopted a resolution confining party membership to whites. At first, because political parties are considered voluntary private organizations, the Court allowed this racial exclusion.[35] But in *Smith v. Allwright* (1944), the Court decided that the party's practice was unconstitutional. The Court reasoned that political primaries are not merely private matters but an integral part of the electoral process. Because the state of Texas regulated many aspects of political parties and primary elections, a political party operating in the state became in effect "an agency of the state," and the party's discrimination constituted a form of state action in violation of the Constitution. The Court concluded that if a state that regulates the election process allows a political party to decide, on the basis of race, who may vote in its primary, the state "endorses, adopts and enforces the discrimination against Negroes." The decision in *Smith v. Allwright* was an important victory for blacks not only in the struggle to win equal voting rights but also provided a precedent for later Court rulings in housing and other areas, broadening the concept of state action to include a number of implicit and explicit discriminatory practices.

Smith v. Allwright aside, by the 1960s, through the use of these legal and extra-legal methods, the southern states had effectively prevented blacks from exercising their right to vote. In a 1961 report, the Civil Rights Commission found that less than one-fourth of all black people of voting age were registered to vote in the southern states. More specifically, the Commission selected seventeen "black belt" counties where blacks constituted a majority of the population and found only 3 percent to be registered in these counties.

CONGRESSIONAL ACTION: THE VOTING RIGHTS ACT OF 1965

Congress passed Civil Rights laws in 1957 and 1960 to secure black voting rights, but these were modest measures that did little to change the voting situations in the South. Spurred by civil rights marches and demonstrations throughout the South, Congress followed up the Civil Rights Act of 1964 with a much stronger voting rights act the next year. The Voting Rights Act of 1965 focused on eliminating the use of voting tests for purposes of discrimination. In any state or political subdivision where less than 50 percent of the persons of voting age had been registered to vote in the November 1964 election, the act specified that the following legal devices would be suspended: literacy and/or constitutional understanding tests; requirements of educational achievement or knowledge in a particular subject; and "good moral character" requirements. Congress believed that the 50-percent test would be a rough index of voting discrimination. A state could challenge the suspensions of these tests, but only if it could prove that they had not been used for purposes of racial discrimination. In addition, the Voting Rights Act of 1965 gave the attorney general of the United States the power to appoint federal "voting examiners" to oversee the process of voter registration in counties with a particularly bad record of discrimination. Moreover, the law shifted the burden of proof onto state registrars to show why a person ought not to vote, whereas before it had been on the individual black citizen to prove why he or she should be allowed to vote.

The Supreme Court ruled the Voting Rights Act (VRA) constitutional in *South Carolina v. Katzenbach* (1966). The affected states (using election data from 1964, the VRA originally applied to nine states—Alabama, Alaska, Arizona, Georgia, Louisiana, Mississippi, South Carolina, Texas, and Virginia—and a number of counties and municipalities in other states) contended that the law invaded their power to set voter qualifications, and that it disregarded "local conditions that have nothing to do with racial discrimination." But the Court cited earlier unsuccessful attempts by Congress to guarantee black people voting rights and concluded that the formula used in the 1965 law was "rational in both practice and theory." Chief Justice Warren premised his opinion for the Court on the following principle: "As against the reserved powers of the States, Congress may use any rational means to effectuate the constitutional prohibition of racial discrimination in voting."

The impact of the Voting Rights Act was dramatic. By 1976, drastic increases in black voter registration in the southern states automatically covered by the act occurred, closing the gap between white and black registration (see Table 9.2). And perhaps most important, in these states 1,100 blacks had been elected to public office by 1974, whereas only a handful had been elected prior to 1965.

When the Voting Rights Act came up for renewal in 1970, Congress suspended literacy tests nationwide, and in subsequent years Congress has extended and toughened the act's requirements even further, most notably requiring bilingual voting information be provided to citizens.

ELECTORAL SYSTEM DISCRIMINATION

In addition to challenging practices that deny the right to vote on the basis of race, individuals have challenged various electoral schemes that have the effect of diluting minority voting strength. Unfair district boundary-drawing, two-stage primary processes, majority versus plurality vote rules, and at-large elections all tend to deny representation in public offices to black candidates even though black citizens may constitute a sizable proportion of the community. But the Supreme Court has consistently ruled that in instances involving such election laws, only a showing of purposeful intent to discriminate renders them unconstitutional.

Mobile v. Bolden (1980) offers a prime example. In Mobile, Alabama, the three-member city commission was elected at large. No black person had ever been elected to the commission even though blacks made up 40 percent of the city's population. A district court judge ruled that the at-large election provision discriminated against blacks, but on appeal the Supreme Court reversed this judgment. The Court held that an electoral system violates the Constitution "only if there is purposeful discrimination" or if the system devised is "motivated by a racially discriminatory purpose." According to the Court, "To prove such a purpose it is not enough to show that the group allegedly discriminated against has not elected representatives in proportion to its numbers." The Equal Protection Clause does not require proportional representation of all identifiable groups, and because black citizens voted freely, no Fifteenth Amendment violation was present.

Questions about racial equality in the U.S. electoral system continue to be perplexing. The VRA provided clear Congressional guidance concerning the general need and specific mechanisms to eliminate racial discrimination in voting and elections. But in recent years, new questions have arisen concerning the extent of legislative authority in rectifying past racial discrimination. On the one hand, the Court majority has tended to interpret the VRA narrowly, making it difficult for the federal government to guarantee proportional representation and power to minority voters (see Brief 9.7). And as this edition goes to press, the Court will be deciding on a case that may overturn a crucial part of the VRA. As discussed in Brief 9.7, Section 5 of the VRA requires those states and localities covered by the law to obtain permission (or "preclearance") from the federal government before making any changes in their voting or election procedures. When Congress renewed the VRA for 25 additional years in 2006, it did not update its "coverage formula," continuing to use data from the 1972 election to determine which states or subdivisions were to be affected by this section of the law.

Table 9.2 Black Voter Registration, 1964–1976

	1964	1976
Alabama	23.0*	58.1
Georgia	44.0	56.3
Louisiana	32.0	63.9
Mississippi	6.7	67.4
South Carolina	38.8	60.6
Virginia	45.7	60.7

*Percentage of black voting-age population registered to vote.

Brief 9.7
BLACK VOTING POWER: REPRESENTATION OR INFLUENCE?

The Voting Rights Act was clearly designed to prevent state and local practices that would keep racial minorities from meaningful participation and power in the political system, as well as to guarantee representation to previously underrepresented minority groups. Accordingly, Section 5 of the Act requires that any jurisdiction originally covered by the law receive "preclearance" from the federal government for any change in election procedures. This is to ensure that the change "does not have the purpose and will not have the effect of denying or abridging the right to vote on account of race or color." In practice, the Supreme Court has determined that preclearance should depend on whether the change will create a "retrogression" in the position of racial minorities with respect to their effective exercise of the right to vote.

Over the past two decades there has been considerable dispute over what constitutes effective representation of minority voters. Some argue that voting districts should be created to ensure the election of minority representatives, as these representatives are best able to represent minority voters' interests. This has led to the creation in many states covered by the Voting Rights Act of a specified number of "majority–minority districts," where the voting-age population of minority groups makes up the majority of the district's overall voting-age population. Others have argued that majority–minority districts do not necessarily maximize minority voter influence, as such representation schemes often dilute minority power by concentrating minority voters into a single district rather than dispersing minority interests across a number of districts. These critics of majority–minority districts have argued that a more effective strategy is the creation of "minority influence districts," where minority voters are not the majority of the population but exist in large enough numbers to ensure that their interests are considered.

This dispute was brought to the Supreme Court in the case of *Georgia v. Ashcroft* (2003). Following the 2000 census, the state of Georgia enacted a new redistricting plan for the state's senate, one that reduced the number of black voters in three previously majority–minority state senate districts but increased the number of districts where minority voters could have significant influence. A federal district court denied Section 5 preclearance, largely on the grounds that the changes in these three districts were retrogressive. But the U.S. Supreme Court, by a 5–4 vote, overruled the district court, saying that it had not considered the totality of the circumstances surrounding this change in the state's plan. Most important, the Court argued that the decrease in minority population in the three majority–minority districts needed to be considered against the increase in the percentage of black voters in many other districts, thus validating the "minority influence district" argument. In fact, the Court suggested that states may legitimately decide to "risk having fewer minority representatives in order to achieve greater overall representation of a minority group by increasing the number of representatives sympathetic to the interests of minority voters."

Shelby County, Alabama, has challenged the preclearance requirement, arguing that, with the great progress that has been made in minority voting rights, Section 5 has outlived its usefulness, and stands as a threat to state sovereignty and a badge of shame on those jurisdictions affected by it. The case of *Shelby County v. Holder* is likely to be decided at the end of the 2012 Term, in June 2013.

At the same time, the Court has been willing to use the Equal Protection Clause to review efforts by state legislatures—particularly those originally targeted by the Voting Rights Act—to reapportion electoral districts with racial considerations in mind (see Brief 9.8). These decisions will leave state legislatures to their own devices in setting up electoral districts and will handcuff the federal government in its attempts to use the Voting Rights Act to achieve more proportional representation of minority voters. Given the tendency of legislatures to protect incumbents, who are, by and large, white, this may signal a halt to the gradual increase in minority representation, especially in Congress. Justice Ginsburg, in her dissent in a recent case, even worried that the Court, "in the name of equal protection, [could] shut out the very minority group whose history in the United States gave birth to the Equal Protection Clause."

Conclusion

Although the beginning of this chapter suggests that equality is cherished by both individualists and communitarians, the issue of racial equality has magnified the tension between the individualist's protection of minority rights and the communitarian's support of majority rule. African Americans in particular have borne the brunt of unbridled majoritarianism, owing to the historical institution of slavery. Constitutionally, the post–Civil War amendments were designed to put an end to that unequal legal treatment of black people by the white majority. But as the historical record shows, neither the Supreme Court nor the various state governments originally had a very generous

Brief 9.8

EQUAL PROTECTION CHALLENGES TO STATE LEGISLATIVE REDISTRICTING

The Supreme Court has been very active in Equal Protection cases challenging state legislative redistricting following changes in the census. For example, three cases involving attempts in Georgia, Virginia, and North Carolina after the 1990 census to create additional majority black congressional districts were challenged by white voters. In *Miller v. Johnson* (1995)—the Georgia case—the justices invalidated a plan to increase by one the number of majority black districts. Applying a strict-scrutiny standard to the apportionment plan, the Court could not find a sufficiently compelling justification to allow the state to assign black populations to certain legislative districts for the purpose of proportional racial representation. In *Meadows v. Moon* (1997), the Court affirmed the judgment of a lower federal court that Virginia's Third Congressional District had been unconstitutionally gerrymandered on the basis of race to achieve proportional representation of black voters.[36]

The state of North Carolina offers a unique case study. Four times beginning in 1993, white voters brought challenges against the North Carolina legislature of unconstitutional "racial districting" in Congressional District 12, challenges that were eventually decided by the U.S. Supreme Court. In the first two cases—*Shaw v. Reno* (1993) (*Shaw I*) and *Shaw v. Hunt* (1996) (*Shaw II*)—the Court ruled that the legislature had violated the Equal Protection Clause in creating a 160-mile-long district, unconventional and "snakelike" in shape, one that split towns and counties to produce a voting population that was predominantly African American in its racial makeup. In its ruling, the Court said "the district was so extremely irregular that it rationally can be viewed only as an effort to segregate the races for purposes of voting, without regard for traditional districting principles and without sufficiently compelling justification." Even though the districting plan did not dilute white citizens' voting strength, the Court decided that it unconstitutionally reinforced "racial stereotypes and threaten[ed] to undermine our system of representative democracy by signaling to elected officials that they represent a particular racial group rather than their constituency as a whole."

Following *Shaw II*, the North Carolina legislature redrew the boundaries of District 12 in 1997. Once again, white plaintiffs challenged the constitutionality of the legislature's efforts. Citing the fact that the district was still unusually shaped, split cities and counties, and contained a heavily African American voting population, they succeeded in getting a District Court to question District 12 on equal protection grounds. The State appealed, claiming that the primary objective in drawing the district lines was political—the creation of a safe seat for the Democratic Party. This time, in two separate rulings—*Hunt v. Cromartie* (1999) and *Hunt v. Cromartie* (2001)—the Supreme Court overturned the lower federal court and let the congressional district stand. Deferring to the legislature's "discretion to exercise the political judgment necessary to balance competing interests," a 5–4 majority ruled that those claiming that a legislature has improperly used race as a criterion in drawing electoral districts must show that race was the "predominant factor" in the districting decision. In this instance, the Court held, district lines correlated with race because they were drawn on the basis of political party affiliation, which also correlated with race. The decisions in the four North Carolina cases may be instructive as state legislatures continually redraw districts following demographic changes, especially given the even stronger tendency in recent elections of African Americans to vote for Democratic Party candidates.[37]

---

vision of black legal and constitutional equality. In the Supreme Court's case, the triple requirement of state action, purposeful discrimination, and reasonableness had the effect of severely narrowing the Fourteenth Amendment's application.

Beginning in the 1930s, the Supreme Court seemingly abandoned its narrow nineteenth-century understanding of equal protection. In many of the school segregation cases including the landmark *Brown vs. Board of Education* decision, and in employment discrimination rulings such as *Griggs v. Duke Power Co.*, the Court looked to the effect or impact of a practice rather than its underlying motivation to rule on the demands of equal protection (thus seemingly discarding the purposeful-discrimination requirement). And justices had so expanded the concept of state action in the *Smith v. Allwright*, *Shelley v. Kraemer*, and *Burton v. Wilmington Parking Authority* rulings that almost any discriminatory practice associated with or encouraged by the government would qualify for protection under the Fourteenth Amendment. In addition, congressional protection of civil rights for racial minorities beginning in the late 1950s provided yet another source of Supreme Court anti-discrimination rulings.

The Supreme Court pendulum, however, may have swung back to a position more consistent with its nineteenth-century understandings. More recent education, employment, and election procedure rulings have once again in effect invoked a strict purposeful-discrimination standard, placing a heavy burden on minorities to prove discriminatory intent on the part of public officials. More recent state-action rulings suggest that the expansive days of *Shelley* have come to an end. Many Supreme Court observers have concluded that the current majority—though a slim majority of five—adheres to a strict "anti-discrimination principle" view of equality (as described at the beginning of this chapter), beyond which it is unwilling to go. More is said about the current majority's propensity to limit the push of constitutional equality in the next chapter, but it may well be that these justices are, to quote Justice Marshall in his *Milliken* dissent, reflecting "a perceived public mood that we have gone far enough in enforcing the Constitution's guarantee of equal justice."

Still, one important component of nineteenth-century equal protection interpretation that has been and remains drastically revised is the rational scrutiny standard. The Court, beginning in the 1930s, has established a new criterion for certain types of equal protection claims, one that automatically requires justices to give "strict scrutiny" (as opposed to "rational scrutiny") to state laws and classifications. The following chapter focuses on the "new equal protection" and what it does and does not entail.

CHAPTER 10
The New Equal Protection

Gender equality remains at the forefront of what has been called "the new equal protection." Elizabeth Cady Stanton, who formally introduces this chapter, was one of the leading advocates of women's equality, helping to organize the first women's rights convention in 1848 in Seneca Falls, New York. It was at this table in the nearby Waterloo home of Mary Ann M'Clintock that convention organizers met and Stanton wrote the Declaration of Sentiments, proclaiming that the ideal of equality found in the Declaration of Independence ought to apply to women as well as to men. This declaration was the centerpiece of demands for gender equality over the next several decades.

▼ Introductory Remarks by Elizabeth Cady Stanton

My name is Elizabeth Cady Stanton, and it is my privilege to introduce this chapter on the new equal protection. As an early advocate of women's equality under the U.S. Constitution, my political activism and writing epitomizes the efforts of many different groups—the elderly, people with disabilities, immigrants, the lesbian gay bisexual transgender (LGBT) community, low-income citizens—in more recent years to secure equal rights and prohibit legal discrimination.

I was born in 1815, in Johnstown, New York. During my time growing up in the first half of the nineteenth century, not only was the right to vote closed off to women, but so, too, were property rights, legal protections during marriage, and most educational opportunities. Like so many other women's-rights advocates of the time, I cut my teeth in the abolitionist movement, although as a woman I was often excluded from participating in or speaking at assemblies and gatherings protesting slavery.

In 1848, I helped organize the first women's-rights convention, in Seneca Falls, New York. I also took the lead in drafting a document that was endorsed by the delegates at the convention, called the Declaration of Sentiments. It was modeled after the Declaration of Independence and, as such, opens with the following statement:

> We hold these truths to be self-evident: that all men and women are created equal; that they are endowed by their Creator with certain inalienable rights; that among these are life, liberty and the pursuit of happiness . . .

Continuing to follow the Declaration of Independence, my Declaration goes on to list the "history of repeated injuries and usurpations on the part of man toward woman," including these charges:

- He has compelled her to submit to laws, in the formation of which she had no voice
- He has made her, if married, in the eye of the law, civilly dead.
- He has taken from her all right in property, even to the wages she earns.
- He has monopolized nearly all the profitable employments, and from those she is permitted to follow, she receives but a scanty remuneration.
- He has denied her the facilities for obtaining a thorough education . . .

After chronicling the ways male-dominated government and society have deprived women of their equal rights, the Declaration of Sentiments continues with a list of "Resolutions," including a demand that women be given "their sacred right to the elective franchise."

The dozens of delegates to the Seneca Falls Convention and the over three hundred who signed the Declaration of Sentiments were hopeful that change would come quickly, and with the end of the Civil War and the abolition of slavery in 1865, we thought the next step would be to secure equality for all people, the promise of the Fourteenth Amendment. Sadly, it would take seventy-two years after Seneca Falls for women to secure a constitutional right to vote. And as this chapter discusses, in the century since the Nineteenth Amendment was passed, women and other groups seeking their rights and the "equal protection of the laws" have struggled to have the Constitution recognize and address the injustices they face. Think about these origins as you read the history of this "new equal protection" and what it has brought to a variety of Americans in our history.

Introduction: Equal Protection Old and New

As Justice Miller declared in the Slaughterhouse Cases (1873), the "pervading purpose" of the Fourteenth Amendment was to protect blacks against state-sponsored discrimination: "We doubt very much whether any action of a State not directed by way of discrimination against the negroes as a class, or on account of their race, will ever be held to come within the purview of this provision." With this understanding in mind, the Supreme Court narrowly construed the Amendment's provisions and applied minimal standards when reviewing any governmental actions under the Equal Protection Clause. As discussed in Chapter 9, "rationality scrutiny" was the standard the Court adopted. Under this standard, justices acted deferentially toward governments seeking to embody the majority's sentiments in law. Individuals challenging the government on equal protection grounds were required to demonstrate the irrationality of the majority's actions, normally presumed reasonable. In fact, the Court was hostile to most equal protection claims prior to the 1930s: Justice Holmes once described them as "the usual last resort of constitutional arguments."[1]

The Fourteenth Amendment's language, however, offers hope of a more expansive, egalitarian constitutional vision. It guarantees equality and due process to "any person." And it announces the goal of federal protection to individuals who may be left out of the processes of representative democracy. In this sense the Fourteenth Amendment brings together in an often uneasy balance the individualist values of protection against majority tyranny with the communitarian values of democratic self-governance. In the beginning decades of this century, the balance was tipped on the side of legislative majorities. By the 1930s, however, the Supreme Court had set its task at tipping the balance in the other direction. The justices began to assert their power of judicial review against popular governments who were unjustly trampling on the rights of individuals and minority groups. In specific areas, the Court has substituted **strict scrutiny** for the more self-restrained rationality scrutiny. In cases in which the Court exercises strict scrutiny, the burden of proof is shifted heavily to the government to justify its actions in attempting to deny equal rights to individuals.

Rather than being the "last resort of constitutional arguments," equal protection claims have outranked just about every other basis of constitutional argument and have been used to rule out countless governmental practices in many substantive areas. In addition to racial minorities, white males (including President Bush!), women, the elderly, noncitizens, disabled persons, gay men and lesbians, and the poor, among others, have brought serious claims under the Fourteenth Amendment. The Supreme Court's consideration of these challenges to government programs based on other than traditional racial discrimination grounds has been termed the **new equal protection**. This chapter discusses the nature of this new equal protection, its expansion beyond racial discrimination, and the ongoing problems and issues such an expansion creates.

Origins of the New Equal Protection

Tracing the origins of a constitutional idea is never easy, but this discussion of the new equal protection begins with Justice Harlan Stone's famous footnote in *United States v. Carolene Products Co.* (1938). In an otherwise inconsequential decision, Justice Stone, in Footnote 4 of his majority opinion, laid out three possible exceptions to the rule that judges ought to presume government actions constitutional. He stated that normal deference toward government should be curbed in favor of a "more exacting judicial scrutiny" in cases (1) "when legislation appears on its face to be within a specific prohibition of the Constitution, such as those of the first ten amendments"; (2) when legislation "restricts those political processes which can ordinarily be expected to [prevent] undesirable legislation" (restrictions on the right to vote and other aspects of the democratic political process); and (3) where "prejudice against discrete and insular minorities . . . tends seriously to curtail the operation of those political processes ordinarily to be relied upon to protect minorities." Stone's footnote invited the Court to exert its authority against the government in these instances and to use the Fifth and Fourteenth Amendments as the basis for such judicial activism.

Four years later, in *Skinner v. Oklahoma* (1942), Justice Douglas used the term "strict scrutiny" (in place of Stone's "more exacting judicial scrutiny") to describe the judicial standard the Court would apply to legislation depriving individuals of their civil rights (see discussion of this case in Chapter 11).

And over the next two years, the Court further clarified this new standard of scrutiny under the Fourteenth Amendment. This was done in cases involving restrictions on Japanese Americans during World War II. In sustaining a curfew order against the Japanese in *Hirabayashi v. United States* (1943), Justice Stone stated:

> DISTINCTIONS BETWEEN CITIZENS SOLELY BECAUSE OF THEIR ANCESTRY ARE BY THEIR VERY NATURE ODIOUS TO A FREE PEOPLE WHOSE INSTITUTIONS ARE FOUNDED UPON THE DOCTRINE OF EQUALITY. FOR THAT REASON, LEGISLATIVE CLASSIFICATION OR DISCRIMINATION BASED ON RACE ALONE HAS OFTEN BEEN HELD TO BE A DENIAL OF EQUAL PROTECTION.

A year later, in sustaining the infamous exclusion order against Japanese Americans in *Korematsu v. United States* (1944) (see Chapter 5), Justice Hugo Black began the Court's opinion by setting out a standard of "rigid scrutiny" for all racially based classifications:

> IT SHOULD BE NOTED TO BEGIN WITH, THAT ALL LEGAL RESTRICTIONS WHICH CURTAIL THE CIVIL RIGHTS OF A SINGLE RACIAL GROUP ARE IMMEDIATELY SUSPECT. THIS IS NOT TO SAY THAT ALL SUCH RESTRICTIONS ARE UNCONSTITUTIONAL. IT IS TO SAY THAT COURTS MUST SUBJECT THEM TO MORE RIGID SCRUTINY.

With these two cases, although it upheld gross intrusions on individual freedoms by the government in both instances, the Court had announced a new jurisprudence of active scrutiny of all governmental classifications on the basis of race. It was only because of what they thought were overriding national security interests that the justices allowed racial classifications to stand in these instances. With the invalidation of racial classification schemes in the segregation cases preceding and including *Brown*, the Court definitely signaled an end to judicial deference to government under the Equal Protection Clause.

THE TWO-TIER APPROACH

From these rather modest beginnings, the Supreme Court came to adopt what has been called a two-tier approach to Fourteenth Amendment questions. Under it, the justices initially place governmental actions and classifications under one of two tiers of judicial review. The lower tier represents judicial review of classifications under the previously discussed rationality-scrutiny standard. Most government classifications fall under this lenient standard, with the Court usually deferring to the judgment of the people's representatives in the legislative or executive branches of government. All the Court requires is that some reasonable relationship exist between the law under review and a valid governmental goal. In practice, this has meant that a statute placed on the lower tier of rationality scrutiny is almost always upheld.

The upper tier of the two-tier approach is reserved for those few instances when a government's laws or actions are held up to a rigorous standard of judicial review. Laws placed on the upper tier draw strict scrutiny from the Supreme Court. Currently the Court applies strict scrutiny to two kinds of laws: (1) laws that threaten "fundamental rights" (see Chapter 11); and (2) laws that use "suspect classifications" to make legal distinctions between people (following Black's statement in *Korematsu*). Only if the government can show a compelling interest for its actions, a close fit between the challenged law and the compelling interest, and evidence that no less drastic means were available other than acting as it did will the Court allow such a law to stand.

The Court's application of the strict-scrutiny standard has been, according to Professor Gerald Gunther, "'strict' in theory and fatal in fact."[2] Professor Gunther's description is apt because the Court has almost always invalidated legislation it believed used "suspect" classifications or interfered with what it believed were fundamental rights. For example, in *Johnson v. California* (2005), the Court ruled constitutionally suspect a California prison policy that temporarily segregated new inmates by race, even in the face of California's claim that the policy was necessary to curb gang violence.

The Supreme Court developed this two-tier approach to aid it in making determinations about the legitimacy of particular classifications under the

Equal Protection Clause. But over the years, the seemingly rigid, all-or-nothing character of two-tier judicial review has drawn criticism from judges and legal scholars, and the Court itself has abandoned the approach in certain instances. Some critics have argued that only the name remains to the Court's two-tier approach to the Fourteenth Amendment. In fact, they contend that the Court has actually used a multiple-tier, or "sliding-scale," approach as the basis for reviewing legislation under the Equal Protection Clause. In addition to covering the Court's two-tier approach as applied in particular cases, this chapter examines the various criticisms justices have faced concerning this new equal protection.

SUSPECT CLASSIFICATIONS AND THE EQUAL PROTECTION CLAUSE

The Court has subjected governmental actions to rigorous inspections when such actions are based on a scheme of **suspect classification**. The question the Court has had to address is: What classifications ought to be considered serious threats to the ideal of equality and, as a result, considered constitutionally illegitimate on their face? True to the intentions of those who framed the Fourteenth Amendment, the Court finally moved to put race and national origin in this category beginning in the 1930s. Discrimination against racial or ethnic minorities continues to be considered "inherently suspect," and the Court subjects such classifications to strict scrutiny. The following passage from Chief Justice Warren's opinion in *Loving v. Virginia* (1967) makes this clear:

> AT THE VERY LEAST, THE EQUAL PROTECTION CLAUSE DEMANDS THAT RACIAL CLASSIFICATIONS, ESPECIALLY SUSPECT IN CRIMINAL STATUTES, BE SUBJECTED TO THE "MOST RIGID SCRUTINY," AND IF THEY ARE EVER TO BE UPHELD, THEY MUST BE SHOWN TO BE NECESSARY TO THE ACCOMPLISHMENT OF SOME PERMISSIBLE STATE OBJECTIVE, INDEPENDENT OF THE RACIAL DISCRIMINATION WHICH IT WAS THE OBJECT OF THE 14TH AMENDMENT TO ELIMINATE.

In the last thirty years, however, other groups have brought equal protection claims against classifications they would like the Court to certify as "suspect" (see Brief 10.1). White males have argued that governmental affirmative action plans that benefit minorities in education and the workplace classify on the basis of race and therefore ought to be considered automatically invalid. Women's-rights advocates contend that laws differentiating on the basis of gender should be considered constitutionally suspect. Aging persons, noncitizens, the poor, lesbians and gay men, and persons with disabilities have all asked the Court to elevate classifications against them to "suspect" status. A look at each of these claims and the Court's response follows.

AFFIRMATIVE ACTION: DENIAL OF EQUAL PROTECTION TO WHITES?

Affirmative action generally refers to a policy whereby racial minorities (or sometimes women) are given preference in admissions, hiring and firing, or promotional practices. The policy rests on the assumption that a history of overt past discrimination against a disadvantaged group of people may require that, to achieve true equality of opportunity, positive action be taken by government and society to bring minority group members to an equal starting place in the competitive social race. Affirmative action has been initiated and undertaken by a variety of institutions in American society: governmental bodies, the courts, private businesses, educational institutions, and labor unions.

The Supreme Court itself called for affirmative action in some of its school desegregation decisions, arguing that merely eliminating discrimination was not enough to end racial segregation in education (see Chapter 9). In the *Swann* case, for example, the Court unanimously concluded that "just as the race of students must be considered in determining whether a constitutional violation has occurred, so also race must be considered in formulating a remedy."

The federal government adopted affirmative action policies beginning in the Johnson administration. President Johnson himself laid the groundwork for affirmative action. In announcing an executive order mandating affirmative action in the federal bureaucracy, Johnson stated that eliminating overt racial discrimination was not enough:

Brief 10.1
WHAT MAKES A CLASSIFICATION SUSPECT?

The raging controversy over classification schemes and equality under the Constitution raises questions about why a classification is considered suspect. The general guidelines applied in Supreme Court opinions have been broad and subject to a great deal of interpretation. Justice Stone's *Carolene Products'* footnote spoke of classifications reflecting "prejudice against discrete and insular minorities," an open-ended invitation to include all sorts of groups, not just *racial* minorities.[3] Justice Powell only added confusion to the controversy in his opinion in *San Antonio School District v. Rodriguez* (1973). He stated that a suspect class is one that has been

> saddled with such disabilities, or subjected to such a history of purposeful unequal treatment, or relegated to such a position of political powerlessness as to command extraordinary protection from the majoritarian political process.

But Powell and others have found this to be insufficient justification for making women, the economically disadvantaged, or disabled persons suspect classes. Other justices have tried to make the reasoning underlying suspect classifications clearer. Justice Brennan, in *Plyler v. Doe* (1982), deemed suspect "legislation imposing special disabilities upon groups disfavored by virtue of circumstances beyond their control [which] suggests the kind of 'class or caste' treatment that the Fourteenth Amendment was designed to abolish." And Justice Marshall defined a number of characteristics contributing to suspectness, in *Cleburne v. Cleburne Living Center* (1985):

> No single talisman can define those groups likely to be the target of classifications offensive to the Fourteenth Amendment and therefore warranting heightened or strict scrutiny; experience, not abstract knowledge, must be the primary guide. The "political powerlessness" of a group may be relevant . . . but that factor is neither necessary, as the gender cases demonstrate, nor sufficient, as the example of minors illustrates. . . . Similarly, immutability of a trait at issue may be relevant, but many immutable characteristics, such as height or blindness, are valid bases of governmental action and classifications under a variety of circumstances.
>
> The political powerlessness of a group and the immutability of its defining trait are relevant insofar as they point to a social and cultural isolation that gives the majority little reason to respect or be concerned with that group's interests and needs.
>
> The discreteness and insularity warranting a "more searching judicial inquiry" must therefore be viewed from a social and cultural perspective as well as a political one. To this task judges are well suited, for the lessons of history and experience are surely the best guide as to when, and with respect to what interests, society is likely to stigmatize individuals as members of an inferior caste or view them as not belonging to the community. Because prejudice spawns prejudice, and stereotypes produce limitations that confirm the stereotype on which they are based, a history of unequal treatment requires sensitivity to the prospect that its vestiges endure. . . . Where classifications based on a particular characteristic have [offended the principles of equality] in the past, and the threat that they may do so remains, heightened scrutiny is appropriate.

Do any of these attempts to define the characteristics of suspect classes clarify the Court's criteria? Has the Court applied these general standards consistently in the specific claims documented in this chapter?

> YOU DO NOT TAKE A PERSON WHO, FOR YEARS, HAS BEEN HOBBLED BY CHAINS AND LIBERATE HIM, BRING HIM UP TO THE STARTING LINE OF A RACE AND THEN SAY YOU ARE FREE TO COMPETE WITH ALL THE OTHERS, AND STILL JUST BELIEVE THAT YOU HAVE BEEN COMPLETELY FAIR.[4]

The Department of Health, Education, and Welfare (HEW) followed suit in 1967. Using its authority under Title VI of the Civil Rights Act of 1964, HEW promulgated regulations ordering all agencies or institutions receiving federal funds to "take affirmative action to overcome the effects of conditions which resulted in limiting participation by persons of a particular race, color, or national origin even in the absence of . . . prior discrimination" by the institution. In line with these regulations, colleges and universities, employers, and state agencies all began consciously to design programs that would increase the number of minority participants.

By the 1970s, whites began challenging these affirmative action programs as an affront to their right to equality under the Fourteenth Amendment. The

Court has subsequently been asked to decide whether government and private efforts to alleviate racism can be color-conscious to the detriment of whites. That is, should the use of racial classifications that burden whites be considered suspect under the two-tier approach? If, as Justice Harlan announced in his *Plessy* dissent, the Constitution is color-blind, then doesn't affirmative action cause the same violation of constitutional equality as the racial discrimination ruled unconstitutional by the Court beginning in the 1950s?

THE COURT'S FIRST ANSWER: THE *BAKKE* DECISION

Having dodged an affirmative action case in 1974,[5] the Court was presented with a controversy four years later that it could not avoid. As part of its affirmative action plan in line with HEW's guidelines, the University of California at Davis established a special admissions program in their medical school for economically and/or educationally disadvantaged persons, specifically defined as members of minority groups. Davis reserved sixteen of the one hundred seats available in the medical school each year for special admissions applicants. The special admissions program would consider for admission minority group members with lower grades and Medical College Admission Test scores than the regular admissions program.

Alan Bakke, a white male, was denied admission to the Davis Medical School in 1973 and 1974, even though his grades and Medical College Admission Test scores were higher than those admitted under the special program. After his second application was rejected, Bakke filed suit in the state courts, claiming primarily that the university's admissions program violated the Equal Protection Clause, as well as Title VI of the Civil Rights Act of 1964. The California Supreme Court, hearing the case on appeal, ruled in Bakke's favor. Because the Davis program classified according to race, the state supreme court applied the strict-scrutiny standard in coming to a decision. The state supreme court believed that though "the goals of integrating the medical profession and increasing the number of physicians willing to serve members of minority groups were compelling state interests," the means the university had adopted were illegitimate.

The California Supreme Court concluded that the Equal Protection Clause required that "no applicant may be rejected because of his race, in favor of another who is less qualified, as measured by standards applied without regard to race" and ordered Bakke's admission to the medical school. The university sought and obtained review from the U.S. Supreme Court in *Regents of the University of California v. Bakke* (1978).

The justices strongly disagreed among themselves on the validity of the Davis program and on the issue of affirmative action in general. Four justices (Brennan, White, Marshall, and Blackmun) approved of the use of affirmative action and believed the Davis Medical School program to be constitutional and legal under Title VI. They voted to deny Bakke's claims. Four justices (Burger, Stewart, Rehnquist, and Stevens) believed that Title VI of the Civil Rights Act of 1964 was sufficient in itself to outlaw the kind of program Davis had established. They agreed with the California Supreme Court that Bakke was discriminated against because of his race and voted to affirm the court's order to admit him. That left Justice Powell to cast the deciding vote.

Justice Powell's opinion, which became the judgment of the Court, is a mixed bag. On the one hand, he agreed with the lower court that strict judicial scrutiny be applied to government programs that classify on the basis of race and ethnic status.

> [THE] GUARANTEE OF EQUAL PROTECTION CANNOT MEAN ONE THING WHEN APPLIED TO ONE INDIVIDUAL AND SOMETHING ELSE WHEN APPLIED TO A PERSON OF ANOTHER COLOR. IF BOTH ARE NOT ACCORDED TO SAME PROTECTION, THEN IT IS NOT EQUAL.... RACIAL AND ETHNIC DISTINCTIONS OF ANY SORT ARE INHERENTLY SUSPECT AND THUS CALL FOR THE MOST EXACTING JUDICIAL EXAMINATION.

For Powell, then, state educational affirmative action plans disadvantaging whites would be subjected to the same degree of judicial scrutiny as a plan disadvantaging racial minorities. And applying this strict scrutiny, he thought the Davis program could not be justified because it set a specific racial quota without compelling state interests to justify it.

On the other hand, Powell was unwilling to say that the state could never take race into account in its educational programs. Powell recognized that "the State has a substantial interest that legitimately may be served by a properly devised admissions program involving the competitive consideration of race and ethnic origin." An admissions program that makes race a plus in a candidate's favor without "insulat[ing] the individual from comparison with all other candidates for the available seats" would meet constitutional muster, according to Powell.

Powell's opinion for the Court agreed that the affirmative action plan at Davis too rigidly drew lines on the basis of race and ethnicity. The program's "principal evil" was its denial to Bakke of his "right to individualized consideration without regard to race." But Powell also affirmed the consideration of race in a "properly devised admissions program" to meet the state's legitimate goals of diversity and countering the effect of past societal discrimination.

Justices Brennan, Marshall, and Blackmun all wrote separate opinions defending the affirmative action program at Davis. Brennan rejected the idea that racial classifications that burden whites are "inherently suspect." Because the classification used in the Davis plan did not disfavor a traditionally mistreated "class" or "stigmatize" any class with a brand of inferiority, Brennan would apply a "heightened-" but not "strict-" scrutiny standard under the Equal Protection Clause. By using the test applied to gender discrimination cases (see the discussion of *Craig v. Boren* in this chapter), Brennan concluded that "racial classification designed to further remedial purposes 'must serve important governmental objectives and must be substantially related to achievement of those objectives.'" He thought the Davis program met this test.

Marshall looked at the question historically:

[THE] POSITION OF THE NEGRO TODAY IN AMERICA IS THE TRAGIC BUT INEVITABLE CONSEQUENCE OF CENTURIES OF UNEQUAL TREATMENT. MEASURED BY ANY BENCHMARK OF COMFORT OR ACHIEVEMENT, MEANINGFUL EQUALITY REMAINS A DISTANT DREAM FOR THE NEGRO.... IN LIGHT OF THE SORRY HISTORY OF DISCRIMINATION AND ITS DEVASTATING IMPACT ON THE LIVES OF NEGROES, BRINGING THE NEGRO INTO THE MAINSTREAM OF AMERICAN LIFE SHOULD BE A STATE INTEREST OF THE HIGHEST ORDER.... [WHILE] I APPLAUD THE JUDGMENT OF THE COURT THAT A UNIVERSITY MAY CONSIDER RACE IN ITS ADMISSIONS PROCESS, IT IS MORE THAN A LITTLE IRONIC THAT, AFTER SEVERAL HUNDRED YEARS OF CLASS-BASED DISCRIMINATION AGAINST NEGROES, THE COURT IS UNWILLING TO HOLD THAT A CLASS-BASED REMEDY FOR THAT DISCRIMINATION IS PERMISSIBLE.

Justice Blackmun's opinion put the pro-affirmative action position most succinctly. After expressing the "hope that the time will come when an affirmative action program is unnecessary," Blackmun admitted that at the present time, "that hope is a slim one." He concluded his support of the Davis program by pointing out a profound paradox of constitutional equality in America: "In order to get beyond racism, we must first take account of race. There is no other way. And in order to treat some persons equally, we must treat them differently."

The Supreme Court decided little beyond the invalidity of the particular affirmative action program challenged in the *Bakke* case. *Bakke* was merely the first word on affirmative action. Since then, the Court has tried to clarify its position.

AFFIRMATIVE ACTION RESOLVED: THE *CROSON* AND *ADARAND* DECISIONS

Following Bakke and through most of the 1980s, the Court's decisions on affirmative action were almost schizophrenic, at times upholding affirmative action plans[6] and other times ruling against them.[7] Finally, at the end of the decade, the Court resolved the question of whether racial classifications aiming to ameliorate the effects of past discrimination ought to draw the same degree of scrutiny as those aimed at traditionally burdened racial minorities. In *City of Richmond v. J. A. Croson Co.* (1989), the majority's answer suggested that *any* use of racial classifications by government would warrant strict scrutiny under the Equal Protection Clause.

Responding to what it saw as a history of discrimination against racial minorities in the construction industry, the City of Richmond had adopted a rule requiring companies awarded city construction contracts to subcontract at least 30 percent of the total public dollars received to Minority Business Enterprises. This ordinance was modeled on a Congressional provision approved in a 1980 case[8] and was similar to affirmative action measures in effect in over thirty states and nearly two hundred localities.

The Supreme Court, by a 6–3 margin, invalidated the ordinance, applying a strict scrutiny standard to the use of race in a way that burdens whites. Writing for the majority, Justice O'Connor began by quoting *Shelley v. Kraemer*, saying that "the rights created by the . . . Fourteenth Amendment are, by its terms, guaranteed to the individual. The rights established are personal rights." Accordingly, any governmental program that would deny individual citizens opportunity solely on the basis of race are suspect and ought to be judged by the strict scrutiny standard. Declaring that "the standard of review under the Equal Protection Clause is not dependent on the race of those burdened or benefited by a particular classification," O'Connor announced that the only permissible governmentally initiated affirmative action—using the "compelling interest" standard—would be to "remedy" the effects of "past discrimination by the governmental unit involved," and only then when the government could clearly prove such a history of its own past discrimination. Furthermore, even if the government could prove such a compelling interest, the program in question would have to be "narrowly tailored" to further that interest. She could find no such compelling interest that Richmond could use to justify such a sweeping—not narrowly tailored, in her mind—30 percent set-aside program.

In a separate concurring opinion, Justice Antonin Scalia went even further, saying that "only a social emergency rising to the level of imminent danger to life and limb" could justify deviation from the Fourteenth Amendment's standard of strict color-blindness. He ruled out the use of racial classifications to make up for the effects of past discrimination:

THE DIFFICULTY OF OVERCOMING THE EFFECTS OF PAST DISCRIMINATION IS NOTHING COMPARED WITH THE DIFFICULTY OF ERADICATING FROM OUR SOCIETY THE SOURCE OF THOSE EFFECTS, WHICH IS THE TENDENCY—FATAL TO A NATION SUCH AS OURS—TO CLASSIFY AND JUDGE MEN AND WOMEN ON THE BASIS OF THEIR COUNTRY OF ORIGIN OR THE COLOR OF THEIR SKIN. A SOLUTION TO THE FIRST PROBLEM THAT AGGRAVATES THE SECOND IS NO SOLUTION AT ALL.

In his dissenting opinion, Justice Marshall continued to argue that a different standard of review be applied to remedial race-conscious programs designed to eliminate the effects of past discrimination against racial minorities. "A profound difference," he wrote, "separates governmental actions that themselves are racist, and governmental actions that seek to remedy the effects of prior racism or to prevent neutral governmental activity from perpetuating the effects of such racism."

The *Croson* case represented the first time that a *majority* of the justices explicitly adopted strict scrutiny as their standard of Equal Protection Clause review of affirmative action programs. But the Court did not apply this standard to *federal* affirmative action under *congressional* statutes. This created the seemingly contradictory decision eighteen months after *Croson* in which a five-justice majority upheld a Federal Communications Commission policy of giving preference to minority applications for new broadcast licenses. In *Metro Broadcasting Inc. v. Federal Communications Commission* (1990), the Court majority applied the lesser "important governmental interest" standard to the congressional goal of promoting broadcast diversity through this racial preference program. Finally, in *Adarand Constructor's Inc. v. Pena* (1995), the Court resolved the contradiction, saying that all racial classifications, by whatever level of government, must be analyzed under a strict scrutiny standard.

In the many years since the *Bakke* decision, affirmative action continues to be a lightning rod, especially on college campuses (see Brief 10.2).[9] In 1996, California voters passed Proposition 209, amending the state constitution to abolish all preferences based on race, gender, and ethnicity in state college admissions and hiring. The states of Florida and Washington followed suit, abolishing all racial, ethnic, and gender preferences. And in light of the Supreme Court cases involving the University of Michigan (see Brief 10.2), voters in Michigan passed a ballot initiative in 2006, ending affirmative action in higher education, public contracting, and hiring. (The Supreme Court recently agreed to hear a case in their 2013

Brief 10.2

BAKKE REVISITED: AFFIRMATIVE ACTION IN HIGHER EDUCATION

Following the *Bakke* decision, many colleges and universities were forced to adjust their affirmative action admissions programs, making sure not to set rigid numerical quotas for students from certain racial or ethnic backgrounds while still taking race and ethnicity into account in the admissions process. The *Bakke* decision did not discourage affirmative action efforts. In fact, the commitment to achieve racial and ethnic diversity in the student body and staff of many colleges and universities grew stronger over the years. Campus officials justified the use of race-conscious admissions policies on the grounds that a diverse group of students produces a community in which student learning is enhanced by the variety of perspectives and life situations.

But many white students, and even some minority students, have come to challenge these assumptions and policies. White student critics of affirmative action have argued for color-blind admissions policies, where academic merit alone is the deciding factor. Minority students critical of affirmative action often think that they are the victims of others' assumptions that they are not qualified or prepared for college work, that they are there only because of affirmative action.

In 2003, the Supreme Court had the opportunity to revisit the question of affirmative action in higher education and their decision in the *Bakke* case. In two cases involving the University of Michigan, the Court at once reaffirmed the principle that affirmative action can be used to achieve racial diversity on college campuses and also set down a blueprint for taking race and ethnicity into account without violating the Constitution's guarantee of equal protection.

Grutter v. Bollinger (2003) involved the admissions practices of the University of Michigan law school. The law school, specifically seeking to comply with Justice Powell's opinion in the *Bakke* decision, had used a candidate's race or ethnicity as one of a number of factors in attempting to enroll a diverse student body. In addition to looking at the applicant's undergraduate grade point average, Law School Admissions Test score, and letters of recommendation, the admissions committee considered how the applicant would contribute to law school life and diversity. The admissions policy did not define diversity solely in terms of racial or ethnic status, but was specifically committed to the inclusion of African American, Hispanic, and Native American students, who would not be represented in enough numbers to enroll a "critical mass" without special consideration.

By a 5–4 majority, the Supreme Court upheld the affirmative action admissions policy. Justice O'Connor, who wrote for the majority, affirmed Justice Powell's argument in *Bakke* and her own position in *Croson* that a university's use of race or ethnic origin must be subjected to strict scrutiny. But, O'Connor argued, the University of Michigan *did* have a compelling interest in creating a diverse student body. "In order to cultivate a set of leaders with legitimacy in the eyes of the citizenry, it is necessary that the path to leadership be visibly open to talented and qualified individuals of every race and ethnicity." Moreover, the fact that the law school used a "highly individualized, holistic review of each applicant's file" in which race counted as a factor but was not part of a "quota system" meant that they met the requirement that an affirmative action plan be "narrowly tailored" to achieve the university's compelling interest in diversity.

At the same time, in *Gratz v. Bollinger* (2003), by a 6–3 majority, the Court invalidated Michigan's affirmative action program for *undergraduate* student admissions. The difference in the undergraduate program lay in the mechanical fashion by which race was considered for admission. Rather than using an individualized, case-by-case approach to considering an applicant's contribution to campus diversity, the College of Literature, Science, and the Arts automatically awarded 20 points on a scale of 150 for an applicant's membership in an underrepresented racial or ethnic minority group. Chief Justice Rehnquist, writing for the majority, argued that the undergraduate admissions policy violated the Equal Protection Clause because it "is not narrowly tailored to achieve the interest in educational diversity that [the University] claims justifies their program."

The Court's two Michigan decisions reaffirmed the principles established in *Bakke* and provided a road map for universities to follow, but they also set limits on the use of affirmative action in higher education, including time limits. Justice O'Connor concluded her opinion in *Grutter* by commenting on the twenty-five years that had passed since the Court first approved the use of race to advance a public university's interest in student body diversity (in the *Bakke* decision). "It has been 25 years since Justice Powell first approved the use of race to further an interest in student body diversity in the context of public higher education," she stated. "We expect that 25 years from now, the use of racial preferences will no longer be necessary."

This twenty-five-year "statute of limitation" on approving affirmative action schemes in higher education suggested by Justice O'Connor may be more than the current Court is willing to allow, however. In a case involving the University of Texas's affirmative action program argued before the Court in the Fall of 2012, the justices indicated that they may be ready to prohibit any use of race in the college admissions process. As this textbook goes to press, the nation awaits the Court's decision in *Fisher v. University of Texas at Austin*.

Term arising out of this attempt by Michigan citizens to eliminate affirmative action programs.) In other states, however, attempts to pass laws or initiatives banning affirmative action failed, and in a few instances states actually enacted policies supporting the use of affirmative action programs.

GENDER-BASED DISCRIMINATION AND THE CONSTITUTION

Next to those based on race and national origin, classifications based on gender have raised the most questions. Sex-based classifications surely share with race and national origin many of the characteristics that caused the Court to consider them suspect. Gender is an essentially unalterable trait that has been the basis of legal and social stereotypes that discriminate against women. For much of our nation's history, women have been "relegated to a position of political powerlessness" (the formula Justice Powell used in determining suspect classifications; see Brief 10.1).

However, women are distinguished from racial and ethnic minorities in certain ways. Women do not constitute a "discrete and insular minority" group; in fact, they are the political majority. Women are found in every class in every neighborhood; they live and work in close physical contact with men. They share economic profits with men, but the same men also have advantages and control over them. Moreover, some generalizations about the differences between the sexes used to make distinctions in law are either benign or "protecting" of women, and a very few are based on factually valid biological distinctions between the sexes. As a result, the Supreme Court was slow in recognizing sex discrimination as a constitutional problem (see Brief 10.3). Table 10.1 presents the important cases, events, and laws that have contributed to the struggle for women's rights and gender equality.

Brief 10.3
THE LONG HISTORY OF WOMEN'S LEGAL INEQUALITY

Although the Declaration of Independence proclaimed all men to be created equal, few of the founding generation believed this generic "men" to include women. At the time, culture and religion required women to marry, and marriage laws denied women their property, their power, and even their identity. A married woman could not bind herself by contract and could not sue or be sued in court. Her husband gained complete control over all her real and personal property. He had the right to any wages she earned, and she was even required by law to assume his name upon marriage.

With its birth at Seneca Falls, New York, in 1848,[10] the women's-rights movement began to redress the subjugation of American women. This nascent feminist movement held out the hope that the Fourteenth Amendment, passed in 1868, was broad enough to cover women as well as newly freed blacks (insofar as it referred to "persons"). But congressional deliberations over the amendment reveal that even its supporters denied that it applied to women. In response to a question on the House floor asking whether the Fourteenth Amendment would put married women on the same footing as men, Thaddeus Stevens replied that as long as all married women were treated equally and all unmarried women treated equally, the demands of the Equal Protection Clause would be satisfied. Senator Poland of Vermont even commented that women would not need political or legal equality because "the fathers, husbands, brothers and sons to whom the right of suffrage is given will in its exercise be as watchful of the rights and interests of their wives, sisters, and children who do not vote as of their own."[11]

The Supreme Court moved quickly to confirm this opinion. In *Minor v. Happersatt* (1875), the justices unanimously decided that the Fourteenth Amendment did not guarantee women the right to vote.[12] And in *Bradwell v. Illinois* (1873), the Court upheld the Illinois Supreme Court's denial to Myra Bradwell of a license to practice law on the grounds that she was a woman. In a concurring opinion, Justice Joseph Bradley gave this now infamous reasoning for his affirmation of the state's sex discrimination:

> *The civil law, as well as nature herself, has always recognized a wide difference in the respective spheres and destinies of man and woman. Man is, or should be, woman's protector and defender. The natural and proper timidity and delicacy which belongs to the female sex evidently unfits it for many of the occupations of civil life. The constitution of the family organization, which is founded in the divine ordinance, as well as in the nature of things, indicates the domestic sphere as that which properly belongs to the domain and functions of womanhood. . . . It is true that many women are unmarried and not affected by any of the duties, complications, and incapacities arising out of the married state, but these are the exceptions to the general rule. The paramount*

destiny and mission of woman are to fulfill the noble and benign offices of wife and mother. This is the law of the Creator. And the rules of civil society must be adapted to the general constitution of things, and cannot be based upon exceptional cases.

Again in *Muller v. Oregon* (1908), the Court used "the woman's physical structure and the performance of maternal functions" as the primary justification for upholding a state maximum-hour law for women only (see Brief 8.4). With the passage of the Nineteenth Amendment in 1920 women won the right to vote, but it would take fifty-one more years for the Supreme Court to begin to extend the principle of equality to other areas of social and political life.[13] By the time the Supreme Court changed its position, Congress had already acted to rectify women's position of inequality, through a number of statutes barring sex discrimination, especially in the workplace (see Table 10.1).

Table 10.1 Development of the Law: Gender Equality

Year	Event	Significance
1873	*Bradwell v. Illinois*	Denied woman license to practice law on basis of sex.
1875	*Minor v. Happersatt*	Court ruled that the Fourteenth Amendment does not guarantee women the right to vote.
1908	*Muller v. Oregon*	Upheld state maximum-hour law applied to women only.
1920	Nineteenth Amendment	Gave women the right to vote in federal and state elections.
1923	Equal Rights Amendment first introduced	Would have granted women "equal rights throughout the United States and in every place subject to its jurisdiction."
1963	Equal Pay Act of 1963	Required equal pay for equal work regardless of sex.
1964	Title VII, Civil Rights Act	Prohibits sex discrimination in employment.
1971	*Reed v. Reed*	First time the Equal Protection Clause was used to strike down a law that classified on the basis of sex.
1972	Equal Rights Amendment reintroduced	Congress passed and sent to states for ratification amendment that would have guaranteed that "equality of rights . . . shall not be denied . . . on account of sex" (see Brief 10.6 for discussion).
1973	*Frontiero v. Richardson*	In ruling unconstitutional a federal law, four justices used the same strict scrutiny standard for sex that they use for race.
1974	*Geduldig v. Aiello*	Allowed state to provide differential treatment for pregnancy, even though only women were affected.
1979	*Mass. v. Feeney*	Upheld gender-neutral statute that had discriminatory disproportionate impact on women.
1981	*Michael M. v. Superior Court of Sonoma County*	Upheld statutory rape law that made criminal for young men what was not criminal for young women.
1982	*MUW v. Hogan*	Rejected decision by all-women's university to deny male admission to nursing school, further articulating the intermediate level of scrutiny used in sex equality cases.
1984	*Heckler v. Mathews*	Upheld Social Security plan that treated nondependent wives more preferentially than nondependent husbands.
1986	*Meritor Savings v. Vinson*	Ruled that sexual harassment was illegal sex discrimination.
1987	*Johnson v. Santa Clara County*	Upheld gender-based affirmative action promotion plan.
1996	*U.S. v. Virginia*	Declared unconstitutional the males-only admissions policy of the Virginia Military Institute.
1998	*Burlington v. Ellerth Farragher v. Boca Raton Oncale v. Sundowner Offshore Services*	Expanded sexual harassment protections under Title VII.
2000	*U.S. v. Morrison*	Ruled attempt by Congress to create federal civil remedies for victims of gender-motivated violence unconstitutional.

The Court's First Steps: *Reed* v. *Reed* and Progeny

The year 1971 marked the turning point in the Supreme Court's extension of equality to women. In *Reed v. Reed* (1971), the Court for the first time used the Equal Protection Clause to strike down a law that classified on the basis of sex. In question was an Idaho law that gave men an absolute preference over women as administrators of estates. When Richard Reed, a minor, died intestate in Ada County, Idaho, his separated parents, Cecil and Sally Reed, filed competing petitions in probate court to be declared administrator of their son's estate. In accord with the Idaho law, the probate court gave preference to Cecil Reed because he was male.

The Supreme Court invalidated the Idaho law. Chief Justice Burger, for the Court, stated:

> To give mandatory preference to members of either sex over members of the other, merely to accomplish the elimination of hearings on the merits, is to make the very kind of arbitrary legislative choice forbidden by the Equal Protection Clause of the Fourteenth Amendment.

Although the Court decided the question presented in *Reed* is based on a rationality-scrutiny standard, the justices' decision implied a stricter constitutional scrutiny toward sex discrimination. Of course, Congress had begun its hearings on the revived and reintroduced the Equal Rights Amendment (ERA) in 1970, and presented the amendment to the states in 1972, so the push for women's equality was all around the Court.

Two years later, in *Frontiero v. Richardson* (1973), the Court (or at least four justices) moved toward adopting a strict-scrutiny position on sex discrimination that would parallel its stance on race. The Court ruled against a federal law that automatically provided benefits to the wives of male members of the armed services but not to the husbands of female military personnel. Justice Brennan, writing on behalf of three other justices, began his opinion by stating:

> There can be no doubt that our Nation has had a long and unfortunate history of sex discrimination. Traditionally, such discrimination was rationalized by an attitude of "romantic paternalism" which, in practical effect, put women, not on a pedestal, but in a cage.

After chronicling the history of women's legal inequality, Justice Brennan reached the conclusion that sex discrimination ought to be regarded as suspect, along with race and national origin:

> With these considerations in mind, we can only conclude that classifications based upon sex, like classifications based upon race, alienage, or national origin, are inherently suspect, and must therefore be subjected to strict judicial scrutiny. Applying the analysis mandated by that stricter standard of review, it is clear that the statutory scheme now before us is constitutionally invalid.

The conclusions Justice Brennan reached in *Frontiero* brought the Court a long way in a short period of time. He did not represent the majority, however. Only four justices concluded that sex ought to be regarded as a suspect classification. For the other four justices who comprised the eight-member majority that declared the law invalid, the rationality standard announced in *Reed* provided ample justification. In fact, Justice Powell's concurring opinion indicated that for the Court to declare sex a suspect classification was premature, given the ratification debate over the ERA going on in the states.

The majority of justices, then, did not place gender classifications in the highest tier of the two-tier approach, to be given strict scrutiny. In 1976, a majority of the Court did accept a new standard of scrutiny for sex-based classifications, somewhere in between rationality and strict scrutiny. In *Craig v. Boren*, the Court invalidated sections of an Oklahoma law that allowed females to purchase 3.2 percent beer at age eighteen but prohibited males from doing so until they reached age twenty-one. For the majority, Justice Brennan declared that sex-based classifications would receive what has been termed "heightened"- or "intermediate"-level scrutiny, governed by the following standards:

> TO WITHSTAND CONSTITUTIONAL CHALLENGE, PREVIOUS CASES ESTABLISH THAT CLASSIFICATIONS BY GENDER MUST SERVE IMPORTANT GOVERNMENTAL OBJECTIVES AND MUST BE SUBSTANTIALLY RELATED TO ACHIEVEMENT OF THOSE OBJECTIVES.

Further articulation of the Court's position on gender discrimination has come from its two lone female justices. In *Mississippi University for Women v. Hogan* (1982), Justice O'Connor gave greater specificity to this "intermediate level of scrutiny" established in *Craig*. In an opinion for a five-justice majority that denied the right to an all women's university to discriminate against a male applicant to its nursing school, she declared that a state must demonstrate a "substantial relationship" between its "important governmental objectives" and the means it uses to achieve them:

> THE PURPOSE OF REQUIRING THAT CLOSE RELATIONSHIP IS TO ASSURE THAT THE VALIDITY OF A CLASSIFICATION IS DETERMINED THROUGH REASONED ANALYSIS RATHER THAN THROUGH THE MECHANICAL APPLICATION OF TRADITIONAL, OFTEN INACCURATE, ASSUMPTIONS ABOUT THE PROPER ROLES OF MEN AND WOMEN. THE NEED FOR THE REQUIREMENT IS AMPLY REVEALED BY REFERENCE TO THE BROAD RANGE OF STATUTES ALREADY INVALIDATED BY THIS COURT, STATUTES THAT RELIED UPON THE SIMPLISTIC, OUTDATED ASSUMPTION THAT GENDER COULD BE USED AS A "PROXY FOR OTHER, MORE GERMANE BASES OF CLASSIFICATION."

Justice Ginsburg, who as a lawyer litigated many of the earlier Court cases involving gender equality, added further clarification in *United States v. Virginia* (1996), in which the Court declared unconstitutional Virginia's attempt to maintain the males-only admission policy at the Virginia Military Institute. Drawing on but extending O'Connor's earlier language in *Mississippi Univ. for Women*, Ginsburg maintained that government classifications based on gender required "an exceedingly persuasive justification." In what some, including Justices Scalia and Rehnquist, saw as a tricky ratcheting up of the bar for gender-based discrimination, Justice Ginsburg called on the courts to take a very hard look at any law classifying on the basis of gender:

> "INHERENT DIFFERENCES" BETWEEN MEN AND WOMEN, WE HAVE COME TO APPRECIATE, REMAIN CAUSE FOR CELEBRATION, BUT NOT FOR DENIGRATION OF THE MEMBERS OF EITHER SEX OR FOR ARTIFICIAL CONSTRAINTS ON AN INDIVIDUAL'S OPPORTUNITY. SEX CLASSIFICATIONS MAY BE USED TO COMPENSATE WOMEN "FOR PARTICULAR ECONOMIC DISABILITIES SUFFERED," TO "PROMOTE EQUAL EMPLOYMENT OPPORTUNITY," TO ADVANCE FULL DEVELOPMENT OF THE TALENT AND CAPACITIES OF OUR NATION'S PEOPLE. BUT SUCH CLASSIFICATIONS MAY NOT BE USED AS THEY ONCE WERE, TO CREATE OR PERPETUATE THE LEGAL, SOCIAL, AND ECONOMIC INFERIORITY OF WOMEN.

Courts must be very skeptical of gender classifications, Ginsburg argued, because sex-segregated institutional arrangements like those at Virginia Military Institute have the tendency to deny to women, simply because they are women, full citizenship stature—"equal opportunity to aspire, achieve, participate in and contribute to society based on their individual talents and capacities."

In a series of cases beginning with *Reed*, then, the Supreme Court established that the Equal Protection Clause of the Fourteenth Amendment guaranteed women's equality. With these rulings, sex-based classifications would be treated as "somewhat suspect" and be given greater scrutiny by the Court than they had been given in the past. There have been setbacks for advocates of gender equality, including the case of *United States v. Morrison* (2000)—already discussed in Chapter 8—in which the Court struck down the Violence Against Women Act, a sweeping piece of legislation guaranteeing the right of "all persons . . . to be free from crimes of violence motivated by gender." Other limitations on women's equality have come in the area of employment discrimination, whose discussion follows.

SEX DISCRIMINATION IN EMPLOYMENT

Although most employment cases involve federal statutes and not the Constitution, the issue is worth exploring here because the workplace has been the biggest legal battleground in the war between the sexes. Title VII of the Civil Rights Act of 1964 prohibits employment discrimination on the basis of sex, as well as race, color, religion, or national origin.[14] Interestingly, sex-based discrimination was not part of the original draft of the bill and was added by southern representatives as an attempt to defeat the civil rights legislation! The biggest question for the courts in confronting claims of sex discrimination in employment has been determining what constitutes sex discrimination. In many cases, the Supreme Court has ruled in ways that limit the scope of Title VII to eliminate gender distinctions. The treatment of pregnancy in the workplace has been one such area (see Brief 10.4). Another area involves **disparate-impact legislation**, laws that are neutral on their face but that have a disproportionate impact on women. In *Personnel Administrator of Massachusetts v. Feeney* (1979), the Court upheld a law giving veterans absolute preference for employment in state civil service jobs, even though at the time 98 percent of Massachusetts veterans were male and a woman who had scored higher on competitive civil service exams was passed over in favor of male veterans. And in *Lorance v. AT & T Technologies* (1991), a Court majority dismissed a Title VII suit filed by women claiming that a facially neutral change in the company's seniority system was adopted for the purpose, and had the clear effect, of discriminating on the basis of sex.

A more recent decision also had the temporary effect of limiting the scope of enforcement of Title VII, specifically as it affects pay discrimination against women. In *Ledbetter v. Goodyear Tire and Rubber Co.* (2007), the Supreme Court made it much harder for women employees to sue for pay discrimination by strictly interpreting the time limitation for claims under the statute. Lily Ledbetter, the lone female supervisor at a Goodyear Tire plant in Alabama, sued after determining that her pay and raises had been lower compared with male colleagues at the company over a nineteen-year period. Although Title VII sets a 180-day limit on filing claims for "unlawful discrimination," the Equal Employment Opportunity

---

Brief 10.4
IS DIFFERENTIAL TREATMENT OF PREGNANCY SEX DISCRIMINATION?

The fact that women and not men can become pregnant is one of the few biological differences between the sexes. As such, the Supreme Court has at times allowed the differential treatment of pregnant women in the workplace. For instance, in *Geduldig v. Aiello* (1974), the Court majority rejected a claim that a California disability insurance plan violated the Equal Protection Clause because it excluded normal pregnancy from the list of disabilities that were covered. The Court's reasoning, in this case, was that an exclusion based on pregnancy was not a sex-based classification per se because the distinction was between pregnant and nonpregnant *persons* (which would include men and women!). The *Geduldig* decision was extended to similar challenges of employer disability schemes under Title VII of the Civil Rights Act in *General Electric Company v. Gilbert* (1976). Again, the majority, led by Justice Rehnquist, ruled that discrimination on the basis of pregnancy was not gender discrimination "as such," and could be shown to be "neutral" with no discriminatory effect under Title VII.

Congress specifically responded to the *Gilbert* decision, however, passing the Pregnancy Discrimination Act (PDA) as an amendment to Title VII. The PDA provides that "women affected by pregnancy, childbirth, or related medical conditions shall be treated the same for all employment-related purposes, including receipt of benefits under fringe benefit programs, as other persons not so affected but similar in their ability or inability to work." The Supreme Court's rulings on pregnancy and employment policy since the passage of the PDA have been mixed. In *California Federal Savings and Loan Association v. Guerra* (1987), the justices held that the PDA did not preempt California from passing legislation that gave preferential treatment to pregnant women. Later that year, the Court ruled that there was no discrimination based on pregnancy involved when the state of Missouri refused to pay unemployment benefits to a woman who lost her job when her employer would not rehire her after she attempted to return to work from a maternity leave.[15] Finally, in *International Union, UAW v. Johnson Controls, Inc.* (1991), the Court ruled against a company's blanket exclusion of all fertile female employees from certain jobs because of its concern for the health of the fetus the woman might conceive. Writing for the Court, Justice Blackmun argued that because

> *fertile men but not fertile women are given a choice as to whether they wish to risk their reproductive health for a particular job . . . [the company's] fetal protection policy explicitly discriminates against women on the basis of their sex.*

Passage in 1993 of the Family and Medical Leave Act, which requires businesses to provide up to twelve weeks a year of unpaid leave to workers caring for children or ill relatives or for their own medical problems, may help resolve some of the thorny legal issues surrounding pregnancy, parenting, and the workplace.

Commission (EEOC) had always interpreted the law, with lower federal court approval, to mean that the time limit would apply to any paycheck that reflected the initial discrimination. Ledbetter, who had not been made aware of her male colleagues' pay discrepancies until the time she filed claims through the EEOC, argued that this interpretation of the time limit ought to apply in her case. But Justice Alito, writing for a 5–4 majority, read Title VII literally, which meant that "any unlawful employment practice, including those involving compensation, must be presented within the [180-day] period prescribed by the statute." Justice Ginsburg, in a strongly worded dissent read directly from the bench, chastised the majority for being oblivious to the real-world employment practices Title VII was meant to cover: "The court does not comprehend, or is indifferent to, the insidious way in which women can be victims of pay discrimination." She urged Congress to correct what she saw as the Court's mistaken interpretation of Title VII. Within weeks, a bill titled the Lilly Ledbetter Fair Pay Act was introduced to reverse the Court's interpretation in this case, stating that the 180-day statute of limitations for filing an equal-pay lawsuit resets with each discriminatory paycheck. Passage of the law finally came early in the days of the Obama administration, in January 2009.

Sexual harassment in the workplace has been the one area in which the Supreme Court has been uniformly strong in its enforcement of laws against sex discrimination. In the 1970s feminists began arguing that sexual harassment is a form of sex discrimination,[16] and in line with this argument, the EEOC promulgated guidelines about what constitutes sexual harassment in the workplace. The Supreme Court first affirmed that sexual harassment was sex discrimination in violation of federal antidiscrimination law in its unanimous ruling in *Meritor Savings Bank v. Vinson* (1986). More important, the Court approved the extension of the definition of impermissible sexual harassment beyond *quid pro quo* sexual demands on the job to include unwelcome verbal or physical conduct of a sexual nature that creates a hostile working environment for the person harassed. Educational institutions have followed the *Meritor Bank* decision with sexual harassment codes that parallel those of the EEOC. Still, more than anything else, it was Anita Hill's charge of sexual harassment against Clarence Thomas—former head of the EEOC—during Senate confirmation hearings on his nomination to the Supreme Court that brought the whole issue of sexual harassment to the forefront of women's equity issues in the 1990s (see Brief 10.5).

What conclusions can be drawn from Table 10.1 and this discussion of cases involving sex discrimination? The Supreme Court has acted ambiguously in interpreting the Fourteenth Amendment's application to gender classifications. A majority of the justices agree that laws differentiating according to gender should receive heightened judicial scrutiny

---

Brief 10.5

THE EXPANSION OF SEXUAL HARASSMENT LAW IN THE 1990s

Although her appearance before the Senate Judiciary Committee in 1991 did not unseat Clarence Thomas from a place on the Supreme Court (see Brief 3.3), Anita Hill did raise public consciousness about the problem of sexual harassment on the job. In the year following her testimony, sexual harassment inquiries at the EEOC increased 150 percent, and actual charges filed jumped 50 percent over those of the previous year.

In a number of decisions in the 1990s, the Court not only affirmed the *Meritor* ruling, but went even farther to preclude harassing behavior in the workplace. In *Harris v. Forklift Systems, Inc.* (1993), the justices unanimously held that an employee does not have to show that harassing conduct seriously affects her or his psychological well-being to win a Title VII lawsuit. All that employees have to demonstrate is that the discriminatory sexual harassment was severe enough to "unreasonably interfere with [their] work performance." The Court followed this reasoning up further in *Burlington Industries Inc. v. Ellerth* (1998), ruling that employees could sue for sexual harassment even when they are unable to show any job-related harm. In *Farragher v. City of Boca Raton* (1998), the Court made it clear that employers are fully responsible for preventing and eliminating sexual harassment. In this case, the city was held liable for the harassing acts of a supervisory employee, even though his actions violated articulated city workplace policies and top management had no knowledge of his harassing behavior.[17] Finally, in *Oncale v. Sundowner Offshore Services* (1998), the justices ruled unanimously that the antidiscrimination provisions of Title VII cover sexual harassment by members of the same sex. Justice Scalia, writing for the Court, said that what matters is the conduct at issue, not the sex of the people involved or the presence or absence of sexual desire.

Brief 10.6

THE EQUAL RIGHTS AMENDMENT AND CONSTITUTIONAL EQUALITY FOR WOMEN

The Equal Rights Amendment (ERA) reads as follows:

1. Equality of rights under the law shall not be denied or abridged by the United States or by any State on account of sex.
2. The Congress shall have the power to enforce, by appropriate legislation, the provisions of this article.
3. This amendment shall take effect two years after the date of ratification.

After a fifty-year struggle to win congressional approval for an equal rights amendment, the House of Representatives (by a vote of 354–23) and the Senate (by a vote of 84–8) passed the ERA in 1972 and sent it on to the states for ratification. Congress gave the states seven years to ratify the amendment. Within the first year of passage, thirty of the required thirty-eight states had ratified the amendment. But there the process broke down. Over the next five years only five additional states had ratified the amendment, and three states sought to rescind their original enthusiastic approval of the ERA. Congress extended the original 1979 deadline by thirty-nine months, but, even at that, no additional states had ratified the ERA by June 1982, and the amendment died.[18] Thus, the U.S. Constitution remains "the only major written constitution that includes a bill of rights but lacks a provision explicitly declaring the equality of the sexes."[19]

What caused such a simple statement of egalitarian principles to fail? One argument holds that the Supreme Court's interpretation of the demands of the Fourteenth Amendment with respect to sex discrimination made an ERA unnecessary and redundant. Others contend that a very vocal minority succeeded in changing the discourse surrounding the ERA, making it into a women's military draft, unisex bathroom, abortion-enhancing, family-wrecking provision. Others partially fault the amendment's supporters, who often made radical claims for what the ERA would do, causing a decline in popular and state legislative support. Attempts have been and are being made to reintroduce the ERA in Congress, but for the present time, it lies dormant.[20] The ERA, if ever passed, would probably clarify the question of how to regard gender consistent with the ideal of equality. But even an ERA would require judicial interpretation and, given the current divisions on the Court, would still leave judges with the difficult task of deciding the difficult issues of pregnancy, affirmative action for women, and disparate-impact legislation.

---

and have invalidated laws containing explicit sex-based classifications that they believe operate to the detriment of women, especially when these laws have treated "similarly situated" men and women differently. But in the absence of explicit constitutional language guaranteeing sexual equality (see Brief 10.6), the Court majority has yet to conclude that gender-based classifications are suspect and, therefore, uniformly subjected to strict judicial scrutiny.

AGE DISCRIMINATION AND EQUALITY

The Court has never considered age-based classifications inherently suspect under the two-tier approach. Two Burger Court decisions exemplify the Court's approach to legislation that classifies by age. In *Massachusetts Board of Retirement v. Murgia* (1976), the Court upheld a state law requiring state police officers to retire at age fifty. Robert Murgia, an officer forced to retire even though he had just passed a rigorous physical and mental examination, challenged the law on equal protection grounds. But the Court, in a *per curiam* opinion, upheld the law using a lower-tier rationality standard:

WHILE THE TREATMENT OF THE AGED IN THIS NATION HAS NOT BEEN WHOLLY FREE OF DISCRIMINATION, SUCH PERSONS, UNLIKE, SAY, THOSE WHO HAVE BEEN DISCRIMINATED AGAINST ON THE BASIS OF RACE OR NATIONAL ORIGIN, HAVE NOT EXPERIENCED A "HISTORY OF PURPOSEFUL UNEQUAL TREATMENT" OR BEEN SUBJECTED TO UNIQUE DISABILITIES ON THE BASIS OF STEREOTYPED CHARACTERISTICS NOT TRULY INDICATIVE OF THEIR ABILITIES. [O]LD AGE DOES NOT DEFINE A "DISCRETE AND INSULAR" GROUP IN NEED OF "EXTRAORDINARY PROTECTION FROM THE MAJORITARIAN POLITICAL PROCESS." INSTEAD IT MARKS A STAGE THAT EACH OF US WILL REACH IF WE LIVE OUT OUR NORMAL LIFE SPAN. EVEN IF THE STATUTE COULD BE SAID TO IMPOSE A PENALTY UPON A CLASS DEFINED AS THE AGED, IT WOULD NOT IMPOSE A DISTINCTION SUFFICIENTLY AKIN TO THOSE CLASSIFICATIONS THAT WE HAVE FOUND SUSPECT TO CALL FOR STRICT JUDICIAL SCRUTINY.

Using a rationality standard, the Court decided that the state's announced purpose of protecting public safety "by assuring physical preparedness of its uniformed police" was a reasonable justification for the mandatory retirement scheme.

Three years later the Court reiterated its position that age was not a suspect classification. In *Vance v. Bradley* (1979), the Court sustained a federal law forcing Foreign Service personnel to retire at age sixty. It was reasonable for Congress to conclude, Justice Byron White said, "that age involves increased risks of less than superior performance in overseas assignments."

In lone dissenting opinions in each case, Justice Marshall took the opportunity to attack the rigid application of a two-tier analysis to equal protection. He claimed that the Court's adherence to this approach has meant that the Court almost always strikes down that limited class of laws subjected to strict scrutiny while almost always upholding all the rest under a rationality-scrutiny test. "The approach presents the danger that," Marshall stated in his *Murgia* dissent, "relevant factors will be misapplied or ignored. All interests not 'fundamental' and all classes not 'suspect' are not the same; and it is time for the Court to drop the pretense that, for the purposes of the Equal Protection Clause, they are." Instead of "suspectness" and "nonsuspectness," Marshall would have the Court focus on "the character of the classification in question, the relative importance to individuals in the class discriminated against of the governmental benefits that they do not receive, and the state interests asserted in support of the classification." Using this more flexible approach, Marshall would have voided automatic retirement for individuals based on their age alone.

While the Court has continued to disregard the aged as a suspect class, Congress has acted to prohibit age discrimination. The Age Discrimination in Employment Act of 1967 forbids employers from discriminating against employees because of age, and the Age Discrimination Act of 1975 prevents age discrimination in any program receiving federal funds.

NONCITIZENS AND THE EQUAL PROTECTION CLAUSE

The Fourteenth Amendment begins by stating that "[a]ll persons, born or naturalized in the United States, are citizens." Equal protection guarantees follow this statement, which begs the question of how to regard the equality claims of "aliens" (the language historically used by courts to describe the legal status of those individuals who are not U.S. citizens).

In the early 1970s, the Supreme Court elevated government classifications based on alienage to the highest tier of scrutiny under the Equal Protection Clause. For example, in *Graham v. Richardson* (1971), the Court ruled that states could not deny welfare benefits to aliens. Justice Blackmun announced the Court's rationale in making alienage a suspect classification:

> [C]LASSIFICATIONS BASED ON ALIENAGE, LIKE THOSE BASED ON NATIONALITY OR RACE, ARE INHERENTLY SUSPECT AND SUBJECT TO CLOSE JUDICIAL SCRUTINY. ALIENS AS A CLASS ARE A PRIME EXAMPLE OF A "DISCRETE AND INSULAR" MINORITY FOR WHOM SUCH HEIGHTENED JUDICIAL SOLICITUDE IS APPROPRIATE.

Blackmun then applied strict scrutiny to examine whether the State had a compelling interest in excluding aliens from receiving welfare benefits:

> [W]E CONCLUDE THAT A STATE'S DESIRE TO PRESERVE LIMITED WELFARE BENEFITS FOR ITS OWN CITIZENS IS INADEQUATE TO JUSTIFY [THE DENIAL OF WELFARE BENEFITS TO ALIENS]. AN ALIEN AS WELL AS A CITIZEN IS A "PERSON" FOR EQUAL PROTECTION PURPOSES; [A]LIENS LIKE CITIZENS PAY TAXES AND MAY BE CALLED INTO THE ARMED FORCES. THERE CAN BE NO "SPECIAL PUBLIC INTEREST" IN TAX REVENUES TO WHICH ALIENS HAVE CONTRIBUTED ON AN EQUAL BASIS WITH THE RESIDENTS OF THE STATE.

Subsequent to the *Graham* decision, the Court struck down a Connecticut law excluding aliens from practicing law,[21] state and federal laws restricting state civil service jobs to American citizens,[22] and a New York law preventing aliens from receiving financial aid for higher education.[23] And in *Plyler v. Doe* (1982), a case referred to earlier, the Court decided that Texas could not deny free public education to the children of undocumented aliens.

However, the Court does not always consider legal distinctions based on citizenship status to be suspect. In *Plyler v. Doe*, for example, Justice Brennan's majority opinion relied on intermediate scrutiny to invalidate Texas' denial of public education to noncitizens. And in numerous other cases, the Court, using the lower-tier rationality standard, has deferred to legislative restrictions on noncitizens. In 1978, the Court allowed a New York law barring aliens from employment as state troopers.[24] And in *Ambach v. Norwick* (1979), the justices sustained a New York statute forbidding state certification as a public school teacher to noncitizens, unless they have "manifested an intention to apply for citizenship." In *Ambach v. Norwick* the Court announced "the general principle that some state functions are so bound up with the operation of the State as governmental entity as to permit the exclusion from those functions of all persons who have not become part of the process of self-government."

Concerns about the export of international terrorism to the United States on the one hand and about employment opportunities in a time of economic hardship on the other have only created more opportunities to restrict the rights of noncitizens. After September 11, 2001, a number of restrictions were placed on both the legal status and the actual activities of foreign nationals. Executive orders and federal laws have been put into place to respond to terrorist threats, and many of these single out individuals—citizens and foreign nationals alike—on the basis of their country of origin. In addition, concerns about illegal immigration have caused many states to pass restrictions on benefits to undocumented foreign nationals. In 2010 in Arizona, the state legislature passed the most restrictive anti-immigration law in the country, making the failure to carry immigration documents a crime and requiring law enforcement officials to detain people they suspect are in the country illegally. In *Arizona v. United States* (2012), the Supreme Court upheld this one part of the Support Our Law Enforcement and Safe Neighborhoods Act (known as Arizona SB 1070), but struck down three other parts of the law, on the grounds that federal power over immigration preempted the state from enforcing such provisions (see Chapter 7 for a more extensive discussion of the Court's ruling). In light of this ruling, other states are considering enacting similar restrictions on suspected undocumented immigrants. At the same time, the 113th session of Congress has begun with a promise to enact major federal immigration reform, including a "path to citizenship" for the millions of undocumented immigrants currently living in the United States.

The current crisis over immigration has led many to question whether noncitizens as a class deserve anywhere near the same kind of "equal protection of the laws" that racial and ethnic minorities have been granted. After all, alienage is not an unalterable trait; noncitizens can voluntarily change their status, and as a result, gain equal rights. Moreover, noncitizens have been completely excluded by both the courts and the Constitution itself from voting and from attaining elected public office. Former Chief Justice Rehnquist once stated his objections succinctly: "[T]here is no language [or] any historical evidence as to the intent of the Framers [of the 14th Amendment], which would suggest in the slightest degree that it was intended to render alienage a 'suspect' classification. . . . [T]he Constitution itself recognizes a basic difference between citizens and aliens."[25]

DISABLED PERSONS AND THE EQUAL PROTECTION CLAUSE

Physically and mentally disabled persons have also pressed claims for equal protection of the laws. Many commentators believe that state actions discriminating against the disabled ought to be subjected to strict judicial scrutiny. After all, a disability is usually unalterable, often subjects its bearer to "invidious discrimination," and usually condemns him or her to a position of economic, social, and political powerlessness. Professor Judith Baer even argues that "the disabled are as powerless and isolated a minority as any group in American society."[26]

The Supreme Court has not yet seen fit to include the disabled as a suspect class, laws aimed at whom would require the Court's strict scrutiny. Still, the Court has come far in recognizing the problem of discrimination against persons with disabilities. Earlier in this century the justices enthusiastically approved a court order authorizing the sterilization of a "feebleminded" woman, proclaiming that "three generations of imbeciles are enough."[27] Today the Court has shown a willingness to invalidate unreasonable actions taken against disabled persons. However, the Court has not been willing to subject differential treatment of the disabled to any type of heightened scrutiny.

Justice White's opinion in *Cleburne v. Cleburne Living Center* (1985) exemplifies the Court's rationale for lower-tier analysis of classifications applying to the disabled:

> [I]T IS UNDENIABLE IN THAT THOSE WHO ARE MENTALLY RETARDED HAVE A REDUCED ABILITY TO COPE AND FUNCTION IN THE EVERYDAY WORLD.... THEY ARE THUS DIFFERENT, IMMUTABLY SO, IN RELEVANT RESPECTS, AND THE STATES' INTEREST IN DEALING WITH AND PROVIDING FOR THEM IS PLAINLY A LEGITIMATE ONE.

The *Cleburne* case is significant because the Court of Appeals for the Fifth Circuit had invalidated a city ordinance discriminating against the mentally challenged using an intermediate level of judicial scrutiny. The Supreme Court rejected the judgment that mental disability was a "quasi-suspect classification," using *Murgia* as its guide:

> THE LESSON OF *MURGIA* IS THAT WHERE INDIVIDUALS IN THE GROUP AFFECTED BY A LAW HAVE DISTINGUISHING CHARACTERISTICS RELEVANT TO INTERESTS THE STATE HAS THE AUTHORITY TO IMPLEMENT, THE COURTS HAVE BEEN VERY RELUCTANT... TO CLOSELY SCRUTINIZE LEGISLATIVE CHOICES AS TO WHETHER, HOW AND TO WHAT EXTENT THOSE INTERESTS SHOULD BE PURSUED. IN SUCH CASES, THE EQUAL PROTECTION CLAUSE REQUIRES ONLY A RATIONAL MEANS TO SERVE A LEGITIMATE END.

A majority of the Supreme Court, then, has concluded that because of real differences between disabled and nondisabled persons, the Equal Protection Clause only requires that judges exercise rationality scrutiny when ruling on legislation affecting persons with disabilities.

Congress, however, has acted forcefully to protect the disabled from discrimination and to provide them with access to various institutions essential to their goal of equal opportunity. For example, in the Rehabilitation Act of 1973, Congress provided that "no otherwise qualified handicapped individual . . . shall, solely by reason of his handicap, be excluded from participation, be denied the benefits of, or be subjected to discrimination under any program or activity receiving federal financial assistance." In 1975, Congress passed the Education of All Handicapped Children Act (since amended as the Individuals with Disabilities Education Act), which establishes for "all disabled children the right to a free appropriate public education," and provides federal funds to ensure that end.[28] The culmination of Congressional activity came in 1990, when the Americans with Disabilities Act (ADA) was passed, a sweeping law aimed at eliminating discrimination against individuals with disabilities (see Brief 10.7).

SEXUAL ORIENTATION AND THE CONSTITUTION

For three decades, gay men and lesbians have challenged laws that discriminate on the basis of a person's sexual orientation. Challenges to the constitutionality of state sodomy laws (which often apply to heterosexuals as well) on the grounds that they violate right to privacy guarantees are discussed in the following chapter. Here we examine equal protection challenges to state and federal statutes that differentiate on the basis of sexual orientation. Advocates of gay rights have asked the courts to consider whether sexual orientation should be a suspect classification calling for heightened scrutiny under the Fourteenth Amendment. Their argument holds that, like racial and ethnic minorities, gay men, lesbians, and bisexuals have been subjected to a history of purposeful discrimination, based on an immutable trait. An individual's sexuality has historically been the basis for legal and social stereotypes that deny equality, and given their minority political status, gay men, lesbians, and bisexuals have been traditionally "relegated to a position of political powerlessness." In addition to the arguments that sexual orientation should be considered a suspect classification, a few constitutional scholars contend that discrimination against homosexuals should be treated as a form of sex discrimination, because laws prohibiting same-sex relationships punish on the basis of the sex of the individuals involved. Under this argument, a law that prohibited or punished sexual relations between persons of the same sex would be guilty of imposing a quasi-suspect, sex-based classification, a reasoning similar to that used to declare miscegenation laws unconstitutional in the 1960s.[30]

Brief 10.7
THE SCOPE AND ENFORCEMENT OF THE ADA

When the ADA went into effect in 1992, disability-rights activists were optimistic about its potential impact on the estimated forty million Americans who have one or more physical or mental disabilities. Title I of the Act sets down enforceable standards to address employment discrimination against the disabled, and Title II provides that "no qualified individual with a disability shall, by reason of such disability, be excluded from participation in or denied the benefits of the services, programs, or activities of a public entity." Title III requires employers, educational institutions, and transportation systems to alter their existing facilities, restructure examinations and other materials, and modify equipment to provide "reasonable accommodations" to disabled persons. Moreover, the law offered disabled citizens who had been discriminated against recourse to sue for damages and equitable relief, and offered an expansive notion of what counted as a disability.[29]

Critics of the law, especially businesses and state officials, are concerned that it is overinclusive in its reach and overly costly in its implementation. (This criticism even spilled into popular culture, where in an episode of *The Simpsons* Homer tried to become so obese that he would be exempt under the ADA from a mandatory workplace fitness program!) But concerns also abound about the effective enforcement of the law, especially in light of studies showing that judges overwhelmingly tend to side with businesses in claims filed by individuals under the ADA. The Supreme Court's decision in the *Garrett* case, where it ruled that a state's sovereign immunity protected it from ADA lawsuits by employees under Title I, suggested that it would limit Congressional authority to prevent discrimination against the disabled (see Chapter 8 for more detailed coverage).

But two more recent decisions have swung the other way. In *Tennessee v. Lane* (2004), the Court, by a slim 5–4 majority, upheld citizens' rights to sue state governments for failures to abide by the demands of Article II of the ADA, even in the face of the Eleventh Amendment. In this case, two paraplegics—a criminal defendant and a court reporter—filed actions for damages against the state of Tennessee. In a decision focused more on the Due Process Clause than the Equal Protection Clause of the Fourteenth Amendment, Justice Stevens, writing for the majority, argued that Congress had the authority to act on behalf of disabled citizens denied their fundamental right of access to the courts (see Chapter 11 for discussion of fundamental rights under the Due Process Clause). In a separate concurring opinion, Justice Ginsburg put it this way:

> Legislation calling upon all government actors to respect the dignity of individuals with disabilities is entirely compatible with our Constitution's commitment to federalism.

And in *Spector v. Norwegian Cruise Line* (2005), the Court ruled that foreign cruise lines operating in U.S. waters had to abide by the accommodations provisions of Title III of the ADA. Justice Kennedy, also for a 5–4 majority, wrote that "to hold that there is no protection for disabled persons who seek to use the amenities of foreign cruise ships would be a harsh and unexpected interpretation of a statute designed to provide broad protection for the disabled."

In 1996, the Supreme Court gave some hope to those fighting discrimination on the basis of sexual orientation, declaring unconstitutional a state's attempt to nullify civil rights protections for gays and lesbians. In question was an attempt by citizens in Colorado to amend the state constitution to disallow all actions at any level of state or local government—past or future—to grant legal protections to persons on the basis of "homosexual, lesbian, or bisexual orientation, conduct, practices, or relationships." Amendment 2, as the provision passed by a 1992 statewide referendum was known in Colorado, was a response by a coalition of groups to local ordinances adopted in Aspen, Boulder, and Denver prohibiting discrimination on the basis of sexual orientation. In *Romer v. Evans* (1996), a six-justice majority ruled that this state constitutional amendment violated the Equal Protection Clause.

Writing for the majority, Justice Kennedy argued that the amendment could not stand up even under a rational scrutiny standard. Quoting Justice Harlan's dissent in *Plessy*, that the Constitution "neither knows nor tolerates classes among citizens," Kennedy ruled that the Colorado amendment was aimed exclusively at disadvantaging a particular group based solely on their sexual orientation, which had to be justified by some rational relationship to a legitimate governmental purpose. Seeing none, the majority was left to infer "that the disadvantage imposed is born of animosity" toward gays and lesbians, something the Court could not countenance consistent with the Fourteenth Amendment.

> WE MUST CONCLUDE THAT AMENDMENT 2 CLASSIFIES HOMOSEXUALS NOT TO FURTHER A PROPER LEGISLATIVE END BUT TO MAKE THEM UNEQUAL TO EVERYONE ELSE. THIS COLORADO CANNOT DO. A STATE CANNOT SO DEEM A CLASS OF PERSONS A STRANGER TO ITS LAWS.

Brief 10.8

EQUAL PROTECTION AND SAME-SEX MARRIAGE

When Vermont passed legislation in 2000 allowing same-sex couples to obtain a certificate of "civil union," granting them "the same benefits, protections, and responsibilities under law . . . as are granted to spouses in a marriage," a national debate was initiated. Because the Vermont law had been ordered by a state supreme court ruling determining that the previous marriage law unconstitutionally discriminated against same-sex couples, it raised questions about whether gays and lesbians might find similar support from federal judges under the U.S. Constitution. In fact, Justice Scalia warned the Court that the reasoning in its 2003 ruling against state sodomy laws (see the discussion of *Lawrence v. Texas* in Chapter 11) "leaves on pretty shaky grounds state laws limiting marriage to opposite-sex couples."

Justice Scalia's somewhat prophetic warning would come true less than a year later. In Massachusetts, the state's highest court ruled that there could be no legal barriers to gay marriage consistent with the equal rights provisions of the state constitution. Gay marriages began taking place May 17, 2004, exactly fifty years after the *Brown* decision. Following the 2012 election, when the citizens of three states approved marriage equality laws and three other state legislatures quickly passed legislation, twelve states and the District of Columbia currently allow couples of the same sex to marry. In six others same-sex civil unions are accorded all or most of the rights and privileges of marriage. As this text goes to press, over 130,000 legally married same-sex couples are living in the United States.

On the other hand, the majority of states in 2013 ban marriage between couples of the same sex, and over the past decade voters in twenty-nine states have overwhelmingly approved state constitutional amendments limiting marriage to heterosexuals, including California, where same-sex marriage had been made legal by the State Supreme Court. And the federal Defense of Marriage Act (DOMA), passed in 1996, defines marriage for purposes of federal law as the legal union between one man and one woman, and protects states from having to recognize same-sex marriages performed in other states.

The Supreme Court recently heard two cases challenging restrictions to same-sex marriage on Equal Protection grounds. In *Hollingsworth v. Perry*, the justices were asked to rule on the constitutionality of California's Proposition 8, the initiative prohibiting same-sex marriage and overturning a State Supreme Court ruling. In *United States v. Windsor*, the Court was presented with the constitutionality of the federal DOMA law. As this textbook goes to press, we await what could be major rulings on the constitutional right to marry for gay and lesbian couples—or not (see Chapter 3).

In a stinging and vigorous dissent, Justice Scalia accused the Court majority of taking sides in the "culture wars" through a subjective "act not of judicial judgment but of political will." Declaring that Amendment 2 had been adopted by the "most democratic of procedures," Scalia argued that Colorado's voters had a legitimate right to prohibit giving gays and lesbians "favored status because of their homosexual conduct," especially in light of the precedent set by *Bowers v. Hardwick*.

Combined with the more recent decision in *Lawrence v. Texas* (to be discussed in Chapter 11), the Court's decision in *Romer v. Evans* may pave the way for more rulings protecting the constitutional rights of gay, lesbian, bisexual, and transgendered citizens. A number of state legislatures have begun to include sexual orientation among the list of characteristics that cannot be the basis of discrimination. Over half of the states (thirty-one states and the District of Columbia) ban at least some forms of workplace discrimination on the basis of sexual orientation or gender identity, and an increasing number now permit marriage or "civil unions" between same-sex couples (see Brief 10.8). Changes also have occurred in the U.S. military, where a long-standing policy barring those who are openly lesbian, gay, or bisexual from military service was recently repealed by Congress.

THE EQUAL PROTECTION CLAUSE AND THE POOR: WEALTH CLASSIFICATIONS, POVERTY, AND THE FUNDAMENTAL "NECESSITIES OF LIFE"

Buoyed by the Court's new equal protection analysis, poor people have tried to redress economic inequalities. To this end, lawyers representing the economically disadvantaged have brought constitutional claims to the courts under the Equal Protection Clause. They have argued that wealth should be regarded as a suspect classification, and that certain "necessities of life" are fundamental rights to be provided to all regardless of ability to pay. As this section indicates, the Court has been reluctant to extend strict-scrutiny status to legislative programs that burden indigent persons. For most purposes, discrimination against the poor on the basis of their wealth alone draws only minimal scrutiny under the Equal Protection Clause.

From one perspective, the Court's refusal to make economic inequality a constitutional issue seems justified. After all, a capitalist society based on a relatively free market is premised on the assumption that persons pay the full market price for the goods they receive. Inequalities in the distribution of wealth and other economic goods are seen as perfectly legitimate. Moreover, looking at the constitutional question of poverty, the framers of the Equal Protection Clause never intended it to touch the unequal distribution of income. Indeed, as Federal Judge Ralph K. Winter commented:

> THE FOURTEENTH AMENDMENT WAS ENACTED AT A POINT IN AMERICAN HISTORY WHEN NOTIONS OF LAISSEZ-FAIRE AND SOCIAL DARWINISM WERE ABOUT TO PEAK.... THE AMENDMENT WAS NOT DESIGNED TO REDUCE INEQUALITY IN THE SOCIETY GENERALLY OR TO SERVE AS A DEVICE BY WHICH GOVERNMENT MIGHT BE COMPELLED TO TAKE STEPS TO BRING ABOUT ECONOMIC EQUALITY. NEITHER THE MEN INVOLVED NOR THE SPIRIT OF THE TIMES FAVORED SOCIAL OR ECONOMIC EQUALITY, MUCH LESS THE NOTION THAT GOVERNMENT HAD RESPONSIBILITIES TO REWORK SOCIETY ALONG EGALITARIAN LINES.[31]

Even under the newer equal protection guidelines of today, wealth-based classifications would not seem to be suspect. Poverty is not an inalterable trait, and economic inequalities in society may indeed act as incentives to increase productivity and economic progress among all classes, including the poor. Unlike race, poverty has not been the basis of laws that systematically discriminate, nor have poor people as a class been "saddled with such disabilities" as to relegate them "to a position of political powerlessness."

From another perspective, however, a case can be made for heightened judicial scrutiny of wealth-based classifications. One's poverty can hamper access to the legal and political processes of American society. Furthermore, certain fundamental rights may be effectively denied if wealth is a criterion for their enjoyment. Frank Michelman, a consistent advocate of "minimum protection" for the poor, puts it this way:

> TO BE HUNGRY, AFFLICTED, ILL-EDUCATED, ENERVATED, AND DEMORALIZED BY ONE'S MATERIAL CIRCUMSTANCES OF LIFE IS NOT ONLY TO BE PERSONALLY DISADVANTAGED IN COMPETITIVE POLITICS, BUT ALSO, QUITE POSSIBLY, TO BE IDENTIFIED AS A MEMBER OF A GROUP—CALL IT "THE POOR"—THAT HAS BOTH SOME CHARACTERISTIC POLITICAL AIMS AND VALUES AND SOME VULNERABILITY TO HAVING ITS NATURAL FORCE OF NUMBERS SYSTEMATICALLY SUBORDINATED IN THE PROCESSES OF POLITICAL INFLUENCE AND MAJORITARIAN COALITION-BUILDING.

With this preliminary discussion in mind, the contemporary judicial history concerning poverty and the Fourteenth Amendment is examined.

POVERTY AS A POTENTIALLY SUSPECT CLASS: THE WARREN COURT

The first suggestion that the Court might regard wealth as a suspect classification occurred in a concurring opinion by Justice Robert H. Jackson in *Edwards v. California* (1941). Jackson argued that a California law that made it a crime to bring a nonresident indigent into the state illegitimately discriminated against the poor:

> WE SHOULD SAY NOW, AND IN NO UNCERTAIN TERMS THAT A MAN'S MERE PROPERTY STATUS, WITHOUT MORE, CANNOT BE USED BY A STATE TO TEST, QUALIFY, OR LIMIT HIS RIGHTS AS A CITIZEN OF THE UNITED STATES.... THE MERE STATE OF BEING WITHOUT FUNDS IS A NEUTRAL FACT—CONSTITUTIONALLY AN IRRELEVANCE, LIKE RACE, CREED, OR COLOR.

The Warren Court built on Justice Jackson's words in a series of cases dealing with wealth-based legislative schemes. *Griffin v. Illinois* (1956) held that states must provide indigent defendants with a free copy of trial transcripts necessary for filing a criminal appeal. Justice Black said, "In criminal trials a state can no more discriminate on account of poverty than on account of religion, race, or color." In *Douglas v. California* (1963), the Court ruled that indigent defendants had a right to court-appointed lawyers on their first criminal appeal. Reiterating its position in *Griffin*, the majority said, "[T]here can be no equal justice where the kind of an appeal a man enjoys 'depends on the amount of money he whas.'"

Justice Douglas's opinion in *Harper v. Virginia Board of Elections* (1966) (discussed in Chapter 11) suggested that the Warren Court was willing to elevate all wealth-based classifications to the highest tier of scrutiny under the new equal protection analysis. In an oft-quoted passage, Douglas stated, "Lines drawn on the basis of wealth, like those of race, are traditionally disfavored." Three years later Chief Justice Warren echoed these sentiments, stating that "a careful examination on our part is especially warranted where lines are drawn on the basis of wealth or race, two factors which independently render a classification highly suspect and thereby demand a more exacting judicial scrutiny."[32] Finally, Justice Brennan's opinion in *Shapiro v. Thompson* (see Chapter 11), which talked of "food, shelter and other necessities of life," gave support to those who would use fundamental rights analysis to guarantee "minimum protection" for the poor.

In retrospect, however, the Warren Court's rhetoric never reflected a majority consensus on the suspect status of wealth classifications. Those seeking equal justice for the poor could only point to possibilities implicit in certain justices' words. In fact, the Court had only applied strict scrutiny to indigency-based classification schemes when such schemes threatened either the right to vote or access to the state's criminal justice system (both declared fundamental interests under the Warren Court). The Warren Court never invalidated a law solely because it had a differential economic impact on citizens. Still, the possibilities existed for heightened judicial scrutiny of economic inequalities during the Warren era. These possibilities were immediately dashed under the Burger Court.

THE RETURN TO RATIONALITY SCRUTINY: THE BURGER COURT

Chief Justice Burger's arrival on the Supreme Court marked the narrowing of equal protection doctrine with regard to the poor. In both its rhetoric and its rulings, the Burger Court denied the claims of equal protection for poor people as a class. This judicial restraint in dealing with statutes differentiating on the basis of wealth can be seen in cases as early as *Dandridge v. Williams* (1970).

The *Dandridge* case involved Maryland's provision under a joint federal–state Aid to Families with Dependent Children program that no matter how large the family seeking aid, the maximum welfare payment could not exceed $250 a month. Linda Williams sued in federal court, contending that the maximum grant regulations denied members of large families both equal protection and the fundamental necessities of life. The Supreme Court upheld Maryland's welfare provision. Justice Stewart, writing for the majority, ruled that because this law "deal[t] with state regulation in the social and economic field, not affecting freedoms guaranteed by the Bill of Rights," rationality scrutiny was all that the Court need employ in making its judgment. Using this standard, Stewart found Maryland's welfare regulations rationally related to legitimate state interests "in encouraging gainful employment, in maintaining an equitable balance in economic status between welfare families and those supported by a wage earner, in providing incentives for family planning, and in allocating available public funds in such a way as fully to meet the needs of the largest possible number of families." Justice Stewart concluded by stating that the Court should not use the Equal Protection Clause to second-guess state legislatures on what constitutes wise economic and welfare policy: "[T]he Equal Protection Clause does not require that a State must choose between attacking every aspect of a problem or not attacking the problem at all."

The Court followed Dandridge with two rulings denying housing rights to indigent citizens,[33] moving quickly to head off any claims by the poor calling for strict scrutiny of state programs that disproportionately burdened them. Probably no case better illustrates the Burger Court's position on wealth-based classifications than *San Antonio School District v. Rodriguez* (1973). A detailed analysis of this case follows.

RATIONALITY SCRUTINY CONFIRMED: *SAN ANTONIO SCHOOL DISTRICT V. RODRIGUEZ*

In 1973, public schools in the United States were financed primarily through local property taxes. State and federal expenditures for education had increased over the years, but large differentials in public school funding still existed, with richer property tax–based districts spending more money on public education and poorer districts spending less. The Rodriguez family lived in the Edgewood district of San Antonio, Texas, a poor, predominantly Hispanic neighborhood. The per-pupil expenditures in Edgewood schools were barely half those spent on students in another part of town, the Alamo Heights district. Demetrio Rodriguez filed a class-action suit on behalf of his children and other children across the state who were being deprived of equal educational opportunities by Texas's property-tax system of school finance. Rodriguez claimed that the Texas system of financing public education violated the Equal Protection Clause, for two reasons: (1) it discriminated on the basis of wealth, by providing children in wealthy districts with a higher-quality education than those in poorer districts; and (2) since public education was acknowledged to be a fundamental interest that the state should provide to all its citizens without regard to their ability to pay for it, inequalities in school finance violated the equal protection rights of poor schoolchildren across Texas.

The Supreme Court, however, rejected the claim that "the Texas system of financing public education operates to the disadvantage of some suspect class or impinges upon a fundamental right explicitly or implicitly protected by the Constitution, thereby requiring strict judicial scrutiny." Justice Powell's majority opinion first disposed of the claim that wealth was a suspect classification. Powell denied that the Texas public school finance system operated to the disadvantage of any "suspect class" of poor persons. The poor, he said, are not always congregated in the poorest property districts; they may live around major industrial or commercial centers that do contribute substantial property tax income to the public schools. Moreover, the alleged discrimination against the poor was relative. No claim was made that children in poorer school districts were denied public education altogether; the only charge made was that "they are receiving a poorer quality education than that available to children in districts having more assessable wealth." In response to the relative deprivation contention, Powell explained that "at least where wealth is involved, the Equal Protection Clause does not require absolute equality or precise equal advantages." He concluded that "the Texas system does not operate to the peculiar disadvantage of any suspect class," leaving a general standard of suspectness against which future justices could measure equal protection claims:

> THE SYSTEM OF ALLEGED DISCRIMINATION AND THE CLASS IT DEFINES HAVE NONE OF THE TRADITIONAL INDICIA OF SUSPECTNESS: THE CLASS IS NOT SADDLED WITH SUCH DISABILITIES, OR SUBJECTED TO SUCH A HISTORY OF PURPOSEFUL UNEQUAL TREATMENT, OR RELEGATED TO SUCH A POSITION OF POLITICAL POWERLESSNESS AS TO COMMAND EXTRAORDINARY PROTECTION FROM THE MAJORITARIAN POLITICAL PROCESS.

Of course, there still remained the question of whether education was a fundamental right, which would also cause the Court to exercise strict scrutiny (see Chapter 11). For this claim the Rodriguez lawyers drew on numerous Supreme Court rulings, most prominently this passage from the original *Brown* decision:

> TODAY, EDUCATION IS PERHAPS THE MOST IMPORTANT FUNCTION OF STATE AND LOCAL GOVERNMENTS. COMPULSORY SCHOOL ATTENDANCE LAWS AND THE GREAT EXPENDITURES FOR EDUCATION BOTH DEMONSTRATE OUR RECOGNITION OF THE

IMPORTANCE OF EDUCATION TO OUR DEMOCRATIC SOCIETY.... IN THESE DAYS, IT IS DOUBTFUL THAT ANY CHILD MAY REASONABLY BE EXPECTED TO SUCCEED IN LIFE IF HE IS DENIED THE OPPORTUNITY OF AN EDUCATION. SUCH AN OPPORTUNITY, WHERE THE STATE HAS UNDERTAKEN TO PROVIDE IT, IS A RIGHT WHICH MUST BE MADE AVAILABLE TO ALL ON EQUAL TERMS.

Justice Powell acknowledged these earlier Court statements about the importance of education, but he denied that they established education as a fundamental constitutional right: "The importance of a service performed by the state does not determine whether it must be regarded as fundamental for purposes of examination under the Equal Protection Clause." Powell then proceeded to put a damper on the Court's use of fundamental rights reasoning under the Fourteenth Amendment:

IT IS NOT THE PROVINCE OF THIS COURT TO CREATE SUBSTANTIVE CONSTITUTIONAL RIGHTS IN THE NAME OF GUARANTEEING EQUAL PROTECTION OF THE LAWS. THUS, THE KEY TO DISCOVERING WHETHER EDUCATION IS "FUNDAMENTAL"... LIES IN ASSESSING WHETHER THERE IS A RIGHT TO EDUCATION EXPLICITLY OR IMPLICITLY GUARANTEED BY THE CONSTITUTION.

Powell concluded that there was not such a constitutional guarantee of education as a fundamental right.

Having dismissed the arguments for strict scrutiny, the Court's only question was whether the Texas system of school finance bore "some rational relationship to legitimate state purposes." Stressing "the traditional limitations of this Court's function," Powell upheld Texas's use of property-tax revenues to fund the public schools. Any educational inequities resulting from such a system, Powell said, would be a legislative, not a judicial, problem; solutions to it "must come from the lawmakers and from the democratic pressures of those who elect them."[34]

In a long and memorable dissent, Justice Marshall attacked the majority on all points of its opinion. Using the *Brown* decision as his backdrop, Marshall began his dissent by saying that "the right of every American to an equal start in life, so far as the provision of a state service as important as education is concerned, is far too vital to permit state discrimination on grounds as tenuous as those presented by this record." Marshall continued by addressing the majority's denial of strict-scrutiny status to the Rodriguez claims. He asserted that Texas's program of public school finance clearly had a discriminatory impact on an identifiable "class" of people. Moreover, he rejected the majority's conclusion that inequalities in education would not deny equal protection so long as children were not completely denied public education.

In addition, Marshall took offense at Powell's claim that only rights explicitly or implicitly guaranteed in the Constitution were fundamental. Where, he queried, does the Constitution "guarantee the right to procreate . . . or the right to vote in state elections . . . or the right to an appeal from a criminal conviction?"—all of which the Court had previously said to be fundamental rights. Marshall believed that equal educational opportunity certainly qualified for constitutional protection under the Fourteenth Amendment and was being denied by Texas in this instance.

The Supreme Court's ruling in *San Antonio School District v. Rodriguez* (1973) did not put an end to litigation aimed at eliminating unequal public school financing, as many might have predicted. Individuals challenging inequities in public school spending have been able to find provisions in state constitutions to support their claims. Since the *Rodriguez* decision, over thirty state supreme courts have ruled on the constitutional adequacy of public school financing schemes, and in half of those decisions the existing educational funding systems have been struck down, including Texas, where the state supreme court has been issuing opinions since 1989. This "judicial federalism" has had a great impact on the equalization of per-pupil expenditures in a number of states, as well as the way legislatures are choosing to finance public education.[35]

Still, as this analysis of cases concerning indigent claimants shows, the Court has generally refused to grant special status to equal protection claims brought by the poor. The Court only acts with strict scrutiny when individuals are denied constitutionally based fundamental rights on the basis of their lack of wealth.[36] To use the justices' own words, "this Court has held repeatedly that poverty, standing alone, is not a suspect classification."[37] And attempts by the poor to make equal protection claims on the basis of implicit fundamental rights (e.g., to welfare, housing, medical care, and education) have uniformly failed to win the Court's acceptance.[38] The Supreme Court's continued reluctance to include the poor among those especially protected by the Equal Protection Clause has puzzled many constitutional scholars. Laurence Tribe has characterized the Court's position on the poor as "minimal protection of the laws, with some of us very much more equal than others."[39]

EQUAL PROTECTION AND REFORM OF THE ELECTORAL SYSTEM: *BUSH V. GORE*

Bush v. Gore (2000) undoubtedly will go down as one of the most significant Supreme Court decisions in recent times, if only because of its impact on the outcome of a presidential election. Chapter 4 already has treated the Court's decision as it affects our understanding of the power of judicial review. The decision also may have consequences for equality in the U.S. electoral system.

As discussed earlier, the Court majority rested its case against the Florida Supreme Court primarily on its violation of the Equal Protection Clause. While the majority's *per curiam* opinion admitted that "[t]he individual citizen has no federal constitutional right" to vote for presidential electors, it stated that "when the state legislature vests the right to vote for President in its people, the right to vote . . . is fundamental." Building on Warren Court–era voting rights rulings (see Chapter 11), the court indicated that equality in the fundamental right to vote means more than merely allocating the franchise on an equal basis. It also extends to how each vote is treated after ballots are cast: "Having once granted the right to vote on equal terms, the State may not, by later arbitrary and disparate treatment, value one person's vote over that of another." In this instance, the Florida Supreme Court had ordered a manual ballot recount without uniform standards, where decisions about which votes to count "might vary not only from county to county, but indeed within a single county from one recount team to another." To the majority of the justices, the equal protection issues were clear: "When a court orders a statewide remedy, there must be at least some assurance that the rudimentary requirements of equal treatment and fundamental fairness are satisfied."

What are the broader Equal Protection implications of this decision? What might need to change in our federal election system to guarantee a citizen's equality in the right to vote and to have that vote count equally in an election? The Court itself tried to downplay any wider impact of this case. "Our consideration is limited to the present circumstances, for the problem of equal protection in election processes generally presents many complexities." Most constitutional scholars agree that the current Court majority—which has generally acted to limit the further reach of the Constitution in advancing the interests of historically burdened groups in the United States—is unlikely to turn to *Bush v. Gore* to launch expansive Equal Protection rulings.[40]

Still, the election of 2000 revealed a number of significant problems in the way different voting systems treat voters differently. From the electoral college to outdated voter registration procedures and lists to often unintelligible voting instructions to variations in ballot design to problems with receiving and recording absentee ballots, the American system is rife with potential equal protection violations. A rash of lawsuits were filed in the aftermath of *Bush v. Gore*, and Congress moved quickly to solve some of these problems by passing the Help America Vote Act in 2002 (see Brief 10.9).

On a related equal protection issue, critics of the Court's decision, including some of the dissenting justices in the case, maintain that the majority's opinion had the effect of privileging some voters' equal protection claims over others. In Florida, votes that remained uncounted after *Bush v. Gore* tended to come from districts in which minority voters were concentrated. The U.S. Commission on Civil Rights study on irregularities in the Florida 2000 election reported that minority voters were ten times more

Brief 10.9

ELECTORAL REFORM IN THE AFTERMATH OF THE 2000 ELECTION

In light of the overall concerns raised by the 2000 presidential election, most publicly—but not exclusively—in Florida, a prestigious National Commission of Federal Election Reform was created, with former presidents Gerald Ford and Jimmy Carter serving as honorary co-chairs. The Commission presented its final report to Congress and President Bush in July 2001. A year later, Congress, with broad bipartisan support, passed the Help America Vote Act (HAVA), adopting most of the commission's recommendations. HAVA requires all the states to reform a number of aspects concerning the way they run elections and appropriates federal funding to help them. The law includes the following reforms:

- Every state must adopt a system of statewide voter registration;
- Every state must permit "provisional voting" by any voter who claims to be qualified to vote in that state;
- Each state must adopt uniform, nondiscriminatory standards for defining what will count as a "vote" on each category of voting equipment certified for use in that state;
- Each state must have at every polling place a voting system that is accessible to individuals with disabilities, and provides such individuals with the same opportunities for participation and privacy afforded to other voters;
- Each state should meet certain requirements for voters who register and/or vote by mail;
- Each state must improve its voter education and poll worker recruitment and training programs.

All of HAVA's provisions went into effect in January 2006, but even new standards regarding voting equipment systems and federal funding to improve election equipment and administration have not stopped critics from questioning how much the law has improved the conduct of elections and the equal protection concerns expressed by many citizens. A number of studies citing failures in state election systems and administration, particularly affecting minority voters and precincts, surfaced problems in each national election since 2002. And two of the national commission's recommendations went unheeded: (1) that each state should restore voting rights to those convicted of felonies once they have served their sentence; and (2) that Congress should enact legislation to hold presidential and congressional elections on a national holiday, to increase the availability of poll workers and suitable polling places as well as to make voting easier for some workers. The question of voting rights for convicted felons is discussed in Chapter 11.

---

likely not to have their votes correctly counted than were nonminority voters. Ironically, then, the Court's equal protection decision may have indicated the interests of politically powerful middle-class voters, at the expense of those who were intended to be the Equal Protection Clause's original benefactors (defined by justices in earlier opinions as the "politically powerless").

CONCLUSION

Originally intended to grant equality to newly freed blacks after the Civil War, the Fourteenth Amendment has been the basis of claims by those alleging discrimination on the basis of gender, age, poverty, noncitizen status, and sexual orientation. From an original understanding that applied a rationality scrutiny standard to all equal protection claims, the Court has evolved a two-tier approach, with strict scrutiny being reserved for those governmental actions based on "suspect classifications" or those denying "fundamental rights." The justices have even added a "middle" tier of intermediate scrutiny for some kinds of classifications (e.g., gender). The Court's divisions over how to interpret and apply the demands of equality remain confusing, although recent decisions suggest that the current Court majority seeks a halt to the expansive nature of claims under this "newer" equal protection.

The main problem, as Justice Stevens once put it, is that "there is only one Equal Protection Clause,"[41] which implies a single standard for all cases. Answers to the question of what that one standard should be abound. When he was on the Court, Chief Justice Rehnquist fought for a return to what he considers the Fourteenth Amendment's original intent. To Rehnquist, modern-day problems with the Fourteenth

Amendment came "not so much from the Equal Protection Clause but from the Court's insistence on reading so much into it." Rehnquist's solution was to go back to the original, deferential standard of rationality scrutiny to solve all equal protection claims, "except in the area of the law in which the Framers obviously meant it to apply—classifications based on race or national origin, the first cousin of race."[42]

Regardless of what standard the Court adopts, the new equal protection is probably here to stay. As Justice Marshall once aptly explained, "it is far too late in the day to contend that the Fourteenth Amendment prohibits only racial discrimination." As the Declaration of Independence did for nineteenth-century women's-rights advocates such as Elizabeth Cady Stanton, the expansive language of the Equal Protection Clause has given sustenance to those who perpetually find themselves disadvantaged by their government. The Court's future problem lies in devising consistent and reasonable standards by which to interpret the idea of equality, ones that also live up to the promises of founding documents like the Declaration, but that have yet to be realized.

CHAPTER 11
The Bill of Rights and Due Process of Law

One of the most controversial provisions of the Bill of Rights is the Second Amendment's guarantee of "the right of the people to keep and bear arms." The Court has recently interpreted this clause as giving individuals the right—against both state and federal governments—to possess weapons for self-defense. This gun shop in Red Lodge, Montana, proudly displays the Second Amendment along with its array of firearms for sale.

▼ Introductory Remarks by Justice Thurgood Marshall

My name is Thurgood Marshall, and although I am most known as the first African American justice on the Supreme Court as well as a strong advocate for civil rights, I was also a fierce defender of civil liberties and of an interpretation of the Constitution that would expand the fundamental rights of citizens. In introducing this chapter I lay out my reasoning for moving beyond a "fixed" meaning of the Constitution based solely on what is explicitly written and thus evolving our understanding of what rights it protects and how far they extend.

My early professional life was dedicated to the cause of civil rights, particularly those of African Americans for whom the promise of the post–Civil War era had not been realized, largely because state laws were discriminating against them. After receiving my law degree from Howard University in 1933 I began working on civil rights cases for the NAACP, where I eventually would become its chief counsel.

In that capacity, I argued and won a number of cases before the Supreme Court, including the landmark *Brown v. Board of Education* decision. After a brief stint as Solicitor General of the United States, President Johnson appointed me the first "descendant of an African slave" to be a Supreme Court justice in 1967.

In addition to fighting against racial discrimination, on the Court I became known for my defense of affirmative action as the main remedy to address histories of past racial discrimination (discussed in Chapter 10) and my staunch opposition to the death penalty (discussed in Chapter 13). I also argued for regarding the Constitution as a living document, one that can recognize and protect "individual freedoms and human rights" as they may be threatened in years and centuries to come, not just as they may have existed in the eighteenth century. As I stated in my famous "Bicentennial Speech,"

> THE GOVERNMENT [THE FRAMERS] DEVISED WAS DEFECTIVE FROM THE START, REQUIRING SEVERAL AMENDMENTS, A CIVIL WAR, AND MOMENTOUS SOCIAL TRANSFORMATION TO ATTAIN THE SYSTEM OF CONSTITUTIONAL GOVERNMENT, AND ITS RESPECT FOR THE INDIVIDUAL FREEDOMS AND HUMAN RIGHTS, WE HOLD AS FUNDAMENTAL TODAY. WHEN CONTEMPORARY AMERICANS CITE "THE CONSTITUTION," THEY INVOKE A CONCEPT THAT IS VASTLY DIFFERENT FROM WHAT THE FRAMERS BARELY BEGAN TO CONSTRUCT TWO CENTURIES AGO.

The question for all of us, and especially those of us who have been specifically charged with interpreting the Constitution as it applies to contemporary "cases and controversies," is how we determine what "fundamental interests" or rights beyond those "explicitly or implicitly guaranteed by the text of the Constitution itself" should be protected from government intervention. This, of course, is a difficult question, but it goes to the heart of the issues presented in this chapter.

In my lengthy dissent in *San Antonio v. Rodriguez* (discussed in Chapter 10), I tried to establish principles for determining which individual rights might be fundamental, subjecting any law or government action seeking to restrict these freedoms to "strict scrutiny." In that dissent, I acknowledged that justices should avoid "an unprincipled, subjective, 'picking and choosing' between various interests" or rights that we might seek to protect against government intervention. I came up with the following guidelines:

> ALTHOUGH NOT ALL FUNDAMENTAL INTERESTS ARE CONSTITUTIONALLY GUARANTEED, THE DETERMINATION OF WHICH INTERESTS ARE FUNDAMENTAL SHOULD BE FIRMLY ROOTED IN THE TEXT OF THE CONSTITUTION. THE TASK IN EVERY CASE SHOULD BE TO DETERMINE THE EXTENT TO WHICH CONSTITUTIONALLY GUARANTEED RIGHTS ARE DEPENDENT ON INTERESTS NOT MENTIONED IN THE CONSTITUTION. AS THE NEXUS BETWEEN THE SPECIFIC CONSTITUTIONAL GUARANTEE AND THE NONCONSTITUTIONAL INTEREST DRAWS CLOSER, THE NONCONSTITUTIONAL INTEREST BECOMES MORE FUNDAMENTAL AND THE DEGREE OF JUDICIAL SCRUTINY APPLIED WHEN THE INTEREST IS INFRINGED ON A DISCRIMINATORY BASIS MUST BE ADJUSTED ACCORDINGLY . . . ONLY IF WE CLOSELY PROTECT THE RELATED INTERESTS FROM STATE DISCRIMINATION DO WE ULTIMATELY ENSURE THE INTEGRITY OF THE CONSTITUTIONAL GUARANTEE ITSELF.

Although these guidelines have never been adopted by a majority of the Supreme Court, I believe they offer clear answers to the kinds of human rights concerns we face with an over two hundred-year-old document that can't possibly have anticipated what civil liberties could be threatened, concerns that Americans going all the way back to Madison have understood (see Brief 11.3). I hope you will keep these ideas in mind while reading this chapter.

SOURCES: Juan Williams, *Thurgood Marshall: American Revolutionary* (New York: Random House, 1998); Remarks of Thurgood Marshall at the Annual Seminar of the San Francisco Patent and Trademark Law Association, Maui, Hawaii, May 6, 1987, www.thurgoodmarshall.com/speeches/constitutional_speech.htm; *San Antonio School District v. Rodriguez*, 411 U.S. 1 (1973), at 70.

THE BILL OF RIGHTS

The evolution of individual rights and liberties in the United States has been a slow, often piecemeal, process. Our experience has demonstrated that the existence of a Bill of Rights, while critical to the protection of individual rights and liberties, does not ensure an end to injustice, and, if anything, the protection of individual rights requires constant vigilance on the part of all citizens. The author of the Bill of Rights himself, James Madison, once said that a bill of rights was nothing but a "paper parapet" in the absence of responsible citizens. To place the development of citizen rights and liberties in clearer perspective, this chapter begins with an examination of the Bill of Rights (particularly the first eight amendments, which contain protections for the individual), and then analyze the process by which these guarantees gradually were expanded to apply to all levels of government in the United States. The chapter concludes with an exploration of possible fundamental rights beyond those found in the Bill of Rights. As might be expected, the Supreme Court has played a prominent role in both the "nationalization" and interpretation of the constitutional rights of citizens.

When the state of Virginia on December 15, 1791, ratified the first ten amendments to the new United States Constitution, it became the eleventh state to do so. As a result, the necessary three-fourths requirement was satisfied, and the Bill of Rights became part of the Constitution.[1] The Bill of Rights, as noted in Chapter 2, owed much of its existence to the ratification struggles between Federalists and Anti-Federalists. According to author Robert Rutland, "a broad base of public opinion forced the adoption of the Bill of Rights upon those political leaders who knew the value of compromise."[2] Actually, the states had been called upon to ratify twelve, not ten, amendments. Two proposals—one dealing with a fixed apportionment of seats in the House of Representatives and the other with congressional salaries—were defeated (see Brief 11.1). Nevertheless, the resulting first ten amendments opened a new dimension in the development of the American Constitution.

Some dispute occurred in the First Congress during the debates over the proposed Bill of Rights and its applicability to the state governments. James Madison, the chief architect of the proposals, actually favored an amendment protecting the rights of conscience, free speech, press, and trial by jury against state action. According to author Edward Dumbauld, "Madison thought this provision important, since some states did not have bills of rights."[3] The Senate, however, refused to include any provision that would apply the rights to the states, so the proposed amendments clearly limited only the new national government.

The Senate view of the Bill of Rights received overwhelming Supreme Court confirmation in the case of *Barron v. Baltimore* (1833). The case stemmed from a dispute concerning the Just Compensation Clause of the Fifth Amendment. The final lines of the

---

Brief 11.1

THE TWENTY-SEVENTH AMENDMENT

The longest ratification period for a constitutional amendment ended on May 7, 1992, when the Michigan legislature approved a proposal first ratified by Maryland in 1789. The amendment, proposed by James Madison and included as the second of the twelve amendments sent to the states in 1789, reads as follows:

> *No law varying the compensation for the services of the Senators and Representatives shall take effect, until an election of Representatives shall have intervened.*

The 1789 Congress placed no time constraints on ratification of the proposals, although most amendments proposed in later years have been sent to the states with a deadline (usually seven years) for ratification. Although constitutional experts disagreed over the legality of the latest amendment's ratification, all agreed that the final decision about acceptance rested with the United States Congress. In several cases decided earlier in the twentieth century, the Supreme Court held that amendments should reflect "a contemporaneous consensus," but it left that determination to Congress. Not surprisingly, under considerable election-year pressure, as well as the public outcry concerning recent congressional pay raises, both houses of Congress quickly agreed not to challenge the legality of the newly enacted Twenty-seventh Amendment. The ideas of Madison and his colleagues continue to influence our constitution's development.

Fifth Amendment state: "Nor shall private property be taken for public use, without just compensation." For John Barron, the co-owner of a wharf located in Baltimore, Maryland, that specific guarantee had been violated by the city's efforts to change the direction of several streams and waterways. In the process of diverting the streams, vast amounts of sediment began to collect around Barron's wharf, making it inaccessible to ships and, therefore, worthless. After winning a judgment at the county level, Barron lost on appeal and asked the Supreme Court to uphold his award of damages.

Writing for a unanimous court, Chief Justice John Marshall refused to hold the provisions of the Bill of Rights applicable to the states. In his view, the question was "not of much difficulty," given what he considered to be clear and convincing historical evidence. First, Marshall emphasized the national character of the Constitution itself:

> THE CONSTITUTION WAS ORDAINED AND ESTABLISHED BY THE PEOPLE OF THE UNITED STATES FOR THEMSELVES, FOR THEIR OWN GOVERNMENT AND NOT FOR THE GOVERNMENT OF THE INDIVIDUAL STATES. EACH STATE ESTABLISHED A CONSTITUTION FOR ITSELF, AND, IN THAT CONSTITUTION, PROVIDED SUCH LIMITATIONS AND RESTRICTIONS ON THE POWERS OF ITS PARTICULAR GOVERNMENT AS ITS JUDGMENT DICTATED.

Second, Marshall's opinion focused on the process by which the first ten amendments were added to the constitution. He rejected Barron's claim that these had been intended to apply additional limitations on state governments, adding the following point:

> HAD THE FRAMERS OF THESE AMENDMENTS INTENDED THEM TO BE LIMITATIONS ON THE POWERS OF THE STATE GOVERNMENTS, THEY WOULD HAVE IMITATED THE FRAMERS OF THE ORIGINAL CONSTITUTION, AND HAVE EXPRESSED THAT INTENTION.... THESE AMENDMENTS CONTAIN NO EXPRESSION INDICATING AN INTENTION TO APPLY THEM TO THE STATE GOVERNMENTS. THIS COURT CANNOT SO APPLY THEM.

In holding that the Bill of Rights could not be applied directly to the states, Marshall's Court established a legal precedent that has not been rejected, even though, as a practical matter, most of the amendments do apply to the states today. Technically, the Bill of Rights was written to apply only to the national government, and that has not changed. As a result of decisions such as *Barron v. Baltimore*, the Bill of Rights did not play a significant role in early American life. According to political scientist Richard Cortner:

> THE BILL OF RIGHTS WAS THUS CONFINED TO BEING A LIMITATION ONLY UPON THE POWER OF THE FEDERAL GOVERNMENT AND PLAYED A VERY LIMITED ROLE IN AMERICAN CONSTITUTIONAL ADJUDICATION PRIOR TO THE CIVIL WAR. FOR THE PROTECTION OF THEIR MOST BASIC POLITICAL AND CIVIL LIBERTIES FROM INVASION BY THE STATES, AMERICANS WERE REQUIRED TO LOOK TO THEIR STATE CONSTITUTIONS AND STATE BILLS OF RIGHTS AND NOT TO THE FEDERAL BILL OF RIGHTS.[4]

THE FOURTEENTH AMENDMENT AND DUE PROCESS OF LAW

Some discussion of the impact of the post–Civil War amendments has been provided in Chapters 7 and 9. As a result, it is unnecessary to examine the entire range of issues underlying these amendments. However, the Fourteenth Amendment in particular raised numerous questions concerning the rights and liberties of individuals that related directly to the guarantees in the Bill of Rights. The historical evidence is not entirely clear with respect to the intentions of the framers of the Fourteenth Amendment. Did they intend for the Privileges and Immunities Clause and the Due Process of Law Clause to change the long-standing relationship between the Bill of Rights and state governments? In other words, did they believe that the amendment would make the individual protections of the first eight amendments binding upon the states in the same manner as it was upon the national government? Much historical analysis has centered on this point, and the results are inconclusive.

Such analyses generally have focused on the important role played by Representative John Bingham in the formation of the post–Civil War amendments, particularly the Fourteenth. Representative Bingham led the fight for proposal of the Fourteenth Amendment in the House of Representatives, and he seemingly favored the idea that the amendment should guarantee fundamental rights on a nationwide basis. According to Henry J. Abraham, sifting through the various points of view regarding the historical evidence, "there seems little doubt that the Amendment's principal framers and managers, Representative Bingham and Senator Howard, if not every member of the majority in the two houses of Congress, did believe the Bill of Rights to be made generally applicable to the several states via Section 1."[5]

Of course, whether the intention of persons such as Bingham, assuming they can be known, should be binding on future generations presents another question. In a turn-of-the-century opinion, Justice Rufus Peckham of the Supreme Court expressed what generally has been the prevailing view of most justices concerning the origins of the Fourteenth Amendment:

> WHAT INDIVIDUAL SENATORS OR REPRESENTATIVES MAY HAVE URGED IN DEBATE IN REGARD TO THE MEANING TO BE GIVEN TO A PROPOSED CONSTITUTIONAL AMENDMENT . . . DOES NOT OFFER FIRM GROUND FOR ITS PROPER CONSTRUCTION.[6]

Despite Justice Peckham's views, later Supreme Court justices kept the issue very much alive.

The years since the ratification have produced considerable disagreement concerning the proper relationship between the protections in the Bill of Rights and the meaning of the Fourteenth Amendment. Table 11.1 provides a chronological overview of several key developments in the gradual march from the situation before the Fourteenth Amendment until the Supreme Court's acceptance of the doctrine of "selective incorporation." These events will provide the basis for the following discussion.

As discussed in Chapter 8, the Supreme Court's ruling in *The Slaughterhouse Cases* (1873) effectively rejected the contention that the Fourteenth Amendment had brought constitutional privileges and immunities under federal control. Similarly, the Court held the due process guarantees of the Fourteenth Amendment as applicable only to the procedural rights of Negroes. While the Due Process Clause gradually served as a limitation on state economic regulation, it was not broadly regarded as a protector of federal constitutional rights. Several cases serve as examples.

In *Hurtado v. California* (1884), the Court held that California's practice of using a prosecutor's "information" in lieu of a grand jury indictment did not deprive a person of due process of law. At issue was a provision of the California Constitution that allowed a person to be tried without the use of a grand jury indictment to initiate a prosecution, despite the Fifth Amendment's guarantee of such a practice in all federal cases. Joseph Hurtado appealed his conviction and death sentence on the ground that they violated the Due Process Clause of the Fourteenth Amendment.

In the majority opinion, Justice Stanley Matthews traced the idea of due process through its English and common law heritage but found no specific list of guarantees to be linked to a due process of law, stating that "it would be incongruous to measure and restrict them by the ancient customary English law." States should be free to shape their own due process guarantees.

Next, Justice Matthews drew attention to the identical wording used in the Due Process Clauses of the Fifth and Fourteenth Amendments. With respect to the Fifth Amendment, he noted, "[T]hat article also makes specific and express provision for perpetuating the institution of the grand jury." As a result, if the Fourteenth Amendment had intended states to require grand jury indictments in all cases, it would have stated that requirement clearly. This reasoning has produced what Richard Cortner terms the "doctrine of nonsuperfluousness."[7] The doctrine is based on the Court's holding that the due process guarantees in the Fifth and Fourteenth Amendments are identical, as stated in *Hurtado*:

> ACCORDING TO A RECOGNIZED CANON OF INTERPRETATION, ESPECIALLY APPLICABLE TO FORMAL AND SOLEMN INSTRUMENTS OF CONSTITUTIONAL LAW, WE ARE FORBIDDEN TO ASSUME, WITHOUT CLEAR REASON TO THE CONTRARY, THAT ANY PART OF THIS MOST IMPORTANT AMENDMENT IS SUPERFLUOUS.

Table 11.1 Development of the Law: Steps in the Nationalization of the Bill of Rights

Date	Event	Significance
1791	Bill of Rights becomes part of Constitution	Guarantee of rights and liberties from the national government.
1833	*Barron v. Baltimore*	Chief Justice Marshall's majority opinion holds that the Bill of Rights applies only to the national government.
1868	Fourteenth Amendment	Presumably the rights of ex-slaves are safeguarded against state governments.
1873	*Slaughterhouse Cases*	The Fourteenth Amendment did not apply the privileges and immunities of national citizenship to state governments. Due Process in the Fourteenth Amendment protects the procedural rights of Negroes.
1884	*Hurtado v. California*	Grand Jury Clause does not apply in states through the Fourteenth Amendment. The Due Process Clauses of the Fifth and Fourteenth Amendments are identical.
1886	*Santa Clara County v. Southern Pacific RR*	Corporations are "persons" for purposes of the Due Process Clause of the Fourteenth Amendment. Corporate property rights can be protected from state interference.
1897	*Chicago, Burlington & Quincy Railroad Co. v. Chicago*	Due Process Clause of Fourteenth Amendment requires states to give "just compensation" for property taken.
1908	*Twining v. New Jersey*	Court refuses to hold Fifth Amendment self-incrimination protections applicable to the Due Process of the Fourteenth Amendment. But the Due Process Clause may guarantee certain "fundamental" rights that are "similar" to those in the Bill of Rights.
1925	*Gitlow v. New York*	Court assumes "for present purposes" that freedoms of speech and the press are found in the liberties guaranteed by the Fourteenth Amendment.
1931	*Near v. Minnesota*	Freedom of the press is applicable to the state governments.
1932	*Powell v. Alabama*	The "right to counsel" for indigents in capital cases is fundamental. The *Hurtado* rule contains some exceptions.
1937	*DeJonge v. Oregon*	The "right of peaceable assembly" is a fundamental liberty and applies to states through the Fourteenth Amendment.
1937	*Palko v. Connecticut*	A majority of the Court recognizes the principle of "selective incorporation" of those rights "implicit in the concept of ordered liberty."

The existence of a Grand Jury Clause in the Fifth Amendment meant that grand jury provisions were not included in the Due Process Clause; to assume otherwise would violate the "nonsuperfluousness" doctrine. Accordingly, if they were not in the Due Process Clause of the Fifth Amendment, grand jury requirements could not be in the Fourteenth either.

Two late-nineteenth-century Supreme Court rulings added new significance to the due process controversy. First, in 1886, the Court held that corporations were "persons" within the meaning of the Due Process Clause. This ruling effectively brought corporate property rights under due process protection, thereby making government regulation especially difficult.[8] A review of the section on substantive due process of law in Chapter 8 provides several examples of this development. Second, in the case of *Chicago, Burlington & Quincy Ry. v. Chicago* (1897), the Supreme Court held the Fifth Amendment's Just Compensation Clause to be contained in the Fourteenth Amendment's Due Process Clause. Ironically, this first instance of applying a provision of the Bill of Rights to the due process guarantees of the Fourteenth Amendment involved the very provision that was unsuccessfully claimed by John Barron against the city of Baltimore. The Court's ruling seemed to be in direct conflict with the *Hurtado* precedent, especially the aspect of nonsuperfluousness.

After all, both the Grand Jury and Just Compensation clauses are part of the same Fifth Amendment. How is it possible that the Grand Jury Clause cannot be contained in due process guarantees while the opposite is true for just compensation? The Supreme Court did not say.

The Court suggested a slightly broader test for determining matters of due process in *Twining v. New Jersey* (1908). In that case, Albert C. Twining and his associate refused to take the witness stand in their own defense. The trial judge, in his instructions to the jury, made note of this fact. Following his conviction, Twining claimed on appeal that his silence had served as a form of self-incrimination. Although it rejected Twining's claim that the Fifth Amendment's self-incrimination protections constitute "due process" in Fourteenth Amendment terms, Justice William Moody's majority opinion wondered

> WHETHER THE EXEMPTION FROM SELF-INCRIMINATION IS OF SUCH A NATURE THAT IT MUST BE INCLUDED IN THE CONCEPTION OF DUE PROCESS. IS IT A FUNDAMENTAL PRINCIPLE OF LIBERTY AND JUSTICE WHICH INHERES IN THE VERY IDEA OF FREE GOVERNMENT AND IS THE INALIENABLE RIGHT OF A CITIZEN OF SUCH A GOVERNMENT?

The *Twining* interest in "fundamental" liberties suggested a possible opening for those hoping to expand the protections of the Bill of Rights into the states. If it could be determined that a particular liberty was indeed fundamental, would it not be logical to hold it as binding against all governments, including the states? Justice Moody's conclusions showed the right to be "a privilege of great value," but not one that had been regarded "as a part of the law of the land of Magna Charta or the due process of law." Importantly, Justice Moody's opinion recognized that fundamental rights, if they should eventually be protected from state action (as was just compensation), would be protected not because they were found in the Bill of Rights, but rather because they fall into the accepted notion of due process of law.

A major step was taken in *Gitlow v. New York* (1925) with respect to the freedoms of speech and press. The *Gitlow* opinion (discussed further in Chapter 14) almost casually announced the following:

> FOR PRESENT PURPOSES WE MAY AND DO ASSUME THAT FREEDOM OF SPEECH AND OF THE PRESS—WHICH ARE PROTECTED BY THE FIRST AMENDMENT FROM ABRIDGEMENT BY CONGRESS—ARE AMONG THE FUNDAMENTAL PERSONAL RIGHTS AND "LIBERTIES" PROTECTED BY THE DUE PROCESS CLAUSE OF THE FOURTEENTH AMENDMENT FROM IMPAIRMENT BY THE STATES.

Although the Court upheld the New York law under which Benjamin Gitlow had been convicted, it forged the link between freedoms found in the Bill of Rights and the "liberties" protected by the Fourteenth Amendment. Yet the Court mentioned no freedoms beyond speech and press. Perhaps speech and press were more "fundamental" than other freedoms, but the *Gitlow* ruling opened the way for new questions concerning the fundamental nature of other rights and liberties.[9]

The Court's ruling in *Powell v. Alabama* (1932) held the Due Process of Law Clause of the Fourteenth Amendment to require that counsel be appointed for indigent defendants in state criminal proceedings involving capital crimes. Accused of raping two white girls, the black defendants, characterized by the Court as "young, ignorant, [and] illiterate," were convicted by a jury and given the death penalty all in a single day. Their appeal contended that they had not received a fair and impartial trial, that they had been denied the right to counsel, and that since blacks had been systematically excluded from their juries, they had not received a proper trial by a "jury of their peers."

Justice George Sutherland, speaking for the majority, held that "the necessity of counsel was so vital and imperative that the failure of the trial court to make an effective appointment of counsel was likewise a denial of due process within the meaning of the Fourteenth Amendment." While the *Powell* ruling did not formally "incorporate" the Sixth Amendment in all cases, it recognized "that there are certain immutable principles of justice which inhere in the very idea of free government which no member of the Union may disregard." In the case at hand, at least, the Supreme Court felt that the right to counsel was one of those principles. Increasingly, the Court was being called upon to consider new due process questions stemming from the guarantees in the Bill of Rights. When the Court held the First Amendment's freedom of assembly to be protected from state action by the Due Process Clause of the Fourteenth Amendment in 1937, it had moved a long way from the nineteenth-century *Slaughterhouse* and *Hurtado* decisions. The Bill of Rights was coming ever closer to a resolution with the Fourteenth Amendment.

THE DOCTRINE OF SELECTIVE INCORPORATION

In *Palko v. Connecticut* (1937), the Court accepted on appeal a case from the Connecticut Supreme Court of Errors involving the first-degree murder conviction of Frank Palko, who had actually been twice convicted of murder. The first trial ended in Palko's conviction for second-degree murder, but the state filed notice of appeal, and the Supreme Court of Errors ordered a new trial. In the second trial, the state was allowed to introduce previously excluded testimony, with the result being a conviction for first-degree murder and a sentence of death. Palko contended that Connecticut's actions violated the Fifth Amendment's guarantee that no person shall "be subject for the same offence to be twice put in jeopardy of life or limb."

Writing for an 8–1 majority, Justice Benjamin Cardozo distinguished between types of rights and liberties found in the Constitution. Those such as freedom of speech, press, and religion, stated Cardozo, "have been found to be implicit in the concept of ordered liberty, and thus, through the Fourteenth Amendment, become valid as against the states." Elsewhere, he described these rights as being "of the very essence of a scheme of ordered liberty." Those rights that qualify as "fundamental" are therefore as binding on the states as they are on the federal government. The process by which such rights are applied to the states has been termed **selective incorporation**, although Cardozo spoke of "absorption":

> WE REACH A DIFFERENT PLANE OF SOCIAL AND MORAL VALUES WHEN WE PASS TO THE PRIVILEGES AND IMMUNITIES THAT HAVE BEEN TAKEN OVER FROM THE EARLIER ARTICLES OF THE FEDERAL BILL OF RIGHTS AND BROUGHT WITHIN THE FOURTEENTH AMENDMENT BY A PROCESS OF ABSORPTION. THESE IN THEIR ORIGIN WERE EFFECTIVE AGAINST THE FEDERAL GOVERNMENT ALONE. IF THE FOURTEENTH AMENDMENT HAS ABSORBED THEM, THE PROCESS OF ABSORPTION HAS HAD ITS SOURCE IN THE BELIEF THAT NEITHER LIBERTY NOR JUSTICE WOULD EXIST IF THEY WERE SACRIFICED.

Using this new standard, Cardozo ruled that double-jeopardy protections are not "fundamental" to due process or liberty, and that Palko's first-degree conviction was proper. The Fourteenth Amendment's due-process guarantees definitely contained those rights "implicit in the concept of ordered liberty." It would be up to future courts to determine just which privileges and immunities should be absorbed or incorporated (see Brief 11.2). In the short term, and certainly from Palko's perspective, the decision was a blow to the expansion of the Bill of Rights, but the long-term effects of selective incorporation, as presented in Table 11.2, tell an entirely different story.

Table 11.2 presents the history of selective incorporation and the Supreme Court decisions that incorporated portions of the Bill of Rights into the liberties of the Fourteenth Amendment. Actually, only six of the ten amendments contain rights and privileges that lend themselves to possible incorporation. For example, the Third (quartering of soldiers during peacetime), Seventh (civil trials), Ninth (other rights), and Tenth (reserved powers) Amendments do not appear likely to be incorporated, primarily because of their subject matter.

INCORPORATION OF THE FIRST AMENDMENT

The First Amendment freedoms were among the earliest to be incorporated into the Fourteenth Amendment, prompting many observers to recognize what they saw as the amendment's "preferred freedoms." The Court's unexpected proclamation in *Gitlow v. New York* holding freedoms of speech and press to be fundamental began the incorporation process. It appeared from that ruling that speech and press freedoms were indeed more important than other liberties. The Court's ringing endorsement of a free press in *Near v. Minnesota* (1931) (see Chapter 16) further added to the idea that First Amendment protections would receive special treatment.

Brief 11.2

THE CASE FOR TOTAL INCORPORATION

The Court's lone dissenter in the *Hurtado* and *Twining* decisions was Justice John Harlan I, who argued that the Fourteenth Amendment's Due Process Clause had nationalized the entire Bill of Rights. The idea of **total incorporation** was given its strongest voice by Justice Hugo Black in his dissenting opinion in *Adamson v. California* (1947). In that case, a majority of the Court refused to incorporate the Fifth Amendment's protection against self-incrimination, largely on the strength of the *Twining* precedent. Black criticized what he called the "natural-law theory" of his colleagues, which gave too much discretion to the whims of individual justices. He even attached an appendix to his opinion supporting his claim that the founders of the Fourteenth Amendment had specifically intended to make the first eight amendments applicable to the states and overturn the *Barron v. Baltimore* precedent. According to Black:

> My study of the historical events that culminated in the Fourteenth Amendment, and the expressions of those who sponsored and favored, as well as those who opposed its submission and passage, persuades me that one of the chief objects that the provisions of the Amendment's first section, separately, and as a whole, were intended to accomplish was to make the Bill of Rights applicable to the states.

Justice Black's opinion drew an almost instant response from the legal community. Harvard Law School Professor Charles Fairman, a leading scholar of the time, wrote a *Law Review* article highly critical of Justice Black's contentions, in which he argued that the Fourteenth Amendment's framers had never intended to incorporate the entire Bill of Rights.[10] The community of American constitutional law scholars was, and to some extent remains, divided over the issue.[11] Among Justice Black's colleagues on the Court, the debate was no less real. Justice Felix Frankfurter took the consistent position of opposing Black's "total incorporation" view, choosing instead to decide due process claims on a case-by-case approach.

The foundation of an even broader view of incorporation, termed by some as **total incorporation plus**, was laid by Justice Frank Murphy in his *Adamson* dissent, in which Murphy was not willing to hold the Fourteenth Amendment's due process guarantees to be "entirely and necessarily limited by the Bill of Rights." It was conceivable, according to Justice Murphy, that:

> Occasions may arise where a proceeding falls so short of conforming to fundamental standards or procedures as to warrant constitutional condemnation in terms of lack of due process despite the absence of a specific provision in the Bill of Rights.

This view generally is associated with the later opinions of Justice William O. Douglas and Justice Arthur Goldberg, which were especially visible in the case of *Griswold v. Connecticut* (1965) concerning a right of privacy (to be discussed later in this chapter).

With incorporation of the religion clauses in *Cantwell v. Connecticut* (1940) and *Everson v. Board of Education* (1947) the Court made virtually the entire First Amendment applicable to the states. Although controversy has continued to surround government efforts to legislate in various First Amendment–related areas, there has been no serious dispute of the First Amendment's applicability to the states in all its individual rights and liberties. The religion issues are discussed in Chapter 18.

Incorporation of the Second Amendment

The Second Amendment reads, "A well regulated Militia, being necessary to the security of a free State, the right of the people to keep and bear Arms, shall not be infringed." There has been great conflict in recent years over what the amendment means, and whether it might apply to the states. Much of the disagreement centers on how one interprets the relationship between the amendment's dependent and independent clauses. A number of citizens and citizen interest groups, such as the National Rifle Association (NRA), focus on the independent clause and assume that the right to bear arms is an individual right like others found in the first eight amendments, to be protected against both federal and state infringement. Until recently, most constitutional interpreters, including the justices of the Supreme Court, have read the Second Amendment in the context of its framers' concerns about national "standing armies" and, as such, see it preventing Congress from disarming state militias. From this perspective the Second Amendment does not confer even a limited individual right to keep and bear arms against government intervention or regulation.

Table 11.2 Selective Incorporation of the Bill of Rights

Amendment/Rights	Supreme Court Case/Year
First Amendment	
❑ Speech	*Gitlow v. New York* (1925)
❑ Press	*Near v. Minnesota* (1931)
❑ Free exercise of religion	*Cantwell v. Connecticut* (1940)
❑ Establishment of religion	*Everson v. Board of Education* (1947)
❑ Assembly	*DeJonge v. Oregon* (1937)
Second Amendment	*McDonald v. City of Chicago* (2010)
Third Amendment	Not incorporated
Fourth Amendment	
❑ Search and seizure	*Wolf v. Colorado* (1949)
❑ Exclusionary rule	*Mapp v. Ohio* (1961)
Fifth Amendment	
❑ Grand jury	Not incorporated
❑ Double jeopardy	*Benton v. Maryland* (1969)
❑ Self-incrimination	*Malloy v. Hogan* (1964)
❑ Just compensation	*Chicago, Burlington & Quincy Ry. v. Chicago* (1897)
Sixth Amendment	
❑ Speedy trial	*Klopfer v. North Carolina* (1967)
❑ Public trial	*In re Oliver* (1948)
❑ Impartial jury	*Parker v. Gladden* (1966)
❑ Jury trial	*Duncan v. Louisiana* (1968)
❑ Notice	*Cole v. Arkansas* (1948)
❑ Confrontation	*Pointer v. Texas* (1965)
❑ Compulsory process	*Washington v. Texas* (1967)
❑ Assistance of counsel	*Gideon v. Wainwright* (1963) *Argersinger v. Hamlin* (1972)
Seventh Amendment	Not incorporated
Eighth Amendment	
❑ Excessive bail and fines	Not incorporated
❑ Cruel and unusual punishments	*Robinson v. California* (1962)
Ninth Amendment	Not incorporated **
Tenth Amendment	Not incorporated **

** The Ninth and Tenth Amendments, although ratified along with the first eight, generally are not considered to contain specific rights that could be incorporated. Many observers do not include them in the Bill of Rights.

Until 2008, the Supreme Court confirmed this opinion about the limited nature of the right conferred in the Second Amendment. For example, in *United States* v. *Miller* (1939), the justices upheld a federal law making it illegal to ship sawed-off shotguns in interstate commerce, saying that such weapons had no relationship "to the preservation or efficiency of a well-regulated militia." And in *Lewis v. United States* (1980), the Court plainly stated:

> THE SECOND AMENDMENT GUARANTEES NO RIGHT TO KEEP AND BEAR A FIREARM THAT DOES NOT HAVE "SOME REASONABLE RELATIONSHIP" TO THE PRESERVATION OR EFFICIENCY OF A WELL-REGULATED MILITIA.

The Court's position had been that even applied to the federal government, the Second Amendment allows for the regulation of private ownership or use of firearms. And given its specific relationship to the prohibition on congressional disbanding of state militias, the amendment had never been incorporated to apply to state regulations of firearms. Justice Douglas's opinion in *Adams v. Williams* (1972) provides strongly worded language to this effect:

> [A] POWERFUL LOBBY DINS INTO THE EARS OF OUR CITIZENRY THAT GUN ... PURCHASES ARE CONSTITUTIONAL RIGHTS PROTECTED BY THE SECOND AMENDMENT.... THERE IS UNDER OUR DECISIONS NO REASON WHY STIFF STATE LAWS GOVERNING THE PURCHASE AND POSSESSION OF PISTOLS MAY NOT BE ENACTED. THERE IS NO REASON WHY PISTOLS MAY NOT BE BARRED FROM ANYONE WITH A POLICE RECORD. THERE IS NO REASON WHY A STATE MAY NOT REQUIRE A PURCHASER OF A PISTOL TO PASS A PSYCHIATRIC TEST. THERE IS NO REASON WHY ALL PISTOLS SHOULD NOT BE BARRED TO EVERYONE EXCEPT THE POLICE.

In 2008, in a stunning reversal of previous precedents, the Court announced that the Second Amendment protects an individual's right to possess firearms in the home for self-defense, and overturned a District of Columbia law restricting such possession. The D.C. law, dating back to 1976, made it a crime to carry an unregistered firearm, and generally prohibited the registration of handguns. It also required residents to keep registered guns "unloaded and dissembled or bound by a trigger lock or similar device." Dick Heller was a D.C. policeman who applied to register a handgun to keep at home. When the District refused, he sued the city on Second Amendment grounds, to keep it from enforcing the ban on registered handguns.

In *District of Columbia v. Heller* (2008), a slim 5–4 majority ruled in Heller's favor. Writing for the majority, Justice Scalia spent the bulk of his lengthy opinion attempting to elicit the historical meaning of the Second Amendment's words. After reviewing the "normal and ordinary" meaning of the amendment's words at the time of its drafting, historical documents such as the English Bill of Rights, and post-ratification commentaries by judges and scholars, Scalia concluded that, in addition to protecting state militias from Congressional disarmament, the Second Amendment "elevates above all other interests the right of law-abiding, responsible citizens to use arms in defense of hearth and home." While this individual right to keep and bear arms "is not unlimited," Scalia declared that "the District's ban on handgun possession in the home violates the Second Amendment [as does] its prohibition against rendering any lawful firearm in the home operable for the purpose of immediate self-defense." Scalia found the city's ban particularly objectionable, since "the American people have considered the handgun to be the quintessential self-defense weapon . . . it can be pointed at a burglar with one hand while the other hand dials the police."

The ideas of the four justices in dissent were captured in two opinions: one by Justice Stevens and the other by Justice Breyer. In his dissent, Stevens challenged Scalia's historical interpretation of the Second Amendment's language. Stevens's own review of the historical record at the time of the Amendment's framing, as well as the commentaries of Blackstone and other jurists, caused him to side with the unanimous Court in *Miller*, concluding that the Amendment "protects only a right to possess and use firearms in connection with service in a state-organized militia." He also invoked Justice Frankfurter to chide the majority for so willingly wiping out seventy years of Supreme Court precedent and "endorsing such a dramatic upheaval in the law."

Breyer's opinion conceded the majority's point that the Second Amendment may protect an individual "interest in possessing guns for self-defense" beyond service in a militia, but concluded that the District's interest in "saving lives, preventing injury, and reducing crime" could reasonably be seen to justify restrictions on the individual liberties the Amendment might protect. Breyer's "interest-balancing inquiry" examined the history of government regulation of firearms, particularly in urban areas, and concluded that the Court should defer to local and state legislatures in their policy conclusions about what compelling public interests exist in dealing with gun-related problems. Like Stevens, Breyer lamented, "the unfortunate consequence . . . that the decision threatens to throw into doubt the constitutionality of gun laws throughout the United States."

Two years later, in *McDonald v. City of Chicago* (2008), the Court, by the same 5–4 majority, extended the Second Amendment right to keep and bear arms to apply against the states through the Fourteenth Amendment. In question here was a 1982 Chicago city ordinance prohibiting possession of handguns by private individuals. After the Court's decision in *Heller*, Otis McDonald and several other Chicago residents challenged the law, claiming that it violated the Second and Fourteenth Amendments.

Writing for the majority, Justice Alito examined the Court's fifty-year history of "incorporation precedent," and concluded that the individual citizen's right to self-defense protected by the Second Amendment was "deeply rooted in this Nation's history and tradition." To accept the argument against incorporation offered by the City of Chicago would treat the Second Amendment guarantee as a "second-class right, subject to an entirely different body of rules than the other Bill of Rights guarantees that we have held to be incorporated into the Due Process Clause." Alito argued that this individual right to keep and bear arms was indeed "fundamental to our scheme of ordered liberty and system of justice," and ordered the cases be returned to the lower courts to determine whether the strict gun control ordinance could be reconciled with the Second Amendment.

In an interesting twist, Justice Thomas, in a concurring opinion, argued that the right to keep and bear arms should apply to the states through the Privileges and Immunities Clause. He even urged the Court to reconsider *Slaughterhouse* and the long-standing precedent concerning the inapplicability of this clause to rights such as those protected by the Second Amendment.

Once again, Justices Breyer and Stevens wrote dissenting opinions, wishing the Court would reconsider the *Heller* decision, and denying that the Due Process Clause could be used to incorporate the Second Amendment right "to keep and bear arms." Justice Stevens argued that whether a right applies to the states turns on one's interpretation of "liberty" under the Due Process Clause; in his analysis, a citizen's interest in keeping a handgun in the home was not "comprised within the term liberty in the Fourteenth Amendment."

While the Court's decisions in *Heller* and *McDonald* are likely to render many state and local gun-control laws invalid, the justices left plenty of room for legislatures to regulate or restrict gun rights. In both cases, the Court indicated that laws prohibiting possession of firearms by felons or the mentally ill, or restricting guns in "sensitive places" like schools or government buildings, would pass constitutional muster. So, too, would laws "imposing conditions and qualifications on the commercial sale of arms." In 2013, Congress contemplated its own gun control regulations, in light of a number of recent mass killings, including one in December 2012 involving twenty-six children and staff at Sandy Hook Elementary School in Newtown, Connecticut.

Still, the decision to interpret the Second Amendment as conferring an individual right to possess firearms for self-defense, and to incorporate that right to apply against the states, was a dramatic departure from past precedent and the latest step toward total incorporation of the Bill of Rights into the Fourteenth Amendment's Due Process Clause.

Incorporation of the Third Amendment

The Third Amendment states that "[n]o Soldier shall, in time of peace be quartered in any house, without the consent of the Owner, nor in time of war, but in a manner to be prescribed by law." About all that can be said of this amendment is that it obviously was of great importance to the framers. The British practice of requiring colonists to make their homes available for soldiers had stirred up violent opposition in the colonies. The First Continental Congress proclaimed that the keeping of a standing army during peacetime without the approval of the colonial legislature violated the law. Also, one of the complaints listed against George III in the Declaration of Independence was "for quartering large bodies of armed troops among us." Since the colonial era, however, the practice of quartering soldiers during peacetime has been largely unimportant in the United States. As a result, the Supreme Court has never been called upon to resolve a dispute concerning the Third Amendment.

Incorporation of the Fourth Amendment

Incorporation of the Fourth Amendment into the Fourteenth Amendment's Due Process of Law Clause actually has occurred in two stages. The first stage involved the amendment's enforcement, a matter that first arose early in the twentieth century. In *Weeks v. United States* (1914), the Supreme Court ruled that evidence seized in violation of the provisions of the Fourth Amendment was inadmissible in a federal court. Known ever since as the **exclusionary rule**, this prohibition operated only at the federal level for many years, creating what amounted to a double standard for law enforcement. In fact, the double standard was responsible for what has been called the "silver-platter doctrine." Under this doctrine, state officials, to whom the Fourth Amendment was inapplicable, could seize evidence illegally and then turn it over to federal officers "on a silver platter" for use in federal courts. This doctrine survived until 1960.

In the second stage, the Court held in *Wolf v. Colorado* (1949) that the Fourth Amendment's protections against unreasonable searches and seizures, but not the exclusionary rule, were applicable to the states, stating "that in a prosecution in a State court for a State crime, the Fourteenth Amendment does not forbid the admission of evidence obtained by unreasonable search and seizure." Therefore, should state authorities conduct an unlawful search and seizure, the tainted evidence could still be used in the courtroom to obtain a conviction.

Although the protections of the Fourth Amendment were binding on states as a result of *Wolf*, they were not the exact, identical provisions that applied to the national government and did not contain the same enforcement mechanism. The Court's refusal to incorporate the exclusionary rule in *Wolf* largely rested on the fact that only seventeen states at that time used the exclusionary rule, a fact noted in Justice Frankfurter's opinion. According to Justice Frankfurter, "it is not for this Court to condemn as falling below the minimal standards assured by the due process clause a state's reliance upon other methods which, if consistently enforced, would be equally effective." In short, the exclusionary rule was but one of several different methods available to state governments.

In 1961, the increasingly activist Earl Warren Supreme Court accepted a case on appeal from Ohio that was destined to extend the protection of the Fourth Amendment, including the exclusionary-rule method of enforcement, to the states by way of the Due Process Clause of the Fourteenth Amendment. The case, *Mapp v. Ohio* (1961), also served as a landmark in selective-incorporation terms, standing as the case that began a decade of wholesale nationalization of nearly all the remaining guarantees in the first eight amendments.

Dolree (Dolly) Mapp, a Cleveland woman with known ties to the boxing world and a questionable reputation, was at her house one day in 1957. Police, acting on a tip that Ms. Mapp was hiding a bombing suspect at her house, arrived at her residence and asked to enter. Ms. Mapp called her attorney, who advised her to refuse entry unless a search warrant was produced. About 4:00 P.M., some three hours after their arrival, the police forced their way into Mapp's house. Following an ensuing scuffle in which Mapp grabbed what police said was a warrant and stuffed it into her blouse, Mapp was handcuffed and the paper was retrieved. At the same time, the police uncovered several "obscene materials." Mapp was charged with possession of obscene materials and subsequently convicted, even though no search warrant was produced at her trial.

Writing for the Court, Justice Thomas Clark brought the exclusionary rule into the Due Process Clause of the Fourteenth Amendment. He explained that the "same sanction of exclusion as is used against the Federal Government" was necessarily applicable to the states, stating:

> WERE IT OTHERWISE, THEN JUST AS WITHOUT THE *WEEKS* RULE THE ASSURANCE AGAINST UNREASONABLE FEDERAL SEARCHES AND SEIZURES WOULD BE "A FORM OF WORDS," VALUELESS AND UNDESERVING OF MENTION IN A PERPETUAL CHARTER OF INESTIMABLE HUMAN LIBERTIES, SO TOO, WITHOUT THAT RULE THE FREEDOM FROM STATE INVASIONS OF PRIVACY WOULD BE SO EPHEMERAL AND SO NEATLY SEVERED FROM ITS CONCEPTUAL NEXUS WITH THE FREEDOM FROM ALL BRUTISH MEANS OF COERCING EVIDENCE AS NOT TO MERIT THIS COURT'S HIGH REGARD AS A FREEDOM "IMPLICIT IN THE CONCEPT OF ORDERED LIBERTY."

Justice Clark was mindful of the inconsistency that the previous, long-standing relationship between federal and state authorities had produced. He said that the Court's decision to incorporate the exclusionary rule was:

> NOT ONLY THE LOGICAL DICTATE OF PRIOR CASES, BUT IT ALSO MAKES VERY GOOD SENSE. THERE IS NO WAR BETWEEN THE CONSTITUTION AND COMMON SENSE. PRESENTLY, A FEDERAL PROSECUTOR MAY MAKE NO USE OF EVIDENCE ILLEGALLY SEIZED, BUT A STATE'S ATTORNEY ACROSS THE STREET MAY, ALTHOUGH HE SUPPOSEDLY IS OPERATING UNDER THE ENFORCEABLE PROVISIONS OF THE SAME AMENDMENT. THUS THE STATE, BY ADMITTING EVIDENCE UNLAWFULLY SEIZED, SERVES TO ENCOURAGE DISOBEDIENCE TO THE FEDERAL CONSTITUTION WHICH IT IS BOUND TO UPHOLD.

The *Mapp* ruling completed the incorporation of the Fourth Amendment by providing for its enforcement in state courts. Today, both state and federal authorities must operate under the same constitutional standards governing searches and seizures. Still, opposition to the restrictions of the exclusionary rule has been on the increase in recent years. These matters are explored in the following chapter.

INCORPORATION OF THE FIFTH AMENDMENT

Of the five provisions in the Fifth Amendment, one—the Due Process Clause—was duplicated in the Fourteenth Amendment, while three others—double jeopardy (*Benton v. Maryland* [1969]), self-incrimination (*Malloy v. Hogan* [1964]), and just compensation (*Chicago, Burlington & Quincy Ry. v. Chicago* [1897])—have been incorporated as fundamental liberties. The lone unincorporated provision is the Grand Jury Clause, which states that "No person shall be held to answer for a capital, or otherwise infamous, crime, unless on a presentment or **indictment** of a Grand Jury." Not all states require grand jury indictments, and many have chosen to allow a prosecutor's **information** in place of an indictment. An information affidavit stipulates that the prosecuting attorney possesses evidence to justify a trial. Of course, all criminal defendants in federal courts must be indicted by a federal grand jury before trial. Given the well-established use of the prosecutor's information, as well as some criticisms of the grand jury system, it is unlikely that the Grand Jury Clause will be incorporated into the Fourteenth Amendment and applied to the states.

The matter of double jeopardy, as noted earlier, was raised by Palko in his unsuccessful 1937 attempt to incorporate the privilege. In *Benton v. Maryland* (1969), the Court addressed the issue again and arrived at quite different results from those in *Palko*. John Benton had been charged with burglary and larceny in a single indictment. The trial resulted in his acquittal for larceny but conviction for burglary. Upon Benton's appeal, the indictment was found to be faulty due to a defect in the grand jury process. The state reindicted him, and this time he was convicted on both counts.

Writing for the Court, Justice Thurgood Marshall held that Benton's conviction for larceny could not be judged "by the watered-down standard enunciated in *Palko*, but under this Court's interpretations of the Fifth Amendment double jeopardy provision." Marshall's opinion clearly applied "federal double jeopardy standards" to the case, and held that the larceny conviction could not stand. Coming more than thirty years after *Palko*, the *Benton* decision stands as a good example of our society's changing understanding of the due process of law.

INCORPORATION OF THE SIXTH AMENDMENT

Of the eight distinct rights presented in the Sixth Amendment, two were incorporated in the late 1940s, and the remaining six were incorporated during the 1960s and the tenure of the Warren Court. In one way or another, all of these rights involve the courtroom and the manner in which a trial is to be conducted. Individuals are entitled to a speedy and public trial by an impartial jury of their peers, with proper notice of the charges, the right to confront witnesses and obtain information held by the prosecution, and the right to an attorney.

In *Duncan v. Louisiana* (1968), a 7–2 majority of the Court held that "trial by jury in criminal cases is fundamental to the American scheme of justice." As such, the majority held that "the Fourteenth Amendment guarantees a right of jury trial in all criminal cases which—were they to be tried in a federal court—would come within the Sixth Amendment's guarantee." In their incorporation of the Sixth Amendment's jury trial provisions, the Court reversed the conviction of Gary Duncan, a black man, for simple battery in a Louisiana court. Duncan, charged with slapping a white person on the elbow, asked for a jury trial, but the judge denied his request on the grounds that Louisiana law provided for jury trials only in cases in which hard labor or capital punishment might be imposed. Although Duncan was sentenced only to sixty days in jail and a fine of $150, state law provided for as much as two years' imprisonment and a $300 fine.

Justice Byron White's majority opinion addressed the question of what constitutes a "petty offense" for purposes of a jury trial. The state of Louisiana had contended that Duncan's sixty-day sentence made the case a minor matter, but White's opinion focused on the "penalty authorized for a particular crime." White noted the existence of "a category of petty crimes or offenses which is not subject to the Sixth Amendment jury trial provision and should not be subject to the Fourteenth Amendment jury trial requirement here applied to the States." Nevertheless, the fact that Louisiana had authorized up to two years' imprisonment for a simple battery conviction served, in White's view, to make it far from a petty offense. He noted that the federal system defined petty offenses "as those punishable by no more than six months in prison and a $500 fine," although his opinion stopped short of precisely defining the "exact location of the line between petty offenses and serious crimes." No matter where the line might fall, the Court was convinced that a crime punishable by two years in prison qualifies as a serious offense. In 1970, the Court defined a "serious crime" as one that involves imprisonment for six months or more.[22]

The Supreme Court incorporated the right to confront witnesses in the case of *Pointer v. Texas* (1965). In that case, Robert Pointer had been charged with robbery and testified against by the victim, Kenneth Phillips, at a preliminary hearing. Since Pointer had no attorney at the hearing, no one cross-examined Phillips, who subsequently moved out of the state. At Pointer's trial, the prosecution introduced a transcript of Phillips's testimony, and Pointer was convicted. On appeal, Pointer claimed that the state of Texas had denied him the Sixth Amendment right to confront witnesses, and the Supreme Court agreed.

The Sixth Amendment's right of compulsory process to secure witnesses allows the accused to call witnesses on his behalf, just as the state has the power to subpoena its witnesses. The Supreme Court incorporated this right in *Washington v. Texas* (1967), striking down a Texas statute that prohibited a codefendant from testifying on behalf of the accused. Texas held that this restriction was intended to reduce the likelihood of perjury in such situations, but the Court found the effect on due process to be too severe. As a result, if a defendant calls an individual to be a witness, that witness may not refuse to testify by citing the accused's self-incrimination rights. Nonetheless, some communications have continued to remain privileged and hence not subject to testimonial requirements, most notably husband–wife and certain lawyer–client privileges.

Finally, the remaining Sixth Amendment guarantee, the assistance of counsel, was incorporated in *Gideon v. Wainwright* (1963), following a rather lengthy process. It is discussed more fully in Chapter 13, along with an overview of more recent Sixth Amendment developments.

INCORPORATION OF THE EIGHTH AMENDMENT

Of the two distinct clauses in the Eighth Amendment, only one has been incorporated into the Fourteenth Amendment and held applicable to the states. The Excessive Bail and Fines Clause remains limited to the national government in its application, but it is not inconceivable that future litigation will bring this clause within the parameters of due process of law. The amendment's other clause, known as Cruel and Unusual Punishments, has been incorporated. While most of the constitutional debate concerning this clause has involved the death penalty (see the following chapter), the case that incorporated the clause dealt with another subject entirely.

The Supreme Court addressed the issue of cruel and unusual punishments in *Robinson v. California* (1962), involving a California statute that made it a misdemeanor to be "addicted to the use of narcotics." The appellant, Lawrence Robinson, had been arrested by a police officer who observed scars and needle marks on Robinson's arms, although he was not under the influence of drugs at that time. Speaking for himself and four other justices, Justice Stewart found that narcotics addiction was an illness and not a criminal offense. Under the illness reasoning, he suggested that no state would consider making it a criminal offense to be "mentally ill, or a leper, or to be afflicted with a venereal disease." Punishment of an affliction such as drug addiction "inflicts a cruel and unusual punishment in violation of the Fourteenth Amendment." By this ruling, the Eighth Amendment's ban on cruel and unusual punishments was incorporated into the Due Process Clause of the Fourteenth Amendment. In dissent, Justice White criticized what he called the "novel" application of cruel and unusual punishment in this case.

BEYOND THE BILL OF RIGHTS: FUNDAMENTAL RIGHTS AND DUE PROCESS OF LAW

The Bill of Rights remains the primary constitutional locus for the protection of individual liberty against governments representing community interests and values. But the Constitution is over two hundred years old, and issues involving individual liberties cannot be confined to the specific protections enumerated in the 1791 landmark. The same Fourteenth Amendment that has been the vehicle for application to the states of provisions found in the Bill of Rights also gives a broad guarantee that individual liberty shall not be deprived without due process of law. And the Bill of Rights itself, specifically the Ninth Amendment, tells us to look beyond the first eight amendments for "the enumeration ... of [other rights] retained by the people" (see Brief 11.3).

Beginning over seventy years ago, the Supreme Court acknowledged that fundamental rights, including those not found in the Bill of Rights, deserved constitutional protection against government intrusion. Chapter 10 discussed Justice Harlan Stone's famous footnote in *United States v. Carolene Products Co.* (1938), where he suggested that a "more exacting judicial scrutiny" should be applied to government actions that individuals claimed deprived them of their constitutional rights, especially those found in the first ten amendments. Four years later, in *Skinner v. Oklahoma* (1942), the Court invalidated an Oklahoma law requiring the sterilization of persons convicted a third time for felonies "involving moral turpitude." Writing for the Court, Justice Douglas invoked the Fourteenth Amendment to speak out against deprivation of an individual's fundamental rights, even though the sterilization law in question

---

Brief 11.3

WHAT DOES THE NINTH AMENDMENT MEAN?

The attempt to locate a right to privacy in the Ninth Amendment raises questions about the uses to which this amendment can be put. In his Senate confirmation hearings in 1987, Judge Robert Bork argued that the Ninth Amendment was originally designed to protect rights found in the various state constitutions in 1791. He disputed the contention that a judge could use the Ninth Amendment to give substance to "newly found" rights and to protect them from government interference. But research into the intentions of the framers of the Bill of Rights suggests that Judge Bork's narrow interpretation of the Ninth Amendment may be misguided. When Madison sat down to draft a Bill of Rights in 1789, one of his main fears, echoed in the words of other political leaders, was that by listing the rights protected against government interference, the implication might be that government could abridge equally important liberties not enumerated in the Bill of Rights. Some of Madison's colleagues held the idea that any such enumeration of certain rights might result in the violation of other basic human rights that were not specifically identified:

> *The conclusion will be that [the framers of the Bill of Rights] have established all which they esteem valuable and sacred. On every principle, then, the people having begun, ought to go through enumerating, and establish particularly all the rights of individuals, which can by any possibility come in question in making and executing federal laws.*[12]

To avoid an extensive, maybe even incessant enumeration of rights in amending the Constitution, Madison fastened on the Ninth Amendment. Madison's own words offer proof of his intent:

> *It has been objected against a bill of rights, that, by enumerating particular exceptions to the grant of power, it would disparage those rights which were not placed in that enumeration; and it might follow by implication, that those rights which were not singled out, were intended to be assigned into the hands of the General Government, and were consequently insecure. This is one of the most plausible arguments I have ever heard urged against the admission of a bill of rights into this system; but I conceive, that it may be guarded against. I have attempted it, as gentlemen may see by turning to the last clause of the fourth resolution (the Ninth Amendment).*[13]

It is clear from this examination of Madison's intent, then, that the Ninth Amendment potentially goes beyond any enumerated rights in either the federal or the various state constitutions of the time. The problem, however, is that to use the Ninth Amendment to create "new fundamental rights," a judge may be opening a Pandora's box of constitutional rights. As such, Supreme Court justices have been reticent to ground fundamental rights arguments in the Ninth Amendment, preferring the language of the Due Process Clause or even the "penumbras" argument of Justice Douglas in *Griswold*.

here failed to directly interfere with protections found in the Bill of Rights. Ordinarily, Douglas wrote, the Court would defer to state criminal statutes, but "we are dealing here with legislation which involves one of the basic civil rights of man. Marriage and procreation are fundamental to the very existence and survival of the race." An individual falling under this law "is forever deprived of a basic liberty." Douglas concluded that in areas like this involving fundamental civil rights, "strict scrutiny" of state laws "is essential."

Since *Skinner*, then, the Supreme Court has used the Constitution to hold that "any classification which serves to penalize the exercise of a fundamental right, unless shown to be necessary to promote a compelling governmental interest, is unconstitutional."[14] Using a fundamental-rights analysis, the Court has not only ruled against laws that deter or penalize the exercise of a fundamental right, but also has invalidated government policies that create inequalities in access to or levels of a fundamental right. Thus, the Court says that the Constitution disallows *relative* deprivations that usurp the power of individuals to exercise rights and make choices in areas that ought to be beyond the majority's control.

Of course, the interpretation of fundamental rights under the Ninth and Fourteenth Amendments is controversial. It involves the judiciary in making determinations about what constitutes a fundamental right, often absent any clear constitutional statement. Beyond the question of what makes a right fundamental (see Brief 11.4), judges have had to decide the limits of such rights. Are fundamental rights absolutely protected, absent a compelling governmental interest? Or can government regulate the exercise of these rights? If so, to what extent can government restrict the individual's fundamental rights?

The Supreme Court's answers to these questions about the nature and scope of fundamental rights have understandably brought it under constitutional criticism. Critics such as Chief Justice Rehnquist and Professor John Hart Ely have argued that elected officials representing the people's will, and not judges, should make determinations about what rights beyond those explicitly listed in the Constitution itself are fundamental.[15] Others have contended that the scope of protection offered to fundamental rights under the Fourteenth Amendment suggests the Court's earlier "substantive due process" decisions like *Lochner v. New York*, where property rights were

---

Brief 11.4
WHAT MAKES A RIGHT FUNDAMENTAL?

In the process of "discovering" fundamental rights, judges have attempted to answer the question of what makes a right fundamental, and what the source of such rights ought to be. For the strict constructionist, of course, the only fundamental rights the Supreme Court can protect are those found explicitly in the text of the Constitution itself. All other rights are determined by popularly elected officials. For most judges and constitutional scholars, however, this strict adherence to the Constitutional text too narrowly defines the area free from governmental intrusion. Most constitutional commentators, therefore, would grant fundamental status to rights beyond those listed in the Constitution. But where do we draw the line between rights that are fundamental and ones that are not? A brief look at judicial reasoning beyond Justice Marshall's comments in the introduction to this chapter may be instructive.

In the *Palko* case discussed earlier in this chapter, Justice Cardozo justified incorporating specific provisions of rights into the Fourteenth Amendment by saying that rights "so rooted in the traditions and collective conscience of our people as to be ranked as fundamental" deserved constitutional protection. Cardozo also spoke of the fundamental nature of rights "implicit in the concept of ordered liberty." In more recent years, justices have sought other lines of reasoning to find sources of fundamental rights. Justice Douglas in *Griswold v. Connecticut* (discussed in a later section of this chapter) found substantive rights emanating from the Bill of Rights that created "penumbras" of protection for rights implied by its specific provisions. In the same decision, Justice Goldberg saw the source of fundamental rights as the "entire fabric of the Constitution and the purposes that underlie its specific guarantees," and Justice Harlan pointed to "history and tradition" as his source for fundamental rights. Chief Justice Warren found the source of fundamental rights in "the evolving standards of decency that mark the progress of a maturing society."[16]

All of these different standards for determining what rights (beyond those explicitly listed in the Constitution) are fundamental may be more confusing than clarifying. And it is hard to escape the conclusion of Justice White, who commented: "What the deeply rooted traditions of the country are is arguable; which of them deserve the protection of the Due Process Clause is even more debatable." Indeed, what makes a right fundamental may ultimately be rooted more in "judges' . . . personal and private notions" than in their disinterested interpretation of the Constitution.[17]

given more or less absolute protection against any government interference.

But whatever the problems with the open-endedness of the search for fundamental rights, with the overextension of judicial authority involved in such a search, and with the usurpation of the power of the people's tribunals (the legislatures) to make policy on such matters, the Court has continued to use fundamental rights reasoning to place certain interests beyond the scope of majority control. The rest of this chapter examines the issues surrounding the expansion of fundamental rights beyond the first eight amendments. What rights have (or have not) been deemed fundamental, their scope of protection by the Court, and the controversies raised by them are all discussed in the case history that follows.

THE RIGHT TO VOTE

One of the first rights beyond those found in the Bill of Rights to be recognized as fundamental is the right to vote. Of course, the right to vote can be said to have textual support in the Constitution, as the Fifteenth, Nineteenth, and Twenty-sixth Amendments all prohibit governmental denial of voting rights based on race, sex, or age. In the past half-century, however, the Court has not only enshrined voting as a fundamental right, it has declared that inequalities in the franchise threaten that fundamental right, and has been willing to invalidate a wide range of governmental practices with respect to the franchise. Chapter 9 discussed the dismantling by both the courts and Congress of racial barriers to equal voting rights. Here we examine how the Supreme Court has used the Constitution to rule against the following practices: (1) legislative apportionment plans that give voters unequal representation, (2) state laws that deny equal access to the franchise, and (3) statutes that restrict candidate and party access to the ballot.

LEGISLATIVE APPORTIONMENT

Chapter 4 examined the Supreme Court's landmark apportionment decisions beginning with *Baker* v. *Carr*. As that discussion revealed, legislative malapportionment raised few constitutional questions before the 1960s. States were generally free from any federal controls over how they set up districts for the purpose of electing representatives to the state legislatures. Left to their own devices, many states deviated from a strict population standard in their legislative apportionment schemes. Voters began to realize that although they had an equal right to vote, districting schemes that diluted their representation in the state legislature in effect made the impact of their vote unequal. In a series of cases culminating in *Reynolds v. Sims* (1964), the Supreme Court decided the Fourteenth Amendment meant that each vote must count equally in a state's legislative apportionment plan.

Reynolds v. Sims challenged the constitutionality of Alabama's legislative apportionment scheme. Alabama's constitution mandated that the legislature reapportion its electoral districts every ten years. It qualified this reapportionment, however, by providing that each county be provided at least one representative in the state's lower house and that each county be allocated only one senator in the upper house. No reapportionment had taken place in Alabama since 1901, resulting in highly skewed representation. Lower house districts ranged in population from 6,700 to 104,000, while state senatorial districts ranged from 15,000 to 634,000. Under this apportionment scheme, it was possible for 25 percent of the state's population to elect a majority in the state senate. A group of citizens challenged the apportionment plan on the grounds that it violated the Equal Protection Clause. The Supreme Court was eventually asked to decide the question after a district court invalidated several reapportionment plans.

The Supreme Court, in an 8–1 decision, decided that all state legislative apportionment plans would have to accord with the standard that each person's vote count equally with another's. Chief Justice Warren's majority opinion began with a statement about the fundamental nature of the right to vote:

> UNDOUBTEDLY, THE RIGHT OF SUFFRAGE IS A FUNDAMENTAL MATTER IN A FREE AND DEMOCRATIC SOCIETY. ESPECIALLY SINCE THE RIGHT TO EXERCISE THE FRANCHISE IN A FREE AND UNIMPAIRED MANNER IS PRESERVATIVE OF OTHER BASIC CIVIL AND POLITICAL RIGHTS, ANY ALLEGED INFRINGEMENT OF THE RIGHT OF CITIZENS TO VOTE MUST BE CAREFULLY AND METICULOUSLY EXAMINED.

Applying this standard, Chief Justice Warren ruled that both houses of a state legislature must be apportioned according to population so as to preserve the standard of "one person, one vote":

> WE HOLD THAT, AS A BASIC CONSTITUTIONAL STANDARD, THE EQUAL PROTECTION CLAUSE REQUIRES THAT THE SEATS IN BOTH HOUSES OF A BICAMERAL STATE LEGISLATURE MUST BE APPORTIONED ON A POPULATION BASIS. SIMPLY STATED, AN INDIVIDUAL'S RIGHT TO VOTE FOR STATE LEGISLATORS IS UNCONSTITUTIONALLY IMPAIRED WHEN ITS WEIGHT IS IN A SUBSTANTIAL FASHION DILUTED WHEN COMPARED WITH VOTES OF CITIZENS LIVING IN OTHER PARTS OF THE STATE.

The Court conceded that it would be impossible as well as undesirable to require strict, mathematical equality in apportioning legislative districts. The Chief Justice noted that "mathematical exactness or precision is hardly a workable constitutional requirement." Nevertheless, the Court *has* made it a constitutional requirement that state legislatures make an honest and good faith effort to construct their districts as equally as possible, not only to give voters their equal rights, but to satisfy basic principles of democracy and majority rule.

EQUAL ACCESS TO THE FRANCHISE

The Court has maintained that a second principle necessary to guarantee the fundamental right to vote is that the franchise must be made available to all citizens on an equal basis. The Court has invalidated a number of state statutes attempting to impede equal access to the voting booth.

For example, in 1966 the Court finally invalidated the poll tax as a requirement for voting in state elections. Poll taxes were yet another method some states adopted at the turn of the century to keep blacks and poor whites from voting. Although poll taxes had fallen into general disuse, the Court had upheld their use in *Breedlove* v. *Suttles* (1939). In 1965, a handful of states still required payment of a small tax to vote in state elections (the Twenty-fourth Amendment to the Constitution, ratified in 1964, outlawed the poll tax in federal elections). But in *Harper v. Virginia State Board of Elections* (1966), the Supreme Court held that the poll tax violated the Constitution. Justice Douglas, writing for the six-justice majority, contended that "the right to vote is too precious, too fundamental to be burdened or conditioned" by the payment of a fee, however small (Virginia's annual poll tax was $1.50). His reasoning for invalidating the poll tax continued:

> [T]HE INTEREST OF THE STATE, WHEN IT COMES TO VOTING, IS LIMITED TO THE POWER TO FIX QUALIFICATIONS. WEALTH, LIKE CREED, OR COLOR, IS NOT GERMANE TO ONE'S ABILITY TO PARTICIPATE INTELLIGENTLY IN THE ELECTORAL PROCESS.... TO INTRODUCE WEALTH OR PAYMENT OF A FEE AS A MEASURE OF A VOTER'S QUALIFICATIONS IS TO INTRODUCE A CAPRICIOUS OR IRRELEVANT FACTOR.

A few years later the Court extended the principle established in *Harper* and rejected New York's attempt to restrict school board elections to property owners and the parents of public school children. In *Kramer v. Union Free School District No. 15* (1969), the Court ruled that "statutes granting the franchise to residents on a selective basis always pose the danger of denying some citizens any effective voice in the governmental affairs which substantially affect their lives." The Court indicated that any restriction on the franchise would be subjected to strict scrutiny.

Another area where the Court has demonstrated hostility to state restrictions on the right to vote is durational residency requirements. *Dunn* v. *Blumstein* (1972), the seminal case here, involved the Court's invalidation of a Tennessee law requiring one year's residence in the state and three months in the county as a condition of voting. The Supreme Court struck down the statute, both because it limited the right to vote and because it burdened interstate travel (to be discussed in a later section of this chapter). The Court (and Congress) basically limited state residency requirements for voting to thirty days.[18] More recently, concerns about transient students skewing the results of local elections in college towns has raised the question of whether college students can be denied access to the vote in the districts where they are attending school (see Brief 11.5).

Brief 11.5
CAN COLLEGE STUDENTS BE RESTRICTED FROM VOTING ON CAMPUS?

College students often create resentment among the permanent residents who live near campus, and "town-gown" relations have been known to be tense in many parts of the country. This often has to do with rowdy or disrespectful student behavior, noisy parties, and failure to clean up the streets or neighborhoods where students live abutting the campus. But in recent years, a growing concern has arisen when political organizers mobilize college students to vote for candidates or issues in state and municipal elections. Long-time residents, property owners, and taxpayers have been angered when students—who are only passing through town for a few years—are turned out on election day to vote for candidates or approve initiatives and referenda that will affect the community for many years. If the students come from another state, or a different district within the state, can they be barred from voting in the district where they are attending college?

This question has been raised by efforts in several communities to prohibit students from voting in the jurisdiction where they are enrolled in college. For example, at the beginning of the 2011 legislative session, the New Hampshire legislature considered a proposal denying voter registration to college students who did not live in the state before attending school and who do not intend to stay. However, the Supreme Court's decision in *Symm v. United States* (1979) would seem to render such efforts unconstitutional. In the *Symm* case, the Court affirmed, without opinion, a district-court ruling that an effort in Waller County, Texas, to keep Prairie View A&M students from registering to vote was a violation of the Twenty-sixth Amendment. This ruling has been interpreted to mean that college students have a choice of where to vote. They can vote either where they attend college, or where they lived with their family before attending college (but not both places!).

The Court is not always hostile to state or local laws challenged on grounds that they restrict voter access. In an important decision with major ramifications today, the Court indicated that state laws requiring voters to show identification at the polling place do not threaten voter access. In *Crawford* v. *Marion County Election Board* (2008), a 6–3 majority upheld Indiana's requirement that all citizens show current state or federal photo identification in order to cast a ballot, in the face of challenges claiming that this would be an unconstitutional burden on the voting rights of many citizens. Right now a majority of states either have laws in effect or have proposed new laws requiring voters to present some type of photo identification to vote. Legal challenges to these laws are pending in several states.

Another area where the Court has been less hostile to state restrictions concerns the voting rights of convicted felons, an issue that has begun to receive substantial attention across the nation (see Brief 11.6). In *Richardson v. Ramirez* (1974), a six-justice majority ruled that California did not have to prove a compelling state interest in permanently disenfranchising felons convicted of "an infamous crime," in part because Section 2 of the Fourteenth Amendment exempts state restrictions on voting rights based on a citizen's "participation in rebellion, or other crime."

EQUAL ACCESS TO THE BALLOT: *WILLIAMS V. RHODES* (1968)

The third principle the Court has enunciated in voting rights questions is that citizens should be able to vote "meaningfully" and "effectively." What this means is that the Court strictly scrutinizes laws that restrict candidate and political party access to elections. The Court first addressed the issue of ballot access in *Williams v. Rhodes* (1968). In question were Ohio election laws that severely burdened the ability of third-party candidates to win a place on the presidential ballot, while automatically including the two major-party candidates. The Court decided that the election laws impaired "the right of qualified voters, regardless of their political persuasion, to cast their votes effectively." Without a showing of a compelling state interest, the Court declared that Ohio could not—consistent with the Equal Protection Clause—establish such burdensome obstacles to a third-party candidacy. The Court's logic in *Williams* has been applied consistently to outlaw a number of restrictive electoral practices in the past two decades.[19]

In short, then, the Court has declared the right to vote to be fundamental, something that must be provided on an equal basis. Moreover, the Court has operated to the detriment of states attempting to carry out policies that were once within their sole

Brief 11.6

THE RIGHT TO VOTE AND CONVICTED FELONS

The past three presidential elections and resulting concerns about voter disenfranchisement have led to greater scrutiny of state policies regarding the voting rights of convicted felons. Advocacy groups estimate that as many as 5.3 million American citizens nationwide are ineligible to vote as a result of laws that prohibit voting by felons or ex-felons, with nearly half being ex-felons who have served their prison time. Only two states (Maine and Vermont) allow prisoners to vote, but in the other 48 and the District of Columbia, policies vary quite dramatically on whether and when ex-felons who have served their sentences can have their voting rights restored. In four states any citizen convicted of a felony is permanently excluded from the voting booth, and in eight others a felony conviction may result in permanent disenfranchisement. Only thirteen states and the District of Columbia allow felons to vote immediately after release from prison; the rest make ex-felons wait until after parole or probation to enter the voting booth. With public demand for longer sentences, including parole and probation, this has the effect of delaying the enfranchisement of many ex-felons. And although state policies regarding felons' voting rights vary dramatically from state to state, in every state laws prohibiting convicted felons from voting have a disproportionate impact on African Americans, particularly African American males. One advocacy group estimates that 13 percent of black men are unable to vote as a result of felony disenfranchisement laws.

Changes have occurred over the last several years, and some ex-felons have regained their voting rights. Since the 2000 election, over a dozen states have consciously liberalized their policies, allowing more citizens who have served prison sentences for felonies to have their voting rights restored. In another handful of states, laws or constitutional amendments restoring voting rights to citizens upon release from prison are pending. Support for reform seems to be growing, reflecting a position that to keep ex-felons from voting not only denies these citizens their rights (some call it a form of taxation without representation), it also isolates them and prevents their full reintegration into the community. On the other side, it is argued that those convicted of a felony have broken the social contract and therefore are not entitled to full citizen rights. And as a practical matter, it is difficult for legislators to restore the voting rights of ex-felons, for fear of being perceived as "soft on crime."

---

authority. The Court has subjected a wide range of state electoral practices to strict scrutiny under the Fourteenth Amendment. The Court's general position is found in a statement by Chief Justice Warren: "Once the franchise is granted to the electorate, lines may not be drawn which are inconsistent with the Equal Protection Clause."[20]

THE RIGHT TO INTERSTATE TRAVEL: *SHAPIRO V. THOMPSON*

Along with the right to vote, the Court has recognized as fundamental the right to travel and migrate from state to state. The Court long ago established the citizen's right to travel. In the *Passenger Cases* (1849), Chief Justice Taney announced that all "citizens of the United States . . . must have the right to pass and repass through every part of [the country] without interruption, as freely as in our own States." This position was echoed by the Court in *United States v. Guest* (1966):

> THE CONSTITUTIONAL RIGHT TO TRAVEL FROM ONE STATE TO ANOTHER . . . OCCUPIES A POSITION FUNDAMENTAL TO THE CONCEPT OF OUR FEDERAL UNION. IT IS A RIGHT THAT HAS BEEN FIRMLY ESTABLISHED AND REPEATEDLY RECOGNIZED.

In *Shapiro v. Thompson* (1969), the Court's protection of the right to travel from state to state took on a broader significance. The justices began to use the Constitution to prevent the states from enacting regulations that would have the *effect* of impairing interstate mobility. *Shapiro* concerned the validity of state laws that denied welfare benefits to people who had not resided in the state for at least one year. Vivian Thompson, a pregnant, nineteen-year-old unwed mother, moved to Connecticut from Massachusetts and subsequently applied for state aid under the Aid to Families with Dependent Children (AFDC) program. Upon being told that she did not meet Connecticut's one-year residency requirement, Thompson sued the state welfare commissioner, claiming a violation of her right to equal protection.

In a 6–3 decision, the Supreme Court invalidated the state's residency requirement as violative of a citizen's equal right to interstate travel and migration. Justice Brennan delivered the opinion of the Court:

> THERE IS NO DISPUTE THAT THE EFFECT OF THE WAITING PERIOD REQUIREMENT . . . IS TO CREATE TWO CLASSES OF NEEDY RESIDENT FAMILIES INDISTINGUISHABLE FROM EACH OTHER EXCEPT THAT ONE IS COMPOSED OF RESIDENTS WHO HAVE RESIDED A YEAR OR MORE, AND THE SECOND OF RESIDENTS WHO HAVE RESIDED LESS THAN A YEAR, IN THE JURISDICTION. ON THE BASIS OF THIS SOLE DIFFERENCE THE FIRST CLASS IS GRANTED AND THE SECOND CLASS IS DENIED WELFARE AID UPON WHICH MAY DEPEND THE ABILITY OF THE FAMILIES TO OBTAIN THE VERY MEANS TO SUBSIST—FOOD, SHELTER, AND OTHER NECESSITIES OF LIFE. . . . [WE AGREE] THAT THE STATUTORY PROHIBITION OF BENEFITS TO RESIDENTS OF LESS THAN A YEAR CREATES A CLASSIFICATION WHICH CONSTITUTES AN INVIDIOUS DISCRIMINATION DENYING THEM EQUAL PROTECTION OF THE LAWS.

Justice Brennan based his conclusions on the statute's interference with a constitutional right to interstate travel. Although he acknowledged that the "right finds no explicit mention in the Constitution," he nevertheless believed it was fundamental, and that the state could not show a compelling interest to restrict the right to interstate travel.

Justice Harlan's dissent took issue with the Court's expansion of the Fourteenth Amendment to protect fundamental rights. Harlan wrote that the "compelling state interest [test] is sound when applied to racial classifications," but unwise when applied under "the more recent extensions" to other classification schemes and to fundamental rights. Contending that "virtually every state statute affects important rights," Justice Harlan objected that:

> TO EXTEND THE "COMPELLING INTEREST" RULE TO ALL CASES IN WHICH SUCH RIGHTS ARE AFFECTED WOULD GO FAR TOWARD MAKING THIS COURT A "SUPER-LEGISLATURE". . . . I KNOW OF NOTHING WHICH ENTITLES THIS COURT TO PICK OUT PARTICULAR HUMAN ACTIVITIES, CHARACTERIZE THEM AS "FUNDAMENTAL," AND GIVE THEM ADDED PROTECTION UNDER AN UNUSUALLY STRINGENT EQUAL PROTECTION TEST.

The Court's decision in *Shapiro* banned the use of residency requirements to penalize a citizen's exercise of the right to travel interstate. But although the Court has protected this fundamental right in certain situations involving durational residency requirements for voting (see the *Dunn v. Blumstein* discussion) and for receiving medical and other welfare benefits,[21] this right is not absolute. The Court has allowed the states to maintain residency restrictions for persons wishing to obtain a divorce, to gain admission to the state bar, to attend free public schools, or to be elected to the legislature. And the Court has refused to extend the same stringent protection to citizens against government interference with their right to travel outside the United States.[22]

A more recent case worth discussing in some detail seemingly expanded the constitutional right to travel. In *Saenz v. Roe* (1999), the Court used the rarely invoked Privileges and Immunities Clause to strike down a California law limiting state welfare benefits to new residents. In question here was the validity of legislation aimed at reducing the state's large welfare budget. California's legislature sought to limit new residents' benefits under the Temporary Assistance to Needy Families (TANF) program, which replaced the AFDC program in the welfare reforms of 1996, for the first twelve months they lived in the state. Benefits were limited to those they would have received in the state of their prior residence. At the time, California's welfare benefits under this program were among the highest in the nation. Congress had authorized states to enact such rules in its 1996 welfare reform legislation. Two women whose prior states of residence offered benefit levels that were substantially lower than California filed a class-action lawsuit challenging the constitutionality of this durational residency requirement.

In a 7–2 decision, the Supreme Court held unconstitutional the California law. In doing so, the justices had to go beyond prior right to travel decisions, as this state action neither prohibited travel to the state nor denied absolutely an important benefit to new residents (as was the case in *Shapiro v. Thompson* and *Dunn v. Blumstein*). Justice Stevens's majority opinion articulated "three different components" to the constitutional right to travel:

> IT PROTECTS THE RIGHT OF A CITIZEN OF ONE STATE TO ENTER AND TO LEAVE ANOTHER STATE, THE RIGHT TO BE TREATED AS A WELCOME VISITOR RATHER THAN AN UNFRIENDLY ALIEN WHEN TEMPORARILY PRESENT IN THE SECOND STATE, AND, FOR THOSE TRAVELERS WHO ELECT TO BECOME PERMANENT RESIDENTS, THE RIGHT TO BE TREATED LIKE OTHER CITIZENS OF THAT STATE.

In this case, the Court argued, California was denying "the right of the newly arrived citizen to the same privileges and immunities enjoyed by other citizens of the same State." Invoking the Privileges and Immunities Clause of the Fourteenth Amendment, Stevens proclaimed that "the right to travel embraces the citizen's right to be treated equally in her new State of residence," and denied California's attempt to create different classes of citizens based on where they last resided.

The two dissenting justices, Rehnquist and Thomas, worried about the expansive nature of the Court's ruling in *Saenz v. Roe*. Opening with the statement that "[t]he Court today breathes new life into the previously dormant Privileges and Immunities Clause," Rehnquist's dissent openly questioned the Court's consistency in this case with prior right to travel decisions. Justice Thomas's opinion retraced the history of the Privileges and Immunities Clause in order to determine its authors' original intent. He concluded from the history that "people understood that 'privileges or immunities of citizens' were fundamental rights, rather than every public benefit established by positive law." He concluded that the Court's decision here "raises the specter that the Privileges and Immunities Clause will become yet another convenient tool for inventing new rights."

THE RIGHT TO PRIVACY

In a series of decisions, the Supreme Court has also enshrined the right to privacy as a fundamental right deserving stringent protection under the Fourteenth Amendment. The right to privacy is unarguably the most discussed and debated of the fundamental rights the Court has singled out for constitutional protection against governmental interference. The Court's establishment of a constitutional right to privacy, and its strict scrutiny of laws invading that right, gave rise to a number of controversies. The first concerns its constitutional locus. Since an expressly protected right to privacy cannot be found in the Constitution's text, where does it originate? A second controversy lies in the extent to which privacy rights are protected. What does the right to privacy protect, and how far does it extend? Finally, the Court's finding of a fundamental right to privacy has generated conflict about judicial authority within our constitutional system. Do the courts have the authority to give substance to certain rights (e.g., privacy), protecting them against almost any interference by government? This final question involves a more specific criticism that the Court, in giving near-absolute protection to the right to privacy, is actually engaging in the same kind of faulty analysis it used early in the twentieth century under the substantive due process doctrine. In the course of the analysis here we attempt to take up these larger questions involving the right to privacy.

RIGHT TO PRIVACY: ORIGINS AND FOUNDATIONS

Louis Brandeis, a future justice on the Supreme Court, was the first to lobby for constitutional protections of the right to privacy. In a seminal 1890 *Law Review* article,[23] and later in a stinging Supreme Court dissenting opinion in *Olmstead v. U.S.* (1928), Brandeis argued that an individual's privacy was a right of significant constitutional concern:

> THE MAKERS OF OUR CONSTITUTION UNDERTOOK TO SECURE CONDITIONS FAVORABLE TO THE PURSUIT OF HAPPINESS.... THEY SOUGHT TO PROTECT AMERICANS IN THEIR BELIEFS, THEIR THOUGHTS, THEIR EMOTIONS AND THEIR SENSATIONS. THEY CONFERRED, AS AGAINST THE GOVERNMENT, THE RIGHT TO BE LET ALONE—THE MOST COMPREHENSIVE OF RIGHTS AND THE RIGHT MOST

> VALUED BY CIVILIZED MEN. TO PROTECT THAT RIGHT, EVERY UNJUSTIFIED INTRUSION OF THE GOVERNMENT UPON THE PRIVACY OF THE INDIVIDUAL, WHATEVER THE MEANS EMPLOYED, MUST BE DEEMED A [CONSTITUTIONAL] VIOLATION.

Thirty-seven years later, Justice Brandeis's opinion was vindicated by the Court majority in *Griswold v. Connecticut* (1965). The *Griswold* case concerned a Connecticut law that made it a crime to use or advise as to the use of "any drug, medicinal article or instrument for the purpose of preventing conception."[24] Estelle Griswold, executive director of the Planned Parenthood League of Connecticut, was found guilty under this law of dispensing contraceptive "information, instruction and medical advice" to married persons throughout the state. She appealed, claiming that the law in question violated the Fourteenth Amendment. In a 7–2 decision, the Court ruled the law unconstitutional. Writing for the Court, Justice Douglas announced that the Constitution protected an individual's right to privacy. Although he acknowledged that this right was not explicitly mentioned in the document, Douglas argued that the "right to privacy [is] older than the Bill of Rights—older than our political parties, older than our school system." Looking to specific provisions in the First, Third, Fourth, Fifth, and Ninth Amendments, Douglas indicated "that specific guarantees in the Bill of Rights have penumbras, formed by emanations from those guarantees that help give them life and substance.... Various guarantees create zones of privacy." Having enunciated this "penumbral" right to privacy, Justice Douglas went on to apply his reasoning to Estelle Griswold's case:

> THE PRESENT CASE, THEN, CONCERNS A RELATIONSHIP LYING WITHIN THE ZONE OF PRIVACY CREATED BY SEVERAL FUNDAMENTAL CONSTITUTIONAL GUARANTEES. AND IT CONCERNS A LAW WHICH, IN FORBIDDING THE USE OF CONTRACEPTIVES RATHER THAN REGULATING THEIR MANUFACTURE OR SALE, SEEKS TO ACHIEVE ITS GOALS BY MEANS HAVING A MAXIMUM DETRIMENTAL IMPACT ON THAT RELATIONSHIP.... WOULD WE ALLOW THE POLICE TO SEARCH THE SACRED PRECINCTS OF MARITAL BEDROOMS FOR TELLTALE SIGNS OF THE USE OF CONTRACEPTIVES? THE VERY IDEA IS REPULSIVE TO THE NOTIONS OF PRIVACY SURROUNDING THE MARRIAGE RELATIONSHIP.

Justice Douglas, relying on the penumbral shadow cast by other constitutional provisions, established the individual's vested right to privacy, free from governmental invasion. But not all justices would go along with Douglas's "astronomical" (penumbras) reasoning. Justice Goldberg, joined by Chief Justice Warren, relied largely on the Ninth Amendment (see Brief 11.3) as the constitutional source for a fundamental right to privacy. And Justices Harlan and White, in concurring opinions, lodged the right to privacy in the Due Process Clause of the Fourteenth Amendment.

In dissent, Justice Black wrote an opinion that would be echoed by other critics in more recent privacy cases. Though he found the Connecticut law "offensive," Black refused to vacate it without a direct conflict with "some specific constitutional provision." Justice Black questioned the majority's use of "natural law" reasoning reminiscent of *Lochner* and other substantive-due-process cases at the turn of the century:

> IF THESE FORMULAS BASED ON "NATURAL JUSTICE," OR OTHERS WHICH MEAN THE SAME THING, ARE TO PREVAIL, THEY REQUIRE JUDGES TO DETERMINE WHAT IS OR IS NOT CONSTITUTIONAL ON THE BASIS OF THEIR OWN OPINION OF WHAT LAWS ARE UNWISE OR UNNECESSARY.... THE USE BY FEDERAL COURTS OF SUCH A FORMULA OR DOCTRINE OR WHATNOT TO VETO FEDERAL OR STATE LAWS SIMPLY TAKES AWAY FROM CONGRESS AND STATES THE POWER TO MAKE LAWS BASED ON THEIR OWN JUDGMENT OF FAIRNESS AND WISDOM AND TRANSFERS THAT POWER TO THIS COURT FOR ULTIMATE DETERMINATION—A POWER WHICH WAS SPECIFICALLY DENIED TO FEDERAL COURTS BY THE CONVENTION THAT FRAMED THE CONSTITUTION.

The Court failed to heed Justice Black's fears, and seven years later expanded the protections of the right to privacy. In *Eisenstadt v. Baird* (1972), the Court ruled unconstitutional a Massachusetts law that prohibited the distribution of contraceptives to unmarried persons. Justice Brennan, writing for the majority, acknowledged that a law making it a crime to *distribute* contraceptives to unmarried persons differed from the law in *Griswold*, which penalized their *use* among married couples. Nevertheless, Brennan reached the conclusion that the fundamental right to privacy could not be impaired in accordance with the Equal Protection Clause:

> IT IS TRUE THAT IN *GRISWOLD* THE RIGHT OF PRIVACY IN QUESTION INHERED IN THE MARITAL RELATIONSHIP. YET THE MARITAL COUPLE IS NOT AN INDEPENDENT ENTITY WITH A MIND AND HEART OF ITS OWN, BUT AN ASSOCIATION OF TWO INDIVIDUALS EACH WITH A SEPARATE INTELLECTUAL AND EMOTIONAL MAKE-UP. IF THE RIGHT OF PRIVACY MEANS ANYTHING, IT IS THE RIGHT OF THE INDIVIDUAL, MARRIED OR SINGLE, TO BE FREE FROM UNWARRANTED GOVERNMENTAL INTRUSION INTO MATTERS SO FUNDAMENTALLY AFFECTING A PERSON AS THE DECISION WHETHER TO BEAR OR BEGET A CHILD.

The *Eisenstadt* decision is important for a number of reasons. First, in contradistinction to *Griswold*, the Court recognized that the right to privacy inheres in the person rather than in a place ("the sacred precincts of marital bedrooms") or in a protected "relationship" (marriage). Second, Justice Brennan employed a broad conception of privacy to outlaw legislation, a practice that has continued since 1972 and has brought the Court under substantial constitutional criticism for using the repudiated substantive-due-process reasoning. And finally, by attaching the right to privacy to the Equal Protection Clause, the Court seemed to be placing privacy questions under the same strict scrutiny given to racial classifications.

The Court was not finished extending the right to privacy. One year after *Eisenstadt*, the Court ruled that the right to privacy would protect women against restrictive abortion statutes, setting off a controversy that continues today. The discussion turns now to the famous case of *Roe v. Wade*.

THE RIGHT TO PRIVACY AND ABORTION

In 1972, most states severely limited a woman's access to legal abortion. Only four states (Alaska, Hawaii, New York, and Washington) allowed abortion with few legal restrictions, and the rest continued to operate under restrictive nineteenth-century statutes. Although a number of states liberalized their abortion laws beginning in 1967, in 1972 twenty-five states allowed an abortion only to save the mother's life. *Roe v. Wade* (1973) challenged one of the most restrictive abortion statutes. The Texas law in question, first enacted in 1854, made it a crime to "procure an abortion" except "by medical advice for the purpose of saving the life of the mother." Jane Roe (the pseudonym of an unmarried woman who wished to terminate her pregnancy) filed suit "on behalf of herself and all other women" similarly situated against Henry Wade, district attorney for Dallas County, Texas, asking the courts to rule the Texas criminal abortion laws unconstitutional. She claimed that the abortion statutes "abridged her right of personal privacy." The Supreme Court was asked to review Ms. Roe's case along with a challenge to a more liberal Georgia abortion statute.

By a 7–2 margin, the Supreme Court ruled that state criminal abortion laws like that of Texas violated a woman's right to privacy.[25] Justice Blackmun, writing for the Court, began his opinion by surveying the history of abortion "for such insight as that history may afford." (Blackmun's prior membership on the board of directors of the Mayo Clinic may explain his intense interest in the medical and legal history behind abortion.) After a lengthy historical survey, Blackmun determined that "at common law, at the time of the adoption of our Constitution, and throughout the major portion of the 19th century, abortion was viewed with less disfavor than under most American statutes [in effect in 1973]."

Justice Blackmun went on to state that the right of privacy, which he founded in the "concept of personal liberty" in the Due Process Clause of the Fourteenth Amendment, "is broad enough to encompass a woman's decision whether or not to terminate her pregnancy." The fundamental right to privacy was involved in a woman's abortion decision, and though her right was not absolute, it could only be abridged by the state if it could show a "compelling interest" (consistent with the strict-scrutiny approach to laws threatening fundamental rights).

The state of Texas contended that it had two compelling interests for enacting abortion restrictions: (1) to safeguard the mother's health and (2) to protect the right to life of the fetus (also guaranteed, the State argued, under the Fourteenth Amendment's Due Process Clause). Blackmun denied both claims, at least in the early stages of pregnancy. With respect to the right of prenatal life, Blackmun uttered these provocative words:

> [T]HE WORD *PERSON* AS USED IN THE FOURTEENTH AMENDMENT DOES NOT INCLUDE THE UNBORN. THE UNBORN HAVE NEVER BEEN RECOGNIZED IN THE LAW AS PERSONS IN THE WHOLE SENSE.... WE NEED NOT RESOLVE THE DIFFICULT QUESTION OF WHEN LIFE BEGINS. WHEN THOSE TRAINED IN THE RESPECTIVE DISCIPLINES OF MEDICINE, PHILOSOPHY, AND THEOLOGY ARE UNABLE TO ARRIVE AT ANY CONSENSUS, THE JUDICIARY, AT THIS POINT IN THE DEVELOPMENT OF MAN'S KNOWLEDGE, IS NOT IN A POSITION TO SPECULATE AS TO THE ANSWER.... WE DO NOT AGREE THAT, BY ADOPTING ONE THEORY OF LIFE, TEXAS MAY OVERRIDE THE RIGHTS OF THE PREGNANT WOMAN THAT ARE AT STAKE.

Still, the Court conceded that Texas had important and legitimate interests in protecting maternal health and the "potentiality of human life" represented in the fetus. Justice Blackmun noted that each of these state interests "grows in substantiality as the woman approaches term and, at a point during pregnancy, each becomes 'compelling.'" He then focused in on the sequence of a woman's pregnancy as the basis for balancing the woman's right to privacy with the state's compelling interests. For the majority, Blackmun reached certain conclusions, which are summarized below:

1. In the first trimester of pregnancy, during which maternal mortality in abortion is actually less than maternal mortality in normal childbirth, the state's interests are minimal. In this period the abortion decision is a private matter left up to the woman in consultation with her physician, free from state interference.
2. During the second trimester of pregnancy, "the State, in promoting its interest in the health of the mother, may, if it chooses, regulate the abortion procedure in ways that are reasonably related to maternal health" (e.g., regulating the facilities in which the abortion operation is performed and the persons performing the procedure). Still, during the second trimester, the decision itself whether or not to have an abortion must remain unfettered, consistent with the pregnant woman's right to privacy.
3. After the second trimester, the states' two interests become compelling. At this stage the fetus is viable, and "the State in promoting its interest in the potentiality of life may, if it chooses, regulate, and even proscribe, abortion except where it is necessary, in appropriate medical judgment, for the preservation of the life or health of the mother."

Blackmun concluded by striking down both the Texas and Georgia laws as too restrictive of the pregnant woman's right to privacy guaranteed by the Fourteenth Amendment.

The Court's opinion in *Roe v. Wade* unleashed a barrage of moral and legal criticism that continues today. Of course, there are those who, on moral grounds, chastise the Court for denying the rights of prenatal life. And some feminists, including Justice Ginsburg, have faulted the Court for lodging abortion rights under the right to privacy, as opposed to granting abortion rights as a part of a woman's right to equal protection under the Fourteenth Amendment. But Justice Blackmun's opinion also draws fire from those concerned about the Court's unjustified exercise of judicial authority. Dissenting opinions by Justices White and Rehnquist sum up this legal criticism best. Justice White said:

> THE COURT SIMPLY FASHIONS AND ANNOUNCES A NEW CONSTITUTIONAL RIGHT FOR PREGNANT WOMEN AND, WITH SCARCELY ANY REASON OR AUTHORITY FOR ITS ACTION, INVESTS THAT RIGHT WITH SUFFICIENT SUBSTANCE TO OVERRIDE MOST EXISTING STATE ABORTION STATUTES. THE UPSHOT IS THAT THE PEOPLE

AND THE LEGISLATURES OF THE 50 STATES ARE CONSTITUTIONALLY DISENTITLED TO WEIGH THE RELATIVE IMPORTANCE OF THE CONTINUED EXISTENCE AND DEVELOPMENT OF THE FETUS, ON THE ONE HAND, AGAINST A SPECTRUM OF POSSIBLE IMPACTS ON THE MOTHER, ON THE OTHER HAND. AS AN EXERCISE OF RAW JUDICIAL POWER, THE COURT PERHAPS HAS AUTHORITY TO DO WHAT IT DOES TODAY; BUT IN MY VIEW ITS JUDGMENT IS AN IMPROVIDENT AND EXTRAVAGANT EXERCISE OF THE POWER OF JUDICIAL REVIEW THAT THE CONSTITUTION EXTENDS TO THIS COURT.

And Justice Rehnquist raised the question of the Court's violation of the separation of powers, stepping into policy areas normally reserved to legislatures:

THE DECISION HERE TO BREAK PREGNANCY INTO THREE DISTINCT TERMS AND TO OUTLINE THE PERMISSIBLE RESTRICTIONS THE STATE MAY IMPOSE IN EACH ONE, FOR EXAMPLE, PARTAKES MORE OF JUDICIAL LEGISLATION THAN IT DOES OF A DETERMINATION OF THE INTENT OF THE DRAFTERS OF THE FOURTEENTH AMENDMENT.

For forty years, Supreme Court decisions have remained faithful to the basic *Roe* precedent, although majorities have voted to allow a variety of government restrictions on abortion.[26] Beginning with decisions allowing state and federal prohibitions on abortion funding and culminating with rulings that allow states substantial power in curbing abortion itself, the Court majority has slowly moved away from its initially strong support of abortion rights.

LIMITATIONS ON ABORTION RIGHTS: STATE AND FEDERAL FUNDING RESTRICTIONS

The one area where anti-abortion activists have won continuous success is in restricting state and federal abortion funding. Beginning with three cases decided in 1977, the Supreme Court has consistently held that neither the Constitution nor federal law requires states to pay for nontherapeutic (not medically necessary) abortions for poor women even though the same states pay for indigent childbirth costs. In one of those cases, *Maher v. Roe*, Justice Powell dispensed with equal protection claims made on behalf of indigent pregnant women. Lawyers challenging Connecticut's abortion funding restrictions contended that states "must accord equal treatment to both abortion and childbirth, and may not evidence a policy preference by funding only the medical expenses incident to childbirth." To deny payment to impoverished women for abortions was to disadvantage them solely on the basis of their indigency (thus operating to the disadvantage of the poor as a suspect class), as well as to interfere with their fundamental right to privacy inherent in the choice to terminate pregnancy.

But Justice Powell dismissed these equal protection claims. He found that the law did not operate to the disadvantage of any suspect class warranting strict judicial scrutiny (see Chapter 10 for a discussion of poverty and the Fourteenth Amendment). Justice Powell also denied that abortion funding restrictions operated to burden any fundamental right. The right established in *Roe v. Wade*, he claimed,

[ONLY] PROTECTS THE WOMAN FROM UNDULY BURDENSOME INTERFERENCE WITH HER FREEDOM TO DECIDE WHETHER TO TERMINATE HER PREGNANCY. IT IMPLIES NO LIMITATION ON THE AUTHORITY OF A STATE TO MAKE A VALUE JUDGMENT FAVORING CHILDBIRTH OVER ABORTION, AND TO IMPLEMENT THAT JUDGMENT BY THE ALLOCATION OF PUBLIC FUNDS.

Powell concluded that since no suspect class or fundamental right was burdened by laws restricting abortion funding to the poor, rationality scrutiny was the appropriate judicial standard. The state's "strong and legitimate interest in encouraging normal childbirth" rationalized such legislation. Exhibiting the kind of deference associated with rationality scrutiny, Powell concluded by saying that:

[W]HEN AN ISSUE INVOLVES POLICY CHOICES AS SENSITIVE AS THE FUNDING OF NONTHERAPEUTIC ABORTIONS, THE APPROPRIATE FORUM FOR THEIR RESOLUTION IN A DEMOCRACY IS THE LEGISLATURE.... CONNECTICUT IS FREE—THROUGH NORMAL

DEMOCRATIC PROCESSES—TO DECIDE THAT SUCH BENEFITS SHOULD BE PROVIDED. WE HOLD ONLY THAT THE CONSTITUTION DOES NOT REQUIRE A JUDICIALLY IMPOSED RESOLUTION OF THESE DIFFICULT ISSUES.

Justice Brennan, writing for Justices Marshall and Blackmun, dissented. He accused the Court majority of "a distressing insensitivity to the plight of impoverished pregnant women." The Court's decision not to apply strict scrutiny to abortion funding restrictions did not make sense to Brennan, given previous rulings: "The Connecticut scheme cannot be distinguished from other grants and withholdings of financial benefits that we have held unconstitutionally burdened a fundamental right." Using a strict scrutiny standard, Brennan concluded that the state regulation "constitutes an unconstitutional infringement of the fundamental right of pregnant women to be free to decide whether to have an abortion [by placing] financial pressures on indigent women that force them to bear children they would not otherwise have."

Despite Justice Brennan's criticisms, the Court has continued to uphold laws that restrict funding for abortions to indigent women, even including medically necessary abortions. *Harris v. McRae* (1980) held that the Hyde Amendment, prohibiting the payment of federal Medicaid funds for even abortions deemed medically necessary, was constitutional. And in *Rust v. Sullivan* (1991), a majority led by Chief Justice Rehnquist upheld a "gag rule" imposing restrictions on abortion counseling in federally funded family practice clinics (see Brief 11.7).

Brief 11.7
USING RESTRICTIONS ON SPEECH TO RESTRICT ABORTION: *RUST V. SULLIVAN*

The Court's decision in *Rust v. Sullivan* raises a number of important issues that not only involve abortion rights but also concern the First Amendment. In question was a reinterpretation of Title X of the Public Health Service Act, which grants federal funding to a variety of family planning projects. When the law was passed in 1970, it specified that no federal funds appropriated for family planning services "shall be used in programs where abortion is a method of family planning." In 1988, the Secretary of Health and Human Services issued new regulations expanding the original prohibition on abortion-related funding by attaching three new conditions on the grant of federal funds for Title X projects: (1) a Title X project "may not provide counseling concerning the use of abortion as a method of family planning or provide referral for abortion as a method of family planning," (2) Title X projects must refer every pregnant client "for appropriate prenatal and/or social services by furnishing a list of available providers that promote the welfare of the mother and the unborn child," and (3) a Title X project is prohibited from referring a pregnant client to an abortion provider, even upon the client's specific request. The response to be given to such an inquiry is that "the project does not consider abortion an appropriate method of family planning and therefore does not counsel or refer for abortion."

In ruling the new regulations constitutional, the majority relied on the *Maher v. Roe* and *Harris v. McRae* precedents. Rehnquist wrote that "when the government appropriates public funds to establish a program it is entitled to define the limits of that program," including, as in this case, what can be said by doctors and health professionals to pregnant women.

Once again Justice Blackmun, joined by Justices Marshall and Stevens, dissented. He was "most disturbed" by the effect the ruling would have on a poor woman's right to choose "without coercion whether she will continue her pregnancy to term." Going back to his original opinion in *Roe*, Blackmun attempted to spell out his concern over the future of abortion rights in light of this decision:

> *Roe v. Wade and its progeny are not so much about a medical procedure as they are about a woman's fundamental right to self-determination. Those cases serve to vindicate the idea that "liberty," if it means anything, must entail freedom from governmental domination in making the most intimate and personal of decisions. . . . Both the purpose and result of the challenged Regulations is to deny women the ability voluntarily to decide their procreative destiny. For these women, the Government will have obliterated the freedom to choose as surely as if it had banned abortions outright.*

The *Rust* decision has a number of important constitutional ramifications. However, the final legal status of this gag order has been the subject of political game playing. In January 1993, President Clinton rescinded the gag order immediately upon taking office. President Bush matched this action on his first day in office in 2001, reinstituting a "global gag rule" applied to information about abortion tied to various forms of foreign aid. And on January 23, 2009, President Obama issued an executive order overturning the ban on funding international groups that provide abortion information.

LIMITATIONS ON ABORTION RIGHTS: GOVERNMENT REGULATIONS ON ABORTION PROCEDURES

The Supreme Court, while upholding the basic ruling in *Roe*, gradually allowed state and local governments to place some restrictions on a woman's right to choose abortion in the first two trimesters of pregnancy. At first, following the 1973 landmark case, the Court was hostile toward any attempt by government, under the guise of regulation, to burden the woman's fundamental right to privacy involved in a choice of abortion. This hostility was evidenced in the 1976 *Danforth* decision (see footnote 26).

But a growing uneasiness with the absoluteness of the *Roe* decision created a willingness on the part of a growing number of justices to allow states to place curbs on abortion without overturning *Roe* altogether. This uneasiness would produce majorities in favor of widespread state restrictions on abortion, beginning in 1989 (see Brief 11.8). Finally, after initially striking down a state's effort to outlaw the procedure, the Court in 2007 upheld a Congressional ban on "partial-birth abortions," the culmination so far of governmental efforts to chip away at the right protected by *Roe*.

State legislatures' initial attempts to prohibit "partial-birth abortion" were ruled unconstitutional in *Stenberg v. Carhart* (2000). In question was a Nebraska law, similar to ones in twenty-nine other states, prohibiting "an abortion procedure in which the person performing the abortion partially delivers vaginally a living unborn child before killing the unborn child and completing the delivery." Violation of this law was classified as a Class III felony and carried a prison sentence of up to twenty years, a fine of up to $25,000, and the automatic revocation of a doctor's license to practice medicine in the state.

In a bitterly divided 5–4 ruling, the Court ruled the Nebraska law unconstitutional. Writing for the majority, Justice Breyer began by recognizing the "controversial nature" of the abortion issue:

> MILLIONS OF AMERICANS BELIEVE THAT LIFE BEGINS AT CONCEPTION AND CONSEQUENTLY THAT AN ABORTION IS AKIN TO CAUSING THE DEATH OF AN INNOCENT CHILD; THEY RECOIL AT THE THOUGHT OF A LAW THAT WOULD PERMIT IT. OTHER MILLIONS FEAR THAT A LAW THAT FORBIDS ABORTION WOULD CONDEMN MANY AMERICAN WOMEN TO LIVES THAT LACK DIGNITY, DEPRIVING THEM OF EQUAL LIBERTY AND LEADING THOSE WITH THE LEAST RESOURCES TO UNDERGO ILLEGAL ABORTIONS WITH THE ATTENDANT RISKS OF DEATH AND SUFFERING.

Using the principles set down in *Casey* (see Brief 11.8), Breyer wrote that Nebraska's prohibition was unconstitutional because it both burdened a woman's decision whether to terminate a pregnancy and failed to provide an exception to the prohibition in cases where the preservation of the mother's health was in question.

Each of the four justices voting in the minority wrote strongly worded dissenting opinions. In a lengthy dissent, Justice Kennedy took painstaking measures to show why Nebraska's partial-birth abortion law "denies no woman the right to choose an abortion and places no undue burden upon the right."

The most biting and bitter dissenting opinion, however, was offered by Justice Scalia. Comparing the Court majority's jurisprudence in this case to *Dred Scott* (see Brief 9.1), Scalia returned to his dissent in *Casey* (see Brief 11.8) to rail against the imperiousness of judicial conclusions about moral matters. Quoting from his *Casey* dissent, he once again criticized the *Roe* precedent for having "fanned into life an issue that has inflamed our national politics in general, and has obscured with its smoke the selection of Justices to this Court in particular, ever since." He concluded by boldly stating that "the Court should return [the issue of abortion] to the people—where the Constitution, by its silence on the subject, left it—and let *them* decide, State by State, where the practice should be allowed."

The dissenters would not have to wait long for their opinions to prevail. The replacement of Justice O'Connor with Justice Alito provided a potential fifth vote in favor of banning the procedure, and in the meantime opponents in Congress sought to ban partial-birth abortions. After two earlier attempts to prohibit the procedure were vetoed by President Clinton, Congress passed the Partial-Birth Abortion Ban Act of 2003, the first federal law to make

Brief 11.8

RESTRICTIONS ON ABORTION RIGHTS: THE WEBSTER AND CASEY DECISIONS

Two Supreme Court cases—*Webster v. Reproductive Health Services* (1989) and *Planned Parenthood v. Casey* (1992)—exemplify the majority's increased willingness to allow state and local regulations that limit abortion rights without abandoning the *Roe* precedent. The *Webster* case involved a Missouri law passed in 1986, which began by stating that "[t]he life of each human being begins at conception" and that "unborn children have protectable interests in life, health, and well-being." The law contained a number of provisions restricting abortion, including a prohibition on the use of public employees or facilities to perform or assist abortions that are not necessary to save the mother's life. In addition, the law required doctors to perform tests of "fetal viability" on all women believed to be at least twenty weeks pregnant.

The Supreme Court upheld all of the controversial provisions regulating abortion. Chief Justice Rehnquist, one of the original *Roe* dissenters, wrote an opinion for the Court that was joined by Justices White and Kennedy. In it, he took the opportunity to "modify and narrow *Roe*" without revisiting its basic holding. Rehnquist contended that the state of Missouri's decision to make value judgments, regulations, and prohibitions on public employees "to encourage childbirth over abortion 'places no governmental obstacle in the path of a woman who chooses to terminate her pregnancy.'"

Justice Scalia, in a separate concurrence, urged the Court to go further and "more explicitly" overturn *Roe*, thus returning all state regulation of abortion to a rational basis standard of judicial scrutiny. Justice O'Connor, while agreeing to uphold the law's provisions, indicated her uneasiness, based on a "fundamental rule of judicial restraint," in directly confronting *Roe* in this case. Justice Blackmun, author of the Court's opinion in *Roe*, sounded a warning that "the fundamental constitutional right of women to decide whether to terminate a pregnancy survive[s] but [is] not secure." Citing the plurality opinions' "winks and nods, and knowing glances to those who would do away with *Roe* explicitly," he chided the Rehnquist and Scalia opinions for being "oblivious or insensitive to the fact that millions of women, and their families, have ordered their lives around the right to reproductive choice, and that this right has become vital to the full participation of women in the economic and political walks of American life."

As Blackmun suggested, the Court's decision in *Webster* gave a clear signal to all sides in the abortion debate that the constitutional right established in *Roe* could be in jeopardy. Pro-life and pro-choice forces lobbied state legislatures, some of which passed laws further regulating abortion. Utah and Louisiana went further, prohibiting all abortions except those necessary to preserve the mother's life.[27]

In the *Casey* decision, the Court stopped short of fulfilling Justice Blackmun's prophecy. In question here was the constitutionality of the Pennsylvania Abortion Control Act, which imposed several constraints on abortion rights by requiring spousal notification, abortion counseling intended to discourage abortions, a twenty-four-hour waiting period, and parental consent for minors seeking an abortion. In a decision that found the justices deeply divided, the Court reaffirmed what it called the "essence" of abortion rights, but it approved new state restrictions. In an unusual opinion for the Court written jointly by Justices O'Connor, Kennedy, and Souter, a 5–4 majority reaffirmed *Roe*, a "rule of law and a component of liberty we cannot renounce." This slim majority abandoned the rigid "trimester" approach and fashioned a new "undue burden" rule to determine whether states could regulate abortion consistent with the fundamental right to privacy announced in *Roe*. The Court said, in effect, that it would only overturn statutes that placed a "substantial obstacle in the path of a woman seeking an abortion before the fetus attains viability." Under this new standard, the Court upheld all the Pennsylvania restrictions except the spousal notification constraint because it offered inadequate protection for women who might face physical or psychological abuse from a spouse. A four-member minority would have upheld all provisions of the Pennsylvania law and would have overturned *Roe*, which Chief Justice Rehnquist referred to as a "facade" based on a standard "not built to last." Justice Scalia sarcastically asserted that "the imperial judiciary lives," and regretted the courts having to decide this contentious issue. In a different minority coalition, Justice Blackmun stated that he would have struck down all the state restrictions, and said, "I cannot remain on this Court forever." The implication of his remark was that his replacement would determine the fate of the *Roe* precedent. But with the election of President Clinton in 1992, the essence of the *Roe* ruling remained intact with his appointment of pro-choice Justice Ginsburg to replace Justice White (one of the two original *Roe* dissenters), and Justice Breyer to replace Blackmun.

---

illegal an abortion procedure. The law, signed by President Bush in November 2003, makes it a crime, punishable by up to two years in prison, for a doctor to perform an abortion in which an intact fetus is partially removed from a woman's body before being terminated. In an effort to overcome the Supreme Court's objection to such laws as evidenced by the *Stenberg* decision, Congress attempted to tighten the definition of prohibited abortions and declared that the banned procedures are dangerous and are never necessary to protect a woman's health. This declaration, which relied on medical testimony from supporters of the law, was Congress's attempt to get around the need for a health exemption that the Supreme Court found lacking in the Nebraska law.

Opponents to the federal partial-birth abortion ban brought suit in federal district courts in California, Nebraska, and New York. The Court of Appeals for the Eighth Circuit held the law unconstitutional in the Nebraska case, which once again involved Dr. Leroy Carhart, a Nebraska physician who performs abortions, as the main plaintiff.

In *Gonzales v. Carhart* (2007), the Court, by another 5–4 vote, reversed its position in *Stenberg* and for the first time upheld an abortion ban that did not contain an exception for a woman's health. Justice Kennedy, this time writing for the majority, argued that the Congressional law, unlike the one in Nebraska, provided specific guidelines about what kind of procedure would be prohibited. Because of its specificity about what was outlawed, Kennedy said that alternative procedures would be left for doctors and their patients, and therefore the law would pose no "undue burden" or "substantial obstacle" for women seeking an abortion prior to fetal viability, the standard set down in *Casey*. With respect to Congress's failure to provide a health exception in the Act, Kennedy's opinion cites the disagreements within the scientific and medical communities on whether the procedure in question is ever necessary to protect a woman's health, concluding that in the presence of "medical uncertainty" it is acceptable for legislatures to act to ban a procedure without exception.

In his deference to Congress and its interests in respecting the "dignity of human life" by banning what the Court agreed was a "brutal and inhumane [medical] procedure," Kennedy laced his opinion in *Gonzales* with moral judgments, describing the fetus as an "unborn child" or "baby" and using the pejorative terms "abortion doctor" or "abortionist" to describe the surgeons who perform abortion procedures. At one point in the opinion, Kennedy implied that the law in question would be good for women, as it bans a method of terminating pregnancy that women might come to regret later:

> RESPECT FOR HUMAN LIFE FINDS AN ULTIMATE EXPRESSION IN THE BOND OF LOVE THE MOTHER HAS FOR HER CHILD. THE ACT RECOGNIZES THIS REALITY AS WELL. WHETHER TO HAVE AN ABORTION REQUIRES A DIFFICULT AND PAINFUL MORAL DECISION [AND] SOME WOMEN COME TO REGRET THEIR CHOICE TO ABORT THE INFANT LIFE THEY ONCE CREATED AND SUSTAINED. SEVERE DEPRESSION AND LOSS OF ESTEEM CAN FOLLOW.... THE STATE HAS AN INTEREST IN ENSURING SO GRAVE A CHOICE IS WELL INFORMED. IT IS SELF-EVIDENT THAT A MOTHER WHO COMES TO REGRET HER CHOICE TO ABORT MUST STRUGGLE WITH GRIEF MORE ANGUISHED AND SORROW MORE PROFOUND WHEN SHE LEARNS, ONLY AFTER THE EVENT, WHAT SHE ONCE DID NOT KNOW: THAT SHE ALLOWED A DOCTOR TO PIERCE THE SKULL AND VACUUM THE FAST DEVELOPING BRAIN OF HER UNBORN CHILD, A CHILD ASSUMING THE HUMAN FORM.

In her blistering dissent, read aloud from the bench, Justice Ginsberg, joined by Justices Breyer, Souter, and Stevens, called the Court's decision "alarming," and criticized Kennedy's failure to heed his own opinion in *Casey* with regard to the need to provide exceptions for a woman's health, especially in light of evidence presented by medical professional associations that this procedure can be safer for women than the alternatives. Rather than focusing in on the right to privacy involved in the abortion decision, Ginsburg located the rights protected by *Roe* and *Casey* in "a woman's autonomy to determine her life's course and thus to enjoy equal citizenship stature," and thus criticized the majority for depriving women of "the right to make an autonomous choice, even at the expense of their safety." She vehemently protested Justice Kennedy's use of what she called "an antiabortion shibboleth" about women's bonds to children and their moral and emotional regrets after abortions. "This way of thinking," she argued, "reflects ancient notions about women's place in the family and under the Constitution—ideas that have long since been discredited." Detecting clear "hostility to the right *Roe* and *Casey* secured," Ginsburg concluded that the Partial-Birth Abortion Ban Act and the majority's opinion upholding it "cannot be understood as anything other than an effort to chip away at a right declared again and again by this Court—and with increasing comprehension of its centrality to women's lives."

Over the last few years, a number of states have passed laws further narrowing abortion rights. Ten states have enacted legislation prohibiting abortions after twenty weeks, on the claim that a fetus can feel pain by this point in a woman's pregnancy. In Mississippi, the state's only remaining abortion clinic may shut down due to a law requiring doctors performing abortions to have visiting privileges at local hospitals (the clinic currently relies on doctors traveling from out of state). In Arkansas, the legislature recently adopted the Human Heartbeat Protection Act, which prohibits abortions at twelve weeks, the point at which an abdominal ultrasound usually can detect a fetal heartbeat. In North Dakota, three laws were passed in the spring of 2013, including a ban on abortion once a fetal heartbeat is "detectable" (as early as six weeks into a pregnancy), making the state the leader in efforts to curb abortion nationwide. And a state constitutional amendment goes on the North Dakota ballot in 2014, declaring that "the inalienable right to life of every human being at any stage of development must be recognized and defendant." These "personhood" bills and amendments have also been introduced in several other states and in Congress, extending full legal protections to "life" at the moment of conception or fertilization. A federal judge in Idaho struck down that state's twenty-week ban, and many other legal challenges are pending.

THE RIGHT TO SEXUAL PRIVACY: *LAWRENCE V. TEXAS*

The intimate association of gay adults was the final frontier of the right to privacy. At first, the Supreme Court refused to go there, upholding a state sodomy law in Georgia against a claim that it interfered with homosexuals' rights to privacy. Speaking for a 5–4 majority, Justice White proclaimed that the Constitution does not confer any fundamental right upon homosexuals to engage in sodomy. Observing that "proscriptions against [sodomy] have ancient roots," White ruled that it was completely within the legislative authority of the state to prohibit such sexual acts, even when done in the privacy of one's home. White denied that precedents existed to support Hardwick's claims, pointing out that previous privacy cases involved "family, marriage, or procreation," none of which could be linked to "homosexual activity."

Furthermore, the Court's conferral of fundamental rights had previously been based on values "deeply rooted in this Nation's history and tradition," or "implicit in the concept of ordered liberty." In light of this principle, White found Hardwick's claim that homosexuals had "fundamental rights" to engage in sodomy "facetious." Justice White's opinion concludes with a general warning to judges against giving substantive content to the Fourteenth Amendment:

> THE COURT IS MOST VULNERABLE AND COMES NEAREST TO ILLEGITIMACY WHEN IT DEALS WITH JUDGE-MADE CONSTITUTIONAL LAW HAVING LITTLE OR NO COGNIZABLE ROOTS IN THE LANGUAGE OR DESIGN OF THE CONSTITUTION. . . . THERE SHOULD BE, THEREFORE, GREAT RESISTANCE TO EXPAND THE SUBSTANTIVE REACH OF [THE DUE PROCESS CLAUSE], PARTICULARLY IF IT REQUIRES REDEFINING THE CATEGORY OF RIGHTS DEEMED TO BE FUNDAMENTAL. OTHERWISE, THE JUDICIARY NECESSARILY TAKES TO ITSELF FURTHER AUTHORITY TO GOVERN THE COUNTRY WITHOUT EXPRESS CONSTITUTIONAL AUTHORITY. THE CLAIMED RIGHT PRESSED ON US TODAY FALLS FAR SHORT OF OVERCOMING THIS RESISTANCE.

In a vigorous dissent, Justice Blackmun, quoting Brandeis, criticized his judicial brethren for failing to see that Hardwick's claim involved "'the most comprehensive of rights and the right most valued by civilized men,' namely, 'the right to be let alone.'" Blackmun contended that the constitutionally protected right to privacy extended to two general areas: (1) the individual's interest in securing independence in making certain private decisions, and (2) "the privacy interest in protecting certain *places* without regard for the particular activities in which the individuals who occupy them are engaged." Hardwick's activity involved "both the decisional and the spatial aspects of the right to privacy." Using a strict-scrutiny standard, Blackmun could not agree that historical condemnation of personal conduct constituted a compelling enough interest for the state to ban that conduct in the present day. Accepting that giving individuals freedom to choose will mean that "different individuals will make different choices,"

Blackmun berated the majority for allowing Georgia to trample on the individual's right to intimate association. He concluded his dissent with the hope that:

> THE COURT SOON WILL RECONSIDER ITS ANALYSIS AND CONCLUDE THAT DEPRIVING INDIVIDUALS OF THE RIGHT TO CHOOSE FOR THEMSELVES HOW TO CONDUCT THEIR INTIMATE RELATIONSHIPS POSES A FAR GREATER THREAT TO THE VALUES MOST DEEPLY ROOTED IN OUR NATION'S HISTORY THAN TOLERANCE OF NONCONFORMITY COULD EVER DO.

Justice Blackmun's hope would be realized a mere seventeen years later, when the Court was given the opportunity to reconsider this decision in *Lawrence v. Texas*. In question was a Texas statute making it a crime for two persons of the same sex to engage in "deviate sexual intercourse." This was defined as "any contact between any part of the genitals of one person and the mouth or anus of another person; or the penetration of the genitals or the anus of another person with an object." At the time, Texas was one of only four states (including Kansas, Oklahoma, and Missouri) to apply a criminal sodomy law exclusively to same-sex couples.

John Lawrence and his partner Tyron Garner were caught having sex in Mr. Lawrence's apartment by police sent to investigate a tip about a "weapons disturbance." The two were arrested, held in jail overnight, and each fined $200 for violating the sodomy statute. They appealed all the way to the Texas Supreme Court, which rejected their challenge to the state law, citing *Bowers* as a precedent.

By a 6–3 majority, the U.S. Supreme Court invalidated the Texas law, with five of the six-justice majority voting to overrule the *Bowers* decision in the process. Justice Kennedy, writing for the majority, declared that the liberty protected by the Due Process Clause of the Fourteenth Amendment allows homosexual persons to express their sexuality through intimate contact with each other free from state interference, especially in the privacy of their own homes. Gay men and lesbians are "entitled to respect for their private lives," Kennedy argued. "The state cannot demean their existence or control their destiny by making their private sexual conduct a crime."

Since the facts and the law in the *Bowers* case were similar to those in *Lawrence*, it forced the justices to reconsider whether their earlier precedent was based on sound constitutional principles. Kennedy concluded that it was not, saying "its continuance as a precedent demeans the lives of homosexual persons. . . . *Bowers* was not correct when it was decided, and it is not correct today. It ought not to remain binding precedent. *Bowers v. Hardwick* should be and now is overruled." As an interesting side note, Justice Blackmun's recently released personal papers reveal that when the justices took their initial vote on *Bowers*, a five-justice majority existed for overturning the Georgia law in question. After further reflection, however, Justice Powell changed his mind and voted to join Justice White's opinion in upholding the statute.

Justice O'Connor was part of the 5–4 majority upholding the Georgia sodomy law in *Bowers*. She contributed a sixth vote to overturn the Texas law, but refused to overrule *Bowers*, writing a separate opinion attacking the law on equal protection grounds because it made "deviate sexual intercourse" a crime only between partners of the same sex, not for heterosexuals.

Justice Scalia wrote a vehement dissent, in which he chided the Court for its "surprising readiness to reconsider a decision rendered a mere 17 years ago." Making comparisons to the Court's refusal to reconsider *Roe v. Wade*, Scalia accused the majority of "sign[ing] on to the so-called homosexual agenda" and thereby "taking sides in the culture war." He reiterated his position that moral matters in particular should be left to the people and their elected representatives, rather than to the courts:

> LET ME BE CLEAR THAT I HAVE NOTHING AGAINST HOMOSEXUALS, OR ANY OTHER GROUP, PROMOTING THEIR AGENDA THROUGH NORMAL DEMOCRATIC MEANS. . . . BUT PERSUADING ONE'S FELLOW CITIZENS IS ONE THING, AND IMPOSING ONE'S VIEWS IN ABSENCE OF DEMOCRATIC MAJORITY WILL IS SOMETHING ELSE. WHAT TEXAS HAS CHOSEN TO DO IS WELL WITHIN THE RANGE OF TRADITIONAL DEMOCRATIC ACTION, AND ITS HAND SHOULD NOT BE STAYED THROUGH THE INVENTION OF A

BRAND-NEW "CONSTITUTIONAL RIGHT" BY A COURT THAT IS IMPATIENT OF DEMOCRATIC CHANGE.

One final note is in order here. Despite Justice Scalia's criticisms of the use of judicial authority to create a right not explicitly granted in the Constitution, the case for a right to privacy has drawn support in circles outside the Supreme Court. Congress expressly acknowledged an individual's right to privacy in legislation passed in 1974, and ten state constitutions now contain explicit right to privacy provisions as part of their Bills of Rights.[28]

FUNDAMENTAL RIGHTS OF PARENTS

Troxel v. Granville (2000) offered the Court yet another opportunity to rule on whether an individual's fundamental rights trump state law. In this case, the justices issued a ruling that could have the effect of expanding substantive rights not explicitly enumerated in the Constitution.

Washington law permits "any person" to petition a state court for visitation rights "at any time." The court, in turn, is authorized to grant such visitation rights whenever "visitation may serve the best interest of the child." Acting under this broadly worded provision, a superior court judge ordered Tommie Granville to make her two children available for mandatory visitation with their paternal grandparents, Jenifer and Gary Troxel. The visitation order was appealed, with the Washington Supreme Court ruling that the state visitation statute swept too broadly, unconstitutionally infringing on the fundamental right of parents to rear their children. The U.S. Supreme Court affirmed, seemingly invoking the infamous substantive due process doctrine in their decision.

While *Troxel v. Granville* contains no majority opinion, Justice O'Connor wrote an opinion joined by three others in which she argued that the visitation order "was an unconstitutional infringement on Granville's fundamental right to make decisions concerning the care, custody, and control of her two daughters." Although she was unwilling to define "the precise scope of the parental due process right" or to rule that nonparental visitation statutes are unconstitutional per se, O'Connor nevertheless cited several *Lochner*-era substantive due process decisions to make her case. In a concurring opinion, Justice Thomas added that "strict scrutiny" should be applied as the standard of review in cases involving infringement on the fundamental rights of parents. The same Justice Thomas who worried about the specter of substantive fundamental rights in *Saenz v. Roe* here was willing to endorse them more or less absolutely.

It is unclear what the long-term impact of this decision might be. Potential significance lies in the fact that a majority of justices were willing to give broad scope under the Due Process Clause to an unenumerated right of parents to care for and guide their children, something that bothered the three dissenting justices. Justices Kennedy and Stevens worried that the Court's decision might prevent states from placing reasonable limits on parental rights. Justice Scalia, echoing his dissent in *Stenberg v. Carhart* and *Lawrence v. Texas*, questioned the wisdom of such judicial pronouncements of absolute rights, especially absent clear textual mandates in the Constitution itself. He concluded that:

IF WE EMBRACE THIS UNENUMERATED RIGHT, I THINK IT OBVIOUS . . . THAT WE WILL BE USHERING IN A NEW REGIME OF JUDICIALLY PRESCRIBED, AND FEDERALLY PRESCRIBED, FAMILY LAW. I HAVE NO REASON TO BELIEVE THAT FEDERAL JUDGES WILL BE BETTER AT THIS THAN STATE LEGISLATURES; AND STATE LEGISLATURES HAVE THE GREAT ADVANTAGES OF DOING HARM IN A MORE CIRCUMSCRIBED AREA, OF BEING ABLE TO CORRECT THEIR MISTAKES IN A FLASH, AND OF BEING REMOVABLE BY THE PEOPLE.

Justice Scalia's dissent in *Troxel v. Granville* takes us back to many of the philosophical questions raised earlier in this chapter about fundamental rights beyond those found in the Bill of Rights. These include questions about what makes a right fundamental, the nature of judicial authority in interpreting the scope of rights not specifically enumerated in the Constitution, and the power of government—attempting to represent a larger public interest—to limit the fundamental rights of individuals.

CONCLUSION

When the first ten amendments became part of the new United States Constitution in 1791, it is unlikely that many of the leaders of that era could have visualized their profound impact on future generations of Americans. The Bill of Rights, after all, had originated largely as the result of a compromise between Federalists and Anti-Federalists during the struggle for constitutional ratification. Moreover, because the new amendments specifically were limited in their application to the national government and not the states, they would not have much significance in the everyday affairs of most Americans. The long-standing precedent established by Chief Justice Marshall's ruling in *Barron v. Baltimore* (1833) added further support to this view.

The ratification of the Fourteenth Amendment in 1868 laid the foundation that ultimately would change the relationship between the Bill of Rights and the states. Provisions in that amendment preventing states from abridging the privileges and immunities of citizens of the United States and denying life, liberty, and property without due process of law were quickly claimed by some persons to guarantee the protections in the Bill of Rights against state governments. The Supreme Court's rulings in *The Slaughterhouse Cases, Hurtado v. California*, and *Twining v. New Jersey*, for example, effectively rejected that contention for many years. Finally, after several important developments between 1925 and 1931 extending First Amendment freedoms to the states, the Court held in *Palko v. Connecticut* (1937) that the "liberties" of the Due Process Clause of the Fourteenth Amendment contained portions of the first eight amendments that were "implicit in the concept of ordered liberty." Under this doctrine, known as "selective incorporation," future Supreme Courts gradually nationalized nearly all the provisions of the Bill of Rights, making them binding against the states. As a result, the rights originally protected from the national government alone became truly nationwide in scope. The final five chapters of this text examine more carefully the specific provisions found in the Bill of Rights, especially those pertaining to criminal procedure (Chapters 12 and 13) and the freedoms found in the First Amendment (Chapters 14–16).

In recent years, the "incorporation controversy" has given way to a series of claims that certain rights beyond those explicitly guaranteed in the Bill of Rights should be protected against both federal and state interference. The Court has had to answer difficult questions about whether the rights to privacy and to travel from state to state are fundamentally protected by the Constitution. In applying strict scrutiny to state government actions denying fundamental rights beyond those found in the first eight amendments, the justices have been accused of bringing substantive due process back into the Fourteenth Amendment. By giving substance to certain unenumerated rights and offering individuals near-absolute protection from government interference with these rights, the Court has been criticized for overstepping the bounds of constitutional interpretation, much as it had been attacked for its economic decisions at the beginning of the twentieth century. As with the new equal protection, ongoing conflicts over fundamental rights often reflect the tension between individualist concerns over minority rights and communitarian interests in majority rule.

CHAPTER 12
The Fourth Amendment: Searches, Seizures, and Privacy

THE FOURTH AMENDMENT PROTECTS CITIZENS "AGAINST UNREASONABLE SEARCHES AND SEIZURES." WHAT CONSTITUTES AN "UNREASONABLE" SEARCH IS CONSTANTLY CHANGING, CREATING TENSIONS IN THE BALANCE BETWEEN INDIVIDUAL RIGHTS AND SOCIETY'S NEEDS FOR SECURITY AND PROTECTION. IN THE NATION'S AIRPORTS, INDIVIDUALS SUBJECT THEIR "PERSONS AND EFFECTS" TO FAIRLY EXTENSIVE SEARCHES BY THE FEDERAL TRANSPORTATION SECURITY ADMINISTRATION, IN ORDER TO TRAVEL MORE SECURELY.

▼ INTRODUCTORY REMARKS BY JAMES OTIS

Library of Congress, Prints & Photographs Division [LC-USZ62-102561].

A man's house is his castle; and whilst he is quiet, he is well guarded as a prince in his castle. Hello, my name is James Otis, and when I uttered those words in 1761, I was defending the rights of my fellow Americans against the illegal practices of the British Crown. Let me tell you about that episode and introduce you to this chapter dealing with the Fourth Amendment to the Constitution.

At that time, the British made extensive use of so-called "Writs of Assistance," a new form of general search warrant that allowed any customs official to enter any dwelling or business to find anything they considered to be "contraband." We challenged those writs in a Boston courthouse, and I did my best to point out that they were unlawful:

This writ, if it should be declared legal, would totally annihilate this privilege. Custom-house officers may enter our houses when they please; we are commanded to permit their entry. Their menial servants may enter, may break locks, bars, and everything in their way; and whether they break through malice or revenge, no man, no court may inquire.

I was told that a young Massachusetts resident, John Adams, was present in that courtroom, and he remarked that "then and there, the child Independence was born." He may be giving me too much credit, but I also believe that the trial changed things forever. Yes, we lost the case, but Americans never looked at the British in the same way after that; and more importantly, we began to demand an end to unreasonable searches and seizures by government—any government!

You will see in this chapter the fruits of our labors: namely, the inclusion of the Fourth Amendment in the United States Constitution. Allow me to quote it for you:

The right of the people to be secure in their persons, houses, papers, and effects, against unreasonable searches and seizures, shall not be violated, and no Warrants shall issue, but upon probable cause, supported by Oath or affirmation, and particularly describing the place to be searched, and the persons or things to be seized.

This was what we demanded in 1761, and it continues to be a work in progress. This chapter introduces such important concepts as probable cause, the exclusionary rule, a reasonable expectation of privacy, and others. The Supreme Court has shaped the meaning of the Fourth Amendment through its rulings; some of the more significant ones presented in this chapter include *Mapp v. Ohio*, *Terry v. Ohio*, *Katz v. United States*, *Arizona v. Gant*, and *United States v. Jones*, among others.

The Fourth Amendment covers searches and seizures that could not have been contemplated by our Founding Fathers, including me. Such things as wiretapping, drug testing, thermal imaging devices, and GPS tracking are commonplace in today's world. With all of these innovations, it is important for a free society to maintain a vigilant watch against overzealous governmental intrusion into our private lives.

Let me remind you, as I stated above, that "a man's house is his castle." Look carefully in this chapter at the difficulty of reconciling government power with individual liberty. Enjoy the chapter. JO

SOURCES: The 4th Amendment, Revolutionary War and Beyond, www.revolutionary-war-and-beyond.com/4th-amendment.html; "Otis was a Flame of Fire," www.foundersofamerica.org/jotis.html

LIBERTY AND SECURITY IN A FREE SOCIETY

One of the central dilemmas in a constitutional political order is the balancing of individual civil liberties with the need to protect society and keep it safe. It is an issue with which the Founding Fathers were familiar, prompting many leaders of that era to support the addition of a "bill of rights." For nearly two hundred years since that addition, Americans have debated, argued, and occasionally fought over the proper balance of individual rights and community rights. Civil libertarians who emphasize the rights of the individual clash repeatedly with those for whom the interests of society are paramount. The controversy has taken varying forms from generation to generation, but the underlying positions have remained remarkably stable. The following statement from Fred E. Inbau, an influential and rather controversial proponent of society's interests at the expense of individual liberties, illustrates one view of the problem:

> WE CANNOT HAVE "DOMESTIC TRANQUILITY" AND "PROMOTE THE GENERAL WELFARE" AS PRESCRIBED IN THE PREAMBLE TO THE CONSTITUTION WHEN ALL THE CONCERN IS UPON "INDIVIDUAL CIVIL LIBERTIES." OUR CIVIL LIBERTIES CANNOT EXIST IN A VACUUM. ALONGSIDE OF THEM WE MUST HAVE A STABLE SOCIETY, A SAFE SOCIETY; OTHERWISE THERE WILL BE NO MEDIUM IN WHICH TO EXERCISE SUCH RIGHTS AND LIBERTIES. TO HAVE THESE LIBERTIES WITHOUT SAFETY OF LIFE, LIMB, AND PROPERTY IS A MEANINGLESS THING. INDIVIDUAL CIVIL LIBERTIES, CONSIDERED APART FROM THEIR RELATIONSHIP TO PUBLIC SAFETY AND SECURITY, ARE LIKE LABELS ON EMPTY BOTTLES.[1]

Supporters of Professor Inbau consider themselves "tough on crime" and advocates of "law and order," believing that excessive concern with liberties results in severe costs for the society as a whole. Supporters of individual civil liberties disagree with the premise of Inbau's remarks, noting that the loss of individual liberties ultimately results in a loss for the overall society. If persons are not protected as individuals, they note, then the constitutional system of limited government becomes uncontrollable and potentially tyrannical. And yet, despite recent declines, the United States does have a problem with crime (Brief 12.1). Throughout the next two chapters, the controversy between the rights of individuals and societal stability surfaces in numerous ways. This chapter focuses on Fourth Amendment issues, and the following chapter explores the other protections of the Bill of Rights.

CRIME IN THE UNITED STATES: THE UNIFORM CRIME REPORT

The Federal Bureau of Investigation (FBI) publishes its annual Uniform Crime Report (UCR), which compiles crime data as reported from over 14,000 law enforcement organizations around the country. The data is reported as the **Crime Index**, which includes eight crimes: murder, forcible rape, robbery, aggravated assault, burglary, larceny-theft, motor-vehicle theft, and arson. The FBI 2010 UCR showed a decline in all violent crimes in the nation for the fifth straight year, with a decrease of 13.6 percent since 2006; and property crimes also declined slightly in 2010, down 9.3 percent since 2006. An estimated 1,246,248 violent crimes were reported, along with an estimated 9,082,887 property crimes The figures represent 403.6 violent crimes and 2,941.9 property crimes per 100,000 population in 2010. A further breakdown shows aggravated assault to be the most reported violent crime (62.5 percent) and murder the lowest at 1.2 percent. Among property crimes, larceny-theft represents the largest number (68.1 percent) with motor vehicle thefts the lowest at 8.1 percent.[2]

Explanations for the slight decrease in crime are plentiful. Some point out that the events of September 11 have placed a high priority on spending for security and safety policies, and this may translate into support for tougher law enforcement. Others point to the increase in the prison population and the basic argument that individuals don't commit crimes when they are locked up in prison. Others argue that tougher sentencing laws act as a deterrent to criminals. No matter the explanation, Americans are concerned about crime, but Americans also are concerned with individual rights and personal freedoms. The difficulty comes in trying to achieve a balance between these values.

FOURTH AMENDMENT

The origins of the Fourth Amendment are quite evident in the reaction of colonial Americans against British invasions of privacy. British violations of the common law produced strong resentment among Americans, who believed that they were also "Englishmen" and entitled to the full protections of the common law. A Boston town meeting in 1772 produced "A List of Infringements and Violations of Rights," which named numerous rights violated by British agents of the Crown. The list included complaints against the so-called "Writs of Assistance" employed by British officials in their search for contraband. Bostonians complained that "our houses and even our bed chambers are exposed to be ransacked, our boxes, chests, and trunks broke open, ravaged and plundered by wretches, whom no prudent man would venture to employ even as menial servants."[3]

The writs of assistance were a type of general warrant authorizing British agents to undertake indiscriminate searches of ships and houses to stop smuggling. While ordinary search warrants describe the object and the specific premises of the search, general warrants offer authorities complete discretion in their search and seizure decisions. Largely as a result of the abuses associated with general warrants, five states in their post-Revolution constitutions prohibited general warrants that did not specify the person, place, or purpose of a search.[4] Other states relied upon different methods to eliminate such abuses. As a result, the proposed Fourth Amendment to the new Constitution caused relatively little debate either in Congress or among the states during ratification. In the minds of most Americans of that period, general warrants were synonymous with "unreasonable searches and seizures."

The Fourth Amendment protects "The right of the people to be secure in their persons, houses, papers, and effects, against unreasonable searches and seizures." The amendment prohibits unreasonable searches and seizures and establishes several criteria for search warrants. One such requirement is that no warrants may be issued "but upon probable cause, supported by Oath or affirmation, and particularly describing the place to be searched, and the persons or things to be seized." The framers probably had more concern for the dreaded writs of assistance and general warrants used by the British than for searches conducted without any warrant whatsoever.

THE FOURTH AMENDMENT AND WARRANTS

The Fourth Amendment does not say that warrants are required for all searches and seizures, but proper warrants provide the necessary reasonableness required by the amendment's provisions. Generally speaking, a search or seizure undertaken under a specifically worded warrant, based on probable cause, and sworn before an impartial judge will not be considered "unreasonable."

The concept of **probable cause** poses problems for law enforcement officials and courts as well. On numerous occasions, the Supreme Court has pointed out that probable cause cannot be easily defined in conventional terms. Rather, as stated in *Ornelas v. United States* (1996), probable cause exists "where the known facts and circumstances are sufficient to warrant a man of reasonable prudence in the belief that contraband or evidence of a crime will be found." More recently, in *Maryland v. Pringle* (2003), the Court suggested that probable cause is based on a degree of probability:

> THE PROBABLE CAUSE STANDARD IS INCAPABLE OF PRECISE DEFINITION OR QUANTIFICATION INTO PERCENTAGES BECAUSE IT DEALS WITH PROBABILITIES AND DEPENDS ON THE TOTALITY OF THE CIRCUMSTANCES. . . . [T]HE SUBSTANCE OF ALL THE DEFINITIONS OF PROBABLE CAUSE IS A REASONABLE GROUND FOR BELIEF OF GUILT, AND THAT THE BELIEF OF GUILT MUST BE PARTICULARIZED WITH RESPECT TO THE PERSON TO BE SEARCHED OR SEIZED.

What the Court has called the "flexible, common-sense standard" of probable cause (*Illinois v. Gates*, 1983), was instrumental in deciding *Florida v. Harris* (2013). In that case, the Court had to decide whether an "alert" by a drug-detecting dog during a traffic stop provides probable cause to search a vehicle.

Officer Wheetley stopped Clayton Harris's truck because of an expired license plate. The officer approached the vehicle, saw that Harris was "visibly nervous" and shaking, with an open beer can in the cup holder. When Harris refused consent to search the truck, Officer Wheetley retrieved Aldo, a trained German Shepherd drug-detecting dog, from the patrol car and walked him around the truck for a "free air sniff." Aldo alerted at the driver's-side door handle, signaling that drugs were present. Officer Wheetley concluded that he had probable cause to search the truck. The search did not reveal any of the drugs Aldo was trained to detect, but it produced 200 loose pseudoephedrine pills, 8,000 matches, a bottle of hydrochloric acid, two containers of antifreeze, and a coffee filter full of iodine crystals—all ingredients used in making methamphetamine. While out on bail following his arrest the following week, Harris again was stopped for a broken brake light, Aldo again alerted on the same door handle, a search was conducted, but nothing was found.

At his hearing, Harris moved to suppress the evidence on the ground that Aldo's alert did not give Officer Wheetley probable cause to search. The officer testified as to Aldo's extensive training in drug detection and his certification by a private group (the certification had expired, but it was not required by the State). The trial court concluded that probable cause justified the search, but the Florida Supreme Court reversed, holding that more "evidence of the dog's performance history" was needed to establish probable cause.

Justice Elena Kagan's opinion for a unanimous Court held that the Florida Supreme Court had gone far beyond the "common-sense" standards of probable cause. What courts must do, she said, is to hold probable cause hearings in which both parties have an opportunity to make their best case within a "totality of circumstances" approach:

> IN ALL EVENTS, THE COURT SHOULD NOT PRESCRIBE, AS THE FLORIDA SUPREME COURT DID, AN INFLEXIBLE SET OF EVIDENTIARY REQUIREMENTS. THE QUESTION—SIMILAR TO EVERY INQUIRY INTO PROBABLE CAUSE—IS WHETHER ALL THE FACTS SURROUNDING A DOG'S ALERT, VIEWED THROUGH THE LENS OF COMMON SENSE, WOULD MAKE A REASONABLY PRUDENT PERSON THINK THAT A SEARCH WOULD REVEAL CONTRABAND OR EVIDENCE OF A CRIME. A SNIFF IS UP TO SNUFF WHEN IT MEETS THAT TEST. . . . AND HERE, ALDO'S DID. THE RECORD IN THIS CASE AMPLY SUPPORTED THE TRIAL COURT'S DETERMINATION THAT ALDO'S ALERT GAVE WHEETLEY PROBABLE CAUSE TO SEARCH HARRIS'S TRUCK.

Justice Kagan concluded by noting that probable cause cannot be evaluated in hindsight, based on what a search does or does not produce. As long as Officer Wheetley had good reason to view Aldo as a reliable detector of drugs, and no special circumstances existed to question that reason, it is clear that probable cause existed to justify the search.

Search warrants also must be specific, describing the place to be searched and the persons or things to be seized. Courts have held that the description of the place must be sufficiently definite to clearly distinguish the premises from all others, and officers must make a reasonable effort to ascertain the correct location (see Brief 12.2). On some occasions, when officers have made a "good-faith" effort (see below), Courts have upheld the legality of a search at the wrong premises.

Because an arrest is considered a "seizure," the Fourth Amendment requires arrest warrants as well as search warrants. Arrest warrants are subject to the same constitutional guidelines as those applicable to searches. Of course, it often is impractical to secure an arrest warrant, particularly since many persons in jeopardy of arrest will take the opportunity to flee the scene to avoid being apprehended. As a result, many arrests occur today without a sworn warrant, but even these warrantless arrests must be based on probable cause. In *Henry v. United States* (1959), Justice William Douglas defined probable cause:

> THE REQUIREMENT OF PROBABLE CAUSE HAS ROOTS THAT ARE DEEP IN OUR HISTORY. . . . AND AS THE EARLY AMERICAN DECISIONS BOTH BEFORE AND IMMEDIATELY AFTER [THE FOURTH AMENDMENT'S] ADOPTION SHOW, COMMON RUMOR OR REPORT, SUSPICION, OR EVEN "STRONG REASON TO SUSPECT" WAS NOT ADEQUATE

Brief 12.2
EXECUTING A SEARCH WARRANT

A valid search warrant must be issued by a neutral judicial officer, one without any sort of involvement in the investigation. The law enforcement official seeking the warrant must swear under oath that the facts being presented are correct. Once the warrant has been issued, several technical steps are required. The following rules are taken from the Federal Rules of Criminal Procedures, Rule 41(f).

1. The officers serving the warrant first are required to note the time of execution.
2. An inventory of items confiscated should be made in the presence of another officer or other credible person.
3. Officers are required to give a copy of the warrant and a receipt for property taken to the person from whom, or from whose premises, the property was taken; or, leave a copy of the warrant and receipt at the location where property was taken. An exception in cases involving terrorism was created in the USA Patriot Act, which authorized so-called "sneak and peek" searches. In these cases, entry occurs without the owner's permission or knowledge, and no copy of the warrant is left behind.
4. Finally, when the search and seizure are completed, officers must promptly return the warrant and a copy of the inventory to the magistrate judge.

The courts have addressed other issues related to the execution of search warrants. In *Michigan v. Summers* (1981), the U.S. Supreme Court held that officers executing a search warrant for contraband have the authority "to detain the occupants of the premises while a proper search is conducted." Justification for such detentions included preventing flight in the event that incriminating evidence is found; minimizing the risk of harm to the officers; and facilitating an orderly search. Based on the *Summers* precedent, the Court ruled in *Muehler v. Mena* (2005) that officers had the right to detain Ms. Mena and others in handcuffs during the three-hour search of their residence. Armed with a proper search warrant, law enforcement authorities may restrain any persons on the premises. But what if the person is not on the premises?

In 2013, the Court was asked to decide whether *Summers* allowed police to follow a person and take him into custody about a mile away from his apartment that was being searched under a warrant at the time. Justice Kennedy's 6–3 majority opinion in *Bailey v. United States* (2013) held that while the search was reasonable, the seizure of Bailey was not:

> *In sum, of the three law enforcement interests identified to justify the detention in Summers, none applies with the same or similar force to the detention of recent occupants beyond the immediate vicinity of the premises to be searched. Any of the individual interests is also insufficient, on its own, to justify an expansion of the rule in Summers to permit the detention of a former occupant, wherever he may be found away from the scene of the search. This would give officers too much discretion. The categorical authority to detain incident to the execution of a search warrant must be limited to the immediate vicinity of the premises to be searched.*

Finally, in *United States v. Grubbs* (2006), a unanimous Supreme Court upheld the use of "anticipatory warrants." An anticipatory warrant is "one based upon an affidavit showing probable cause that at some future time certain evidence of a crime will be located at a specified place." In this case, police knew that Grubbs had ordered a child pornography videotape from a website run by an undercover postal inspector. The Postal Inspection Service arranged a controlled delivery of the videotape to Grubbs's residence. A warrant was obtained that became effective only upon the delivery and receipt of the videotape. Writing for the unanimous Court, Justice Scalia said that anticipatory warrants must meet the same standards as other warrants: They require the magistrate to determine (1) that it is now probable that (2) contraband evidence of a crime or a fugitive will be on the described premises (3) when the warrant is issued. The warrant would have been unconstitutional had the delivery not occurred.

TO SUPPORT A WARRANT FOR ARREST.... PROBABLE CAUSE EXISTS IF THE FACTS AND CIRCUMSTANCES KNOWN TO THE OFFICER WARRANT A PRUDENT MAN IN BELIEVING THAT THE OFFENSE HAS BEEN COMMITTED.... TO REPEAT, AN ARREST IS NOT JUSTIFIED BY WHAT THE SUBSEQUENT SEARCH DISCLOSES. UNDER OUR SYSTEM SUSPICION IS NOT ENOUGH FOR AN OFFICER TO LAY HANDS ON A CITIZEN. IT IS BETTER, SO THE FOURTH AMENDMENT TEACHES, THAT THE GUILTY SOMETIMES GO FREE THAN THAT CITIZENS BE SUBJECT TO EASY ARREST.

THE EXCLUSIONARY RULE AND THE FOURTH AMENDMENT

The **exclusionary rule** holds that evidence seized in violation of a defendant's constitutional rights is inadmissible for a criminal prosecution in a court of law. The rule was formulated by the Supreme Court in *Weeks v. United States* (1914) and has undergone considerable revision since (see Table 12.1).

The exclusionary rule was devised by the Supreme Court to prevent wrongdoing by police. The rule focuses on the way in which evidence is obtained, and not the nature of the evidence itself. In cases when an illegal action by police results in the recovery of even more evidence later on, this evidence is known as "fruit of the poisonous tree" and can be excluded as well.

The most famous expression of the controversy surrounding the exclusionary rule, in all likelihood, was phrased by Judge (later Justice) Benjamin Cardozo in *People v. DeFore* (1926): "Is the criminal to go free because the Constable has blundered?" In recent years, arguments over the exclusionary rule have become more intense. Supporters of the rule have argued for its continuation as a means of ensuring that protections of the Fourth Amendment are upheld. Under this view, the exclusionary rule is required by the Constitution to protect specific rights from being violated.[5]

Table 12.1 Development of the Law—The Exclusionary Rule

Year	Event	Significance
1914	*Weeks v. United States*	Held that the admission of illegally obtained evidence at trial would violate a defendant's Fourth Amendment Rights. Established the "exclusionary rule."
1949	*Wolf v. Colorado*	Held the Fourth Amendment protection from unreasonable searches and seizures to be a fundamental right and applicable to the states but did not apply the exclusionary rule to the states.
1951	*Rochin v. California*	Held that narcotics retrieved from a suspect's body (see Brief 12.7) illegally could not be admitted as evidence due to the shocking nature of the conduct. Did not apply the exclusionary rule to the states, however.
1961	*Mapp v. Ohio*	Held the exclusionary rule was an "essential ingredient of the right" to be secure from unreasonable searches and seizure. Required states to abide by the exclusionary rule.
1974	*United States v. Calandra*	Illegally obtained evidence could be presented to a grand jury without violating the Fourth Amendment.
1975	*United States v. Janis*	Allowed federal tax authorities to introduce illegally obtained evidence in a civil trial.
1984	*United States v. Leon*	Held that the exclusionary rule did not prevent the use of illegally obtained evidence based on a flawed search warrant if the authorities acted in "good faith."
1984	*Nix v. Williams*	Held that evidence obtained through an unlawful search is admissible in court if a high degree of probability exists that the evidence would have been discovered anyway. Known as the "inevitable discovery doctrine."
1984	*Segura v. United States*	Evidence obtained from a valid warrant following an illegal entry into a dwelling is admissible if the warrant came from sources wholly unconnected with the initial entry and was known to the agents well before that entry.
1995	*Arizona v. Evans*	Held that evidence obtained by police acting on an arrest warrant that had been quashed by a judge but not entered into the computer by court officials was admissible. The exclusionary rule was designed to prevent police misconduct, not mistakes by other court employees.
2006	*Hudson v. Michigan*	Evidence seized in violation of a "knock-and-announce" search rule should not be suppressed. The Court said that many new methods exist other than the exclusionary rule to ensure police compliance with the Fourth Amendment.
2008	*Herring v. United States*	Held that a police clerk's negligent error wrongly confirming the existence of an arrest warrant was not the kind of conduct deterred by the exclusionary rule. The negligent error was not related to the arrest itself.

Brief 12.3

THE "GOOD-FAITH" EXCEPTION TO THE EXCLUSIONARY RULE

The "good-faith" exception pertains primarily to the issue of whether evidence should be admissible following a search that was admittedly flawed. The exception was first noted in *United States v. Peltier* (1975) and has been raised several times since. The argument goes like this: Why should evidence obtained in good faith, even though later determined unlawful, be suppressed from the trial? As Justice Rehnquist stated in his *Peltier* majority opinion, "If the purpose of the exclusionary rule is to deter unlawful police conduct, then evidence obtained from a search should be suppressed only if it can be said that the law enforcement officer had knowledge, or may properly be charged with knowledge, that the search was unconstitutional under the Fourth Amendment."

A major development in the good-faith exception to the exclusionary rule occurred in *United States v. Leon* (1984), when police conducted a search pursuant to a facially valid search warrant (a warrant that seems correct but contains unseen errors or omissions). The searches produced large quantities of drugs and other evidence. Alberto Leon and other defendants were indicted by a grand jury and charged with a variety of drug-related counts.

Writing for the 6–3 Court, Justice White reversed the court of appeals and held that "the exclusionary rule can be modified somewhat without jeopardizing its ability to perform its intended functions." His majority opinion stressed the fact that officers had acted reasonably in obtaining a warrant from a "neutral and detached magistrate." Because the affidavit reflected the officers' good faith, their reliance upon the magistrate's determination of probable cause was reasonable. The seized evidence should not have been suppressed.

Joined by Justice Marshall (Justice Stevens dissented separately), Justice Brennan's dissent was blunt in its concern for what the majority had done, stating that "The majority ignores the fundamental constitutional importance of what is at stake here." According to Brennan, the courts were given the "sometimes unpopular task" of protecting individual rights. Pessimistically, he concluded that he would not be surprised if, in the future, "my colleagues decide once again that we simply cannot afford to protect Fourth Amendment rights."

In *Arizona v. Evans* (1995), a 7–2 Court used the "good-faith" exception to allow the admission of marijuana seized following a routine traffic stop. When police stopped Isaac Evans's car, they discovered that a misdemeanor arrest warrant was outstanding. What they didn't know was that the warrant had been quashed by a judge seventeen days earlier but never entered into the computer by court officials. Chief Justice Rehnquist noted that the exclusionary rule was designed to deter police misconduct, not mistakes by other court employees. The police had acted in good faith, thereby making the seizure of marijuana acceptable.

A narrower 5–4 majority found no exclusionary rule violation in *Herring v. United States* (2008), even though the search took place because of an outstanding warrant that did not exist. A police clerk's negligent error caused authorities to believe such a warrant was active. Chief Justice Roberts wrote for the majority that police searches that result from negligence and not systematic error or reckless disregard of constitutional rights are not barred by the exclusionary rule. In this case, the criminal should not "go free because the constable has blundered."

In the 2011 case of *Davis v. United States*, a 7–2 majority opinion by Justice Alito upheld a search by police that was initiated under the belief that an existing precedent allowed the search. The precedent, *New York v. Belton*, was overturned subsequently by the Supreme Court in *Arizona v. Gant* (see "Search-Incident-to-Arrest Exception"). Justice Alito found that the officers acted in good faith by following what had been legal precedent, stating that an officer who conducts a search in reliance on binding appellate precedent does no more than act "as a reasonable officer would and should act" under the circumstances.

The Warren Court expanded the exclusionary rule to state governments in the case of *Mapp v. Ohio* (1961). As a result, state authorities were no longer free to ignore the limitations of the exclusionary rule and hand illegally obtained evidence over to federal officials on a "silver platter," as the prevailing practice was then known. Since *Mapp*, most law enforcement searches and seizures in the United States are subject to the exclusionary rule.

With the onset of the Burger Court, the new chief justice, often joined by Justice White, frequently expressed his opposition to the restrictions of the exclusionary rule.[6] An important first step in limiting the exclusionary rule was taken in *United States v. Calandra* (1974). In that case, the Court upheld the use of improperly obtained evidence for a grand jury investigation, noting that the exclusionary rule's deterrent effect on police misconduct must be balanced against society's need to gather and obtain crucial evidence. Following similar reasoning in the case of *United States v. Janis* (1976), the Court allowed evidence illegally obtained by state officials to be used by the Internal Revenue Service in a civil case. The evidence could not be used in the state criminal matter for which it had been obtained originally.

To summarize, the problems associated with applying the exclusionary rule are difficult. Consider the words of Justice Powell in *Stone v. Powell* (1976):

> APPLICATION OF THE RULE THUS DEFLECTS THE TRUTHFINDING PROCESS AND OFTEN FREES THE GUILTY. THE DISPARITY IN PARTICULAR CASES BETWEEN THE ERROR COMMITTED BY THE POLICE OFFICER AND THE WINDFALL AFFORDED A GUILTY DEFENDANT BY APPLICATION OF THE RULE IS CONTRARY TO THE IDEA OF PROPORTIONALITY THAT IS ESSENTIAL TO THE CONCEPT OF JUSTICE . . . THUS, ALTHOUGH THE RULE IS THOUGHT TO DETER UNLAWFUL POLICE ACTIVITY IN PART THROUGH THE NURTURING OF RESPECT FOR FOURTH AMENDMENT VALUES, IF APPLIED INDISCRIMINATELY IT MAY WELL HAVE THE OPPOSITE EFFECT OF GENERATING DISRESPECT FOR THE LAW AND ADMINISTRATION OF JUSTICE.

Justice Powell called for the application of the exclusionary rule to be balanced against the "acknowledged costs to other values vital to a rational system of criminal justice." But it may not be easy to ascertain the true "costs and benefits" associated with the rule.

EXCEPTIONS TO THE FOURTH AMENDMENT'S WARRANT REQUIREMENTS

In *Draper v. United States* (1959), the Court ruled that it is impractical to obtain a warrant in an emergency or "exigency." These emergencies might include believing the suspect will escape if an arrest is not made immediately or believing evidence is in danger of being destroyed by the suspect. In short, the realities of law enforcement often demand officers to act quickly and without the guidance of a magistrate (Brief 12.4). The following exceptions offer clear evidence of the problem's complexity.

THE "AUTOMOBILE" EXCEPTION

The United States is a highly mobile society, and this mobility can cause problems for law enforcement officials. Table 12.2 provides an overview of the major decisions involving the automobile and police searches.

Stated first in *Carroll v. United States* (1925), the automobile exception permits authorities to stop and search a moving vehicle on probable cause without a warrant. This exception is necessary, according to the Court, because of the ease with which an automobile can be moved away from law enforcement authorities and the jurisdiction of the court issuing the warrant. The authorities should have probable cause to believe that the car is being used to commit a crime or contains evidence of a previously committed crime.

The Court clarified the moving vehicle exception in *United States v. Ross* (1982). In that case, rather than focusing on the "nature of the container in which the contraband is secreted," the Court said that if the search was justified by probable cause, then every part of "the vehicle and its contents" would be subject to search. *United States v. Ross* did not completely resolve the questions surrounding the search of closed containers found inside a car. That step occurred in *California v. Acevedo* (1991), when the Court formally announced a single rule to govern searches of automobiles and containers found inside automobiles. This case originated when police observed Acevedo carrying a brown paper bag the size of marijuana packages, which the police had seen earlier. He placed the bag in his trunk and drove off. Police stopped the car, opened the trunk, searched the bag, and found marijuana. Finding the officers had probable cause to believe that the bag contained drugs but lacked probable cause to suspect that the car, itself, otherwise contained contraband, the California Court of Appeals ordered the marijuana suppressed as evidence.

Justice Harry Blackmun's 6–3 majority opinion established a new principle:

> WE THEREFORE INTERPRET *CARROLL* AS PROVIDING ONE RULE TO GOVERN ALL AUTOMOBILE SEARCHES. THE POLICE MAY SEARCH AN AUTOMOBILE AND THE CONTAINERS WITHIN IT WHERE THEY HAVE PROBABLE CAUSE TO BELIEVE CONTRABAND OR EVIDENCE IS CONTAINED.

In an emotional dissent, Justice Stevens questioned the majority's contention that warrant requirements have hindered law enforcement efforts in the war against drugs by pointing out that the Court had upheld twenty-seven of thirty Fourth Amendment

Brief 12.4

TWO CASES ON THE COMMON LAW AND ARRESTS

The Fourth Amendment grew out of understandings of a "common law" protecting the rights of an individual's property, possessions, and person. This common law had come to America through the decisions of British courts over many years. In the more than two hundred years since the Fourth Amendment's ratification, the Supreme Court frequently has been called upon to clarify the framer's intentions. In *Wilson v. Arkansas* (1995), Justice Clarence Thomas wrote for a unanimous Supreme Court that the common law "knock-and-announce" rule was among the factors that the amendment's framers thought should be considered in assessing the reasonableness of a search. Even though the constitution does not formally require police officers to knock and announce themselves, the principle is so well established and documented in our common-law tradition that it must be given great weight in determining whether a search is reasonable and, therefore, constitutional. A unanimous Court reaffirmed *Wilson* in *Richards v. Wisconsin* (1997), but indicated that no-knock searches, if justified by the circumstances, would be permissible. A 2006 decision in *Hudson v. Michigan* weakened the knock-and-announce rule somewhat by holding that evidence seized in violation of the knock-and-announce provisions should not be suppressed. The exclusionary rule does not apply to knock-and-announce searches.

In *Atwater v. City of Lago Vista, Texas* (2000), a closely divided 5–4 majority held that the Fourth Amendment does not forbid a warrantless arrest for a minor criminal offense—in this case, a seat belt violation. The arrest occurred when Lago Vista police officer Bart Turek observed Gail Atwater driving her pickup truck with her two young children in the front seat. None of them was wearing a seat belt. Following a verbal exchange, the officer handcuffed Atwater, placed her in his squad car, and drove her to the police station. Officers had her remove her shoes, jewelry, and eyeglasses and empty her pockets. They took her "mug shot," placed her alone in a jail cell for about one hour, and then took her to a magistrate where she was released on $310 bond. She eventually pleaded no contest to the misdemeanor seat belt offenses and paid a $50 fine. All other charges were dropped.

Atwater contended that the common law had always prohibited warrantless arrests for misdemeanors except for cases of "breach of the peace." Justice Souter's majority opinion traced the pre-founding era common law and found that the rules "were not nearly as clear as Atwater claims." He noted that some of the major common-law commentators (Lord Halsbury, James Fitzjames Stephen, Sir William Blackstone, and Sir Edward East) seemed to support Atwater's position, while others (Sir Matthew Hale, Sergeant William Hawkins) did not. Souter concluded that no consensus can be found in the common law to support Atwater's argument:

> *The point is that the statutes riddle Atwater's supposed common-law rule with enough exceptions to unsettle any contention that the law of the mother country would have left the Fourth Amendment's Framers of a view that it would necessarily have been unreasonable to arrest without warrant for a misdemeanor unaccompanied by real or threatened violence.*

Because Texas law authorizes an officer to arrest "for any offense committed in his presence or within his view," and because no one disputed that the officer had probable cause to arrest Atwater and did so without unusual harm to her privacy interests, the majority held the arrest to be "not unreasonable for Fourth Amendment purposes."

Justice O'Connor's dissent found the majority's rule to be "not only unsupported by our precedent, but . . . contrary to the principles that lie at the core of the Fourth Amendment. . . . When a full custodial arrest is effected without a warrant, the plain language of the Fourth Amendment requires that the arrest be reasonable."

---

searches and seizures involving narcotics searches since 1982. He concluded on a somber tone: "It is too early to know how much freedom America has lost today."

The *Acevedo* rule was broadened in *Wyoming v. Houghton* (1999), when a 6–3 majority ruled that when police have probable cause to believe a car contains contraband, they may search a passenger's personal belongings. This case stemmed from a traffic stop for speeding and a faulty brake light. When the officers asked the driver why he had a syringe in his shirt pocket, the driver, "with refreshing candor," said that he used it to take drugs. The officer ordered the driver and two female passengers out of the car and asked for identification. Sandra Houghton identified herself as Sandra James and said she had no identification. The officer found a purse in the back seat, searched it, and found Houghton's identification and syringes filled with methamphetamine. She was convicted of felony drug possession.

Justice Scalia held the search of Houghton's purse to be legal, citing the long line of cases that allow officers to search all cars and all containers for contraband. This rule applies regardless of ownership of the container and

Table 12.2 Development of the Law—The Automobile Exception

Year	Event	Significance
1925	*Carroll v. U.S.*	Established the "automobile exception" to the search warrant requirement, citing likelihood of mobility.
1977	*U.S. v. Chadwick*	Luggage in an automobile is not searchable under the automobile exception because a person's "expectations of privacy" in personal luggage are greater than in the automobile.
1979	*Arkansas v. Sanders*	Ruled a suitcase in an automobile was not subject to warrantless search under an "automobile exception."
1981	*Robbins v. California*	Held a search of plastic-wrapped packages in a car as unreasonable.
1982	*U.S. v. Ross*	In upholding a drug dealer's conviction for selling out of his car, the Court seemed to allow searches of containers within automobiles depending on the presence of probable cause.
1985	*California v. Carney*	A motor home is an automobile for purposes of the automobile exception, since a motor home can become mobile with the turn of a key.
1991	*California v. Acevedo*	Announcement of a single rule to govern all automobile searches. If based on probable cause, automobile exception allows search of the auto and all containers within.
1999	*Wyoming v. Houghton*	When officers have probable cause to believe an automobile contains contraband, they may search a passenger's personal belongings inside the automobile.
2000	*Bond v. United States*	Authorities are prohibited from "feeling" the outside of a bag belonging to a bus passenger to determine the contents.
2003	*Maryland v. Pringle*	Police officers had probable cause to arrest Pringle for possession of cocaine, although he had been a front-seat passenger and the drugs were found in a rear-seat armrest.
2005	*Illinois v. Caballes*	A dog sniff during a legal traffic stop revealing the presence of marijuana in the trunk does not violate the Fourth Amendment.
2007	*Brendlin v. California*	A passenger in a car that has been stopped by police is considered "seized" for Fourth Amendment purposes and therefore is able to challenge the constitutionality of the stop and ask for evidence to be suppressed.

includes even the personal belongings of passengers. Justice Breyer concurred but expressed concern about the search of a purse, saying that it essentially was like a man's billfold.

An even more unusual scenario occurred in the case of *Maryland v. Pringle* (2003), in which a unanimous Court ultimately concluded that police officers had probable cause to arrest Pringle for possession of cocaine, even though he had been a front-seat passenger and the drugs were found in a rear-seat armrest. Police had stopped the car for speeding around 3:00 A.M., searched the car, seized $763 from the glove compartment and cocaine from behind the back-seat armrest, and arrested the three occupants. Later, Pringle confessed and claimed that the others did not know about the drugs. His ten-year sentence was reversed by the appellate court on the ground that officers did not have probable cause to arrest Pringle for possession when the drugs were elsewhere in the car.

In its ruling, the Court said it was reasonable for the officer to infer a common enterprise among the three men, and the quantity of drugs and cash in the car indicated the likelihood of drug dealing. Chief Justice Rehnquist concluded: "We hold that the officer had probable cause to believe that Pringle had committed the crime of possession of a controlled substance."

The Court added to the long line of automobile cases in *Brendlin v. California* (2007). That decision focused on the rights of passengers who are riding in a car that is stopped by the authorities. Previous decisions generally had held the driver was considered "seized" for Fourth Amendment purposes, but not the passenger. Accordingly, the passenger possessed no rights to challenge the action. In *Brendlin*, the Court concluded that a reasonable person in a passenger's position would not feel free to leave during a traffic stop. As such, the passenger should be considered "seized" and consequently has the right to challenge the constitutionality of the stop and the admissibility of evidence.

The automobile exception becomes even more complex when drug-sniffing dogs are introduced into the picture. A 2005 Supreme Court ruling in *Illinois v. Caballes* upheld the use of drug-sniffing dogs around a vehicle that has been stopped for a routine traffic violation. Evidence obtained from that sniff may be used at trial. In other words, if a dog reacts to a substance on or in the vehicle, probable cause to search is established. As this book goes to press, the Supreme Court is deciding *Florida v. Harris*, in which Aldo, a highly trained and certified narcotics detection dog, sniffed a car's door handle and indicated the presence of narcotics. The search produced all of the material needed to produce methamphetamine but no drugs. The trial court upheld the search, and the Florida Supreme Court reversed on the grounds that a dog's training and certification are not sufficient to establish probable cause. The Court's ruling could have a significant impact on the widespread use of drug-sniffing dogs.

The automobile exception does not extend to mass transit conveyances, and the Court made that clear in *Bond v. United States* (2000), when a 7–2 majority held that the physical manipulation of a bus passenger's carry-on luggage violated the Fourth Amendment. At issue was a standard police practice of "feeling" the outside of soft luggage to assist in determining the contents. Chief Justice Rehnquist wrote that the passenger had a reasonable expectation that people would not touch the carry-on bag in a probing manner. He noted that "[p]hysically invasive inspection is simply more intrusive than purely visual inspection. . . . Obviously, petitioner's bag was not part of his person. But travelers are particularly concerned about their carry-on luggage; they generally use it to transport personal items that, for whatever reason, they prefer to keep close at hand."

Bond's carry-on bag was protected from physical manipulation, but Houghton's purse was not. Both were used to transport highly personal items. In *Houghton*, however, the police officers had probable cause to search the automobile for contraband. In *Bond*, no probable cause or even reasonable suspicion existed. More recently, however, the Court has eased restrictions on bus searches (see "Consent Exception" below).

THE "BORDER" EXCEPTION

Given the ongoing controversy surrounding the movement of illegal aliens into the United States, the U.S. Border Patrol has been involved in numerous search and seizure cases. On this issue, the Supreme Court gradually has brought border searches into the coverage of the Fourth Amendment, while maintaining the long-standing practice of not requiring search warrants for searches at border crossings. However, in *Almeida-Sanchez v. United States* (1973), a 5–4 majority held that a roving search of an automobile by Border Patrol agents approximately twenty miles from the border without a warrant and lacking probable cause was unconstitutional. Two years later, in *United States v. Ortiz* (1975), the Court extended the probable cause requirement to vehicle searches at check points away from the border (Brief 12.5).

In *United States v. Martinez-Fuerte* (1976), however, a 7–2 majority ruled that a permanent checkpoint situated at San Clemente, California, was properly within the border patrol's authority to administer, that the location of checkpoints was a matter properly left to the border patrol's discretion, and that the practice of referring some persons for secondary inspections at the checkpoint did not violate the Fourth Amendment. The concern with our national borders after September 11 was reflected in the Court's 9–0 decision in *United States v. Arvizu* (2002). The ruling approved a Border Patrol agent's stop of a vehicle some thirty miles from the border, largely because of the "stiff posture" of alien drug smugglers. Based on the "totality of the circumstances," said the Court, the trained officer had the reasonable suspicion required to stop the suspect.

Brief 12.5
POLICE CHECKPOINTS AND REASONABLE SUSPICION

The Supreme Court has upheld certain types of police checkpoints and invalidated others, largely depending on whether the roadblocks are designed to serve some "special needs" beyond law enforcement. These special needs might include highway safety or preventing smuggling at the border. In *Michigan Dept. of State Police v. Sitz* (1990), a 6–3 Court upheld a Michigan pilot program of highway sobriety checkpoints at which all motorists were stopped. During the only operation conducted before the practice was halted, 126 vehicles passed through the checkpoint, the average delay per vehicle was twenty-five seconds, and two drivers were arrested for driving under the influence. Chief Justice William Rehnquist's opinion held that the checkpoints in this case were constitutional because officers followed clearly established guidelines and stopped every car. The fact that 1.5 percent of the drivers stopped were arrested for alcohol impairment demonstrated that the program was sufficiently effective to justify the State's interest in implementing the program.

But what about checkpoints that are established for the primary purpose of discovering and interdicting illegal narcotics? In *City of Indianapolis v. Edmond* (2000), a 6–3 Court struck down a program in which a certain number of drivers were stopped on the highway, asked for license and registration, and then checked for signs of driver impairment. Drug-sniffing dogs were also present to walk around and examine every vehicle stopped at the checkpoint. If the dog indicated the presence of drugs, the police claimed probable cause to search the car.

Justice O'Connor's majority opinion indicated that a search or seizure is ordinarily unreasonable without some sort of individualized suspicion, unless the suspicionless stops are designed to serve "special needs." But suspicionless stops solely to determine evidence of criminal wrongdoing are clearly unreasonable.

An example of the "special needs" referred to by Justice O'Connor became clear in *Illinois v. Lidster* (2004). Police set up a highway checkpoint to obtain information from motorists about a hit-and-run accident occurring about one week earlier at the same location and time of night. Officers stopped each vehicle for ten to fifteen seconds, asked the occupants whether they had seen anything happen there the previous weekend, and handed each driver a flyer describing and requesting information about the accident. As Robert Lidster approached, his minivan swerved, nearly hitting an officer. One officer smelled alcohol on Lidster's breath, and another officer administered a sobriety test. Lidster was arrested and convicted in Illinois state court of driving under the influence of alcohol. He then challenged the arrest and conviction on the ground that the government obtained evidence through use of a checkpoint stop that violated the Fourth Amendment. The trial court rejected that challenge, but the state appellate court reversed, and the State Supreme Court agreed, holding that, in light of *Indianapolis v. Edmond*, the stop was unconstitutional.

Writing for a 6–3 majority, Justice Breyer held that *Edmond* did not govern the outcome of this case. The checkpoint in *Edmond* was designed to ferret out drug crimes committed by the motorists themselves, but the primary law enforcement purpose in *Lidster* was not to determine whether a vehicle's occupants were committing a crime, but to ask the occupants, as members of the public, for help in providing information about a crime in all likelihood committed by others. An information-seeking stop is not the kind of event that involves suspicion, or lack thereof, of the relevant individual. Most importantly, according to Justice Breyer, the stops interfered only minimally with liberty of the sort the Fourth Amendment seeks to protect. As a result, the checkpoint, although a "seizure," was reasonable.

THE "HOT-PURSUIT" EXCEPTION

Police authorities often must react to the fleeing suspect who seeks to avoid capture by any number of methods. The issue of "hot pursuit" arose in *Warden v. Hayden* (1967), a case in which police entered a residence that an armed robbery suspect had been seen entering previously. Upon entering, police discovered a shotgun and pistol in a running flush tank, a jacket and trousers that matched the description, and assorted ammunition. Hayden was arrested, the items of evidence were introduced at his trial, and he was convicted.

Justice William Brennan's majority opinion upheld the validity of the entry and search without a warrant, stating that "speed here was essential," and the authorities were required to make a thorough search of the house for persons and weapons. Police officers, he stated, are not required "to delay in the course of an investigation if to do so would gravely endanger their lives or the lives of others." In *United States v. Santana* (1976), a 7–2 majority upheld the arrest of a felony suspect who, having been seen on her front porch, ran inside the house. According to Justice William Rehnquist, "a suspect may not defeat an arrest which has been set in motion in a public place . . . by the expedient of escaping to a private place" (see Brief 12.6).

THE "STOP-AND-FRISK" EXCEPTION

The police officer on patrol may encounter what he regards as a suspicious person or situation. With no time to obtain a warrant, the officer may be operating

Brief 12.6
WHEN POLICE COME TO THE DOOR

The Fourth Amendment provides paramount protection for the "home," called by the Court "first among equals" in its importance. The home also includes the area "immediately surrounding and adjacent to the home," what the common law calls "curtilage," as part of the home itself. Law enforcement authorities are not permitted to use the curtilage in order to obtain evidence from within the home, but it would appear reasonable that police be able to walk to and knock on the front door to ask questions. At what point have the police engaged in a search when they enter the curtilage? The cases of *Kentucky v. King* (2011) and *Florida v. Jardines* (2013) provide differing answers, although the circumstances of the cases differ somewhat.

In *Kentucky v. King*, police set up a controlled drug buy in a parking lot outside an apartment complex in Lexington, Kentucky. An undercover officer watched the drug deal take place and radioed officers to hurry because the suspect was moving quickly toward a breezeway in the complex and might enter an apartment. Officers in a nearby parking lot ran to the breezeway, where they heard a door shut and detected a strong odor of marijuana. They were facing two apartments, one on the left and one on the right, but they did not know which one the suspect had entered. They smelled marijuana coming from the left apartment, so they banged on the door and announced, "This is the police," or "Police, police, police." They immediately heard the sounds of things being moved inside the apartment, so they kicked in the door and entered. Inside, they found three people in the front room smoking marijuana, one of whom was Hollis King. A protective sweep revealed cocaine and marijuana in plain view, and a subsequent search produced crack cocaine, cash, and drug paraphernalia. Eventually, police also entered the apartment on the right and found the initial suspect. Hollis King was convicted and received an eleven-year sentence. The Kentucky Supreme Court held the search unreasonable and reversed.

Writing for an 8–1 Court, Justice Samuel Alito reasoned that the real question is whether the police acted "reasonably" and did not engage in or threaten illegal conduct in order to cause the exigency. When the police went to the door and knocked, they were behaving in a reasonable and professional manner. They did not threaten to break down the door, nor did they do so until it was clear that the destruction of evidence inside the apartment was imminent. Justice Alito concluded:

> *Where, as here, the police did not create the exigency by engaging or threatening to engage in conduct that violates the Fourth Amendment, warrantless entry to prevent the destruction of evidence is reasonable. . . . For these reasons, we conclude that the exigent circumstances rule applies when the police do not gain entry to premises by means of an actual or threatened violation of the Fourth Amendment.*

Justice Ruth Bader Ginsburg, the lone dissenter, argued that the police had ample time and opportunity to obtain a search warrant. The fact that the suspect had entered that building along with the smell of marijuana provided sufficient probable cause to justify a search warrant. Police could have posted on the premises until the warrant was obtained.

In *Florida v. Jardines*, a police officer received an unverified tip that Jardines was growing marijuana in his home. The officer went to the home and watched for several minutes. He was then joined by a canine officer and his drug-sniffing dog, and they went to the front porch. On the porch, the officer allowed the dog to sniff for drugs, and the dog "alerted" on the front door—suggesting that this was the strongest source of the odor. The officers returned later that day with a search warrant, found marijuana growing in the house, and arrested Jardines. The lower courts suppressed the evidence, considering the search to be unreasonable.

Justice Scalia, writing for a five-member majority, held that the actions of the officers and dog on the front porch constituted a "search" under the Fourth Amendment, which requires a warrant. He noted that when "the Government obtains information by physically intruding" on persons, houses, papers, or effects, "a search within the original meaning of the Fourth Amendment" has "undoubtedly occurred." He continued by pointing out the exalted place of the home and the surrounding curtilage, emphasizing that authorities may not enter private property illegally to conduct a search. Justice Scalia also wrote the opinion in *United States v. Jones* (2012), discussed later in this chapter, in which he emphasized that the "trespass rule" forbids authorities from entering private property without permission to engage in a search. In his view, this was a very similar situation.

So, whereas *Kentucky v. King* held that officers could knock on the door of a home, hear noses, and then enter, *Florida v. Jardines* does not allow officers to use a drug dog on the front porch to obtain evidence. In part, officers knocking on a front door are doing nothing different from any other visitor, but most visitors don't bring drug-sniffing dogs with them.

---

on something considerably less than probable cause. In response to these situations, the courts have established the standard of **reasonable suspicion** to justify a warrantless search and seizure when probable cause is lacking (see Brief 12.7).

Most of the cases involving reasonable suspicion have dealt with "stop and frisk" matters related to questioning suspects. The leading case among these was *Terry v. Ohio* (1968). In that case, Detective Martin McFadden was on afternoon patrol in downtown

Brief 12.7
WOULD YOU CALL THIS "REASONABLE SUSPICION"?

In *United States v. Sokolow* (1989), the Supreme Court was called on to determine whether reasonable suspicion must include at least some indication of "ongoing criminal activity" before officials can detain a suspect. The case began when DEA agents stopped Sokolow on his arrival at Honolulu International Airport. They found 1,063 grams of cocaine in his carry-on luggage. The agents did not know that criminal activity was "afoot," but they knew the following facts: (1) Sokolow paid $2,100 for two round-trip tickets with a roll of $20 bills; (2) he traveled under a name that did not match the name under which his telephone number was listed; (3) his destination was Miami, a source city for illicit drugs; (4) he stayed in Miami for only forty-eight hours, although a round-trip flight takes twenty hours; (5) he appeared nervous during his trip; and (6) he checked none of his luggage.

Based on these facts, the District Court found the stop justified by "reasonable suspicion," but the Court of Appeals disagreed, stating that some finding of "criminal activity" was necessary. Writing for a 7–2 majority, Chief Justice Rehnquist reversed the Court of Appeals. He noted that, "although each of the six factors listed above is not by itself proof of illegal conduct and is quite consistent with innocent travel, taken together, they amount to reasonable suspicion that criminal conduct was afoot." The stop and subsequent seizure were justified by "reasonable suspicion."

The *Sokolow* ruling can be contrasted with an earlier decision in *Reid v. Georgia* (1980), in which the Court found no reasonable suspicion. In *Reid*, the DEA agent stopped the defendant, knowing only that (1) the defendant flew into Atlanta from Fort Lauderdale, a source city for cocaine; (2) he arrived early in the morning, when police activity might be less; (3) he did not check his luggage; and (4) the defendant and his traveling companion appeared to be trying to hide the fact that they were traveling together. These facts, said the Court, did not produce reasonable suspicion of criminal activity.

Cleveland. While observing John W. Terry and a companion, McFadden noticed that something about the men "didn't look right," so he decided to watch them from a distance of a few hundred yards. He watched as one of the men walked down the street, stopped to look in a store window, walked past, looked back in the window, and eventually returned to his starting place. These actions were repeated several times and, when a third man arrived, McFadden decided to investigate further, believing that the men might be planning to rob the store. Approaching the men, he identified himself, asked the men their names, and received only a mumbled reply. At that point, McFadden grabbed Terry, turned him around, and patted down the outside of his clothing. Detecting what felt like a pistol, McFadden moved the men inside the store, ordered Terry to remove his coat, and confiscated the pistol. A "pat-down" search of the other men produced another gun. Terry and his companion were booked and subsequently convicted for carrying concealed weapons.

In *Terry v. Ohio* (1968), an 8–1 majority held the search to be reasonable. Chief Justice Earl Warren's opinion clarified the "difficult" issues:

> WE MERELY HOLD TODAY THAT WHERE A POLICE OFFICER OBSERVES UNUSUAL CONDUCT WHICH LEADS HIM REASONABLY TO CONCLUDE IN LIGHT OF HIS EXPERIENCE THAT CRIMINAL ACTIVITY MAY BE AFOOT AND THAT THE PERSONS WITH WHOM HE IS DEALING MAY BE ARMED AND PRESENTLY DANGEROUS, WHERE IN THE COURSE OF INVESTIGATING THIS BEHAVIOR HE IDENTIFIES HIMSELF AS A POLICEMAN AND MAKES REASONABLE INQUIRIES, AND WHERE NOTHING IN THE INITIAL STAGES OF THE ENCOUNTER SERVES TO DISPEL HIS REASONABLE FEAR FOR HIS OWN OR OTHERS' SAFETY, HE IS ENTITLED FOR THE PROTECTION OF HIMSELF AND OTHERS IN THE AREA TO CONDUCT A CAREFULLY LIMITED SEARCH OF THE OUTER CLOTHING OF SUCH PERSONS IN AN ATTEMPT TO DISCOVER WEAPONS WHICH MIGHT BE USED TO ASSAULT HIM. (EMPHASIS ADDED)

In two companion cases to *Terry*, the Court showed the importance of specific facts in each "stop-and-frisk" encounter. A policeman who stuck his hand into a suspect's pocket to obtain narcotics he suspected to be there conducted an unreasonable search, according to the decision in *Sibron v. New York*. However, in *Peters v. New York*, a police officer who observed two unfamiliar men tiptoeing past his apartment door was justified in apprehending the suspects and patting them down. When he felt a hard object that "might have been a knife" in one suspect's pocket, the officer reached into the pocket and removed a small set of burglary tools. According to the Court, the burglary tools were discovered in a valid search and as such were properly admissible as evidence in court.

Two cases in 2000 produced contrasting "stop and frisk" rulings. In *Florida v. J.L.* (2000), a unanimous court held that a "stop and frisk" is not permissible when it is based solely on an anonymous tip that a person is carrying a gun. *Illinois v. Wardlow* (2000), on the other hand, established that police can detain and frisk a person solely because he runs away from them. This 5–4 decision placed heavy reliance on the fact that the suspect was in a "high crime area" known for heavy narcotics trafficking. Chief Justice Rehnquist stated that while "headlong flight" from police is not necessarily indicative of wrongdoing, it is suggestive of such. Nervous and evasive behavior, he said, is an important element in determining reasonable suspicion. The dissenting justices noted that in some areas citizens do not view the police as friendly or supportive of the community, and some persons may seek to avoid contact at all costs (see Brief 12.8).

THE "SEARCH-INCIDENT-TO-ARREST" EXCEPTION

Today in America, probably a majority of all searches occur following, or incident to, an arrest. The long-recognized reasons for such searches include the need to protect the officer from being harmed by weapons held by the suspect, as well as the need to prevent evidence from being destroyed. Table 12.3 illustrates the development of the "search-incident-to-arrest" exception.

Chimel v. California (1969) marked a distinct change in the Court's treatment of the valid arrest exception. Ted Chimel, the appellant, had been arrested at home on burglary charges. Despite his objections, the police undertook a complete search of the house, including the attic and garage. Certain items obtained in the search were introduced as evidence in Chimel's trial, in which he was convicted.

Justice Potter Stewart's majority opinion reversed Chimel's conviction and enunciated new standards governing the scope of searches incident to a lawful arrest, significantly narrowing their permissibility in the process. According to Stewart, a lawful arrest provides "ample justification" for a search of the person

---

Brief 12.8

"STOP AND FRISK" IN NEW YORK CITY

According to a *New York Times* analysis of data provided by the NYPD and other organizations, New York City police registered a record-setting 685,724 citywide "stop and frisks" in 2011, up from 97,000 in 2002. While many urban police departments rely heavily on such stops, New York City appears to be in a league of its own. Of course, supporters point to the waves of violence that require aggressive community policing strategies in the high crime areas.

In one approximate eight-block area of Brownsville, Brooklyn, police logged nearly 52,000 stops during 2009. The department policy known as "Stop, Question, Frisk" focuses on persons who may fit the description of a suspect or who were stopped for "furtive movements." Critics of the police policy argue that these categories can be interpreted so broadly as to allow the police to conduct a stop for really almost any reason. Many of the stops occur within the numerous housing projects in Brooklyn, and anyone who does not enter with a key is likely to be stopped. New York Housing Authority rules prohibit anyone from being in a housing project who does not live there or is visiting someone. The *New York Times* data showed that 109 of these stops occurred on a single day. Some of those arrested were actual residents of the building in which they were stopped.

Neighborhood activists and concerned citizens argue that the police are necessary, but that they need to be more selective in their use of stops. Some charge that the police operate under a "quota" system to produce more stops—a charge denied by NYPD. At least three lawsuits challenging the "stop-and-frisk" policy are moving through the courts, and the Bronx District Attorney's Office notified NYPD that it would no longer prosecute people stopped for trespassing unless police could show the arrests were justified. At any rate, the controversy surrounding "stop-and-frisk" tactics in New York City underscores the fundamental difficulty in policing in a free society—protecting the innocent while apprehending the guilty.

SOURCE: Ray Rivera, Al Baker, and Janet Roberts, "A Few Blocks, 4 Years, 52,000 Police Stops," *New York Times*, July 11, 2010; "Losing Faith in Stop-and-Frisk," Editorial, *New York Times*, September 26, 2012; Julie Dressner and Edwin Martinez, "The Scars of Stop-and-Frisk," *New York Times*, June 12, 2012; "Stop-and-Frisk, Part 3," Editorial, *New York Times*, October 7, 2012.

Table 12.3 Development of the Law—"Search Incident to Arrest"

Year	Event	Significance
1914	*Weeks v. U.S.*	Classic case establishing exclusionary rule but also recognizing the need to allow a warrantless search following a lawful arrest.
1950	*U.S. v. Rabinowitz*	Court upheld warrantless one-and-one-half-hour search of a one-room office following a valid arrest.
1969	*Chimel v. California*	Court drastically restricted permissible "incident-to-arrest" searches, limiting them to the person arrested and the area within his immediate control.
1973	*U.S. v. Robinson* *Gustafson v. Florida*	Stop for routine traffic violation constitutes "custodial arrest," which justifies search of the person and surrounding area. Searches produced quantities of drugs.
1977	*Pennsylvania v. Mimms*	Police officer making valid stop is entitled to order the driver out of the vehicle, based on the possible threat to the officer's safety.
1981	*New York v. Belton*	Held that police may search the passenger compartment of a vehicle and any containers therein as a contemporaneous incident of an arrest of the vehicle's recent occupant.
1990	*Maryland v. Buie*	Court upheld a "protective-sweep" search in which officers with arrest warrant fanned out throughout a house and found evidence. Court said the sweep should extend only to a cursory inspection of the spaces where a person may be found.
1996	*Whren and Brown v. U.S.*	An observed traffic violation is sufficient to justify a stop and search even if the violation poses no immediate threat to the safety of others.
1997	*Maryland v. Wilson*	Extended the *Mimms* rule to passengers. Police officers may order a passenger out of the car following a valid traffic stop.
1998	*Knowles v. Iowa*	Police who issue a traffic citation do not have powers to conduct a "full-blown search" of a motorist and the automobile.
2009	*Arizona v. Gant*	The precedent set in *New York v. Belton* does not authorize a vehicle search incident to a recent occupant's arrest after the arrestee has been secured and cannot access the interior of the vehicle.
2012	*Florence v. County of Burlingtonç*	The 5–4 ruling allows officials to strip-search persons arrested for any offense, however minor, before admitting them to the general jail population.
2013	*Maryland v. King*	When a person is arrested under probable cause and brought to the police station, police may take and analyze a cheek swab of the arrestee's DNA—a booking procedure that is like fingerprinting and photographing and is reasonable under the Fourth Amendment.

arrested and the area "within his immediate control," but no further.

While *Chimel* has not been overturned by the Court, considerable attention has been directed at the issue of searches conducted following a valid arrest. Court decisions in the 1970s established the rule that a valid arrest, including a traffic violation, justifies a search of the person and the immediate environment surrounding the person (see Brief 12.9). More recent decisions such as *Maryland v. Buie* (1990), upholding a "protective sweep" of a house, and *Maryland v. Wilson* (1997), allowing the search of a passenger in an automobile during a traffic stop, illustrate the complex issues raised by this exception.

The "search-incident-to-arrest" exception was significantly narrowed in *Arizona v. Gant* (2009), when a 5–4 majority held that the search of an automobile once the arrestee was fully secured and unable to access the vehicle was invalid. This decision clarified *New York v. Belton* (1981) that had authorized the contemporaneous search of a vehicle once its occupant had been arrested, largely on the premise that a suspect might obtain a weapon or destroy evidence. But *Arizona v. Gant* involved a different set of facts: Rodney Gant was arrested for driving on a suspended license, handcuffed, and locked in a patrol car before officers searched his car and found cocaine in a jacket pocket. The lower court upheld the search and Gant was

Brief 12.9

SEARCHES AND CITATIONS: KNOWLES V. IOWA (1998) AND VIRGINIA V. MOORE (2008)

Patrick Knowles was driving forty-three in a twenty-five mph zone when an Iowa police officer pulled him over and gave him a speeding ticket. The officer then ordered Knowles out of the car and searched it, finding a bag of marijuana and pipe under the driver's seat. Knowles was then arrested and charged with drug offenses. Knowles moved to suppress the evidence because he had not been placed under arrest, and the search could not be upheld under the search-incident-to-arrest exception. Knowles had not consented to the search, and the officer admitted that he did not have probable cause. However, the officer claimed that the Iowa law authorized the search. The Iowa law allows an officer to give a citation or to arrest for a traffic violation, and it then says that the decision to give a citation does not affect the officer's authority to conduct a search.

A unanimous Supreme Court in *Knowles v. Iowa* (1998) held that the search-incident-to arrest-exception does not authorize a search following a citation. The Court noted two rationales for the exception—to disarm the suspect and take him into custody and to preserve evidence for trial—and neither was present in this case. The Court stated that police who are concerned for their safety during routine traffic stops can take less intrusive steps when issuing a ticket: ordering the driver and passengers out of the car, pat-down searches based on reasonable suspicion, or even arresting the suspect and then conducting a full-blown search. While the search of Knowles's car was permissible under Iowa law, it violated the Fourth Amendment.

Ten years later, the Supreme Court addressed the constittionality of a search following an arrest, despite the fact that the state (Virginia) law required that only a citation be issued for the offense. *Virginia v. Moore* (2008) occurred because police heard that Moore was driving with a suspended license, an offense for which Virginia law required issuance of a summons. Instead, the officers arrested Moore, searched his person, and found 16 grams of crack cocaine and $516 in cash. According to Chief Justice Roberts writing for a unanimous Court (Justice Ginsburg concurred in the judgment), *Knowles* did not apply in this case because police arrested Moore—they did not issue a summons as was done in *Knowles*:

> We reaffirm against a novel challenge what we have signaled for more than half a century. When officers have probable cause to believe that a person has committeda crime in their presence, the Fourth Amendment permits them to make an arrest, and to search the suspect in order to safeguard evidence and ensure their own safety.

Since the arrest did not violate the Fourth Amendment, it did not matter that it was inconsistent with Virginia law.

---

convicted of drug offenses. The Arizona Supreme Court, however, held that *Belton* did not answer the question of whether officers may conduct such a search once the arrestee is secured. Since *Chimel* requires that a search incident to arrest must be justified either by officer safety or the preservation of evidence, it was unclear whether either was relevant in *Gant*.

Justice Stevens held that police may search the passenger compartment of a vehicle incident to a recent occupant's arrest only if it is reasonable to believe that the arrestee might access the vehicle at the time of the search, or that the vehicle contains evidence of the offense of arrest. Since Rodney Gant was handcuffed and locked in a police car, it was not reasonable to believe that he could access the vehicle. Moreover, he had been arrested for a suspended license—not for drugs—and the search was not related to the offense of arrest. The search was unreasonable.

THE "CONSENT" EXCEPTION

A person may waive the Fourth Amendment requirement for a warrant, but such waiver should be completely voluntary. *Schneckloth v. Bustamonte* (1973) raised the issue of whether such a waiver is ever truly voluntary if the person being searched is not aware that he has the right to refuse permission to authorities. In that ruling, Justice Stewart held for the majority that explicit notice of the right to refuse a warrantless search is not required to establish proof of voluntary consent. The Court reaffirmed that principle in *Ohio v. Robinette* (1996) and most recently in *United States v. Drayton, et al.* (2002). In *Drayton*, two officers boarded a commercial passenger bus and asked permission to search luggage and passengers. One of the officers stood at the front of the bus without blocking the door. Justice Kennedy's 6–3 majority opinion concluded that no coercion was present, and the Fourth Amendment does not require authorities to warn passengers of their right to refuse consent.

The Court has created a standard of "objective reasonableness," that is, "What would a reasonable person think or do?" to guide police in consent-based searches. Using this standard, the Court upheld the search of a paper bag in an automobile (*Florida v. Jimeno*, 1991) and an apartment search for which consent was given by a third party who police mistakenly thought was a resident (*Illinois v. Rodriguez*, 1990). However, in *Georgia v. Randolph* (2006), the Court addressed the somewhat unusual situation of having both occupants present at the time consent to search a dwelling is sought, with one giving consent and the other refusing to do so. In *Randolph*, the wife gave consent but the husband refused. The police entered based on the wife's consent, found cocaine, and arrested the pair. The wife later withdrew her consent. The Supreme Court held the search to be unreasonable. Police are under no obligation to locate all occupants to obtain their consent prior to entering, but they cannot enter if an occupant who is present refuses to give consent.

A unanimous Court held in *United States v. Knights* (2001) that a probation agreement containing a "consent-to-search" clause provides reasonable consent for a warrantless search. Chief Justice Rehnquist noted that "probationers do not enjoy the absolute liberty to which every citizen is entitled." The same logic was applied to parolees in *Samson v. California* (2006). In that case, a 6–3 majority found that parolees "have lesser expectations of privacy than probationers," and the parolee is aware of the condition that allows such searches. Persons on probation and parole essentially give their "consent" to be searched by virtue of their legal status.

THE "PLAIN-VIEW" EXCEPTION

In *Harris v. United States* (1968), the Court issued the following announcement: "It has long been settled that objects falling in the plain view of an officer who has a right to be in the position to have that view are subject to seizure and may be introduced into evidence." This plain-view exception was given further elaboration in *Coolidge v. New Hampshire* (1971). Justice Stewart's plurality opinion reversed the conviction and emphasized three requirements for the plain-view search or seizure: first, the police must enter lawfully; second, the evidence must be discovered "inadvertently"; and third, it should be "immediately apparent" to the police that the items in question are contraband or evidence of a crime.

These three elements were central issues in *Arizona v. Hicks* (1987), one of the Court's recent attempts to clarify the plain-view exception. The facts of the case are summarized as follows:

POLICE ENTERED AN APARTMENT TO SEARCH FOR THE PERSON WHO HAD FIRED A SHOT THROUGH THE FLOOR AFTER THE BULLET HAD STRUCK AND INJURED A PERSON IN THE DOWNSTAIRS APARTMENT. INSIDE, THREE WEAPONS AND A STOCKING-CAP MASK WERE DISCOVERED. ONE OF THE POLICE OFFICERS, OFFICER NELSON, NOTICED TWO SETS OF EXPENSIVE-LOOKING STEREO COMPONENTS. AS HE SUSPECTED THE STEREOS MIGHT BE STOLEN, HE RECORDED THEIR SERIAL NUMBERS, AN ACTION THAT REQUIRED THAT HE MOVE SOME OF THE COMPONENTS. HE REPORTED THESE NUMBERS TO HEADQUARTERS. SHORTLY AFTERWARD, HEADQUARTERS REPORTED BACK THAT A BANG AND OLUFSEN TURNTABLE HAD BEEN STOLEN IN AN ARMED ROBBERY. OFFICER NELSON SEIZED IT IMMEDIATELY AND TOOK IT TO THE STATION. IT WAS LATER DETERMINED THAT SOME OF THE OTHER EQUIPMENT HAD BEEN TAKEN IN THE SAME ARMED ROBBERY, AND A WARRANT WAS EXECUTED TO SEIZE THAT EQUIPMENT AS WELL. HICKS WAS SUBSEQUENTLY INDICTED FOR THE ROBBERY.

In writing for a 6–3 Court, Justice Scalia held that "probable cause" is required to invoke the plain-view doctrine, and that the "reasonable suspicion" (less than probable cause) that the stereo equipment was stolen was not enough to justify the seizure. As a result, the plain-view doctrine did not make the search "reasonable" under the Fourth Amendment. Interestingly, the Court held that, while the policeman's actions were covered by the Fourth Amendment, the mere recording of serial numbers was not a "seizure" under the amendment's meaning. However, moving the equipment was a search unrelated to the "exigency" (the shooting), which justified the entry.

Finally, the plain-view exception has been applied to certain uses of aerial surveillance, especially those uses designed to detect the cultivation of marijuana. In *California v. Ciraolo* (1986), police, acting on an informant's tip, flew over the defendant's fenced property, saw the marijuana, and then obtained a search warrant. The majority's ruling emphasized the use of public air space to observe the property in question, holding that the Fourth Amendment was not violated by such activity. The Court has upheld similar uses of aerial surveillance by environmental enforcement agents to detect violations.

DRUG TESTING

Government efforts to obtain evidence from a person's body have led to conflicts over the constitutionality of drug testing policies and procedures (Brief 12.10). The primary issue in most drug testing cases is whether testing can be random or should be based on something similar to probable cause, generally referred to as "individualized suspicion" (i.e., some reason exists to suggest that a particular individual may be using drugs). In *National Treasury Employees Union v. Von Raab* (1989), a 5–4 Court upheld a U.S. Customs Service program requiring urinalysis tests from employees seeking transfer or promotion to positions having a direct involvement in drug interdiction, requiring the carrying of firearms, or the handling of classified material. In a strong dissent, Justice Antonin Scalia pointed out that the employees affected by the program had no demonstrated frequency of drug use.

A 7–2 majority upheld drug testing in the same-day-case of *Skinner v. Railway Labor Executives' Association* (1989). That case involved regulations established by the Federal Railroad Administration (FRA) that required that blood and urine tests of employees be conducted following certain major train accidents or incidents. The act also authorized railroads to administer breath and urine tests or both to covered employees who violate certain safety rules. When the Court of Appeals held that the tests could not be required without individualized suspicion, the Supreme Court accepted the appeal. Justice Kennedy's majority opinion, joined by Justice Scalia, held that, although the Fourth Amendment is applicable to the drug and alcohol testing required by the FRA, "the compelling governmental interests" served by the regulations outweigh employees' privacy concerns. Railroad employees work in an industry subject

---

Brief 12.10
ENTERING THE BODY TO OBTAIN EVIDENCE

The practice of entering the body of a suspect to obtain evidence raises both Fourth and Fifth Amendment (self-incrimination) issues, and the Supreme Court has ruled several times that such intrusions must be reasonable. According to the Court, an individual's privacy and security interests must be weighed against society's need for evidence on a case-by-case basis. The case law offers some help in understanding which types of intrusions may be upheld as permissible.

In *Rochin v. California* (1952), the Court overturned a conviction based on the forced pumping of the suspect's stomach after authorities reportedly saw him swallow two capsules. When the officers "jumped upon him" and were still unable to extract the capsules, they took him to the hospital and forced him to have his stomach pumped. The capsules were used as evidence to obtain the conviction. Justice Felix Frankfurter's opinion called the actions "conduct that shocks the conscience" and "too close to the rack and screw" to be allowable under the Due Process Clause.

However, in *Breithaupt v. Abram* (1957), the Court upheld the taking of a blood sample from an unconscious person who had been involved in a fatal traffic accident, primarily on the grounds that a blood test conducted under the authority of a physician was safe and inoffensive. In *Schmerber v. California* (1966), a compulsory blood test was upheld as reasonable even though the suspect was awake and opposed the test on advice of his lawyer. The Court applied the *Schmerber* guidelines to the case of *Winston v. Lee* (1985) and ruled that a person cannot be compelled to submit to a surgical procedure requiring use of a general anesthetic to obtain evidence of a crime. At issue was a bullet lodged beneath the suspect's collarbone, which presumably would have confirmed that he had been involved in a shooting with a shopkeeper. Writing for the Court, Justice William Brennan noted that factors such as the difficulty of the surgery and its likely effect on the health or safety of the suspect must be considered along with the community's interest in obtaining the evidence.

A narrow 5–4 ruling in *Missouri v. McNeely* (2013) pulled back from the *Schmerber* guidelines somewhat by holding that a warrantless search is not justified in a drunk-driving investigation due to the natural dissipation of alcohol in the bloodstream. The dissipation does not constitute an "exigency" in every case. McNeely's Fourth Amendment rights were violated when a Missouri state trooper took him to a hospital and ordered a blood draw without a warrant, even though McNeely refused. Justice Sotomayor's opinion held that a warrantless search must fall within a recognized exception and also emphasized that obtaining a warrant can now be done much more quickly than in the past.

In recent years, a growing number of courts have upheld "strip searches" of all persons who are admitted to a jail's general population—even those arrested for such offenses as violating a leash law, driving without a license, or failure to use a turn signal. The Supreme Court held such searches to be constitutional in *Florence v. County of Burlington* (2012). That case is discussed in the following chapter's section dealing with prisoners.

to pervasive safety regulation and one in which the traveling public has a strong interest.

School districts also have established drug testing programs aimed at curtailing the harmful effects of drugs on their students. A 6–3 majority in *Vernonia School District 47J v. Acton* (1995) upheld a school policy under which all students participating in interscholastic athletics were required to sign a form consenting to drug testing with parental approval. All student athletes were tested prior to the sport season and randomly thereafter. According to Justice Antonin Scalia, the school plan did not violate the constitutional rights of students who, as he noted, "were committed to the temporary custody of the State as schoolmaster." He added that the school setting allows a "degree of supervision and control that could not be exercised over free adults." But what about the privacy intrusion involved in obtaining the sample? Scalia said that the intrusions in this case were not much different from those "typically encountered in public restrooms, which men, women, and especially school children use daily." He termed the privacy interests of students in this case "negligible."

Justice Sandra Day O'Connor dissented, joined by Justices Stevens and Souter, stating that such blanket searches were "not part of any traditional school function of which I am aware." She thought that a far more reasonable choice would be to focus on the students who had been identified as violating school rules and disrupting classes.

The limits of *Vernonia* were surpassed in *Board of Education of Independent School District No. 92 of Pottawatomie County v. Lindsay Earls* (2002). A 5–4 majority upheld the Tecumseh, Oklahoma, district's Student Activities Drug Testing Policy, which required all middle and high school students to consent to urinalysis testing as a condition for participating in extra-curricular activities. The district applied the policy to students seeking to participate in competitive extra-curricular activities, such as the Academic Team, Future Farmers of America, Future Homemakers of America, band, choir, pom pon, cheerleading, and athletics. Lindsay Earls, a member of the choir, band, Academic Team, and National Honor Society, alleged that the policy violated the Fourth Amendment and that the school district (unlike *Vernonia*) had failed to identify a drug problem in the school.

Citing the minimal privacy interests of students and the custodial responsibilities of the state, Justice Thomas found the Tecumseh plan virtually indistinguishable from *Vernonia*. The distinction between athletics and all extracurricular activities was not significant, according to the Court, especially since participation was voluntary in both. The dissenting justices would have confined drug testing to athletes, given their increased safety needs and chance of injury. The *Earls* decision opens the possibility that the next step will be the testing of all students within a school district. While the Court did not specifically address that possibility, the five-justice majority gave great weight to the state's custodial responsibilities and the limited expectation of privacy by students. On the other hand, drug testing programs are expensive and difficult to administer, possibly explaining why relatively few school districts have established such programs since *Vernonia*.

Outside of schools, the Supreme Court has placed limitations on some drug testing programs. In *Chandler v. Miller* (1997), an eight-person majority struck down a 1990 Georgia law requiring drug testing of candidates for certain elected state offices: governor, lieutenant governor, secretary of state, attorney general, and others. Reversing the Georgia courts, the Supreme Court found the law "diminishes personal privacy for a symbol's sake." The Court distinguished this case from the *Skinner*, *Von Raab*, and *Vernonia* decisions by pointing out that those cases involved "special needs beyond ordinary law enforcement," while no such interests were present in this case. Georgia had no evidence of a drug problem among its statewide political candidates.

Society's interest in reducing the number of "cocaine babies" has led some hospital authorities to impose drug testing on pregnant women without their consent. *Ferguson v. City of Charleston* (2001) stemmed from a similar policy at a South Carolina public hospital requiring pregnant women to be tested for cocaine use. Positive test results were then shared with law-enforcement authorities. Some women were arrested and threatened with prosecution if they failed to complete the drug treatment program. Ten women sued the hospital, contending that the tests violated the Fourth Amendment as nonconsensual searches without a warrant.

A 6–3 Supreme Court agreed with the women and overruled the appellate court. Justice Stevens noted in his majority opinion that, although hospitals and employees may have an obligation to provide evidence to the police that they obtain during treatment, "when they undertake to obtain such evidence from their patients for the specific purpose of incriminating those patients, they have a special obligation to make sure that the patients are fully informed about their constitutional rights. . .". It was the use of the warrantless drug tests for law enforcement purposes that violated the Fourth Amendment.

WIRETAPPING AND ELECTRONIC SURVEILLANCE

Perhaps no issue contributes to the view of government as a prying "big brother" more than the use of wiretapping and electronic eavesdropping. In the first such case, *Olmstead v. United States* (1928), a 5–4 majority failed to see wiretapping as a Fourth Amendment issue. Chief Justice William Howard Taft gave the following, rather traditional interpretation of the amendment:

> THE AMENDMENT ITSELF SHOWS THAT THE SEARCH IS TO BE OF MATERIAL THINGS—THE PERSON, THE HOUSE, HIS PAPERS, OR HIS EFFECTS. . . . THE AMENDMENT DOES NOT FORBID WHAT WAS DONE HERE. THERE WAS NO SEARCHING. THERE WAS NO SEIZURE. THE EVIDENCE WAS SECURED BY THE USE OF THE SENSE OF HEARING AND THAT ONLY. THERE WAS NO ENTRY OF THE HOUSES OR OFFICES OF THE DEFENDANTS. . . . THE LANGUAGE OF THE AMENDMENT CANNOT BE EXTENDED AND EXPANDED TO INCLUDE TELEPHONE WIRES, REACHING TO THE WHOLE WORLD FROM THE DEFENDANT'S HOUSE OR OFFICE. THE INTERVENING WIRES ARE NOT PART OF HIS HOUSE OR OFFICE, ANY MORE THAN ARE THE HIGHWAYS ALONG WHICH THEY ARE STRETCHED.

A famous dissenting opinion by Justice Louis Brandeis focused on the dangers inherent in the majority's position. The framers, he argued, "sought to protect Americans in their beliefs, their thoughts, their emotions and their sensations." Any unjustifiable government invasion of an individual's privacy, "whatever the means employed," would be unconstitutional. Justice Brandeis termed it "immaterial where the physical connection with the telephone wires leading into the defendants' premises was made."

The dissenting view came to be accepted by a majority in *Katz v. United States* (1967), in which the FBI had "bugged" several public telephone booths in Los Angeles to obtain evidence of interstate gambling against Charles Katz. The listening device was attached to the outside of the phone booths, a distinction relied upon by the government in defense of its actions. Katz was convicted largely on the basis of the recordings made of his telephone conversations.

The *Katz* opinion, written by Justice Potter Stewart, was significant for two reasons. First, it enunciated a notion that has come to be associated with the workings of the Fourth Amendment—namely, the idea of a **reasonable expectation of privacy**. According to Justice Stewart, Katz had entered the telephone booth and closed the door so as to avoid being heard. It did not matter, as the Government contended, that Katz could be seen through the glass-enclosed telephone booth:

> WHAT HE SOUGHT TO EXCLUDE WHEN HE ENTERED THE BOOTH WAS NOT THE INTRUDING EYE—IT WAS THE UNINVITED EAR. HE DID NOT SHED HIS RIGHT TO DO SO SIMPLY BECAUSE HE MADE HIS CALLS FROM A PLACE WHERE HE MIGHT BE SEEN. NO LESS THAN AN INDIVIDUAL IN A BUSINESS OFFICE, IN A FRIEND'S APARTMENT, OR IN A TAXICAB, A PERSON IN A TELEPHONE BOOTH MAY RELY UPON THE PROTECTION OF THE FOURTH AMENDMENT. ONE WHO OCCUPIES IT, SHUTS THE DOOR BEHIND HIM, AND PAYS THE TOLL THAT PERMITS HIM TO PLACE A CALL IS SURELY ENTITLED TO ASSUME THAT THE WORDS HE UTTERS INTO THE MOUTHPIECE WILL NOT BE BROADCAST TO THE WORLD.

The Court's ruling in *Katz* was significant also for its effect upon the long-standing **trespass rule** (see below), which can be traced to the much earlier *Olmstead* case. Under the trespass rule, an unreasonable search and seizure could only occur when authorities invaded or physically intruded into some enclosure. Justice Stewart's statement that the Fourth Amendment "protects people, not places" set the

Brief 12.11

THE EXPECTATION OF PRIVACY IN YOUR HOME (OR SOMEONE ELSE'S HOME)

Two 1999 decisions shed new light on the privacy interests of property owners and effectively limited the popular practice of allowing the media to accompany authorities while serving warrants. In *Wilson v. Layne* (1999), the Court held that the Fourth Amendment forbids police officers from bringing media representatives along while executing an arrest warrant in a private home. Police entered the Wilson home to arrest Dominic Wilson, accompanied by a photographer and a reporter from the *Washington Post*. The photographer took several photographs of the inside of the house and Wilson's parents in their nightclothes, but the photos were never published. Dominic Wilson's parents sued the officers, arguing that their Fourth Amendment rights were violated by bringing the media into their home. The Court agreed, noting that while the officers were entitled to enter the Wilsons' home to execute the arrest warrant, bringing the media representatives exceeded the scope of the warrant. The Court was not persuaded by the officers' argument that media "ride-alongs" contribute to the law enforcement mission of the police.

On the same day, a unanimous Court held in *Hanlon v. Berger* (1999) that officials of the United States Fish and Wildlife Service who brought along a crew of photographers and reporters from Cable News Network (CNN) while executing a search warrant had violated the Fourth Amendment. In this case, the warrant authorized the search of the entire 75,000-acre ranch and appurtenant structures, but not the residence. The authorities were looking for evidence of the taking of wildlife in violation of federal law. As in *Wilson*, the Court held that police violate the Fourth Amendment rights of homeowners when they bring the media with them to record the search. In both cases, the homeowners were suing for money damages, but the Supreme Court held that the officials had "qualified immunity" because law on this issue was not clearly established when the events occurred.

But does one have an expectation of privacy while in someone else's home? The Court had earlier ruled in *Morrison v. Olson* (1990) that an overnight guest staying in another's residence did have a legitimate expectation of privacy, but it had not addressed the issue of someone merely visiting. In *Minnesota v. Carter* (1998), two men from Chicago were visiting an apartment in Eagan, Minnesota. An informant came up to a police officer and reported that he had just seen people in an apartment putting white powder into plastic bags. The officer went to the apartment, peered through a small gap in the blinds, saw the two men and a woman bagging what looked like cocaine, and radioed his superiors to obtain a search warrant. The men soon left in a Cadillac and were stopped and arrested by police. The search of the apartment and the Cadillac produced evidence of cocaine. Was the officer's peek through the blinds a "search"? Was it reasonable? Were the men entitled to an expectation of privacy in a home?

Writing for a 5–4 majority, Chief Justice Rehnquist focused on the latter question and concluded that the Fourth Amendment did not apply in this case. These men were not overnight guests, he noted, but were "merely present with the consent of the householder. . .". The Fourth Amendment does not convey an expectation of privacy to a person who is merely visiting for a few hours to conduct a "business transaction." Justice Scalia wrote a concurring opinion to emphasize that he believed the Fourth Amendment protections extend only to a person's "residence."

---

tone for a sweeping change in the Court's thinking (Brief 12.11).

Despite the government's objections, the Court held that it was of "no constitutional significance" that the electronic device used to eavesdrop on Katz did not happen to penetrate the wall of the telephone booth. Hence, the electronic eavesdropping constituted a "search and seizure" within the meaning of the Fourth Amendment, and it did not matter that there had been no trespass or physical intrusion. As a protection of the "person," *Katz* also contributed to the growing "right of privacy" line of decisions (see *Griswold v. Connecticut* [1965] in Chapter 9).[7]

Technological advances have further complicated the issue of electronic surveillance. In *United States v. Knotts* (1983), the Court upheld the use of an electronic beeper—a sort of "homing device"—without a warrant. That case involved a beeper placed in a drum of chloroform purchased by one of the suspects. The drum was placed in the suspect's car, and the electronic signals led authorities to a secluded cabin that was being used to manufacture illegal drugs. After visual surveillance of the cabin, the authorities obtained a search warrant and obtained evidence of the illegal activity. The Supreme Court unanimously rejected the contention that the suspects' expectation of privacy had been violated, although the *Knotts* opinion did not specifically address the question of whether a beeper could be installed without a warrant. Similarly, in *Hoffa v. United States* (1966), the Court held that a government informant wearing a "wire" without a warrant is not a Fourth Amendment violation.

With the growing sophistication and prevalence of electronic monitoring throughout society, it was just a matter of time before the Court would accept a case like *United States v. Jones* (2012). Government agents obtained a search warrant permitting it to install a global positioning system (GPS) tracking device on a vehicle registered to Antoine Jones's wife. The warrant authorized installation in the District of Columbia and within ten days, but the GPS device was not installed until the eleventh day in Maryland, not Washington, D.C. The Government tracked the vehicle's movements for twenty-eight days, compiling nearly two thousand pages of data over the twenty-eight-day period. Jones was indicted on drug trafficking and conspiracy charges. The District Court suppressed data while the vehicle was parked at Jones's residence but allowed all other information because Jones had no "reasonable expectation of privacy" while driving a vehicle. The D.C. Circuit reversed, finding the search unreasonable. All nine Supreme Court justices believed the search was unreasonable, but some differences emerged.

Justice Scalia wrote for a five-person majority and found the search to be unreasonable because it violated the "trespass rule" that lay at the heart of the Fourth Amendment when the Constitution was written. By going onto private property, installing the device on a private vehicle, and monitoring its movements for twenty-eight days, the government had engaged in a "search" for Fourth Amendment purposes. Justice Scalia held that the text of the Fourth Amendment was closely tied to property rights, with any unauthorized entry onto another's property constituting a "trespass." The Government committed a trespass when it installed the GPS device on Jones's (wife's) vehicle. It was the trespass that rendered the search unreasonable.

The four other justices concurred in the judgment but did not like Justice Scalia's emphasis on the trespass rule. Justice Samuel Alito's concurrence, joined by Justices Breyer, Ginsburg, and Kagan, took the majority to task for deciding the case "based on eighteenth-century tort law." The proper approach, Alito stated, is to use the Katz "expectation of privacy" test, which has largely governed Fourth Amendment law since 1967. According to Justice Alito,

> THE BEST THAT WE CAN DO IN THIS CASE IS TO APPLY EXISTING FOURTH AMENDMENT DOCTRINE AND TO ASK WHETHER THE USE OF GPS TRACKING IN A PARTICULAR CASE INVOLVED A DEGREE OF INTRUSION THAT A REASONABLE PERSON WOULD NOT HAVE ANTICIPATED. UNDER THIS APPROACH, RELATIVELY SHORT-TERM MONITORING OF A PERSON'S MOVEMENTS ON PUBLIC STREETS ACCORDS WITH EXPECTATIONS OF PRIVACY THAT OUR SOCIETY HAS RECOGNIZED AS REASONABLE. BUT THE USE OF LONGER TERM GPS MONITORING IN INVESTIGATIONS OF MOST OFFENSES IMPINGES ON EXPECTATIONS OF PRIVACY. . . . WE NEED NOT IDENTIFY WITH PRECISION THE POINT AT WHICH THE TRACKING OF THIS VEHICLE BECAME A SEARCH, FOR THE LINE WAS SURELY CROSSED BEFORE THE 4-WEEK MARK.

With the proliferation of GPA devices and cellular phones, more cases in this area appear inevitable. Whether the Court will continue to regard the "trespass rule" or the "expectation of privacy" as the primary protection of individual privacy rights may be uncertain, but it is clear that technological innovations will continue to place stress on the Fourth Amendment (see Brief 12.12).

WIRETAPPING AND NATIONAL SECURITY

Governments around the world routinely engage in electronic surveillance and eavesdropping, often in the name of protecting national security. But when government eavesdropping extends to the nation's own citizens, the Fourth Amendment becomes a central issue. How is it possible to give the government enough secrecy to protect national security while safeguarding the rights of citizens to be free from unconstitutional intrusions? In the post-9/11 world we live in, the question has taken on an even greater sense of urgency.

The United States Congress first addressed the issue by enacting the Foreign Intelligence Surveillance Act (FISA) in 1978. Passed as a response to President Nixon's illegal spying on political opponents, FISA allowed warrantless surveillance within the U.S. for up to one year unless "a United States person is a party." If a United States person is involved, FISA required judicial authorization within seventy-two hours after the initiation of surveillance. The Act also created a court that meets in secret, approving or denying applications for search warrants. The Foreign

Brief 12.12

HIGH-TECH THERMAL IMAGING: KYLLO V. UNITED STATES (2001)

Police in Florence, Oregon, used a thermal imager, a video camera–like device that detects infrared radiation and displays images based on their relative warmth. Driving down the street, the police could scan buildings (including residences) for signs of suspicious "hot spots" that might indicate the growing of marijuana indoors with the use of high-intensity grow lights. When they came to Danny Kyllo's residence the scan showed several "hot spots" in the garage roof and side wall. Actually, the police had scanned Kyllo's house following an informant's tip and a review of his utility records, which showed he was using an unusual amount of electricity. However, the police did not obtain a warrant prior to the imaging, although they probably could have done so,

Based on the results of the thermal imaging, police obtained a warrant, searched Kyllo's house, and discovered a marijuana-growing operation. Kyllo argued that his expectation of privacy in his home had been violated and asked "whether the Fourth Amendment's guarantee of personal security in your home must yield to scientific advances that make traditional barriers of privacy obsolete." The Ninth Circuit ruled against Kyllo, refusing to consider the thermal scan a "search" within the terms of the Fourth Amendment.

Writing for an unusual 5–4 majority, which included both conservative and liberal justices, Justice Scalia found the power of technology to be a serious threat to personal privacy. He was especially concerned with the use of "sense-enhancing technology" that was not in "general public use":

Where, as here, the Government uses a device that is not in general public use, to explore details of the home that would previously have been unknowable without physical intrusion, the surveillance is a "search" and is presumptively unreasonable without a warrant.

Perhaps as thermal imaging becomes more readily available to the general public, the technology may not pose the constitutional problems noted by the majority in this case.

Justice Stevens distinguished between "off the wall" and "through the wall" electronic surveillance, pointing out that thermal imaging is not like x-ray technology and does not penetrate the wall of a dwelling. Because it merely allows police to monitor temperatures "off the wall," it cannot be considered a search. Police should not be required to obtain a warrant before engaging in surveillance that does not involve physical penetration of the premises.

The discussion of "off the wall" and "through the wall" surveillance is in some ways reminiscent of the Supreme Court's initial wiretapping decision in *Olmstead*. Nearly seventy-five years after that ruling, our highest court continues to try to balance the need for effective law enforcement with the very precious right of privacy in one's home. Justice Scalia saw the *Kyllo* ruling as designed to protect "that degree of privacy against government that existed when the Fourth Amendment was adopted." That is likely to be difficult as technology provides new and more invasive forms of electronic surveillance.[8]

Intelligence Surveillance Court (FISC) is located within the Department of Justice and consists of eleven judges appointed by the Chief Justice of the United States. Under this arrangement, the president has wide discretion to authorize electronic surveillance without a court order, as long as it is only for foreign intelligence information.

President George W. Bush asked Congress in 2007 to amend FISA to make it easier to spy on terrorist suspects where one party (or both parties) is located overseas. Congress passed the Protect America Act of 2007, which removes from the definition of "electronic surveillance" in FISA any person who is believed to be located outside the United States. No request for a warrant is required from FISC. The Act also granted immunity from liability in any federal or state court for any entity providing information, facilities, or assistance. The issue of immunity was at the center of controversy when it became known that the major telecommunication companies in the United States apparently had cooperated with the government and in all likelihood provided information on private citizens.

Because the Protect America Act amendments expired after 180 days, President Bush urged Congress to pass new amendments that would make many of the earlier amendments permanent. That step was taken in July 2008, when President Bush signed the new FISA amendments into law. The law provided legal immunity for phone companies that cooperated with the National Security Agency wiretapping program following the September 11 terrorist attacks. The new amendments give the executive branch broader powers in eavesdropping on people both at home and abroad, and it removes some issues from the FISA court's docket.

The new law sets up a seven-day period for wiretapping foreigners without a court order in "exigent" circumstances, and it expands to seven days the period for emergency wiretaps on Americans without a court order. The latter requires the attorney general to certify the existence of a probable cause to terrorism. The FISA law now stands as the "exclusive" guide to conducting government wiretapping and surveillance, and Americans certainly have not heard the last of it.

The Fourth Amendment and Administrative Searches

Government at all levels is empowered to carry out administrative rules and requirements, many of which involve periodic inspections and visits. The social worker, health inspector, revenue agent, and safety engineer are but a few examples of government employees whose jobs involve entering and inspecting both commercial and private premises on occasion. As government regulation has increased, the matter of the administrative inspection has grown ever more controversial.

Generally speaking, Fourth Amendment warrant requirements apply to administrative searches with certain exceptions and limitations. For one thing, an administrative search warrant is considerably easier to obtain than one in a criminal matter. Rather than showing "probable cause," an administrator must prove to a magistrate only that an inspection is authorized by law and that it is part of a reasonable enforcement policy.[9]

Wyman v. James (1971) established the principle that caseworker visits to welfare recipients' homes do not require a warrant. Justice Harry Blackmun's majority opinion listed numerous reasons for upholding the home visit—including the fact that the welfare recipient is in no danger of criminal prosecution for refusing entry by authorities and has the right to refuse the caseworker's visit, knowing that she would probably suffer the loss of benefits—"The choice is entirely hers, and nothing of constitutional magnitude is involved."

The issue of searches by public authorities has extended into the nation's schools. In *New Jersey v. T.L.O.* (1985), a fourteen-year-old girl, T.L.O., was caught smoking in a restroom and brought to the principal's office. When she denied having been smoking, the assistant vice principal demanded to see her purse, which he then opened to look for cigarettes. He found the cigarettes, but he also found a small amount of marijuana, money, a list of students who owed money, and some letters implicating T.L.O. in the dealing of marijuana. The state sought to have T.L.O. declared a delinquent on the basis of the seized evidence. The juvenile court allowed the evidence to be used and determined T.L.O. to be delinquent. Later, the New Jersey Supreme Court reversed the lower courts and held that the evidence should be suppressed as the result of an unreasonable search.

Justice White's majority opinion began by holding that the Fourth Amendment applies to searches conducted by school authorities, and such searches must be reasonable. However, he noted also that it is necessary to balance schoolchildren's privacy interests with the school's "need to maintain an environment in which learning can take place." As a result, the standards required of a "reasonable" search may be quite different in the school setting. First, on the issue of warrants, Justice White stated:

> THE WARRANT REQUIREMENT, IN PARTICULAR, IS UNSUITED TO THE SCHOOL ENVIRONMENT: REQUIRING A TEACHER TO OBTAIN A WARRANT BEFORE SEARCHING A CHILD SUSPECTED OF AN INFRACTION OF SCHOOL RULES (OR OF THE CRIMINAL LAW) WOULD UNDULY INTERFERE WITH THE MAINTENANCE OF THE SWIFT AND INFORMAL DISCIPLINARY PROCEDURES NEEDED IN THE SCHOOLS. . . . (W)E HOLD TODAY THAT SCHOOL OFFICIALS NEED NOT OBTAIN A WARRANT BEFORE SEARCHING A STUDENT WHO IS UNDER THEIR AUTHORITY.

The Court held that the school setting "does not require strict adherence to the requirement that searches be based on probable cause to believe that the subject of the search has violated or is violating the law." Even the decision by the vice-principal to read the list of people who owed money to T.L.O. and the letters—both of which were found in a separate, zippered compartment—were within the standards of a reasonable search. While searches by school officials fall under the Fourth Amendment, they clearly are not subject to the strict guidelines applied to other areas of the law.

Conclusion

Several of the first eight amendments apply to the rights of persons suspected, accused, or convicted of crimes against society. The Fourth Amendment, protecting against "unreasonable searches and seizures" and requiring the issuance of warrants based on probable cause, has provoked much debate between the individualist interest in privacy and the communitarian interest in law, order, and society. With the decision in *Mapp v. Ohio* (1961) incorporating the controversial exclusionary rule, the debate intensified even more. Although all searches and seizures without warrants are not automatically "unreasonable," to be legal they must fall within a specific but growing list of exceptions, including searches of a moving automobile, those made following "hot pursuit," so-called "stop-and-frisk" incidents, and seizure of materials in the "plain view" of authorities, to name but a few. Evidence of the dynamic nature of the Constitution can be found in court rulings holding that wiretapping and other types of electronic surveillance unknown to the framers are subject to the provisions of the Fourth Amendment. Ongoing disagreements over the continued application of the exclusionary rule serve as evidence that the Fourth Amendment is likely to produce more rather than less controversy in coming years.

In concluding this treatment of the Fourth Amendment, it is important to recognize that no area of the law is more fluid than the matter of searches and seizures. Because no two situations involving police and suspects are ever likely to be identical, it is difficult to foresee the Court's ability to reduce the workload produced by the Fourth Amendment. Balancing the interests of individual privacy with society's concern with protection and security will remain one of the difficult tasks facing the Court in coming years. In the words of Justice Blackmun's concurring *Leon* opinion, the exclusionary rule and its effect upon the Fourth Amendment remain "subject to change."

CHAPTER 13
Criminal Procedure and Due Process of Law

ACCUSED SUSPECTS IN CRIMINAL PROCEEDINGS AS WELL AS STATE AND FEDERAL PRISONERS INCREASINGLY LOOK TO THE CONSTITUTION TO PROTECT THEIR RIGHT TO "DUE PROCESS OF LAW." FIVE OF THE TEN AMENDMENTS AND THIRTEEN OF THE TWENTY-THREE PROVISIONS THAT MAKE UP THE BILL OF RIGHTS SET DOWN THE PROCEDURAL GUARANTEES OF CITIZENS IN THE AREA OF CRIMINAL JUSTICE.

▼ Introductory Remarks by Chief Justice Earl Warren

Greetings. My name is Earl Warren, and I served as the fourteenth Chief Justice of the United States Supreme Court from 1953 until 1969. I am pleased to introduce a subject that is so important, namely, the protections of the Bill of Rights as applied to persons who face prosecution by the government.

I am a Californian, having been raised in that great state. I got my start in politics in California, rising to the post of state attorney general in 1938, followed by three terms as the governor of California. Part of my job in the early years involved the implementation of the government-exclusion orders against Japanese Americans. At the time, I believed that detention of those people was absolutely the right thing to do, and I have taken some criticism for that over the years. I almost became Vice President of the United States in 1948, running alongside Tom Dewey in an effort to defeat President Harry Truman. But my happiest times were spent on the bench of the U.S. Supreme Court. Some of that work is discussed in this chapter.

You have already seen some of my decisions in earlier chapters (e.g., *Brown v. Board of Education* and *Baker v. Carr*), but I feel especially good about my decisions relating to persons accused of committing crimes. I was disgusted by police conduct in *Spano v. New York* (1959), when I held that a confession had been obtained illegally:

"*The abhorrence of society to the use of involuntary confessions does not turn alone on their inherent untrustworthiness. It also turns on the deep-rooted feeling that the police must obey the law while enforcing the law; that, in the end, life and liberty can be as much endangered from illegal methods used to convict those thought to be criminals as from the actual criminals themselves.*"

But I certainly received more criticism for my majority opinion in *Miranda v. Arizona* (1966) (see later in this chapter), holding that before a defendant can be interrogated:

"*He must be warned prior to any questioning that he has the right to remain silent, that anything he says can be used against him in a court of law, that he has the right to the presence of an attorney, and that, if he cannot afford an attorney one will be appointed for him prior to any questioning if he so desires. Opportunity to exercise these rights must be afforded to him throughout the interrogation. After such warnings have been given, and such opportunity afforded him, the individual may knowingly and intelligently waive these rights and agree to answer questions or make a statement. But unless and until such warnings and waiver are demonstrated by the prosecution at trial, no evidence obtained as a result of interrogation can be used against him.*"

I was especially gratified by the Court's 2000 decision in *Dickerson v. United States*, in which a majority proclaimed that our *Miranda* rules had become "constitutional" rules. We've taken a lot of criticism for the *Miranda* decision over the years, but it now appears to be firmly entrenched. I realize that my time on the Court, the so-called "Warren Court," has been controversial—even President Eisenhower who appointed me as Chief Justice later apparently called the appointment "the biggest damfool mistake I ever made."

You can't make progress without making some people upset. Notice throughout this chapter how society continues to wrestle with the problem of balancing the rights of individuals with the need to protect and safeguard society at large. It is not an easy task. Enjoy the chapter. EW

SOURCES: "Earl Warren," Earl Warren College, University of California at San Diego, http://warren.ucsd.edu/about/biography.html; *Spano v. New York* (1959); *Miranda v. Arizona* (1966).

Due Process Guarantees in the Bill of Rights

When James Madison and his colleagues in Congress began identifying various liberties to include in a promised Bill of Rights, they paid close attention to issues of fairness and justice. One of the most important areas, protection from unreasonable searches and seizures, was discussed in the previous chapter. Additional liberties eventually found their way into other proposed amendments. Most of these guarantees focus on the need for fair and just procedures to be followed—hence, the concept of due process. This chapter focuses on three constitutional amendments—Fifth, Sixth, and Eighth—that contain the core protections that Americans have come to depend on.

Fifth Amendment

The Fifth Amendment stands as a powerful protector of individuals in their dealings with government. Under its provisions, the amendment prevents government from taking property without just compensation (see Chapter 8), trying a person twice for the same offense in the same jurisdiction, and forcing an individual to reveal information involuntarily. The two provisions discussed in this section—Double Jeopardy and Self-Incrimination Clauses—have been responsible for more than their share of controversy over the years.

Double Jeopardy

In spite of double jeopardy's incorporation in 1969, the subject has remained both controversial and uncertain. In its most basic sense, the Double Jeopardy Clause protects a person from being tried twice for the same offense in the same jurisdiction.[1] An interesting example of the Clause's complexity can be seen in *Sattazahn v. Pennsylvania* (2003). In that case, a 5–4 Supreme Court held that double jeopardy did not bar the imposition of a capital sentence on a person who had successfully appealed his first murder conviction. After Sattazahn was convicted of murder, the jury deadlocked 9–3 in the punishment phase, resulting in a requirement of life imprisonment. Sattazahn successfully appealed his conviction and obtained a reversal as a result of errors in jury instructions. Pennsylvania then retried him, and this time he was convicted and received the death penalty. According to the Supreme Court, capital cases contain two trials—one dealing with guilt or innocence, the other with the sentence. A rejection of death by jury in the punishment phase "amounts to an acquittal on the merits and . . . bars any retrial of the appropriateness of the death penalty." It should be noted that this ruling does not apply to all state death penalty laws. Some provide for different procedures, and some do not divulge the jury vote against the death penalty, so it would be impossible to know if the jury rejected it unanimously. However, double jeopardy does not prevent a new trial following a hung jury (see Brief 13.1), and Table 13.1 indicates that the clause does not always prevent the retrial of criminal defendants. But an 8–1 Supreme Court majority in *Evans v. Michigan* (2013) reaffirmed that a directed verdict of acquittal, even if based on an incorrect reading of a statute, prohibits a retrial.

Historically, the Double Jeopardy Clause has worked to ensure that no person is punished twice for the same offense. It can become confusing when an action carries both criminal and civil penalties. Criminal penalties constitute punishment for having committed an illegal act against the state, whereas civil penalties generally are regarded as "nonpunitive," although the distinction may be fuzzy. The Comprehensive Drug Abuse Prevention and Control Act of 1970 provides for the forfeiture of any property involved in or traceable to any illegal drug activity. Another statute applies forfeitures to illegal money laundering. What happens when a person is assessed a criminal punishment and also required to forfeit his property for the same offense?

The Supreme Court clarified the issue of criminal punishment and civil forfeitures in two cases decided simultaneously: *United States v. Ursery* (1996) and *United States v. $405,089.23* (1996). In *Ursery*, the government sought to forfeit Ursery's home after discovering he grew marijuana there. Ursery settled the forfeiture for $13,250. Shortly thereafter, he was indicted, found guilty of manufacturing marijuana, and sentenced to a sixty-three-month prison term. In the other case, Charles Arlt and James Wren were arrested for various drug-trafficking and money-laundering offenses. Forfeiture proceedings were delayed until after their criminal trials, at which both men received life sentences. A year later, the government prevailed at forfeiture,

Brief 13.1
JURIES AND DOUBLE JEOPARDY: BLUEFORD V. ARKANSAS (2012)

The state of Arkansas charged Alex Blueford with capital murder for the death of a one-year-old child. That charge included the lesser offenses of first-degree murder, manslaughter, and negligent homicide. Before the start of deliberations, the trial judge instructed the jury to consider the offenses as follows: "If you have a reasonable doubt of the defendant's guilt on the charge of capital murder, you will consider the charge of murder in the first degree. . . . If you have a reasonable doubt of the defendant's guilt on the charge of murder in the first degree, you will then consider the charge of manslaughter. . . . If you have a reasonable doubt of the defendant's guilt on the charge of manslaughter, you will then consider the charge of negligent homicide." The court presented the jury with a set of verdict forms, which allowed the jury either to convict Blueford of one of the charged offenses, or to acquit him of all of them. Acquitting on some but not others was not an option.

After deliberating for a few hours, the jury reported that it could not reach a verdict. When asked by the court to provide information on the jury's progress, the foreperson disclosed that the jury was unanimous against guilt on the charges of capital murder and first-degree murder, was deadlocked on manslaughter, and had not voted on negligent homicide. The court told the jury to continue deliberations, but it still could not reach a verdict and the court declared a mistrial. Later, when the State sought to retry Blueford, he moved to dismiss the capital and first-degree murder charges on double jeopardy grounds.

Chief Justice John Roberts, writing for a 6–3 majority in *Blueford v. Arkansas* (2012), noted that "[a]ll agree that the defendant may be retried on charges of manslaughter and negligent homicide. The question is whether he may also be retried on charges of capital and first-degree murder." He answered that question with a resounding yes—Blueford could be retried on both grounds because the jury did not acquit him of capital or first-degree murder charges. The foreperson's report that the jury was unanimous against guilt on the murder offenses "was not a final resolution of anything." The jury's deliberations had not yet concluded, the jurors went back to the jury room to deliberate further, and nothing in the court's instructions prohibited them from reconsidering their votes on capital and first-degree murder. The Chief Justice believed that the foreperson's report "lacked the finality necessary to amount to an acquittal on those offenses."

Justice Sotomayor wrote a dissent in which she was joined by Justices Ginsburg and Kagan. She charged the majority with misapplying two key principles of double jeopardy jurisprudence: first, an acquittal occurs if a jury's decision, "whatever its label, actually represents a resolution, correct or not, of some or all of the factual elements of the offense charged" (*United States v. Martin Linen Supply Co*, 1977); and, second, a trial judge may not defeat a defendant's entitlement to "the verdict of a tribunal he might believe to be favorably disposed to his fate" by declaring a mistrial before deliberations end (*United States v. Jorn*, 1971). Justice Sotomayor concluded:

"This case demonstrates that the threat to individual freedom from reprosecutions that favor States and unfairly rescue them from weak cases has not waned with time. Only this Court's vigilance has."

Table 13.1 | Can a Defendant Be Retried if . . .

A. A trial ends in acquittal .... No

B. A trial ends with a guilty verdict... No, **unless**
  1. Defendants request judge to set aside the verdict, OR
  2. Defendants appeal to a higher court.

C. A trial is halted before a final verdict .... It depends
  1. If indictment is dismissed due to insufficient evidence........... No
  2. If the interruption occurs for another reason.......................... Yes
  3. If the jury cannot agree on a verdict....................................... Yes
  4. If the defendant requests a stop to the trial for reasons which do not relate to guilt or innocence............................ Yes
  5. If the prosecutor asks for a mistrial to prevent the defeat of "the ends of public justice." .... Yes
  6. If the jury is deadlocked on some but not all charges when it is not possible to acquit on some charges. Yes

Note: These outcomes are the result of several Court decisions, the most significant being *North Carolina v. Pearce* (1969); *United States v. Scott* (1975); *United States v. Martin Linen Supply Co.* (1977); *Arizona v. Washington* (1978); *Blueford v. Arkansas* (2012); *Evans v. Michigan* (2013).

obtaining property worth $405,089.23. In both cases, the forfeiture decisions were reversed by the Courts of Appeals as violations of the Double Jeopardy Clause.

The Supreme Court reversed the Courts of Appeals decisions, allowing both the criminal and civil forfeiture actions to stand and holding that civil forfeiture is not "punishment" under the Double Jeopardy Clause. The Court noted a two-part test to determine whether forfeiture is punishment for double jeopardy purposes: first, whether Congress intended the particular forfeiture to be a remedial civil sanction or a criminal penalty; and, second, whether the forfeiture proceedings are so punitive in fact as to establish that they are not civil in nature. In other words, both the intent of Congress and the effect of the forfeiture would be examined. The Court did note that a forfeiture might be so excessive as to violate the Excessive Bail and Fines Clause of the Eighth Amendment (see below), but neither of these cases was excessive.

SELF-INCRIMINATION

The privilege against self-incrimination, though acquired from British law and part of the Fifth Amendment, probably "became widely known by many Americans during the 1950s, when legislative committees were conducting hearings in two major areas—political belief and activity, and organized crime."[2] Senator Joseph McCarthy's questionable tactics during committee hearings forced many persons to invoke their Fifth Amendment protections, prompting McCarthy to call them "Fifth Amendment Communists."[3]

Actually, the Fifth Amendment does not forbid all self-incrimination, only that which is considered compulsory. People are free to confess or provide otherwise incriminating evidence if they choose, as long as they are not forced to do so. However, as Table 13.2 illustrates, the protections against self-incrimination are limited. It is fairly clear that a man yelling out his guilt while being stretched on the rack is being compelled to incriminate himself—but what, say, of the woman who offers a confession after a lengthy police interrogation? What if she asks for a lawyer to be present but is refused? The matter of compulsory self-incrimination is not always clear-cut.

SELF-INCRIMINATION AND CONFESSIONS

Nothing is as beneficial to a prosecutor's case as a confession signed by the defendant. However, a confession is expected to be voluntary rather than compulsory. Unfortunately, the line between voluntary and compulsory is not always clear. While physical torture or beating might be clear evidence of coercion, other, more subtle, methods are often difficult to judge. Table 13.3 provides an overview of developments in the law relating to the issue of voluntary confessions, and the variety of cases has been extraordinary.

The Court's earliest rule governing involuntary confessions emphasized a **totality of circumstances** approach. This approach looked at the circumstances on a case-by-case basis to determine whether the

Table 13.2 When Do Self-Incrimination Protections *Not* Apply and Why?

When	Why
Immunity from prosecution is granted	If punishment cannot result from incriminating testimony, the threat of self-incrimination is removed. Still, a narrower "use" immunity common today excludes only evidence obtained directly or indirectly from the testimony itself. Prosecution is still possible using evidence obtained by other means.
"Nontestimonial" evidence is used	Evidence other than direct testimony (fingerprints, blood samples, handwriting, etc.) is "nontestimonial" and not protected by the Self-Incrimination Clause. Refusal to submit, say, to a breath test may be introduced as incriminating evidence. In *Pennsylvania v. Muniz* (1990), the Court held that answers to "routine booking questions" while in custody were nontestimonial and therefore not subject to self-incrimination protections.
Nonpersonal evidence is involved	Self-incrimination protections apply only to the individual. They do not extend to corporate, partnership, or other records that are not the "private" papers of the individual.
The evidence is held by someone else	Records and papers in the possession of another person are not protected, and the other person (e.g., accountant) holding the papers (e.g., tax records) may not claim self-incrimination protection on behalf of someone else.

Table 13.3 Development of the Law—Self-Incrimination and Confessions

Year	Event	Significance
1936	Brown v. Mississippi	Court outlawed physical torture as means of extracting confessions.
1940	Chambers v. Florida	Overturned confession obtained by isolation from friends and attorneys and long interrogations by rotating teams of police officers.
1959	Spano v. New York	Used "totality of circumstances" approach to overturn confession obtained by nearly twelve hours of "official pressure, fatigue and sympathy falsely aroused."
1964	Escobedo v. Illinois	Court reversed a conviction based on a confession given without a lawyer present, despite suspect's repeated appeals for one. An important step toward the *Miranda* ruling.
1966	Miranda v. Arizona	Established firm rule governing proper interrogation procedural safeguards, including right to remain silent, right to an attorney.
1971	Harris v. New York	An improperly obtained confession may be used in Court to impeach the credibility of a witness who takes the stand and commits perjury.
1975	Oregon v. Hass	Relied on *Harris* to allow use of a confession obtained without a lawyer to be used to impeach the defendant's credibility on the witness stand.
1980	Rhode Island v. Innis	Upheld use of suspect's voluntary statements made as a result of listening to the police talking to each other in "good faith" about the dangers that a weapon might pose to a child who stumbled upon it.
1981	Edwards v. Arizona	Police questioning of a suspect must cease after he invokes his *Miranda* rights.
1984	New York v. Quarles	Created "public safety" exception to *Miranda* rule, holding that police may not have to give *Miranda* rights in narrow instances when a danger exists to public safety.
1986	Colorado v. Connelly	To be involuntary, a confession must be the result of police coercion.
1989	Duckworth v. Eagan	Police may depart from actual *Miranda* wording. Upheld "We have no way of giving you a lawyer, but one will be appointed for you, if you wish, if and when you go to court."
1990	Illinois v. Perkins	Undercover officer posing as a fellow inmate is not required to give *Miranda* warnings to an incarcerated suspect before asking questions.
1991	Arizona v. Fulminante	Ruled that a confession made to an undercover informant in prison was the result of coercion, based on fear of retaliation. But, majority also held that coerced confessions are subject to "harmless error rule" (i.e., as long as a conviction would have been obtained by other evidence, the admission of a coerced or improper confession is harmless).
2000	Dickerson v. United States	*Miranda* is a "constitutional rule" that cannot be overruled by legislation. It has become part of our national culture.
2003	Chavez v. Martinez	Even if police use coercive tactics, a person's self-incrimination rights are not violated until legal proceedings are initiated. In this case, authorities declined to prosecute Martinez. He could not sue for damages.
2003	Kaupp v. Texas	Unanimous ruling overturns Texas courts and holds that a confession following an illegal, middle-of-the-night arrest, even though *Miranda* warnings were given, violated self-incrimination protections.
2010	Berghuis v. Thompkins	A suspect's right to remain silent must be invoked "unambiguously." The same standards exist for determining when a suspect has invoked his *Miranda* right to remain silent and the *Miranda* right to counsel. In short, he must say so.
2010	Maryland v. Shatzer	Held that the *Edwards* protections expire after fourteen days, allowing police to question a suspect who has invoked his *Miranda* rights after the fourteen-day period has passed.
2011	J.D.B. v. North Carolina	Held that a child's age is a relevant factor in determining when a person is in custody. A child is less likely to feel free to leave or refuse to answer questions.
2012	Howes v. Fields	A prisoner taken from his cell, questioned privately in a room by sheriff's deputies about criminal activity he was allegedly engaged in before coming to prison, and who later confesses, is not in a custodial situation for *Miranda* purposes.

confession was voluntary. One such case was *Spano v. New York* (1959), in which the suspect had endured more than twelve straight hours of questioning and trickery by a friend who was also a police officer. Using the "totality of circumstances," Chief Justice Earl Warren reversed Spano's conviction and found the confession to be involuntary. While providing case-by-case fairness, the "totality of circumstances" approach gave police and prosecutors little guidance in formulating acceptable procedures. Eventually, the Court would abandon the case-by-case approach in favor of a firm rule governing the admissibility of confessions.

The rule was established in *Miranda v. Arizona* (1966), a case that was heard along with three other cases, all of which involved the admissibility of statements obtained by authorities during custodial interrogation. In all instances, the suspect provided a confession following police interrogation, and the confession was then introduced as evidence in the trial. Ernesto Miranda, a twenty-three-year-old indigent, educated through half of the ninth grade and suffering what one doctor termed "an emotional illness," was arrested for kidnapping and rape. After being picked out of a lineup, he was interrogated by two police officers. In less than two hours, apparently without any warnings of his rights to silence or counsel, *Miranda* "gave a detailed oral confession and then wrote out in his own hand and signed a brief statement admitting and describing the crime."

Chief Justice Warren's opinion for the 5–4 majority focused on the nature of the custodial setting, calling it "incommunicado interrogation of individuals in a police-dominated atmosphere." In such a setting, individual liberties are jeopardized and subjected to great pressure, he stated, adding that ". . . without proper safeguards the process of in-custody interrogation of persons suspected or accused of crime contains inherently compelling pressures which undermine the individual's will to resist and to compel him to speak where he would not otherwise do so freely."

The opinion called for procedural safeguards to protect the privilege against self-incrimination. These safeguards were spelled out in this now-familiar passage:

> PRIOR TO ANY QUESTIONING, THE PERSON MUST BE WARNED THAT HE HAS A RIGHT TO REMAIN SILENT, THAT ANY STATEMENT HE DOES MAKE MAY BE USED AS EVIDENCE AGAINST HIM, AND THAT HE HAS A RIGHT TO THE PRESENCE OF AN ATTORNEY, EITHER RETAINED OR APPOINTED. THE DEFENDANT MAY WAIVE EFFECTUATION OF THESE RIGHTS, PROVIDED THE WAIVER IS MADE VOLUNTARILY, KNOWINGLY AND INTELLIGENTLY.

Miranda's conviction, based on the improperly obtained confession, was thereby reversed. Perhaps anticipating to some degree the storm of protest by critics of the decision, the Chief Justice stated that the ruling would not be "an undue interference" with law enforcement and noted that it would "not in any way preclude police from carrying out their traditional investigatory functions." Despite these words, the *Miranda* ruling produced a strong reaction in some circles (Brief 13.2).

Other Court decisions have further defined and, in most cases, limited the effect of the *Miranda* ruling. A strong 8–1 majority, with Justice Marshall dissenting, held in *Illinois v. Perkins* (1990) that an undercover law enforcement officer, posing as a fellow inmate, is not required to give *Miranda* warnings to an incarcerated suspect before asking questions that may produce an incriminating response. In *Arizona v. Fulminante* (1991), the Court held that the so-called **harmless error rule** should be applied to coerced confessions just as it is applied to other "trial errors." Fulminante had confessed to an undercover prison informant in a manner that was later determined to be coercive.

The harmless error rule holds that some errors that occur in the course of a trial do not have an adverse effect on the outcome of the case. Writing for the majority in this section of the *Fulminante* opinion, Chief Justice Rehnquist stated that as long as the conviction would have been obtained through other evidence, the error resulting from admission of a coerced confession is harmless. In *Fulminante*, however, five justices felt that Arizona had not met its burden of demonstrating that the admission of the coerced confession was harmless to the outcome of the case. As a result, the Arizona Supreme Court's reversal of Fulminante's conviction was upheld.

In summary, despite some rather confusing shifts within the Court itself, a basic principle seems to have taken hold in *Fulminante*: the introduction as evidence of a confession later shown to be coerced does

Brief 13.2

MIRANDA IS A "CONSTITUTIONAL RULE". . . BUT IT MAY BE LIMITED

Two years after *Miranda*, Congress passed a statute attempting to overturn the decision and substitute the "voluntariness" test. This test had been in existence prior to *Miranda* and continued to be required alongside the new rules. However, the Warren Court believed the voluntariness requirement to be inadequate by itself. For most of the next thirty years, the Department of Justice virtually ignored the statute and required *Miranda* warnings in all cases. Opponents of *Miranda* continued to regard it as a "court-made" or "prophylactic" rule that was not part of the Constitution.

Dickerson v. United States (2000) represented an effort by opponents of *Miranda* to see whether the Supreme Court might finally conclude that the rules were no longer required under the Constitution. They had some reason to be optimistic, as five of the justices in earlier written opinions had indicated their belief that *Miranda* went beyond the requirements of the Constitution or that it was merely a "prophylactic" rule.

A 7–2 majority, headed by Chief Justice Rehnquist, himself on record as a *Miranda* critic, put the issue to rest by holding that *Miranda* "has become embedded in routine practice to the point where the warnings have become part of our national culture." In other words, *Miranda* is a constitutional rule that cannot be overturned by legislation—only by a constitutional amendment. The majority concluded that the voluntariness test alone did not adequately protect individual rights and that *Miranda* was supported by *stare decisis*. While the majority decision suggested that the issue was closed and would not be reopened, the opinion clearly stated that some of the majority justices would not vote in favor of *Miranda* if it were a new issue before the court. Precedent can be a powerful force.

Two 2010 decisions further restricted the *Miranda* rules. In *Berghuis v. Thompkins*, a 5–4 majority held that Van Chester Thompkins had not been denied his *Miranda* rights by police continuation to question him over nearly a three-hour period. During that time, Thompkins refused to sign a statement indicating that he understood his rights, only occasionally responding to a question with a single word or a nod. Finally, an officer asked Thompkins, "Do you believe in God?" Thompkins said, "Yes." The officer then asked Thompkins whether he prays to God. Again, he responded yes. Then the officer asked, "Do you pray to God for shooting that boy down?" Thompkins again said, "Yes." The three "yes" answers were admitted against Thompkins at trial and helped in obtaining his conviction. Did the use of these statements deny Thompkins his Fifth Amendment rights? According to Justice Kennedy's majority opinion, a suspect's silence is not sufficient to invoke the right to remain silent. There must be an "unambiguous" invocation of the right to remain silent, just as is required for the right to counsel.

A unanimous Court ruled in *Maryland v. Shatzer* (2010) that a suspect's invocation of the right to counsel does not last forever. Michael Shatzer was in prison when police questioned him about molesting a child. He invoked his *Miranda* right to counsel and police ceased questioning. Three years later, police gave him his *Miranda* warnings, and Shatzer waived them and made incriminating statements. Did his earlier invocation of silence prevent further police questioning? Justice Scalia's opinion for the court explained that some sort of expiration must exist, and he indicated that fourteen days is the appropriate time period. Police may attempt to question a suspect who has invoked his constitutional rights after waiting for fourteen days. Justice Scalia's opinion pointed out that the fourteen-day period is necessary to end the "custodial interrogation" atmosphere. A 2012 ruling in *Howes v. Fields* further reduced prisoner protections under *Miranda* by holding that a prisoner taken from his cell to be questioned in a private conference room about activities occurring prior to his incarceration was not in custody for *Miranda* purposes. His confession, even without *Miranda* warnings, was admissible.

Quite a few exceptions to the *Miranda* requirements have been recognized by the Court in recent years. By a 5–4 vote in *Harris v. New York* (1971), the Court held that use of the improperly obtained evidence to impeach the credibility of the defendant was valid. Harris, said the Court, was under an obligation to speak truthfully once on the witness stand. The *Miranda* precedent "cannot be perverted into a license to use perjury by way of a defense, free from the risk of confrontation with prior inconsistent utterances." Other exceptions have upheld confessions that, although improper, were the result of "good-faith" efforts on the part of the police; confessions which were involuntary but nevertheless justified by the need to protect the public safety; and confessions "coerced" by a higher power (see Brief 13.3).

---

not automatically make a conviction impossible. When this occurs, the state must show that the improperly introduced confession did not contribute to the conviction. If the state is successful, the conviction will be upheld.

SIXTH AMENDMENT

The provisions of the Sixth Amendment relate directly to the procedural rights of criminal defendants, with primary emphasis on courtroom practices. At least eight separate privileges are stated in the amendment, and these can be grouped into three broad categories: those guarantees relating to the nature of the trial, jury considerations, and the defendant's right to mount a defense.

THE NATURE OF A FAIR TRIAL

The first two clauses in the Sixth Amendment guarantee a person's rights to a speedy and public trial.

Brief 13.3

CAN GOD COERCE A CONFESSION?: COLORADO V. CONNELLY (1986)

Francis Connelly approached a uniformed Denver police officer on the street and stated that he had murdered someone and wanted to talk about it. The policeman, off duty at the time, advised Connelly of his *Miranda* rights, and Connelly said he understood and wanted to talk. A detective arrived, new *Miranda* warnings were given, and Connelly told of a murder he had committed in 1982. Later, he took officers to the location of the crime. While being interviewed the next morning, however, Connelly became "visibly disoriented" and began giving confused answers to questions. He stated that "voices" had told him to confess. A psychiatrist later testified that Connelly was following the "voice of God," and he believed that Connelly's psychosis had motivated his confession. The trial court, although finding the police to have done nothing wrong or coercive, held that the confession was inadmissible because it was not completely voluntary—not a product of Connelly's free will. The Colorado Supreme Court affirmed the ruling.

The Supreme Court reversed, with Chief Justice Rehnquist stating that before a confession can be held involuntary, it must be shown to result from police coercion. Only coercive behavior on the part of authorities can make a confession "involuntary." Rehnquist added that the Fifth Amendment privilege against self-incrimination is not concerned with "moral and psychological pressures" to confess—even if the "voice of God" is the source of those pressures.

Justice Brennan, joined by Justice Marshall, dissented, holding that due process recognizes "the right to make vital choices voluntarily." However, despite the strong dissent, the law of the land, as a result of the *Connelly* decision, holds that all confessions made without official coercion are deemed to be voluntary.

Both provisions were incorporated into the due process guarantees of the Fourteenth Amendment and applied to the states at quite different times: speedy trial by *Klopfer v. North Carolina* (1967) and public trial by *In Re Oliver* (1948). Both issues, along with others related to the nature of a "fair trial," have arisen numerous times since their incorporation (see Brief 13.4).

One reason that the right to a speedy trial has proven such a difficult area is the vague nature of the concept itself. Through several decisions, the Supreme Court has refused to apply a specific time frame to "speedy" trials, although the justices have helped to define its parameters.[4] In *Smith v. Hooey* (1969), for example, the Court held that the state of Texas had denied due process to the defendant by its failure to bring him to trial for six years, during which time he had been in a federal penitentiary. Accordingly, Texas authorities were required to drop the charge against him.

In 1974 Congress passed the Speedy Trial Act providing for a maximum of one hundred days between arrest and trial, although the law remains cumbersome and confusing. Under the statute, if the one-hundred-day limitation is not met, the judge is to dismiss the charges, either with or without prejudice. Charges dismissed with prejudice prohibit the defendant's being prosecuted again, but those without prejudice allow the prosecution to begin anew. A number of states have enacted their own statutes dealing with acceptable standards for speedy trials.

Overloaded court dockets are likely to cause significant problems for prosecutors in meeting speedy trial requirements both at the state and federal levels. Such delays, however, are part of the price of a system that provides the accused with numerous procedural safeguards and guarantees. In fact, since delay often works to the advantage of the accused, it should not be surprising to know that the prosecution often may be ready for trial long before the defense. A recent decision in *Bloate v. United States* (2010) underscored the complexity of determining when the speedy trial clock is ticking and when it is not. And in *United States v. Tinklenberg* (2011), a seven-person majority held that the seventy-day trial clock stops when a pretrial motion is filed, even if it does not delay the trial.

JURY TRIALS

The tradition of using an impartial body of people to determine guilt or innocence originated in Britain, and there is a reference to the "lawful judgment of his peers" in the Magna Carta of 1215. For centuries, however, the right to such a jury of one's peers generally was reserved to noblemen.[5] Early American colonists considered trial by jury to be a fundamental right, and it was commonly mentioned in early colonial charters. The Massachusetts Body of Liberties, adopted in 1641, recognized numerous liberties and privileges that were to be enjoyed by all.[6] The list of liberties was comprehensive, blending rights found in the common law and Puritan theology. The right to trial by jury seemingly was among the most important, as it was

Brief 13.4

WHAT MAKES A TRIAL "UNFAIR"?

The fairness of a trial depends on many factors, quite a few of which are specifically required by the Constitution (i.e., right to counsel, confrontation of witnesses, cross-examination, jury of one's peers, speedy trial, public trial, etc.). But the fairness of a trial might be affected by any number of practices that prove prejudicial to the defendant, even if everything required by the Constitution is provided. The Supreme Court has addressed numerous situations in which a defendant's rights arguably were placed at risk.

For example, in *Estelle v. Williams* (1976), the Court held that a Texas policy of requiring a defendant to stand trial in prison clothes was likely to raise questions for the jury concerning the defendant's presumed innocence. Ten years later in *Williams v. Taylor* (1986), the Court struck down the practice of seating uniformed state troopers in the row of trial spectators directly behind the defendant. Both of these practices were considered by the Court to be so inherently prejudicial that they must be justified by an "essential state" policy or interest.

But what about conduct undertaken not by the state but by others in the courtroom? In *Carey v. Musladin* (2006) the Court had to decide whether members of the victim's family could sit in the courtroom wearing buttons displaying an image of the victim. The trial court allowed the buttons, but the Ninth Circuit Court of Appeals found the judge's decision to be "contrary to . . . clearly established federal law." Overturning the Ninth Circuit, the Supreme Court held that federal law in this area was not "clearly established," and the earlier Estelle and Williams precedents were not applicable. Those cases involved state-sponsored conduct, while this case involved private actors. As a result, the Supreme Court could find no evidence that the trial court had denied Musladin a fair trial.

A 7–2 Court sided with the defendant in *Presley v. Georgia* (2010) and overturned his conviction following the trial court's decision to exclude his uncle from the public gallery during the jury *voir dire*. The majority opinion noted that there might be "circumstances" where a judge could conclude that threats or improper communications involving jurors are significant enough to justify the closing of *voir dire*. However, those circumstances require clearly articulated and specific findings that a reviewing court can properly determine. No such factors could be found in this case.

---

mentioned in no fewer than six different sections. Given the importance of jury trials to Americans, it is not surprising that the Supreme Court has been called upon numerous times to address the subject. In recent years, three important issues have occupied much of the Court's attention.

JURY SIZE

Not long after *Duncan v. Louisiana* (Chapter 11), the Court gave strong indication that not all of the traditional requirements associated with a jury trial were necessarily binding upon the states. One of these issues concerned the size of juries and the traditional requirement for twelve persons to determine guilt or innocence. The case of *Williams v. Florida* (1970) concerned a robbery conviction handed down by a six-person jury allowed under Florida law for all non-capital cases. Justice White's opinion sought to ascertain the basis for the twelve-person jury, but it ultimately concluded the requirement to be nothing more than a "historical accident, unnecessary to effect the purposes of the jury system and wholly without significance." Florida's use of a six-person jury did not violate the defendant's due process right, because the twelve-person requirement "cannot be regarded as an indispensable component of the Sixth Amendment." Since the *Williams* decision, thirty-three states have authorized juries of fewer than twelve members in a least some types of cases.[7]

In *Colgrove v. Battin* (1973), the Court ruled that a six-person jury did not violate the Seventh Amendment right to a jury trial in a civil case, a decision seemingly consistent with the *Williams* ruling. However, in *Ballew v. Georgia* (1978), the Court was required to address the question of less than six-person juries. The state of Georgia had implemented a five-person jury for misdemeanor cases, in part to save both time and money. Writing for a fragmented plurality, Justice Blackmun stated that a jury should be large enough "to promote group deliberation, to insulate members from outside intimidation, and to provide a representative cross-section of the community." Using these criteria, along with several empirical studies conducted on jury size and noted by the Court, Justice Blackmun concluded that "the purpose and functioning of the jury in a criminal trial is seriously impaired, and to a constitutional degree, by a reduction in size to below six members." Apparently, while the Court can find no "bright line" to identify a minimum jury size, it will accept a jury of six but not five persons as consistent with the demands of due process. It should be pointed out that a unanimous Court held in *Berghuis v. Smith* (2010), that there is no clearly established Supreme Court precedent to determine what the fair cross-section requirement really means.

Jury Verdicts

The second important issue related to the jury trial requirement is unanimity. Under American criminal justice procedure, a person is innocent until proven guilty "beyond a reasonable doubt." Does the "beyond a reasonable doubt" standard require that a jury be unanimous in its verdict to convict, or is a verdict of 11–1 or, say, 10–2 equally free of doubt? In *Apodaca v. Oregon* (1972), the Court upheld the jury convictions of Apodaca and two co-defendants on votes of 11–1, 11–1, and 10–2. Under Oregon law, the 10–2 split was the minimum verdict allowable for conviction. Apodaca and the others appealed their convictions on the ground that the Sixth and Fourteenth Amendments required convictions only by a unanimous jury vote.

Once again, the Court showed real signs of division. Justice White, joined only by three others, delivered the judgment of the Court, which upheld the nonunanimous verdicts as long as the jury "consists of a group of laymen representative of a cross-section of the community who have the duty and the opportunity to deliberate, free from outside attempts at intimidation, on the question of a defendant's guilt." Four justices (Stewart, Douglas, Brennan, and Marshall) dissented, leaving Justice Powell squarely in the middle. According to Justice Powell, the requirement for unanimity is not applicable to juries in state courts, but it should be maintained in federal courts. He indicated that not "all of the elements of jury trial within the meaning of the Sixth Amendment are necessarily embodied in or incorporated into the Due Process Clause of the Fourteenth Amendment." Justice Powell could not accept what he considered to be the Court's primary assumption—namely, that the Sixth Amendment's trial by jury provisions "must be identical in every detail" in both federal and state courts. Such an assumption, according to Powell, was inconsistent with our federal form of government:

> In holding that the Fourteenth Amendment has incorporated "jot-for-jot and case-for-case" every element of the Sixth Amendment, the Court derogates principles of federalism that are basic to our system. . . . [T]he Court has embarked upon a course of constitutional interpretation that deprives the states of freedom to experiment with adjudicatory processes different from the federal model.

As a result, state juries need not convict only upon unanimous vote. Using the same reasoning, the Court in *Johnson v. Louisiana* (1972) upheld a 9–3 jury vote for conviction. On the other hand, in *Burch v. Louisiana* (1979), a state law that allowed conviction by a 5–1 vote for a petty offense, was struck down. Obviously, due process is not simply a matter of percentages.

Jury Selection

The selection of jurors ranks as one of the most important stages of any trial, and the Constitution offers little guidance in the matter. The process typically begins with lists of potential jurors created by government officials. From these lists, smaller numbers are then summoned for jury duty, where they are questioned during a process known as *voir dire*. They can be removed for cause—perhaps they are acquainted with the defendant—and dismissed from jury duty. In addition, both prosecution and defense can use a predetermined number of **peremptory challenges**. These may be used without any explanation or stated reason and historically have allowed both sides to exclude certain types of persons from the jury.

In *Batson v. Kentucky* (1986), the Court held that the Fourteenth Amendment's Equal Protection Clause forbids the prosecutor's use of peremptory challenges to remove potential jurors solely because of their race, and later cases prohibit peremptory strikes to exclude racial groups of a different race from the defendant.[8] Two 2005 decisions found racial bias in jury selection and ordered new trials for the defendants. In *Miller-El v. Dretke* (2005), Dallas, Texas, prosecutors had used peremptory strikes to exclude 91 percent of the eligible black panelists. In *Johnson v. California* (2005), the prosecutor removed the only three black potential jurors. According to the U.S. Supreme Court, both situations violated *Batson*. A 7–2 Court strengthened *Batson* in *Snyder v. Louisiana* (2008) by striking down a conviction obtained by an all-white jury after the prosecutor had struck all five black potential jurors.

The much-awaited case of *J.E.B. v. Alabama ex rel T.B.* (1994) involved a civil action brought by the state of Alabama on behalf of T.B. for paternity and child support against J.E.B. From a list of thirty-six potential jurors, twenty-four females and twelve males, three were released for cause. J.E.B. had eleven peremptory challenges, and one was used to remove a male juror. The state had ten challenges and used nine to remove males, leaving a jury of twelve females. The jury returned a verdict finding that J.E.B. was the father of T.B.'s child, and J.E.B. appealed.

In a 6–3 judgment, the Court ruled that the Equal Protection Clause prohibits discrimination in jury selection on the basis of gender, or on the assumption that an individual will be biased in a particular case solely because that person happens to be a woman or a man. Writing for a five-member majority (Justice Kennedy filed a separate concurring opinion), Justice Blackmun took aim at discrimination that "serves to ratify and perpetuate invidious, archaic, and overbroad stereotypes about the relative abilities of men and women." Such discrimination, he argued, "causes harm to the litigants, the community, and the individual jurors who are wrongfully excluded from participation in the judicial process."

Calling the decision a "vandalizing of our people's traditions," Justice Scalia, in a dissent joined by Chief Justice Rehnquist and Justice Thomas, characterized the majority's reasoning as "largely obscured by anti-male-chauvinist oratory."

NOTICE, CONFRONTATION, AND SECURING OF WITNESSES

The Sixth Amendment's concern with procedural guarantees is further evident in the Notice, Confrontation, and Compulsory Process Clauses. These clauses state:

> IN ALL CRIMINAL PROSECUTIONS, THE ACCUSED SHALL ENJOY THE RIGHT . . . TO BE INFORMED OF THE NATURE AND CAUSE OF THE ACCUSATION; TO BE CONFRONTED WITH THE WITNESSES AGAINST HIM; TO HAVE COMPULSORY PROCESS FOR OBTAINING WITNESSES IN HIS FAVOR.

The right to be informed of the nature and cause of the accusation is commonly referred to as **notice**. In effect, the clause requires that laws be specific with respect to what constitutes a criminal act, thereby eliminating the use of overly vague laws to prosecute suspected violators. From a practical standpoint, the notice clause requires that a person be presented with a copy of all charges, including a copy of the indictment.

The right to confront witnesses stems from a long-standing tradition that recognizes that a defendant must be given the opportunity to see his accusers publicly and to cross-examine them. Under this rule, all testimony is to be given in open court, subject to intense cross-examination by the other party, although some very rare situations such as death-bed confessions may allow testimony by an absent witness to be introduced. Since *Pointer v. Texas* (Chapter 9), the Court has refined the Confrontation Clause.[9]

As growing numbers of child molestation and sexual abuse cases enter the judicial system, efforts have been made to provide some protections for the child who is required to testify against a defendant in a face-to-face situation. In *Coy v. Iowa* (1988), the Supreme Court struck down an Iowa statute that allowed child victims of alleged sexual abuse to testify from behind a screen in the courtroom. The Court observed that "the Confrontation Clause guarantees the defendant a face-to-face meeting with witnesses appearing before the trier of fact." Furthermore, the Court indicated that any exception to this right would be allowed "only when necessary to further an important public policy."

Such an exception was found in the case of *Maryland v. Craig* (1990). The defendant in this case was convicted of sexual offenses and assault and battery against a six-year-old child in her preschool. Under Maryland law, if a judge determines that a child's courtroom testimony would result in the child suffering serious emotional distress, such that he or she could not reasonably communicate, the judge may allow the following procedure: the child, prosecutor, and defense counsel withdraw to another room where the child is examined and cross-examined; the judge, jury, and defendant remain in the courtroom, where the testimony is displayed on one-way closed-circuit television; the child cannot see the defendant, although the defendant remains in contact with counsel. Sandra Craig appealed her conviction as violative of her Sixth Amendment right to confrontation of witnesses.

In a narrow 5–4 ruling, Justice O'Connor, writing for the majority, reviewed the history of the Confrontation Clause and concluded: "We have never held, however, that the Confrontation Clause guarantees criminal defendants the *absolute* right to a face-to-face meeting with witnesses against them at trial." According to Justice O'Connor, the main concern of the Confrontation Clause is to ensure the reliability of the evidence "by subjecting it to rigorous testing in the context of an adversary proceeding before the trier of fact." In this context, four elements were identified as central to confrontation: (1) physical presence, (2) testimony under oath, (3) submission to cross-examination, and (4) ability of the jury to observe the demeanor of the witness making the statements.

Holding that in some cases the State's interest in the physical and psychological well-being of child abuse victims outweighs a defendant's right to face his or her accusers in court, Justice O'Connor drew attention to the following statistics: thirty-seven states permit the use of videotaped testimony of sexually abused children; twenty-four states have authorized the use of one-way closed-circuit television testimony; and eight states authorize the use of a two-way system in which the child witness is permitted to see the courtroom and the defendant on a video monitor and in which the jury and judge are permitted to view the child during the testimony. In this context, the Maryland procedures were clearly justified. Stating that exceptions to face-to-face confrontation must be "case specific," Justice O'Connor vacated the Court of Appeals judgment and remanded the case for further proceedings. In a strong dissent, Justice Scalia argued that face-to-face confrontation is the central element of the Confrontation Clause.

Justice Scalia's emphasis on face-to-face confrontation prevailed in *Crawford v. Washington* (2004). In that case, Michael Crawford was on trial for assault and attempted murder after stabbing a man who allegedly tried to rape his wife, Sylvia. The couple had gone to the man's apartment, a fight ensued, and the man was wounded. At trial, prosecutors wanted to play a recorded statement taken from Sylvia at the police station that cast some doubt on the self-defense claims of her husband. Under Washington law, she did not testify at the trial because of the marital privilege law, under which one spouse may not testify without the other spouse's permission. The statement was played in the trial.

Justice Scalia wrote for a seven-person majority, with two concurring justices, that the wife's statement should not have been played at the trial. The State's use of Sylvia's statement violated the Confrontation Clause because, where testimonial statements are involved, the only method to establish reliability sufficient to satisfy constitutional demands is confrontation. The Confrontation Clause history supports two principles. First, the Clause's primary object is testimonial hearsay, and interrogations by law-enforcement officers fall squarely within that class. Second, the framers would not have allowed testimonial statements of a witness who did not appear at trial unless he was unavailable to testify and the defendant had had a prior opportunity for cross-examination.

In the following term, the Supreme Court found itself again embroiled in the Confrontation Clause. Two cases, *Davis v. Washington* (2005) and *Hammon v. Indiana* (2005), were decided on the same day and reached different conclusions. In the *Davis* case, a woman, Michelle McCottry, made a 911 call complaining that Adrian Davis was punching her. She did not take the stand at the trial but the 911 tape was admitted over defense objections. Davis was convicted. In the *Hammon* case, police responded to a domestic disturbance of Hershel and Amy Hammon. The police found Amy on the front porch "somewhat frightened." Police asked for permission to enter the home, observed property damage, kept the two Hammons apart, and questioned them. During questioning, Amy stated that Hershel had pushed her face into broken glass. She was subpoenaed but did not appear in court. Her statements were entered into evidence over defense objection, and Hershel was convicted.

The Supreme Court upheld the conviction of Davis but reversed Hammon's. According to the majority, the evidence presented in *Davis* was "nontestimonial" because the 911 statements were made in the course of an ongoing emergency, and the crime had not been completed. In *Hammon*, however, the actions had been completed and the parties were separated and questioned in what was really an interrogation. The resulting statements were "testimonial" because they were obtained in the course of investigating a crime that was no longer occurring. Testimonial statements must be subjected to cross-examination to ensure a fair trial (see Brief 13.5).

The Court further refined the "testimonial–nontestimonial" dispute in the case of *Michigan v. Bryant* (2011). When police were dispatched to a gas-station parking lot, they found Anthony Covington mortally wounded. He told police that he had been shot by Bryant outside Bryant's house and had driven himself to the gas station. At Bryant's trial, officers testified as to Covington's description of Bryant, and Bryant was subsequently convicted. Although the trial occurred prior to the Supreme Court's *Crawford v. Washington* decision, the appellate court relied on *Crawford* to strike down the conviction on Confrontation Clause grounds.

Writing for a five-person majority, joined in a concurrence by Justice Thomas, Justice Sotomayor held that Covington's identification and description of the shooter, along with the location of the shooting, were not "testimonial" and therefore did not violate the Confrontation Clause. The statements were not testimonial, she noted, because "they had a primary purpose . . . to enable police assistance to meet an ongoing emergency." Justice Sotomayor also noted that because all of this occurred during an "ongoing emergency," the statements had to be considered within that context. Justice Scalia, the author of the *Crawford* decision, issued a scathing dissent in which he said that the decision "destroys our Confrontation Clause jurisprudence and leaves it in a shambles."

RIGHT TO COUNSEL

The final procedural guarantee in the Sixth Amendment has been perhaps the most controversial and certainly one of the most heavily litigated. A person's right to be assisted by counsel generally has been available to those able to afford such assistance for some time, but in recent years the right to appointed counsel has emerged in instances when the accused is unable to pay. The earliest recognition by the Supreme Court that the Due Process Clause of the Fourteenth Amendment required the appointment of counsel in some circumstances occurred in *Powell v. Alabama* (1932) (discussed in Chapter 9). Although the circumstances in the *Powell* case were clearly unusual, the movement for appointed counsel was well underway

---

Brief 13.5
FORENSIC ANALYSIS, LAB REPORTS, AND CSI: SEE YOU IN COURT

The Supreme Court's increasing enforcement of the Confrontation Clause took another large step in the case of *Melendez-Diaz v. Massachusetts* (2009). Writing for a somewhat unusual five-person majority, Justice Scalia struck down the Massachusetts law that required police laboratory tests to be certified, sworn before a notary public, and then submitted as *prima facie* evidence what they asserted to a court. In this case the reports indicated that the material seized by police from Melendez-Diaz was cocaine of a certain composition, quality, and net weight. However, no one was required to appear to testify to those facts. Justice Scalia's opinion pointed out that the lab reports constituted "testimonial" evidence that must be subjected to cross-examination as would all other testimony. He rejected the government's argument that only "accusatory" witnesses are required to testify, finding no support for that position in either the Sixth Amendment or in the Court's precedents.

Under *Melendez-Diaz*, all analysts and forensic scientists who participate in preparing lab tests and other procedures that ultimately are introduced as evidence in court must testify and be subjected to cross-examination. Critics point to the burden that such a rule will place on overworked police labs and analysts, requiring them to spend much of their time in court. While some states have been requiring direct analyst testimony without widespread evidence of a slowdown in productivity, others are not so sure. Justice Kennedy's dissenting opinion emphasized the fact that scientific analysis has been introduced into evidence without testimony for at least ninety years in some thirty-five states and six Federal Courts of Appeal.

The Court reaffirmed its stance toward laboratory tests in *Bullcoming v. New Mexico* (2011). During the trial of Donald Bullcoming on DUI charges, the lab analyst that performed the tests and signed the certification did not come to court. Instead, a supervisor who had played no part in the testing or certification provided the testimony from the witness stand. A 5–4 majority overturned Bullcoming's conviction on the grounds that the Confrontation Clause requires the analyst who conducted the test and signed the certification to offer the testimony.

by the early 1960s, despite the Supreme Court's refusal in *Betts v. Brady* (1942) to incorporate the right to counsel as a part of the Fourteenth Amendment's guarantees. That major step occurred in *Gideon v. Wainwright* (1963), as a unanimous court reversed its earlier ruling and held the right to counsel to be a fundamental right. In that case, only two states sided with Florida in asking that *Betts* be upheld, while twenty-two states argued for its reversal.

The celebrated case of Clarence Gideon's conviction for breaking and entering a poolroom with intent to commit a misdemeanor (a felony under Florida law) has been the subject of a well-known book and movie, undoubtedly in large part because it highlighted such an obvious inequality in the criminal justice system. On one hand, the state of Florida provided appointed counsel only in capital cases, yet it relied heavily upon its own lawyers to prosecute defendants. Gideon, on the other hand, was penniless and certainly not skilled in the workings of the legal system. Gideon's request for a lawyer was dismissed by the trial court, so Gideon conducted his own defense "about as well as could be expected for a layman." In spite of his opening statement, cross-examination of witnesses, calling of his own witnesses, and a final argument, Gideon was convicted by a jury and sentenced to five years in prison. Following an unsuccessful appeal to the Florida Supreme Court, Gideon asked the U.S. Supreme Court, in a handwritten request, to reverse his conviction. Because of Gideon's lack of funds, the Court accepted his petition *in forma pauperis* and appointed legal counsel.

Justice Black's opinion tied a defendant's prospects for a fair trial strongly to the right to counsel, calling *Betts v. Brady* "an abrupt break" with the Supreme Court's precedents upholding due process guarantees. The right to a lawyer, according to Justice Black, had become essential to our system of justice:

> THAT GOVERNMENT HIRES LAWYERS TO PROSECUTE AND DEFENDANTS WHO HAVE THE MONEY HIRE LAWYERS TO DEFEND ARE THE STRONGEST INDICATIONS OF THE WIDESPREAD BELIEF THAT LAWYERS IN CRIMINAL COURTS ARE NECESSITIES, NOT LUXURIES. THE RIGHT OF ONE CHARGED WITH CRIME TO COUNSEL MAY NOT BE DEEMED FUNDAMENTAL AND ESSENTIAL TO FAIR TRIALS IN SOME COUNTRIES, BUT IT IS IN OURS.

In *Argersinger v. Hamlin* (1972), the Court extended the right of counsel to all cases, including misdemeanors, involving imprisonment. While some observers believed the *Argersinger* holding was applicable to all cases involving the possibility of imprisonment, the Court in *Scott v. Illinois* (1979) stated otherwise. In that case, a defendant was given only a fine, although imprisonment had been a possibility. The Court held that under such conditions, a conviction would not be reversed simply because no counsel had been provided. Finally, the right to counsel has been extended into both pre- and post-trial areas, as presented in Table 13.4.[10]

The Rehnquist Court had not addressed the right to counsel until its ruling in *Alabama v. Shelton* (2002). In that case, the Court required appointed counsel for any indigent defendant who requests representation and receives a suspended sentence. LeReed Shelton, the defendant, received a suspended thirty-day sentence, so he would spend no time in jail unless he violated the terms of probation over the next two years. In that case, the court could send him to jail for up to thirty days. A narrow 5–4 majority held that counsel is required in those situations in which imprisonment is a possibility, and Shelton indeed faced possible jail time.

Justice Ruth Bader Ginsburg's majority opinion pointed out that only sixteen states would be affected by the ruling, and ten of those states already provided counsel in most misdemeanor cases. She also noted that states could legally avoid appointed counsel by using "pretrial probation," in which a defendant and prosecutor agree to probation before trial. Charges are dismissed if probation is satisfied, but a trial will be held if they are not.

Calling Shelton a "low-profile case," Professor Alan Raphael argues that is one of the most significant right-to-counsel rulings in recent years:

> THE DECISION IS NOTEWORTHY BECAUSE IT IS THE COURT'S FIRST SIGNIFICANT EXTENSION OF THE IMPORTANT RIGHT TO COUNSEL IN TWO DECADES, BECAUSE IT EXTENDS THE RIGHT TO COUNSEL IN AT LEAST A SIGNIFICANT MINORITY OF STATES, AND BECAUSE IT WILL CAUSE THE EXPENDITURE OF SIGNIFICANT SUMS OF MONEY AND/OR CHANGES IN COURT PROCEDURES IN MANY STATES.[11]

Table 13.4 Recent Supreme Court Rulings on the Assistance Of Counsel

Stages at Which Assistance of Counsel Is Required	Case
First appeal after felony conviction	*Douglas v. California* (1963); *Halbert v. Michigan* (2005)
Arraignment	*Massiah v. U.S.* (1964)
"Accusatory" setting; pre-indictment	*Escobedo v. Illinois* (1964)
Custodial setting	*Miranda v. Arizona* (1966)
Post-indictment lineup	*U.S. v. Wade* (1967)
Preliminary hearing	*Coleman v. Alabama* (1970)
Probation and parole revocation	*Gagnon v. Scarpelli* (1973)
Post-indictment tactics that "deliberately elicit" testimony in the absence of counsel	*Fellers v. United States* (2004)
Stages at Which Assistance of Counsel Is *Not* Required	**Case**
Fingerprinting	*Davis v. Mississippi* (1969)
Pre-indictment lineup	*Kirby v. Illinois* (1972)
Mugshot session	*U.S. v. Ash* (1973)
Second appeal after felony	*Ross v. Moffitt* (1974)
Civil contempt proceeding	*Turner v. Rogers* (2011)

INEFFECTIVE COUNSEL

Defendants generally have a difficult time successfully challenging convictions on the basis of "ineffective" counsel, but it is not impossible. In *Strickland v. Washington* (1984), the Court laid out a two-step process for determining whether counsel had been ineffective. First, the criminal defendant must show that the counsel's performance was grossly deficient. Second, there must be some evidence of "prejudice," meaning that the case outcome likely would have been different with a better lawyer. The Supreme Court has now become more involved in determinations of ineffective counsel.

In *Wiggins v. Smith* (2003), Justice O'Connor wrote for a 7–2 Court that the performance of counsel is deficient "if it falls below an objective standard of reasonableness, which is defined in terms of prevailing professional norms." Wiggins had wanted his attorney to look into his background—which he argued would show mitigating factors related to his life history—alcoholic mother, problems in foster care—in preparing for the punishment phase of a death penalty trial. The majority agreed with Wiggins, finding that "any reasonably competent attorney would have realized that pursuing such leads was necessary to making an informed choice among possible defenses, given the apparent absence of aggravating factors from Wiggins' background." Then, the Court found a "reasonable probability" that without the counsel's unprofessional errors, the result would have been different.

A unanimous Supreme Court reached the opposite conclusion in *Yarborough v. Gentry* (2003). Gentry's defense counsel gave a lengthy closing statement expressing a general theme that the jury, like the prosecutor and defense counsel himself, were not at the scene of the crime and so could only speculate about what had happened and who was lying. The U.S. Supreme Court agreed that "Gentry's lawyer was no Aristotle or even Clarence Darrow," but it was not comfortable in making the subjective judgment that the closing arguments had been deficient.

The Court's 2004–05 term continued the growing number of ineffective counsel cases. *Florida v. Nixon* (2004) involved a defendant who refused to cooperate with his lawyer. When the lawyer decided to concede the defendant's guilt in hopes of obtaining a better result during the punishment phase of the trial, the defendant refused to give his express consent to the strategy. The Supreme Court felt that the defendant who refused to cooperate with his lawyer could not later use the ineffective counsel argument. But, in *Rompilla v. Beard* (2005), the Court found counsel to be ineffective for failing to examine court files dealing with the defendant's earlier rape and assault convictions. The next term, in *United States v. Gonzalez-Lopez* (2005), a 5–4 majority reversed a conviction after a judge denied the defendant the right to use his preferred lawyer. The lawyer, according to the judge, had violated a rule of professional conduct in a separate case and could not practice in his court. Justice Scalia's majority opinion held that denial of counsel of choice is not "harmless error," and will lead to reversal of a conviction.

The cases seem to keep coming. In *Padilla v. Kentucky* (2010), the majority found that a lawyer who failed to tell his client that he would likely be deported if he entered a guilty plea was grossly deficient, and the case was remanded to see if the trial court could find "prejudice." The Court found "prejudice" in *Porter v. McCollom* (2010), a death penalty case, in which the defense counsel had failed to uncover or present mitigating evidence of the defendant's childhood abuse, mental impairment, and, most significantly, distinguished military service during the Korean War. And in *Sears v. Upton* (2010), the Court unanimously overturned another death sentence after finding that the lawyer spent less than a day attempting to uncover mitigation evidence and had missed significant evidence of child abuse. And finally, the ruling in *Missouri v. Frye* (2012) held Frye's counsel to be ineffective under the *Strickland* standard because the lawyer neglected to tell Frye about two possible plea bargains, including an offer to reduce the charge to a misdemeanor and to recommend, with a guilty plea, a ninety-day sentence. The Sixth Amendment right to effective assistance of counsel extends to the consideration of plea offers that lapse or are rejected.

Eighth Amendment

The protection against excessive bail and fines has not been nationalized, although the Supreme Court has addressed the matter of bail as "excessive." In *Stack v. Boyle* (1951), the Court held "excessive" to mean "set at a figure higher than an amount reasonably calculated" to ensure that the defendant will be present at his trial. Whether bail is viewed as excessive depends on various factors such as the nature of the offense, any potential threat to society, the defendant's own safety, and the likelihood of flight from the jurisdiction. In some states, bail may be denied for certain felonies.

Preventive Detention

The Bail Reform Act of 1984 was intended to reduce the number of crimes committed by defendants awaiting trial. The law allows federal courts to keep in jail defendants who are determined to be threats to the community. These may include defendants charged with offenses for which the sentence is life imprisonment or death, certain drug offenses, or repeat offenders whose release would jeopardize the safety of others or the community. The act requires that specific factors be considered in each instance, supported by written findings and reasons, and subject to review. The length of detention may not exceed the limits of the Speedy Trial Act.

This practice, known as "preventive" or pretrial detention, was tested in *United States v. Salerno* (1987). That case concerned Anthony Salerno and Vincent Cafaro, charged in a twenty-nine-count indictment for numerous offenses such as fraud, extortion, gambling, and conspiracy to commit murder. The government argued that Salerno was a "boss" in the Genovese Crime Family of La Cosa Nostra, and that Cafaro also was a participant. The defendants sought their release on due process grounds as well as on Eighth Amendment excessive bail arguments.

Writing for a 6–3 majority, Chief Justice Rehnquist upheld the Bail Reform Act as part of the government's legitimate interest in preventing crime. His assessment of the balance between governmental regulation and individual rights touched on the key issues of individualism and communitarianism:

> While the government's general interest in preventing crime is compelling, even this interest is heightened when the government musters convincing proof that the arrestee, already indicted or held to answer for a serious crime, presents a demonstrable danger to the community. Under these narrow circumstances, society's interest in crime prevention is at its greatest.
>
> On the other side of the scale, of course, is the individual's strong interest in liberty. We do not minimize the importance and fundamental

NATURE OF THIS RIGHT. BUT, AS OUR CASES HOLD, THIS RIGHT MAY, IN CIRCUMSTANCES WHERE THE GOVERNMENT'S INTEREST IS SUFFICIENTLY WEIGHTY, BE SUBORDINATED TO THE GREATER NEEDS OF SOCIETY.

Justices Marshall and Brennan joined in a dissenting opinion attacking the majority's reasoning on several fronts, but most forcefully on the matter of a defendant's presumed innocence. According to Marshall's opinion:

THE STATUTE NOW BEFORE US DECLARES THAT PERSONS WHO HAVE BEEN INDICTED MAY BE DETAINED IF A JUDICIAL OFFICER FINDS CLEAR AND CONVINCING EVIDENCE THAT THEY POSE A DANGER TO INDIVIDUALS OR TO THE COMMUNITY. . . . BUT OUR FUNDAMENTAL PRINCIPLES OF JUSTICE DECLARE THAT THE DEFENDANT IS AS INNOCENT ON THE DAY BEFORE HIS TRIAL AS HE IS ON THE MORNING AFTER HIS ACQUITTAL.

In a separate dissent, Justice Stevens also held the pretrial detention of persons based on their "future dangerousness" to be unconstitutional.

THE DEATH PENALTY

Whereas the bail and fines provision of the Eighth Amendment has produced relatively little constitutional debate, the amendment's ban on "cruel and unusual punishments" has been a different matter entirely. Most of the attention given cruel and unusual punishments in recent years has involved the punishment of death for certain crimes (but see Brief 13.6 for other issues). Table 13.5 provides a chronological overview of the Supreme Court's decisions regarding the death penalty.

The Supreme Court did not address the death penalty issue until 1972, although executions had been part of American justice for years. Critics of the practice, however, sought to draw attention to the arbitrary and discriminatory way in which the death penalty had been administered. In *Furman v. Georgia* (1972), the Court voted 5–4 to strike down the use of the death penalty as then practiced, but no single majority opinion was written. Justices Brennan and Marshall held the death penalty *per se* to be unconstitutional, while three others—Douglas, Stewart and White—found fault with the manner in which the death penalty had been administered. While Douglas noted the impact upon minorities, all were concerned with the system of arbitrariness and unguided discretion available to judges and juries. To summarize: of the five separate opinions, three justices opposed the absence of clear standards and the resulting arbitrariness of death penalty use but stopped short of deciding on the legality of the death penalty itself; two justices opposed the death penalty in all circumstances; and four justices dissented.

The four dissenters, all Nixon appointees, found that legislatures, more so than courts, should decide on the appropriateness of the death penalty. Chief Justice Burger's opinion called upon legislatures "to make a thorough re-evaluation of the entire subject of capital punishment." Burger's call for legislative activity took little time to show results. Many of the states revised their death penalty statutes, spurred on by public opinion polls that showed a majority of Americans in favor of such laws. In 1976 the Court addressed the new laws in five separate cases. Four justices (Burger, White, Rehnquist, and Blackmun) found all five state laws acceptable, while two (Brennan and Marshall) held all five to be invalid. The crucial "swing" votes were held by Justices Stewart, Powell, and Stevens, all of whom delivered a joint opinion in each of the five cases—upholding three laws (Georgia, Texas, and Florida) and striking down two (North Carolina and Louisiana).

In *Gregg v. Georgia* (1976), a 7–2 majority upheld Georgia's new death penalty statute. Justice Stewart's plurality opinion held that the death penalty "does not invariably violate the Constitution," adding that it "is not a form of punishment that may never be imposed. . . ." The new Georgia law provided for several important factors to be considered before the death penalty could be imposed. First, the law requires that the guilt–innocence phase of the trial be completely separate from the punishment phase. In effect, this creates two separate trials, one right after the other. Second, Georgia specified ten "aggravating circumstances, one of which must be found by the jury during the punishment phase to exist beyond a reasonable doubt before a death sentence can ever be imposed" (e.g., Was the crime committed upon a peace officer or judicial officer? Was it committed in

Brief 13.6
SOME NON–DEATH PENALTY "CRUEL AND UNUSUAL PUNISHMENTS" CASES

The Supreme Court has been called upon numerous times to determine whether specific practices constitute cruel and unusual punishments. Historically, the amendment has been regarded as banning such barbaric practices as drawing and quartering, crucifixion, burning at the stake, and use of the rack. In *Weems v. United States* (1910) the Court held the sentence of fifteen years of *cadena temporal*, a punishment of Spanish origin that required the prisoner to spend the entire sentence at hard labor and bound by heavy chains around his wrists and ankles, to be cruel and unusual punishment.

Students. In *Ingraham v. Wright* (1977), a 5–4 majority held that the use of corporal punishment (paddling of students) does not constitute cruel and unusual punishment in Eighth Amendment terms. Speaking for the Court, Justice Powell stated that the Eighth Amendment was "designed to protect those convicted of crimes." Schoolchildren, he said, are free to leave the school, which is "an open institution," unlike those criminals confined in prison.

Prisoners. *Hudson v. McMillian (1992)* revolved around a beating administered to Keith Hudson, a Louisiana prison inmate, by two prison guards. Hudson was handcuffed and shackled during the beating, which resulted in minor bruises, facial swelling, loosened teeth, and a cracked dental plate. Hudson filed suit under 42 U.S.C. § 1983, alleging that he had been the victim of cruel and unusual punishment. Writing for a 7–2 Court, Justice O'Connor held that the use of excessive physical force against a prisoner may constitute cruel and unusual punishment even though the inmate does not suffer serious injury. What is important is whether the use of force was "wanton and unnecessary" and whether the force was applied "maliciously and sadistically to cause harm." Justice O'Connor pointed out that not every "malevolent touch by a prison guard" constitutes cruel and unusual punishment, and the "good-faith" use of force to maintain or restore discipline certainly poses no constitutional problems. A 2010 ruling in *Wilkins v. Gaddy* held that even "*de minimis*" injuries might constitute excessive force.

In *Helling v. McKinney* (1993), the Court was asked to rule on a petition by William McKinney, a Nevada state prisoner, alleging that his involuntary exposure to environmental tobacco smoke (ETS) from his cellmate's and other inmates' smoking posed an unreasonable health risk, thereby subjecting him to cruel and unusual punishment in violation of the Eighth Amendment. The Supreme Court remanded the case for trial, holding that McKinney should have been permitted to prove that ETS was an unreasonable danger to his health. While the Court did not rule on the effects of cigarette smoke, it held that the prisoner might indeed have a case if he could show that his particular situation was dangerous and that exposure to cigarette smoke is a risk that today's society does not choose to tolerate. McKinney was transferred to a new prison with a no-smoking section.

Mandatory "three-strikes" sentencing laws. Today, more than 2 million people are behind bars in the United States. Much of the increase can be attributed to stiffer prison sentences. But can these sentences constitute "cruel and unusual" punishments? During the 2002–03 term, the Supreme Court decided two cases effectively guaranteeing that state legislatures can establish almost any sentence as punishment for a crime. In *Ewing v. California* (2003) and *Lockyer v. Andrade* (2003), a 5–4 Court upheld California's "three-strikes" law. That law provides that any person convicted of a felony who has two previous felony convictions is subject to a prison term of twenty-five years to life. Ewing received twenty-five years without parole for stealing three golf clubs, while Leandro Andrade stole videotapes from two California K-Mart stores. The value of the tapes taken in the two thefts was $84.70 and $68.85. Andrade previously had been convicted of misdemeanor theft, residential burglary, transportation of marijuana (twice), and escape from prison. He was charged with "theft with a prior conviction," a charge that could be either a misdemeanor or a felony. The state chose the felony charge, he was convicted, and he received two twenty-five-year-to-life sentences—one for each of the thefts.

On appeal, the Ninth Circuit reversed the convictions, holding that they were disproportionate "contrary to . . . clearly established Federal law, as determined by the Supreme Court of the United States." In the majority opinion, Justice O'Connor rejected this holding, pointing out that:

> . . . [O]ur precedents in this area have not been a model of clarity. Indeed, in determining whether a particular sentence for a term of years can violate the Eighth Amendment, we have not established a clear or consistent path for courts to follow. . . . Our cases exhibit a lack of clarity regarding what factors may indicate gross disproportionality.

The Court did not attempt to provide that clarity in these cases, choosing instead to defer to the California legislature (and state legislators in general). So, does the Eighth Amendment provide any limits on criminal sentencing? One observer concludes:

> With this decision, the Supreme Court has stated that it will almost never find a sentence authorized by a legislature as punishment for crime to violate the Eighth Amendment to the United States Constitution. Both the majority and the dissent in this case (*Andrade*) would agree that the overwhelming bulk of decisions regarding sentencing should be made by legislative bodies and that the courts should only rarely find a sentence to be unconstitutionally disproportionate.[13]

Juveniles. In *Graham v. Florida* (2010), a 5–4 majority (Chief Justice Roberts concurred in the result) held that imposing a life sentence without the possibility of parole for a nonhomicide crime committed by a juvenile violates the Cruel and

Unusual Punishment Clause of the Eighth Amendment. The majority pointed out that only 129 individuals were serving such sentences, and seventy-seven of these were in Florida. The Court recognized the differences between adults and juveniles with respect to rehabilitation and change, holding that juveniles under this system would spend a much higher percentage of their life behind bars than would an adult. The ruling was not retroactive but allowed those serving life-without-parole sentences to a meaningful hearing. The Supreme Court extended the *Graham* precedent through a 5–4 decision in *Miller v. Alabama* (2012), holding that a mandatory life sentence without parole for those committing a homicide under the age of eighteen constitutes cruel and unusual punishment in violation of the Eighth Amendment. Taking together the rulings in *Roper*, *Graham*, and *Miller*, the Supreme Court has found that juveniles may not be subject to death or life-without-parole sentences.

Table 13.5 Development of the Law—The Death Penalty

Year	Event	Significance
1972	*Furman v. Georgia*	With no majority opinion, a 5–4 Court struck down the death penalty because of the "arbitrary and capricious" manner in which it was being administered.
1976	*Gregg v. Georgia*	Georgia's new death penalty law is upheld; requires separate punishment phase, consideration of aggravating and mitigating circumstances, and automatic appeal. Similar laws were upheld in *Proffitt v. Florida* and *Jurek v. Texas*.
1976	*Woodson v. North Carolina; Roberts v. Louisiana*	Mandatory death sentences are held unconstitutional because they omit consideration of the character and record of the offender and the circumstances of the particular offense.
1977	*Coker v. Georgia*	The death penalty is not appropriate for a crime (rape) in which a human life is not taken.
1986	*Ford v. Wainwright*	The Eighth Amendment prohibits a state from carrying out a sentence of death on a prisoner who is insane.
1987	*McCleskey v. Kemp*	Even though clear statistical evidence showed that killers of white people are more likely than killers of blacks to receive the death penalty, a defendant must prove racial discrimination in his particular case.
1987	*Booth v. Maryland*	Struck down a state law requiring victim-impact statements to be included in capital sentencing decisions.
1988	*Thompson v. Oklahoma*	Reversed death sentence for a crime committed at age fifteen, although Court suggested that state laws may specify a legal execution age.
1989	*Stanford v. Kentucky Wilkins v. Missouri*	Upheld death sentences for crimes committed at ages seventeen and sixteen, respectively, noting that a majority of states with capital punishment allow executions of sixteen- and seventeen-year-olds.
1989	*Penry v. Lynaugh*	Upheld execution of the mentally retarded.
1989	*South Carolina v. Gathers*	Upheld *Booth*; restricted the use of victim-impact statements.
1989	*Hildwin v. Florida*	Even if the jury fails to find an aggravating circumstance, a judge may do so and impose the death penalty.
1990	*Walton v. Arizona Blystone v. Pennsylvania Boyde v. California*	Upheld requirement that accused must bear burden of proof in showing mitigating circumstances; upheld requirement that death sentence must be given if aggravating circumstances out-weigh mitigating; upheld mandatory jury instruction language.
1990	*McKoy v. North Carolina*	Struck down requirement that mitigating circumstances must be found unanimously by the jury before they can be considered.
1991	*Payne v. Tennessee*	Reversed *Booth* and *Gathers*, upholding use of victim-impact statements in the sentencing phase of death penalty trials.
1995	*Harris v. Alabama*	Upheld a judge's sentence of death even though the jury's advisory verdict called for life imprisonment.
2000	*Weeks v. Angelone*	When a jury told the judge that it did not understand the instructions concerning mitigating circumstances, the judge simply directed the jury's attention to the relevant paragraph. The Court held this to be sufficient.

2001	Shafer v. South Carolina	When considering the future dangerousness of a defendant, a jury must be informed that a life sentence carries no possibility of parole.
2001	Penry v. Johnson	A jury must be told to consider a capital defendant's mental retardation and abusive childhood.
2002	Atkins v. Virginia	The Eighth Amendment prevents states from executing mentally retarded offenders. Overruled Penry v. Lynbaugh.
2002	Ring v. Arizona	Juries rather than judges must determine the facts necessary to subject a convicted person to the death penalty. Overruled Walton v. Arizona.
2005	Deck v. Missouri	The Constitution prohibits the use of visible shackles during a capital trial's penalty phase, as it does during the guilt phase, unless that use is "justified by an essential state interest."
2005	Roper v. Simmons	Execution of persons who commit crimes under the age of eighteen is prohibited by the Eighth Amendment.
2006	Kansas v. Marsh	Upheld Kansas law that requires jurors in capital cases to impose a death sentence if they conclude that mitigating and aggravating circumstances are equal.
2007	Brewer v. Quarterman / Cole v. Quarterman	Reversed Texas death conviction for state's failure to allow consideration of mitigating evidence related to defendant's mental illness or family experiences.
2007	Panetti v. Quarterman	Prior findings of competency to stand trial do not prevent a prisoner from proving he is incompetent to be executed because of his present medical condition.
2008	Medellin v. Texas	Held an international treaty signed by the U.S. does not have automatic effect on domestic law. Upheld Texas death sentence for Mexican national.
2008	Baze v. Rees	Upheld Kentucky "three-drug protocol" for lethal injection, allowing executions to resume.
2008	Kennedy v. Louisiana	Struck down Louisiana law allowing death penalty for child rape when the crime did not result in the victim's death.

the course of another capital crime? Was it committed for money?). Second, the jury must consider "mitigating circumstances" as well, including such items as the defendant's youth, emotional state, and the extent of his cooperation with authorities. The statute provides that the jury is not required to find a mitigating circumstance to recommend mercy, but it must find an aggravating circumstance to recommend a death sentence. Third, all death sentences carry automatic appeal to the Georgia Supreme Court, which reviews each sentence of death to determine if the sentence is disproportionate compared to other cases.

In recent decisions, the Court has strengthened the use of the death penalty through the general procedures announced in *Gregg v. Georgia* (Brief 13.7). These rulings have focused on four main issues: sentencing guidelines, execution of minors and the mentally retarded, "victim-impact" statements, and methods of execution.

SENTENCING GUIDELINES

Much of the Court's recent death penalty work has involved sentencing guidelines, focusing on such issues as instructions to the jury, findings of aggravating and mitigating circumstances, and whether a judge or jury should make findings of fact. In *Hildwin v. Florida* (1989), a judge found an aggravating circumstance authorizing the death sentence even though the jury did not specifically note such a circumstance. An 8–1 Court went even further in *Harris v. Alabama* (1995) in upholding a judge's sentence of death even though the jury's advisory verdict called for life imprisonment. But in *Ring v. Arizona* (2002), a 7–2 majority ruled that juries must determine the existence of any fact necessary to subject a person convicted of murder to the death penalty (unless the defendant waives a jury trial). The ruling essentially overturned *Walton v. Arizona* (1990), under which the judge determines whether an aggravating

Brief 13.7

TRENDS IN THE DEATH PENALTY

Since the Supreme Court allowed the resumption of executions in 1976, the nation's death-row population has increased dramatically. By the end of 2012, some 3,146 persons were awaiting execution on death row, with almost one-half of that total in three states: California (724), Florida (411), and Texas (304). Nearly 98 percent are male, but sixty-one females live on death row as well. In all, twelve women have been executed since 1976. In terms of race, the death row population is nearly 43 percent white, 42 percent black, and 12 percent Hispanic. These figures roughly correspond to the race of those persons convicted of murder in the United States. Yet, cries of racial discrimination have been associated with the death penalty for many years, often by focusing on the race of the murder *victim* rather than the murderer. For example, 76 percent of murder victims for which individuals receive the death penalty were white, but only 50 percent of all murder victims generally are white. A 2005 *Santa Clara Law Review* article found that those killing whites were more than three times likely to receive the death penalty than those who killed blacks and four times more than those who killed Hispanics.[12] In *McCleskey v. Kemp* (1987) the Court held Georgia's capital punishment system to be constitutional, despite a statistical study by Professor David C. Baldus of the University of Iowa that showed that killers of whites were more than four times as likely to get the death sentence than killers of blacks. Justice Powell assumed the validity of the study, but he described it as "clearly insufficient to support an inference that any of the decision makers in McCleskey's case acted with discriminatory purpose." Despite acknowledging the discretion and possible disparities inherent in the criminal justice system, Powell added that a defendant "must prove that the decision makers in his case acted with a discriminatory purpose."

By the start of 2013, 1,320 persons had been executed since resumption of the death penalty in 1976. More than half of these have occurred since 1999 when executions reached their peak (98). Most of the executions are concentrated in a handful of states. Texas leads with 492 executions, slightly more than one-third of the total, followed by Virginia (109), Oklahoma (102), Florida (74), Missouri (68), Alabama (55), Georgia (52), Ohio (49), North Carolina (43), South Carolina (43), Arizona (34), Louisiana (28), and Arkansas (27). These thirteen states account for nearly 90 percent of all executions in the country, while more than half of all executions have occurred in just three states.

Source: *Facts About the Death Penalty*, Death Penalty Information Center, *www.deathpenaltyinfo.org*, December 28, 2012.

---

circumstance has been proven and then whether that should result in the death penalty. The *Ring* ruling now requires that juries find any fact that would allow for a death sentence.

EXECUTION OF MINORS AND THOSE WITH MENTAL PROBLEMS

MINORS

The issue of executing minors has become more heated in recent years, following several well-publicized schoolyard shootings by teenage murderers. The Court first encountered the issue in *Thompson v. Oklahoma* (1988), when a 5–3 majority reversed the death sentence of William Wayne Thompson, who had committed a murder when he was only fifteen years old. Justice O'Connor, in a concurring opinion, indicated that states could not execute persons for crimes committed under the age of sixteen unless the state's capital punishment statute specified a minimum age. Because of the plurality and concurring opinions, however, the ruling's effect was unclear.

Some questions raised by *Thompson* were answered in *Stanford v. Kentucky* and *Wilkins v. Missouri* (1989), two cases that were decided together. In the Kentucky case, Kevin Stanford had committed murder as a seventeen-year-old, while Heath Wilkins had committed murder in Missouri as a sixteen-year-old. Both states authorized procedures allowing a juvenile to be certified for trial as an adult. In both cases, the defendants were tried as adults, convicted, and sentenced to death. The question facing the Supreme Court was whether the execution of an individual for a crime committed at age sixteen or seventeen constitutes cruel and unusual punishment under the Eighth Amendment.

Writing for a 5–4 majority, Justice Scalia noted that capital punishment for sixteen- or seventeen-year-olds was not one of the types of punishment considered cruel and unusual at the time the Bill of Rights was adopted. Therefore, if such punishment is cruel and unusual in modern times, it could only be the result of "evolving standards of decency that mark the progress of a maturing society." Justice Scalia pointed out the fact that, of the thirty-seven states whose laws permitted capital punishment, only fifteen declined to impose it on sixteen-year olds and twelve declined to impose it on seventeen-year-olds. In other words, a majority of states that allow capital punishment also allow it for sixteen- and seventeen-year-olds. As a result, a national consensus cannot be found against such punishments. Perhaps a consensus was emerging, however, as a May 2002 Gallup Poll showed that 69 percent of Americans opposed capital punishment for juvenile offenders.[13]

About three years after that poll, in *Roper v. Simmons* (2005), a 5–4 Supreme Court majority recognized the consensus and banned all executions of persons who committed crimes under the age of eighteen. The Court's ruling rejected the death sentence for Christopher Simmons, who was seventeen when he tied and gagged the murder victim and threw her off a bridge into a river where she drowned. Since 1976, two persons had been executed for crimes they committed while under the age of eighteen, and some seventy-one juvenile offenders were on death row as of 2005. Prior to *Roper v. Simmons*, some nineteen states with the death penalty actually prohibited the execution of juvenile offenders. These factors convinced Justice Stevens and other members of the Court's majority that a national consensus did in fact exist against such executions (see the discussion of *Graham v. Florida* [2010], in Brief 13.5).

Mentally Retarded

The Supreme Court first approved execution of mentally retarded defendants in *Penry v. Lynbaugh* (1989). Apparently reacting to what the majority considered an "emerging consensus," however, the Court reversed *Penry* and banned the execution of the mentally retarded in *Atkins v. Virginia* (2002). Daryl Atkins, convicted of abducting a man, forcing him to withdraw money from an ATM, and shooting him eight times, also had an IQ of 59. In the *Atkins* decision, the Supreme Court did not decide whether Atkins himself falls under the accepted definition of retardation, and it did not provide much in the way of guidelines for states to follow. State juries must decide whether defendants are retarded under the state's standard.

But different standards have evolved in different states. Early in 2004, the Texas Court of Criminal Appeals held that defendants on death row must prove that their "adaptive functioning" is limited, a task that would examine whether the crime involved "forethought, planning and complex execution of purpose." Seven other states have enacted laws following the *Atkins* decision, and most require low intelligence (below 70 or 75 generally) and evidence of difficulty in living independently.[14] In some states, the retardation decision is made by a judge in a pretrial hearing, but others have placed it in the punishment phase of the trial and left it to the jury. While the principle may be clear, its application certainly is not.

Victim-Impact Statements

In deciding whether a sentence of death is appropriate in a given case, the judge and/or jury are required to consider numerous factors, including aggravating and mitigating circumstances, as discussed earlier. As victims'-rights groups have become more active, however, pressure to consider information about the victim has also increased in capital murder trials. In *Payne v. Tennessee* (1991), the Court reversed its earlier precedents and upheld the use of **victim-impact statements**. Pervis Tyrone Payne had been convicted of murdering a young mother and her two-year-old daughter. A three-year-old son had survived. During the sentencing phase, the prosecutor called the young child's grandmother to the stand. She testified that the boy missed his murdered mother and sister. The prosecutor then commented to the jury on the effects of the crimes on the family. The jury sentenced Payne to death on each of the murder counts.

Writing for a 6–3 majority, Chief Justice Rehnquist noted that earlier cases had been based on two premises. First, that evidence relating to a particular victim or to the harm that a capital defendant causes a victim's family do not in general reflect on the defendant's "blameworthiness." Second, that only evidence relating to "blameworthiness" is relevant to the capital sentencing decision. Rehnquist noted that Payne's parents and a girlfriend had been called to testify as to Payne's character during the sentencing phase, and none of this testimony was related to the circumstances of Payne's crimes. He concluded that "(t)here is no reason to treat such evidence differently than other relevant evidence is treated."

In an emotional dissent, Justice Marshall stated what he saw as the real reasons for the Court's reversal of the *Booth* and *Gathers* precedents.

> Four Terms ago, a five-justice majority of this Court held that "victim-impact" evidence of the type at issue in this case could not constitutionally be introduced during the penalty phase of a capital trial. By another 5–4 vote, a majority of this Court

REBUFFED AN ATTACK UPON THIS RULING JUST TWO TERMS AGO. . . . NEITHER THE LAW NOR THE FACTS SUPPORTING BOOTH AND GATHERS UNDERWENT ANY CHANGE IN THE LAST FOUR YEARS. ONLY THE PERSONNEL OF THIS COURT DID.

METHODS OF EXECUTION

The method of execution employed to carry out the death penalty has always been a matter of state preference. The 1,320 executions since 1976 break down as follows: lethal injection, 1,146; electrocution, 157; gas chamber, 11; hanging, 3; and firing squad, 3. Of the 34 states plus the federal government that allow the death penalty, all now employ lethal injection as the primary method. Nebraska's Supreme Court ruled its primary method, electrocution, unconstitutional in 2008.

Despite the overwhelming preference for lethal injection, many observers point to possible problems with the procedure. The Supreme Court was finally drawn into the lethal injection debate in the case of *Baze v. Rees* (2008). At issue in that case was Kentucky's so-called "three-drug cocktail" method of lethal injection. In that procedure, the inmate is sedated with sodium thiopental, producing unconsciousness. Then, the inmate is injected with a paralyzing agent, pancuronium bromide, which stops the breathing muscles. Finally, a dose of potassium chloride stops the heart. Death penalty opponents claim that the procedure can be excruciatingly painful if not properly done. A 7–2 majority held in *Baze v. Rees* that Kentucky's method did not constitute cruel and unusual punishment, with Chief Justice Roberts writing that the risks of giving someone the wrong dosage "are not so substantial or imminent as to amount to an Eighth Amendment violation." Justices Ruth Bader Ginsburg and David Souter dissented. Justice John Paul Stevens, who concurred in the judgment, nevertheless expressed his views opposing the death penalty and suggesting that the Court was not finished with the lethal injection issue.

THE CHANGING NATURE OF DUE PROCESS OF LAW

Judge Henry J. Friendly, in a widely cited 1975 law review article, suggested that the due process "explosion" had produced a situation in which Americans felt entitled to "some kind of hearing" before facing any government action.[15] Judge Friendly's thesis drew heavily upon two influential Supreme Court decisions of the early 1970s. In *Goldberg v. Kelly* (1970), a majority held that the Due Process Clause requires that a welfare recipient be given an evidentiary hearing before benefits are terminated, even though welfare procedures provided for a "constitutionally fair proceeding" following termination. The right to "some kind of hearing" was expanded in *Goss v. Lopez* (1975). Justice White's 5–4 majority opinion held that school suspensions of ten days or less "may not be imposed in complete disregard of the Due Process Clause. . . ." Students facing such suspensions are entitled to "effective notice and informal hearing permitting the student to give his version of the events." In both the *Goldberg* and *Goss* decisions, the majority stopped short of requiring formal trial-type hearings complete with appointed counsel.

Beginning in 1976, however, the Court seemingly shifted toward a "balancing test" in ascertaining the necessity of a hearing. In *Matthews v. Eldridge* (1976), Justice Powell's majority opinion denied a hearing for George Eldridge prior to the termination of his Social Security disability benefit payments. Finally, an important step was taken in *Dixon v. Love* (1977) upholding an Illinois statute that authorized the revocation of a driver's license for repeated traffic offenses without a pre-revocation hearing, although a post-hearing was provided.

As the two sets of cases suggest, the Supreme Court's response to the demand for "some kind of hearing" increasingly has tended to balance due process considerations with broader societal and governmental concerns. The "individualist" right to be heard, while an integral principal of American justice, must be viewed alongside broader "communitarian" interests in safety, government efficiency in administration, and school discipline. A few of the more controversial areas are discussed next.

DUE PROCESS FOR JUVENILES

A young person who breaks the law usually is brought before a juvenile court, as opposed to a regular trial court. These juvenile courts were developed late in the nineteenth century "by reformers who were appalled that children were being treated like adult criminals."[16] This reform movement basically held that youthful offenders were in need of guidance rather than punishment, correction rather than imprisonment. As a result, each of the states established a system of juvenile courts to treat the problems of young people. Seemingly, such a system would provide help for troubled young people without turning them into hardened criminals (see Brief 13.8).

In the landmark case of *In re Gault* (1967), the Warren Court addressed the issue of juvenile defendants and guarantees of due process. Gerald Gault, age fifteen, and a friend were picked up by an Arizona county sheriff after receipt of a complaint from a neighbor that the boys had called her on the phone and made lewd or indecent remarks. The boys were taken to a detention home and kept overnight, pending a hearing in juvenile court the next day. No record of the hearing was made, no decision was reached, and Gerald Gault was taken back to the detention home. He was released several days later, along with a note setting the date and time for another hearing. This time, following some questions and answers (again, no record of the testimony was kept), the judge committed Gault to Fort Grant, the state industrial school, for delinquency. Under the terms of the ruling, Gault would remain in detention until the age of majority (twenty-one), "unless sooner discharged by due process of law." In practical terms, Gerald Gault was probably looking at a six-year detention.

After unfavorable rulings through the Arizona courts, the Gaults and their attorney appealed to the U.S. Supreme Court. The appeal contended that the Arizona Juvenile Code was unconstitutional because

Brief 13.8
THE CHANGING JUVENILE JUSTICE SYSTEM

In 2009, law enforcement agencies in the United States arrested an estimated 1.91 million persons younger than age eighteen. While this number appears staggering, it actually represents a 9 percent decline from the previous year and a 17 percent drop since 2000. Nevertheless, the problem of juvenile crime continues to concern observers. Since the mid-1990s, numerous states have begun to emphasize punishment over rehabilitation and prosecuted increasing numbers of juveniles as adults. On January 1, 1996, the state of Texas implemented a significant new law pertaining to its juvenile justice system. The state was attempting to deal with the problem of violent juvenile crimes, an increasing number of which are being committed by younger and younger persons. The act contains a strong emphasis on public safety, protection, and the concept of punishment. Under the law, violent juvenile offenders may be certified to adult court at age fourteen for a capital felony, aggravated controlled substance felony, or any first-degree felony. Certification to an adult court is mandatory if the juvenile has been previously certified and is currently accused of a felony offense.

The law also places accountability on the parents of juvenile offenders and provides for the rights of victims. For example, each parent or guardian is required to attend all juvenile hearings, and the court can order parents to perform community service restitution along with the child. As for victims, all juvenile court proceedings are open to the public, and the victim may not be excluded from the hearing unless appearing as a witness. Victims are given all rights that would be available to victims of adult criminals.

Beyond Texas, some forty-five states have made it easier to prosecute juveniles as adults. Fifteen states now allow prosecutors complete discretion to transfer juveniles into adult courts for certain offenses, and twenty-nine states allow automatic transfer for some types of crimes. Connecticut, at one extreme, treats anyone over age fifteen as an adult, regardless of the crime. While some states allow only children fourteen and older to be prosecuted as adults (seventeen states), twenty-two states and the District of Columbia have no minimum statutory age, and others have set younger minimum ages (age ten in Vermont and Kansas; age twelve in Colorado, Missouri, and Montana). As a result of these changes, an estimated 200,000 juveniles entered the adult criminal justice system, an increase of more than 200 percent since the 1990s.[17]

The debate over treating juveniles as adults appears to be intensifying. Research shows that minors incarcerated in adult facilities are at a very high risk of being assaulted or abused, and they tend to have higher recidivism rates than minors in the juvenile system. Some states have begun to review their policies, but others see the tougher stance toward juveniles as a primary reason for the drop in violent crime across the country.

Despite the movement toward blurring the boundary between juvenile and adult systems, the Supreme Court has recently acted to reinforce the boundary. As noted elsewhere in this chapter, decisions in *Roper v. Simmons* (2005), *Graham v. Florida* (2010), and *Miller v. Alabama* (2012) reinforced the notion that adult punishments (death penalty and life without parole, respectively) are not appropriate for juveniles. The juvenile–adult boundary continues to confound many Americans.

Additional Sources: U.S. Department of Justice, Office of Juvenile Justice and Delinquency Prevention, *Juvenile Arrests 2009*, December 2011; Office of Juvenile Justice and Delinquency Prevention, *Trying Juveniles as Adults: An Analysis of State Transfer Laws and Reporting*, September 2011.

it did not provide juveniles with due process of law under the Fourteenth Amendment. Writing for an 8–1 Court, Justice Abe Fortas noted that the juvenile justice system, although based on "the highest motives and most enlightened impulses," had produced results not entirely satisfactory. The Court took note of the fact that, had Gault been eighteen instead of fifteen, he would have come under the jurisdiction of the criminal court, been subject to a small fine or two months in jail, and, most importantly, been entitled to all the rights and privileges of the U.S. Constitution. "Neither the Fourteenth Amendment nor the Bill of Rights is for adults alone," stated the Fortas opinion.

In the ruling, the majority laid down several specific requirements for juvenile courts. First, the juvenile and his parents have the right to notice of the specific charges and of each scheduled court proceeding. Second, self-incrimination protections must be provided to a juvenile in Gault's situation, despite the fact that juvenile proceedings technically are not "criminal" in nature. When proceedings may lead to imprisonment, the Court said, the privilege against self-incrimination must be respected. Third, when commitment to an institution is possible, "the child and his parents must be notified of the child's right to be represented by counsel retained by them, or if they are unable to afford counsel, that counsel will be appointed to represent the child." Finally, the Court held that the rights to confront and cross-examine witnesses were essential in such a proceeding, ruling that reliance on hearsay evidence was improper. In summary, the *Gault* decision brought certain guarantees of the Due Process Clause of the Fourteenth Amendment to bear on juvenile proceedings.

Mental Patients

In the case of *O'Connor v. Donaldson* (1975), the Supreme Court addressed a situation in which a state mental hospital superintendent, an agent of the state, knowingly confined a mental patient who was not dangerous and who was capable of surviving safely in freedom by himself or with the help of willing family members or friends. Looking at the virtual absence of due process protections for such a confined person, a majority of the Court held that the superintendent had indeed violated the patient's constitutional right to liberty as guaranteed in the Fourteenth Amendment.

The Court did not allege a constitutional right to treatment, but it did hold that patients, nondangerous to others and capable of surviving safely on their own or with the willing help of others, may not be confined arbitrarily. Such confinement violates that patient's constitutional right to liberty.

Sex Offenders

Kansas enacted the Sexually Violent Predator Act in 1994, which defined a sexually violent predator (SVP) as one who (1) has been convicted of or charged with committing a sexually violent act and who (2) has a mental abnormality (i.e., the inability to control one's sexual conduct to the extent that the individual poses a menace to the health and safety of others). The Act provides for the involuntary and indeterminate commitment of any person determined to be a sexually violent predator. If committed, an individual is placed in a mental health facility, not a prison, for treatment. Safeguards for the individual include the State must prove beyond a reasonable doubt that the individual is a sexually violent predator; the individual is entitled to counsel and a mental health examination at the State's expense if indigent; the person is entitled to a jury trial, the right to review State's evidence, and present and cross-examine witnesses; the individual is entitled to annual judicial review at which the State must prove beyond a reasonable doubt that the person is still a SVP; and finally, the individual has a right at any time to petition a court for release.

Leroy Hendricks, an avowed pedophile with a forty-year history of molesting children, both male and female, was convicted in 1984 of indecency with two thirteen-year-old boys. Shortly before his scheduled release in 1994, Kansas sought to commit him under the act. A jury found Hendricks to be a SVP beyond a reasonable doubt, and he was placed in a mental health facility. He appealed his civil commitment to the Supreme Court of Kansas, which struck down the act as a violation of the Due Process Clause. The Kansas court said that a person must be dangerous and mentally ill, not just suffering from a mental abnormality, before involuntary commitment can be justified.

In *Kansas v. Hendricks* (1997), the United States Supreme Court reversed by a 5–4 vote, holding that the Kansas act does not violate the Due Process Clause. The Court majority said that due process considerations are satisfied if the state establishes the individual's dangerousness and mental incapacity, whether an illness or an abnormality. Hendricks's own admission that he cannot control the urge to engage in sex acts with children establishes his future dangerousness and incapacity. The majority also rejected Hendricks's claims that civil commitment constitutes a second punishment and thus violates the Double Jeopardy Clause. Double jeopardy is only implicated when punishment is imposed, and commitment is not punishment (see the discussion on double jeopardy earlier in this chapter). Commitment has only one purpose—to protect society from a narrowly defined category of persons who are sexually dangerous beyond a reasonable doubt. The Court made it easier for states to commit a sexual offender in *Kansas v. Crane* (2002), holding that a state must prove only that the offender has "serious difficulty" controlling his or her behavior.

The United States Congress enacted a law authorizing court-ordered civil commitment by the federal government of "sexually dangerous" federal prisoners near the end of their original sentence as well as "sexually dangerous" persons who are in federal custody because they are mentally incompetent to stand trial. The law was challenged by those who claimed that Congress had exceeded its authority under the Necessary and Proper Clause of the Constitution. A six-person majority along with two concurring opinions strongly held that Congress indeed possesses the powers to enact such legislation. The decision in *United States v. Comstock* (2010) rested on the long-standing congressional involvement in mental health care for federal prisoners and civil commitment.

PROBATIONERS, PAROLEES, AND PRISONERS

In the case of *Morrissey v. Brewer* (1972), the Supreme Court ruled that a person on probation or parole may only be returned to prison after notice and a hearing. At the hearing, the probationer or parolee must be given "a written statement by the factfinders as to the evidence relied on," as well as the reasons for the hearing. Other due process requirements include the disclosure of evidence; the opportunity to be heard; the right to present evidence and witnesses; the right to confront and cross-examine witnesses (although subject to limitation if a good cause is presented); and a neutral hearing body.[18] The following year, in *Gagnon v. Scarpelli* (1973), the Court extended a limited right to counsel in such revocation hearings. While the probationer or parolee is entitled to be represented by counsel, the state is not required to appoint counsel for indigents unless the hearing would not be fair otherwise.

The due process of law moved inside prison gates in the case of *Wolff v. McDonnell* (1974). At issue was the legality of a Nebraska prison's system of disciplinary proceedings for determining whether a prisoner could be deprived of "good time credits" or placed in confinement for serious misconduct. The Court held that proceedings inside prison must be governed by a mutual accommodation between institutional needs and generally applicable constitutional requirements. Specifically, the due process requirements for prison disciplinary hearings, the Court stated, should include advanced written notice of the charges no less than twenty-four hours before the adjustment committee meets; a written statement of the evidence relied on and the reasons for the disciplinary action; and the inmate's right to call witnesses and present documentary evidence in his defense if this will not jeopardize "institutional safety or correctional goals." Significantly, the Court held that the inmate has no constitutional right to confrontation or cross-examination of witnesses in prison disciplinary hearings; furthermore, there is no right to retained or appointed counsel in such hearings, although counsel substitutes should be provided in certain instances.

The Supreme Court further strengthened the powers of correctional officials in the case of *Florence v. Board of the County of Burlington* (2012), when a 5–4 majority held that officials may strip-search any person arrested for any offense before admitting them to jails. The case involved the arrest of Albert Florence who was riding as a passenger in his vehicle when his wife was stopped for speeding. A search of the records showed an outstanding warrant for an unpaid fine by Mr. Florence, although it was later learned that the fine had actually been paid. Mr. Florence was arrested and held for nearly a week in jails in two counties, where he was strip-searched in both jails. In general terms, he was made to stand naked in front of guards and required to move various parts of his body.

Justice Kennedy's majority opinion said, "Correctional officials have a legitimate interest, indeed a responsibility, to ensure that jails are not made less secure by reason of what new detainees may carry in on their bodies." He pointed to several examples in other settings in which inmates were carrying contraband in body cavities. However, Justice Breyer's dissent took issue with the majority, arguing that there was almost no empirical evidence supporting the usefulness of strip searches in detecting contraband.

It is likely that the Supreme Court will be called upon to hear even more due process claims, as the number of persons in jails and state and federal prisons has increased from less than 200,000 in 1970 to nearly 2.3 million people in 2009. The United States 2009 incarceration rate of 743 inmates per 100,000 persons now exceeds that of all other countries. Russia, in second place, imprisons 568 persons per 100,000. Other industrialized nations have much lower rates, including England (151), China (122), France (96), Germany (85), and Japan (58).[19]

Experts point out that the United States does not significantly outpace other countries when it comes to annual prison admissions. American prison policy differs most from other countries in the length of sentences served by those behind bars. And, of course, there is the issue of drugs. More than one-half of all inmates in U.S. federal prisons are serving a sentence for some type of drug offense. These figures demonstrate a conscious American effort to put more criminals behind bars and suggest that the constitutional guarantees of due process will face future challenges from inside our nation's prisons (see Brief 13.9).

Conclusion

Numerous rights of the accused in the Fifth and Sixth Amendments have been found among the "liberties" of the Fourteenth Amendment and applied to the states, although not necessarily in the same way as to the national government. The Sixth Amendment right to a jury trial exemplifies a kind of nonexact "selective incorporation," specifically in matters such as jury size and jury unanimity. Other provisions such as the Fifth Amendment's protection against self-incrimination and the Sixth Amendment's right to counsel have come together to establish a solid core of protection for the person accused of a crime. Decisions such as *Gideon v. Wainwright* (1963) and *Miranda v. Arizona* (1966) have helped to expand constitutional rights to all persons, regardless of whether they can afford or understand them. These rights have become entrenched in our system of law, as evidenced by the Court's finding that the *Miranda* warnings must be considered "constitutional rules," thereby effectively ending the debate over that issue. Overall, the plethora of Supreme Court rulings, doctrines, and holdings dealing with criminal procedure suggests that our nation's emphasis on protecting individual rights while serving society's interests is not an easy task. Individualists and communitarians have argued their respective positions for centuries, and elements of each view remain firmly rooted in our nation's approach to justice.

Brief 13.9

DUE PROCESS AND THE "SUPERMAX" PRISON

"Supermax" prisons are maximum-security facilities with extreme restrictions placed on inmates. Their use has increased in recent years, in part due to the increase in prison gangs and prison violence. The state of Ohio opened its only Supermax facility, the Ohio State Penitentiary (OSP), following a riot in one of its other prisons. Life in the OSP is very difficult. Inmates in the OSP are prohibited any contact with other humans, including a ban on cell-to-cell conversations. Lights must be left on for twenty-four hours, and inmates may exercise for only one hour each day in a small indoor room. But two other conditions have more serious implications: first, placement in the OSP is indefinite and, after an initial thirty-day review, the prisoner is reviewed only annually; second, placement disqualifies an otherwise eligible inmate for parole consideration. Obviously, prisoners have a strong incentive to avoid transfer to the OSP, but are they entitled to due process before being transferred?

In *Wilkinson v. Austin* (2005), a unanimous Supreme Court agreed that inmates do have a "liberty interest" that requires some level of due process protection. The Court reviewed Ohio's "new policy" for transfer to the OSP and found that it provided sufficient protection for inmates. Among other protections, the new policy provides for a three-tier review process after a recommendation that an inmate be placed in the OSP. The inmate must receive notice of the factual basis leading to consideration for the OSP placement and a fair opportunity for rebuttal at a hearing, although he may not call witnesses. In addition, the inmate is invited to submit objections prior to the final level of review. If a single reviewer votes against the OSP placement, the transfer will not take place. Finally, each placement is reviewed thirty days after transfer and annually thereafter. These protections, reasoned the Court, are sufficient to satisfy due process.

Finally, our society's concern with what constitutes "cruel and unusual punishment" has forced Americans to address the monumental issue of taking a human life as punishment for certain serious crimes. The effect has been to require quite exacting procedural requirements before the death penalty may be administered, thereby involving courts in often long appellate actions. Meanwhile, prisons continue to grow more crowded in general, and death row populations expand as well. Like those issues stemming from other provisions in the Bill of Rights, the choices with respect to capital punishment are not easy.

The attacks of September 11 have brought the issue of due process to the forefront of our national agenda. While Americans worry about terrorism and national security, they also know that individual rights and liberties must be preserved. Public opinion polls indicate that growing numbers of Americans are worried about the threat to personal privacy and freedom resulting from the government's war on terrorism, although they also overwhelmingly favor the government's efforts. The indefinite detentions of numerous suspects and material witnesses by federal authorities since September 11, for example, has placed a strain on our national understanding of due process of law, and the likelihood is great that more such controversies will emerge with each new terrorist threat. Americans have faced grave threats to their security in the past, and they likely will face more in the future, but they have thus far managed to strike a workable balance between liberty and security. That is the ongoing struggle that faces citizens and leaders within a constitutional government.

Chapter 14

The First Amendment in a Democratic Society: Political Speech and Other Forms of Expression

In addition to political speech, the First Amendment protects peaceful assembly and protest demonstrations. Pictured here is a group of protesters convening at the State House in Providence, Rhode Island, demonstrating against a bill before the state legislature that would grant marriage rights to same-sex couples.

An Introductory Conversation Between Justices Hugo Black and Felix Frankfurter

Background: During a time in United States constitutional history where citizens and public officials were struggling to develop workable theories of free expression, two justices with contrasting views sat on the Supreme Court. Although both Justices Hugo Black and Felix Frankfurter were appointees of President Franklin Roosevelt and each compiled a distinguished career on the Court (Black, 1937–71; Frankfurter, 1939–62), they held contrasting views of First Amendment rights, which partially reflected the turmoil both on the Court and in American society over these several decades.

Justice Black read the First Amendment guarantee of free speech (and of the press) literally, requiring absolute protection from governmental restraints. Though supportive of some regulation of speech during World War II, he became a judicial activist on the First Amendment, increasingly critical of any government attempting to limit these essential guarantees. Justice Frankfurter was a proponent of judicial self-restraint and an advocate of balancing the all-important rights of society against those of the individual. Frankfurter felt that an absolutist stance on free speech oversimplified very complex issues involving liberty and national security. He believed that judges must frequently balance one provision of the Constitution against another, and in doing so, they should pay particular attention to the preferences of popularly elected majorities that are responsible for enacting the laws of society.

The dialogue between them that follows, often real and disputatious, seems an appropriate way to introduce the contentious constitutional debate over the history and meaning of freedom of expression.

Justice Felix Frankfurter: My dear friend and colleague Hugo, after all of our time together on the Court, I still can't understand how you come to the conclusion that the First Amendment protects all speech from interference or regulation by government.

Justice Hugo Black: It's very simple, Felix my friend. As I said in a concurring opinion in 1959, the First Amendment "provides in simple words that Congress shall make no law . . . abridging freedom of speech or of the press. I read 'no law abridging' to mean no law abridging. The First Amendment, which is the supreme law of the land, has thus fixed its own value on freedom of speech and press by putting these freedoms wholly beyond the reach of federal power to abridge."[1]

FF: I find your position on the First Amendment not only dangerous, but incompatible with what the Constitution says the Court's role in our system should be. Dangerous because there are often times, as I once said in my opinion for the Court in *Minersville School District v. Gobitis* (1940)—an opinion in which you joined—when society legitimately compels us "to do what [it] thinks necessary for the promotion of some great common end," or penalizes individuals "for conduct which appears dangerous to the general good." And for we justices on the Court to strike down laws any time we think they abridge freedom of speech would be to make ourselves a superlegislature for the country. We must exercise judicial self-restraint, and balance the First Amendment guarantees against reasonable regulations undertaken by society to advance the common good.

HB: What is dangerous, Felix, is this idea of "balancing" the values of freedom in the First Amendment against the majority's ideas about the common good. As I said in a dissenting opinion, "I believe that the First Amendment's unequivocal command that there shall be no abridgment of the rights of free speech and assembly shows that the men who drafted our Bill of Rights did all the 'balancing' that was to be done in the field. . . . [T]he very object of adopting the First Amendment, as well as the other provisions of the Bill of Rights, was to put the freedoms protected there completely out of the area of any congressional control that may be attempted through the exercise of precisely those powers that are now being used to 'balance' the Bill of Rights out of existence."[2]

FF: But Hugo, we always are asked to balance principles in the Constitution against laws and cases before us, even against other principles in the Constitution itself. "The Constitution does not give us greater veto power when dealing with one phase of 'liberty' than with another."[3] In fact, as I said in the Minersville opinion, "[t]he ultimate foundation of a free society is the binding tie of cohesive sentiment," and the government must therefore be given leeway to bind its people in ways that some of us might find mildly restrictive of absolute freedom of expression. But it isn't our role to substitute our judgment for that of a legislature or school board.

HB: It's clear that we disagree on this, and luckily for the First Amendment, the majority of the justices have been closer to my position than to yours.

FF: I don't know about this, Hugo, but there is one thing on which I think we agree, and that is when an individual's actions go beyond "pure speech" into the area of conduct or behavior, especially when it involves sensitive areas like the public schools. In the *Tinker* case, which will be discussed in this chapter, you almost sounded like me when you stated that "uncontrolled and uncontrollable liberty is an enemy to domestic peace,"[4] and argued for judicial self-restraint lest the power to control students be "transferred to the Supreme Court."

HB: Yes, my literalism in reading the First Amendment caused me to balk at extending its protections to what other justices have called "symbolic speech" or expression. In these instances, I allowed the government to place reasonable restrictions on the expressive behavior of individuals, as long as this was consistently applied to all individuals.

FF: We have discussed our positions on freedom of speech under the Constitution. Students can read this chapter to see how the Supreme Court has understood First Amendment provisions in the wake of controversy over time.

SOURCES: Steve Suitts, *Hugo Black of Alabama: How His Roots and Early Career Shaped the Great Champion of the Constitution* (Montgomery, AL: New South Books, 2005); Melvin Urosky, *Felix Frankfurter: Judicial Restraint and Individual Liberties* (Boston: Twayne, 1991); *Konigsberg v. State Board of California*, 366 U.S. 36 (1961), at 61; *Minersville School District v. Gobitis,* 310 U.S. 586 (1940); *Smith v. California,* 361 U.S. 147 (1959), at 157; *Tinker v. Des Moines Independent Community School District,* 393 U.S. 503 (1969), at 515.

THE THEORY AND SCOPE OF FIRST AMENDMENT FREEDOMS

Of all the liberties guaranteed by the Bill of Rights, perhaps none are more widely cited and cherished than those of the First Amendment: the freedoms of religion, speech, press, assembly, and petition. For generations, these guarantees have been considered essential to individual freedom and dignity, citizen development, and the practice of enlightened self-government. The ability of individuals to express themselves freely on a wide range of subjects reflects the widespread belief that only through an open and robust public forum—where all are encouraged to consider different ideas, preferences, and values—can democracy be realized. As Justice Louis Brandeis observed long ago, "the freedom to think as you will and to speak as you think are means indispensable to the discovery and spread of political truth."[5]

But as this chapter reflects, a formal Bill of Rights does not always ensure the protection and enjoyment of these rights. James Madison, author of the U.S. Bill of Rights, believed that bills of rights were but "paper parapets" whose provisions ultimately cannot be defended in the absence of engaged citizens. American history holds numerous examples of intolerance toward political, racial, and religious minorities who have been frustrated by the popular majority when they have tried to exercise their First Amendment rights. For majorities of Americans, extending free expression to gays and lesbians, atheists, neo-Nazis, Ku Klux Klansmen, anarchists, or other unpopular minorities is asking too much. This ambivalence about some basic provisions of the Bill of Rights has existed for a long time and reflects the continuing difficulty of applying abstract principles in concrete cases. A recent survey by The First Amendment Center indicates a surprising ignorance of these vital guarantees.[6] For example, although 65 percent of the respondents could specifically name freedom of speech as one of the freedoms guaranteed by the First Amendment, far fewer could specifically identify freedom of religion (28 percent), freedom of the press (13 percent), the right of peaceable assembly (13 percent), and the right to petition (4 percent).

FREEDOM OF EXPRESSION IN HISTORICAL PERSPECTIVE

Because First Amendment freedoms occupy so prominent a position in American constitutional law, one might assume that these "preferred" freedoms have always had central importance in American history.[7] This is definitely not the case. Actually, most litigation relating to First Amendment rights, especially free expression, has occurred over the past several decades. Some very important precedents that still secure freedom of speech and political association emerged during the heated climate of World War I.

Although freedom of expression can be traced to classical times,[8] in both the Greek and Roman empires, it was severely limited by restrictions upon the speaker, content, and place of communication. Such restrictions allowed only a small minority of the population to express itself openly. The Roman Republic emphasized civic responsibility and public order. As a result, freedom of speech was a communal right and responsibility rather than an individual civil liberty. The emphasis was on the social or communitarian aspects of public discourse, rather than the individual's entitlement to free expression, as is stressed today. From these classical times and until the Middle Ages, no Western nation extended freedom of speech to its citizens in any modern sense.

The signing of Magna Carta in 1215 by King John of England was an early recognition of the principle of limited government that took root in Great Britain and eventually in the United States (see Chapter 1). Although freedom of speech was not specifically mentioned in Magna Carta, the word "liberty" appeared several times in the document, and Magna Carta occupies a prominent place in the development of the idea of limited government, personal liberty, and the rule of law.

In the centuries following Magna Carta, freedom of speech in England extended gradually from monarch, to members of Parliament, and eventually to commoners in an evolutionary process that was not completed until nearly 1900.[9] On one level, the adoption of the writ of *habeas corpus* protected persons with unpopular ideas or views from arbitrary arrest and imprisonment. On a second level, freedom of speech was gradually expanded in three distinct phases. Originally only monarchs and members of the high clergy could speak without restraint. Then, with the passage of the English Bill of Rights in 1689, members of Parliament in their official capacity could speak freely (see Brief 1.8). Finally, with the passage of Foxe's Libel Act in 1792, the Reform Bill in 1832, and the full implementation of these laws by the mid-1800s, most efforts to control the written and spoken word had faded. Freedom of speech for English citizens had slowly become a reality.

As noted earlier, freedom of speech in the United States is a relatively recent phenomenon. In his study of free speech in America, Leonard Levy notes:

> THE PERSISTENT IMAGE OF COLONIAL AMERICA AS A SOCIETY IN WHICH FREEDOM OF EXPRESSION WAS CHERISHED IS A HALLUCINATION OF SENTIMENT THAT IGNORES HISTORY. . . . THE AMERICAN PEOPLE SIMPLY DID NOT UNDERSTAND THAT FREEDOM OF THOUGHT AND EXPRESSION MEANS EQUAL FREEDOM FOR THE OTHER FELLOW, ESPECIALLY THE ONE WITH HATED IDEAS.[10]

Intolerance in colonial America was transplanted from England and flourished long after independence from Great Britain. Like the English experience, early American practice found only high government officials and the clergy being able to enjoy freedom of expression. Repression of political and religious thought was very common before the adoption of the Bill of Rights in 1791. Members of the colonial assemblies who enjoyed much freedom made certain that the masses did not have the same privilege. Colonial authorities vigorously suppressed opinions that criticized the church or government. In some of the colonies, most notably Massachusetts, New York, Pennsylvania, and Virginia, the press was limited in what it could print by a colonial licensing system that survived until the 1720s.

The original Constitution, as stated in earlier chapters, included no formal bill of rights. By the time the Constitution had been ratified in 1788, many were insisting upon a national bill of rights. But even in the presence of constitutional protections found in the Bill of Rights, for the next 150 years both the states and the federal government passed laws designed to regulate civil liberties and punish individuals suspected of sedition, blasphemy, defamation of character, or obscenity. In summary, American experience before the early 1900s had a rather dismal record of protecting many of the sacred freedoms that today are taken for granted, especially a constitutional right to free expression.

CONTRASTING VIEWS OF FREEDOM OF EXPRESSION

Saying that most Americans value freedom of expression, at least in the abstract, does not address the question of what the amendment that protects this important freedom actually means. Despite the literal wording of the First Amendment ("Congress shall make no law . . . "), the Supreme Court has never held that the amendment prohibits all regulations of free speech. Some forms of speech are not protected, such as obscene, libelous, lewd, or "fighting-words" remarks, as is discussed here. Throughout the past century, the justices on the Court disagreed greatly about the proper standards to apply to First Amendment claims and what actions by government are legitimate. Much of this disagreement merely reflects the long-standing diversity of opinion on the subject through many generations.

Defenders of free speech today, as might be expected, are indebted to a few champions of independent thought and the right of free expression. Such notables as John Milton, Thomas Jefferson, and John Stuart Mill had an important impact on building this tradition of free discourse in both the written and spoken word. Jefferson's views on freedom of expression are well known, and are discussed more fully in the context of freedom of the press (Chapter 15) and freedom of religion (Chapter 16, particularly Brief 16.1). The discussion here centers on Britons John Milton and John Stuart Mill.

In his *Areopagitica*, written in 1644, Milton argued that restrictions upon an open press were wrong for four reasons:

❏ they were used by tyrants not deserving allegiance or respect;
❏ they inhibited the development of individual character and potential;
❏ they were ultimately ineffective because suppressed ideas will eventually become known; and
❏ they discouraged learning and the search for truth.[11]

The fact that Milton was advancing these justifications for honoring free expression in the early seventeenth century attests to how powerful ideas were emerging in the European Enlightenment. Once unleashed, they would resonate to the present day as critical safeguards for personal freedoms.

In his 1859 essay *On Liberty*, John Stuart Mill authored what many consider to be one of the most eloquent defenses of free speech ever written. If societies were to succeed in their search for moral truth and enlightened self-governance, freedom of expression was necessary for several important reasons. Mill first argued that censored ideas may be true and the majority opinion may be in error. Since human beings are fallible and occasionally prone to follow a false sense of "truth," it is important to consider the worth of all expressions. Second, even though the censored opinion may be wrong in certain respects, it may contain some elements of truth. The prevailing view rarely captures all elements of truth, which can only be achieved through the healthy exchange of differing views. Third, even if it constitutes the entire truth, prevailing opinion must be tested periodically and defended on rational and open grounds in order to avoid prejudice and deceit. Mill went so far as to state, "If all mankind minus one, were of one opinion, and only one person were of the contrary opinion, mankind would be no more justified in silencing that one person, than he, if he had the power, would be justified in silencing mankind." Still, Mill believed that speech could be restricted if it directly infringed upon the personal rights of others.

After World War I, the federal courts began struggling with more controversies involving freedom of expression. During the next few decades, several different views of free speech emerged that influenced how judges would resolve disputes involving governmental authority and personal freedoms. One of the first attempts to document the history of freedom of expression in the United States was authored by Harvard law professor Zechariah Chafee, Jr. Chafee published an important work in 1942, *Free Speech in the United States*, in which he distinguished between expression that serves a personal interest and that which serves a more general social and public interest. Speech that is not intrinsically valuable to a community (i.e., profanity, obscenity, defamation of personal character) can be restricted because it is neither useful to the community nor contributing in any meaningful way to public discourse or decision making. Chafee's work was very useful to what would soon become known as a two-tier system of speech—"worthwhile" and "worthless." However, as subsequent cases and discussion revealed, attempting to distinguish speech on the basis of social utility can be subjective and controversial. One person's useful speech may be another's threat to order and stability.

Another academic whose discussion of freedom of speech closely resembled that of Chafee was Alexander Meiklejohn. In his work *Free Speech and its Relationship to Self-Government*, first published in 1948, Meiklejohn, like Chafee, developed a theory that provided for two types of speech: one absolute and entitled to complete protection, and the other, conditional and subject to regulation by government. Meiklejohn distinguished between public or **political speech**, which discusses political issues and important public topics, and that which consisted of private communications dealing with personal matters. Political speech should be protected absolutely under the First Amendment, according to Meiklejohn. All other speech deserves protection by the Fifth Amendment (from national encroachment) and the Fourteenth Amendment (from state regulation), but it can be regulated if basic due process standards are satisfied. According to Meiklejohn:

> INDIVIDUALS HAVE . . . . A PRIVATE RIGHT OF SPEECH WHICH MAY ON OCCASION BE DENIED OR LIMITED, THOUGH SUCH LIMITATIONS MAY NOT BE IMPOSED UNNECESSARILY OR UNEQUALLY. . . . BUT THIS LIMITED GUARANTEE OF THE FREEDOM OF A MAN'S WISH TO SPEAK IS RADICALLY DIFFERENT IN INTEREST FROM THE UNLIMITED GUARANTEE OF THE FREEDOM OF PUBLIC DISCUSSION, WHICH IS GIVEN BY THE FIRST AMENDMENT. THE LATTER, CORRELATING THE FREEDOM OF SPEECH IN WHICH IT IS INTERESTED WITH THE FREEDOM OF RELIGION, OF PRESS, OF ASSEMBLY, OF PETITION FOR REDRESS OF GRIEVANCES, PLACES ALL THESE ALIKE BEYOND THE REACH OF LEGISLATIVE LIMITATION . . . .[12]

Meiklejohn's **absolutist theory** of political speech was quite controversial for many decades, especially in the context of national security challenges of the 1940s and 1950s. It was instrumental in the thinking and writing of Justice Black, as the introduction indicates, but it was also roundly criticized by many others, including Chafee (a former student of

Meiklejohn) and several writers and legal scholars who supported government regulation of some public speech. According to these critics, this absolutist theory neither reflects accurately the thinking and writings of the framers of the Constitution nor the practical necessities of living in an often dangerous world. The threat international terrorism presents to public safety and organized government is a more recent example of the need for limits to political speech.

One other student of the First Amendment who was prominent in the mid-twentieth century is Thomas I. Emerson. A former Yale law professor, Emerson's theory of free speech first appeared in 1966 and was republished in 1970, under the title, *The System of Freedom of Expression*. Emerson maintained that freedom of expression is essential to a free society. By the late 1960s, when freedom of expression was sharply tested by public protests against the Vietnam War, Emerson advanced what has been termed the **expression-action theory** of First Amendment rights. He argued that freedom of expression includes the right to form and maintain beliefs on any subject and to communicate those beliefs by whatever medium one desires: speech, press, music, art, literature, poetry, and film. Furthermore, freedom of expression includes the right to hear the opinions of others, and the correlative rights to inquire about and gain access to information, and to associate with others. In a manner strongly reminiscent of Milton, Mill, and Meiklejohn, Emerson maintained that freedom of expression is a necessary means of personal self-fulfillment, discovering truth, deciding issues democratically, and achieving a better, more stable community by balancing between "a healthy cleavage and necessary consensus." Referring to what he saw as the "chaotic state of First Amendment theory" in the 1960s, Emerson criticized the Supreme Court for its failure to maintain any clear and consistent rule of law on the subject.[13] He recommended that an important distinction must be drawn between conduct that consists of "expression" and conduct that consists of "action." Whereas the latter might be regulated on rare occasions that threaten public order, the former should be left free to flourish in democratic societies.

The distinction between free expression and action that can be regulated is still unclear. As Judge Learned Hand stated in a case decided during World War I, "words are not only the keys of persuasion, but the triggers of action,"[14] and it is those expressions that fall on the fault line between "persuasion" and "action" that a government might have a need to prevent that raise the most questions for First Amendment jurisprudence. As Supreme Court precedents for nearly a century indicate, trying to protect the fundamental right to freedom of expression has frequently found the justices temporarily suspending it in the face of more immediate public needs. At least part of the reason for these questions over the scope of the First Amendment can be attributed to the sharp differences of opinion that have sometimes existed on the Supreme Court, as our introductory conversation indicates. The discussion now turns to some distinct categories of free speech law that the Court has constructed over the past several decades.

POLITICAL SPEECH AND NATIONAL SECURITY: CONFLICTING STANDARDS OF REGULATION

Governmental restraints upon freedom of speech have existed throughout much of American history. They have occurred most frequently during periods of real or perceived national emergency when the political or economic system seemed more vulnerable. The states and the federal government have historically sought to restrict selected political activities and punish dissenters during four notable periods of American history[15]:

❑ In the 1790s, when Congress passed the Alien and Sedition Acts
❑ Several years prior to, during, and after the Civil War, when both Union and Confederate authorities suppressed free speech and press in many instances
❑ During World War I, with the passage of federal laws severely limiting free expression
❑ After World War II, when Congress and segments of the American public sought to limit and punish political dissenters

Although the first two periods generated several trials and convictions of persons considered to have violated certain federal laws, none of these incidents ever found the Supreme Court ruling on the constitutionality of these government actions on First Amendment grounds. But the latter two periods of increased governmental censorship during the twentieth century presented several opportunities for the Court to create important precedents respecting the limits to government regulation of freedom of expression.

Shortly after the United States declared war against Germany in 1917, Congress passed the Espionage Act. The law made it a federal crime to interfere in any way with the armed forces; to cause insubordination, disloyalty, or mutiny in the military services; or to obstruct recruiting and enlistment efforts. One year later, passage of the Sedition Act in 1918 made it a federal crime to obstruct the sale of government war bonds; to say, print, write, or publish anything intended to cause contempt or scorn for the federal government, the Constitution, the flag, or the uniform of the armed forces; or to say or write anything that interfered with defense production. The patriotic climate then sweeping the country, plus the public hysteria concerning the Russian Revolution of 1917, accelerated passage of similar criminal anarchy laws in approximately two-thirds of the American states by 1925.

Under the Espionage and the Sedition Acts, more than 2,000 Americans were prosecuted for various violations of these two federal laws. Several prominent cases emerged from this litigation (see Table 14.1), a few of which carried special significance. A key question arising in these cases was whether the right of free speech, as granted by the

Table 14.1 Development of the Law—Political Speech and National Security

Year	Case	Significance
1919	Schenck v. U.S.	Upheld the Espionage Act of 1917 against persons convicted of having obstructed draft; Justice Holmes created "clear-and-present danger" test for weighing federal government's right to regulate free speech.
1919	Frohwerk v. U.S.	Again used "clear-and-present danger" test to uphold conviction of defendant who had placed articles in several German-language newspapers that U.S. Government felt might cause disloyalty/insubordination in military services.
1919	Debs v. U.S.	Used "clear-and-present danger" test in upholding conviction of Socialist Eugene Debs for violating Espionage Act (1917) for delivering speech that federal government felt was intended to interfere with recruitment in armed services.
1919	Abrams v. U.S.	First divided Court ruling concerning seditious speech against the federal government; upheld conviction of five Russian immigrants in New York for criticizing federal government for sending troops to Russia in 1918; decision reflects emergence of "bad tendency" test, allowing greater restriction of speech and less freedom for speech.
1920	Schaefer v. U.S.	Conviction of five officers of German-language newspaper for publishing false material intended to enhance German war effort and disrupt recruiting of U.S. armed forces; majority held that articles presented no immediate danger but did have a bad effect; Holmes and Brandeis dissented.
1920	Pierce v. U.S.	Upheld conviction of several defendants who had distributed anti-war pamphlet written by Episcopal priest and published by Socialist Party; seven-member majority held that pamphlet was intended to obstruct war effort, not recruit members to Socialist Party; Holmes and Brandeis dissented, saying that pamphlet contained political opinions and should be protected.
1951	Dennis v. U.S.	Upheld conviction of Dennis and other American Communist Party leaders under the Smith Act (1940), which prohibited violent overthrow of the government, organizing or belonging to any group advocating revolution; "bad tendency" test used to justify restrictions.
1957	Yates v. U.S.	Overturned conviction of Yates and other Communist Party members under the Smith Act (1940); majority distinguished between advocacy of direct action to overthrow government and advocacy of abstract doctrine; former is punishable under the Act, whereas latter is not.

First Amendment, was absolute or open to regulation by Congress. If Congress could regulate such speech, under what circumstances and to what extent? The answers provided by the Court proved very significant, both to the parties involved and to American society at large. It should be noted that all of the cases were decided by the Supreme Court only after World War I had ended in November 1918.

RESTRICTING SPEECH DURING WAR: "A QUESTION OF PROXIMITY AND DEGREE"

In the first of several related cases, Justice Oliver Wendell Holmes, Jr. spoke for a unanimous court in *Schenck v. United States* (1919) and upheld the conviction of Charles T. Schenck for violation of the Espionage Act. As the general secretary of the Socialist party, Schenck had been convicted on three counts of conspiring to obstruct military recruitment and conscription by circulating leaflets urging civil resistance to the draft and using the mail to circulate that material. In upholding Schenck's conviction, Justice Holmes qualified First Amendment protection of free speech by stating that it was not an absolute right:

> WE ADMIT THAT IN MANY PLACES AND IN ORDINARY TIMES THE DEFENDANTS, IN SAYING ALL THAT WAS SAID IN THE CIRCULAR, WOULD HAVE BEEN WITHIN THEIR CONSTITUTIONAL RIGHTS. BUT THE CHARACTER OF EVERY ACT DEPENDS UPON THE CIRCUMSTANCES IN WHICH IT IS DONE. . . . THE MOST STRINGENT PROTECTION OF FREE SPEECH WOULD NOT PROTECT A MAN IN FALSELY SHOUTING FIRE IN A THEATRE, AND CAUSING A PANIC.

According to Holmes, "[t]he question in every case is whether the words used are used in such circumstances and are of such a nature as to create a clear-and-present danger that they will bring about the substantive evils that Congress has a right to prevent." To Holmes, it was "a question of proximity and degree." The defendant's words, printed during wartime and with the intent to persuade men not to enlist in the armed forces, presented an obvious and immediate danger to the successful prosecution of the war. Unfortunately, the **"clear-and-present danger"** test created in *Schenck* would soon be forgotten by the Court as additional claims contesting government restraints on free expression required the justices to reevaluate the preferred compromise between freedom and security.

THE AFTERMATH OF SCHENCK: A NEW STANDARD EMERGES

Following the *Schenck* decision, the justices dealt with several cases involving important free speech rights and the Espionage Act. Two rulings a week after *Schenck* upheld the convictions of two defendants convicted of having criticized the American war effort and the military draft. In both instances, Justice Holmes referred to the "clear-and-present danger" posed by the defendants' actions.[16] Based on his reading of Socialist leader Eugene Debs's political speech and Jacob Frohwerk's published articles in a German newspaper, Holmes emphasized the *tendency* of both actions to obstruct conscription of men then being recruited for the armed forces. The irony here is that Holmes himself had suggested a new test regulating political speech with which he would soon take exception.

Eight months after these decisions, and after considerable reflection by Holmes and Brandeis on the real meaning of "clear-and-present danger," the important case of *Abrams v. United States* (1919) was decided. Rather than using the more stringent "clear-and-present danger" test and over the objections of Justices Holmes and Louis Brandeis, the majority ruled that even actions that might have a less detrimental effect on the country violated the law. *Abrams* involved five Russian immigrants living in the United States. They had been convicted for writing, publishing, and distributing two allegedly seditious pamphlets criticizing the federal government for sending American military personnel to Russia in 1918. One of the pamphlets described President Woodrow Wilson as a coward and a hypocrite, and implied that the real reason for sending the troops was to aid anti-Communist forces then trying to overthrow the Bolshevik regime. The pamphlet also described capitalism as an "enemy of the workers." The trial court convicted the five defendants and sentenced them to twenty-year prison terms.

In a 7 to 2 majority opinion, Justice John H. Clarke stated what was soon to become a rationale for the **bad-tendency doctrine**:

> THE PLAIN PURPOSE OF THEIR PROPAGANDA WAS TO EXCITE, AT THE SUPREME CRISIS OF WAR, DISAFFECTION, SEDITION, RIOTS, AND . . . REVOLUTION IN THIS COUNTRY FOR THE PURPOSE OF EMBARRASSING AND IF POSSIBLE DEFEATING THE MILITARY PLANS OF THE [U.S.] GOVERNMENT IN EUROPE. . . .[17]

In dissent, Justices Holmes and Brandeis thought that the majority had ignored one of the free speech standards in the clear-and-present danger doctrine—"proximity" as well as "degree"—that more properly protected First Amendment rights. For Holmes, only the danger of immediate evil or an intent to bring it about warranted governmental efforts to limit individual expression. Holmes's prominent dissent in *Abrams* did not attract a majority of justices until the late 1930s, when the Court reverted once again to "clear-and-present danger" as a substitute for the more restrictive bad-tendency doctrine.

The final case prosecuted under the Espionage Act, *Pierce v. United States* (1920), concerned an antiwar, anti-conscription pamphlet titled, "The Price We Pay." It had been written by a prominent Episcopal clergyman and was published by the Socialist Party of the United States. Four defendants had been convicted in Albany, New York, on charges that the pamphlet was a deliberate attempt to cause insubordination in the armed forces and thus interfere with the war effort. The defendants alleged that the pamphlet was little more than an attempt to recruit members to the Socialist Party and its philosophy, and thus was protected by the First Amendment.

In the *Pierce* ruling, seven justices, with Holmes and Brandeis again dissenting, upheld the convictions. Justice Mahlon Pitney's majority opinion clearly applied the bad-tendency test when it noted that a jury might reasonably conclude that the pamphlet contained several false statements and "would have a tendency to cause insubordination, disloyalty and refusal of duty in the military and naval forces." Justice Brandeis disagreed with the majority's ruling. He argued that the defendants' remarks involved merely individual opinions and conclusions about public issues, and therefore did not present any clear-and-present danger of causing military insubordination.

The *Pierce* case was the last of the major seditious libel cases prosecuted under the Espionage and Sedition Acts. Although the *Schenck* precedent had generated the clear-and-present danger standard to judge the limits of individual speech, it was soon forgotten in favor of the bad-tendency doctrine that enabled government to intervene earlier and more extensively in the speech process.

THE EARLY COLD WAR AND NATIONAL SECURITY CONCERNS: HOW SERIOUS IS THE THREAT?

During World War I and its aftermath, civil liberties were very much under siege, and few organizations were willing to risk alienating federal and state authorities (see Brief 14.1 for an important exception). Following World War II, the Supreme Court tried to strike a balance between individual freedom and national security during a time when new threats to national security were apparent.

Over a span of nearly two decades, the Court considered several cases involving federal laws restricting free speech and political association. However, just as it had made clear in several rulings following World War I, the Court emphasized that the right of political association can be curtailed in times of national peril.

Immediately following World War II, a new threat arose that posed both a military and ideological challenge to democratic governments everywhere: Communism. Congress passed four major federal laws during and after World War II to deal with the threat of subversion by Communist organizations in the United States: the Alien Registration Act (known as the Smith Act), the Taft-Hartley Amendments to the National Labor Relations Act, the Internal Security Act (known as the McCarran Act), and the Communist Control Act.

The Smith Act (1940) made it illegal to advocate the violent overthrow of government or to organize or to belong to any group advocating such revolutionary activity. It also forbade the publication or distribution of any materials advocating or teaching the overthrow of government by force. Also in language directly limiting freedom of political

Brief 14.1

THE AMERICAN CIVIL LIBERTIES UNION

Americans have always been preoccupied with freedom. The principles of liberty, equality, individualism, democracy, and constitutionalism compose basic tenets of what some have called "American exceptionalism." Since its creation in 1920 by Roger Baldwin, the American Civil Liberties Union (ACLU) has epitomized the struggle to ensure that these principles are not merely promised in theory but rigorously enforced and protected in practice. Although many other organizations have also contributed to the protection of civil rights and liberties, the ACLU has few rivals in the field. As the nation's oldest and largest public-interest organization devoted to protecting civil liberties, the ACLU works in three major areas of the law: First Amendment freedoms (particularly speech and religion), due process, and equality before the law.

Since its inception, the ACLU has fought tens of thousands of cases in state and federal courts. It was instrumental in influencing many landmark Supreme Court decisions—*Mapp v. Ohio, Gideon v. Wainwright, Miranda v. Arizona, Tinker v. Des Moines Independent School District*—and it typically submits important "friend of the court" briefs defending basic civil liberties. Nationwide, the primary work of the organization is done by a national office located in New York and a large legislative office in Washington, D.C. It also maintains local chapters in all fifty states, where normally 80 percent of the organization's workload is managed. Referred to by some as "the nation's largest law firm," the ACLU appears before the Supreme Court more often than most other organizations. Around one hundred staff attorneys work with some two thousand volunteer, "cooperating attorneys," who provide the backbone of the ACLU's litigation.

Membership in the ACLU has fluctuated over the past several decades, in part because of debates over the causes that the ACLU defends. When the organization decided in 1977 to represent members of the National Socialist Party who had been denied a permit to march in Nazi uniforms in Skokie, Illinois, home to many Jewish concentration camp survivors, the organization lost more than 60,000 members who protested its involvement in that case. But today, the ACLU lists over 500,000 members nationally, and participates in nearly 6,000 cases each year.

The ACLU has been involved in most speech and religion controversies argued before the Supreme Court over the past few decades. It also has played a prominent role in some specialized activities, such as the National Prison Project, which monitors prison conditions to ensure that prisoner rights are not violated, and the Reproductive Freedom Project, a pro-choice group dedicated to protecting reproductive rights for women. Another of its more prominent activities is the Women's Rights Project, which has been active since the 1970s, and in which Ruth Bader Ginsburg, now associate justice on the Supreme Court, was active from 1973 until 1980, when she argued six gender-discrimination cases before the Supreme Court. (For contrasting views of this controversial public interest organization, see Samuel Walker, *In Defense of American Liberties: A History of the ACLU* [New York: Oxford University Press, 1990]; and William A. Donohue, *The Politics of the American Civil Liberties Union* [New Brunswick, NJ: Transaction Books, 1985].)

---

association, the law made it illegal to organize any group committed to teaching, advocating, or encouraging the overthrow or destruction of government by force.

Growing concern in Congress during the 1940s over Communist infiltration of the American labor movement and the fear of "political strikes" against key elements of American industry spurred passage of the Taft-Hartley Act in 1947. A key component of this legislation was a provision requiring officers of all labor organizations in the United States to sign sworn statements (affidavits) verifying that they were not members of or affiliated with the Communist party in any way, nor did they believe in or hold membership in any organization that advocated violent overthrow of the federal government. Any union official refusing to sign such an affidavit was denied all protections afforded under the National Labor Relations Act, which was the primary collective bargaining statute affecting organized labor. By 1950, the Supreme Court had upheld these affidavit provisions of the Taft-Hartley Act.[18]

Fearing that the Smith Act did not provide enough protection against the domestic Communist movement, Congress passed the McCarran Act in 1950 over President Truman's veto. This particular law required all Communist-action or Communist-front organizations to register with the Justice Department and to disclose their membership lists. It further penalized members of such groups by prohibiting them from holding any government- or defense-related position of employment. Somewhat naively, sponsors of the law assumed that subversive organizations would obey the law and register with the federal government. Title I of the McCarran Act established a five-member Subversive Activities Control Board (SACB) appointed by the president. The mission of the board was to determine, subject to judicial review, whether a particular organization was affiliated with the Communist party in any way. Once labeled as a subversive organization, the group had to turn over its membership lists to the federal government, and any federal employees of such an organization could lose their government employment. The ineffectiveness of the law is demonstrated by the fact that never during the next fifteen years did the Communist party ever register with the SACB as a subversive organization. By the mid-1960s, the SACB and the law passed into obscurity.

The last major statute passed by Congress in the 1950s to limit speech and association of Communist party sympathizers was the Communist Control Act of 1954. This statute branded the Communist party as a treasonable conspiracy against the United States government. As such, the party had none of the rights and privileges of political parties in the United States. The act went farther than any of the preceding federal laws in denying constitutional rights to members of certain political organizations. With these several laws in force and much of the country harboring considerable political paranoia over possible Communist conspiracies, the Supreme Court found itself once again ruling on the constitutionality of a federal law that had important implications for political speech and freedom of association.

Dennis v. United States (1951)

In 1948, with Congress and the American public growing increasingly alarmed about the threat of an international Communist conspiracy, the federal government indicted Eugene Dennis, secretary general of the Communist Party of the United States, and ten other top-level members of the central committee of the party. After a six-month trial, the defendants were convicted for violating Section 2 of the Smith Act, which punished speech advocating the overthrow of government by force, and Section 3, which prohibited any person from conspiring to organize any group advocating the forceful overthrow of government. Their conviction was upheld by a federal appellate court, which asserted that sufficient evidence had been presented during the trial to demonstrate that the defendants had conspired to overthrow the government by force. In the appellate ruling, Chief Judge Learned Hand dramatically revised the clear-and-present danger test, when he declared: "In each case [courts] must ask whether the gravity of the 'evil,' *discounted by its improbability*, justifies such invasion of free speech as is necessary to avoid the danger" (emphasis added).

Dennis and his fellow defendants appealed their conviction to the Supreme Court on the grounds that the Smith Act violated the First and Fifth Amendments to the Constitution. On a vote of 6 to 2, the Supreme Court in *Dennis v. United States* (1951) upheld the convictions. Most of the opinions for a divided Court reflected very different assessments of how serious a threat the Communist party posed to the nation. In writing for the majority, Chief Justice Fred Vinson insisted that the government must decide what the words "clear-and-present danger" actually meant as guidelines for congressional action:

> IF GOVERNMENT IS AWARE THAT A GROUP AIMING AT ITS OVERTHROW IS ATTEMPTING TO INDOCTRINATE ITS MEMBERS AND TO COMMIT THEM TO A COURSE WHEREBY THEY WILL STRIKE WHEN THE LEADERS FEEL THE CIRCUMSTANCES PERMIT, ACTION BY THE GOVERNMENT IS REQUIRED. . . . CERTAINLY AN ATTEMPT TO OVERTHROW THE GOVERNMENT BY FORCE, EVEN THOUGH DOOMED FROM THE OUTSET BECAUSE OF INADEQUATE NUMBERS OR POWER OF THE REVOLUTIONISTS, IS A SUFFICIENT EVIL FOR CONGRESS TO PREVENT.

Vinson argued that since the Communist party was dedicated to the overthrow of the government, a more stringent rule for protecting government was necessary. His remedy was to adopt the device used by Judge Learned Hand and quoted earlier about the "gravity of the 'evil' discounted by its improbability." The Vinson opinion thus gave symbolic support to "clear-and-present danger" but actually used the "bad-tendency" test for regulating the First Amendment rights of these defendants. Concurring opinions by Justices Felix Frankfurter and Robert Jackson strongly endorsed the view that a Communist conspiracy existed and that the federal government was justified in prosecuting these persons under the Smith Act.

The two dissenters in *Dennis*, Justices Black and Douglas, insisted that the government had no right to punish political speech and association in this instance. Allowing Congress to "water down" the First Amendment by regulating free speech and political association as it did here was wrong, according to Justice Black. His dissent left little doubt about why the First Amendment was being ignored by the Court in this instance:

> PUBLIC OPINION BEING WHAT IT NOW IS, FEW WILL PROTEST THE CONVICTION OF THESE COMMUNIST PETITIONERS. THERE IS HOPE, HOWEVER, THAT IN CALMER TIMES, WHEN PRESENT PRESSURES, PASSIONS AND FEARS SUBSIDE, THIS OR SOME LATER COURT WILL RESTORE THE FIRST AMENDMENT LIBERTIES TO THE HIGH PREFERRED PLACE WHERE THEY BELONG IN A FREE SOCIETY.

Within a few years, Black's view would be vindicated.

YATES V. UNITED STATES (1957)

Six years after *Dennis*, in the case of *Yates v. United States* (1957), the Court overturned the conviction of fourteen more subordinate members of the Communist party by distinguishing between abstract doctrine and action taken to overthrow the government. Oleta Yates and thirteen other members of the Communist party in California had been convicted in federal court of conspiring to violate the Smith Act by advocating the forcible overthrow of the federal government. By a 6 to 1 vote, the Supreme Court overturned the convictions of these defendants and in so doing, made a major shift in interpreting how the Smith Act was to be interpreted and applied.

The key issue addressed in a majority opinion written by Justice John Harlan was that the trial judge had not properly distinguished between advocacy of an *abstract doctrine*, a protected activity under the First Amendment, and actual incitement of illegal *action*, a prosecutable offense under the Smith Act.

> WE RECOGNIZE THAT DISTINCTIONS BETWEEN ADVOCACY AND TEACHING OF ABSTRACT DOCTRINES WITH EVIL INTENT, AND THAT WHICH IS DIRECTED TO STIRRING PEOPLE TO ACTION, ARE OFTEN SUBTLE AND DIFFICULT TO GRASP, FOR IN A BROAD SENSE, AS MR. JUSTICE HOLMES SAID IN HIS DISSENTING OPINION IN GITLOW, "EVERY IDEA IS AN INCITEMENT . . .". BUT THE VERY SUBTLETY OF THESE DISTINCTIONS REQUIRED THE MOST CLEAR AND EXPLICIT INSTRUCTIONS WITH REFERENCE TO THEM.

Harlan's distinction here between abstract doctrine and direct action reflected a new majority moving away from much of the *Dennis* precedent, and closer to the "clear-and-present danger" test in earlier decades. As they had in the *Dennis* case, Justices Black and Douglas urged that all of the charges against the defendants should have been dropped. According to Justice Black, the Smith Act provisions on which the charges had been based "abridge freedom of speech, press and assembly in violation of the First Amendment."

Although the Court in *Yates v. United States* did not declare the Smith Act unconstitutional, as Justices Black and Douglas had urged it to do, the majority's holding that future prosecutions by the federal government would have to prove that the accused advocated illegal conduct was an important change. Absent such a finding, *Yates* established that it would be very difficult to prosecute Communist Party members unless "their actions spoke far louder than their words." A few cases in the early 1960s found members of the Communist party still being prosecuted and occasionally convicted under rather narrow readings of Smith Act provisions or the McCarran Act.[19] The registration provisions of the McCarran Act were finally repealed in 1968 and the Subversive Activities Control Board was never reauthorized thereafter by Congress.

POLITICAL SPEECH, THE STATES, AND INTERNAL SECURITY

Throughout much of American history, many states have felt their internal security threatened by radical political forces and, like the federal government, they have on occasion felt compelled to limit First Amendment freedoms. In the twentieth century, the model for many of these state sedition laws was a 1902 New York law that prohibited advocacy of criminal anarchy by speech and the printing and distribution of any materials advocating or teaching the violent overthrow of government. Following the Russian

Revolution in 1917 and World War I, some thirty-three states enacted peacetime **criminal syndicalism** laws, which made it illegal to advocate, teach, or assist in the violent overthrow of the political or economic systems.

For a brief period following World War I, the Supreme Court upheld these state sedition laws in a few notable cases, but by the late 1930s, a different blend of justices on the Court began to invalidate them on grounds that they were either overly broad or that the defendants posed no imminent danger to organized government (see Table 14.2). Two cases over the decades warrant extended mention here.

MODERNIZATION OF THE BILL OF RIGHTS BEGINS: GITLOW V. NEW YORK (1925)

The first of several state sedition laws to be tested in court was New York's criminal anarchy law. Benjamin Gitlow, a radicalized member of the Socialist Party of the United States, had been convicted in state court for printing and distributing pamphlets that urged realization of the "Communist Revolution" based on "the class struggle," and that called for the staging of mass political strikes and destruction of the parliamentary state. Gitlow appealed to the U.S. Supreme Court, arguing that the state law unconstitutionally restricted his right of free speech. Implicit in Gitlow's appeal was an important assertion—that certain rights guaranteed by the First Amendment against infringement by Congress are also applicable to the states by virtue of the Fourteenth Amendment Due Process Clause.

Writing for a seven-member majority, Justice Edward Sanford upheld Gitlow's conviction in a majority opinion, which argued that the pamphlet had urged the staging of mass strikes in order to foment industrial strife and revolutionary action aimed at the overthrow of organized government. Regardless of how remote the likelihood of disruption and revolution were, Sanford insisted that the state had every right to intervene:

> THE STATE CANNOT REASONABLY BE REQUIRED TO MEASURE THE DANGER FROM EVERY UTTERANCE IN THE NICE BALANCE OF A JEWELER'S SCALE. A SINGLE REVOLUTIONARY SPARK MAY KINDLE A FIRE THAT, SMOLDERING FOR A TIME, MAY BURST INTO A SWEEPING AND DESTRUCTIVE CONFLAGRATION. [THE STATE] MAY, IN THE EXERCISE OF ITS JUDGMENT, SUPPRESS THE THREATENED CHANGES IN ITS INCIPIENCY.

Table 14.2 Development of the Law— Political Speech, the States, and Internal Security

Year	Case	Significance
1925	*Gitlow v. N.Y.*	Six-member majority upheld conviction of Socialist Party member, for his role in distributing "Left Wing Manifesto" calling for overthrow of government by force, in violation of state criminal anarchy act; decision incorporated *speech* and *press* rights in the First Amendment into 14th Due Process Clause.
1927	*Whitney v. Calif.*	Unanimous court upheld conviction of member of Communist Labor Party, for belonging to organization that advocated violent overthrow of government, which was prohibited by state criminal anarchy law; ruling often remembered for Justice Brandeis's eloquent defense of First Amendment values of expression.
1927	*Fiske v. Kansas*	Decided same day as *Whitney*, Court for first time reversed conviction for violating state criminal syndicalism law; defendant was an organizer for International Workers of the World; justices ruled that no evidence existed that proved IWW advocated violent or criminal actions.
1937	*Herndon v. Lowry*	Defendant convicted of violating Georgia law making it unlawful to attempt to persuade others to participate in any insurrection against organized government; divided Court overturned conviction; Court abandoned "bad tendency" test, moved closer to reinstating "clear-and-present danger" doctrine.
1969	*Brandenburg v. Ohio*	Majority overturned conviction of Ohio leader of Ku Klux Klan; in response to several new state criminal syndicalism laws in the 1960s, Court established the "incitement" standard, which distinguishes between advocating use of force as abstract doctrine (protected by First Amendment) and actual incitement to use force (unprotected); decision also overturned *Whitney* (1927).

Because of the majority's implicit recognition of a more restrictive standard protecting freedom of speech, Justices Holmes and Brandeis dissented in the ruling.

Notwithstanding Gitlow's conviction being upheld, the most important aspect of the ruling was the majority's recognition that "freedom of speech and of the press—which are protected by the First Amendment from abridgment by Congress—are among the fundamental personal rights . . . protected by the due process clause of the Fourteenth Amendment from impairment by the states . . . ". This was a truly momentous development that launched the so-called nationalization process of the Bill of Rights. But in spite of this important recognition of the sanctity of speech and press guarantees, the next couple of decades were not always kind to voices of political dissent (see Brief 14.2). Increasingly, in the decade following *Gitlow*, the Supreme Court viewed itself primarily as an economic policymaker, rather than a protector of civil liberties. Following the Supreme Court Revolution of 1937, however, the Court more consistently began to support First Amendment guarantees.

Over the next three decades, as the nation mellowed somewhat in its views toward political dissent and the Supreme Court allowed more freedom to debate differing philosophies, state concerns about internal security began to subside. But many of these criminal syndicalism laws remained on the statute books into the 1960s when many states used such legislation to regulate growing public debate over the civil rights movement and the Vietnam War. An important case in the late 1960s established a new standard concerning freedom of expression.

A NEW STANDARD: BRANDENBURG V. OHIO (1969)

The case of *Brandenburg v. Ohio* (1969) involved a leader of the Ohio Ku Klux Klan, Clarence Brandenburg, who had spoken at a public rally in the state. A short speech by Brandenburg was carried on a local television broadcast in which he stated, "[If] our President, our Congress, our Supreme Court, continues to suppress the white, Caucasian race, it's possible that there might have to be some revengence [sic] taken." For that statement, and on the basis of other evidence introduced at his trial, Brandenburg was tried and convicted of having violated Ohio's Criminal Syndicalism Act, which made it illegal to advocate the use of violence or terrorism to accomplish industrial or political reform. Brandenburg appealed his conviction to the U.S. Supreme Court.

A unanimous Supreme Court overruled Brandenburg's conviction, and in the process, established a new standard for safeguarding freedom of speech. In a *per curiam* opinion the Court emphasized that

> THE CONSTITUTIONAL GUARANTEE OF FREE SPEECH AND FREE PRESS DO NOT PERMIT A STATE TO FORBID OR PROSCRIBE ADVOCACY OF THE USE OF FORCE OR OF LAW VIOLATION EXCEPT WHERE SUCH ADVOCACY IS DIRECTED TO INCITING OR PRODUCING IMMINENT LAWLESS ACTION AND IS LIKELY TO INCITE OR PRODUCE SUCH ACTION. . . . MEASURED BY THIS TEST, OHIO'S CRIMINAL SYNDICALISM ACT CANNOT BE SUSTAINED.

THE TRIAL AND EXECUTION OF SACCO AND VANZETTI

The famous murder trial in the 1920s of two Italian immigrants reflected the political, economic, and social biases afflicting much of American society. Nicola Sacco and Bartolomeo Vanzetti were arrested on May 5, 1920, for the murder of two persons in South Braintree, Massachusetts. Known for their leftist political views and prominent in socialist political causes at the time, Sacco and Vanzetti were convicted on July 14, 1921, in a judicial proceeding that by most accounts was badly conducted and politically biased. In addition to prejudicial statements made privately by the presiding judge, no procedural concessions were made to the defense, and the climate of the entire trial reflected anti-immigrant feelings and hostility toward political agitators. From the time of their conviction in 1921 until August 23, 1927, when they were both executed, Sacco and Vanzetti became symbols of oppressed immigrants denied fairness in the American criminal justice system. To the present day, the Sacco-Vanzetti case represents to many the travesty of how minority political views can convict those who hold them in a distorted court proceeding because of deep bias and prejudice on the part of judge and jury who are quick to twist the evidence presented in the courtroom.

With the *Brandenburg* ruling, the Court went beyond previous uses of the "clear-and-present danger" test and established an **incitement standard**. This new doctrine meant that government had to prove that the danger presented in provocative speech was real, not imagined, and that it was directed toward inciting or producing *immediate* illegal activity. In effect, the Court assumed responsibility for judging intent and deciding if the speaker were likely to incite immediate hostile action against government, rather than simply trying to impress his audience. In the *Brandenburg* case, the Court apparently thought that the defendant did not pose a serious threat of imminent hostile action that the state was entitled to repress. In retrospect, the Court had entered a new era with a higher standard with which to protect political speech in civil society.

Other Political Expression Issues Before the Supreme Court

Thus far, the concept of free speech has only dealt with pure political speech—oral statements that are intended to communicate a particular political message (i.e., stop the war, resist the draft, or overthrow the government). However, when certain nonverbal forms of expression are also designed to convey a particular message or idea, different questions and standards are implicated.

Are Political Symbols Included in the Meaning of "Speech"?

Symbolic speech, the expression of ideas and beliefs through symbols rather than words, has generally been thought to be protected by the First Amendment. Because the variations on symbolic speech are as abundant as the ingenuity of the "speaker" and the audience, efforts to develop a coherent and comprehensive philosophy reflecting a definitive constitutional standard have been somewhat disappointing over the decades. Many Supreme Court cases have emerged over several decades that again have found the justices struggling with the difficult task of balancing competing interests in a free society (see Table 14.3).

The Supreme Court first dealt with symbolic speech in *Stromberg v. California* (1931), where it invalidated a state law that made it a crime to use certain symbols to demonstrate opposition to organized government. This case reflected the public's aversion to socialist ideas and teachings that existed during the 1930s. Yetta Stromberg, a member of the Youth Communist League in California, had led a group of league members in saluting a Russian flag. Recognizing the communicative element of a flag as a political symbol, the state law made it a felony to "display a red flag and banner in a public place and in a meeting place as a sign, symbol and emblem of opposition to organized government." In its first mention of the **vagueness doctrine** against legislation considered too restrictive because it limited both protected and unprotected speech, the Court held that the California law unconstitutionally infringed upon free expression. The majority opinion maintained that displaying any banner or symbol that advocated a change in government through even peaceful means conceivably could be penalized under the California law. Writing for the majority, Chief Justice Charles Evans Hughes said that ". . . a statute which upon its face . . . is so vague and indefinite as to permit the punishment of the fair use of this opportunity [of free political discussion] is repugnant to the guarantee of liberty contained in the Fourteenth Amendment."[20]

Although they are usually discussed in the context of religious freedom, the Flag Salute Cases of the early 1940s (discussed more fully in Brief 16.2 in Chapter 16) relate to political symbolism and free speech. The relevance of these cases to this discussion of symbolic expression is reflected in the majority opinion of Justice Robert Jackson in *West Virginia State Board of Education v. Barnette* (1943) striking down the law:

> THERE IS NO DOUBT THAT IN CONNECTION WITH THE PLEDGES, THE FLAG SALUTE IS A FORM OF UTTERANCE. SYMBOLISM IS A PRIMITIVE BUT EFFECTIVE WAY OF COMMUNICATING IDEAS. THE USE OF AN EMBLEM OR FLAG TO SYMBOLIZE SOME SYSTEM, IDEA, INSTITUTION, OR PERSONALITY, IS A SHORT CUT FROM MIND TO MIND. . . . SYMBOLS OF STATE OFTEN CONVEY POLITICAL IDEAS JUST AS RELIGIOUS SYMBOLS COME TO CONVEY THEOLOGICAL ONES.[21]

Table 14.3 Development of the Law—Symbolic Expression as Protected Speech

Year	Case	Significance
1931	*Stromberg v. Calif.*	Court for first time acknowledged that symbolic speech may receive First Amendment protection; Calif. law had outlawed raising a red flag as a protest against organized government; Court declared the law void for vagueness of regulation.
1943	*W. Va. State Bd. of Educ. v. Barnette*	Six-member majority struck down state law compelling schoolchildren to salute daily the American flag; reaffirmed that a person may not be coerced to participate in any symbolic activity; specifically overruled *Minersville v. Gobitis* (1940).
1961	*Garner v. Louisiana*	Dealt with student sit-ins at segregated lunch counters; Court held that nonviolent silent protest of segregated public accommodation is part of "free trade in ideas" and is protected by First Amendment.
1968	*U.S. v. O'Brien*	Seven-member majority upheld conviction of defendant for burning his draft card as symbolic protest against Vietnam War and the draft; Congress had substantial interest in maintaining draft registration system.
1969	*Tinker v. Des Moines School District*	Court ruled that school officials improperly suspended students for wearing black armbands in symbolic protest against Vietnam War; noted that the "undifferentiated fear . . . of disturbance is not enough to overcome the right to freedom of expression."
1969	*Street v. New York*	Five-justice majority overturned conviction of person who verbally protested and burned American flag, thereby violating state law that was overly broad because it punished words that were protected by First/Fourteenth Amendment.
1971	*Cohen v. California*	Landmark ruling held that defendant's wearing a jacket, on the back of which appeared "Fuck the Draft," was entitled to First Amendment protection; expression was neither aimed at any particular individual nor intended to create civil disturbance.
1974	*Smith v. Goguen*	Court overturned conviction of Massachusetts defendant who wore a small American flag on seat of his trousers, in violation of state ban against contemptuous treatment of the flag; Court held that statute was unconstitutionally vague because it failed to distinguish between " . . . the kinds of non-ceremonial treatment . . . that are criminal and those that are not."
1974	*Spence v. Washington*	Six-member majority held that First Amendment protected student who had displayed American flag upside down from apartment window, with a superimposed peace symbol on the flag, in protest of U.S. invasion of Cambodia and Kent State shootings in 1970; Court declared that state law was unconstitutional because it regulated the content of symbolic speech.
1989	*Texas v. Johnson*	Closely divided Court overturned Texas law prohibiting flag desecration, which had been used to convict defendant for burning American flag at Republican National Convention in 1984 in Dallas; soon led to passage of Federal Flag Protection Act (1989).
1990	*U.S. v. Eichmann*	Court declared the Federal Flag Protection Act unconstitutional; decision prompted many to call for constitutional amendment banning flag-burning.
2007	*Morse v. Frederick*	Court upheld a public school's punishment of a student for holding up a banner with the words "Bong Hits 4 Jesus" across the street from the school; justices ruled that students in public schools do not have the same level of constitutional protection as adults, and since the expression—as part of a school-sanctioned event—could be construed as promoting drug use, the school had the power to restrict it.

According to Justice Jackson, the compulsory flag salute and pledge required affirmation of a belief and attitude that infringed upon the First Amendment. He closed with an impassioned plea to recognize the negative consequences of trying to effect the "compulsory unification of opinion." Given the fact that it came during wartime amid frequent displays of patriotism, the *Barnette* decision still stands as a remarkable testament to the need for toleration of political and religious difference in a free society.

SYMBOLIC PROTEST AGAINST FEDERAL POLICIES

As the following cases indicate, although the First Amendment protects some instances of symbolic speech, that protection is qualified. The period in question here is the late 1960s and the American public's growing disenchantment with the Vietnam War. The conflict generated several cases concerning symbolic speech, especially among draft-age men.

One case involved David Paul O'Brien, who burned his Selective Service registration card in March 1966 on the steps of a Boston courthouse as a symbolic protest against the draft and the Vietnam War. Following the protest, O'Brien was convicted of having violated a 1965 federal law making it unlawful to alter, forge, knowingly destroy, or mutilate a draft card. A federal appellate court reversed the conviction on First Amendment grounds, accepting O'Brien's claim that the Constitution protected such symbolic expression. The federal government appealed the ruling to the Supreme Court and in 1968, in a 7–1 opinion in *United States v. O'Brien*, the justices reversed the appellate ruling and upheld O'Brien's conviction. The majority opinion authored by Chief Justice Earl Warren stated that a governmental regulation limiting speech was justified if it were (1) within the constitutional power of the government, (2) furthered an important or substantial governmental interest, (3) were unrelated to the suppression of free expression; and (4) was an incidental restriction on a First Amendment freedom that was no greater than was essential to the furtherance of that governmental interest. According to the Court, the 1965 Amendment to the Universal Military Training and Service Act met all of these requirements.

Tinker v. Des Moines Independent Community School District (1969) was another case in which symbolic speech was used to protest United States involvement in the Vietnam War. In *Tinker*, the Supreme Court reviewed a suit brought by three high school students who had been suspended from their Iowa public high school for violating a local school ban on wearing armbands as a symbol of protest against the war. The suspended students argued in court that the First Amendment protected their right to protest against the war. In a 7 to 2 decision, with only Justices Black and Harlan dissenting, the Supreme Court upheld the students' alleged right of symbolic expression as protected by the First Amendment.

Writing for the majority, Justice Abe Fortas stressed that for more than half a century, First Amendment rights had been available to teachers and students in public schools. According to Fortas, "It can hardly be argued that either students or teachers shed their constitutional rights to freedom of speech or expression at the schoolhouse gate." The fact that the school officials had sought to suspend the students for their silent and passive expression of opinion was contrary to constitutional protections afforded by the First Amendment. The majority struck down the Des Moines school regulation and upheld the students' rights in this important symbolic expression case.

In these cases involving symbolic speech, two points should be emphasized. First, although some nonverbal communication is protected under the First Amendment, the Court has never said that symbolic speech is entitled to exactly the same degree of protection as verbal communication. Pure speech becomes more susceptible to regulation as it seeks to include particular *conduct*. Second, in incidents involving what is usually referred to as "speech-plus"—actions that combine verbal speech mixed with conduct as a form of protest— "pure" speech has received more protection under the First Amendment than has "speech plus" conduct, the latter of which usually seeks to dramatize the intensity of one's feelings and protest. The best example of this is *O'Brien*, where the Warren Court maintained that the government had a justifiable interest in preventing the destruction of draft cards.

In the late 1960s and early 1970s, some other symbolic speech cases dealt with issues such as desecration of the American flag. In one of the last symbolic protest cases dealt with by the Warren Court, a sharply divided Court in *Street v. New York* (1969) overturned the conviction of a New York protestor who had both burned an American flag and uttered derogatory remarks about it. A five-member majority said that the state law under which he was convicted was overly broad in its punishment of verbal speech.[22]

In the late 1980s, the Supreme Court returned to the issue of whether flag-burning *per se* was protected under the First Amendment. Previous rulings by the justices had not directly addressed this question. When they did in 1989, a sharply divided Court ruled against government restrictions on flag-burning and in so doing, unleashed sustained public criticisms of the justices' interfering with legislation passed by democratic majorities.

The first of these controversial rulings involved a flag-burning incident that took place during a political protest in 1984 at the Republican National Convention in Dallas. Demonstrators protesting the policies of the Reagan administration and certain Dallas-based corporations marched through the city and participated in a rally in front of Dallas City Hall. Gregory Lee Johnson, a member of the Revolutionary Socialist party, doused an American flag with kerosene and set it on fire, while protesters chanted, "America, the red, white, and blue, we spit on you." No one was physically injured or threatened with injury, although several bystanders said they were deeply offended by Johnson's action. Johnson was convicted of a misdemeanor for intentionally desecrating a venerated object (defined by the law to include "a national or state flag"), sentenced to one year in prison, and fined $2,000. After his conviction was reversed by the Texas Court of Criminal Appeals on the ground that flag-burning was symbolic expression protected by the First Amendment, the state appealed the ruling to the Supreme Court in *Texas* v. *Johnson* (1989).

Justice Brennan wrote for a five-justice majority that argued that Johnson's act of burning the flag was clearly expressive conduct protected under the First Amendment, occurring as it did as part of a political demonstration. The question then was whether Texas had an interest compelling enough to justify restricting Johnson's right to symbolic speech and protest. Since no breach of the peace occurred in response to the flag-burning, Texas could not justify its prosecution as a necessary step toward preventing public disorder. In subjecting Texas's other stated claim—the interest in preserving the flag "as a symbol of national unity"—to strict scrutiny, Brennan concluded that this interest could not be served by a means that prohibited a particular political expression toward the flag. According to Brennan, "if there is a bedrock principle underlying the First Amendment, it is that the government may not prohibit the expression of an idea simply because society finds the idea disagreeable." Justice Kennedy concurred in the result, stating that "it is poignant but fundamental that the flag protects those who hold it in contempt." In dissent, Chief Justice Rehnquist wrote that Johnson's act "was no essential part of an exposition of ideas," and he insisted that the state had ample justification for prosecuting him.

Public reaction to the *Johnson* decision was swift and quite critical, and President George H. W. Bush immediately called for either federal legislation to prohibit flag-burning. Congress immediately passed the Flag Protection Act of 1989 by large margins (House, 380–38; Senate, 91–9), making it illegal to mutilate, deface, physically defile, burn, or trample upon the United States flag. In 1990, in *U.S.* v. *Eichman*, the same five-justice majority held the act unconstitutional under the First Amendment, since Congress was attempting to suppress "expression out of concern for its likely communicative impact." In response to the government's argument that Congress was responding to a "national consensus" favoring a prohibition on flag-burning following *Johnson*, Justice Brennan wrote: "Even assuming such a consensus exists, any suggestion that the Government's interest in suppressing speech becomes weightier as popular opposition to that speech grows is foreign to the First Amendment." But the volatile issue of flag-burning continued to fuel several legislative attempts (ultimately unsuccessful) in Congress over the next two decades to overturn the ruling in *Texas v. Johnson* via constitutional amendment.

The *Johnson* and *Eichmann* decisions are significant because they indicate the very slim margin of protection afforded both pure and symbolic speech. If these flag-burning cases are any indication, laws

Brief 14.3

THE STUDENT'S RIGHT TO FREE SPEECH CAN BE REGULATED

In the landmark case of *Tinker v. Des Moines School District* (1969), the Supreme Court moved to protect the First Amendment rights of students in public schools, stating that students do not "shed their constitutional rights to freedom of speech or expression at the schoolhouse gate." Moreover, the Court said that students' symbolic speech could not be prohibited or punished simply because school officials disagreed with its content. Over the past four decades, however, the Court has moved to limit the impact of the *Tinker* decision. A recent example of this more restrictive approach to freedom of speech as it affects students can be found in *Morse v. Frederick* (2007).

The case involved an incident outside of Juneau-Douglas High School in Juneau, Alaska. On January 23, 2002, the school's students and staff were allowed to leave school to view the passing of the Olympic Torch on its way to Salt Lake City. Joseph Frederick and his friends stood on a sidewalk across the street from the high school, and when television cameras came by them, they unfurled a 14-foot banner reading "BONG HiTS 4 JESUS." Deborah Morse, the school's principal, ran across the street and seized the banner, later suspending Frederick for ten days for violating the school's anti-drug policy. After an appeal to the Juneau School Board failed, Frederick filed a federal civil rights lawsuit, claiming that the principal and school board violated his state and federal constitutional rights to free speech. In a 5–4 decision, the Supreme Court ruled in favor of the school principal, saying that the principal had the authority to restrict speech promoting drug use at a school-sponsored event.

Writing for the majority, Justice Roberts cited *Tinker* but argued that even that decision allowed the suppression of student expression if school officials determine that such expression will "materially and substantially disrupt the work and discipline of the school." In this case, Frederick's expression at an event that the school sponsored, even though off school grounds, interfered with the school's important educational mission "to educate students about the dangers of illegal drugs and to discourage their use." Roberts went on to say that "[b]ecause schools may take steps to safeguard those entrusted to their care from speech that can be reasonably regarded as encouraging drug use, the school officials in this case did not violate the First Amendment by confiscating the pro-drug banner and suspending Frederick." In a concurring opinion, Justice Thomas went even further, arguing that *Tinker* should be overturned because public school students do not have free speech rights: "In my view, the history of public education suggests that the First Amendment, as originally understood, does not protect student speech in public schools."

In a sharply worded dissenting opinion, Justice Stevens expressed his concern that "the Court does serious violence to the First Amendment in upholding—indeed, lauding—a school's decision to punish Frederick for expressing a view with which it disagreed." Stevens lamented the Court's watering down of the "cardinal principles" found in the *Tinker* decision, by "uphold[ing] a punishment meted out on the basis of a listener's disagreement with her understanding (or, more likely, misunderstanding) of the speaker's viewpoint." He argued that "carving out pro-drug speech for uniquely harsh treatment finds no support in our case law and is inimical to the values protected by the First Amendment."

Although the consequences of this decision are not clear for future First Amendment cases, *Morse v. Frederick* stands in a line of cases since 1986[23] limiting the constitutional rights of public school students, and is consistent with the Court's 1988 student free press rights ruling in *Hazlewood School District v. Kuhlmeier* (see Brief 15.4).

---

used to suppress the expression of particular political ideas continue to draw the Court's strictest scrutiny and the public's condemnation when the justices strike down criminal statutes seeking to punish such conduct. More recently, in the context of a drug-related message in a public school setting, the Court moved to restrict protections of symbolic speech for students (see Brief 14.3).

"SPEECH PLUS" AND THE FIRST AMENDMENT

As Chapter 11 emphasized, the process whereby most of the federal Bill of Rights was selectively applied to the several states during the twentieth century had enormous consequences for the personal freedoms of Americans. Nowhere was this process more significant than in the area of First Amendment freedoms, as more and more activities were seen as entitled to protection from the restrictive hand of government. Private citizens, either individually or in groups, increasingly challenged the actions of government concerning what has been known for decades as "speech plus," namely speech that is accompanied by personal conduct. As much of the following discussion will reflect, many "expression-action" phenomena have found the courts ruling that governments at various levels can intervene and limit certain conduct for a variety of reasons with reasonable "time–place–manner" restrictions. One of the best known areas of "speech-plus" law involves labor organizations and their struggle for decades to petition government for the right to organize and bargain collectively.

LABOR PICKETING AND THE FIRST AMENDMENT

A form of speech-plus that has long been protected by the First Amendment involves picketing by labor organizations. A series of decisions by the Supreme Court over the last several decades has established an important though sometimes confusing line of precedents (see Table 14.4). In 1940, peaceful picketing was brought under the protection of free speech with the Court's decision in *Thornhill v. Alabama*. In this case, the Court struck down an Alabama law as too broad because it prohibited all labor picketing in the area of a labor dispute. Writing for the Court majority soon after being appointed by President Roosevelt in 1940, Justice Frank Murphy stated in terms reminiscent of the "clear-and-present danger" test that abridging free speech in labor disputes was permissible "only where the clear danger of substantive evils arises under circumstances affording no opportunity to test the merits of ideas by competition for acceptance in the market of public opinion."

After *Thornhill*, the Court reviewed several labor-picketing cases that involved the limits of "time–place–manner" restrictions on picketing and free speech. In *Marsh v. Alabama* (1946), the Court upheld the guarantees of the First Amendment against attempts by an Alabama deputy sheriff to limit picketing and literature distribution in a section of town largely owned and controlled by a private shipbuilding company. Justice Hugo Black noted that despite the fact that a private company had legal title to the

Table 14.4 Development of the Law—Picketing and the First Amendment

Year	Case	Significance
1940	*Thornhill v. Alabama*	Court overturned state law prohibiting all picketing by labor organizations in area of a labor dispute; dissemination of information concerning labor dispute is guaranteed by freedoms of speech, peaceable assembly, and petition.
1941	*AFL v. Swing*	Court struck down state law that limited picketing to cases where union members had dispute with employer; justices ruled that state could not forbid organizational picketing by unions trying to persuade nonunion members to join.
1946	*Marsh v. Alabama*	Involved issue of picketing on private property; Court struck down city ordinance that forbade picketing and distribution of literature in company-owned town; justices said that town had all attributes of other public arenas and First Amendment–protected activity.
1950	*Hughes v. Superior Ct. of Calif.*	Court upheld injunction against picketing by black protestors trying to force employer to hire a certain percentage of black employees; judge held that picketing was harmful to state policy of supporting nondiscrimination.
1953	*Local Plumbers Union #10 v. Graham*	Court held that speech aspects of picketing did not exempt it from time, place and manner restrictions; Court ruled that picketing by union was intended to force employer to replace nonunion with union workers, which would violate state "right-to-work" law.
1968	*Amalgamated Food Employees Union Local 590 v. Logan Valley Plaza*	Six-member Court majority upheld right of union members to picket outside a store in a privately owned shopping center in protest to hiring of nonunion workers; justices ruled that center was equivalent of a public forum for union to publicize its labor dispute.
1972	*Lloyd Corp. v. Tanner*	Divided court moved away from *Logan Valley* precedent; ruled that private shopping mall could prohibit distribution of anti-war leaflets unrelated to business conducted in mall.
1976	*Hudgens v. NLRB*	Confused ruling that denied striking union members the right to protest on private property, holding that uninvited speech on private property could be banned by owners.
1980	*PruneYard Shopping Ctr. v. Robins*	Unanimous Court upheld Calif. constitutional right to free speech; said that students could collect petition signatures over objections of private owner of shopping mall; allowed state courts to decide balance between free speech and property rights on private property.

town, it was not authorized to impair "channels of communication" of its inhabitants or persons passing through the community. Black also observed that when owners, for their own advantage, make available their property for public use in general, they are obligated to honor the statutory and constitutional rights, including free expression, of those using that property.

Over two decades later, in *Amalgamated Food Employees v. Logan Valley Plaza* (1968), a 6 to 3 Court majority used the "company-owned town" analogy of *Marsh* to uphold the right of union members to picket a privately owned shopping center that employed nonunion workers. Justice Thurgood Marshall said that the owners could not exclude "those members of the public wishing to exercise their First Amendment rights on the premises in a manner and for a purpose generally consonant with the use to which the property is actually put." One of the dissenters in the case was Justice Black, who insisted that the *Marsh* analogy was inappropriate because the shopping center had little resemblance to a town:

> [TO] HOLD THAT STORE OWNERS [IN *LOGAN VALLEY*] ARE COMPELLED BY LAW TO SUPPLY PICKETING AREAS FOR PICKETS TO DRIVE STORE CUSTOMERS AWAY IS TO CREATE A COURT-MADE LAW WHOLLY DISREGARDING THE CONSTITUTIONAL BASIS ON WHICH PRIVATE OWNERSHIP OF PROPERTY RESTS IN THIS COUNTRY.

The case of *Hudgen v. National Labor Relations Board* (1976) involved several striking employees of a shoe company warehouse who decided to picket the company's retail stores. One of the stores was located in a privately owned shopping center whose owners threatened to have the picketers arrested and removed unless they stopped picketing the store. The picketers challenged the owners' threat as an unfair labor practice under the National Labor Relations Act. A six-member Court majority held that picketing on uninvited private property was not entitled to First Amendment protection. Therefore, the owners did not have to abide by the same First Amendment guarantees barring discrimination on public property. One problem with the *Hudgens* ruling is that it is somewhat difficult to reconcile with a long line of decisions related to nonunion peaceful protest and demonstrations. It is to that category of federal cases that the narrative now turns.

PEACEFUL ASSEMBLY AND THE FIRST AMENDMENT

For many decades, the Court has been asked to deal with the extent to which the First Amendment protects peaceful protest and demonstrations on a wide array of public issues. Those who seek such protection argue that the First Amendment guarantees of free speech and peaceable assembly should safeguard the individual, whether acting alone or in concert with others. In *De Jonge v. Oregon* (1937), the Supreme Court first moved to make peaceable assembly applicable to the states, when it confronted a state regulation that attempted to punish members of leftist organizations for both speech and assembly rights. The *De Jonge* case involved a member of the Communist Party who had been convicted under an Oregon law that, like the New York statute in *Gitlow* discussed earlier in this chapter, forbade criminal syndicalism. Dirk De Jonge had been arrested after making a speech at a public rally of union members. In his speech, he had criticized law enforcement officials of Portland, Oregon, and their treatment of striking longshoremen. In this case, it is important to note that the defendant was convicted and given a seven-year sentence for merely participating in and speaking at a public meeting sponsored by the Communist Party. He appealed his conviction to the U.S. Supreme Court, arguing that the First Amendment protection of peaceable assembly should apply to the states under the Fourteenth Amendment Due Process Clause.

A unanimous Supreme Court overturned De Jonge's conviction, thereby recognizing that the right of free assembly was on an equal status with the rights of free speech and free press, and applicable to the states under the Fourteenth Amendment. Writing for the majority, Chief Justice Charles Evans Hughes stated:

> FREEDOM OF SPEECH AND OF THE PRESS ARE FUNDAMENTAL RIGHTS WHICH ARE SAFEGUARDED BY THE DUE PROCESS CLAUSE OF THE FOURTEENTH AMENDMENT OF THE FEDERAL CONSTITUTION. . . . THE RIGHT OF PEACEFUL ASSEMBLY IS A RIGHT COGNATE TO THOSE OF FREE SPEECH AND

FREE PRESS AND IS EQUALLY AS FUNDAMENTAL.

According to Hughes, under the Federal Constitution, "the holding of meetings for peaceable political action cannot be proscribed." The Court struck down the Oregon statute as an unconstitutional invasion of freedom of assembly protected by the First and Fourteenth Amendments.

Two years later, in *Hague v. Committee for Industrial Organization* (1939), the Court clarified what governments were permitted to do in regulating public assembly consistent with the First Amendment. In question here was a Jersey City, New Jersey, ordinance requiring anyone seeking to assemble in public to obtain a permit from the Director of Public Safety of the city. Under Mayor Hague, the city denied the Committee for Industrial Organization (CIO) a permit, on the grounds that it was a "communist organization." The Supreme Court struck down the ordinance, but allowed for some regulation of public assemblies. In his majority opinion, Justice Owen Roberts asserted:

WHEREVER THE TITLE OF STREETS AND PARKS MAY REST THEY HAVE [LONG] BEEN USED FOR PURPOSES OF ASSEMBLY, COMMUNICATING THOUGHTS BETWEEN CITIZENS, AND DISCUSSING PUBLIC QUESTIONS. SUCH USE OF THE STREETS AND PUBLIC PLACES HAS, FROM ANCIENT TIMES, BEEN A PART OF THE PRIVILEGES, IMMUNITIES, RIGHTS AND LIBERTIES OF CITIZENS. THE PRIVILEGE TO USE THE STREETS AND PARKS FOR COMMUNICATION OF VIEWS ON NATIONAL QUESTIONS MAY BE REGULATED IN THE INTEREST OF ALL; BUT IT MUST NOT, IN THE GUISE OF REGULATION, BE ABRIDGED OR DENIED.

So while governments cannot use laws to deny equal access to groups to assemble peaceably, they can, through what are referred to as "time–place–manner" laws, regulate access in the public interest, knowing that public places serve other purposes in addition to communication. As long as such freedoms are not totally denied, municipalities are allowed to enforce reasonable time, place, and manner restrictions upon public assembly in order to protect public safety and order.

The line of decisions controlling this important claim has generally reflected growing support for First Amendment freedoms, although just as it did with respect to labor picketing cases, the Court has occasionally handed down rulings that do not fit neatly into any consistent pattern (see Table 14.5 on peaceful protest). Soon after the *Hague* precedent, the Court addressed the right of a state to require parade permits of all groups wanting to participate in such an activity. In *Cox v. New Hampshire* (1941), a unanimous Court held that the permitting process could not be used to deny particular views of marchers, although it could be a reasonable and permissible regulation to ensure that parades would not interfere with a public thoroughfare. The 1960s produced several cases involving civil rights demonstrators in several Southern states in which the Court normally found in favor of persons convicted under invalid laws that infringed upon First Amendment rights of free speech and assembly, as Table 14.5 reflects.

Since the early 1970s, one of the most divisive issues in American society has been the volatile subject of abortion rights and in recent years the limits of public protest against those rights. As Brief 14.4 indicates, the Supreme Court reviewed three cases in the 1990s that involved both a woman's right to terminate a pregnancy and the right of those opposed to the *Roe* precedent to demonstrate peaceably. In all probability, the balance that was struck satisfied few parties in the controversy.

A more recent case involving peaceful protest concerned a different type of tension: between a group's right to communicate its religious and public policy beliefs and the grief caused by sometimes hateful expression for families attending the funeral of a fallen soldier. The Westboro Baptist Church, based in Topeka Kansas, has been picketing at military funerals for the past twenty years, to protest what it considers an overly tolerant U.S. policy toward homosexuality. Carrying signs like "Thank God for Dead Soldiers," "God Hates Fags," and "America is Doomed," members of the church travel around the country to appear outside the locations of military funerals. In 2006, church founder Fred Phelps and six other members of the Westboro Baptist Church (all relatives of Phelps) protested at the Maryland funeral of Marine Lance

Table 14.5 Development of the Law—Peaceful Protest and the First Amendment

Year	Case	Significance
1937	*DeJonge v. Oregon*	Communist Party member had been convicted of having made a political speech at a public meeting sponsored by party; Court unanimously overturned his conviction, thereby incorporating First Amendment freedom of assembly into 14th Due Process Clause.
1941	*Cox v. New Hampshire*	Court unanimously upheld conviction of demonstrators who had failed to obtain a permit to protest on a public street; "time–place–manner" restrictions were intended only to ensure that paraders would not unduly interfere with others using the streets.
1963	*Edwards v. S. Carolina*	First of several civil rights demonstrations; Court overturned conviction of demonstrators who had conducted a nonviolent protest on the state capitol steps; ruled that law under which they had been convicted was unconstitutionally broad.
1965	*Cox v. Louisiana*	Cox had demonstrated in Baton Rouge against segregated lunch counters near courthouse and state capitol; convicted for disturbing the peace; Court found ordinance to be overly broad.
1966	*Brown v. Louisiana*	Court overturned conviction of five civil rights demonstrators at public library who had staged a peaceable, nonviolent protest inside a segregated facility; justices found the protest to be protected by First Amendment.
1966	*Adderly v. Florida*	Five-member majority ruled against several blacks who had demonstrated at a county jail in support of students who had tried to integrate a theater; Court ruled that jail was not a public forum.
1969	*Gregory v. City of Chicago*	Unanimous Court upheld right of peaceful demonstrators to parade in a residential neighborhood on public sidewalks, if peaceful and orderly.
1972	*Lloyd Corp. v. Tanner*	Five-member Court majority upheld banning of distribution of anti–Vietnam War leaflets inside an enclosed, privately owned shopping mall; justices held that mall was not a public forum.
1984	*Clark v. Community for Creative Non-Violence*	Court ruled against a group demonstrating peacefully and sleeping overnight in Lafayette Park in Washington, D.C.; National Park Service had reasonable regulations prohibiting such demonstrations.
1994	*Madsen v. Women's Health Center*	Case dealt with anti-abortion demonstrators protesting against women having an abortion; justices upheld abortion rights, but struck down several limitations on anti-abortionists' right to protest.
1997	*Schenck v. Pro-Choice Network of Western New York*	Decision reaffirmed right of anti-abortion activists to demonstrate at abortion clinics; also reflected continued right of women seeking pregnancy-related, family planning services, including abortions.
2011	*Snyder v. Phelps*	Ruled that members of the Westboro Baptist Church protesting at military funerals to communicate the belief that God hates the United States for allowing homosexuality were protected by the First Amendment from lawsuits by families of the dead soldiers claiming emotional distress.

Corporal Matthew Snyder, who was killed while serving in Iraq. Snyder's father, seeing what was written on the signs of the protesters, sued for intentional infliction of emotional distress, and was initially awarded $5 million in damages by a jury. Phelps appealed, and in an 8–1 decision, the Supreme Court ruled in *Snyder v. Phelps* (2011) that the First Amendment protected the church from such state tort claims.

Writing for the majority, Chief Justice Roberts argued that a determination about whether the First Amendment protected Westboro Baptist Church in this case hinged on the nature of the speech, and if it was "of public or private concern." It was clear to the Court majority that the content of the protest, and the signs that caused the Snyder family such distress, "plainly related to broad issues of interest to society at large [and] matters of public import." Although the

Brief 14.4
ANTI-ABORTIONISTS AND THE FIRST AMENDMENT

In recent years, the ugly spectacle of abortion clinic bombings, physical assaults upon clinic personnel and women seeking an abortion, and fatal shootings of physicians who administer abortions have taken peaceful protest far beyond legal protection. Although it has consistently disclaimed any responsibility for violence at abortion clinics, the organization known as Operation Rescue has been a fiercely committed and outspoken opponent of abortion rights.

On January 24, 1994, the Supreme Court handed down a decision that has important implications for organized protests at family planning clinics in the United States. In *National Organization for Women v. Scheidler*, a unanimous Supreme Court ruled that abortion clinics can invoke the Racketeer-Influenced and Corrupt Organizations Act (known as RICO) to sue violent anti-abortion protest groups for damages. In an opinion written by Chief Justice William Rehnquist, himself a staunch abortion opponent, the Court gave family planning and abortion clinics a potentially powerful legal weapon to combat and deter the violence that has made it increasingly more dangerous and expensive for the clinics to remain open. Whereas anti-abortion groups such as Operation Rescue, the Pro-Life Action League, and Project Life—defendants in the suit—all claimed that RICO applied only to activities motivated by a desire for *economic* gain, the Court ruled that Congress had not required an economic motive when it passed the law in 1970. Rehnquist noted in his opinion that the economic motive requirement was "neither expressed nor . . . fairly implied" in the law.

Another decision by the Court in June 1994 found the justices dealing more directly with so-called "time–place–manner" restrictions on protesters at family planning clinics. At issue in the case of *Madsen v. Women's Health Center, Inc.* (1994) was what, if any, limits can be placed on the efforts of anti-abortion activists to discourage women from choosing to end a pregnancy. The specific focus of the appeal concerned several constraints upon anti-abortionists in Melbourne, Florida, which (1) barred anti-abortion protesters from a thirty-six-foot buffer zone around the clinic; (2) prohibited protesters from approaching staff and patients within three hundred feet of the clinic unless the persons being approached "indicate a desire to communicate" with the protesters; (3) prohibited such activities as chanting, shouting, yelling, or the use of amplification equipment that might be audible to patients; and (4) prohibited picketing, demonstrating, or using amplification equipment within three hundred feet of staff residences.

The Court majority seemed to support the government's purposes in protecting a woman's right to end a pregnancy, in ensuring public safety and the free flow of vehicular traffic near the clinics, and in protecting the privacy of patients and staff inside the clinic. The Court also upheld the anti-noise restrictions around the clinic and the staff residences, as well as the thirty-six-foot buffer zone around the entrance and exit of the clinic. But it struck down the buffer zone around other areas of clinic property, the three-hundred-foot prohibition near staff residences, and the prohibition against visual images carried or shown by protesters to patients, noting that the patients could avoid seeing these images by having the blinds or shades drawn during operating hours.

In the case of *Schenck v. Pro-Choice Network of Western New York* (1997), the justices reaffirmed the right of anti-abortionists to demonstrate peacefully, while at the same time protecting a woman's right to have access to a full array of family planning services, including abortion procedures. The *Schenck* case involved family planning clinics in Buffalo and Rochester that had been increasingly the target of large-scale demonstrations by anti-abortionists. After countless protests against the clinics that degenerated into verbal and physical confrontations between patients, staff, and protestors, a network of clinics obtained a court injunction that allowed for a 15-foot buffer zone between patients entering the clinic and protestors, as well as a 15-foot floating buffer zone around any person or vehicle approaching the clinic. In a somewhat mixed ruling, the justices upheld the fixed 15-foot buffer zone and struck down the floating buffer zone.

At the end of its 1999 term, in the case of *Hill v. Colorado* (2000), the Court had to decide if a Colorado law that prevented protesters outside abortion clinics from "knowingly approach[ing] another person within eight feet" without that person's consent was constitutional. The justices decided 6 to 3 that the state law did not violate the free-speech rights of abortion protesters. Writing for the majority, Justice Stevens said that the statute was content-neutral and therefore did not violate the First Amendment. As he observed in his majority opinion,

> *The Colorado statute passes [that] test for three independent reasons. First, it is not a "regulation of speech." Rather, it is a regulation of the places where some speech may occur. Second, it was not adopted "because of disagreement with the message it conveys . . . ". Third, the State's interests in protecting access and privacy, and providing the police with clear guidelines, are unrelated to the content of the demonstrators' speech.*

In essence, the majority here gave substantial support to the right of private citizens to decide independently what they wish to read and, within some limits, what oral messages they want to avoid. It is clearly within state power to equip private citizens seeking abortion counseling or other services to enter a health care facility and to be protected from a speaker with a message that they do not want to hear.

protest was planned to coincide with the funeral, it did not disrupt the funeral proceedings. Roberts concluded by stating:

> SPEECH IS POWERFUL. IT CAN STIR PEOPLE TO ACTION, MOVE THEM TO TEARS OF BOTH JOY AND SORROW, AND—AS IT DID HERE—INFLICT GREAT PAIN. [BUT] WE CANNOT REACT TO THAT PAIN BY PUNISHING THE SPEAKER. AS A NATION WE HAVE CHOSEN A DIFFERENT COURSE—TO PROTECT EVEN HURTFUL SPEECH ON PUBLIC ISSUES TO ENSURE THAT WE DO NOT STIFLE PUBLIC DEBATE.

In a lone dissenting opinion, Justice Alito likened the case to others where the Court used a "fighting-words" rationale to uphold restrictions on expression (see the discussion later in this chapter). "In order to have a society in which public issues can be openly and vigorously debated, it is not necessary to allow the brutalization of innocent victims." Alito asserted that the "profound national commitment" to free public expression "is not a license for the vicious verbal assault that occurred in this case."

What seems clear from decisions stretching back over more than five decades is that peaceful protest enjoys substantial protection under the First Amendment. The Court has basically upheld this vital constitutional guarantee, even when the potential for civil disorder has existed, because people hold differing opinions and policy preferences and public debate is inevitable. As long as these protests do not infringe upon equally valid constitutional rights of other citizens, they should be allowed in a free society. But what about the free expression of private businesses? Are these forms of commercial speech equally protected by the First Amendment?

COMMERCIAL SPEECH AND THE FIRST AMENDMENT

Although it was originally unprotected by the First Amendment, the courts have recognized commercial speech for many years as worthy of protection. Clearly part of the reason for this change has been the increasing recognition that commercial speech should be part of the free flow of information that is necessary for informed consumer choice and democratic participation in a free society. At its core, commercial speech involves the advertising of goods and services by corporations and business organizations. For a century, American consumers have come to expect fairness and integrity from businesses marketing their products and services. The passage by Congress of pure food and drug legislation in 1906, followed by the establishment of the Federal Trade Commission in 1914, reflected a more expectant public and a more responsive federal government in monitoring these important aspects of the commercial marketplace. Commercial speech is subject to much more governmental regulation than other kinds of speech, particularly political speech. Government can forbid advertising the sale of anything illegal, false, or misleading with respect to how companies market their products and services. Whether government can realistically implement this ideal is another question.

Not until the 1970s did the Supreme Court begin to apply the First Amendment to commercial speech (see Table 14.6). When asked during World War II to consider the issue, the Court said that "purely commercial speech" was not entitled to constitutional protection (*Valentine* v. *Chrestensen* [1942]). But that precedent began eroding during the 1960s, especially with the Court's ruling in the important libel law judgment in *New York Times v. Sullivan (1964)*, where the justices unanimously ruled that a paid political advertisement had limited protection under the First Amendment (see Chapter 15).

The Burger Court handed down two important commercial speech cases during the 1970s. In *Bigelow v. Virginia (1975)*, the Court extended First Amendment protection to an advertisement for an abortion referral service. And in *Virginia State Board of Pharmacy v. Virginia Citizens Consumer Council* (1976), the Court said that the First Amendment also protected advertising of prescription drugs. The justices held in this second decision that fair and accurate advertising were necessary in order for consumers to make wise decisions, and that benefits would attend the larger market by honest and accurate marketing of products and services.

The Court's decision in *Central Hudson Gas & Electric Corp. v. Public Service Commission* (1980) established a stringent four-part test to determine

Table 14.6 Development of the Law—Commercial Speech and the First Amendment

Year	Case	Significance
1939	*Schneider v. Irvington*	First time that Court discussed the issue of commercial speech; majority ruled that First Amendment prohibited a city from requiring a person soliciting for religious purposes to first obtain permission from city officials; left open the question of whether such permission could be applied to commercial solicitation.
1942	*Valentine v. Chrestensen*	Court suggested that commercial speech might be less protected than other kinds of speech; upheld a New York ordinance prohibiting distribution of commercial advertising material.
1975	*Bigelow v. Virginia*	Court held that Virginia violated First Amendment when it punished a local newspaper editor for printing an advertisement concerning the availability of legal abortions in New York; effect of ruling was to protect advertisement for abortion referral service.
1976	*Virginia State Bd. of Pharmacy v. Virginia Citizens Consumer Council*	Court said that First Amendment protected advertising price of prescription drugs; justices based ruling on need to disseminate economic information to consumers in order for them to make informed decisions.
1977	*Bates v. Arizona State Bar*	Court ruled that lawyers could not be prohibited from advertising the prices of "routine legal services."
1995	*Rubin v. Coors Brewing Co.*	Company claimed that 1935 federal law prohibiting labeling on beer and malt liquor products violated free speech; Court ruled in favor of brewing company, based on what it saw as irrational and inconsistent alcohol-content regulations on beer, wine, and other distilled spirits.
1996	*44 Liquormart, Inc. v. Rhode Island*	Court ruled that the state's ban on price advertising for liquor violated First Amendment right to truthful commercial speech; suggests that similar bans in other states may be unconstitutional.
2001	*Lorillard Tobacco v. Reilly*	Court ruled that a Massachusetts law prohibiting all tobacco advertising within 1,000 feet of schools violated First Amendment.

whether a regulation of commercial speech meets the demands of the First Amendment:

❑ The advertisement falls within lawful activity and is not misleading or fraudulent
❑ The governmental interest being asserted to justify some restriction is substantial
❑ The regulation being invoked directly advances the governmental interest being asserted
❑ Any restrictions on commercial speech being applied are no more extensive than necessary to serve the government's interest[24]

As several decisions under the Rehnquist Court reflect, some changes have occurred in the area of commercial speech.

Another issue concerns long-standing advertising bans within the brewing industry in the United States.

The case of *Rubin v. Coors Brewing Company* (1995) involved the Federal Alcohol Administration Act of 1935, which prohibits disclosure by brewing companies of alcohol content on the labels of malt beverages, such as beer and ale, and in advertising unless such disclosure is specifically required by state law. The same federal law, conversely, requires the disclosure of alcohol content on other wines and distilled spirits that contain more than 14 percent alcohol by volume. Coors Brewing sued in federal court claiming that the disclosure prohibition on beer and ale violated freedom of speech of the First Amendment.

When the case reached the Supreme Court in 1995, the justices held that the federal government's interest in suppressing "strength wars" might be an interest substantial enough to warrant restricting commercial speech. But they also concluded that the regulatory framework constructed incrementally since passage of the 1935 law did not materially advance that government purpose. An integral part of the Court's finding against the labeling prohibition were the contradictory requirements under which labels for distilled spirits and wine require disclosure of alcohol content, but the same information on malt beverage labels was prohibited. The justices reasoned that strength wars could conceivably occur throughout the alcohol industry, and to restrict commercial speech (statements on alcohol content) in one segment of the industry while requiring it in another was irrational and unjustified.

Over the next few court terms, additional commercial speech rulings collectively held significance for selected areas of social policy and public health. One case concerned Section 1304 of the Communications Act of 1934, which prohibits radio and television broadcasting of "any advertisement of or information concerning any lottery, gift enterprise, or similar scheme, offering prizes dependent in whole or part upon lot or chance . . . ". The complicated law contains several exceptions that apply only to broadcast stations in states where gambling is illegal. In *Greater New Orleans Broadcasting Assoc. v. United States* (1999), the justices ruled unanimously that the federal ban on gambling advertisements in Louisiana (where gambling is legal), which was intended to prevent broadcast in Texas and Arkansas (where casino gambling is illegal), did not comply with several provisions of the *Central Hudson* test. The advertisements were neither misleading nor fraudulent, the federal government's interest in banning the broadcasts did not overcome some economic benefits that might result, the prohibition did not materially advance an asserted governmental interest, and the ban was far more extensive than it needed to be. In his opinion for the Court in *Greater New Orleans*, Justice Stevens noted that the federal government's asserted interest in minimizing the social costs of gambling was discounted by its long-standing support for casino gambling on Indian reservations in the United States.

Two rulings by the Court in the 2000 term had other commercial speech implications under the First Amendment. One case involved the federal Mushroom Promotion, Research, and Consumer Information Act of 1990, and the Department of Agriculture's practice of requiring mushroom growers to contribute to a national advertising program that encourages the public to buy and consume more mushrooms. Some mushroom growers objected to the mandatory-contributions provisions of the program, claiming that they constituted "compelled speech" that violated the First Amendment. In *United States v. United Foods* (2001), a six-member majority represented by Justice Kennedy agreed with that claim. As Kennedy noted in his opinion,

> [J]UST AS THE FIRST AMENDMENT MAY PREVENT THE GOVERNMENT FROM PROHIBITING SPEECH, THE AMENDMENT MAY PREVENT [IT] FROM COMPELLING INDIVIDUALS TO EXPRESS CERTAIN VIEWS . . . OR FROM COMPELLING CERTAIN INDIVIDUALS TO PAY SUBSIDIES FOR SPEECH TO WHICH THEY OBJECT. . . .

This ruling has constitutional, as well as economic and political, implications. First, it upholds the right against compelled speech in commercial speech controversies, which was cast in doubt in 1997 when the Court upheld mandatory contributions by California raisin growers for advertising.[25] Second, the decision most likely requires the Department of Agriculture, which oversees several marketing programs with a mandatory-contributions budget of some $500 million annually, to ensure that these programs do not constitute compelled speech. Whether the executive branch will do this remains to be seen.

One of the more significant commercial-speech cases in recent times, certainly with respect to the beleaguered tobacco industry, is *Lorillard Tobacco Co. v. Reilly* (2001). In a complicated decision that contained several voting coalitions, the justices sided with the tobacco industry and overturned restrictions by state and local governments to regulate tobacco advertising. At issue in this case was a 1999 Massachusetts law, one of the most restrictive in the country, which prohibited all tobacco advertising within a 1,000-foot radius of schools and playgrounds. Several tobacco companies challenged the law because they said it violated the terms of a 1998 settlement between four major tobacco companies and forty-six states. They also claimed that it violated a federal statute, the Cigarette Labeling and Advertising Act of 1965, which states that "no requirement or prohibition based on smoking and health shall be imposed under state law with respect to the advertising or promotion of any cigarettes . . . ". At issue here was whether this federal law effectively preempted all state-local regulations of tobacco advertising.

A unanimous Court felt that smoking by young people was a very serious public health problem that governments needed to address in an appropriate and legal manner. However, they also thought that the Massachusetts ban on outdoor advertising violated the manufacturers' First Amendment right because the restrictions, which were aimed at protecting children, interfered with the industry's right to market its product to adult consumers, thus violating the fourth component of the *Central Hudson* test. The *Lorillard* ruling suggests that those wanting to limit tobacco advertising to teens may have to rely upon municipal zoning regulations of playgrounds and schools, rather than state restrictions of commercial speech.

These several rulings on commercial speech suggest that the Rehnquist Court was more likely to scrutinize state or federal legislation that failed to comply with the several requirements of the *Central Hudson* test of 1980—lawful advertising, substantial government interest, direct advancement of that interest, and minimally restrictive of First Amendment rights. Taken together, the rulings collectively tend to endorse the virtue of a free market philosophy and decentralized government, although there have been some strong differences of opinion on the Supreme Court in this area of First Amendment law.

ADULT ENTERTAINMENT AND THE FIRST AMENDMENT

In a more specific area of "commercial speech," the adult entertainment industry has sought protection under the First Amendment for what it claims is "artistic expression." Two rulings involving adult entertainment dealt with whether public nudity is protected under the First Amendment. In *Barnes v. Glen Theatre, Inc.* (1991), the Rehnquist Court divided 5 to 4 and upheld an Indiana law that prohibited public nudity in a controversy that involved totally-nude dancing in two adult establishments in South Bend, Indiana.[26] Three justices in the majority (Rehnquist, O'Connor, and Kennedy) argued that the state's power to protect the moral climate of the community and prohibit public nudity was sufficient to justify the law and override any claim to "expressive conduct" under the First Amendment. Justices Souter and Scalia upheld the state law for other reasons.

Following the *Barnes* ruling, many municipalities, including Erie, Pennsylvania, passed ordinances that banned totally-nude dancing in the belief that such conduct encouraged increased criminal activity. An adult-oriented club in the city challenged the ordinance on the grounds that it violated the First Amendment, an argument with which the state supreme court agreed when it heard the case on appeal. The city then appealed the adverse judgment to the U.S. Supreme Court in a case known as *City of Erie v. Pap's A. M.* (2000). In a plurality opinion for a 6 to 3 court, Justice Sandra Day O'Connor said that the ordinance was a constitutionally permissible way of combating the "negative secondary effects" often associated with nude dancing. According to O'Connor, the ordinance was content-neutral in that it was carefully aimed at all public nudity, regardless of whether such nudity was accompanied by expressive activity. She also stated that the city did not have to present any evidence "independent of that already generated by other cities" to demonstrate that nude dancing was likely to produce negative effects in the community. In a dissenting opinion, Justice David Souter, who was actually in the majority in the *Barnes* ruling in 1991, disagreed with the Court. He argued that without supporting evidence that clearly linked nude dancing to secondary criminal activity, the ordinance should not have been allowed under the First Amendment. The other dissenters, Justices Stevens and Ginsburg, argued that the city had a right to regulate the location of these adult businesses but it could not prohibit nude dancing itself because it was a form of protected artistic expression under the First Amendment.

Campaign Finance and the First Amendment: Corrupted Politics or Free Speech?

For over one hundred years, Congress has attempted to regulate the sources and amounts of money going to candidates for public office in federal elections. In the Tillman Act of 1907, for example, Congress prohibited corporations from donating directly to those seeking federal office, and in the Corrupt Practices Act of 1910, it limited the amount of money that congressional candidates could contribute to their own campaigns for nomination or election to office. In all of these years of campaign finance regulation, Congress has struggled with balancing two worthy goals: (1) the right of citizens to make monetary contributions to political campaigns and elections; and (2) the need to protect these critically important instruments of democratic participation from corrupting influences. The Supreme Court has frequently entered the political debate over the nexus between money and elections (see Table 14.7), and the consequences have often been confusing, unintended, and unsatisfactory to the many parties involved.

Part of the ongoing problem with constitutional interpretation concerning campaign finance regulation is that there are competing conceptions of freedom of speech applied to this area of First Amendment jurisprudence, as well as competing understandings of the kind of political corruption that the government may need to prevent. Constitutional scholar and former Stanford Law School Dean Kathleen Sullivan has argued that Supreme Court justices are split between what she calls "libertarian" and "egalitarian" views about what constitutes "free speech" in electoral politics.[27] The "libertarian strand" within this free speech tradition (which aligns with what we have called the individualist theory of politics) holds that government interference with any element of the system of freedom of speech as applied to campaigns and elections is a constitutional problem. Whether it is individuals, private corporations, labor unions, or not-for-profit organizations, all "speakers" should be free to contribute financially to the electoral process. The "egalitarian strand" (which aligns more with what we have called the communitarian theory of politics), on the other hand, sees freedom of speech rights "as belonging to individual speakers," and thus will allow government restrictions when aimed at equalizing the overall electoral playing field, "redistributing speaking power to reduce some speakers' disproportionate influence" (as with wealthy or corporate contributors).[28] On top of these competing conceptions of free speech in the electoral context, different views about political corruption influence how judges have ruled on congressional campaign finance legislation. One view holds that the government can act to prevent the kind of *quid pro quo* arrangements that come when "candidates ingratiate themselves with their wealthy backers," or even when there might be a perception of such corruption when wealthy contributors have unlimited ability to influence potential public office holders.[29] An alternative view of political corruption holds that government can act to prevent "large expenditures capturing the marketplace of political ideas," influencing the overall political process and making it hard for voters to sift through all the messages tainted by campaign cash, especially when economic and social inequalities skew the electoral process in particular ways.[30] Efforts by the federal government to regulate campaign contributions often cross the lines between these different views of free speech and political corruption, and make constitutional interpretation more difficult.

Campaign Contributions versus Expenditures: Buckley v. Valeo

This area of First Amendment law has been problematic for many years, in part because of the escalating costs of federal campaigns and elections and the valued right of candidates to communicate their message to voters. Whether federal legislation has actually improved the process is debatable. Following the Watergate scandal of the early 1970s, public concerns increased about political corruption and the unfair advantage that money and wealth might provide to candidates in federal elections. This prompted Congress to make changes in campaign expenditure requirements under the Federal Election Campaign Act (FECA) Amendments of 1974. The 1974 legislative amendments (1) limited the amount of money that candidates could spend in political campaigns; (2) restricted the size of individual and group contributions to federal candidates to $1,000 and $5,000, respectively; (3) required

Table 14.7 Development of the Law: Campaign Finance and Elections

Year	Case/Law	Significance
1921	*Newbury v. U.S.*	Court struck down portion of Federal Corrupt Practices Act limiting amount of money congressional candidates could spend in primaries; infringed on state powers over nominating process.
1934	*Burroughs v. U.S.*	Court upheld power of Congress to require political committees to keep detailed accounts of all financial contributions in federal contests and to report all contributors to Congress.
1941	*U.S. v. Classic*	Upheld Congress's power to regulate primary and general elections.
1971	Federal Election Campaign Act	Congress's first major effort to limit campaign contributions by corporate and banking organizations; created a Presidential Election Campaign Fund to provide federal subsidies to presidential candidates in the general election.
1972	*Pipefitters v. U.S.*	Court ruled that selected bans on labor contributions to political campaigns did not prohibit "voluntary" contributions to political action committees (PACs).
1974	Federal Election Campaign Act Amendments	Following Watergate scandal, Congress placed new limits on campaign contributions and expenditures, created the Federal Election Commission to enforce the law, and provided optional public funding for presidential (but not congressional) elections.
1976	*Buckley v. Valeo*	Court upheld limits on how much individuals and PACs may contribute to candidates; new disclosures and record-keeping requirements; public financing of presidential campaigns. Candidates accepting federal funding had to abide with limits on campaign costs. Struck down limits on what candidates could spend overall, and of their own money.
1985	*FEC v. National Conservative PAC*	Court struck down provision of the 1974 FECA limiting PACs from making "independent expenditures" above $1,000 if supporting presidential candidates who had accepted federal funding.
1990	*Austin v. Michigan Chamber of Commerce*	Court upheld Michigan law restricting corporations from making independent expenditures from their general coffers to directly support or oppose candidates in elections.
1996	*Colorado Republican CC v. FEC*	Ruled that First Amendment prohibits Congress from placing limits on amounts that political parties can spend "independently" (not at direction of or coordination with) of congressional candidates.
2000	*Nixon v. Shrink Mo. Gov't PAC*	Court upheld state ceiling of $1,000 on individual contributions to candidates, over arguments that inflation had made limits derived in 1976 legislation obsolete.
2001	*FEC v. Colorado Republican CC*	Court dealt with issue of candidate coordination of independent contributions; upheld federal limits on amount of money parties can spend in coordination with candidates.
2002	Bipartisan Campaign Reform Act	Known as McCain-Feingold, federal law prohibits national political parties from raising and spending "soft money," but places no limits on independent (so-called 527 groups); also bans "issue ads" by parties, often thinly disguised attacks on opposition candidates.
2003	*McConnell v. FEC*	Upheld soft-money limits of law; raised new questions about 527 groups.
2003	*FEC v. Beaumont*	Court ruled that FECA ban on direct corporate contributions to federal candidates also applied to ad hoc corporate entities created specifically for ideological advocacy in federal elections.
2006	*Randall v. Sorrell*	Vermont law imposed expenditure and contribution limits on state/local candidates; first time that plurality of Court struck monetary limits on contributions to candidates

2007	*FEC v. Wisconsin Right to Life*	Court ruled that Sec. 203 of BCRA prohibiting corporations from using general treasury funds on broadcasts that refer to federal candidates inside thirty days (primary contests) or sixty days (general elections) were unconstitutional.
2008	*Davis v. FEC*	Divided Court struck down "millionaire's amendment" in BCRA, which allows opponents of wealthy congressional incumbents who spend more than $350,000 of their own money to raise triple the usual amounts of individual contributions; law violated First Amendment.
2010	*Citizens United v. FEC*	Court overturned *Austin* and parts of the *McConnell* ruling, striking down that part of BCRA that prohibited expenditures by corporations on communications about candidates within thirty days of a primary or sixty days of a general election.

full disclosure of campaign contributions and expenditures; (4) provided for public financing of presidential campaigns; and (5) created the Federal Election Commission to administer the act.

Several of these provisions were challenged in federal court soon after the legislation went into effect and in the midst of the 1976 presidential election. In *Buckley v. Valeo* (1976), the Court upheld the provisions of the act dealing with public financing of presidential campaigns, the president's power to appoint members to the Federal Election Commission, and limitations on campaign *contributions* by individuals and groups. In upholding the contribution ceilings under the act, the opinion for the Court stated:

> THE OVERALL EFFECT OF THE ACT'S CONTRIBUTION CEILINGS IS MERELY TO REQUIRE CANDIDATES AND POLITICAL COMMITTEES TO RAISE FUNDS FROM A GREATER NUMBER OF PERSONS AND TO COMPEL PEOPLE WHO WOULD OTHERWISE CONTRIBUTE AMOUNTS GREATER THAN THE STATUTORY LIMITS TO EXPEND SUCH FUNDS ON DIRECT POLITICAL EXPRESSION.

However, the Court said that "the governmental interest in preventing corruption and the appearance of corruption is inadequate to justify [the] ceiling on independent expenditures." The limits imposed by the act on what candidates could spend of their own personal funds and cumulative campaign assets violated the First Amendment. According to the Court,

> THE FIRST AMENDMENT DENIES GOVERNMENT THE POWER TO DETERMINE THAT SPENDING TO PROMOTE ONE'S POLITICAL VIEWS IS WASTEFUL, EXCESSIVE, OR UNWISE. IN THE FREE SOCIETY ORDAINED BY OUR CONSTITUTION IT IS NOT THE GOVERNMENT, BUT THE PEOPLE . . . WHO MUST RETAIN CONTROL OVER THE QUANTITY AND RANGE OF DEBATE ON PUBLIC ISSUES IN A POLITICAL CAMPAIGN.

An underlying premise of *Buckley v. Valeo* was that there is a fundamental difference between *contributions* and *expenditures*: Congress can limit the former but not the latter. This premise reinforces the notion that the potential for political corruption is most serious when well-heeled contributors can give large amounts of money to support specific political candidates, thus raising the specter of *quid pro quo* arrangements between the donor (and the donor's special interests) and the public official beholden to such large contributions. The other form of potential corruption, the overall flooding of federal elections with increasing amounts of campaign dollars (expenditures), is overridden by the First Amendment interests of candidates and their supporters in having their voices fully heard—without government limitation—in an election campaign (the "libertarian strand" detailed above). Since 1976 most judicial rulings have sought to sustain this distinction, but often with disappointing results. Serious gaps in the FECA amendments led to the proliferation in political action committees, an explosion in nonregulated campaign contributions to political parties ("soft money"), and ever more expensive political campaigns, all of which entered the election process via loopholes in FECA and *Buckley*.

CAMPAIGN FINANCE REFORM, THE BCRA, AND THE *CITIZENS UNITED* DECISION

In the campaigns for Congress in 2000, some $500 million found its way into the campaign coffers of candidates. And by 2002, the average expenditure (in current dollars) by the winning House of Representatives candidate had risen ten-fold over the preceding generation, from about $87,000 in 1976 to $891,000 in 2002.[31] Calls by the general public and public interest groups for reform of the jaded campaign finance landscape finally led to passage of the Bipartisan Campaign Reform Act (BCRA), otherwise known as "McCain-Feingold."

The legislation that passed Congress in March 2002 (see Brief 14.5) was aimed at curbing "soft money" contributions, the unlimited funds given to

---

Brief 14.5
THE STRUGGLE TO ABOLISH "SOFT MONEY"

Under the 1974 Federal Election Campaign Act and the subsequent ruling in *Buckley v. Valeo (1976)*, national political parties had virtually unlimited chances to raise and spend campaign funds, provided that the funds were not funneled directly to federal candidates. A party could legally give up to $10,000 directly to a House candidate and $17,500 to a Senate candidate. The money that a candidate received from individual contributors ($1,000 maximum per contributor per election) and interest groups (up to $5,000 per group) is termed "hard money." Before 2002 party organizations could provide what is generally known as "soft money" without federal dollar caps or source prohibitions. Although the 1974 law and subsequent amendments limit how much an individual or group could give directly to a federal candidate, the law permits that contributor to give an unlimited amount to a political party. Whereas wealthy contributors can give only $1,000 to the candidate, that same contributor can give unlimited amounts to the political party that can legally be spent on "party activities" or "issue advocacy" such as voter registration drives, advertising campaigns, and get-out-the-vote efforts. For many years, Democrats relied more on soft money contributions, in part because they lagged so far behind Republicans who were more adept at raising hard money contributions.

Efforts to close this "soft money" loophole prior to 2002 failed to win approval in Congress or the White House for reasons that relate to electoral competition, ideological preferences, and economic advantage. In 1992, after a bill imposing spending limits on campaigns and partial public subsidies in federal elections passed Congress, President George H. W. Bush vetoed the legislation, in part because of concerns about losing the enormous Republican advantage in "hard money" contributions. Some of that advantage spurred the Democrats under Bill Clinton and Al Gore, particularly in the 1996 presidential election, to solicit huge caches of campaign contributions with rather lavish appeals for money at White House sleepovers. The excesses of such activity eventually found Senator John McCain (R-AZ) making campaign finance reform his signature issue in the 2000 presidential campaign, with substantial support from public opinion polls.

In part because of the economic collapse of Enron Corporation in December 2001 and the companion issue of corporate giving to federal candidates, in February 2002 legislation sponsored by Representatives Martin Meehan (D-MA) and Christopher Shays (R-CT) passed the House of Representatives by a margin of 240 to 189. In late March 2002, the Senate approved of virtually identical legislation co-sponsored by Senators John McCain and Russell Feingold (D-WI) on a convincing vote of 60 to 40 that promised important changes in the funding of federal election campaigns. The main features of the new law, signed by President George W. Bush in March 2002, included the following changes:

a. *Soft Money*—prohibited national political parties from accepting or spending any of the large, unlimited contributions made by corporations, labor unions, or individuals; leaves state and local party organizations to accept up to $10,000 per year per individual for "get-out-the-vote" efforts or voter registration drives in federal elections.

b. *Hard Money*—increased the total contributions that individuals can make during each two-year election cycle to all federal candidates, political action committees, and political parties from $50,000 to a total of $95,000 (indexed to inflation); also raises the amount individuals may contribute directly to candidates from $1,000 to $2,000 (also indexed to inflation rate; $2,400 in 2010) for each election.

c. *"Electioneering Communications"*—prohibits unions, corporations, and nonprofit organizations from paying for broadcast advertisements if those ads refer to a specific candidate and are broadcast within thirty days of a primary contest or sixty days of a general election; such ads could be paid for only with regulated hard money through PACs.

d. *Disclosure and Disclaimer Rules*—requires persons, corporations, or other groups dispersing an aggregate of $10,000 or more for the production and/or airing of electioneering communications to file a report with the FEC, including the names and addresses of persons who have contributed $1,000 or more to accounts funding the communication.

The law took effect after the November 2002 elections.

national political parties by individuals, corporations, unions, and political action committees for party-building registration drives, mailings, and advertising, and which do not specify a particular candidate by name. The new law also:

- Raised the limit from $1,000 to $2,000 that any person can give to a House or Senate candidate in each of the primary and general elections.
- Set a limit of $5,000 per candidate in the primary and another $5,000 limit in the general election for PACs.
- Set an overall limit of $37,500 for individuals over a two-year election cycle.
- Banned soft money except for $10,000 per state and local party committee for voter registration and political activism.
- Banned the use of corporate and union treasury money for all "electioneering communication," including issue advocacy.[32]

Consistent with the *Buckley* decision, the BCRA set no limit on the amount that individuals or groups could spend independently, that is, the expenses of a person, political committee, or group free of any coordination with a candidate's official campaign committee.

After an initial decision in *McConnell v. Federal Election Commission* (2003), where a razor-thin (5 to 4) majority of the Court upheld the two main provisions of the law—the Title I ban on soft money contributions to national parties and Title II restrictions on broadcast ads by corporations and labor unions that are aimed at opposition candidates—the Supreme Court majority began to show a "libertarian" hostility to many of the provisions of the BCRA (see Table 5.4 for details on this case history). This would culminate in the highly publicized decision in *Citizens United* v. *FEC* (2010). In question here was an effort during the 2008 presidential campaign by Citizens United—a conservative group organized as a nonprofit corporation—to release a feature-length documentary, *Hillary: The Movie*, criticizing Senator Hillary Rodham Clinton, who was then seeking the Democratic nomination for President of the United States. Because the release was scheduled for a date within the thirty days of a primary election, it ran afoul of the restrictions on "electioneering communications" under the BCRA. Citizens United brought suit against the FEC, seeking to have both the prohibitions on corporate funding of electioneering communications and the disclosure and disclaimer requirements for campaign advertisements declared unconstitutional. After initially refusing to hear the case on appeal, and then ordering the sides to reargue the case in October 2009, in January 2010 the Supreme Court ruled, overturning an earlier decision in *Austin v. Michigan State Chamber of Commerce* (1990) and parts of their decision in *McConnell* (see Table 14.7 for details).

Justice Kennedy, writing for a five-justice majority, held that the BCRA restriction on independent corporate electioneering communication violated the First Amendment, thus overturning that portion of their ruling in *McConnell*. "If the First Amendment has any force," Kennedy stated, "it prohibits Congress from fining or jailing citizens, or associations of citizens, for simply engaging in political speech." Quoting the Court's decision in *First National Bank of Boston v. Bellotti* (1976), Kennedy stated that "the First Amendment does not allow political speech restrictions based on a speaker's corporate identity." Fully consistent with the "libertarian" view of electoral free speech, the Court majority held that the only government interest strong enough to overcome the First Amendment would be to prevent *quid pro quo* corruption or its appearance, which is consistent with the contributions-versus-expenditures distinction established by the *Buckley* ruling. Expenditures limitations, even upon corporate entities, restrict the freedom to speak, and the citizens ability to hear, a wide variety of campaign messages:

> WHEN GOVERNMENT SEEKS TO USE ITS FULL POWER, INCLUDING THE CRIMINAL LAW, TO COMMAND WHERE A PERSON MAY GET HIS OR HER INFORMATION OR WHAT DISTRUSTED SOURCE HE OR SHE MAY NOT HEAR, IT USES CENSORSHIP TO CONTROL THOUGHT. THIS IS UNLAWFUL. THE FIRST AMENDMENT CONFIRMS THE FREEDOM TO THINK FOR OURSELVES.

While overturning the ban on corporate electioneering communications, an 8–1 majority upheld the disclosure requirements of BCRA, as a way for "citizens and shareholders to react to the speech of corporate entities in a proper way."

In a passionate 90-page dissenting opinion (he concurred only with the majority's ruling on disclosure requirements), Justice Stevens denied that the pre-election corporate communications ban infringed on speech, since corporations could still spend on campaign advertisements through their associated PACs. He further argued that the majority got it wrong—and got the framers of the First Amendment wrong—in equating corporate campaign spending with individual free speech. He expressed grave concern that the decision would open the floodgates to corporate campaign spending, thus unleashing a huge potential for political corruption and distortion of the democratic process. "The Court's ruling," he concluded, "threatens to undermine the integrity of elected institutions across the nation. The path it has taken to reach its outcome will, I fear, do damage to this institution."

The Court's ruling in *Citizens United* was immediately criticized, perhaps most vehemently by President Obama, who called it "a major victory for big oil, Wall Street banks, health insurance companies, and the other powerful interests that marshal their power every day in Washington to drown out the voices of everyday Americans."[33] The hysteria with which the decision was and has been greeted, especially on the political left, is probably overblown, as the ruling does not radically depart either from the line of campaign finance decisions that preceded it or from established free speech principles. Although it reflects the more libertarian approach to First Amendment jurisprudence regarding campaign and election expenditures, it also maintains the distinction between contributions (which can be regulated) and expenditures (which, increasingly, cannot) established over thirty years ago in *Buckley*. Whether this distinction can be realistically maintained in a truly libertarian framework remains to be seen. And whether any restrictions on contributions matter, in light of the use of the Internet and social media to organize and solicit campaign support, is a question many pundits and scholars have been asking. After the 2012 elections—where most critics of *Citizens United* predicted that unleashed independent expenditures would determine electoral outcomes—the jury is out on this question, as the massive amounts of campaign funding seem not to have had a real impact on who won and who lost. The real question, however, is how Congress might enact campaign finance reform legislation that deals with ongoing public concerns about the corruptive influence of money in politics without running afoul of the First Amendment.[34]

COERCED SPEECH AND THE "CULTURE WARS"

For many decades the Supreme Court has been sympathetic to citizens claiming that they ought not to be coerced to support an expression or ideology with which they disagree. In 1943 this very important rationale was endorsed by the Court when it struck down a mandatory flag salute law that Jehovah Witness parishioners claimed offended their religious beliefs (see Chapter 16, Brief 16.2, and discussion of *West Virginia State Board of Education v. Barnette*). A similar claim was central in another case brought in the 1970s by the same religious minority concerning New Hampshire's requirement that all noncommercial vehicles had to display license plates with the state motto, "Live Free or Die." When Jehovah Witnesses in the state objected to the motto and state requirement because they were contrary to their moral, religious, and political beliefs, the Supreme Court supported their claim in *Wooley v. Maynard* (1977). In its ruling, the Court said that the state could not require persons to advertise an ideological message with which they disagree by using a private vehicle as a "mobile billboard."

By the 1990s, the same principle involving compelled speech appeared in the context of homosexual rights and anti-discrimination laws. A decision by the Court in 1995 dealt with parade permits and whether the private sponsor of a parade could deny participation to a homosexual rights group based on the content of any message that might reasonably be expected to be transmitted (see Brief 14.6). In this more recent example, the Court again ruled in favor of those not wanting to be associated with a particular message.

Two additional decisions by the Court concern this same issue of coerced speech and the right of individuals or groups not to be associated with particular messages. The first had far-reaching implications for administrative discretion and academic integrity in American higher education. In *Board of Regents of the University of Wisconsin v. Southworth* (2000), the Court upheld a public university's

Brief 14.6

GAY RIGHTS AND FREE SPEECH

At the end of the 1994 term, the Supreme Court announced a decision that found the justices upholding the right of those who sponsor a parade to control the message that might be communicated. The case of *Hurley v. Irish-American Gay, Lesbian and Bisexual Group of Boston* (1995) involved the South Boston Allied War Veterans' Council, which, since 1947, had organized and conducted the annual St. Patrick's Day Parade in South Boston. In 1992 and 1993, the Gay-Lesbian and Bisexual Group of Boston (GLIB) was denied permission to march in the parade. GLIB filed suit in court claiming that the denial violated a Massachusetts public accommodation law, which prohibited "any disturbance, discrimination or restriction on account of sexual orientation." GLIB further claimed that it had a right to "express pride in their Irish heritage as openly gay, lesbian, and bisexual individuals . . . and to express their solidarity with like individuals . . . ". Against this claim, the War Veterans' Council claimed that the First Amendment protected the right of a "speaker"—in this case, the Council—to choose the content of its own message. Both the trial court and the Massachusetts Supreme Court ruled in favor of GLIB and against the parade organizers' exclusion of the group.

When the case was appealed to the Supreme Court, the justices ruled 9–0 that the state law was incorrectly interpreted and applied in this instance. According to Justice Souter's opinion for the unanimous Court, inherent in the protection provided by the First Amendment to parade participants is the organizer's right to shape any message that might be associated with the parade. That right of autonomy includes the right to exclude, as well as include, certain viewpoints. Since the First Amendment applies to a parade, the parade sponsor cannot be compelled by the government to express a viewpoint with which it disagrees. The justices reasoned that the War Veterans' Council had not attempted to exclude homosexuals or bisexuals who might participate in the parade as *individual* participants in bands or any number of other groups. The Court maintained, therefore, that the Council's decision was related to GLIB's message, not to the sexual orientation of the individual members. The Court's decision means that the sponsor of such events can exclude particular groups or organizations precisely because of the content of the message that might be conveyed, a right that can extend to any parade organizer. If GLIB wants to communicate a particular collective message, it can then organize its own parade and choose participants on the basis of the messages it wishes to convey. It is important to note here that the Court's deference to message content associated with a private organization does not apply when public bodies, such as local or state governments, are involved. The latter may not tailor the message and thereby discriminate against the messenger.

---

charging mandatory student fees over objections of a few students who claimed that the practice amounted to coerced speech. The University of Wisconsin at Madison assessed the student fees to subsidize various academic activities, student health services, intramural sports, and some two hundred campus organizations during the school year. Three law students challenged the policy of mandatory fees, claiming that the fees were a form of "compelled speech" that violated the First Amendment. Most of the controversy here was motivated by the fact that some of the money collected by the university was used one year to finance three activities with which the law students ideologically disagreed: an abortion-rights program presented at the Campus Women's Center, a gay-rights film festival, and a gay-rights conference held on campus and sponsored by two student groups.

Writing for a unanimous Court, Justice Anthony Kennedy said that a public university can charge its students a mandatory activities fee that helps to fund student organizations, even those that engage in ideological speech that some might find objectionable. In his opinion for the Court, Kennedy stated:

> THE UNIVERSITY MAY DETERMINE THAT ITS MISSION IS WELL SERVED IF STUDENTS HAVE THE MEANS TO ENGAGE IN DYNAMIC DISCUSSIONS OF PHILOSOPHICAL, RELIGIOUS, SCIENTIFIC, SOCIAL AND POLITICAL SUBJECTS IN THEIR EXTRACURRICULAR CAMPUS LIFE OUTSIDE THE LECTURE HALL. IF THE UNIVERSITY REACHES THIS CONCLUSION, IT IS ENTITLED TO IMPOSE A MANDATORY FEE TO SUSTAIN AN OPEN DIALOGUE TO THESE ENDS.

The justices did find fault with one feature of the Wisconsin system for charging student fees—namely, an alternative method of obtaining financing, or of denying an organization its funding, through a student-held referendum. The justices found this feature quite worrisome from a constitutional standpoint because it provided insufficient protection for minority viewpoints. As Kennedy observed, "[t]he whole theory of viewpoint neutrality is that minority views are treated with the same respect as are majority views." As a consequence, the justices considered that this feature of the Wisconsin system needed to be reexamined by a federal appeals court in Chicago.

In the same year, the Supreme Court was asked to decide whether a New Jersey anti-discrimination public accommodations law had been violated by the Boy Scouts of America (BSA), a private organization engaged in instilling in its members values that were contrary to a homosexual lifestyle. The specific question addressed in *Boy Scouts of America v. Dale* (2000) was whether James Dale, a gay-rights activist and assistant scoutmaster, could be excluded from membership in the organization. At issue here was the claim by the Boy Scouts of America that, given Dale's avowed sexual orientation, allowing him to serve in a leadership position would violate the organization's First Amendment associational right not to be affiliated with a message it strongly opposed. The justices divided 5 to 4, and ruled that the Boy Scouts did have an expressive associational right to exclude Dale and that the New Jersey law violated the Boy Scouts' right to freedom of speech. The majority opinion written by Chief Justice Rehnquist gave great deference to the BSA's claimed opposition to homosexual conduct and its right to exclude any scout leader who might impair its ability to preserve its organizational identity. The dissenters in the ruling, led by Justice Stevens, insisted that the Boy Scouts had never taken a definitive public stance against homosexual conduct, that the state law did not impose any serious burden upon the organization, and that Dale's continued membership would not have conveyed the message that the Boy Scouts necessarily endorsed homosexuality.

Given the prevalence of anti-discrimination laws similar to the New Jersey law, some feared that there might be a backlash against the Boy Scouts following the decision from corporations and state governments withdrawing their support because they might not want to be accused of intolerance. Running somewhat counter to this anti-discrimination trend at the state level, but testifying to the emotional and political volatility of the issue of membership in the BSA, Congress passed in 2002 the Boy Scouts of America Equal Access Act, which requires that no public school or state educational agency receiving federal funding shall deny equal access to any group officially affiliated with the Boy Scouts. Failure to comply with the law and allow these groups to meet on school property before or after school hours would result in the termination of federal assistance. At the same time, the BSA has been debating whether to change its policy and allow gay scouts and scoutmasters in the organization.

THE "FIGHTING-WORDS" DOCTRINE: IS SOME SPEECH NOT PROTECTED?

First Amendment freedoms, like all constitutional rights, have never been interpreted by any majority of the Supreme Court as absolute, meaning that under some circumstances (usually involving the time, place, and manner under which the claimed right can be exercised), these guarantees must yield to more important societal goals imposed by government. But for many decades, when government imposes a restriction under these basic rights, it must prove a compelling interest for doing so. For a long time, however, courts have honored what has been termed the "fighting-words" doctrine to exclude certain categories of speech altogether, although the line of precedents surrounding this doctrine has been at times confusing and inconsistent. In *Chaplinsky v. New Hampshire* (1942), the Supreme Court ruled that a state could prohibit public speech that is offensive or derisive of another person. A few years later, the justices divided closely in *Terminiello v. Chicago* (1949) when they struck down a Chicago ordinance that prohibited any speech that "stirs the public to anger" or "invites disputes." In this ruling, the majority insisted that a key function of free speech is to invite disputes, and [i]t may indeed best serve its high purpose when it induces a condition of unrest, creates dissatisfaction with conditions as they are, or even stirs people to anger." The justices seemed to retreat somewhat from these early precedents when it upheld a New York law two years later that prohibited incitement of a breach of the peace in the case of *Feiner v. New York* (1951). Twenty years later, the *Cohen v. California* ruling in 1971 discussed earlier under symbolic speech found another slim five-member majority overturning the conviction of a man wearing a jacket with "Fuck the Draft" emblazoned on the back. In this ruling, the majority reasoned that this protest was aimed at no one individual but was intended to lodge a strong condemnation against conscription into the military during the Vietnam War.

In a few recent cases involving alleged "fighting-words" doctrine, the issue of **hate speech** has arisen, especially as it involves prejudicial expressions of derision or hateful prejudice against racial minorities. Some have argued successfully that government needs to legislate against such speech for two legitimate reasons. First, they claim that such expressions have no legitimate place in the exposition of ideas that ought to be considered in a democratic society. Additionally, as reflects the self-fulfilling prophecy of some "fighting-words" doctrine, racial minorities as the more vulnerable target of such epithets can oftentimes be the most immediate, though not the only, victims of such expressions. As one observer of the "fighting-words" doctrine has noted:

> [R]ACIST SPEECH FUNCTIONS AS A BLOW, NOT AS A PROFFERED IDEA. AND ONCE THE BLOW IS STRUCK, A DIALOGUE IS UNLIKELY TO FOLLOW. RACIAL INSULTS ARE PARTICULARLY UNDESERVING OF FIRST AMENDMENT PROTECTION, BECAUSE THE PERPETRATOR'S INTENTION IS NOT TO DISCOVER TRUTH OR INITIATE DIALOGUE BUT TO INJURE THE VICTIM.[35]

In the 1970s, one of the more intense episodes involving this issue concerned the request by the American Nazi Party to march in Skokie, Illinois, a community with a large number of Holocaust survivors. Party members argued that they should be entitled to march in their party uniforms, display the Nazi swastika, and distribute literature promoting hatred against Jews. After many separate court rulings, including one by the U.S. Supreme Court that denied a petition for certiorari to hear the case, a compromise was eventually reached whereby the party held a rally in Chicago's Marquette Park further from the Skokie community.

Incidents involving hate speech and the Ku Klux Klan merit attention in the sometimes confusing context of "fighting-words" doctrine. The case of *R.A.V. v. City of St. Paul* (1992) involved a white juvenile in Minnesota who had been charged with violating a city ordinance in St. Paul after he had participated in a late-night cross-burning at the home of an African American family. After the law was challenged as a violation of his First Amendment right to freedom of speech, a unanimous Supreme Court struck it down and said that the city could not single out "racial" fighting words or punish those who utter them. In his opinion for the Court, Justice Scalia insisted that

> [S]ELECTIVITY OF THIS SORT CREATES THE POSSIBILITY THAT THE CITY IS SEEKING TO HANDICAP THE EXPRESSION OF PARTICULAR IDEAS. THE POINT OF THE FIRST AMENDMENT IS THAT MAJORITY PREFERENCES MUST BE EXPRESSED IN SOME FASHION OTHER THAN SILENCING SPEECH ON THE BASIS OF ITS CONTENT.

Perhaps in order to win support for the Court's reasoning rather than its holding, Scalia noted that while he found cross-burning to be "reprehensible," the community "has sufficient means at its disposal to prevent such behavior without adding the First Amendment to the fire."

In a confusing sequel to *R.A.V. v. St. Paul*, the Supreme Court addressed a question not actually raised in the 1992 ruling: whether a state can specifically prohibit cross-burning, not as a protected symbolic expression, but as part of calculated intimidation against an individual or group. In *Virginia v. Black* (2003), a six-member majority struck down a Virginia law passed in 1952 because it allowed a jury to infer that *any* cross-burning was clear and convincing evidence of the intent to intimidate. But the majority also concluded that "a state, consistent with the First Amendment, may ban cross-burning carried out with the intent to intimidate." In her opinion for the majority, Justice O'Connor seemed especially sensitive to the intimidation of racial minorities:

> THE FIRST AMENDMENT PERMITS VIRGINIA TO OUTLAW CROSS BURNINGS DONE WITH THE INTENT TO INTIMIDATE BECAUSE BURNING A CROSS IS A PARTICULARLY VIRULENT FORM OF INTIMIDATION. INSTEAD OF PROHIBITING ALL INTIMIDATING MESSAGES, VIRGINIA MAY CHOOSE TO REGULATE THIS SUBSET OF INTIMIDATING MESSAGES IN LIGHT OF CROSS BURNING'S LONG AND PERNICIOUS HISTORY AS A SIGNAL OF IMPENDING VIOLENCE.

Justice Thomas's concurring opinion argued that cross-burning itself should be granted a First

Brief 14.7
DOES THE FIRST AMENDMENT PROTECT FALSE SPEECH?

In recent years the Supreme Court has been hostile to government efforts to place content-based restrictions on speech, even expression deemed harmful or offensive (the decision in *Snyder v. Phelps* discussed earlier in this chapter is a good case in point). But what about congressional efforts to protect the integrity and value of military awards and medals, by making it a crime to lie about winning such an honor? This was the question for the justices in *United States v. Alvarez* (2012).

Congress passed the Stolen Valor Act in 2006, attempting to uphold "the reputation and meaning of military awards" by making it a misdemeanor for anyone to "falsely representing himself or herself, verbally or in writing, to have been awarded any decoration or medal authorized by Congress for the Armed Forces of the United States." Xavier Alvarez, who was serving as an elected member of a local water board in California, violated the law by making the following statement to his fellow members at a board meeting:

I'm a retired marine of 25 years. I retired in the year 2001. Back in 1987, I was awarded the Congressional Medal of Honor. I got wounded many times by the same guy. I'm still around.

His statement was a lie. Not only did Alvarez never receive this highest military honor awarded by the United States, he never even served in the military! He was charged with and convicted of violating the Stolen Valor Act. Alvarez moved to dismiss his conviction, arguing that the law was unconstitutional on its face.

By a 6–3 vote, the Court held the act an unconstitutional infringement on freedom of speech. In his plurality opinion joined by three other justices (Roberts, Ginsburg, and Sotomayor), Justice Kennedy rejected the notion that false speech is categorically unprotected, saying that intentional lies can only be punished when tied to some harm, such as defamation of character or fraud. He argued for applying strict scrutiny to the law in question, and did not think the government had satisfied the demands of showing a "compelling interest" for issuing this prohibition on speech. The government had not provided evidence that

the public's general perception of military awards is diluted by false claims such as those made by respondent. And it has not shown, and cannot show, why counterspeech, such as the ridicule respondent received online and in the press, would not suffice to achieve its interest.

Justices Breyer and Kagan concurred in the decision, but wanted to apply an intermediate level of scrutiny to determine where the balance lies between the government's interest in preventing the undermining of military decorations and the First Amendment harm done by punishing even false factual statements, which can "serve useful human objectives in many contexts." They concluded that the Stolen Valor Act was unconstitutional because a more finely tailored law would have imposed less harm to free speech while still achieving the government's legitimate objectives.

Justice Alito, joined by Justices Scalia and Thomas, dissented, claiming that "false factual statements possess no intrinsic First Amendment value." Although he conceded that it may sometimes be necessary to accord protection to false speech in order to give "breathing space" for protected or true speech, in this case the law specifically targeted a particularly odious kind of lie, one that tarnished the heroic actions of men and women, dead and alive, who courageously served their country.

Once again, the Court found itself opposing content-based censorship of speech, even false speech that most would consider harmful to society and nation. Like the decision the year before to protect offensive picketing at military funerals, the justices ruled against a government seeking what they considered an overbroad and overly speech-restrictive solution to a problem better handled by means other than repressing the First Amendment.

Amendment exception, as the practice was uniquely associated with racial and religious supremacy, and therefore properly banned by the state. Three justices (Souter, Ginsburg, and Kennedy) dissented in the judgment on First Amendment grounds that the Court here permitted the state to single out one especially potent symbol for criminal treatment. Justice Kennedy insisted that this ruling on cross-burning is very difficult to reconcile with the *R. A. V.* ruling and the complete message neutrality that it required.

The following chapter explores additional categories of expression (i.e., obscenity and libel) that are not protected by the First Amendment, but a recent decision raised questions about whether false and harmful expression could be restricted by public officials consistent with free speech principles (see Brief 14.7).

CONCLUSION

The First Amendment's guarantees of freedom of expression seek to fulfill a multitude of individual and communal functions. Freedom of expression strengthens personal growth and the intellectual faculties that citizens need to function responsibly in a democratic society. It compels the discerning citizen to separate truth from fiction, just from unjust, in the cacophony of voices that are aired in the public square. It protects the marketplace of ideas that citizens need to consider in a community as diverse and pluralistic as the United States.

As Justice Oliver Wendell Holmes, Jr. observed decades ago that "if there is any principle of the Constitution that more imperatively calls for attachment than any other it is the principle of free thought—not free thought for those who agree with us but freedom for the thought that we hate."[36] But many of the clashes over freedom of speech covered in this chapter demonstrate that this reminder by Justice Holmes can be a difficult precept for many private citizens and public officials to live with, even in the best of times. On many occasions in America's political history, the Supreme Court has had to enter the political arena and establish guidelines regarding legal limits to freedom of expression, especially political speech.

There is little doubt that for many decades, the Court has been increasingly more vigilant about protecting political speech in American society, although the degree of protection accorded it has varied with the magnitude of perceived threats to internal order and national security, and occasionally with prevailing public opinion. Paralleling these developments in free speech law have been some important freedom of assembly cases before the Supreme Court. Symbolic speech has not enjoyed precisely the same degree of protection as pure speech, although many of the cases in this area, such as *Texas v. Johnson*, demonstrate the Court's continuing sympathy for persons expressing themselves through symbolic behavior. In such areas as labor picketing, commercial speech, electoral campaign expenditures, and hate speech, the Supreme Court has had more difficulty establishing a clear and coherent body of First Amendment law.

Having examined several Supreme Court decisions on free speech and assembly guarantees, two general observations are appropriate. First, nothing in First Amendment case history has found a majority of the justices adopting an absolute view of these critical freedoms. When national security issues have arisen, the Court has normally deferred to the federal government in its struggle to accomplish strategic ends in a free but sometimes fragile society. The justices have also tried to balance the guarantees of free expression against the community's interest in avoiding violence, preventing electoral corruption, and protecting the rights of others who may be negatively affected by such free expression.

Second, although the developments discussed in this chapter might suggest broader protections for self-expression, the Court has not devised a single, uniform standard for deciding First Amendment controversies. Instead, it has avoided making a broad, encompassing legal doctrine and resorted to a case-by-case approach with standards limited to the time, place, and manner regulations of free expression. This approach may be the most pragmatic one to accommodating the widely divergent political views of a population that now numbers over 315 million citizens, but it also highlights the difficulties that the Supreme Court must face in dealing with this broad diversity.

Chapter 15
Freedom of the Press

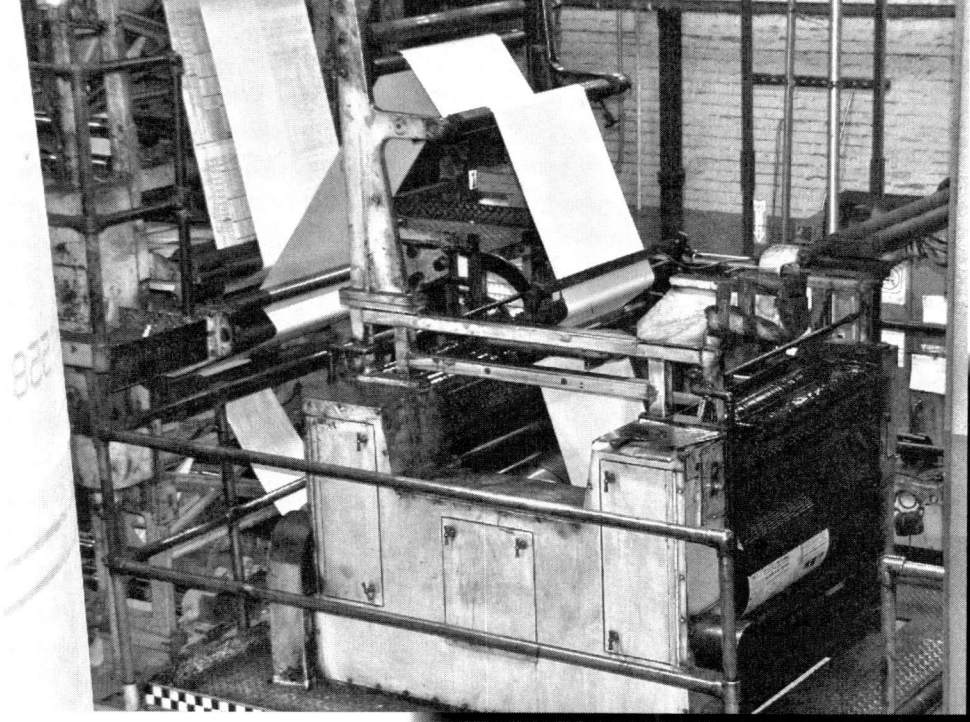

The printing press stands as a vivid representation of a vigorous press, free from government censorship—a tradition that predates even the First Amendment. Today, the traditional press faces challenges, especially from new media, that the Constitution's framers could not have imagined.

▼ Introductory Remarks by Benjamin Franklin

Library of Congress, Prints & Photographs Division [LC-USZ62-90398].

Hello, readers, my name is Benjamin Franklin. I was more than eighty years old when we wrote the great Constitution of the United States, but my interest in freedom of the press began long before that. I learned to be a printer as an apprentice in Boston under my brother, James. In 1729, when I was 23 years old, I began publishing my first newspaper, the *Pennsylvania Gazette*, in Philadelphia. Some people have called it the first modern newspaper because I combined many different features—news, opinion, gossip, and even some sensationalism when it came to sex and crime.

During those years, I was often criticized and censured by all kinds of persons for printing things they didn't like. I finally answered my critics in a *Gazette* editorial that I called "Apology for Printers." In my editorial, I made it clear that we printers are in the business of printing "*mens opinions*," which "*are almost as various as their Faces.*" As I went on to say, "*if all Printers were determined not to print any thing till they were sure it would offend no body, there would be very little printed.*" Frankly, you can't have a free press if you are afraid of offending someone.

I never believed that the role of the press was to stay out of trouble, but I firmly believed that the press should be truthful and fair. As I stated once: "*Printers are educated in the belief that when men differ in opinion, both sides ought equally to have the advantage of being heard by the public; and that when Truth and Error have fair play, the former is always an overmatch for the latter.*"

But, of course, the "press" has changed a lot since my day. Americans today are subjected to such a wide array of news sources and other information, including your new so-called "social media," that it is difficult to keep up with it all. I still pay attention to the workings of the "press" but I haven't figured out Twitter or Facebook yet.

Pay attention in this chapter to the many issues that surround a free press in a free society. The role of prior restraint, or government censorship, has always been a problem for supporters of a free press, as you will see in the discussion of the *New York Times v. United States*. Also, remember that sometimes allowing free rein to the press may compromise other freedoms—such as the right to a fair trial. This is a tough call in a democracy, but it is one that judges need to make. Readers of this chapter also face the issue of a reporter's privilege to protect sources of confidential information through so-called "shield laws."

And finally, I was always known as a little "earthy" when it came to issues involving sex. We had our troubles with people who were offended by too much "skin" or even sexual innuendos, just as you do today. Pay particular attention to the discussions of obscenity and libel in the chapter to see just how far our society will allow a free press to go. As society has become more open with regard to sex, however, it has also found the need to draw the line when protecting vulnerable Americans, especially children, from pornography and exploitation.

Finally, let me say that the newspaper business was very good to me. I sold the *Gazette* and made a very good living from my other project, *Poor Richard's Almanack*. Pick it up sometime and see if you learn anything. BF

Sources: Benjamin Franklin and His Printing Press, *The Franklin Institute*, http://sln.fi.edu/franklin/printer/printer.html; Benjamin Franklin: Apology for Printers, www.jprof.com/history/franklin-apologia.html.

THE BASIC THEORY OF FREEDOM OF THE PRESS

Important connections exist between freedom of speech and freedom of the press. Much of the value of free speech would be lost if ideas and expressions could not be circulated freely in a democratic society through a free press. Although its several freedoms are normally discussed in individualist terms, the First Amendment also serves an important communal purpose of informing the public. People are vitally dependent upon a free press—including the broadcast media, the cable television and film industries, and online information systems—in order to obtain sufficient information to make responsible judgments about public affairs and to disseminate enlightened ideas and analysis about those affairs. This reciprocal process must be open and free from governmental censorship (see Brief 15.1).

The public's right to a free press has stronger historical roots than the right to free speech. Of the eleven original states that adopted constitutions during the Revolutionary War, nine of them protected freedom of the press, and only Pennsylvania protected free speech. Freedom of the press carries two very important rights: the right to publish free of government censorship; and the right to publish without fear of being prosecuted or punished for the views advanced.

When government imposes a **prior restraint** upon the dissemination of information and ideas, it restrains or forbids expression before it is communicated. Obtaining governmental approval for expression prior to publication, dissemination, or broadcast has several

---

Brief 15.1

FREEDOM OF THE PRESS AT HOME AND AROUND THE WORLD

The First Amendment Center's 2012 survey on "State of the First Amendment" contained some predictable and some surprising news about how a random sample of respondents view the role of a free press in America. When asked if the First Amendment goes too far in the rights that it guarantees, only 13 percent agreed, while 81 percent felt it does not go too far. However, public awareness of the First Amendment is still surprisingly low. When asked to name the five specific freedoms in the First Amendment, 65 percent of respondents could name freedom of speech, followed by 28 percent who could name the freedom of religion, 13 percent the freedom of the press, 13 percent the right to assemble, and 4 percent the right to petition. Twenty-seven percent could not list any of the First Amendment rights.

The majority of American respondents are suspicious of government control of the Internet, with a majority (59 percent) believing that government should not be allowed to take control of the Internet in the event of a national emergency. The survey revealed that higher numbers of Americans than ever before are supportive of more freedom: 85 percent believe that people should be allowed to record or photograph the activities of the police in public as long as they do not interfere with police actions; and 69 percent agree that musicians should be allowed to sing potentially offensive songs.

When asked about their most useful sources of news about candidates in the 2012 election, 40 percent of Americans indicated that they relied on television broadcast news, followed by newspapers and their websites (30 percent), TV news organization websites (29 percent), the Internet (14 percent), and radio (10 percent). These figures have moved consistently in recent years away from print journalism toward electronic and broadcast sources.

While Americans probably tend to take a free press for granted, this freedom is not a given throughout most of the world. In its annual report on global press freedom, Freedom House reported a decline in 2009 for the eighth year in a row. The most negative direction for press freedom has occurred in China, the Middle East, and even in parts of Latin America. China specifically stands out as a "poor performer," earning Freedom House's lowest score in this regard. While the "new media," including the Internet, helped to lead the expansion of press freedom in the 1990s, governments have become more effective in limiting Internet access and global technologies. The ongoing dispute between China and Google stands as an example, but other countries such as Russia and Venezuela also have launched strong efforts against bloggers and certain websites. The Freedom House study also found that one of the most alarming losses of press freedom occurred in Mexico, where drug cartels and gangs effectively threaten journalists into not reporting the news.

Parts of the world are increasingly dangerous places for journalists to do their jobs. American reporter Daniel Pearl, who was kidnapped and beheaded while on assignment in Pakistan in 2002, was the South Asia Bureau Chief for the *Wall Street Journal*. His murder drew international attention and started a bipartisan movement within the United States to help journalists in these situations. In May 2010, President Barack Obama signed into law the Daniel Pearl Freedom of the Press Act. The Act requires the State Department in its annual Human Rights Reports to publicize threats to journalists by listing countries and governments that commit crimes against them.

SOURCES: Howard La Franchi, "Press freedom falls around the world," *Christian Science Monitor*, April 29, 2010, www.csmonitor.com; *Freedom of the Press*, Freedom House, www.freedomhouse.org; The First Amendment Center, "State of the First Amendment 2012," www.firstamendmentcenter.org.

negative implications for thought and communication. It presumes that the material is harmful to society in some respect and thereby prevents it from being judged fairly under normal due process procedures. Prior restraints also deprive the community of the chance to evaluate openly whether the information will actually harm society in any way.

Another difficulty with imposing a prior restraint upon publications is that it violates the principle that an author is entitled to be judged by one's peers for opinions and information that are distributed freely. When a prior restraint occurs, the government declares the defendant guilty without the benefit of society judging for itself the accuracy or worth of the censored material, thereby violating due process safeguards of both the Fifth and Fourteenth Amendments. Finally, prior restraint has a chilling effect upon all speech, protected and unprotected. As the Supreme Court has said, "The special vice of a prior restraint is that communication will be suppressed, either directly or by inducing excessive caution in the speaker, before an adequate determination that it is unprotected by the First Amendment."[1]

THE ANGLO-AMERICAN CONTEXT OF A FREE PRESS

Notwithstanding the admonition of William Blackstone, English jurist and author, that the "liberty of the press consists in laying no previous restraints upon publication,"[2] early Anglo-American practice exhibited many instances of prior restraints and relatively few successful protests against its imposition. The classical prior restraints on publication were the English licensing laws that began in the early sixteenth century under King Henry VIII (1509–47), Edward VI (1547–53), and Queen Mary I (1553–58). The reign of Queen Elizabeth I (1558–1603) was memorable for many things, including a strengthened prior restraint system begun under Queen Mary with the passage in 1557 of England's first monopoly copyright law. The English Parliament eventually allowed the copyright law to expire in 1694, and in 1710 it passed a law that granted the right to publish to the author, rather than the publisher. However, any individual publishing material that was deemed to be "seditious libel," a vague category of press law referring to virtually anything that offended or annoyed the government, could be tried and punished by the government. In summary, the history of censorship in England from 1538 to 1695, and the government's pervasive control of religious and political publications, was a deliberate attempt to censor what the English citizenry wrote and read.

Licensing of the press in the American colonies existed in some areas until the early eighteenth century, although it was never as pervasive as that in England. Prior restraints upon printing existed in Virginia until the late seventeenth century and in Massachusetts, New York, and Pennsylvania until the 1720s. But by 1725, licensing of the press by colonial legislatures had been abolished as inconsistent with increasing public pressure for more freedom from official constraints (see Brief 15.2).

Thomas Jefferson and James Madison played very prominent roles in the early American movement to protect freedom of the press. With his unlimited faith in "the good sense of the people" and their capacity for self-correction, Jefferson was well aware of the critical role performed by a free press. He noted in a letter to his friend Edward Carrington in 1787, "[w]ere it left to me to decide whether we should have a government without newspapers, or newspapers without a government, I should not hesitate a moment to prefer the latter."[3] He deeply regretted the omission of any reference to a free press in the new Constitution and why it was so vital to society:

> THE WAY TO PREVENT... IRREGULAR INTERPOSITIONS OF THE PEOPLE IS TO GIVE THEM FULL INFORMATION OF THEIR AFFAIRS THROUGH THE CHANNEL OF THE PUBLIC PAPERS, AND TO CONTRIVE THAT THOSE PAPERS SHOULD PENETRATE THE WHOLE MASS OF THE PEOPLE.[4]

When the First Congress began drafting a formal bill of rights in the summer of 1789, James Madison's original proposal to protect free communication read in part, "[t]he people shall not be deprived or abridged of their right to speak, to write, or to publish their sentiments, and the freedom of the press, as one of the great bulwarks of liberty, shall be inviolable."[5] As it was modified by the new Congress and eventually embodied in the First Amendment, freedom of the press was widely assumed to mean freedom from any prior restraint upon the press. Somewhat ironically, the early American press was rather primitive and partisan, compared to what much of mass media have become in the contemporary era (see Brief 15.3). Throughout American history,

Brief 15.2

THE ZENGER TRIAL AND THE QUEST FOR A FREE PRESS

In the 1730s, an important trial took place in what is today Federal Hall National Memorial next to the present-day New York Stock Exchange. The trial involved a German-born publisher named John Peter Zenger, who by 1733 owned and operated the *New York Weekly Journal*. Zenger was part of a political faction in New York City that was opposed to the British Royal Governor, William Cosby. Zenger began to publish in his newspaper articles that accused Cosby of incompetence, favoritism, jury tampering, and election fraud. In 1734, Zenger, as publisher of the newspaper, was arrested and prosecuted for sedition. In the 1735 trial, Zenger's lawyers were highly critical of both Governor Cosby's administration and the trial judge's political bias in the case. They were dismissed and disbarred from practicing law in the colony, and a prominent Quaker attorney from Philadelphia, Andrew Hamilton, decided to defend Zenger in the trial.

Early in the trial, the judge explained to members of the jury that, under common law, their task was only to decide the factual basis of the publication, and that he, as judge, would decide whether or not Zenger's published articles were seditious. As part of Zenger's defense, Hamilton argued that Zenger's publications were true and if he were not allowed to demonstrate the truthfulness of the material, then the jury should acquit the defendant. In what today would fall under the label of "jury nullification," the jury ignored the judge's instructions as to how the law should be interpreted and applied, and found Zenger not guilty of seditious libel. Although the Zenger trial and verdict did not immediately change the common law that prevailed at that time, it established a very significant precedent for citizens' rights to freedom of speech and press, and against governmental censorship. Specifically, the press should not be restrained or punished for publishing stories about matters of public interest and public affairs.

SOURCE: Leonard Levy, ed., *Freedom of the Press from Zenger to Jefferson* (New York: Bobbs-Merrill, 1966); Thomas L. Tedford, *Freedom of Speech in the United States* (New York: Random House, 1985).

THE "PRESS" THEN AND NOW

At the time of the founding, the press consisted of exclusively print media (magazines, newspapers, pamphlets, tabloids) that were irregular in their publication, relatively expensive in their production, and very partisan in what they conveyed to their readers. Even though such political leaders as John Adams, Alexander Hamilton, Thomas Jefferson, and James Madison recognized the critical need to keep citizens informed, the newspapers of this era were quite primitive and unprofessional compared to much of the contemporary mass media. The politically savvy and calculating Alexander Hamilton prevailed upon his Federalist friend, John Fenno, to begin publishing the *Gazette of the United States*, an early newspaper which unabashedly promoted Federalist policies of President George Washington's administration, partly in exchange for government printing contracts arranged by Hamilton, Secretary of the Treasury. To counter the Federalist Party agenda and administration, the nascent political movement of Jefferson and Madison, which was the forerunner of what became the Democratic Party in the 1820s, launched its own partisan newspaper. Jefferson convinced one Philip Freneau to begin publishing the *National Gazette* to answer Fenno's paper. Taking a cue from Hamilton, Freneau was able to win a contract to print documents from the State Department, largely because of Jefferson's position as Secretary of State until 1793. Freneau's *National Gazette* soon disappeared with the loss of its financial base. In many respects, in spite of the strong principle of a free and operating press, most newspapers in this early founding era were decades away from being professionally objective and financially successful.

Over the next century, the working press in the United States gradually became less financially dependent on political parties, more objective in how it covered the public's business, and more professionally skilled in gathering and reporting news and public affairs. Newspaper circulation by the 1990s rested at over 60 million subscribers, and many reputable nationwide newspapers, such as the *Wall Street Journal*, the *New York Times*, *USA Today*, the *Los Angeles Times*, and the *Washington Post*, each had circulations near or beyond 1 million daily readers. In television, the field has expanded noticeably in recent years. Whereas the three main commercial networks of Columbia Broadcasting System, National Broadcasting Company, and American Broadcasting Company dominated television in the early 1950s, by the 1970s several new challengers to these big three networks appeared, the most successful of which were Cable News Network and Fox News Network. For many "news junkies" today, the federally owned and operated Corporation for Public Broadcasting and C-SPAN, along with National Public Radio, have become increasingly more popular with an attentive and alert American citizenry that strongly supports a publicly funded media network. Added to this media mix that tries to enlighten the public on political issues is an equally elaborate cable television industry. These mass media instruments compete for the public's eyes and ears with an endless run of broadcasts focused on major professional sports, movie reruns, syndicated situation comedies, and talk shows, some of which sometimes test the viewers' patience and aptitude for boredom.

relatively few prior restraints have been imposed by government upon the press (see Table 15.1), unlike the several efforts by government

discussed in the previous chapter to regulate free speech, especially seditious speech. As this chapter indicates, free press doctrine varies with the particular medium at issue, the circumstances surrounding the exercised press guarantee, and the balancing of different rights of individuals and society at large.

THE CLASSIC CASE: NEAR V. MINNESOTA (1931)

In 1931, the U.S. Supreme Court reviewed for the first time a case specifically dealing with prior restraint of the press and ruled that a free press is within the liberty safeguarded by the Due Process Clause of the Fourteenth Amendment against impairment by the states. The statutory grounds for the case began in 1925, with the passage of the Minnesota Public Nuisance Law, prohibiting any publication of "malicious, scandalous and defamatory" newspapers, magazines, or other periodicals. Two years later, a Minneapolis tabloid known as *The Saturday Press* began publishing several articles charging that various Minneapolis public officials had failed to expose and punish alleged criminals responsible for the gambling, bootlegging and racketeering prevalent in the city. The publisher of the newspaper was one Jay M. Near, who two authors of a prominent book on controversial cases have portrayed as notoriously "anti-Catholic, anti-Semite, anti-black, and anti-labor."[6]

Acting upon the basis of the state law, a court in 1927 issued a temporary injunction against Near because of the prejudicial nature of several articles appearing in *The Saturday Press*. The trial court convicted Near over his objections that the law violated the First and Fourteenth Amendments. The Minnesota Supreme Court upheld the conviction, stating that, "our Constitution was never intended to protect malice, scandal and defamation when untrue or published with bad motives or without justifiable ends." Near then appealed to the U.S. Supreme Court, which held 5 to 4 that the state law violated both the First and Fourteenth Amendments. The majority opinion drafted by Chief Justice Charles Evans Hughes argued that even though freedom of the press was not absolute, restraint was the exception:

THE FACT THAT FOR APPROXIMATELY ONE HUNDRED AND FIFTY YEARS THERE HAS BEEN ALMOST AN ENTIRE ABSENCE OF ATTEMPTS TO IMPOSE PREVIOUS RESTRAINTS UPON PUBLICATIONS RELATING TO THE MALFEASANCE OF PUBLIC OFFICERS IS SIGNIFICANT OF THE DEEP-SEATED CONVICTION THAT SUCH RESTRAINTS WOULD VIOLATE CONSTITUTIONAL RIGHT.

According to Hughes, only four circumstances might justify invoking prior restraint under the First Amendment: the publication of critical military information in wartime; obscene publications; publications inciting "acts of violence" or the violent overthrow of the government; or finally, publications that invade "private rights." Since none of these special circumstances existed in *Near*, Hughes wrote that "liberty of the press... has meant, principally although not exclusively, immunity from prior restraints or censorship." According to the Chief Justice, the "fact that the liberty of the press may be abused by miscreant purveyors of scandal does not make any the less necessary the immunity of the press from previous restraint in dealing with official misconduct." Hughes also indicated that public officials who felt that they or their official conduct had been defamed could still seek remedy and damages through then-existing libel laws.

A key principle established in *Near v. Minnesota* is that a prior restraint upon the press is an extreme measure that should be allowed only in rare circumstances, all of which would be the subject of future controversies before the Court. At the center of Hughes's argument was his insistence that libel laws, not suppression of the press, provided the best protection against false accusations and defamation of character. (For a case of censorship of a student newspaper, see Brief 15.4.)

PRIOR RESTRAINT AND THE VIETNAM WAR: *NEW YORK TIMES V. UNITED STATES* (1971)

Before the summer of 1971 the federal government had never asked the federal courts to suppress the publication of material deemed a threat to national security. Some reports had circulated during the early 1960s that the Kennedy administration had persuaded both the *New York Times* and the *Washington Post* to

Table 15.1 Development of the Law Doctrine of Prior Restraint: Censorship and the Press

Year	Case	Significance
1931	*Near v. Minnesota*	First time that Court reviewed case of prior restraint on press; struck down state "public nuisance" law prohibiting malicious, scandalous, or defamatory publications as an unconstitutional restraint upon publication; free press nearly absolute.
1936	*Grosjean v. American Press*	Court ruled that Louisiana law taxing gross receipts on newspapers was a discriminatory burden upon newspaper because it restrained amount of revenue realized from advertising and restricted circulation.
1938	*Lovell v. Griffin*	Liberty of free press not limited to newspapers or periodicals; also includes leaflets, handbills, and pamphlets; municipal ordinance in Georgia banned distribution of leaflets without first obtaining permission; Court struck down ordinance as prior restraint upon the press.
1939	*Schneider v. Irvington*	Jehovah Witness convicted of canvassing and distributing religious tracts; Court declared local ordinance unconstitutional violation of First Amendment.
1960	*Talley v. California*	Los Angeles ordinance required all handbills distributed to include the name and address of person preparing, sponsoring, and distributing them; Court said that identification of authorship restricted freedom to distribute and violated freedom of expression.
1966	*Mills v. Alabama*	Alabama law prohibited solicitation of votes on election day; newspaper editor printed editorial on election day encouraging readers to vote a particular way on proposition and was convicted under law; Court overturned law as violation of free press.
1971	*Organization for a Better Austin v. Keefe*	Circulation of handbills by citizens' group opposed real estate agent's effort to sell property to minority buyers; injunction tried to restrain further distribution of material; Court declared that injunction was an unconstitutional restraint upon First Amendment rights.
1971	*New York Times v. U.S.*	Court denied attempt by federal government to impose a prior restraint upon publication of *Pentagon Papers* study; justices ruled that government had failed to meet heavy burden of showing justification for restraint on national security grounds.
1980	*Snepp v. U.S.*	Involved issue of indirect prior restraint; divided Court upheld right of CIA to require prospective employees to take lifetime oath never to release any material without first obtaining agency approval prior to publication.
1988	*Lakewood v. Plain Dealer Publishing*	City ordinance giving mayor near total discretion over granting of vending racks on public sidewalks was struck down; city of Lakewood, Ohio, could regulate sale of materials but criteria must be neutral and not based on point of view of material.
1988	*Hazelwood School Dist. v. Kuhlmeier*	Held that public school administrators can impose prior restraint upon articles in student newspapers considered inconsistent with "basic educational mission" of school
1991	*Simon & Schuster v. New York State Crime Victims Bd.*	Struck down New York law denying criminals the right to profit from any publication written about their crimes and diverting the monies to a victim's fund.

Brief 15.4

THE STUDENTS' RIGHT TO PUBLISH CAN BE REGULATED

In May 1983, the principal of the high school in Hazelwood, Missouri, deleted two pages from the student newspaper entitled *Spectrum*, published as part of the school curriculum, on the grounds that they were inappropriate for publication in a campus newspaper. One of the purged articles reported interviews with three anonymous, but possibly identifiable, students concerning their pregnancies and personal experiences with sex and birth control. Another article discussed divorce and included a student's complaints about her father, naming the student. Neither article contained any graphic accounts of sexual activity, violence, or illegal activities.

Student staff members of *Spectrum* sued in federal court claiming that their right to a free press under the First Amendment had been violated. In 1988 in the case of *Hazelwood School District v. Kuhlmeier*, the Supreme Court ruled 5–3 that public school officials have extensive authority to censor student newspapers and other "school-sponsored expressive activities." The ruling argued that the activities that are part of the school curriculum carry the imprint of school authority and legitimacy; therefore, officials have a right to regulate the dissemination of information relating to drugs, sexual activity, pregnancy, birth control, and other contentious political and social issues.

The majority opinion in this speech-press case was authored by Justice Byron White, who recognized the school authorities' right to intervene and limit publication of information inconsistent with the school's "basic educational mission." White reaffirmed the longtime principle that had emerged in *Tinker v. Des Moines School District* (1969; see Chapter 14) guaranteeing students the right of free expression on school grounds. But he also said that the *Tinker* principle did not pertain in *Hazelwood* because the latter occurred as incident to the school curriculum and carried the "imprimatur of the school." Among three dissenting justices in this case, Justice William Brennan criticized the "blanket censorship authority" assumed by the school principal in this case, and the rule that apparently jeopardized a large body of student expression channeled through the campus newspaper.

---

delay or alter their coverage of the Bay of Pigs fiasco and the Cuban Missile Crisis, but these alleged incidents did not involve direct government censorship.[7] In June 1971, the publication in both of these newspapers of a series of articles based on a top-secret history of American involvement in the Vietnam War created an immediate clash between national security interests and free press guarantees. The main focus of the controversy, which arose and was settled in an uncharacteristically brief three-week period,[8] was a 47-volume, 7,000-page document titled "History of U.S. Decision-Making Process on Viet Nam Policy." Initiated in the late 1960s by then–Secretary of Defense Robert S. McNamara, the lengthy report, usually referred to as the *Pentagon Papers*, documented the nation's growing involvement in Indochina during the Truman–Eisenhower–Kennedy–Johnson administrations. In addition to its top-secret classification, the study revealed that the United States had been more deeply involved in the Vietnamese civil war during the 1950s and 1960s than American public officials had ever disclosed.

Copies of the classified study had been obtained by former Defense Department analysts Daniel Ellsberg and Anthony Russo, who had helped prepare the survey. By 1969–70, Ellsberg and Russo had grown increasingly disillusioned with the war effort and had become active in the anti-war movement. Upon leaving government employment in 1970, they apparently gave the report to the *New York Times*, which began on June 13, 1971, to serialize various excerpts from the study. The *Washington Post* began publishing its own account of the survey soon thereafter, and the Nixon administration sued in two federal courts to stop publication of the study. In an effort to resolve differing federal court rulings, the Supreme Court agreed to hear the case.

In a very brief *per curiam* opinion, the Supreme Court decided on June 30, 1971, to deny the U.S. government's request for a permanent restraining order because it had failed to show sufficient justification for why prior restraint was necessary to preserve national security. The precise ruling in this case is important to understand because the decision meant that government might impose a prior restraint in cases where it can prove that a particular publication will pose a serious threat to national security (in accordance with one of the circumstances established in *Near*). However, in the *Pentagon Papers Case*, the government did not meet the stringent standard, with the justices dividing 6 to 3 against the government's request for an injunction. Interestingly, all nine justices authored separate opinions explaining their respective votes.

In separate concurring opinions, Justices Hugo Black and William O. Douglas adopted an absolutist stance, arguing that under no circumstances should prior restraint be tolerated by the First Amendment. In what would be his last opinion in a long and very distinguished Supreme Court career, Justice Black stated:

> [F]OR THE FIRST TIME IN THE 182 YEARS SINCE THE FOUNDING OF THE REPUBLIC, THE FEDERAL COURTS ARE ASKED TO HOLD THAT THE FIRST AMENDMENT DOES NOT MEAN WHAT IT SAYS, BUT RATHER MEANS THAT THE GOVERNMENT CAN HALT THE PUBLICATION OF CURRENT NEWS OF VITAL IMPORTANCE TO THE PEOPLE OF THIS COUNTRY.

Four other justices authored concurring opinions, stating that, under some circumstances, they might be willing to support restraining orders upon the two newspapers. Justice Brennan stated that the government could conceivably impose prior restraint if the conflict involved a declared war and if the government could unequivocally prove that irreparable damage would be inflicted upon American military forces, but the government had not met that heavy burden of proof. In separate concurring opinions, Thurgood Marshall focused on the separation of powers principle and congressional refusal in the past to provide the president with broad authority to restrain the press. To him, the delineation of constitutional powers was clear and unequivocal:

> THE CONSTITUTION PROVIDES THAT CONGRESS SHALL MAKE LAWS, THE PRESIDENT EXECUTE LAWS, AND COURTS INTERPRET LAWS. . . . IT DID NOT PROVIDE FOR GOVERNMENT BY INJUNCTION IN WHICH THE COURTS AND THE EXECUTIVE "MAKE LAWS" WITHOUT REGARD TO THE ACTION OF CONGRESS.

Chief Justice Warren Burger, along with Justices John Harlan and Harry Blackmun, each authored dissenting opinions in which they emphasized the unfortunate urgency with which the Court was being asked to consider important issues affecting national security. Chief Justice Burger referred specifically to the "unwarranted deadlines and frenetic pressures" under which the majority seemed compelled to act. Justice Harlan criticized the "irresponsibly feverish" manner in which the Court was being asked to deal with the case. Both Harlan and Blackmun indicated their support for the "inherent powers" doctrine, which, as Blackmun stated, gave the president "primary power over the conduct of foreign affairs and . . . responsibility for the Nation's safety."

In essence, *New York Times v. United States* (1971) reinforced the principle articulated earlier in *Near* that in times of national crisis, when the government can prove that publications will result in irreparable damage to national security or the national interest, prior restraint upon publication might be justified. Because the absolutist position endorsed by Justices Black and Douglas has never been fully endorsed by a Court majority since this important decision, one wonders how the Supreme Court would handle a similar case today (see Brief 15.5).

FREE PRESS AND FAIR TRIAL: PROBLEMS WHEN RIGHTS COLLIDE

Society depends on an extensive communications network to keep citizens informed of a wide range of news stories and public issues. The United States exhibits a media audience that can receive hourly updates on news events occurring on the other side of the world.[9] However, communications technology also raises some important questions about how to safeguard the rights of persons who may be the focus of criminal investigations or defendants in a trial. What happens when an evening news program informs the public of fast-breaking news developments relating to a sordid murder scene where a suspect has been taken into custody? What about high-profile trials of prominent celebrities like O.J. Simpson, Kobe Bryant, Martha Stewart, or Lewis "Scooter" Libby where the public is bombarded with daily updates on the latest developments, some of which might be potential grounds for appeal of a conviction?[10]

Much of the dilemma concerning media publicity of a criminal setting arises because the Constitution provides its citizens with competing rights—the First Amendment's guarantee of a free press and the Sixth Amendment's promise of a "speedy and public trial by an impartial jury." The provision for a fair trial based solely on the presentation of evidence legally obtained can be difficult to guarantee, especially in an

Brief 15.5

PRIOR RESTRAINT AS A CONDITION FOR GOVERNMENT EMPLOYMENT: *SNEPP V. UNITED STATES* (1980)

In *Snepp v. United States* (1980), the Supreme Court dismissed a First Amendment challenge to the Central Intelligence Agency's long-standing practice of requiring employees and former employees to submit any authored material to the agency for prepublication review. Frank W. Snepp had worked for the CIA since 1968 and had signed a secrecy agreement promising not to publish any material without first obtaining clearance from the agency. When he resigned from the agency in 1976, he reaffirmed his obligation never to divulge any classified information or any material without first obtaining approval from the agency director. He later wrote a book based on his experiences titled *Decent Interval*, without submitting the manuscript to the agency for clearance in accordance with the signed agreement. The book was very critical of the agency but contained no classified information.

The federal government sued Snepp for breach of contract and the district court found in favor of the government, ordering him to refrain from publishing any further material without first obtaining agency clearance. The trial court also granted the government's request to establish a trust for the government to receive all book royalties. An appellate court upheld the ruling against Snepp, affirming that he had violated the terms of his contract with the CIA, but it disagreed with the constructive trust arrangement. Because of the narrow ruling on contract grounds, the First Amendment issue of free press and prior restraint was not specifically decided. In a 6–3 *per curiam* opinion handed down in *Snepp v. United States* (1980), the Supreme Court upheld the decision of the district court in all respects, including the breach of contract, the establishment of a trust, and the obligation of Snepp not to publish anything in the future without agency clearance. The opinion noted that ". . . undisputed evidence in this case shows that a CIA agent's violation of his obligation to submit writings about the Agency for prepublication review impairs the CIA's ability to perform its statutory duties. . . ."

---

era when journalists and media organizations can significantly influence how viewers perceive events beyond their personal experience.

Over the past few decades, the Supreme Court has frequently dealt with several aspects of pretrial and trial publicity (see Table 15.2 for a list of relevant cases). Many of the cases have taken place alongside television's growth as the primary source of information (see Brief 15.6). Television, however, is not the only medium affecting the collision between a free press and a fair trial. In 1961, the case of *Irwin v. Dowd* marked the first time that the Supreme Court struck down a state court conviction solely on the grounds of prejudicial pretrial coverage. In that case, a unanimous Supreme Court overturned the conviction of a person found guilty of murdering six people because the trial court had not done enough to ensure the selection of an unbiased jury capable of rendering a decision based solely on the evidence presented in the courtroom.

PRETRIAL PUBLICITY AND "GAG ORDERS"

Two prominent murder trials—one in a large metropolitan area in the 1950s and the other in the rural Midwest in the 1970s—compelled the Supreme Court to deal with the questions of pretrial publicity and media "gag rules." In one of the most famous "trial-by-newspapers" cases in the twentieth century, a prominent Cleveland physician, Dr. Samuel Sheppard, was implicated in the brutal murder of his pregnant wife in their suburban home in 1954. In some of the most sensationalized news coverage ever to accompany a murder investigation, newspaper reporters questioned witnesses and prosecutors before the trial began and published important information on the state's case. During the trial, reporters were seated a few feet from the jury box. Throughout the proceedings, the defendant, jurors, defense counsel, and witnesses were accessible to reporters and photographers as they entered and left the courtroom.

More than a decade later, the U.S. Supreme Court reversed the Sheppard conviction in *Sheppard v. Maxwell* (1966), comparing the atmosphere at the original trial to that of a "Roman holiday" created by the news media. In an 8–1 opinion authored by Justice Tom Clark, the Court noted that "bedlam reigned" at the courthouse, and it placed much of the blame for the blundered trial upon the court itself, especially the presiding judge. Had steps been taken to obtain a change of venue to a more neutral setting, or to delay the trial or limit the number of reporters covering the trial, a more neutral environment might have been ensured. But the Court also indicated its reluctance to impose any direct limitations on a free press, for "what transpires in the courtroom is public property." According to Clark, the press "does not

Table 15.2 | Development of the Law—Free Press, Fair Trial, and Newsgathering

Year	Case	Significance
1941	*Bridges v. California*	Raised issue of whether the press can be cited for contempt of court because of criticism of a judge's actions in a case; Court divided 5–4 and overturned contempt rulings against a labor leader and an anti-union Los Angeles newspaper.
1961	*Irvin v. Dowd*	First time that Court struck down a state court conviction on basis that pretrial publicity had denied defendant due process; after police sent out press releases, media covered alleged confession and previous crimes in which defendant had been implicated, Court ruled that trial was unfair.
1965	*Estes v. Texas*	Court overturned conviction of defendant on grounds that presence of TV cameras, radio microphones, and newspaper photographers at both pretrial hearing and trial had prejudiced the judicial process; television can be present at trial but it must be carefully monitored.
1966	*Sheppard v. Maxwell*	Famous murder trial in 1950s involving Cleveland doctor accused of killing his pregnant wife; extraordinary pretrial publicity and latitude given to press at trial; Court overturned conviction, saying that trial violated defendant's right to a fair trial.
1972	*Branzburg v. Hayes*	Issue of whether reporters had to comply with grand jury subpoena ordering them to testify and divulge confidentiality of news sources; Court divided 5–4, said that journalists had to comply.
1975	*Cox Broadcasting v. Cohn*	Court held the First Amendment protects publication of accurate information (name of a deceased rape victim) obtained lawfully from a public record.
1976	*Nebraska Press Assn. v. Stuart*	Court for first time addressed constitutionality of protective orders on media; said that they should be used only as a last resort after other means to ensure fair trial have been considered.
1978	*Zurcher v. Stanford Daily*	Issue of whether First Amendment protects newpaper offices from warranted police searches for information or evidence; Court ruled 5–3 that search warrant based on probable cause was sufficient to enter offices in search of material.
1979	*Smith v. Daily Mail Publ. Co.*	Newspapers may publish the name of a juvenile charged with a crime obtained through interviews, despite a state law banning such publications.
1979	*Gannett Co. v. DePasquale*	Court held that judge could bar media from pretrial proceedings.
1980	*Richmond Newspapers v. Virginia*	Court ruled 7–1 that formal trials must be open to public.
1981	*Chandler v. Florida*	Court held that nothing in Constitution prevented a state from allowing television cameras in a courtroom to broadcast trial.
1984	*Press-Enterprise v. Superior Ct of California*	Extended the *Richmond Newspapers* ruling to jury selection, although access to jury selection is not absolute.
1986	*Press-Enterprise v. Superior Ct*	Public has a right to attend preliminary hearing in criminal cases.

simply publish information about trials but guards against the miscarriage of justice by subjecting the police, prosecutors, and judicial processes to extensive public scrutiny and criticism."

In the years following the *Sheppard* ruling and the Court's insistence that state courts should seek to minimize the chances of prejudicial media coverage of trials, local jurisdictions increasingly imposed protective orders that limited media coverage of investigations and trials in order to prevent adverse publicity that might jeopardize a fair trial. These protective orders for judicial proceedings, sometimes referred to as **gag orders**, are intended to limit or prohibit the publication of material about ongoing trials and

Brief 15.6

TELEVISION IN THE COURTROOM

Despite rapid technological advancements and the popularity of "reality" television, the courts have refused to recognize a First Amendment right to televise trials. Two cases in the 1960s extended the analysis of pretrial publicity to media coverage of the trial itself. *Estes v. Texas* (1965) raised the issue of whether the presence of working journalists in or near the courtroom adversely affects the trial proceedings and the rendering of a fair verdict. The case involved flamboyant Texas financier Billy Sol Estes and his conviction for fraud in a nationally publicized trial. Both the pretrial and trial phases of the proceeding involved extensive television and radio coverage. At the trial, the media equipment was encased in a booth to minimize any disturbance in the courtroom, although film footage of the trial was regularly shown to local, state, and even national audiences. After he was convicted, Estes appealed to the U.S. Supreme Court on the grounds that the publicity before and during the trial effectively denied him a fair trial as guaranteed under the Sixth Amendment.

In 1965, the Supreme Court overturned the Estes conviction. In a 5 to 4 opinion authored by Justice Tom Clark, the Court said that "the defendant is entitled to his day in court—not in a stadium or city or nationwide arena." Clark and three other members of the majority (Chief Justice Warren, Justices Douglas and Goldberg) considered the introduction of television into the courtroom to have seriously prejudiced the ability of the judge and jury to achieve an impartial verdict. But Justice Harlan, the fifth member of the majority, thought that the television ban should only pertain to "criminal trials of great publicity," and the Estes trial in his view did not initially fall into that category. Importantly, the majority opinion in *Estes v. Texas* found nothing in the First Amendment to justify banning television from courtrooms.

The four dissenting justices (Stewart, Black, Brennan, and White) had reservations about televising courtroom proceedings, but they were more concerned about restricting information to the public. Writing for the minority, Justice Stewart said that, notwithstanding his concern about introducing television into the courtroom, he could not recommend a general constitutional rule that banned television, primarily because of the precedent that would be established for future trials and the resultant chilling effect upon First Amendment freedoms. As Stewart wrote in his dissent,

> The idea of imposing upon any medium of communication the burden of justifying its presence is contrary to where I had always thought the presumption must lie in the area of First Amendment freedoms. And the proposition that non-participants in a trial might get the "wrong impression" from unfettered reporting and commentary contains an invitation to censorship which I cannot accept.

Following *Estes*, many states began experimenting with television in the courtroom, and inevitably, some defendants challenged the use of certain types of media coverage in their trials. Florida is one state where only the approval of the presiding judge is necessary for televised court proceedings. In *Chandler v. Florida* in 1981, two former Miami police officers had been convicted of conspiracy to commit burglary and grand larceny. Over the defendants' objections, the trial court permitted television coverage of the proceedings. A Florida appeals court upheld their conviction, the Florida Supreme Court denied review, and the defendants appealed the ruling to the U.S. Supreme Court on the grounds that their Sixth and Fourteenth Amendment rights had been violated. In 1981, the Supreme Court upheld their convictions and ruled 7 to 2 that media coverage for public broadcast of a state criminal trial does not inherently deprive a defendant of constitutional guarantees. The *Estes* and *Chandler* precedents allow states and local governments to experiment with the visual media so long as they did not jeopardize the constitutional rights of the defendants.

Since *Chandler*, some states have broadened access to courtrooms, and it is now possible to watch a trial on television nearly all the time. But, no state thus far has recognized a "right" to televise or broadcast trials or judicial proceedings, and nowhere has the resistance to televising court proceedings been more intense than in the United States Supreme Court itself.

---

investigations. Refusal by the press to comply with such orders can result in a contempt-of-court citation.

In 1976, the Supreme Court reviewed for the first time the constitutionality of a judge-imposed gag order, and the result was an incomplete victory for the press. The case involved the trial and eventual conviction of Edwin Charles Simants, who had been apprehended, questioned, and indicted for the grisly murder of six family members in Sutherland, Nebraska, in October 1975. Because of the nature of the crimes and the isolated location of the trial, the trial court prohibited the release or publication of any information, testimony, or evidence introduced at the preliminary hearing and trial of Simants.[11] The initial gag order was modified somewhat by a state judge, but it still prohibited the media from reporting any alleged confessions or incriminating statements by the defendant to law enforcement officials or to any third parties. The order was to remain in effect until a jury could be selected and protected from the press and the public. The Nebraska Press Association challenged the protective order, and after losing its claim at both the trial and appellate levels, it appealed to the U.S. Supreme Court.

A unanimous Supreme Court in the case of *Nebraska Press Association v. Stuart* (1976) struck down the gag order as a violation of both the First and the Fourteenth Amendments. In an opinion drafted by Chief Justice Warren Burger, the Court referred to both *Near* and *New York Times v. United States* and insisted that the sanctity of a free press must be safeguarded:

> THE THREAD RUNNING THROUGH [THESE CASES], IS THAT PRIOR RESTRAINTS ON SPEECH AND PUBLICATION ARE THE MOST SERIOUS AND THE LEAST TOLERABLE INFRINGEMENT ON FIRST AMENDMENT RIGHTS.... [A] PRIOR RESTRAINT [HAS] AN IMMEDIATE AND IRREVERSIBLE SANCTION. IF IT CAN BE SAID THAT A THREAT OF CRIMINAL OR CIVIL SANCTIONS AFTER PUBLICATION "CHILLS" SPEECH, PRIOR RESTRAINT "FREEZES" IT AT LEAST FOR THE TIME.

In overturning the gag order, the Court held that before imposing such restraints upon the press, courts should use less drastic means to preserve the integrity of the court process, such as changing the location for the trial, delaying the trial until public sentiment subsides, taking more care to select an impartial jury, and giving more detailed instructions by the trial judge to the jury on the need to preserve objectivity. The trial judge should also instruct the prosecutor, defense counsel, police, and witnesses to use great discretion when talking to the media. The *Stuart* ruling placed gag orders at a distinct disadvantage, and state courts have had little success since 1976 in imposing them.

MEDIA ACCESS TO PRETRIAL HEARINGS

Does the public have a constitutional right of access to a pretrial hearing, even though the defendant, the prosecutor, and the trial judge have all agreed to bar the media from the proceeding? In 1979, the Supreme Court answered this question in the negative. In *Gannett Company v. DePasquale*, at issue was a series of stories by two newspapers in Rochester, New York, which had implicated two suspects in the abduction, disappearance, and murder of a Rochester police officer. The defendants pleaded not guilty to the charges and tried to have their confessions suppressed in a pretrial hearing. At the suppression hearing, defense attorneys argued that the adverse publicity surrounding the case was jeopardizing their clients' chances of receiving a fair trial, and they requested that the public and the media be barred from the hearing. Neither the prosecutor nor the judge objected to this request, and the proceedings were closed to the public and media. When one of its reporters was among those excluded from the proceedings, the newspaper argued that such action violated both the media's and the public's right of access to the judicial process.

Justice Stewart, for a 5–4 majority, held that the Sixth Amendment's guarantee of a right to a public trial applied only to the *defendant*, and not to the general public or to the press. Since both defendants in this case had requested the closed hearing, Stewart maintained that the circumstances of the case suggested that the defendant's right to a fair trial may well have been safeguarded by the closed hearing.

The Court cracked open the courthouse doors a little wider in two decisions involving the Press-Enterprise Company. In *Press-Enterprise Co. v. Superior Court of California* (1984), the Supreme Court extended its *Richmond Newspapers* ruling (see below) to include jury selection. Two years later, in *Press-Enterprise Co. v. Superior Court* (1986), the majority extended their ruling to include preliminary hearings in criminal cases. Access to civil trials has not yet been addressed by the United States Supreme Court, but lower courts have repeatedly done so.

MEDIA ACCESS AT THE TRIAL STAGE

The *Gannett* decision was a setback for the press, for it encouraged many local and state courts to close their proceedings in order to avoid public scrutiny. Recognizing that its decision may have precipitated this closure trend, the Supreme Court moved quickly to correct it. Whereas *Gannett* dealt with public access to pretrial hearings, the case of *Richmond Newspapers, Inc. v. Virginia* (1980) involved a defendant whose attorney, without objections from either the prosecutor or two reporters that were present, requested to have the trial closed to the public. The trial judge granted the motion, in accordance with the discretion allowed him by state law, and the trial eventually resulted in the acquittal of the defendant. Richmond Newspapers, Inc., which had objected to being barred from the trial, appealed to the Supreme Court for a definitive ruling on the question of media access to criminal trials.

Chief Justice Warren Burger wrote for a 7–1 majority that the Sixth Amendment required that formal trials must be open to the public, noting that "the administration of justice cannot function in the dark." As a consequence,

> WE HOLD THAT THE RIGHT TO ATTEND CRIMINAL TRIALS IS IMPLICIT IN THE GUARANTEES OF THE FIRST AMENDMENT; WITHOUT THE FREEDOM TO ATTEND SUCH TRIALS, WHICH PEOPLE HAVE EXERCISED FOR CENTURIES, IMPORTANT ASPECTS OF FREEDOM OF SPEECH AND OF THE PRESS COULD BE EVISCERATED.

The media's reaction to the *Gannett* and *Richmond Newspapers* decisions prompted comments by two different justices concerning the mandate of a free press.[12] Justice William Brennan argued in 1979 that society needed to consider two different models for a free press. The first one—a "speech" model—"more or less absolutely . . . prohibit[s] any interference with freedom of expression." But this absolutist model clashes noticeably with a "structural" model, which sees the interests of the press to gather and disseminate the news competing with other societal interests. The Supreme Court on various occasions must weigh the effects of imposing restraints upon the press against different societal interests that are sometimes served by such impositions. After the *Gannett* decision, Brennan said that the press tended to treat many cases involving freedom of the press as if they involved only the absolutist model:

> [IT] MATTERS A GREAT DEAL WHETHER THE PRESS IS ABRIDGED BECAUSE RESTRICTIONS ARE IMPOSED ON WHAT IT MIGHT SAY, OR WHETHER THE PRESS IS ABRIDGED BECAUSE ITS ABILITY TO GATHER THE NEWS OR OTHERWISE PERFORM COMMUNICATIVE FUNCTIONS NECESSARY FOR A DEMOCRACY IS IMPAIRED. . . . THE TENDENCY OF THE PRESS TO CONFUSE THESE TWO MODELS HAS . . . BEEN AT THE ROOT OF MUCH OF THE RECENT ACRIMONY IN PRESS–COURT RELATIONS.

In other words, the press occasionally overreacts as if its role as a public spokesman has been improperly, if not permanently, impaired.

In another post-*Gannett* comment, Justice John Paul Stevens distinguished between "the dissemination of information or ideas," which composes the core of First Amendment press freedom, and the "acquisition of newsworthy matter," which needs further legal clarification by the courts. To these two staunch defenders of a free press, the media often treat all "anti-press" decisions as contrary to the "absolutist" banner, which ignores some occasional restrictions upon the news-gathering process that have been upheld by the Court using another set of legitimate societal interests (see Brief 15.7).

FREE PRESS ISSUES AND CRIMINAL JUSTICE

Three separate cases since 1990 involving the mass media have raised some issues that collide with different aspects of the criminal justice system. In all three instances, the Court was generally supportive of free press rights.

GRAND JURY TESTIMONY

One case, *Butterworth v. Smith* (1990), involved Michael Smith, a reporter for the *Charlotte Herald-News* in Charlotte County, Florida, who had written several newspaper articles on alleged improprieties at the State Attorney's Office and the Sheriff's Department in Charlotte County. A special prosecutor appointed to investigate the allegations subpoenaed Smith to testify before a special grand jury that had been convened as part of the investigation. After testifying, Smith was directed to remain silent about his testimony and informed that his failure to do so could result in his criminal prosecution under state law.

After the grand jury completed its investigation, Smith wanted to author a news story and possibly a book about the investigation, but he feared prosecution under the state law. He sued the county, alleging that the statute was an infringement of his First Amendment freedom. The district court found in favor of the state law but its decision was reversed by the U.S. Court of Appeals for the Eleventh

Brief 15.7
THE LIMITS OF PRESS REGULATION

The latter half of the twentieth century bore several narrow rulings about what types of regulations upon the press were legitimate and which were considered as unconstitutional restraints upon the press. These decisions have established the following precedents that government and the press have had to accommodate themselves to in an oftentimes tense relationship:

Valid Regulations—Ruling Against the Press

Gov't can prohibit media from distributing agency materials to private homes if resident has posted warnings to the contrary
—*Martin v. Struthers*, 319 U.S. 141 (1943)

Uninvited door-to-door solicitations or canvassing by a publishing representative can be prohibited
—*Breard v. Alexandria*, 341 U.S. 622 (1951)

Publishers are not exempt from agency subpoena powers
—*Oklahoma Press Pub. Co. v. Walling*, 327 U.S. 186 (1946)

Prison officials may prohibit interviews of inmates and reporters investigating and publicizing prison conditions
—*Houchins v. KQED Inc*, 438 U.S. 1 (1978)

Invalid Regulations—Ruling For the Press

Congress can exclude certain materials from the mails, but Postmaster cannot act as a censor by deciding which items may be mailed
—*Hannegan v. Esquire*, 327 U.S. 146 (1946)

Laws prohibiting electioneering or soliciting of votes on election day cannot be applied to newspapers publishing interviews on election day
—*Mills. v. Alabama*, 384 U.S. 214 (1966)

Gov't cannot prohibit distribution of magazines on vague grounds claiming criminal activity of subjects
—*Winters v. New York*, 333 U.S. 507 (1948)

Public officials cannot be given unlimited authority in granting or denying newspapers right of access to news-racks on public property
—*City of Lakewood v. Plain Dealer Publishing Co.*, 486 U.S. 750 (1988)

Circuit on the grounds that the grand jury term had expired.

In his opinion for a unanimous Supreme Court, Chief Justice Rehnquist emphasized the importance of secret grand jury deliberations in preserving the candor and integrity of witnesses and the need to protect individuals who are accused but exonerated in the course of an investigation. However, against these important considerations, Rehnquist emphasized that "... the invocation of grand jury interests is not 'some talisman that dissolves all constitutional protections.'" Grand juries are supposed to operate "within the limits of the First Amendment," as well as other provisions of the Constitution. Rehnquist also observed how Federal Rules of Criminal Procedure expressly exempt grand jury witnesses from the obligation of secrecy. And although fourteen states had joined Florida in imposing an obligation of secrecy on such witnesses, of the remaining thirty-five states, twenty-one of them either explicitly or implicitly exempted witnesses from abiding by a general secrecy obligation. Thus, the Court overturned the Florida law.

PUBLISHING AND PROFITING FROM CRIME

One year after the *Butterworth* decision, the Supreme Court declared unconstitutional a New York law that attempted to compensate victims of crimes with funds obtained from the published accounts of criminal activities. Under this "Son of Sam" law (named for notorious serial killer David Berkowitz, who had terrorized New York City in 1977), the New York Crime Victims Board was created to receive monies from any company contracting with a person accused or convicted of a crime for the production of a book or other work describing the crime. These monies were then deposited in escrow and payment was to be made to any victim who, within five years, obtained a civil judgment against the accused or convicted person.

The case of *Simon & Schuster, Inc. v. New York State Crime Victims Board* (1991) began in 1986 when the Crime Victims Board first became aware of a contract between Simon & Schuster Publishers and an admitted organized crime figure, Henry Hill. Arrested in 1980, Hill was promised immunity from prosecution in exchange for his testimony against many of his former syndicate colleagues. In 1981, he and a co-author contracted with Simon & Schuster to publish a detailed narrative account of Hill's day-to-day existence in organized crime, which eventually was turned into the movie *GoodFellas*. Soon after publication of a book, the Crime Victims Board informed Simon & Schuster that the company had violated the state law by not turning over all payments owed Hill to the Board. Simon & Schuster sued and lost in federal district court in 1987. A divided Court of Appeals affirmed the decision.

On appeal to the Supreme Court, the justices ruled unanimously that the state law was unconstitutional. Writing for the Court, Justice O'Connor first observed that the law imposed a financial burden on speakers because of the content of their speech. Examining the effect of the law, O'Connor said that it "singles out income derived from expressive activity for a burden the State places on no other income, and it is directed only at works with a specified content."

O'Connor further insisted that states had a "compelling interest" in ensuring that victims of crime were compensated and in preventing criminals from profiting from stories about their criminal behavior, but such laws must be sufficiently tailored to compensate actual victims from the fruits of crimes. Those assurances were not evident in this particular state law.

Intercepting Private Conversations

In accordance with the Omnibus Crime Control and Safe Streets Act of 1968 and its subsequent amendments, federal law prohibits the interception of wire, electronic, and oral communications and imposes civil and criminal liability on anyone who discloses a conversation knowing that it was illegally intercepted. Some cell-phone conversations between two teachers' union negotiators were intercepted and recorded as they were plotting against a local school board. What made these conversations matters of particular concern to public officials was the fact that the persons were overheard clearly suggesting that some violent acts might be warranted against members of the board.

In the case of *Bartnicki v. Vopper* (2001), recorded conversations were given first to a community leader, who then gave them to a local radio show host who broadcast them on the air. The union negotiators whose conversations were intercepted sued the community leader, the radio station, and the talk-show host for violating their alleged First Amendment rights under the 1968 federal law. The Supreme Court then had to decide whether the First Amendment protects the repeated intentional disclosure of an illegally intercepted cell-phone conversation about a matter of public concern. A six-member majority, speaking through Justice Stevens, said that the radio station could not be held liable for publishing illegally intercepted information if the matter is of "public importance" and the press did not participate in any act of interception. In effect, the majority in this case created a narrowly defined First Amendment exception to the federal wiretap law, which imposes liability on anyone who discloses the contents of illegally tapped communications.

Confidentiality of Sources: Privilege for Journalists?

Journalists have long maintained that the First Amendment entitles them to preserve the confidentiality of sensitive news sources, a privilege that they say is essential to protecting against government wrongdoing and fulfilling the public's right to know. They insist that the public is more likely to be deprived of newsworthy information if these sources cannot be guaranteed anonymity. Sources with sensitive information are more likely to come forward and talk with reporters if they are assured that their identity will be protected from government officials who might retaliate against them. Those who advance this view of press privilege assert that the relationship between journalist and source parallels that of "doctor–patient" or "lawyer–client." Some argue that it even extends to protecting information that may be relevant to a criminal investigation. Based on this claim that media organizations can better perform their function of informing the public about public affairs if they can protect their news sources, state legislatures throughout the United States have normally passed **shield laws** that protect journalists' sources from judicial scrutiny.

As of 2010, thirty-seven states and the District of Columbia had shield law protections for journalists.

Texas became the thirty-seventh state to add a shield law in May 2009. Varying levels of protection exist in other states.

By early 2008, support was building in Congress to advance a federal shield law. In December 2009, the Free Flow of Information Act was approved in committee and placed on the Senate Legislative Calender awaiting action by the entire chamber, but the massive leak of 75,000 classified Afghanistan war documents by the foreign website WikiLeaks effectively stopped the bill.[13]

In the early 1970s, *The Pentagon Papers* and the Watergate scandal in different ways enhanced the public's perception of the vital role that the media play in a democratic society in uncovering the truth. In both instances, major newspapers relied upon anonymous sources for some of the most prominent information involving possible wrongdoing by government officials. For example, the information provided by "Deep Throat" (later identified as Mark Felt) helped bring down the Nixon administration.

Three separate decisions announced on the same day in 1972 by the Supreme Court addressed the issue of confidential sources. *Branzburg v. Hayes* involved a reporter for the *Louisville Courier-Journal* who had written several articles, based on personal observations, about the processing of hashish. Branzburg was subpoenaed to testify before a grand jury but refused to appear on First Amendment grounds. The second case, *In re Pappas,* involved a Massachusetts television reporter who had visited a Black Panther headquarters after promising not to reveal its location or activities. Like the *Branzburg* case, the state court refused to honor Pappas's refusal to testify before a grand jury. Finally, in the case of *United States v. Caldwell*, Earl Caldwell, a *New York Times* journalist, also refused to reveal the sources for his information on the Black Panthers organization.[14] On appeal to the U.S. Supreme Court, the justices in all three instances said that reporters do not have an unqualified right to shield information and evidence needed in a criminal investigation.

In the lead case *Branzburg v. Hayes* (1972), Justice Byron White wrote the opinion of the Court, which represented the views of four of the five justices in the majority, and narrowly confined the key issue decided to the press' obligation to respond to a grand jury subpoena (an order to appear in court and testify under oath) relating to an ongoing criminal investigation. White emphasized that the First Amendment did not protect journalists from performing the same duty required of private citizens—namely, appearing before and providing information in a grand jury proceeding. White stated that it would be absurd to "seriously entertain the notion that the First Amendment protects a newsman's agreement to conceal the criminal conduct of his source. . . on the theory that it is better to write about crime than to do something about it." In an important concurring opinion by Justice Lewis Powell, the press seemed to be justified in occasional refusals to testify:

> IF THE NEWSMAN IS CALLED UPON TO GIVE INFORMATION BEARING ONLY A REMOTE AND TENUOUS RELATIONSHIP TO THE SUBJECT OF THE INVESTIGATION, OR IF HE HAS SOME OTHER REASON TO BELIEVE THAT HIS TESTIMONY *IMPLICATES CONFIDENTIAL SOURCE RELATIONSHIPS WITHOUT A LEGITIMATE NEED OF LAW ENFORCEMENT*, HE WILL HAVE ACCESS TO THE COURT ON A MOTION TO QUASH AND AN APPROPRIATE PROTECTIVE ORDER MAY BE ENTERED.

Over the next three decades, this very narrow 5 to 4 ruling by the Court in 1972 left considerable room for journalists to avoid the clutches of grand jury subpoenas and snatch victory from what many would characterize as a judicial defeat for the press. Since the early 1990s journalists frequently have defied court orders to divulge information provided by confidential sources, and as a consequence they have been jailed for their noncompliance. The most prominent case involved Vanessa Leggett, a journalist for the *Houston Chronicle*, who in 2001 served 168 days in jail for refusing to surrender research notes and information for a book she was writing about a federal murder-for-hire case.[15] In a more recent incident, popularly known as "Spygate," Judith Miller of the *New York Times* was jailed for refusing to reveal a confidential source, and a key member of the Bush administration, Lewis "Scooter" Libby, had been convicted of perjury and other charges.[16] The fallout from this episode seemed to rekindle an active interest in protecting journalists and their anonymous sources on the premise that the ultimate casualty of not doing so will be the public's right to know what is really happening in their government.

Obscenity and the First Amendment

No area of the First Amendment and free press law has exhibited as much debate and diversity of viewpoint over the past several decades as that dealing with obscenity. Throughout much of this period, the Supreme Court has struggled with numerous cases involving allegedly obscene materials in search of constitutional protection, and the result has usually been a divided Court and a confusing line of precedents (see Table 15.3).

Early Attempts to Define Obscenity

One of the earliest attempts in Anglo-American history to define obscenity occurred before a British court in 1868, in the case of *Regina v. Hicklin*, and involved an anti-Catholic pamphlet titled, "The Confessional Unmasked." In ruling that the publication was not legally obscene, a British judge said that the test of obscenity should be whether the material tends to "deprave and corrupt those whose minds are open to such immoral influences."[17] Although there was no attempt to define "immoral influences," the "*Hicklin* rule" would have a substantial impact on the future regulation of obscenity. As Professor Thomas Emerson observed in 1970, the rule allowed government to ban any publication containing even isolated passages that courts felt might exert "immoral influences on susceptible persons."[18] Although it was never specifically endorsed by the U.S. Supreme Court, Harry Clor has observed that the vague guideline became for many decades "the predominant test of obscenity in American courts."[19]

By 1873, the U.S. Congress joined the anti-obscenity bandwagon by passing the Obscene Literature

Table 15.3 Development of the Law: Obscenity and the First Amendment

Year	Case	Significance
1957	*Roth v. U.S. Alberts v. California*	Held that all ideas having slightest redeeming social importance are protected; national standard would be "whether to the average person applying contemporary community standards, the dominant theme of the material taken as a whole appeals to the prurient interest."
1962	*Manual Enterprises v. Day*	*Roth* test was expanded to include materials that appeal to the prurient interest in a "patently offensive way"; materials that are so offensive as to affront current community standards of decency.
1966	*"Memoirs" v. Mass.*	Held that obscene material could be excluded from First Amendment protection if it had a prurient interest, appealed in a patently offensive way, and lacked redeeming social value.
1966	*Ginzburg v. v. U.S.*	Developed a "pandering" element of test used to define obscenity; specifically, material that might not be obscene *per se* could become so if it were placed "against a background of commercial exploitation of erotica solely for . . . prurient interest."
1969	*Stanley v. Georgia*	Struck down state law that allowed for prosecution of persons possessing obscene materials in privacy of home.
1973	*Miller v. California*	Ruled for first time that a state/local community standard for judging obscenity was constitutional; majority said that offensive sexual conduct must be defined by applicable state law, must appeal to prurient interest in sex, and when considered as a whole, lacks serious literary, artistic, political, or scientific value.
1974	*Jenkins v. Georgia*	Overturned a jury's finding that movie *Carnal Knowledge* was obscene, after holding that local juries do not have "unbridled discretion" to determine what is patently offensive.
1982	*New York v. Ferber*	Upheld state law banning child pornography under state's "compelling interest" in protecting children.
1990	*Osborne v. Ohio*	Upheld state law prohibiting private possession of child pornography.

and Articles Act, known as the Comstock Act, which made it illegal to sell, give away, exhibit, import, or mail any "obscene book, pamphlet, paper, writing, advertisement, circular, print, picture, drawing, or other representation, figure, or image on or of paper or other material, or any cast, instrument, or other article of an immoral nature, ..."[20] An obvious difficulty with the law was its silence on how one might define "obscene" or "immoral nature," though its passage indicates that the United States also had its own Victorian tendencies in such matters.

By the early twentieth century, the *Hicklin* rule came under increasing scrutiny by those advocating less regulation of the press. By the mid-1930s, an appellate court judge found that James Joyce's book, *Ulysses*, was not obscene, and in the process, mentioned that the proper test of whether a book is obscene is its "dominant effect":

> IN APPLYING THIS TEST, RELEVANCY OF THE OBJECTIONABLE PARTS TO THE THEME, THE ESTABLISHED REPUTATION OF THE WORK IN THE ESTIMATION OF APPROVED CRITICS, IF THE BOOK IS MODERN, AND THE VERDICT OF THE PAST, IF IT IS ANCIENT, ARE PERSUASIVE PIECES OF EVIDENCE, FOR WORKS OF ART ARE NOT LIKELY TO SUSTAIN A HIGH POSITION WITH NO BETTER WARRANT FOR THEIR EXISTENCE THAN THEIR OBSCENE CONTENT.[21]

The appellate court noted that the real problem with the *Hicklin* rule was that it weighed too heavily in favor of moral considerations and isolated passages, and tended to ignore or underestimate scientific or literary values of the work. For the next two decades, the prevailing standard was the "dominant effect" of the objectionable material, rather than the narrow nature of the *Hicklin* rule.

During World War II the Supreme Court decided a case that had significance for the struggle over obscenity for the next several decades. *Chaplinsky v. New Hampshire* (1942) did not deal directly with obscenity, but rather involved the limits of free speech in provoking a public disturbance. In the majority opinion, Justice Frank Murphy referred to certain "limited classes of speech," such as the lewd and obscene, the profane, the libelous, and the insulting or "fighting" words that were not entitled to constitutional protection:

> SUCH UTTERANCES ARE NO ESSENTIAL PART OF ANY EXPOSITION OF IDEAS, AND ARE OF SUCH SLIGHT SOCIAL VALUE AS A STEP TO TRUTH THAT ANY BENEFIT THAT MAY BE DERIVED FROM THEM IS CLEARLY OUTWEIGHED BY THE SOCIAL INTEREST IN ORDER AND MORALITY.

This stance by the Supreme Court in 1942 held obscenity, once proven, to be unprotected by the First Amendment. The idea that some classes of speech are undeserving of protection has produced other efforts to broaden the category of unprotected speech (see Brief 15.8).

SEARCH FOR A NATIONAL STANDARD: THE *ROTH* TEST

By the 1950s, the Supreme Court became more involved in reviewing obscenity cases, in part because of the proliferation of ambiguous and divergent standards generated by state legislation. In 1952, the Court unanimously struck down a New York law that banned the showing of "sacrilegious movies," on the grounds that the law was an unconstitutional prior restraint, as well as an attempt to implement state policy with religious purposes.[22] The Warren Court in 1957 struck down a Michigan law that prohibited "obscene books" from the general public when the book might have a potentially deleterious effect on youth. A unanimous Court ruled that the law would "reduce the adult population of Michigan to reading only what is fit for children."[23]

Over the next several years, the justices veered in different directions in their attempts to define the nature of obscenity. Competing philosophies ranged from the absolutist view of Justices Hugo Black and William O. Douglas who insisted that the First Amendment prohibited all attempts at regulation, to Justices William Brennan (beginning in the 1950s) and Arthur Goldberg (by the 1960s) who insisted on defining obscenity on the basis of a recognizable "national" community standard of decency, to Chief Justice Warren and Justice Clark who seemed to be more comfortable with a contemporary local community standard.

Speaking for a six-member majority in *Roth v. United States* (1957), Justice Brennan stated that the First Amendment was intended to protect *ideas* and

Brief 15.8

ANIMAL CRUELTY AND VIOLENCE: PROTECTED OR UNPROTECTED SPEECH?

Life in a free society exposes individuals to numerous things that they may find offensive, troublesome, or even dangerous. When that occurs, pressure is often put on government leaders to ban or limit those activities. But the history of the First Amendment clearly shows that government may not censor or limit free expression because of the content of that speech. And yet, the *Chaplinsky* doctrine holds that some classes of speech are "unprotected" by the First Amendment. Perhaps government can create new classes of unprotected speech. Two recent episodes suggest that the Court is not receptive to such efforts.

Section 48 of the United States Code criminalizes the "commercial creation, sale, or possession of certain depictions of animal cruelty." Although designed to address the so-called "crush" videos, in which small animals are crushed to death, the Act establishes a penalty of five years in prison for anyone who knowingly creates or possesses "a depiction of animal cruelty" for financial gain. At issue in *United States v. Stevens* (2010) were videotapes depicting animal fighting, including some showing pit bulls engaging in dogfights and attacking other animals. Robert Stevens ran a business selling those videotapes. He was convicted of violating Section 48 and sentenced to three consecutive thirty-seven-month sentences. Writing for an 8–1 majority, Chief Justice Roberts held that Section 48 was an unconstitutional violation of the First Amendment because of its overly broad ban on expression. The Chief Justice acknowledged the long history of prohibiting animal cruelty in America, but he found no similar history of banning depictions of animal cruelty.

The following year in *Brown v. Entertainment Merchants Association* (2011), a 7–2 Court struck down a California law banning the sale of violent video games to minors, with up to $1,000 for each violation. The statute defined a violent video game as one showing the "killing, maiming, dismembering, or sexually assaulting the image of a human being" and that appeals to "a deviant or morbid interest." The state of California's efforts to have the Court find violence to be an unprotected class of speech were rejected by Justice Scalia's majority opinion:

> Like the protected books, plays, and movies that preceded them, video games communicate ideas—and even social messages—through many familiar literary devices (such as characters, dialogue, plot, and music) and through features distinctive to the medium (such as the player's interaction with the virtual world). That suffices to confer First Amendment protection. . . . [G]overnment has no power to restrict expression because of its message, its ideas, its subject matter, or its content. . . . Because the Act imposes a restriction on the content of protected speech, it is invalid unless California can demonstrate that it passes strict scrutiny—that is, unless it is justified by a compelling government interest and is narrowly drawn to serve that interest. . . . California cannot meet that standard.

Justice Scalia's opinion noted that California would have a stronger case if it could point to a long-standing tradition in this country of restricting children's access to violent materials. But he then reviewed numerous children's books, including *Grimm's Fairy Tales* and high school readings such as Homer's *Odyssey* and *Lord of the Flies*. The California law is unconstitutional.

---

their "unfettered interchange," but obscenity was not worthy of protection, since it was "utterly without redeeming social importance." Brennan then fashioned a new standard that drew heavily upon earlier historical antecedents. He stated that obscene material involved "whether to the average person, applying contemporary community standards, the dominant theme of the material taken as a whole appeals to prurient interest."

Of the three justices (Douglas, Black, Harlan) who dissented in the *Roth* decision, Justice Douglas stated that this new test for determining what is obscene "gives the censor free range over a vast domain." As a result of this subjective judgment of what is obscene, "the test that suppresses a cheap tract today can suppress a literary gem tomorrow."

Like Jefferson, Mill, and Meiklejohn, Douglas was more comfortable with the innate ability of people to reject worthless literature in the same way that they might discount false theology, politics, economics, or others fields of thought.

Over the next several years, the Supreme Court struggled in numerous cases with this *Roth* test, which placed major emphasis on "redeeming social importance," the "average person," "contemporary community standards," and the "dominant theme" of the material in question. The ambiguity of these phrases prevented any consistent majority from adopting any one standard. It also meant that the Court had to look at the materials on a case-by-case basis. By the early 1970s, the Court would adopt a new standard, but until then, the 1957 precedent generated what one author has referred to as "the Grapes of Roth."²⁴

Modifications to *Roth*

By the early 1960s, the *Roth* standard was being changed incrementally. In one ruling in 1962, the Supreme Court overturned the lower court conviction of a defendant who had published magazines that had been deliberately designed to appeal to homosexuals. In a majority opinion drafted by Justice Harlan in *Manuel Enterprises v. Day* (1962), the Court spoke of "patent offensiveness," which meant materials "so offensive on their face as to affront current community standards of decency." In overturning the lower court conviction, Harlan wrote that the photographs of male nude models in the magazines were no more objectionable than many portrayals of female models, which society tolerates. And since the magazines were presumably read almost entirely by male homosexuals, they would not appeal to the average adult, which was a major element of *Roth*.

Two years later, another obscenity decision added to the growing confusion surrounding the topic. In *Jacobellis v. Ohio* (1964), an Ohio court had convicted a theater manager for showing an allegedly obscene film in violation of a state anti-obscenity law. Dividing 6 to 3, the Supreme Court overturned the conviction, although the six-member majority could not agree on a single majority opinion that summarized their rationale. Perhaps the most memorable, was from Justice Stewart and indicated the continuing difficulty of defining obscenity:

> I HAVE REACHED THE CONCLUSION THAT... UNDER THE FIRST AND FOURTEENTH AMENDMENTS, CRIMINAL LAWS IN THIS AREA ARE LIMITED TO HARD-CORE PORNOGRAPHY. I SHALL NOT TODAY ATTEMPT TO FURTHER DEFINE THE KINDS OF MATERIAL I UNDERSTAND TO BE EMBRACED WITHIN THAT SHORT HAND DESCRIPTION; AND PERHAPS I SHALL NEVER SUCCEED IN DOING SO. BUT I KNOW IT WHEN I SEE IT....²⁵

And the cases kept coming and coming. In *Memoirs of a Woman of Pleasure v. Massachusetts* (1966), the Court overturned a lower court judgment against distribution of the novel *Fanny Hill* as an obscene book. Sharp disagreements emerged among the justices in this case concerning how to define obscenity. In a concurring opinion joined by two other justices, Justice Brennan wrote that if material had "some minimal literary value," it was not obscene under the new test, which essentially saved the material here from further restriction. On the same day, the Court announced *Ginzburg v. United States* (1966), upholding the conviction of Ginzburg for "pandering," which is "purveying textual or graphic matter openly advertised to appeal to the erotic interests" of consumers. The *Ginzburg* ruling established the precedent that publishers and vendors were responsible for the manner in which they marketed particular materials. In a strong dissent in which he criticized the Court for suspending First Amendment protection, Justice Stewart said that the Court was forsaking "a government of law" and replacing it with "government by Big Brother" (see Brief 15.9).

In the few years following these three cases, the Court overturned several lower court convictions unless they dealt with the distribution of obscene materials to juveniles, nonconsenting adults, or consumers who had been attracted by pandering.²⁶ In a rare display of unity in an obscenity case, the Court delivered a unanimous decision in *Stanley v. Georgia* (1969) that was applauded by many civil libertarians. Stanley had been convicted after police, armed with a search warrant for gambling materials, had found movie film in his possession that was later judged to be obscene. The Georgia law under which he was convicted made *private possession* of such materials illegal. But a unanimous Supreme Court overturned the conviction. In a strongly worded majority opinion, Justice Thurgood Marshall insisted that government "has no business telling a man, sitting alone in his own house, what books he may read or what films he may watch." Over the next two decades, as the Court and much of American society sought more restrictive regulation of obscene materials, *Stanley* came under scrutiny in the area of child pornography (see Brief 15.10).

Confusion, Politics, and Obscenity Law

By the late 1960s, the Supreme Court had constructed a confusing and imprecise *national* standard dealing with obscenity. To be judged obscene, materials had to be utterly without redeeming social value

Brief 15.9

WHO IS THE "AVERAGE PERSON"?

On March 21, 1966, in tandem with the *Memoirs* and *Ginzburg* rulings, the Supreme Court also disposed of *Mishkin v. New York* (1966). This case involved a New York publisher who had been convicted of distributing such works as *Screaming Flesh, Mistress of Leather, Stud Broad, Queen Bee, Swish Bottom,* and *The Whipping Chorus Girls*. The books described unorthodox sexual behavior that the defendant contended would not appeal to any "average person" within the meaning of the *Roth* test.

The trial court did not agree with this rationale, nor did the Supreme Court on appeal. In a majority opinion upholding Mishkin's conviction on a 6–3 vote, Justice Brennan reasoned that the *Roth* test still applied in this instance, since the prurient appeal requirement must be assessed "in terms of the sexual interests of its intended and probable recipient group." But this focus on an "intended and probable recipient group" was a definite addition to the distant *Roth* test, and the justices in the minority did not like the change effected by the majority. Among the three dissenters, Justice Black regretted the Court's performance as a "national board of censors." He also reiterated his insistence that the First Amendment should be interpreted in an absolutist manner:

> I think the Founders of our Nation in adopting the First Amendment meant precisely that the Federal Government should pass "no law" regulating speech and press but should confine its legislation to the regulation of conduct. [T]he First Amendment . . . leaves the States vast power to regulate conduct but no power at all, in my judgment, to make the expression of views a crime.

(*Jacobellis*) and sexually lewd, meaning that to the average person (*Roth*) or the intended and probable recipient group (*Mishkin*), applying contemporary community standards, the dominant theme of the material as a whole appeals to a prurient sexual interest (*Roth*) or is advertised to appeal to prurient interests (*Ginzburg*). However, government could not punish a citizen for mere *private* possession of

Brief 15.10

PRIVATE POSSESSION OF CHILD PORNOGRAPHY

Courts and legislatures attempting to limit the incidence of sexual abuse against children have frequently been challenged on First Amendment grounds. This tension has been especially evident in governmental efforts to ban the private possession of child pornography in light of the Court's ruling in *Stanley v. Georgia* (1969). The Supreme Court confronted this conflict in the case of *Osborne v. Ohio* (1990), upholding an Ohio law banning the private possession of child pornography, and thereby eroding much of *Stanley*.

Clyde Osborne was convicted in state court in 1985 of possessing four photographs of nude male adolescents in violation of Ohio's law prohibiting any person from possessing or viewing any material or performance that depicted a nude minor. Osborne ultimately appealed his conviction to the Ohio Supreme Court, arguing that the state law that defined "nudity" was unconstitutionally broad, and that the trial court judge had improperly instructed the jury on that definition. His conviction was upheld at the next appellate level.

On April 18, 1990, the U.S. Supreme Court ruled 6 to 3 that the state law was not unconstitutional under the First Amendment, but it reversed Osborne's conviction on due process grounds because the trial court failed to properly instruct the jury. In the majority opinion, Justice Byron White said that even under the *Stanley* precedent, "compelling interests" to protect the well-being of minors and to combat child pornography may at times override the individual's right to possess pornographic materials. He insisted that the law's ban on photographs of "nude" adolescents was not overly broad. Its several exceptions allowed for scientific, medical, and educational uses that ensured that it would be aimed specifically at child pornography, rather than at photographs that were "morally innocent." But after rejecting the *Stanley* and overbreadth objections, White stated that the trial court's failure to inform the jury that "nudity" included the lewd or graphic depiction of genitals meant that due process rights were violated at the trial stage, and he reversed the conviction.

In dissent, Justice Brennan agreed that Osborne's conviction should have been reversed because of the imprecise definition of "nudity" under which he was convicted. As he noted, "'nudity alone' does not place otherwise protected material outside the mantle of the First Amendment." He concluded what would be his last opinion in an obscenity case before retiring from the Court in June 1990, with these words:

> When speech is eloquent and the ideas expressed lofty, it is easy to find restrictions on them invalid. But were the First Amendment limited to such discourse, our freedom would be sterile indeed. Mr. Osborn's pictures may be distasteful, but the Constitution guarantees both his right to possess them privately and his right to avoid punishment under an overbroad law.

obscene materials that were used for personal use (*Stanley*).

On September 30, 1970, the President's Commission on Obscenity and Pornography (appointed by former President Johnson in 1967) released its final report. Among other things, the report recommended that federal, state, and local regulations prohibiting the distribution of sexually explicit materials to consenting adults be repealed. President Richard Nixon characterized the conclusions and recommendations contained in the report as "morally bankrupt." He maintained that as president, there would be "no relaxation of the national effort to control and eliminate smut from our national life."[27] Nixon's major contribution to that goal was his appointment of three new conservative Supreme Court justices: Warren Burger as chief justice, and Justices William Rehnquist and Lewis Powell as associate justices.

ADVENT OF A NEW STANDARD: *MILLER V. CALIFORNIA* (1973)

In a key ruling in 1973, the justices revised the "utterly without redeeming social value" guideline and also stated that a single uniform national standard for judging obscenity was not necessary under the First Amendment. In *Miller v. California* (1973), Chief Justice Burger announced three new guidelines that had to be satisfied in order for contested materials to be regulated as obscene:

> A) WHETHER THE "AVERAGE PERSON, APPLYING CONTEMPORARY COMMUNITY STANDARDS" WOULD FIND THAT THE WORK, TAKEN AS A WHOLE, APPEALS TO THE PRURIENT INTEREST; B) WHETHER THE WORK DEPICTS OR DESCRIBES, IN A PATENTLY OFFENSIVE WAY, SEXUAL CONDUCT SPECIFICALLY DEFINED BY THE APPLICABLE STATE LAW; AND C) WHETHER THE WORK, TAKEN AS A WHOLE, LACKS SERIOUS, LITERARY, ARTISTIC, POLITICAL, OR SCIENTIFIC VALUE.

This new standard meant that the new majority was rejecting the "utterly without redeeming social value" element of *Jacobellis* and *Memoirs*. Equally important, Chief Justice Burger explicitly stated that the First Amendment did not require any "hypothetical and unascertainable 'national standards'" for judging what is obscene. As he noted,

> IT IS NEITHER REALISTIC NOR CONSTITUTIONALLY SOUND TO READ THE FIRST AMENDMENT AS REQUIRING THAT THE PEOPLE OF MAINE OR MISSISSIPPI ACCEPT PUBLIC DEPICTION OF CONDUCT FOUND TOLERABLE IN LAS VEGAS, OR NEW YORK CITY.... PEOPLE IN DIFFERENT STATES VARY IN THEIR TASTES AND ATTITUDES, AND THIS DIVERSITY IS NOT TO BE STRANGLED BY THE ABSOLUTISM OF IMPOSED UNIFORMITY.

In addition to state obscenity standards now being authorized, another important new direction stated by the Court in *Miller* was that forbidden sexual conduct had to be "specifically defined by the applicable state law." In other words, if states or local communities were going to impose their own standards for defining obscenity, they had to state very carefully what kinds of depicted sexual conduct would be unlawful.

Of the four dissenters in the decision, Justice Douglas insisted that the decision was rank censorship at the state and local levels. "To send men to jail for violating standards they cannot understand, construe, and apply," said Douglas, "is a monstrous thing to do in a Nation dedicated to fair trials and due process." To Douglas, an absolutist on such matters, it was immaterial whether the guideline for evaluating what is "obscene" was national, state, or local.

In another case decided the same day as *Miller*, *Paris Adult Theatre v. Slaton* (1973), the Court upheld the conviction of an Atlanta theater owner for showing obscene films to consenting adults, Chief Justice Burger spoke for the majority when he stated that consenting adults viewing such conduct does not

> [B]ECOME AUTOMATICALLY PROTECTED BY THE CONSTITUTION MERELY BECAUSE THE CONDUCT IS MOVED TO A BAR OR A "LIVE" THEATER STAGE, ANY MORE THAN A "LIVE" PERFORMANCE OF A MAN AND WOMAN LOCKED IN A SEXUAL EMBRACE AT HIGH NOON IN TIMES SQUARE IS PROTECTED BY THE CONSTITUTION BECAUSE THEY SIMULTANEOUSLY ENGAGE IN A VALID POLITICAL DIALOGUE.

A dissenting opinion in *Paris Adult Theatres*, authored by Justice Brennan, concluded that regulation should not be allowed except in situations involving juveniles or "obtrusive exposure to nonconsenting adults." On the same day as *Miller* and *Paris Adult Theatres*, the Court also released three other decisions, which held that (1) a book consisting only of narrative was obscene under the new *Miller* standard; and (2) material destined for private use could be denied entry into the United States as obscene material.[28]

The advent of a state-local community standard under *Miller* did not relieve the Supreme Court from frequently having to interpret and apply anti-obscenity laws that some contend are violations of the First Amendment. Although a few of these cases have required that the justices must still decide whether the material in question is obscene,[29] many of the Court's deliberations in this area have concerned the regulatory means by which various levels of government have tried to limit access to the materials in question. Four main areas of conflict have required the justices to weigh in with their collective views on whether the First Amendment protects certain activities: federal grants for artistic expression, telephone communications (see Brief 15.11), child pornography, and the Internet.

GOVERNMENT SUBSIDIES AND FREE EXPRESSION: NEA GRANTS

In 1990 Congress amended legislation passed one year earlier requiring the National Endowment for the Arts to consider decency standards when deciding which artists should receive grants from the NEA. In the case of *National Endowment for the Arts v. Finley* (1998), Justice O'Connor wrote for the majority in an 8 to 1 judgment that upheld the law. She argued that the legislation does allow the agency to consider "general standards of decency and respect for the diverse beliefs and values of the American public" when awarding grants to artists, and that it would not "compromise First Amendment values." Justice Souter wrote in dissent that "a statute disfavoring speech that fails to respect Americans' 'diverse beliefs and values' is the very model of viewpoint discrimination."

CHILD PORNOGRAPHY

For many years governments have treated children differently from adults with respect to the parameters of obscenity law. The Supreme Court has said that states may restrict minors below seventeen years of age from reading materials that are not obscene for adults.[31] The Court has also decided, with some

---

Brief 15.11
FEDERAL REGULATION OF "DIAL-A-PORN"

Congressional efforts in the 1980s to prohibit sexually explicit prerecorded telephone messages (popularly known as "dial-a-porn") would eventually be challenged in federal courts, and the Supreme Court had to decide on the constitutionality of the laws. Congress first passed legislation on this subject in 1983 prohibiting any party in interstate or foreign communication from transmitting by telephone "any obscene or indecent communication for commercial purposes . . ." to any person below eighteen years of age. The law [97 Stat. 1469, Sec. 8 (1983)] had the obvious problem of preventing the provider of the message from knowing the age of the caller, and the Federal Communications Commission had great difficulty enforcing the legislation. By 1988, Congress amended the Federal Communications Act and imposed a blanket ban on indecent as well as obscene interstate commercial telephone messages, regardless of the age of the caller. Sable Communications had been transmitting sexually explicit telephone messages since 1983, and soon after the 1988 amendments to the law went into effect, the company sued in federal court, claiming that the law violated the First Amendment. After an adverse ruling at the lower court level, the company appealed to the Supreme Court.

In June 1989, on a vote of 6 to 3, the Supreme Court ruled in *Sable Communications of California, Inc. v. F.C.C.* that banning obscene telephone messages was constitutional, but denying adult access to telephone messages that were merely "indecent" violated the First Amendment. In writing for the majority, Justice White observed that while the federal government has a legitimate interest in protecting children from exposure to indecent messages, the 1988 amendment was overbroad and not sufficiently designed to accomplish that purpose, even though the FCC determined after lengthy proceedings that its credit card, access code, and scrambling rules properly kept indecent messages out of children's hands.

According to Justice White, the 1988 amendment "has the invalid effect of limiting the content of adult telephone conversations to that which is suitable for children to hear. It is another case of 'burn[ing] up the house to roast the pig.'" After the *Sable* ruling, Congress again amended the legislation to require telephone companies to block access to dial-a-porn messages unless customers specifically asked in writing to receive them. A federal appellate court upheld these amendments, and in 1992 the Supreme Court refused to hear the case on appeal, thereby allowing the amendments to stand.[30]

confusion, that certain materials can be restricted if there is a likelihood that such material reaches "the impressionable young and [has] a continuing impact."[32] Disputes have also arisen regarding how sexual material and magazines that might be harmful to children can be displayed by booksellers.[33]

Heightened concern about child abuse, sexual molestation, and kidnapping galvanized much of the public to demand the eradication of sexual exploitation of adolescents in American society by the 1980s. In July 1982, the Supreme Court upheld a New York law that made it illegal for persons to knowingly promote a sexual performance by a child under sixteen years of age and by distributing any material that depicts a real or simulated act. In *New York v. Ferber* (1982), a unanimous Court, with Justice White writing a majority opinion, noted that child pornography had become a "serious national problem," and that Congress and forty-seven states had enacted laws restricting it. Nearly one-half of these states, including New York, prohibited the distribution of material depicting children engaged in sexual acts without requiring that the material itself be legally obscene. In upholding the New York law and the conviction of an individual prosecuted under that law, Justice White said that states have a "compelling" state interest in curbing materials that encourage continued sexual abuse of minors because "the evil to be restricted so overwhelmingly outweighs the expressive interests . . . at stake." In a later case, *United States v. X-Citement Video, Inc.* (1994), a 7–2 Court upheld the 1977 Protection of Children Against Sexual Exploitation Act.

The protracted battle between the courts and Congress to enact a federal law that would protect minors from pornographic material on the Internet began first with two provisions of the Communications Decency Act (CDA) of 1996. One provision made it a federal crime to use a telecommunication device to knowingly make an indecent communication to any person below eighteen years of age. A second provision criminalized the use of an interactive computer service to make available any "patently offensive communication" to minors. The legislation was challenged in federal court soon after passage as a violation of free speech guarantees under the First Amendment (see Table 15.4).

In *Reno v. American Civil Liberties Union* (1997), the Court said that the Internet, as "the most participatory form of mass speech yet developed, deserves the highest protection from governmental intrusion." All nine justices said that the CDA was defective in several ways. First, unlike broadcast communications, the Internet is not especially invasive in the sense that potentially harmful programming can be thrust upon unsuspecting listeners or viewers without warning. Furthermore, the Court said that the terms "indecent" and "patently offensive" as defined in the law were too vague, and the very ambiguity of these terms raises the risk that they would be applied to speech that is clearly protected by the First Amendment.

Congress responded in 1998 by passing the Child Online Protection Act (COPA), which its supporters maintained was narrower in scope than the CDA. The new law made it a federal crime for the operator of a commercial website on the Internet to knowingly make available to children below seventeen years of age any sexually explicit material considered "harmful to minors."

When the case reached the Supreme Court, the justices ruled 5 to 4 in *Ashcroft v. American Civil Liberties Union* (2002) that COPA's reference to "contemporary community standards" did not, by itself, render the law unconstitutionally overbroad. Following this very narrow ruling, the case was sent back to the appellate court to rule on the broader First Amendment issues of the overbreadth and vagueness standards.

Upon its second appearance before the Court in 2004, *Ashcroft v. American Civil Liberties Union*, the justices divided in a new 5–4 majority, with Justice Kennedy writing that because COPA "effectively suppresse[d] a large amount of speech that adults have a constitutional right to receive" and was "a content-based speech restriction," Congress had yet to prove that there was no less restrictive means to suppress the proscribed material. Kennedy also maintained that filtering software would be less restrictive than the methods employed by the federal law, which has a "potential chilling effect."

The Children's Internet Protection Act (CIPA; 2000) was enacted by Congress so that schools and libraries could receive federal Internet grants only if they install filtering technology that blocked access to obscenity, child pornography, and material unsuitable for minors when children have access to computers.

Table 15.4 Development of the Law—Obscenity, Child Pornography, and the Internet

Year	Case	Significance
1997	*Reno v. ACLU*	Court declared the Communications Decency Act (1996), which outlawed transmitting "indecent" or obscene material on the Internet, unconstitutional.
2002	*Ashcroft v. Free Speech Coalition*	Court declared some provisions of the Child Pornography Prevention Act (1996), outlawing "virtual," computer-generated pornography, unconstitutional.
2002	*Ashcroft v. ACLU*	Court ruled that Child Onlne Protection Act (1998), which outlawed placing on the Internet sexually explicit material to anyone under 17 years of age, was not overbroad in its reliance on a contemporary community standard for determining what is harmful to minors; but Court did not rule on whether its law was sufficiently narrowly tailored or vague on First Amendment grounds; sent back to lower court for clarification.
2003	*U.S. v. American Library Assoc.*	Court majority ruled that Children's Internet Protection Act requiring installation of filtering devices on library computers to block material deemed unsuitable for minors was not unconstitutional.
2004	*Ashcroft v. ACLU 2*	Second review of case from 2002; narrow majority found law too restrictive of protected speech and therefore not enforceable.
2008	*U.S. v. Williams*	Court upheld PROTECT Act (2003), which outlaws any real or computer-generated images of children; seven-member majority held that law was neither overbroad nor a violation of due process because it was clear what was proscribed by law.

Several libraries, library associations, library patrons, and website publishers sued the federal government, alleging that CIPA's filtering requirements violated the First Amendment by denying otherwise legitimate users access to the Internet.

In 2003, a 6 to 3 Court majority ruled in *United States v. American Library Association* that CIPA did not violate the First Amendment by funding Internet access only in public libraries that installed software designed to block obscene and pornographic material. Chief Justice Rehnquist argued that the law simply reflects "Congress' decision not to subsidize libraries that do not comply. . . . To the extent that libraries wish to offer unfiltered access, they are free to do so without federal assistance."

One final issue relating to pornography on the Internet involves "virtual" or computer-generated images of graphic sexual conduct. Two cases involving "virtual porn" reached the Supreme Court in recent years with differing results. At issue in *Ashcroft v. Free Speech Coalition* (2002) was the Child Pornography Prevention Act (CPPA) of 1996, which prohibited any computer-generated images of minors engaged in sexually explicit conduct. Because the new law criminalized the "virtual" or computer-generated depiction of minors engaged in sex, instead of actual minor actors engaging in such conduct, the legislation raised a First Amendment question of unlawfully abridging free expression. In the ruling announced on April 16, 2002, a 6–3 Court struck down the law in question. In an opinion joined by four other justices, Justice Kennedy said that sexual activity of minors is a fact of modern society and an age-old theme of literature and artistic expression. Insisting that government "cannot constitutionally premise legislation on the desirability of controlling a person's private thoughts," Kennedy said that under CPPA, the Shakespearean classic, *Romeo and Juliet*, as well as such movies as *Traffic* and *American Beauty*, all of which involve actors under eighteen years of age engaged in sex, could potentially be outlawed under the statute. In summary, the majority thought that the law was too restrictive of a basic constitutional right and therefore unconstitutional.

Following the *Ashcroft v. Free Speech Coalition* ruling, Congress soon passed the Prosecutorial Remedies and Other Tools to end the Exploitation of Children Today (PROTECT) Act of 2003, which, among other things, prohibited the pandering of "any material or purported material in a manner that reflects the belief, or that is intended to cause another to believe" that the material is illegal child pornography. The case known as *United States v. Williams* (2007) began in 2004 when a Florida resident, Michael Williams, was apprehended in a federal sting operation offering child pornography in an Internet chat room. When federal agents executed a search warrant of his residence, they found several explicit images of real children on his computer hard drives. He appealed his conviction and won in appellate court in Atlanta where the judges found that the statute was overbroad and unconstitutionally vague.

On October 30, 2007, the Supreme Court upheld the PROTECT Act as a legitimate effort by Congress to police the Internet against "virtual pornography." Justice Scalia's 7–2 majority opinion upheld the Act and said that by limiting the crime to the "pandering" of child pornography, the new statute was "a carefully crafted attempt to eliminate the First Amendment problems we identified" in the earlier 2002 decision. Under this most recent interpretation of the PROTECT Act, any person offering material as child pornography can be convicted on either of two grounds: for believing that the material depicts real children; or for intending to convince a would-be recipient of the material that it does (see Brief 15.12).

THE LAW OF LIBEL

The Supreme Court has even said that the First Amendment "requires that we protect some falsehood in order to protect speech that matters."[34] Laws that punish individuals for defamation of character by either the spoken or written word (slander and libel, respectively) have ancient origins. Ancient Greece and Rome prohibited accusations against the dead or criticism of public officials or private citizens in any manner that tended to damage the personal reputation of the individual. Fifteenth- and sixteenth-century England also had laws that punished those who criticized the policies of political or religious leaders. Although disagreement exists about whether the First Amendment's guarantee of a free press was supposed to prevent Congress from passing seditious libel laws that prohibited criticism of government policy, some of the most controversial legislation ever passed in the United States were the Alien and Sedition Acts by the Federalist-controlled Congress in 1798, which partially explains why the legislation expired in 1800. The legality of these acts was never determined by the Supreme Court, and later justices on the Court considered them to be unconstitutional.[35]

Brief 15.12
IS "SEXTING" CHILD PORN?

The practice of "sexting," or sending nude or semi-nude pictures via text message, reportedly has become very popular among teenagers across the country. In early 2009, three Pennsylvania teenage girls who allegedly sent nude photos of themselves were charged with child pornography along with the three male classmates who received them. A seventeen-year-old Wisconsin boy was charged with possessing child pornography after he posted naked pictures of his sixteen-year-old ex-girlfriend online. A 16-year-old in New York faced prison for forwarding a nude picture of a fifteen-year-old girlfriend to others. And a Texas eighth-grader was sent to juvenile detention when his football coach found a nude photo on his cell phone. According to a survey by the National Campaign to Support Teen and Unplanned Pregnancy, roughly 20 percent of teenagers admit to some form of "sexting."

Experts note that these practices place many teens at risk of a major felony conviction, while others argue that the laws were not intended to work in this fashion. State legislatures have recently become involved with the issue. For example, the Texas Legislature took action in 2011 to reduce the offense of minors intentionally and knowingly promoting or processing text messages that contain explicit images of those seventeen years old or younger from a felony to a Class C misdemeanor. The charge can be upgraded to a Class A misdemeanor for a third offense. The new legislation also contains several defenses to prosecution: communications between minor spouses or minors within two years of age who are engaged in a dating relationship. Finally, the new law requires minors and their parents to appear in court to answer the charges and to complete an educational program about sexting's long-term, harmful repercussions. Minors who complete the program can apply to have their record expunged when they turn seventeen.

SOURCE: "'Sexting' Shockingly Common Among Teens," January 15, 2009, www.cbsnews.com; "'Sexting' Teens Can Go Too Far," March 13, 2009, www.abcnews.go.com; "Sexting Prevention Legislation Signed Into Law, Attorney General of Texas Greg Abbott," August 1, 2011, https://www.oag.state.tx.us/alerts/alerts_view.php?id=262&type=3.

LIBEL LAW IN THE TWENTIETH CENTURY

By the 1950s, no national standard or guideline had been announced by the Supreme Court that properly balanced press rights and irresponsible defamation of character. A few earlier rulings by the Supreme Court are relevant to this discussion of an evolving law of libel. In addition to *Near*, the Court in *Chaplinsky v. New Hampshire* (1942) found libelous statements, obscenity, profanity, "fighting words," and statements threatening national security to be beyond First Amendment protection, since they were not an "essential part of any exposition of ideas." A decade later, in the case of *Beauharnais v. Illinois* (1952), a 5 to 4 Supreme Court majority upheld the conviction of a private citizen who had been convicted under a state libel law prohibiting any publication that made defamatory or derogatory remarks about "a class of citizens of any race, color, creed or religion." Writing for the majority, Justice Felix Frankfurter reiterated that libelous statements did not constitute protected speech.

In *Barr v. Matteo* (1959), the Court held that federal officials, even if acting "within the outer perimeter" of their official duties, have an absolute immunity from libel suits for statements made by them against other individuals. Of course, if they are found to be acting *beyond* their official duties, they can be prosecuted as private citizens for having violated libel laws.

Historically, the truth of a particular statement by a publisher was an adequate defense in a libel suit brought by an individual claiming to have been libeled. But the truth is sometimes hard to prove in certain instances. Demanding that a publisher "prove" the truth of political opinion or judgment can result in self-censorship and a constraint upon the airing of ideas and issues in a newspaper or magazine article. As a result, several states passed laws in the twentieth century that protected publishers from libel suits. If a defamatory statement were false but made in "good faith" that it was true, it was known as *simple malice*. If it were deliberately false or displayed a reckless disregard for the truth, it was known as *actual malice*. This particular rule, which was eventually adopted by the U.S. Supreme Court nearly sixty years later, was stated by the Kansas Supreme Court in 1908 in a libel suit brought by a political candidate against a newspaper publisher (*Coleman v. McLennan*, 98 P 281 [1908]). Political criticism of public officials was virtually outside the realm of libel law, except in those instances where deliberate, malicious falsehoods could be proven. But for the first half of the twentieth century, libel law had been almost entirely a matter for *state* courts to decide, and the states applied their libel law responsibilities in a variety of ways, resulting sometimes in a patchwork of legislation, considerable media expense to defend their actions in libel suits, and substantial penalties if the press were found guilty of libel.

THE "ACTUAL-MALICE" DOCTRINE: *NEW YORK TIMES V. SULLIVAN* (1964)

Prior to the early 1960s, public officials could successfully sue for libel damages if they could prove that statements made about them were false. The deliberate intent to malign or ridicule the official was not necessary to prove as long as the material contained false statements or characterizations. In much the same manner that it dramatically changed judicial precedents relating to civil rights, church–state separation, legislative apportionment, and criminal procedure, the Warren Court transformed libel law (see Table 15.5) with its landmark decision of *New York Times v. Sullivan* in 1964. The case involved L. B. Sullivan, a city commissioner in Montgomery, Alabama, who had responsibilities for managing the municipal police department.

Sullivan had sued the *New York Times* and four black clergymen for allegedly libelous statements made in a March 1960 issue of the newspaper. The *Times* had carried a paid advertisement titled "Heed Their Rising Voices," which stated that "truckloads of police armed with shotguns and tear-gas ringed Alabama State College Campus" in the city and that "the Southern violators [had] bombed [Dr. Martin Luther King, Jr's] home, assaulted his person [and] arrested him seven times." Some of the statements in the advertisement were later found to have been false, and Sullivan was able to prove in state court that he had not participated in the incidents attributed to him or his department. Under Alabama libel law, an official had only to prove that some of the challenged statements were false. Upon such a finding in this case, the court awarded Sullivan $500,000 in damages, a finding that was later upheld by the Alabama Supreme Court. Claiming protection under the First

Table 15.5 Development of the Law—Libel and the First Amendment

Year	Case	Significance
1952	*Beauharnais v. Illinois*	Dealt with group libel laws that made it illegal for anyone to publish anything defamatory or derogatory about a group based on race, color, creed, or religion; Court upheld Illinois law against head of the White Circle League in Chicago.
1959	*Barr v. Matteo*	Court held that statements by federal administrative officials are absolutely immune from libel suits, even if made within the "outer perimeters" of their official duties.
1964	*New York Times v. Sullivan*	First time that Court established a national standard for awarding libel damages; public officials have to prove "actual malice," that is, with knowledge that publication is false or a demonstrated reckless disregard for truth or falsity.
1964	*Garrison v. La.*	Court ruled that "actual malice" rule limited state power to impose both criminal and civil sanctions against persons criticizing official conduct of public officials; punishment could only be applied to false statements made with knowledge of their falsity or a reckless disregard for their falsity or truth.
1966	*Rosenblatt v. Baer*	Court held that former ski instructor/county commissioner was a public official who had to prove actual malice in reports concerning his involvement with city corruption; disagreement on Court over definition of "public official" and whether actual malice must be proven.
1967	*Curtis Publishing v. Butts/ Associated Press v. Walker*	Raised issue of "actual malice" standard being applied in libel cases involving "public figures"; divided Court could not agree on whether doctrine should apply or if First Amendment absolutely bars libel damages being awarded.
1967	*Time Inc. v. Hill*	Raises question of whether freedom of press may be punished for publishing stories that invade "private rights"; Court overturned libel damages award to family claiming invasion of privacy, after novel, play, and film depicted experience; Court held that "actual malice" applied due to public nature and newsworthiness of story.
1974	*Gertz v. Welch*	New standard for "private individual" being awarded libel damages; must prove only that publisher was "negligent" in failing to exercise normal care in reporting; Court also held that liability of publisher in private-persons suits limited only to actual, not punitive, damages.
1975	*Cox Broadcasting v. Cohn*	Court struck down Georgia law that made it illegal to broadcast name of rape victim obtained from open court record; unconstitutional to "impose sanctions for the publication of truthful information . . . open to public inspection."
1976	*Time Inc. v. Firestone*	Court reaffirmed principle in *Gertz*, that "actual malice" doctrine does not apply in private-person libel suits.
1979	*Herbert v. Lando*	Raised issue of the editorial process being subjected to judicial scrutiny when one is trying to prove "actual malice"; members of press had no special immunity from interrogation about prepublication process; Court here rejected a CBS producer's claim of protection under First Amendment.
1986	*Phila. Newspapers v. Hepps*	Narrow Court majority ruled that private persons suing for libel damages must demonstrate the falsity of stories that touch upon matters of public concern.
1989	*The Florida Star v. B.J.F.*	Court held that First Amendment protected newspaper from being sued for libel damages because it published name of rape victim obtained from publicly released police report; state law prohibiting such disclosure was violation of free press.
1990	*Milkovich v. Lorain Journal*	A 7–2 majority held that the First Amendment does not contain a separate "opinion" privilege limiting state defamation laws.
1991	*Masson v. New Yorker*	Court held that fabricated quotations may be libelous if they are published with knowledge of their falsity or if they convey a meaning different from what the speaker actually said.

Amendment and the right to publish material that criticized public officials, the *New York Times* appealed the adverse judgment to the U.S. Supreme Court.

In 1964, the Court ruled unanimously that the First Amendment protects publishers from those seeking libel damages, although that protection is not unlimited. Writing for six of the nine justices, Brennan emphasized both the crucial role and function of the press in a free society and the civil rights debate then preoccupying much of the country:

> WE CONSIDER THIS CASE AGAINST THE BACKGROUND OF A PROFOUND NATIONAL COMMITMENT TO THE PRINCIPLE THAT DEBATE ON PUBLIC ISSUES SHOULD BE UNINHIBITED, ROBUST, AND WIDE-OPEN, AND THAT IT MAY WELL INCLUDE VEHEMENT, CAUSTIC, AND SOMETIMES UNPLEASANTLY SHARP ATTACKS ON GOVERNMENT AND PUBLIC OFFICIALS.... THE PRESENT ADVERTISEMENT, AS AN EXPRESSION OF GRIEVANCE AND PROTEST ON ONE OF THE MAJOR PUBLIC ISSUES OF OUR TIME, WOULD SEEM CLEARLY TO QUALIFY FOR THE CONSTITUTIONAL PROTECTION. THE QUESTION IS WHETHER IT FORFEITS THAT PROTECTION BY THE FALSITY OF SOME OF ITS FACTUAL STATEMENTS AND BY ITS ALLEGED DEFAMATION OF [SULLIVAN].

Brennan maintained that a rule compelling a publisher to prove the absolute truth of all statements made in print would be comparable to "self-censorship," and thereby "[dampen] the vigor and [limit] the variety of public debate." Relying heavily upon a restated *McLennan* rule from 1908, Brennan stated what has become known as the "actual-malice" or the *Times-Sullivan* doctrine. Before public officials can be awarded libel damages for any statement made about their official conduct, they must first prove that the statement was made with "actual malice—that is, with knowledge that it was false or with reckless disregard of whether it was false or not." Applying this rule to the *Sullivan* case, the Court was unable to find grounds for actual malice.

As with many landmark decisions, the *Times-Sullivan* case immediately raised new legal questions. The case involved *civil* libel, meaning that it was initiated by Sullivan for financial damages. Had the newspaper been found guilty of libel, it would have had to pay a fine and a monetary award to Sullivan, but no jail term could have been imposed. Thus, it left unanswered the question of whether actual malice must be proven in *criminal* libel suits.

The Supreme Court addressed this important question very soon in the case of *Garrison v. Louisiana* (1964). The role of the press was indirect in this case in that the newspapers were reporting charges made by Jim Garrison, a controversial district attorney of New Orleans, against state judges he accused of being lazy, inefficient, and hindering his investigation of crime in the city. As a consequence of his charges, he was convicted under a state criminal libel law that prohibited statements made with "actual malice" or false statements made with ill will or a reasonable belief that they were inaccurate. In reviewing this case, the U.S. Supreme Court ruled unanimously that Garrison's conviction was illegal under the actual-malice doctrine, and the Louisiana law was declared unconstitutional. As a result of this decision, the *Times-Sullivan* doctrine was applied to both civil and criminal libel suits.

"PUBLIC FIGURES" AND ACTUAL MALICE

Although the Court's ruling in *New York Times v Sullivan* established a precedent that said libel controversies would finally be resolved through application of a national standard, it also left many questions unanswered. For example, what does "actual malice" really mean, how far down the public hierarchy does the label "public official" reach, and does the doctrine apply to others who might sue claiming that the press had defamed or ruined their reputation? Justice Brennan defined "public official" in a 1966 case as including "those among the hierarchy of government employees who have, or appear to the public to have, substantial responsibility for or control over the conduct of government affairs."[36] Since 1971, the Court has considered candidates for public office to be "public officials" as well.[37]

Soon after the *Times-Sullivan* case, the Court was asked to apply the actual-malice test to libel suits brought by individuals that were not public "officials" as defined by previous precedents, but were allegedly "public figures" by virtue of publicity or notoriety in their profession or industry. Two cases in 1967 addressed themselves to this question. *Curtis Publishing Co. v. Butts* involved a suit brought by the athletic director at the University of Georgia, Wallace Butts, against the publisher of *The Saturday Evening Post*. The magazine had printed a story in which it had accused Butts of "fixing" a football game by revealing significant portions of his team's strategy to Coach Paul "Bear" Bryant of the University of Alabama. Since the original trial was conducted prior to the *Times-Sullivan* decision, Butts was able convince the jury that the magazine's investigation and preparation of the story were careless, and he was awarded $480,000 in damages. In a related case, *Associated Press v. Walker* (1967), a trial court had awarded libel damages to a retired Army general, Edwin A. Walker, the commander of federal troops policing the integration of the University of Mississippi in 1958. The Associated Press had alleged in a copyrighted story that Walker had contributed to a riot at the school as a consequence of his official conduct. The Supreme Court accepted both cases on appeal, unanimously reversing the award given in the *Walker* case, but dividing 5 to 4 and upholding the libel award to Butts.

In the opinion for the Court, Justice Harlan said that a public figure could recover damages for a defamatory falsehood

> WHOSE SUBSTANCE MAKES SUBSTANTIAL DANGER TO REPUTATION APPARENT, ON A SHOWING OF HIGHLY UNREASONABLE CONDUCT CONSTITUTING AN EXTREME DEPARTURE FROM THE STANDARDS OF INVESTIGATION AND REPORTING ORDINARILY ADHERED TO BY REASONABLE PUBLISHERS.

Harlan said that the magazine had ignored professional standards before printing the story about Butts and exhibited a reckless disregard for the truth. However, the libel award to Walker had to be overturned because there was no "departure from accepted journalistic standards." The major difference in these two cases, from Harlan's perspective, was that the *Post*, being a magazine, was not under the same press deadlines as a wire service, and it should have verified the facts before printing the story.

In a later libel case, *Herbert v. Lando* (1979), a 6–3 Court held that the First Amendment does not protect the editorial process. The majority opinion written by Justice White mentioned that plaintiffs in libel cases must be allowed to prove their case by resorting to "direct as well as indirect evidence" in order to discourage the publication of "erroneous information known to be false or probably false." The justices in the majority did not think that frank discussion among reporters and editors would be endangered by requiring them to answer in libel suits occasional inquiries aimed at proving actual malice. Three dissenters in this case (Justices Brennan, Stewart, and Marshall), for different reasons, felt that the editorial process should be shielded from such inquiries.

PRIVATE CITIZENS AND LIBEL LAW

The Supreme Court has decided that private individuals who thrust themselves temporarily into some public activity or who speak out on a public issue do not have to adhere to the same rigorous standard as either public officials or public figures that occupy positions of "persuasive power and influence." The ruling in which the Court altered the standard by which states can award libel damages in cases involving private citizens began with an inflammatory article appearing in a 1969 issue of *American Opinion*, published by the John Birch Society. The article in question referred to Chicago attorney Elmer Gertz as a "Leninist" with a criminal record, an "architect" in a "communist frameup" of a policeman accused of shooting a teenager, and a "communist fronter" seeking to discredit local law enforcement. Gertz sued the magazine for libel. During the trial, the judge informed the jury that since Gertz was neither a public official nor a public figure, actual malice need not be proven. The jury found in favor of Gertz and against the magazine, but the presiding judge dismissed the judgment in light of a case then pending before the U.S. Supreme Court, which ruled that the actual-malice doctrine extended to subjects of general public interest, even when the person seeking damages was a *private citizen*.

In accepting *Gertz v. Welch* (1974) for review, the Supreme Court had to deal with the issue of whether a newspaper, magazine, or broadcaster that proclaims a **defamatory falsehood** about a private citizen is immune from liability in libel suits. A five-member majority in the decision ruled that the actual-malice doctrine did not apply in libel cases brought by private citizens. In this instance, *American Opinion* was liable for its statements under a less rigorous standard. In a majority opinion, Justice Powell stated that many private citizens have not *voluntarily* thrust themselves into the spotlight, nor sought greater public scrutiny for their actions. A private person, said Powell,

> HAS NOT ACCEPTED PUBLIC OFFICE NOR ASSUMED AN "INFLUENTIAL ROLE IN ORDERING SOCIETY . . .". HE HAS RELINQUISHED NO PART OF HIS INTEREST IN THE PROTECTION OF HIS OWN GOOD NAME, AND CONSEQUENTLY HE HAS A MORE COMPELLING CALL ON THE COURTS FOR REDRESS OF INJURY INFLICTED BY DEFAMATORY FALSEHOOD.

Gertz v. Welch established that states should have more latitude in defining the appropriate liability standard in libel suits brought by private citizens against the media. First, because private individuals are entitled to more protection from media statements than public officials or public figures, actual malice need not be proven to award damages in a libel suit. Second, since media defendants must be protected under the First Amendment, each state can establish its own minimum standard of fault, as long as that standard can demonstrate "negligence" by the media. Finally, in order to limit liability of the media in such suits, only actual damages to one's reputation can be awarded, rather than punitive damages that punish the media offender. Hypothetical or possible damage to reputation is immaterial; demonstration of actual damage is necessary.

In early 1986, a 5–4 Supreme Court ruled in *Philadelphia Newspapers, Inc. v. Hepps* that a private individual suing a newspaper for libel must prove that damaging statements are false, at least on "matters of public concern." In citing several of the precedents discussed above (*Sullivan, Gertz, Garrison,* and *Herbert*), O'Connor stated that "to ensure that true speech on matters of public concern is not deterred, we hold that the common-law presumption that defamatory speech is false cannot stand." She also recognized that, in some instances, falsehoods would be published but cited *Gertz* to reinforce the principle that "the First Amendment requires that we protect some falsehood in order to protect speech that matters." In dissent, Justice Stevens likened the majority ruling to an "obvious blueprint for character assassination," and trading "on the good names of private individuals with little First Amendment coin to show for it" (see Brief 15.13).

REFINING THE LAW OF LIBEL

Since *Gertz*, the Supreme Court generally has adhered to past precedents, but several interesting cases have emerged. *Florida Star v. B.J.F.* (1989) involved a

---

Brief 15.13
LARRY FLYNT VS. THE REVEREND JERRY FALWELL

In 1983, *Hustler* magazine ran an ad parody on Reverend Jerry Falwell in which it portrayed the prominent Baptist minister as having had a drunken and incestuous rendezvous with his mother in an outhouse. The fictionalized interview with Falwell quoted the former head of Moral Majority as saying,"I always get sloshed before I go out to the pulpit." Falwell sued the magazine and its controversial publisher, Larry Flynt, for libel damages, and a Virginia court ruled in Falwell's favor, awarding him $200,000 in damages for what the jury considered to be "emotional distress." Later, a divided federal appellate court in Richmond upheld the damage award to Falwell. Even though the interview parody was not libelous under the actual-malice doctrine of *Times-Sullivan*, inasmuch as it was not intended to be interpreted as factually correct, the appellate court said that it was "sufficiently outrageous" to justify damages on grounds of "intentional infliction of emotional distress."

In February 1988, in a ruling that surprised many court watchers and encouraged civil libertarians, the U.S. Supreme Court unanimously overturned the lower court judgment. In *Hustler v. Falwell* (1988), the Court ruled 8–0 (Justice Kennedy had not joined the Court in time to hear oral argument) that the First Amendment protects even "vehement, caustic and sometimes unpleasantly sharp attacks." Chief Justice Rehnquist, who often took a more constricted view of First Amendment protection of speech and press rights, stated that "we must decide whether a public figure may recover damages for emotional harm caused by the publication of an ad parody offensive to him, and doubtless gross and repugnant in the eyes of most." In citing and quoting liberally from the long line of libel law decisions since the *Roth* decision in 1957, Rehnquist thus cut off any chance that the actual-malice test would be modified when publications involved obviously fictitious caricatures of social or political events or persons. As might be expected, Rev. Falwell expressed dismay at the Court ruling, saying that "no sleaze merchant like Larry Flynt should be able to use the First Amendment as an excuse for maliciously and dishonestly attacking public figures as he has so often done."[38]

Jacksonville, Florida, weekly that published the full name of a rape victim in a featured section of the newspaper. In doing so, the paper violated both its own internal policy and a state law against such a practice. In what was generally seen as a victory for the media, the Supreme Court ruled 6 to 3 that, except in unusual circumstances, imposing libel damages on a newspaper for publishing the victim's name violates the First Amendment.

Another libel decision, *Harte-Hanks Communications v. Connaughton* (1989), announced by the Court the day after the *Florida Star* decision, involved a candidate for judicial office, Daniel Connaughton, who had sued *The Journal News* of Hamilton, Ohio, a local newspaper that supported the incumbent who was running for reelection. About a month before the election, the incumbent's Director of Court Services resigned and was soon arrested on bribery charges. A grand jury investigation of the charges was in progress in November 1983, when the newspaper ran a front-page story quoting one of the witnesses before the grand jury as stating that Connaughton had used various "dirty tricks" and offered her and her sister jobs and a "victory trip" to Florida "in appreciation" for their help in the investigation.

Connaughton sued in federal court for libel damages, alleging that the article was false, that it had significantly damaged his personal and professional reputation, and that it had been published with actual malice. Connaughton was awarded $5,000 in compensatory damages and $195,000 in punitive damages. The Court of Appeals for the Sixth Circuit affirmed the judgment and the ruling, and a unanimous Supreme Court affirmed the lower court decision and concluded that the evidence warranted a finding of actual malice against the newspaper. Stevens emphasized that public figure libel cases are governed by the *Times-Sullivan* standard, but he also noted that after examining all the evidence in this particular case, it was clear that *The Journal News* had deliberately refused to listen to some critical evidentiary tapes of personal interviews with witnesses whose testimony would have confirmed Connaughton's charges.

Finally, the Court ultimately had to make a decision about whether statements labeled as "opinions" could also constitute defamation. In the case of *Milkovich v. Lorain Journal* (1990), which Chief Justice Rehnquist noted had been before the Court "for the third time in an odyssey of litigation spanning nearly 15 years," the Court held that the First Amendment does not contain a separate privilege for "opinions." Writing for a seven-person majority, Chief Justice Rehnquist noted that:

> "IF A SPEAKER SAYS, 'IN MY OPINION JOHN JONES IS A LIAR,' HE IMPLIES A KNOWLEDGE OF FACTS WHICH LED TO THE CONCLUSION THAT JONES TOLD AN UNTRUTH. . . . . SIMPLY COUCHING SUCH STATEMENTS IN TERMS OF OPINION DOES NOT DISPEL THESE IMPLICATIONS; AND THE STATEMENT, 'IN MY OPINION JONES IS A LIAR,' CAN CAUSE AS MUCH DAMAGE TO REPUTATION AS THE STATEMENT, 'JONES IS A LIAR.'"

GOVERNMENT REGULATION OF THE AIRWAVES

With the advent of electronic mass media in the twentieth century, several technological and constitutional issues have emerged that often require all three branches of government to intervene in policy disputes. Unlike the print media where the number of products is virtually unlimited and is determined by a straight publisher–reader transaction that is normally determined by quality and price, the number of broadcast frequencies on radio and television is limited. As a consequence, the federal government has found it necessary to allocate scarce availability to these channels via a licensing system. Furthermore, because of limited access and the belief that mass media have a public-trust responsibility to serve a common good, questions have also arisen about the government's right and obligation to monitor the airwaves in order to protect the public from "obscene" or offensive material, whatever those terms might mean. Several cases have reached the Supreme Court over the past four decades (see Table 15.6), a few of which are reviewed here.

Until the late 1980s, through the regulatory effort of the Federal Communications Commission (FCC), the federal government required broadcasters who editorialized on the air to allow speakers with opposing views a chance to respond. Historically, this

Table 15.6 Development of the Law: Broadcast Regulation

Year	Case	Significance
1969	*Red Lion Broadcasting Co. v. FCC*	Court upheld constitutionality of the fairness doctrine requiring broadcasters to give air time to different points of view.
1973	*CBS v. DNC*	First Amendment does not require radio and televisions to sell air time to all individuals and groups who desire to express themselves on public issues across the airwaves.
1978	*FCC v. Pacifica Foundation*	Upheld Federal Communications Commission's power to limit the hours during which radio stations may broadcast material that, although offensive to many listeners, is not obscene.
1978	*FCC v. National Citizens Comm. for Broadcasting*	Upheld power of FCC to decree an end to common ownership of a community's single newspaper and its only radio or television station; Court held that such regulation was in the "public interest."
1984	*FCC v. League of Women Voters of Calif.*	Struck down a federal law prohibiting editorials on public radio and television programs that received federal grants.
1994	*Turner BroadCasting v. FCC*	Extended First Amendment protections historically confined to print journalism to cable television; cable television is not subject to same regulations as regular broadcast industry because scarcity of channels does not apply; ruling left unanswered question of "must-carry" provisions of 1992 federal law.
1996	*Denver Area Educ. Telecommunications Consortium v. FCC*	Upheld provision of 1992 federal law that authorized cable operators to implement written policy that prohibits indecent or sexually explicit programming to children.
1997	*Turner Broadcasting v. FCC*	Held that "must-carry" provisions of 1992 Cable Television Consumer Protection and Competition Act serve important governmental interests that warrant regulation.
2000	*U.S. v. Playboy Entertainment*	Struck down a provision in the Telecommunications Act of 1996 that required cable TV operators to either fully scramble "adult entertainment" channels or broadcast them only at night. Majority held these were not the "least restrictive alternatives" available.
2009	*FCC v. Fox Television Station*	Upheld FCC indecency enforcement policy under the Administrative Procedure Act but did not rule on its constitutionality.
2012	*FCC v. Fox Television Station*	Ruled FCC policies not unconstitutional for vagueness but held that FCC failed to give broadcasters fair notice that fleeting expletives and momentary nudity would be found indecent. Court seemed to be encouraging the FCC to review its policies.

opposing-viewpoints policy was called the "fairness doctrine." In the case of *Red Lion Broadcasting v. FCC* (1969), broadcasters challenged the constitutionality of the fairness doctrine as a violation of the First Amendment. Over the objections that the doctrine interfered with the broadcasters' constitutional right to determine the content of programs, a unanimous Court in *Red Lion* said that limited access on radio and television compelled some modification in First Amendment rights. In writing for the majority, Justice Byron White noted that in this instance, the right of viewers and listeners to diverse viewpoints on political, social, and economic issues outweighed the rights of the mass media to determine content. However, four years later, the Court ruled in *CBS v. Democratic National Committee* (1973) that media stations are not required under the First Amendment to sell air time to all individuals and groups who want to expound their views on the air. Radio and television stations can have some control over what it chooses to broadcast. The FCC abandoned the fairness doctrine in 1987.

The case of *Federal Communications Commission v. Pacifica Foundation* (1978) dealt with a recorded monologue by humorist George Carlin, whose "Filthy Words" performance satirized society's attitude toward well-known four-letter words that are normally banned from the airwaves, but which found prominent place in Carlin's twelve-minute on-air monologue. When the performance was rebroadcast by a New York radio station in 1973, a complaint was lodged with the FCC and the agency issued an order to stations restricting the hours that such offensive material could be aired. Pacifica Foundation challenged the ruling on grounds that the restriction violated the First Amendment. A bare majority of the Court upheld the FCC ban on offensive material on the rationale that the "uniquely pervasive presence" of the broadcast media enabled them to reach the public in their homes where they have the right to be left alone (see Brief 15.14).

In the 1990s, two decisions handed down by the Supreme Court dealt with the burgeoning cable industry and the Cable Television Consumer Protection and Competition Act of 1992. One provision of the law required cable television operators with more than twelve channels to set aside one-third of their channel capacity for use by over-the-air broadcast television stations at no cost to the broadcast stations. Another provision permitted cable operators to implement a written and published policy prohibiting programming that the operator reasonably believed was indecent or sexually explicit. In *Denver Area Educational Telecommunications Consortium v. FCC* (1996), the justices upheld the provision authorizing operators to prohibit sexually explicit programming via a written policy as long as it grants adults access to such programming. The following term found the justices dealing with the "must-carry" provision noted above. In *Turner Broadcasting System v. FCC* (1997), the Court ruled that the provision serves three important governmental interests: (1) preserving the benefits of free over-the-air broadcast television; (2) promoting widely disseminated information from a wide variety of sources; and (3) promoting fair competition in television programming. The justices held that these important government interests would be seriously jeopardized without some form of regulation by the FCC.

Finally, in *United States v. Playboy Entertainment Group, Inc.* (2000), the Court held that a provision of the Telecommunications Act of 1996, Section 505, requiring scrambling of "adult entertainment" programs was unconstitutional. In his opinion, Justice Kennedy observed that the government should have required cable operators to block undesired channels at individual households upon request because that technique was less restrictive of First Amendment rights. The government had not proved its case.

Conclusion

Like the other First Amendment liberties of the people, freedom of the press did not gain much attention, at least before the Supreme Court, until the post–World War I era, with the seminal ruling in *Near v. Minnesota* (1931). This case and a few others at the time demonstrated that the rights of speech, assembly, and press freedom were essential bulwarks of a democratic society. Furthermore, restraints upon these freedoms should be rare and carefully justified by government at any level.

The constitutional landscape in the United States has been surprisingly free of government censorship of the media. But like other First Amendment freedoms, the courts have never interpreted press rights as absolute guarantees that government can never regulate. On rare occasions, prior restraints are tolerated, as several of the cases in this chapter have indicated. *New York Times v. United States* (1971) serves as a beacon to those who value the right of a free press in a democratic society to inform its citizens of secret decisions made by its leaders that might involve the use of military force and the loss of human life.

The contemporary student of the press freedom in the United States should remember that unlike other First Amendment freedoms of expression, the generic "press" actually includes different mediums—a newspaper, film, photograph, or broadcast—to transmit the message from the sender to the receiver. This dependence upon a particular medium can complicate protection of this important constitutional right. While the medium can either enhance or detract from the message, depending on the context, purpose, and professional competence of the messenger, reliance upon various mediums can also make it more difficult to devise any one standard that will adequately protect the audience. The several dimensions of press freedom that have been covered in this chapter attest to this continuing dilemma.

Brief 15.14
REGULATING "FLEETING EXPLETIVES"

In the more than 30 years since George Carlin's "Filthy Words" monologue, the Federal Communications Commission (FCC) has generally regulated the airwaves without generating too much criticism—at least until it changed its policy in 2004 and began fining broadcasters up to $325,000 every time certain words were uttered on the air. The real impetus for the policy change was the famous "wardrobe malfunction" during the 2004 Super Bowl involving Janet Jackson and Justin Timberlake. The FCC fined CBS $550,000, a verdict that was later voided by the appellate court. The Supreme Court's ruling in the following case, however, upheld the FCC policy and remanded the CBS case to the circuit court. Several uses of the "F" word on air by celebrities such as Cher and Nicole Richie also contributed to the FCC's policy change.

Fox Television Stations and other broadcasters challenged the FCC change in policy because the FCC had never explained its reasons. When the Second Circuit Court of Appeals held that the FCC policies were not justified, the case arrived for consideration by the Supreme Court. In *FCC v. Fox Television Stations* (2009), a 5–4 majority held that the FCC has the authority to penalize even the occasional or "fleeting" use of certain words on the airwaves. The Court actually confined its ruling to the FCC's authority and left untouched the broader, and more significant, question of whether regulation of such words is constitutional. The case came back to the Court in 2012 with a seven-person majority refusing to find the FCC policy overly vague but upholding the broadcasters. The Court held that the FCC rules were not in place when the violations occurred, so the television stations did not receive fair notice of the policy. Justice Ginsburg's concurring opinion called for reconsideration of the *Pacifica* standard.

SOURCE: Robert Barnes, "Supreme Court Rules that Government can Fine for 'Fleeting Expletives'"; *Washington Post*, April 29, 2009.

Obscenity law seems at first glance to be preoccupied with the definitional and moral questions surrounding what people see, hear, and view, and what the role of government should be in regulating this activity. Technological developments in cable networks, satellite dishes, home videos, and fiber optics, and especially personal computers, all raise difficult questions about privacy, ownership, copyright, and access to the airwaves that judges and juries must consider carefully and decide fairly. Finally, libel law has undergone some change over the past forty years with the advent of television and potentially ruinous character assassination for personal, political, or economic gain. But the courts have insisted that, particularly with public officials, the public is entitled to a full debate on and criticism of their leaders, without which an important check upon irresponsible power would eventually disappear.

In summary, the presence of a free press in the twenty-first century is a credit to the framers more than two centuries ago who recognized its critical role in building a strong American democracy. The modern press serves several key roles in society—communicating information about important public affairs and problems, providing an important conduit for political leaders to communicate with the citizenry, exposing improper or corrupt political behavior, and on some occasions, entertaining the public. In all of these essential arenas of communication performed by the mass media, they must be accountable to their different publics, their stockholders, and ultimately, the rule of law.

Chapter 16
Freedom of Religion

Freedom to worship according to the dictates of individual conscience was a primary motivation for many to immigrate to America's shores and is a key provision in the Bill of Rights. Pictured here is Trinitarian Congregational Church, with roots going back to the first settlers of Concord, Massachusetts, in 1636.

▼ INTRODUCTORY REMARKS BY PRESIDENT JOHN F. KENNEDY

Greetings. My name is John F. Kennedy, and I served as the thirty-fifth President of the United States from 1961 until 1963. All U.S. presidents before and after me have been members of Protestant denominations. When I ran for president in 1960, some people worried that my Roman Catholic faith would cause me to be unduly influenced by or deferential toward the Catholic Church. On September 12, 1960, I delivered a major speech concerning my faith to the Greater Houston Ministerial Association, a group of Protestant ministers.

I am pleased to introduce this chapter on the freedom of religion, as it is a subject with which I have some familiarity. From my vantage point today, far removed from the American political scene, I see that the 2012 presidential election raised some of the same issues as 1960—but this time it was a Mormon candidate, Governor Mitt Romney, and not a Roman Catholic. When I heard Governor Romney deliver his "faith speech" at the George Bush Presidential Library in 2007, it took me back to an earlier time, and Governor Romney talked of my speech: "Almost 50 years ago another candidate from Massachusetts explained that he was an American running for president, not a Catholic running for president. Like him, I am an American running for president. I do not define my candidacy by my religion." Here is an excerpt from my 1960 Houston speech:

I believe in an America where the separation of church and state is absolute, where no Catholic prelate would tell the president (should he be Catholic) how to act, and no Protestant minister would tell his parishioners for whom to vote; where no church or church school is granted any public funds or political preference; and where no man is denied public office merely because his religion differs from the president who might appoint him.

The Houston speech allowed me to express my belief in religious tolerance and my firm opposition to any kind of religious test for public office. The United States Constitution specifically prohibits such tests, but it was important for me to emphasize that point. Our nation's progress, in my opinion, has been strengthened by our willingness to accept differing religious viewpoints.

As you read this chapter, you will see that my vision of the First Amendment is not shared by all and has not been followed in every instance. For example, we do allow government funds to flow into religious schools on a neutral basis, tax deductions for religious organizations, and even public display of certain religious symbols. However, the Supreme Court has drawn a clear line limiting compulsory school prayer, Bible reading, and laws teaching evolution. The debate over the precise meaning of "an Establishment of Religion" is still as relevant today as it was in 1960 and, indeed, even as it was when the Constitution was written.

As a Supreme Court justice once said, "We are a religious people," so it is not unusual that we take very seriously the role of religion in our nation. It may be America's greatest strength. Enjoy the chapter. JFK

SOURCES: Transcript: JFK's Speech on His Religion, National Public Radio, www.npr.org/templates/story/story.php?storyId=16920600.

The Constitution, Religious Freedom, and American Culture

Over 150 years ago, Alexis de Tocqueville described religion in America as "a political institution which powerfully contributes to the maintenance of a democratic republic among the Americans" by supplying a strong moral consensus amid incremental change.[1] Several religious historians have noted the unique place that religion occupies in American public life.[2] Robert Bellah has noted how American presidents since George Washington have consistently referred to images of God, a "chosen" people, thanksgiving, redemption, and rebirth to both establish their own legitimacy and inspire the American people. To Bellah, religion in America has always had both a private and a public face: a *publicly* expressed belief in God (which may mean many different things to many people) and *personal* belief in the liberty of conscience and the right to worship. It has been a virtual prerequisite for American political leaders to articulate this belief in God. According to Bellah,

> ... ALTHOUGH MATTERS OF PERSONAL RELIGIOUS BELIEF, WORSHIP, AND ASSOCIATION ARE CONSIDERED TO BE STRICTLY PRIVATE AFFAIRS, THERE ARE, AT THE SAME TIME, CERTAIN COMMON ELEMENTS OF RELIGIOUS ORIENTATION THAT THE GREAT MAJORITY OF AMERICANS SHARE. THESE HAVE PLAYED A CRUCIAL ROLE IN THE DEVELOPMENT OF AMERICAN INSTITUTIONS AND STILL PROVIDE A RELIGIOUS DIMENSION FOR THE WHOLE FABRIC OF AMERICAN LIFE, INCLUDING THE POLITICAL SPHERE.[3]

Bellah calls this set of symbols, beliefs, and rituals the American "civil religion," which allows secular American politics to exhibit an important religious dimension. This dichotomy between private and public religion in the United States during the past half-century partially explains the existence of several theories advanced to explain church–state separation. These theories are discussed later.

Early English and American Colonial Experience

The dualistic approach to religion in the United States has both historical and constitutional antecedents. In many respects, contemporary religious controversies in the United States derive from Anglo-American culture and experience. One of the reasons that English settlers emigrated to the New World in the early seventeenth century was to escape religious persecution. When the British Parliament adopted the Book of Common Prayer in 1548–49, it fueled great debate about the inability of individuals to worship freely. The Church of England was the established church, and those wishing to deviate from official teachings did so at considerable risk.

Following the settlement of the Jamestown Colony in Virginia in 1607, and the arrival of the Pilgrims at Plymouth Colony on the rugged coast of Cape Cod in 1620, a succession of religious groups flowered and sought to worship in a free and undisturbed manner. One irony of this settlement pattern and the variety of groups espousing particular religious ideas was the frequent intolerance toward and sometimes punishment of religious minorities that refused to conform to the tenets of the prevailing majority. Early American colonial history is filled with portrayals of the Puritans' impatience with religious dissenters, especially in Massachusetts Bay Colony founded in 1630, that eventually led to later settlements in Rhode Island and the Connecticut River valley. Subsequent colonizations in New York, Pennsylvania, and Maryland established religious pluralism as an early characteristic in the American colonies.[4]

American Experience During and After the Founding

Religious intolerance was not unique to the Puritans. Prior to the American Revolution, only three American colonies (Pennsylvania, Rhode Island, and Delaware) had no established church. In Connecticut, Massachusetts, and New Hampshire, the Congregational church was the officially recognized order, with some provision for Anglicans and others to form their own churches. In New York, New Jersey, Georgia, North and South Carolina, Maryland, and Virginia, the officially established church was the Anglican Church. Not until the early 1800s did the states finally abolish officially sanctioned churches or religions, with New Hampshire and Massachusetts being the last to do so in 1819 and 1833, respectively.

Virginia was the first American colony that acted to protect religious freedom in the United States. Through the efforts of individuals like George Mason, Thomas Jefferson, and James Madison during the 1770s and 1780s, religious toleration became a prominent objective of the fledgling American Republic. When a state constitutional convention convened in Williamsburg in 1776, George Mason, a liberal Anglican, proposed a bill of rights with a provision granting "the fullest Toleration in the Exercise of Religion." A young James Madison also offered a substitute amendment stating that "all men are equally entitled to the full and free exercise of religion." The Virginia Declaration of Rights adopted that same year held that "all men are equally entitled to the free exercise of religion according to the dictates of conscience; and . . . it is the mutual duty of all to practice Christian forebearance, love and charity toward the other . . . ."[5] Probably more than anything else, the efforts of Madison and Jefferson to influence the legislative battle in Virginia over state support for established religion were crucial to contemporary religious freedom in the United States (see Brief 16.1).

Although Madison and Jefferson played the most prominent role in the defense of religious liberty, other political leaders of the era also warrant brief comment. Varying greatly in their degree of personal piety, such people as Benjamin Franklin, George Washington, Alexander Hamilton, and John Adams all recognized the need for religion as an important

---

Brief 16.1
TWO SONS OF VIRGINIA LABOR FOR RELIGIOUS FREEDOM

Of the multitude of writings by Thomas Jefferson and James Madison that had a crucial impact on the drafting of the First Amendment and the place of religious freedom, three are of special note. In 1784, the state of Virginia was considering a bill to reinstate direct state financial support for the Christian religion. As an outspoken opponent of this plan, James Madison, in 1785, authored his famous *Memorial and Remonstrance Against Religious Assessments*. He contended that "the Religion . . . of every man must be left to the conviction and conscience of every man; and it is the right of every man to exercise it as these may dictate." Madison argued that a tax to support organized religion should be defeated because "the same authority which can establish Christianity, in exclusion of all other Religions, may establish with the same ease any particular sect of Christians, in exclusion of all other Sects." He also reflected tolerance for nonbelievers when stating, "[w]hilst we assert for ourselves a freedom to embrace, to profess and to observe the Religion which we believe to be of divine origin, we cannot deny an equal freedom to those whose minds have not yet yielded to the evidence which has convinced us." Madison's broadside attack on religious assessments was vehemently criticized by many Baptists, Presbyterians, Quakers, Catholics, and Methodists, but it was directly responsible for defeat of the assessments bill, which died in committee in December 1785.

A second document, which reflected the combined efforts of both Madison and Jefferson, was the Virginia *Bill for Establishing Religious Freedom*. The bill was originally introduced into the Virginia General Assembly in 1779 and soon thereafter defeated. But it attracted renewed attention following the defeat of the assessments bill in 1785. Commonly referred to as the "Virginia Statute of Religious Freedom," this important plea for liberty of conscience reaffirmed that "Almighty God hath created the mind free . . . ." A key provision of the bill was found in Clause 2:

> *Be it enacted by the General Assembly, That no man shall be compelled to frequent or support any religious worship, place or ministry whatsoever, nor shall be enforced, restrained, molested, or burthened in his body or goods, nor shall otherwise suffer on account of his religious opinions or belief; but that all men shall be free to profess, and by argument to maintain, their opinions in matters of religion, and that the same shall in no wise diminish, enlarge, or affect their civil capacities.*

The Virginia Statute was passed by the state assembly in January 1786. Along with Madison's *Memorial and Remonstrance*, the "Virginia Statute of Religious Freedom" was vitally important to the drafting of the religion clauses of the First Amendment.

A final document that has frequently been referred to by authorities, including Supreme Court justices, for defining the meaning and intent of the First Amendment religion clauses is Jefferson's letter to the Danbury Baptist Association of Connecticut. The letter, written in 1802, when Jefferson was serving as president, said that "religion is a matter which lies solely between man and his God, that he owes account to none other for his faith or his worship, [and] that the legitimate powers of government reach actions only, and not opinions. . . ." But the most memorable passage in the letter appears where Jefferson states that the religion clauses of the First Amendment were intended to erect "a wall of separation between Church & State."[6] That brief passage has generated an immense amount of both conjecture and constitutional law during the past two centuries.

foundation for cohesive, republican government. They generally agreed that government served to check the natural tendency in human nature toward self-interest, but they also thought that government itself was to be distrusted (see Chapter 3). Finally, in recognizing the practical utility of religion for constructing a more moral polity, they were convinced that government should be kept largely secular, in part because no single religious group composed the majority in American society during the late 1700s.[7] The dilemma then became how to balance the need for a largely secular state with the reality of a society that had, even then, been strongly shaped by religion This task was eventually addressed in the First Amendment of the Bill of Rights.

THE BILL OF RIGHTS AND THE RELIGION CLAUSES

The only mention of religion in the Constitution of 1787 was in Article VI, Section 3. This passage states that "no religious Test shall ever be required as a Qualification to any Office or public Trust under the United States." As noted in Chapter 3, one of the key arguments of those opposing ratification of the new constitution in 1787 was that it lacked protections for the liberties of the people; consequently, the states were promised that the Constitution would be amended. When the First Congress convened in 1789, the legislators sought to make good on their promise; by September, the Congress had completed work on what would soon become the first ten amendments to the Constitution. In conference committee, Madison won agreement on the opening passage of the crucial First Amendment: "Congress shall make no law respecting an establishment of religion, or prohibiting the free exercise thereof. . . ."

Not until the early twentieth century did there arise much question over precisely what the two religion clauses—Free Exercise and Establishment—actually meant. Thomas Jefferson's reference to a "wall of separation between church and state" has generated great debate among scholars who maintain that there is little evidence to support the contention that the framers ever insisted upon a *strict*, complete separation.[8] Given their insistence that religion both informed and ordered representative government, the question was not whether there should be some relation between the two, but rather, what the nature of that relationship should be. As happened with so many aspects of the new Constitution, precise definition was allowed to drift as the new nation set out to consolidate government under a document that contained many hidden meanings. It fell to the Supreme Court to search for these meanings within the words and phrases used to structure this noble experiment in responsible government.

THE FREE EXERCISE CLAUSE AND RELIGIOUS FREEDOM

The Free Exercise Clause involves governmental interference with the practice of a citizen's faith, while the Establishment Clause involves alleged governmental support for or hostility toward religion. For 150 years, the Supreme Court had few occasions to interpret the meaning of the Free Exercise or the Establishment Clauses. Since the clauses did not apply to the state governments, very few controversies emerged requiring the Court to render an opinion. Table 16.1 presents an overview of the Free Exercise Clause, and it demonstrates that the clause has become very visible since the 1940s. In most free exercise cases cited in the table, the Supreme Court has tried to reconcile secular governmental regulations with the demands of persons claiming sincere religious beliefs, pitting the individualist and communitarian theories of politics against one another.

EARLY CONFLICTS WITH THE FREE EXERCISE OF RELIGION

The first freedom of religion case heard by the Supreme Court dealt with the Free Exercise Clause, and the Court's handling of the issue in question held great significance for future government regulation of religious behavior. The case was *Reynolds v. United States* (1878), which involved the right of Mormons to practice polygamy, then an accepted tenet of the Mormon faith. George Reynolds, convicted of violating a federal law prohibiting polygamy, appealed to the Supreme Court claiming a violation of the Free Exercise Clause. A unanimous Supreme Court upheld his conviction. In the majority opinion, Chief Justice Morrison Waite stated that monogamous marriage was a practice of Western moral tradition and a

Table 16.1 | Development of the Law—The Free Exercise Clause

Year	Event	Significance
1786	Virginia Statute of Religious Freedom	Approved in Virginia and based on the efforts of Madison and Jefferson, this law had a major impact on the religion clauses later added to the Constitution.
1878	*Reynolds v. U.S.*	First free exercise case heard by Supreme Court, upheld conviction of Morman for violating federal anti-polygamy law. Held that government may regulate actions but not opinions.
1905	*Jacobson v. Massachusetts*	Upheld state law requiring smallpox vaccinations as part of state's valid secular police power policies.
1925	*Pierce v. Society of Sisters*	Struck down Oregon law requiring public school attendance for all children ages eight to eighteen; decided on due process grounds.
1940	*Cantwell v. Connecticut*	Free exercise clause is incorporated into Fourteenth Amendment and applied to states. Court reversed Jehovah's Witness conviction for disturbing the peace.
1940	*Minersville School District v. Gobitis*	Court (8–1) upheld a mandatory Pennsylvania flag salute law for public schools over Jehovah's Witnesses free exercise claims.
1943	*West Virginia State Board v. Barnette*	A 6–3 Court overruled a West Virginia flag salute law nearly identical to the *Minersville* case. Government may not compel persons to swear allegiance or utter personal opinions.
1944	*U.S. v. Ballard*	Religion held to be a private matter not susceptible to being defined by an outside group, including a jury.
1961	*Torcaso v. Watkins*	Unanimous Court ruled that a Maryland law requiring a religious test for public office was unconstitutional; a personal belief in God is not an essential component of all religions.
1961	*Braunfeld v. Brown*	Upheld state Sunday-closing laws as minor burden on religion.
1963	*Sherbert v. Verner*	Held that denial of unemployment benefits to a Seventh Day Adventist for refusal to work on Saturday violated Free Exercise Clause; established compelling interest test.
1965	*U.S. v. Seeger*	Created "parallel-place doctrine" for evaluating the sincerity of religious beliefs for conscientious objection. The test is whether nonreligious beliefs are sincere and meaningful.
1970	*Welsh v. U.S.*	Allowed conscientious objector status to a person who denied that religion had anything to do with his opposition to military service.
1971	*Gillette v. U.S.*	Persons may not be conscientious objectors to specific wars.
1971	*Clay v. U.S.*	Cassius Clay (Muhammad Ali) wins his case as a conscientious objector; persons must be conscientiously opposed to all wars; based on genuine religious training and sincere belief.
1972	*Wisconsin v. Yoder*	Amish may be exempted from state mandatory education laws due to the devout and sincere nature of their beliefs. Recognized "areas of conduct" protected by Free Exercise Clause.
1989	*Frazee v. Illinois Dept. of Employment Security*	Unanimous Court expanded *Sherbert* to persons who were not members of particular religious sects.
1990	*Oregon v. Smith*	Ruled that *Sherbert* principle did not apply to require exemptions from a generally applicable criminal law. Removed the compelling interest requirement.
1993	Religious Freedom Restoration Act	Law passed in reaction to *Smith* decision requiring compelling interest test whenever religious freedom is restricted.

1993	*Church of the Lukumi Babalu Aye v. City of Hialeah*	Invalidated municipal ordinance that banned certain types of animal killings or sacrifices. Because ordinances pertained only to religious sacrifices, the law was not generally applicable.
1997	*City of Boerne, Texas v. Flores*	Court struck down Religious Freedom Restoration Act's applicability to state governments as beyond the statutory authority of Congress.
2004	*Locke v. Davey*	Upheld Washington's refusal to provide scholarships to college students who chose to pursue religious degrees while providing scholarships to students who chose other majors.
2006	*Gonzales v. O Centro Espirita Beneficente Uniao De Vegetal*	Held that RFRA protects sacramental use of hoasca tea, containing dimethyltryptamine (DMT), a Schedule I drug in the Controlled Substances Act, and requires judges to evaluate the harm posed by its use in communion. Court held that sacramental use was an exception to the "rule of general applicability."

foundation upon which "society may be said to be built." As a result, Congress had acted properly in outlawing polygamy. According to Waite, "Congress was deprived of all legislative power over mere opinion, but was left free to reach actions which were in violation of social duties or subversive of good order." This reference was important because it implied that people are free to believe but not necessarily to act on those beliefs in all instances. Religious freedoms, like others, are not absolute, but must be balanced against other competing societal rights.

In *Jacobson v. Massachusetts* (1905), the Supreme Court found that the state law requiring vaccinations had a valid secular purpose. Two decades later, in *Pierce v. Society of Sisters* (1925), the Supreme Court struck down an Oregon law compelling attendance in a public school for all children from ages eight to sixteen on the grounds that the statute interfered with the "liberty" protected by the Fourteenth Amendment. The Court reasoned that this liberty included the right of parents to supervise the education of their children, including having them enrolled in church-related schools.

In *Cantwell v. Connecticut* (1940), the Supreme Court unanimously held that Newton Cantwell, a Jehovah's Witness, had been wrongly convicted of disturbing the peace in New Haven, Connecticut, for playing a record that attacked the Roman Catholic religion. The main significance of *Cantwell* was that the Court incorporated the Free Exercise Clause into the Fourteenth Amendment's Due Process Clause, thereby making it applicable to the American states (see the discussion of selective incorporation in Chapter 11). *Cantwell* became the first of several important cases in the 1940s involving the Jehovah's Witnesses challenging state regulations that allegedly infringed upon their religious beliefs (see Brief 16.2).

INTERPRETING THE FREE EXERCISE CLAUSE: TWO COMPETING STANDARDS

Until the early 1960s, the Court relied upon the **secular-legislation rule** in evaluating free exercise cases. Under this rule, state legislation had to serve some legitimate secular purpose and could not discriminate against particular religious groups. If those stipulations were met, though, the fact that the legislation might conflict with some person's perceived religious obligations did not necessarily invalidate it. According to this pre-1960 interpretation, the First Amendment did not require government to give special recognition to religious beliefs or religiously motivated behavior. Two decisions in the early 1960s resulted in a new standard for evaluating state legislation being challenged on free exercise grounds, one that required a **compelling state interest** whenever religious freedom was jeopardized.

COMPELLING STATE INTEREST STANDARD

In 1961, the Supreme Court upheld Pennsylvania's Sunday Closing Law in the case of *Braunfeld v. Brown*, despite the fact that laws that mandate

Brief 16.2

JEHOVAH'S WITNESSES, FREE EXERCISE, AND THE FLAG SALUTE CASES

The vast majority of free exercise cases have involved America's so-called "marginal or nonconventional religions." In this regard, no religious group can claim more free exercise involvement than the Jehovah's Witnesses. According to noted church–state scholar James E. Wood, Jr., the Jehovah's Witnesses were involved in the first eleven cases to be decided on the basis of the Free Exercise Clause, coming in the period between 1940 and 1944. Overall, the Supreme Court heard some twenty-five cases involving the Jehovah's Witnesses between 1938 and 1948. As Wood states:

> Far out of proportion to their numerical membership or institutional strength, Jehovah's Witnesses have been responsible for more cases concerned with religious liberty than any other religious body in the United States. The result of these decisions, as in others resulting from the application of the Free Exercise Clause to nonconventional religions, has been a broadening of the meaning and protection of the Free Exercise Clause.[9]

In the same year as *Cantwell*, the Supreme Court was asked to consider a Pennsylvania law requiring public school students to salute the American flag daily. The Jehovah's Witness parents of a child that had been expelled for refusing to salute the flag on religious grounds challenged the state law as a violation of the First Amendment. The district court upheld the law, but the federal Court of Appeals struck it down as a violation of the First Amendment. On appeal, an 8–1 majority of the Supreme Court ruled in *Minersville School District v. Gobitis* (1940) that the statute did not violate the First Amendment.

During the next three years, two developments resulted in an unusually quick reversal of a Supreme Court decision. First, Justices Black, Douglas, and Murphy, who had ruled with the eight-member majority in the *Minersville* judgment, changed their minds about their earlier vote. In a three-member dissent in *Jones v. Opelika* (1942), the three justices stated that both the *Minersville* and *Opelika* decisions were, in their minds, wrongly decided, and that the First Amendment required greater protection for religious minorities than those two decisions reflected. The Court appointments of Robert Jackson in 1941 and Wiley Rutledge in 1943, along with the change in attitude by three justices, meant that, if given an opportunity to reconsider the *Minersville* decision, the Court might handle the issue differently.

The Court did not have to wait very long. Following the *Minersville* decision, several other states, including West Virginia, passed similar flag salute and pledge of allegiance laws. In 1943, in *West Virginia State Board of Education v. Barnette*, the Supreme Court overruled the flag salute precedent of three years earlier. The facts of the *Barnette* case were virtually identical to the 1940 case, with the parents of children claiming that the compulsory flag salute law violated their religious beliefs under the Free Exercise Clause. In a 6–3 decision, Justice Jackson wrote a majority opinion that is often quoted to exemplify the new attitude that had been emerging on the New Deal Court. According to Jackson, First Amendment freedoms are not absolute, but they are to be safeguarded by a very high standard:

> [F]reedoms of speech and of press, of assembly, and of worship may not be infringed on . . . slender grounds. They are susceptible of restriction only to prevent grave and immediate danger to interests which the state may lawfully protect. . . . If there is any fixed star in our constitutional constellation, it is that no official, high or petty, can prescribe what shall be orthodox in politics, nationalism, religion, or other matters of opinion or force citizens to confess by word or act their faith therein. [emphasis added]

The *Barnette* case established a significant civil liberties principle. Rather than narrowly interpreting the status of Jehovah's Witnesses before the law and exempting that religious minority from the law on religious grounds, the Court actually said that *no one* should be required to salute the flag or, more broadly, be forced to utter any belief or opinion against his will. Therefore, this case won rights for all citizens and upheld the view that government cannot compel personal beliefs.

---

business closings on Sunday may discriminate against persons, for example, Jews and Seventh-Day Adventists, who recognize their sabbath on another day. Writing for a six-member Court, Chief Justice Earl Warren argued that:

> IF THE STATE REGULATES CONDUCT BY ENACTING A GENERAL LAW WITHIN ITS POWER, THE PURPOSE AND EFFECT OF WHICH IS TO ADVANCE THE STATE'S SECULAR GOALS, THE STATUTE IS VALID DESPITE ITS INDIRECT BURDEN ON RELIGIOUS OBSERVANCE UNLESS THE STATE MAY ACCOMPLISH ITS PURPOSE BY MEANS WHICH DO NOT IMPOSE A BURDEN.

In dissent, Justice William Brennan criticized the majority's use of a "compelling state interest" to justify the "mere convenience of having everyone rest on the same day." Justice Potter Stewart, like Brennan, was disturbed by the Court's ruling, which compelled a "cruel choice" between practicing their religion or their trade, all "in the interest of enforced Sunday togetherness." In these cases, the Court was comfortable with resolving the controversies on statutory, rather than constitutional, grounds; as a result, no precise standard was devised for defining acceptable and unacceptable secular purpose. In more recent years, states generally have relaxed or even abandoned Sunday-closing laws, presumably in response to the voices of consumers for more shopping opportunities.

The clear step to a "compelling state interest" standard was taken by the Court in *Sherbert v. Verner* (1963). Adell Sherbert, a resident of South Carolina, belonged to the Seventh-Day Adventist church, but was fired by her employer of thirty-five years when she refused to work on Saturday, her sabbath. Unable to find work that allowed her to worship on Saturday, she applied for state unemployment benefits. Her claim was denied, primarily because she refused to accept jobs requiring Saturday employment. Following her defeat in state courts, Sherbert appealed to the Supreme Court. Writing for the majority, Justice Brennan ruled that the denial of state benefits violated the First and Fourteenth Amendments—"to condition the availability of benefits upon [Sherbert's] willingness to violate a cardinal principle of her religious faith effectively penalizes the free exercise of her constitutional liberties." The Brennan opinion reflected the view that the state had not sufficiently considered alternative means for ensuring financial integrity and preventing fraud in dismissing Sherbert's claim before the state board.

For all practical purposes, the *Sherbert* doctrine required evidence of a compelling state interest before any state could limit religious freedom: "Only the gravest abuses endangering paramount interest, give occasion to permissible limitation" of the Free Exercise Clause. In dissent, Justice John Harlan felt that the *Sherbert* ruling, in effect, overruled *Braunfeld*, and compelled a state, attempting to condition unemployment benefits on an applicant's availability for work, to "carve out an exception" and make benefits available to those refusing to work on religious grounds.

Sherbert cases marked a major shift in the Supreme Court's interpretation of the Free Exercise Clause. Laws that adversely affected religious practices and behavior would be upheld only if they served a compelling state interest. That standard promised religious minorities significant protections for both their beliefs and actions. Nevertheless, conflicts were inevitable, and free exercise claims continued to contend against state laws that attempted to apply the same rules to all citizens, regardless of religion.

THE "GENERALLY APPLICABLE LAW" STANDARD

Perhaps more than any case in recent years, the ruling in *Employment Division, Dept. of Human Resources of Oregon v. Smith* (1990) significantly altered the nature of Free Exercise protections. Because of the importance of this ruling, a review of the facts is helpful in understanding the major issues. Alfred Smith and another person, both members of the Native American Church, were fired by a drug treatment organization because they used the hallucinogenic drug peyote during religious ceremonies. They were denied unemployment compensation on the basis of an Oregon law that disallows benefits to persons dismissed for work-related misconduct. The Oregon appellate and Supreme Courts held the denial of benefits to violate the Free Exercise Clause. The U.S. Supreme Court granted certiorari but first remanded the case to the Oregon Supreme Court to determine whether Oregon anti-drug laws prohibited the sacramental use of peyote. After the Oregon Supreme Court held that peyote use did violate these laws but still upheld Smith's free exercise claims, the U.S. Supreme Court again granted certiorari. Under *Sherbert*, the Oregon law would be upheld only if it could be justified by some "compelling governmental interest" and balanced against free exercise of religion considerations.

But according to Justice Antonin Scalia, writing for a 6–3 Court, *Sherbert* should not be applied to require exemptions from a generally applicable criminal law. The right of free exercise, according to Justice Scalia, does not relieve an individual of the obligation to comply with a valid or neutral law of general applicability on the ground that the law prohibits or requires conduct that conflicts with his religious practice. If such were to be the case, he argued, individuals would be permitted to decide which laws to obey depending on their religious beliefs and conscience. Justice Sandra Day O'Connor concurred in the judgment but refused to join the majority opinion because it "dramatically departs from well-settled First Amendment jurisprudence, appears unnecessary to resolve the question presented, and is incompatible with our Nation's fundamental commitment to individual religious liberty."

Justices Blackmun, Brennan, and Marshall joined parts of Justice O'Connor's opinion but dissented from the judgment. Blackmun's opinion noted that twenty-three states provide some exemption in their drug laws for the religious use of peyote. He also addressed the numerous concerns raised by the majority's ruling:

> THIS DISTORTED VIEW OF OUR PRECEDENTS LEADS THE MAJORITY TO CONCLUDE THAT STRICT SCRUTINY OF A STATE LAW BURDENING THE FREE EXERCISE OF RELIGION IS A "LUXURY" THAT A WELL-ORDERED SOCIETY CANNOT AFFORD, AND THAT THE REPRESSION OF MINORITY RELIGIONS IS AN "UNAVOIDABLE CONSEQUENCE OF DEMOCRATIC GOVERNMENT." I DO NOT BELIEVE THE FOUNDERS THOUGHT THEIR DEARLY BOUGHT FREEDOM FROM RELIGIOUS PERSECUTION A "LUXURY," BUT AN ESSENTIAL ELEMENT OF LIBERTY—AND THEY COULD NOT HAVE THOUGHT RELIGIOUS INTOLERANCE "UNAVOIDABLE," FOR THEY DRAFTED THE RELIGION CLAUSES PRECISELY IN ORDER TO AVOID THAT INTOLERANCE.

The *Smith* ruling provoked outspoken opposition from many scholars, jurists, and religious groups (see Brief 16.3). Shortly after the decision, groups such as the American Civil Liberties Union, the American Jewish Committee, Americans United for the Separation of Church and State, the Baptist Joint Committee on Public Affairs, the National Council of Churches, and numerous legal scholars petitioned the Court for a rehearing. The petition was denied, but opponents were determined to take action. According to James E. Wood, Jr.:

> IT WAS WIDELY AGREED BY MANY CIVIL LIBERTARIANS AND PROFESSORS OF CONSTITUTIONAL LAW THAT THE PRACTICAL EFFECT OF *SMITH* WAS TO GUT THE FREE EXERCISE CLAUSE. THE COURT'S DECISION WAS A SWEEPING REPUDIATION OF FIVE DECADES OF ITS OWN INTERPRETATION OF THE FREE EXERCISE CLAUSE AND THREE DECADES OF ITS TIME-HONORED "COMPELLING STATE INTEREST" TEST.[10]

Despite the mounting criticisms of the Court's "generally applicable law" standard by religious liberty advocates, the Court used the standard to hand down a strongly pro–free exercise decision in the case of *Church of the Lukumi Babalu Aye v. City of Hialeah* (1993). This case involved the Santeria religion, a group with African origins that had absorbed certain elements of Roman Catholicism along the way. Santeria means "the way of the saints," and the group's religious ceremonies involve devotion to spirits, often through Catholic saints. Specifically, the church engages in animal sacrifice—including chickens, ducks, pigeons, guinea pigs, goats, sheep, and turtles. The animals are killed by cutting their carotid arteries and are cooked and eaten following all Santeria rituals, except healing and death rites. When the church leased land in Hialeah, Florida, the city council held an emergency session, passed an ordinance expressing "great concern regarding the possibility of public ritualistic animal sacrifices," and promised to prosecute any person or organization that engaged in animal sacrifice. Three additional ordinances were passed that defined sacrifices, prohibited the sacrifice of animals, and banned the slaughter of animals outside specific areas. Numerous exemptions were granted.

The church challenged the ordinances, alleging violations of the Free Exercise Clause of the First Amendment, but the district court, while acknowledging that the ordinances were not "religiously neutral," ruled in favor of the city. The Court of Appeals affirmed the ruling, and the case was appealed to the Supreme Court. Justice Anthony Kennedy wrote for a unanimous Court in holding the Hialeah ordinances unconstitutional on the grounds that they were not religiously neutral, not of general applicability, and that they singled out only one type of conduct—religious—and made it illegal. Because the ordinances did not stop other types of animal killings, they could be seen only as directly intended to hinder or burden religion. Even though the ruling was unanimous, several justices wrote concurring opinions and took an opportunity to express their reservations with the Smith precedent. Justice Harry Blackmun restated his belief that Smith "ignored the value of religious freedom as an affirmative individual liberty," and Justice David Souter called upon the Court to reexamine the decision. Just a few years later, of course, the Court's Boerne ruling would seemingly give even more weight to *Smith*.

Brief 16.3

RISE AND FALL OF THE RELIGIOUS FREEDOM RESTORATION ACT

The movement to overturn *Smith* gathered momentum when religious leaders and organizations were successful in having the Religious Freedom Restoration Act (RFRA) introduced in the U.S. House of Representatives in 1990. The proposed act was designed to restore the compelling governmental interest test whenever any action was taken that restricted "any person's free exercise of religion." RFRA applied to governments at all levels and required that any law, rule, or regulation that substantially burdens religious conduct must satisfy strict scrutiny (i.e., be supported by compelling interest and constitute the least restrictive means of achieving the identified compelling interest). The 101st Congress adjourned before any action could be taken. The RFRA was reintroduced in 1991 and 1992, the latter time with more than 150 House co-sponsors. In early 1993, the U.S. Catholic Conference, which had opposed the bill because of fears that it could be used to strike down restrictions on abortion, dropped its opposition after bill sponsors convinced them otherwise.

With the opposition to RFRA declining, the bill was reintroduced in both the House and Senate in early 1993. It was unanimously approved by a voice vote in the House in April 1993. A final stumbling block in the Senate concerned whether the legislation should apply to prisoners. A memorandum from the Bureau of Prisons called upon the Senate to exempt prisoners from the law on the grounds that it might undermine prison discipline and force officials to allow prisoners to engage in unacceptable, or even illegal, practices. Nevertheless, on October 27, 1993, by a vote of 97–3, the U.S. Senate passed the Religious Freedom Restoration Act. It also refused to exempt prisoners by a vote of 58 to 41. President Bill Clinton, an avowed supporter of the legislation, formally signed the bill into law on November 16, 1993.

The euphoria of RFRA supporters came to an abrupt halt when the Supreme Court handed down its decision in *City of Boerne, Texas v. Flores* (1997), a case that pitted a municipal government against a powerful church hierarchy. The City of Boerne adopted an ordinance authorizing the City's Historic Landmark Commission to develop a preservation plan for the downtown area. Under the ordinance, the commission would be required to preapprove any construction affecting historic landmarks or buildings within the historic district. St. Peter Catholic Church was located in the historic district as established by the city. Church attendance at St. Peter had grown too large for the existing sanctuary, so Archbishop Flores authorized expansion of the church and requested a building permit. The commission, relying on the historic preservation ordinance, denied the permit. Archbishop Flores sued the city, alleging that the commission's decision failed the strict scrutiny test embodied in the RFRA. The District Court sided with city but the Fifth Circuit sided with Archbishop Flores.

A 6–3 Supreme Court decided in favor of the city, ruling that the RFRA was an unconstitutional expansion of congressional power as applied to state and local governments. Justice Anthony Kennedy's majority opinion emphasized that insofar as RFRA is construed to affect a change in the interpretation of the Free Exercise Clause, it is beyond the constitutional authority of Congress. Kennedy's opinion reaffirmed the rule of *Marbury v. Madison* that "it is emphatically the province and duty of the judicial department to say what the law is." Distinguishing the RFRA from other congressional enforcement legislation such as the Voting Rights Act of 1965 (see Chapter 9), the majority pointed out that little or no evidence existed to show that states were persecuting religious minorities in the same ways that they had in the area of minority voting rights. Finally, the Court noted that, because the RFRA touches every legislative and administrative act by every level of government as soon as someone alleges a free exercise of religion claim, it constitutes a substantial intrusion into the daily operation of state and local governments. As such, the RFRA is unconstitutional. The decision left *Oregon v. Smith* and the "generally applicable law" standard intact with respect to free exercise matters. However, opponents pledged to work with Congress to propose new legislation.

THE ISSUE OF EXCEPTIONS TO GENERALLY APPLICABLE LAWS

To what extent can one claim exemption to universally applicable laws on religious freedom grounds? Can government compel behavior that is contrary to people's sincere religious beliefs or, conversely, prohibit behavior that is claimed to be an integral part of their religion? Until the 1990 *Smith* ruling, the Court apparently was willing to grant certain exemptions to religious groups based on their claim of free exercise rights under the First Amendment. These exemptions raise numerous questions concerning the meaning of "religion" itself as well as the wisdom of allowing specific religious groups to be treated differently. Two of the most controversial examples—compulsory school attendance and conscientious objection—are examined more carefully here.

COMPULSORY SCHOOL ATTENDANCE AND THE OLD AMISH ORDER

Wisconsin v. Yoder (1972) involved Jonas Yoder and other believers belonging to the Old Amish faith who defied Wisconsin's compulsory school attendance law requiring students to attend school until the age of sixteen, while Wisconsin argued that it had a compelling duty to educate children within its jurisdiction. The Amish, known to be industrious, self-sufficient, law-abiding citizens, have usually considered themselves far removed from contemporary society. Amish doctrine holds that members must withdraw from most worldly aspects of modern society and commit themselves to a life of hard work, a simple lifestyle, and a deep commitment to religious values. Although committed to educating their children, the Amish historically have supplemented the first few years of public schooling with in-home education that reinforces their religious values and have shunned high school in the belief that such an educational environment debases their culture and religion. The Wisconsin Supreme Court found in favor of Yoder, and the state appealed the decision to the U.S. Supreme Court.

In a landmark 6–1 ruling, the Supreme Court ruled in favor of the Amish respondents. Chief Justice Warren Burger's majority opinion first considered whether the Amish claim for an exemption from the law was motivated by a deep religious belief or merely a personal preference. The Court was comfortable with the conclusion that the Amish lifestyle was not merely personal preference, but a sincere religious conviction that was reflected in the Biblical injunction to "be not conformed to this world." To comply with the compulsory attendance policy, the Court reasoned, would compel the Amish to "perform acts undeniably at odds with fundamental tenets of their religious beliefs."

The Court then weighed the state's interest—educating its citizens—against Yoder's religious beliefs. On this point, the justices found that if education is vital to self-sufficiency and self-reliance, then the Amish display an exemplary record, inasmuch as they have been industrious, have refused to accept public welfare, and have already been exempted from Social Security taxation. On the point that education is essential to developing job skills, the Court felt that, here too, the Amish system of "learning by doing" was "ideal" for preparing Amish children to live as adults in their religious community. Finally, Wisconsin argued that its compulsory school attendance law recognized the substantive right of all children to a secondary education. But the law did not say that parents must consult with their children about whether they want to attend public school. After noting that the state cannot hold Amish parents to a stricter standard than non-Amish parents of consulting their children about whether they want to attend public school, Burger invoked the *Pierce* precedent of 1925 to emphasize the discretion of parents:

> [*PIERCE*] STANDS AS A CHARTER OF THE RIGHTS OF PARENTS TO DIRECT THE RELIGIOUS UPBRINGING OF THEIR CHILDREN.

> AND, WHEN THE INTERESTS OF PARENTHOOD ARE COMBINED WITH A FREE EXERCISE CLAIM OF THE NATURE REVEALED BY THIS RECORD, MORE THAN MERELY A "REASONABLE RELATION TO SOME PURPOSE WITHIN THE COMPETENCY OF THE STATE" IS REQUIRED TO SUSTAIN THE VALIDITY OF THE STATE'S REQUIREMENT UNDER THE FIRST AMENDMENT.

Wisconsin v. Yoder is significant for two reasons. Ever since the *Reynolds* case in 1878, the Court had recognized that religious beliefs were inviolable but that actions based on those beliefs could be regulated by government in order to protect society. In *Yoder*, the Court rejected this pattern and held that, without totally ignoring a state's compelling interest in some instances, "there are areas of conduct protected by the Free Exercise Clause . . . beyond the power of the State to control."

The second novelty introduced by the *Yoder* case was that, for the first time, by granting certain privileges to persons under the Free Exercise Clause, the Court was obligating itself to consider for future claims that government might be violating the Establishment Clause.[11] By exempting the Amish from compulsory school attendance laws, was Wisconsin granting special support for that religious group in violation of the other religion clause? This issue would arise in many future cases (see Brief 16.4).

THE MEANING OF "RELIGION" AND CONSCIENTIOUS OBJECTORS

Serious conflicts over the definition of religion developed during the late 1960s, when numerous social, political, and economic norms were under siege in American society. During the Vietnam War, the issue of conscientious objection (CO) produced several cases involving persons opposed to the selective service system and American participation in an "immoral" war. Prior to 1965, the Court required that, in order to claim CO status and exemption from military service, the person had to prove sustained "religious training and belief" in a particular pacifist sect, such as the Quakers or the Mennonites. Under the Universal Military Training and Service Act passed by Congress in 1948, persons had to prove that they were "conscientiously opposed to participation in war in any form." Furthermore, this religious training and belief had to involve a person's "belief in a relation to

Brief 16.4

MAY A RELIGIOUS SECT HAVE ITS OWN SCHOOL DISTRICT?

The Village of Kiryas Joel, located in New York State, is totally inhabited by members of the Satmar Hasidic sect of Judaism. The religious sect limits all contact with the secular world and educates its children in sex-segregated private schools. Since the entire village is comprised of sect members, the New York Legislature created a separate school district that would give the group complete authority over all school-related matters, including attendance, teachers, textbooks, and taxes. The school board operated only a special education program for handicapped children, however, with all other village children attending private religious schools. The arrangement was challenged as violating the Establishment Clause, and the state courts ruled against the school district.

In the *Board of Education of Kiryas Joel v. Grumet* (1994), a 6–3 majority affirmed the lower court rulings and found the special school district to be a violation of the Establishment Clause. Justice Souter's opinion for the Court stressed the need for government to steer a course of neutrality in these matters. He also noted that the New York Legislature had made no provision for other religious groups that might want their own school district, a step that would be required to satisfy the Establishment Clause requirement that government should not prefer one religion to another, or religion to irreligion. The majority also noted that bilingual and bicultural special education may be provided through existing public school districts to children of a religious enclave, rather than through a separate special district, without violating the Establishment Clause, as long as the plan is administered according to neutral principles.

Justice Scalia's dissenting opinion, joined by Chief Justice Rehnquist and Justice Thomas, criticized the majority for "calling religious toleration the establishment of religion." He questioned whether the educating of religious students in a public school was really all that different from providing services to these students on a neutral site or allowing public employees to serve as sign-language interpreters (see the *Zobrest* case below) for children in parochial schools. Justice Scalia concluded that no evidence existed to show that New York had favored the Satmar religion.

---

a Supreme Being involving duties superior to those arising from any human relation . . . ."

In 1965, this provision of the Universal Military Training and Service Act was challenged on the grounds that it discriminated against nonreligious conscientious objectors and certain kinds of religious expression. In *United States v. Seeger* (1965), the Supreme Court ruled that three individuals, none of whom claimed a personal belief in God, were entitled to be exempted from compulsory military service on religious grounds. In ruling this way, the Court concluded that when Congress referred in the federal law to a Supreme Being, rather than to God, it was only trying to clarify the meaning of religious training and beliefs so as to include all religions and exclude mere philosophical, political, or sociological views. In writing for the majority, Justice Thomas Clark said that the test of one's beliefs was based on whether those beliefs are "sincere and meaningful, and occupy a place in the life of its possessor parallel to that filled by the orthodox belief in God . . . ."

Seeger was significant because it created the **parallel-place doctrine** for evaluating the sincerity of religious beliefs. Although the Court retained the demand for "religious motivation" to be exempt from the draft, the new standard eliminated formal religious *instruction* as a requirement. This tactical definition avoided the criticism that by exempting pacifist sects, the Court was discriminating against religious beliefs that might lead some to morally oppose war. After *Seeger*, there was no longer an exclusive exemption for Quakers and Mennonites, but for others as well who could claim a parallel religious motivation, regardless of a belief in God or formal religious training.[12]

Although the Free Exercise Clause has caused some difficulties in trying to define "religion" and determining whether certain individuals should be exempt from universal rules, the Establishment Clause has posed even more problems for the courts in the twentieth century. The chapter now turns to an examination of those issues.

THE ESTABLISHMENT OF RELIGION

The First Amendment begins with a deceptively simple prohibition that, "Congress shall make no law respecting the establishment of religion," but the meaning of "establishment" is not clear. Some have argued that the phrase should be interpreted in the context of the times in which it was drafted, and that it was intended to ensure that the new national government would not allow an official, established church supported at public expense. This view would still allow the states to support religious institutions as long as that support did not prefer any one religion or church over another (see Brief 16.5).

The inevitable tension between America's "civil" religion and the ever-present "wall of separation"

Brief 16.5

COMPETING THEORIES OF THE ESTABLISHMENT CLAUSE

For the past four decades, the Supreme Court has been struggling with the meaning of the Establishment Clause, and constitutional scholars have differed greatly over what the Clause compels in contemporary society.[13] Several authorities have noted at least three constitutional theories to explain the large majority of Establishment Clause cases.[14]

The **strict-separation** or **no-aid theory** incorporates Thomas Jefferson's reference to a "wall of separation" and reflects a rigid division between secular and religious authorities and structures. This first theory was implicit in *Everson v. Board of Education* in 1947, but more explicitly stated by Justice Hugo Black in *McCollum* in 1948 and *Engel v. Vitale* in 1962. This "no aid" theory has also been occasionally displayed by the Court in decisions that have prohibited fifty-foot lighted crosses being displayed on public property[15] and prevented the military service academies from requiring that cadets attend chapel religious services.[16]

A second theory used to explain how the Court has applied the Establishment Clause is known as the **governmental-neutrality theory**. It requires that government be neutral in various matters involving religion in the public order. It maintains that government must do nothing either to aid or hamper religion. Perhaps the first articulation of this theory came in 1963 with the *Abington v. Schempp/Murray v. Curlett* Bible Reading cases. As Justice Thomas Clark then wrote for the majority, "[i]n the relationship between man and religion, the state is firmly committed to a position of neutrality." The Rehnquist Court relied extensively on the neutrality principle in its Establishment Clause rulings.

A third test that has been very prominent in recent years is the **government-accommodation theory**. This view of the church–state relationship was prominent in Justice Douglas's majority opinion in *Zorach v. Clausen* in 1952, wherein he referred to Americans as "a religious people." It was also hinted at in Brennan's concurring opinion in *Abington v. Schempp*. In that decision, he noted that only some form of secular accommodation of religion can reconcile the inherent clash between the two religion clauses of the First Amendment. Several of the matters sustained by the Court over the past few decades, such as the reference to God on U.S. coinage, the Pledge of Allegiance, tuition tax credits, legislative chaplains, nativity displays, and tax exemptions for religious organizations are all embedded in the "accommodationist" school.

These three theories attest to the fact that the Supreme Court has left a rather confused path to follow through the church–state maze. One author recently referred to the body of constitutional law concerning permissible state aid to parochial schools as being "clearly in a shambles."[17]

---

between church and state has forced the American public to look to the Supreme Court for "final" answers, but the Court has itself often generated new disagreements over the preferable interpretation of the law. In the following sections, these theories will be applied to the Supreme Court decisions that have helped to define establishment issues. For four decades, several cases concerning the Establishment Clause have focused on two primary areas: public financial *assistance* to parochial institutions and religious *practices* in the public schools. The following narrative will first discuss public aid to parochial institutions, since that topic prompted the application of the Establishment Clause to the states. Table 16.2 provides an overview of the key developments.

PUBLIC ASSISTANCE TO PAROCHIAL SCHOOLS: THE CONSTITUTIONAL FOUNDATION

Few cases concerning the Establishment Clause came before the Supreme Court prior to 1947. In 1930, the Supreme Court upheld a Louisiana law that authorized public funding for nonsectarian textbooks to be used by students in parochial schools.[18] A major feature of this decision was the **child-benefit theory**, which held that a law allowing textbooks to be purchased with public money did not violate the Establishment Clause because it was the child, and not the religious institution, that benefited from the book purchases.

An important case after World War II finally applied the Establishment Clause to the states. *Everson v. Board of Education* (1947) involved a taxpayer in New Jersey who challenged the constitutionality of a state law that allowed local school districts to reimburse parents for expenses incurred in using public transportation to send their children to parochial schools. Justice Hugo Black's majority opinion provided an explanation of the Establishment Clause, noting that it "requires the state to be a neutral in its relations with groups of religious believers and non-believers; it does not require the state to be their adversary." He also invoked Thomas Jefferson's words, that the clause "was intended to erect 'a wall of separation between Church and State.'" This was all prelude to Black's opinion for a five-member majority upholding the constitutionality of the New Jersey law.

According to the justices, New Jersey contributed no money to parochial schools, but instead, provided a general program to allow parents to get their children safely to and from accredited schools.

Table 16.2 Development of the Law—Public Aid to Religion

Year	Event	Significance
1785	Memorial and Remonstrance Against Religious Assessments	Madison's powerful statement against a Virginia plan to provide financial support for the Christian religion. It was criticized by most religious groups but helped defeat the proposed assessments bill.
1930	*Cochran v. Louisiana State Board of Education*	Upheld state law authorizing public funding for nonsectarian textbooks for students in parochial schools.
1947	*Everson v. Board of Education*	Incorporated Establishment Clause into the Fourteenth Amendment. Upheld reimbursement for transportation expenses to and from private school under "child benefit."
1968	*Board of Education v. Allen*	Upheld New York law requiring local school districts to loan books to children in private and parochial schools.
1970	*Walz v. Tax Commission*	Upheld state tax exemption of property used exclusively for religious purposes since no specific religion was singled out.
1971	*Lemon v. Kurtzman*	Struck down law to pay salaries of parochial school teachers as "excessive entanglement" between church and state. Along with purpose and effect, became basis for *Lemon* test.
1971	*Tilton v. Richardson*	Upheld 5–4 Federal Higher Education Facilities Act of 1963 providing funds for academic buildings on private sectarian and secular colleges.
1972	*Essex v. Wolman*	Ohio law giving tuition rebates was "excessive entanglement."
1973	*Hunt v. McNair*	Upheld state bond issue for construction and financing of nonreligious buildings on *all* institutions of higher learning.
1973	*Committee for Public Education v. Nyquist*	Struck down various state programs providing broad aid for parochial schools (e.g., tuition, testing, remedial classes).
1975	*Meek v. Pittenger*	Upheld textbook loan portion only of a broad Pennsylvania law but struck down counseling, testing, and equipment.
1976	*Roemer v. Maryland Public Works Board*	Allowed funding for church-affiliated colleges even if the colleges require religion and theology courses.
1977	*Wolman v. Walter*	Confusing decision upholding certain publicly funded services for private schools (textbooks, diagnostic services performed off school grounds), but striking down funds for field trips.
1981	*Widmar v. Vincent*	Used free speech to strike down Missouri law prohibiting use of university buildings for religious purposes. Equal access.
1983	*Mueller v. Allen*	Allowed parents of all (public and private) students to receive up to $700 tax deduction for education expenses incurred.
1983	*Bob Jones University v. U.S.*	Racially discriminatory private schools are not eligible for federal tax-exempt status.
1984	Equal Access Act	Extended *Widmar* precedent to public schools.
1985	*Grand Rapids School District v. Ball*	Struck down programs offered in private schools paid for by school district as promoting religion.
1985	*Aguilar v. Felton*	New York City may not provide instruction to parochial schools on school premises using public school teachers.
1986	*Witters v. Washington*	State vocational rehabilitation funds may be used by a blind student for studies at a Christian college; the funds were paid to the student.

1989	*Texas Monthly, Inc. v. Bullock*	Struck down a state sales tax exemption that applied only to religious publications.
1990	*Jimmy Swaggart Ministries v. Board of Equalization*	Generally applicable sales taxes that also apply to religious organizations do not violate the religion clauses. States are not required to grant tax-exempt status to religious organizations.
1990	*Board of Education of Westside v. Mergens*	Upheld Equal Access Act of 1984, requiring public high schools to allow student religious groups to meet on school premises.
1993	*Lamb's Chapel v. Center Moriches Free Union School District*	Public schools may not prevent church groups from using their facilities after hours when facilities are available to others. Decided on free speech grounds.
1993	*Zobrest v. Catalina School District*	Court relied on *Witters* to uphold use of government funds to hire a sign language interpreter for a deaf child in parochial school under Individuals with Disabilities Education Act.
1995	*Rosenberger v. Rector and visitors of the University of Virginia*	Public university engages in "viewpoint discrimination" when it denied funding only to student publications with religious content.
1997	*Agostini v. Felton*	Narrow 5–4 ruling overturning the 1985 *Aguilar* and *Grand Rapids* decisions. Majority said that on-premises instructional programs do not violate Establishment Clause.
1998	*Board of Education v. Mergens*	Court upheld Equal Access Act as applied to public schools noting that a school does not endorse student speech merely by permitting it on a nondiscriminatory basis.
2000	*Mitchell v. Helms*	Upheld government program lending computers, software, and library books to public and private schools if done neutrally and without religious indoctrination.
2001	*Good News Club v. Milford Central School*	Upheld permission for a religious club to meet on school premises after hours as protection of free speech rights.
2002	*Zelman v. Simmons-Harris*	Upheld Ohio's voucher program that provides tuition for poor families to send their children to public or private schools.
2004	*Locke v. Davey*	Upheld Washington's refusal to provide scholarships to college students who chose to pursue religious degrees while providing scholarships to students who chose other majors.
2005	*Cutter v. Wilkinson*	Upheld the Religious Land Use and Institutionalized Persons Act of 2000 allowing accommodation of religion within institutions unless the state can show "compelling interest."
2007	*Hein, et al. v. Freedom from Religion Foundation, Inc.*	Taxpayers have no standing to challenge the actions of the Executive Branch in creating a faith-based initiative when no prior or subsequent act of Congress authorized such programs. Tax-payers can challenge government spending statutory violation exists.only when a statutory violation exists.
2010	*Christian Legal Society Chapter of the University of California, Hastings College of Law, aka, Hastings Christian Fellowship v. Martinez*	Upheld a public university law school's refusal to recognize a religious student organization for its refusal to take "all comers" into its membership.
2012	*Hosanna-Tabor Evangelical Lutheran Church and School v. Equal Employment Opportunity Commission, et al.*	Held that a "ministerial exception" bars government legislation from interfering with the employment relationship between a religious institution and its ministers.

Undoubtedly, a major rationale of the *Everson* majority opinion was, once again, the child-benefit explanation. The state was providing an important service to the parents and children, not to any religious denomination. The New Jersey law did not even "slightly breach" the wall separating church and state.

Justice Wiley Rutledge, who cast one of four dissenting votes in the *Everson* case, was troubled by the decision, arguing that providing aid would leave the door open to expand that assistance in the future. Rutledge stated that this was "the very thing Jefferson and Madison experienced and sought to guard against, whether in its blunt or in its more screened form."

With the *Everson* case, the Court for the first time confronted the difficult issue of what constitutes government aid to religion. At the time, some considered the public transportation subsidies to parents as clearly encouraging and facilitating attendance at parochial schools, which Black's "no-aid" reference would seem to preclude. Those who supported state aid to church schools argued that for New Jersey to deny transportation to students attending parochial schools would have reflected governmental hostility, not neutrality, toward religion. During the next two decades, the question of state aid to church schools and its questionable status under the Establishment Clause subsided and was overshadowed by the issue of religious activities in public schools. When state aid returned to prominence in the 1970s, the Supreme Court was not prepared to follow a clear line of reasoning.

EMERGENCE OF THE THREE-PRONGED TEST

As parochial schools found it increasingly more difficult to meet their financial obligations in the 1960s and 1970s, parents and church authorities became more vocal in pressing state legislatures to authorize subsidies for church school operations. In 1968, the Supreme Court ruled that a New York law requiring local school districts to lend textbooks on secular subjects to parochial school students at no cost was not a violation of the Establishment Clause. In *Board of Education v. Allen* (1968), the Court ruled 5–4 that the law had both "a secular legislative purpose and a primary effect that neither advances nor inhibits religion."

This two-pronged guideline—secular purpose and neutral effect—had been created six years earlier in the Bible Reading Cases of 1963 (to be discussed below, as the "*Schempp* test"). Writing for the majority, Justice Byron White invoked the familiar child-benefit theory, stating that the financial benefit provided by New York State was to the parents and the children, not to the religious schools.

The 1970s were especially active years regarding aid to parochial schools and court challenges to those programs. In several decisions concerning the parochial aid issue, the Burger Court gradually moved away from the earlier emphasis upon benefits being provided to the *students* involved, and toward the nature of the relationship between government and religion. The most prominent case, *Lemon v. Kurtzman* (1971), involved two separate state aid-to-schools programs. Under a 1968 Pennsylvania law, the state directly reimbursed parochial schools for expenditures incurred for teacher salaries, textbooks, and various instructional materials in selected secular subjects. Under a similar law passed by the Rhode Island legislature in 1969, that state contributed up to 15 percent of the salaries for teachers in parochial schools who were engaged in teaching only secular subjects offered in the public schools.

With Chief Justice Burger delivering the majority opinion in *Lemon*, the two state laws were declared unconstitutional. After reviewing the background of the two state laws, Burger observed that this "extraordinarily sensitive area of constitutional law" had to pass three important elements:

> FIRST, THE STATUTE MUST HAVE A SECULAR LEGISLATIVE PURPOSE; SECOND, ITS PRINCIPAL OR PRIMARY EFFECT MUST BE ONE THAT NEITHER ADVANCES NOR INHIBITS RELIGION, *ALLEN*; FINALLY, THE STATUTE MUST NOT FOSTER "AN EXCESSIVE GOVERNMENT ENTANGLEMENT WITH RELIGION," *WALZ*.

The third element—excessive entanglement—condemned both of the state aid programs in Pennsylvania and Rhode Island. The Court said that both programs involved an unacceptably close relationship between government and religion. In Rhode Island, the Court thought that some teachers involved might find it virtually impossible "to make a total separation between secular teaching and religious doctrine." Also, because the state education board had to inspect and evaluate the religious content of the curriculum in order to ensure secularism, the program was "fraught with the sort of entanglement that the Constitution forbids." The Pennsylvania program was burdened by basically the same aspects as the plan in Rhode Island, with the additional problem of providing direct financial aid to the parochial schools. Although drawn from earlier precedents, the **Lemon** test—secular purpose, primary effect, and excessive entanglement—would be very important to future aid-to-parochial-schools controversies (see Brief 16.6).

THE MOVEMENT TOWARD NEUTRALITY AND ACCOMMODATION

In *Zelman v. Simmons-Harris* (2002), a divided Supreme Court upheld the Ohio Pilot Project Scholarship Program, a program providing vouchers for students to attend public or private schools. The *Zelman*

Brief 16.6

THE "MINISTERIAL EXCEPTION": AVOIDING EXCESSIVE ENTANGLEMENT

Disputes within religious denominations and churches are far from uncommon, and resolution of these disputes may raise constitutional problems. Over the years, denominations and churches have used courts to resolve conflicts disputing ownership of church property. The United States Supreme Court has required courts to use "neutral principles of law" in adjudicating these disputes, meaning that courts will not inquire into doctrinal or political issues. Similar disputes have evolved concerning the employment of ministers and other clerical workers.

The case of *Hosanna-Tabor Evangelical Lutheran Church and School v. Equal Employment Opportunity Commission, et al.* (2012) raised such a dispute and produced a unanimous Supreme Court ruling upholding the right of religious denominations to control the employment relationship that exists for ministers and other clerical leaders. The case originated when Cheryl Perich, a teacher at Hosanna-Tabor Evangelical Lutheran School (Hosanna) was terminated following an illness and disability leave. Hosanna classifies its teachers as either "called" or "lay" teachers. To be considered "called," a teacher must complete some academic requirements and a course of theological study. The teacher then is called "Minister of Religion, Commissioned." A "lay" teacher, on the other hand, is not required to be trained by the Synod or even to be Lutheran. Both teachers perform essentially the same duties.

When Ms. Perich developed narcolepsy and went on disability leave, she notified the principal that she would return in February, but the principal responded that the school already had a lay teacher to replace her for the remainder of the school year. When she appeared at school in February, Ms. Perich indicated that she would pursue her legal rights. Subsequently, the school board rescinded her "call" for insubordination and disruptive behavior, followed by a letter of termination. She filed a charge with the EEOC, claiming that she had been terminated in violation of the Americans with Disabilities Act (ADA). The EEOC filed suit in federal district court, but the court granted summary judgment to Hosanna. On appeal, the Sixth Circuit vacated and remanded the case on the basis that Perich did not qualify as a "minister." The U.S. Supreme Court accepted the case.

Writing for a unanimous Court, Chief Justice Roberts made the strong case for a "ministerial exception" to employment laws:

> We agree that there is such a ministerial exception. The members of a religious group put their faith in the hands of their ministers. Requiring a church to accept or retain an unwanted minister, or punishing a church for failing to do so, intrudes upon more than a mere employment decision. Such action interferes with the internal governance of the church, depriving the church of control over the selection of those who will personify its beliefs. By imposing an unwanted minister, the state infringes the Free Exercise Clause, which protects a religious group's right to shape its own faith and mission through its appointments. According the state the power to determine which individuals will minister to the faithful also violates the Establishment Clause, which prohibits government involvement in such ecclesiastical decisions.

The Chief Justice then turned to the question of whether the "ministerial exception" applies to Ms. Perich. He noted that every court of appeals to consider this question have concluded the ministerial exception is not limited to the head of a religious congregation. He refused, however, to adopt a rigid formula to determine when an employee qualifies as a minister. "It is enough for us to conclude, in this our first case involving the ministerial exception, that the exception covers Perich, given all the circumstances of her employment." Because Perich had received a significant degree of religious training, because Hosanna held her out as a minister, because Perich held herself out as a minister, and because her job duties involved conveying the Church's message and carrying out its mission, "we conclude that Perich was a minister covered by the ministerial exception." The Chief Justice concluded that, when employment disputes develop between a church and a minister, "The church must be free to choose those who will guide it on its way."

decision illustrates a clear pattern in which the Court puts crucial emphasis on the principle of neutrality and private choice. In this view, government's primary responsibility is to ensure neutrality in its actions and not favor one type of school (public or private) over another. If neutrality is preserved, government aid can flow to all types of recipients without limitation. The *Zelman* decision can be best understood by looking at several precedents leading up to the eventual ruling.

MUELLER V. ALLEN (1983)

Mueller v. Allen (1983) was a Minnesota case in which a 5–4 Court upheld a state law allowing taxpayers to deduct from their gross income up to $700 for expenses they incurred for school tuition, textbooks, transportation, and other supplies for dependents who attended elementary and secondary schools within the state. Although the state law specifically extended this benefit to all parents, regardless of whether the children were attending public or private institutions, the court record indicated that over 95 percent of the parents taking advantage of the tax credit had children enrolled in religious schools (this would also be an important issue in *Zelman*). Some Minnesota taxpayers contested the law, arguing in federal court that it violated the Establishment Clause. Both the trial and the appellate courts upheld the constitutionality of the law and the judgment was appealed to the Supreme Court.

In writing the majority opinion, Justice William Rehnquist distinguished this case from several other parochial aid controversies of the preceding two decades. He said *Mueller* was "vitally different" from *Nyquist* because the New York law in 1973 had allowed tuition deductions only for parents with children in *nonpublic* schools, whereas the Minnesota law was designed to benefit *both public and private school parents*. In response to critics claiming only a "facial neutrality" in the law, Rehnquist said that the Court would not establish a rule requiring annual reports attesting to how many parents took advantage of the law. In dissent, where he was joined by Justices Brennan, Blackmun, and Stevens, Justice Thurgood Marshall found no appreciable difference between the defective New York law struck down in 1973 and the Minnesota law upheld in *Mueller*. To him, both had "a direct and immediate effect of advancing religion."

ZOBREST V. CATALINA FOOTHILLS SCHOOL DISTRICT (1993)

Individuals with disabilities may qualify for government support in various areas, including education. When the individual takes those government funds and applies them in a religious school, however, questions can be raised related to an establishment of religion. The Supreme Court held in *Witters v. Washington Department of Services for Blind* (1986) that the Establishment Clause does not prohibit a blind person receiving government support from studying to become a pastor at a Christian college. The key element, stated the Court, was that while some aid would ultimately flow to the religious school, it did so "only as a result of the genuinely independent and private choices of aid recipients."

The same rationale can be found in the Individuals with Disabilities Education Act (IDEA) of 1991. This act provides benefits to any child qualifying as "handicapped," without regard to the nature of the school the child attends. The case of *Zobrest v. Catalina Foothills School District* (1993) originated when the parents of James Zobrest, who was deaf since birth, brought suit in U.S. District Court for the reimbursement of more than $7,000 they had paid a sign-language interpreter for their son. James Zobrest had attended first through fifth grades in a school for the deaf and then transferred to a public school for the sixth, seventh, and eighth grades. The public school had provided a sign-language interpreter. In the ninth grade, James enrolled at Salpointe Catholic High School. Under the federal Individuals with Disabilities Education Act, the parents asked the Catalina Hills School District to pay for the sign-language interpreter helping their son at the parochial school. When the county and state authorities ruled that such aid would violate the Establishment Clause, the Zobrests filed suit.

Chief Justice Rehnquist, writing for the majority, reversed the lower courts and found no establishment of religion violation. According to Rehnquist, the IDEA was a "neutral government program dispensing aid not to schools but to individual handicapped children." As such, the Establishment Clause would not prevent a school district from furnishing a sign-language interpreter for the student "to facilitate his education."

Justice Blackmun's two-part dissent argued that the majority's characterization of a sign-language interpreter as a "neutral hearing aid" was incorrect, adding that there was not much difference between the function of a teacher and an interpreter. Both, he said, serve as a "conduit" for religious messages. Particularly, in the "pervasive religious" atmosphere of Salpointe Catholic High School, Blackmun stated, the use of an interpreter "involves ongoing, daily, and intimate governmental participation in the teaching and propagation of religious doctrine."

AGOSTINI V. FELTON (1997)

In two same-day decisions, *Grand Rapids School District v. Ball* and *Aguilar v. Felton* (1985), a 5–4 Court struck down programs that used public funds to pay for public school teachers providing remedial or enrichment instruction in parochial schools. These plans were funded by Title I of the Elementary and Secondary Education Act of 1965, which provides funds for remedial educational services to economically disadvantaged students attending public and private schools, whether sectarian or nonsectarian. The Act provides that Title I services must be secular, neutral, nonideological, and must supplement, not replace, educational services already being provided.

Supporters of these programs refused to give up. In New York City, the board modified its plan, sending some private school students to nearby public schools, nearby leased sites, or to mobile units parked adjacent to private schools. As a result, public funds were supporting education for private school students as long as they were not on private school property. In 1995, the New York City Board of Education and a group of parents asked the federal district court to lift the injunction on providing on-premises instructional services, arguing that the law surrounding the Establishment Clause had changed since 1985.

Apparently, they were right. In a rare step, a 5–4 majority of the Supreme Court held in *Agostini v. Felton* (1997) that the law had indeed changed, and the 1985 *Grand Rapids* and *Aguilar* precedents were overruled. Justice O'Connor's majority opinion emphasized that public money made available to all eligible students for secular educational purposes does not violate the Establishment Clause. Citing the ruling in *Zobrest,* she rejected the argument that the mere physical presence of public employees on private school property results in an impermissible union between government and religion. *Agostini* largely collapsed the three-prong *Lemon* test into two elements: whether the statute results in religious indoctrination and whether it defines the recipients by reference to religion.

MITCHELL V. HELMS (2000)

The shift on the Supreme Court became even more clear with the decision in *Mitchell v. Helms* (2000). In that case, the Court upheld the use of federal funds to support the lending of educational materials and equipment such as computers, software, and library materials to public and private elementary and secondary schools to implement "secular, neutral and nonideological" programs. A 6–3 majority upheld the federal law, but four of the justices joined in a plurality opinion expressing the view that some direct government aid to religious schools is permissible when it is administered with neutrality toward both religious and secular schools on a nondiscriminatory basis. The plurality also held that even the "diversion" of the aid for religious purposes would not violate the Establishment Clause. Justices O'Connor and Breyer, part of the broad majority, could not accept the plurality's notion that "neutrality" was sufficient to qualify the aid as constitutional. They also believed that actual "diversion" of the aid to religious purposes was unconstitutional, but they found no significant evidence of diversion in the present case.

The significance of *Mitchell v. Helms* is difficult to overstate. According to Derek Davis, the plurality opinion in Helms is "unique . . . not in its determination that a government aid program that encompasses religious schools is constitutional, but for its sweeping rejection of past tests of government establishment and its almost exclusive reliance on the 'principle of neutrality' as a constitutional determinant."[19] Professor Davis adds that the Court's almost exclusive reliance on the neutrality principle, when tied to the emphasis on "private choice" by individuals, will greatly expand the government funding of private schools. He cautions, however, that "there must certainly exist a level at which these institutions will begin to lose their religious identities and assume more secular ones based upon the level of public funding."[20]

ZELMAN V. SIMMONS-HARRIS (2002)

The movement for increased parental and student choice has gathered momentum in recent years, and debates over vouchers have proliferated. Various voucher programs in cities such as Milwaukee and Cleveland have drawn nationwide attention as alternatives to public schooling. Both proponents and opponents of vouchers believe that the Constitution favors their position: proponents of vouchers arguing that vouchers simply give parents and students a choice among various school alternatives; opponents contending that government monies cannot flow to religious schools without violating the Establishment Clause. While debates over vouchers focus on various issues—the quality of public schools, equality in education, and educational policy—the primary constitutional issue revolves around the Establishment Clause and the movement of tax-generated dollars from government to private, often religious, schools. That was the central aspect in *Zelman v. Simmons-Harris* (2002).

Chief Justice William Rehnquist's opinion for a 5–4 majority upheld the Ohio Pilot Project Scholarship Program, which gives educational choices to families in any Ohio school district that is under state control pursuant to a federal court order. Cleveland was the only covered district in Ohio, and students there were eligible to receive either tutorial assistance grants (for students staying in public school) or tuition aid scholarships (for students opting to attend magnet, community, or private schools). Opponents argued that the plan simply supported private religious schools, despite the program's preference for magnet schools or independent community schools. Their arguments were based on the fact that in the 1999–2000 school year, 82 percent of the participating private schools had a religious affiliation, none of the adjacent public schools participated, and 96 percent of the students participating in the scholarship program were enrolled in religiously affiliated schools. In short, although the program provided more money for students to attend magnet and community schools, most chose to attend religiously affiliated private schools. Opponents did not see this as a real choice.

In his opinion, Chief Justice Rehnquist began by noting that the program was enacted for the "valid secular purpose of providing educational assistance to poor children in a demonstrably failing public school system." With that established, the primary issue was whether the plan had the effect of promoting or hindering religion. That question, he said, is clearly answered by the Court's recent precedents:

> *MUELLER, WITTERS,* AND *ZOBREST* THUS MAKE CLEAR THAT WHERE A GOVERNMENT AID PROGRAM IS NEUTRAL WITH RESPECT TO RELIGION, AND PROVIDES ASSISTANCE DIRECTLY TO A BROAD CLASS OF CITIZENS WHO, IN TURN, DIRECT GOVERNMENT AID TO RELIGIOUS SCHOOLS WHOLLY AS A RESULT OF THEIR OWN GENUINE AND INDEPENDENT PRIVATE CHOICE, THE PROGRAM IS NOT READILY SUBJECT TO CHALLENGE UNDER THE ESTABLISHMENT CLAUSE. A PROGRAM THAT SHARES THESE FEATURES PERMITS GOVERNMENT AID TO REACH RELIGIOUS INSTITUTIONS ONLY BY WAY OF THE DELIBERATE CHOICES OF NUMEROUS INDIVIDUAL RECIPIENTS. THE INCIDENTAL ADVANCEMENT OF A RELIGIOUS MISSION, OR THE PERCEIVED ENDORSEMENT OF A RELIGIOUS MESSAGE, IS REASONABLY ATTRIBUTABLE TO THE INDIVIDUAL RECIPIENT, NOT TO THE GOVERNMENT, WHOSE ROLE ENDS WITH THE DISBURSEMENT OF BENEFITS.

The Chief Justice went on to say that the Ohio program, consistent with *Mueller, Witters,* and *Zobrest,* was a program of "true private choice" and was "neutral in all respects toward religion." By conferring benefits to all individuals with children in the Cleveland City School District without reference to religion, the program cannot be said to violate the Establishment Clause.

Justice Sandra Day O'Connor concurred to point out that the decision was entirely consistent with the Court's earlier rulings and also to argue that the Cleveland program indeed allowed broad parental and student choice. She noted that the broad pattern of tax exemptions for religious organizations (see *Walz v. Tax Commission of City of New York* below) results in far greater financial benefits for religion than vouchers, and other federal programs such as Medicare, Medicaid, the G.I. Bill, and Pell Grants provide federal dollars to religiously affiliated organizations. As for the issue of parental choice, Justice O'Connor noted that far more students opted for magnet and community schools than religious schools.

The dissenters, Justices Stevens, Souter, Breyer, and Ginsburg, focused on the undeniable fact that government dollars were being paid to religious schools to provide education to children, something that they believe was clearly outlawed in *Everson* and later rulings. Justice Souter questioned the "choice" existent within the program, noting that 82 percent of the private schools participating in the program were religious schools (the $2,250 tuition voucher, he argued, was simply inadequate to provide tuition at the private, nonreligious schools).

Finally, Justice Breyer provided a stern warning for his majority colleagues:

THE COURT, IN EFFECT, TURNS THE CLOCK BACK. IT ADOPTS, UNDER THE NAME OF "NEUTRALITY," AN INTERPRETATION OF THE ESTABLISHMENT CLAUSE THAT THIS COURT REJECTED MORE THAN HALF A CENTURY AGO. IN ITS VIEW, THE PARENTAL CHOICE THAT OFFERS EACH RELIGIOUS GROUP A KIND OF EQUAL OPPORTUNITY TO SECURE GOVERNMENT FUNDING OVERCOMES THE ESTABLISHMENT CLAUSE CONCERN FOR SOCIAL CONCORD. . . . IN A SOCIETY COMPOSED OF MANY DIFFERENT RELIGIOUS CREEDS, I FEAR THAT THIS PRESENT DEPARTURE FROM THE COURT'S EARLIER UNDERSTANDING RISKS CREATING A FORM OF RELIGIOUSLY BASED CONFLICT POTENTIALLY HARMFUL TO THE NATION'S SOCIAL FABRIC.

Zelman energized the supporters of voucher programs across the country, and state legislatures have begun to address the issue. In January 2004, Congress passed the first federally funded school voucher program, providing $14 million for low-income students in the District of Columbia. While a number of states have constitutional provisions prohibiting the distribution of public funds to religious institutions or for religious purposes (see Brief 16.7), the federal government, which has jurisdiction over Washington, D.C., has no such limitation following *Zelman*.

THE NEUTRALITY PRINCIPLE IN EQUAL ACCESS AND TAXATION

The principle that government must be neutral with respect to religion has been applied in ways other than tuition, vouchers, and learning accommodations. In fact, neutrality has been at the heart of two significant areas of Establishment Clause interpretation: access to public facilities and taxation.

EQUAL ACCESS AND PUBLIC FACILITIES

In an effort to encourage on-campus activities, the University of Missouri at Kansas City (UMKC) had for many years recognized over one hundred student organizations, providing them with meeting facilities on the UMKC campus. Between 1973 and 1977, Cornerstone, a registered religious group, conducted its meetings on the campus, but in 1977, the administration told the group that it could no longer use campus facilities. In *Widmar v. Vincent* (1981), an 8–1 Court said that public universities that made their facilities generally available for the activities of registered student organizations cannot exclude religious groups from such facilities because of the content of their speech. Having created a "forum generally open" for use by student groups, UMKC then had to justify why it had discriminated against Cornerstone. The university claimed that it had a compelling interest in maintaining strict separation of church and state.

This ruling created momentum for the "equal access" of religious groups to public facilities. Substantial majorities in both houses of Congress passed the Equal Access Act by late July 1984, which President Reagan signed into law on August 11, 1984. This legislation allowed primary and secondary public school groups, religious and nonreligious, the same right to meet in public facilities, thus extending the principle established in *Widmar* to public schools.

In *Board of Education of Westside Community Schools v. Mergens* (1990), an 8–1 Court upheld the Equal Access Act. Justice O'Connor's opinion found that Westside High School's policy of requiring student

Brief 16.7

WHEN FREE EXERCISE AND ESTABLISHMENT CLASH: LOCKE V. DAVEY (2004)

By a 7–2 ruling, the Supreme Court held in *Locke v. Davey* (2004) that states may refuse to subsidize or provide scholarships for students preparing for the ministry, even if the states provide scholarships for all other courses of study. The state of Washington initiated its Promise Scholarship program in 1999. The program was tailored to be consistent with a provision in the Washington Constitution that prohibits the use of public funds to support "any religious worship, exercise or instruction." As a result, students who were otherwise qualified for the scholarship were ineligible if they wanted to use the money to major in theology and/or train for the ministry. And yet, the program did not discriminate against students who took religion courses or who attended a religious college, as long as they majored in a secular subject.

Joshua Davey was awarded a Promise Scholarship and chose to attend Northwest College, a private, Christian college affiliated with the Assemblies of God denomination. As an accredited institution, Northwest was an eligible institution for the Promise Scholarship program. When he enrolled at Northwest, Davey decided to pursue a double major in pastoral ministries and business management. As a result of his decision to major in pastoral ministries, he did not receive any Promise Scholarship funds. He filed suit in federal court claiming that the denial of his scholarship because of his decision to pursue a theology degree violated the Free Exercise, Establishment, and Free Speech Clauses of the First Amendment, as incorporated by the Fourteenth Amendment, and the Equal Protection Clause of the Fourteenth Amendment.

The District Court rejected Davey's constitutional claims, but the Ninth Circuit Court reversed, concluding that the State had singled out religion for unfavorable treatment. Interestingly, the circuit court relied heavily on the Supreme Court's 1993 decision in *Church of Lukumi Babalu Aye, Inc. v. Hialeah*.

Chief Justice Rehnquist, a consistent supporter of various forms of government aid to religion, wrote the majority opinion upholding the Washington law and its exclusion for theology and religious studies. The Chief Justice zeroed in on the tension that often exists between the Free Exercise and Establishment Clauses, noting that "we have long said that 'there is room for play in the joints' between them. In other words, there are some state actions permitted by the Establishment Clause but not required by the Free Exercise Clause."

This case, he said, involves that "play in the joints." While the state of Washington could permit Promise Scholars to pursue a degree in devotional theology under the Federal Constitution, its own Constitution did not permit state funds to be spent for that purpose. The question then became: Can Washington deny such funding without violating the Free Exercise Clause of the Federal Constitution? The answer, according to the Chief Justice, was yes, and Washington's decision should not be interpreted, he said, as hostility toward religion. Chief Justice Rehnquist concluded:

> In short, we find neither in the history or text of Article I . . . of the Washington Constitution, nor in the operation of the Promise Scholarship Program, anything that suggests animus towards religion. Given the historic and substantial state interest at issue, we therefore cannot conclude that the denial of funding for vocational religious instruction alone is inherently constitutionally suspect. . . . The State's interest in not funding the pursuit of devotional degrees is substantial and the exclusion of such funding places a relatively minor burden on Promise Scholars. If any room exists between the two Religion Clauses, it must be here.

Justice Scalia, joined by Justice Thomas, dissented vocally: "Let there be no doubt: This case is about discrimination against a religious minority. . . . What next? Will we deny priests and nuns their prescription-drug benefits on the ground that taxpayers' freedom of conscience forbids medicating the clergy at public expense?" The ruling, while significant, was focused quite narrowly on training for the ministry at the college level. Proponents and opponents of broader voucher plans had differing views on the outcome, but both agreed that this would not be the Court's last word on the subject.

---

groups and clubs to have a faculty sponsor in order to meet after school hours on school premises violated the Act. She also noted that the Congressional purpose behind the legislation was to prevent discrimination against religious and other types of speech, goals that she described as "undeniably secular." As to the claim that the Act had the effect of advancing religion, particularly by the school itself, Justice O'Connor held that the Establishment Clause prohibits "government" but not "private" speech endorsing religion, adding that "a school does not endorse or support student speech that it merely permits on a nondiscriminatory basis."

The free speech rights of students were central to the Court's eagerly awaited ruling in *Rosenberger v. Rector and Visitors of the University of Virginia* (1995). The University of Virginia (UVA) maintains a Student Activities Fund (SAF) to pay outside contractors for printing costs of various publications issued by student groups called "contracted independent organizations (CIOs)." The money comes from mandatory student fees and is designed to support a broad range of extracurricular student activities. The CIOs must sign a disclaimer that they are independent of UVA and the university is not responsible for their content. The UVA administration refused to pay the printer on behalf of Wide Awake Productions (WAP), solely because its student newspaper, *Wide Awake: A Christian Perspective at the University of Virginia*, "primarily promotes or manifests a particular belief in or about a deity or an ultimate reality." Rosenberger and his organization contended that UVA had violated their First Amendment rights to freedom of speech, while UVA claimed it was required to comply with the Establishment Clause.

A 5–4 majority opinion written by Justice Anthony Kennedy zeroed in on the free speech rights of the students, holding that UVA was practicing "viewpoint discrimination." Justice Kennedy explained that "viewpoint discrimination" occurred because, while UVA had not excluded religion as a subject matter for student publications, it denied funding to student journalistic efforts with religious editorial viewpoints. As such, it was discriminating against a religious viewpoint. The Court concluded by noting that the significant factor in upholding government programs in the face of possible Establishment Clause violations should be neutrality toward religion (see Brief 16.8)

The Court's concern with neutrality was strongly apparent in *Good News Club v. Milford Central School* (2001). That case involved a Milford policy that authorized district residents to use the school building after school for educational, social, civic, recreational, and entertainment activities. When Stephen and Darleen Fournier, sponsors of the Good News Club, a private Christian organization for children ages six to twelve, sought permission to use the school, they were turned down.

In a 6–3 decision, Justice Thomas held that Milford had discriminated against the Good News Club because of its religious viewpoint in violation of the Free Speech Clause, just as the Court had found in the *Lamb's Chapel* and *Rosenberger* cases. Justice Thomas also drew attention to the neutrality principle expressed in *Mitchell v. Helms* (discussed earlier):

> THE GOOD NEWS CLUB SEEKS NOTHING MORE THAN TO BE TREATED NEUTRALLY AND GIVEN ACCESS TO SPEAK ABOUT THE SAME TOPICS AS ARE OTHER GROUPS. BECAUSE ALLOWING THE CLUB TO SPEAK ON SCHOOL GROUNDS WOULD ENSURE NEUTRALITY, NOT THREATEN IT, MILFORD FACES AN UPHILL BATTLE IN ARGUING THAT THE ESTABLISHMENT CLAUSE COMPELS IT TO EXCLUDE THE GOOD NEWS CLUB.

Justice Souter's dissent focused on the club's use of the "challenge" and the "invitation," during which "saved" children who "already believe in the Lord Jesus as their Savior," are challenged to ask God for strength to obey Him. He characterized this as an "evangelical Christian" worship service and said the majority's ruling completely ignored reality. Otherwise, he stated, "this case would stand for the remarkable proposition that any public school opened for civic meetings must be opened for use as a church, synagogue, or mosque."

TAXATION AND RELIGION: RENDERING UNTO CAESAR

Should churches be required to pay taxes to help support the government, or are they deserving of special treatment? This question, in one form or another,

---

Brief 16.8
HASTINGS CHRISTIAN FELLOWSHIP V. MARTINEZ (2010)

The Supreme Court ruled 5–4 in *Hastings Christian Fellowship v. Martinez* (2010) that a law school (Hastings) may refuse to recognize a student organization (Christian Legal Society) that does not allow non-Christians and practicing gays to join. The Hastings so-called "all comers" policy required that recognized student organizations must "allow any student to participate, become a member, or seek leadership positions in the organization, regardless of status or beliefs." Justice Ginsburg, writing for the majority, pointed out that in so-called "limited public forums" such as the law school, government policies need only be "reasonable" and viewpoint-neutral to be acceptable. The CLS argued that Hastings's policy discriminated against religious groups on the basis of their viewpoint, but the Court pointed out that the policy applied to all organizations. The law school had the right to prohibit discrimination based on religion and sexual orientation, and since the policy applied to "all comers," it passed constitutional muster. As a result, the CLS would not be a recognized student organization and not entitled to the benefits (limited funding, email access) that are available to such groups. While CLS has the First Amendment right to hold its views, it does not have a constitutional right to state funding and support of its position.

has been the cause of numerous conflicts between religious and secular authorities over the years. Even Jesus was presented with the "taxing" question at least on one occasion. In the United States, the issue of taxation has direct Establishment Clause implications. The arguments on both sides are easily understandable. Strict separationists argue that granting tax-exempt status to churches and other religious organizations violates the Establishment Clause by providing yet another benefit to religion. Furthermore, tax exemption also denies an important source of tax revenue to governments, inasmuch as much church-owned property is often located in valuable urban and suburban settings. Those who favor an accommodation of religion argue that religious groups, along with certain other entities, contribute to the betterment of the overall community and should not be subjected to the burdens of taxation.

In the case of *Walz v. Tax Commission of City of New York* (1970), the Supreme Court addressed the issue for the first time. The case originated when a New York taxpayer challenged the city's policy of granting tax exemptions on property used solely for purposes of religious worship. Chief Justice Burger's majority opinion stated that, under the First Amendment, the Court would tolerate neither state-established religion or governmental interference with religion. Short of these prohibited governmental acts, said Burger, "there is room for play in the joints productive of a *benevolent neutrality* which will permit religious exercise to exist without sponsorship [or] interference" [emphasis added]. He argued that the tax exemptions neither advanced nor inhibited religion, and were granted in the same manner that many other nonprofit properties, such as libraries, hospitals, and a host of community organizations, enjoyed. Finally, given the particular demands of the Establishment Clause, Burger emphasized that these tax exemptions had to be provided in a way that did not result in "an excessive government entanglement with religion." The Court's ruling in *Walz* upheld tax exemptions for religious organizations as long as the exemptions neither advanced nor inhibited religion, were granted in the same way as for other nonprofit groups, and did not result in "excessive" government and religious entanglement. Justice Douglas, in a solitary dissent, wondered how the Court could uphold a tax exemption while it most certainly would not allow government to subsidize religion directly:

A TAX EXEMPTION IS A SUBSIDY. IS MY BROTHER BRENNAN CORRECT IN SAYING THAT WE WOULD HOLD THAT STATE OR FEDERAL GRANTS TO CHURCHES, SAY, TO CONSTRUCT THE EDIFICE ITSELF WOULD BE UNCONSTITUTIONAL? WHAT IS THE DIFFERENCE BETWEEN THAT KIND OF SUBSIDY AND THE PRESENT SUBSIDY?

On March 24, 1983, the Supreme Court ruled 8–1 that racially discriminatory private schools are not eligible for federal tax-exempt status. In the case of *Bob Jones University v. United States* (1983), the majority said that the IRS's anti-discrimination policy was a proper interpretation of federal tax law, the agency had proper congressional authority to carry out its policy, and the policy did not violate any constitutional rights of the schools or their students. Not everyone was pleased with the decision. Reverend Bob Jones, president of the university, observed in a sermon to the student body in the school chapel that "[w]e're in a bad fix when eight evil old men and one vain and foolish woman can speak a verdict on American liberties."

The Court has handed down several other significant decisions concerning the religious taxation issue. In *Texas Monthly, Inc. v. Bullock* (1989), a 6–3 majority struck down a Texas law that exempted from the state sales tax periodicals that advance a religious faith. Since the exemption applied only to religious publications, the majority held that it placed a burden on nonreligious publications and amounted to a subsidy for religion. The division of the Court in *Texas Monthly* was interesting, particularly since the case involved both Establishment and Free Exercise Clauses. Writing for a plurality of three, Justice Brennan found the exemption in violation of the Establishment Clause and further stated that the Free Exercise Clause does not prevent a state from taxing the sale of publications, religious or otherwise. Justice White, concurring in the judgment, concluded that the exemption violated the Free Press Clause because the content of the publication determined its tax-exempt status. Justices Blackmun and O'Connor concurred in the plurality's Establishment Clause holding but reserved judgment on whether the Free Exercise Clause requires a tax exemption for the sale of religious materials by a religious organization.

A unanimous Court answered that question in *Jimmy Swaggart Ministries v. Board of Equalization of California* (1990). At issue in this case was the California sales tax law requiring a 6 percent sales tax on in-state sales of tangible personal property and a 6 percent use tax on property bought outside the state, with no exemption for religious organizations. Jimmy Swaggart Ministries had made substantial sales of both religious and nonreligious merchandise during crusades in California as well as through a large mail-order business. When the California Board of Equalization notified Swaggart Ministries that it owed total taxes, interest, and penalties of $166,145.10 on those sales, Swaggart Ministries paid the taxes on what it considered "nonreligious merchandise," but it claimed that taxes on specifically religious materials violate the Free Exercise and Establishment Clauses.

According to Justice O'Connor's opinion for a unanimous Court, the only taxes that violate the Free Exercise Clause are those that exert a "prior restraint on the exercise of religious liberty." In other words, a tax placed on religions as a precondition for their right to operate—for example, a license tax—would be unacceptable. However, the California tax, said O'Connor, was neutral, nondiscriminatory, and generally applicable to all activities, religious and secular, in the state. In summarizing her ruling, Justice O'Connor concluded that "the collection and payment of the generally applicable tax in this case imposes no constitutionally significant burden on appellant's religious practices or beliefs. The Free Exercise Clause accordingly does not *require* the State to grant appellant an exemption from its generally applicable sales and use tax" (original emphasis).

Religious Activities in Public Schools and Society

The Establishment of Religion Clause has been applied to a wide range of religious activities, including religious education classes, school prayer, legislative chaplains, and the teaching of "creationism." Because religious activities generally represent deeply held beliefs, the controversies have often become emotional and heated. The Supreme Court has found itself at the center of this storm, as Table 16.3 indicates. Although fewer in number than aid to religion cases, religious activities controversies are among the most difficult matters the Court has faced.

As soon as the Supreme Court applied the Establishment Clause to the states in *Everson*, an issue arose in Illinois involving possible violations of the First Amendment. *McCollum v. Board of Education* (1948) dealt with the validity of the Champaign, Illinois, "released time" program for religious instruction for public school students. In 1940, an interfaith group of religious leaders in Champaign petitioned the municipal school board to offer classes in religious instruction to public school students in grades four through nine. Privately employed religious teachers were invited into the public schools to offer weekly classes to children of parents who had signed a permission slip authorizing the inclusion of their children in the weekly exercises. Nonparticipating students studied various secular subjects elsewhere in the public schools. Some students not pursuing secular study were required to sit among the students receiving religious instruction.

Scarcely one year after applying the Establishment Clause to the states, the Court overturned the Champaign released-time program as a violation of the First Amendment. Justice Hugo Black rested most of the Court's decision on the fact that the Champaign program utilized the state's tax-supported facilities for disseminating religious teachings and the state's compulsory school attendance law to ensure a readily available audience.

Given the conservative climate of post-war United States and the American public's perception of a serious threat from international communism, *McCollum* was not a popular decision. Whether influenced by the heat of public opinion or the circumstances of the case, four years later, in *Zorach v. Clausen* (1952), the Supreme Court upheld a released-time program in New York City. The New York City program was held in church buildings, rather than the public schools, with no visible expenditure of public funds. Curiously, the *Zorach* decision found Justice Douglas, one of the most liberal justices on the Court, authoring the majority opinion for a 6–3 decision. In his opinion, Douglas listed several examples of how the Establishment Clause did not require a complete separation of church and state, such as tax exemptions, police and fire protection for churches, prayers in legislative assemblies, and courtroom oaths that include the reference "so help me God" (see Brief 16.9). In a quote often

Table 16.3 Development of the Law—Religious Activities

Year	Event	Significance
1948	McCollum v. Board of Education	Overturned in-school religious education program funded and staffed by the public school system.
1952	Zorach v. Clausen	Allowed program to release students to attend nearby religious education classes off school premises.
1962	Engel v. Vitale	Struck down state-written twenty-two-word nondenominational prayer as violative of purpose and effects tests.
1963	Abington School Dist v. Schempp; Murray v. Curlett	Struck down Pennsylvania and Maryland mandatory bible reading and Lord's Prayer requirements.
1968	Epperson v. Arkansas	Unanimous Court held Arkansas law banning teaching of evolution unconstitutional as promotion of religion.
1980	Stone v. Graham	Struck down a Kentucky law requiring posting of Ten Commandments in every public school classroom, even though paid for by private funds.
1981	Hall v. Bradshaw	Struck down North Carolina "motorist's prayer" on an official map.
1983	Marsh v. Chambers	Upheld Nebraska's state-employed chaplain who prayed before each legislative session as "part of the fabric of our society."
1984	Lynch v. Donnelly	City-owned nativity scene in a private park is a "passive" symbol and useful reminder of the holidays. No violation of Establishment Clause.
1985	Wallace v. Jaffree	Alabama's minute of silence in all public schools for "meditation or voluntary prayer" was clearly religious in purpose. Struck down.
1987	Edwards v. Aguillard	Louisiana may not require the teaching of "creationism" as balanced treatment with respect to "evolution."
1989	County of Allegheny v. American Civil Liberties Union	Held a creche in a courthouse to be in violation of Establish-ment Clause but a menorah located just outside was not.
1992	Lee v. Weisman	Nonsectarian benedictions and invocations at public school graduation ceremonies violate the Establishment Clause, even though students are not required to attend the ceremonies.
2000	Santa Fe Independent School District v. Doe	Held unconstitutional a Texas school district's policy authorizing high school student's delivery of a prayer before home varsity football games.
2004	Elk Grove Unified School District v. Newdow	Refused to rule on the constitutionality of the words "under God" in the Pledge of Allegiance because the plaintiff lacked standing to sue.
2005	Van Orden v. Perry	Held that a granite monument containing the Ten Command-ments on the grounds of the Texas State Capitol had historical meaning and did not violate the Establishment Clause.
2005	McCreary County v. American Civil Liberties Union	Held framed copies of the Ten Commandments on the walls of two Kentucky courthouses were part of a religious agenda by authorities and violated the Establishment Clause.
2009	Pleasant Grove City v. Summum	Placement of a monument in a public park is a form of government speech and is not subject to scrutiny under the Free Speech Clause of the First Amendment. The city may decide which monuments it chooses to accept.
2010	Salazar v. Buono	Upheld the congressional transfer of land to the VFW that allowed a five-foot white cross to continue being displayed in the Federal Mojave National Preserve. The cross now sits on private land.

Brief 16.9
ACCOMMODATING RELIGION IN PRISON: *CUTTER V. WILKINSON* (2005)

Section 3 of the Religious Land Use and Institutionalized Persons Act of 2000 (RLUIPA) provides in part: "No government shall impose a substantial burden on the religious exercise of a person residing in or confined to an institution," unless the burden furthers "a compelling governmental interest," and does so by "the least restrictive means." Current and former inmates of Ohio state institutions who were members of Satanist religions and other unconventional sects alleged that prison officials violated that law by failing to accommodate the prisoners' free exercise of religion in various ways. Prison officials responded by arguing that accommodating religious practices actually advances religion in violation of the First Amendment's Establishment Clause. They also argued that safety and security interests were "compelling interests" that outweighed prisoner rights.

In *Cutter v. Wilkinson* (2005), a unanimous U.S. Supreme Court upheld the constitutionality of RLUIPA and confirmed that state accommodation of religion does not automatically constitute a violation of the Establishment Clause. Justice Ginsburg's opinion for the Court emphasized that the Act did not force states to establish or promote religion, but rather simply to recognize the religious practices of institutionalized persons. She noted that the Act did not elevate accommodation of religious beliefs over an institution's need to maintain order and security, as courts would be particularly sensitive to security concerns within prisons. Finally, she stated, the Act did not confer a privileged status on any particular religious sect, differentiating this case from the decision in *Board of Education of Kiryas Joel Village School District v. Grumet* (see Brief 16.4).

The *Cutter* decision says that government accommodation of religious beliefs and practices is constitutionally permissible (but not absolutely required), even for persons who are confined in state institutions. Justice Ginsburg pointed out also that other state accommodations such as providing chaplains for "traditionally recognized" religions would be illegal if all accommodation of religion were banned. But what if authorities find themselves deluged by prisoner requests for accommodation? According to Justice Ginsburg:

> Should inmate requests for religious accommodations become excessive, impose unjustified burdens on other institutionalized persons, or jeopardize the effective functioning of an institution, the facility would be free to resist the imposition. In that event, adjudication in as-applied challenges would be in order.

Justice Clarence Thomas, in a concurring opinion, also noted that Ohio's acceptance of federal funds under RLUIPA for support of its prisons "undercuts Ohio's argument that congress is encroaching on its turf."

---

cited to counter criticisms that the Supreme Court was anti-religious and working to "banish God from the classroom," Justice Douglas stated:

> WE ARE A RELIGIOUS PEOPLE WHOSE INSTITUTIONS PRESUPPOSE A SUPREME BEING.... WHEN THE STATE ENCOURAGES RELIGIOUS INSTRUCTION OR COOPERATES WITH RELIGIOUS AUTHORITIES BY ADJUSTING THE SCHEDULE OF PUBLIC EVENTS TO SECTARIAN NEEDS, IT FOLLOWS THE BEST OF OUR TRADITIONS.

Justices Black and Jackson dissented in the *Zorach* case, Black because he found no meaningful differences between *McCollum* and *Zorach*, and Jackson because he thought that the wall being erected between church and state was "even more warped and twisted than I expected." The latter felt that *Zorach* would be more valuable to "students of psychology and the judicial processes than to students of constitutional law."

THE DELICATE ISSUE OF SCHOOL PRAYER

By the 1960s, the public debate over the role of religion in public schools became more heated, as the Court tackled one of its most controversial subjects: prayer in public schools. The furor began with the Court's decision in *Engel v. Vitale* in 1962, that state-sponsored prayer in public schools was a violation of the Establishment Clause. At issue in this landmark decision was a nondenominational prayer of twenty-two words that had been recommended by the New York Board of Regents in 1951, for recitation at the beginning of each school day in New York public schools. The prayer read: "*Almighty God, We acknowledge our dependence upon Thee, and we beg Thy blessings upon us, our parents, our teachers, and our country.*" Although not required by the state, in 1958 the New Hyde Park school district on Long Island decided to make the prayer mandatory and have it read or recited each day in the presence of a teacher. Those children whose parents did not want them to participate in the prayer exercise could be excused from the classroom.

A group of parents in the district, led by Steven Engel, brought suit in federal court, claiming that the prayer exercise violated the First and the Fourteenth Amendments of the Constitution. Writing for a six-member majority, Justice Hugo Black explained the meaning of the Establishment Clause:

> [T]HE CONSTITUTIONAL PROHIBITION AGAINST LAWS RESPECTING AN ESTABLISHMENT OF RELIGION MUST AT LEAST MEAN THAT IN THIS COUNTRY IT IS NO PART OF THE BUSINESS OF GOVERNMENT TO COMPOSE OFFICIAL PRAYERS FOR ANY GROUP OF THE AMERICAN PEOPLE TO RECITE AS PART OF A RELIGIOUS PROGRAM CARRIED ON BY GOVERNMENT....

According to Black, the prayer had definite religious content, and its nondenominational and voluntary nature did not save it from limitations imposed by the First Amendment. The only dissenting vote in Engel was that of Justice Stewart, who regretted the Court's denying the schoolchildren the opportunity to share "in the spiritual heritage of our Nation."

This particular decision was immediately condemned by citizens, church leaders and many members of Congress. Clearly, if oral prayer in public schools were unconstitutional, other religious activities would most likely be scrutinized soon. In two same-day decisions—*Abington School District v. Schempp* (1963) and *Murray v. Curlett* (1963)—an 8–1 Court invalidated a Pennsylvania law requiring ten verses from the bible each day and a Maryland law requiring a chapter from the bible or the Lord's Prayer.

Justice Clark's majority opinion articulated two of the three requirements that would several years later compose the *Lemon* test used to judge alleged Establishment Clause violations:

> THE TEST MAY BE STATED AS FOLLOWS: WHAT ARE THE *PURPOSE* AND THE *PRIMARY EFFECT* OF THE ENACTMENT? IF EITHER IS THE ADVANCEMENT OR INHIBITION OF RELIGION THEN THE ENACTMENT EXCEEDS THE SCOPE OF LEGISLATIVE POWER.... THAT IS TO SAY THAT TO WITHSTAND THE STRICTURES OF THE ESTABLISHMENT CLAUSE THERE MUST BE A SECULAR LEGISLATIVE PURPOSE AND A PRIMARY EFFECT THAT NEITHER ADVANCES NOR INHIBITS RELIGION.

When the activities prescribed by these state laws were compared to previous exercises in public schools, the violations were clear: Pennsylvania and Maryland were requiring religious exercises as part of the curricular activities of students compelled to attend public school; the activities were held in public facilities; and they were supervised by government employees. Again, the only dissenter in the cases was Justice Stewart, who felt that banishing these religious exercises from the public classroom placed religion at an "artificial and state-created disadvantage" and violated students' rights.

In the more than thirty years since these three decisions, a firestorm of public criticism has hit the Court for "expelling God from American classrooms." With the possible exception of the period following *Brown v. Board of Education* in 1954 and 1955, and the massive civil resistance accompanying those decisions, perhaps no other Supreme Court rulings of the twentieth century have met with as much noncompliance as have the *Engel*, *Schempp*, and *Murray* decisions. Public opinion polls have consistently shown that between 70 and 75 percent of the American people favor the return of "voluntary" prayer to the classroom. Deliberate violations of the rulings have persisted in some school districts, and have in fact been encouraged by public officials at all levels of government. Over 380 proposed constitutional amendments designed to reverse the Court's prayer and Bible reading decisions had been introduced in Congress prior to 1990, some of which nearly passed.[21]

Approximately one-half of the states have passed what are usually referred to as "moment-of-silence" laws, which allow public school students to set aside a brief period at the beginning of each school day for meditation or reflection. Alabama passed such a law in 1981, under which "a period of silence not to exceed one minute in duration shall be observed for *meditation or voluntary prayer*" [emphasis added]. Ishmael Jaffree, the father of three children enrolled in the Mobile public school system, sued in federal court, claiming that the prayers violated his First and Fourteenth Amendment rights.

In *Wallace v. Jaffree* (1985), Justice John Paul Stevens's opinion for a 6–3 Court held that the Alabama law was unconstitutional, having failed the purely "secular purpose" prong of *Lemon*. He pointed to the fact that the key sponsor of the bill in the Alabama legislature had indicated that the legislation was an "effort to return voluntary prayer" to the public classroom. Stevens added that since the law specifically allowed for "meditation or voluntary prayer," the state fully intended to characterize prayer as a favored practice. In separate concurring opinions, Justices Lewis Powell and Sandra Day O'Connor each noted that the Alabama law did not display a clear secular purpose because of its specific reference to "voluntary prayer." Justice O'Connor emphasized that the Establishment Clause does not prohibit the states from allowing schoolchildren to voluntarily pray silently during a moment of silence, but the Alabama law had crossed the line between an allowable period of silence and the state's endorsement of a religious practice. As O'Connor noted, "this line may be a fine one, but our precedents and the principles of religious liberty require that we draw it."

In separate dissenting opinions, Chief Justice Burger and Justices Rehnquist and White criticized the majority ruling. Emphasizing that both the U.S. Congress and the Supreme Court commence their daily proceedings with oral prayer, the Chief Justice regretted the "mistaken understanding of constitutional history" and Jefferson's "misleading metaphor" about a "wall of separation" between church and state. He insisted that the Establishment Clause does not require government "to be strictly neutral between religion and irreligion," nor does it prevent the states from pursuing secular ends through "nondiscriminatory sectarian means."

Religious Invocations and Benedictions

In 1992, the Supreme Court was asked to directly overrule the *Lemon* test and substitute a new and less restrictive "government coercion" test in the case of *Lee v. Weisman* (1992). The case involved religious invocations and benedictions at public school promotional and graduation ceremonies in the Providence, Rhode Island, school district. Generally, the middle school promotional exercises were held on school property, while the high school graduation ceremonies took place at rented facilities. Those students graduating were given the option of asking members of the clergy to offer an invocation and a benediction, and attendance at the exercises was voluntary. The practice was challenged by Deborah Weisman, a student in the system, and her father after a rabbi delivered an invocation at her middle school promotional exercises.

The Weismans alleged the practice to be in violation of the Establishment Clause by virtue of its efforts to advance religion. The school district countered with the argument that the clause was intended to prevent government from forcing religion on society, and it should not prevent the free expression of all religious beliefs. Since attendance at the ceremonies was voluntary, school authorities contended that no government coercion was involved and that no violation of the Establishment Clause had occurred.

In a surprisingly broad 5–4 decision, the Court struck down the practice of school-sponsored religious activities as violative of the Establishment Clause. Writing for the majority, Justice Anthony Kennedy stated that the Court's precedents dealing with prayer and religious exercises in schools virtually required that the Providence practice be struck down:

> THE LESSONS OF THE FIRST AMENDMENT ARE AS URGENT IN THE MODERN WORLD AS IN THE 18TH CENTURY WHEN IT WAS WRITTEN. ONE TIMELESS LESSON IS THAT IF CITIZENS ARE SUBJECTED TO STATE-SPONSORED RELIGIOUS EXERCISES, THE STATE DISAVOWS ITS OWN DUTY TO GUARD AND RESPECT THAT SPHERE OF INVIOLABLE CONSCIENCE AND BELIEF WHICH IS THE MARK OF A FREE PEOPLE.

In a dissenting opinion joined by Chief Justice Rehnquist and Justices White and Thomas, Justice Scalia struck an angry and, at times, somewhat sarcastic tone. Scalia accused the majority of engaging in a "psycho-journey" through the minds of students to determine whether they were being psychologically coerced to participate in religious exercises, but his primary focus was on what he saw as the majority's inattention to "a tradition that is as old as public-school graduation ceremonies themselves" (Brief 16.10).

Brief 16.10

PRAYER AND FOOTBALL GAMES: *SANTA FE INDEPENDENT SCHOOL DISTRICT V. DOE*

In *Santa Fe Independent School District v. Doe*, a 6–3 Supreme Court majority struck down a Texas school district's policy which authorized a high school student to deliver an "invocation and/or message" before home that games. The case originated when two sets of former students and their mothers brought suit alleging that the school district had allowed students to read overtly Christian prayers at graduation ceremonies and home football games in violation of the Establishment Clause. When a district court entered an interim order that a nondenominational prayer could be presented by students at graduation, the only remaining issue was the football games. The school district subsequently implemented a new policy that allowed students to vote in two elections: first, to determine whether invocations ought to be delivered at home football games and, second, to select to the student spokesperson. The new policy said that the student should promote good sportsmanship, solemnize the event, and establish the appropriate environment for competition, but it did not require that the content be nonsectarian and nonproselytizing.

Justice Stevens's majority opinion found that the student invocation violated the Establishment Clause for several reasons: (1) such invocations were not private student speech but rather public speech; (2) minority views were not protected by the system of elections; (3) the school policy actually endorsed religion; and (4) the practice of student elections did not remove the element of coercion from the practice. The opinion went on to say that even if every high school student's decision to attend a home football game were interpreted as voluntary, the delivery of a pregame prayer had the effect of coercing those present to participate in an act of religious worship. The dissenting justices (Rehnquist, Scalia, and Thomas) would have allowed the policy because the students were free to choose prayer, the speech resulting from the election would be "private," and the policy had plausible secular purposes apart from religion.

TALE OF TWO THEORIES: EVOLUTION VERSUS CREATIONISM

In the 1986 term, the Supreme Court tackled an issue that had been dormant for decades—the teaching of evolution in public schools. Nearly twenty years earlier, the Court had struck down as unconstitutional an Arkansas law patterned somewhat after the Tennessee law at issue in *Scopes v. State of Tennessee* in 1925 (see Brief 16.11). By 1968, Arkansas had made it a crime to teach that humans were descended from a lower order of animals or to use any textbook that taught that theory. A unanimous Supreme Court, in *Epperson v. Arkansas* (1968) said that the Arkansas law violated the Establishment Clause by embodying a specific religious belief and prohibiting all others. The state's power to determine the public school curriculum did not include the right to ban the teaching of established scientific theory simply because it conflicted with Biblical teachings or a particular religious doctrine.

After the *Epperson* decision, opponents resorted to another strategy to inject their views into the public classroom. One tactic was to ask for "equal time" — if evolutionary theory (and they emphasized the *theory*) were taught, so must what they termed "creation science." This theory argues that Genesis accurately details the origins of mankind as occurring with a single spontaneous event between 6,000 and 10,000 years ago, and it deserves to be covered in the classroom along with evolution. One of several states that passed laws after *Epperson* to allow for the teaching of "creation science" in public schools was Arkansas. In 1982, a federal district court in Little Rock struck down that state law as a violation of the Establishment Clause.

In an effort to prevent a succession of challenges to state laws and the possibility of courts handing down conflicting decisions, the Supreme Court accepted for review a Louisiana case, *Edwards v. Aguillard* (1987), involving a state law that two lower federal courts had said conflicted with the Establishment Clause because it sponsored a religious belief. At issue in the case was the Louisiana Balanced Treatment for Creation-Science and Evolution-Science in Public School Instruction Act, the so-called Creationism Act, passed in 1981, but never put into effect because of a succession of court challenges. The law did not require the teaching of creationism, but instead mandated that if either evolution or creationism was taught in the public schools, *both* had to be taught. The case became the *cause celebre* for a large assortment of parents, civil libertarians, scientists, religious leaders, and school teachers and administrators on both sides of the evolution–creationism debate.

Brief 16.11
THE SCOPES "MONKEY TRIAL": IN THE IMAGE OF MAN OR MONKEY?

The battle among different religious and scientific groups over the teaching of the evolution of living species began with the first printing of Charles Darwin's *The Origin of Species* in 1859, but it was not until the 1920s that the matter received much publicity in the United States. During the 1920s, John T. Scopes, a biology teacher in Tennessee, was indicted for violating a state law that forbade teaching in public schools of the state "any theory which denies the story of the divine creation of man as taught in the Bible" which holds instead that "man is descended from a lower order of animals." The state of Tennessee retained three-time Democratic presidential nominee and famous orator William Jennings Bryan, to prosecute Scopes and to proclaim his own personal and the state's belief in the literal truth of the Book of Genesis. Defending John Scopes was the equally celebrated lawyer Clarence Darrow, who argued valiantly that the then-cumulative body of evidence established that man was, indeed, descended from a long line of primates.

Despite the efforts of Darrow and national publicity that portrayed Tennessee as an intellectual backwater, Scopes was convicted of violating the state law and fined $100. A subsequent state appellate court reversed that conviction because of a technical procedural error in sentencing, and as a result, the case was never appealed to the U.S. Supreme Court. The primary effect of the trial was the widespread ridicule of religious opponents of evolutionary theory, and the ultimate vindication of Scopes, scientific theory, and academic freedom.

In June 1987, the Supreme Court, with only two justices dissenting, declared the law to be a violation of the Establishment Clause. After reviewing the well-worn path of *Lemon v. Kurtzman*, Justice Brennan wrote for the majority that parents with children in the public schools expect both a quality education and the "understanding that the classroom will not purposely be used to advance religious views that may conflict with the private beliefs of the student and his or her family." He concluded that law limited academic freedom because it had "the distinctly different purpose of discrediting 'evolution by counterbalancing its teaching at every turn with the teaching of creation science.'" To Brennan, "[t]he preeminent purpose of the Louisiana Legislature was clearly to advance the religious viewpoint that a supernatural being created humankind."

The *Edwards v. Aguillard* decision drew comments from both supporters and opponents. The high school principal in Lafayette, Louisiana, who originally brought the suit challenging the law said that he was pleased with the Court's decision. Said Donald Aguillard, "[w]e just don't have the money now to spend on bad science." The executive director of the Louisiana Interchurch Conference, Reverend James L. Stovall, who argued against the law, said that he was glad that the state would not have another Scopes trial. But the original sponsor of the legislation, former state senator Bill Keith, showed dismay at the decision. Said Keith, "evolution is no more than a fairy tale about a frog that turns into a prince, but this is what we are teaching our schoolchildren today."[22]

The years since *Edwards* have produced changes in the tactics of anti-evolution groups, primarily by emphasizing the theory of **intelligent design** (ID). Intelligent design posits that the complexity and sophistication of the universe simply could not have evolved without the guidance or direction of an outside, intelligent force. According to a 2005 survey, 60 percent of Americans believe that humans were created or evolved under the direction of a Supreme Being, while only 26 percent believe Darwin was correct. Moreover, nearly 64 percent support teaching creationism or intelligent design along with evolution in the classroom.[23] While most scientists do not accept these challenges to evolution, a smaller group of researchers are working to legitimize ID as science.

Some states have attempted to move ID into the classroom by insisting on "disclaimers" when evolution is taught. In 2005, a federal district court held in *Selman v. Cobb County School District* that the following disclaimer, attached to textbooks, promoted religion:

> THIS TEXTBOOK CONTAINS MATERIAL ON EVOLUTION. EVOLUTION IS A THEORY, NOT A FACT, REGARDING THE ORIGIN OF LIVING THINGS. THIS MATERIAL SHOULD BE APPROACHED WITH AN OPEN MIND, STUDIED CAREFULLY AND CRITICALLY CONSIDERED.

Intelligent design finally found itself in federal court in the case of *Kitzmiller v. Dover Area School District* (2005). The Dover, Pennsylvania, school board enacted a policy requiring brief instruction on ID in the high school science curriculum. Eleven parents filed suit, claiming the policy violated the Establishment Clause. In his ruling, Judge John Jones, a George W. Bush appointee, held that intelligent design is not science and cannot be separated from its reliance on creationism. As such, it is a religiously based theory and must be prohibited in public school classrooms. A possible appeal of the decision became most unlikely when all eight Dover school board members who had voted for the requirement were defeated in the November 2005 election. The new school board indicated that it would not seek an appeal.

PUBLIC RELIGIOUS DISPLAYS

For four decades, the city of Pawtucket, Rhode Island, had cooperated with downtown merchants in erecting a nativity scene as part of its Christmas holiday season observance. The display included both secular and religious figures, including Santa's sleigh and reindeer, a Christmas tree, carolers, and a creche consisting of the traditional nativity figures of the Christ child, Mary, and Joseph. All the components of the display were owned by the city of Pawtucket and erected at public expense in a privately-owned park. A group in the city challenged the constitutionality of the display, and both the federal district and appellate courts said that it violated the Establishment Clause.

The case was appealed to the Supreme Court, and, in *Lynch v. Donnelly* (1984), the Court upheld the nativity display. In a 5–4 judgment, Chief Justice Burger began by stating that Establishment Clause cases involved an "inescapable tension" between church and state, and a realization that "total separation of the two is not possible . . . ." In Burger's mind, the Constitution "affirmatively mandates *accommodation*, not merely tolerance, of all religions, and forbids hostility toward any." He characterized the display as a "passive" symbol only remotely benefiting any religion, and insisted that it served as a useful reminder of a national holiday's early roots:

> [IT] ENGENDERS A FRIENDLY COMMUNITY SPIRIT OF GOOD WILL IN KEEPING WITH THE SEASON. . . . THAT THE DISPLAY BRINGS PEOPLE INTO THE CENTRAL CITY, AND SERVES COMMERCIAL INTERESTS AND BENEFITS MERCHANTS AND THEIR EMPLOYEES, DOES NOT, . . . DETERMINE THE CHARACTER OF THE DISPLAY.

In a dissenting opinion, Justice William Brennan faulted the majority for its distorted application of the *Lemon* test. Also, Brennan was troubled by the majority's attempt to "explain away the clear religious import" of the nativity scene:

> TO SUGGEST, AS THE COURT DOES, THAT [THE CRECHE] IS MERELY "TRADITIONAL" AND THEREFORE NO DIFFERENT FROM SANTA'S HOUSE OR REINDEER IS NOT ONLY OFFENSIVE TO THOSE FOR WHOM THE CRECHE HAS PROFOUND SIGNIFICANCE, BUT INSULTING TO THOSE WHO INSIST FOR RELIGIOUS OR PERSONAL REASONS THAT THE STORY OF CHRIST IS IN NO SENSE A PART OF "HISTORY" NOR AN UNAVOIDABLE ELEMENT OF OUR NATIONAL "HERITAGE."

A short accompanying dissent by Justice Harry Blackmun echoed Brennan's sentiments, saying that the majority "does an injustice to the creche and the message it manifests."

Five years after the *Lynch v. Donnelly* ruling, the Court had an opportunity to rule again on the subject of Christmas displays located on public property. In *County of Allegheny v. American Civil Liberties Union* (1989), the Supreme Court came to a conclusion that differed from the earlier Pawtucket case. The 1989 case involved two holiday displays located on public property in downtown Pittsburgh. The first was a creche depicting the nativity scene located on the grand staircase of the Allegheny County Courthouse. The creche was donated by the Holy Name Society, a Roman Catholic group, and a sign identified it as such. The manger had a crest with an angel holding a banner that proclaimed, "Gloria in Excelsis Deo," or "Glory to God in the Highest." The second of the displays was an eighteen-foot Chanukah menorah or candelabrum, which was located just outside the City-County Building next to the city's forty-five-foot decorated Christmas tree. A sign at the foot of the tree gave the Mayor's name and a text that declared the city's "salute to liberty." The menorah was owned by Chabad, a Jewish group, but the city was responsible for storing, erecting, and removing it each year.

An obviously divided Court held the creche to be in violation of the Establishment Clause but upheld the use of the menorah. Chief Justice Rehnquist, along with Justices Kennedy, Scalia, and White, believed that both displays should be upheld, arguing that the symbols posed no serious risk leading to an establishment of religion. Justices Brennan, Marshall, and Stevens thought that both displays, which constituted clear religious symbols, violated the Establishment Clause. It was left to Justices Blackmun and O'Connor to tip the balance. In his opinion announcing the judgment of the Court, Justice Blackmun drew attention to the banner over the manger which announced a purely Christian message. Since this message was located on public property, it amounted to governmental preference and endorsement of religion. Accordingly, the creche failed the "primary effect" test by advancing religion. As for the menorah, Justice Blackmun emphasized that the "particular physical setting," along with the Christmas tree and the sign saluting liberty did not amount to an endorsement of either Christianity or Judaism. Rather, he stated, the symbols illustrated the different ways in which the holiday season can be celebrated. The mayor's sign underscored the display's emphasis on liberty and cultural diversity.

Justice O'Connor's separately written opinion argued that not all use of religious objects by government amounts to an endorsement, depending on the context and purpose of the display (see Brief 16.12). In this case, Justice O'Connor saw the creche as a religious object used in a way to send a religious message, while the menorah was placed in a display that conveyed a secular theme.

The controversy concerning religious displays was renewed in two recent cases. A unanimous court held in *Pleasant Grove City, Utah, et al. v. Summum* (2009),

---

Brief 16.12

THE TEN COMMANDMENTS: RELIGIOUS, HISTORICAL, OR BOTH?

The first time that the United States Supreme Court confronted the issue of the Ten Commandments, it held in *Stone v. Graham* (1980) that Kentucky could not post copies in each public school classroom in the state. To do so was to endorse or promote religion, even though the actual posters had been paid for by private contributions. That ruling emphasized the religious nature of the Ten Commandments. Two decisions handed down on the last day of the Court's 2004–05 term, however, raised new questions about whether the Ten Commandments might be permissible on government property under certain circumstances. The fact that the Court ruled differently in the two cases gave some hope to both sides but did not provide the guidance that many legal observers had hoped for.

The grounds of the twenty-two-acre Texas Capitol in Austin contain seventeen monuments and twenty-one historical markers. One of those is a granite monument containing the Ten Commandments. The monument was one of many erected in public places around the country in the 1950s and 1960s by the Fraternal Order of Eagles, a national civic organization, that believed exposure to the Ten Commandments would help reduce juvenile delinquency. The monument was challenged as a violation of the Establishment Clause by Thomas Van Orden, a homeless law school graduate, who walked past the monument regularly. Both the district court in Austin and the Fifth Circuit Court of Appeals in New Orleans found that the monument had a valid secular purpose and did not violate the Establishment Clause.

In the other case, the Pulaski and McCreary county courthouses in Kentucky had initially placed framed copies of the Ten Commandments on display. Faced with litigation, both courthouses added other "historical" documents, allegedly in hopes of convincing critics that the Ten Commandments was simply part of a broader historical display. The Sixth Circuit Court of Appeals in Cincinnati had ruled that the display of the Ten Commandments did not have a valid secular purpose and was unconstitutional.

In two 5–4 decisions, the Supreme Court upheld the constitutionality of the Texas monument in *Van Orden v. Perry* (2005) but struck down the Kentucky displays in *McCreary County v. American Civil Liberties Union* (2005). Only Justice Stephen Breyer agreed with both decisions. The other justices were divided into two camps, those that found nothing wrong with either display (Rehnquist, Scalia, Thomas, Kennedy), and those that found both to be unconstitutional (Stevens, O'Connor, Souter, Ginsburg). The distinction in the two cases came down to the circumstances, context (one was inside a building, the other outside), and the judgment of the justices. Justice Breyer called the Texas case "borderline," but he also emphasized factors such as the monument's physical setting (which he said suggested "little or nothing of the sacred"), the fact that forty years had passed since the monument's erection without dispute, and the very negative impact that would follow if all depictions of the Ten Commandments had to be removed from their settings nationally.

In his majority opinion in *McCreary*, Justice Souter called the claim by the Kentucky counties that the Ten Commandments had a secular purpose "an apparent sham." He emphasized the fact that the courthouse displays had begun with only the Ten Commandments. Other items were added after legal challenges were mounted. In what turned out to be her final opinion, Justice Sandra Day O'Connor concurred by stating:

Voluntary religious belief and expression may be as threatened when government takes the mantle of religion upon itself as when government directly interferes with private religious practices. When the government associates one set of religious beliefs with the state and identifies nonadherents as outsiders, it encroaches upon the individual's decision about whether and how to worship.

Chief Justice Rehnquist dismissed the argument that the Ten Commandments represented only codes of secular law, but he also saw them as something more than religious. "Of course," he stated, "the Ten Commandments are religious," but he noted that they also have "an undeniable historical meaning." He then summed up the effect of the two cases: "Simply having religious content or promoting a message consistent with a religious doctrine does not run afoul of the Establishment Clause." For now, displays of the Ten Commandments similar to those at the Texas Capitol are permissible, but those in courthouses likely are not.

Other challenges of a similar nature are also pending: May the national motto established by Congress in 1956—"In God We Trust"—be displayed on or in public buildings? Can states distribute "In God We Trust" posters in school classrooms and other public places? Apparently the Supreme Court will be called upon in the near future to address these and other related issues.

---

that the placement of a permanent monument in a public park is a form of government speech that is not subject to the Free Speech Clause. The case originated when Summum, a religious group, requested that the city place a monument to the "Seven Aphorisms of Summum" inside the park, pointing out that the park already contained a Ten Commandments monument. When city officials rejected Summum's request, the religious group filed suit, claiming a violation of their First Amendment rights. Justice Alito's opinion for the Court indicated that governments have long used monuments to speak to the public and, as such, clearly represent government speech. The city's "final approval authority" over all monuments in the parks satisfied the Court that it was indeed a matter of government speech.

The following term, a 5–4 majority divided over several issues, including some technical concerns about standing to sue and injunctive relief. However, the primary thrust of the opinion focused on the question of whether Congress had acted properly in enacting a land-transfer law that allowed a small parcel of land located inside the Mojave National Preserve to be exchanged with the Veterans of Foreign Wars (VFW) for other lands nearby. The land in question, since 1934, had been the site of a five-foot Latin cross erected to honor soldiers who died in World War I. In *Salazar, Secretary of the Interior v. Buono* (2010), the Court held that the transfer of land from the government to the VFW effectively ended any concern about government-sponsored religious activity.

Conclusion

The Establishment and Free Exercise Clauses reflect the concern that existed in late eighteenth-century America about preserving liberty of conscience in the young republic. A history of religious persecution in England and colonial America, as well as the specter of established religions in most of the American states, convinced Founders such as Madison that they had to devise certain "auxiliary precautions" to protect religious freedom in the United States from the power and influence of the state. If religious liberty were to flourish, guarantees protecting the people from an encroaching state were essential. That is why the two religion clauses were inserted into the First Amendment in the late 1780s.

It took a century and a half to apply the two clauses to the American states, but since that process began in the 1940s, the Supreme Court has been besieged with numerous cases dealing with church–state issues. The Free Exercise Clause has generally been interpreted as affording absolute protection for religious *beliefs* and qualified protection for religious *actions* based on those beliefs. Beginning in the 1960s, with a more liberal Warren Court, and later affirmed by the Burger Court in the 1970s, the justices granted some individuals and groups exemptions from universal laws, mainly on the grounds of religious conscience and tradition. As the United States has become a more religiously diverse nation in the past half-century, the Supreme Court has been at the center of having to define "religion" and what actions justified on religious principle qualify for protection.

Since applying the Establishment Clause to the states in 1947, the Supreme Court has contended with two main areas of debate: what constitutes acceptable *aid* to parochial schools and what religious *activities* are prohibited by the Clause. Although decisions by the Court in the activities area have probably generated the most public hostility and noncompliance, the Court has had the greatest difficulty constructing a consistent legal and judicial philosophy for the "aid-to-schools" controversy. The Supreme Court has gradually retreated from a "strict separationist" stance that emerged in *Everson* in 1947, and has continued to allow some governmental assistance to parochial schools. Its justification for doing so has usually been based on what selected justices interpret "establishment" in the First Amendment to mean, and whether the state aid in question violates the shifting consensus on the meaning of that term.

How the Supreme Court has interpreted and applied the religion clauses raises the question of where the particular decisions reside on the "individualist–communitarian" continuum. One might argue that being able to have "voluntary" prayer or a daily bible reading in public school is in the best tradition of individuals practicing religious freedom, or that vouchers, a nativity display at Christmas, or religious clubs meeting in public facilities reflect harmless accommodations of popular religious preferences. All of these examples might be justified as legitimate exercises of religious faith of various persons or concessions to spiritual traditions in the United States, and thus they lie within the "individualist" tradition.

But one could also argue that all these examples contain the potential for divisiveness and discord in society and, as such, they are counterproductive to building a sense of community. They also have the serious potential for enabling government at various levels to tell people how they can pray, what they should read for spiritual enlightenment, and what body of religious beliefs and traditions are better than all others. Eventually, as a people strive to act on their religious beliefs, they discover that the state has expropriated their freedom to believe or not believe. That is why the framers were so vigilant about protecting religious freedom. They knew that unless there were specific limits upon what the State could do vis-à-vis the freedom of conscience, that freedom would be jeopardized. Religious freedom was best insured by keeping government largely out of the realm of religion. The real strength of an enduring democratic system lies in nurturing diversity and open debate, not in coercion and conformity. Nowhere is that more important than in protecting religious freedom for all Americans.

As the justices have noted in numerous opinions over several decades, there is inevitable tension between the Establishment and the Free Exercise Clauses. One compels government, at a minimum, to neither favor nor disfavor religion, and the other insists that government allow individuals to act on the basis of their religious beliefs with a minimum of governmental constraints. Many argue that to protect the latter violates the former, and others insist that the justices have too narrowly interpreted and applied one or the other of the two religion clauses. The criticisms of the Court›s actions will most likely continue to reflect the disagreements that have existed ever since the Bill of Rights was drafted in 1789.

Appendix

The Constitution of the United States of America

We the People of the United States, in Order to form a more perfect Union, establish Justice, insure domestic Tranquility, provide for the common defence, promote the general Welfare, and secure the Blessings of Liberty to ourselves and our posterity, do ordain and establish this Constitution for the United States of America.

Article I.

Section 1. All legislative Powers herein shall be vested in a Congress of the United States, which shall consist of a Senate and House of Representatives.

Section 2. The House of Representatives shall be composed of Members chosen every second Year by the People of the several States, and the Electors in each State shall have the Qualifications requisite for Electors of the most numerous Branch of the State Legislature.

No Person shall be a Representative who shall not have attained to the Age of twenty-five Years, and been seven Years a Citizen of the United States, and who shall not, when elected, be an Inhabitant of that State in which he shall be chosen.

Representatives and direct [Taxes][2] shall be apportioned among the several States which may be included within this Union, according to their respective Numbers [which shall be determined by adding to the whole Number of free Persons, including those bound to Service for a Term of Years, and excluding Indians not taxed, three-fifths of all other Persons].[3] The actual Enumeration shall be made within three Years after the first Meeting of the Congress of the United States, and within every subsequent Term of ten Years, in such Manner as they shall by Law direct. The Number of Representatives shall not exceed one for every thirty Thousand, but each State shall have at Least one Representative; and until such enumeration shall be made, the State of New Hampshire shall be entitled to chuse three, Massachusetts eight, Rhode Island and Providence Plantations one, Connecticut five, New York six, New Jersey four, Pennsylvania eight, Delaware one, Maryland six, Virginia ten, North Carolina five, South Carolina five, and Georgia three.

When vacancies happen in the Representation from any State, the Executive Authority thereof shall issue Writs of Election to fill such Vacancies.

The House of Representatives shall chuse their Speaker and other Officers; and shall have the sole Power of Impeachment.

Section 3. The Senate of the United States shall be composed of two Senators from each State [chosen by the Legislature thereof][4] for six Years; and each Senator shall have one Vote.

---

[1]The spelling, capitalization, and punctuation of the original have been retained here. Brackets indicate passages that have been altered by amendments to the Constitution.
[2]Modified by the Sixteenth Amendment.
[3]Modified by the Fourteenth Amendment.
[4]Repealed by the Seventeenth Amendment.

Immediately after they shall be assembled in Consequence of the first Election, they shall be divided as equally as may be into three Classes. The Seats of the Senators of the first Class shall be vacated at the Expiration of the second Year, of the second Class at the Expiration of the fourth Year, and of the third Class at the Expiration of the sixth Year, so that one third may be chosen every second Year [and if Vacancies happen by Resignation, or otherwise, during the Recess of the Legislature of any State, the Executive thereof may make temporary Appointments until the next Meeting of the Legislature, which shall then fill such Vacancies].[5]

No Person shall be a Senator who shall not have attained to the Age of thirty Years, and been nine Years a Citizen of the United States, and who shall not, when elected, be an Inhabitant of that state for which he shall be chosen.

The Vice President of the United States shall be President of the Senate, but shall have no Vote, unless they be equally divided.

The Senate shall chuse their other Officers, and also a President pro tempore, in the Absence of the Vice President, or when he shall exercise the Office of President of the United States.

The Senate shall have the sole Power to try all Impeachments. When sitting for that Purpose, they shall be on Oath or Affirmation. When the President of the United States is tried, the Chief Justice shall preside: And no Person shall be convicted without the Concurrence of two thirds of the Members present.

Judgment in Cases of Impeachment shall not extend further than to removal from Office, and disqualification to hold and enjoy any Office of honor, Trust, or Profit under the United States: but the Party convicted shall nevertheless be liable and subject to Indictment, Trial, Judgment, and Punishment, according to Law.

SECTION 4. The Times, Places and Manner of holding Elections for Senators and Representatives, shall be prescribed in each State by the Legislature thereof; but the Congress may at any time by Law make or alter such Regulations, except as to the Places of chusing Senators.

[The Congress shall assemble at least once in every Year, and such Meeting shall be on the first Monday in December, unless they shall by Law appoint a different Day.][6]

SECTION 5. Each House shall be the Judge of the Elections, Returns, and Qualifications of its own Members, and a Majority of each shall constitute a Quorum to do Business; but a smaller Number may adjourn from day to day, and may be authorized to compel the Attendance of absent Members, in such Manner, and under such Penalties as each House may provide.

Each House may determine the Rules of its Proceedings, punish its Members for disorderly Behaviour, and, with the Concurrence of two thirds, expel a Member.

Each House shall keep a journal of its Proceedings, and from time to time publish the same, excepting such Parts as may in their Judgment require Secrecy; and the Yeas and Nays of the Members of either House on any question shall, at the Desire of one fifth of those Present, be entered on the journal.

Neither House, during the Session of Congress, shall, without the Consent of the other, adjourn for more than three days, nor to any other Place than that in which the two Houses shall be sitting.

SECTION 6. The Senators and Representatives shall receive a Compensation for their Services, to be ascertained by Law, and paid out of the Treasury of the United States. They shall in all Cases, except Treason, Felony and Breach of the Peace, be privileged from Arrest during their Attendance at the Session of their respective Houses, and in going to and returning from the same; and for any Speech or Debate in either House, they shall not be questioned in any other Place.

No Senator or Representative shall, during the Time for which he was elected, be appointed to any civil Office under the Authority of the United States, which shall have been created, or the Emoluments whereof shall have been encreased during such time; and no Person holding any Office under the United States, shall be a Member of either House during his Continuance in Office.

---

[5]Modified by the Seventeenth Amendment.

[6]Changed by the Twentieth Amendment.

Section 7. All Bills for raising Revenue shall originate in the House of Representatives; but the Senate may propose or concur with Amendments as on other Bills.

Every Bill which shall have passed the House of Representatives and the Senate, shall, before it become a Law, be presented to the President of the United States; If he approve he shall sign it, but if not he shall return it, with his Objections to the House in which it shall have originated, who shall enter the Objections at large on their Journal, and proceed to reconsider it. If after such Reconsideration two thirds of that House shall agree to pass the Bill, it shall be sent together with the Objections, to the other House, by which it shall likewise be reconsidered, and if approved by two thirds of that House, it shall become a Law. But in all such Cases the Votes of both Houses shall be determined by Yeas and Nays, and the Names of the Persons voting for and against the Bill shall be entered on the Journal of each House respectively. If any Bill shall not be returned by the President within ten Days (Sundays excepted) after it shall have been presented to him, the Same shall be a Law, in like Manner as if he had signed it, unless the Congress by their Adjournment prevent its Return in which Case it shall not be a Law.

Every Order, Resolution, or Vote to which the Concurrence of the Senate and House of Representatives may be necessary (except on a question of Adjournment) shall be presented to the President of the United States; and before the Same shall take Effect, shall be approved by him, or being disapproved by him, shall be repassed by two thirds of the Senate and House of Representatives, according to the Rules and Limitations prescribed in the Case of a Bill.

Section 8. The Congress shall have Power To lay and collect Taxes, Duties, Imposts and Excises, to pay the Debts and provide for the common Defence and general Welfare of the United States; but all Duties, Imposts and Excises shall be uniform throughout the United States;

To borrow Money on the credit of the United States;

To regulate Commerce with foreign Nations, and among the several States, and with the Indian Tribes;

To establish a uniform Rule of Naturalization, and uniform Laws on the subject of Bankruptcies throughout the United States;

To coin Money, regulate the Value thereof, and of foreign Coin, and fix the Standard of Weights and Measures;

To provide for the Punishment of counterfeiting the Securities and current Coin of the United States;

To establish Post Offices and post Roads;

To promote the Progress of Science and useful Arts, by securing for limited Times to Authors and Inventors the exclusive Right to their respective Writings and Discoveries;

To constitute Tribunals inferior to the supreme Court;

To define and punish Piracies and Felonies committed on the high Seas, and Offences against the Law of Nations;

To declare War, grant Letters of Marque and Reprisal, and make Rules concerning Captures on Land and Water;

To raise and support Armies, but no Appropriation of Money to that Use shall be for a longer Term than two Years;

To provide and maintain a Navy;

To make Rules for the Government and Regulation of the land and naval Forces;

To provide for calling forth the Militia to execute the Laws of the Union, Suppress Insurrections and repel Invasions;

To provide for organizing, arming, and disciplining the Militia, and for governing such Part of them as may be employed in the Service of the United States, reserving to the States respectively, the Appointment of the Officers, and the Authority of training the Militia according to the discipline prescribed by Congress;

To exercise exclusive Legislation in all Cases whatsoever, over such District (not exceeding ten Miles square) as may, by Cession of particular States, and the Acceptance of Congress, become the Seat of the Government of the United States, and to exercise like Authority over all Places purchased by the Consent of the Legislature of the State in which the Same shall be, (or the Erection of Forts, Magazines, Arsenals, dock-Yards, and other needful Buildings;—And

To make all Laws which shall be necessary and proper for carrying into Execution the foregoing Powers, and all other Powers vested by this Constitution in the Government of the United States, or in any Department or Officer thereof.

Section 9. The Migration or Importation of such Persons as any of the States now existing shall think proper to admit, shall not be prohibited by the Congress prior to the Year one thousand eight hundred and eight, but a Tax or duty may be imposed on such Importation, not exceeding ten dollars for each Person.

The privilege of the Writ of Habeas Corpus shall not be suspended, unless when in Cases of Rebellion or Invasion the public Safety may require it.

No Bill of Attainder or ex post facto Law shall be passed.

[No Capitation, or other direct, Tax shall be laid, unless in Proportion to the Census or Enumeration herein before directed to be taken.][7]

No Tax or Duty shall be laid on Articles exported from any State.

No Preference shall be given by any Regulation of Commerce or Revenue to the Ports of one State over those of another: nor shall Vessels bound to, or from, one State, be obliged to enter, clear, or pay Duties in another.

No Money shall be drawn from the Treasury, but in Consequence of Appropriations made by Law; and a regular Statement and Account of the Receipts and Expenditures of all public Money shall be published from time to time.

No Title of Nobility shall be granted by the United States: And no Person holding any Office of Profit or Trust under them, shall, without the Consent of the Congress, accept of any present, Emolument, Office, or Title, of any kind whatever, from any King, Prince, or foreign State.

Section 10. No State shall enter into any Treaty, Alliance, or Confederation; grant Letters of Marque and Reprisal; coin Money; emit Bills of Credit; make any Thing but gold and silver Coin a Tender in Payment of Debts; pass any Bill of Attainder, ex post facto Law, or Law impairing the Obligation of Contracts, or grant any Title of Nobility.

No State shall, without the Consent of the Congress, lay any Imposts or Duties on Imports or Exports, except what may be absolutely necessary for executing its inspection Laws; and the net Produce of all Duties and Imposts, laid by any State on Imports or Exports, shall be for the Use of the Treasury of the United States; and all such Laws shall be subject to the Revision and Controul of the Congress.

No State shall, without the Consent of Congress, lay any Duty of Tonnage, keep Troops, or Ships of War in time of Peace, enter into any Agreement or Compact with another State, or with a foreign Power or engage in War, unless actually invaded, or in such imminent Danger as will not admit of delay.

ARTICLE II.

Section 1. The executive Power shall be vested in a President of the United States of America. He shall hold his Office during the Term of four Years, and, together with the Vice President, chosen for the same Term, be elected, as follows.

Each State shall appoint, in such Manner as the Legislature thereof may direct, a Number of Electors, equal to the whole Number of Senators and Representatives to which the State may be entitled in the Congress; but no Senator or Representative, or Person holding an Office of Trust or Profit under the United States, shall be appointed an Elector.

[The Electors shall meet in their respective States, and vote by Ballot for two Persons, of whom one at least shall not be an Inhabitant of the same State with themselves. And they shall make a List of all the Persons voted for, and of the Number of Votes for each; which List they shall sign and certify, and transmit sealed to the Seat of the Government of the United States, directed to the President of the Senate. The President of the Senate shall, in the Presence of the Senate and House of Representatives, open all the Certificates, and the Votes shall then be counted. The Person having the greatest Number of Votes shall be the President, if such Number be a Majority of the whole Number of Electors appointed; and if there be more than one who have such Majority, and have an equal Number of Votes, then the House of Representatives shall immediately chuse by Ballot one of them for President; and if no Person have a Majority, then from the five highest on the List the said House shall in like Manner chuse the President. But in chusing the President, the Votes shall be taken by States, the Representation from each State having one Vote; A quorum for this Purpose shall consist of a Member or Members from two thirds of the States, and a Majority of all the States shall be necessary to a Choice. In every Case,

---

[7]Modified by the Sixteenth Amendment.

after the Choice of the President, the Person having the greater Number of Votes of the Electors shall be the Vice President. But if there should remain two or more who have equal Votes, the Senate shall chuse from them by Ballot the Vice President.]8

The Congress may determine the Time of chusing the Electors, and the Day on which they shall give their Votes; which Day shall be the same throughout the United States.

No person except a natural born Citizen, or a Citizen of the United States, at the time of the Adoption of this Constitution, shall be eligible to the Office of President; neither shall any Person be eligible to that Office who shall not have attained to the Age of thirty five Years, and been fourteen Years a Resident within the United States.

[In Case of the Removal of the President from Office, or of his Death, Resignation or Inability to discharge the Powers and Duties of the said Office, the same shall devolve on the Vice President, and the Congress may by Law provide for the Case of Removal, Death, Resignation or Inability, both of the President and Vice President, declaring what Officer shall then act as President, and such Officer shall act accordingly, until the Disability be removed, or a President shall be elected.]9

The President shall, at stated Times, receive for his Services, a Compensation, which shall neither be encreased nor diminished during the Period for which he shall have been elected, and he shall not receive within that Period any other Emolument from the United States, or any of them.

Before he enter on the Execution of his Office, he shall take the following Oath or Affirmation: "I do solemnly swear (or affirm) that I will faithfully execute the Office of President of the United States, and will to the best of my Ability, preserve, protect and defend the Constitution of the United States."

Section 2. The President shall be Commander in Chief of the Army and Navy of the United States, and of the Militia of the several States, when called into the actual Service of the United States; he may require the Opinion, in writing, of the principal Officer in each of the executive Departments, upon any Subject relating to the Duties of their respective Offices, and he shall have Power to grant Reprieves and Pardons for Offences against the United States, except in Cases of Impeachment.

He shall have Power, by and with the Advice and Consent of the Senate, to make Treaties, provided two thirds of the Senators present concur; and he shall nominate, and by and with the Advice and Consent of the Senate, shall appoint Ambassadors, other public Ministers and Consuls, Judges of the supreme Court, and all other Officers of the United States, whose Appointments are not herein otherwise provided for, and which shall be established by Law; but the Congress may by Law vest the Appointment of such inferior Officers, as they think proper, in the President alone, in the Courts of Law, or in the Heads of Departments.

The President shall have Power to fill up all Vacancies that may happen during the Recess of the Senate, by granting Commissions which shall expire of their next Session.

Section 3. He shall from time to time give to the Congress Information of the State of the Union, and recommend to their Consideration such Measures as he shall judge necessary and expedient; he may, on extraordinary Occasions, convene both Houses, or either of them, and in Case of Disagreement between them, with Respect to the Time of Adjournment, he may adjourn them to such Time as he shall think proper; he shall receive Ambassadors and other public Ministers; he shall take Care that the Laws be faithfully executed, and shall Commission all the Officers of the United States.

Section 4. The President, Vice President and all civil Officers of the United States, shall be removed from Office on Impeachment for, and Conviction of, Treason, Bribery, or other high Crimes and Misdemeanors.

Article III.

Section 1. The judicial Power of the United States, shall be vested in one supreme Court, and in such inferior Courts as the Congress may from time to time ordain and establish. The Judges, both of the supreme and inferior Courts, shall hold their Offices during good Behaviour, and shall, at stated Times, receive for their Services a Compensation, which shall not be diminished during their Continuance in Office.

8Changed by the Twelfth Amendment.
9Modified by the Twenty-fifth Amendment.

SECTION 2. The judicial Power shall extend to all Cases, in Law and Equity, arising under this Constitution, the Laws of the United States, and Treaties made, or which shall be made, under their Authority;—to all Cases affecting Ambassadors, other public Ministers and Consuls;—to all Cases of admiralty and maritime jurisdiction;—to Controversies to which the United States shall be a Party;—to Controversies between two or more States; [—between a State and Citizens of another State;—][10] between Citizens of different States; between Citizens of the same State claiming Lands under Grants of different States, [and between a State, or the Citizens thereof, and foreign States, Citizens or Subjects.][11]

In all Cases affecting Ambassadors, other public Ministers and Consuls, and those in which a State shall be a Party, the supreme Court shall have original jurisdiction. In all the other Cases before mentioned, the supreme Court shall have appellate Jurisdiction, both as to Law and Fact, with such Exceptions, and under such Regulations as the Congress shall make.

The Trial of all Crimes, except in Cases of Impeachment, shall be by Jury; and such Trial shall be held in the State where the said Crimes shall have been committed; but when not committed within any State, the Trial shall be at such Place or Places as the Congress may by Law have directed.

SECTION 3. Treason against the United States, shall consist only in levying War against them, or, in adhering to their Enemies, giving them Aid and Comfort. No Person shall be convicted of Treason unless on the Testimony of two Witnesses to the same overt Act, or on Confession in open Court.

The Congress shall have Power to declare the Punishment of Treason, but no Attainder of Treason shall work Corruption of Blood, or Forfeiture except during the Life of the Person attainted.

ARTICLE IV.

SECTION 1. Full Faith and Credit shall be given in each State to the public Acts, Records, and judicial Proceedings of every other State. And the Congress may by general Laws prescribe the Manner in which such Acts, Records and Proceedings shall be proved, and the Effect thereof.

SECTION 2. The Citizens of each State shall be entitled to all Privileges and Immunities of Citizens in the several States.

A Person charged in any State with Treason, Felony, or other Crime, who shall flee from Justice, and be found in another State, shall on Demand of the executive Authority of the State from which he fled, be delivered up, to be removed to the State having Jurisdiction of the Crime.

[No Person held to Service or Labour in one State, under the Laws thereof, escaping into another, shall, in Consequence of any Law or Regulation therein, be discharged from such Service or Labour, but shall be delivered up on Claim of the Party to whom such Service or Labour may be due.][12]

SECTION 3. New States may be admitted by the Congress into this Union; but no new State shall be formed or erected within the Jurisdiction of any other State; nor any State be formed by the junction of two or more States, or Parts of States, without the Consent of the Legislatures of the States concerned as well as of the Congress.

The Congress shall have Power to dispose of and make all needful Rules and Regulations respecting the Territory or other Property belonging to the United States; and nothing in this Constitution shall be so construed as to Prejudice any claims of the United States, or of any particular State.

SECTION 4. The United States shall guarantee to every State in this Union a Republican Form of Government, and shall protect each of them against Invasion; and on Application of the Legislature, or of the Executive (when the Legislature cannot be convened) against domestic Violence.

ARTICLE V.

The Congress, whenever two-thirds of both Houses shall deem it necessary, shall propose Amendments to this Constitution, or on the Application of the Legislatures of two-thirds of the several States, shall call a Convention for proposing Amendments, which, in either Case, shall be valid to all Intents and Purposes, as part of this Constitution, when ratified by

---

[10] Modified by the Eleventh Amendment.
[11] Modified by the Eleventh Amendment.
[12] Repealed by the Thirteenth Amendment.

the Legislatures of three-fourths of the several States, or by Conventions in three fourths thereof, as the one or the other Mode of Ratification may be proposed by the Congress; Provided that no Amendment which may be made prior to the Year One thousand eight hundred and eight shall in any Manner affect the first and fourth Clauses in the Ninth Section of the first Article; and that no State, without its Consent, shall be deprived of its equal Suffrage in the Senate.

ARTICLE VI.

All Debts contracted and Engagements entered into, before the Adoption of this Constitution shall be as valid against the United States under this Constitution, as under the Confederation.

This Constitution, and the Laws of the United States which shall be made in Pursuance thereof; and all Treaties made, or which shall be made, under the Authority of the United States, shall be the supreme Law of the Land; and the judges in every State shall be bound thereby, any Thing in the Constitution or Laws of any State to the Contrary notwithstanding.

The Senators and Representatives before mentioned, and the Members of the several State Legislatures, and all executive and judicial Officers, both of the United States and of the several States, shall be bound by Oath or Affirmation, to support this Constitution; but no religious Test shall ever be required as a Qualification to any Office or public Trust under the United States.

ARTICLE VII.

The Ratification of the Conventions of nine States shall, be sufficient for the Establishment of this Constitution between the States so ratifying the Same.

Done in Convention by the Unanimous Consent of the States present the Seventeenth Day of September in the Year of our Lord one thousand seven hundred and Eighty seven and of the Independence of the United States of America the Twelfth. IN WITNESS whereof we have hereunto subscribed our Names,

Go. WASHINGTON
Presid't. and deputy from Virginia

Attest
WILLIAM JACKSON
Secretary

DELAWARE
Geo. Read
Gunning Bedford jun
John Dickinson
Richard Bassett
Jaco. Broom

PENNSYLVANIA
B. Franklin
Thomas Mifflin
Robt. Morris
Geo. Clymer
Thos. FitzSimons
Jared Ingersoll
James Wilson
Gouv. Morris

VIRGINIA
John Blair
James Madison Jr.

MASSACHUSETTS
Nathaniel Gorham
Rufus King

CONNECTICUT
Wm. Saml. Johnson
Roger Sherman

NEW YORK
Alexander Hamilton

NEW JERSEY
Wh. Livingston
David Brearley
Wm. Paterson
Jona. Dayton

NEW HAMPSHIRE
John Langdon
Nicholas Gilman

MARYLAND
James McHenry
Dan of St. Thos. Jenifer
Danl. Carroll

NORTH CAROLINA
Wm. Blount
Richd. Dobbs Spaight
Hu. Williamson

SOUTH CAROLINA
J. Rutledge
Charles Cotesworth Pinckney
Charles Pinckney
Pierce Butler

GEORGIA
William Few
Abr. Baldwin

Articles in addition to, and amendment of the Constitution of the United States of America, proposed by Congress and ratified by the Legislatures of the several states, pursuant to the Fifth Article of the original Constitution.

AMENDMENT I[13]

Congress shall make no law respecting an establishment of religion, or prohibiting the free exercise thereof; or abridging the freedom of speech or of the press or the right of the people peaceably to assemble, and to petition the Government for a redress of grievances.

AMENDMENT II

A well regulated militia, being necessary to the security of a free State, the right of the people to keep and bear arms, shall not be infringed.

AMENDMENT III

No Soldier shall in time of peace, be quartered in any house, without the consent of the owner, nor in time of war, but in a manner to be prescribed by law.

AMENDMENT IV

The right of the people to be secure in their persons, houses, papers, and effects, against unreasonable searches and seizures, shall not be violated, and no warrants shall issue, but upon probable cause, supported by oath or affirmation, and particularly describing the place to be searched, and the persons or things to be seized.

AMENDMENT V

No person shall be held to answer for a capital, or otherwise infamous crime, unless on a presentment or indictment of a Grand Jury, except in cases arising in the land or naval forces, or in the militia, when in actual service in time of war or public danger; nor shall any person be subject for the same offence to be twice put in jeopardy of life or limb; nor shall be compelled in any criminal case to be a witness against himself, nor be deprived of life, liberty, or property, without due process of law; nor shall private property be taken for public use, without just compensation.

AMENDMENT VI

In all criminal prosecutions, the accused shall enjoy the right to a speedy and public trial, by an impartial jury of the State and district wherein the crime shall have been committed which district shall have been previously ascertained by law, and to be informed of the nature and cause of the accusation; to be confronted with the witnesses against him; to have compulsory process for obtaining witnesses in his favor, and to have the assistance of counsel for his defence.

AMENDMENT VII

In suits at common law, where the value in controversy shall exceed twenty dollars, the right of trial by jury shall be preserved, and no fact tried by jury, shall be otherwise re-examined in any Court of the United States, than according to the rules of the common law.

AMENDMENT VIII

Excessive bail shall not be required, nor excessive fines imposed, nor cruel and unusual punishments inflicted.

AMENDMENT IX

The enumeration in the Constitution, of certain rights, shall not be construed to deny or disparage others retained by the people.

AMENDMENT X

The powers not delegated to the United States by the Constitution, nor prohibited by it to the States, are reserved to the States respectively, or to the people.

---

[13]The first ten amendments were passed by Congress on September 25, 1789, and were ratified on December 15, 1791.

AMENDMENT XI
(Ratified on February 7, 1795)

The Judicial power of the United States shall not be construed to extend to any suit in law or equity, commenced or prosecuted against one of the United States by Citizens of another State, or by Citizens or Subjects of any Foreign State.

AMENDMENT XII
(Ratified on June 15, 1804)

The Electors shall meet in their respective states, and vote by ballot for President and Vice-President, one of whom, at least, shall not be an inhabitant of the same state with themselves; they shall name in their ballots the person voted for as President, and in distinct ballots the person voted for as Vice-President, and they shall make distinct lists of all persons voted for as President, and of all persons voted for as Vice-President, and of the number of votes for each, which lists they shall sign and certify, and transmit sealed to the seat of the government of the United States, directed to the President of the Senate; The President of the Senate shall, in the presence of the Senate and House of Representatives, open all the certificates and the votes shall then be counted; The person having the greatest number of votes for President, shall be the President, if such number be a majority of the whole number of Electors appointed; and if no person have such majority, then from the persons having the highest numbers not exceeding three on the list of those voted for as President, the House of Representatives shall choose immediately, by ballot, the President. But in choosing the President, the votes shall be taken by states, the representation from each state having one vote, a quorum for this purpose shall consist of a member or members from two-thirds of the states, and a majority of all states shall be necessary to a choice. [And if the House of Representatives shall not choose a President whenever the right of choice shall devolve upon them, before the fourth day of March next following, then the Vice-President shall act as President, as in the case of the death or other constitutional disability of the President.][14]— The person having the greatest number of votes as Vice-President, shall be the Vice-President, if such number be a majority of the whole number of Electors appointed, and if no person have a majority, then from the two highest numbers on the list, the Senate shall choose the Vice-President; a quorum for the purpose shall consist of two-thirds of the whole number of Senators, and a majority of the whole number shall be necessary to a choice. But no person constitutionally ineligible to the office of President shall be eligible to that of Vice-President of the United States.

AMENDMENT XIII
(Ratified on December 6, 1865)

Section 1. Neither slavery nor involuntary servitude, except as a punishment for crime whereof the party shall have been duly convicted, shall exist within the United States, or any place subject to their jurisdiction.

Section 2. Congress shall have power to enforce this article by appropriate legislation.

AMENDMENT XIV
(Ratified on July 9, 1868)

Section 1. All persons born or naturalized in the United States, and subject to the jurisdiction thereof, are citizens of the United States and of the State wherein they reside. No State shall make or enforce any law which shall abridge the privileges or immunities of citizens of the United States; nor shall any State deprive any person of life, liberty, or property, without due process of law; nor deny to any person within its jurisdiction the equal protection of the laws.

Section 2. Representatives shall be apportioned among the several States according to their respective numbers, counting the whole number of persons in each State, excluding Indians not taxed. But when the right to vote at any election for the choice of electors for President and Vice-President of the United States, Representatives in Congress, the Executive and judicial officers of a State, or the members of the Legislature thereof, is denied to any of the male inhabitants of such State, being [twenty-one][15] years of age, and citizens of the United States, or in any way

---

[14]Changed by the Twentieth Amendment.

[15]Changed by the Twenty-sixth Amendment.

abridged, except for participation in rebellion, or other crime, the basis of representation therein shall be reduced in the proportion which the number of such male citizens shall bear to the whole number of male citizens twenty-one years of age in such State.

SECTION 3. No person shall be a Senator or Representative in Congress, or elector of President and Vice-President, or hold any office, civil or military, under the United States, or under any State, who having previously taken an oath, as a member of Congress, or as an officer of the United States, or as a member of any State legislature, or as an executive or judicial officer of any State, to support the Constitution of the United States, shall have engaged in insurrection or rebellion against the same, or given aid or comfort to the enemies thereof. But Congress may by a vote of two-thirds of each House, remove such disability.

SECTION 4. The validity of the public debt of the United States, authorized by law, including debts incurred for payment of pensions and bounties for services in suppressing insurrection or rebellion, shall not be questioned. But neither the United States nor any State shall assume or pay any debt or obligation incurred in aid of insurrection or rebellion against the United States, or any claim for the loss or emancipation of any slave, but all such debts, obligations and claims shall be held illegal and void.

SECTION 5. Congress shall have power to enforce, by appropriate legislation, the provisions of this article.

AMENDMENT XV
(RATIFIED ON FEBRUARY 3, 1870)

SECTION 1. The right of citizens of the United States to vote shall not be denied or abridged by the United States or by any State on account of race, color, or previous condition of servitude.

SECTION 2. The Congress shall have power to enforce this article by appropriate legislation.

AMENDMENT XVI
(RATIFIED ON FEBRUARY 3, 1913)

The Congress shall have power to lay and collect taxes on incomes, from whatever source derived, without apportionment among the several States, and without regard to any census or enumeration.

AMENDMENT XVII—
(RATIFIED ON APRIL 8, 1913)

The Senate of the United States shall be composed of two Senators from each State, elected by the people thereof, for six years; and each Senator shall have one vote. The electors in each State shall have the qualifications requisite for electors of the most numerous branch of the State legislatures.

When vacancies happen in the representation of any State in the Senate, the executive authority of such State shall issue writs of election to fill such vacancies: *Provided*, That the legislature of any State may empower the executive thereof to make temporary appointments until the people fill the vacancies by election as the legislature may direct.

This amendment shall not be so construed as to affect the election or term of any Senator chosen before it becomes valid as part of the Constitution.

AMENDMENT XVIII
(RATIFIED ON JANUARY 16, 1919)

SECTION 1. After one year from the ratification of this article the manufacture, sale, or transportation of intoxicating liquors within, the importation thereof into, or the exportation thereof from the United States and all territory subject to the jurisdiction thereof for beverage purposes is hereby prohibited.

SECTION 2. The Congress and the several States shall have concurrent power to enforce this article by appropriate legislation.

SECTION 3. This article shall be inoperative unless it shall have been ratified as an amendment to the Constitution by the legislatures of the several States, as provided in the Constitution, within seven years from the date of the submission hereof to the States by the Congress.[16]

AMENDMENT XIX
(RATIFIED ON AUGUST 18, 1920)

The right of citizens of the United States to vote shall not be denied or abridged by the United States or by any State on account of sex.

---

[16]The Eighteenth Amendment was repealed by the Twenty-first Amendment.

Congress shall have power to enforce this article by appropriate legislation.

AMENDMENT XX
(RATIFIED ON JANUARY 23, 1933)

SECTION 1. The terms of the President and Vice-President shall end at noon on the 20th day of January, and the terms of Senators and Representatives at noon on the 3d day of January, of the years in which such terms would have ended if this article had not been ratified; and the terms of their successors shall then begin.

SECTION 2. The Congress shall assemble at least once in every year, and such meeting shall begin at noon the 3d day of January, unless they shall by law appoint, a different day.

SECTION 3. If, at the time fixed for the beginning of the term of the President, the President elect shall have died, the Vice-President elect shall become President. If a President shall not have been chosen before the time fixed for the beginning of his term, or if the President elect shall have failed to qualify, then the Vice-President elect shall act as President until a President shall have qualified; and the Congress may by law provide for the case wherein neither a President elect nor a Vice-President elect shall have qualified, declaring who shall then act as President, or the manner in which one who is to act shall be selected, and such person shall act accordingly until a President or Vice-President shall have qualified.

SECTION 4. The Congress may by law provide for the case of the death of any of the persons from whom the House of Representatives may choose a President whenever the rights of choice shall have devolved upon them, and for the case of the death of any of the persons from whom the Senate may choose a Vice-President whenever the right of choice shall have devolved upon them.

SECTION 5. Sections 1 and 2 shall take effect on the 15th day of October following the ratification of this article.

SECTION 6. This article shall be inoperative unless it shall have been ratified as an amendment to the Constitution by the legislatures of three-fourths of the several States within seven years from the date of its submission.

AMENDMENT XXI
(RATIFIED ON DECEMBER 5, 1933)

SECTION 1. The eighteenth article of amendment to the Constitution of the United States is hereby repealed.

SECTION 2. The transportation or importation into any State, Territory, or possession of the United States for delivery or use therein of intoxicating liquors, in violation of the laws thereof, is hereby prohibited.

SECTION 3. This article shall be inoperative unless it shall have been ratified as an amendment to the Constitution by conventions in the several States, as provided in the Constitution, within seven years from the date of the submission hereof to the States by the Congress.

AMENDMENT XXII
(RATIFIED ON FEBRUARY 27, 1951)

No person shall be elected to the office of the President more than twice, and no person who has held the office of President, or acted as President, for more than two years of a term to which some other person was elected President shall be elected to the office of President more than once. But this Article shall not apply to any person holding the office of President when this Article was proposed by the Congress, and shall not prevent any person who may be holding the office of President, or acting as President, during the term within which this Article becomes operative from holding the office of President or acting as President during the remainder of such term.

AMENDMENT XXIII
(RATIFIED ON MARCH 29, 1961)

SECTION 1. The District constituting the seat of Government of the United States shall appoint in such manner as the Congress may direct:

A number of electors of President and Vice-President equal to the whole number of Senators and Representatives in Congress to which the District would be entitled if it were a State, but in no event more than the least populous State; they shall be in addition to those appointed by the States, but they shall be considered, for the purposes of the election of President and Vice-President, to be electors appointed by a State; and they shall meet in the District and perform such duties as provided by the twelfth article of amendment.

Section 2. The Congress shall have power to enforce this article by appropriate legislation.

Amendment XXIV
(Ratified on January 23, 1964)

Section 1. The right of citizens of the United States to vote in any primary or other election for President or Vice-President, for electors for President or Vice-President, or for Senator or Representative of Congress, shall not be denied or abridged by the United States, or any State by reason of failure to pay any poll tax or other tax.

Section 2. The Congress shall have power to enforce this article by appropriate legislation.

Amendment XXV
(Ratified on February 10, 1967)

Section 1. In case of the removal of the President from office, death or resignation, the Vice President shall become President.

Section 2. Whenever there is a vacancy in the office of the Vice-President, the President shall nominate a Vice-President who shall take office upon confirmation by a majority vote of both Houses of Congress.

Section 3. Whenever the President transmits to the President pro tempore of the Senate and the Speaker of the House of Representatives his written declaration that he is unable to discharge the powers and duties of his office, and until he transmits to them a written declaration to the contrary, such powers and duties shall be discharged by the Vice-President as Acting President.

Section 4. Whenever the Vice-President and a majority of either the principal officers of the executive departments or of such other body as Congress may by law provide, transmit to the President pro tempore of the Senate and the Speaker of the House of Representatives their written declaration that the President is unable to discharge the powers and duties of his office, the Vice-President shall immediately assume the powers and duties of the office as Acting President.

Thereafter, when the President transmits to the President pro tempore of the Senate and the Speaker of the House of Representatives his written declaration that no inability exists, he shall resume the powers and duties of his office unless the Vice-President and a majority of either the principal officers of the executive department or of such other body as Congress may by law provide, transmit within four days to the President pro tempore of the Senate and the Speaker of the House of Representatives their written declaration that the President is unable to discharge the powers and duties of his office. Thereupon Congress shall decide the issue, assembling within forty-eight hours for that purpose if not in session. If the Congress, within twenty-one days after receipt of the latter written declaration, or, if Congress is not in session, within twenty-one days after Congress is required to assemble, determines by two-thirds vote of both Houses that the President is unable to discharge the powers and duties of his office, the Vice-President shall continue to discharge the same as Acting President; otherwise, the President shall resume the powers and duties of his office.

Amendment XXVI
(Ratified on July 1, 1971)

Section 1. The right of citizens of the United States, who are eighteen years of age or older, to vote shall not be denied or abridged by the United States or by any State on account of age.

Section 2. The Congress shall have power to enforce this article by appropriate legislation.

Amendment XXVII
(Ratified on May 7, 1992)

No law varying the compensation for the services of the Senators and Representatives shall take effect, until an election of Representatives shall have intervened.

Chapter 1

Endnotes

1. Quoted in Carl J. Friedrich, *Limited Government: A Comparison* (Englewood Cliffs, NJ: Prentice-Hall, 1974), p. 16.
2. "Federalist No. 51," Alexander Hamilton, John Jay, and James Madison, *The Federalist Papers* (New York: Modern Library, 1937), p. 337.
3. The United States is one of the few sovereign states in the world that has failed to ratify any of these major international human rights conventions.
4. *www.state.gov/r/pa/ei/bgn/*.
5. Freedom House, "Democracy's Century: A Survey of Global Political Change in the 20th Century," *www.freedomhouse.org/reports/century.html*.
6. Amartya Sen, "Democracy as a Universal Value," *Journal of Democracy 10*, no. 3 (1999), p. 4.
7. Samuel P. Huntington, "Democracy's Third Wave," in *Comparative Politics 93/94, Annual Editions*, 11th ed. (Guilford, CT: Dushkin, 1993).
8. Samuel Huntington, *The Clash of Civilizations and the Remaking of World Order* (New York: Simon & Schuster, 1996), p. 71.
9. Freedom House, "Freedom in the World 2012," *www.freedomhouse.org/report/freedom-world-2012*.
10. See Daniel A. Bell, *East Meets West: Human Rights and Democracy in East Asia* (Princeton, NJ: Princeton University Press, 2000).
11. Amartya Sen, *Development as Freedom* (New York: Alfred A. Knopf, 1999), p. 147.
12. Ted Robert Gurr, "America as a Model for the World?: A Skeptical View," *PS: Political Science and Politics 24* (December 1991), 659.
13. Ibid., p. 666.
14. Cass Sunstein, *Designing Democracy: What Constitutions Do* (New York: Oxford University Press, 2001), pp. 6, 10.
15. Ivo D. Duchacek, *Rights and Liberties in the World Today: Constitutional Promise and Reality* (Santa Barbara, CA: ABC-CLIO, 1973), p. 25.
16. Ivo D. Duchacek, *Power Maps: Comparative Politics of Constitutions* (Santa Barbara, CA: ABC-CLIO, 1973), p. 3.
17. *Federalist No. 51*, p. 337.
18. See William E. Hudson, *American Democracy in Peril*, 7th ed. (Washington, DC: Congressional Quarterly Press, 2012), pp. 25–62.
19. Douglas V. Verney, *British Government and Politics*, 3rd ed. (New York: Harper & Row, 1976), pp. 37–38.
20. Charles Evans Hughes, Speech at Elmira, New York, March 3, 1907, quoted by Sanford Levinson, "On Interpretation," *Southern California Law Review 58* (1985), 724.
21. "Federalist #51," in Alexander Hamilton, John Jay, & James Madison, *The Federalist* (New York: The Modern Library), p. 337.
22. The best example of Friedman's individualism can be found in his book *Capitalism and Freedom*, where he argues against such governmental intrusions into personal liberty as Social Security, public education, and civil rights legislation. The most famous work embodying the radical individualism of Ayn Rand is her novel *The Fountainhead*.
23. See, e.g., Benjamin Barber, *Strong Democracy* (Berkeley: University of California Press, 1984); Robert Bellah, et al., *Habits of the Heart: Individualism and Commitment in American Life* (New York: Harper & Row, 1985) and *The Good Society* (New York: Harper & Row, 1989).
24. "Federalist #51," in *The Federalist*, p. 339.
25. Edward S. Corwin, "The 'Higher Law' Background of American Constitutional Law," *Harvard Law Review 42* (1928), 149.
26. Quoted in Corwin, "The 'Higher Law' Background," p. 368.
27. Thomas Paine, *Rights of Man* (New York: Penguin Books, 1969), p. 187.
28. "The Mayflower Compact, November 11, 1620," in Henry Steele Commager, ed., *Documents of American History*, 8th ed. (New York: Meredith, 1963), pp. 15–16.
29. See Wilson Carey McWilliams, *The Idea of Fraternity in America* (Berkeley: University of California Press, 1973), pp. 496–498.

Chapter 2

Endnotes

1. James Otis, "The Rights of the British Colonies Asserted and Proved," in Merrill Jensen, ed., *Tracts of the American Revolution, 1763–1776* (Indianapolis, IN: Bobbs-Merrill, 1967), pp. 19–40.
2. "Resolution for Independence, June 7, 1776," in Henry Steele Commager, ed., *Documents of American History*, 8th ed. (New York: Meredith, 1963), p. 100.

3. "Jefferson's Third Draft of a Virginia Constitution," quoted in Gordon S. Wood, *The Creation of the American Republic, 1776–1787* (Chapel Hill: University of North Carolina Press, 1969), p. 136.
4. Merrill Jensen, *The Articles of Confederation: An Interpretation of the Social-Constitutional History of the American Revolution, 1774–1781*, (Madison: University of Wisconsin Press, 1940).
5. "Resolution for Independence, June 7, 1776," in Commager, *Documents of American History*, p. 100.
6. Quoted in Andrew C. McLaughlin, *A Constitutional History of the United States* (New York: Appleton-Century-Crofts, 1935), p. 139.
7. "The Annapolis Convention, September 14, 1786," in Commager, *Documents of American History*, p. 133.
8. James Madison, "Letter to Thomas Jefferson, October 17, 1788," in Julian Boyd, ed., *The Papers of Thomas Jefferson* (Princeton, NJ: Princeton University Press, 1950), Vol. XIV, pp. 19, 20.
9. Thomas Jefferson, *Notes on the State of Virginia*, ed. William Peden (Chapel Hill: University of North Carolina Press, 1955), p. 120.
10. "Resolution of Congress, February 21, 1787," quoted in Herbert J. Storing, *What the Anti-Federalists Were For* (Chicago: University of Chicago Press, 1981), p. 7.
11. "The Virginia Plan," in Commager, *Documents of American History*, p. 134.
12. Ibid.
13. "Vices of the Political System of the U.S.," quoted in Wood, *The Creation of the American Republic*, p. 410.
14. Quoted in Storing, *What the Anti-Federalists Were For*, p. 17.
15. "Letter to James Madison, July 31, 1788," quoted in Wood, *The Creation of the American Republic*, p. 537.
16. "Speech on a Plan of Government," in Harold C. Syrett, *The Papers of Alexander Hamilton* (New York: Columbia University Press, 1961), Vol. IV, p. 200.
17. Merrill Jensen, *The Articles of Confederation: An Interpretation of the Social-Constitutional History of the American Revolution, 1774–1781* (Madison: University of Wisconsin Press, 1940), p. 243.
18. Robert Dahl, *How Democratic is the American Constitution?* (New Haven, CT: Yale University Press, 2002).

CHAPTER 3

ENDNOTES

1. *The Federalist No. 78*, edited with Historical and Literary Annotations and Introduction by J. R. Pole (Indianapolis, IN: Hackett, 2005).
2. Ibid.
3. PL 107-273, 21st Century Department of Justice Appropriations Authorization Act, passed on November 2, 2002.
4. Data drawn from Administrative Office of the United States Courts, *2010 Federal Court Management Statistics*; U.S. District Court—Judicial Caseload Profile, 12-month period ending March 31, 2011, *www.uscourts.gov/Statistics/FederalJudicialCaseloadStatistics/FederalJudicialCaseloadStatistics2011.aspx*.
5. Op.cit., U.S. Court of Appeals—Judicial Caseload Profile, 12-month period ending March 31, 2011, *www.uscourts.gov/Viewer.aspx?doc=/uscourts/Statistics/FederalJudicialCaseloadStatistics/2011/tables/B00Mar11.pdf*.
6. During the 1970s, in part because of Chief Justice Warren Burger's frequent pleas for judicial reform, several calls emerged for the addition of a National Court of Appeals that would ease the increasing workload of the U.S. Supreme Court. Support for this new court level subsided when critics claimed that it might dramatically change the nature and potency of Supreme Court rulings. The Burger Court tried to manage its workload by limiting standing of certain parties to bring suit in federal courts. See the cases of *Laird v. Tatum*, 408 U.S. 1 (1972); *Schlesinger v. Reservists Committee to Stop the War*, 418 U.S. 208 (1974); *United States v. Richardson*, 418 U.S. 166 (1974); *Warth v. Seldin*, 422 U.S. 490 (1975); and *Simon v. Eastern Kentucky Welfare Rights Organization*, 426 U.S. 26 (1976).
7. This discussion is drawn from several sources: Thomas G. Walker and Lee Epstein, *The Supreme Court of the United States: An Introduction* (New York: St. Martin's Press, 1993), pp. 71–74; Howard Ball, *Courts and Politics: The Federal Judicial System*, 2nd ed. (Englewood Cliffs, NJ: Prentice-Hall, 1987), pp. 122–123; Stephen L. Wasby, *The Supreme Court in the Federal Judicial System*, 3rd ed. (Chicago: Nelson-Hall, 1988), p. 191; David G. Barnum, *The Supreme Court in the American Judicial System* (New York: St. Martin's Press, 1993), pp. 59–66; and Lawrence Baum, *The Supreme Court*, 6th ed. (Washington, DC: Congressional Quarterly Press, 1998), pp. 121–127.
8. Lawrence Baum, *The Supreme Court*, 9th ed. (Washington, DC: Congressional Quarterly Press, 2007), p. 98.
9. The first example arose in the case of *Ex Parte McCardle* (1869). In 1867, Congress authorized federal courts to grant writs of habeus corpus to persons detained illegally. Persons claiming illegal detention could appeal any adverse ruling to the U.S. Supreme Court. William McCardle had been imprisoned following the Civil War for publishing allegedly libelous statements criticizing the reconstruction government in Mississippi. After losing in a lower court in Mississippi, McCardle appealed to the Supreme Court. Fearing that its reconstruction policy would soon be declared unconstitutional, the Radical Republican Congress repealed the habeus corpus law, thus denying McCardle the right to appeal his conviction. The major question raised in *McCardle* was whether the Supreme Court could hear the case after the repeal of the statute. The Court ultimately ruled that it had no authority to hear the case because Congress had repealed its appellate jurisdiction in the matter.

The other case found Congress voting to limit the Court's appellate jurisdiction in *Yakus v. United States* (1944). Soon after declaring war against Japan and Germany in 1941, Congress repealed the Emergency

Price Control Act of 1942, which instituted price controls on various priority items needed in wartime. It also created the Emergency Court of Appeals, giving it "exclusive jurisdiction to determine the validity of any regulation or order of the Price Administrator." The legislation also declared that "no Court, Federal, State or Territorial, shall have jurisdiction or power to restrain, enjoin, or set aside any provision of this Act." In *Yakus*, the Supreme Court held, on a vote of 6 to 3, that the Act was a broad, but legal, delegation of legislative authority to the Office of Price Administration.

10. Thomas G. Walker and Lee Epstein, *The Supreme Court of the United States: An Introduction* (New York: St. Martin's Press, 1993), p. 49. Walker and Epstein also note that of the twenty-nine nominees rejected by the Senate from 1793 to 1987, three of them (William Paterson, Roger B. Taney, and Stanley Matthews) later won confirmation.

11. Much of this discussion of the blue slip procedure relies heavily upon a recent article by Brannon P. Denning, in "The Judicial Confirmation Process and the Blue Slip," *Judicature 85*, no. 5 (March–April 2002).

12. Sarah Binder and Forrest Maltzman, "Advice and Consent During the Bush Years: The Politics of Confirming Federal Judges," *Judicature* 92, no. 6 (May–June 2009), 327.

13. From 1956 to 1970, the ABA Committee used two evaluative categories: "professionally qualified" and "unqualified"; between 1970 and 1990, it used the three ratings of "highly qualified," "not opposed," or "not qualified."

14. Quoted in Sarah Binder and Forrest Maltzman, "Advice and Consent During the Bush Years: The Politics of Confirming Federal Judges," *Judicature* 92, no. 6 (May–June 2009), 320.

15. Associate Justices Hughes, Stone, and Rehnquist were initially appointed to the Court without prior judicial experience, but later were nominated and confirmed as Chief Justice.

16. Interestingly, during the Nixon and Reagan years the ABA Committee was frequently charged with being too liberal and biased against prospective nominees made by these two presidents, especially with respect to the Committee's evaluations of the Clarence Thomas nomination in 1990.

17. For a historical glance at this practice, see Howard Ball, *Courts and Politics: The Federal Judicial System*, 2nd ed. (Englewood Cliffs, NJ: Prentice-Hall, 1987), p. 176. For a look at the appointment practices of Presidents Bush and Clinton, see Sheldon Goldman, "Bush's Judicial Legacy: The Final Imprint," *Judicature 76*, no. 6 (April–May 1993), 287, 293; Sheldon Goldman and Matthew D. Saronson, "Clinton's Nontraditional Judges: Creating a More Representative Bench," *Judicature 78*, no. 2 (September–October 1994), 72; and Sheldon Goldman and Elliot Slotnick, "Clinton's First Term Judiciary: Many Bridges To Cross," *Judicature 80*, no. 6 (May–June 1997), 261, 269.

18. Sheldon Goldman, Elliot Slotnick, Gerard Gryski, and Gary Zuk, "Clinton's Judges: Summing Up the Legacy," *Judicature 84*, no. 5 (March–April 2001), 244, Table 3.

19. See Lee Epstein, Kevin Quinn, Andrew D. Martin, and Jeffrey A. Segal, "On the Perils of Drawing Inferences about Supreme Court Justices From Their First Few Years of Service," *Judicature 91*, no. 4 (January–February 2008), 179.

20. Sheldon Goldman, Elliot Slotnick, Gerard Gryski, Gary Zuk, and Sara Schiavoni, "W. Bush Remaking the Judiciary: Like Father Like Son?" *Judicature 86*, no. 6 (May–June 2003), 294, Table 1.

21. Jennifer Segal Diascro and Rorie Spill Solberg, "Policy in the Face of Diversity," *Judicature 92*, no. 6 (May–June 2009), 291.

22. Quoted in Peter Baker and Jeff Zeleny, "Obama Hails Judge as 'Inspiring'," *New York Times*, May 27, 2009.

23. Peter Baker and Jeff Zeleny, "Obama Hails Judge as 'Inspiring,'" *New York Times*, May 27, 2009.

CHAPTER 4

ENDNOTES

1. Alexis de Tocqueville, *Democracy in America* (New York: The New American Library, 1956), p. 76.
2. Quoted from Edwin Meese speech, as reprinted in *The Great Debate: Interpreting Our Written Constitution* (Washington, DC: The Federalist Society, 1986), pp. 1–10.
3. Ibid., p. 29.
4. This discussion of constitutional interpretation relies heavily upon the discussion in Walter F. Murphy, James E. Fleming, Sotirios A. Barber, and Stephen Macedo, *American Constitutional Interpretation*, 4th ed. (Mineola, NY: Foundation Press, 2008).
5. Linda Greenhouse, "Judicial Intent: The Competing Visions of the Role of the Court," *New York Times*, July 7, 2002.
6. *District of Columbia v. Heller*, 554 U.S. 570 (2008).
7. One of the first constitutional scholars to use these two terms was C. Herman Pritchett in his book, *The Roosevelt Court* (New York: Macmillan, 1948).
8. Although this seminal article has been reprinted in numerous publications over the decades, it first appeared in *Harvard Law Review 7* no. 3 (1893).
9. Lawrence Baum, *The Supreme Court*, 7th ed. (Washington, DC: Congressional Quarterly Press, 2001), p. 197, Table 5-3; and p. 199, Table 5-4.
10. From Harlan dissent in *Reynolds v. Sims*, 533 at 624–625 (1964).
11. From Holmes's dissent in *Hammer v. Dagenhart*, 247 U.S. 251 (1918), at 280.
12. *United States v. Butler*, 297 U.S. 1 (1936), at _____.
13. From Senate Report, 75th Congress, 1st sess., Document #711.
14. Relevant to this point about the other coordinate branches looking to the courts to resolve complex, controversial issues is a rather candid interview in 1979 between Professor Harry M. Clor and Associate Justice Lewis F. Powell Jr., when Powell was still on the Supreme Court. An excerpt of the Clor–Powell

interview is contained in Louis Fisher, *American Constitutional Law: Constitutional Structures, Separated Powers and Federalism*, Vol. I, 6th ed. (Durham, NC: Carolina Academic Press, 2005). Contained here one finds Justice Powell's response to a question from Clor concerning whether the Court remakes the Constitution by reading into the document meanings that might not have been originally there. Powell responds: ". . . [A] good many people think the legislative branch bucks tough decisions to the judicial branch by drawing statutes in quite general and vague terms. Thus, a role sometimes viewed as legislative . . . is thrust upon us. . . . It has been said a number of times that Congress does that, and perhaps if I were there I'd think it was a good idea on some issues. In this way members of Congress do not have to go on record on a tough issue." Id., pp. 61–62.

15. This discussion of federal, state and local laws declared unconstitutional by the U.S. Supreme Court relies heavily upon Lawrence Baum, *The Supreme Court*, 7th ed. (Washington, DC: Congressional Quarterly Press, 2001), pp. 195–202.
16. Abraham, *The Judiciary*, op. cit., 71.
17. Carr, *The Supreme Court and Judicial Review*, 1942, documents over 460 cases of the Privy Council in London overruling laws adopted by American colonial assemblies during the seventeenth and eighteenth centuries. Charles G. Haines discusses eight occasions in which American state courts between 1778 and 1788 had either claimed or used this power (see his *American Doctrine of Judicial Supremacy*, reprint, 1959). In the 1790s, national laws were reviewed by the U.S. Supreme Court in four instances (*Hayburn's Case* in 1792, *Chandler v. Secretary of War* and *U.S. v. Yale Todd* in 1794, and *Hylton v. U.S.* in 1796). Had any of these four instances found the Court invalidating the federal law in question, *Marbury v. Madison* in 1803 would have had much less historical significance.
18. Alexander Hamilton, *The Federalist No. 78*, Edited, with Introduction and Historical Commentary, by J. R. Pole (Indianapolis, IN: Hackett, 2005), p. 415.
19. Jesse Choper, "The Supreme Court and the Political Branches: Democratic Theory and Practice," *University of Pennsylvania Law Review 122* (1974), 848.
20. The other three instances in which a constitutional amendment overruled a Court decision are the Fourteenth Amendment, ratified in 1868, which overruled *Dred Scott v. Sandford* and made blacks citizens of the United States; the Sixteenth Amendment, ratified in 1913, which overruled *Pollack v. Farmers' Loan & Trust* and authorized passage of a federal income tax; and the Twenty-Sixth Amendment, adopted in 1971, which overruled *Oregon v. Mitchell* and guaranteed eighteen-year-olds the right to vote.
21. This important case suggests a serious conflict of interest that was never addressed adequately. As the outgoing Secretary of State, John Marshall had played an instrumental role in the Marbury appointment, but for some unexplained reason, he never actually delivered the commission to William Marbury. Under modern Court protocol, any justice sitting on the Supreme Court who had played as important a role as Marshall had in the case would have "recused" himself from participating in *Marbury v. Madison* in 1803. Undoubtedly, with John Marshall's strong assertion of judicial power and persuasive reasoning, *Marbury* would not have been the significant precedent that it was. But Marshall never disqualified himself from either hearing the case or assigning the opinion to himself, and his decision and reasoning in the case had a lasting impact on American law.
22. ames Madison, *The Federalist No. 51*, op. cit., p. 281.
23. In *Gray v. Sanders* 372 U.S. 368 (1963), the Court applied the "one person–one vote" principle to invalidate a Georgia county unit system of primary elections for statewide offices that greatly disfavored urban counties. In *Wesberry v. Sanders* 376 U.S.1 (1964), the Court extended the same principle to congressional districts in the U.S. House, arguing that Article I of the Constitution had the "plain objective of making equal representation for equal numbers of the people the fundamental goal for the House of Representatives." And finally, in *Reynolds v. Sims* 377 U.S. 533 (1964), the justices ruled that both houses of bicameral state legislatures must be based on the "one person–one vote" principle.
24. Herbert Wechsler, "Toward Neutral Principles of Constitutional Law," *Harvard Law Review 73* (1950), 15.
25. Arthur S. Miller and Ronald F. Howell, "The Myth of Neutrality in Constitutional Adjudication," *University of Chicago Law Review 27*, no. 4 (Summer 1960), 661.
26. Eugene V. Rostow, "The Democratic Character of Judicial Review," *Harvard Law Review 66* (1952), 195.

CHAPTER 5

ENDNOTES

1. James Bryce, *The American Commonwealth*, Abridged ed. (New York: Macmillan, 1917), p. 14.
2. See Arthur M. Schlesinger, Jr., *The Imperial Presidency* (Boston: Houghton Mifflin, 1973); Nathan Glazer, "Toward An Imperial Judiciary," *The Public Interest* (1975), 104–123.
3. See C. Herman Pritchett, *The Federal System in Constitutional Law* (Englewood Cliffs, NJ: Prentice-Hall, 1978).
4. James Madison, *The Federalist No. 37*, Edited, with Introduction and Historical Commentary by J. R. Pole (Indianapolis, IN: Hackett, 2005), p. 193.
5. Ibid., p. 195.
6. From *The Federalist Papers* (New York: New American Library, 1961), at 308.
7. Richard Pious, *The American Presidency* (New York: Basic Books, 1978).
8. Harry A. Bailey, Jr., and Jay M. Shafritz, eds., *The American Presidency: Historical and Contemporary Perspectives* (Chicago: Dorsey Press, 1988), p. vii.
9. John C. Hamilton, *Works of Alexander Hamilton* (New York: C.S. Francis and Co., 1851).

10. Phillip R. Fondall, ed., *Letters and Other Writings of James Madison* (Philadelphia: J. P. Lippincott, 1865), p. 621.
11. William Howard Taft, *Our Chief Magistrate and His Powers* (New York: Columbia University, 1916), pp. 139–140.
12. Theodore Roosevelt, *Autobiography* (New York: Macmillan, 1913), p. 389.
13. William Safire, *The New Language of Politics* (New York: Collier Books, 1972), pp. 79–80.
14. Laurence H. Tribe, *American Constitutional Law* (Mineola, NY: Foundation Press, 1978), p. 157.
15. Harry S. Truman, *Years of Trial and Hope* (New York: Signet, 1956), p. 535.
16. See Clement Fatovic, "Constitutionalism and Presidential Prerogative: Jeffersonian and Hamiltonian Perspectives," *American Journal of Political Science 48*, no. 3 (July 2004), 429–444.
17. "Vetoes by President George W. Bush," *www.senate.gov/reference/Legislation/Vetoes/BushGW.htm*.
18. George Edwards and Stephen Wayne, *Presidential Leadership*, 8th ed. (Boston: Wadsworth, 2010), p. 344.
19. For a comparison of treaties and executive agreement statistics, see Lyn Ragsdale, *Vital Statistics on the Presidency*, 3rd ed. (Washington, DC: Congressional Quarterly Press, 2009), pp. 447–460.
20. Quoted in Anthony Lewis, "An Ingenious Structure," *New York Times Magazine*, September 13, 1987, p. 41.
21. William Safire, "Tug of War," *New York Times Magazine*, September 13, 1987, p. 66.
22. Quoted from *New York Times*, April 21, 1988, p. A1.
23. Julie Johnson, "President Signs Law to Redress Wartime Wrong," *New York Times*, August 11, 1988, pp. A1, 8.
24. In the Nixon administration, both the *New York Times v. United States* (1971), to be covered in Chapter 16 on freedom of the press, and *United States v. United States District Court* (1972) found the Supreme Court finding against the federal government in its claim that extraordinary powers were warranted to protect national security. During the administration of Jimmy Carter in the late 1970s, the Court ruled in *United States v. The Progressive, Inc.* (1979) that a free press should not be enjoined from publishing an article on building a tactical nuclear device.
25. Arthur M. Schlesinger, Jr., *The Imperial Presidency* (Boston: Houghton Mifflin, 1973).
26 Richard E. Neustadt, "The Weakening White House," *British Journal of Political Science 31* (2001), 1–11.
27. Michael Beschloss, "The End of the Imperial Presidency," *New York Times*, December 18, 2000, Op-Ed.
28. Elisabeth Bumiller and David E. Sanger, "Bush, As Terror Inquiry Swirls, Seeks Cabinet Post on Security," *New York Times*, June 7, 2002.
29. Michael R. Gordon, "U.S. Weighs Fewer Troops After 2014 in Afghanistan," *New York Times*, January 5, 2013.
30. Linda Greenhouse, "Justices Face Decision on Accepting 9/11 Cases," *New York Times*, November 3, 2003, pp. A1, A15.
31. Howard Ball, *Bush, the Detainees, and the Constitution: The Battle over Presidential Power in the War on Terror* (Lawrence: University Press of Kansas, 2007), p. 184.
32. The White House, "President Bush Signs Military Commissions Act of 2006," *www.whitehouse.gov/news/releases/2006/10/print/20061017-1.html*.
33. Charles Babington and Jonathan Weisman, "Senate Approves Detainee Bill Backed by Bush," *Washington Post*, September 29, 2006, p. A1.
34. "Military Commissions Act of 2006--Turning Bad Policy into Bad Law," *http://web.amnesty.org/library/print/ENGAMR511542006/*.

CHAPTER 6

ENDNOTES

1. Roger H. Davidson, Walter J. Oleszek, and Frances E. Lee, *Congress and Its Members* 12th ed. (Washington: Congressional Quarterly Press, 2010), pp. 126–127.
2. Woodrow Wilson, *Congressional Government* (Boston: Houghton Mifflin, 1885), p. 303.
3. Walter Lippman, *Public Opinion* (New York: Harcourt, Brace, 1922), p. 289.
4. For a recent commentary on this so-called "RIP" syndrome and "political combat by other means," see Theodore J. Lowi and Benjamin Ginsberg, *Democrats Return to Power: Politics and Policy in the Clinton Era* (New York: W. W. Norton, 1994), pp. 33ff.
5. *Federalist #65*, original emphasis.
6. Alexander Hamilton, *The Federalist Papers*, p. 423.
7. To emphasize that impeachment and conviction do not necessarily bar the individual from high political office, Alcee Hastings is currently a member of the House of Representatives, representing the 20th congressional district from Florida.
8. The Watergate scandal is generally credited with accelerating the passage of at least four prominent federal laws: the War Powers Resolution (1973); the Budget Impoundment and Control Act (1974); the Special Prosecutor Law (1978); and the Foreign Intelligence Surveillance Act (1978). All four of these laws sought to curtail presidential authority in war powers, budgetary policy, internal investigations, and intelligence gathering.
9. Jones claimed that on May 8, 1991, while working as an employee of the Arkansas Industrial Development Commission and attending a state-sponsored conference at the Excelsior Hotel in Little Rock, she had been summoned to a room in the hotel where Clinton had made improper sexual advances toward her. She asserted in her suit that she resisted his advances and left the room but that her refusal to comply with his requests eventually resulted in work difficulties, a change in her job duties, and the creation of a hostile working environment.
10. Gerald R. Ford and Jimmy Carter, "A Time to Heal Our Nation," *New York Times*, December 22, 1998, p. A31.
11. Davidson, Oleszek, and Lee, pp. 343–344.
12. Jay M. Shafritz, E. W. Russell, and Christopher Borick, *Introducing Public Administration*, 6th ed. (New York: Pearson, 2009), pp. 430–432.

CHAPTER 7

ENDNOTES

1. Alexis de Tocqueville, *Democracy in America*, Vol. I (New York: Vintage Books, 1945), p. 173.
2. The comparison of federal and unitary systems requires some awareness of the difference between formal and actual distribution of power. See Gabriel A. Almond and G. Bingham Powell, eds., *Comparative Politics Today: A World View*, 3rd ed. (Boston: Little, Brown, 1984), pp. 88–89.
3. For a discussion of the Indian pattern, see Robert L. Hardgrave and Stanley A. Kochanek, *India: Government and Politics in a Developing Nation*, 5th ed. (New York: Harcourt Brace Jovanovich, 1993).
4. The "logical" approach to Constitutional interpretation is discussed in Harold J. Spaeth, *An Introduction to Supreme Court Decision-Making*, Revised ed. (New York: Chandler, 1972), pp. 49–52.
5. Alfred H. Kelly, Winfred A. Harbison, and Herman Belz, *The American Constitution: Its Origins and Development*, 6th ed. (New York: W.W. Norton, 1983), p. 140.
6. Forrest McDonald, *A Constitutional History of the United States* (New York: Franklin Watts, 1982), p. 97.
7. Allen Johnson, "Jefferson and His Colleagues," in Allen Johnson, ed., *The Chronicles of America States*, Vol. 9 (New Haven, CT: Yale University Press, 1921), p. 168.
8. "The Hartford Convention," in Thomas A. Bailey, ed., *The American Spirit: United States History as Seen by Contemporaries* (Boston: Heath, 1963), pp. 203–204.
9. "The Webster–Hayne Debate," in Bailey, pp. 246–249.
10. John C. Calhoun, *A Disquisition on Government and Selections from the Discourse*, (New York: The Liberal Arts Press, 1953), pp. 22–31. (Original work published 1853)
11. Woodrow Wilson, *A History of the American People*, Vol. IV (New York: Harper & Brothers, 1902), Appendix.
12. For an excellent treatment of the history of the federal–state relationship, see Deil S. Wright, "Federalism, Intergovernmental Relations, and Intergovernmental Management: Historical Reflections and Conceptual Comparisons," *Public Administration Review 50*, no. 2 (March–April 1990), 168–178.
13. Richard A. Brisbin, Jr. "The Reconstitution of American Federalism?: The Rehnquist Court and Federal–State Relations, 1991-1997," *Publius: The Journal of Federalism 28*, no. 1 (Winter 1998), 189–215, argues that the Rehnquist Court "has not initiated a sea change in American federalism." Brisbin characterizes the changes initiated by the Rehnquist Court as more than a "bump in the road," but he believes that the Court continues to maintain basic constitutional traditions regarding federalism. On the other hand, Susan Gluck Mezey, "The U.S. Supreme Court's Federalism Jurisprudence: *Alden v. Maine* and the Enhancement of State Sovereignty." *Publius: The Journal of Federalism 30*, nos. 1–2 (Winter/Spring 2000), 21–38, paints a very different picture. She believes that the Court has used the sovereign immunity doctrine to cast doubt on the federal government's power to provide relief for federally protected rights. She believes the Rehnquist Court has drastically altered the federal balance.
14. Total Outlays for Grants to State and Local Governments by Function, Agency, and Program: 1940-2014, Table 12.3; Office of Management and Budget, Historical Tables; www.whitehouse.gov/omb/budget/historicals

CHAPTER 8

ENDNOTES

1. See, for example, the treatment of Charles Beard in Chapter 3.
2. The Marshall Court consistently resisted changes in the creditor–debtor relationship, despite the fact that several states had begun in the early nineteenth century to legislate in the areas of bankruptcy and other forms of debtor relief. In *Sturges v. Crowninshield* (1819), the Marshall Court invalidated a New York bankruptcy law that was passed after the contractual obligations were established; but, with Marshall dissenting, in *Ogden v. Saunders* (1827), the Court upheld a bankruptcy statute already in effect before contractual obligations were created. The Marshall Court expanded the meaning of the Contract Clause in *Fletcher v. Peck* (1810) to include contracts in which the state was a party.
3. Benjamin F. Wright, Jr., *The Contract Clause and the Constitution* (Westport, CT: Greenwood Press, 1938), p. 62.
4. Wright, pp. 94–95.
5. Henry J. Abraham and Barbara A. Perry, *Freedom and the Court: Civil Rights and Liberties in the United States*, 8th ed. (New York: Oxford University Press, 2003), p. 95
6. Joseph B. James, *The Framing of the Fourteenth Amendment* (Urbana: University of Illinois Press, 1956), p. 197.
7. Felix Frankfurter, *The Commerce Clause Under Marshall, Taney and Waite* (Chapel Hill: University of North Carolina Press, 1937). Frankfurter considers the *Munn* case to have "laid the foundation for Congressional entry into fields of comprehensive regulation of economic enterprise," p. 83.
8. James, p. 199.
9. Frankfurter, pp. 66–67.
10. The Marshall view can be seen in court decisions upholding the regulation of telegraphs (*Pensacola Telegraph Company v. Western Union Telegraph Company* [1878]), railroads (*Wabash, St. Louis & Pacific Ry. Co. v. Illinois* [1886]), as well as radio, airplanes, and television.
11. Frankfurter, p. 19.
12. Ibid., p. 50.
13. See *Southern Pacific Company v. Arizona*, 325 U.S. 761 (1945).

14. The Commerce Clause also conflicts with efforts by states to protect their own economic interests. Several recent examples of state "economic protectionism" struck down by the U.S. Supreme Court include *Oregon Waste Systems, Inc. v. Oregon Department of Environmental Quality* (1994), in which the Court struck down a 1989 Oregon law that levied a surcharge of $2.25 per ton on all solid waste generated outside of the state and disposed of at an Oregon site, but only 85 cents a ton for "in-state" waste; *C & A Carbone, Inc. v. Town of Clarkstown, New York* (1994), striking down a town ordinance that required that all solid waste be disposed of in a town recycling center at the mandatory rate of $81 per ton. A private company had the capability of doing the job for around $70 per ton; *Associated Industries of Missouri v. Missouri Director of Revenue* (1994) struck down a state sales tax that allowed some counties to charge a higher rate for goods purchased outside the state; and *West Lynn Creamery, Inc. v. Commissioner of the Massachusetts Department of Food and Agriculture* (1994), struck down a Massachusetts law that paid subsidies only to Massachusetts milk producers.

    A 5–4 majority struck down Michigan and New York laws in *Granholm v. Heald* (2005) that allowed in-state wineries to sell directly to consumers but denied that right to out-of state wineries. The state laws were considered to be discriminatory against interstate commerce.
15. Earl W. Kintner, *An Antitrust Primer*, 2nd ed. (New York: Macmillan, 1973), p. 18, notes that anti-monopoly feelings ran so deeply in Congress that the Sherman Act passed with only one dissenting vote.
16. Edward S. Corwin, *The Commerce Power Versus States Rights* (Gloucester, MA: Peter Smith, 1962), pp. 152–153.
17. Kintner, p. 11, considers the "flow-of-commerce" ruling in *Swift* to be the first significant change to the narrow, late-nineteenth-century view of commerce.
18. A series of labor relations cases in 1938 and 1939 resulted in the Court's willingness to consider "potential" effects upon commerce as sufficient to justify regulation, it no longer being necessary to show a current of commerce or a significant volume of business. In these cases, the Court upheld NLRB orders governing a fruit-packing business moving only 37 percent of its products in interstate commerce (*Santa Cruz Fruit Packing Co. v. NLRB*), a power company that sold power only within a single state (*Consolidated Edison Co. v. NLRB*), and a garment-maker who sold his entire output within the state (*NLRB v. Fainblatt*). Quite clearly, while the current-of-commerce doctrine had laid the foundation for these changes, the commerce power had moved beyond it.
19. Including employees involved in the maintenance of a building in which others produce and sell clothing in interstate commerce [*A.B. Kirschbaum v. Walling* (1942)], a night watchman [*Walton v. Southern Package Corporation* (1944)], and elevator operators in an office building [*Borden Co. v. Borella* (1945)].
20. The Pure Food and Drug Act was upheld in *Hipolite Egg Co. v. United States* (1911), while the Mann Act was upheld in *Hoke v. United States* (1913). Along this line, the Court upheld a federal law prohibiting the interstate transportation of stolen cars [*Brooks v. United States,* (1925)] and one, popularly known as the "Lindberg Act," prohibiting the movement of kidnapped persons [*Gooch v. United States,* (1936)].
21. Stephen B. Wood, *Constitutional Politics in the Progressive Era: Child Labor and the Law* (Chicago: University of Chicago Press, 1968).
22. Richard A. Brisbin, Jr., "The Reconstitution of American Federalism?: The Rehnquist Court and Federal–State Relations, 1991–1997," *Publius: The Journal of Federalism 28*, no. 1 (Winter 1998), 205, notes that Justice Thomas, although isolated in this interpretation, "appears bent on reading congressional power to include only the powers contained in what he claims is the historical meaning of the Constitution's text."
23. R. Alton Lee, *A History of Regulatory Taxation* (Lexington: The University Press of Kentucky, 1973).
24. Lee, pp. 57–59. Despite broadened federal taxing and spending powers, certain limitations continue to be placed upon their use. In *Marchetti v. United States* (1968), the Court declared a federal occupational tax on gamblers to be an unconstitutional violation of the self-incrimination protections in the Fifth Amendment. In making the decision, the Court specifically noted that only constitutional prohibitions such as the protection against self-incrimination would justify the striking down of tax statutes. Federal tax laws that do not violate specific provisions of the Constitution are essentially beyond judicial scrutiny.

Chapter 9

Endnotes

1. See Paul Brest, "The Supreme Court—1975 Term: Foreword: In Defense of the Antidiscrimination Principle," *Harvard Law Review 90*, no. 1 (1976), 1–54.
2. Shelby Steele, *The Content of Our Character: A New Vision of Race in America* (New York: St. Martin's Press, 1990), p. 111.
3. See Owen M. Fiss, "Groups and the Equal Protection Clause," *Philosophy and Public Affairs* (1976), 107–177.
4. Don E. Fehrenbacher, *Slavery, Law, and Politics: The Dred Scott Case in Historical Perspective* (New York: Oxford University Press, 1981), p. 12.
5. Quoted in Staughton Lynd, *Class Conflict, Slavery, and the United States Constitution* (Westport, CT: Greenwood Press, 1980), p. 154.
6. Luther Martin, quoted in Derek Bell, *And We Are Not Saved: The Elusive Quest for Racial Justice* (New York: Basic Books, 1987), p. 35.
7. Quoted in Lynd, p. 159.
8. Herbert J. Storing, "Slavery and the Moral Foundations of the American Republic," in Robert Horwitz, ed., *The Moral Foundations of the American Republic* (Charlottesville: University Press of Virginia, 1977), p. 225.

9. Richard Kluger, *Simple Justice* (New York: Vintage Books, 1975), p. 626.
10. Black slaves weren't the only people affected by the federal government. Even free blacks were denied a number of things considered basic to equal citizenship, such as serving in the militia, becoming naturalized citizens, or receiving a passport for travel outside the United States.
11. *Strauder v. West Virginia*, 100 U.S. 303 (1880).
12. However, in the same opinion the Court recognized the legitimacy of limiting jury service to males.
13. Walter F. Murphy, James E. Fleming, & William F. Harris, II, *American Constitutional Interpretation* (Mineola, NY: Foundation Press, 1986), p. 744.
14. C. Vann Woodward, *The Strange Career of Jim Crow* (New York: Oxford University Press, 1966). In fact, Supreme Court Justice Bradley had been the deciding vote on the special commission that resolved the Hayes-Tilden deadlock.
15. *Pace v. Alabama*, 106 U.S. 583 (1883). For a general understanding of the Court's interpretation of the Equal Protection Clause, see Tussman & TenBroek, "The Equal Protection of the Laws," *California Law Review* 37 (1949), 341.
16. Some scholars have argued, by contrast, that Reconstruction Era congressional action on civil rights actually reflected the sentiments of more conservative Republicans and, as such, a more limited reading of the scope of the post–Civil War amendments is appropriate; see Earl Maltz, *Civil Rights, The Constitution, and Congress, 1863–1869* (Lawrence: University of Kansas Press, 1990).
17. Ironically, the Court had allowed the use of the Fourteenth Amendment to protect business corporations from state government regulation.
18. See the Court's ruling in *Corrigan v. Buckley*, 271 U.S. 323 (1926).
19. Five years later, in *Barrows v. Jackson* (1953), the Court extended its position to include civil suits brought by property owners in a restricted neighborhood to gain damages from another owner who sold his property to a black person in violation of the restrictive covenant. The Supreme Court said that a California court's order to a property owner to pay damages for failing to observe a racially restrictive covenant was also a form of state action violative of the Constitution.
20. In California, white homeowners revolted against state laws prohibiting such discrimination. Exercising their initiative power, California voters passed a state constitutional amendment in 1964 providing that the state could not deny the right of any person "to sell, lease or rent any part or all of his real property to such persons as he, in his absolute discretion, chooses." Known as Proposition 14, this amendment in effect repealed state laws providing for fair housing. In *Reitman v. Mulkey* (1967), the Supreme Court put an end to these kinds of actions by ruling that Proposition 14 was a form of state action violating the Fourteenth Amendment.
21. In addition to *Runyon v. McCrary*, see *Sullivan v. Little Hunting Park, Inc.*, 396 U.S. 229 (1969). The two recent cases involving Arabs and Jews are *St. Francis College v. Majid Gaidan Al-Khazraji* and *Shaare Tefila Congregation v. Cobb*, 107 S.Ct. 2019 (1987), respectively.
22. *Roberts v. Boston*, 59 Mass. 198, 5 Cush.198 (1849).
23. *Cumming v. Richmond County Board of Education* (1899), *Berea College v. Kentucky* (1908), and *Gong Lum v. Rice* (1927).
24. The most important of these early victories were *Missouri ex rel. Gaines v. Canada*, 305 U.S. 337 (1938), where the Court decided that the state of Missouri had to furnish Gaines, a black applicant to the state university law school, substantially equal legal education within the state's borders and could not offer to pay his tuition at an out-of-state law school that accepted blacks; and *McLaurin v. Oklahoma State Regents for Higher Education*, 339 U.S. 637 (1950), where the Court decided that to separate a black graduate student from his fellows within a state university was to violate his rights to equal protection.
25. The Court had invited parties in addition to the original litigants to file arguments in *Brown II*. Six states that were practicing school segregation filed separate briefs: Arkansas, Florida, Maryland, North Carolina, Oklahoma, and Texas. In addition, the federal government filed a separate brief that included its findings and recommendations about implementation of desegregation.
26. Quoted in Kluger, *Simple Justice*, p. 753.
27. In addition to the *Griffin*, *Green*, and *Alexander* cases cited in Brief 7.4, the Court's rulings in *Goss v. Board of Education*, 373 U.S. 683 (1963) and *Monroe v. Board of Commissions*, 391 U.S. 450 (1968) all make this point clear.
28. Quoted in Gerald N. Rosenberg, *The Hollow Hope*. Chicago: University of Chicago Press, 1991, p. 43.
29. Charles Clotfelter, in *After Brown: The Rise and Retreat of School Desegregation* (Princeton, NJ: Princeton University Press, 2004), beautifully documents changes in interracial contact in public schools over the past fifty years, in different regions and cities across the United States.
30. For example, in *Oklahoma City Schools v. Dowell* (1991) and *Freeman v. Pitts* (1992), the Court majority allowed federal judges to remove themselves from ongoing supervision of racial desegregation in districts that they believe to be in basic compliance with original court orders to desegregate, even though large numbers of students attended predominantly one-race schools. The majority of justices in both cases contended that as long as a district had eliminated the vestiges of past discrimination "to the extent practicable," it was neither possible nor desirable to have desegregation orders "operate in perpetuity." And in *Missouri v. Jenkins* (1995), the Supreme Court limited what a federal judge could do to advance extensive new desegregation solutions to combat the vestiges of *de jure* segregation. Building on a seven-year effort to

desegregate Kansas City schools, Federal District Judge Russell Jenkins authorized the implementation of an expensive magnet school program that would desegregate by drawing white suburban students, through various incentives, into urban Kansas City schools. The Supreme Court ruled that such a program went beyond the scope of federal judicial authority, usurping local control over education. In his concurring opinion, Justice Thomas foreshadowed the mood of the current Court majority, saying that although the justices "should never approve a state's efforts to deny students, because of their race, an equal opportunity for an education, [they] also should avoid using racial equality as a pretext for solving social problems that do not violate the Constitution."

31. The Court's decision in *Ricci v. DeStefano* (2009) raises the possibility that the disparate-impact requirements of Title VII may themselves be deemed a violation of the Equal Protection Clause. Justice Scalia's concurrence in a decision favoring white firefighters challenging the City of New Haven's throwing out the results of promotional examinations due to their disparate impact on minority firefighters, asked "Whether . . . the disparate-impact provisions of Title VII [are] consistent with the Constitution's guarantee of equal protection."

32. *Village of Arlington Heights v. Metropolitan Housing Development Corp.* (1977).

33. *Minor v. Happersett*, 21 Wall. 162 (1875).

34. *Lane v. Wilson*, 307 U.S. 268 (1939).

35. *Grovey v. Townsend*, 295 U.S. 45 (1935).

36. One exception to these rulings narrowing application of the Voting Rights Act came in *Quilter v. Voinovich* (1998), in which the justices upheld an Ohio redistricting plan that took race into consideration, "in conjunction with and not in predomination over other demographic data and traditional districting criteria." This consideration of race in congressional redistricting, the majority said, was in line with a legitimate state interest, and the resulting plan was reasonably related to that interest.

37. A more recent case from Texas, *League of United Latin American Citizens v. Perry* (2006), offers a similar ruling in favor of Republican Party efforts, under the direction of former House majority leader Tom DeLay, to redraw House districts in their favor. While the Court ruled that the plan diluted Latino voting strength in two West Texas congressional districts, it ruled that in another Dallas-area district, it was acceptable to redraw lines in favor of Republicans, even though this had the effect of diluting African-American influence.

CHAPTER 10

ENDNOTES

1. *Buck v. Bell*, 274 U.S. 200 (1927).
2. Gerald Gunther, "The Supreme Court, 1971 Term—Foreword: In Search of Evolving Doctrine on a Changing Court: A Model for a Newer Equal Protection," *Harvard Law Review* 86 (1972), 1.
3. Justice Rehnquist, in his dissenting opinion in *Sugarman v. Dougall*, 413 U.S. 634 (1973), stated that "it would hardly take extraordinary ingenuity for a lawyer to find 'insular and discrete' minorities at every turn of the road."
4. Quoted in *Affirmative Action to Open the Doors to Job Opportunity* (Washington, DC: Citizen's Commission on Civil Rights, 1984), p. 27.
5. In *Defunis v. Odegaard*, 416 U.S. 312 (1974), the Court ruled moot a claim by Mr. Defunis that an affirmative action program at the University of Washington discriminated against him (see further discussion in conjunction with the mootness doctrine in Chapter 4).
6. See, for example, *United Steelworkers v. Weber* (1979), *Fullilove v. Klutznick* (1980), *Sheet Metal Workers v. EEOC* (1986), *Firefighters v. Cleveland* (1986), and *United States v. Paradise* (1987).
7. See *Firefighters Local Union No. 1784 v. Stotts* (1984) and *Wygant v. Jackson Board of Education* (1986).
8. *Fullilove v. Klutznick* (1980).
9. Affirmative action plans involving women have also come to the federal courts for approval. In 1987, in its first gender-based affirmative action ruling, the Court upheld a government-sponsored affirmative action plan for women in the case of *Johnson v. Transportation Agency, Santa Clara County*, saying that a woman's gender could be taken into account in this county's promotion plan, especially given that there appeared to be a history of past discrimination against women in the particular job classification in question. The implications of the *Croson* and *Adarand* cases for gender-based affirmative action are not yet clear.
10. Feminists met at a women's-rights convention in Seneca Falls in 1848, culminating in the drafting of the Declaration of Sentiments, which follows the form of the Declaration of Independence: "We hold these truths to be self-evident: that all men and women are created equal. . . ."
11. Quoted in Judith Baer, *Equality Under the Constitution: Reclaiming the Fourteenth Amendment* (Ithaca, NY: Cornell University Press, 1983), p. 91.
12. Interestingly enough, a woman was able to run for president during the nineteenth century. Belva Lockwood garnered over four thousand votes as the National Equal Rights Party candidate in both 1884 and 1888. Although women were denied the right to vote, the Constitution has never prohibited women from becoming president.
13. Even the otherwise progressive Warren Court unanimously held constitutional—in *Hoyt v. Florida* (1961)—a jury selection scheme that excluded women, on the grounds that since "woman is still regarded as the center of home and family life, [w]e cannot say that it is constitutionally impermissible for a State, acting in pursuit of the general welfare, to conclude that a woman should be relieved from the civic duty of jury service unless she herself determines that such service is consistent with her own special responsibilities."

14. In 1972 the law was amended to cover educational institutions and state and local governments.
15. *Wimberly v. Labor and Industrial Relations Commission of Missouri*, 479 U.S. 511 (1987).
16. See Catharine A. MacKinnon, *Sexual Harassment of Working Women* (New Haven, CT: Yale University Press, 1979).
17. At the same time, the Court has set a highly restrictive standard for determining when a school district can be held liable under federal law for a teacher's sexual harassment of a student. In *Gebser v. Lago Vista Independent School District* (1998), the Court ruled that a student victim of a teacher's harassing behavior can only recover damages from the school district if a school official with authority to intervene knew of the situation and failed to stop the harassment.
18. The issues of how much control Congress has over the amending process and whether a state can rescind its original ratification of an amendment were both raised as a result of the Equal Rights Amendment battle. Although a federal district judge declared the Congressional attempt to extend the period for ratification unconstitutional and the state of Idaho's rescission valid (*Idaho v. Freeman*, 507 F. Supp. 706 [1981]), the Supreme Court vacated this ruling in *National Organization for Women v. Idaho*, 459 U.S. 809 (1982). The case challenging the ERA extension legislation came to the Supreme Court on appeal after the extension deadline had passed, and so the Court declared the entire controversy moot.
19. Kathleen M. Sullivan, "Constitutionalizing Women's Equality," *California Law Review* 90 (2002), 735.
20. For a comprehensive account of the struggle for and the final defeat of the ERA, see Jane Mansbridge, *Why We Lost the ERA* (Chicago: University of Chicago Press, 1986).
21. *In re Griffiths*, 413 U.S. 717 (1973).
22. *Sugarman v. Dougall* (1973).
23. *Nyquist v. Mauclet*, 432 U.S. 1 (1977).
24. *Foley v. Connelie*, 435 U.S. 291 (1978).
25. *Sugarman v. Dougall* (1973), dissenting opinion. Former Governor Pete Wilson of California even went so far as to call on Congress to change the Fourteenth Amendment, to prohibit the U.S.-born children of illegal aliens from receiving state welfare benefits and other "citizen" entitlements, a position that is reflected to a certain extent in current welfare policy.
26. Judith Baer, "The Burger Court and the Rights of the Handicapped," *Western Political Quarterly* 35 (1982), 357.
27. *Buck v. Bell* (1927).
28. In *Florence City School District Four v. Carter* (1993), the Court allowed the use of the Individuals with Disabilities Education Act to require the state to reimburse parents who withdrew their learning-disabled child from the public schools for the cost of providing "appropriate education" in a private school.
29. In fact, one of the legal battlegrounds over the Americans with Disabilities Act (ADA) has been the scope of conditions covered by the law. In its first substantive decision regarding the ADA, the Supreme Court ruled—in *Bragdon v. Abbott* (1998)—that the law covered a woman with asymptomatic human immunodeficiency virus infection. The Court's analysis in this case suggests that the ADA may also cover conditions—including infertility, insulin-controlled diabetes, cancer in full remission—that lower courts have regarded as beyond the law's scope.
30. So far, no federal court has accepted the sex discrimination claim. However, a plurality of the Hawaii Supreme Court has held that a statute denying marriage to same-sex couples discriminated on the basis of sex and was therefore subject to strict scrutiny under the state's equal rights amendment; see *Baehr v. Lewin*, 1993 Hawaii Lexis 26.
31. Ralph K. Winter, "Poverty, Economic Equality, and the Equal Protection Clause," in *Contemporary Debates on Civil Liberties*, eds. Glenn A. Phelps and Robert A. Poirier (Lexington, MA: Heath, 1985), p. 221.
32. *McDonald v. Board of Election*, 394 U.S. 802 (1969).
33. in *James v. Valtierra* (1971) and *Lindsey v. Normet* (1972).
34. Powell was not entirely correct. In the past fifteen years, the courts in a number of states, *including Texas*, have invalidated unequal public school funding on the grounds that they violated provisions of the *state* (rather than the federal) constitution.
35. See Douglas S. Reed, *On Equal Terms: The Constitutional Politics of Educational Opportunity* (Princeton, NJ: Princeton University Press, 2001).
36. Most recently, in *M.L.B. v. S.L.J.* (1997), the Court affirmed this position and its decision in the *Griffin* case, ruling that the state of Mississippi could not condition a woman's appeal of a termination of her parental rights on her ability to prepay court record fees of over $2,000.
37. *San Antonio School District v. Rodriguez* (1973).
38. For example, the Court more recently turned aside a poor family's challenge of a North Dakota school district policy requiring parents to pay for their children's bus transportation to and from school. In *Kadrmas v. Dickinson Public Schools* (1988), the Supreme Court used the *Rodriguez* precedent to uphold the school district's policy. Justice O'Connor's opinion for a five-justice majority continued to deny that "statutes having different effects on the wealthy and the poor should on that account alone be subjected to strict equal protection scrutiny." O'Connor ruled that it was "manifestly rational" for North Dakota to allow local school boards to charge user fees for school bus service.
39. Tribe, *American Constitutional Law* (Mineola, NY: Foundation Press, 1988), p. 1136.
40. See, e.g., Tribe, "Comment: *Erog v. Hsub* and its Disguises: Freeing *Bush v. Gore* from its Hall of Mirrors," *Harvard Law Review* 115 (2001), 170.
41. *Craig v. Boren* (1976), Stevens, J., concurring opinion.
42. *Trimble v. Gordon* (1977), Rehnquist, J., dissenting opinion.

CHAPTER 11

ENDNOTES

1. Robert Allen Rutland, *The Birth of the Bill of Rights* (New York: Collier Books, 1962), p. 217.
2. Ibid., p. 218.
3. Edward Dumbauld, *The Bill of Rights and What It Means Today* (Norman: University of Oklahoma Press, 1957), p. 41.
4. Richard C. Cortner, *The Supreme Court and The Second Bill of Rights: The Fourteenth Amendment and the Nationalization of Civil Liberties* (Madison: University of Wisconsin Press, 1981), p. 5.
5. Abraham, *Freedom*, p. 41.
6. *Maxwell v. Dow*, 176 U.S. 581, 601 (1900).
7. Cortner, *op. cit.*, pp. 20–21.
8. *Santa Clara County v. Southern Pacific Railroad Company*, 118 U.S. 394 (1886).
9. In *Grosjean v. American Press Co.*, 297 U.S. 233, 244 (1936), Justice Sutherland stated that the freedoms of speech and press had been held to be guarantees of the Due Process Clause in "a series of decisions of this court, beginning with *Gitlow v. New York* . . . and ending with *Near v. Minnesota* . . ."
10. Charles Fairman, "'Legislature History,' and the Constitutional Limits on State Authority." *University of Chicago Law Review* 1 (1954).
11. Several influential sources include J. B. James, *The Framing of the Fourteenth Amendment* (Urbana: University of Illinois Press, 1956): Horace Flack, *The Adoption of the Fourteenth Amendment* (Baltimore: Johns Hopkins University Press, 1908); and Raoul Berger, *Government by Judiciary: The Transformation of the Fourteenth Amendment* (Cambridge, MA: Harvard University Press, 1977).
12. "Federal Farmer No. 16, January 20, 1788," in Philip B. Kurland and Ralph Lerner, eds., *The Founders' Constitution* (Chicago: University of Chicago Press, 1987), Vol. V, p. 399.
13. James Madison, "Speech Before the House of Representatives, June 8, 1789," in Kurland and Lerner, *The Founders' Constitution*, Vol. V, p. 399.
14. *Shapiro v. Thompson* (1969).
15. See John Hart Ely, *Democracy and Distrust* (Cambridge, MA: Harvard University Press, 1980).
16. *Trop v. Dulles*, 356 U.S. 86 (1958).
17. See Justice White's dissenting opinion in *Moore v. East Cleveland*, 431 U.S. 494 (1977).
18. However, the Court did allow fifty-day residency requirements, in *Marston v. Lewis*, 410 U.S. 679 (1973), on the grounds that such a period served the state's important interest in accurate voter lists.
19. See *Lubin v. Panish*, 415 U.S. 709 (1974), and *Anderson v. Celebr ezze* (1983) for two examples.
20. *Kramer v. Union Free School District No. 15* (1969).
21. See *Memorial Hospital v. Maricopa County*, 415 U.S. 250 (1974).
22. See *Sosna v. Iowa*, 419 U.S. 393 (1975), residency requirement for divorce; *Martinez v. Bynum*, 461 U.S. 321 (1983), residency restrictions on attending public schools; *Vlandis v. Kline*, 412 U.S. 441 (1973), residency requirement for receipt of in-state tuition benefits at state colleges. On the subject of restrictions of foreign travel, see *Haig v. Agee* (1981) and *Regan v. Wald* (1984).
23. Louis D. Brandeis and Samuel D. Warren, "The Right to Privacy," *Harvard Law Review* 4 (1890), 193.
24. The same Connecticut statute had been challenged in two previous instances, in *Tileston v. Ullman*, 318 U.S. 44 (1943) and *Poe v. Ullman*, 367 U.S. 497 (1961). In *Poe v. Ullman*, the Court invoked the ripeness doctrine (see Chapter 4) and refused to review the law upon a challenge by doctors and their patients on the grounds that it had not been enforced for nearly a century.
25. The state of Texas asked the Court to declare the case moot, on the grounds that Ms. Roe's claim for access to an abortion was moot by the time the Court heard the case four years later. But the Court agreed to hear the case, largely on the grounds that this was a condition (pregnancy) that could recur and present Ms. Roe with the same dilemma.
26. In the early years following *Roe*, the Court even expanded the scope of the decision in one instance. In *Planned Parenthood of Central Missouri v. Danforth* (1976), the Court ruled that states could not require a married woman to obtain her husband's consent before attaining an abortion, nor could they require parental consent as a requirement for unmarried minors seeking an abortion. On the former question of spousal consent, Justice Blackmun's majority opinion argued that "since the state cannot [prohibit] abortion during the first stage [of pregnancy], the State cannot delegate authority to any particular person, even the spouse, to prevent abortion during that same period." Despite the husband's "deep and proper concern and interest in his wife's pregnancy . . . [the woman] is the more directly and immediately affected by the pregnancy [and], as between the two, the balance weighs in her favor." On the more sensitive issue of parental consent for a minor's abortion, Blackmun stated that "any independent interest the parent may have in the termination of the minor daughter's pregnancy is no more weighty than the right of privacy of the competent minor mature enough to have become pregnant."
27. Meanwhile, the Supreme Court decided, beginning one year after *Webster*, to support parental notification requirements for minors seeking abortions, in the cases of *Hodgson v. Minnesota* (1990), *Ohio v. Akron Center for Reproductive Health* (1990), and *Lambert v. Wicklund* (1997). These decisions overrode the earlier majority opinion in the *Danforth* case.
28. The states that have express protections of a right to privacy in their state constitutions are Alaska, Arizona, California, Florida, Hawaii, Illinois, Louisiana, Montana, South Carolina, and Washington.

CHAPTER 12

ENDNOTES

1. Fred E. Inbau, "Law Enforcement, The Courts, and Individual Civil Liberties," in Yale Kamisar, Fred E. Inbau, and Thurman Arnold, eds., *Criminal Justice in Our Time* (Charlottesville: University Press of Virginia, 1965), p. 134.
2. Federal Bureau of Investigation, *Crime Summary – Crime in the United States, 2010,* Department of Justice. www.fbi.gov/about-us/cjis/ucr/crime-in-the-u.s/2010/crime-in-the-u.s.-2010/index-page.
3. Robert Allen Rutland, *The Birth of the Bill of Rights* (New York: Collier Books, 1962), p. 25.
4. Glenn A. Phelps and Robert A. Poirier, eds., *Contemporary Debates on Civil Liberties: Enduring Constitutional Questions* (Lexington, MA: Heath, 1985), p. 123.
5. A defense of the exclusionary rule can be found in Timothy Lynch, "In Defense of the Exclusionary Rule," *Cato Policy Analysis* 319 (October 1, 1998). www.cato.org.
6. Chief Justice Burger stated perhaps his most ambitious critique of the exclusionary rule while dissenting in the case of *Bivens v. Six Unknown Named Agents of the Federal Bureau of Narcotics* (1971). The six agents unlawfully and without a warrant broke into Bivens's apartment, arrested and shackled him, searched the apartment, and took him to their headquarters for questioning. Bivens sought $15,000 in damages from each agent, as compensation for the violation of his Fourth Amendment rights, and the Court majority held that he was entitled to the damages. In dissent, the Chief Justice noted that *Bivens* illustrated the problems with the exclusionary rule, and he then proposed a system that would compensate victims of police wrongdoing without necessarily excluding the evidence obtained in the process of an illegal search and seizure.
7. Since *Katz*, the Supreme Court has reviewed several electronic search and seizure cases (see Brief 10.6). In *United States v. United States District Court for Eastern District of Michigan* (1972), the Court rejected the government's contention that domestic aspects of national security were exempt from the provisions of the Omnibus Crime Control and Safe Streets Act of 1968. Title III of the act authorized the attorney general to request wiretaps for specific listed crimes. This case involved numerous, nonjudicially approved wiretaps undertaken to gather information concerning the bombing of a CIA office. Speaking for the Court, Justice Lewis Powell swept aside the government's claims that prior judicial approval was not required for national security investigations. However, Powell's opinion limited itself to domestic aspects of national security, leaving open the matter of surveillance against foreign powers or their agents.
8. Charles F. Williams, "Return of the Fourth Amendment," *Preview of United States Supreme Court Cases,* Issue 8 (August 2, 2001), 442–444.
9. In *Camara v. Municipal Court* (1967), the Court overturned a section of the San Francisco Housing Code, which provided for warrantless inspections of buildings by authorized employees of city departments. Justice White's majority opinion noted that *Frank v. Maryland*, 359 U.S. 360 (1959), which allowed administrative inspection requirements without warrants, had become outmoded. In a companion case, *See v. Seattle*, the Court broadened the requirement of a warrant to inspect business and commercial properties.

   Several decisions upholding warrantless inspections followed shortly after the *Camara* and *See* rulings. In *Colonnade Catering Corp. v. United States* (1970), the Court held that an establishment that had a liquor license could be searched by an inspector without a warrant. The Court's ruling was based heavily upon the long history of government regulation of the liquor industry. Two years later, in *United States v. Biswell* (1972), the Court upheld a warrantless search by a treasury agent of a licensed gun dealer's premises. Such inspections, said the Court, are necessary to support governmental efforts at preventing violent crime and regulating firearms traffic.

CHAPTER 13

ENDNOTES

1. It should be noted that the double jeopardy clause does not prevent different governments (national and state) from trying a person for the same criminal activities. If a person violates both state and federal laws, he or she may be tried by both jurisdictions. Should a trial in one jurisdiction end in acquittal, the person may still be tried in the other. However, the Court held in *Waller v. Florida* (1970) that the relationship between a state and its subdivisions is not analogous to the relationship that exists between a state and the federal government. Because local subdivisions owe their existence to the state, they are considered to be part of a single government.

   One area of controversy relating to double jeopardy concerns the theory of **collateral estoppel**, or the so-called "single frolic" argument found in *Ashe v. Swenson* (1970). Bob Fred Ashe had been acquitted of robbing one of six poker players, primarily because of problems in identification. Authorities later tried Ashe for robbing another one of the same six players, and this time he was convicted. The Court set aside Ashe's conviction by considering the robbery of the poker players to be a single transaction, and since he had already been acquitted of robbing one of the victims, he could not be prosecuted again.
2. Ann Fagan Ginger, *The Law, The Supreme Court and The People's Rights* (Woodbury, NY: Barron's, 1977), p. 283.
3. *Ibid.*, p. 284.
4. In other decisions, the Court has clarified some aspects of the speedy trial. On several occasions the Court has

held that the speedy trial requirement applies only from the time of a person's indictment (see *United States v. Lovasco*, 1977). Of course, considerable delays in a trial are acceptable when they are requested by the counsel for the accused, and the many procedural safeguards built into our criminal justice system virtually guarantee that delays are inevitable.

5. David W. Neubauer, *Judicial Process: Law, Courts, and Politics in the United States* (Pacific Grove, CA: Brooks-Cole, 1991), pp. 308–309.
6. David J. Bodenhamer, *Fair Trial: Rights of the Accused in American History* (New York: Oxford University Press, 1992), p. 16.
7. Harry P. Stumpf, *American Judicial Politics* (San Diego, CA: Harcourt Brace Jovanovich, 1988), p. 348.
8. *Powers v. Ohio* (1991) prohibited peremptory challenges against racial groups *different* from the race of the defendant, while later cases have prohibited racially discriminatory strikes in criminal cases and race-based strikes in a civil action.
9. The Court reversed a conviction resulting from the state's refusal to allow its chief witness, a juvenile delinquent on probation for burglary, to be cross-examined (*Davis v. Alaska* [1974]); it refused to allow the use of a co-defendant's confession as evidence when the co-defendant refused to take the stand (*Burton v. United States* [1968]); yet, the Court ruled that the right to confront witnesses may be lost if the defendant engages in disruptive behavior that will not allow the trial to continue without interruption (*Illinois v. Allen* [1970]) or if the defendant is voluntarily absent from the proceedings (*Taylor v. United States* [1973]).
10. Political scientist Andrea Bonnicksen has examined the Court's decisions concerning appointed counsel, and argues that the Court has insisted upon counsel at "critical" stages of the accusatory process, including custodial interrogation, post-indictment lineup, and preliminary hearing; Andrea Bonnicksen, *Civil Rights and Liberties: Principles of Interpretation* (Palo Alto, CA: Mayfield Publishing, 1982), p. 248.
11. Alan Raphael, "Criminal Procedure: From the Right to an Attorney to the Right to a Jury," *Preview of United States Supreme Court Cases*, American Bar Association, no. 8 (July 29, 2002).
12. Pierce and Radelet, *Santa Clara Law Review*, 2005.
13. "National Polls," DPIC, *www.deathpenaltyinfo.org*.
14. Adam Liptak, "New Challenge for Courts: How to Define Retardation," *New York Times*, March 14, 2004, p. 12.
15. Henry J. Friendly, "Some Kind of Hearing," *University of Pennsylvania Law Review* 123 (1975), 1267.
16. Ginger, *op. cit.*, p. 367.
17. Alexandra Marks, "States Rethink Trying Juveniles as Adults," *Christian Science Monitor*, March 22, 2007.
18. The 1997 ruling in *Young v. Harper* applied the *Morrissey* precedent to Oklahoma's preparole conditional supervision program.
19. Roy Walmsley, *World Prison Population List*, 9th ed. International Centre for Prison Studies, 2011.

CHAPTER 14

ENDNOTES

1. *Smith v. California*, 361 U.S. 147 (1959), at 157.
2. *Konigsberg v. State Board of California*, 366 U.S. 36 (1961), at 61.
3. *West Virginia State Board of Education v. Barnette*, 319 U.S. 624 (1943), at 648.
4. *Tinker v. Des Moines Independent Community School District*, 393 U.S. 503 (1969), at 524.
5. Quoted in *Whitney v. California*, 274 U.S. 357 (1927), at 375.
6. The First Amendment Center, "State of the First Amendment 2010," *www.firstamendmentcenter.org*.
7. Although a few references in Chief Justice Charles Evans Hughes's opinion in *DeJonge v. Oregon* (1937) and the famous Footnote Four reference of Justice Harlan Fiske Stone in *U.S. v. Carolene Products* (1938), the first specific reference to the "preferred place" that such freedoms have in the American Constitution arises in Justice Wiley Rutledge's opinion in *Thomas v. Collins*, 323 U.S. 516 at 529–530 (1945).
8. For a history of free expression in ancient Greece and Rome, see Herbert J. Muller, *Freedom in the Ancient World* (New York: Harper & Row, 1961); Robert J. Bonner, *Aspects of Athenian Democray* (New York: Russell & Russell, 1967), reprint of the 1933 edition; and Charles Wirszubski, *"Libertas" as a Political Idea at Rome During the Late Republic and Early Principate* (Cambridge, MA: Cambridge University Press, 1950).
9. To understand better the evolving concept of liberty and free speech, see Leonard Levy, *Freedom of Speech and Press in Early American History: Legacy of Suppression* (New York: Harper & Row, 1963) and Frederick S. Siebert, *Freedom of the Press in England: 1476–1776* (Urbana: University of Illinois Press, 1952).
10. Levy, *Freedom of Speech and Press in Early American History*, 18.
11. These several justifications of free speech and a free press as advanced by Milton would be reiterated by prominent Supreme Court justices in the twentieth century in several famous espionage and sedition cases following World War I, such as the concurring opinion by Justice Brandeis in *Whitney v. California*, to be discussed later.
12. Alexander Meiklejohn, *Free Speech and Its Relation to Self-Government* (New York: Oxford University Press, 1965), reprint, 37.
13. This criticism by Emerson is especially valid with respect to the topic of obscenity, as is discussed in the next chapter. A long line of judicial precedents relating to what might be defined as "obscene" and how governmental authority might be justified in limiting access to pornography has generated an enormous amount of litigation and a rather tortured path of legislation and limitations upon what the public should have access to in a free society.
14. *Masses Publishing Co. v. Patten*, 244 F. 535 (S.D.N.Y. 1917)

15. One might be tempted to add a fifth period here, following the September 11, 2001, attacks on the United States and such legislation as the USA PATRIOT Act of 2001, Detainee Treatment Act of 2005, Military Commissions Act of 2006, and amendments to the Foreign Intelligence Surveillance Act in 2008. But these laws implicated other provisions of the Bill of Rights and thus will not be examined here.
16. *Frohwerk v. United States*, 249 U.S. 204 (1919) and *Debs v. United States*, 249 U.S. 211 (1919).
17. *Abrams v. United States*, 250 U.S. 616 at 623 (1919).
18. *American Communications Association v. Douds*, 339 U.S. 382 (1950).
19. See *Scales v. United States*, 367 U.S. 203 (1961); *Communist Party v. Subversive Activities Control Board*, 367 U.S. 1 (1961); *Aptheker v. Secretary of State*, 378 U.S. 500 (1964); *Communist Party v. Subversive Activities Control Board*, 382 U.S. 70 (1965).
20. *Stromberg v. California*, 283 U.S. 359 at 369 (1931).
21. *West Virginia State Board of Education v. Barnette*, 319 U.S. 624 at 632-33 (1943).
22. *Street v. New York*, 394 U.S. 576 (1969).
23. In *Bethel School District v. Frazier*, 478 U.S. 675 (1986), the Court upheld the suspension of a student who made a sexually suggestive speech at a school assembly, noting that "the constitutional rights of students in public school are not automatically coextensive with the rights of adults in other settings."
24. *Central Hudson Gas v. Public Service Commission*, 447 U.S. 557 (1980).
25. See *Glickman v. Wileman Brothers & Elliott, Inc.*, 521 U.S. 457 (1997).
26. See *Barnes v. Glen Theatre, Inc.*, 501 U.S. 560 (1991).
27. Kathleen M. Sullivan, "Two Conceptions of Freedom of Speech," *Harvard Law Review* 124(2010), 143–177.
28. Ibid., p. 176.
29. Samuel Issacharoff, "On Political Corruption," *Harvard Law Review* 124(2010), 118–142 (quote at p. 122).
30. Ibid., p. 122.
31. Cited in Louis Fisher, *American Constitutional Law: Constitutional Rights*, 6th ed. (Durham, NC: Carolina Academic Press, 2005), Volume 2, p. 1009.
32. "Electioneering communication" is defined by the BCRA as "any broadcast, cable, or satellite communication that refers to a clearly identified candidate for Federal office and is made within 30 days of a primary or 60 days of a general election."
33. Quoted in Adam Liptak, "Justices, 5–4, Reject Corporate Spending Limit," *New York Times*, January 22, 2010.
34. Since 2010, the Supreme Court has also moved to restrict what states can do to counter the effects of unequal and corporate campaign spending, consistent with the *Citizens United* decision. In *Arizona Free Enterprise Club's Freedom Club PAC v. Bennett* (2011), a 5–4 majority invalidated an Arizona campaign finance law that increased the amount of public funding available to candidates running against well-healed privately or independentlyfunded opponents. And in *American Tradition Partnership v. Bullock* (2012), the same majority struck down a century-old Montana law prohibiting corporations from using their funds to influence the outcome of state elections, reiterating their support for the free speech principles underlying the *Citizens United* decision.
35. Charles R. Lawrence, III, "If He Hollers Let Him Go: Regulating Speech on Campus," *Duke Law Journal* (1990), 452.
36. *United States v. Schwimmer*, 279 U.S. 644 (1929), at 654–655.

CHAPTER 15

ENDNOTES

1. *Pittsburgh Press Co. v. Pittsburgh Commission on Human Rights*, 413 U.S. 376 (1973), at 390.
2. Quoted in *Near v. Minnesota*, 283 U.S. 697 (1931), at 713.
3. Thomas Jefferson to Col. Edward Carrington, January 16, 1787; by the early 1800s, Jefferson was extremely frustrated with the working press.
4. Quoted in Julian Boyd, ed., *The Papers of Thomas Jefferson*, Vol. 2 (Princeton, NJ: Princeton University Press, 1950), p. 49.
5. Quoted in Thomas L. Tedford, *Freedom of Speech in the United States* (New York: Random House, 1985), p. 38.
6. Fred W. Friendly and Martha J. H. Elliott, *The Constitution: That Delicate Balance* (New York: Random House, 1984), p. 32.
7. Ibid., pp. 51–63.
8. Seldom has the federal court system disposed of a case as quickly as it did in the Pentagon Papers Case. Because of the gravity of the issue, the Court moved very quickly in this case once the government invoked national security as the justification for imposing prior restraint. On June 12–14, 1971, the *New York Times* (and on June 18, the *Washington Post*) began publishing excerpts from this top-secret Pentagon study of American involvement in the Vietnam War. Government attempts to obtain temporary restraining orders and permanent injunctions to stop further publication progressed through two district courts and two courts of appeal between June 15 and 23, with the appellate tribunals allowing publication by the *Post* and suspending publication by the *New York Times*. The Supreme Court consented to hear arguments in the *Times* case, scheduled for June 26, and four days later, a divided Court handed down its decision in a judgment that included one *per curiam* opinion, six concurring opinions, and three dissenting opinions. All of this activity transpired barely three weeks after the initial publication of the excerpts in the *New York Times*.

9. For an interesting account of some of the different ways in which the major commercial television networks in the United States covered selected crises in the late 1970s and early 1980s, see Dan Nimmo and James E. Coombs, *Nightly Horrors: Crisis Coverage in Television Network News* (Knoxville: University of Tennessee Press, 1985).
10. Several trials come to mind here, some dealing with very serious crimes, others not so serious. O. J. Simpson, a former professional football player, acquitted of murdering his wife and a companion in 1995; the Oklahoma City bombing defendants, Terry McVeigh and Terry Nichols, convicted of the crimes, in 1996;and the alleged Unabomber, Theodore J. Kaczynski, in 1996, were all very high-profile trials. Robert Blake was accused of killing his wife in 2002 but after a long detention and much publicity in his 2004 trial, he was eventually acquitted. The trials in 2005 involving Martha Stewart for alleged insider trading (for which she was convicted), and Michael Jackson for child molestation (for which he was acquitted) both raised questions about overexposure of both defendant and process. Finally, the March 2007 conviction of Lewis "Scooter" Libby, former top aide to Vice President Dick Cheney, on four counts of lying to investigators and misleading a grand jury in the Valerie Plame outing case, found President George W. Bush eventually commuting his 30-month prison sentence.
11. One of the more incriminating statements reported prior to the gag order being imposed was a purported statement by the defendant—a retarded neighbor of the murdered family members—to his father the morning after the murders that he had, in fact, killed the six people in question.
12. See William J. Brennan, Jr., "Address," in *Rutgers Law Review* 32 (1979), 173–183; and John Paul Stevens, "Some Thoughts About a General Rule," *Arizona Law Review* 21 (1979), 599–605.
13. "First Amendment Law Center," *www.firstamendmentcenter.org*; and"Texas Free Flow of Information Act,"*Austin American-Statesman*, May 13, 2009, *www.statesman.com/ffoia/content/ffoia/index.html*.
14. Unlike the first two cases, Caldwell's earlier conviction was reversed by a federal court of appeals, which held that the First Amendment protected the journalist from having to testify or appear before the grand jury. The Department of Justice appealed the *Caldwell* case to the U.S. Supreme Court.
15. Adam Liptak, "Reporter Jailed After Refusing to Name Source," *New York Times*, July 7, 2005, p. A1.
16. Spygate is described in several articles that appeared in the *New York Times* in 2003–05 that included the following: Douglas Jehl, "Iraq Arms Critic Reacts to Report on Wife," *New York Times*, August 8, 2003, p. A9; James Risen, "How Niger Uranium Story Defied Wide Skepticism," *New York Times*, July 14, 2004; Adam Liptak, "Court Declines to Rule on Case of Reporters' Refusal to Testify," *New York Times*, June 28, 2005, pp. A1, A16; _____, "Judge Gives Reporters One Week to Testify or Face Jail," *New York Times*, June 30, 2005, p. A12; _____, "Time Inc. to Yield Files on Sources, Relenting to U.S.," *New York Times*, July 1, 2005; _____, "Prosecutor in Leak Case Calls for Reporters' Jailing, *New York Times*, July 6, 2005; Richard W. Stevenson, "At White House, A Day of Silence on Role of Rove," *New York Times*, p. A14; Douglas Jehl, "Case of C.I.A. Officer's Leaked Identity Takes New Turn," *New York Times*, p. A19; Anne E. Kornblut, "Columnist Hints Who's Who Source That Led to Use of Officer's Name," *New York Times*, A10.
17. Quoted in Harry M. Clor, *Obscenity and Public Morality: Censorship in a Liberal Society* (Chicago: University of Chicago Press, 1969), p. 15.
18. Thomas Emerson, *The System of Freedom of Expression* (New York: Random House, 1970), p. 469.
19. Clor, *Obscenity and Public Morality*, p. 17.
20. 18 U.S. Code, Section 1461.
21. *United States v. One Book Entitled "Ulysses,"* 72 F. 2d 705 (2d Circ., 1934).
22. *Joseph Burstyn, Inc. v. Wilson*, 343 U.S. 495 (1952).
23. *Butler v. Michigan*, 352 U.S. 380, 383 (1957).
24. See C. Peter Magrath, "The Obscenity Cases: Grapes of Roth," in Phillip Kurland, ed., *The Supreme Court Reporter* (Chicago: University of Chicago Press, 1966), p. 7–77.
25. *Jacobellis v. Ohio*, 378 U.S. 84 (1964).
26. See *Redrup v.New York*, 386 U.S. 767 (1967) and *Ginsberg v. New York*, 390 U.S. 629 (1968).
27. Ibid., October 25, 1970, p. 71.
28. *Kaplan v. United States*, 413 U.S. 115 (1973); *United States v. 12,200-Foot Reels of Super 8mm Film*, 413 U.S. 123 (1973); and *United States v. Orito*, 413 U.S. 139 (1973).
29. See *Jenkins v. Georgia*, 418 U.S. 153 (1974), where the Court ruled that the popular film, *Carnal Knowledge*, starring Jack Nicholson and Ann-Margret, did not depict or describe "hard-core" sexual conduct that could be banned by local government merely because it contained scenes of frontal nudity
30. *Dial Information Services Corporation of New York v. Barr*, 502 U.S. 1072 (1992).
31. *Ginsberg v.New York*, 390 U.S. 629 (1968).
32. *Kaplan v. California*, 413 U.S. 115, (1973), at 120.
33. *Virginia v. American Booksellers Association*, 484 U.S. 383 (1988).
34. See *Gertz v. Robert Welch, Inc.*, 418 U.S. 323, 341 (1974).
35. See the Holmes dissent in *Abrams v. United States*, 250 U.S. 616 (1919), at 630; opinions by Black and Douglas in *Beauharnais v. Illinois*, 343 U.S. 250 (1952), at 272.
36. *Rosenblatt v. Baer*, 383 U.S. 75 (1966), at 85-86.
37. *Monitor Patriot Co. Roy*, 401 U.S. 265 (1971) and *Ocala Star-Banner Co. v. Dameron*, 401 U.S. 295 (1971).
38. Quoted in the *New York Times*, February 25, 1988, p. A-14.

CHAPTER 16

ENDNOTES

1. Alexis de Tocqueville, *Democracy in America* (New York: Random House, 1945), Vol. 1, p. 310.
2. See Edwin S. Gaustad, "Church, State, and Education in Historical Perspective," *Journal of Church and State 26*, no. 1 (Winter, 1984), 17–29; and for a more elaborate analysis, see Martin E. Marty, *A Nation of Behavers* (Chicago: University of Chicago Press, 1976).
3. Robert Bellah, "Civil Religion in America," *Daedalus 96* (1967), 3–4.
4. For a thorough discussion of some distinctions between the Puritans, Pilgrims, Anabaptists, and a succession of other religious colonizers in early America, see A. James Reichley, *Religion in American Public Life* (Washington, DC: Brookings Institution, 1985), Chapter 3.
5. Ibid., p. 86.
6. Quoted in *Basic Documents Relating to the First Amendment* (Washington, DC: Americans United for the Separation of Church and State, 1965).
7. Reichley notes that Congregationalists and Presbyterians comprised the largest followings, though neither was a majority, followed by Baptists, Episcopalians, Dutch and German Calvinist Reformed, Lutherans, Roman Catholics, and a smattering of Jews. There were also smaller groups of Quakers and Methodists, the latter of which would become the most prominent denomination during the early 19th century.
8. See Walter Berns, *The First Amendment and the Future of American Democracy* (New York: Basic Books, 1970); Paul Weber, "James Madison and Religious Equality: The Perfect Separation," *Review of Politics 44* (April 1982), 179–183; and A. James Reichley, *Religion in American Public Life* (Washington, DC: Brookings Institution, 1985).
9. James E. Wood, Jr., "Editorial: The Restoration of the Free Exercise Clause," *Journal of Church and State 35*, no. 4 (Autumn 1993), 718.
10. Ibid., p. 720.
11. During the mid-1980s, two U.S. District Court decisions [*Mozert v. Hawkins County Public Schools* (1986) and *Smith v. Board of School Commissioners, Mobile County, Alabama* (1987)] upheld claims by parents of schoolchildren that certain textbooks promoted "secular humanism" and therefore violated their religious beliefs. Both decisions were later overturned by U.S. Courts of Appeals.
12. In the early 1970s, with public opposition to the Vietnam War continuing under the Nixon administration, three other cases before the Supreme Court required the justices to clarify further conscientious objection status and how it qualified under the Free Exercise Clause. In *Welsh v. United States* (1970), the Court allowed CO status to an individual even though he denied that religion had anything to do with his opposition to military service. But two cases in 1971 indicated some limits to how far the Court would go in granting these exemptions. In *Gillette v. United States* (1971), the Court denied a draft exemption to a person who selectively opposed American involvement in the Vietnam War, refusing to allow individuals to make personal distinctions between the *types* of war in which they would participate. Finally, in *Clay v. United States* (1971), involving the famous heavyweight boxing champion Cassius Clay (his name had already been changed to the more recognizable Muhammed Ali), the Court awarded CO status to Clay after stating that three conditions had to be satisfied: individuals must show that they are conscientiously opposed to all wars; that the opposition is based on genuine religious training and belief; and that the objection is sincere.
13. For two very different views of this debate over the meaning of the Establishment Clause, see Leonard Levy, *The Establishment Clause: Religion and the First Amendment* (New York: Macmillan, 1986). Levy believes that the clause prohibits not only an established church or religion, but any aid, benefit, exercise, or law that attends to favor one religion over another, or religion over irreligion. He also argues that the Court was correct in applying the Establishment Clause to the states in 1947, regardless of the intentions of the Founding Fathers. For a very different view that the Establishment Clause should only prohibit an established church, and not a broad array of state actions that may accommodate religion without favor to one particular denomination, see A. James Reichley, *Religion in American Public Life* (Washington, DC: Brookings Institution, 1985). Reichley also maintains that the Establishment Clause should not have been applied to the states as of 1947, but only to the federal government, as the framers intended in 1791.
14. These theories, along with several others, are discussed extensively in Paul Kauper, *Religion and the Constitution* (Baton Rouge: Louisiana State University Press, 1964), Chapter 3; Richard E. Morgan, *The Supreme Court and Religion* (New York: Free Press, 1972), Chapter 3; Jesse C. Choper, "The Religion Clauses in the First Amendment: Reconciling the Conflict," *University of Pittsburgh Law Review 41*, no. 4 (Summer 1980); and Henry J. Abraham, *Freedom and the Court*, 6th ed. (New York: Oxford University Press, 1995), Chapter 6.
15. *Eugene Sand and Gravel v. Lowe*, 397 U.S. 591 (1970).
16. *Laird v. Anderson*, 409 U.S. 1071 (1972).
17. Gibney, "State Aid to Religious-Affiliated Schools," supra., p. 153.
18. *Cochran v. Louisiana State Board of Education*, 281 U.S. 370 (1930). Decades later, the Supreme Court would disallow the same sort of textbook aid law for parochial students. One possible explanation for this apparent

disparity is that the Cochran case came before the Establishment Clause had been applied to the states.

19. Derek H. Davis, "Editorial: The U.S. Supreme Court as Moral Physician: *Mitchell v. Helms* and the Constitutional Revolution to Reduce Restrictions on Governmental Aid to Religion,"*Journal of Church and State 43*, no. 2 (Spring 2001), 217.
20. Ibid., p. 227.
21. Henry J. Abraham, *The Judiciary: The Supreme Court in the Governmental Process*, 7thed. (Boston: Allyn and Bacon, 1987), p. 148.
22. Quoted in *New York Times*, June 20, 1987, p. 7
23. "*From Darwin to Dover: An Overview of Important Cases in the Evolution Debate*," Legal Backgrounder. The Pew Forum on Religion and Public Life, PewResearch Center, September 2005.

Glossary

ABSOLUTIST THEORY OF FREE SPEECH—The view that certain forms of expression are protected absolutely by the First Amendment from governmental encroachment, normally associated with such persons as Zechariah Chafee, Alexander Meiklejohn, and Justice Hugo Black.

ACTUAL MALICE—The principle, derived from *New York Times* v. *Sullivan* (1964) wherein one suing for libel damages must prove that statements were made with either the knowledge that they were false or demonstrated a reckless disregard for their truth or falsity.

AMICUS CURIAE—"Friend of the Court"; an interested third party who presents a brief to the Court on behalf of one or the other parties in a case.

APPEAL, WRIT OF—A writ identifying the type of case brought to the Supreme Court as a matter of right such as those coming from federal courts or highest state courts when state or federal laws are found to conflict with the Constitution or a treaty. Such cases are brought to the Court "on appeal."

APPELLATE JURISDICTION—The power and authority to review and, if necessary, to correct errors of law that may have occurred in the trial court. Most cases heard by the U.S. Supreme Court each year are reviewed under its appellate jurisdiction, which can be regulated by Congress according to Article III.

BAD-TENDENCY DOCTRINE—A test devised by the Supreme Court in *Abrams* v. *United States* (1920) to determine the permissible bounds of free speech; holds that First Amendment freedoms can be limited if there is a possibility that their exercise might lead to some harm or evil to government.

BILL OF ATTAINDER—The direct infliction of punishment by a legislature upon a person without benefit of a trial or other due process of law guarantees.

BILL OF RIGHTS—A list of guaranteed individual rights and liberties normally attached to a constitution. The first ten amendments to the U.S. Constitution constitute a bill of rights, protecting freedoms such as speech, press, religion, and jury trial.

CERTIFICATION, WRIT OF—A method of taking a case from an appellate court to the Supreme Court in which the lower court asks that some question or interpretation of law be certified or clarified.

CERTIORARI, WRIT OF—Literally, "to make sure"; a Writ issued at the discretion of the Supreme Court which orders the lower court to send the record of a case to the Court for review. This route is the normal procedure for appealing a case to the Supreme Court.

CHILD-BENEFIT RATIONALE—The view that government aid to parochial schools is justified and no violation of the Establishment Clause occurs if the aid is judged to be beneficial to the child and not the religious denomination.

CLEAR-AND-PRESENT DANGER TEST—A test devised by Justice Homes in *Schenck* v. *U.S.* (1919) to measure the permissible bounds of free speech; individual expression may be restrained only if it is likely to lead to imminent violence or serious, immediate harm to national security.

COLLATERAL ESTOPPEL—A concept, first developed in civil litigation, which holds that when an issue of ultimate fact (such as guilt or innocence) has been determined by a valid and final judgment (such as a jury verdict), that issue cannot again be litigated between the same parties in any future lawsuit; see *Ashe v. Swenson* (1970).

COMITY—A term from international law which refers to friendly and cooperative relations among independent states. This principle underlay the Articles of Confederation and accounted for the relatively calm dealings among the several states.

COMMUNITARIAN APPROACH TO GOVERNMENT—One of the twin foundations of American constitutionalism; a theory which stresses the public interest and community values over those of the individual. Government is seen as a positive force in achieving the common good.

CONCURRENT JURISDICTION—The type of jurisdiction which might find a case being heard in either a federal or state court, depending upon the nature of laws allegedly violated. Examples might include bank robbery or fraud cases.

CONCURRENT-SENTENCE DOCTRINE—The judicial doctrine which holds that a person serving concurrent sentences for different offenses should not be entitled to judicial review of one of the convictions, since even if he prevailed, he would still have to serve the sentences for the other charges; see *Benton v. Maryland* (1969).

CONFEDERATION—A loosely organized grouping of independent states or other units in which sovereignty is retained by the states. The result, as in the Articles of Confederation, is a weak central government.

CONSTITUTIONAL COURTS—Federal courts established under the authority of Article III, Section 1 of the Constitution; examples include the U.S. Supreme Court, the U.S. Courts of Appeal and the U.S. District Courts.

CONSTITUTIONALISM—The principle that government should be limited in its scope and functions and accountable for its actions, based on the underlying idea that unlimited governmental power can become corrupt and tyrannical.

CREATIVE FEDERALISM—The approach taken by the administration of President Lyndon B. Johnson in structuring national-state relations. In creative federalism, the role of the national government was expanded, and national grants-in-aid programs grew rapidly.

CRIMINAL SYNDICALISM—The doctrine that advocates that organized government should be overthrown by force or violence, including the assassination of the chief executive or any of the executive officials of government; laws prohibiting such criminal activity became prominent in the early twentieth century with the passage initially of a criminal anarchy law in New York State in 1902; see *Gitlow v. New York* (1925).

CURRENT (STREAM) OF COMMERCE—A judicial doctrine first stated by Justice Holmes in the *Swift* case which held that commerce was not a technical legal conception, but a concept drawn from the course of business. The doctrine played a large role in the expansion of the federal commerce power.

DEFAMATORY FALSEHOOD—Statements made about a private citizen which, if untrue and injurious to one's reputation, can be grounds for the awarding of damages; in recent years, states have been given more latitude to award libel damages for defamatory falsehoods. See *Gertz v. Welch* (1974).

DE JURE—"Of right"; lawful. Applied to questions of race, *de jure* segregation refers to separation of the races resulting from some past or present government action; see *Swann v. Charlotte-Mecklenburg Board of Education* (1971).

DIRECT-INDIRECT EFFECTS DOCTRINE—The principle, first noted by the Court in the *E. C. Knight* case, holding that only those activities with a direct effect upon commerce could be reached by Congress. In *Knight*, manufacturing was held to be only indirectly related to commerce.

DISPARATE-IMPACT LEGISLATION—Laws which on their face are fair but when applied have a disproportionate impact on one group (e.g., racial minorities or women); see *Personnel Administrator of Massachusetts v. Feeney* (1979).

DIVERSITY CASES—Lawsuits involving citizens of different states; the Constitution (Art. III, Sec. 2) confers jurisdiction in such cases on the federal courts, which generally apply relevant state law in resolving the issue. If the controversy involves more than $50,000, federal courts customarily settle the dispute.

DOUBLE JEOPARDY—From the Fifth Amendment, the idea that a person may not be tried by the same jurisdiction twice for the same offense.

DUAL FEDERALISM (DUAL SOVEREIGNTY)—The theory of federalism associated originally with Chief Justice Taney which held that the national and state governments each were sovereign in their respective spheres of authority.

EMINENT DOMAIN—The government's power to take property for public use by providing just compensation, as noted in the Fifth Amendment.

EQUAL ACCESS—A principle, endorsed by both the Supreme Court and the Congress, which says that public schools granting access to nonreligious groups for the purpose of meetings and activities must also provide the same access to religious groups. Equal access cannot be denied on the basis of the content of a group's speech; see *Westside Community Schools* v. *Mergens* (1990).

EXCLUSIONARY RULE—A Supreme Court-created rule in which illegally obtained materials may not be used as evidence to obtain a conviction at trial (see *Weeks* v. *United States*, [1914]). The rule has been limited by numerous exceptions.

EXCLUSIVE JURISDICTION—The type of jurisdiction in which only a particular court can hear a case or controversy that arises. Examples in which the Supreme Court has exclusive jurisdiction are cases involving ambassadors, U.S. consuls, or one of the fifty states.

EXECUTIVE AGREEMENT—An agreement with foreign heads of state concluded by presidents under their power as commander in chief and their general authority in foreign affairs. An executive agreement does not need senatorial approval.

EXECUTIVE PRIVILEGE—The right of executive officials to refuse to appear before or withhold information from a legislative committee or a court on the grounds that certain communications between a president and his advisors are protected from disclosure. Limited executive privilege was recognized in *U.S.* v. *Nixon* (1974).

EX POST FACTO LAWS—A retroactive criminal law that makes a particular act committed before the law was passed a crime, or one that retroactively reduces the proof necessary to convict an individual of a crime that occurred before the act's passage; see *Calder* v. *Bull* (1798).

EXPRESSION-ACTION THEORY OF FIRST AMENDMENT RIGHTS—The concept sometimes associated with Professor Thomas Emerson which maintains that individual expression should not be limited by government and is completely protected by the First Amendment, whereas some actions that threaten national security might be regulated by government.

EXTRADITION—In international relations, the returning by one nation to another of a person who has fled from justice. Article IV of the Constitution establishes a general obligation for a state to return a fugitive to another state, although this practice, sometimes called interstate rendition, cannot be compelled.

FEDERALISM—The method of organizing government in which a constitution divides powers between different levels of government, usually national and state governments.

FREEDOM OF CONTACT—A Supreme Court-created liberty holding that each person has the constitutional right to make his or her own economic arrangements, including wages, hours and working conditions. Found in the "liberties" of the Due Process Clauses, this freedom owed a strong debt to laissez-faire economic theory; see *Allgeyer* v. *Louisiana* (1897).

GAG (PROTECTIVE) ORDERS—Governmental restrictions upon what the press may write about a case prior to a trial; see *Nebraska Press Association* v. *Stuart* (1976).

HABEAS CORPUS, WRIT OF—An order to an official having custody of a person to produce the prisoner before a court to determine the legality of the prisoner's detention.

HATE SPEECH—Expression that insults, defames, or harasses individuals or groups based on characteristics such as race, color, ethnic origin, sex, religion, age, or sexual orientation; considered by many as not entitled to constitutional protection; has spawned the implementation of speech codes on several college campuses; see *R. A. V.* v. *St. Paul* (1992).

Horizontal Federalism—The relationships among state governments themselves. Article IV addresses state-to-state cooperation in matters of full faith and credit, privileges and immunities, and extradition.

Impeachment power—The power derived from Article I of the constitution, which gives Congress the power to remove, under certain conditions, various federal officials from office. More formally, impeachment is an accusation or indictment by the lower house of a legislative body which commits an accused civil official for trial in the upper house.

Implied powers—Powers not specifically delegated to the national government but which can reasonably be inferred. Implied powers stem from the Necessary and Proper Clause and were first given official recognition in *McCulloch v. Maryland* (1819).

Impoundment—The process whereby the president either defers spending or refuses to spend money appropriated by Congress; see *Train v. City of New York* (1975).

Incitement standard—In limiting speech and assembly rights, government must prove that the danger presented in provocative speech is real, not imagined, and that it is directed toward producing or inciting *immediate* illegal activity; see *Brandenburg v. Ohio* (1969).

Indictment—A formal charge by a grand jury which results in the person being bound over for trial. The Fifth Amendment requires a grand jury indictment for all federal crimes.

Individualist approach to government—One of the twin foundations of American constitutionalism; a theory based on the assumption that individuals and their interests take precedence over the larger community. Government exists to preserve and protect individual rights.

Information—An affidavit presented by a prosecutor to a judge in lieu of a grand jury indictment in some instances. An information affidavit cannot be used in the federal judicial process.

Interposition—A states' rights concept which holds that states may exercise their sovereignty to block, or interpose themselves between, an unjust national law and their own citizens. Interposition was asserted in Virginia and Kentucky Resolutions.

Judicial activism—The view that judges must, on occasion, overrule the actions of popularly-elected representatives if those actions are either "unwise" public policy or contrary to some specific provision of the Constitution.

Judicial nationalism—The judicial philosophy associated with Chief Justice John Marshall; articulated in several decisions advancing such principles as popular sovereignty, supremacy of the national government, an authoritative role for the Supreme Court to interpret the Constitution, and the need for flexibility in interpreting that document.

Judicial restraint—The view that judges should defer to the officials in the legislative and executive branches, because they are more politically responsible to the voters. This view also maintains that judges should not inject their own views of "good" or "wise" public policy into their decision making, but rather leave that determination to popularly-elected representatives of the people.

Judicial review—The power of courts to determine the validity of governmental acts. Though not specifically mentioned in the Constitution, this principle was firmly established in *Marbury v. Madison* (1803), and it has given the Supreme Court, in particular, vast power to determine whether legislative or executive acts conform to the Constitution.

Jurisdiction—Literally, "to say the law" authority vested in a court to hear and decide a case; the jurisdiction of federal courts is determined by the Constitution and the Congress.

Legislative courts—Federal courts established under the authority of Article I, Sec. 8, Clause 9, of the Constitution which gives Congress the power to "constitute Tribunals inferior to the supreme Court." Examples include the U.S. Court of Claims and the U.S. Court of International Trade.

Legislative veto—The rejection of an executive action or that of an administrative agency by either one or two houses of the legislature without the consent of the chief executive. The legislative veto was declared unconstitutional in *I.N.S. v. Chadha* (1983).

LEMON TEST—A concept dealing with controversies involving separation of church and state, wherein governmental policies that allocate public aid to parochial schools must demonstrate three elements: a valid secular purpose; a primary effect that neither advances nor inhibits religion; and no excessive entanglement between government and religion.

LIBEL—The defamation of character or reputation by the written word; libelous statements expose a person to hatred, contempt, ridicule, or injury to one's character by imputing to one a criminal act or harming one's trade or profession; see *New York Times* v. *Sullivan* (1964).

LINE-ITEM VETO—A power exercised by most state governors to veto portions of a bill and accept others. The president of the United States cannot exercise line-item veto authority (see *Clinton* v. *City of New York* [1998]).

MANDAMUS, WRIT OF—literally, "we command" a court order commanding a public official or government department to do something, particularly as it relates to the official duties of that position or office.

MIXED CONSTITUTION—A form of government dating back to ancient Greek and Roman times, whereby different institutions of government reflective of the different classes of society share governmental power; the form of government present in England at the time of the American Revolution.

MOOTNESS—The situation that arises when an individual brings a case or controversy to a court after the issue presented has already been settled elsewhere or by other means, thus making the matter "moot."

NEGATIVE FREEDOM—The absence of external restraint (e.g., law) on individual choice; associated with the individualist approach to government.

NEUTRAL PRINCIPLES—The ideal where judges search for the impartial and objective principles that transcend the immediate case under consideration and which might be useful for resolving future cases.

NEW EQUAL PROTECTION—The use of the Equal Protection clause of the Fourteenth Amendment to secure rights for persons other than the racial minorities for whom the clause was originally intended.

NOTICE—From the Sixth Amendment, the right of persons to be informed of charges and other legal matters for which they may be held accountable.

NULLIFICATION—John C. Calhoun's doctrine of extreme state sovereignty which holds that state governments can legally nullify unjust national laws. Tried by South Carolina in the early 1830s, nullification failed as a device for settling constitutional disputes.

ORIGINAL JURISDICTION—The jurisdiction of a court of first instance or a trial court where the legal action begins. The U.S. Supreme Court has original jurisdiction under Article III of the Constitution, which cannot be regulated by the Congress; see *Marbury* v. *Madison* (1803).

OVERBREATH DOCTRINE—governmental restrictions upon free expressions that are struck down because they sweep aside both speech and actions that are legal, as well as other actions that are illegal; see *Street* v. *New York* (1969).

PARALLEL-PLACE DOCTRINE—A test for evaluating the sincerity of a person's religious beliefs with reference to a claim of CO (conscientious objector) status; the Supreme Court held in *United States* v. *Seeger* (1965) that persons without formal or traditional religious training or belief could qualify as conscientious objectors if their beliefs occupy "a place parallel to that filled by the God of those admittedly qualifying for the exemption."

PARLIAMENTARY SYSTEM OF GOVERNMENT—A form of government in which executive and legislative powers are fused rather than separated. The British parliamentary system has served as a model for many other nations.

PAUPER'S PETITION—A request by an indigent or poor defendant that an appellate court review one's conviction; this has accounted for much of the increased workload of the Supreme Court in recent years.

PER CURIAM—"By the court" an opinion of the Supreme Court which is authored collectively by the justices.

POLICE POWERS—The obligation and authority of a government to protect the health, safety, morals, and welfare of its people. The national government has generally relied upon its commerce and taxation powers to police these matters.

POLITICAL QUESTIONS—Questions considered more appropriate for resolution by elected officials in the legislature or the executive branches. In recent years, federal courts have become more prone to intervene in controversies involving these matters, as the issue of legislative apportionment indicated; see *Baker v. Carr* (1962).

POLITICAL SPEECH—Expression dealing with public affairs which is generally seen as worthy of a greater level of protection under the First Amendment because it allows citizens to deliberate openly in arriving at approximations of truth in political discourse.

POSITIVE FREEDOM—Liberty devoted to achieving the public good and to carrying out the community's values; associated with the communitarian approach to government.

PREFERRED-POSITION DOCTRINE—A position taken by several Supreme Court justices, especially Wiley Rutledge and Frank Murphy in the 1940s, which held that First Amendment freedoms deserved a "preferred" place among protected rights and liberties; see *Thomas v. Collins* (1945). The doctrine has largely remained a minority view on the Court.

PREVENTIVE (PRE-TRIAL) DETENTION—The practice of denying bail to a person in custody before trial on the grounds that the public safety would be endangered by the person's release. The practice was upheld by the Court in *U.S. v. Salerno* (1987).

PRIOR RESTRAINT—The power of the government to restrain or forbid individual expression prior to publication or broadcast; see *Near v. Minnesota* (1931).

PROCEDURAL DUE PROCESS—The view that due process guarantees are confined to specific procedural protections (such as notice, confrontation of witnesses, and counsel) rather than to substantive rights. In general, procedural due process holds that persons are entitled to their "day in court."

PROCEDURAL JUSTICE—A condition which exists when society's rules are fair and apply equally to all persons.

RATIONALITY SCRUTINY—An approach applied by the Supreme Court to most equal protection challenges of legislative classifications. Judges ask if the distinction made by law or government is reasonable; the burden of proof falls upon the individual claiming unequal treatment.

RIPENESS—The situation which occurs when a case is ready for adjudication and decision by a court. The issues presented must not be hypothetical, and the parties must have exhausted all other routes of appeal and resolution. The federal cases of *United Public Workers v. Mitchell* (1947) and *Poe v. Ullman* (1961) found the Supreme Court refusing to decide the cases because the issues presented were not "ripe" for judicial resolution.

RULE OF LAW—A system of government in which the highest authority is the law, not one person or a group of persons; no one is above the law.

RULE OF REASON—The judicial doctrine appearing in the early twentieth century by which certain monopolies and trusts could by held "reasonable" and thereby escape dissolution under the Sherman Anti-Trust Act.

SECESSION—The ultimate weapon of advocates of states' rights; the power of a state to leave the Union; was ruled unconstitutional in *Texas v. White* (1869).

SECULAR-LEGISLATION RULE—State legislation which may conflict with one's perceived religious obligations, but which may not necessarily violate the Free Exercise Clause as long as it can be demonstrated as serving some legitimate secular purpose and not discriminate against particular religious groups. See *Braunfeld v. Brown* (1961).

SELECTIVE EXCLUSIVENESS—The doctrine associated with Chief Justice Taney's opinion in the *Cooley* case holding that, while the congressional commerce power is exclusive, it is only exclusive in those areas in which Congress has selected to exercise it. As a result, states are free to regulate certain matters relating to interstate commerce when not in conflict with congressional authority.

SELECTIVE INCORPORATION—The judicial doctrine, first enunciated in *Palko v. Connecticut,* (1937) which provided for the expansion of certain guarantees in the Bill of Rights to the states via the Due Process Clause of the Fourteenth Amendment. Only those guarantees "implicit in the concept of ordered liberty" were selected to be incorporated.

SENATORIAL COURTESY—An unwritten agreement that requires the president to confer with the senators of his party from a particular state before he nominates an individual to fill a federal position within that state.

SEPARATE-BUT-EQUAL DOCTRINE—An approach to the Equal Protection Clause, beginning with *Plessy* v. *Ferguson* (1896), that allowed states to segregate the races in schools and other public facilities as long as the separate facilities were "equal." The doctrine was overruled by the Court in *Brown* v. *Board of Education* (1954).

SEPARATION OF POWER—The division of governmental powers between legislative, executive, and judicial branches on the premise that each has some unique characteristics and each keeps the others from becoming too powerful; reflected in the first three articles of the Constitution.

SHIELD LAWS—Laws passed by several states that protect journalists from having to disclose their news sources in certain instances; journalist-source relationship has been compared with that of lawyer-client, doctor-patient, and priest-penitent; see *Branzburg* v. *Hayes* (1972).

SIMPLE MALICE—Defamatory statements about a person which are false but made in "good faith" that they are true; insufficient for public officials or public figures to be awarded libel damages.

SOCIAL CONTRACT—A theory that bases the authority of a government upon the consent of the governed, who enter into a hypothetical covenant or contract with those who rule.

SOVEREIGNTY—The final and ultimate authority of the state to make binding decisions and resolve conflicts. Arguments over whether the national or state governments were sovereign have raged throughout significant portions of American constitutional history.

STANDING—A person's right to bring a lawsuit because he or she is directly affected by the issues raised; having the appropriate characteristics to bring or participate in a case.

STARE DECISIS—Literally, "Let the decision stand" the principle of adherence to settled cases; the doctrine that principles of law established in earlier cases should be accepted as authoritative in subsequent cases that are similar.

STRICT CONSTRUCTION—The idea that the Constitution should be read narrowly so as to limit the expansion of national powers. Originally embraced by Jeffersonians and Anti-Federalists, this position was contrasted with the so-called "loose construction" of the Federalists.

STRICT SCRUTINY—The approach taken by the Supreme Court in those few equal protection cases where the government uses a suspect classification scheme (e.g., one based upon race or national origin) or interferes with a fundamental right. The government bears the burden of showing a compelling state interest before the Court will allow the program to stand.

SUBPOENA—An order by a court to present oneself before a grand jury, court, or legislative hearing to present evidence in a case.

SUBSTANTIVE DUE PROCESS—The idea that clearly identifiable, concrete rights can be found among due process guarantees. This view holds that the due process of law goes beyond mere procedural fairness, and includes specific rights and liberties. Examples of substantive due process included freedom of contract and corporate property rights.

SUBSTANTIVE JUSTICE—A results-oriented approach which calls for governmental power to adjust inequalities among individuals in society.

SUSPECT CLASSIFICATION—A condition which arises when government or the law distinguishes between persons on the basis of an illegitimate characteristic, such as race or national origin.

SYMBOLIC SPEECH—The expression of ideas and symbols (i.e., armbands, sit-ins, signs) rather than spoken words; generally seen as protected by the First Amendment, although it can be regulated under time, place, and manner guidelines.

TOTAL INCORPORATION—A judicial doctrine, never accepted by a majority of the Supreme Court, which holds that the Due Process Clause of the Fourteenth Amendment incorporated the entire Bill of Rights and applied it to the states. Primary supporters of this view were the first Justice Harlan and Justice Black.

TOTAL INCORPORATION PLUS—The concept which holds that the Fourteenth Amendment's Due Process Clause contains liberties beyond those in the first eight amendments. Justices Goldberg and Douglas, for example, argued that the Ninth Amendment might contain a "right to privacy" which could be applied to the states.

UNITARY SYSTEM OF GOVERNMENT—A centralized governmental organization in which all power stems from central authorities. Although local governments usually exist, they do so at the pleasure of national authorities.

VAGUENESS DOCTRINES—Governmental restrictions on free expression normally struck down by courts because they are not written precisely enough to indicate whether actions are legal or illegal; see *Stromberg* v. *California* (1931).

VESTED RIGHTS—Rights which are held to be so fundamental as to be inseparable from the individual and therefore beyond the reach of any government.

VICTIM-IMPACT STATEMENTS—Testimony provided during the punishment phase of a capital trial which emphasizes the effect of the crime upon the victim, as well as on friends and family members, rather than upon the blameworthiness of the defendant. The Supreme Court upheld the use of victim-impact statements in *Payne* v. *Tennessee* (1991).

Index

Note: Figures are indicated by an italic '*f*'; tables are indicated by an italic '*t*'; notes are indicated by an italic '*n*'.

A

ABA Committee. *See* American Bar Association (ABA) Committee
Abortion rights and right to privacy
   criminal laws, 296
   due process clause, Fourteenth Amendment, 296–297
   equal protection, 297–298
   government restrictions, 298
   legal restrictions, 296, 297
   limitations. *See* Limitations of abortion rights
   maternal health protection, 297
   moral and legal criticism, 297
   Roe v. Wade, 296
   violation of separation of powers, 298
   woman's right, 297
Actual malice
   New York Times v. Sullivan. *See New York Times v. Sullivan*
   and public figures, 434–435
AFDC. *See* Aid to Families with Dependent Children (AFDC)
Affirmative action
   Bakke decision. *See Bakke* decision, affirmative action in higher education
   denial of equal protection, 245–247
   resolution, Croson and Adarand decisions, 247–251
Age discrimination and equality, 257–258
Aid to Families with Dependent Children (AFDC), 176
Amendatory articles and supreme law
   ages and origins, 14, 15*t*
   Chisholm v. Georgia, 14
   constitution's framers, 13
   "Post-Mao" constitution, 15
   ratification, 13
   two-stage process, 13
   "unwritten" British constitution, 14
   World War II, 14
American Bar Association (ABA) Committee
   court nominees, 74
   Federal Judiciary, 74
American Constitutionalism
   amendatory articles and supreme law, 13–15
   American Revolution, 32
   articles of confederation, 38–41
   auxiliary precautions, 7
   Bills of Rights, 16
   colonial documents and writings, 32
   colonial influences, 24–27
   communitarian theory of politics, 19–21
   and comparative constitutions, 8–10
   critical period and state governments, 41–43
   declaration of independence, 34–36
   emergence, 32–34
   federal judiciary and individual rights, 47
   government and people, 6
   historical influences. *See* Historical influences, American Constitutionalism
   individual rights, 8
   James Madison statements, 30–31

John Locke and Jean-Jacques Rousseau, 4–5
liberties of individuals, 7
Madison, 7
organization and operation, 6
organizational chart. *See* Organizational chart
powers of congress, 44–45
The Preamble, 10–11, 11*t*
ratification, 47–52
revolutionary state constitutions, 36–38
rule of law, 7
separation of powers and presidency, 45–47
Twin Pillars, 16–18
universal declaration, human rights, 7
Virginia plan, 43–44

Anglo-American context, free press
censorship, 408, 411*t*
First Amendment, 408
licensing, 408
monopoly, copyright law, 408
omission, 408
prior restraints, publication, 408
protection, 408
Zenger trial, 408, 409

Anti-Federalist position
Constitution in 1791, 170
Gibbons v. Ogden, 170
Jeffersonianism and the Virginia and Kentucky Resolutions, 170–171
McCulloch v. Maryland, 170

Appointment of Judges and Justices
judicial selection. *See* Judicial selection
prerequisites—nomination, 72

Articles of confederation
congress and enforcement powers, 39
federal constitution, 38
multi-tiered united government, 39
Northwest ordinance, 40
Revolutionary War, 40
Robert Morris description, 41
separation-of-powers principle, 39
United States and foreign governments, 41
western-territories, 39

Articulation, neutral principles
Bush v. Gore, 102–103
judicial decision making, 102
judicial impartiality, 103

'Automobile' exception
Acevedo rule, 316
Blackmun's opinion, 315
Bond v. United States, 318
Brendlin v. California, 318
Carroll v. United States, 315
development, law, 315, 317*t*
drug dealing, 317
Houghton's purse, 316
Illinois v. Caballes, 318
Maryland v. Pringle, 317
United States v. Ross, 315

B

Bail Reform Act of 1984, 351
Bakke decision, affirmative action in higher education
affirmative action plan, 247–248
Davis program, 248
Negro, 248
race discrimination and ethnic status, 247
racial classifications, 248
requirement, 247
revisits, 250
strict-scrutiny standard, 247
BCRA. *See* Bipartisan Campaign Reform Act (BCRA)
Bills of Rights, 16, 17*t*, 337
Bipartisan Campaign Reform Act (BCRA)
campaign finance decisions, 399
corporate electioneering communication, 398
McCain-Feingold, 397
McConnell v. Federal Election Commission, 398
national political parties, 397–398
struggle to abolish "soft money", 397
Black voting power, 237
Broadcast regulation
cable industry, 439
development of law, 437, 438*t*
electronic mass media, 20th century, 437
FCC, late 1980s, 437–439
fleeting expletives, 439, 440
public-trust responsibility, 437
publisher–reader transaction, 437

C

Cable Television Consumer Protection and Competition Act of 1992, 439
Campaign finance and first amendment
Buckley v. Valeo, 394–396
constitutional interpretation, 394
and elections, 394, 395–396*t*

FECA, 394
Federal Election Commission, 396
Reform, The BCRA and Citizens United Decision, 397–399
CCC. *See* Civilian Conservation Corps (CCC)
CDA. *See* Communications Decency Act (CDA)
Child labor, freedom of contract, 199
Child Online Protection Act (COPA), 429
Child pornography
    CDA, 429
    CIPA, 429–430
    COPA, 429
    CPPA, 430
    development of law, 430*t*
    eradication, sexual exploitation, 429
    internet, 429
    national problem, 429
    obscenity law, 428
    PROTECT Act, 430–431
    protection, 429
    reading materials, 428–429
    sexting, 431
    telecommunication, 429
    United States v. American Library Association, 430
Child Pornography Prevention Act (CPPA), 430
CIA. *See* The Central Intelligence Agency (CIA)
CIO. *See* Committee for Industrial Organization (CIO)
Civil Rights Act of 1964, 247
Civilian Conservation Corps (CCC), 176
Colonial influences, American constitutionalism
    religious ideas and practices, 24–26
    structure of government, 26–27
Combatant Status Review Tribunals (CSRT), 136–137
Commerce
    definition, 191, 193
    development of the law—the federal commerce power, 191–192*t*
    federal police power, 198–200
    John Marshall and the commerce power, 193–194
    manufacturing, monopolies and the economy, 195–198
    "Obamacare", 201–202
    Roger Taney and Dual Federalism, 194–195
    and spending powers, 200–201

Commercial speech and First amendment
    brewing industry, 391
    commercial-speech cases, 392
    democratic participation, 390
    disclosure prohibition, 391
    paid political advertisement, 390
    regulation, commercial speech, 390–391
    regulatory framework, 391–392
    Rehnquist Court, 393
    Rubin v. Coors Brewing Company, 391
    social policy and public health, 392
    state-local regulations of tobacco advertising, 393
Committee for Industrial Organization (CIO), 387
Communications Decency Act (CDA), 429
Communitarian theory of politics
    contemporary liberals and conservatives, 20, 21
    democratic government, 19
    and individualists contrasted, 20*t*
    republican tradition, 20
    substantive, justice, 19
Comparative constitutions and constitutionalism
    anti-democratic forces, 8–9
    "checks and balances", 9
    core ingredients, national documents, 10
    democracy as governance, 8, 491*n*6
    Gurr argument, 9–10
    nonprofit organization Freedom House, 8
    restricted democratic practices, 8
    Sunstein argument, 10
Comprehensive Drug Abuse Prevention and Control Act, 337
Confederate Constitution
    executive power, 175
    slaves and property rights, 175
    sovereignty issue, 175
    taxation, 175
Confidentiality, freedom of press, 420–421
Constitution
    Amendment I, 486
    Amendment II, 486
    Amendment III, 486
    Amendment IX, 486
    Amendment V, 486
    Amendment VI, 486
    Amendment VII, 486
    Amendment VIII, 486
    Amendment X, 486

Amendment XI, 487
Amendment XII, 487
Amendment XIII, 487
Amendment XIV, 487–488
Amendment XIX, 488–489
Amendment XV, 488
Amendment XVI, 488
Amendment XVII, 488
Amendment XVIII, 488
Amendment XX, 489
Amendment XXI, 489
Amendment XXII, 489
Amendment XXIII, 489–490
Amendment XXIV, 490
Amendment XXV, 490
Amendment XXVI, 490
Amendment XXVII, 490
Article I, 479–482
Article II, 482–483
Article III, 483–484
Article IV, 484
Article V, 484–485
Article VI, 485
Article VII, 485
Constitution and Detainees' Rights
   British colonial rule, 138
   CSRT, 136–137
   executive imprisonment, 135
   federal law, 136
   Guantanamo Bay, 134
   Hamdan v. Rumsfeld, 136
   Hamdi v. Rumsfeld., 135
   historical development, 138
   Johnson v. Eisentrager, 135
   judicial activism, 137–138
   Military Commissions Act in 2006, 136, 137
   unlimited presidential power and authority, 138
Constitutional equality
   the Civil Rights Act of 1875, 215
   Congress in the Civil Rights Act of 1875, 216–217
   Fourteenth Amendment's sponsors, 215–216
   "Jim Crow" law, 217
   judicial ratification, Compromise of 1877, 217
   laundries and jury boxes, 215, 216
   Louisiana legislature, 217
   political equality, 215
   ringing defense, 217–218
   "social" inequalities, 217
COPA. *See* Child Online Protection Act (COPA)
Counsel rights, criminal procedure
   appointment of counsel, 348
   assistance of Counsel, 349, 350*t*
   fair trial, 349
   ineffective counsel, 350–351
   misdemeanor cases, 349
   Powell v. Alabama, 348–349
   pre-and post-trial areas, 349
   right to appoint, accused, 348
   rulings, 349
CPPA. *See* Child Pornography Prevention Act (CPPA)
Criminal justice system and free press
   grand jury testimony, 418–419
   mass media, 1990, 418
   private conversations, 420
   publishing and profiting, 419–420
Criminal procedure
   attacks of September 11, 363
   Bill of Rights, 337
   confront witnesses, 346–347
   constitutional rules, 362
   Counsel rights. *See* Counsel rights, criminal procedure
   death penalty. *See* Death penalty
   double jeopardy. *See* Double jeopardy
   due process of law. *See* Due process of law, criminal procedure
   forensic analysis, lab reports, and CSI, 348
   jury trials. *See* Jury trials, criminal procedure
   nature of fair trial, 342–343
   notice, 346
   preventive detention, 351
   privileges, 342
   procedural rights of criminal defendants, 342
   punishment, 363
   rights of accused, 362
   selective incorporation, 362
   self-incrimination. *See* Self-incrimination
   unfair trail, 343, 344
   witnesses security, 347–348
Critical period and state governments
   constitutional convention, 42–43
   governors, 42
   majority tyranny and democratic despotism, 41

postwar depression, 42
reform state governments, 42
State legislatures, 41
CSRT. *See* Combatant Status Review Tribunals (CSRT)

D

Death penalty
  cruel and unusual punishments cases, 352, 353
  execution of mentally retarded defendants, 357
  execution of minors, 356–357
  Furman v. Georgia, 352
  Gregg v. Georgia, 352, 355
  methods of execution, 358
  sentencing guidelines, 355–356
  trends, 355, 356
  victim-impact statements, 357–358
Declaration of Independence
  abolitionists and women's rights, 35
  British trade restrictions, 34
  individualism and communitarianism, 35
  Jefferson's declaration, 34
  John Locke's argument, 35
  Lee's resolution, 34
  natural-rights foundation, 35
  post-revolutionary constitutionalism, 35–36
Direct taxes and federal income tax, 202
Disabilities Act, 260, 261
Disabled persons and equal protection clause, 259–260
Disenfranchisement methods
  elections and voting qualifications, 234, 499*n*33
  literacy tests, 234
  white primary laws, 234–235
Doctrine of selective incorporation, 279, 281*t*
DOMA. *See* The Defense of Marriage Act (DOMA)
Double jeopardy
  in 1969, 337
  Clause protection, 337
  criminal punishment and civil forfeitures, 337, 339
  and hung juries, 337, 338
  illegal drug activity, 337
  no person punished twice for same offense, 337
  prevention, retrial of criminal defendants, 337, 338*t*
  Sattazahn v. Pennsylvania, 337

Drug testing and Fourth Amendment
  Chandler v. Miller, 327
  constitutional rights, 328
  Ferguson v. City of Charleston, 327
  FRA, 326
  National Treasury Employees Union v. Von Raab, 326
  Pottawatomie County v. Lindsay Earls, 327
  railroad employees, 326
  school districts, 327
Due process of law, criminal procedure
  "balancing test", 358
  early 1970s, 358
  explosion, 358
  hearing, 358
  juveniles, 358–360
  mental patients, 360
  parolees and prisoners, 361–362
  probationers, 361
  sex offenders, 360–361
  "supermax" prison, 362

E

Early Cold War and National Security Concerns
  Alien Registration Act, 374
  American Civil Liberties Union, 374, 375
  federal laws, 374
  McCarran Act, 375
  political speech and freedom of association, 376
  SACB, 375
  Smith Act (1940), 374
  Taft-Hartley Act., 375, 508*n*18
Education, racial discrimination
  Brown v. Board of Education, 224–225
  positive duty to desegregation and court-ordered busing, 225–228
  school desegregation after fifty years, 228–232
  Sweatt v. Painter, 223–224
EEOC. *See* Equal Employment Opportunity Commission (EEOC)
Electronic surveillance
  GPS, 330
  Katz v. United States, 328
  Olmstead v. United States, 328
  privacy, home, 329
  reasonable expectation, privacy, 328
  trespass rule, 328
  United States v. Jones, 329

Environmental Protection Agency (EPA), 176
EPA. *See* Environmental Protection Agency (EPA)
Equal access and public facilities
    Board of Education of Westside Community Schools v. Mergens, 463–464
    encourage on-campus activities, 463
    Equal Access Act, 463
    free speech rights, students, 464–465
    Good News Club v. Milford Central School, 465
    Hastings Christian Fellowship v. Martinez, 465
    neutrality principle, 465
    prevention, discrimination, 464
    undeniably secular, 464
    Widmar v. Vincent, 463
    worship service, 465
Equal access franchise
    Harper v. Virginia State Board of Elections, 290
    photo identification, 291
    poll taxes, 290
    state restrictions, rights to vote, 290, 291
    voting booth, 290
    voting restriction, college students, 291
Equal access to the ballot, 291–292
Equal Employment Opportunity Commission (EEOC), 255–256
Equal protection
    affirmative action. *See* Affirmative action
    age discrimination and equality, 257–258
    Bakke decision, 247–249
    clause, 245
    constitutional argument, 243
    disabled persons, 259–260
    Fourteenth Amendment's language, 243
    gender-based discrimination, 251, 252*t*
    noncitizens, 258–259
    origins, new equal protection, 243–244
    and poor, 262–263
    poverty, 263–264
    rationality scrutiny standard, claims, 268–269
    Reed v. Reed and Progeny, 253–254
    and reforms, electoral system, 267–268
    return, rationality scrutiny, 264–265
    in 1930s, 243
    and same-sex marriage, 262
    San Antonio School District v. Rodriguez, 265–267
    sex discrimination, employment, 254–257
    sexual orientation and Constitution, 260–262
    Strauder v. West Virginia, 216
    strict scrutiny, 243
    and suspect classification, 245, 246
    two-tier approach, 244–245
    women's legal inequality, 252–253
    Yick Wo v. Hopkins, 216
Establishment of religion
    avoiding excessive entanglement, 459
    First Amendment, 454
    governmental-neutrality and accommodation theory, 455
    governmental-neutrality theory, 455
    interpretation, 455
    Lemon test, 459
    meaning, 454
    public aid, 455, 456–457*t*
    religious practices, public schools, 455
    secular teaching and religious doctrine, 459
    state aid programs, 458–459
    strict-separation/no-aid theory, 455
    subsidies, church school operations, 458
    support religious institutions, 454
Exclusionary rule
    development, law, 312, 313*t*
    "good-faith" exception, 313
    People v. DeFore, 313
    Stone v. Powell, 315
    United States v. Calandra, 314

F

Fair trial and free press
    communications technology, 413
    criminal investigations, 413
    guarantee, 413
    media audience, 413
    and newsgathering, 414, 415
    and pretrial publicity, 414
    pretrial publicity and "gag orders". *See* Pretrial publicity
    primary source of information, 414
    television, courtroom, 414, 416
FBI. *See* The Federal Bureau of Investigation (FBI)
FECA. *See* Federal Election Campaign Act (FECA)
Federal Election Campaign Act (FECA), 394
Federal Emergency Management Agency (FEMA), 155–156, 495*n*11
Federal minimum wage, 198

Federal police power
    Champion v. Ames, 198–199
    child labor, 199
    civil rights and liberties, 199
    Heart of Atlanta Motel, Inc. v. United States, 200
    Katzenbach v. McClung, 200
    powerful anti-gambling lobby, 198
Federal power and economic regulation
    the Civil War primary effect, 205
    commerce. *See* Commerce
    Commerce Clause, 205
    congressional power to tax and spend, 202–204
    Contract Clause, 205
    Due Process of Law Clauses, 205
    Franklin D. Roosevelt and Ronald Reagan, 184–185
    freedom of contract, 189–191
    property rights and economic liberty, 186–188
    Slaughterhouse Cases, 188–189
    Taxing and Spending Clause, 205
    West Coast Hotel vs. Parrish, 205
Federal preemption, 180–181
Federal Railroad Administration (FRA), 326
Federalism. *See* Federal power and economic regulation
Federalism issues
    Eleventh Amendment and sovereign immunity, 177–180, 179*t*
    federal preemption of state law, 180–181
    the Homeland Security Grant Programs (HSGP), 181, 182
    "preemption", 177
    September 11, 2001, 181
Federalism theory
    American constitutional development, 165
    American federalism, 166–167
    the Civil War, 165
    comparative perspective, 165–166, 166*t*
    horizontal federalism, 167
    principles, 165
    sovereignty, 165
Federalist political theory
    constitutional amendments, 50
    "extended republic" government, 49–50
    Hamilton statement, 50
    political conflict, 51–52
    "progressives", 49
    ratification battle, 50, 51
    U.S. Constitution, 51
FEMA. *See* Federal Emergency Management Agency (FEMA)
Fifth Amendment
    double jeopardy. *See* Double jeopardy
    self-incrimination. *See* Self-incrimination
Filibuster, 145
First Amendment, Democratic Society
    and adult entertainment, 393
    The Aftermath of Schenck, 373–374
    and campaign finance, 394–399
    "Culture Wars", 399–401
    Dennis v. United States (1951), 376–377
    Early Cold War and National Security Concerns, 374–376
    elements, truth, 370
    European Enlightenment, 369
    expression-action theory, 371
    "Fighting-Words" Doctrine, 401–403
    freedom of expression, historical perspective, 368–369
    jurisprudence, 371
    Meiklejohn's absolutist theory, 370
    personal self-fulfillment, 371
    political speech and national security, 371–373
    public/political speech, 370
    restricting speech during war, 373
    and "Speech Plus", 384–393
    states and internal security, 377–380
    symbolic behavior, 404
    symbolic protest against federal policies, 382–384
    symbolic speech, 380–382
    theory and scope, 368
    two-tier system, speech, 370
    Yates v. United States (1957), 377
FMLA. *See* The Family and Medical Leave Act (FMLA)
Fourteenth Amendment and due process of law
    appointment of counsel and rights, 278–279
    Chicago, Burlington & Quincy Ry. v. Chicago, 277–278
    doctrine of "selective incorporation", 276
    freedoms of speech and press, 278
    fundamental liberties, 278
    guarantee, fundamental rights, 276
    Hurtado v. California, 276

impact of post–Civil War, 275
late-nineteenth-century, 277
nationalization, bill of rights, 276, 277t
origins, 276
privileges and immunities, 275
ratification, 306
self-incrimination protections, 278
The Slaughterhouse Cases, 276
state criminal proceedings, capital crimes, 278
Twining v. New Jersey, 278

Fourth Amendment
and administrative searches, 332
"automobile" exception, 315–318
"border" exception, 318
"consent" exception, 324–325
drug testing, 326–328
"Englishmen", 309
and Exclusionary Rule. *See* Exclusionary rule
"hot-pursuit" exception, 319
James Otis, 308
liberty and security, 308
"plain-view" exception, 325–326
post-Revolution constitutions, 309
searches and seizures, 309
"search-incident-to-arrest" exception, 322–324
"stop-and-frisk" exception, 319–322
and warrants. *See* Warrants and Fourth Amendment
wiretapping and electronic surveillance, 328–330
wiretapping and national security, 330–332

FRA. *See* Federal Railroad Administration (FRA)

Free Exercise Clause and religious freedom
Cantwell v. Connecticut, 448
compelling state interest, 448–450
development of law, 446, 447–448, 447t
early conflicts, 446–448
Fourteenth Amendment, 448
generally applicable laws standard. *See* Generally applicable laws standard, religious freedom
governmental support and regulation, 446
parents liberty, 448
restoration act, 452
Reynolds v. United States, 446, 448
societal rights, 448
witnesses, free exercise, and the flag salute cases, 448, 449

Freedom of press

Anglo-American. *See* Anglo-American context, free press
broadcast regulation. *See* Broadcast regulation
censorship, student newspaper, 410, 412
child pornography. *See* Child pornography
confidentiality, 420–421
and criminal justice system. *See* Criminal justice system and free press
dangerous places, 407
effects, technological developments, 440
electronic and broadcast sources, 407
and fair trial, 413–415
First Amendment rights, 407
global press, 407
government censorship, 439
government employment, prior restraint, 414
government subsidies, 428
guarantees, 439
Law of libel. *See* The Law of libel
mass media, 409
media access. *See* Media access
national emergency, 407
Near v. Minnesota, 410, 412
Obscenity. *See* Obscenity and First Amendment
pretrial publicity and "gag orders", 414–417
print media, 409
prior restraint, 407–408
prior restraint and Vietnam War. *See New York Times v. United States*
public's business, 409
public's right, 407
Revolutionary War, 407
safeguards, 408
and speech, 407
student, 439
twenty-first century, 440

Fundamental rights and due process of law
analysis, 288
civil rights of man, 288
guarantee, individual liberty, 287
interpretation, 288
limits, 288
Lochner v. New York, 288
making, 288
marriage and procreation, 288
nature and scope, 288–289
parents rights, 305

protection, individual liberty against governments, 287
right to privacy. *See* Right to privacy
right to privacy, Ninth Amendment, 287
Skinner v. Oklahoma, 287
United States v. Carolene Products Co., 287

G

Gay rights, 260
Gender-based discrimination and equal protection, 251, 252*t*
Generally applicable laws standard, religious freedom
 Church of the Lukumi Babalu Aye v. City of Hialeah, 451
 civil liberties, 451
 compulsory school attendance and old Amish order, 452–453
 conflicts, 453–454
 drug laws, 451
 Employment Division, Dept. of Human Resources of Oregon v. Smith, 450–451
 nature of free exercise protections, 450
 ordinances, church, 451
Government subsidies and free expression, 427–428

H

Hamiltonian Economic Program, 168–169
Historical influences, American constitutionalism
 ancient, 21–22
  English common law and parliamentary practice, 23–24
  medieval, 22–23
Holmes-Brandeis-Stone model
 Agricultural Adjustment Act of 1933, 92
 civil rights/liberties, 93
 forms, economic regulation, 92
 processes, democratic government, 93, 493*n*12
 Supreme Court Revolution of 1937, 93
Homeland Security Grant Programs (HSGP)
 OPSG, 182
 SHSP, 182
 UASI, 182
Horizontal federalism
 extradition, 167
 full faith and credit clause, 167
 privileges and immunities clause, 167
HSGP. *See* Homeland Security Grant Programs (HSGP)

HUAC. *See* The House Un-American Activities Committee (HUAC)

I

Impeachment power, Congress
 Article II, section 4, 149
 Clinton Presidency and impeachment, 152–154
 incumbent president, 149–150
 Nixon Presidency, 150–152
 qualification, impeachment power, 149
Individualist theory of politics, 19–20
Investigative power, Congress
 anti-Communist turmoil, 147–148
 Barenblatt v. United States, 148
 congressional investigations, 147
 HUAC, 147
 Kilbourn v. Thompson, 147
 McGrain v. Daugherty, 147
 public cynicism and criticism, 147
 senate investigations since 1860, 146–147, 146*t*
 Vietnam era, 148
 Watkins v. United States, 148

J

Jeffersonianism, 170–171
"Jim Crow" law, 217
Judicial activism
 economic regulation, 94
 judicial role behavior, 95
 merits, restraint and activism, 94
 politics, judicial decision-making, 94, 94*f*
Judicial Power
 Constitution, Congress and Federal Court Jurisdiction, 61–62, 61*t*
 Courts of Appeal, United States, 63–64
 District Courts, U.S., 63
 federal judiciary, 60–61
 Judges and Justices. *See* Appointment of Judges and Justices
 limitations, 70–72
 organizational structure, 62, 62*f*
 Rehnquist, 59
 Roberts Court and Ongoing Judicial Confirmation Concerns, 82, 83
 United States Supreme Court. *See* United States Supreme Court

Judicial restraint and activism
    constitutional interpretation, 91, 493*n*7
    and Holmes-Brandeis-Stone Prescription, 92–93
    and Thayer-Frankfurter-Harlan Prescription, 91–92

Judicial Review in the American System
    activism, John Marshall to John Roberts, 94–95
    and articulation, neutral principles, 101–103
    "auxiliary precautions", 100
    Baker v. Carr, 100
    decision making, 90–93
    democratic political system., 98
    democratic system, 88
    electoral districts, 100–101
    federal statutes declared unconstitutional, 95, 96*t*
    Framers' Intentions and Judicial Review, 95–97
    historical acceptance, 97–98
    John Marshall statements, 86–87
    Marbury v. Madison, 98, 99
    policymaking function, 88–90
    political assemblies, 88
    preeminent judicial conscience, country, 104
    principles of liberty and justice, 98
    societal conflicts, 103
    Supreme Court decisions, 100

Judicial selection
    ABA Committee, 74
    "advice and consent", 72
    "blue slips", 74
    Constitutional Convention, 72
    contentious confirmation process, 74, 75
    federal judgeship, 72
    historic battles, Supreme Court confirmation, 72, 73
    lower-court nominees, 74
    Senatorial courtesy, 73
    variables. *See* Variables, Judicial selection

Jury trials, criminal procedure
    Court's attention, 344
    determination, guilty, 343
    fundamental right, 343
    selection, 345–346
    size, 344–345
    verdicts, 345

Juveniles
    adults, 360
    courts, 358
    guarantees of due process, 359–360
    jurisdiction, 360
    justice system, 359
    reform movement, 358–359
    specific requirements, 360

L

Lawrence v. Texas, 303–305

Legislative apportionment
    Baker v. Carr., 289
    equal right to vote, 289
    malapportionment, 289
    "one person, one vote", 290
    plans, 289
    reapportionment, 289
    Reynolds v. Sims, 289

Legislative power, Congress, 145

Limitations of abortion rights
    government regulations, abortion procedures, 300–303
    state and federal funding restrictions, 298–299

M

Media access
    limitation, press regulation, 418, 419
    Pretrial hearings, 417
    trial stage, 417–418

Merit Systems Protection Board (MSPB), 156
Military Commissions Act of 2006, 136, 137
Modern civil service system, 117–118
MSPB. *See* Merit Systems Protection Board (MSPB)

N

NAACP. *See* The National Association for the Advancement of Colored People (NAACP)

National and state governments
    American federalism, 181–182
    anti-Federalist position. *See* Anti-Federalist position
    federalism issues. *See* Federalism issues
    federalism theory. *See* Federalism theory
    individualist and communitarian perspectives, 182
    John C. Calhoun, 164
    Missouri compromise, 172–173
    northern states' population, 172

post–Civil War. *See* The Civil War
    state sovereignty and nullification, 173–174
    states, territories and federalism, 172
    supremacy. *See* National supremacy
    the Union, 174–175
National bank
    Congress, 168
    federalists *v.* anti-federalists, 169
    Maryland tax, 170
    states' rights, 169
National supremacy
    federal system, 168
    Federalists, 168
    Hamiltonian Economic Program, 168–169, 169*t*
    John Marshall's federalism, 169–170
    the Judiciary Act of 1789, 168
Neutrality and accommodation movement
    Agostini v. Felton, 461
    Locke v. Davey, 463, 464
    Mitchell v. Helms, 461–462
    Mueller v. Allen, 460
    Zelman v. Simmons-Harris, 462–463
    Zobrest v. Catalina Foothills School District, 460–461
Neutrality principle, equal access and taxation
New York Times v. Sullivan
    civil and criminal libel law, 434
    early 1960s, 432
    effect, libelous statements, 432
    financial damages, 434
    libel and First Amendment, 432, 433*t*
    publishers protection, First Amendment, 432, 434
    self-censorship, 434
New York Times v. United States
    conflicts, 413
    delineation, constitutional powers, 413
    early 1960s, 410, 412
    First Amendment, 413
    government censorship, 412
    government employment, 412
    national security, 413
    prior restraint, government employment, 412, 414
    Vietnam War, 412
Noncitizens and equal protection clause, 258–259

O

Obscenity and First Amendment
    animal cruelty and violence, 423, 424
    anti-obscenity, 422–423
    and child pornography. *See* Child pornography
    Comstock Act, 423
    confusion, politics, and law, 425–427
    definition, 422
    development of law, 422*t*
    federal regulation, telephone communications, 428
    free press law, 422
    "Hicklin rule", 422, 423
    immoral influences, susceptible persons, 422, 505*n*18
    material, 423
    national standard. *See* Roth test
    new standard, *Miller v. California*, 427–428
    Regina v. Hicklin, 422
    World War II, 423
Office of Management and Budget (OMB), 158, 159
Office of Personnel Management (OPM), 156
OMB. *See* Office of Management and Budget (OMB)
Omnibus Crime Control and Safe Streets Act of 1968, 420
Operation Stonegarden (OPSG), 182
OPM. *See* Office of Personnel Management (OPM)
OPSG. *See* Operation Stonegarden (OPSG)
Organizational chart
    "constitutional" governments, 11
    federalism, 12
    judicial review, 13
    principles, 11
    separation of powers, 12

P

Parents rights, 305
Peaceful assembly and the first amendment
    anti-abortionists, 387, 389
    CIO, 387
    civil disorder, 390
    criminal syndicalism, 386
    De Jonge v. Oregon, 386
    Hague v. Committee for Industrial Organization, 387

"profound national commitment", 390
religious and public policy beliefs, 387
Snyder v. Phelps, 388
Persian gulf conflict, 129, 130
Policymaking function, U.S. Supreme Court
    authoritative interpretation, 89, 493n4
    constitutional interpretation, 88–90
    evolutionary interpretation, 90
    Fourth Amendment, 90
    judicial role, 89
    judicial system, 90
    social and political consensus, 90
    "victims' rights", 90
Political speech and national security
    Espionage and Sedition Acts, 372
    federal laws, 371–372
    law development, 372, 372t
    political activities, 371
    Russian Revolution of 1917, 372
Political speech, states and internal security
    Brandenburg v. Ohio, 379–380
    criminal syndicalism laws, 377–378
    internal security, 377
    modernization, bill of rights, 378–379
    Russian Revolution in 1917, 377–378
    state sedition laws, 377
Poverty and equal protection, 263–264
Pre–Civil War, 214
Prerogative theory, 115, 116
Presidential war power, 129, 130
Pretrial publicity
    contempt-of-court, 416
    and "gag orders", 414–416
    murder trials, 414
    prejudicial media coverage, 415
    Sheppard v. Maxwell, 414–415
    "trial-by-newspapers", 414
Preventive detention, 351–352
Prosecutorial Remedies and Other Tools to end the Exploitation of Children Today (PROTECT) Act of 2003, 430–431
Protection of Children Against Sexual Exploitation Act, 429
Public funding, religion
    after World War II, 455
    child-benefit theory, 455
    in 1930, 455
Punishment, criminal procedure, 363

R

Racial equality
    American Dilemma, 211–212
    "anti-discrimination principle", 238–239
    Brown v. Board of Education, 238
    color blindness, 219, 220t
    disenfranchisement methods. *See* Disenfranchisement methods
    in education. *See* Education, racial discrimination
    in employment, 232–233
    framers intention, 218–219
    franchise, 233–234
    Frederick Douglass, 210
    Griggs v. Duke Power Co., 238
    in housing, 219–222
    individualists and communitarians, 237
    post–Civil War amendments, 213–215
    race and constitutional equality, 215–218
    slavery and race, 212–213
    "strict scrutiny", 239
    the Voting Rights Act of 1965. *See* The Voting Rights Act of 1965
Ratification, constitution
    anti-federalist argument, 48–49
    constitution's adoption, 48
    federalist response, 49–52
    nine-state requirement, 47
Rationality scrutiny, 218
Religious activities, public schools and society
    accommodating religion, prison, 467, 469
    anti-religious, 469
    "creationism", 467
    development of law, 467, 468t
    Establishment Clause, 467
    evolution *v.* creationism, 472–474
    invocations and benedictions, 471
    McCollum v. Board of Education, 467
    monkey trial, 472, 473
    public religious displays, 474–476
    released-time program, 467
    Santa Fe Independent School District v. DOE, 471–472
    school prayer, 469–471
    Zorach v. Clausen, 467, 469
Religious freedom
    Bill of Rights and religion clauses, 446
    constitution and American culture, 444
    early English and colonial experience, 444

early 1800s, 444
equal access and public facilities, 463–465
and Establishment Clauses. *See* Free Exercise Clause and religious freedom
Free Exercise Clause. *See* Free Exercise Clause and religious freedom
government protection, 446
late 1700s, 446, 506*n*7
movement, neutrality and accommodation. *See* Neutrality and accommodation movement
place of, 445
public schools and society. *See* Religious activities, public schools and society
recognition, churches, 444
and taxation, 465–467
virginia labor, 445
Religious Freedom Restoration Act, 452
Revolutionary state constitutions
bicameral legislature, 37
Committees of Correspondence, 38
constitutional and legal colonial resistance, 36
democratic equality, 38
"free and independent states", 36
governors, 37
home rule, 38, 492*n*4
people's representatives, 37
separation-of-powers theory, 36
State constitutions, 38
Right to privacy
and abortion. *See* Abortion rights and right to privacy
constitutional protections, 294
controversy, 294
due process clause of Fourteenth Amendment, 295
equal protection clause, 296
Griswold v. Connecticut, 295
guarantees, 295
individual's, 294–295
penumbral, 295
protections, 295–296
sexual, 303–305
substantive due-process, 295
Right to sexual privacy
deviate sexual intercourse, 304
"deviate sexual intercourse", 304
Fourteenth Amendment, 303
gay men and lesbians, 304

homosexual activity, 303
homosexuals, 304–305
individual's right, 304
protection, right to privacy, 303–304
weapons disturbance, 304
Right to vote, 289
Roth test
average person, 425, 426
determination, 424
implement state policy with religious purposes, 423, 505*n*22
materials, 424–425
modifications, 425
private possession, child pornography, 425, 426
proliferation, ambiguous and divergent standards, 423
Roth v. United States, 423–424

S

SACB. *See* Subversive Activities Control Board (SACB)
School desegregation
"American Dilemma", 231
Brown decision, 226
Brown v. Board of Education, 228
"colorblindness", 229
Court's decision, 230, 232
de jure and *de facto* segregation, 229–230
educational diversity, 229
Parents Involved in Community Schools v. Seattle School District No. 1, 228–229
Sweatt v. Painter, 223–224
Search warrant, execution, 311, 312
Search-incident-to-arrest exception
"ample justification", 322
Arizona v. Gant, 323
Chimel v. California, 322
development of law, 322, 323*t*
Maryland v. Buie, 323
occupant's arrest, 324
searches and citations, 323, 324
Second Iraq War, 133–134
Self-incrimination
Colorado v. Connelly, 343
communists, Fifth Amendment, 339, 502*n*3
and confessions, 339–342
Miranda's conviction, 341, 342
protections, 339*t*

Separation of powers
- Article II, section 4, 149
- borrowing and debt, 158–161, 160*t*
- challenges, twenty-first century, 161
- Clinton presidency and impeachment, 152–154
- colonial legislatures, 141
- and Constitution and Amendments, 143, 144*t*
- Constitutional Convention, 1787, 141
- core functions, 154–155
- domestic and foreign policy commitments, 161
- the European settlers, 141
- fairness, legislative branch, 141–142
- federal government, 45
- federal legislature control, 46–47
- Federalists and Anti-Federalists, 141
- financing and funding, 156
- Glorious Revolution, 17th century, 141
- the House of Representatives, grounds, 153
- incumbent president, 149–150
- institutionalization, 141
- investigative power of, 146–149, 146*t*
- legislative power of, 145
- Nixon presidency, 150–152
- old-line republicans, 46
- organizing and staffing government, 155–156
- powers and composition, 46
- Presidential electors, 46
- qualification, impeachment power, 149
- Robert C. Byrd, 140
- spending, 158, 158*t*
- 1st *v.* 112th congresses, 142–143
- taxation, 157, 157*t*

Sex discrimination, employment
- determination, 255
- differential treatment of pregnancy, 255
- disparate-impact legislation, 255
- EEOC, 255–256
- Equal Rights Amendment (ERA) and constitutional equality, 257
- Fourteenth Amendment, 256–257
- harassment, 256
- *Personnel Administrator of Massachusetts v. Feeney*, 255
- workplace, 254–255

Sex offenders, 360–361

Sexual orientation and equal protection
- *Bowers v. Hardwick*, 262
- civil rights protections, 261
- constitutional rights, 262
- culture wars, 262
- discrimination, gay men and lesbians, 260
- Fourteenth Amendment, 261
- gay rights, 260
- prohibition, 260
- *Romer v. Evans*, 261
- same-sex marriage, 262
- suspect classification, 260

Sexually Violent Predator (SVP) Act, 360
Sherman anti-trust Act, 196
Shreveport Rate Cases, 194
SHSP. *See* State Homeland Security Program (SHSP)
Slaughterhouse Cases, 188–189
Sovereign immunity, 178
"Speech Plus" and First Amendment
- and commercial speech, 390–393
- and labor picketing, 385–386, 385*t*
- and peaceful assembly, 386–390

Spending powers, commerce
- *Gonzalez v. Raich*, 201
- *Reno v. Condon*, 201
- *United States v. Lopez*, 200–201

SSI. *See* The Supplemental Security Income (SSI)
State Homeland Security Program (SHSP), 182
States' Rights position
- anti-Federalist position. *See* Anti-Federalist position
- extension, 172

Stewardship theory, 115
Stop-and-frisk exception
- *Florida v. J.L.*, 322
- McFadden decision, 321
- in New York, 322
- *Peters v. New York*, 321
- police officer, 319
- "reasonable suspicion", 320, 321
- *Terry v. Ohio*, 320, 321

Subversive Activities Control Board (SACB), 375
Symbolic protest against federal policies
- constitutional protections, 382
- flag-burning incident, 383
- Johnson's act of burning the flag, 383
- Justice Abe Fortas, 382
- state law, 383, 504*n*22
- student's right, free speech, 384
- *Texas v. Johnson*, 383
- Universal Military Training and Service Act, 382

Symbolic speech
    expression, protected speech, 380, 381
    flag salute and pledge, 382
    political symbolism, 380
    vagueness doctrine, 380

T

Taxation and religion
    anti-discrimination policy, 466
    churches, 465–466
    exemptions, 466
    implications, Establishment Clause, 465–466
    Jimmy Swaggart Ministries v. Board of Equalization of California, 467
    monthly taxes, 466
    sales tax, 466, 467
    tax-exempt status, 466
The Bill of Rights and due process of law
    amendments, 274
    Barron v. Baltimore case, 274–275
    college students voting, campus, 291, 501*n*19
    Eighth Amendment, 286
    equal access to franchise. *See* Equal access franchise
    equal access to the ballot, 291–292
    existence, 274
    Fifth Amendment, 285
    and Fourteenth amendment. *See* Fourteenth Amendment and due process of law
    Fourth Amendment, 283–285
    freedoms of speech and press, First Amendment, 279–280
    fundamental rights. *See* Fundamental rights and due process of law
    legislative apportionment. *See* Legislative apportionment
    limitations on abortion rights. *See* Limitations of abortion rights
    parents rights, 305
    proposals, 274
    right to interstate travel, 292–294
    right to privacy. *See* Right to privacy
    right to sexual privacy, 303–305
    right to vote, 289
    right to vote and convicted felons, 274
    selective incorporation and controversy, 279, 281*t*, 306
    self-defense, Second Amendment, 280–283
    Sixth Amendment, 285–286
    Third Amendment, 283
The Central Intelligence Agency (CIA), 150
The Civil War
    federal–state relations, 175
    Lyndon B. Johnson and "Great Society", 176
    New Deal and federalism, 175–176
    primary effect, 175
    Ronald Reagan's federalism and "devolution", 176–177
The Defense of Marriage Act (DOMA), 167
The Family and Medical Leave Act (FMLA)
    Chief Justice, explanations, 178–179
    "family-care", 180
    Hibbs on Eleventh Amendment grounds, 177–178
    "prophylactic legislation", 178
    "self-care", 180
The Federal Bureau of Investigation (FBI), 150
The House Un-American Activities Committee (HUAC), 147–148
The Judiciary Act of 1789, 168
The Korean War, 127–128
The Law of libel
    "actual-malice" doctrine. *See* Actual malice
    Alien and Sedition Acts, 431
    criticism of public officials, 431
    First Amendment, 431
    guarantee of free press, 431
    Larry Flynt v. The Reverend Jerry Falwell, 436
    and private citizens, 435–436
    refining, 436–437
    in twentieth century, 432
The National Association for the Advancement of Colored People (NAACP)
    the Legal Defense and Education Fund, 224
    school desegregation, 223–224
    Sweatt v. Painter, 223
The Supplemental Security Income (SSI), 176
The Supreme Court
    Buchanan v. Warley, 219
    constitutional equality. *See* Constitutional equality
    Cooper v. Aaron, 226
    Equal Protection cases, 238
    federal and state legislation, 221
    Georgia v. Ashcroft, 237

Griffin v. County School Board of Prince Edward County, 226
Jones v. Alfred H. Mayer Co., 222
Milliken case, 228
school segregation cases, 224
Shelley v. Kraemer, 220–221
Sweatt v. Painter, 223
the Voting Rights Act (VRA), 235–236
The Thayer-Frankfurter-Harlan prescription
constitutional law, 92
Federal Statutes, Supreme Court-1789-2010, 91, 91*t*
State and Local Statutes, Supreme Court-1789-2010, 91, 91*t*
The Vietnam War
presidential war power and Persian gulf conflict, 129, 130
war powers resolution, 129, 130
The Voting Rights Act of 1965
black voting power, 236, 237
civil rights, 235
electoral system discrimination, 236–237
legal devices, 235
South Carolina v. Katzenbach, 235–236
Theories of executive power
constitutional/Whig theory, 115
prerogative theory, 115, 116
presidential power, 115, 495*n*11
president's constitutional powers, 114
stewardship theory, 115
Twin Pillars of American Constitutionalism
Fourteenth Amendment, 17
individualist/communitarian, 18
Madison acknowledgement, 18
political game, 18
principles and provisions, 16

U

UASI. *See* Urban Areas Security Initiative (UASI)
United States Presidency
anatomy, 2012 presidential election, 114
Constitution and Detainees' Rights, 134–138
constitutional amendments and presidency, 112
contrasting theories, executive power, 114–116
early writings and the founding, 108–110
electing the president, 112–113
executive branch of government, 117, 119
executive war power and national emergencies, 124
Korean War and the Steel Seizure Case, 127–128
legislative and executive agreement, 119, 120
Legislative Leader, 116
modern civil service system, 117–118
presidential power to pardon, 121
presidential powers, 113–114
Presidential Vetoes, 1900–2012, 116, 117*t*
presidential war power and Persian gulf conflict, 129, 130
presidents, US, 110–111*t*
quasi-legislative/quasi-judicial tasks, 120
removing the president, 113
rise and fall of the line-item veto, 116, 118
Second Iraq War, 133–134
separation, powers, 108
September 11 and the War on Terror, 131–133
State of the Union, 116–117
Theodore Roosevelt, 106–107
treaties and executive agreements, 121–123
The Vietnam War, 128–129
war powers resolution, 129, 130
World War II and Internment of Japanese-American, 126–127
United States Supreme Court
American Civil Liberties Union, 70
annual term, 64–66
Appellate Docket, 69
clerking, 66
Court's discretionary jurisdiction, 67
Federal census data, 70
interpretation and application, Constitution, 64
Judiciary Act of 1789, 67
justices, 64, 65*t*
operational changes, 67
primary routes, appeal, 67, 68*f*
Shrinking Docket, Expanding Demands, 67, 67*t*
"standing to sue", 69
writ of certiorari, 70
Urban Areas Security Initiative (UASI), 182

V

Variables, Judicial selection
ideological/policy views, 77–78
political affiliation, 76–77
professional competence, 76
race, gender and ethnic origin, 79–82

W

War powers resolution, 129, 130
Warrants and Fourth Amendment
    drug-detecting dog, 310
    Florida Supreme Court, 311
    "free air sniff", 311
    "good-faith" effort, 311
    Henry v. United States, 311
    iodine crystals, 311
    Ornelas v. United States, 310
    probable cause poses, 310
    search warrant execution, 311, 312
    "totality of circumstances", 311
Watergate scandal, 151
Webster–Hayne debate, 173
White primary laws, 234–235
Wiretapping
    and electronic surveillance, 328–330
    and national security, 330–332
Woman's right, 297
Women and wages, freedom of contract, 190
Women's legal inequality
    history, 251–252
    Reed v. Reed and Progeny, 253–254
Works Progress Administration (WPA), 176
World War II
    and Internment of Japanese-Americans, 126–127
    unilateral presidential activity., 124
WPA. *See* Works Progress Administration (WPA)